MW01014428

A COMMENTARY ON THE JEWISH ROOTS OF

GALATIANS

A COMMENTARY ON
THE JEWISH ROOTS OF

GALATIANS

Hilary Le Cornu
with
Joseph Shulam

ACADEMON

© Netivyah Bible Instruction Ministry
All rights reserved. Published 2005.
Printed in Jerusalem by Academon Ltd.
Cover design by Academon Ltd.
Cover photo: 4QMMT ff14-17 col. 1; used by permission of the Israel
Antiquities Authority

Le Cornu, Hilary, 1959–
A commentary on the Jewish roots of Galatians / Hilary Le
Cornu, Joseph Shulam
Includes bibliographical references and indices.
ISBN   965-350-102-X
Bible. N.T. Galatians – Commentaries. 2. Bible. N.T. Galatians –
Chronology.   3. Bible. N.T. Epistles of Paul – Theology.
4. Judaism–Relations–Christianity.
I.   Shulam, Joseph, 1946–. II. Title

Netivyah Bible Instruction Ministry
P.O. Box 8043
Jerusalem 91080
Israel
www.netivyah.org

TABLE OF CONTENTS

GLOSSARY

Aggada:
The term denotes all Scriptural interpretation which is non-halakhic (non-legal) in character and came to refer mainly to homiletic material and stories.

Amora (Amoraim):
Literally, lecturer or translator. The term is used more widely to designate the Sages – Eretz Israel and Babylonian – who taught in the period following the compilation of the Mishna (200-500 C.E.). Their comments on the Mishna and Tosefta constitute the bulk of the Talmud. Eight generations of Amoraim were in the amoraic period.

Halakhah:
The term comes from the Hebrew root "to walk" and refers generally to the body of legal rulings derived by various forms of exegesis from Scripture. A (one) halakhah is a specific ruling given regarding a particular issue, "the halakhah" being the ruling accepted and observed by the community.

Intertestamental Literature:
The body of literature ascribed to the post-biblical period until the New Testament writings. It traditionally includes the apocryphal literature – documents preserved in the Greek Old Testament (the Septuagint) but not in the Hebrew Tanakh – and the pseudepigrapha – extra-and post-canonical Jewish and Christian texts whose authorship is ascribed to biblical characters (cf. "with false superscription").

The apocrypha includes the books of 1 Esdras (= 2 Ezra) and 2 Esdras (= 4 Ezra), Tobit, Judith, Additions to Esther, Wisdom of Solomon, Sirach (Ecclesiasticus), 1 Baruch, Letter of Jeremiah, Prayer of Azariah with the Song of the Three Men, Susanna, Bel and the Dragon, 1 and 2 Maccabees, and the Prayer of Manasseh.

The pseudepigrapha (under which the apocrypha is sometimes subsumed) includes nine collections: The works of Philo (c. 20 B.C.E. – 50 C.E.); the writings of Josephus Flavius (c. 37 C.E. – c. 100 C.E.); the Qumran texts; the Targumim or Aramaic translations of the Tanakh; Jewish magical papyri; the Hermetica, texts of the first few centuries C.E. attributed to Hermes which describe the means to personal salvation; the Coptic codices from Nag Hammadi (C1-4 C.E.), which are mostly gnostic writings; and the New Testament apocrypha and pseudepigrapha, usually legendary expansions of the New Testament texts.

LXX (Septuagint):
The "official" Greek translation of the Tanakh, dating from the third century B.C.E. through the fourth century C.E. The original translation was of the Torah (Pentateuch, the first five books), which the Letter of Aristeas records was allegedly made by seventy(-two) Jewish scholars in Alexandria (Egypt) from which it gained its name (Septuaginta). It is commonly referred to by the abbreviation, LXX (70).

Masoretic Text:
The "official" text of the Hebrew Bible (Tanakh) edited by the "Massoretes" or Jewish grammarians during the sixth to tenth centuries C.E. This text is "pointed" with vowel signs (and accents) which were lacking in the previous texts.

Midrash:
Midrash is a comprehensive term for the Jewish exegesis of Scripture and individually collected works of scriptural interpretation (cf. "Genesis Rabbah" or "Midrash Psalms"). It also refers to a specific mode of interpretation, based primarily on "verbal analogy" in which one scriptural text is interpreted through a second text (cf. commentary on 13:32-41, 17:2-3). It can then refer to a specific midrash on a specific scriptural verse or theme (cf. commentary on 7:30-34). According to the context it thus refers either to a text (textual tradition) or a mode of interpretation. The term comes from the post-biblical root "to search out" or "expound".

Mishna:
The first body of the "oral Torah" which comprises the Talmud. It is composed of halakhah (halakhot) or traditional and categorical statements of law and aggada (aggadot), Scriptural expositions in the form of narrative, parables and proverbs. The Mishna is attributed to the Tannaim or early Sages (Rabbis) and its editing is usually ascribed to Judah haNasi around 200 C.E. It is divided into six Orders which contain a number of tractates. The tannaitic material is complemented by two further sources:

The Tosefta – "addition" or "supplement" – which is a collection of tannaitic statements and traditions not included in the Mishna, which follows the divisional order of the Mishna; and baraitot (baraita), tannaitic statements "extraneous" to R. Judah's Mishna.

Qumran:
The documents which were discovered at Khirbet Qumran on the Dead Sea and frequently known as the Dead Sea Scrolls. These texts include copies of most of the biblical books, apocryphal writings (such as Enoch), and texts produced by the community itself (cf. the manual of Discipline and the Thanksgiving Hymns). The texts are referred to according to the number of the cave in which they were discovered (e.g., 1QS [Community Rule], 11QTemp [Temple Scroll]).

Talmud:
The major body of rabbinic literature which embodies the "oral law" of Jewish tradition. The name is given both to the whole corpus of the "oral Torah" (mishna and gemara) and to the gemara alone. The mishna was written in Hebrew by the tannaim and is generally held to have been edited around 200 C.E. It consists of legal rulings based on the Tanakh; the gemara is a later commentary upon the mishna, written in Aramaic by several generations of Amoraim (as well as some Savoraim [C6] and Geonim). The Talmud exists in two recensions, the earlier Jerusalem (Palestinian) Talmud and the later Babylonian Talmud (c. 500 C.E.). The Babylonian Talmud is often considered more authoritative in the Western Jewish intellectual tradition, which is reflected in the fact that only the Palestinian Talmud is noted as such in the present volume (e.g., JPe'ah, JSotah). The Talmud is divided into six Orders (e.g., Mo'ed, Nashim) which contain a number of tractates (e.g., Shabbat, Ketubot). Some tractates contain only mishna with no gemara (e.g., Pe'ah, Shekalim). Each talmud page is divided into a folio page and numbered "a" and "b," although the Palestinian Talmud is referred to according first to the chapter, then to the halakhah, and finally to the folio page (e.g., JNed. 9, 1, 41b). Each page contains, in addition to the mishna and gemara, Rashi's commentary on the text, written in "Rashi script" and found on the inner side of the page, the commentary of the Tosafot (medieval commentators), printed on the outer column of the page, and several other commentaries. The capital letters which the Soncino English translation uses to designate the Mishna as a piska have normally been replaced with ordinary text.

Tanakh:
The Hebrew acronym denoting the three sections of the Hebrew Bible: the Torah, the Prophets (nevi'im), and the Writings (ketuvim).

Tanna (tannaim):

Literally, the one who repeats or recites. The term designates those Sages mentioned either in the Mishna or braitot (a saying external to the Mishna, frequently found in the Tosefta). Six generations of these Sages, preceded by the "pairs" (200 B.C.E-20 C.E.), were active in the tannaitic period between 20-200/220 C.E.

Targumim:

The Aramaic translations of the Tanakh, which were read aloud in the synagogue as a vernacular aid to understanding the biblical text.

Torah:

The term refers comprehensively to the Hebrew Bible in its entirety. More strictly speaking, it is restricted to the first five books of Moses (the Pentateuch or Chumash). In Jewish thought, the Torah is primarily used in the latter sense, and is also divided into the "Written Torah" and the "Oral Torah." The latter is embodied in the Talmud (mishna and gemara) and its halakhah, and constitutes the "tradition" or commentary of later generations on the original biblical text. In Jewish tradition both the Written and the Oral Torah are regarded as "inspired" and authoritative texts, the Oral Torah being held to be have been given to Moses on Mount Sinai simultaneously with the Written Torah.

ABBREVIATIONS

Apocrypha (KJV):

Ap.Bar.	Apocalypse of Baruch
Esd.	Esdras (1 and 2)
Jud.	Judith
Sir.	Ben Sirach (Ecclesiasticus)
Macc.	Maccabees (1 and 2)

Pseudepigrapha (J. Charlesworth [ed.], *The Old Testament Pseudepigrapha* (NY: Doubleday, 1985):

Apoc.Abr.	Apocalypse of Abraham
Artapanus	Artapanus
Ass.Mos.	Assumption of Moses
Bar.	Baruch (2, 3, and 4)
En.	Enoch (1, 2, and 3)
Ep.Arist.	Letter of Aristeas
4 Ez.	4 Ezra
Hell.Syn.Pray.	Hellenistic Synagogal Prayers
Hist.Rechab.	History of the Rechabites
Jos.Asen.	Joseph and Aseneth
Jub.	Jubilees
Macc.	Maccabees (3 and 4; Charlesworth)
Odes Sol.	Odes of Solomon
Ps.-Philo	Pseudo-Philo
Ps.Sol.	Psalms of Solomon
Sib.Or.	Sibylline Oracles
Test.Abr.	Testament of Abraham
Test.Asher	Testament of Asher (Testament of Twelve Patriarchs)
Test.Ben.	Testament of Benjamin "
Test.Dan	Testament of Dan "
Test.Gad	Testament of Gad "

Test.Isaac	Testament of Isaac
Test.Iss.	Testament of Issachar (Test. Twelve Patriarchs)
Test.Jac.	Testament of Jacob
Test.Job	Testament of Job
Test.Jos.	Testament of Joseph (Test. Twelve Patriarchs)
Test.Jud.	Testament of Judah (Test. Twelve Patriarchs)
Test.Levi	Testament of Levi "
Test.Naph.	Testament of Naphtali (Test. Twelve Patriarchs)
Test.Reuv.	Testament of Reuben "
Test.Sim.	Testament of Simeon "
Test.Sol.	Testament of Solomon
Test.Zev.	Testament of Zebulun (Test. Twelve Patriarchs)
Tob.	Tobit
Wis.Sol.	Wisdom of Solomon (KJV)

Qumran (F. García Martínez and E. Tigchelaar, *The Dead Sea Scrolls Study Edition* [Leiden/Grand Rapids: Brill/Eerdmans, 1997]):

CD-A	Damascus Document
CD-B	Damascus Document, manuscript B
1QapGen.	Genesis Apocryphon
1QH^a	(Thanksgiving) Hymns
1QpHab	Commentary on Habakkuk
1QM	War Rule
1QS	Rule of the Community
1Q28a	Rule Annexe
1QS28b	Book of Blessings
4QFlor	Florilegium (= 4Q174)
4QMMT	Miktzat Ma'asei ha-Torah/Halakhic Letter (4Q394-399)
4QNab	Prayer of Nabonidus (= 4Q242)
4QpHos	Commentary on Hosea (= 4Q166/167)
4QpIsa	Commentary on Isaiah (= 4Q161-165)
4QpMic	Commentary on Micah (= 4Q168)
4QpNah	Commentary on Nahum (= 4Q169)
4QpPs37	Commentary on Psalm 37 (= 4Q171-173)
4QPat.Bless.	Patriarchal Blessings (= 4Q252)
4QTest	Testimonia (= 4Q175)
11QMelch	Melchizedek text (= 11Q13)
11QTemp	Temple Scroll (= 11Q19)

Josephus (Loeb Classical Library):

Ant.	Antiquities of the Jews
CA	Contra Apion (Against Apion)
Life	Life
War	Jewish War

Philo (Loeb Classical Library):

Conf.Ling.	De Confusione Linguarum (On the Confusion of Tongues)
De Abr.	De Abrahamo (On Abraham)
De Agr.	De Agricultura (On Husbandry)
De Cher.	De Cherubim (On the Cherubim)
De Sac.	De Sacrificiis Abelis et Caini (On the Sacrifices of Abel and Cain)
De Sob.	De Sobrietate (On the Prayers and Curses uttered by Noah when he became Sober)
Dec.	De Decalogo (On the Decalogue)
Hypoth.	Hypothetica (Apologia pro Iudaeis)
In Flac.	In Flaccum (Flaccus)
Jos.	De Iosepho (On Joseph)
Leg.	De Legatione ad Gaium (On the Embassy to Gaius)
Leg.All.	Legum Allegoriae (Allegorical Interpretation)
Mig.Abr.	De Migrationes Abrahami (On the Migration of Abraham)
Mut.Nom.	De Mutatione Nominem (On the Change of Names)
Opif.Mun.	De Opificio Mundi (On the Creation)
Praem.	De Praemiis et Poenis (On Rewards and Punishments)
Quis Rerum	Quis Rerum Divinarum Heres (Who is the Heir of Divine Things)
Quod Omnis	Quod Omnis Probus Liber sit (Every Good Man is Free)
Somn.	De Somniis (On Dreams)
Spec.Leg.	De Specialibus Legibus (On the Special Laws)
Virt.	De Virtutibus (On the Virtues)
Vit.Cont.	De Vita Contemplativa (On the Contemplative Life)
Vit.Mos.	De Vita Moses (On the Life of Moses)

Targumim:

Targ.	Targum
Targ.Onk.	Targum Onkelos
Targ.Ps.-Jon.	Targum Pseudo-Jonathan
Targ.Jon.	Targum Jonathan

Midrashim:

Cant.R.	Canticles Rabbah (Song of Solomon) (Shir Hashirim Rabbah)
Cant.Zuta	Canticles Zuta
Dt.R.	Deuteronomy Rabbah (Devarim Rabbah) (Midrash Rabbah, Soncino)
Eccl.R.	Ecclesiastes Rabbah (Kohelet Rabbah) "
Esth.R.	Esther Rabbah "
Ex.R.	Exodus Rabbah (Shemot Rabbah) "
Gen.R.	Genesis Rabbah (Bereshit Rabbah) "
Lam.R.	Lamentations Rabbah (Eikha Rabbah) "
Lev.R.	Leviticus Rabbah (Midrash Rabbah, Soncino) (Yayikra Rabbah)
Meg.Ta'anit	Megillat Ta'anit (Lichtenstein; HUCA 1931/2)
Mekh.	Mekilta de-Rabbi Ishmael (Lauterbach; JPS: 1961)
Mekh.de SbY	Mekilta de-Rabbi Shimon bar Yochai (Horowitz)
Mid.Prov.	Midrash on Proverbs
Mid.Ps.	Midrash Psalms (Braude; Yale University Press: 1959)
Mid.Sam.	Midrash on Samuel
Num.R.	Numbers Rabbah (Midrash Rabbah, Soncino) (Bamidbar Rabbah)
Pes.Rab.	Pesikta Rabbati (Braude; Yale University Press: 1968)
PRE	Pirkei de Rabbi Eliezer (Friedlander; Sepher-Hermon Press: 1981)
PRK	Pesikta de-Rab Kahana (Braude and Kapstein; JPS: 1975)
Ruth.R.	Ruth Rabbah (Midrash Rabbah, Soncino)
Sifra	Sifra on Leviticus (Torat Cohanim)
Sifre	Sifre Numbers
Sif.Dt.	Sifre Deuteronomy (Hammer; Yale University Press, 1986)
Sif.Zuta	Sifre Zuta on Numbers (Horowitz)
SOR	Seder Olam Rabbah
Tanh.	Tanhuma
Tanh.B.	Tanhuma, ed. S. Buber

| TBE | Tanna debe Eliyyahu (Braude and Kapstein; JPS: 1981) (EZ = Eliyyahu Zuta) |
| Yalk. | Yalkut Shimoni |

Mishna and Talmud (London: Soncino Press, 1952; Mishna also from H. Danby [London: OUP, 1933]):

The Babylonian Talmud is cited without any further identifying marks (e.g., San. 43a). The Jerusalem Talmud is marked "JSan." It is cited from two sources and in two alternative forms: When the text has been derived from the Bar Ilan DBS CD-Rom, the citation corresponds to the Babylonian system (e.g. JSan. 43a). Otherwise, the text refers to the Ms. Or. 4720 (Scal. 3) of the Leiden University Library, published by The Academy of the Hebrew Language (Jerusalem: 2001) (cf. JMeg. 4, 3, 75b).

Abbr.	Tractate	Order
Arak.	Arakhin (Vows of valuation)	Kodashim (Holy things)
AZ	Abodah Zarah (Idolatry)	Nezikin (Damages)
BB	Baba Bathra (Last Gate)	Nezikin
Bek.	Bekhoroth (Firstlings)	Kodashim
Ber.	Berakoth (Benedictions)	Zera'im (Seeds)
Betza	Betzah (Festival days)	Mo'ed (Festivals)
Bik.	Bikkurim (First fruits)	Zera'im
BK	Baba Kamma (First Gate)	Nezikin
BM	Baba Mezia (Middle Gate)	Nezikin
Dem.	Demai (Uncertainly-tithed produce)	Zera'im
Eduy.	Eduyoth (Testimonies)	Nezikin
Eruv.	Erubin (Shabbat boundaries)	Mo'ed
Git.	Gittin (Bills of divorce)	Nashim (Women)
Hag.	Hagigah (Festal offering)	Mo'ed
Hal.	Hallah (Dough offering)	Zera'im
Hor.	Horayoth (Instructions)	Nezikin
Hul.	Hullin (Animals killed for food)	Kodashim
Kel.	Kelim (Vessels)	Toharoth (Purity)
Ker.	Kerithoth (Extirpations)	Kodashim
Ket.	Ketuboth (Marriage contracts)	Nashim
Kid.	Kiddushin (Betrothals)	Nashim
Kil.	Kil'ayim (Diverse kinds)	Zera'im
Maas.	Maaseroth (Tithes)	Zera'im
Maas.Sheni	Maaser Sheni (Second Tithe)	Zera'im
Mak.	Makkoth (Stripes)	Nezikin
Maksh.	Makshirin (Predisposers)	Toharoth

Meg.	Megillah (Scrolls of Esther)	Mo'ed
Me'ilah	Meilah (Sacrilege)	Kodashim
Men.	Menahoth (Meal offerings)	Kodashim
Mid.	Middoth (Measurements)	Kodashim
Mikv.	Mikwaoth (Immersion pools)	Tohoroth
MK	Moed Katan (Mid-festival days)	Mo'ed
Naz.	Nazir (Nazirite vows)	Nashim
Ned.	Nedarim (Vows)	Nashim
Neg.	Negaim (Leprosy signs)	Tohoroth
Nid.	Niddah (Menstruant)	Tohoroth
Ohal.	Ohalot (Tents)	Toharoth
Orla	Orla (Fruit of young trees)	Zera'im
PA	(Pirkei) Avot (Sayings of the Fathers)	Nezikin
Par.	Parah (Red Heifer)	Toharoth
Pe'ah	Peah (Corners/gleaning)	Zera'im
Pes.	Pesahim (Passover)	Mo'ed
RH	Rosh Hashanah (New Year)	Mo'ed
San.	Sanhedrin (Sanhedrin)	Nezikin
Shab.	Sabbath (Shabbat)	Mo'ed
Shek.	Shekalim (Shekel dues)	Mo'ed
Shevu.	Shebuoth (Oaths)	Nezikin
Shevi.	Shebiith (Seventh year)	Zera'im
Sot.	Sotah (Suspected adulteress)	Nashim
Suk.	Sukkah (Tabernacles)	Mo'ed
Ta'anit	Taanith (Fast days)	Mo'ed
Tam.	Tamid (Daily whole-offering)	Kodashim
Tem.	Temurah (Substituted offering)	Kodashim
Ter.	Terumoth (Heve offerings)	Zera'im
Toh.	Tohoroth (Cleannesses)	Tohoroth
Yad.	Yadaim (Hands)	Toharoth
Yev.	Yebamoth (Sisters-in-law)	Nashim
Yoma	Yoma (Day of Atonement)	Mo'ed
Zav.	Zabim (Fluxes)	Tohoroth
Zev.	Zebahim (Animal offerings)	Kodashim

Minor Tractates:

ARN	Aboth D'Rabbi Nathan, version A (ARNᵃ) (Soncino); version B (ARNᵇ), The Fathers According to Rabbi Nathan, ed. A. Saldarini (Leiden: Brill, 1975)
DER	Derek 'Erez Rabbah (Soncino)
DEZ	Derek 'Erez Zuta (Soncino)
Ger.	Gerim (Soncino)

Kal.   Kallah (Soncino)
Kal.Rab.   Kallah Rabbathi (Soncino)
Sem.   Semahot (Soncino)
Sof.   Soferim (Soncino)

Tosefta (Zuckermandel):
Tos.   Tosefta

Prayer Book (Artscroll, Ashkenaz):
PB   Prayer Book

New Testament Apocrypha, Early Christian and Patristic Writings:
1 Clem.   First Letter of Clement (Loeb Classical Library)
Aug.   Augustus
Clem.   Clement of Alexandria
Did.   Didache (Loeb Classical Library)
Dio Chrys.   Dio Chrysostom
Epiph.   Epiphanius
Ep.Barn.   Epistle of Barnabas (Loeb Classical Library)
Eus.   Eusebius (Loeb Classical Library)
Gos.Thom.   Gospel of Thomas
Hipp.   Hippolytus
Ignat.   Ignatius
Iren.   Irenaeus
Just.   Justin Martyr
Ps.-Clem.   Pseudo-Clement
Tert.   Tertullian

Greek and Latin Authors:
Arist.   Aristotle
Demos.   Demosthenes
Diog.Laert.   Diogenes Laertius
Epict.   Epictetus
Juv.   Juvenal
Lact.   Lactantius
Plut.   Plutarch
Suet.   Suetonius
Tac.   Tacitus

Maimonides (Rambam):
Guide   Guide for the Perplexed
Yad   Mishneh Torah

HOW TO USE THE
COMMENTARY

The Commentary's primary purpose is to provide a reading of the text of Galatians in its Jewish context. A correlation of the New Testament material with the literature of the time offers an important tool for understanding both the larger context of the biblical events and the telling of the story in its natural setting and circumstances. Where the actual quote from contemporary sources was felt to be of benefit to the reader, it has been cited in full. Perhaps the most difficult passages will be those dependent upon halakhic explanations – together with the methodology employed in these texts. The reader is asked to have patience with these, since they are generally important for the argument. Although those who find the intricacies rather too heavy may need to satisfy him/herself with a more general understanding, it is hoped that wherever possible, s/he will devote some time to reach an understanding of these difficult passages.

In order to make the explanation intelligible, it was considered prudent to include much of the background material which would otherwise be found in a biblical dictionary or other aid. These are found in the excursi inserted into the body of the text – such as those on Gentiles and godfearers in 2:1-10. The reader who understands the interpretation may skip the contextualised detail. If s/he does not know any ancient languages, s/he may ignore the footnotes which cite the original language. Although pains have been taken to explain arguments which are dependent on the original language, some passages will prove more difficult than others. Some perseverance is called for on the part of the non-Hebrew speaker, and will hopefully be rewarded. The more scholarly reader will gain much from the language notes and cross-references.

The Commentary's format includes the following features:

- All bibliographical references have been included in the text. Thus (Hemer: 208), for example, refers to C. Hemer, *The Book of Acts in the Setting of Hellenistic History*, the full bibliographical details being given in the Bibliography. Where an author has more than one publication or where more than one author shares the same surname, an abbreviated reference to the title is added (e.g., Lichtenstein, Studies). The original text of primary sources (Aramaic, Greek, Hebrew, Latin) has largely been confined to footnotes.

- The use of italics reflects the NASB text, which employs italics to denote words which have been supplied in the English translation but do not appear in the Greek. Bold emphases, on the other hand, mark stresses indicated by the present authors. Bold marking in the English/Hebrew text indicates particular words for identification and/or emphasis. The same purpose is served in the Greek text by italics.

- Internal cross-references – i.e., to other places within the Commentary – have been developed in order to enable the reader to gain a full picture of the topic under discussion. Where a particular verse deals with a specific subject, the reader is directed to those verses where other aspects of the same subject are covered. In this way, it is important to consider that parts of the argument in later chapters are at times dependent on discussions brought in earlier sections. This format also enables the reader who wishes to make a comprehensive study of any particular theme thereby has at his fingertips a list of passages where the topic is reviewed.

- The above cross-references relate to the verses which the Commentary treats as a unit. These are marked in the text, in brackets, by "see" – e.g., "see 2:1-10 (n136), 15-21 (n292), 3:1-5 (nn14, 28), 4:12-20, 5:2-12 (verse 11), 24-26, 6:1f (verses 11, 15, 17), and verses 15-16b, 21-24." References to other chapters include the chapter and verse unit and, where appropriate, a footnote number. Verses within the same chapter are marked as "verses 2-12." References in square brackets (e.g., [3:19-20]) indicate a passage of less immediately direct relevance.

- External cross-references are marked in the text, also in brackets, by "cf."

- The external cross-references follow a consistent order and are separated by a semi-colon: a) Tanakh and New Testament (not separated); b) Apocrypha and Pseudepigrapha (not separated); c) Qumran; d) Josephus; e) Philo; f) Strabo; g) Targumim; h) Rabbinic texts – Midrashim, Mishna, Tosefta, Jerusalem Talmud, Babylonian Talmud, Prayer Book, Yad (Mishneh Torah); i) New Testament apocrypha; j) Patristics; k) Classical writers.

While the glossary is confined to primary sources and terms, the reader is encouraged to use the Index as a source of basic definitions. The Index gives both Hebrew and English versions of terms where both are used (e.g., Passover and Pesach), and a rudimentary definition of Hebrew, Greek, and Latin terms (e.g., matan Torah – the giving of the Torah).

We have endeavoured to make the Index as detailed as possible to give the reader the maximum information and to aid him/her in understanding which ideas and concepts occupy the Commentary, are central to its focus, and serve as hermeneutical building blocks. By adding sub-references (*See also*) it is also hoped that readers will be able to broaden their knowledge of specific themes/topics.

INTRODUCTION

Author

Paul's name appears in the epistolary preface (cf. 1:1) and his authorship is one of the least controverted issues in the whole study of the letter. Pauline authorship of Galatians was an unquestioned postulate in antiquity, overwhelming even Marcion's drastically anti-pauline sentiments. Modern scholarship, which has established for itself a corpus of "authentic" pauline literature, employs Galatians as the criterion for inclusion or exclusion: "If Galatians is not by Paul, no NT letter is by him, for none has better claim" (Longenecker, Galatians: lviii).[1]

While we know Paul from his letters – some would say exclusively so – we then allow this information to determine what of Paul's thought is authentic to him and what is not.[2] The paradox of this circumstance does not appear to generate permanent perplexity. The typical assumption posits that the theological argument of Galatians is characteristically pauline in both method and content, the particularity expressing itself in an anti-Jewish, antinomian attitude – the assertion of the latter having turned Paul, over generations, into the archetypal "Christian."[3]

---

[1] For a list of scholars who do not accept pauline authorship, cf. Betz, Galatians: 1n1; for the implications of an amanuensis on pauline authorship, see below, **Form**.

[2] This, of course, is the best-case scenario, where Marcion's influence has been rejected and Paul is at least accepted as a legitimate New Testament representative. Once this position has been allowed, academic convention subsequently confronts scholars with the necessity of determining whether they accept the pauline corpus and Acts as essentially contradictory or as essentially harmonious texts (see also below, **Form**).

[3] The irony here is also almost universally missed – that the author of the quintessentially "Christian" fruit of "love, peace, patience, kindness, goodness" should be made to demonstrate the opposite attributes of enmity, strife, jealousy, anger, disputes, dissensions, factions, and envyings towards his fellow Jews – and, moreover, to foster such sentiments in his followers.

The general picture which has emerged from Christian commentary on the corpus of this celebrated "founder of Christianity" is that of an intellectually and emotionally confused, conflicted, convoluted, contradictory figure – all traits of his Jewishness which converge into resolution in his "conversion." This Paul is frequently depicted as able to achieve his "true" nature only by repudiating his "former life" – which, being in the Messiah, he then turns into a caricature, devoid of any possible redeeming features (in both senses of the phrase). As the "father of Christian anti-Judaism," Paul has also – irrespective of the fact that Romans 8-11 (*sic*) remains in every scholar's Bible – become the supercessionist *par excellence*: the author and founder, as it were, of replacement theology.[4]

The tentacles of academia proving so pervasive and tenacious, it has taken pauline scholarship until the most recent of years to understand that this is indeed its prevalent picture of Paul and to comprehend the need to "reinvent" him, as it were.[5] The outstandingly self-evident nature of the statements which such a scholar as Gager employs to portray the "New Paul" witnesses to the depth of the "blindness" which Christian commentators have traditionally displayed towards the New Testament texts:

> . . . I will rigorously avoid the term *Christianity* when speaking of Jesus, his early followers, and Paul. Instead I will employ the term *Jesus-movement* . . . Behind this shift of terms, from Christian to Jesus-movement, lies a much broader contention, namely, that there was no Christianity at all until well after the time of Jesus, his earliest followers, and Paul. In the case of Jesus and his early followers, this position is now taken for granted – they belong totally within the context of first-century Judaism in Roman

---

[4] The fact that Romans 9-11 has routinely been treated in such a "Christianly" pauline fashion as to turn Paul's argument on its head is further evidence of the strength to which his "Christian" character has been developed. For recent "New Pauline" readings of Romans, cf. Nanos, *Mystery*; Stowers. While those commentators who have insisted that Paul actually means what he says in Romans 9-11 are to be commended, the focus on these three chapters has frequently obscured the fact that they form the point of the letter as a whole and that the proper unit is not 9-11 but an extended argument which starts in 3:1 and climaxes in 11, the following chapters constituting the halakhic (practical) outworking of the intellectual excursus (cf. Shulam and Le Cornu: 149n4, 303ff, 325ff).

[5] Cf. Gager. It is unfortunate that Gager's book should carry such an ambiguous title ("Reinventing Paul") when he appears to precisely apprehend the point that Paul needs to be "rehabilitated" (in the sense of bringing him back home) – not invented a second time round. The fact may reflect the circumstance that even now, in the "New Pauline" era, scholars find it inordinately difficult to extricate themselves from the original invention.

Palestine and not to the history of later Christianity. To use the term Christian is anachronistic and misleading. The argument here is simple and convincing: the fact that his followers proclaimed Jesus the Messiah (Christ is simply the Greek word used by Jews for the Hebrew *Mashiach*/Messiah) does not place them outside the pale of Judaism. They become Christians only when they begin to view themselves, and are viewed by others, as standing outside, above, or even against Judaism. In other words, this is not a book about early Christianity. In fact, it is not about Christianity at all. Along with others, I hold that this position must be extended to Paul – and beyond. He, too, belongs to the history of first-century Judaism. (Gager: viii)[6]

While not convinced by Gager's particular solution – that Paul consistently and exclusively addresses Gentiles (as if that would in itself diminish the effect of his so-called denigration of the Torah in Jewish ears) – the recognition that the New Testament writings are Jewish texts constitutes the guiding principle of this series of commentaries on the Jewish background of the New Testament.[7] "Christian" understandings of Paul regularly understand Paul to stand in dichotomous opposition to Judaism and all things Jewish. Once an assumption of such a basic proportion is made it cannot but colour every aspect of pauline exegesis. It becomes the standard against which Paul's thought is measured and

---

[6] This is not the place to enter into a discussion of Gager's interpretative position, with which we find ourselves in serious disagreement. Suffice it to say that the erudite scholar's endeavours to reinvent Paul continue, in our opinion, to be made at Jewish expense. The argument that Paul is exclusively addressing Gentiles – itself a very difficult claim to sustain – effectively denies Paul involvement in any Jewish discussion or content. Just as significantly, Gager's criticism of his predecessors, whose debt he fully acknowledges, appears to equate their acceptance of *anything* Christian – but peculiarly Jesus as Israel's redeemer – as a betrayal of the New Paul. This smacks very heavily of two covenant theology.

[7] For the present exegetical understanding of Paul's attitude towards the Torah (already an expression which betrays a "Christian" bias, but necessary because the weight of past history demands that the issue be addressed rather than taken as a given) as expressed in Galatians, see Appendix and below, **Argument**. Even the title of this series reflects a certain accommodation to Christian convention. The proper designation would avoid "Background," which implies that the book is not Jewish but can be explained by certain Jewish ideas and beliefs. The position which the series adopts is precisely that the New Testament documents *per se* are Jewish texts. Segal's comment regarding Strack-Billerbeck is very revealing in this respect: "In spite of the handbook's sometimes unappreciated erudition, its methodology is entirely suspect. Rather a commentary to the Mishnah should be written, using the New Testament as marginalia that demonstrates antiquity" (Segal, Paul: xv).

authentically pauline views and terminology determined.[8] It should be evident that approaching Paul as a Jew – appropriately to his own witness – leads to a very different perspective. His context is then governed by Jewish rather than so-called "Christian" principles, ideas, and methods.[9] It subsequently behoves the Christian commentator and reader alike to endeavour to familiarise themselves with this milieu. Once Paul and his texts are placed within such a framework, work can begin in attempting to apprehend Paul and his communications with those around him in the worlds in which he lived.[10]

Date and destination
The dating of Galatians (cf. 1:2, 3:1) – which has been identified as "one of the most knotty problems in Pauline studies" (Longenecker, Galatians: lxxiii, and for the following discussion) – has traditionally hinged on three independent but interrelated issues: a) the location of "Galatia"; b) Paul's visits to Jerusalem according to Acts and Galatians; and c) Galatians' relation to other pauline literature, specifically to Romans (and 1 Thessalonians).

The term "Galatia" (Γαλατία) possesses two distinct usages in ancient texts, one relating to an ethnic population, the other to Roman provincial boundaries. Greek and Latin writers identify the Γαλάται ("Galatians") interchangeably with the Κέλται/Κελτοί (*Celtae*; Celts) and *Galli* (Gauls) (cf. Pausanius, *Desc. of Greece*, 1.4.1, 10.3.3). The various terms reflect the places to which, having originated in the Danube basin in central Europe, the Celts migrated – Switzerland, southern Germany, northern Italy, and thence into France and Britain, eventually making their way southeastwards into the Balkan peninsula and Asia Minor. The name "Celt" is characteristic to Britain, the people being known in France as "Gauls" and their territory "Gallia." In Asia Minor, they were designated

---

[8] This is the positive side of Gager's argument, even where we do not see that he truly "saves" Paul. Rather than placing decisive weight on what appear to be "anti-Jewish" passages, as if they gave the final word, treating the "pro-Jewish" passages as inconsistent, Gager suggests that Paul's readers can – and should – just as properly begin with the "pro-Israel" set and work in the other direction (cf. ibid: 9). For an extended biography of Paul's life and ministry, see Appendix.

[9] We would go so far as to say – in conjunction with Gager as quoted above – that Paul has no connection with "Christianity," his whole thought, including his focus on Jesus, his death and resurrection, remains Jewish. To the extent that no Roman persecution of the early community as distinctive from Judaism exists prior to Nero, Galatians itself witnesses to this perspective. For the present understanding of the persecution of which Paul speaks in the letter, see below, **Occasion and circumstances**.

[10] For a brief explication of this effort in relation to Paul's hermeneutics, see below, **Theological pointers**.

"Galatians (Gallograeci; Γαλλογραικοί)" living in Gallograecia – "the land of the Greek-speaking Gauls."[11]

The Galatians crossed from Europe (Greece) to Asia Minor in 278/77 B.C.E., some 20,000 traversing the Hellespont to join the forces of the Bithynian king Nicomedes as mercenaries (cf. Pausanius, *Desc. of Greece* 7.6.8).[12] They were renowned warriors of impressive physical stature, whose barbarian ways greatly intimidated their enemies (cf. Livy, *Hist.* 38.17.3-9). Having settled in Ancyra (modern Ankara), in the heartland of Asia Minor, they proceeded to take control over an area of 200 miles southwest to northeast in the arid steppes of central Anatolia. Following a series of battles, they finally lost much of their power to Attalus I, king of Pergamum, c. 232. Although they retained their independence, their territory was restricted to northern Asia Minor, bounded by Bithynia and Paphlagonia to the north, Pontus to the east, Phrygia to west, and Cappadocia and Lycaonia to the south.

In the wake of the seleucid king Antiochus III's defeat by the Romans at Magnesia in 190 B.C.E., the whole of Asia Minor also fell to the Romans in 189 B.C.E. Despite their prior support of Antiochus, the Galatian leaders transferred their allegiance to the Romans, their subsequent loyalty during the Roman wars against Mithridates VI of Pontus (95-63 B.C.E.) gaining them important territorial grants. In 64 B.C.E., Pompey changed Galatia's status from that of a dependent to a client kingdom. Some twenty years later Mark Antony conferred the kingdom, together with the eastern part of Paphlagonia, on the late Galatian king Deiotaros' son-in-law, Kastor. On Kastor's death, Rome placed Galatia in the hands of Amyntas, Deiotaros' former secretary. Amyntas not only preserved the Phrygio-Pisidian territory but also gained a part of Pamphylia and, subsequently, also a substantial segment of Lycaonia – to which Augustus added Cilicia Tracheia and much of Pisidia and Isauria as a reward for Amyntas' aid during the battle of Actium (31 B.C.E.). During his reign Amyntas controlled the whole of central Turkey, reaching to the Mediterranean, while other Galatian peoples occupied territory in northeastern Anatolia.

The Galatians were composed of three tribes: The Trocmi – the most powerful – settled in the east around Tavium. The Tectosages possessed the fortress of Ancyra, while the Tolistobogii occupied the territory in the west around Pessinus (cf. Strabo, *Geog.* 12.5.1f; Appian, *Syr.* 6.31, 7.42) (cf. Gill and Gempf: 380ff, and for the following discussion). Although the Celtic dialect survived, in rural areas, until the fourth century C.E., and the tribes possessed their own military/political organisation, Livy speaks of them as "degenerates, of mixed race (degeneres sunt, mixti)" (*Hist.*

---

[11] Cf. Livy, *Hist.* 38.17.3-9; Strabo, *Geog.* 12.5.1; Appian, *Mith.* 114.
[12] For the pre-history of the region (Phrygians, Cimmerians, and Persians), cf. Scott: 182-84.

38.17.9). Despite the name "Gallogrecians (Γαλλογραικοί)" which he gives them, the Galatians appear to have been more influenced by local Phrygian than hellenistic culture, participating in the temple of the Phrygian goddess Cybele, the Mother of gods, in Pessinus, for example (cf. Strabo, *Geog.* 12.5.3). The Galatian nobility apparently ruled over the native population, the three tribal kings governing in the first century B.C.E. and Deiotaros gaining power ·of all Galatia following the civil war of 42 B.C.E. At Amyntas' death in 25 B.C.E., the territory of Galatia included a large region of southern Asia Minor which had never been ethnically Galatian.

When Amyntas was killed in battle against the Homanadenses, rather than instating Amyntas' son in power, Augustus chose to reorganise the Galatian kingdom as a Roman province (*Provincia Galatia*), under the authority of a Roman governor. Writing around the turn of the first centuries, Strabo remarks: "At the present time the Romans possess both this country [i.e., Galatia] and the whole of the country that became subject to Amyntas, having united them into one province"[13] (*Geog.* 12.5.1). The Roman province consequently included the original Galatian territory – from Pessinus in the west to Tavium in the east – with the addition of substantial areas of Isauria, Pisidia, and Phrygia, including Pisidian Antioch, Iconium, Lystra, and Derbe (cf. Acts 13:14-14:25).

When the province was further enlarged in 5 B.C.E. through the annexation of a large section of Paphlagonia to the north, and again c. 2 B.C.E. with the addition of part of Pontus (Pontus Galaticus), it effectively extended from the Black Sea to the Mediterranean (Pamphylia) (cf. Pliny, *Nat.Hist.* 5.42.147). The province was reduced in size by Vespasian's detachment of most of Pisidia c. 74 C.E., only returning to its ancient ethnological dimensions c. 297 C.E. when, portions having already been ceded to the province of Cilicia, the remainder of the southern regions became part of the province of Pisidia, with Pisidian Antioch as its capital and Iconium as its second city.

Strabo describes the population of the Roman province of Galatia as composed of numerous tribal groups, including the Trocmi, Tolistobogii, and Tectosages, "each speaking the same language and differing from each other in no respect (τριῶν δὲ ὄντων ἐθνῶν ὁμολώττων καὶ κατ' ἄλλο οὐδὲν ἐξηλλαγμένων)" (*Geog.* 12.5.1). This assertion is corroborated by evidence of linguistic independence: Acts 14:11 indicates that the Lycaonians spoke Lycaonian, Pisidian and Phrygian possibly also having been spoken (cf. Mitchell: 1:172). Within the province, autonomous city states in large regional territories were established, such as the constitution of the Celtic tribes in Pessinus, Tavium, and Ancyra, the last serving as the chief provincial city (cf. ABD: 2:870). Despite these distinctions, Strabo also

---

[13] νῦν δ' ἔχουσι ῾Ρωμαῖοι καὶ ταύτην καὶ τὴν ὑπὸ τῷ ᾿Αμύνα γενομένην πᾶσαν εἰς μίαν συναγαγόντες ἐπαρχίαν.

maintains that the Roman failure to divide them according to tribes made the various groups difficult to identify (cf. *Geog.* 12.4.4, 13.4.12). Simultaneously, colonies were also set up, thirteen in all and primarily in the south, including those of Pisidian Antioch, Iconium, and Lystra. The colonies were primarily inhabited by discharged Roman veterans, adding a Roman element to the local ethnic mix. Garrison legions were further stationed in the south of the province, around Pisidian Antioch.

Two points emerge clearly from this discussion. The ethnic designation – Galatians as a Celtic tribe settled in central Anatolia – relates Galatia exclusively to a northern location. This fact serves in New Testament circles as the basis for what is known as the "north Galatia" theory. While relatively straightforward in geographical terms, this thesis runs into serious difficulties when integrated into the framework of Acts – especially in terms of establishing any correspondence between Galatians 2:1-10 and Acts 15 (see below).[14] Recognition of Galatia as a Roman *province*, on the other hand, allows for the identification of the "congregations of Galatia (ταῖς ἐκκλησίαις τῆς Γαλατίας)" (1:2) as the places Paul visited in Acts 13-14: Pisidian Antioch, Iconium, Lystra, and Derbe. This provincial rather than ethnic designation determines southern Galatia as the location of Paul's addressees.

Under a south Galatian theory, the first exigency imposed is to address the objections raised against: a) the very existence of an extensive Galatian province; b) the usage of "Galatia" in reference to the/a province; and c) the identity of any "Galatians" within such a province (cf. Hemer: 290f, and for the following discussion).

The primary designation of the Latin *provincia* was in fact to a "sphere of duty," the concept only secondarily bearing a geographical connotation. Galatia appears in this respect to have served as the functional inheritor of the province of Cilicia, charged with the task of safeguarding Rome's eastern connections. Like Cilicia (cf. Cicero, *Verr.* 1.38.95) – which at one point omitted Cilicia proper – the Galatian province's territorial aspect accommodated to fluctuating needs.

Ancient sources provide clear evidence that the name "Galatia" referred to the whole province (cf. Eutropius 7.10; *ILS* 9499 ll. 6f; *IG Rom.* 3.263; *CIG* I 3991). Various inscriptions witness to the presence of benefactors in south Galatian cities who are designated as officials in "Galatia." References to dating according to Roman officials and to the latter themselves are available from Lycaonian, Isaurian, and Phrygian cities (Iconium), where the men in question are known independently to have held office in the province of Galatia. The province possessed

---

[14] It should be evident that this approach presumes the legitimacy of attempting to "harmonise" Acts with Paul's letters – an endeavour which does not find universal favour amongst all New Testament scholars. For an excellent review of the literature, cf. Riesner: 1-32; Hemer.

provincial officials known as "Galatarchs" – corresponding to the better-known Asiarchs (cf. Acts 19:31) – as well as a Galatian league of cities (κοινὸν Γαλατῶν; koinon Galatōn).

This testimony can be adduced in relation to the charge that reference to Pisidians, Phrygians, and Lycaonians as "Galatians" – if Paul is addressing south Galatian congregations – would be counterproductive, conveying offense by ethnically misidentifying his audience. Yet if the communities were spread over various ethnic regions, the provincial name is not only a proper and legitimate designation but may have constituted the sole method of inclusive address. The aggressive propagation of the imperial cult in the temples of Ancyra, Pessinus, and Antioch may have constituted part of an attempt to promote a provincial identity (cf. Riesner: 289). It is generally noted, if with caution, that Paul displays an unmistakable preference for reserving proper names to designate provinces (cf. ibid).[15]

Physical evidence of provincial status can be found in the road linking Ancyra to Pisidian Antioch, officially maintained by the Galatian legate irrespective of its passage for a considerable distance through proconsular Asia. Boundary stones discovered in the extreme south and west evidently mark not merely city confines but also provincial territory, clearly distinguishing the provinces of Galatia and Asia.

The central difficulty posed to this provincial theory is the presence of Galatia as one component in a list of other territorial units – a custom reflected among both Greek and Latin provincial formulations. Such usage gives the distinct impression that "Galatia" carries a narrow, regional/ethnic (non-provincial) sense. The force of this argument is, however, mitigated by the variability of the lists and their divergences and omissions. These anomalies – which appear to relate to the constant shifting of provincial boundaries and which seem to occur most frequently during a period when Galatia and Cappodocia and their various appendages were united in a larger entity – demand a cautious use of the evidence they provide.

Against objections that the province was always referred to as the "Galatic province (*provincia Galatica*)," numerous examples can be produced of the usage Galatia/Γαλατία (cf. Ptolemy, *Geog.* 5.14; Tac.*Hist.* 2.9; *Ann.* 13.35) (cf. ibid: 287). Josephus identifies the Galatians with the descendants of Japhet's son Gomer (cf. Gen. 10:2f) and ascribes their

---

[15] Cf. Rom. 15:26, 16:5; 1 Cor. 16:15, 19; 2 Cor. 1:8, 8:1, 9:2, 11:9-10; 1 Thess. 1:7, 4:10. The geographical theory proposed by Scott attributes the steps of Paul's itinerary to (half of) the territory of Japhet – which approximately corresponds to the contemporary Roman empire, the land inhabited by the Kittim according the table of nations tradition (cf. Gen. 10:4) (cf. Scott: 144). Scott also suggests that the table of nations tradition lies behind Paul's usage of Roman provincial nomenclature (cf. ibid: 181).

homeland to the Roman province of Galatia (cf. *Ant.* 1.123, 126) (cf. Scott: [40-49], 201-8).

If Galatia is allowed as a province, definitive proof is still lacking to identify Galatia and "Galatians" (cf. Hemer: 299f, and for the following discussion). Various ancient sources appear to bestow the designation on peoples not ethnically Galatian. Such is Pausanius' description of the habit of "the Gauls who inhabit Pessinus (Γαλατῶν ... οἱ Πεσσινοῦντα ἔχοντες)" of abstaining from pork (*Desc. of Greece* 7.17.10) – a reference to a religious custom and a time framework both specifically *Phrygian*. A first-century inscription from Pednelissus – a city on the southern edge of Pisidia – appears to designate it unequivocally as "the city of the Galatians (ἡ πόλις Γαλατῶν)." A number of slaves mentioned in a group of inscriptions at Delphi, not one bearing a Celtic name and many associated with Phrygian elements, are also identified as "Galatian (Γαλάτης/Γαλάτισσα)." Conversely, many names in southern Galatia reflect a markedly Anatolian (north Galatian), especially Phrygian, cultural and religious influence. The statistics in fact indicate that the mix of populations in northern and southern Galatia corresponded fairly closely, seriously mitigating the claim for "Galatians" as strictly "north Galatian."

The above discussion suggests that no conclusive evidence exists to exclude an identification of Galatia with the Roman province which, during Paul's lifetime, stretched from Pontus to Pamphylia on the Mediterranean. The central New Testament texts upon which the identification of the Galatian location – and therefore communities – rests are three in Acts: Paul's journey through Pisidian Antioch, Iconium, Lystra, and Derbe in 13:14-14:25, and two specific allusions to Galatia in 16:6 and 18:23.

The Greek of Acts 16:6 is notoriously awkward to translate (cf. Hemer: 282f, and for the following discussion). Literally, it reads "the Phrgyian and [unarticled] Galatian region (τὴν Φρυγίαν καὶ Γαλατικὴν χώραν)." Scholars have long debated whether Φρυγίαν (Frygian) is a noun or an adjective, the difference producing an allusion either to two distinct places (Phrygia and Galatia) or to one place (Phrygian Galatia). It has traditionally been objected that no sources witness to the use of "Phrygia" as an adjective and that so understanding the term pushes the meaning of καὶ (kai), which normally means "and," into an untenable sense of "or" – the adjectival form demanding a type of hyphen ("the Phrygian or, that is, Galatian, region"). Despite such arguments, numerous examples of Phrygia as an adjective (and in the feminine, as in Acts) can in fact be derived from Pseudo-Aristotle, the Sibylline Oracles, Strabo, Apollodorus, Dio Chrysostom, Pollux, Alciphron, Arrian, Aelian, Diogenes Laertius, Pseudo-Lucian, and Athenaeus – as well as from numerous inscriptions dating from almost every period from Alexander the Great to the fourth century C.E. Here, too, examples are readily available, drawn up partly to parry the difficulty anticipated by this verse.

On a dual-reference theory (Phrygia and Galatia), Paul, Barnabas, and Timothy leave Lystra and the cities to which they were delivering the apostolic encyclical and travel northwards, first to Phrygia and then to Galatia – obviously a north Galatian perspective. Not having been ruled out on the grounds of Greek grammar, the south Galatian theory can, however, appeal to further known usage in understanding the phrase as referring to "Phrygia Galatica." This method invokes the analagous forms of "Pontus Galaticus" and "Phrygia Asiania," both well attested in ancient sources.[16] Such an area corresponds to Phrygia Paroreius, lying on either side of Sultan Dağ, the mountainous range separating Pisidian Antioch and Iconium. Ethnically Phrygian, this region was divided between the Roman provinces of Asia and Galatia (cf. ABD: 871).

This location is geographically consistent with the route which Luke describes the group as following: Leaving Derbe and Lystra, the party reaches Mysia whence they descend to Troas (cf. Acts 16:7-8). To have travelled through ethnic (north) Galatia at this point would have entailed a 125 mile (200 km) passage northeastward of any natural route from Lystra to Mysia in southwest Asia Minor (cf. ibid). (This argument holds true also for Acts 18:22-23, 19:1.) Nor does any logic exist in turning westward towards Mysia if the intended destination is Bithynia in the north (cf. Acts 16:7) (cf. Riesner: 283).

The northern Galatian identity is frequently defended on the grounds that it makes good sense of Paul's double journey to the region as intimated in Galatians 4:13: ". . . it was because of a bodily illness that I preached the gospel to you the first time (δι᾽ ἀσθένειαν τῆς σαρκὸς εὐηγγελισάμην ὑμῖν τὸ πρότερον)." Paul's statement clearly implies that he has visited the communities at least once. On a north Galatian reading, the initial visit refers to Acts 16:6 and the second to Acts 18:23, τὸ πρότερον (to proteron) being taken in the strict sense of the "former" of two (cf. ibid: 290). Here too, however, Greek usage fails to lie on the north Galatian side. The idea of the "first of two" was generally conveyed by the term πρῶτος (prōtos). The most accurate meaning of τὸ πρότερον is "at the first" or "originally" – without any specific indication of further events (cf. Hemer: 305n73).[17]

---

[16] Cf. Jos.*Ant.* 1.201-8; Ptolemy, *Geog.* 5.2, 4.

[17] North Galatianists at times contend that Gal. 4:14, wherein Paul declares that he was received "as an angel of God, as the Messiah Jesus *himself* (ὡς ἄγγελον θεοῦ ἐδέξασθέ με, ὡς Χριστὸν Ἰησοῦν)" cannot be reconciled with Luke's portrait of Paul and Barnabas' reception by the Lycaonians as Hermes and Zeus, failing to allow for the possibility that the "illness" may either allude to the effects of his stoning (cf. Acts 14:5, 19) or to a more generalised "human frailty" (cf. Longenecker, Galatians: lxv, lxix; Gill and Gempf: 57).

Arguments regarding strategy may be adduced at this point. Scholars researching the motives behind Paul's choice of itinerary – where he possessed the freedom of decision and was not compelled into visits either by *force majeure* or by human duress – have indicated that the most significant factors appear to include visiting places with Jewish communities and/or the local synagogue, the latter with its combined Jewish and godfearing elements; clement or inclement travelling conditions; attention to Roman provinces and their centres; the welcome or hostility extended him; avoidance of areas already served by others; and the creation and strengthening of congregations (cf. Riesner: 255-256).

With regard to the first point, the evidence concerning the Jewish communities of the region is mixed. On the one hand, the abundance of information relating to the strength and vibrancy of the Jewish population of Asia Minor in general is such that it occupies an exclusive section in a recent book devoted to Jewish-gentile relations in the ancient world (cf. Feldman, Jew: 69-74). When specific communities are detailed, however, their overwhelming majority fall into regions in southern Galatia, including Pamphylia, Phrygia, Pisidia, and Lycaonia (cf. Safrai and Stern: 148-150).[18] References to places in north (ethnic) Galatia appear to be non-existent, the one possible allusion to Ancyra being uniformly dismissed as a mis-reconstruction and the presence of a Jewish community not even being discussed by the foremost research (cf. Schürer: 3:34-35).

While 2 Maccabees 8:20 speaks of the people of Israel fighting with the Seleucids against "the Galatians (τοὺς Γαλάτας)" in Babylon, little is known of the event. Although rabbinic texts refer quite frequently to גליא (Gallia), the geographic specifications are very vague. R. Akiva went to Gallia – as also to Africa and Arabia, quite likely as an envoy to the Jewish communities there (cf. RH 26a: . . . כשהלכתי לגליא). Several Sages are identified as "Galatians": Nachum (or Menachem) [נחום/מנחם איש גליא], whose shabbat (sabbath) halakhah was followed[19] – although the allusion here may be either to Gaul or the Galilee[20] (cf. Lichtenstein, Geography: 92).[21] The general statistics indicate that Jewish settlement in Asia Minor during the period under question was concentrated in four commercial centres and ten towns located at important crossroads (cf. Safrai and Stern: 718). Epigraphical evidence from north Galatia from the third to sixth centuries C.E. indicates that small Jewish communities existed in rural districts (cf. ABD: 2:871).

---

[18] Cf. Acts 2:9-10, 13:14, 14:1, 19-25, 16:1-2; 1 Macc. 15:23; Jos.*Ant.* 12.147-53; *CA* 1.176-82; Philo, *Leg.* 281; Cicero, *Pro Flac.* 28-68.

[19] Cf. Tos.Eruv. 11[8]:10; JBer. 4, 4, 8b; Ket. 60a.

[20] Cf. Tanh.Emor 14; Yalk.Lev. 493, 643. Cf. also R. Yudan (Gen.R. 51:9; Lev.R. 9:7, 20:4).

[21] This confusion makes the identity of any decisive reference to Gaul extremely uncertain.

Two further factors devolve from the Jewish presence in northern and southern Galatia. The southern communities' accessibility – particularly from the coast, whence Paul's party arrived – contrasts with the north's geographical and linguistic isolation. If a Jewish presence existed in both halves of the extended territory, it is strange that those whose views Paul is countering – whoever they are determined to be – should have confined their activities to the north, the north Galatia theory maintaining that the communities in the south are not addressed in Galatians.[22] The northern territory was remoter and thus more difficult to reach – a fact of significance in determining whether or not the "influencers" are local or outsiders to the region (see below, **Occasion and circumstances**).[23] Once there, moreover, they may have faced a graver language difficulty in the local preference of pre-Graeco/Roman (neo-Phrygian) dialects, the interior regions becoming hellenized at a far later date than those in greater proximity to the coast (cf. Riesner: 283n8, 286; Hemer: 286n28).

The issue may be further pursued in reference to the presence/absence of biographical allusions in Galatians and Acts (cf. Longenecker, Galatians: lxx-lxxii, and for the following discussion). The most noteworthy of these is Paul's silence in Galatians regarding Timothy. The latter was a native of Lystra or Derbe and, having impressed Paul on their first meeting, accompanied him and Silas as the party continued to Europe (cf. Acts 16:1ff), proving a constant and faithful disciple throughout Paul's ministry.[24] In contrast to other letters and other figures,[25] Paul fails to include greetings from Timothy to those who would presumably know him well – either from his home region (on a south Galatian theory) or from his participation in Paul's later travels (cf. Acts 16:1-3, 18:23, 20:4). Taken with the considerations listed above, this fact may suggest that Timothy was yet unknown to Paul when he penned Galatians.[26] While Timothy's referential absence creates certain difficulties for both theories, it appears capable of carrying a more constructive role with respect to the south Galatian theory (see below).

---

[22] For the relation of these people to Paul, see below, **Occasion and circumstances**.

[23] The term "influencers" is, of course, adopted from Nanos (Irony) (see below, **Occasion and circumstances**).

[24] Cf. Acts 17:14-15, 18:5, 19:22, 20:4; Rom. 16:21; 1 Cor. 4:17, 16:10; 2 Cor. 1:19; Phil. 2:19; 1 Thess. 3:2; 2 Thess. 1:1; 1 Timothy; 2 Timothy. This evidence is supported by Acts (Luke) and Paul (in his letters) alike.

[25] Cf. Rom. 16:21; 1 Cor. 1:1; 2 Cor. 1:1; Phil. 1:1; Col. 1:1; 1 Thess. 1:1; 2 Thess. 1:1; Phlm 1.

[26] This circumstance must be weighed against the fact that Paul conveys no greetings whatsoever in the letter, a phenomenon most likely derivating from its pressing point of rebuke and request (see below, **Argument**). While Timothy may be included in the reference to "all the brethren who are with me (οἱ σὺν ἐμοὶ πάντες ἀδελφοὶ)" (1:2), would Paul not have made a point of mentioning Timothy personally?

Paul's relatively frequent allusion to Barnabas in Galatians (cf. 2:1, 9, 13) works to a similar effect – in the reverse direction. Barnabas' participation in the journey through southern Galatia is well established by Acts (cf. 13:2, [13], 42-51, 14:12-28), Paul equally appearing to assume his readers' acquaintance with him (cf. 2:13: "even Barnabas [καὶ Βαρναβᾶς]"). While the references do not locate Barnabas in southern Galatia itself (as is true also of 1 Cor. 9:6), Paul's manner of reference to him matches Barnabas' presence during the foundation of the congregations. Acts places Barnabas in Antioch in 11:26-30, 12:25-13:3, and 14:26-15:2 (see below). The probability that the occasion of Barnabas' "stumbling" took place almost immediately following the "council" in Acts 15 – if Galatians 2:11-14 is identified with his falling out with Paul in Acts 15:36-39 – is also logically far remoter than its occurrence at some, as yet undefined, time prior to the meeting.

The case of Titus presents slightly greater complications. Since a north Galatian theory demands that the letter was written subsequent to Acts 15, its proponents also frequently assume that Galatians 2:1-10 and Acts 15 refer to the same event, the so-called "apostolic council." On the present reading, which sees no justification for considering that Titus was actually circumcised, no discrepancy exists on such account between Acts and Galatians, irrespective of whether Acts 15 and Galatians 2:1-10 are to be linked. At the same time, the claim that the two texts cannot relate to the same incident on the grounds that "it is hard to believe that pressure for the circumcision of a single individual would have been mounted in the midst of a meeting called to deal with the whole issue of Jewish-Gentile relations. One would have thought that the principles involved would have been treated first and a decision reached before demands for the circumcision of a particular person were made" (Longenecker, Galatians: lxxii) displays an ignorance of the nature and form of halakhic decision-making.[27]

While Titus may theoretically have been among the "certain others (τινας ἄλλους)" who went up to Jerusalem with Paul and Barnabas in Acts 15:2, his whereabouts are most evident in 2 Corinthians (c. 56), where he directly participated in the Achaian collection for Jerusalem (cf. 2 Cor. 2:13, 7:6-7, 8:6, 12:18). The fact that mention of him is entirely absent in 1 Corinthians suggests that his involvement with the Corinthian community began after Paul had already sent that letter (c. 55). The dating of Galatians in this regard makes the period during which his actions are unknown longer or shorter. If Galatians 2 is associated with Acts 11:27-30, Titus arrives in Jerusalem with Paul in 42/43 and then disappears until Paul

---

[27] For the Cornelius incident as a halakhic precedent (מעשה; ma'aseh) upon which the council's decision in Acts 15 was founded, cf. Le Cornu and Shulam: 609, 828-34.

charges him with the Achaian collection around 12 years later.[28] If Galatians 2 is rather connected with Acts 15 (48 C.E.), the interval of Titus' absence is shortened to around 6 years. The weight attached to this argument must remain fairly insignificant, however, given that ignorance over 12 years or over 6 is of little consequence in and of itself.

The final biographical details concern Peter's presence in Antioch. The chronological possibilities for this include, theoretically, following the incident with Cornelius; prior to Peter's return to Jerusalem (cf. Acts 11:2); the interval following his subsequent departure from the city "to another place (εἰς ἕτερον τόπον)" (Acts 12:17); once Paul and Barnabas returned (cf. Acts 12:25); and any time during Acts 13-15 – although nothing indicates that Peter was in Antioch when Paul and Barnabas returned (cf. Acts 14:26-15:2). The period is narrowed down to 12:25-13:3 and chapter 15, these being the possible time-frameworks during which Peter and Barnabas were together in Antioch.[29]

On internal grounds, the preference between these two periods may incline towards Acts 15. Luke's allusion to "some men . . . from Judea (τινες . . . ἀπὸ τῆς 'Ιουδαίας)" in 15:1 may correspond to "certain men from James (τινας ἀπὸ 'Ιακώβου)" in Galatians 2:12 but does not necessarily do so (see also below, **Occasion and circumstances**). If Peter's virtually verbatim "quote" of Paul (cf. Gal. 2:16) in 15:11 – "But we believe that we are saved through the grace of the Lord Jesus, in the same way as they also are (ἀλλὰ διὰ τῆς χάριτος τοῦ κυρίου 'Ιησοῦ πιστεύομεν σωθῆναι καθ' ὃν τρόπον κἀκεῖνοι)" – suggests Peter's acceptance of Paul's rebuke, Peter demonstrating clear affinities with the gentile position at the "council," the more logical assignation of Galatians 2:11-14(f) is to Acts 15:1-2.[30] His conduct having very recently been called on, Peter

---

[28] For the chronology of Acts assumed here, cf. Le Cornu and Shulam: xxiii-xxv. No inherent reason exists for excluding Titus from Paul's Antioch-to-Jerusalem journey in Acts 11. Moreover, his participation in the delivery of these funds may have given Paul reason to entrust him with the Achaian collection from Corinth. Rather surprisingly, Titus appears not to have travelled with the Achaian and Macedonian "delegates" in taking the monies to Jerusalem (cf. Acts 20:4-5). Tit. 1:4 suggests that he was originally one of Paul's disciples, although the occasion of their acquaintance remains otherwise obscure.

[29] The three men may also have found themselves together in Antioch immediately subsequent to the "council," although Acts gives no indication that Peter either accompanied Paul, Barnabas, and those travelling with them to the city or arrived later. The problems with this hypothesis correspond to those relating to a post-"council" dating of Galatians, addressed below. For the correspondence between Galatians 2 and Luke's account of Paul's visits to Jerusalem, see below.

[30] This would presumably also hold true for Barnabas, whom Luke portrays as supporting Paul's testimony regarding the Gentiles at the council (cf. Acts 15:12). Despite the various theories which attempt to account for the bitter relations

reinforces his acknowledgement of Paul's position publicly at the "council."

While Galatians 2:1-10 may still, on this reading, refer to Acts 11:27-30, the passage can only refer to Acts 15:6-29 if Galatians 2 does not represent a chronological account.[31] Paul would also have had opportunity to compose the letter subsequent to the incident with Peter and prior to the trip to Jerusalem. The greatest difficulty with this approach is its implication that Peter was in Antioch when Paul and Barnabas were sent up to Jerusalem to discuss the circumcision issue with "the apostles and elders (τοὺς ἀποστόλους καὶ πρεσβυτέρους)" (Acts 15:2). Had Peter – an Apostle himself, and one of the "pillars" – been present it might be imagined that the Antiochian community would have had no need to appeal to Jerusalem. This claim may perhaps, however, be mitigated precisely by the fact that Peter himself had demonstrated an ambivalence regarding the Gentiles' status.[32] No inherent reason prevents Peter from having gone up to Jerusalem with Paul and Barnabas, especially if he had accepted Paul's rebuke.

Although the absence of any intention on Paul's part to immediately return to the Galatian communities to deal with the problems personally (cf. Riesner: 394-95) may, in this context, reflect a preoccupation with the imminent journey to Jerusalem, this solution raises difficulties of its own. If the conflict over the Gentiles' status could be resolved through a competent and authoritative halakhic ruling, Paul could then communicate this – as he later did – to the Galatian congregations.[33] But why not then delay with a letter until he could provide a definitive decision? While this may constitute an obstruction for the proponents of Paul's independence from the Jerusalem Apostles, it does not do so for those who hold that the latter approved his position (cf. Howard, Crisis: 7-9).[34] In answer to these

---

between Paul and Barnabas, Paul appears to demonstrate no antagonism towards his colleague in 1 Cor. 9:6.

[31] For the possible relations between the two sections, see below.

[32] For the sake of this argument, it matters little whether Peter's conduct involved eating with gentile believers or the matter of their circumcision. On the present reading of Gal. 2:11(-21), Paul's point appears to be that Peter's withdrawal from their company is tantamount to asserting that they must convert.

[33] For the council's halakhic competence, cf. Le Cornu and Shulam: [36, 44-45, 793], 812ff, 843-51.

[34] In contrast to the majority perception of Galatians 1-2 as Paul's defence of his apostleship and gospel against accusations made by the "influencers," the present understanding of Galatians sees Paul's reference to his apostleship as a function of the affirmation of his authority, in preparation for the "request" he intends to make of his disciples in 4:12ff (see below, **Argument**). Recognition of the influencers' local origin obviates the need to introduce Jerusalem or the Apostles as players in Paul's narrative in chapters 1-2 (see below, **Occasion and circumstances**). For the terms

objections, Paul cannot have possessed the ability to definitively predict the outcome of the discussion in Jerusalem. His complete omission of any reference to the upcoming meeting may be ascribed to a prudential caution in this respect, it being a safer course to articulate his views irrespective of the consultation.

Much the same argument regarding Acts 15:1-3 holds with respect to Acts 12:25-13:3 – minus the possible textual links. Here too, Galatians 2:1-10 may relate to Acts 11:27-30 but not to Acts 15.

This brings us to the much-discussed topic of Paul's various visits to Jerusalem. The basic difficulty which arises derives from the disparity displayed between Luke in Acts and Paul's account in Galatians, with Luke recording five journeys whose correspondence with Galatians, where Paul mentions two alone, is most arduously, if impossibly, arrived at.[35] While many scholars are content to identify Galatians 1 with Acts 9 (Paul's first return visit following his trip to Damascus), both Acts 11:29-30 and Acts 15 have variously been related to Galatians 2.[36] The critical discrepancy here is between Paul's explicit statement – made on oath – that the first time he went up to Jerusalem following his calling was after three years' residence in Damascus, subsequent to his return there from Arabia (cf. Gal. 1:18-20), and the chronological difficulties attendant on the implied dating.[37] Paul's assertion is made in conjunction with his contention that when he thence travelled to Syria and Cilicia he was "still unknown by sight to the congregations of Judea which were in the Messiah . . . (ἀγνοούμενος τῷ προσώπῳ ταῖς ἐκκλησίαις τῆς Ἰουδαίας ταῖς ἐν

---

adopted to describe those whose views Paul is countering, see below, **Occasion and circumstances**.

[35] The common scholarly consensus assumes Paul's letters as primary evidence for his *curriculum vitae*, Acts constituting – at best – a secondary source (cf. Longenecker, Galatians: lxxiii; Hemer: 245ff). While not intending to minimise problems where they genuinely occur, we prefer to hold the grounds of perspective and motivation as a "primary" explanation and to assume, as far as possible, the integrity of both Paul's letters and Luke's account in Acts (cf. Hemer: 247). Paul's final visit – for the purpose of delivering the Achaian and Macedonian collection – indicated in Rom. 15:25-33, 1 Cor. 16:1-4, and 2 Cor. 1:16 – can readily be identified with Acts 24 (cf. Le Cornu and Shulam: 1318-22). For the three-visit hypothesis, which almost completely disengages itself from Acts, cf. Longenecker, Galatians: lxxv-vii; for a general review of New Testament/pauline chronological theories, cf. Riesner: 3-28.

[36] For the problems associated with the Acts 9/Galatians 1 correspondence, cf. Hemer: 248-51.

[37] These difficulties arise irrespective of the problem of integrating Luke's and Paul's account if it is granted that Luke's reference to Gallio in Acts 18 is historic. The latter – which places Paul in Corinth in 51 – is generally accepted as the one firm pauline date available confirmed by external sources in the entire New Testament corpus (cf. Hemer: 251-53; Riesner: 202-11, 318-26).

Χριστῷ)" (Gal. 1:21-22) and that he next went up to the city "after an interval of fourteen years ("Επειτα διὰ δεκατεσσάρων ἐτῶν ʿπάλιν ἀνέβην)" (Gal. 2:1).

Whatever the oath specifically refers to, it cannot but hold great significance regarding the accuracy of Paul's account, which then contends that Paul went back up to Jerusalem on two occasions only. Giving the oath its full weight, the correspondences remaining open to the commentator also committed to Acts are either Acts 11:27-30 or Acts 15. The most significant problem lies in the fact that the latter simultaneously constitutes the most logical and appropriate chronological identification and the most serious "theological" obstacle while the former encounters chronological but no necessary textual difficulties.

While it is theoretically possible to explain why Paul should have omitted all allusion to an upcoming consultation in Jerusalem if he penned the letter from Antioch prior to going up to Jerusalem, his failure to communicate an authoritative halakhic decision directly pertinent to the Gentiles' status constitutes a serious objection to the association of Galatians 2:1-10 with Acts 15 – as well as to any post-council dating of the letter (48 C.E.).[38] With one stroke of his pen, appeal to the council's ruling would have provided an unequivocal settlement of the Galatians' dilemma.[39] Secondly, identifying Galatians 2:1-10 and Acts 15 forces Paul into an intractable contradiction with Luke, denying by implication (but still under oath) that his delivery of the Antiochian contribution to the Jerusalem community occurred.

A third, less weighty but nevertheless significant factor, can be adduced in respect of Timothy. The fact that Paul neither includes greetings nor mentions Timothy at all to those (if the communities he is addressing are those in Antioch, Iconium, Lystra, and Derbe) who "spoke well of him" (Acts 16:2) would seem to intimate that Paul and Timothy

---

[38] Paul specifically designates his meeting as "in private[,] to those who were of reputation (κατ᾽ ἰδίαν δὲ τοῖς δοκοῦσιν)" (2:2). While Acts 15:6 indicates that, following the initial pharisaic appeal, the "apostles and the elders came together to look into this matter (οἱ ἀπόστολοι καὶ οἱ πρεσβύτεροι)," the continuation suggests that the congregation as a whole was involved in the convention. Paul and Barnabas' report is in fact directly linked to the "all the multitude (πᾶν τὸ πλῆθος)" (Acts 15:12). Unfortunately, the identity of the "elders" remains uncertain – although the double reference *per se* inclines against associating Gal. 2:1-10 with Acts 15. It is equally difficult to collate the apostolic encyclical with the "right hand of fellowship (δεξιὰς . . . κοινωνίας)" (Gal. 2:9), even when Paul and Barnabas are entrusted (together with Silas and Judas) with the encyclical's delivery. For the elders and "pillars," cf. Bauckham, Acts: 427ff.

[39] While theoretically possible, the suggestion that Paul wrote the letter between his "private" meeting with James, Peter, and John (Gal. 2:1-10 = Acts 15:6) and the convening of the council is hardly practical. It would also seem to demand a chronological displacement of Gal. 2:1-10 and 11-14(f).

A Commentary on the Jewish Roots of Galatians

were as yet unacquainted (see above). If Paul composed the letter following the council, he must have done so either immediately, while still in Jerusalem, or having arrived back in Antioch (cf. Acts 15:30-35). Although not impossible, this window of communication is extremely narrow and its immediacy sharpens the question why, if he has just been charged with delivering the encyclical, Paul makes no mention of the ruling – or of an imminent visit, which he evidently anticipated (cf. Acts 15:36).

The chronological problem is directly linked to Paul's account of his movements in Galatians (cf. Hemer: 261f, and for the following discussion). Paul's temporal notations indicate that having reached Damascus and then travelled to Arabia – for an undetermined period – he then resided in Damascus for three years. The subsequent interval of fourteen years may refer either to his original arrival in Damascus (i.e., inclusive of the three years) or to the end of the period he has just cited – i.e., fourteen years following his first visit to Jerusalem (exclusive of the three years). The calculations then run either concurrently – fourteen years in total – or consecutively, seventeen years in all. These periods must be accommodated on the one end to the single firm date of 51, when Paul appears before Gallio in Corinth, and his calling on the other. Although these proceedings should logically be reversed, not only is the precise date of Paul's calling unknown but its correlative counter – the date of Jesus' crucifixion – is itself uncertain, as also the interval between these two events.[40]

If the crucifixion is dated to 30 C.E., a calculation based on a number of variables and argued by reputable scholars, and Paul's calling to 31/32, supported by ancient patristic tradition – the most probable date for the council, working backwards from 51, seems to be 48 (cf. Riesner: 319-20).[41] Two options present themselves on this basis: An identification between Galatians 2:1-10 and Acts 15 on a consecutive (17 years) reading, the letter being written prior to the council's convention. Or: an identification

---

[40] The association of 2 Cor. 12:2, in which Paul refers to a "vision" experienced "fourteen years ago," with Paul's calling is generally dismissed. (Segal remains one of the theory's prominent proponents [cf. Paul].) 2 Corinthians can be fairly accurately dated to 55/56, giving a date for Paul's encounter with Jesus outside Damascus of 42, an untenable provenance on all accounts.

[41] For a detailed examination of the arguments regarding the dating of the crucifixion, including Pilate's accession and dismissal, John the Baptist's emergence and execution, the jubilee year, Pesach (Passover), and astronomical considerations, cf. Riesner: 35-58. The latter concludes: "Therefore, the fourteenth of Nisan (7 April) of the year A.D. 30 is, apparently in the opinion of the majority of contemporary scholars as well, far and away the most likely date of the crucifixion of Jesus" (p. 58).

between Galatians 2:1-10 and Acts 11:27-30 on a concurrent (13/14 year) reading. At least theoretically, the three years of Galatians 1:18 may be ascribed to the period immediately following Paul's calling (Arabia being a very brief visit), leading to a date c. 33/35 for Paul's first return visit to Jerusalem (cf. ibid: 322). Here, the chronology begins to run into more serious difficulties. Identifying Galatians 2:1-10 and Acts 11:27-30 on the basis of a concurrent calculation brings Paul's second visit to Jerusalem, delivering the Antiochian community's contribution to the community in Jerusalem, to c. 46 (cf. Hemer: 267). While the independent dating of this event is uncertain in and of itself, Luke presents it as taking place before Agrippa I's death in 42/43. If this were to be extended to 44, Paul referring to the duration of the visit to Jerusalem, possibly following the royal death, and Paul's calling kept as early as possible (31/32 rather than 32/33, as Hemer suggests), the calculations may just be allowed.[42]

Once the chronological problems have been mitigated, some textual markers may associate Galatians 2:1-10 with Acts 11. Paul asserts in Galatians that he "went up again to Jerusalem . . . because of a revelation (᾽πάλιν ἀνέβην⟩ εἰς ῾Ιεροσόλυμα . . . κατὰ ἀποκάλυψιν)" (Gal. 2:1-2). In the context of Agabus' prophetic indications of famine – the grounds for the collection and delivery of the Antiochian contribution to the community in Jerusalem – mention of a "revelation" fits quite well.[43] While James', Peter's, and John's request to "remember the poor – the very thing I also was eager to do (τῶν πτωχῶν ἵνα μνημονεύωμεν, ὃ καὶ ἐσπούδασα αὐτὸ τοῦτο ποιῆσαι)" (2:10) may not in fact directly relate to financial assistance, it certainly does not exclude it and actually highlights Paul's established concern for the Jerusalem community.[44] Less certain but also of some interest is Paul's other allusion to a "spiritual" experience in 2 Corinthians 12:1-4. On a date of 55/56 for this letter, the fourteen years to which it refers relates to c. 42, similarly around the time of Agabus' prophesying.

Despite cautions that Paul's awareness of his calling to the Gentiles may not have emerged until later in his lifetime, Galatians clearly posits a direct correlation between his original encounter with Jesus and his commission to the Gentiles.[45] This is most prominent in 1:16, where Paul

---

[42] Absence of any mention of the council visit in Acts 15 in Galatians on this reading is readily countered by the fact that the letter was written before it took place.

[43] The appeal is made of both Paul and Barnabas, the latter being commissioned, with Paul, to deliver the donation to Jerusalem (cf. Acts 11:30).

[44] For the proposed reading of this text, see 2:1-10.

[45] While countering Kim's dispute with James Dunn and the "New Perspective on Paul," the former can be applauded for identifying and elucidating the biblical

asserts that God was "pleased to reveal His son in me, that [lit.: in order that] I might preach him among the Gentiles (εὐδόκησεν . . . ἀποκαλύψαι τὸν υἱὸν αὐτοῦ ἐν ἐμοί, ἵνα εὐαγγελίζωμαι αὐτὸν ἐν τοῖς ἔθνεσιν)." That he should wish for approval of this commission amongst the Jerusalem leadership at such an early date as Acts 11 does not in this respect constitute any serious problem. The "and" joining the revelation and the submission of his gospel in Galatians 2:2 is not necessarily explicative – i.e., it does not demand an interpretion of the revelation in terms of the submission. If in fact no inherent connection links the two clauses, Paul is possibly simply indicating that he took the opportunity once in Jerusalem to speak with the leaders.[46] This reading also makes good sense both of the apprehension which he exhibits (cf. 2:2d) and of his ambivalence towards the "reputation" of those with whom he shared his message (cf. 2:6).

Various scholars have appealed to theological affinities between the pauline letters to demonstrate chronological proximity, particularly the relation between Galatians and Romans, whose substantive resemblances are traditionally employed as proof of pauline authorship of both letters (cf. Bruce, *Galatians*: 43-56; Longenecker, *Galatians*: lxxxiii-lxxxviii). Without going as far as Howard's claim of theological development from Galatians to Romans in support a pre-council date for Galatians,[47] we would argue for a correspondence which reflects some of the central themes of Paul's thought upon which he elaborated at various junctures and under diverse circumstances (cf. Hemer: 249-50).[48] At the same time, positing a date of 48 for the letter assumes that the Galatian "influencers" emerged shortly on the heels of Paul's departure. This circumstance directly impacts identification of these figures. Not only does it mitigate against their arriving from outside Galatia but it also suggests that the Galatians themselves were at a stage where they understood, and actively sought, circumcision, suggesting a pre-existing well-defined Jewish

---

bases of Paul's self-understanding as "apostle to the Gentiles" in his Damascus experience (cf. Origin/Paul).

[46] Again, we would remind the reader that the present view of Galatians does not perceive Paul's argument as directed against charges made by his so-called opponents – either of dependence on or independence from Jerusalem (see below, **Occasion and circumstances; Argument**). For a critique of the way in which this claim allows for assertions of both dependence and independence on Paul's part, cf. Howard, *Crisis*: 7-8 (without accepting Howard's alternative suggestion) (see also **Occasion and circumstances** [nn54, 121]).

[47] In the second edition, 1990: ix.

[48] For a discussion of the implications of an early Galatians date for 1 Thessalonians, otherwise Paul's first letter, cf. Bruce, *Galatians*: 53-55. On the present chronological scheme, Galatians and Romans are separated by a span of approximately 9 years.

sensibility (cf. Nanos, Irony: 77, 183, 203ff) (see also below, **Occasion and circumstances**).

In the cautious and balanced spirit demanded by the evidence, we present the following chronological scheme:

Crucifixion	30
Paul's calling	31/32
First Jerusalem visit	33/35
(Galatians 1 = Acts 9)	
Second Jerusalem visit	44/46
(Gal. 2:1-10 = Acts 11:27-30)	
Gal. 2:11-14(f)	48
(Antioch, prior to the council)	
Galatians (south) written from	48
Antioch, prior to the council[49]	

[49] Cf. Bruce, Galatians: 55. Even more precisely, presumably also prior to the arrival of the Judaean teachers, the vociferous debate with whom precipitated the trip to Jerusalem. At this point, Paul was not purposing to visit Jerusalem or to consult with the Jerusalem community. Perceptive readers will notice that this scheme differs from that assumed in *A Commentary on the Jewish Roots of Acts*, primarily in its rejection of the identification between Acts 15 and Galatians 2:1-10. The date of Galatians in the former volume was posited, by force of the association, to (Jerusalem or) Antioch following the council but prior to Paul's acquaintance with Timothy (cf. Le Cornu and Shulam: 809). North Galatian options for the provenance of the letter include Ephesus, Macedonia, and Corinth (cf. Betz, Galatians: 12).

Occasion and circumstances

Even when one is disinclined to accept Gager's attempt to save Paul from anti-Jewish tendencies by referring all his remarks (concerning the Torah) to Gentiles, the most obvious conclusion regarding Paul's addressees' identity remains that they are Gentiles.[50] Whatever connotation is put upon his argument, the endeavour against which Paul is striving so mightily is his audience's temptation to be circumcised. The fact that Paul considers his disciples to be vulnerable to such provocation demonstrates that they have not themselves yet taken the step of full conversion.[51]

The source of the inducement has traditionally been considered "Jewish Christian" – i.e., "judaisers" whose tendency is to enforce Torah-observance by/on all. The insistence of such people is that Gentiles who wish to be "saved" must, in addition to becoming Jesus' followers, be circumcised and commit themselves to performance of all the commandments. In other words, they are attempting to compel the gentile believers in Galatia – against Paul's express teaching – to join the Jewish community in order to become full members of the messianic community. This Paul feels as a direct slight on the Messiah's death and resurrection, the seeking of any other condition making of his sacrifice an inadequate procedure (see below).[52]

---

[50] Acts witnesses to gentile audiences in Galatia (cf. Acts 13:16, 26, 43, 48, 14:1, [8f]). Paul also explicitly identifies his readers as former pagans in 4:8 and implicitly implies such a status throughout the letter (cf. 2:2-5, 3:8f, 4:21, 5:2f, 6:12-15). (He also emphasises his calling to the Gentiles [cf. 2:7, 9, 12-15].) Despite Timothy's example (cf. Acts 16:1-3), historical circumstances make it very difficult to maintain that Paul's audience were Jews who had not been circumcised at birth (cf. Nanos, Irony: 77-78). Interpretation of the much-disputed passage in 4:1ff revolves around whether Paul's pronounal usage should be regarded as strictly distinctive of Jews ("we/us") and Gentiles ("you") or as indiscriminate. The fact that Paul's usage is specific and discriminate in Galatians, Romans, and – notably – Ephesians, indicates that in speaking of "you" he is generally to be understood as referring to Gentiles (see the commentary on 3:10-14 and 4:1-7). For Ephesians, cf. McRay, Paul: 340-48; for Gentiles as idolators, cf. Le Cornu and Shulam: 573ff.

[51] This is accomplished through circumcision (for males), immersion, and a sacrifice (cf. Yev. 45b ff; Ger. 1:3f, 2:5). Given the understanding of circumcision as the "seal of the covenant" (cf. Rom. 4:11; Jub. 15:33-34; TBE p. 124), however, "circumcision" is regularly used as a shorthand for "conversion" (cf. 5:3) (see 2:1f [excursi]). It is not impossible that some have, in fact, already taken this step (cf. 5:4). For the meaning of the participle in 6:13, see below.

[52] For the sake of clarity, we would emphasise, even at this initial stage, that it is the seeking of social status which Paul finds so offensive – not circumcision *per se*. The Galatians' persuasion to undergo circumcision/conversion must be understood in light of their specific circumstances. Having already found "standing" in Jesus' faithfulness, he does not wish them to "exchange" this for approval in the eyes of the Jewish community according to the prevailing social norms. Such an action is to

When combined with the theory of Paul's defence of his apostleship in 1:11ff, this assertion casts direct implications on the identity of those troubling his disciples.[53] Since this "defence" is primarily conceived by the majority of commentators in terms of Paul's dependence on/independence from the Apostles in Jerusalem, those promoting judaising ideas have frequently been linked with the Jerusalem leadership. Notwithstanding divergences in particulars, the broad picture painted by New Testament scholars of Galatians has been that:

Paul's teaching to the Galatian communities when he first visited the region was that they had no need to convert to Judaism in order to become Jesus' followers. Following his departure, Jewish believers arrived from Jerusalem and wielded a considerable amount of influence on these communities in persuading them that the status of "godfearer" was untenable and that they must undergo full conversion, the distinguishing mark of which being circumcision. Paul's letter is occasioned by news of this situation, which he is at great pains to counter, defending his authority and his gospel in relation to the Apostles in Jerusalem on the one hand and the Gentiles' right to a "law-free gospel" on the other.[54]

Recent application of rhetorical criticism to Galatians has begun to direct this interpretation into new avenues. At the same time as the rhetorical approach has instituted a long-overdue appreciation of Paul's finely-wrought and carefully-structured argument in Galatians - a marked improvement over earlier denigrations of Paul's epistolary skills - it has also aptly introduced a distinction between the diverse genres employed in the letter. One of its most significant achievements in this regard lies in the proposal of a method whereby the identity of those whose view Paul is

---

put stock in the "flesh" (literally), rather than seeking identity according to "spiritual" criteria. For this idea in full, see below and **Argument**.

[53] The concept of "apostleship" so frequently bandied around by Christian scholars constitutes, to a large extent, a "legal fiction." While the office of "apostle" - "agent" - is clearly evident from New Testament texts, the term usually takes on a far broader sense when applied to Paul in Galatians. This incidence appears to lie in direct correlation to the traditional assumption of Paul's defence of his independence of/conformity with the Jerusalem Apostles. It behoves us to remember, however, that since the original word simply signifies "one who is sent," the source (authority) of Paul's commission (task) is more likely to stand at the center of Paul's argument than ideas of position or status (cf. 1:8ff). The characteristic use of such expressions as the "approval" of Paul's apostleship consequently bear revision in favour of focusing upon the person to whom he is responsible and what commission he carries.

[54] Excellent surveys of the history of Galatians scholarship in this regard may be found in Longenecker, Galatians; Howard, Crisis. Variant views ascribe the "Jerusalem influence" to the Galatian believers' own assumptions regarding Jerusalem and the Apostles - irrespective of their truth or of any direct contact (see also below).

countering may accurately be established.[55] Once we are enabled to pinpoint legitimate material for character-identification, the subsequent identity is likely to possess considerably greater plausibility.

In proposing that much of Paul's intent in Galatians is informed by – and expressed in – irony, Nanos suggests that the body of the letter, traditionally appealed to for his so-called adversaries' identity, be divided into sections of narrative discourse, autobiographical material, transitional seams, and "situational discourse" (cf. Nanos, Irony: 62ff, and for the following discussion). Since the latter directly relates to the circumstances in Galatia it may be adduced as proper (strictly relevant) evidence for the "situation" there. To the extent to which they move either from or to situational discourse, so also may certain transitional passages. In contrast, while obviously important to Paul's argument, neither the narrative nor the autobiographical information (which may overlap to the degree that Paul narrates past events) should be employed as immediate evidence for identifying the "influencers" – both lacking any direct situational connection with Galatia and the Galatians.

Since in most instances Paul brings "historical examples" – such as the incident with Peter in Antioch – in order to build his argument, the points these embody reflect Paul's position and the rhetorical function he intends them to serve in the letter. They should not, consequently, be adduced as representative of the influencers' viewpoint.[56] As precedents to which Paul appeals in application to the Galatians' current circumstances, neither should narratives be regarded as identity statements about the precise parties influencing the Galatian addressees. Significantly, the passages in which Paul alludes to the meeting with the Jerusalem leadership (2:1-10) and to the "men from James (τινας ἀπὸ 'Ιακώβου)" (2:12) both fall outside the genre of situational discourse. On the rhetorical grounds established above, Nanos argues that these verses may only provide secondary evidence regarding the influencers' identity.

The most significant segment of situational discourse with respect to the influencers' identity is 6:11-17, a section in which Paul makes direct

[55] The problem of ascertaining Paul's so-called opponents' identity has long plagued Galatians scholars. While much caution has correctly been advised with regard to the use of "mirror-imaging" – determining a person's views from the counterattack mounted against them – commentators have found it very difficult to extricate themselves from this methodological trap. Nanos' adoption of the term "influencers" speaks directly to the problems raised by the assumption that those troubling the gentile Galatians were Paul's direct opponents. Such a presumption – before their identity has even been established – prejudges the very identity which if purports to define (see also below).
[56] This does not exclude such portions of the letter from playing an important structural and substantive role in Paul's argument, however. For the significance attributed to Paul's reproof of Peter in the present work, see below, **Argument**.

statements concerning the conduct of those disturbing Paul's gentile disciples in Galatia: "Those who desire to make a good showing in the flesh try to compel you [the Galatians] to be circumcised, simply that they may not be persecuted for the cross of the Messiah. For those who are circumcised do not even keep the Torah themselves, but they desire to have you circumcised, that they may boast in your flesh"[57] (6:12-13).[58]

The first question which may profitably lead to a clarification of the influencers' identity is: What may we understand by "persecution"? Or to put it more broadly: How (under whatever circumstances) would advocating the circumcision/conversion of gentile believers enable other believers – themselves circumcised – to avoid being persecuted?[59] The most logical "historical" answer to such a query is that the early believing community was being troubled by the Roman authorities who perceived that its members were no longer part of the Jewish community. While Judaism was recognised as a *religio licita* during the period under discussion – a religion whose members were licensed to live "in accordance with their ancestral customs," even where these affronted Roman religious sensibilities (cf. Jos.*Ant.* 14.202-264, 16.160-178), nascent Christianity possessed neither status as an independent religion nor Roman recognition as one (cf. Ferguson, Backgrounds: 342-43, 480-81). The best way to avoid persecution was therefore to formally convert to Judaism – a move of expediency rather than of conviction, and one which put a "good showing in the flesh" over and above recognition of a "law-free gospel."

The lucidity of this argument notwithstanding, it fails to hold water historically. Even dating Galatians according to a north Galatian theory,

---

[57] Ὅσοι θέλουσιν εὐπροσωπῆσαι ἐν σαρκί, οὗτοι ἀναγκάζουσιν ὑμᾶς περιτέμνεσθαι, μόνον ἵνα τῷ σταυρῷ Χριστοῦ μὴ διώκωνται. οὐδὲ γὰρ οἱ περιτεμνόμενοι αὐτοὶ νόμον φυλάσσουσιν ἀλλὰ θέλουσιν ὑμᾶς περιτέμνεσθαι, ἵνα ἐν τῇ ὑμετέρᾳ σαρκὶ καυχήσωνται.

[58] In addition to the traditional passages appealed to in 1:6-9, 4:17, 5:10-12, and 6:12-13 for "direct" identification of the influencers, we are currently proposing the supplement of what appear to be veiled (or not so veiled) pauline warnings against allowing the influencers any place in the community. These include a series in 4:30, 5:7-10, [26], and 6:3-8. The nature of these sections, however, precludes reference to them for elaboration of any further details concerning the influencers' identity (see below, **Argument**).

[59] The meaning of οἱ περιτεμνόμενοι (hoi peritemnomenoi – NASB "those who are/have been circumcised") is greatly disputed (cf. Nanos, Irony: 234-42), and whole theses regarding the influencers' identity have been built around the phrase (cf. Munck). Whatever its precise significance, the initial implication is clearly that the influencers are closely associated with the act of circumcision, whether in their own bodies or in that of others. For the question of whether or not the influencers should be regarded as believers – and whether they are themselves circumcised – see below.

the latest the letter could have been written is the early 50's – and the
southern theory places it at the end of the 40's (see above, **Date and
destination**). No historical evidence exists to indicate that Roman
recognition of "Christianity" as distinct from a Jewish sect occurred before
Nero's campaign against the community of believers in Rome in 64 – the
earliest extant witness to an official Roman persecution of Jesus' followers
(cf. Stern: 114; Nanos, Mystery: 68f, 372f).[60] The whole tenor of Acts, from
Gallio's reaction to the Corinthian Jewish accusation against Paul to Felix
and Festus' response to the Sanhedrin's charges, moreover, corroborates
the assertion that the Romans – not to speak of the Jewish community –
were ignorant of the early believing community as an entity distinct from
Judaism.[61]

   A second possible "historical" circumstance attributes the persecution
to zealot sources (cf. Jewett, Agitators). This theory also possesses merit on
"theological" grounds, as it were. Zealot antagonism towards gentile
elements in general is well attested. The shammaite institution of the
Eighteen Decrees – a comprehensive prohibition against gentile foods and
relations – was apparently effected in the years immediate to the outbreak
of the War in 66, the revolt being sparked by the Jewish refusal to continue
to accept gentile offerings (cf. JShab. 1, 4, 3c) (cf. Ben-Shalom; Hengel,
Zealots: 200f). The zealot insistence that a Gentile should not be permitted

---

[60] The suggestion that Claudius' expulsion of the Jewish community from Rome
only involved the "Christians" (cf. Feldman, Jew: 97, 304) is highly doubtful,
Feldman himself dismissing the claim before subsequently proposing it (p. 47). The
witnesses to the event and their interpretation are subject to such difficulties as to
preclude their use as conclusive historical evidence. The most "obvious" argument,
that the persecution derives from the Jewish community hostile to Jesus' name, falls
prey to similar considerations. None of the incidents which Luke reports in Acts
detailing conflict between the early community and the local Jewish communities
(in the diaspora) appear to be "theological" in nature – with the possible exception
of Corinth (Acts 18) – which proves the rule. The bases of the variance can be traced
in most cases to economic factors, specifically godfearing patronage of diaspora
Jewish communities (cf. Le Cornu and Shulam: 747-49, 55-59, 1004-12, 38-40, 1181)
(see also below [nn99, 105]).
[61] A second argument may be raised in regard to Roman persecution of gentile
believers who, by virtue of their new identity in the Messiah, began to refuse to
participate in civic-religious pagan practices. One way to escape such persecution
lay in joining the officially-recognised Jewish community, whose members were
exempt from such participation (cf. Nanos, Irony: 268). While this proposition
would, like the former, posit a literal/physical persecution of Jesus' followers,
making sense both of their "return" to pagan practices in 4:9-10 (as one way of
avoiding the persecution) and their expediency in only "pretending" to observe the
Torah (their adherence being merely to avert harassment), it is – for this period –
equally as unattested in historical terms as a Roman distinction, at this early point,
between Judaism and nascent "Christianity." For the present understanding of the
"return" in 4:8-11, see below, **Argument**.

to study Torah unless he was circumcised appears to be symptomatic of the zealot conviction that Gentiles interested in Judaism must convert rather than remain "godfearers"[62] (cf. Ben-Shalom: 162f).

According to this reading of Galatians, the leaders of the Jerusalem believing community were experiencing pressure from zealot sources to disassociate themselves from all gentile contact. The violence attendant on zealot activities was known to be fierce, the sicarii indiscriminately assassinating people on no more than mere pretexts of justice (cf. Jos.*War* 4.356, 363, 365). A reasonable solution to remove themselves from imminent threat would have been for the Jerusalem believing community to send representatives urging gentile believers throughout the diaspora to convert. In this way, they could demonstrate their "loyalty" to zealot tendencies.

Notwithstanding the logical sense this interpretation imparts to the text of Galatians, it encounters several serious difficulties (cf. Nanos, Irony: 209-11). No evidence exists of zealot intimidation of the early community. If any links may be suggested, they in fact lie in the reverse direction, some of the Eretz Israel believing community demonstrating affinities with – rather than opposition to – zealot causes[63] (cf. Le Cornu and Shulam: 639-41, 726). While it is true that Luke's account in Acts suggests that the early community in Jerusalem responded to rumours concerning Paul's "apostasy" in a fashion very compatible with zealot sensibilities (cf. Acts 21:20) – reports which are more likely to have derived from his lenient attitude towards the Gentiles than from any assumed separation from Judaism on his part – it is in precisely the same context that James reiterates the council's halakhic acceptance of the Gentiles' godfearing status (cf. Acts 21:25).[64]

More seriously, if Paul wrote Galatians immediately prior to the council in 48, the decision not to require gentile conversion taken at that meeting represents an attitude calculated to disturb zealot sensibilities.[65] The likelihood that the Jerusalem Apostles would attempt to impose

---

[62] Cf. Jos.*Ant.* 20.41f; [Ex.R. 30:12, 33:7]; Yalk.Lev. 587; Yalk.Dt. 951; AZ 3:8; Tos.Shab. 17:1; J AZ 3, 8, 43b; Hag. 13a; San. 59a; Hipp.*Ref.Omn.Her.* 9.21.

[63] Cf. Mt. 10:4, [16:17; Acts 1:6]; Git. 56a; Acts of Philip 107; Eus.*EH* 3.32.1 (cf. Liebes: Tosefet).

[64] Cf. Le Cornu and Shulam: 483-44, 1182, 88-91, 1303-4.

[65] Due to the 2-4 years Jewett assigns to Paul's second journey, dating Paul's arrival in Corinth in the winter of 49/50, he is compelled to argue for the council's convention subsequent to Paul's ministry in Greece (51), identifying the visit to Jerusalem of Galatians 2:1-10 (= Acts 15) with Acts 18:22 (cf. Jewett, Chronology: 91f). While Jewett's chronological scheme admittedly greatly differs from the present one (as does his adoption of a "north Galatian" provenance), such a 3-5 year disparity remains relatively negligible in terms of zealot influence within the general time period. For the present dating of Galatians, see above, **Date and destination.**

conversion on gentile believers in far-flung diaspora communities rather than demonstrating their gentile antipathies locally also seems very slim.[66] While the presence of "zealots" is attested in diaspora communities (cf. Acts 15:1; Jos.*War* 7.418), the reference in Josephus is much later, to refugees from the Revolt in 73 C.E.. The "men . . . from Judea (τινες· . . . ἀπὸ τῆς 'Ιουδαίας)" in Acts 15:1 are also most likely members of the early community and not Zealots (cf. ibid: 797ff).[67]

With these circumstances dismantled, two highly significant points emerge. The first relates to the meaning attached to "persecution for the cross of the Messiah (τῷ σταυρῷ τοῦ Χηριστοῦ διώκωνται)" (6:12). To the extent that no historical circumstances can be adduced for any persecution of the early believing community – either by Roman authorities or by the Jewish community – no other recourse appears available than to argue that the influencers were *non-believers*.[68] A second extrapolation indicates that since the "persecution" cannot represent a literal harassment, it must be interpreted "metaphorically" in some way. An example of such a figurative comprehension is that the influencers were concerned not to be considered Jesus' followers (see below).

A second derivative from the discussion of persecution relates to the traditional argument that those whose views Paul is countering were

---

[66] Cf. Nanos' perceptive remark that such a construction "assumes that any such [zealot] group, if it existed, would have had an interest in, or the ability to affect [*sic*], the circumcision of Gentiles in Antioch, which would seem to be counterintuitive for Judean anti-Roman politic-interest groups anyway" (Galatians: 291).

[67] Here again, Nanos' argument (Irony: 209-11) that Jewett's thesis fails primarily because it addresses the "influencers of the influencers" is telling. Focusing attention on Zealots in Judaea is not only one step removed from Galatia but two steps removed from the influencers and three from the Galatians themselves. Jewett's scheme presents the additional problem of proposing a circumstance in which the influencers' Judaean commissioners are Torah-observant Jewish believers who wish to *avert suspicion* of non-zealot-like sympathies by making sure that none of their associates remain Gentiles. In acting expediently to placate zealot appeals they behave as though they do not value Torah-observance for themselves – despite the fact that the Galatians' godfearing status is precisely what is potentially casting doubt on their own Torah-observant standards. Any identity of the influencers as Torah-observant must present a convincing explanation of their implied expediency and ulterior motives with regard to the "works of the Torah" in 6:12-13 (see below). Paul's accusation that they "do not even keep the law themselves (οὐδὲ . . . αὐτοὶ νόμον φυλάσσουσιν)" indicates that Jewish believers would have been unlikely to obligate as observance something to which themselves did not subscribe. For a reading of the Jewish antagonism to the early community as almost exclusively representing economic *versus* religious considerations, cf. Le Cornu and Shulam: 747-51, 1036-40.

[68] For additional arguments asserting the influencers' identity as non-believers, see below.

associated in some way with the early community in Jerusalem.[69] This claim rests primarily on Paul's relation to the latter as an apostle, in conjunction with the reference to "certain men from James (τινας ἀπὸ Ἰακώβου)" in 2:12. Since rhetorical criticism has deprived the latter allusion of its immediate contribution, being autobiographical material not directly connected to the Galatian circumstances, the necessity of contending that the influencers are foreigners rather than locals loses much of its force.[70] The dating currently being posited for Galatians (immediately prior to the council in 48) suggests that very little time has elapsed since Paul's visit, allowing only a brief opportunity for outsiders to have arrived and begun persuading the Galatian communities to desert Paul's teaching.[71]

While itinerant teachers, prophets, envoys, and "proselytisers" are known from the period,[72] they too remain undemanded by the context. In this respect, although the "some men . . . from Judea (τινες . . . ἀπὸ τῆς Ἰουδαίας)" (Acts 15:1) is a lukan construct and cannot, on those grounds, be compared directly with Paul's "certain men from James (τινας ἀπὸ Ἰακώβου)" (2:12), neither can the former figures be conclusively identified with the Jerusalem believing community solely on the basis of the internal witness of Galatians (see also above, **Date and destination**). In similar fashion, the imprecise identity of the "false brethren (ψευδαδέλφους)" (cf. 2:4) and their appearance in a narrative section notwithstanding, Paul explicitly distinguishes them from the inner Jerusalem leadership (the "private" meeting with James, Peter, and John) – indicating not only that the Jerusalem believing community was troubled by inconsistencies but also that those whose views Paul is countering in Galatia do not necessarily need to be identified with the (position of the) Apostles.[73]

---

[69] This assocation, too, might have been either literal or assumed, some in the Galatian communities possibly (mistakenly) appealing to Jerusalem in support of their pro-circumcision position (see above [n54]).

[70] For the debate regarding Paul's "apostleship," see below.

[71] The compulsion of the reverse claim, that a certain period would have been required in order for this inducement to have prevailed, derives from the assumption that the Galatian believers were Gentiles unacquainted with Judaism. It is then asked: How could they have achieved such a familiarity to be swayed towards conversion in such a short time? The force of the assertion breaks down, however, if it is accepted that these believers were already godfearers.

[72] Cf. Jos.*Ant.* 20.34-48; RH 1:3, 2:2; Yev. 16:7; RH 26a; Did. 11:1f (cf. Le Cornu and Shulam: 405, 78-79, 528, 681, 834-35). For a thorough discussion of Judaism as a proselytising force in the ancient world, cf. Feldman, Jew: 288-382; Goodman; McKnight.

[73] If the "men from Judea" are identified as envoys from the Jerusalem community, they were presumably authorised to teach that "unless you are circumcised according to the custom of Moses, you cannot be saved (ἐὰν μὴ περιτμηθῆτε τῷ ἔθει τῷ Μωϋσέως, οὐ δύνασθε σωθῆναι)" (Acts 15:1). The council's decision then

The fact that almost immediately following the council, on the present chronology, Judas and Silas are commissioned to accompany Paul and Barnabas in delivering an encyclical containing the decision regarding the Gentiles' status, and that the two men convey it to the Galatian communities in addition to Antioch, Cilicia, and Syria (cf. Acts 15:22f, 41, 16:1-5), would appear to suggest that the leaders in Jerusalem had not previously sent any official delegates.[74] Nothing in the letter itself establishes any direct link between the influencers and Jerusalem (cf. Nanos, Irony: 143f-158).[75] Reading Galatians as a "halakhic letter" along the lines of 4QMMT, moreover, provides an alternative understanding of Paul's "defence" of his apostleship. This structuring of Galatians frames the epistle as a communication of combined "rebuke" and "request": Paul's reprimand of his disciples for transferring their loyalty to another, and his stipulation that they return (or be brought back) to their original allegiance to the Messiah in his teaching – the authority for both of which he sets out in the letter's opening (see below, **Form; Argument**).

The determination that Paul's antagonists are likely *not* to have been "non-locals" – people extraneous to Galatia in origin – does not necessarily preclude their status as "outsiders" with respect to the Galatian communities themselves (cf. Nanos, Irony: 171).[76] This fact – which may

---

represents an 180 degree *volte face*, asserting that the Gentiles may remain godfearers. While a theoretical possibility, Acts 15 gives no indication of such a violent swing. "Those who were circumcised (οἱ ἐκ περιτομῆς)" in Jerusalem had already demonstrated their approval of Peter's acceptance of Cornelius' immersion/baptism – without circumcision (cf. Acts 11:2-18). Peter himself supports the godfearers' side and had, a mere brief period prior to the council according to the present chronology, displayed his acceptance of the gentile believers in Antioch (cf. 2:12) – as had all the "pillars" over approximately five years earlier. No necessity in fact exists for understanding this group to be directly responsible for the conflict, an assumption frequently associated with the identification – arbitrary again – of "the men from James" with "the party of the circumcision" (see on 2:10-14). (For the dating of Galatians and Paul's Jerusalem visits, see above, **Date and destination**.)

[74] Paul's participation in the promotion of the encyclical has traditionally caused commentators no little confusion in this respect, some emphasising that Silas – not Paul – delivered the letter, Acts 16:4 representing a gloss derived from the doublet in δ in 15:41 (cf. Bruce, Acts: 352-53).

[75] Commentators who have proposed that the linkage is with Antioch rather than with Jerusalem appear to assume the subjection of the Antiochian community to Jerusalem, leaving the same objections in force (cf. Nanos, Irony: 143n79). In discussing the contention that the influencers are "outsiders" *unattached* to Jerusalem, Nanos concludes that it represents "a logical result of the other conclusions about their provenance, interests, and activities" (p. 159).

[76] The evidence for the mixed tribal, Greek, Roman colonist, and Jewish population in Galatia is clear (see above, **Date and destination**). To the extent that the evidence of Acts indicates that the Galatian communities were at least partly composed of

serve as a corroboration of the assertion that the influencers were not Jesus' followers (see above) – itself receives confirmation from the indication that once a Jerusalem connection has been dismissed, the Jewish-believing identity of the influencers appears highly unlikely.[77] Put positively, if those whose views Paul is countering were not sent from Judaea, little evidence exists to substantiate their status as (Jewish) believers.[78]

A further point in favour of forging a non-believing identity for the influencers may transpire from Paul's diverse treatment of the influencers in Galatians and the "opponents" in his Corinthian correspondence. In the latter, Paul directly addresses those whose actions he denounces within the Corinthian believing community (cf. Walter: 355/366).[79] In 1 Corinthians 5:1-5 he declares not only that "*I have decided* to deliver such a one [as engages in incest] to Satan for the destruction of his flesh" but also signifies that this conduct is conducive to repentance – "that his spirit may be saved in the day of the Lord Jesus"[80] (1 Cor. 5:5). In 1 Corinthians 11:17-34, he remonstrates with those participating in the Lord's supper "in an unworthy manner (ἀναξίως)" (1 Cor. 11:27). In neither case – as also in 2 Corinthians 10-13 – does he curse those whom he opposes as he does in Galatians.[81] The lack of these circumstances – of immediate appeal and of

---

godfearers (cf. Acts 13:16, 26, 43), they presumably possessed already-existing ties with the local Jewish population. (For the problematic reference in Acts 13:43, cf. Le Cornu and Shulam: 720.)

[77] Even exegetes who propose a gentile influence – whether local or foreign – seem unable to avoid linking the activities of the "troublers" to Jerusalem (cf. Nanos, Irony: 135n62). Precisely how, or why, the Jerusalem leadership would have wished to employ Gentiles – or why Gentiles should have desired to be so occupied – on Jerusalem business is quite obscure.

[78] Nanos' engagement of the prevailing interpretations of the influencers' identity classifies the category of "Christ-believers with a different gospel of Christ" as the "virtually unchallenged" consensus of historical interpretation. Despite its differentiation from those "oriented toward a Jerusalem Christ-believing coalition," this group lacks any inclusion of non-Jerusalem-based "judaising" Jewish interests. The two scholars whom Nanos cites as proffering alternative options – Muddiman and Walter – in fact argue that Paul's opponents are "*non-Christ-believing* Jews" (cf. Nanos, Irony: 138; emphasis added).

[79] The point is well taken that the influencers may not be responding directly to Paul's teaching but to an (imputed) claim on behalf of the gentile Galatian believers to have become part of God's covenant with Israel (see above). For the origin of the issue at stake, see below.

[80] παραδοῦναι τὸν τοιοῦτον τῷ σατανᾷ εἰς ὄλεθρον τῆς σαρκός, ἵνα τὸ πνεῦμα σωθῇ ἐν τῇ ἡμέρᾳ τοῦ κυρίου.

[81] His request for "restoration" in 6:1 is of those within the community who are succumbing to the influencers' persuasion. It does not refer to the influencers themselves – although other parts of that section do. See below, **Argument**.

seeking repentance – in Galatians strongly suggests that they did not belong to any of the local believing communities.[82]

Scholarly consensus has traditionally argued that Galatians 1:6: "I am amazed that you are so quickly deserting Him who called you . . . for a different gospel · (θαυμάζω ὅτι οὕτως ταχέως μετατίθεσθε ἀπὸ τοῦ καλέσαντος ὑμᾶς . . . εἰς ἕτερον εὐαγγέλιον)" – interpreted as a distortion of the true gospel by people with Christian views different and opposed to those of Paul – unambiguously signifies the influencers' status as believers. Despite clear evidence of the use of εὐαγγέλιον (euangellion – "gospel") external to the New Testament, it has regularly been assumed that the term, within the New Testament texts, carries a meaning exclusively specific to Jesus' death and resurrection: "He [Paul] calls their message *'another* gospel' because it was significantly different from his own; but he calls it *'gospel'* because that was the term they [Paul's antagonists] no doubt also used in their capacity as missionaries like Paul" (Dunn, Galatians: 41-42; original emphasis).

The Greek word, which derives from ἄγγελος (angelos – "messenger/one sent"), simply means "good news" (εὐ- [eu-] = "good"), the verbal form εὐαγγελίζω (euangelizō) forming a compound from ἀγγέλλω (angellō – "to tell/announce") (cf. 1 Thess. 3:6) (cf. Nanos, Irony: 284ff, and for the following discussion). The LXX employs the term to render the common Hebrew root בשר (basar), which carries the basic meaning of "to herald."[83] While the concept's messianic import is clear,[84] its usage in other contexts is equally well attested.[85] The LXX plays on the ironic meaning of good news in effect being bad in 2 Kings 4:10 (MT 2 Sam. 4:10), and both Philo and Josephus adopt the term in biblical settings where the LXX does not.[86] Josephus also applies it in a politically-charged sense (cf. *War* 2.420, 4.618). Paul's use of the word is itself variegated, not being appropriated exclusively to designate preaching of the gospel. In describing the latter Paul employs several equivalent verbs, including καταγγέλω (katangellō – "to announce"), κηρύσσω (kēryssō – " to

---

[82] Cf. the claim – albeit made for other purposes – that Paul always addresses the Galatians directly ("you") to the exclusion of their antagonists, to whom he always alludes in the third person impersonal ("they") (cf. Dunn, Theology: 8). For a discussion of the contention that Paul is "avoiding the use of names and [thus] the providing of free publicity," cf. Nanos, Irony: 176-78.

[83] Cf. 1 Kings 31:9; 3 Kings 1:42; Jer. 20:15.

[84] Cf. Ps. 96:2; Isa. 40:9, 41:27, 52:7-10, 61:1f; Nah. 1:15; Mt. 4:23, 9:35, 11:5, 24:14, 26:13; Mk. 1:15, 8:35, 10:29, 13:10, 14:9, 16:15; Lk. 4:16-21, 7:22; Acts 10:36-38; Rom. 1:1f, 16-17, 10:15; [Eph. 2:17]; Ps.Sol. 11:1; 1QHᵃ 23:14-15; 4Q521 f2ii:12; 11QMelch 2:15-25; Gen.R. 63:8; Ex.R. 15:1; Lev.R. 9:9, 30:16; Pes.Rab. 15:14/15, 35:4, 51:3; Mid.Ps. 29:2.

[85] For 11QMelch, see 1:1f, 3:21-25, and 4:1-7.

[86] Cf. Jos.*Ant.* 5.24, 277, 11.65; Philo, *Jos.* 245.

proclaim"), and λαλέω (laleō - "to speak"), sometimes in parallel in the same verse.[87] He also - most significantly for the whole argument of Galatians - depicts the blessing which comes to the nations through Abraham as "good news" (cf. 3:8) (see 3:6-9).

Reading the phrase "another gospel" through the lense of irony removes it a further step from any "literal" reference to the good news of Jesus' death and resurrection. The effect which Paul is endeavouring to elicit is that this "other" good news is in fact - as in the case of 4 Kings - bad. On this understanding, the adjective ἕτερος (heteros - "different") (1:6) does not mean a gospel "of another kind" but a gospel which is not good but bad news - and therefore not the "good news of the gospel."[88] This force also includes the terms ἄλλο (allo - "another"; here, "not another") and παρά (para - "contrary"). Paul explains his purpose in the final clause: "only [except that] there are some who are disturbing you, and want to distort the gospel of the Messiah (εἰ μή τινές εἰσιν οἱ ταράσσοντες ὑμᾶς καὶ θέλοντες μεταστρέψαι τὸ εὐαγγέλιον τοῦ Χριστοῦ)" (1:7b). By alluding to teaching which he makes abundantly clear is *not* appropriate to Jesus' good news Paul may well be intending to shock his readers into realising that they have in fact been relating to as if it were. It is not "gospel" in any sense and can masquerade as such only because the Galatians are willing to grant it such a status.

Having established the difficulties attendant on claiming believing status for the influencers, the remaining question regarding their identity to be asked is: Are they Jewish or gentile?

While Paul never states his adversaries' Jewish identity explicitly, the influencers' Jewish thrust is abundantly clear: They wish (for reasons still to be discussed) the Galatian communities' gentile members to be circumcised and convert. This is indubitably a Jewish concern, and one fully documented - notwithstanding the vociferous scholarly debate over whether or not Judaism was a proselytising religion during this period.[89] Paul portrays the influencers as those who "desire to make a good

---

[87] Cf. Rom. 10:8, 14-15; 1 Cor. 1:23, 2:1, 9:14, 27, 11:26, 15:11; Gal. 2:2; Phil. 1:14-18; 1 Thess. 2:2, 4, 9, 16.
[88] The analogy which springs to mind is the biblical description of "gods which are not gods" (cf. Jer. 2:11, 16:20: אלהים והמה לא אלהים).
[89] Cf. Bamberger; Feldman, Jew: 288-382; Goodman; McKnight. We have argued, in the Commentary, that Paul's assumption that his "apostleship ("agency") to the Gentiles" was intelligible to his audiences suggests that such an activity was familiar in the period under discussion (see the commentary on 1:15-16b). The problem ostensibly raised by Gal. 4:8-9, where Paul suggests that his readers are simultaneously attempting to "turn back to weak and worthless elemental things, to which you desire to be enslaved all over again," is perhaps best resolved when the "back" is referred not to a resumption of a previous lifestyle (either pagan or Jewish - both of which are problematic in the context) but to the "period" of bondage from which the Messiah's death and resurrection sets one free (see below, **Argument**).

showing in the flesh ... simply that they may not be persecuted for [because of] the cross of the Messiah (θέλουσιν εὐπροσωπῆσαι ἐν σαρκί ... μόνον ἵνα τῷ σταυρῷ τοῦ Χριστοῦ μὴ διώκωνται)" (6:12). This statement suggests that, whatever the motive behind the "good showing" – whether "in the flesh (ἐν σαρκί)" as referring to "before men" or literally to circumcision "in the flesh of the foreskin [בשר ערלתו]" – its fulfilment is bound up with circumcision.[90]

Nanos argues that the influencers are non-believing Jews from the local Galatian Jewish community (cf. Irony: 199ff). Two primary factors indicate to him that they are Jewish: It is precisely their Torah-observance which makes their appeal for conversion to the Galatian gentile believers persuasive; and it is upon this fact which Paul bases his remonstration of them (cf. Irony: 229, 232).[91] More specifically, he claims that they were "social control agents" – people "probably involved in the administration of the ritual conversion process" – and may well themselves have been proselytes.[92] As non-believers, their desire to elude persecution, suggests Nanos, rests upon their eagerness to avoid granting "legitimacy to the addressees' claims made on the basis of the meaning of 'the cross of

---

[90] Verses 12-13 give the strong impression of chiasmus. The "boasting in the flesh" in 6:13 corresponds to the "good showing in the flesh" in 6:12, the result of both being persuasion towards circumcision. In similar fashion, the reverse order of the two purpose clauses in the two verses ("simply that [μόνον ἵνα] ... /that they may boast [ἵνα] ...") indicates that the purpose of the circumcision is to boast, just as circumcision is the outcome of the boasting. In other words, irrespective of the order in which the motive and effect are stated, they remain constant: The purpose of circumcision is to "boast in the flesh." The chiasmus also establishes a parallelism between avoidance of persecution and lack of Torah-observance (see below, Argument).

[91] Nanos' explanation of the substantive *non sequitur* of 6:13 – "those who are circumcised do not even keep the Law themselves (οὐδὲ γὰρ οἱ περιτεμνόμενοι αὐτοὶ νόμον φυλάσσουσιν)" – runs along the idea of "violation of the spirit of Torah by seeking their own honor at the addressees' expense ... when, by Paul's reckoning, they should be reconsidering their norms in the face of the demonstration of God's Spirit at work among these Gentiles." They are not "doing the law lawfully" because they are excluding the Gentiles' claims of having become part of the people of Israel through Jesus' inauguration of the messianic age (cf. Irony: 229).

[92] A further ground of Nanos' identification appears to lie on his understanding of the Galatians' circumstances within the framework of "agonistic communities" who, in struggling for "zero sum" product, tend to contend with potential rivals through the exercise of the evil eye (cf. Social). To the extent that the propriety of this context is questioned, less compulsion exists to see the influencers as proselytes who are "invested in convincing the addressees of the relevance of Scripture and revelation-based traditions for becoming proselytes in order to gain what they seek to claim," the influencers themselves "fitting the model of Ishmael as a type of proselyte" (Present: 14).

Christ,' that is, predicated upon an appeal to the present end of ages meaning of a Judean martyr's purpose for themselves, because they do not share the addressees' belief in this meaning. The influencers thus do not want to have to answer for their failure to bring about compliance as though they accepted the legitimacy of this claim" (p. 223) (cf. p. 268). Out of the convoluted sense of this sentence, Nanos appears to be asserting that the statement "simply that they may not be persecuted for the cross of Christ" signifies that the influencers wish not to be identified as believers in Jesus.[93]

Despite Nanos' evident desire to locate Paul's thought and expression within its rightful Jewish context, no evidence exists to support his assertions.[94] Recent research on the form of conversion in the tannaitic period suggests that no ceremony at all was followed, a person wishing to convert doing so at his/her own initiative – save for the actual circumcision.[95] At the same time, later evidence – which frequently reflects earlier practice – goes directly against the grain of Nanos' supposition. To avow that proselytes could administer these is tantamount to contending

---

[93] The contention contains a hint of tautology: The influencers are not Jesus' followers (i.e., are Jewish non-believers) because they desire not to be considered believers in Jesus (by the Jewish community). This is rescued by the further claim that, with regard to the pagan authorities, the influencers (proselytes, according to Nanos) do not acknowledge the early community's claim (that of Paul and/or of his disciples) to "aggregated identity" – i.e., to recognised status as part of the Jewish community, a standing which grants them exclusion from civic cultic practices (cf. Irony: 268).

[94] This is, of course, a problem which most, if not all, commentators share, material relative to conversion processes and procedures during this period being very scarce and scanty.

[95] Cf. Tos.Shab. 8[9]:5; Tos.Dem. 2:4 – the emphasis laying on the fact that no other person is mentioned and the Gentile takes the step independently (cf. Cohen, Rabbinic; Kulp; Samet). While several arguments are marshalled in support of the thesis, it is noteworthy that precisely the same criteria are applied in the discussions between Beit Hillel and Beit Shammai (c. 30 B.C.E. – 20 C.E.) to an עם הארץ (am ha-aretz – an unlearned person) seeking to become a חבר (chaver – "associate"): "Our Rabbis taught: If one is prepared to accept the obligation of a *haber* except one religious law, we must not receive him as a *haber*. If a heathen is prepared to accept the Torah except one religious law, we must not receive him [as an Israelite] . . . One who desires to accept the obligations of a *haber* is required to accept them in the presence of three *haberim*, and even a *talmid hakam* [a scholar] is required to accept the obligations in the presence of three *haberim* ת"ר : הבא לקבל דברי חבירות חוץ מדבר אחד, אין מקבלין אותו. עובד ככבים שבא לקבל דברי תורה חוץ מדבר אחד, אין מקבלין אותו . . . הבא לקבל דברי חבירות, צריל לקבל בפני ג' חבירים ואפילו תלמיד חכם צריך לקבל בפני שלשה חבירים" (Bek. 30b) (cf. Tos.Dem. 2:4-5). (Here, too, it seems likely that the practice related to the suspicion of "hypocrisy" – that the person seeking superior status might not in fact be willing to abide by his commitment. See below, **Argument**.) At the same time, the proselyte's lack of inclusion in this ordinance may indicate his exemption from the statute.

that proselytes could sit on the beit din (בית דין – [law] court) of three which was required to witness the rites of conversion.[96] Even though known proselytes achieved positions of prestige (Shemaiah and Avtalion were said to be Sennacherib's descendants, and the scriptural translator Onkelos/Aquila was a convert[97]), a proselyte could not be appointed to any public office: *"Thou shalt in any wise set him king over thee . . . one from among thy brethren* (Dt. 17:15): all appointments which you make must be made only *'from among thy brethren'"* (Yev. 45b).[98] A proselyte was thus ineligible to hold the office of judge in a criminal court, and most authorities bar a proselyte from acting as a judge even in a civil court, despite the ruling which permitted it, or restrict his jurisdiction to that over a fellow proselyte (cf. San. 4:2; Hor. 1:4; San. 36b).

Although the final act of conversion – the offering of a sacrifice – required the proselyte's presence in the Temple in Jerusalem (cf. Ker. 2:1; Ker. 8b-9a; Ger. 2:5), conversion outside Eretz Israel was recognized. Here, too, however, the Sages required proof that circumcision had been performed at the beit din for the specific purpose of conversion (cf. Yev. 47a; Ger. 4:3). Although batei din (law courts) existed in such diaspora communities as Alexandria (cf. Tos.Pe'ah 4:6; Tos.Ket. 3:1), Josephus also witnessing that the Jewish communities of Sardis (or Ephesus) "had a place of their own in which they decide their affairs and controversies with one another (τόπον ἴδιον, ἐν ᾧ τά τε πράγματα καὶ τὰς πρὸς ἀλλήλους ἀντιλογίας κρίνουσι)" (*Ant.* 14.[117], 235), it is not clear whether these would have exercised authority in regard to proselytes.[99]

If the influencers are neither Jesus' followers (whether from Jerusalem or local Galatians), nor yet (proselytes) from within the local Jewish

---

[96] "R. Hiyya b. Abba stated in the name of R. Johanan: The initiation of a proselyte requires the presence of three men; for *law* has been written in his case אמר רבי חייא בר אבא אמר רבי יוחנן : גר צריך ג' ; משפט כתיב בה" (Yev. 46b) (cf. Num. 15:16). A court of three men is required to authoritatively determine a point of law, and talmudic sources demonstrate the existence of a "beit din of [for] proselytes בית דין של גרים" (cf. Kid. 14a; Yev. 101b).
[97] Cf. Lev.R. 30:8; Num.R. 8:9; Eccl.R. 7.8.1; JMeg. 1, 9, 71a; Meg. 3a; Ber. 19a; Pes. 70b; San. 96b; Git. 56b.
[98] For the discussion of "brethren," see 1:1-5.
[99] Several indications regarding Judaean/diaspora relations can be obtained from ancient sources. Acts 15:1 and Josephus' report of Izates give information concerning itinerant teachers (cf. *Ant.* 20.34-48). Acts 9:21, 21:21, [27-28], 28:21, and Gal. 1:23 suggest that an effective communications network existed between widespread Jewish communities (Damascus, [Asia], Rome), corroborated by the envoys and encyclicals known from rabbinic literature. Despite its measure of obscurity, Acts 16:1-3 indicates that Timothy was circumcised "because of the Jews (διὰ τοὺς Ἰουδαίους)" and Gal. 2:3 implies that Titus was not. For an analysis of the *economic* basis of Jewish antagonism to the early community, see above (n60) and below (n105).

community, their identity appears to be reduced to gentile non-believers.[100] Do the two motives which Paul attributes to his antagonists permit them this status? What persecution could non-believing Gentiles fear, and what meaning can be attributed in such a case to being persecuted "for/because of the cross of the Messiah"?

A possible answer suggests itself in the circumstances in Galatia which Luke reports in Acts 13-14. Acts 13:50 states: "But the Jews aroused the devout women of prominence and the leading men of the city [Pisidian Antioch], and instigated a persecution against Paul and Barnabas, and drove them out of their district."[101] Luke specifically designates this incident as a form of "persecution (διωγμὸν)" – instigated by Gentiles (godfearing women and the leading men of the city). While the measures affect Paul and Barnabas, Luke's comment in Acts 14:21-22 suggests that the south Galatian communities also faced local opposition: ". . . they returned to Lystra and to Iconium and to Antioch, strengthening the souls of the disciples, encouraging them to continue in the faith, and *saying* 'Through many tribulations we must enter the kingdom of God.'[102"]103]

Acts 13:50 presents an exegetical difficulty which requires explanation: Why should *godfearers* (σεβομένας; sebomenas) take sides against Paul and Barnabas? Luke clearly suggests that the warm welcome with which Paul's teaching was received in the synagogue came in part from the local godfearing audience (cf. Acts 13:16, 26, 42-43).[104] Who then were the "devout women of prominence and the leading men of the city" who joined a campaign to drive Paul and his companions out of Antioch, and what motives could they have possessed for doing so?

The initial conclusion is that this group of Gentiles did not accept Paul and Barnabas' teaching – i.e., they did not esteem the gospel. Their collusion with the local Jewish community suggests that they possessed Jewish sympathies – but ones which did not extend to Paul and Barnabas.[105] A second deduction may be that this opposition to the gospel

---

[100] For the influencers' possible pharisaic identity, see 2:15-21 (n269).

[101] οἱ δὲ Ἰουδαῖοι παρώτρυναν τὰς σεβομένας γυναῖκας τὰς εὐσχήμονας καὶ τοὺς πρώτους τῆς πόλεως καὶ ἐπήγειραν διωγμὸν ἐπὶ τὸν Παῦλον καὶ Βαρναβᾶν καὶ ἐξέβαλον αὐτοὺς ἀπὸ τῶν ὁρίων αὐτῶν.

[102] . . . ὑπέστρεψαν εἰς τὴν Λύστραν καὶ εἰς Ἰκόνιον καὶ εἰς Ἀντιόχειαν ἐπιστηρίζοντες τὰς ψυχὰς τῶν μαθητῶν, παρακαλοῦντες ἐμμένειν τῇ πίστει καὶ ὅτι διὰ πολλῶν θλίψεων δεῖ ἡμᾶς εἰσελθεῖν εἰς τὴν βασιλείαν τοῦ θεοῦ.

[103] The evidence of Galatians regarding persecution of the communities does not decide unambiguously whether it derived from an external source or from the influencers (cf. 3:4?, 4:29). On the present reading, these two factors are identical, the godfearers remaining outside – and opposed to – the Galatian communities.

[104] For Acts 13:43, see n76.

[105] The "jealousy" displayed by the Jewish community over Paul and Barnabas' teaching in Antioch seems best attributed to *economic* considerations. Godfearers – women in particular – frequently served as patron/esses to the local Jewish

derived from the implicit or explicit contention that gentile believers have relinquished their pagan status in some way through their commitment to the Jewish Messiah.

The problem posed by Acts 13:50 lies in the fact that godfearers could be expected to *welcome* Paul's teaching of a so-called "law-free gospel." Two problems arise here: Why should such godfearers oppose a message which supported their own godfearing status; and, if they are to be identified with the influencers, why, as godfearers, should they counsel circumcision and conversion – an activity more to be expected of proselytes eager to make other converts?

A possible explanation may lie in an unwillingness on the part of some godfearers to accept the claim (based on Paul's teaching) that becoming faithful to Jesus removes people from their idolatrous pagan status.[106] Such godfearers, while not wishing to compromise their own gentile genesis, may not have been prepared to entertain the notion that others could say that they were no longer pagans without either joining their ranks (as godfearers) or undergoing circumcision in order to become official members of the Jewish community.[107] This attitude may have derived from their own conviction (jealousy?) or may have arisen in conjunction with the position displayed by the Jewish community to which they were attached.[108] [109]

---

community. The threat of losing financial support if the synagogues' supporters transferred their patronage to a new community could have been sufficient to generate the conflict which erupted (cf. Le Cornu and Shulam: 747-49, 755f) (see above [nn60, 99]).

[106] While a merely "theological" debate for Jews – who are circumcised at birth (and therefore not an object of persuasion for the influencers) – the question of circumcision is of a most practical nature for Gentiles. For a godfearer, the issue of whether he (*sic*) can "become Jewish" through faithfulness to Jesus or whether he must undergo a rite of conversion which will not only mark him for life but also mark the whole of his life by observance of the Torah and commandments (cf. 5:3) is of paramount pragmatic import.

[107] This is not to say that Paul's disciples are not, at this point, godfearers, the evidence pointing to the fact that they in fact *are* such and most likely were so even before Paul's arrival in Galatia. Recognition of the influencers' godfearing status requires understanding the participle οἱ περιτεμνόμενοι (hoi peritemnomenoi – NASB: "those who are/have been circumcised") of 6:13 as present middle causative, to be translated as "the advocates of circumcision" (cf. Nanos, Irony: 234). See the commentary on 6:12-16.

[108] If Galatians is to be understood in the context of Acts 13-14, a certain degree of tension between two groups of godfearers – one of whom accepted the gospel, the other of which did not – may be assumed as a natural outcome. It remains a possibility that the assumption of all *external* pressure, of whatever form, is redundant in explaining the Galatian circumstances, especially when the "persecution" is not taken as literal in any form. See the commentary on 6:12-16.

The question of the claim's origin is very difficult to ascertain with exactitude. Did Paul teach that gentile believers in Jesus were no longer pagans? Or did his disciples misunderstand him to? Or did the idea exist in the minds of the influencers alone, who imputed assertions to the gentile believers non-existent in reality?

The first possibility, that Paul explicitly taught that those Gentiles who become faithful to God in Jesus thereby obtained normatively-legitimate Jewish identity, seems highly implausible. Even in the context of the "messianic age" – which he does maintain Jesus to have inaugurated (cf. 1:4) – Gentiles are not considered in Jewish sources to have gained Jewish status or identity without being circumcised, either becoming proselytes or remaining (non-idolatrous) "Gentiles" (cf. Sif.Dt. 354; J AZ 2, 1, 40c) (cf. Keener: 518). Nor does Paul appear to be countering authorship of such a view in the letter.

Could the Galatians then have *misunderstood* Paul to be implying that they had now "officially" (i.e., according to "normative" Jewish standards) become members of the covenant? To the extent that Paul is thought to have anticipated, on his original visit, that his disciples would encounter challenges to the claim that the messianic age had arrived, room for misapprehension diminishes, Paul presumably having originally taken pains to clarify his position on the Gentiles' standing in the Messiah. Notwithstanding the allusions which imply that he is reemphasising something he has already taught (cf. 1:6-9, [13], 5:3, 21), human nature allows for the possibility that, for whatever reason, the Galatians may have chosen to believe that, in ascribing to them status as "sons of Abraham" Paul was thereby also recognizing them as "sons of the covenant"– or failed to comprehend that he was not.[110]

---

[109] While we do not adopt the concept of the "evil eye" and "envy" as an explanation of Paul's argument and, in fact, perceive in it a great difficulty for the influencers' identity as proselytes, jealousy or envy may perhaps play a part between godfearers, some of whom see Jesus' death and resurrection as claiming a Jewish status which they otherwise find available only in the taxing and painful process of circumcision/conversion. It could be imagined that such an emotion would lead to bad feelings and attempts to "sabotage" the gains implicit in the constitution of Jesus' followers. For the evil eye, cf. Nanos, Social; Irony: 181-92, 251-52, 279-80.

[110] On this reading, Paul's focus on the identity of the "sons of Abraham" speaks directly to the issue facing the Galatians: While they are to understand themselves as "sons of the promise" they are not to confuse this status with that of "sons of the covenant," the latter belonging exclusively to Israel. To the extent, however, that a proper definition of the "sons of the covenant" includes the "sons of the promise," the latter now have access to God's Kingdom in he who fulfilled the promise (cf. 3:16). Yet this inclusivity is precisely that which precludes any necessity on their part to seek "natural-born" (proselyte) status within the Jewish community. This is precisely the argument which Paul employs in chapter 3.

As with Nanos' theory, this argument perceives aspersion being cast upon the Galatians' assumed status. While Nanos' identification of the influencers as proselytes supports a circumstance in which the Galatians are denounced as *not being* Jewish – and therefore in need of formal conversion – the present volume perceives the godfearing influencers' insistence to be that gentile believers *should* convert if they wish to be recognised as Jewish in conformity with the prevailing ("present age") norms. On both readings, the influencers call the gentile Galatian believers' alleged era/status into question, causing them to doubt whether Paul has instructed them correctly, and to suffer a sense of "marginalisation" on the part of the Jewish community, of which they had assumed they were now members.[111]

At this point, Paul's disciples are very vulnerable to the influencers' persuasion, sensing not only an absence of recognition but also its availability at the influencers' hands. Their gullibility arouses Paul's ire, in its obvious implications, simultaneously, that Jesus' death and resurrection do not gain Gentiles full access to God's Kingdom and that, in entertaining such a notion, his disciples are exchanging the freedom of redemption from sin and death bought by Jesus for renewed bondage to the dominon of Belial in this present evil age (cf. 1:4, 4:1-7).[112]

Although the third circumstance differs little practically from the second, it relieves some of the pressure concerning what Paul taught and when he did so. Doubt having been sown concerning the Galatians' actual status, the influencers are able to persuade Paul's disciples that, if their faithfulness to God in Jesus has *not* brought them into the messianic age, they must join the commonwealth of Israel by the legitimate means of circumcision-conversion.[113]

Jesus not only has no importance in the influencers' eyes, but is to be opposed because, according to their understanding of Paul's teaching, his

---

[111] The fine nuance between the two views reflects the affinities which they share in their view of the influencers' *intention*. The divergence between them is largely a consequence of a difference in opinion regarding their *identity* – the latter deriving, in substantial part, from historical criteria, together with the difficulty in attributing laxity in Torah-observance to proselytes (cf. 6:13) (see above and below).

[112] Paul further identifies this problem in speaking of the "desire of the flesh" in literal terms – i.e., circumcision – in 5:13f, wherein he sets social norms against those of the messianic age (living in the Spirit). See the commentary on 5:13-18.

[113] Such an argument may have exercised a certain logic upon godfearers – as evidenced in the influencers' own activities. While no prescribed conversion ceremony can be conclusively claimed for this early period (see above), tannaitic sources witness to the need to "make friends" with prospective converts, which may well be construed as teaching them Torah (cf. Mekh.Amalek 3 [R. Eliezer]; Tanh.Yitro 6) (cf. Kulp: 443). For the discussion concerning Jewish proselytising during this period, see above (nn72, 89).

death and resurrection bring Gentiles into Judaism without conversion.[114] Their horizon is determined by "physical" rather than by "spiritual" boundaries, their estimation of Jewish identity weighing more heavily than the radicality of the "one new man" in overcoming paganism.[115] In this sense, they simultaneously oppose the gospel and resist all identification as believers.[116] This factor presumably accounts for the vehemence with which Paul attacks them: They reject the gospel and directly impugn the

---

[114] While the godfearers could affirm their own status and that of converts, a new category, as it were, may have lain beyond the bounds of their credibility or acceptance, potentially threatening the conventional norms by which both those within the Jewish community and those without recognise the boundaries and the proper rites of passage by which they are to be crossed (cf. Nanos, Social: 29). The argument here differs from Nanos' proposition that the early community contended that "because of Christ the age to come had begun in the midst of the present age, and they [gentile believers] can participate in this eschatological reality *as Gentiles*" (Nanos, Inter: 403; original emphasis) only in the identification of the "influencers" as proselytes and thus members of the Jewish community (cf. ibid, for the clearest expression of the argument). Laying aside the questionability of such an identification, it seems clear that the council's decision in Acts 15 approved recognition of the Gentiles' transformation, through the Messiah's righteousness, from "resident aliens [גרי תושב]" (who are not "brothers") to "righteous proselytes [גרי צדק]" who share in Israel's heritage (cf. Ezek. 47:22) (cf. Lichtenstein, Studies: 166). This clarification made, we merely wish to substitute gentile non-believers in place of proselytes (within the Jewish community), while retaining Nanos' general scheme.

[115] Cf. 3:28, 6:15; Eph. 2:11-22, 4:24; Col. 3:10-11. A certain "irony" lies in this interpretation itself. While "in the flesh" means precisely what it says – i.e., the physical act of circumcision (cf. Gen. 17:11, 14, 23-27; Lev. 12:3) – it also places "flesh" in dichotomy to "spirit." Although commentators are accustomed to speaking of these as "pauline terms" (cf. 2:20, 3:3, 29, 5:13ff, 6:8), the so-called opposition between "flesh and spirit/works and faith/Law and grace" is foreign in every way to the normative Jewish framework. Thus while understanding "in the flesh" literally appears to juxtapose Judaism and Christianity in a negative valence, this clearly does not represent the viewpoint of the present authors. As will hopefully become clear, the comparison between flesh/spirit in Galatians is peculiar to the specific context of gentile non-believers who wish to impose circumcision/conversion upon the gentile believers in Galatia. Where it carries a "theological" character, it finds this in the context of "hypocrisy" or outward observance without inward "intent" or "faithfulness" (see below, **Argument**; **Theological pointers**).

[116] Here, too, we concur, with slight variation, with Nanos' reading of the influencers' wish to avoid persecution as a wish not to be considered believers, although being less convinced that they are unwilling "to suffer for the cross of Christ, which they do not believe legitimates the addressees' claim to aggregated identity, and thus to the rights and privileges of Jewish communial life ... in exclusion from civic cultic practices" (Irony: 268) (see above).

A Commentary on the Jewish Roots of Galatians

power of Jesus' death and resurrection in denying it any relevance for the Gentiles' standing.[117]

At the same time, Paul's charge that they are not themselves Torah-observant (cf. 6:13) – an awkward assertion when simultaneously advocating circumcision – may simply (and quite accurately) describe the influencers' godfearing status. On this reading, they are in fact not proselytes, and despite campaigning for circumcision, are not – as mere godfearers – bound in any way to perform the commandments[118] Why then, indicates Paul, should his disciples seek conversion and Torah-observance for themselves?

The local Jewish community may possibly have been pressuring their godfearering patron/esses to express their loyalty to the Jewish community as their clients. These godfearers may have sought to demonstrate such affinity by promoting an attitude calculated to find approval in Jewish eyes. Their position may well have been a vulnerable one in this context. To the extent that they shared, in Jewish considerations, the same status as the believing gentile godfearers, they may have anticipated being the object of suspicion that they would become infected by the same ideas as promoted by Paul.[119]

In summary, the argument presently proposed runs as follows: Acts 13-14 suggests the existence of a group of Gentiles convinced that godfearers did not become part of the people of Israel (as a distinct social community) through faithfulness to the Jewish Messiah. When understood in the context of Galatians, these godfearers – either from their own volition or under the influence of the Jewish community – appear to have put pressure on the local Galatian communities by insisting that, to the extent that they sought Jewish status, gentile believers must undergo circumcision and thereby obtain official social standing. The influencers' opposition was moreover directly to Paul's presentation of the gospel, Jesus' death and resurrection, in their consideration, being imputed to make conversion unnecessary and to grant gentile believers the status of Jews without the official rite of circumcision and entry into the Jewish

---

[117] On this reading, Paul does not oppose proselytism *per se* but the claim that gentiles can only become part of the Jewish community by way of full conversion. For the contention that Paul followed Beit Shammai in practice – including its repulsion regarding proselytes (cf. Shab. 31a) – while being a Hillelite in his halakhah, cf. Hugger: 271-79; Wright, What; and Appendix.

[118] Reading lack of Torah-observance as an accusation demands an act of expediency on the part of the influencers which is made superfluous if the assertion is merely a statement of fact. This relieves many of the difficulties attendant on the traditional reading of 6:12-13.

[119] Ultimately, if the persecution is "metaphorical," no specific third party is required at all, the godfearers simply being unwilling to be recognised – by anyone – as faithful to Jesus and finding their "boast" in Jewish identity (circumcision).

community. The Galatian communities were apparently receptive to such arguments, having initially been attracted to Judaism as godfearers.[120] Paul writes to them, having learnt of the pressure they are experiencing, warning them not to be swayed by the influencers' arguments, specifically because the latter are more concerned with "rites of passage" and Jewish identity than with the gospel and thus dismissing Jesus' death and resurrection as invalid. The letter is structured, halakhically, around a "rebuke" of the Galatian disciples' willingness to be persuaded away from the gospel on the one hand, and Paul's "request" on the other, that they remove the unwholesome influence and remain loyal to himself and to his gospel (see below, **Form**).

One of the most striking implications of this view is that Paul's argument is not an inner-"Christian" one of "faith *versus* circumcision" but a claim exerted against non-believing Gentiles who insist that Gentiles attracted to Judaism must fully convert, dismissing the status of the "new man." His disagreement is consequently with non-believers who seek to convince the Galatian gentile believers that their attachment to Judaism must be expressed through proselytism. The campaign arouses Paul's antagonism because it simultaneously devalues Jesus' death and resurrection and dismisses the status of gentile godfearers. A second implication relates to Paul's defence of his apostleship. If his adversaries are unrelated in any way to Jerusalem or the Apostles – are in fact local, non-believing Gentiles – the necessity of linking Galatians 1:11-24 with the Jerusalem leadership loses its cogency.[121]

While Howard's claim that Paul "got his gospel directly from Christ because no man had it beforehand to pass it on to him . . . The point is that Paul was the first one to receive this particular [non-circumcision] form of the gospel and his recent disclosure of it to the apostles had not yet 'trickled down' to the church at large" (Crisis: 35) is hardly tenable in this respect, its orientation is surely correct.[122] Paul's purpose is to demonstrate

---

[120] In some sense, the Galatians' predisposition to circumcision/conversion makes the Jewish or gentile identity of the influencers irrelevant.

[121] For the inconsistencies involved in identifying the influencers as "Jewish Christians" insistent that Paul is dependent upon the Jerusalem Apostles, cf. Howard, Crisis: 7-8 (see above [nn46, 54]). Commentators must deal with the fact that Paul explicitly acknowledges his need to seek affirmation of his gospel from the Jerusalem leaders in 2:2. (While Howard's own rather ingenuous thesis that the influencers assumed Paul's association with Jerusalem and therefore presumed that he was "preaching circumcision" – being of the same school themselves – merits some attention, it fails to explain how such "allies" were motivated by the attempt to avoid "persecution for the cross of the Messiah.") For the present understanding of Galatians 1-2 as Paul's affirmation of the spiritual authority on the basis of which he intends to rebuke and to request of his disciples, see below, **Argument**.

[122] Assertion of the uniqueness of Paul's "non-circumcision gospel" involves the indefensible assumption not only that the Apostles in Jerusalem were ignorant of

that - unlike the influencers, whose understanding of the essence of Judaism is expressed in the concretely physical terms of circumcision in the flesh - he is not "seeking the favor of men (ζητῶ ἀνθρώποις ἀρέσκειν)" but the will of God received "through a revelation of Jesus the Messiah (δι' ἀποκαλύψεως Ἰησοῦ Χριστοῦ)" (1:10, 12). To the extent that the influencers are "boasting in the flesh" - in conversion to Judaism - they are not "bond-servants of the Messiah (Χριστοῦ δοῦλος)" - they are not working for God.[123]

---

such a view but also that it was unknown amongst other Jewish circles. Howard's thesis (in *Crisis*) falters in failing to acknowledge that Jewish attitudes towards Gentiles were dual and included acceptance of godfearers as well as the insistence that they convert. Howard's claim itself - that "no one, not even the apostles, was privy to the terms of his commission which he received at his conversion" (p. 35) until Paul re-visited Jerusalem fourteen years later - is likewise implausible. It implies on the one hand that on his first return to the city, following three years' residence in Damascus, Paul declared nothing regarding his teaching to either Peter or James, despite staying for two weeks with the former and meeting the latter (cf. 1:18-19); and on the other hand that no word had reached Jerusalem concerning Paul's pedagogy over a period of fourteen years, including an indeterminate sojourn in Arabia (cf. 1:17), where many scholars suggest he engaged in a "Nabatean outreach." Even when Howard attempts to explain the former circumstances, they remain obdurate of understanding - especially in light of Luke's report in Acts and Paul's own version (albeit given a different interpretation in Acts 26:14-18) that his commission was conveyed through Ananias (cf. Acts 9:10-19, 22:12-16). Furthermore, the frequency with which Paul points to the revelation of God's mysterious redemptive purpose which he received in his Damascus experience (cf. Kim, Origin/Paul) mitigates against any muting of his ministry in such an immense measure.

[123] Here again it needs to be stressed that Paul's opposition is not to Judaism *per se* or in general. The view being presented here is categorically not meant to suggest - as has so entrenchedly been the attitude of traditional Christian scholarship - that Judaism is equivalent to the "deeds of the flesh" in all their baseness - in abject and dire comparison to the "fruit of the Spirit" in all the latter's comeliness. Paul's objection is to *gentile* insistence that Jewishness for gentiles can only be expressed in proselytism. To this extent - and with exclusive respect to the circumstances of Galatians - we concur with Gager's claim that Paul is addressing *Gentiles*, with the result that none of his (Paul's) remarks concerning Torah-observance and "faith and works" engage Jews/Judaism. (That this is not Gager's position in general may be surmised from his suggestion that Paul's so-called antagonists may be - perhaps probably are - "Jewish followers of Jesus, like those whom the book of Acts calls the 'circumcision party' and 'believers from the Pharisees'" [p. 79] [cf. p. 96]. Gager also applies Paul's discussions of Torah, circumcision, and salvation to the Gentiles *as believers* - where the view currently being proposed precludes the possibility of Galatians representing an inner-messianic debate on the grounds that the influencers are not themselves Jesus' followers.)

Form

Galatians 6:11 - "See with what large letters I am writing to you with my own hand ("Ἴδετε πηλίκοις ὑμῖν γράμμασιν ἔγραψα τῇ ἐμῇ χειρί)" - suggests that Paul employed an amanuensis - a scribe or "secretary" was frequently used to pen written communications[124] (cf. Longenecker, Galatians: lix f, and for the following discussion). While such literati as Cicero regarded dictation of literary works an expedient to be used only under the force of illness or the press of duty, papyrus evidence witnesses to the fact that ordinary correspondence was routinely conveyed by means of an amanuensis, the sender regularly - but not necessarily - adding personal greetings, a word of farewell, and the date in his own hand.[125]

The act of putting another's thought on paper (or parchment, as the case may be) carries significant implications with respect to "authorship." Scholarly opinion is sharply divided over the extent of an ancient amanuensis' "freedom of expression." The available evidence makes it virtually impossible to determine whether an epistoler would demand word for word dictation or convey the gist of his/her message, leaving the scribe to express the thought in his own turn of phrase. It is feasible that a writer may at times have requested a written communication on a particular subject without providing explicit directions for the development of the theme, perhaps relying on the scribe's discretion and/or on his familiarity with the subject and the writer's views. The existence of a shorthand system in both Latin and Greek may have allowed a secretary to inscribe his client's words verbatim and "edit" them when he wrote out the text to be sent.[126]

While this debate is difficult to settle on the extant data, the custom of adding a personal subscription to a formal letter may suggest a degree of scribal liberty, the author's signature not only signifying his authorship but also validating the conformation of the wording to his intentions - thereby indirectly witnessing to scribal involvement.[127] Within the epistolary

---

[124] Cf. Jer. 36:4, 17-18, 27ff, 45:1; Rom. 16:22; 1 Pet. 5:12; Gen.R. 75:5; San. 11b (cf. Stone: 591n48).

[125] Cf. 1 Cor. 16:21; Col. 4:18; 2 Thess. 3:17; Phlm 19.

[126] These systems may have been the creation of slaves/freedmen (cf. Seneca, *Ep.Mor.* 90.25; P. Oxy. 724).

[127] The confirmed participation of an amanuensis in Paul's letters should perhaps make scholars more wary of attributing chronological proximity to the epistles on the basis of assumed theological affinity and more aware of the characteristics peculiar to individual scribes. Surely preferring theological pointers - on the assumption that these are clearly delineated and open to unambiguous interpretation - over historical markers (even where these are uneven) for determining chronological details is a dubious device. (A similar argument may also be adduced with respect to the establishment of a body of "authentic" pauline letters, a determination which demands an identifiable pauline style [see above, **Author**].)

framework of Galatians (see below), amanuensal participation guarantees a well-composed construction, necessitating as it does a first draft or even a sequence of draft, composition, and copy. Any "haphazard" composition is precluded (cf. Betz, Galatians: 1, 312).

The implications of a scribal presence for the question of authorship are further associated with the naming of co-senders in the prescript, here named as "... and all the brethren who are with me (καὶ οἱ σὺν ἐμοὶ πάντες ἀδελφοὶ) ..." (1:2).[128] These are not merely those who send greetings but co-authors of the letter with Paul – of whom the secretary may even be a member. The participation of several people in the letter's composition suggests that the letter's character should be recognised as that of an official document rather than a personal communication. The fact that it is also addressed to "the churches of Galatia (ταῖς ἐκκλησίαις τῆς Γαλατίας)" (1:2) – in the plural – further indicates that it functioned as a form of (en)cyclical letter, designed for several groups rather than one specific community (cf. McRay, Paul: 247-48).[129]

Recent scholarly volumes on Galatians have focused upon its epistolary and rhetorical structure – the Graeco-Roman conventions which gave letters their particular form and enabled them to convey a specific message (cf. Longenecker, Galatians: ci ff, and for the following discussion).[130] Despite the argument that form and content are inseparable in a written document, some commentators – most strikingly Betz – argue that Galatians' epistolary framework can be detached from the letter's body, leaving (in Betz's case) an "apologetic letter" best understood within the rubric of forensic speech, the rules of which are set out in the classical rhetorical handbooks.[131]

---

[128] Cf. Rom. 16:22; [1 Cor. 16:20-21].

[129] If Paul wrote Galatians from Antioch prior to the council (see above, **Date and destination**), the co-senders may be the Antiochian community. Since it would seem more likely that Paul would identify them in some way if so, it may be better to refer the allusion to those who had accompanied him through Galatia – Timothy, Barnabas, and some unidentified others (cf. Acts 13:2, 13) (see above, **Date and destination**); for Barnabas, see also below.

[130] Paul's (spoken) rhetorical skills are clearly on display in his "trial" speeches (cf. Acts 22:1-21, 23:6, 24:10-21, 26:2-23). For Jewish rhetoric and attitudes towards Greek wisdom, cf. Lieberman, Greek/Hellenism; Le Cornu and Shulam: 72-73, 466-68, 1028-30, 1293-1324.

[131] As should become clear in the commentary, the present approach exhibits closer affinities with Hays' search for a narrative substructure in Galatians than with Betz's forensic/apologetic framework: "The central thesis of the book is stated forthrightly in the opening pages and reiterated in the concluding chapter: *a story about Jesus Christ is presupposed by Paul's argument in Galatians, and his theological reflection attempts to articulate the meaning of that story*" (Hays, Faith: xxiv; original emphasis).

Others – notably Longenecker – assert that this approach emphasises the style of argument to the neglect of the significance of the epistolary form. While Longenecker endeavours to redress the balance by stressing that Galatians' proper literary *Gattung* is the common letter tradition and faults Betz for forcing the latter chapters into the forensic mode when their Jewish rhetorical conventions are clear, he himself fails to appeal to Jewish epistolary forms. The most prominent example of these is surely the Halakhic Letter (4QMMT/4Q394-99) from Qumran (cf. Kampen and Bernstein). The parallels between this document and Galatians, which are of general chronological, epistolary, rhetorical, hermeneutical, and halakhic character, demand close attention and analysis, some of which we hope to provide below as well as in the commentary itself.[132]

The corpus of Jewish letters is divided into literary and non-literary letters (cf. Stone: 583f). While encyclicals generally fall under the latter category as representing issuance of specific orders, where they are intended for a wider audience and provide a broader "philosophical" elucidation behind the ordinances they may also be considered as "literary." In a Jewish context, letters may have originated as the written analogy of the sermon given in the synagogue setting, the latter essentially constituting an exhortatory address (cf. ibid). Letters functioned as a substitute for direct communication, providing the vehicle for a direct second-person appeal to the readers in their peculiar context.[133]

To the extent that Galatians constitutes an encyclical it bears comparison with other encyclicals known to us from contemporary Jewish literature. Many of these are specifically halakhic in nature, detailing the rulings to be followed regarding particular issues: "May your peace be great! We beg to inform you that the time of 'removal' has arrived for setting aside [the tithe] from the olive heaps" . . . "May your peace be great! We beg to inform you that the time of 'removal' has arrived for setting aside the tithe from the corn sheaves" . . . "May your peace be great for ever! We beg to inform you that the doves are still tender and the lambs

---

[132] If Longenecker and Betz may be excused for not having the benefit of 4QMMT's availability, Nanos cannot appeal to the same pretext. Gager refers to the text in a footnote to his argument that the phrase "works of the law" alludes "specifically to the ambiguous status of *Gentiles* under the law" (p. 174n15; emphasis added). His biographical reference to Kampen and Bernstein in this respect appears very odd, given that the latter volume provides no evidence – indeed supplies contraindications – of such usage of the term with regard to Gentiles. Qimron and Strugnell (DJD X), 4QMMT's original editors, date the scroll's provenance to 159-52 B.C.E., referring the six extant fragments to c. 75 B.C.E.

[133] Romans represents an excellent example of this form, embodying a communication of "religious thought" articulated in characteristically rabbinic fashion, accompanied by halakhic instruction (cf. Shulam and Le Cornu). For Galatians in this regard, see below, **Argument; Theological pointers.**

still too young and that the crops are not yet ripe. It seems advisable to me and to my colleagues to add thirty days to this year"[134] (San. 11b).

The authors of 4QMMT also call on their addressee(s) to repent and renounce their error in halakhic observance: "And also we have written to you some of the works of the Torah which we think are good for you and for your people, for we s[a]w that you have intellect and knowledge of the Law. Reflect on all these matters and seek from him that he may support your counsel and keep far from you the evil scheming{s} and the counsel of Belial, so that at the end of time, you may rejoice in finding that some of our words are true. And it shall be reckoned to you as justice when you do what is upright and good before him, for your good and that of Israel"[135] (4QMMTᵉ ff14-17ii:2-8).[136]

Since its wider public accessibility in the 1990's, much of the attention paid to 4QMMT within the New Testament scholarly world has centred around issues directly related to Galatians, the very title given to the scroll demonstrating a hope that it might shed light on Paul's phrase "works of the law (ἔργων νόμου)" (cf. Abegg, Paul).[137] Notwithstanding, interest in its *genre* – peculiarly in relation to Galatians – has been curiously and conspicuously lacking. 4QMMT was termed a "halakhic letter" in the first publications, and while this designation may be disputed on various grounds, none of these preclude its comparison with Galatians on epistolary grounds (cf. ABD: 4:843-45; Kampen and Bernstein: 5, and for the following discussion).

Some of the objections raised relate to the text's halakhic status which, in citing opposing halakhic opinions, differs from such prescriptive legal texts as CDC and 1QS. It is also acknowledged that the halakhic section (B)

---

[134] שלומכון יסגא! מהודעין אנחנא לכון דזמן ביעורא מטא לאפרושי מעשרא ממעטנא דזיתא . . .
שלומכון יסגא! מהודעין אנחנא לכון דזמן ביעורא מטא לאפרושי מעשרא מעומרי שיבליא . . .
שלומכון יסגא לעלם! מהודעין אנחנא לכון דגוזליא רכיכין ואימריא ערקין וזמנא דאביבא לא מטא.
ושפרא צילתא באנפאי ובאנפי חברייי ואוסיפית על שתא דא יומין תלתיו.

[135] אנחנו כתבנו אליך מקצת מעשי התורה שחשבנו לטוב לך ולעמך שר[א]ינו עמך ערמה ומדע תורה הבן בכל אלה ובקש מלפנו שיתקן את עצתך והרחיק ממך מחשב[ו]ת רעה ועצת בליעל בשל שתשמח באחרית העת במצאך מקצת דברינו כן ונחשבה לך לצדקה בעשותך הישר והטוב לפנו לטוב לך ולישראל.

[136] Cf. Lk. 1:3; Acts 15:22f; Rom. 7:1; 1 Macc. 15:19; 2 Macc. 1:1-10; Jos.*Ant.* 16.163 (Greek); Tos.San. 2:6; JSan. 1, 2, 18d; JMaas.Sheni 5, 8, 56c. For the apostolic encyclical, cf. Le Cornu and Shulam: 840-51. Identification of Galatians with a halahkic model carries with it significant implications regarding Paul's influence, a central issue within the letter itself (however it may be interpreted). Encyclicals are by nature official and afford their senders a direct measure of responsibility over a community whose submission to their authority is assumed. If Barnabas is one of the co-senders, he would be included within the authority-bearing status (cf. Acts 13:2ff), a fact of considerable importance for 2:13. For Barnabas, see above, **Date and destination**.

[137] Cf. Rom. 3:20, 28; Gal. 2:16, 3:2, 5, 10.

lacks an epistolary opening.[138] In both cases, however, the document's very polemical (dialogical) character – especially conjoined with the so-called "hortatory epilogue" – is precisely what upsets these definitional attempts. One of the scroll's most striking features is its first and second person address. Not only does it possess a sender (consistently expressed in the first person plural – "we") and an addressee ("you" – plural in section B, singular in section C), but its author also characteristically expresses "himself" through the expression חושבים/אומרים אנחנו (anachnu choshvim/omrim – "we think/say"),[139] the prevailing second-person address being . . . אתם יודעים (atem yodim – "you know [that] . . .").[140] The text also implies the existence of a third party – a group from whom the senders have separated themselves and with whom they wish not to be identified by the addressees (cf. 4Q397 ff14-21:7-9). The specific cause of the division is explicitly described as a halakhic dispute, the ordinances listed in section B suggesting these to be primarily related to purity, the Temple, sacrifices, and festivals.[141]

The importance of "influence" – which Nanos has recently brought out so succinctly – is clearly common to both 4QMMT and Galatians.[142]

---

[138] The effect of this argument is somewhat compromised in light of the debate concerning the authenticity of the preceding calendrical section. Scholars are divided over whether or not this segment should be regarded as an integral part of the text. The opening formula of the document as a whole is also unfortunately missing.

[139] Cf. Rom. 16, 7:1; Gal. 1:11, 3:7; 4Q394 ff3-7ii:16, f8iii:12, f8iv:5; 4Q396 2:6-7; 4Q397 f5:3, ff6-13:6.

[140] Cf. 4Q396 3:8, 4:9; 4Q397 ff6-13:14, ff14-21:7f.

[141] The historical situation to which 4QMMT refers is debated amongst scholars, as is the identity of the three groups, although the "we" group clearly represents the sending community. Rabbinic sources indicate that the halakhot disputed by the sect represent pharisaic rulings, those espoused by them being identified in rabbinic literature as sadducean (cf. Baumgarten). It is quite likely that the sender(s) and addressee(s) shared a general common ethos, upon the basis of which they had both "separated" themselves from others – a concurrence endangered, in the eyes of the author of this scroll, by the "they" group's attitude towards the Temple and priesthood (cf. Kampen and Bernstein: 75-80). The polemical tone of the letter is mitigated by the conciliatory tone adopted in the final section, indicating that relations between the correspondents were reasonably amicable. The concluding appeal suggests that the senders were relatively confident of a positive response to their request.

[142] The coinage of "influencers" to describe those who are upsetting the gentile Galatian believers directly also gains Nanos a solution to the problems engendered by the traditional concept of "judaisers" as considered in the sense of "opponents" or "rivals" (cf. Irony: 115-27) (see above, **Occasion and circumstances**). Despite the historical problems dependent on Nanos' identification of these personages, the concept of "influence" is singularly appropriate. See the commentary on 2:10f, 4:21-31, and 5:2-12.

Both texts reflect and represent attempts by one group to exert pressure upon another in an effort to convince the second of the propriety and priority of their views, and the shadow of a third party over both "influencers" and those influenced.[143] The propriety of reading Galatians as a "rebuke-request" letter, as suggested by Longenecker on the Greek epistolary model, is strengthened by the understanding that, when placed within a Jewish context, such a genre becomes "halakhic" in a very similar sense as that attributed to 4QMMT. Both Paul and the author of the "Halakhic Letter" are writing in an effort to persuade their readers to act in accordance with their perception of the truth (their interpretation of Scripture).[144]

A second point relates to 4QMMT's style of biblical usage (cf. Kampen and Bernstein: 29-51). Having noted that the polemical tone of the document may weigh against its inclusion within the letter genre and shift it towards a description of legal controversies, it is also suggested that the variant halakhic formulatory style the text exhibits may be due to its epistolary nature (cf. ibid: 33). The implications of this point for Galatians are highlighted when it is recognised that the form is directly associated with a particular handling of the biblical text and idiom. While this issue is specifically related to the way biblical laws are phrased and interpreted in the Qumran text, the question of biblical exegesis is expressly relevant to Paul's use of Scripture in Galatians.[145] Thus, for example, 4QMMT demonstrates clear evidence that the author at times employs biblical vocabulary and at times deviates from the latter.[146] The formula כתוב (katuv – "it is written") also occurs in 4QMMT in citation of a paraphrase

---

[143] A similar dynamic to 4QMMT appears to be in play in Galatians with regard to Paul's "apostleship." The authors of 4QMMT are at pains to prove their sincerity to the addressees – on the basis of which he can also expect them to consider seriously the legal positions defended in the letter (see 2:1-10).

[144] For the centrality of Scripture for Paul, see below, **Theological pointers** (Scripture).

[145] See below, **Theological pointers**.

[146] While not directly linked to the question of genre, it is noteworthy that 4QMMT and Galatians share an appeal to Gen. 15:6, albeit in different contexts. (Abegg's suggestion [Paul] that the reference is not to Abraham in Gen. 15:6 but to Pinchas in Ps. 106:31 is not entirely convincing, given the immediately preceding reference to David [cf. Ps. 32:1-2] [see on 3:10-14].) Additional linguistic "parallels" between the two texts may be adduced in the pauline corpus. Paul's reference to "knowledge of the law" (cf. Rom. 7:1) resembles 4Q398 ff14-17ii:4. If 4QMMT is to be identified with the "[la]w and the Torah והתורה ק[ח]חנ]" which the Teacher of Righteousness sent to the Wicked Priest (cf. 4Q171 4:8-9), the Wicked Priest is said there to have "spied [צפה]" on the Teacher of Righteousness and attempted to kill him (cf. Gal. 2:4) (cf. Kampen and Bernstein: 53ff). (The exegesis derives from Ps. 37:32, a verse which Paul may also have had in mind.) For a discussion of the "works of the Torah" in the two texts, see the commentary on 2:15-21 and 3:10-14.

rather than a direct quotation of a scriptural passage – a fact which may help explain citations at variance with the masoretic text (cf. ibid: 39-40). May the ostensible independence from Scripture reflected in 4QMMT also be attributed to its particular genre?

Although research into the relation between 4QMMT and Galatians is still in its early stages, Abegg submits that "Paul, using the same terminology, is rebutting the theology of documents such as MMT. I do not mean to suggest that Paul knew of MMT or of the zealous members of the Qumran community, but simply that Paul was reacting to the kind of theology espoused by MMT, perhaps even by some Christian converts who were committed to the kind of thinking reflected in MMT" (p. 54). The findings of the present volume seem to indicate that this claim does not bear out. The "works of the law" of which the Halakhic Letter speaks are mentioned in the context of David's "piety [חסידים איש]," a case being arguably made that the phrase consequently arises in the context of an "hypocrisy" deriving from outward observance similar to that with which Paul charges Peter.[147]

Affinities between Galatians and 4QMMT also arise in relation to Paul's "allegory" in 4:22-31, a section in which Paul, "quoting" Scripture, urges his disciples to adopt his advice and conduct themselves according to it by "casting out the bondwoman and her son."[148] While not strictly pesher in form, 4QMMT demonstrates affinities with that genre so favoured in the Qumran literature, giving to Paul's otherwise "perverse" reading and use of Scripture an understanding which helps structure the letter as a whole and provides a proper perception of the "allegory" *per se.*

Argument
The presently proposed reading of Galatians regards the epistle along the lines of 4QMMT – namely, as a "halakhic letter" in which Paul sets out his authority, on the basis of which he proceeds to first rebuke his disciples for straying from the gospel and then lays out for them the "path in which they should walk" (see above, **Form**). The epistle divides into two sections, the first – consisting of 1:1-4:11 – forming the background for the second – 4:12-6:18. The initial unit constitutes Paul's "rebuke" of his Galatian disciples, the second his "request" of them.[149] Peter's hypocrisy in 2:11-21 establishes the letter's conceptual framework.[150]

---

[147] See the commentary on 2:15-21 and 3:10-14.
[148] For Galatians' structural composition, see below, **Argument**; for Paul's use of Scripture, see below, **Theological pointers**.
[149] Cf. Longenecker, Galatians: cviii-cix. While reflecting Longenecker's general thesis, this reading places Galatians specifically within a "halakhic" frame – in epistolary, rhetorical, and conceptual terms. The correspondence between the present work and Longenecker's volume similarly extends to the structural

The rebuke is of the gentile Galatians' willingness to listen to people who are promoting Jewish identity *as a social standing*.[151] The reprimand expresses itself on two complementary planes. Most significantly, according to Paul such seduction "severs" the Galatian believers from the Messiah, the influencers' intention being to convince the former that, if they are seeking Jewish identity, their attachment to Judaism must be formalized. As "godfearers" – Gentiles – themselves, the influencers are unwilling to accept the claim that faithfulness to the (Jewish) Messiah Jesus bestows any "official" Jewish identity. If Paul's disciples are seeking the latter, they have one choice only – to undergo circumcision and conversion.[152] Parallel to this circumstance is the fact that, in listening to the influencers and allowing them expression, the Galatians are in fact turning away from Paul himself – he who "fathered" them in faithfulness to God through Jesus.[153]

Paul's request of the Galatians is correspondingly composed of two analogous halves. Paul urges his disciples to remain faithful to the gospel by renewing their loyalty to him: "Become as *I am*" (4:12). In order so to do, he vehemently and repeatedly warns them, in different ways, to "remove the leaven which is permeating the dough" (5:9) (cf. 4:[17], 30, 5:26, 6:3-8).[154]

On this reading, Paul opens the letter with an "affirmation" of his apostleship, establishing the authority on the basis of which he intends to make the request – rather than with a "defence" against the counter-claims

---

argument – and excludes any real substantive affinity. Nor do we necessarily concur in all the specific details of Longenecker's structural famework.

[150] For the theories assumed in this section regarding the identity of the players involved in Galatians and the issues addressed, see above in the segments devoted to **Date and destination** and **Occasion and circumstances**.

[151] The question whether the Galatians were seeking social standing within the Jewish community irrespective of the influencers' presence, or whether their interest was sparked and kindled by the influencers, is virtually unanswerable (see above, **Occasion and circumstances**). To the extent that determination of this issue is inconclusive, we have spoken indiscriminately of the "Galatians' seeking" and the "influencers' persuasion."

[152] The above comment having been noted, it seems clear that, the Galatians' interest in Judaism having presumably already manifested itself in a godfearing status, the influencers are playing on a *social standing* whose aspiration is goaded *by the influencers themselves*. While it is difficult to ascertain whether the gentile Galatian believers claimed Jewish status for themselves in the Messiah, the influencers clearly considered some such entitlement implicit in Paul's teaching. Under such circumstances, the "troublers" were endeavouring to persuade the Galatians that recognised social status within the Jewish community was not merely optional but obligatory. It could not be gained through identity with the Messiah.

[153] For the issue of "faithfulness," see below, **Theological pointers**.

[154] It should be noted here that this reading of 6:1ff understands Paul's addressees as both his Galatian disciples and (indirectly) the influencers (see below).

of the influencers. Since he is going to ask the Galatians to imitate him and to cast out those who are "troubling" them with "another gospel" (cf. 1:6-9, 5:7-10), he wishes to assure them of his integrity and of his status. Having done this in 1:1-5, he launches immediately into an ironic expression of "surprise" that his disciples should so quickly be deserting him and his gospel (1:6-9) – followed by a second validation of his (apostolic) legitimacy (1:11-17), aimed at rousing them from their "bewitchment" (3:1). Thence he progresses into an account of his early "ministry," a report designed to lead up to the incident in Antioch – an episode possessed of immediate relevance and import to the circumstances in which his Galatian disciples currently find themselves.[155]

The significance of the Antioch episode is here understood according to a particular understanding of Peter's hypocrisy. Paul's rebuke – paralleling and patterning that of the Galatians themselves – is that Peter has "forgotten" that Jewish believers need the Messiah to enter God's Kingdom. The hypocrisy entailed in his conduct is composed of three elements. It is, on the most outward level, an act of expediency – undertaken in order to conform to the standards of others (cf. 2:12). More fundamentally, it constitutes a violation of Peter's personally-held conviction that the Gentiles have been purified before God (cf. Acts 10:34-48). Paul then takes the issue one step deeper, identifying hypocrisy itself with human sinfulness.

Rabbinic texts speak of hypocrisy in terms of possessing the keys to the "inner chamber" of God's Kingdom while lacking access to the "outer chamber": "Every man who possesses learning without the fear of heaven is like a treasurer who is entrusted with the inner keys but not with the outer: how is he to enter [the Kingdom of heaven]? כל אדם שיש בו תורה ואין בו יראת שמים דומה לגזבר שמסרו לו מפתחות הפנימיות ומפתחות החיצוניות לא מסרו לו. בהי עייל?" (Shab. 31b). The "fear of heaven" is frustrated precisely because of human beings' "created" status, being merely human and thus limited by sin: "Because of his sinfulness man has not the power to comprehend the Form on high; otherwise he would have been entrusted with the keys [of the unknown] and discover how heaven and earth had been created אין ספק לאדם לידע מה דמות למעלה ואלמלא כן היו מוסרין לו מפתחות וידע במה נבראו שמים וארץ" (ARNᵃ 39:1).

While it may come easily to people to speak of God's will, the doing of it does not constitute a natural human capacity. The disparity between "hearing and doing" under these circumstances can be discerned as a consequence of the impediment of sinful human nature, such iniquities creating "a separation between you and your God, and your sins have hid

---

[155] Students of Galatians will recognise that this reading does not accord with any of the standard positions. Since, for reasons of clarity and brevity, we do not directly discuss the latter, those wishing to familiarise themselves with them are advised to go to the pertinent commentaries – Burton, Betz, Longenecker, et al.

His face from you כי אם-עונׂתיכם היו מבדלים ביננכם לבין אלהיכם וחטאותיכם
הסתירו פנים מכם" (Isa. 59:2).

This is the motif upon which Paul proceeds to elaborate throughout
the letter. The "bondage to sin" bound up in such hypocrisy is common to
Jews and Gentiles alike. Both are in need of God's deliverance in His
Messiah, whom He sent into the world to "deliver us out of this present
evil age" (1:4), giving "himself for our sins" (1:4) in order to ransom us
from enslavement to the "elemental things of the world" (4:3). Here, Paul's
thought throughout the letter can be read in the light of Isaiah 61:1-3, God
having anointed His Messiah "to bring good news to the afflicted; He has
sent me to bind up the brokenhearted, to proclaim liberty to captives, and
freedom to prisoners; to proclaim the favorable year of the LORD . . ."[156] On
the model of 11QMelch, Paul presents Jesus as releasing wo/mankind
from the "debt" of their sin in the year of jubilee.[157]

In Jesus, both Jews and Gentiles find full access to God's Kingdom,
Jesus' death and resurrection overcoming human sin through the bestowal
of the Spirit. It is this which imparts the necessary ability – the "intention"
– to perform God's will which must accompany human deeds if they are to
be "real" rather than "ritual": "But he who doubts is condemned if he eats
[for example], because his eating is not from faith ["intention"]; and
whatever is not from faith is sin"[158] (Rom. 14:23).

On this reading, Galatians may be conceived as a "commentary" on
Matthew 23. Jesus' words concerning the "neglect of the weightier
provisions of the Torah: justice and mercy and faithfulness (ἀφήκατε τὰ
βαρύτερα τοῦ νόμου, τὴν κρίσιν καὶ τὸ ἔλεος καὶ τὴν πίστιν)" (Mt.
23:23) are themselves an "interpretation" of such prophetic passages as

---

[156] משח ה' אׂתי לבשר ענוים שלחני לחבׁש לנשברי-לב לקרׂא לשבוים דרור ולאסורים פקח-קוח:
לקרׂא שנת-רצון לה' . . .

[157] " And as for what he said: *Lev* 25:13 «In [this] year of jubilee, [you shall return,
each one to his respective property» . . . [Its interpretation] for the last days refers to
the captives, who [. . .] . . . and they are the inherita[nce of Melchize]dek, who will
make them return. And liberty will be proclaimed for them, to free them from [the
debt of] all their iniquities . . . Melchizedek will carry out the vengeance of Go[d's]
judgments, [and on that day he will fr]e[e them from the hand of] Belial and from
the hand of all the sp[irits of his lot] . . . This [. . .] is the day of [peace about whi]ch
he said [. . . through Isa]iah the prophet, who said: [*Isa* 52:7 «How] beautiful upon
the mountains are the feet [of] the messen[ger who] announces peace, the
mess[enger of good who announces salvati]on, [sa]ying to Zion: your God [reigns.»]
ואשר אמר בשנת היובל [הזאת תשובו איש אל אחוזתו . . . [פשרו] לאחרית הימים על השבויים
אשר . . . והמה נחלׂת מלכי צׂדק אשר ישיבמה אליהמה וקרא להמה דרור לעזוב להמה [משׂא] כול
עוונותיהמה . . . ומלכי צדק יקום נקם משפטי א[ל וביום ההוא יצי[לׂמה מיד] בליעל ומיד כול
ר[וחי גורלו] . . . הזאת הואה יום ה[שלום א]שר אמר [. . . ביד ישע[יׂה הנביא אשר אמר [מה] נאוו
"על ההרים רגל[י] מבש[ר מ]שמיע שלום מב[שר טוב משמיע ישוע[ה א]וׂמר לציון [מלך] אלוהיך
(11QMelch 2:2, 4-6, 13, 15-16).

[158] ὁ δὲ διακρινόμενος ἐὰν φάγῃ κατακέκριται, ὅτι οὐκ ἐκ πίστεως· πᾶν δὲ οὐ
οὐκ ἐκ πίστεως ἁμαρτία ἐστίν.

Micah 6:6-8, which demand intention together with practice: "With what shall I come to the LORD and bow myself before the God on high? Shall I come to him with burnt offerings, with yearling calves? Does the LORD take delight in thousands of rams, in ten thousand rivers of oil? Shall I present my first-born *for* my rebellious acts, the fruit of my body for the sin of my soul? He has told you, O man, what is good; and what does the LORD require of you but to do justice, to love kindness, and to walk humbly with your God."[159]

On the basis of similar texts, rabbinic literature speaks of the principle of acting "within the margin of the judgment" – or "go[ing] beyond the law, which in itself is right and good, in order to do what is right and good" (Berkovits: 27). Paul speaks of this concept in Romans in terms of the "spirit" of the Torah, in contrast to its "letter": "For indeed circumcision is of value, if you practice the Torah; but if you are a transgressor of the Torah, your circumcision has become uncircumcision . . . For he is not a Jew who is one outwardly; neither is circumcision that which is outward in the flesh. But he is a Jew who is one inwardly; and circumcision is that which is of the heart, by the Spirit, not by the letter"[160] (Rom. 2:25, 28-29).

The significance of Paul's rebuke of Peter – which, on the current reading, occurred very shortly prior to the penning of the epistle – lies in its resolution of the problem of human hypocrisy for Gentiles as for Jews. If Peter will not acknowledge that, as a Jew, he also is in need of the "outer keys," as it were – the Spirit – his actions are tantamount to denying the validity of the Gentiles' entrance into the Kingdom, they who do not even possess the "inner keys" (Torah-study) but are without hope and without God in the world (cf. Eph. 2:12). Paul's argument with Peter turns, in this respect, on the defining "Israel": Who are truly the "sons of Abraham"? His answer – in line with other Jewish texts of the period – is that Abraham's "disciples" are those who possess his qualities – those who combine Torah-study with the fear of heaven, who act "beyond the margin of the judgment" in the Spirit, who seek after and act according to the "weightier provisions of the Torah: justice and mercy and faithfulness" (Mt. 23:23).[161]

---

[159] במה אקדם ה' אכף לאלהי מרום האקדמנו בעולות בעגלים בני שנה: הירצה ה' באלפי אילים ברבבות נחלי-שמן האתן בכורי פשעי פרי בטני חטאת נפשי: הגיד לך אדם מה-טוב ומה-ה' דורש ממך כי אם-עשות משפט ואהבת חסד והצנע לכת עם-אלהיך.

[160] Περιτομὴ μὲν γὰρ ὠφελεῖ ἐὰν νόμον πράσσῃς· ἐὰν δὲ παραβάτης νόμου ἦς, ἡ περιτομή σου ἀκροβυστία γέγονεν . . . οὐ γὰρ ὁ ἐν τῷ φανερῷ 'Ιουδαῖός ἐστιν οὐδὲ ἡ ἐν τῷ φανερῷ ἐν σαρκὶ περιτομή, ἀλλ' ὁ ἐν τῷ κρυπτῷ 'Ιουδαῖος, καὶ περιτομὴ καρδίας ἐν πνεύματι οὐ γράμματι, οὗ ὁ ἔπαινος οὐκ ἐξ ἀνθρώπων ἀλλ' ἐκ τοῦ θεοῦ.

[161] From Romans 14-15, in which "faith" serves the function of "intention," we may add "love" to the parallels between "intention," "faithfulness," and "acting within the margin of the judgment" in the Spirit: "For if because of food your brother is

Having addressed Peter's hypocrisy in this way, Paul then turns directly to his readers in Galatia, in 3:1, with the exclamation that, being equally "foolish," they have been "bewitched" in a similar way as was Peter.[162] The section 3:1-4:11 subsequently constitutes an extended exegetical excursus, reminding the Galatians' of their status as "sons of Abraham" – which, Paul argues, they have gained through their faithfulness to Jesus' obedience to death on the cross.[163] Having experienced the working of the Spirit, how can they now be persuaded to (or be seeking) a social standing which will negate their existing status in Jesus?

3:6-14 demonstrates how the Gentiles' acceptance before God has been established on the basis of Jesus' faithfulness, verses 10-13 forming a "digression" into Jesus' relation to the Torah. This leads to the dialectical conclusion of 3:14, in which Paul elucidates the fact that the realization of Abraham's blessing to the Gentiles has enabled Israel also to partake of the Spirit through Jesus' faithfulness.[164]

Rather than constituting an *ad hominem* argument, in which Paul emotionally attacks his disciples' disturbers personally, 3:15-18 is presently read as evidencing further scriptural proof, brought this time in respect of the relative status of faithfulness and Torah-observance (as representive of circumcision/ conversion) in temporal terms. Here again, Paul emphasises the significance of Jesus' faithfulness, this time in his status as the "seed" in whom Abraham's blessing to the nations of the world was promised. Paul's argument is that Jesus has fulfilled this promise, spoken to Abraham of himself, embodying in his person the seed/promise through whom the blessing would be realized. Understanding God's initial "covenant" with Abraham as a "will and testament," Paul establishes that the gentile Galatians' newly-established status as "sons of Abraham" through Jesus' fulfilment of the promise constitutes them – together with Israel – as proper and legitimate co-"heirs" of the promise to Abraham's "descendants."

---

hurt, you are no longer walking according to love . . . for the kingdom of God is not eating and drinking, but righteousness and peace and joy in the Holy Spirit (εἰ γὰρ διὰ βρῶμα ὁ ἀδελφός σου λυπεῖται, οὐκέτι κατὰ ἀγάπην περιπατεῖς . . . οὐ γάρ ἐστιν ἡ βασιλεία τοῦ θεοῦ βρῶσις καὶ πόσις ἀλλὰ δικαιοσύνη καὶ εἰρήνη καὶ χαρὰ ἐν πνεύματι ἁγίῳ)" (Rom. 14:15, 17).

[162] This reading of 3:1 specifies the direct relationship between this section of the letter and Paul's preceding rebuke of Peter.

[163] The extended passage from 2:10-4:11 thus focuses on the identity of the "sons of Abraham." The most important divergence between 2:1-21 and 3:1ff lies in the fact that while with Peter Paul addresses the issue of Torah-observance in relation to Jesus' faithfulness, he elaborates that faithfulness in respect to the gentile Galatians in relation to their seeking after circumcision.

[164] For "the faith of Jesus the Messiah" as representing Jesus' own faithfulness, see below, **Theological pointers**.

On this reading, Gentiles are considered as "heirs according to promise" and Israel "heirs according to the covenant." In being of the seed of Isaac, both qualify equally as "sons of Abraham." Both, as Paul cautions in Romans, remain in God's favour as long as they act as Abraham's "disciples" (cf. Rom. 2:12-29, 9:6-11:32). Whatever transpires subsequent to this covenant – i.e., with God's election of Israel – cannot remove or annul the conditions of the original covenant (verses 17-18).[165]

3:19-25 arises as a natural consequence of the historical relationship between God's promise to Abraham and His giving of the Torah.[166] Through the dual ideas of the "mediator" and "tutor" Paul elaborates his understanding that the Torah "accommodates" itself to human nature. God's sovereignty being most explicitly expressed in His unity, it is love which affirms both to the deepest extent: "It is a weighty commandment, the most weighty of the Torah, the command to love God, *Thou shalt love the Lord thy God* (Dt. 6:5) being conjoined with the verse which affirms His sovereignty, *Hear O Israel: the Lord is our God, the Lord alone* (Dt. 6:4)"[167] (TBE p. 140).

In so comprehending the Torah's nature as "condescending" to the level of achievement attainable by human beings, Paul considers that God did not intentionally design the Torah to assist human beings in overcoming their natural inclination and bondage to sin. Its function is rather to serve as a custodian in order to insure Israel's survival until the proper mode of deliverance might come – in God's faithfulness in Jesus. In so acting, God reinforces, once again, the equality of all wo/men – first under hypocrisy/sin and, with Jesus' advent, under "faithfulness" manifested in love for God. Participation "in Jesus" designates Jews and Gentiles alike as "Abraham's disciples."

In 4:1-11 Paul elaborates the difference between the two "aeons" which Jesus' advent has created. The first – modeled on 11QMelchizedek – is one of bondage to "Belial," release from which has come in the "year of jubilee." Through Jesus's death and resurrection, all wo/men are redeemed from slavery to sin and brought into the actuality of their inheritance ("freedom"). Jesus' obedience unto death destroys the world of sin and death characterised by Belial's domination over the "elemental things of the world" and brings into existence a "new creation" (cf. 3:26-29,

---

[165] Once again, we take this opportunity to emphasise that Paul is speaking here of the "grafting in" of the Gentiles into the "commonwealth of Israel" – not of their *replacement* of Israel.

[166] While the issue of Torah-observance is of importance to Gentiles seeking Jewish status, Paul's argument also serves Jewish believers in elaborating the Torah's task (see also above [n163]).

[167] אהבת אדם למקום מנין? אלא אהבת אדם למקום היא מצוה חמורה מן התורה, דהא עול מלכות שמים כתיב בצד האהבה, שנאמר: שמע ישראל ה' אלהינו ה' אחד.

6:15).[168] Rather than continuing to be enslaved, the Galatians have been redeemed and delivered from "the dominion of Satan to God" in their participation in Jesus' faithfulness (cf. Acts 26:18; Col. 1:12-14). Having "matured" and come into their inheritance, why should either Jews or Gentiles seek to return to the status of minors and slaves?

Adoption of the view which attributes significance to Paul's pronounal usage leads here also to the distinction which Jesus' death and resurrection effects with regard to Jews and Gentiles respectively, despite the fundamental address to Gentiles in the passage. Most significantly, it is suggested that the "turning back" of which Paul accuses his disciples in 4:9 has reference primarily neither to Torah-observance nor to imperial cult worship but to the dominion of Belial under which all human beings were formerly bound.[169] It is, in this sense, a return to the bondage of sin and a renunciation of the freedom found in Jesus' faithfulness – 4:1-7 picking up Habakkuk 2:4's (LXX) language of "coming."

4:11 forms the pivot on which Paul shifts from his "rebuke" to his "request" of his Galatian disciples. Having laid out the grounds on which the Gentiles (as also Israel) have come into God's favour – through their faithfulness to Jesus' obedience – he now appeals to them not to "turn back" to this prior "period" – thereby putting all his "birthpangs" to vanity. He has brought them into the gospel, as it were, and wishes, with of all his heart, that they remain in it. To do so, they must continue to act as his disciples – and thus remove any "disturbance" to their faithfulness to God in Jesus by keeping faith with him as their "master" (mentor). Paul plays here on the description of the relationship between the Sage and his disciples as one of "father and son."

Like 1:1-4:11, the section 4:12-6:18 comprises one continuous unit (see above). While the first part of the letter has focused principally on the Galatians' own status, this segment primarily addresses the influencers' effect on the Galatian communities.[170] Following his plea ("request") in 4:11-12, Paul proceeds to justify the exercise of his authority with respect to his disciples. Despite evidences of the "evil eye" – in his "bodily weakness" and the suspicion that as a victim, Paul might impugn their

---

[168] Within this extended unit, Paul "digresses" at points to address issues pertaining to the relation of *Jewish* believers to the "elemental things of the world" in respect of the Torah. Specifically in 3:14 and 4:5-7, he elaborates the "dialectical" relation between Israel's and the Gentiles' redemption. See below, **Theological pointers**.

[169] In its "secondary" sense, namely the specific reference to be attributed to the "days and months and seasons and years," these are currently understood in terms of pagan – not Jewish – practices.

[170] It is perhaps here, more than in the first unit, that the present commentary diverges from other works, in its referencing of particular passages to the influencers in place of the traditional ascriptions.

own health – the gentile believers had welcomed him on his initial visit with open arms ("eyes"). If his absence, or the tone is he is presently taking with them, have allowed his disciples to become his "enemies," he wishes to correct the mistake. In doing so, he contrasts his concern for the Galatians with the motives evidenced by the influencers, a pattern which he repeats (with variations) in 5:7-12 and 6:3-17. He accompanies this move – again with parallels in 5:9-10, 26, 6:3-5, 8, 14, 16-17 – with stringent warnings to remove these "troublers" from within the community.

The climax of this section comes in verses 21-31 where Paul employs an "allegory" in pesher style whereby he interprets various biblical texts in reference to contemporary circumstances. Reading Genesis 21 through Canticles and Isaiah 54:1 – apparently following an established practice – Paul asserts, once again, his gentile disciples' standing in the Messiah as sons of the promise, begotten by God in purity and freedom from sin. In so turning to Scripture for authority, he garners basis and sanction for the stricture which he wishes to impose on his disciples: "Cast out the bondwoman and her son" (4:30). The scriptural command constitutes and authorizes, as it were, his demand ("request") that his gentile Galatian disciples banish the influencers from their midst.[171]

5:1-12 recapitulates for the Galatians the consequences of yielding to the influencers' persuasion towards social status. If his disciples do not "stand firm" (5:1), they will be drawn back into the position of minors and slaves, in which bondage they were found until the Messiah's advent. Utilising an argument drawn from proselytising procedures, Paul goes on to warn the gentile Galatians of the ramifications of obtaining official Jewish status. On the one hand, they will be obligated to full Torah-observance – the performance of which it is far from certain that they will be able to achieve.[172] On the other, in seeking social standing they will have turned their backs on their already-established status in the Messiah.

Verse 6 anticipates verse 13, Paul indicating that the purpose of Torah-observance is "faithfulness working through love." As in 4:12-20, Paul follows this elaboration of his "request" with an imprecation against those seeking (in his eyes) to "sever" his disciples from their Lord (and thus also from him) (verses 7-12). This passage further picks up the theme of 1:6-9, Paul presenting himself as personal example to his disciples, whose conduct they should imitate (verses 10-11).

In contrast to the majority of commentators, who conceive 5:13ff an anomalous discussion of the dangers of "libertinism,"[173] the present work

---

[171] If this is not a physical expulsion it is at least a "cognitive dissociation" from the views which the influencers are promoting.
[172] The potential for hypocrisy in this regard is quite clear.
[173] "The exhortations of 5:13-6:10 are to be seen as intimately connected with the circumstances in Galatia. They disclose a further problem in the churches of that province [sic]. The failure of the Galatians to maintain 'the truth of the gospel' (2:5,

perceives this section as directly continuous with the previous unit. Paul admonishes his disciples that if they are advancing Torah-observance through their wish for circumcision/conversion (cf. 4:21, 5:2-3), the true goal of the latter is in fact to be sought in the love of God, expressed in love to one's neighbour – enabled through the indwelling of God's Spirit. In this, the fulfilment of the whole Torah, and this alone, can his disciples preserve and maintain their liberty from sin through participation in Jesus' faithfulness – not in looking for social standing in circumcision of the "flesh."[174] In explication of this "law of love," Paul appeals to the idea of serving God out of love rather than out of fear, the latter being associated with sin and death. This motif goes hand in hand with that of the Two Ways and "two masters." Two "paths" are available for the walking in, the "good" and the "evil" – one directed by the Spirit of light, the other by the Spirit of darkness. Characteristic of this motif is its demand of a choice: One cannot walk on the one path by serving one Spirit/master without "angering" or rebelling against the other.

At the end of this section, and on the basis of its argument, Paul picks up – once again – his appeal to his disciples to act properly towards him (cf. 4:12-20) by turning their backs on those who are disturbing them (5:26). This leads him directly into an address to those within the Galatian communities who are truly "walking in the Spirit," asking them to restore those who have fallen under the persuaders' "spell" (cf. 3:1). Here, for the first time, he evidences a concern that the wayward be returned to the "fold," giving it as the duty and responsibility of those able to bring those who have been "caught in trespass" back to the obedience of the truth (6:1-2) (cf. 5:7).

The awkwardness and incoherence which commentators have traditionally attributed to 6:1-10 is resolved in the present contribution by

---

14) in their proposed acceptance of Jewish nomism was accompanied by their failure to enter fully into the ethical quality of life consonant with that gospel. Loveless strife was evidently present within the Galatian churches, with such attitudes and actions evidencing the dominance of 'the flesh' and certain libertine tendencies within the church – probably not 'libertinism' as a conscious, articulated philosophy, but libertine tendencies that took the form of self-promotion, self-vindication, and the disregard of others, with the result that Christian freedom was not being expressed in loving service to others. So Paul in upholding Chiristian freedom not only speaks of the Spirit as the effective answer to the Judaizers' call for a nomistic lifestyle, but also argues for the Spirit as the effective power for overcoming the flesh and such libertine attitudes as had arisen in the church" (Longenecker, Galatians: 238).

[174] It is characteristic of the present volume that it construes Paul's allusion to the "flesh" first and foremost in relation to (physical) circumcision, in 4:22-31 and 6:8 in the same way also as here, Paul playing on the analogy created by contrast between the "flesh" understood as the seat of the desires of the human mind and will and the exercise of God's Spirit in "faithfulness working through love."

reading it as direct continuation of 5:26, itself dependent on 5:9-10, which in turn develops the "allegory" of 4:21-31. On this understanding, the section reiterates, one final time, Paul's initial admonition to his disciples, first to imitate and keep faith with him (cf. 4:12ff) and then to remove the influencers' presence (cf. 4:30, 5:7-12).

On the current interpretation, 6:3-5 represents a further caution to his disciples by way of indicating the judgment which the influencers will receive in regard to their deeds: Each person is ultimately responsible for his/her own actions, and boasting on the basis of *others* can "reap" no good reward (cf. 6:4, 7-8, 13).[175] As he has throughout the letter, Paul conjoins this "negative" warning to his disciples with a "positive" one of commitment to himself, this time in the form of support for his teaching (6:6) – a theme which directly picks up 4:12f.[176] Verse 2 returns to 5:6, 13 in speaking of the "law of the Messiah" which consists of the love demanded of one's fellows. Here, it is suggested that Paul's thought reflects the idea of hypocrisy which has dominated the letter through an indirect reference to the influencers as "hypocrites" – bound to the sphere of the "flesh" rather than seeking the Kingdom of God, and desiring proselytes for expedient reasons of social standing in place of acting from the fear of God. Rather than bestowing benefits on the gentile Galatian believers, they are in fact "burdening" them (cf. Mt. 23:1ff).[177]

Verse 6 calls his disciples directly back to their responsibilities to Paul himself as their "father" or "master." As he who has "laboured" over them and given them birth in the Messiah, as it were, they are obligated to keep faith with him, to follow his example, and to walk in his teaching. While it is possible that "all good things" includes financial support, the idea appears to derive from the principle that s/he who shares in spiritual benefits is obligated to return the favour in material form (cf. 1 Cor. 9:11; Did. 1:5, 4:8).

---

[175] The parallels with 5:7-12 are clearly evident on this reading, Paul utilizing the same language of "bearing judgment." The concept of "boasting" – Paul's attribution of which to the influencers in 6:12-13 ties these latter verses together with 6:3-5 – in itself represents a form of "hypocrisy" when viewed through Jer. 9:23-26: "'But let him who boasts boast of this, that he understands and knows Me, that I am the LORD who exercises lovingkindness, justice, and righteousness on earth, for I delight in these things,' declares the LORD כי אם-בזאת יתהלל המתהלל השכל וידע אותי כי אני ה' עשה חסד משפט וצדקה בארץ כי-באלה חפצתי נאם ה'."
[176] The theme of "sowing and reaping" is itself common to both passages.
[177] This association is strengthened by James' description of the "law of liberty" in the framework of hypocritical conduct (cf. Jas. 1:25, 2:12-26). Invocation of Mt. 23:23 also reasserts the theme of walking "within the margin of the judgment" by performing the "weightier provisions of the Torah: justice and mercy and faithfulness" (see above). It is here that this latter principle can be identified with "walking the Spirit" (cf. 5:16ff) and "faithfulness working through love" (cf. 5:6, 13ff, 6:1f).

The following verses (6:7-8) serve as a caution to both the influencers and those whom they have succeeded in disturbing, repeating the thought of verses 3-4 in elaborating the consequences of one's actions.[178] The transition to 6:9, which has so troubled commentators, is herein explained by the suggestion that Paul is following a tradition in which the motif of "sowing" is associated not only with performing deeds of lovingkindness (gmilut chasadim) but also with proselytism – the "winning" or "gathering" of converts. 6:9-10 represents, on this reading, further encouragement to "those who are spiritual" to restore those from "the household of faith" who have stumbled – as part of a general promotion of the gospel.

While 6:11 is generally regarded as the opening of the subscription, it equally as importantly forms the transition between 6:1-10 and the "summation" of Paul's major points in the subscription. Verses 12-13 have been explicated above in the section on **Occasion and circumstances,** as godfearers who, finding an ostensible Jewish status in Jesus inadmissible, are attempting to persuade Paul's disciples that to gain Jewish identity they must undergo circumcision and officially convert. The "persecution" which they are attempting to avoid not being found to possess any historical evidence, it is suggested that it consists of the godfearers opposition to being considered, in any way, shape, or form, Jesus' followers. Their persuasion in relation to the early community is grounded precisely in the fact that they do not recognise Jesus as the bestower of Jewish standing. In Paul's eyes they therefore constitute a danger to his disciples in threatening to "sever" them from God's Kingdom, from His Messiah, and from His apostle.[179]

6:14 represents Paul's personal pattern – which he has already proposed as exemplary (cf. 2:18-21, 4:12f, 5:11, 6:17) – of what a person may properly boast of – in contrast to the influencers' boasting "in the flesh" – leading him to a repetition of the "rule" of the "new creation" which he has set forth in 3:28-29.

Paul concludes the letter with a benediction, reminiscent of the Amidah and the priestly blessing, on those who are willing to listen to his words – reestablishing those who participate in Jesus' faithfulness as the "sons of Abraham." The "Israel of God" are those of the "household of faithfulness" (verse 10) – those who are "out of [the] faithfulness" of Habakkuk 2:4. They are Israel according to the promise, the descendants of Abraham who act as his disciples – both Jews and Gentiles. The blessing

---

[178] One of the merits of this reading is its mitigation of the ostensible contradiction between 6:2 and 6:5, the first calling people to carry each other's burdens, the second warning that each person is responsible for his own.
[179] The additional motif of Torah-observance – or the influencers' lack thereof – is explained in light of the fact that, as godfearers, they are not in any way bound to perform the commandments.

having been given, Paul extends one final implied "curse" on those who
are wielding an adverse influence (6:16-17), thereby closing the letter with
the same blessing of peace and curse of judgment with which he opened it
(cf. 1:3-9) and appealing to that authority in the Messiah with which he has
made his rebuke and request of the Galatians. In the concluding
benediction of grace, Paul summons God's favour on his disciples and
asks, in their response of "Amen," that his disciples confirm his authority,
accept his reprimand, and accede to his request, by declaring with him:
"God's will be done."

Theological pointers
Faithfulness
It will have been noted in the foregoing that the present commentary
adopts the view of "faithfulness" as definitive of the **"faith of Jesus"** –
understanding it as a "subjective genitive" which attributes faithfulness to
Jesus, rather than as an "objective genitive" signifying "faith in him" on
the part of believers. This argument has been made by (among others)
Richard Hays, whose reference to narrative, while not necessary to the
subjective reading, further contributes, in our eyes, to its cogency:

> A second suggestion for readers of this book is to observe its
> insistent claim that we are caught up into the story of Jesus
> Christ. *In a mysterious way, Jesus has enacted our destiny, and those*
> *who are in Christ are shaped by the pattern of his self-giving death. He*
> *is the prototype of redeemed humanity* ... *'The faithfulness of Jesus*
> *Christ' refers first of all to his gracious, self-sacrificial death on a cross.*
> The cross is the dramatic climax of the Jesus-story, and Paul uses
> the expression πίστις 'Ιησοῦ Χριστοῦ by *metonymy* to suggest
> and evoke that focal moment of the narrative ... *Jesus Christ*
> *embodies the new creation and embraces us in his life.* All who are
> baptized into union with him share his destiny and his character.
> His fidelity to God is the pattern for the new life that he has
> inaugurated ... *The cross, as Christ's saving action, is God's action of*
> πίστις, *God's demonstration of fidelity to the promise made to*
> *Abraham.* (Hays, Faith: xxix-xxxiii; original emphasis)[180]

---

[180] As Hays notes in the preface to the second edition to the book, the original
volume did not engage in the question, "how does the story of Jesus fit into the
wider story of Israel, the story of election and promise told in the Old Testament?"
While differing from the narrative role he ascribes to both Torah and people, his
acknowledgement that "I would want to widen the frame of reference beyond the
seleced kerygmatic formulae and grapple more extensively with the problem of
how to understand the story of Christ's faithfulness in relation to the story of Israel"
(ibid: xxxvi) is timely. The present series is intended precisely to place the New
Testament texts as a whole within their biblical and Jewish context.

Most specifically, we have followed Hays' exegesis of Habakkuk 2:4 which takes the phrase ἐκ πίστεως (ek pisteōs – "out of faithfulness") as a "shorthand" for Jesus' obedience to the Father in giving his life for the redemption of others. Those who participate in his faithfulness (through baptism – dying to self and to the world [cf. 2:20, (3:27), 5:24, 6:14]) partake of the redemption which he has effected, being himself the embodiment of the "seed" in whom the blessing promised to Abraham was realized. Thereafter, those who have committed themselves to him are also known as "out of faithfulness" – imitators of his example and followers of his obedience. In similar fashion, the "new creation" which his death and resurrection inaugurate is characterised by the liberty from sin which those "of faithfulness" enjoy – in distinction to bondage to the "elemental things of the world" which are fear and death.

Readers will, no doubt, wonder if this commentary is on the book of Galatians as it is included in their Bible, the word "justification" – with its corrolary "justification by faith" – scarcely appearing at all in its pages. The absence can partially be accounted for on the above account, "faith" not being designated as an assent (whether "mental" or "heartfelt") or "belief in" Jesus but as a response to Jesus' own faithful obedience. At the same time, two other factors play a major role in the circumstance.

The first lies in the scenario which we have ascribed to Galatians, the influencers being identified as non-believing gentile godfearers, opposed to the gospel as infringing on Jewish standards of identity (see above, **Occasion and circumstances**). The disconnection of this party from commitment to Jesus by definition removes the discussion from an internal "theological" debate to a "sociological" plane. Once one group is dissociated from the gospel, the terms can no longer be assumed to carry a common signification and/or to possess the meanings understood by the members of the community involved.

The second reflects the fact that "faithfulness" is associated here with the idea of hypocrisy and entrance to God's Kingdom (see above, **Argument**). On the grounds that it is precisely Jesus' obedience which obtains release from bondage to sin and death, emphasis must lie on his death and resurrection as the means whereby all wo/mankind – Jews and Gentiles alike – are delivered from the "dominion of Belial." Concurrence with ("belief in") the latter, however much it might be true, will not, in and of itself, gain one entrance to God's Kingdom. That can only be achieved through Jesus' own faithfulness to God – itself an expression of God's faithfulness to His creation. Faithfulness is, in this sense, always an act: On God's part, the sending and resurrection of His son; on Jesus' part, his obedience to death; and, on the part of the "believer," participation in that death and resurrection (through baptism).

Justification

In light of the above, "justification" represents a person's possession of the keys to God's Kingdom – firstly through Jesus' death and resurrection, and secondly in his/her faithfulness to God in loving his/her neighbour in walking in God's Spirit: "For the kingdom of God is not eating and drinking, but righteousness and peace and joy in the Holy Spirit. For he who in this *way* serves the Messiah is acceptable to God and approved by men. So then let us pursue the things which make for peace and the building up of one another"[181] (Rom. 14:17-19).

Structurally, Paul's understanding of "justification" is based, in Galatians, upon his rebuke of Peter's hypocrisy – this being the place in which Paul himself introduces the term. On analogy with rabbinic texts which speak of hypocrisy as constituted by an emphasis on Torah-study to the neglect of the "fear of heaven," Paul stresses that both – Torah-study *and* the fear of heaven – are necessary for access to God's Kingdom.[182]

Paul's remarks – according to this reading of the text – rely heavily (conceptually, if not historically) upon Jesus' denunciation of pharisaic hypocrisy in Matthew 23.[183] Jesus himself appears to be quoting Micah 6:8 in the latter passage – with a hint towards Habakkuk 2:4 in the mention of "faithfulness": "hypocrites . . . [you] have neglected the weightier provisions of the law: justice and mercy and faithfulness; but these are the things you should have done **without neglecting the others**" (Mt. 23:23). Jesus defines hypocrisy as putting undue preference upon the "minor commandments" – at the expense of the "major" ones.

Precisely this prophetic emphasis lies behind certain rabbinic statements which define the "sons of Abraham" as those who exhibit his qualities and thereby demonstrate themselves to be his "disciples."[184] Such texts as Micah 6:8, Exodus 18:20, and Proverbs 2:20 also serve as the basis of the principle of לפנים משורת הדין (lifnim mi-shurat ha-din – "within the margin of the judgment") wherein a person is expected to "go beyond the law, which in itself is right and good, in order to do what is right and

---

[181] Οὐ γάρ ἐστιν ἡ βασιλεία τοῦ θεοῦ βρῶσις καὶ πόσις ἀλλὰ δικαιοσύνη καὶ εἰρήνη καὶ χαρὰ ἐν πνεύματι ἁγίῳ· ὁ γὰρ ἐν τούτῳ δουλεύων τῷ Χριστῷ εὐάρεστος τῷ θεῷ καὶ δόκιμος τοῖς ἀνθρώποις. Ἄρα οὖν τὰ τῆς εἰρήνης διώκωμεν καὶ τῆς οἰκοδομῆς τῆς εἰς ἀλλήλους.

[182] For the implications of this argument for Jewish-gentile relations within the congregation of believers, see below.

[183] No compelling reason exists to dismiss the historical dependence as possible either. For an excellent review of Paul's relation to Jesus and his teaching, cf. Wenham, *Paul*.

[184] Paul employs these passages as speaking to the issue of Jewish identity, thereby delimiting the criteria according to which membership in Israel is determined.

good" (Berkovits: 27).[185] It is herein suggested that when Paul speaks of "faithfulness" in 2:15-21, he does not imply a "belief in" Jesus but refers to the "intention" with which a person is enabled to serve God. The Jewish believer will be hypocritical in saying that his Torah-observance is sufficient to gain him/her entry into God's Kingdom without the "fear of heaven" or "intention" which gives practice its purpose (cf. Rom. 2:12-29). The Gentile – who is "by nature a sinner " – has now, by God's grace, been given access to God's Kingdom by Jesus' removal of the barrier of sin in human nature. "Justification" on this interpretation is tantamount to inheritance in the Kingdom, walking "within the margin of the judgment" being equivalent to "walking in the Spirit."[186]

The issue of "hypocrisy" recurs in chapter 5, associated with Paul's discursus on love.[187] As the "fulfilment (summation)" of the Torah, love of God is expressed through love of one's neighbour. To the extent that this latter motif is based on the second half of the Decalogue, which addresses human relationships, Paul's discussion here recalls the Sermon on the Mount. One of the guiding motifs of Jesus' teaching there may be seen as the principle of acting "within the margin of the judgment." Paul's call to "walk in the liberty of the Spirit" (cf. 5:1, 13, 16-18, 25) is to serve God out of love – not out of fear. Fear leads to apprehension over correct observance of His commandments; love seeks ways to serve Him in order to please Him. "Hypocrisy" in these terms reflects the inability of the "flesh" to obey God out of love – the Spirit alone bestowing upon a person such "fruit worthy of repentance" (cf. Mt. 3:8).

The same idea reemerges again in 6:1-16, here again in respect to "boasting" (cf. Romans 2). The "fruit" by which a person is judged is not only that which he "does" – rather than merely "hears" – but also that which he reaps from his/her sowing. The latter motif may well be associated with the "Golden Rule" in the sense that "the [sow]er that sows goodness, harvests good, and whoever sows evil, against him his seed turns זרעה תאיב עלוהי ביש טאב מהנעל ודי זרע די זרע [זר]עא" (4Q213 1:8-9). The latter principle – which can be read as informing the whole of the Sermon on the Mount – is itself associated with the principle of performing "light"

---

[185] We prefer this definition to that of "acting according to the Spirit of the law" rather than according to the "letter of the law," especially in light of the "bad press" given to the latter in traditional Christian theology.

[186] In substantive terms, we are not suggesting that "justification" changes the basic meanings traditionally attributed to it by Protestant theology. At the same time, however, we are proposing that perceiving "justification" in terms of "Kingdom language" provides a new prism through which to view Paul's thought in Galatians. This should constitute an important factor in discussions of Paul's use of the Kingdom motif, together with the ways in which he reflects Jesus' words and/or gospel traditions.

[187] Traces of this theme may also be found in 5:9, in association with "leaven."

commandments equally with "heavy" ones, a parallel to acting "within the margin of the judgment."

In speaking of "burdens" in 6:2, 5, Paul further recalls Jesus' condemnation of the pharisaic hypocritical tendency to "tie up heavy loads, and lay them on men's shoulders; but they themselves are unwilling to move them with *so much as* a finger"[188] (Mt. 23:4). In asking "those who are spiritual" to restore their brethren who are in the process of surrendering to the influencers' persuasion, Paul may thus be phrasing his request in such a way as to demand such action from those who are willing to "act within the margin of the judgment."[189] If the influencers are acting "hypocritically" in seeking proselytes for fleshly motives (cf. 6:12-13), laying burdens on Paul's disciples rather than giving them access to God's Kingdom, Paul's reference to the "law of the Messiah" may possibly allude to Jesus' teaching in contrast to that of the Pharisees (cf. Mt. 23:1ff). The "boasting" against which he inveighs further invokes Jeremiah 9:23f, closely allied to Micah 6:6-8: "'But let him who boasts boast of this, that he understands and knows Me, that I am the LORD who exercises lovingkindness, justice, and righteousness on earth; for I delight in these things' . . . 'Behold, the days are coming,' declares the LORD, 'that I will punish all who are circumcised and yet uncircumcised'"[190] (Jer. 9:24-25). This passage, which underlies both 6:4, 12-14 and Romans 2, links the former passages back to 2:15-21 and 5:13-18.

While "justification" may consequently infrequently appear in the pages of the present work, the notion of "hypocrisy" constitutes its analogy, calling for "walking in the Spirit" as obeying God out of love and not out of fear of punishment and death.[191] Such action is an expression of

---

[188] δεσμεύουσιν δὲ φορτία βαρέα [καὶ δυσβάστακτα] καὶ ἐπιτιθέασιν ἐπὶ τοὺς ὤμους τῶν ἀνθρώπων, αὐτοὶ δὲ τῷ δακτύλῳ αὐτῶν οὐ θέλουσιν κινῆσαι αὐτά.

[189] For Acts 15:10 in relation to Galatians, see above, **Date and destination**. Matthew 23 is possibly significant for Galatians also in relation to 4:17, where Paul employs the same root as "shutting people off" from the Kingdom of heaven in reference to the influencers' "proselytising" of the Galatians.

[190] כי אם-בזאת יתהלל המתהלל השכל וידֹע אותי כי אני ה' עֹשה חסד משפט וצדקה בארץ כי-באלה חפצתי נאֻם ה' . . . הנה ימים באים נאם-ה' ופקדתי על-כל-מֹוּל בערלה.

[191] In terms of the distinction made by Christian theologians between the "forensic" and "moral" grounds of righteousness, it should be clear that, in its analogous relationship with hyprocrisy, we see righteousness as tending more towards a "quality of life," lived within God's Kingdom, than towards a "declaratory, forensic status." The former is certainly not exclusive of the latter, which is primarily established through Jesus' obedience and faithfulness: "The greatest strength of the exegesis set forward in [Hays'] *Faith of Jesus Christ* – and in the work of others who have come to understand the expression πίστις 'Ιησοῦ Χριστοῦ as a shorthand reference to Christ's action – is that it explains how Paul's understanding of the πίστις of Jesus is integrally related to his understanding of δικαιοσύνη [righteousness]. As Leander Keck has commented, 'in every case, construing πίστις

acting according to the "spirit of the law" or "within the margin of the judgment" - seeking "justice and mercy and faithfulness" rather than emphasising the so-called "externals."[192] Faithfulness to Jesus' power of deliverance from sin in one's own dying to the "old man" is complemented in the bestowal of the Spirit as the "intention" of the love which is the summation of the Torah. It is precisely Jesus' faithfulness in his unity with the Father which overcomes, for those who are obedient to him, the breach between "saying and doing" - of wishing to do what is right and of being able to perform it (cf. Rom. 7:14-25).[193]

In this sense, Galatians may be seen to revolve around a matrix of prooftexts, composed of such passages as Genesis 12:3, Jeremiah 9:23-25, Hosea 6:6, Micah 6:6-8, and Habakkuk 2:4. The latter establishes that God's covenant with His people is predicated on faithfulness - His own, His Messiah's, and those who follow Jesus in his death and resurrection. This faithfulness is one of the "great principles in the Torah" - which Jesus conjoins with justice and mercy as a "gloss" on Micah 6:8 (cf. Mt. 23:23).[194] Those whom God accepts before Him, who truly compose His people, are those ἐκ πίστεως (ek pisteōs) - "of faithfulness." These it is, among both Jews and Gentiles who, through God's Messiah, have received Abraham's blessing in receipt of God's Spirit. Such people, Paul says, compose the "household of the faithful" (cf. 6:10). As the "Israel of God" (cf. 6:16), the members of this household are commanded to fulfil the "law of the Messiah" (cf. 6:2), not in seeking God's will through observance of the "minor commandments" but in performing the "weightier commandments" in "faithfulness working through love" (5:6) (cf. Mt. 23:23) - love, faithfulness, and "walking in the Spirit" being parallel entities.[195]

'Iησοῦ as the fidelity of Jesus ... clarifies the key point - the role of Jesus in salvation" (Hays, Faith: xxix; citing L. Keck, "'Jesus' in Romans," *JBL* 108 [1989], 454).

[192] Here again, we would point out that Paul is not outlawing Torah-observance *per se* or relating it, as so many Christian commentators have been accustomed to assume, to "ritual" or the "letter of the law" versus "faith." What God seeks is *obedience* - from the heart.

[193] This, as Wright remarks, constitutes "one particular outworking of what theologians have called the problem of nature and grace" (Climax: 15).

[194] For the "great principle," see below, **Hermeneutics**.

[195] This represents an account of Paul's address to his *gentile* disciples - whose seeking after social status impinges on their already-achieved standing in the Messiah. With regard to Jewish believers it can be understood that *both* Torah-observance *and* intention compile their "faithfulness working through love" (see below).

Scripture

Commentaries which have placed Galatians in the perspective of "Galatia" and/or Graeco-Roman thought have frequently endeavoured to contextualise the letter in those surroundings. Many of them, in the process, have, whether wittingly or unwittingly, devalued the status which Paul ascribes to Scripture. The argument that, in speaking *ad hominem*, Paul must use terms familiar and intelligible to his readers has led many writers to "de-Judaise" Galatians by explaining Scripture without its biblical and Second Temple Jewish context. The presupposition that Paul remained Jewish, however, throughout his life is central to the whole of the present enterprise (see Appendix and above, **Author**).

To the objection that the Galatians – being Gentiles, and possibly not even godfearers – would have understood neither the Tanakh nor biblical arguments (to state the obvious, the canon of the "New Testament" not yet having been established, and Galatians – on the present reading – being the earliest extant pauline letter), we would assert that scriptural exegesis in fact constitutes Paul's natural mode of argument, by training and by inclination.[196] Nothing for him is more authoritative, with the Spirit's confirmatory and vivifying role. While the methods of exegesis and hermeneutical principles which he employs are varied, they all relate to the scriptural text – elucidating, elaborating, and applying it in specific contexts, circumstances, and cases. The most outstanding evidence for this may perhaps be adduced in the "allegory" of 4:22-31, wherein he adopts a biblical story in order to convey his command: "Cast out the bondwoman and her son" (see below).

Hermeneutics

A second point, collateral to the insistence on Scripture's centrality for Paul, lies, as Hays has masterfully demonstrated, in the importance of listening for the "echoes of Scripture" in Paul's letters. In this sense, while hermeneutics do not, perhaps, constitute a strictly "theological" issue, Paul's Jewish context extends not merely to the foundation of his thought in Scripture but also to the hermeneutical and exegetical modes with which he treats the Tanakh (the so-called "Old Testament").

The prevalence with which Paul's exegetical practices have represented a stumbling point in which Christian scholarship has consistently deprec(i)ated Paul's thought is thoroughly lamentable. Paul is so frequently charged with "contradictions, tensions, inconsistencies, antinomies and other worrying things," in N.T. Wright's succinct summary (Climax: 4ff), due (at best) to misperception of his hermeneutics

---

[196] Galatians being the third in a series of commentaries on the books of the New Testament as Jewish texts, the reader is referred to the previous volumes on Romans and Acts as evidence and examples of the approach adopted.

and (at worst) to their complete dismissal (largely a factor of ignorance), his "theology" has possessed sparse chances of emerging in any constructive or confirmatory light.

The logical assumption that a person's arguments should be evaluated in light of the methods characteristic of his/her time and place notwithstanding, Paul has consistently been denied this privilege by Christian presumptions that "he was asking or answering the same questions that subsequent interpreters have brought to him" (ibid: 258). Specifically, much of Christian scholarship has ridiculed Paul's writings on the grounds of an – utterly unwarranted – derision of the Jewish hermeneutical principles which organise his exegetical moves.

As Hays gives witness, Paul's language is thoroughly and fundamentally scriptural. The first task devolving on the reader of his letters is consequently the development of an ear for scriptural allusions. Once noted, these attach to Paul's discussion the original context in which the biblical passage is found. Most outstanding, in this respect, is Paul's description of his calling and his commission as an "apostle to the Gentiles" in terms of the Servant figure of Isaiah. In a less direct sense, in speaking of those who have come to "spy out" the early community's "liberty" in 2:4, the application of Psalm 37 to a similar situation encountered by the Qumran community suggests that Paul may have in mind Psalm 37:32: "the wicked spies on the righteous [צופה רשע לצדיק]."[197]

Paul further shares the ascription of sanctity to Scripture which characterises classical Jewish sources, an attribution which leads directly to a close, tight, and minute scrutiny of the biblical text. This comes to expression in the type of exegesis in which Paul engages in 3:16. Given the authority credited to the biblical passage, what does God mean when He says "seed" in the singular, seeing that He could have used the plural? Out of a profound respect for the "literal" meaning of Scripture, this text, in Paul's hands, enlarges the biblical vision to include the Messiah.[198] It is

---

[197] This latter example further indicates the propriety of placing Paul's thought within the context of other contemporary Jewish texts.

[198] A similar example may be brought from San. 4:5, which adduces both "theological" and halakhic (legal) conclusions from Gen. 4:10: "Know ye, moreover, that capital cases are not as non-capital cases: in non-capital cases a man may pay money and so make atonement, but in capital cases the witness is answerable for the blood of him [that is wrongfully condemned] and the blood of his posterity [that should have been born to him] to the end of the world. For so have we found it with Cain that slew his brother, for it is written, *The bloods of thy brother cry* [Gen. 4:10]. It says not 'The blood of thy brother', but *The bloods of thy brother* – his blood and the blood of his posterity ... Therefore but a single man was created in the world, to teach that if any man has caused a single soul to perish {from Israel} Scripture imputes it to him as though he had caused a whole world to perish הוו יודעין שלא כדיני ממונות דיני נפשות. דיני ממונות, אדם נותן ממון ומתכפר לו. דיני נפשות, דמו ודם זרעיותיו תלויין בו עד סוף העולם, שכן מצינו בקין שהרג את אחיו, שנאמר: דמי אחיך צעקים. אינו אומר

precisely, albeit somewhat paradoxically, commitment to the words, letters, and "punctuation" of Scripture which permits an exegesis of its text which broadens (or deepens) its signification.[199] A second point to be emphasised is the Jewish hermeneutical practice of explicitly citing a segment of the biblical text whose *entirety*, while not quoted in full, is being exegeted. Hand in hand with this method goes the principle that passages carry with them the context in which they originally occur. Where Paul quotes, therefore, in chapter 3, from Genesis 12:3, 15:6, Leviticus 18:5, Deuteronomy 27:26, and Habakkuk 2:4, any understanding of his argument which neglects the covenant framework in which these texts stand in their immediate circumstances is likely to miss Paul's intent. The biblical background sets Paul's thought within the history of God's dealings with His people, its texts serving him as building blocks, as it were, in defining the identity of God's community.

Being a member of a living "interpretative community," Paul employs many of the hermeneutical principles characteristic of that particular community's traditions. In speaking of the "fulfilment of the Torah in one word" (5:14), Paul adopts the motif of כלל גדול בתורה (klal gadol ba-Torah) or "a great principle of/in the Torah." This "rule" is adduced in pointing to a commandment which as it were "sums up" the Torah and its purpose. Paul, as Jesus before him and R. Akiva after him, states that the declaration "You shall love thy neighbour as thyself" constitutes the whole of the Torah – just as Hillel, before all three, declared "What is hateful to you, do not to your neighbour: that is the whole Torah, while the rest is commentary thereof; go and learn it"[200] (Shab. 31a). The fact that Habakkuk 2:4 also serves to "reduce" the Torah to its one "great principle" – "The righteous shall live by his faith" – further places "love" and "faithfulness" as parallel qualities in Paul's eyes.

Paul's most complex usage of Scripture lies in the "allegory" of 4:22-31. Notwithstanding later Christian hermeneutical developments of the "allegorical" interpretation of Scripture, Paul can be read very differently when invoked in his proper (in both senses of the word) Jewish environment. Here, by "allegory" Paul may mean the "mashal" by means of which one portion of Scripture is employed to interpret another. Traditionally, rabbinic literature employs Solomon's "proverbs" in

---

"דם" אחיך אלא "דמי" אחיך "דמי" - דמו ודם זרעיותיו ... לפיכך נברא אדם יחידי, ללמדך, שכל המאבד נפש אחת {מישראל}, מעלה עליו הכתוב כאלו אבד עולם מלא."

[199] Rather than creating a slavishly literal understanding of Scripture, such attention to detail opens up the text to virtually endless interpretative implications, as the example in the previous note, based on the difference of two letters (plural *versus* singular), indicates.

[200] מעשה בנכרי אחד שבא לפני שמאי. אמר לו: גיירני על מנת שתלמדני כל התורה כולה כשאני עומד על רגל אחת. דחפו באמת הבנין שבידו. בא לפני הלל גייריה. אמר לו: דעלך סני לחברך לא תעביד: זו היא כל התורה כולה ואידך פירושה הוא. זיל גמור.

Canticles as a "prism" through which to understand the rest of Scripture (in particular, Exodus). According to a midrashic interpretation, the allusion to "my mother's house" in Canticles 8:2 refers to Sinai – "Because there Israel became like a new-born child"[201] (Cant.R. 8.2.1).[202]

Having established that he is speaking with/through the authority of Scripture, Paul next juxtaposes two additional biblical themes – the story of Sarah and Hagar in Genesis and Isaiah's description of Jerusalem's "sons" as the offspring of she who is barren, interpreting the former text through the latter. In the seven-shabbat cycle of consolation, Isaiah 54:1-10 serves as the haftarah (prophetic reading) for Deuteronomy 21:10-25:19 (Ki Tetzei), a parasha (Torah portion) which contains the ordinance concerning the inheritance of the "hated" and "beloved" wives. Adopting what appears to be an established tradition, Paul understands the relation between Isaac and Ishmael in terms of God's promise that the "older shall serve the younger" (cf. Gen. 25:23) – the children of the "promise" being those whom God gives to Sarah's "barren" womb.

In a final exegetical move, Paul turns this scriptural catena into a "pesher" in order to "decode" the biblical events and to apply them to present circumstances. «Hagar» represents the "flesh" – the "troublers" who are promoting Jewish identity over the gospel. Since his disciples know that they are born of «Sarah» and are therefore "children of promise," Paul admonishes them that they are to "listen to the Torah" – both in the sense of affirming their status as "children of the free woman" (liberated from their "debts/sins" through the Spirit), and in obeying Sarah's voice (which is also that of Scripture), which says: "Cast out the bondwoman and her son" (4:30).[203] In this sense, the "allegory" (mashal) serves as a scriptural injunction, first to listen to its definition of Abraham's rightful heir(s), in Isaac; and, secondly, to follow its directive and to remove the influence of those who are attempting to arrogate this inheritance to the "flesh" through circumcision/conversion.

Jewish-gentile relations

A final point to be noted concerns the issue raised by the inner and outer keys of God's kingdom (see above, **Argument**). The particular reading of Galatians proposed here revolves around the central principle of hypocrisy. Rabbinic texts speak of hypocrisy in terms of persons who hold

---

[201] אביאך אל בית אמי - זה סיני. אמר ר' ברכיה: למה קוראין לסיני "בית אמי"? שמשם נעשו ישראל כתינוק בן יומו.

[202] This point is important in establishing that Paul is not dealing with the text in such an allegorical fashion as that of Philo, for example. He is rather interpreting Scripture through Scripture (see below).

[203] It is important to stress here that reading the mashal in this fashion remains dependent on the mashal's integrated role within the epistle's overall structure as a "halakhic letter" of rebuke and request (see above, **Form**; **Argument**).

the "keys" to the "inner court" of God's Kingdom through Torah-study
but do not hold the keys to the "outer court," lacking as they do the "fear
of heaven" which must accompany deeds: "Every man who possesses
learning without the fear of heaven is like a treasurer who is entrusted
with the inner keys but not with the outer: how is he to enter [the Kingdom
of heaven]? כל אדם שיש בו תורה ואין בו יראת שמים דומה לגזבר שמסרו לו מפתחות
הפנימיות ומפתחות החיצוניות לא מסרו לו. בהי עייל?" (Shab. 31b).[204]

Placed within the context of Galatians, this simile may be taken by
some to imply that, although the Gentiles obtain access to the "outer court"
through participation in Jesus' obedience, which bestows upon them, in
the Spirit, the means to seek the "weighty provisions of the law – justice
and mercy and faithfulness" (Mt. 23:23), they are nonetheless barred from
the "inner court." Entry to the latter court, it may be understood, is
restricted to Jewish believers who, in consequence, retain a status superior
to that of gentile believers, being admitted – in contrast to gentile believers
– to both the inner and the outer courts of the Kingdom.

It is important to signify that *this reading cannot be supported from
Galatians*. Paul's address in the letter is almost exclusively to his gentile
disciples (see above, **Occasion and circumstances**). The issue does indeed
arise from Paul's rebuke of Peter – and to that extent applies to the Jewish
believer's need for Jesus' obedience to allow her/him to avoid the
hypocrisy of those who "say, 'We are wise, and the law of the LORD is with
us' . . . But behold the lying pen of the scribes has made *it* into a lie איכה
תאמרו חכמים אנחנו ותורת הי אתנו אכן הנה לשקר עשה עט שקר ספרים" (Jer. 8:8) –
people who "boast in the Torah, through your breaking the Torah, do you
dishonor God? (ἐν νόμῳ καυχᾶσαι, διὰ τῆς παραβάσεως τοῦ νόμου τὸν
θεὸν ἀτιμάζεις;)" (Rom. 2:23). Yet this idea is not intended to promote
disparity between Jewish and gentile believers.

While Paul does indeed address issues related to Jewish believers at
certain points in the letter – notably 3:10-14, 19f, and 4:3-6, [5:2-3] – he does
so strictly in the context of the overcoming of sin. In this sense, the
metaphor of the "inner" and the "outer" courts speaks to hypocrisy as it
represents the human incapacity to please God in a natural state, a
circumstance which divides people from God: "But your iniquities have
made a separation between you and your God, and your sins have hid His
face from you כי אם־עונתיכם היו מבדלים ביניכם לבין אלהיכם וחטאותיכם הסתירו
פנים מכם" (Isa. 59:2).

As understood in the light of rabbinic texts, hypocrisy represents not
only the disparity between saying and doing – between speech and acts –
but also expresses a fundamental state of "sinfulness" within human

---

[204] Cf. Mt. 16:19, 23:13; Lk. 11:52; ARNᵃ 39:1. For this verse in connection with Peter
in verses 7-8, see there (verses 1-10). Paul engages in a similar admonition against
hypocrisy in Romans 2, where intention again forms the central theme.

beings: "Because of his sinfulness man has not the power to comprehend the Form on high; otherwise he would have been entrusted with the keys [of the unknown] and discover how heaven and earth had been created" [205] (ARN[a] 39:1).

Paul's epistle is designed specifically to demonstrate to the gentile believers in Galatia that their disbarment from God's presence has been removed through Jesus' faithfulness to death on the cross. Through their participation in his death and resurrection, in baptism, they have been given entrance to God's Kingdom, *in its fulness*, because the barrier of their sinfulness has been removed. Paul does not wish to compare Jewish believers against gentile believers. On the contrary, his rebuke of Peter lies precisely in the fact that Peter, notwithstanding his possession of the "inner keys," possesses as little access to the fulness of the Kingdom as the Gentiles who, in their natural state, are without "hope and without God in the world (ἐλπίδα μὴ ἔχοντες καὶ ἄθεοι ἐν τῷ κόσμῳ)" (Eph. 2:12).

To the extent that both Jews and Gentiles alike have been, up until the Messiah's coming, in bondage to the "elemental things of the world" (4:3), both require God's deliverance.[206] This He has supplied in His Messiah – Jesus. To extend the ramifications of Paul's argument to a discursus on the Jewish believer's relation to the Torah is unjustifiable from a reading of Galatians. This is an issue which Paul does not address in this particular letter – although he does so in Romans.[207]

---

[205] אין ספק לאדם לידע מה דמות למעלה ואלמלא כן היו מוסרין לו מפתחות ויודע במה נבראו שמים וארץ.

[206] While not the point of the argument here, we would stress that the "elemental things of the world" are not inclusive of Torah – for which see the commentary on 4:1-7.

[207] This comment applies to all those places in Galatians in which Paul does speak of the Torah's role (cf. 3:10-14, 19-25, 4:3-6, [5:3]). While he evidently relates to the Torah's role in these passages he does so exclusively in the framework of gentile redemption.

GALATIANS
1

Verses 1-5: Salutation

PAUL, an apostle (not *sent* from men, nor through the agency of man, but through Jesus the Messiah, and God the Father, who raised Him from the dead), and all the brethren who are with me, to the communities of Galatia: Grace to you and peace from God our Father, and the Lord Jesus the Messiah, who gave Himself for our sins, that He might deliver us out of this present evil age, according to the will of our God and Father, to whom *be* the glory forevermore. Amen.

Verses 1-5 constitute Paul's salutation to his readers.[1] Greek letters in this period customarily opened with the sender's name (and title), the name of the addressee(s), and a greeting – *superscriptio, adscriptio,* and *salutatio* (cf. Ezra 7:12) (cf. Stone: 584f, and for the following discussion). The Hanukkah letter from 2 Maccabees provides a good example of contemporary usage: "To the brethren, the Jews in Egypt, greeting. The brethren, the Jews in Jerusalem and the country of Judaea, good peace"[2] (2 Macc. 1:1).[3] The designation of the senders and recipients by name – here, Paul and companions to the communities in Galatia – is characteristic of

---

[1] For Paul, see Appendix. The present work being designed to draw out the Jewish character and context of the letter, readers are referred to Betz and Longenecker (in particular) for the classical (Roman and Greek) sources regarding epistolary and rhetorical traditions.

[2] Τοῖς ἀδελφοῖς τοῖς κατ' Αἴγυπτον Ιουδαίοις χαίρειν οἱ ἀδελφοὶ οἱ ἐν Ιεροσολύμοις Ιουδαῖοι καὶ οἱ ἐν τῇ χώρᾳ τῆς Ιουδαίας εἰρήνην ἀγαθήν.

[3] Cf. Ezra 4:17, 5:7; Lk. 10:6, 24:36 [variant]; Rom. 1:7; Jas. 1:1; 1 Pet. 1:1; 1 Macc. 11:32, 12:6, 20; Jos.*Ant.* 16.166f, 17.137f; *Life* 217; Tanh.Vayishlach 3; Gen.R. 75:5.

Greek/Aramaic epistolary style.[4] The infinitive χαίρειν (chairein – lit.: "to greet")[5] is likewise good epistolary Greek usage, corresponding to the Hebrew שלום (shalom)/Aramaic שלם (shlam) – "peace."[6]

To the extent that this letter represents an encyclical – sent to several communities in Galatia rather than to one specific congregation (cf. verse 2) – it evidences correspondence with the letters sent by Gamaliel (II?) as Nasi and those concerning the observance of Hanukkah in Maccabees.[7] Three Aramaic letters have been recorded which are attributed to Rabban Gamaliel (II) as encyclicals, being addressed respectively to "our brethren in Upper Galilee and to those in Lower Galilee לאחנא בני גלילאה עילאה ולאחנא בני גלילאה תתאה," "to our brethren of the South לאחנא בני דרומא," and "to our brethren the Exiles in Babylon and to those in Media, and to all the other exiled [sons] of Israel לאחנא בני גלוותא בבבל ולאחנא דבמדי ולשאר כל גלוותא דישראל."

The texts of these letters run: "May your peace be great! We beg to inform you that the time of 'removal' has arrived for setting aside [the tithe] from the olive heaps שלומכון יסגא! מהודעין אנחנא לכון דזמן ביעורא מטא לאפרושי מעשרא ממעטנא דזיתא." "May your peace be great! We beg to inform you that the time of 'removal' has arrived for setting aside the tithe from the corn sheaves שלומכון יסגא! מהודעין אנחנא לכון דזמן ביעורא מטא לאפרושי מעשרא מעומרי שיבליא." "May your peace be great for ever! We beg to inform you that the doves are still tender and the lambs still too young and that the crops are not yet ripe. It seems advisable to me and to my colleagues to add thirty days to this year שלומכון יסגא לעלם! מהודעין אנחנא לכון דגוזליא רכיכין ואימריא ערקין וזמנא דאביבא לא מטא ושפרא מילתא באנפאי ובאנפי חביריי ואוסיפית על שתא דא יומין תלתין" (San. 11b).[8]

Perhaps most importantly, Galatians displays significant affinities with 4QMMT, the so-called Halakhic Letter from Qumran – although the latter unfortunately lacks a salutation.[9] The notion that a letter represents its sender, substituting for an address by the author in person, was widespread in antiquity. Encyclicals were frequently intended to be read publicly.[10] The fact that Paul urges his readers to observe "with what large letters I am writing to you with my own hand (πηλίκοις ὑμῖν γράμμασιν

---

[4] This usage contrasts with that of Hebrew letters, which customarily employ the expression "From X to Y": "From Shimon ben Kosibah to Yeshua ben Galgulah מן שמעון בר כוסבה לישוע בן גלגלה" (Mur 43).

[5] Cf. Acts 23:26; Rom. 12:15; Jas. 1:1.

[6] Cf. Gen.R. 100:7; Num.R. 21:1 (see also below).

[7] Cf. 2 Macc. 1:1-2:18; Tos.San. 2:6; JSan. 1, 2, 18d; JMaas.Sheni 5, 8, 56c; San. 11b. For Galatians as an encyclical, see Introduction, Form.

[8] Cf. 1 Macc. 15:19; Tos.San. 2:6; JSan. 1, 2, 18d; JMaas.Sheni 5, 8, 56c.

[9] For Galatians as a "halakhic letter" along the lines of 4QMMT, see Introduction, Form; Argument.

[10] Cf. Col. 4:16; 1 Thess. 5:27; 2 Bar. 86:1.

ἔγραψα τῇ ἐμῇ χειρί)" (6:11) may indicate that each community was meant to receive the original letter, delivered by an envoy from congregation to congregation (cf. Bruce, Galatians: 74).[11]

According to his accustomed usage, Paul first identifies himself – here as an "apostle (ἀπόστολος)."[12] While the Greek word is relatively rare, the concept of agency [שליחות] – of being "sent" – is well established in Judaism. In Jewish texts it designates a legal principle whereby a person – the principal [הִמְשַׁלֵחַ] – is enabled to perform a legal act through another – the agent – in order to extend his possible field of legal activity (cf. Elon: 167f, and for the following discussion). The two basic conditions required in agency are the principal's conscious consent and the agent's legal competence.[13] Halakhah (Jewish law) establishes that "A man's agent is like to himself [וְשָׁלוּחוֹ שֶׁלָּאָדָם כְּמוֹתוֹ]" (Ber. 5:5) in the areas of heave offerings [תרומה], sacrifices, civil law [ממונות], recovery of debts, betrothal, and divorce.[14] The agent possesses precisely and exactly the same authority as his commissioner – at the same time as that authority is completely prescribed by the mandate he receives. Any actions he commits without this fiat lack the principal's authority.

Tannaitic sources indirectly indicate that a shaliach may be appointed orally – as Jesus (or Ananias) directed Paul.[15] Only in the matter of wrongdoing (and of testimony regarding his mandate) is an agent held to be unlike his commissioner: "There is no agent in wrongdoing דאין שליח לדבר עבירה" (Kid. 42b-43a). In other words, where the principal commands his agent to commit an unlawful act, the *agent* is liable under criminal law.[16]

---

[11] For Paul's use of an amanuensis, see Introduction, **Form**; for the postscript itself, see 6:1-11.

[12] Cf. Rom. 1:1, 11:13; 1 Cor. 1:1, 9:1f, 15:9; 2 Cor. 1:1; Eph. 1:1; Col. 1:1; 1 Tim. 1:1, 2:7; 2 Tim. 1:1, 11; Tit. 1:1. The noun derives from the verb ἀποστέλλω (apostellō), meaning "to send out, away" (cf. BAGD: 89-89; TDNT: 1:398). In 3 Kings 14:6, the LXXᴬ understands the passive participle שָׁלוּחַ as a noun and renders it as ἀπόστολος (apostolos).

[13] While the Sages recognised that the principle lacks scriptural basis, its validity went unchallenged (cf. Elon: 158). Although women may act as agents for betrothal (cf. Kid. 23b), this area appears to constitute the extent of female rights of agency (cf. Le Cornu and Shulam: 990).

[14] Cf. Jn. 13:16; Mekh.Pischa 3, 5; Yalk.Ex. 192, 196; Ter. 4:4; Kid. 2:1; Eruv. 7:6; Git. 3:6, 4:1; Hag. 10b; Ned. 72b; Kid. 43a; BK 102a-b, 113b; BM 96a; Naz. 12b; [Shevu. 47b]; Git. 21a, 23a-23b.

[15] Cf. Acts 9:3ff, 22:6ff, 26:12ff; verses 12, 16.

[16] This ruling is derived from the hypothetical/"rhetorical" question: "[When] the words of the master [God] and the words of the pupil [are in conflict], whose are obeyed? דברי הרב ודברי תלמיד - דברי מי שומעים?" (Kid. 42b). If A instructs B to do wrong, B acts of his own accord, for were he fulfilling the directions required of him he would obey God's behests in preference. In answering the query in Acts 5:29 –

The person commissioned is required to act strictly within the scope of his mandate and to fulfil it to the smallest detail. If he exceeds his authority, all his actions are rendered null and void. His commission may also be revoked by the principal.[17] Paul states the terms of his commission clearly in verses 15-16: "He who had set me apart ... and called me through His grace, was pleased to reveal His son in me, that I might preach him among the Gentiles."[18]

Paul's frequent epistolary practice – at times reflecting his prison circumstances – is to introduce himself as Jesus' agent and "bond-servant (δοῦλος)."[19] Agents and slaves possess several common elements in terms of halakhic status, both being commanded by their master's commission (cf. BM 8:3; BM 44a) (cf. ibid: 309-15) (see also 4:1-7). The servant's contract is typically effected by commencement of the task (cf. BM 76b) and s/he may withdraw from his/her employment at any moment, not being susceptible to compulsion against his/her will (cf. BM 10a). If the slave has been hired for a specific task, s/he may not be forced to do anything other than that particular job without consent. S/he is bound to work faithfully, with his/her full strength, absenteeism being allowed only on adequate cause. If not explicitly agreed upon between the parties, the duration of the servant's service is determined by custom. In the case of certain public appointments, a contract of undetermined period was considered as life-long. In terms of accountability, the servant is liable for damage resulting from departure from custom or from the terms of his/her employment, from failure to take proper care, or from lack of familiarity with the work (cf. Tos.BK 10:29; BK 98b-100b).

While many biblical figures are characterised as servants (עבדים; avadim)[20] the terms "bond-slave" and "apostle" may be associated here through the idea of the prophet. Contrary to the argument that

---

"We must obey God rather than men" – Peter and the Apostles indicate that they are God's agents and are engaged in no wrongdoing.

[17] This concept simultaneously explains Jesus' calling and his commissioning of the Apostles/disciples (cf. Mt. 4:19, 10:1ff; Mk. 1:16-20, 2:14, 6:7f; Lk. 5:10, 27, 6:13-16, 9:1f, 10:1ff, 17:5, 22:14; Jn. 3:17, 34, 4:34, 5:19ff, 6:27, 29, 38ff, 70, 7:18, 28-29, 33, 8:26, 29, 10:18, 36-38, 12:44f, 13:20, 14:10, 24, 16:5, 28, 17:4, 8, 21f, 18:37, 20:21; Acts 1:2, 26; Heb. 3:1).

[18] εὐδόκησεν ... ὁ ἀφορίσας με ... καὶ καλέσας διὰ τῆς χάριτος αὐτοῦ ἀποκαλύψαι τὸν υἱὸν αὐτοῦ ἐν ἐμοί, ἵνα εὐαγγελίζομαι αὐτὸν ἐν τοῖς ἔθνεσιν. Cf. Acts 9:15, 22:15, 26:16-18; Rom. 1:1-5, 11:13; [1 Tim. 2:4-7; Tit. 1:3].

[19] Cf. Rom. 1:1; [2 Cor. 4:5]; Gal. 1:10; Phil. 1:1; Tit. 1:1. In this way, he sets forth the authority on which he makes his rebuke/request of his disciples (see Introduction, Argument; verses 15-16b, and below). For Paul's "exemplary" role, calling for imitation of his conduct on the part of his disciples, see 2:1-10 (n136), 15-21 (n292), 3:1-5 (nn14, 28), 4:12-20, 5:2-12 (verse 11), 24-26, 6:1f (verses 11, 15, 17), and verses 15-16b, 21-24.

[20] Cf. Gen. 26:24; Num. 12:7; 1 Kings 14:8; Ezra 9:11; Isa. 42:1, 49:5-6.

prophets are never called שליחים (shlichim) in rabbinic literature (cf. TDNT: 1:420), a passage in Avot de Rabbi Natan lists ten terms by which prophets are known in the Tanakh, including both שליח (shaliach) and servant: "By ten terms is a prophet designated, viz. ambassador, the faithful one, servant, messenger [i.e., shaliach], visionary, watchman, seer, dreamer, prophet, and man of God ,עשרה שמות נקרא נביא. ואלו הו: ציר, נאמן אלהים איש ,נביא ,חלום רואה ,צופה ,חוזה ,שליח ,עבד" (ARNª 34:8).[21] Moses and Aaron – the former the prophet *par excellence* – represent themselves to Pharaoh as "the ambassadors of the Lord שלוחיו של הקדוש ברוך הוא אנו" (Ex.R. 5:14).[22]

Prophets are also said to resemble angels (מלאכים; malakhim), the latter specifically being God's "messengers": "The prophets are called *'mal'akim'*. This is indicated by what is written, *And he sent a messenger* (mal'ak), *and brought us forth out of Egypt*, etc. (Num. 20:16). Was it then an angel of the Lord? Surely it was Moses! Why then does it call him *'mal'ak'*? In fact, from this one learns that the prophets are called *'mal'akim'*. Similarly it says, *And the messenger* (mal'ak) *of the Lord came up from Gilgal to Bochim* (Judg. 2:1). Was it then an angel? Surely it was Phinehas! Why then does it call him *'mal'ak'*? The truth is, said R. Simon, that the face of Phinehas, when the Holy Spirit rested upon him, flamed like a torch . . . R. Johanan said: There is a decisive passage which shows that the prophets were called *'mal'akim'*, namely, *Then spoke Haggai, the Lord's messenger* (mal'ak) *in the Lord's message* – mal'akuth (Hag. 1:13). Thus we are bound to conclude from this decisive passage that the prophets are called *'mal'akim'*"[23] (Lev.R. 1:1).[24]

While "proselytisers" (missionaries) are not designated "shlichim," the Sages themselves are associated with the prophets: "The prophet and the scribe, to whom shall we liken them? To a king who sent two messengers from his entourage . . . נביא וזקן למי הן דומין? למלך ששולח ב׳

---

[21] Cf. Ex. 14:31; Num. 12:7; 2 Kings 9:7, 17:13; Jer. 25:4, 26:5; Ezek. 38:17; Heb. 3:5; Rev. 10:7, 15:3; 1 Esd. 8:82 [79]; 2 Esd. 1:32, 2:1; 1QS 1:3; 1QpHab 2:9, 7:5; 4QpHos 2:5; 4Q390 f2i:5.

[22] For Elijah, Elisha, and Ezekiel as שליחים (schlichim) by virtue of their holding the keys to birth, rain, and resurrection – tasks normally reserved for God – cf. Ezekiel 37; Mid.Ps. 78:5; Ta'anit 2a; San. 113a.

[23] נקראו הנביאים מלאכים, הדא הוא דכתיב: וישלח מלאך ויוציאנו ממצרים וגו׳. וכי מלאך ה׳ היה והלא משה היה? ולמה קורא אותו מלאך? אלא מכאן שהנביאים נקראים מלאכים. ודכוותיה: ויעל מלאך ה׳ מן הגלגל אל הבוכים. וכי מלאך היה והלא פנחס היה? ולמה קורא אותו מלאך? אלא אמר ר׳ סימון: פנחס בשעה שהיתה רוח הקדוש שורה עליו היו פניו בוערות כלפידים . . . אמר רבי יוחנן: מבית אב שלהן נקראו הנביאים מלאכים, הדא הוא דכתיב: ויאמר חגי מלאך ה׳ במלאכות ה׳. הא על כן אתה למד שמבית אב שלהן נקראו הנביאים מלאכים.

[24] Cf. Rev. 22:6, 9; Jos.*Ant.* 15.136; Num.R. 10:5, 16:1. For the importance of Paul's receipt of the Spirit for his commission, see verses 15-16b; for teachers with faces like angels, see 4:12-20.

פלמטרין שלו" (JBer. 9a).[25] The scribes (Sages) gather around themselves pupils to whom they pass on their teaching (see 4:12-20). Heirs of the prophets, they derive their authority from their knowledge of God's will, which they declare through their preaching, teaching, and exhortation – which, in the case of the Sages, comes to take precedence over the actual prophetic source (cf. Jeremias, Jerusalem: 241f) (see verses 11-12, 15-16b).

Sirach describes the Sage in words very appropriate to Paul: "But he that giveth his mind to the law of the most High, and is occupied in the meditation thereof, will seek out the wisdom of all the ancients, and be occupied in prophecies . . . He shall serve among great men, and appear before princes. He will travel through strange countries; for he hath tried the good and the evil among men . . . Nations shall show forth his wisdom, and the congregation shall declare his praise"[26] (Sir. 39:1, 4, 10) (cf. Acts 9:15).

Paul clearly describes his calling in prophetic language, the essence of the prophet's task being to speak God's word.[27] The reference to being "set apart, even from my mother's womb (ἀφορίσας με ἐκ κοιλίας μητρός μου)" (verse 15) is modeled after God's appointment of Jeremiah as "a prophet to the nations [נביא לגוים]" (Jer. 1:5), God promising to "deliver (ἐξαιρούμενός; להצילך)" Paul from Jewish and gentile opposition in similar fashion to his assurance to Jeremiah (cf. Jer. 1:8; Acts 26:17) (see verses 15-16b).[28]

On a congregational level, Paul (and Barnabas) were commissioned by the community in Antioch, representing it and carrying its authority (cf. Acts 13:2-3). On this basis, they are both called "apostles" in the Messiah's

---

[25] Cf. Gen.R. 42:3; Cant.R. 1.2.2; JSan. 51a, 55b; J AZ 15a. For proselytism in Galatia, see Introduction, Occasion and circumstances; Theological pointers (n188), 2:15-21 (n269), and 4:12-20 (verse 17).

[26] Πλὴν τοῦ ἐπιδιδόντος τὴν ψυχὴν αὐτοῦ καὶ διανοουμένου ἐν νόμῳ ὑψίστου, σοφίαν πάντων ἀρχαίων ἐκζητήσει καὶ ἐν προφητείαις ἀσχοληθήσεται . . . ἀνὰ μέσον μεγιστάνων ὑπηρετήσει καὶ ἔναντι ἡγουμένων ὀφθήσεται· ἐν γῇ ἀλλοτρίων ἐθνῶν διελεύσεται, ἀγαθὰ γὰρ καὶ κακὰ ἐν ἀνθρώποις ἐπείρασεν . . . τὴν σοφίαν αὐτοῦ διηγήσονται ἔθνη, καὶ τὸν ἔπαινον αὐτοῦ ἐξαγγελεῖ ἐκκλησία.

[27] Cf. Jer. 23:21-22; Amos 3:7-8; [2 Cor. 5:19]; 1QHᵃ 14:9ff, 15:10f, 16:16, 35-36; 4Q436 f1i:7-9. The parallelism of Paul's phraseology with 2 Pet. 1:21 here is surely not coincidental: "For no prophecy was ever made by an act of human will, but men moved by the Holy Spirit spoke from God (οὐ γὰρ θελήματι ἀνθρώπου ἠνέχθη προφητεία ποτέ, ἀλλὰ ὑπὸ πνεύματος ἁγίου φερόμενοι ἐλάλησαν ἀπὸ θεοῦ ἄνθρωποι)."

[28] Cf. Isa. 49:1, 5; Amos 7:14-15; 1QHᵃ 17:29f; Philo, Virt. 63 (cf. Le Cornu and Shulam: 500f, 1126, 1214, 1402-3, 1458; Betz, Galatians: 38). For the link with "amazement," see below; for the further implications of being "set apart," see verses 15-16b.

service[29] – i.e., are sent as "agents," equal to their commissioners until they return to them. Their "work (ἔργον)" (Acts 13:2) was the service of the Kingdom of God – having been commissioned to preach the gospel throughout the diaspora. In this respect, they further resembled the rabbinic envoys whose tasks included teaching Tanakh and Mishnah in the various diaspora communities; intercalating the calendar; and collecting money (cf. Yev. 16:7; Tos.Meg. 2:5). Luke describes Paul and Barnabas' commissioning in Acts 14:26 as being "commended to the grace of God (παραδεδομένοι τῇ χάριτι τοῦ θεοῦ)" – a phrase which recalls both the "word of His grace (τῷ λόγῳ τῆς χάριτος αὐτοῦ)" (cf. Acts 14:3, 20:32) – i.e., the good news which conveys God's grace – and the authority which they received as agents.[30]

Immediately after identifying himself here as an apostle, Paul "digresses" (what Longenecker designates as a characteristic pauline methodological feature of "going off at a word" [Galatians: 2] – actually a typically midrashic associative technique) and begins to explain precisely what he means by the term. While in his later letters Paul regularly regards his calling as being "by the will of God (διὰ θελήματος θεοῦ)"[31] he here employs a more elaborate articulation which simultaneously claims God and Jesus as his principals and disclaims any human element.[32] This move has traditionally been understood to mark the definition as a "defence." Although the latter is typically understood to represent Paul's countering his Jewish-Christian opponents' questioning of his authority, reading Galatians as a halakhic "rebuke-request" letter suggests that Paul is here

---

[29] Cf. Acts 14:4, 14; Rom. 1:1, 16:7; 2 Cor. 8:23 (Greek).

[30] Barnabas had originally been commissioned by the Jerusalem community to oversee the newly-founded and growing community in Antioch (cf. Acts 11:22) (see 2:1-10 [excursus]).

[31] Cf. 1 Cor. 1:1; 2 Cor. 1:1; Eph. 1:1; Col. 1:1; 1 Tim. 1:1; 2 Tim. 1:1; Tit. 1:1-3. God is the person who has commissioned Paul, as the variant "according to the commandment of God (κατ' ἐπιταγὴν θεοῦ)" in 1 Tim. 1:1 makes clear. For the dating of Galatians, see Introduction, **Date and destination**.

[32] Cf. "I [Moses] did not of my own free-will choose to superintend and preside over public affairs, nor did I receive the office through appointment by some other of mankind, but when God by oracles and manifest declarations made clear to me His will and bade me take command, considering the greatness of the task I held back with prayers and supplications, until, when He many times repeated the command, I trembled but obeyed (τὴν γοῦν ἐπιμέλειαν καὶ προτασίαν τῶν κοινῶν οὔτ' αὐτὸς ἐθελοντὴς εἱλόμην οὔθ' ὑπ' ἄλλου τινὸς ἀνθρώπων χειροτονηθεὶς ἔλαβον, ἀλλὰ καὶ τοῦ θεοῦ χρησμοῖς ἐναργέσι καὶ λογίοις ἀριδήλοις ἐμφαβῶς θεσπίζοντος καὶ προστάττοντος ἄρχειν ἀνεδυόμην ἱκετεύων καὶ ποτνιώμενος, εἰς τὸ μέγεθος ἀφορῶν τοῦ πράγματος, ἕως, ἐπειδὴ πολλάκις ἐκέλευε, δείσας ἐπειθάρχησα)" (Philo, *Virt.* 63).

establishing his authority in the eyes of his disciples – from whom he is about to demand conformity (cf. 4:12).[33]

Paul employs a "negative argument [דרך השלילה]" here, positing first of all what he is *not*: "For the overseer must be above reproach as God's steward, not self-willed, not quick-tempered, not addicted to wine, not pugnacious, not fond of sordid gain, but hospitable, loving what is good, sensible, just, devout, self-controlled . . ."[34] (Tit. 1:7-8) (cf. verses 16b-17).[35] In the context of commissioning, the ἀπ' (ap; "from [men]") most probably signifies "*sent* from" (cf. NASB) (cf. Lk. 1:26; Acts 11:11), a verb of direction being implicit. The second prepositional phrase "through man (δι' ἀνθρώπου)" directly implies agency ("by means of"). The play on words here is much clearer in Hebrew, where אדם (adam – "[a] man"), בני אדם (bnei adam – "men"), and אדם (Adam) are variations one on another, both "adam" and Adam representing collective "wo/mankind." Where the first clause "from men" represents a human mandate, the second recalls Paul's wordplay on the first and second Adams in Romans 5: "For if by the transgression of the one the many died, much more did the grace of God and the gift by the grace of the one man, Jesus the Messiah, abound to the many"[36] (Rom. 5:15) (cf. Shulam and Le Cornu: 191-99) (see 3:19-20, 26-29).[37]

In this way, Paul indicates that his commission devolves neither from human beings nor from the "father of mankind" – the first Adam in all his transgression and mortality. Its source is rather in the "Second Adam," the One through whose obedience "the many will be made righteous" (Rom.

---

[33] For the structure of Galatians, see Introduction, Form; Argument.

[34] δεῖ γὰρ τὸν ἐπίσκοπον ἀνέγκλητον εἶναι ὡς θεοῦ οἰκονόμον, μὴ αὐθάδη, μὴ ὀργίλον, μὴ πάροινον, μὴ πλήκτην, μὴ αἰσχροκερδῆ, ἀλλὰ φιλόξενον φιλάγαθον σώφρονα δίκαιον ὅσιον ἐγκρατῆ . . .

[35] Cf. Amos 7:14: "Then Amos answered and said to Amaziah, 'I am not a prophet, nor am I the son of a prophet; for I am a herdsman and a grower of sycamore figs' (cf. ויען עמוס ויאמר אל-אמציה לא-נביא אנכי ולא בן-נביא אנכי כי-בוקר אנכי ובולס שכמים" Judg. 8:23). Note also the rhetorical effect of negations: ". . . in contrast to positive propositions, 'negations are much richer in presuppositions.' That is, negations of a proposition presuppose rhetorically that someone has affirmed or might affirm it; consequently the very act of negation suggests some sort of metaphorical truth, or it at least allows the negated statement to open a door into areas of indefinite metaphorical possibility" (Hays, *Echoes*: 141; quoting J. Culler, *The Pursuit of Signs* [Ithaca: Cornell University Press, 1981], 115) (see also 5:2).

[36] εἰ γὰρ τῷ τοῦ ἑνὸς παραπτώματι οἱ πολλοὶ ἀπέθανον, πολλῷ μᾶλλον ἡ χάρις τοῦ θεοῦ καὶ ἡ δωρεὰ ἐν χάριτι τῇ τοῦ ἑνὸς ἀνθρώπου Ἰησοῦ Χριστοῦ εἰς τοὺς πολλοὺς ἐπερίσσευσεν.

[37] Cf. 1 Cor. 15:20-49. A similar usage of positives/negatives is reflected in John 1:1-13, the last verse of which also clarifies the disparity between the human and divine: ". . . were born not of blood, nor of the will of the flesh, nor of the will of man, but of God (οἳ οὐκ ἐξ αἱμάτων οὐδὲ ἐκ θελήματος σαρκὸς οὐδὲ ἐκ θελήματος ἀνδρὸς ἀλλ' ἐκ θεοῦ ἐγεννήθησαν)."

5:19) (cf. 2 Cor. 4:5 [Greek]).³⁸ Jesus is the person who has mandated Paul in his task of being "a minister and a witness not only to the things which you have seen, but also to the things in which I will appear to you . . . the Gentiles, to whom I am sending you, to open their eyes so that they may turn from darkness to light and from the dominion of Satan to God, in order that they may receive forgiveness of sins and an inheritance among those who have been sanctified by faithfulness to me"³⁹ (Acts 26:16-18).⁴⁰

Paul's witness, "untimely" as he considered it to have been (cf. 1 Cor. 15:8-9), was in line with that of the Twelve, who were appointed on the basis of their personal testimony to Jesus' resurrection.⁴¹ It was the resurrected Jesus who appeared to Paul – thanks to God who raised him from the dead.⁴² Witness to Jesus' resurrection lies at the heart of Paul's commission: "But if there is no resurrection of the dead, not even the Messiah has been raised; and if the Messiah has not been raised, then our preaching is in vain, your faith also is vain"⁴³ (1 Cor. 15:13-14).⁴⁴ As becomes clear in the course of the letter, Paul's affirmation of his commission establishes, simultaneously, the authority on which he calls his Galatian disciples to return their loyalty to him and the power of his influence in comparison to those who are merely "human agents," yet who

---

³⁸ The motif of "one" is also applied to Abraham in Isa. 51:2: "Look to Abraham your father and to Sarah who gave birth to you in pain; when he was one, I called him, then I blessed him and multiplied him הביטו אל-אברהם אביכם ואל-שרה תחוללכם כי-אחד קראתיו ואברכהו ואברהו." Not only does this passage allude to Abraham's blessing (cf. 3:8-14) but it also precedes and forms part of the larger picture of Isaiah 52-54, themes from which also pervade Galatians (see 3:1f, 26-29 and 4:21-31).

³⁹ Προξειρίσασθαί σε ὑπηρέτην καὶ μάρτυρα ὧν τε εἶδές [με] ὧ τε ὀφθήσομαί σοι, ἐξαιρούμενός σε ἐκ τοῦ λαοῦ καὶ ἐκ τῶν ἐθνῶν εἰς οὓς ἐγὼ ἀποστέλλω σε ἀνοῖξαι ὀφθαλμοὺς αὐψῶν, τοῦ ἐπιστρέψαι ἀπὸ σκότους εἰς φῶς καὶ τῆς ἐξουσίας τοῦ σατανᾶ ἐπὶ τὸν θεόν, τοῦ λαβεῖν αὐτοὺς ἄφεσιν ἁμαρτιῶν καὶ κλῆρον ἐν τοῖς ἡγιασμένοις πίστει τῇ εἰς ἐμέ.

⁴⁰ Cf. Acts [1:17], 20:24, 21:19; Rom. 1:5, 15:16f; 1 Cor. 4:1-4; 2 Cor. 4:1, 5:18[f]; [Col. 4:17]; 1 Tim. 1:12; [2 Tim. 4:11]. For Paul's priestly ministry, cf. Le Cornu and Shulam: 500, 522-23, 591, 1216-20, 1319-22.

⁴¹ Cf. Acts 1:21-22. Paul's concern appears to have been not so much that he had not accompanied Jesus during his earthly ministry but that he had actively attempted to destroy his followers – and hence Jesus himself (cf. Acts 8:1-3, 9:1-2, 21, 22:19-20, 26:9-12; 1 Cor. 15:8-9; Gal. 1:13; Phil. 3:6) (cf. Le Cornu and Shulam: 1393). See Appendix, **Persecutor** and verses 13-14.

⁴² Cf. Rom. 1:1-5; 1 Cor. 9:1, 15:8; verses 12, 16.

⁴³ εἰ δὲ ἀνάστασις νεκρῶν οὐκ ἔστιν, οὐδὲ Χριστὸς ἐγήγερται· εἰ δὲ Χριστὸς οὐκ ἐγήγερται, κενὸν ἄρα [καὶ] τὸ κήρυγμα ἡμῶν, κενὴ καὶ ἡ πίστις ὑμῶν.

⁴⁴ Cf. Acts 13:28-41, 17:3, 18-32, 23:6-9, 26:6-8; Rom. 4:14, 24-25; 6:4, 9, 8:11, 10:9; 1 Cor. 15:3-58; Eph. 1:20; Col. 2:12; 1 Thess. 1:10. The reference to the vanity of Paul's preaching is apt here. See also 2:1-10 and 4:8f.

are endeavouring to draw his disciples away from his gospel according to "fleshly" conventions (see Introduction, **Argument**).[45]

While Paul regularly refers first to God the Father and subsequently to Jesus, the reverse order here may reflect his desire to identify God as the raiser from the dead, on the one hand (cf. Betz, Galatians: 41), and Jesus as the immediate principal, on the other.[46] While these are the two natural persons to name in contrast with human agents – the One who raises people from the dead and the one raised – Paul also appeals to the biblical principle of affirming evidence by the mouth of two witnesses: "A single witness shall not rise up against a man on account of any iniquity or any sin which he has committed; on the evidence of two or three witnesses a matter shall be confirmed לא-יקום עד אחד באיש לכל-עוון-לכל-חטאת בכל-חטא אשר יחטא על-פי שני עדים או על-פי שלושה-עדים יקום דבר" (Dt. 19:15) (cf. Elon: 605).[47] The fact that God has raised Jesus from the dead attests to Jesus' fitness as a heavenly principal (cf. Acts 2:22) – just as Paul speaks of the apostle being witnessed "by signs and wonders and miracles"[48] (2 Cor. 12:12) (cf. Rom. 15:19) (cf. Le Cornu and Shulam: 97-101, 117). The phrase "God the Father (θεοῦ πατρός)" (cf. verse 3) is common in other contemporary Jewish sources: "On whom can we stay ourselves? – on our Father in heaven על מי לנו להשען? על אבינו שבשמים" (Sot. 9:15).[49]

---

[45] "Paul struggles to ensure that the authority with which he addresses his converts from afar will not be undermined by those nearby who are 'unsettling' them: 'Paul an apostle – not from human agents nor through a human agency, but through Jesus Christ and God the Father, who raised him from the dead ones' (1:1; cf. 1:10). How can his converts now question what he made so clear to them before (1:9; 5:3), speaking with the authority he had directly from God?" (Nanos, Inter: 399).

[46] Cf. Hos. 6:2; Acts 2:24, 3:15, 26, 4:10, 5:30, 10:40, 13:30f, 17:31; Rom. 4:24, 8:11, 10:9; 1 Cor. 15:15; 2 Cor. 1:9, 4:14; Eph. 1:20; Col. 2:12; 1 Thess. 1:10; Heb. 13:20; 1 Pet. 1:21; 4Q521 f2ii:6ff; Amidah no. 3. The conjunction of Jesus and the Father together serves as at least one reason why the charge that Paul's gospel is not from God cannot lie in the suggestion that "it is precisely that Paul appeals to Jesus the Christ" – i.e., "Not even the Jesus-believing Jews in Jerusalem, who had acknowledged Jesus of Nazareth as the Messiah, would have called him a 'Son of God' in the sense of the Christology of preexistence. Even less could the Jews who did not believe in Jesus see in him anything other than a 'human being'" (Walter: 352/363). For the doctrine of the resurrection, cf. Le Cornu and Shulam: 218-19, 1247-48, 1315-17, 87-89.

[47] Cf. Num. 30:35; Dt. 17:6; 2 Cor. 13:1; Sif.Dt. 188; Sot. 2b; San. 30a. This does not necessarily contradict or exclude the chiasmus between the two initial negative and subsequent dual positive statements concerning the source of Paul's commission in verse 1 (cf. Betz, Galatians: 38-39).

[48] τὰ μὲν σημεῖα τοῦ ἀποστόλου κατειργάθη ἐν ὑμῖν ἐν πάσῃ ὑπομονῇ, σημείοις τε καὶ τέρασιν καὶ δυνάμεσιν.

[49] Cf. Mt. 5:16, 45, 6:9; Mk. 1 1:25; Lk. 11:2; Tob. 13:4; Wis.Sol. 14:3; Sir. 23:1, 4; 4Q372 f1:16; TBE p. 115 [beg.]; Tos.Hag. 2:1; JSot. 46b-47a; JHag. 9a; Sot. 49a-b.

In 1 Corinthians, Paul appeals to that community as testimony of his commissioning, asserting that they constitute "the seal of my apostleship in the Lord (ἡ γὰρ σφραγίς μου τῆς ἀποστολῆς ὑμεῖς ἐστε ἐν κυρίῳ)" (1 Cor. 9:2). The seal serves as affirmation of the authenticity of Paul's agency – "living proof" of the first fruits of the "ministry of reconciliation (τὴν διακονίαν τῆς καταλλαγῆς)" which he has received as an "ambassador for the Messiah, as though God were entreating through us (πρεσβεύομεν ὡς τοῦ θεοῦ παρακαλοῦντος δι' ἡμῶν)" (2 Cor. 5:18, 20) (cf. Shulam and Le Cornu: 164, 502-3).[50] He designates as "false apostles (ψευδαπόστολοι)" those who are "deceitful workers, disguising themselves as apostles of the Messiah (ἐργάται δόλιοι, μετασχηματιζόμενοι εἰς ἀποστόλους Χριστοῦ)" (2 Cor. 11:13). These he harshly characterises as "servants of Satan" who "disguise themselves as servants of righteousness (μετασχηματίζονται ὡς διάκονοι δικαιοσύνης)" (2 Cor. 11:15) (see also verses 11-12).

The context of 2 Corinthians 11 suggests that people whom Paul recognises as "eminent apostles (ὑπερλίαν ἀποστόλων)" have been teaching "another Jesus (ἄλλον Ἰησοῦν)" and "a different gospel (εὐαγγέλιον ἕτερον)" (2 Cor. 11:4-5) and, adding insult to this injury, taking payment for doing so. The Didache affirms such conduct as the mark of the false apostle: "But if the teacher himself be perverted and teach another doctrine to destroy these things [which have just been laid out above], do not listen to him, but if his teaching be for the increase of righteousness and knowledge of the Lord, receive him as the Lord ... when an Apostle goes forth, let him accept nothing but bread till he reach his night's lodging; but if he ask for money, he is a false prophet[51] (Did. 11:2, 6).[52] As elsewhere in Paul, this passage assumes a multiplicity of apostles, not dependent upon the authority of the Twelve (cf. 1 Cor. 12:28-29; Eph. 4:11).

The apostle and prophet are regarded as closely resembling one another also in this text. According to the Didache, the two distinguishing

---

[50] The "through us (δι' ἡμῶν)" of this passage picks up, as it were, the διὰ Ἰησοῦ Χριστοῦ καὶ θεοῦ πατρὸς ("through Jesus the Messiah and God the Father") of the present verse.

[51] ἐὰν δὲ αὐτὸς ὁ διδάσκων στραφεὶς διδάσκη ἄλλην διδαχὴν εἰς τὸ καταλῦσαι, μὴ αὐτοῦ ἀκούσητε· εἰς δὲ τὸ προσθεῖναι δικαιοσύνην καὶ γνῶσιν κυρίου, δέξασθε αὐτὸν ὡς κύριον ... ἐξερχόμενος δὲ ὁ ἀπόστολος μηδὲ λαμβανέτω εἰ μὴ ἄρτον, ἕως οὗ αὐλισθῇ· ἐὰν δὲ ἀργύριον αἰτῇ, ψευδοπροφήτης ἐστί.

[52] For receiving payment for teaching, cf. DEZ 4:3 (Le Cornu and Shulam: 674). Paul appears to adapt the principle to suit the context in which he is currently working. While in 1 Cor. 9:12 Paul asserts that "Nevertheless, we did not use this right [to remuneration], but we endure all things, that we may cause no hindrance to the gospel of the Messiah (ἀλλ' οὐκ ἐχρησάμεθα τῇ ἐξουσίᾳ ταυτη, ἀλλὰ πάντα στέγομεν, ἵνα μή τινα ἐγκοπὴν δῶμεν τῷ εὐαγγελίῳ τοῦ Χριστοῦ)," in 6:6 he directly calls for the Galatians' support (see 4:12-20 and 6:1-11).

characteristics of the agent were mobility – the essence of being "sent" – and teaching (cf. van de Sandt and Flusser: 354). A third central element was the collection of funds. This function was later notable in the mainstream Jewish diaspora in the sending of tributes to the Patriarch, following the destruction of the Temple in 70, possibly as a replacement for the half-shekel tithe.[53] Paul's initial commissioning by the Antiochian community was to deliver a contribution to the Jerusalem community (cf. Acts 11:30), and if that visit is identified with 2:1-10, when the Jerusalem leaders affirmed his status, he and Barnabas were further commissioned to "remember the poor (τῶν πτωχῶν ἵνα μνημονεύωμεν)" (2:10) (see 2:1-10).[54] Paul terms those who accompany him "apostles of the communities (ἀπόστολοι ἐκκλησιῶν)" (2 Cor. 8:23), Epaphroditus, sent with a donation on behalf of the Philippian congregation, likewise being named an ἀπόστολον (apostolon) (Phil. 2:25).[55]

In laying out his authority as the ground for his request for loyalty from his disciples, Paul is also, by definition, countering that of those who are "disturbing" the Galatian communities (cf. verse 7). Even if the "influencers" are not "agents of men" in the sense of having been sent by the Apostles in Jerusalem – the argument here being that they are local, non-believing Gentiles – their persuasion is based on a human principle which, moreover, denies the import of Jesus' death and resurrection.[56] Their purpose is defined by considerations of community – identification with and thereby identity within – כלל ישראל (klal Yisrael – the Jewish commonwealth) *to the exclusion of Jesus.* Paul, on the contrary, has been commissioned directly by Jesus and represents him "as himself" among the Gentiles (cf. verse 16) (see also verses 11-12).

---

[53] Cf. Epiph.*Adv.Haer.* 30.11 (cf. Alon, Land: 2:713; Avi-Yonah: 61).

[54] It was the fulfilment of this task – in delivering the contribution from Macedonia and Achaia to Jerusalem, accompanied by the gentile "delegates" – which brought Paul to Jerusalem, where he was arrested and eventually transferred to Rome for trial, having appealed to Caesar (cf. Acts 20:3-28:31) (cf. Le Cornu and Shulam: 1091-97, 1165-68, 1318-22).

[55] The association here with the Didache may corroborate the claim, currently being made, that Paul is here laying out his authority as the basis of his plea/instruction: "I beg of you, brethren, become as *I am* (Γίνεσθε ὡς ἐγώ . . . δέομαι ὑμῶν)" (4:12) (see above).

[56] Right at the outset (cf. Introduction), it must be stressed that no intention hereby exists to define Judaism itself as a "human principle" – in contrast to the "spirituality" of the Gospel/Christianity (one of the traditional perspectives on Galatians in particular and on Paul in general). Paul's "denunciation" of circumcision arises in the specific context of people who are affirming conversion in place of godfearing status in such a way as to deny the effects of Jesus' death and resurrection for the Gentiles. The debate between conversion/godfearers was naturally an inner-Jewish discussion (cf. Jos.*Ant.* 20.34-48), and despite the gentile nature of his antagonists, Paul's disagreement is also an inner-Jewish argument.

Having satisfactorily established his credentials – at least temporarily – Paul now returns to the epistolary conventions common to the period, specifying the "co-senders" of the letter. Identifying these is a process dependent on the epistle's provenance – where Paul was when he sent it, and who was "with him (οἱ σὺν ἐμοὶ)." On the thesis that Paul penned the letter in Antioch, just prior to the council in 48 (see Introduction, **Date and destination**), the "brethren" may be the Antiochian community at large; its prominent figures (such as Simeon Niger, [Barnabas], Lucius, and Manaen – cf. Acts 13:1); and/or Paul's traveling companions – Barnabas, John Mark, and possibly unnamed others (cf. Acts 12:25, 13:2-6, 13).[57]

No intrinsic reason exists why members of the Antiochian community should have known any of the Galatian believers personally, the city's ties being generally closer with Jerusalem than with Asia Minor (cf. Le Cornu and Shulam: 615-16). The fact that Paul fails to mention any of those associated with him at the time of the letter's composition by name[58] here, merely giving the general "all the brethren (πάντες ἀδελφοί)," may function as a source of endorsement: Paul has the solid backing of "all" the persons who are "with him (οἱ σὺν ἐμοὶ)" not only geographically but also substantively ("theologically").[59] If his amanuensis (scribe) (cf. 6:13) is among the brethren, Paul does not name him, nor does the amanuensis name himself (see Introduction, **Form**). The brevity of address is quite likely a reflection of the agitation disturbing the Galatian communities – and hence himself – with the treatment of which the letter is intended to deal (see below [verse 5]).

Verse 2 introduces the epistolary *adscriptio* signifying the addressees – "to the communities of Galatia (ταῖς ἐκκλησίαις τῆς Γαλατίας)" (verse 2).[60] The Greek term ἐκκλησία (ekklēsia – "church") originally represented the name of the citizen body in its legislative capacity (cf. TDNT: 3:513). The LXX uses the word as the regular rendering of קהל (kahal), the

---

[57] While Stirewalt's arguments are of great interest in this respect, they are ultimately not completely convincing (pp. 94ff). Allowing for his assumption of a post-council date – but ignoring his dating of Galatians following 1 Corinthians, Philippians, and Philemon – identification of the brethren with a "Galatian delegation" must acknowledge that Paul is addressing several communities rather than a single one. Nor does it seem likely that an appeal by Paul to the same brethren who (presumably) brought news of the situation to him (and may have returned with Paul's letter) would carry much weight with the communities – who would regard such "delegates" as hostile witnesses. For the lack of mention of Barnabas and Timothy, see Introduction, **Date and destination**.

[58] Cf. 1 Cor. 1:1; 2 Cor. 1:1; Phil. 1:1; Col. 1:1; 1 Thess. 1:1; 2 Thess. 1:1; Phlm 1.

[59] The "all" is unique in Paul's letters (cf. Stirewalt: 87-98). He otherwise includes epithets and courtesies (cf. Rom. 1:7; 1 Cor. 1:2; 2 Cor. 1:1; Phil. 1:1; 1 Thess. 1:1) (cf. Betz, Galatians: 40) (see 6:1f [verses 11, 16]).

[60] Cf. 1 Cor. 1:2; 2 Cor. 1:1; 1 Thess. 1:1; 2 Thess. 1:1. For the location of Galatia, see Introduction, **Date and destination**.

"assembly" of Israel as a religious body - except in Genesis-Numbers, Jeremiah, and Ezekiel, where it renders the Hebrew with the term συναγωγή (synagōgē - "synagogue")[61] (cf. also עדה [edah - "congregation"]) (cf. Bruce, Galatians: 166).[62] In its early stages, the "congregation" connoted a military camp composed of the twelve tribes with their standards and ensigns, the Tent of Meeting at its centre (cf. Num. 2:2). It also represented Israel in its sacerdotal aspects, convening for holy gatherings and religious ceremonies such as Pesach (Passover) (cf. Ex. 12:43f; Num. 9:2f), covenantal assemblies,[63] holy days, and sacred occasions (cf. Ex. 23:14ff; Lev. 23:4ff). The congregation further wielded judicial and executive power with regard to such violations of the Torah as blasphemy, desecration of shabbat (sabbath), violation of taboos, major cultic deviations, and grave immoral behaviour.[64]

Although the designation fell into disuse during the monarchical period, it was revived by the community at Qumran, which regarded itself as the "true Israel" patterned after the generation of the Exodus before the rest of Israel went astray.[65] In this sense, the early community was part of the assembly of Israel, now further bound together internally through the Messiah, Jesus.[66] If the letter was written prior to the council in 48, the communities are presumably those of Pisidian Antioch, Iconium, Lystra, and Derbe (cf. Acts 13-14), the first three being linked by the Via Sebaste (cf. Gill and Gempf: 52). Although it is difficult to ascertain what relationship(s) obtained between the various communities, Acts 14:19 witnesses to the Jewish network in the area.[67]

The designation "brethren (ἀδελφοὶ)" is a primary marker of Jewish ethnic solidarity, the nation being spread throughout Eretz Israel and the diaspora: "'Brothers' is a designation for Israel, as it is said: 'For my

---

[61] Cf. LXX Gen. 28:3; Ex. 16:3; Num. 20:4f; Dt. 9:10, 18:16; Josh. 9:2f; Judg. 20:2; Ps. 21:23, 39:10, 106:32; Ezek. 26:7.

[62] While "kahal (assembly)" encompasses the whole population of Israel, including men, women, and strangers (cf. Dt. 31:12; Jer. 44:15; Joel 2:16; 2 Chron. 20:13ff), עדה (edah - "congregation") denotes the indigenous, mostly arms-bearing population in the Tanakh (cf. Ex. 16:22; Lev. 4:15, 8:3, 24:16; Num. 10:1f, 15:35, 27:21; Josh. 9:15, 20:6; Judg. 20:1, 21:10; 1 Kings 12:20).

[63] Cf. Ex. 24:3f; Leviticus 19; Dt. 4:10f, 31:12.

[64] Cf. Lev. 24:14ff; Num. 15:32ff; Dt. 13:1f, 17:5; Judges 19-20; Josh. 7:1ff, 22:9ff.

[65] Cf. 1Q28a 1:1f; CD-A 6:19; CD-B 20:12 (see 6:12-16 [n186]).

[66] Although, on the present reading, the Galatian communities need not have included Jews, the evidence of Acts suggests that many of the congregations were mixed (cf. Acts 13:16, 26, 43-48, 14:1, 19, 21). The term ekklēsia was applied to an actual building only much later (cf. Ferguson, Backgrounds: 76; Gill and Gempf: 119ff).

[67] The fact that Jews from Antioch and Iconium travelled to Lystra implies that the latter city possessed no Jewish community of its own (cf. Le Cornu and Shulam: 773-74, 779, 786).

brethren and companions' sakes,' etc. (Ps. 122:8) : אחים אלו ישראל, שנאמר
"למען אחי ורעי וגו'" (Mekh.Be-shall. 4). "Our brother Israelites ... our
brethren, hearken unto us אחינו שמעונו ... "אחינו ישראל" (Sem. 8:8-9). "R.
Zadok came and stood upon the steps of the Hall and called out: Hear me,
our brethren of the House of Israel : בא ר' צדוק ועמד על מעלות האולם ואמר
"שמעוני אחינו בית ישראל" (Tos.Yoma 1:12).[68] The epithet in the singular (cf.
Acts 9:17, 21:20, 22:13) corresponds to the designation of the members of
the community as "brethren (ἀδελφοί)."[69] In rabbinic literature it serves as
an affectionate form of respectful address: "R. Eleazar b. Azariah said to
him, Ishmael my brother, it is not I that have changed the order of the
years: Tarfon, my brother, has changed it, and he must bring forth proof
אמר לו רבי אלעזר בן עזריה : ישמעאל אחי, אני לא שניתי מסדר השנים, טרפון אחי שנה,
ועליו ראיה ללמד" (Yad. 4:3).[70]
    While the epithet is used as an address between equals in Aramaic
letters from the Persian period, its usage in the New Testament – both in
the plural and the singular – suggests that the early community, as Bar
Kokhva's followers later, called one another "brother" as a sign of
fellowship (cf. Stone: 590n38). Paul's use of the term in Galatians (cf. verse
1, 3:15, 4:12, 28, 31, 5:11, 6:1, 18) is nevertheless significant because his
addressees are primarily Gentiles and not Jews. As an ethnic designation,
its employment for non-Jews demands explanation.
    Despite the fact that the גר תושב (ger toshav – "resident alien") was
included in the community of Israel in the biblical period (cf. Num. 14:15),
s/he was not designated as a "brother": "Then I charged your judges at
that time, saying, 'Hear *the cases* between your fellow-countrymen, and
judge righteously between a man and his fellow-countryman, or the alien
who is with him' ואצוה את-שפטיכם בעת ההוא לאמר שמע בין-אחיכם ושפטתם צדק
"בין-איש ובין-אחיו ובין גרו" (Dt. 1:16). In Acts, Luke is careful to designate the
early gentile believers as "disciples (μαθηταὶ)" (cf. Acts 13:52, 14:20f, 28).
The first time he applies the term "brethren" to Gentiles is in Acts 15:1 (cf.
Pfann; Le Cornu and Shulam: 766, 801-2). The grounds which permit the
extension – which is reflected in the continuation of Acts – appear to be
that these Gentiles wish to be circumcised, thereby becoming full members
of the people of Israel and observing the Torah and commandments. In so
doing, they as it were become "brethren" (cf. Lichtenstein, Commentary:

---

[68] Cf. Gen. 13:8; Lev. 19:17; Dt. 1:16, 3:18; 4 Macc. 8:19; Lev.R. 17:5; Sifre, Masa'ei
161; Yalk.Ex. 271; Tos.Shevi. 8:2; Sem. 8:13; MK 21b; Ket. 28b. (Cf. שכל ישראל ערבים זה
בזה ["all Israel are sureties one for another"] – Tanh.Nitzav. 2; TBE p. 56; Sifra, Be-
chuk. 7; Num.R. 10:5; San. 27b; Shevu. 39a.)

[69] Cf. Acts 6:3, 9:30, 10:23, 11:1, 12, 12:17, 14:2, 15:1, 3, 7, 13, 33, 16:2, et al.

[70] Cf. Sif.Dt. 34; AZ 2:5; ARNa 38:3; Yoma 35b.

175).[71] Paul's usage in Galatians would seem to support the chronological time framework when the switch was introduced and began to become general practice, gradually extending not only to those who expressed a wish to become part of the Jewish community but also to those who, by virtue of Jesus' advent, were now included in God's Kingdom in the "messianic age."[72]

Verse 3 represents the epistolary greeting convention of *salutatio*, known from ancient letters, couched here in the form of a prayer or blessing (benediction) (cf. Betz, Galatians: 40). While the Greek customarily used the form χαίρειν (chairein – lit.: "greetings"), the biblical style – carried through into later periods – employs the concept of peace. The latter served as the regular form of oral greeting: "Peace (be upon you) שלום (עליך/עליכם)" – returned in kind depending on the particular relationship.[73] The same formula is reflected in contemporary letters: "The brethren, the Jews in Jerusalem and the country of Judaea, good peace"[74] (2 Macc. 1:1) (cf. Shab. 12b). If "peace" was the standard Hebrew greeting and χαίρειν the Greek, the joint formula "grace and peace (χάρις καὶ εἰρήνη)" may have arisen through the addition of χάρις (charis) under the influence of χαίρειν (chairein – "greetings") (cf. Betz, Galatians: 40), although other Jewish texts employ ἔλεος (eleos – "mercy") rather than grace (cf. 6:16; 2 Bar. 78:2). At the same time, grace and peace appear together in the aaronic blessing: "The LORD bless you, and keep you; the LORD make His face shine on you, and be gracious to you; the LORD lift up His countenance on you and give you peace יברכך ה' וישמרך : יאר ה' פניו אליך ויחנך : ישא ה' פניו אליך וישם לך שלום" (Num. 6:24-26) (cf. Ps. 67:1-7) (see 6:12-16).[75]

The LXX employs χάρις (charis – "grace") almost exclusively to render the Hebrew חן (chen – "favour"), rather than חסד (chesed –

---

[71] Although the change occurs in proximity to the council in Acts 15 and would appear quite naturally under the circumstances to be directly associated with the meeting, the reference strictly precedes the decision regarding the Gentiles' status.

[72] In this sense, the Gentiles were included in the designation "brethren" as participants in an already-existent "brotherhood," as it were. It should be stressed – yet again – that this attitude should always be one of "fellow-citizens" rather than as substitutes for the original members (cf. Rom. 11:17ff; Eph. 2:11f).

[73] Cf. Jub. 12:29, 18:16; Gen.R. 100:7; Num.R. 21:1; PA 4:15; [Ber. 2:1]; Ber. 3a, 27b; Ta'anit 14b, 20b; MK 15a; BK 73b (see also above).

[74] οἱ ἀδελφοὶ οἱ ἐν Ἱεροσολύμοις Ἰουδαῖοι καὶ οἱ ἐν τῇ χώρᾳ τῆς Ἰουδαίας εἰρήνην ἀγαθήν (cf. Ezra 5:7, 7:12; Dan. 4:1; Rom. 1:1; Jas. 1:1; 1 Pet. 1:1; 1 Macc. 11:32, 12:6, 20; Jos.Ant. 16.166f, 17.137f; Life 217; Tanh.Vayishlach 3; Gen.R. 75:5; Mur 42, 43, 44, 46, 48; 5/6 Hev 1, 10, 12) (see also above). The Hebrew is שלום (shalom), the Aramaic שלם (shlam) (cf. Stone: 590) (see above).

[75] For the link with Isa. 61:2, see verses 6-10 and below. It may be no coincidence that the priestly blessing appears in such close proximity to texts associated with Melchizedek, the "priest of God Most High כהן לאל עליון" (Gen. 14:18) (see below). For the reverse order (peace and mercy) in 6:16, see 6:12-16.

"lovingkindness"), which might more normally have been expected. The root also occurs in God's description of his character: "I will be gracious to whom I will be gracious, and will show compassion on whom I will show compassion ורחמתי את-אשר ארחם את-אשר אחן ורחמתי את-אשר "וחנתי (Ex. 33:19) (cf. Ex. 34:6). From the verb derives the adverb חִנָּם (chinam) meaning "free, gratuitously": "For thus says the LORD, 'You were sold for nothing and you will be redeemed without money' תגאלו בכסף ולא נמכרתם חנם הי אמר "כי-כה (Isa. 52:3).[76]

In its biblical context, the root שלם (shalam) includes the ideas of peace (שלום; shalom), wholeness or perfection (שָׁלֵם; shalem), and reconciliation (being made at peace with another (להשלים; le-hashlim). In this sense it is synonymous with the "welfare" of God's salvation: "How lovely on the mountains are the feet of him who brings good news, who announces peace and brings good news of happiness, who announces salvation . . . ישועה משמיע טוב מבשר שלום משמיע מבשר רגלי על-ההרים "מה-נאוו (Isa. 52:7)[77] (cf. Le Cornu and Shulam: 242).[78] In 2 Corinthians 6:2, Paul associates the "the acceptable time/day of salvation" with God's grace in His "ministry of reconciliation" (cf. 2 Cor. 5:18-19). The passage from Isaiah 49:8 which he quotes there also describes salvation as release from bondage: "Thus says the LORD, 'In a favorable time I have answered you [my Servant], and in a day of salvation I have helped you; and I will keep you and give you for a covenant of the people, to restore the land, to make *them* inherit the desolate heritages; saying to those who are bound, "Go forth," and to those who are in darkness, "Show yourselves"'"[79] (Isa. 49:8-9).[80]

---

[76] Cf. Num.R. 11:6; Dt.R. 2:1. The Aramaic equivalent of חנם is מַגָּן (maggan). A midrash understands this to be the meaning of Abraham's shield: "The Holy One, blessed be He, reassured him: '*Fear not, Abram, I am thy shield* (magen), meaning, a gift of grace (*maggan*) to thee, all that I have done for thee in this world I did for nought; but in the future that is to come, Thy reward shall be exceeding great', even as you read, *Oh how abundant is Thy goodness, which Thou hast laid up for them that fear Thee, etc.* (Ps. 31:19) בעולם עמך שעשיתי מה וכל - לך מגן אנכי תירא אל :הוא בקוד הקדוש אמר רב מה :אמר דאת מה היך ,מאד הרבה שכרך לבא לעתיד מתוקן שכרך אבל .עמך עשיתי חנם הזה ליראיך צפנת אשר "טובך (Gen.R. 44:4). For Abraham, so prominent in Paul's account of the gospel for the Gentiles, see 2:15-21 and 3:10f.

[77] Cf. Ps. 27:1; 1QM 1:9, 12:3, 17:7; 4Q504 ff1-2iv:13.

[78] The texts from Isa. 52:7f, 61:1-3 appear to constitute the central background of Paul's thought here (see verses 6-10 and below). In the context of his commission, Paul himself serves as an example of the מבשר (mevaser – "herald") – the figure who brings the good news/gospel to the Galatians (see 2:1-10 and verses 15-16b, 21-24). For the connection between peace and cursing, see verses 6-10.

[79] להנחיל ארץ לבדית עם להקים ואתנך ואצרך עזרתיך ישועה וביום עניתיך רצון בעת הי אמר כה הגלו. בחשך לאשר צאו לאסורים לאמר :שממות נחלות

[80] Cf. the parallels in Isa. 42:6-7, 22, 61:1. Paul clearly contrasts "grace (χάριν)" with being in "debt (ὀφείλημα)" in Rom. 4:4, further asserting in Rom. 13:8 (cf. Rom. 8:12f) that the only "debt" one should carry is of love, "for he who loves his

Verse 4: Paul retains the normal order of "God our father and the Lord Jesus the Messiah" in verse 3, adding a parallel to his elaboration in verse 1 relating to God's raising Jesus from the dead, speaking here of Jesus' obedience. The grace and peace which he wishes upon his readers derive from Jesus' willingness to "give himself for our sins (τοῦ δόντος ἑαυτὸν ὑπὲρ τῶν ἁμαρτιῶν ἡμῶν)" (cf. 1 Cor. 15:3). While the New Testament texts employ several formuli for this idea, they all focus on the idea of "delivering": The Messiah gave himself up; God gave him up; the Messiah was given up.[81]

This motif reflects the gravity of handing over ("betraying") a Jew to the Roman government to be executed (cf. Flusser, Jesus: 195ff; Le Cornu and Shulam: 104-5, 1287-89). It also denotes Jesus' submission to his own principal, having been sent to do his Father's will, becoming "obedient to the point of death (ὑπήκοος μέχρι θανάτου)" (Phil. 2:8).[82] This latter idea expresses the notion that the death of the righteous atones: "*And He said to the Angel that destroyed the people, It is enough* [rab] (2 Sam. 24:16). R. Eleazar said: The Holy One, blessed be He, said to the Angel: Take a great man [*rab*] among them, through whose death many sins can be expiated for them ויאמר למלאך בעם רב. אמר ר' אלעזר: אמר ליה הקדוש ברוך הוא למלאך: טול לי רב שבהם, שיש בו ליפרע מהם כמה חובות" (Ber. 62b).[83]

Having delivered himself into the hands of death, Jesus can "deliver" others from its power.[84] The phrase "for our sins (ὑπὲρ τῶν ἁμαρτιῶν ἡμῶν)" echoes Isaiah 53:5: "But he was pierced through for our transgressions, he was crushed for our iniquities והוא מחלל מפשענו מדכא

---

neighbor has fulfilled *the* law (ὁ γὰρ ἀγαπῶν τὸ ἕτερον νόμον πεπλήρωκεν)" (cf. 5:3, 13-14) (see 5:13-18 and 6:1-11). The idea of bondage displays definite affinities with the motif of exile, one of the determining themes of Israel's history (cf. Gen. 15:13; Ex. 2:23; Dt. 4:27, 28:64, 29:28; Ezra 8:35; Ps. 106:46, 107:3-14; Isa. 45:13, 51:14; Jer. 16:13f, 29:18, 30:8-17; Ezek. 11:16, 12:11; Wis.Sol. 17:2; Ps.Sol. 11:1ff; 4Q385b f16i:7-8; 4Q387a f3ii:5-12, iii:4-5; 4Q389a f3; 4QMMTᵉ ff11-13:2; Gen.R. 75:8; Ex.R. 23:5, 30:19; Lev.R. 18:5; Num.R. 7:10) (cf. Wright, Climax: 140ff; Dunn, Theology: 37) (see also 3:15-18 [n188], 4:21-31, and 5:2-12 [n37]).

[81] Cf. Mt. 20:17-19, 27:2, 18, 26; Mk. 9:31, 10:33, 45; Lk. 9:44, 18:32, 24:7, 20; Jn. 18:35-36; Acts 3:13; Rom. 4:25, 8:32; 1 Cor. 11:23; Eph. 5:2, 25; 1 Tim. 2:6; Tit. 2:14. The Greek is normally expressed either by the simpler δίδωμι (didōmi – "to give") or by the more usual παραδίδωμι (paradidōmi – 'to give/hand over"). For Jesus' "representative role," see Introduction, **Theological pointers** (Faithfulness).

[82] Cf. Mt. 26:39-42; Mk. 14:36; Lk. 22:42; Jn. 6:38-40, 10:15-18, 15:13; Rom. 5:19; Heb. 5:7-9, 12:2; 1 Jn. 3:16.

[83] Cf. 2 Macc. 7:38; 4 Macc. 6:27-28, 17:21-22; 4Q504 ff1-2ii:9-10; Mekh.Pischa 1; Lev.R. 20:12; Shab. 33b; Yoma 42a; MK 28a.

[84] Cf. Mt. 6:13; Acts 26:18; Rom. 7:6, 24, 8:15-32; 2 Cor. 1:10; Col. 1:13; 1 Thess. 1:10; Heb. 2:15.

מְעוֹנֹתֵינוּ."[85] While the language of "giving himself" does not appear directly
in Isaiah 53, the passage describes how "the chastening for our well-being
[peace] *fell* upon him, and by his scourging we are healed מוסר שלומנו עליו
ובחברתו נרפא-לנו" (Isa. 53:5).[86]

The idea of "rescuing/releasing" human beings from their sins is
frequently found in the Qumran texts in relation to the sabbatical and
jubilee years (cf. Lev. 25:10ff). The author(s) of the Dead Sea Scrolls appear
to have extended the idea of physical bondage to "slavery to sin":
"[Behold, for] our [in]iquities were we sold, but in spite of our sins you did
call us [...] and you freed us from sinning against you ןהן בעֵ[וונותינו נמכרנו
ובפשעינו קרתנו [. . .] והצלתנו מחטוא לכה" (4Q504 ff1-2ii:15-16).[87] The most
developed application of this interpretation is found in the
11QMelchizedek text:

> [Its interpretation] for the last days refers to the captives, who
> [. . .] . . . and they are the inherita[nce of Melchize]dek, who will
> make them return. And liberty will be proclaimed for them, to
> free them from [the debt of] all their iniquities. And this [wil]l
> [happen] in the first week of the jubilee which follows the ni[ne]
> jubilees. And the d[ay of aton]ement is the e[nd of] the tenth
> [ju]bilee in which atonement shall be made for all the sons of
> [light and] for the men [of] the lot of Mel[chi]zedek . . . accor[ding
> to] a[ll] their [wor]ks, for it is the time for the «year of grace» [Isa.
> 61:2] of Melchizedek . . . Melchizedek will carry out the
> vengeance of Go[d's] judgments, [and on that day he will fr]e[e
> them from the hand of] Belial and from the hand of all the sp[irits
> of his lot] . . . This [. . .] is the day of [peace about whi]ch he said
> [. . . through Isa]iah the prophet, who said: [*Isa 52:7* «How]
> beautiful upon the mountains are the feet [of] the messen[ger
> who] announces peace, the mess[enger of good who announces
> salvati]on, [sa]ying to Zion: your God [reigns.»] Its interpretation:
> The mountains [are] the prophet[s . . .] . . . and the messenger i[s]
> the anointed of the spir[it] as Dan[iel] said [about him: *Dan 9:25*
> «Until an anointed, a prince, it is seven weeks.»] . . . [«Zi]on» i[s]
> [the congregation of all the sons of justice, those] who establish
> the covenant, those who avoid walking [on the pa]th of the

[85] For the usage of ὑπέρ as "on behalf of," cf. Burton: 12. This sense may quite
easily correspond to the signification of the Hebrew preposition מֵ (mē = מן [min])
as "on account of" (cf. BDB: 580).

[86] The idea of the "echo" is developed masterfully by Hays, Echoes.

[87] Cf. Ps. 44:9-16; Isa. 42:6-7, 49:8-13, 52:2-3; Isa. 61:1f ("proclaim liberty to
captives"); Mt. 11:2f; Lk. 4:16f, 7:22; Jn. 8:34; Acts 26:16-18; Rom. 6:6, 16f , 7:14; 1 Cor.
6:20, 7:23; 2 Cor. 4:4-6; Gal. 4:3, 7-9, 24, 5:1; Test.Zev. 9:8; [1QpHab 8:2]; 4Q504 ff1-
2vii:2; 4Q521 f2ii:5-iii:1; 11Q5 19:10. Again, it may not be accidental that John the
Baptist receives Jesus' answer, based on Isa. 61:1-3, while imprisoned.

people. And «your God» is [. . . Melchizedek, who will fr]e[e them from the ha]nd of Belial.[88] (11QMelch 2:4-9, 13, 15-18, 23-25)[89] (cf. Le Cornu and Shulam: 594, 739-41) (see 3:21-25 and 4:1-7)[90]

The "debts" which are to be returned every seventh year and forty-ninth year are the people's sins – which are "forgiven" like debts (cf. Mt. 6:12; Rom. 8:12) (see also 3:21-25 and 4:1-7).[91] The author of this text also

---

[88] ‏[פשרו] לאחרית הימים על השבויים אשר . . . והמה נחל‏[ת מלכי צ‏]דק אשר ישיבמה אליהמה‏
‏וקרא להמה דרור לעזוב להמה ‏[משא] כול עוונותיהמה ו‏]כן יהי‏]ה הדבר הזה בשבוע היובל הראישון‏
‏אחר תש‏[ע]ת הי‏]ובלים ויו‏]ם הכפ‏]ורים וי‏]ו‏]א‏]ה ס‏]ו‏]י‏]ן] הי‏]י‏]ו‏]בל העשירי לכפר בו על כול בני ‏[אור‏
‏ו‏]אנש‏]י] גורל מל‏]כי] צדק . . . לפני‏] כו‏]ל עש‏]ו‏]תמה כיא הואה הקץ לשנת הרצון למלכי צדק . . .‏
‏ומלכי צדק יקום נקם משפטי א‏]ל וביום ההואה יצי‏]ל‏]מה מיד‏] בליעל ומיד כול ר‏]וחי גורל‏]ו‏]‏
‏הזאת הואה יום ה‏]שלום א‏]שר אמר . . . ביד ישע‏]יה הנביא אשר אמר ‏[מה] נאוו על ההרים רגלי‏]ו‏
‏מבש‏]ר מ‏]שמיע שלום מב‏]שר טוב משמיע ישוע‏]ה א‏]ומר לציון ‏[מלך] אלוהיך פשרו ההרים ‏[המה‏
‏הנביא‏]י‏]ן‏]ם‏] המה . . . והמבשר הו‏]אה‏] משיח הרו‏]ח] כאשר אמר דנ‏]יאל עליו עד משיח נגיד שבועים‏
‏שבעה‏] . . . ‏[צ‏]י‏]ו‏]ן] הי‏]אה‏] ‏[עדת כול בני הצדק המה‏] מקימי‏]ן] הברית הסרים מלכת ‏[בד‏]רך העם‏
‏ואלו‏]ה‏]יך הואה .‏] . מלכי צדק אשר יצי‏]ל‏]מה מי‏]ד בליעל.‏

[89] Cf. Heb. 5:10-7:28; Test.Zev. 9:8; Test.Dan 5:11; 1QH[a] 23:13-15; 4Q387a f3ii:1f; 4Q390; 4Q504 ff1-2ii:16, vii:2; 4Q521 f2ii:7-iii:1. For Melchizedek, cf. Flusser, Judaism: 186-92, 256-60; Kobelski.

[90] The author understands the jubilee through the motif of "seven," the Hebrew serving both as the number (שבע; sheva) and the signification of a "week (שבוע; shavua). Daniel interprets the "seventy-year" figure of the exile (cf. Jer. 25:11-12, 29:10; [Ezek. 4:5-6]; Zech. 1:12) as 7 times 70, i.e., 490 years (= ten jubilees [49 x 10]), identifying its end with the events following the Temple's desecration (cf. Dan. 9:2, 24-27). Once this connection has been made, the "messenger [מבשר]" of Isa. 52:7 is associated with the messianic figure of Daniel (cf. Dan. 9:24-27, 11:31f, 12:11; Mt. 24:15ff; Revelation 6ff). The reference to the "year of grace" further ties Isa. 61:2 to the Day of Atonement (cf. 4Q504 ff1-2vi:2ff; Lev.R. 20:4; Tanh.Acharei mot 3; PRK 26:4), Isa. 61:1 itself speaking about the liberation of captives [לקרא לשבוים דרור ולאסורים פקח-קוח]. The prisoner motif recurs throughout Galatians 3-5. Although the idea of forgiveness naturally introduces the Day of Atonement, a midrashic tradition associates the "one day" of creation with Jacob, the "one night" belonging to Esau (= Edom = Rome), the first day of the world corresponding to Yom Kippur, on which Satan, in the guise of Esau, has no power over Jacob (cf. Gen.R. 2:3, 3:8). (For the atonement of "peace offerings," cf. Lev. 4:26, 31, 35. The late midrash reflecting the idea that the Messiah would appear at the end of a seven-year period [cf. PRK 5:9; TBE (EZ) S p. 11; San. 97a; Meg. 17b] may be linked to the "new priest" expected to arise in the seventh jubilee and to bind Beliar, in the Testament of Levi 17-18. The number seven is also associated with the messianic reign via the seven days of the bridegroom's rejoicing [cf. San. 99a]. For Esau and Rome, see 4:21-31.)

[91] The Aramaic root חוב (chuv) signifies "to sin, incur guilt." Although ἐξαιρέω (exaireō) is a pauline hapax legomenon, the verb regularly translates the Hebrew נצל (natzal), used in the Qumran texts. It also renders the root חלץ (chalatz). The latter is used of a woman's release from levirate marriage (יבום; yibbum), a process known as חליצה (chalitza) (cf. Dt. 25:5-10). If the levir (deceased husband's brother) refuses to marry his childless sister-in-law, she only becomes eligible to marry again if the levir releases her by allowing her to "loose" his shoe and to "curse" him. This

associates the jubilee with the "day of peace" (cf. payment of debts) spoken of in Isaiah 52:7. This presentation corresponds, in Paul's phrase, to "this present evil age (τοῦ αἰῶνος τοῦ ἐνεστῶτος πονηροῦ)," which the Scrolls understand to be under the dominion of Belial, or the Angel of Darkness:

> And in the hand of the Angel of Darkness is total dominion over the sons of deceit; they walk on paths of darkness. From the Angel of darkness stems the corruption of all the sons of justice, and all their sins, their iniquities, their guilts and their offensive deeds are under his dominion in compliance with the mysteries of God, until his moment; and all their afflictions and their periods of grief are caused by the dominion of his enmity; and all the spirits of his lot cause the sons of light to fall.[92] (1QS 3:20-24)[93]

While such language is common to dualist and eschatological thought of the period, it is also hinted at in the "ceremony" later instituted to regulate the conversion process (cf. Cohen, Rabbinic; Daube, New: 113-40). The candidate, who "at the present time desires to become a proselyte" is warned that "Israel at the present time are persecuted and oppressed, despised, harassed and overcome by afflictions", גר שבא להתגייר בזמן הזה, אומרים לו: ... ישראל בזמן הזה דוויים דחופים סחופים ומטורפין (Yev. 47a) (cf. Ger. 1:1). This "present time" is contrasted with the future when the

---

is another form of "bondage" from which a person is released – although the act which liberates here is performed in this case by the woman herself (cf. Elon: 403-7). Paul uses a similar analogy with regard to the Torah in Rom. 7:1ff (cf. Shulam and Le Cornu: 235-38) (see 2:15-21), and the New Testament speaks of the Messiah's body – like Israel – as his "bride" (cf. Canticles; Isa. [5:1-7], 49:18, 61:10, 62:5; Jer. 2:32; Mt. 9:15, [25:1ff]; Lk. 5:35; Jn. 3:29; Rev. 21:9, 22:17). The biblical imagery frequently portrays Israel's idolatry as adultery – going after false gods constituting unfaithfulness to one's husband (cf. Isa. 1:21; Jer. 2:20-3:25, 31:32; Ezekiel 16; Hosea) (see 5:2-12). Paul speaks in Acts 26:18 of Jesus' deliverance as effecting a transfer (rescue) "from darkness to light and from the dominion of Satan to God (τοῦ ἐπιστρέψαι ἀπὸ σκότους εἰς φῶς καὶ τῆς ἐξουσίας τοῦ σατανᾶ ἐπὶ τὸν θεόν)" in such a way as to place it in the context of God's Kingdom, a motif which he also directly links with justification (see 2:15-21, 4:1-7, and 5:2ff).

[92] וביד מלאך חושך כול ממשלת בני עול ובדרכי חושך יתהלכו ובמלאך חושך תעות כול בני צדק וכול חטאתם ועוונותם ואשמתם ופשעי מעשיהם בממשלתו לפי רזי אל עד קצו וכול נגועיהם ומועדי צרותם בממשלת משטמתו וכול רוחי גורלו להכשיל בני אור.

[93] Cf. Jn. 12:31, 14:30, 16:11; 2 Cor. 4:4; Eph. 2:2f, 6:12; 1 Jn. [4:4], 5:19; Jub. 1:20; Test.Dan 1:7, 3:6, 4:7; [Test.Asher 1:3f]; Test.Ben. 6:1, 7:1f; 1QS 1:18; 1QM 13:4, 10f, 14:9; CD-A 12:2; 4Q177 3:8, 4:12f; 4Q390 f2i:3f. This list of "vices" (cf. 1QS 4:9-11) obviously corresponds to Paul's description of the "deeds of the flesh" in 5:19-21 (see 5:13f). For the conception of the world as divided according to ages ("jubilees"), cf. Jub. 50:4; 1 En. 89:9-90:27, 91:12-17, 93:1-10; Test.Levi 16:1-17:11; 4Q180-181; 4Q387a f3ii:1f; 4Q390 (cf. Kobelski: 14, 49-51). Kobelski suggests that 11QMelchizedek originally formed part of a longer pesher on the "Periods of History" (cf. p. 51). A similar scheme appears to lie behind Paul's argument in 4:1ff.

reward will be granted for fulfilment of the commandments: "Be it known
to you that the world to come was made only for the righteous העולם הבא
אינו עשוי אלא לצדיקים." Paul's purpose and point in writing to the Galatians
is to warn them that the "reward" which they are seeking is to be found
through Jesus' death and resurrection – not in formal membership in the
Jewish people.[94] It is precisely Jesus' obedience to God's will in giving
himself as a ransom that gives the Gentiles access to God's righteousness,
enabling them – here and now – to join themselves to God's people
through His Messiah.[95]

Jesus' obedience expresses itself in the fulfilment of his commission
from the Father, whose will he came to perform.[96] It is possible that the
imputation of sin and God's curse to Jesus[97] conjure up the need for
reassurance that, despite the qualities ascribed to him, Jesus' actions were
indeed pleasing before God (cf. Isa. 49:7, 53:10-12). The phrase "according
to the will of our God and Father (κατὰ τὸ θέλημα τοῦ θεοῦ καὶ πατρὸς
ἡμῶν)" may also indicate that Jesus' submission also enables those who
follow him to live in conformity with God's will: ". . . in those *sacrifices*
there is a reminder of sins year by year. For it is impossible for the blood of
bulls and goats to take away sins. Therefore, when he comes into the
world, he says, SACRIFICE AND OFFERING THOU HAST NOT DESIRED, BUT A
BODY THOU HAST PREPARED FOR ME; IN WHOLE BURNT OFFERINGS AND *sacrifices*
FOR SIN THOU HAST TAKEN NO PLEASURE. THEN I SAID, 'BEHOLD, I HAVE COME
(IN THE ROLL OF THE BOOK IT IS WRITTEN OF ME) TO DO THY WILL, O GOD' [Ps.
40:6-8] . . . By this will we have been sanctified through the offering of the
body of Jesus the Messiah once for all . . . For by one offering he has

---

[94] With regard to his gentile audience, Paul's claim is that they cannot let
themselves be persuaded to deny Jesus' death and resurrection in favour of a social
convention (circumcision, in its proper context, being valid and legitimate). With
respect to his Jewish brethren – those whom he designates as "false" – his claim is
that circumcision without the proper intention is invalid (see 2:1-10, 15-21).

[95] This theme is worked out more fully in 2:11-14. Jesus' faithfulness (obedience)
forms the framework and background within which Paul sets his whole argument
of freedom, Jesus' representative act constituting the means whereby human beings
– Jews and Gentiles alike – are delivered from bondage to sin to walk in the liberty
of love bestowed in the Spirit (see 2:15-21, 3:10-14, 26-29, 4:1f, and 5:13f).

[96] Cf. Mt. 26:39; Jn. 5:19, 30, 8:28, 12:49, 14:10; Rom. 5:19; Phil. 2:5-8; Heb. 5:8. In
drawing from the Servant Songs, Paul represents himself as an agent of the Servant
– like him in all things. In this way he extends the Servant's authority and task to
himself (cf. Kim, Paul: 101-27) (see 2:1-10, [4:12-20, 6:1-11], and verses 15-16b).

[97] Cf. Isa. 53:5-6; Rom. 8:3; 2 Cor. 5:21; Gal. 3:13; Heb. 2:14-18, 9:28; 1 Pet. 2:24. For
Jesus' "representative role," see Introduction, **Theological pointers** (Faithfulness)
and below.

perfected for all time those who are being sanctified"[98] (Heb. 10:3-7, 10, 14).[99]

This account of God's working through Jesus' faithfulness exalts God to His highest throne. If Paul's language is liturgical here (cf. Betz, Galatians: 40-43), the doxology recited in the Temple is its most likely source (cf. Stone: 554).[100] The Mishnah relates how the High Priest entered the Holy of Holies on the Day of Atonement and interceded on behalf of himself and the whole people: "And thus used he to say: 'O God, I have committed iniquity, transgressed and sinned before thee, I and my house, as it is written in the Law of thy servant Moses, *For on this day shall atonement be made for you to cleanse you; from all your sins shall you be clean before the Lord* (YHWH)' (Lev. 16:30). And they answered after him [on hearing God's name expressly pronounced], 'Blessed be the name of the glory of his kingdom for ever and ever!'"[101] (Yoma 3:8)[102]

Paul presents himself here as a form of successor to Isaiah: "In the year of King Uzziah's death, I saw the Lord sitting on a throne, lofty and exalted, with the train of His robe filling the temple. Seraphim stood above

---

[98] ἐν αὐταῖς ἀνάμνησις ἁμαρτιῶν κατ᾽ ἐνιαυτόν· ἀδύνατον γὰρ αἷμα ταύρων καὶ τράγων ἀφαιρεῖν ἁμαρτίας. Διὸ εἰσερχόμενος εἰς τὸν κόσμον λέγει· θυσίαν καὶ προσφορὰν οὐκ ἠθέλησας, σῶμα δὲ κατηρτίσω μοι· ὁλοκαυτώματα καὶ περὶ ἁμαρτίας οὐκ εὐδόκησας. τότε εἶπον· ἰδοὺ ἥκω, ἐν κεφαλίδι βιβλίου γέγραπται περὶ ἐμοῦ, τοῦ ποιῆσαι ὁ θεὸς τὸ θέλημά σου . . . ἐν ᾧ θελήματι ἡγιασμένοι ἐσμὲν διὰ τῆς προσφορᾶς τοῦ σώματος Ἰησοῦ Χριστοῦ ἐφάπαξ . . . μιᾷ γὰρ προσφορᾷ τετελείωκεν εἰς τὸ διηνεκὲς τοὺς ἁγιαζομένους.

[99] Such expressions as these, and others in Hebrews, fit very well with the idea of Jesus' "representative role" in redeeming and sanctifying those who share in his faithfulness (cf. Hays, Faith) (see 2:15-21, 3:10-14, 4:1-7, 21-31, and below).

[100] Here again, Melchizedek may figure in the background, being the representative of a priestly line (cf. Gen. 14:18; Ps. 110:4; Heb. 5:6, 10; [Test.Levi 18:2-14]; 11QMelchizedek; [Lev.R. 25:6]; Cant.R. 2.13.4; PRK 5:9; TBE p. 96; Yalk.Zech. 569; Yalk.Cant. 986; ARNᵃ 34:4; Suk. 52b; Ned. 32b) (cf. Kobelski: 64-71). For Melchizedek and the angelic tradition, see verses 6-10. It is striking that Melchizedek may be seen in the scroll to fill a similar (narrative) role to Jesus' "representative" function in Hays' description: "Jesus Christ is the archetypical (or prototypical) hero (ἀρχηγός) who, through his faithfulness unto death on the cross, wins deliverance and access to God for his people . . . [he is] the representative figure in whom the drama of salvation is enacted, in whose destiny the destiny of all is carried" (Faith: 217, 151) (cf. Flusser, Judaism: 186-92). Not only do both Galatians and Hebrews also speak of Jesus as God's heir (cf. Gal. 3:15-29; Heb. 1:2) but both texts also witness to a "theology of mountains" (cf. Gal. 4:22-31; Heb. 12:18-29) (cf. ibid: 265, 271n67) (see also 4:1-7, 21-31).

[101] וכך היה אומר: אנא השם, עויתי פשעתי חטאתי לפניך אני וביתי. אנא השם, כפר נא לעונות ולפשעים ולחטאים, שעויתי ושפשעתי ושחטאתי לפניך אני וביתי, ככתוב בתורת משה עבדך: כי ביום הזה יכפר עליכם לטהר אתכם מכל חטאתיכם לפני יי תטהרו. והן עונין אחריו, ברוך שם כבוד מלכותו לעולם ועד.

[102] Cf. Isa. 6:1-7; Hymn of the Three Young Men 3f, 28f; 4Q403 f1i:25; Yoma 4:1-2, 6:2. For Paul's "doxology" at the letter's close, see 6:18.

Him . . . And one called out to another and said, 'Holy, Holy, Holy is the LORD of hosts, the whole earth is full of His glory' . . . Then I said, 'Woe is me, for I am ruined! Because I am a man of unclean lips, and I live among a people of unclean lips; for my eyes have seen the King, the LORD of Hosts.' Then one of the seraphim flew to me, with a burning coal in his hand which he had taken from the altar with tongs. And he touched my mouth *with it* and said, 'Behold, this has touched your lips; and your iniquity is taken away, and your sin is forgiven.' Then I heard the voice of the Lord, saying: 'Whom shall I send, and who will go for Us?' Then I said, 'Here am I. Send me!'"[103] (Isa. 6:1-8).[104]

If the salutation replaces the usual thanksgiving[105] with this doxology, Paul's purpose is clearly served in summoning his readers' confirmation in the usual response of "Amen" (cf. Bruce, *Galatians*: 78). As in the biblical doxologies,[106] the amen "seals" the benediction and requires recital by all those listening as the indication of their agreement: "R. Jose b. Hanina said: 'Amen' implies oath, acceptance of words, and confirmation of words. It implies oath, as it is written: *And the woman shall say, Amen, amen* (Num. 5:22). It implies acceptance of words, as it is written: *Cursed be he that confirmeth not the words of this law to do them, and all the people shall say, Amen* (Dt. 27:26). It implies confirmation of words, as it is written: *And the prophet Jeremiah said, Amen, the Lord do so! The Lord perform thy words!* (Jer. 28:6)"[107] (Shevu. 36a) (see also 6:18).[108]

Most commentators concur that a note of thanksgiving would be inappropriate at this juncture, given the harsh words which Paul is about to pronounce. Having expressed their unity with Paul in acknowledging

---

[103] ‏בשנת-מות המלך עזיהו ואראה את-אדני ישב על-כסא רם ונשא ושוליו מלאים את-ההיכל:‏
‏שרפים עמדים ממעל . . . וקרא זה אל-זה ואמר קדוש קדוש קדוש ה' צבאות מלא כל-הארץ כבודו‏
‏. . . ואמר אוי-לי כי נדמיתי כי איש טמא-שפתים אנכי ובתוך עם-טמא שפתים אנכי ישב כי-את‏
‏המלך ה' צבאות ראו עיני: ויעף אלי אחד מן-השרפים ובידו רצפה במלקחים לקח מעל המזבח: ויגע‏
‏על-פי ויאמר הנה נגע זה על-שפתיך וסר עונך וחטאתך תכפר: ואשמע את-קול אדני אמר את-מי‏
‏אשלח ומי ילך-לנו ואמר הנני שלחני.‏

[104] For Paul's usage also of the following verses (Isa. 6:9f) in his understanding of the "mystery" of God's redemptive purpose for the Gentiles, cf. Betz, *Vision*; Kim, *Origin*: 74-99; Paul: 239-57 (see also 3:10-14 and 5:2-12).

[105] Cf. Rom. 1:8ff; 1 Cor. 1:4ff; Phil. 1:3ff; Col. 1:3ff; 1 Thess. 1:2ff; 2 Thess. 1:3ff; 2 Tim. 1:3ff; Phlm 4ff.

[106] Cf. Ps. 41:13, 72:19; 89:52, 106:48.

[107] ‏רבי יוסי ברבי חנינא: אמן בו שבועה, בו קבלת דברים, בו האמנת דברים, דכתיב:‏
‏ואמרה האשה אמן אמן. בו קבלת דברים, דכתיב: ארור אשר לא יקים את דברי התורה הזאת‏
‏לעשות אותם ואמר כל העם אמן. בו האמנת דברים, דכתיב: ויאמר ירמיה [הנביא] [אל חנניהו] אמן‏
‏כן יעשה ה' יקם ה' את דבריך.‏

[108] The reference in 3 Macc. 7:22-23 – "The great God had perfectly accomplished great things for their salvation. Blessed be the deliverer of Israel forever and ever ! Amen (τὰ μεγαλεῖα τοῦ μεγίστου θεοῦ ποιήσαντος τελείως ἐπὶ σωτηρίᾳ αὐτῶν. εὐλογητὸς ὁ ῥύστης Ισραηλ εἰς τοὺς ἀεὶ χρόνους. ἀμην)" (originally an allusion to the physical release of Jews from heathen captivity) – also suggests how deliverance could be transferred to spiritual bondage (cf. verse 4) (see verses 1-5).

God's glory and sovereignty, he can then go on to call them to task for "deserting their calling" so hastily (cf. Eph. 4:1).

Verses 6-10: *Exordium*

I am amazed that you are so quickly deserting Him who called you by the grace of the Messiah, for a different gospel; which is *really* not another; only there are some who are disturbing you, and want to distort the gospel of the Messiah. But even though we, or an angel from heaven, should preach to you a gospel contrary to that which we have preached to you, let him be accursed. As we have said before, so I say again now, if any man is preaching to you a gospel contrary to that which you received, let him be accursed. For am I now seeking the favor of men, or of God? Or am I striving to please men? If I were still trying to please men, I would not be a bond-servant of the Messiah.

Having laid out the grounds of his own agency, and Jesus' commission from God on which it is modelled, Paul introduces, without further ado, the issue which constitutes the occasion for the letter.[109] The urgency and severity of the matter at hand allows him no leeway to commend and encourage his readers, as is his subsequent custom (cf. Longenecker, Galatians: 13) (see verses 1-5).[110] Despite themselves having been "called (καλέσαντος)" (cf. 5:8), the Galatians are deserting their Caller – and to this Paul's response can only be "amazement" – not thanksgiving (cf. Dahl: 13).

The notation θαυμάζω (thaumazō – "I am amazed") serves as an overt rhetorical mark of irony (cf. Nanos, Irony: 32ff, and for the following discussion). In such a framework, the expression of "surprise and astonishment" may reflect hurt or disapproval. In the latter case, the amazement represents an artificial devise designed to establish the grounds for a reprimand, the person articulating the "perplexity" indicating thereby that s/he interprets something amiss in the conduct of those over whom s/he is exclaiming. The irony here takes the form of a "guilt trip," as it were, establishing a sense of unease or shame in those addressed. It may also convey a false feeling of ignorance when the person is in fact in full possession of the facts. The basic motif behind the "ironic rebuke" is that its issuer knows better or occupies a higher moral ground than his/her addressees, and hopes by means of sarcasm to alert them to their defect.

The concept occurs in rabbinic literature, usually indicated by the verb תמה (tamah – "to wonder, marvel, be astonished"): "R. Simeon observed: I am amazed that the fathers of the world [i.e., the Sages] engage in controversy over this matter [whether heaven or earth was created first], for surely both were created [simultaneously] like a pot and its lid : ר׳ שמעון

---

[109] The transition from one theme to the next again supports the suggestion that Paul's "defence" of his apostleship is rather an elaboration of his authority as the grounds for demanding loyalty from his Galatian disciples (see verses 1-5).

[110] For Galatians as Paul's first letter, and for its epistolary characteristics, see Introduction, **Date and destination; Form**.

תמיה אני היאך נחלקו אבות העולם על בריית שמים וארץ. אלא שאני אומר: שניהם לא
נבראו אלא כאלפס וכסויה" (Gen.R. 1:15). "R. Eliezer ... had a disciple who
once gave a legal decision in his presence: 'I wonder [I would be
surprised]', remarked R. Eliezer to his wife, Imma Shalom, 'whether this
man will live through the year'; and he actually did not live through the
year. 'Are you', she asked him, 'a prophet?' 'I', he replied 'am neither a
prophet nor the son of a prophet, but I have this tradition: Whosoever
gives a legal decision in the presence of his Master incurs the penalty of
death'"[111] (Eruv. 63a).[112]

The object of Paul's marvelling is the Galatians' apparent
misconviction that they are being presented with "good news" by other
people, a misprision which has led them to "desert God (μετατίθεσθε ἀπὸ
τοῦ καλέσαντος)." The rhetorical function of the phrase "so quickly
(οὕτως ταχέως)" makes it difficult to deduce from it any firm
chronological significance. The notation serves both as an indicator of the
promptness with which the event appears to have occurred and as an echo
of the people's rebelliousness towards God: "They have quickly turned
aside from the way which I commanded them. They have made for
themselves a molten calf, and have worshiped it, and have sacrificed to it,
and said 'This is your god, O Israel, who brought you up from the land of
Egypt!' ... And yet they did not listen to their judges, for they played the
harlot after other gods and bowed themselves down to them. They turned
aside quickly from the way in which their fathers had walked in obeying
the commandments of the LORD; they did not do as *their fathers*"[113] (Ex. 32:8;
Judg. 2:17) (cf. Dt. 9:16).

The middle form of μετατίθημι (metatithēmi) signifies the "turning
away from" from God to worship idols of which the biblical texts so
characteristically accuse the people.[114] Even though Paul's intended readers
are themselves Gentiles, they are liable to the same rebuke for turning
aside from Jesus to social convention (see Introduction, **Occasion and
circumstances**). The significance of the Gentiles' calling by God turns on
the fact that "formerly" they were "not-My-people [לא עמי]" and He not
their God. God has now, in sending His son (cf. 4:4) extended His

---

[111] תלמיד אחד היה לו לרבי אליעזר שהורה הלכה בפניו. אמר רבי אליעזר לאימא שלום אשתו:
תמיה אני אם יוציא זה שנתו - ולא הוציא שנתו. אמרה לו: נביא אתה? אמר לה: לא נביא אנכי ולא
בן נביא אנכי אלא כך מקובלני: כל המורה הלכה בפני רבו חייב מיתה.

[112] Cf. PRK 19:4; Yalk.Lev. 613; Mid.Sam. 5; BM 6:8; Tos.Kel. BK 6:4; Tos.Ohal. 12:1;
JHag. 10b; JYoma 7a; J BM 27a; ARNᵃ 25:3; Yev. 96b; San. 68a. The prophetic
element in R. Eliezer's story is coincidental neither to the Galatians' specific
situation nor to ironic surprise in general.

[113] סרו מהר מן-הדרך אשר צויתם עשו להם עגל מסכה וישתחוו-לו ויזבחו-לו ויאמרו אלה אלהיך
ישראל אשר העלוך מארץ מצרים ... וגם אל-שפטיהם לא שמעו כי זנו אחרי אלהים אחרים
וישתחוו להם סרו מהר מן-הדרך אשר הלכו אבותם לשמע מצות-ה' לא-עשו כן.

[114] Cf. Dt. 11:16, 28, 30:17, 31:20; 1 Sam. 12:20f; 1 Kings 8:33; Neh. 1:9; Jer. 25:5f; Lam.
3:40; Ezek. 14:6; 1 Thess. 1:9.

compassion to those who "were at that time separate from the Messiah, excluded from the commonwealth of Israel, and strangers to the covenants of promise, having no hope and without God in the world"[115] (Eph. 2:12)[116] and given them existence and life (cf. Shulam and Le Cornu: 165-74; Le Cornu and Shulam: 573-88) (see 2:10-14 and 4:1f).

In keeping with the theme of agency, Paul emphasizes that it is God – not wo/men – who has called the gentile believers in Galatia (cf. 5:8). At this initial point, Paul introduces the theme of God's sovereignty in choosing whom He wills, His impartiality leading to the circumstance that "in every nation the man who fears Him and does what is right, is welcome to Him" (Acts 10:35): "But *it is* not as though the word of God has failed. For they are not all Israel who are *descended* from Israel; neither are they all children because they are Abraham's descendants, but: 'THROUGH ISAAC YOUR DESCENDANTS WILL BE NAMED' . . . And not only this, but there was Rebekah also, when she had conceived *twins* by one man, our father Isaac; for though *the twins* were not yet born, and had not done anything good or bad, in order that God's purpose according to *His* choice might stand, not because of works, but because of Him who calls . . . So then it *does* not *depend* on the man who wills or the man who runs, but on God who has mercy"[117] (Rom. 9:6-7, 10-11, 16) (see 3:6f).[118]

The gentile believers' calling is to serve God – not those motivated by human concerns.[119] Paul makes this point most clearly in 1 Corinthians

---

[115] ἦτε τῷ καιρῷ ἐκείνῳ χωρὶς Χριστοῦ, ἀπηλλοτριωμένοι τῆς πολιτείας τοῦ Ἰσραὴλ καὶ ξένοι τῶν διαθηκῶν τῆς ἐπαγγελίας, ἐλπίδα μὴ ἔχοντες καὶ ἄθεοι ἐν τῷ κόσμῳ.

[116] Cf. Isa. 55:5; Hos. 1:9, 2:23; Zech. 2:11; Rom. 1:18-32; Gal. 4:8-9; Eph. 2:1-13, 4:17-19; Col. 1:21, 3:5-9.

[117] Οὐχ οἷον δὲ ὅτι ἐκπέπτωκεν ὁ λόγος τοῦ θεοῦ. οὐ γὰρ πάντες οἱ ἐξ Ἰσραὴλ οὗτοι Ἰσραήλ· οὐδ' ὅτι εἰσὶν σπέρμα Ἀβραὰμ πάντες τέκνα, ἀλλ' ἐν Ἰσαὰκ κληθήσεταί σοι σπέρμα . . . Οὐ μόνον δὲ ἀλλὰ καὶ Ῥεβέκκα ἐξ ἑνὸς κοίτην ἔχουσα, Ἰσαὰκ τοῦ πατρὸς ἡμῶν· μήπω γὰρ γεννηθέντων μηδὲ πραξάντων τι ἀγαθὸν ἢ φαῦλον, ἵνα ἡ κατ' ἐκλογὴν πρόθεσις τοῦ θεοῦ μένῃ, οὐκ ἐξ ἔργων ἀλλ' ἐκ τοῦ καλοῦντος . . . ἄρα οὖν οὐ τοῦ θέλοντος οὐδὲ τοῦ τρέχοντος ἀλλὰ τοῦ ἐλεῶντος θεοῦ.

[118] This passage in Romans comes to address the fact that some of Israel have failed to accept God's Messiah. Paul is at pains to point out to the Roman gentile believers, however, that this does not mean that God has utterly rejected His people, and goes on to warn them that God's sovereignty means that those whom He has grafted in may also be lopped off again (cf. Rom. 9:19ff, 11:17ff). The theme of the "true" "sons of Abraham" is that which informs the whole letter (see Introduction, **Argument**; **Theological pointers**). For God's sovereignty/unity in relation to sin, see 3:19-20.

[119] Again, it must be stressed that Paul's disapproval is not of Judaism *per se* – only of the influencers' insistence that Gentiles must convert (rather than remain godfearers) if they desire official Jewish status. Even this is unacceptable to Paul when it comes at the expense of Jesus' death and resurrection (see Introduction, **Occasion and circumstances**).

7:17f: "Only, as the Lord has assigned to each one, as God as called each, in this manner let him walk. And thus I direct in all the communities. Was any man *already* circumcised? Let him not become uncircumcised. Has anyone been called in uncircumcision? Let him not be circumcised" (1 Cor. 7:17-18).[120]

God's calling to the Gentiles is made through Jesus. Here again (see verses 1-5), the text from the Melchizedek scroll elaborates the source of the "grace (χάριτι)" of which Paul's readers are beneficiaries: "And the d[ay of aton]ement is the e[nd of] the tenth [ju]bilee in which atonement shall be made for all the sons of [light and] for the men [of] the lot of Mel[chi]zedek . . . accor[ding to] a[ll] their [wor]ks, for it is the time for the «year of grace» [Isa. 61:2] of Melchizedek . . . Melchizedek will carry out the vengeance of Go[d's] judgments, [and on that day he will fr]e[e them from the hand of] Belial and from the hand of all the sp[irits of his lot] . . . This [. . .] is the day of [peace about whi]ch he said [. . . through Isa]iah the prophet, who said: [*Isa 52:7* «How] beautiful upon the mountains are the feet [of] the messen[ger who] announces peace, the mess[enger of good who announces salvati]on, [sa]ying to Zion: your God [reigns.»]"[121] (11QMelch 2:7-9, 13, 15-16).[122]

Rather than turning aside to idols, Paul accuses his charges of being persuaded by "another gospel (ἔτερον εὐαγγέλιον)." If the thought of the Melchizedek text lies behind Paul's present articulation, the first reference of the "good news" is again to Isaiah 61: "The Spirit of the Lord GOD is upon me, because the LORD has anointed me to bring good news to the afflicted . . . רוח אדני ה' עלי יען משח ה' אתי לבשר ענוים" (Isa. 61:1).[123] The Hebrew root בשר (basar), especially in Isaiah 40-66, serves as the basis for

---

[120] Εἰ μὴ ἑκάστῳ ὡς ἐμέρισεν ὁ κύριος, ἕκαστον ὡς κέκληκεν ὁ θεός, οὕτως περιπατείτω. καὶ οὕτως ἐν ταῖς ἐκκλησίαις πάσαις διατάσσομαι. περιτετμημένος τις ἐκλήθη, μὴ ἐπισπάσθω· ἐν ἀκροβυστίᾳ κέκληταί τις, μὴ περιτεμνέσθω.

[121] וי]נום הכפ]ורים ה]וא]ה ס]וף] ה]יו]בל העשירי לכפר בו על כול בני [אור ו]אנש]י] גורל מלכי] צדק . . . לפני] כ]ול עש]ו]תמה כיא הואה הקץ לשנת הרצון למלכי צדק . . . ומלכי צדק יקום נקם משפטי אנ]ל וביום ההואה יצי]ל]מה מיד] בליעל ומיד כול ר]וחי גורלו] . . . הזאת הואה יום ה]שלום א]שר אמר [. . . ביד ישע]יה הנביא אשר אמר [מה] נאוו על ההרים רגלי] מבש]ר מ]שמיע שלום מבשר טוב משמיע ישוע]ה א]ומר לציון [מלך] אלוהיך.

[122] The text returns to the passage in Isaiah 61 towards its end, with a tantalisingly obscure and fragmented exegesis of verses 2-3. For the centrality of Isaiah 40-66 in Paul's thought in this chapter, see verses 1-5, 15-16b. Isa. 61:1-3 may also lie behind 3:1-2, where it is linked to "justification" (see 3:1-5).

[123] It may in fact be true that the "afflicted [עֲנָוִים]" in Isa. 61:1 should be understood in relation to sins through the phrase ועניתם את נפשתיכם ("and you shall humble your souls"), which describes the conduct required from the people on Yom Kippur (the Day of Atonement) (cf. Lev. 16:31, 23:27, 32; Num. 29:7). (Contemporary texts interpret the verb ועניתם [ve-initem] in terms of fasting [cf. Ps. 35:13; Isa. 58:3, 5; Acts 27:9; Yoma 74b].) For Isaiah 61 and the "fruit of the Spirit," see [4:12-20 (verse 15)] 5:13-18 (n148) (Sermon on the Mount).

the Greek εὐαγγέλιζομαι / εὐαγγέλιον (euangelizomai/euangelion) = "proclaim good news/gospel" (cf. Bruce, Galatians: 81).[124]

Since the term is not used exclusively of Jesus' death and resurrection (see Introduction, **Occasion and circumstances**), it may bear the full weight of Paul's ironical force: There is no other gospel, and it is only (εἰ μή; ei mē - "except that") the Galatians' complicity with the influencers which makes it appear to them as though it were "gospel truth."[125] On an ironical reading, the grammatical distinction between ἕτερον (heteron - "of a different kind") and ἄλλος (allos - "an additional one") (verses 6-7) loses much of its significance, the nuance only being important if both teachings are regarded as "gospel(s)." The irony may further mitigate the assumption that the "influencers" whom Paul is countering are Jesus' followers, the prevalent presupposition being that they are promulgating a "different" gospel - but a "gospel" no less - to that which Paul conveyed to the communities on his initial visit.[126] The irony lies specifically in attributing to someone a quality not regularly recognised as befitting them - here not a person but the message, which is "*really* not another [gospel] (οὐκ ἔστιν ἄλλο)" (verse 7) (see also 5:2-12).[127]

---

[124] Cf. Isa. 40:9, 52:7, 60:6.

[125] Delitzsch felicitously translates ἕτερον εὐαγγέλιον (heteron euangelion - "a different gospel") as בשורה זרה (besora zara - "a strange/foreign gospel") on analogy with עבודה זרה (avoda zara), the rabbinic term for "idolatry." The term also recalls the אש זרה (esh zara - "strange fire") whose offering before God led to Nadav's and Avihu's death (cf. Lev. 10:1; Num. 3:4, 26:61). The penalty for declaring a message not from God - one of the signs of a false prophet - was death (cf. Dt. 13:5, 18:20; [Jer. 23:16ff]) (cf. Keener: 520) (see also below [n132]). For the commandment to "purge the evil [one] from among you ובערת הרע מקרבך" (Dt. 13:5), see 6:1-11 and verses 11-12.

[126] This has of course been the traditional view of those commentators who consider the influencers to be "Jewish Christian judaisers" - Jewish believers (persistently perceived to represent the Jerusalem Apostles) who are convinced that Gentiles must be circumcised and fully convert to Judaism in order to be "saved" (cf. Nanos, Irony: 284-316).

[127] Nanos' dramatic use of the irony derives from his assignation of an "intra-Jewish context" (p. 287) to Galatians: It is precisely because the influencers are non-believing Jews familiar with the term that Paul's ascription of it to their message (thereby associating them with Jesus) would be so shocking - both to them and to the Galatian believers. This understanding is an extrapolation from Nanos' argument, since apart from making the original statement, he nowhere else in *Irony* appears to explicate from the Jewish perspective "the unexpected inter-Jewish rhetorical emphasis it [the term 'gospel'] provides" (p. 287). The present proposal reflects Nanos' focus on the addressees' response, diverging only to the extent that it presupposes a *gentile* non-believing identity for the influencers, the force of the irony thereby being directed towards the Galatian believers who are acting as though the influencers' message was "gospel." For the content of "Paul's gospel," see verses 15-16b.

Verse 7 provides the epistle's earliest indicator of the influencers' identity, albeit through Paul's prism. They – "some (τινές)" in the plural – are "disturbing (ταράσσοντες)" the Galatians, motivated by an intention to "distort the gospel of the Messiah (θέλοντες μεταστρέψαι τὸ εὐαγγέλιον τοῦ Χριστοῦ)."[128] The present tense in all these verses indicates that these are current circumstances, underlining the urgency with which Paul is penning the epistle, hoping to correct things before it becomes too late. The weight of the "wanting (θέλοντες)" may lie wholly on Paul's side – an attribution of intention where none exists on the influencers' part.[129] Yet if the "some" are indeed non-believers, the notation may indicate a deliberation – hitherto presumably unexpressed explicitly – towards inducing the gentile Galatian believers away from Jesus.[130]

The language of "disturbing (ταράσσοντες)" (cf. 5:10) – like that of the verb μεταστρέψαι (metastrepsai – "distort") – reflects a strong political bias in the Greek, signifying agitators who generate confusion and turmoil (cf. Betz, Galatians: 49-50).[131] The biblical referent is most obviously to Achar/Achan, the "troubler of Israel, who violated God's ban עכר עוכר ישראל אשר מעל בחרם" (1 Chron. 2:7).[132] In the biblical incident, the "trouble" alludes to the fact that the community as a whole bore the punishment for one person's transgression[133] (see 5:2-12).[134] Achan himself is accused in

---

[128] Paul may or may not be "avoiding the use of names and [thus] the providing of free publicity" here (Betz, Galatians: 49n65) (see Introduction, **Occasion and circumstances** [n82]). The use of "code names" is particularly striking in the Qumran pesher texts, albeit influenced by the biblical text which they are interpreting (cf. 4Q163 f2:4-5, ff4-6i:5-19; 4QpHos; 4QpNah; 1QpHab) (see 4:21-31). For furter passages – on the present reading – reflective of the influencers' identity, see 4:12f, 5:2-12, [24-26], and 6:1f; for the singular reference (in place of the plural), see 5:2-12.

[129] For a discussion of the origin of the "other gospel," see Introduction, **Occasion and circumstances**.

[130] The argument being made here is that the aggression on the part of the gentile group in Galatia was on behalf of full conversion, in opposition to godfearing status. To the extent that the gospel promoted the latter and not the former, it was an object of hostility.

[131] This may reflect the incident in Acts 13:50 which, involving the "devout women of prominence and the leading men of the city (τὰς σεβομένας γυναῖκας τὰς εὐσχήμονας καὶ τοὺς πρώτους τῆς πόλεως)," was presumably possessed of (semi-)political qualities. Paul uses similar political demagoguery – "military language turned into political metaphors" (Betz, Galatians: 90) – to describe the "false brethren" in 2:4.

[132] Cf. Josh. 6:18, 7:18-26; 1 Kings 18:17. It is striking, in this context, to find that all the inhabitants of a town who are seduced by a false prophet are to be destroyed and the city itself "accursed" or "put under a ban," for the purpose of ridding all potential for complicity (cf. Dt. 13:12-18) (see above [n125]).

[133] Cf. Lev.R. 9:1; Num.R. 23:6; San. 44b. Cf. also Jephthah's daughter who, on coming to meet Jephthah on his return, became one of "those who trouble me; for I

rabbinic literature of violation of the Torah, adultery, and epispasm – removing his circumcision (cf. San. 44a-b).

Taken in conjunction with Paul's designation of the Galatians as "foolish (ἀνόητοι)" in 3:1, "troubling" can also be understood in a moral context (cf. Nanos, Irony: 184f, and for the following discussion). Those who are "troubled" can, in some sense, be said to be sick, biblically-related texts making an association between sin and illness: ". . . with all (our) heart and with all (our) soul and to implant your law in our heart, [so that we do not stray from it,] either to the right or to the left. For, you heal us of madness, /blindness/ and confusion [of heart . . .] בכול לב ובכול נפש ולטעת תורתכה בלבנו [לבלתי סור ממנה ללכת] ימין ומשמאל כיא תרפאנו משגעון עׄוׄרׄוׄןׄ ותמהון [ולבב]" (4Q504 ff1-2ii:13-15)[135] (see 3:1-5).

מעל (ma'al – "violation of a ban") is one of the crimes from which the community of 4QMMT disassociated themselves in separating from the "multitude of the people" – whom they accuse of "misappropriation of holy property" (the literal translation of ma'al) and fornication: "And concerning the wom[en . . .] and the disloyalty [. . .] for in these matters [. . . because of] violence and fornication many places have been ruined . . . [And you know that] we have segregated ourselves from the multitude of the peop[le . . . and] from mingling in these affairs, and from associating wi[th them] in these things. And you k[now that there is not] to be found in our actions disloyalty [lit.: misappropriation] or deceit or evil . . ."[136] (4QMMT[d] ff14-21:4-6, 7-9).[137]

---

have given my word to Lord, and I cannot take it back פי פציתי ואנכי בעכרי היית ואת אל-ה׳ ולא אוכל לשוב" (Judg. 11:35).

[134] For a fascinating reading of "no one to disturb him [מחריד ואין]," see Zakovitch.

[135] Cf. Dt. 28:60f; Ps. 41:4, 107:17-20; Isa. 19:19f, 53:4-5; Jer. 3:22, 14:19, 30:14ff; Hos. 6:1f, 7:1f; Mal. 4:2; Mt. 9:2; Mk. 2:5, 17; Lk. 5:20; Jn. 9:2; Wis.Sol. 17:8; 4QpHos[a] 1:8-9; 4Q387a 3ii:4-5; Ned. 41a; Amidah no. 8 (cf. Le Cornu and Shulam: 172-73). The association of this idea with the phenomenon of the "evil eye" has been taken to suggest that Paul is intimating that the influencers are casting (perhaps even inadvertently) a malicious eye at his disciples, causing them to see things in a distorted, blind, confused manner – casting a "spell" over them – an idea which denotes envy in both Graeco-Roman and Jewish texts (cf. Ex.R. 31:17; Lev.R. 16:8; PA 2:9, 5:13; Nid. 66a; BM 107b; Herodotus 1.32.1, 3.40.2) (cf. Nanos, Social) (see 4:12-20). This motif is frequently linked to 4:12-14, where "spitting (ἐκπτύω)" is understood as a defence against evil spirits. While the motif may be present in 4:12-14, we do not see it as a device exegetically determinative of Paul's argument, as Nanos proposes (cf. ibid; Irony: 184-92) (see 3:1-5). (For the motif in relation to 4:12f, see 4:12-20; for the "leaven" of 5:9, also at times associated with this theme, see 5:2-12; for the structure of Galatians as a whole, see Introduction, **Argument**.)

[136] ועל הנשי[ם . . .] והמעל [. . .] כי באלה [. . . בגלל] החמס והזנות אבד[ו הרבה] מקומות . . . [ואתם יודעים ש]פרשנו מרוב העם . . . [ו]מהתערב בדברים האלה ומלבוא ע[מהם] לגב אלה ואתם י[ודעים שלוא] [י]מצא בידנו מעל ושקר ורעה . . .

[137] Cf. 1QpHab 1:6, [8:11, 9:3-9, 11:17-12:10]. For 4QMMT's affinities with Galatians, see Introduction, **Form**.

Paul applies the ban which Achan violated to those who are now "troubling" his disciples – "let him be accursed (ἀνάθεμα ἔστω)" (verse 8) (cf. 4Q280). The חרם (cherem) represents that which is proscribed for destruction or consecration to God.[138] In the Second Temple period, the נדוי (niddui) (cf. Num. 12:14; Sifre, Be-he'al. 104) was employed as a ban in a social setting in which excommunication meant isolation from the community and enforced contempt at large (cf. 1 Cor. 5:2, 13) (cf. Elon: 540f; Schiffman, Sectarian: 168-173). While it appears to have implied expulsion from scholarly or purity orders for failure to observe purity rules or to accept the majority ruling (cf. Eduy. 5:6; BM 59b), the niddui also served as a general sanction, applicable also to laypersons, at the discretion of the court (see also below).[139]

Verse 8: The fact that Paul includes himself under the possibility both of excommunication (cf. Rom. 9:3) and of false teaching (the "we" may either be "royal" or inclusive of other teachers like Paul) indicates that no greater authority exists than that of the gospel of the Messiah[140] (cf. Flusser, Judaism: 246-69, and for the following discussion). The reference to "an angel from heaven (ἄγγελος ἐξ οὐρανοῦ)" may derive from a variant reading of Isaiah 63:9, attested by the LXX and 1QM 13:14, which suggests that it was neither an emissary nor an angel (מלאך ושר; malakh ve-sar) which saved the people during the Exodus but God's own face (MT: מלאך פניו [malakh panav – the "angel of His presence"]).[141] In Exodus 33:14-15 –

---

[138] Cf. Lev. 27:28-33; Num. 18:14, 21:2-3; Dt. 7:26, 13:16-17, 20:17-18; Ezek. 44:29; Lk. 21:5 [Greek]; Ned. 5:4; Arak. 8:6; MK 15a ff.

[139] Cf. Ta'anit 3:8; Ber. 19a; Pes. 53a; Shab. 130a; Kid. 72a.

[140] Cf. Mt. 7:28-29, 16:18-19; Jn. 5:19-47, 6:26-59, 7:28-29, 8:38, 42-58, 10:14-38, 14:10-14, 15:5, 16, 16:15, 17:1ff; Heb. 1:2-3:11; Tanh.Tol. 14. For the Messiah's teaching, see 6:1-11.

[141] Cf. Passover Haggada: "'The Lord brought us out of Egypt [with a mighty hand and outstretched arm and with great terror and with signs and wonders]' [Dt. 26:8] – not by a ministering angel, not by a fiery angel, not by a messenger [i.e., Moses], but by Himself, in His glory, did the Holy One, blessed be He עַל לֹא. וַיּוֹצִאֵנוּ מִמִּצְרַיִם. The ".יְדֵי מַלְאָךְ, וְלֹא עַל-יְדֵי שָׂרָף, וְלֹא עַל-יְדֵי שָׁלִיחַ. אֶלָּא הַקָּדוֹשׁ בָּרוּךְ הוּא בִּכְבוֹדוֹ וּבְעַצְמוֹ Aramaic form of שר (sar – [angelic] ruler) stands for the heavenly messenger/angel (עיר; ir) in Dan. 4:10, 14, 20 and elsewhere in the pseudepigrapha. The same argument, based in this case on the suggestion of an intermediary (בינו ובין – beino u-vein) in Lev. 26:46, is found with respect to Moses' receipt of the Torah directly from God (cf. ARN[b] 1) (see 3:19-20). Given the wealth of associations in this verse with Melchizedek (see verses 1-5 and above), it is interesting to note that the latter's role is described in contemporary literature in terms of the functions attributed to the angel Michael in Daniel and other ancient texts (cf. Dan. 12:1-3; 1 En. 10:11-12, 20:5, 24:6, 90:22-23; Ass.Mos. 10:1-2; Test.Levi 5:6; Test.Dan 6:2; 3 Bar. 11:4; 11QMelchizedek; 1QS 3:20, 4:2-8; 1QM 13:9-10, 17:6-7) (cf. Kobelski: 71-83). Even should this be an angel "according to the order of Melchizedek" (equally as unlikely as Paul) . . .

where the Greek translates פנים (panim – God's "face") as αὐτὸς (autos – "Himself") – the angel is associated with Israel's rebelliousness.

Angels are specifically associated with מתן תורה (matan Torah – the giving of the Torah) on Sinai in numerous texts, the idea that they coveted it themselves and wished God not to give it to human beings being widespread:

> R. Joshua b. Levi also said: At every single word which went forth from the mouth of the Holy One, blessed be He, the Israelites retreated twelve *mil*, but the ministering angels led them back [*medaddin*], as it is said, *The hosts of angels march, they march* [yiddodun yiddodun]: read not *yiddodun* but *yedaddun* [they lead]. R. Joshua b. Levi also said: When Moses ascended on high, the ministering angels spake before the Holy One, blessed be He, 'Sovereign of the Universe! What business has one born of woman amongst us?' 'He has come to receive the Torah,' answered He to them. Said they to Him, 'That secret treasure, which has been hidden by Thee for nine hundred and seventy-four generations before the world was created Thou desirest to give to flesh and blood! *What is man, that thou art mindful of him, And the son of man, that thou visitest him? O Lord our God, How excellent is thy name in all the earth! Who hast set thy glory* [the Torah] *upon the Heavens!*'[142] (Ps. 8:4, 1). (Shab. 88b)[143] (see also 3:19-20)[144]

Angelic revelations are staple fare in contemporary Jewish literature[145] (cf. Urbach, Sages: 135-83). Human beings – especially the righteous and Israel – frequently being considered superior to the angels, the latter were also said to represent the image of the person teaching God's word: "If the teacher is like an angel of the Lord of hosts, they should seek the Law at his mouth, but if not, they should not seek the Law at his mouth אם דומה הרב

---

[142] רבי יהושע בן לוי: כל דיבור ודיבור שיצא מפי הקדוש ברוך הוא חזרו ישראל לאחוריהן שנים עשר מיל והיו מלאכי השרת מדדין אותן, שנאמר: מלאכי צבאות ידודון ידודון. אל תיקרי "ידודון" אלא "ידדון": ואמר רבי יהושע בן לוי: בשעה שעלה משה למרום אמרו מלאכי השרת לפני הקדוש ברוך הוא: רבונו של עולם, מה לילוד אשה בינינו? אמר להן: לקבל תורה בא. אמרו לפניו: חמודה שגנוזה לך תשע מאות ושבעים וארבעה דורות קודם שנברא העולם אתה מבקש ליתנה לבשר ודם? "מה אנוש כי תזכרנו ובן אדם כי תפקדנו ה' אדנינו מה אדיר שמך בכל הארץ אשר תנה הודך על השמים".

[143] Cf. 1 Kings 13:18; Ex.R. 28:1, 29:8; Lev.R. 31:5; Dt.R. 7:9; Cant.R. 8.11.2; ARNᵃ 2:3; Shab. 88a.

[144] For Moses, see 3:19-20 and 4:1-7; for angels, see 3:19-20; for "flesh and blood," see verses 16c-17; for "every word," see 5:13-18 (verse 14); for the Torah's preexistence, see 3:6-9 (verse 9).

[145] Cf. Mt. 1:20-24, 2:13, 28:2-7; Lk. 1:11-22, 26-38, 2:9-15, 24:4-9; Acts 1:10-11, 5:19, 12:7-11, 23:11, 27:23-24; Hist.Rechab. 1:3; Jos.Asen. 14:1ff; 2 Bar. 22:1-30:5; Apoc.Abr. 10:4ff; 1 En. 21:5, 64:1-2, 80:1ff; 2 En. [J] 1:4ff; 4 Ez. 4:1ff; Jos.*Life* 208-9.

"למלאך ה׳ צבאות יבקשו תורה מפיהו ואם לאו אל יבקשו תורה מפיהו" (Hag. 15b) (cf. MK 17a) (see 4:12-20 [verses 1-5]).[146]

According to the example of Joshua 6:26, the anathema may also take the form of an oath: "Then Joshua made them take an oath at that time, saying, 'Cursed [arur] before the LORD is the man who rises up and builds this city Jericho' וישבע יהושע בעת ההיא לאמור ארור האיש לפני ה׳ אשר יקום ובנה את-העיר הזאת את-יריחו." "A Tanna taught: *Arur* may imply excommunication, curse, or oath תנא: ארור - בו נידוי בו קללה בו שבועה (Shevu. 36a). Upon the Qumran novitiate's entrance into the community, a curse was pronounced before the assembled gathering on the "sons of Belial" from whom the sectarians pledged to separate themselves:

> And the levites shall curse all the men of the lot of Belial. They shall begin to speak and shall say: «Accursed are you for all your wicked, blameworthy deeds ... Cursed by the idols which his heart reveres whoever enters this covenant, and places the obstacle of his iniquity in front of himself to fall over it. When he hears the words of this covenant, he will congratulate himself in his heart, saying: «I will have peace, in spite of my walking in the stubbornness of my heart».[147] However, his spirit will be obliterated, the dry with the moist, without mercy. May God's anger and the wrath of his verdicts consume him for everlasting destruction. May stick fast to him all the curses of this covenant. May God separate him for evil, and may he be cut off from the midst of all the sons of light because of his straying from following God on account of his idols and obstacle of his iniquity. May he assign his lot with the cursed ones for ever». And all those who enter the covenant shall respond and shall say after them: «Amen, Amen».[148] (1QS 2:4-5, 11-18) (see also 3:10-14 and 5:2-12)[149]

---

[146] It is in this context, of teaching, that we understand Paul's reference to the Galatians' "spitting" at the trial of his "bodily weakness" (see 4:12-20).

[147] Cf. Jer. 23:16-17 – see below.

[148] והלווים מקללים את כול אנשי גורל בליעל וענו ואמרו ארור אתה בכול מעשי רשע אשמתכה ... ארור בגלולי לבו לעבור הבא בברית הזות ומכשול עוונו ישים לפניו להסוג בו והיה בש'מעו את דברי הברית הזות יתברך בלבבו לאמור שלום יהי לי כיא בשרירות לבי אלך ונספתה רוחו הצמאה עם הרויה לאין סליחה אף אל וקנאת משפטיו יבערו בו לכלת עולמים ידבקו בו כול אלות הברית הזות ויבדילהו אל לרעה ונכרת מתוך כול בני אור בהסוגו מאחרי אל בגלוליו ומכשול עוונו יתן גורלו בתוך ארורי עולמים וכול באי הברית יענו ואמרו אחריהם אמן אמן.

[149] Cf. Leviticus 26; Deuteronomy 27. For "amen," see 6:18 and verses 1-5.

Paul may wish his disciples to take a similar oath disassociating themselves, as he wishes, from the influencers – his authority to invoke such an imprecation deriving from the gospel itself, its truth validating the one who proclaims it (see 4:21-31, 5:2-12, 24-26, 6:1ff, and below).[150]

Verse 9 may refer either to the previous verse or to a prior statement to the same effect.[151] Although Paul has evidently visited the communities to whom he is now writing (see Introduction, **Date and destination**), an allusion to such a warning while there seems unlikely, even if Paul's amazement is largely ironic.[152] Whatever the occasion, the effect is to doubly reinforce the curse.[153] The covenantal context is reinforced by Paul's language of "receiving (παρελάβετε)," which indicates the transmission of tradition from one generation to the next: "Moses received the Torah at Sinai and transmitted it to Joshua, Joshua to the elders, and the elders to the prophets, and the prophets to the men of the Great Synagogue משה קבל תורה מסיני ומסרה ליהושע ויהושע לזקנים וזקנים לנביאים ונביאים מסרוה לאנשי כנסת הגדולה ..." (PA 1:1).[154]

The direct address "I say (λέγω)" – here repeated since this statement is itself a reiteration – is a common epistolary marker, employed to emphasise the instruction given: "And also [concerning liquid str]ea[ms, we] say that in these there is no [purity] . . . **to you we have [written]** that you must understand the books of Moses [and] the book[s of the pr]ophets

---

[150] Despite reservations regarding the classification of Galatians as a "magical letter" whose curses and blessings are meant to be actualized (cf. Betz, Galatians: 25, 50), the curse constitutes the direct opposite of the blessing of peace: "May God not be merciful [when] you entreat him. [May he lift the countenance of his anger] upon you for a curse. May there be no peace for you by the mouth of those who intercede. [Be cursed,] without a remnant; and be damned, without a survivor. And accursed be those who act . . . against the covenant of God לוא יחונכה אל נב]קוראכה]וישא פני אפון לכה לזעמה ולא יהיה לכה שלום בפי כול אוחזי אבונת ארור אתה] לאין שרית וזעום אתה לאין על ברית אל ... פליטה וארורים עושנין]" (4Q280 1:3-6). This passage is evidently based on Num. 6:25 (see verses 1-5), and places peace and accursedness in immediate antithesis. The curse-blessing motif is also central to the Abraham texts (cf. 3:8-14) (see 3:6f, 6:12f, and verses 1-5).

[151] It may also be possible that the reference is to a warning issued not to the Galatians themselves but to others (cf. 2 Cor. 11:4).

[152] To the extent that the "we" is taken literally – in reference to other figures – the presence of the latter would presumably also need to be assumed on the earlier occasion (cf. Betz, Galatians: 52).

[153] Cf. Judg. 5:23; Mal. 2:2.

[154] Cf. Mt. 5:21-48; 1 Cor. 11:23; Gal. 1:12; 1 Thess. 2:13; 2 Thess. 3:6; Eccl.R. 12.11.1; ARNᵃ 1:1-3; ARNᵇ 1. The biblical context of blessings and curses makes it unnecessary to classify Galatians as a "magical letter" (*pace* Betz, Galatians: 25, 50) – despite Betz's own pronouncement of its content as "sacred law" and the propriety of recognising the epistle's enclosure within the opening curse and concluding blessing (cf. 6:16). For a criticism of Betz's argument, cf. Longenecker, Galatians: cx-cxiv.

and Davi[d ...] ... [טהרה] [בהם אומרים שהם שאין בהם אומרים שהם אנחנו]ות המוצק]ון[על]ואף
"[כתב]נו אליכה שתבין בספר מושה ו[בספר]י הנ[ב]יאים ובדוי[ד ...] (4QMMTᶜ 2:6-7,
4QMMTᵈ ff14-21:10).[155]

Verse 10 constitutes Paul's proof or justification for invoking such a
dire threat.[156] Here again he returns to his status as a commissioned agent,
this time adopting the language of servanthood (cf. Col. 3:22f) (see 2:1-10,
3:10-14, 4:1ff, 6:17, and verses 1-5, 21-24).[157] The idea of serving a master is
interpreted in a midrashic tradition in terms of "pleasing" or "angering"
either God or one's (evil) inclination, no one being able to simultaneously
serve two masters: "This [the idea that it is too late to repent after death] is
the meaning of the Scriptural verse, *The small and great are there alike; and the
servant is free from his master* (Job 3:19). R. Simon said: This is one of four
similar Scriptural verses. *'The small and great are there alike.'* In this world he
who is small can become great and he who is great can be rendered small,
but in the world to come he who is small cannot become great nor he who
is great small. *'And the servant is free from his master'*: he who performs the
will of his creator (*yozer*) angers his evil inclination (*yezer*), but once he is
dead he emerges into freedom, as it is said, *'And the servant is free from his
master'*"[158] (Ruth R. 3:1)[159] (see also 2:15-21 and 5:13-18).[160]

---

[155] Cf. Rom. 12:3; 1 Cor. 7:29, 15:50; 2 Cor. 13:2; Gal. 5:3, 16; Eph. 4:17; 4QMMTᶜ 4:2;
4QMMTᵈ ff6-13:11.

[156] For the argument that verses 10-11 constitute a *transitus* or *transgressio* from the
exordium to the *narratio*, cf. Betz, Galatians: 46.

[157] Substantial commentarial disagreement exists over the meaning of the Greek
πείθω (peithō) here. Where it is understood in the sense of "persuading," rhetorical
structure is seen to lie at the fore (cf. Betz, Galatians; 54-56; Schmithals). Since the
idea of "persuading God" makes little sense in a Jewish context, and despite the
meaning of "persuasion" in relation to Paul's teaching (cf. Acts 19:8, 28:23; 2 Cor.
5:11), the notation may carry overtones of "obeying" – notwithstanding the
following accusative rather than dative case. Significantly in this regard, the verb
πειθαρχέω (peitharcheō – "to obey") appears in Peter's assertion "We must obey
God rather than men (πειθαρχεῖν δεῖ θεῷ μᾶλλον ἢ ἀνθρώποις) (Acts 5:29) – a
dictum resembling the rabbinic rationale for rebutting wrongdoing in agency:
"[When] the words of the master [God] and the words of the pupil [are in conflict],
whose are obeyed? דברי הרב ודברי תלמיד - דברי מי שומעים?" (Kid. 42b) (see verses 1-5).
[158] זה שאמר הכתוב: קטן וגדול שם הוא ועבד חפשי מאדניו. אמר רבי סימון: זה אחד מארבעה
מקראות שדומין זה לזה. קטן וגדול שם: הוא העולם הזה: מי שהוא קטן יכול להעשות גדול ומי
שהוא גדול יכול להעשות קטן. אבל לעתיד לבא, מי שהוא קטן אינו יכול להעשות גדול ומי שהוא
גדול אינו יכול להעשות קטן. ועבד חפשי מאדוניו: זה הוא שעושה רצון יוצרו מכעיס את יצרו. מת -
יצא לחירות, שנאמר: ועבד חפשי מאדוניו.
[159] Cf. Mt. 6:24; Lk. 16:13; Rom. 12:9; [2 Cor. 6:14f]; 1 Thess. 5:21-22; Test.Dan 4:7;
Ruth R. 8:1; Yalk.Job 886; Ber. 61a; Eruv. 18a; Haggada (see n141) (cf. Shulam and Le
Cornu: 24, 209-33; Flusser, Judaism: 169-72). This constitutes a further variation on
the theme of wrongdoing in agency (see above).
[160] This motif corresponds precisely to Paul's declaration of the freedom from sin
achieved through God's sending of His faithfulness in Jesus, enabling human

As God's agent, Paul is responsible to God alone – not in any way to men or women. He bears God's authority and must declare God's intentions and desires even when they fit neither human sensibilities nor creaturely sensitivities: "Thus says the LORD of hosts, 'Do not listen to the words of the prophets who are prophesying to you. They are leading you into futility; they speak a vision of their own imagination, not from the mouth of the LORD. They keep saying to those who despise Me, "The LORD has said, 'You will have peace'"; and as for every one who walks in the stubbornness of his own heart, they say, "Calamity will not come upon you." But who has stood in the council of the LORD, that he should see and hear His word? Who has given heed to His word and listened?'"[161] (Jer. 23:16-18).

Had Paul been unable to assure the Ephesian elders when parting from them that "I did not shrink from declaring to you the whole purpose of God (οὐ γὰρ ὑπεστειλάμην τοῦ μὴ ἀναγγεῖλαι πᾶσαν τὴν βουλὴν τοῦ θεοῦ ὑμῖν)" (Acts 20:27), he would have been vulnerable to the charge of seeking to please men: "But just as we have been approved by God to be entrusted with the gospel, so we speak, not as pleasing men but God, who examines our hearts"[162] (1 Thess. 2:4).[163] The most convincing proof that he

---

[161] כה-אמר ה' צבאות אל-תשמעו על-דברי הנבאים הנבאים לכם מהבלים המה אתכם חזון לבם ידברו לא מפי ה': אמרים אמור למנאצי דבר ה' שלום יהיה לכם וכל הלך בשררות לבו אמרו לא-תבוא עליכם רעה: כי מי עמד בסוד ה' וירא וישמע את-דברו מי-הקשיב דברי {דברו} וישמע.

[162] ἀλλὰ καθὼς δεδοκιμάσμεθα ὑπὸ τοῦ θεοῦ πιστευθῆναι τὸ εὐαγγέλιον, οὕτως λαλοῦμεν, οὐχ ὡς ἀνθρώποις ἀρέσκοντες ἀλλὰ θεῷ τῷ δοκιμάζοντι τὰς καρδίας ἡμῶν.

[163] The Psalms of Solomon contain a quite vicious indictment of leaders motivated by the desire to impress people: "May God expose the deeds of those who try to impress people; (and expose) their deeds with ridicule and contempt ... those who please men, who deceitfully quote the Law. And their eyes are on a man's peaceful house, as a serpent destroys the wisdom of others with criminal words. His words are deceitful that (he) may accomplish (his) evil desires; he did not stop until he succeeded in scattering (them) as orphans. He devastated a house because of his criminal desire; he deceived with words; (as if) there were no one to see and to judge. He is satiated with lawless actions at one (place), and (then) his eyes are on another house to destroy it with agitating words. With all this his soul, like Hades, is not satisfied ... Let crows peck out the eyes of the hypocrites, for they disgracefully empty many people's houses and greedily scatter (them). They have not remembered God, nor have they feared God in all these things; but they have angered God, and provoked him. May he banish them from the earth, for they defrauded innocent people by pretense" (Ps.Sol. 4:6-13, 20-22). Here the motif of hypocrisy, which informs the whole of Galatians, can already be discerned (see Introduction, **Argument**). The affinities of this passage with Hab. 2:4ff may indicate that Paul's extensive use of Hab. 2:4, both here and in Romans, has itself associations with hypocrisy (see 3:10ff and 4:1f).

is not seeking to please wo/men is his willingness to excommunicate his disciples' persuaders – to declare them undesirable and unwelcome elements within the community.[164] While the "still (ἔτι)" contrasts his "former life" with his present service of Jesus, Paul's point derives almost exclusively from his present commission (10a: ἄρτι – "now") on behalf of the Messiah and says little, if anything, substantive regarding what commentators are so fond of calling his "pre-Christian existence" (cf. Betz, Galatians: 56).

Verses 11-12: *Narratio* (*transitio*)

For I would have you know, brethren, that the gospel which was preached by me is not according to man. For I neither received it from man, nor was I taught it, but *I received it* through a revelation of Jesus the Messiah.

This verse commences an extended autobiographical section reaching through to 2:21, the *narratio* being employed rhetorically to present a "statement of facts" (cf. Betz, Galatians: 16-18, 58-62).[165] The heart of Paul's teaching – his "gospel" – is that it represents not a man-made artifact but a divinely-authored and supernaturally-conveyed "mystery." In the words which he later employs in Ephesians, "the mystery of the Messiah, which in other generations was not made known to the sons of men, as it has now been revealed to His holy apostles and prophets in [by] the Spirit; *to be specific*, that the Gentiles are fellow-heirs and fellow-members of the body, and fellow-partakers of the promise in the Messiah Jesus through the gospel, of which I was made a minister, according to the gift of God's grace which was given to me according to the working of His power"[166] (Eph. 3:4-7) (see 3:10-14).[167]

---

[164] In this sense, verse 10 anticipates 4:16: "Have I therefore become your enemy by telling you the truth? (ὥστε ἐχθρὸς ὑμῶν γέγονα ἀληθεύων ὑμῖν;)" (see 4:12-20). For Paul's reiterated warnings to this effect, see Introduction, **Argument**.

[165] Betz characterizes verses 10-11 as a *transitio* or *transgressio* – a smooth transition from the *exordium* to the *narratio* (pp. 46, 60). He therefore sees the *narratio* proper beginning in verse 12, verse 11 announcing the argument to be proved in the "statement of facts." While his discussion of the *narratio*'s purpose is highly instructive from a forensic perspective, it claims much of its force from Betz's prior assumption that Galatians constitutes an apologetic letter (see Introduction, **Form**). Placing the letter as a whole under a Graeco-Roman rhetorical rubric distances Paul from his primary biblical and Jewish setting – whose centrality the remainder of the epistle demonstrates (cf. Longenecker, Galatians: cx-cxiii; Davies, Jewish: 172-88) (see 2:15-21, 3:1-5, and 4:1-7). For Galatians as a halakhic "rebuke-request" letter along the lines of 4QMMT and for the narrative function of 1:11-2:21, see Introduction, **Form; Argument**; for the biographical genre in rabbinic literature, cf. Alexander; Le Cornu and Shulam: 163-65.

[166] τῷ μυστηρίῳ τοῦ Χριστοῦ, ὃ ἑτέραις γενεαῖς οὐκ ἐγνωρίσθη τοῖς υἱοῖς τῶν ἀνθρώπων ὡς νῦν ἀπεκαλύφθη τοῖς ἁγίοις ἀποστόλοις αὐτοῦ καὶ προφήταις ἐν πνεύματι, εἶναι τὰ ἔθνη συγκληρονόμα καὶ σύσσωμα καὶ συμμέτοχα τῆς

The notation Γνωρίζω γὰρ ὑμῖν, ἀδελφοί (gnōrizō gar hymin, adelfoi – "For I would have you know, brethren") is a customary epistolary "disclosure" formula designed to convey a point of significance: "[And you know that] we have segregated ourselves from the multitude of the peop[le . . .] . . . And you k[now that there is not] to be found in our actions disloyalty or deceit or evil ואתם יודעים ו]ודעים. . . .[. . . מרוב הע]ם ו[אתם יודעים ש]פרשנו מרוב ה ורעה ושלוא"] [ומצא בידנו מעל ושקר "[4QMMT[d] ff14-21:7-9).[168] The textual variants γάρ (gar – "for") and δέ (de – "but") are both well attested, Paul using the latter when introducing a new subject (cf. 1 Cor. 15:1; 2 Cor. 8:1) (cf. Longenecker, Galatians: 22). While the δέ is also preferable when verses 11, 13 are recognized as commencing the *narratio*, the statement of facts is intimately linked with Paul's commission to spread the gospel, supporting a causal connection ("for").[169]

While his addressees are Gentiles (see Introduction, **Occasion and circumstances**), Paul consistently refers to them as "brethren (ἀδελφοί)" (see verses 1-5). Their divergence from his teaching notwithstanding, the Galatian believers remain Paul's partners as long as they remain faithful to the will of the One who has called them (cf. verse 6), disciples of the one master (cf. Mt. 23:8; Mk. 3:35). The context of discipleship clearly lies in the background here, the word "disciple (μαθητής)" constituting Luke's normal term in the first half of Acts for non-Jewish believers.[170] Here in Galatians, Paul wishes the communities to know of their standing in the Messiah and of his devotion to them alike – the first being linked to the second (see 4:12-20). Right at the beginning of his letter he stresses the authority with which he stands in relation to his disciples – and thereby his responsibility towards them on the one hand and their loyalty to him on the other (see 4:12-20).[171]

The rather cumbersome phrase τὸ εὐαγγέλιον τὸ εὐαγγελισθὲν ὑπ' ἐμοῦ (to euangelion to euangelisthen hyp emou – "the gospel which was preached by me") is in fact a precise expression of the facts. To say that "I preached the gospel" would have admitted a possibility that the gospel was "Paul's." The passive emphasizes, to the contrary, that while it was

---

ἐπαγγελίας ἐν Χριστῷ ʼΙησοῦ διὰ τοῦ εὐαγγελίου, οὗ ἐγενήθην διάκονος κατὰ τὴν δωρεὰν τῆς χάριτος τοῦ θεοῦ τῆς δοθείσης μοι κατὰ τὴν ἐνέργειαν τῆς δυνάμεως αὐτοῦ.

167 Cf. Rom. 11:25, 16:25-26; Eph. 3:2-10; Col. 1:26-27.

168 Cf. Rom. 1:13, 11:25; 1 Cor. 12:3, 15:1; 2 Cor. 8:1; Phil. 1:12. For 4QMMT's literary relation to Galatians, see Introduction, **Form**.

169 In this sense, a "conflation" of the two particles may best render Paul's meaning.

170 Cf. Pfann; Le Cornu and Shulam: 801. For discipleship in general, cf. Safrai, Master; Alon, Land: 476-78; EJ: Talmudic Discipleship [CD-Rom]; Le Cornu and Shulam: 301-2, 788.

171 For Galatians as a "halakhic letter" of rebuke and request, see Introduction, **Form; Argument**.

transmitted through him, it did not originate with him.[172] It derives in fact from no human source – the preposition κατά (kata – "according to/after the manner of") denoting "stemming from the will or authority of"[173] (cf. Longenecker, Galatians: 23) (see verses 1-5).[174]

Verse 12 reinforces the "general principle" (כלל; klal) with the "details" (פרטים; pratim): The "good news" which Paul passed on to the Galatians is not the fruit of tradition and teaching but of a divine revelation.[175] The significance which this carries for Paul may be gathered from its sharp divergence from the teaching ethos in which he had been nurtured at the feet of Gamaliel (cf. Acts 22:3) (see Appendix, **Gamaliel**). While the Sages unequivocally declared the supra-human and divine nature and source of halakhah (the application of biblical precepts to historical circumstances) they simultaneously insisted on their exclusive authority to develop halakhah and give it shape (cf. Berkovits; Elon: 53f). These two convictions are expressed in two, as it were contradictory, tenets: תורה מן השמים (Torah min ha-shamayim – "the Torah is from heaven") and תורה לא בשמים היא (Torah lo be-shamayim hee – "the Torah is not in heaven") (cf. San. 10:1; BM 59b).

The transfer of exegetical authority into human hands is expressed in this framework both by the denial of halakhic authority to the "bat kol" and in the importance attributed to tradition. Although the bat kol (literally: "daughter of a voice") constituted God's voice heard in place of prophecy when the latter ceased with Haggai, Zechariah, and Malachi, it was considered to be devoid of authority within the halakhic decision-making process because God had instituted within the Torah itself that rulings are to follow the majority opinion (determined by the Sages)[176] (cf. Le Cornu and Shulam: 568-69; Urbach, Halakha; Safrai, Literature).[177] A

---

[172] For the discussion of "gospel," see verses 1-5.

[173] Cf. Rom. 3:5, 6:19; 1 Cor. 3:3, 9:8, 15:32; Gal. 3:15.

[174] The phrase also recurs in Paul's assertion that he is "speaking in human terms (κατὰ ἄνθρωπον λέγω)" (3:15). This idea is related – as Rom. 6:19 states explicitly – to God's condescending to the human level, thereby "accommodating" wo/man's weakness (cf. Mt. 19:7-8) (cf. Dreyfus) (see 3:19f).

[175] Although these verses do not constitute a strict example of כלל ופרט (klal u-frat – the general and the specific), they do bring the principle to mind. The hermeneutical rule is applied when a biblical passage first gives a general concept, subsequently followed by a specific one (cf. Lev. 1:2). In such a case, the general expression is assumed to signify only what is specified in the detail (cf. Steinsaltz, Talmud: 152-53) (see also verses 13-14).

[176] Cf. 1 Macc. 4:46, 9:27, 14:41; 1QS 9:10-11; Jos.CA 1.41; TBE [EZ] p. 172; Tos.Sot. 13:2; Ber. 52a; BM 59b; Pes. 114a; San. 11a; Yoma 9b; Sot. 48b; Men. 29b.

[177] The "super-apostles" whom Paul later encounters in Corinth appear in this regard to repudiate his authority as based on a revelation. Other of the objections they seem to have raised also recall qualifications demanded by the Sages and the Sanhedrin: Physical fitness, rhetorical power, payment for teaching, and possibly

prophet – as the bearer of a divine vision – is likewise deprived of any halakhic authority: "*These are the commandments* (Lev. 27:34): henceforth a prophet may no longer make any innovations אלה המצות: אין נביא רשאי לחדש עוד דבר מעתה" (Sifra, Be-chuk. 13:7) (cf. Tem. 16a).[178] Rabbinic tradition also revolves around the principle of handing down one's teaching in the name of the master from whom one learnt it: "Rabbah b. Shila [once] met Elijah. He said to him: What is the Holy One, blessed be He, doing? He answered: He utters traditions in the name of all the Rabbis . . . אשכחיה רבה בר שילא לאליהו. אמר לו: מאי קא עביד הקדוש ברוך הוא? אמר לו: קאמר שמעתא מפומייהו דכולהו רבנן . . ." (Hag. 15b).[179]

In contrast to the human "chain of tradition" in which he had been educated and of which he was part (cf. Acts 22:3), Paul refers his ultimate authority to his commissioner (see verses 1-5, 15-16b).[180] Despite the denial of authority to "revelation" in pharisaic texts, both Elijah, the Messiah's precursor, and the Messiah himself were considered to be mediators of the truth: "*Thus saith the Lord God, In the first month, in the first day of the month thou shalt take a young bullock without blemish, and thou shalt offer it as a sin-offering in the sanctuary* (Ezek. 45:18). 'A sin-offering'? But surely it is a burnt-offering? – R. Johanan said, This passage will be interpreted by Elijah in the future כה אמר ה' אלהים בראשון באחד לחודש תקח פר בן בקר תמים וחטאת את המקדש. חטאת? עולה היא! אמר ר' יוחנן: פרשה זו אליהו עתיד לדורשה" (Men. 45a) (cf. EJ: 6:635-36).[181]

A specific midrashic tradition anticipates that the Messiah will propound new meanings and interpretations of Torah, and links this task with the bestowal of commandments also on the Gentiles:

> *His foal and his colt* (Gen. 49:11) intimate: when he will come of whom it is written, *Lowly, and riding upon an ass, even upon a colt the foal of an ass* (Zech. 9:9). *He washeth his garments in wine* (Gen.

---

signs and wonders (cf. Kim, Paul: 228; Le Cornu and Shulam: 457-59, 267-70, 673-74) (see verses 1-5).

[178] To the extent that the *bat kol* is frequently associated with the Holy Spirit in rabbinic literature (cf. Tos.Sot. 13:3f; JSot. 9, 15, 24c; Sot. 48b; Meg. 32a), this hermeneutical principle also contrasts sharply with Paul's appeal to the Holy Spirit's authority (see 3:1f).

[179] Cf. PA 6:6; Meg. 32a; Suk. 28a. Jesus' revelation (as both subjective and objective) is the fulfilment of Scripture and must be so in order not only to be recognised as valid but also to be preached as such. For the sake of clarity, it must be stressed yet again here that Paul is not negating his whole heritage but merely putting earthly things into proper perspective (cf. Phil. 3:2ff).

[180] For Paul as a prophet, modelled on the isaianic Servant, see 2:1-10, 4:1f, 6:17, [verses 1-5], 15-16b, 21-24, and below.

[181] Cf. Eduy. 8:7; BM 1:8, 2:8, 3:4-5; Tos.Eduy. 3:4; Sif.Dt. 41; Num.R. 3:13; ARNᵃ 34:5; Ber. 3a, 35b; Shab. 108a-109b; Eruv. 43b; Pes. 13a, 15a, 20b, 34a; Hag. 25a; Yev. 102a; Git. 42b; Kid. 70a; BM 3a, 29b; Bek. 33b.

49:11), intimates that he [the Messiah] will compose for them words of Torah. *And his vesture in the blood of grapes* (Gen. 49:11), that he will restore to them their errors [point out their misinterpretations]. R. Hanin said: Israel will not require the teaching of the royal Messiah in the future, for it says, *Unto him shall* the nations *seek* (Isa. 11:10), but not Israel. If so, for what purpose will the royal Messiah come, and what will he do? He will come to assemble the exiles of Israel and to give them [the Gentiles] thirty precepts, as it says, *And I said unto them: If ye think good, give me my hire; and if not, forbear. So they weighed for my hire thirty pieces of silver* (Zech. 11:12).[182] (Gen.R. 98:9) (cf. Tanh.Vaychi 10) (cf. Urbach, Sages: 310-14)[183]

Paul himself acknowledges that he "received" - the technical word of transmission - knowledge of Jesus from others, including the facts that "the Messiah died for our sins according to the Scriptures, and that he was buried, and that he was raised on the third day according to the Scriptures"[184] (1 Cor. 15:3-4) (cf. 1 Cor. 11:23-25). Here, however, he appears to refer to his "insight into the mystery of the Messiah (τὴν σύνεσίν μου ἐν τῷ μυστηρίῳ τοῦ Χριστοῦ)" - derived "by revelation (κατὰ ἀποκάλυψιν)" - which "in other generations was not made known to the sons of men (ἑτέραις γενεαῖς οὐκ ἐγνωρίσθη τοῖς υἱοῖς τῶν ἀνθρώπων)" (Eph. 3:4-5).

Although this mystery is intimated in Scripture[185] - whence it gains its legitimacy - it was not understood by those reading "in the synagogue every shabbat (ἐν ταῖς συναγωγαῖς κατὰ πᾶν σάββατον)" (Acts 15:21) until "the fulness of the time" had come (cf. Kim, Paul: 124-25, 239-57).[186] Initially, the revelation is of Jesus himself (cf. 1 Cor. 9:1, 15:8; verse 16). Although the genitive here ("of") is most commonly taken to be objective - i.e., Jesus constituting the content of the revelation - it may also be subjective, Jesus serving as the revelator (cf. Acts [9:15-16, 22:14-15], 26:15-

---

[182] עירו והאתונו: לכשיבא אתו שכתוב בו: עני ורוכב על חמור וגו'. כבס ביין לבושו: שהוא מחוור להן דברי תורה. ובדם ענגים סותה: שהוא מחוור להם טעותיהן. אמר ר' חנין: אין ישראל צריכין לתלמודו של מלך המשיח לעתיד לבוא, שנאמר: אליו גוים ידרושו - לא ישראל. אם כן, למה מלך המשיח בא ומה הוא בא לעשות? לכנס גליותיהן של ישראל וליתן להם ל' מצות הדא הוא דכתיב: ואמר אליהם אם טוב בעיניכם וגו'.

[183] See also 6:1-11 (verse 2).

[184] Παρέδωκα γὰρ ὑμῖν ἐν πρώτοις, ὃ καὶ παρέλαβον, ὅτι Χριστὸς ἀπέθανεν ὑπὲρ τῶν ἁμαρτιῶν ἡμῶν κατὰ τὰς γραφὰς καὶ ὅτι ἐτάφη καὶ ἐγήγερται τῇ ἡμέρᾳ τῇ τρίτῃ κατὰ τὰς γραφάς.

[185] Cf. Mt. 16:17; 1 Pet. 1:10-12; Yalk.Dt. 898; Yalk.Isa. 508; Ber. 34b; San. 99a; Shab. 63a.

[186] Cf. Mk. 1:15; Gal. 4:4; 1 Tim. 2:6, [6:15]; Tit. 1:3. "Mystery" and "fulness" are naturally-related terms to the extent that the former anticipates its revelation at some (future) date (cf. 1QpHab 7:4-6).

18) and thus as Paul's commissioner (see verses 1-5). In similar fashion, the "revelation" may signify content and/or means, Jesus both embodying the "mystery" and functioning as the representative through whom its redemptive purpose is conveyed to humankind – first to Israel and then "also to the Greek" (cf. Rom. 1:16). In this sense, the plethora of scriptural passages which pervade Paul's prose suggest that the "revelation" which he received included an explicitly exegetical element: Insight into the significance of Isaiah 40-66 and other texts relating to the inclusion of the Gentiles in God's kingdom (cf. Rom. 10:5-15, 15:9-12; 1 Cor. 2:4-10) (see 3:1-5, 10-14).[187]

Verses 13-14:

For you have heard of my former manner of life in Judaism, how I used to persecute the community of God beyond measure, and tried to destroy it; and I was advancing in Judaism beyond many of my contemporaries among my countrymen, being more extremely zealous for my ancestral traditions.

If verses 11-12 constitute the *transitio* to the "statement of facts," verse 13 appears to introduce the *narratio* proper, a section extending to 2:14 (21) and consisting primarily of autobiographical witness (cf. Longenecker: 26; Betz, Galatians: 56-66).[188] Here the γάρ (gar – "for") carries its full causal weight, providing the justification for Paul's claim that his gospel derives directly from the Messiah (see verses 1-5, 11:12).

The ἠκούσατε (ēkousate – "you have heard") reflects a standard epistolary disclosure formula (cf. verse 11: "For I would have you know, brethren") (see verses 11-12). While the most logical assumption is that Paul had narrated (parts of) his history to the Galatian communities when he had visited them, the term resonates with Paul's (later) claim before Agrippa II that the course of his life is public knowledge: ". . . all Jews know my manner of life from my youth up, which from the beginning was

---

[187] The "inspiration of the Spirit" in imparting insight appears most strikingly in the Qumran literature: "And I, the Instructor, have known you, my God, through the spirit which you gave in me, and I have listened loyally (faithfully) to your wonderful secret through your holy spirit. You have [op]ened up within me knowledge of the mystery of your wisdom . . . ואני משכיל ידעתיכה אלי ברוח אשר נתתה בי ונאמנה שמעתי לסוד פלאכה ברוח ק'דשכה [פ]תחתה לתוכי דעת ברז שלככה . . ." (1QHᵃ 20:11-13) (see also verses 13-14). For the affinities of this account with Paul's claim that God revealed His son "in me," see verses 15-16b. This view may help bridge the gap between those who hold that Paul's understanding of the "mystery" of God's redemptive purpose for the Gentiles (cf. Rom. 11:25; 1 Cor. 2:6-10; Eph. 3:9; Col. 1:27) was purely exegetical and those who see it as part and parcel of his calling (cf. Kim, Paul: 242ff). For the centrality of Scripture for Paul, see Introduction, **Theological pointers**, 2:15-21, 3:1ff, 4:1-7, 21-31, and verses 15-16b.

[188] For the present structural reading of Galatians 1-2, which perceives Paul's narrative argument as leading up to the incident in Antioch, see Introduction, **Argument**.

spent among my *own* nation and at Jerusalem; since they have known about me for a long time previously, if they are willing to testify, that I lived *as* a Pharisee according to the strictest sect of our religion"[189] (Acts 26:4-5) (cf. Le Cornu and Shulam: 1385-86).[190] No intrinsic reason exists to preclude the possibility that the Galatian communities had at some stage heard rumours/reports of Paul's campaign similar to those which had filtered down to the community in Damascus (cf. Acts 9:21) and reached the communities in Judaea (cf. verse 23).[191]

While the ποτε (pote – "once/formerly") modifies his "manner of life (ἀναστροφήν)," it does not stand in opposition to "in Judaism (ἐν τῷ Ἰουδαϊσμῷ)."[192] Just as his "former way of life" did not include faithfulness to Jesus – the very contrary – and was yet Jewish, so his "present way of life" – which is characterised by commitment to Jesus – remains Jewish.[193] The distinction is merely between two forms of Jewish life.[194]

---

[189] Τὴν μὲν οὖν βίωσίν μου [τὴν] ἐκ νεότητος τὴν ἀπ' ἀρχῆς γενομένην ἐν τῷ ἔθνει μου ἔν τε Ἱεροσολύμοις ἴσασι πάντες [οἱ] Ἰουδαῖοι προγινώσκοντές με ἄνωθεν, ἐὰν θέλωσι μαρτυρεῖν, ὅτι κατὰ τὴν ἀκριβεστάτην αἵρεσιν τῆς ἡμετέρας θρησκείας ἔζησα Φαρισαῖος.

[190] Cf. Acts 22:1-3; Rom. 9:3, 11:1; 2 Cor. 11:22; Phil. 3:5-6. For Paul's background, education, affiliation, persecution of the early community, and calling, see Appendix; for his demonstration of the Messiah's crucifixion and life in his own, see 2:15-21, 3:1-5, and 6:12f. The phrase also recalls Jesus' hermeneutical display in Mt. 5:21-48. As Daube notes of the latter, "The tone [of the antitheses] is not academic but final, prophetic, maybe somewhat defiant" (Daube, New: 57-58). If the suggestion that Jesus' argument most closely resembles the legal form reflected in 4QMMT is correct (cf. Kampen and Bernstein: 133-35), this may indicate a further affinity between 4QMMT and Galatians (see Introduction, **Form**). For Galatians' affinities with the Sermon on the Mount, see Introduction, **Theological pointers** (Justification) and 5:13-18.

[191] For the difficulties attendant on Paul's assertions in this regard, see verses 21-24; for Paul as persecutor, see Appendix (**Persecutor**).

[192] The use of the particle in the future (cf. Lk. 22:32) precludes necessarily understanding the meaning of "once" here to be irrevocably in the past and now "no longer."

[193] This point is nicely made by Kim in his application of the "covenant to the people" in Isaiah 42:6/49:8 to Paul's self-understanding as bound "to the Jew first and also to the Greek" (Rom. 1:16): "Regarding the dual role of the Ebed [Servant], Paul seems to be convinced that the latter is his primary task and the means of fulfilling the former as well . . . since he would ultimately fulfill the role of being a covenant to Israel only by means of fulfilling his gentile mission, he could not emphasize the former" (Paul: 114).

[194] This perception naturally stands in unqualified opposition to the Christian tenet that Paul conclusively broke with Judaism, rejecting all its precepts, and "converted" to Christianity: "you have heard of my conduct *when I was still in Judaism . . .* according to your former (*i.e., pre-Christian*) way of life" (BAGD: 61; emphasis added). For a review of the "traditional" view of Paul, cf. Gager: 3-42; for recent discussions of Paul's "conversion," cf. Longenecker, Road. In many ways, the

It is difficult to ascertain whether the following clause, in conjunction with verse 14, represents an elaboration of this "former life" or whether Paul is making three separate points. Here again (see verses 11-12), it may be possible to appeal to the principle of klal u-frat (the general and the specific). If "my former manner of life in Judaism" is conceived as the כלל (klal – generalisation), Paul then means by it peculiarly his resistance to the early community (the פרט [prat] – detail). To the extent that verses 13-14 represent a klal u-frat u-klal, the same meaning is derived: The generalisation may only be extended to include items which resemble the specific items mentioned (cf. Steinsaltz, Talmud: 153) (see also below).[195]

On this reading, Paul's reference to his early life is not drawn in order to denigrate it but to illustrate how "the gospel which is preached by me" cannot be "according to man" because his actions on the human level sought the unmitigated *destruction* of the gospel's adherents.[196] Both the verb (ἀναστρέφω; anastrefō) and the noun ἀναστροφή (anastrofē) – originally signifying an "(over)turning" – later took on the figurative sense of "conduct, way of life" (cf. BAGD: 61).[197] The rare Ἰουδαϊσμός (Ioudaïsmos – "Judaism") (only in these two verses in the New Testament) is witnessed to as a respected term for Jewish practice and living in contemporary Jewish sources (cf. ibid: 379).[198] The "community of God (τὴν ἐκκλησίαν τοῦ θεοῦ)" stands opposite to "Judaism" here not in the sense of being "Christian" – despite its more universal than local sense[199] –

---

claim made by the author of the Ascension of James – that Paul met a Jewish girl in Jerusalem, converted in order to marry her, and turned his enthusiasm for things Jewish into anger when she refused him (cf. Epiph.*Pan.* 30.16, [25]) – provides a more reasonable psychological (albeit historically unsupported) explanation than many modern speculations.

[195] The imperfect tense of "persecuted (ἐδίωκον)" may indicate a habitual action in this respect (cf. NASB: "used to persecute") (cf. Longenecker, Galatians: 27).

[196] Paul adduces these examples not to collapse an argument but to build his case. His allusion should not therefore be taken as an argument against his "former life" *per se*.

[197] The idea of "turning" is central to Israel's "turning away" from God to idolatry and "returning" in repentance (cf. Dt. 4:30, 5:32, 11:28, 30:9-10; 2 Kings 17:13; 2 Chron. 30:6, 9; Ps. 22:27; Jer. 3:14, 31:18-19; Lam. 3:40; Ezek. 14:6; Joel 2:12-13; Acts 11:21; 1QS 5:1, 8; Philo. *Spec.Leg.* 4.178). Jewish life is thence characterised by "walking [וללכת]" in God's ways, the term הלכה (halakhah) signifying the way in which one "walks" (cf. Lk. 1:6; 1QS 1:8, 13f, 3:9f, 18f, 4:6f; PA 2:1, 9) (cf. Strack: 6f; Safrai, Literature: 121ff; Berkovits) (see 5:13f).

[198] Cf. 2 Macc. 2:21, 8:1, 14:38; 4 Macc. 4:26. For ἰουδαΐζω (ioudaïzō – "living as a Jew"), see 2:11-14.

[199] Cf. 1 Cor. 1:2; 2 Cor. 1:1; Gal. 1:2, 22; 1 Thess. 1:1; 2 Thess. 1:1.

but within the context of an inner-Jewish struggle over the proper expression of Jewish identity (see Appendix, **Persecutor** and 6:12-16).[200]

Verse 14 adduces a second example of how Paul's gospel cannot be apprehended as "human." Here again, the hermeneutical structure of these verses helps their proper apprehension. If they constitute an example of klal u-frat u-klal, this statement – like the initial clause in verse 13 – must be limited by the specific. On this reading, Paul's "zealous[ness] for my ancestral traditions (ζηλωτὴς ὑπάρχων τῶν πατρικῶν μου παραδόσεων)" can only signify items which closely resemble his persecution of the early community. This interpretation is strengthened by Paul's own association between zeal and persecution.[201] Up until Jesus' revelation to (in) him, he had been "progressing" along a "human" trajectory, his zeal having been misplaced, being directed *against* the gospel.[202]

Verses 15-16b:

But when He who had set me apart, *even* from my mother's womb, and called me through His grace, was pleased to reveal His Son in me, that I might preach Him among the Gentiles . . .

The conjunctival δὲ (de) better carries the meaning of "Even" than "But" here: "Even when" Paul responds to God's call in Jesus, the gospel remains within divine bounds, removed from human authority.[203] Paul presents himself as having been prefigured for servanthood, on the model of the long line of biblical prophets, including the Servant of God: "Now the word of the LORD came to me saying, 'Before I formed you in the womb I knew you, and before you were born I consecrated you; I have appointed you a prophet to the nations' ויהי דבר-ה' אלי לאמר : בטרם אצורך בבטן ידעתיך

---

[200] The phrase also anticipates the "Israel of God (τὸν Ἰσραὴλ τοῦ θεοῦ)" in 6:16 (see 6:12-16). For the nature and extent of the persecution, see Appendix, **Persecutor**.

[201] Cf. Acts 22:3-4, [26:9]; Phil. 3:6.

[202] Philippians 3:1-14 serves as a palpable parallel to Paul's phraseology here. As in Galatians, his argument in this passage is that "whatever things were gain to me, those things I have counted as loss for the sake of the Messiah (ἅτινα ἦν μοι κέρδη, ταῦτα ἥγημαι διὰ τὸν Χριστὸν ζημίαν)" (Phil. 3:7). In comparison to his "confidence in the flesh" (i.e., his Jewish identity) – never to be related to as an absolute – he sets "the power of [Jesus'] resurrection (τὴν δύναμιν τῆς ἀναστάσεως αὐτοῦ)" through which he too attains to a resurrected status. The zeal of persecution in Philippians is an affirmative Jewish attribute. For Paul's credentials, see Appendix.

[203] *Contra* Betz (p. 69) – "Paul's conversion to Christianity [sic] was entirely the work of God" – Paul's reference here is to the gospel's status, not his own calling (which, as with all the prophets, comes directly from God; see verses 1-5).

"ובטרם תצא מרחם הקדשתיך נביא לגוים נתתיך" (Jer. 1:4)[204] (cf. Ps. 139:13-16) (see 2:1-10, 3:10-14, 4:1ff, 6:17, and verses 1-5, 21-24).[205]

The verb ἀφορίζω (aforizō) contains the same idea of consecration as signified in the Hebrew קדש (kadash) (cf. Lev. 20:26). Here too, Paul's thought may reflect the Servant Songs of Isaiah, which stress his selection for the task: "But you, Israel, My servant, Jacob whom I have chosen . . . Behold My servant, whom I uphold; My chosen one *in whom* My soul delights ואתה ישראל עבדי יעקב אשר בחרתיך . . . הן עבדי אתמך-בו בחירי רצתה נפשי" (Isa. 41:8, 42:1) (cf. Kim, Paul: 104-6).[206] The same calling is explicitly connected with the Servant's role as "a covenant to the people, as a light to the nations לברית עם לאור גוים" (Isa. 42:6, 49:6). As Jesus' agent (see verses 1-5), Paul is aware of Jesus "working through me, resulting in the obedience of the Gentiles . . . in the power of the Spirit (κατειργάσατο Χριστὸς δι' ἐμοῦ εἰς ὑπακοὴν ἐθνῶν . . . ἐν δυνάμει πνεύματος)" (Rom. 15:18-19). This presentiment permits him to apply passages from the Servant Songs to his own vocation (cf. ibid: 127) (see 2:1-10, 3:10-14, 4:1ff, 6:17, verses 21-24, and below).[207]

The author of the Thanksgiving Psalms utilises passages from the Servant texts in similar fashion: "[For you, O God, are] my refuge, my protection, the rock of my strength, my fortress. In you I will be guarded from every [. . .] salvation for me unto eternity. *Blank* For you have known me since my father, from the womb [. . ., . . . of] my mother you have rendered good to me, from the breasts of her who conceived me your

---

[204] Cf. Isa. 49:1, 5, 8, 52:15; Amos 7:14-15; Acts 9:15, 13:47, 22:21; Rom. 15:20f; 2 Cor. 6:2; Gal. 1:24, [2:2; Phil. 2:17, 3:17]; 1QH[a] 11:8ff; Philo, *Virt.* 63 (cf. Sandnes). For Paul's prophetic calling, see verses 1-5. Both Jeremiah and Amos, for reasons other than Paul's, were reluctant to accept God's call.

[205] Albeit expressed in traditionally anachronistic terms, the point that "Both his [Paul's] life in Judaism and his life as a Christian are viewed as having been under God's sovereignty, for he was 'set apart from birth'" (Longenecker, Galatians: 35) is well taken. It remains unfortunate, nonetheless, that the claim that Paul "converted" to Christianity from Judaism is so ensconced in Christian conception that the counterindication is called for.

[206] It seems solely a sense of Christian bias to suppose that "If . . . the ἀφορίζειν in Gal 1:15 was also intended to allude to Paul's present true set-apart-ness in contrast to his Pharisee (פרוש) days, we can understand even better why he chose the word instead of using the ἐκλέγειν/ἐκλεκτός [eklegein/eklektos - "chosen"] from Isa 41:8-9 and 42:1" (Kim, Paul: 105). The usage is even better apprehended as a form of continuity with the biblical tradition, Paul also nowhere indicating that he had ceased to be a Pharisee.

[207] For Paul's setting forth of his authority and appeal to his personal example as the grounds for his rebuke/request of his disciples, see Introduction, **Argument**; 2:1-10, 15-21 (n292), 3:1-5 (nn14, 28), 4:12-20, 5:2-12 (verse 11), 6:1ff (verses 11, 15, 17), and verses 1-5, 21-24; for Galatians as a "halakhic letter" along the lines of 4QMMT, see Introduction, **Form**; **Argument**.

compassion has been upon me, on the lap of my wet-nurse [. . .] from my youth you have shown yourself to me in the intelligence of your judgment, and with certain truth you have supported me. You have delighted me with your holy spirit . . . You have opened a [spr]ing in the mouth of your servant . . . to [be,] according to your truth, a herald [. . .] of your goodness, to proclaim to the poor the abundance of your compassion, [. . .] . . . from the spring [. . . the bro]ken of spirit, and the mourning to everlasting joy [Isa. 61:1-3]"[208] (1QHᵃ 17:28-32, 23:10, 14-15).[209]

In the context of Jesus' revelation, the verb "pleased (εὐδόκησεν)" (cf. 2 Sam. 22:20) recalls his baptism, at which time God applies to him words reminiscent of Isaiah 42:1: "This is my beloved son, in whom I am well-pleased (οὗτός ἐστιν ὁ υἱός μου ὁ ἀγαπητός, ἐν ᾧ εὐδόκησα) (Mt. 3:17) . . . Behold, My Servant, whom I uphold; My chosen one in whom My soul delights הן עבדי אתמך-בו בחירי רצתה נפשי" (cf. 1 Thess. 2:4).[210] In light of the use which Paul makes of Habakkuk 2:4, both here and later in Romans, we might also hear echoes of the LXX rendering of this verse, which translates the masoretic text to say "because a Coming One will arrive and will not linger; if he draws back, my soul shall have **no pleasure** in him (ὅτι ἐρχόμενος ἥξει καὶ οὐ μὴ χρονίσῃ. ἐὰν ὑποστείληται, οὐκ εὐδοκεῖ ἡ ψυχή μου ἐν αὐτῷ)" (see 2:1-10 [n18], 3:10ff, and 4:1-7).[211]

Paul adopts the same verb to describe how "it was the *Father's* good pleasure for all the fulness to dwell in him (ἐν αὐτῷ εὐδόκησεν πᾶν τὸ πλήρωμα κατοικῆσαι)" (Col. 1:19).[212] This verse, with its link to Jesus' receipt of the Spirit (cf. Isa. 61:1; Mt. 3:16-17) – and very possibly also the announcement of the commencement of his public ministry – anticipates 2

---

[208] *vacat* כי אתה אל[מנוסי משגבי סלע עוזי ומצודתי בכה אחסיה מכול מנ. . .] לי לפלט עד עולם
כי אתה מאבי ידעתני ומרחם [. . .] אמי נמלתה עלי ומשדי ה֯רותי רחמיך עלי ובחיק אומנתי [. . .]ה.
ומנעורי הופעתה לי בשכל משפטכה ובאמת נכון סמכתני וברוח קודשכה . . . [מק]ור פתחתה בפי
. . . ל[היות] כאמתך מבשר [. . .]. טובכה לבשר עניים לרוב רחמיכה [. . .] . . .[. . .] ממקור[. . .] דכ]אי רוח
ואבלים לשמחת עולם.

[209] For Isaiah 61:1-3, see verses 1f. The idea of being set apart from the womb obviously indicates a calling independent of Paul's own volition, coming thus directly from God. The phrase resonates with Israel's being set apart as God's holy people (cf. Ex. 19:5-6; Dt. 7:6f, 14:2), the nazirite's separation (cf. Numbers 6; Judg. 16:17; Lk. 1:15), and the division of the Qumran community from the "sons of darkness" and the "dominion of Belial" (cf. 1QS 1:1-5:22, 8:11, 13, 9:3-11; CD-A 6:14-19; 4Q418 81:1-5; 4QMMTᵈ ff14-21:7; 4Q504 ff1-2iii:5-7) (see also verses 1-5).

[210] The association with Mt. 3:17 leads naturally to the designation "son," while the quote obviously echoes Gen. 22:2, 16 and thus also bears the marks of the akedah (the binding of Isaac – the son of promise), leading back again to Isaiah 53 (see 2:15-20, 3:1ff, 4:21-31, and verses 1-5). For Isaiah 42, see below.

[211] In this sense, Paul has not "drawn back" but followed the Messiah's calling and found his being in him (cf. Acts 9:3ff, 22:3ff, 26:9ff; Phil. 1:21, 3:7-11) (see 2:1-10). The combined themes of Paul's imitation and representation of Jesus thread throughout the letter (see 2:1-10, 15-21, 3:1-5, 4:12f, 5:2-12, [24-26], 6:1ff, and above).

[212] For being "called by grace," see verses 6-10.

Corinthians 1:21-22, where Paul speaks of having been "anointed (χρίσας)" by God who "also sealed us and gave *us* the Spirit in our hearts as a pledge (ὁ καὶ σφραγισάμενος ἡμᾶς καὶ δοὺς τὸν ἀρραβῶνα τῶν πνεύματος ἐν ταῖς καρδίαις ἡμῶν)" (cf. Kim, Paul: 117-21).

Both Isaiah 42:1 and Colossians 1:19 also focus on the concept of being "in" which seems rather awkward in Paul's phrase "was pleased to reveal His son **in me** (ἀποκαλύψαι τὸν υἱὸν *ἐν ἐμοί*)" here – as if Jesus' stature were being manifested in Paul.[213] The affinities – prophetic calling and revelation – with Ezekiel's experience are certainly apt: "Such *was* the appearance of the likeness of the glory of the LORD. And when I saw *it*, I fell on my face and heard a voice speaking. Then He said to me, 'Son of man, stand on your feet that I may speak with you!' And as He spoke to me the Spirit entered me and set me on my feet; and I heard *Him* speaking to me מראה דמות כבוד-ה' ואראה ואפל על-פני ואשמע קול מדבר: ויאמר אלי בן-אדם עמד על-רגליך ואדבר אתך: ותבא בי רוח כאשר דבר אלי ותעמדני על-רגלי ואשמע קול מדבר אלי" (Ezek. 1:28-2:2).[214]

Not only are the prophets sent in the power of the Spirit but s/he who is sent is also commissioned in the bestowal of the Spirit.[215] "This experience of the endowment of the Spirit at his [Paul's] conversion/call explains best both his constant practice of connecting the *Gläubigwerden* [coming to faith] of his converts with the endowment of the Spirit and the

---

[213] The idea of pleasure is associated with revelation in Mt. 11:25-27//Lk. 10:21-22: "I praise Thee, O Father, Lord of heaven and earth, that Thou didst hide these things from *the* wise and intelligent and didst reveal them to babes. Yes, Father, for thus it was well-pleasing in Thy sight. All things have been handed over to me by my Father; and no one knows the son, except the Father; nor does anyone know the Father, except the son, and anyone to whom the son wills to reveal *Him* (ἐξομολογοῦμαί σοι, πάτερ, κύριε τοῦ οὐρανοῦ καὶ τῆς γῆς, ὅτι ἔκρυψας ταῦτα ἀπὸ σοφῶν καὶ συνετῶν καὶ ἀπεκάλυψας αὐτὰ νηπίοις· ναὶ ὁ πατήρ, ὅτι οὕτως εὐδοκία ἐγένετο ἔμπροσθέν σοι. Πάντα μοι παρεδόθη ὑπὸ τοῦ πατρός μου, καὶ οὐδεὶς ἐπιγινώσκει τὸν υἱὸν εἰ μὴ ὁ πατήρ, οὐδὲ τὸν πατέρα τις ἐπιγινώσκει εἰ μὴ ὁ υἱὸς καὶ ᾧ ἐὰν βούληται ὁ υἱὸς ἀποκαλύψαι).

[214] Cf. Le Cornu and Shulam: 1402. Paul's calling is associated not only with that of Ezekiel but also with Jonah's, the "verbal analogy" of the invocation to "arise" linking all three (cf. Jon. 1:2, 3:2; Acts 9:6). Jonah is, of course, the biblical prophet commanded to go to the "Gentiles" – bound to Paul by the further association with "Tarshish" (cf. Jon. 1:3) (cf. Le Cornu and Shulam: 490, 521) (see also verses 21-24). For Jesus as (the) "representative" of human destiny, see Introduction, **Theological pointers** (Faithfulness); for the language of "revealing," see also 3:22-25; for the motif of glory, see below.

[215] Cf. Num. 11:29; 1 Sam. 10:5-10; Neh. 9:30; Isa. 48:16, 61:1; Joel 2:28; Zech. 7:12; Jn. 3:34; Eph. 3:5; 2 Pet. 1:21; 1QS 8:16; 4Q381 f69:4. For Paul's call to his disciples to imitate him in the Messiah, see 4:12-20 and 6:1f (verses 11, 17) [verses 1-5].

overwhelming importance that the Holy Spirit had in his life, thought, and work" (Kim, Paul: 126).[216]

The thought of Jesus being revealed in Paul may also be allied with Paul's declaration of ambassadorship in 2 Corinthians 5:18f: "... we are ambassadors for the Messiah, as though God were entreating through us; we beg you on behalf of the Messiah, be reconciled to God ... And working together *with him*, we also urge you not to receive the grace of God in vain – for He says, 'AT THE ACCEPTABLE TIME I LISTENED TO YOU, AND ON THE DAY OF SALVATION I HELPED YOU'; behold, now is 'THE ACCEPTABLE TIME,' behold now is 'THE DAY OF SALVATION'"[217] (2 Cor. 5:20, 6:1-2).[218]

The reference to the revelation appears primarily to relate to Paul's experience on the road to Damascus.[219] His proclamation of Jesus as the Son of God (ἐκήρυσσεν τὸν Ἰησοῦν ὅτι οὗτός ἐστιν ὁ υἱὸς τοῦ θεοῦ; ekēryssen ton Iēsoun hoti houtos estin ho huios tou theou) (Acts 9:20) – based on "proof (συμβιβάζων)" (cf. Acts 9:22) – demonstrates his pharisaic training and acquaintance with the biblical texts. "Son of God" appears to have become an accepted title of the Messiah during this period as an extension of Israel's status as God's collective "son" – focusing on the king as God's anointed leader.[220] If Psalm 2 – a text which simultaneously identifies the king as God's anointed and as His son – lies behind Jesus' words in Acts 9:15 in its reference to the "nations," "peoples," "kings of the earth," and "rulers," Paul may have understood his task as declaring God's Son before all those who take counsel against God and His Anointed,

---

[216] For the Spirit as the imparter of knowledge, see verses 11-12; for the Spirit as the inspiration of Scripture and the fulfilment of God's promise to Abraham, see 3:1ff. Instructive in this regard is the Thanksgiving psalmist's claim regarding "the mystery which you have concealed in me בי חבת ואתה" (1QHᵃ 13:25). The fact that Isaiah 42 plays a central role in the "Jesus tradition" may also feed into the "narrative sub-structure" of Paul's gospel (cf. Hays, Faith; Kim, Paul: 126).

[217] Ὑπὲρ Χριστοῦ οὖν πρεσβεύομεν ὡς τοῦ θεοῦ παρακαλοῦντος δι᾿ ἡμῶν· δεόμεθα ὑπὲρ Χριστοῦ, καταλλάγητε τῷ θεῷ ... Συνεργοῦντες δὲ καὶ παρακαλοῦμεν μὴ εἰς κενὸν τὴν χάριν τοῦ θεοῦ δέξασθαι ὑμᾶς· λέγει γάρ· καιρῷ δεκτῷ ἐπήκουσά σου καὶ ἐν ἡμέρᾳ σωτηρίας ἐβοήθησά σοι. ἰδοὺ νῦν καιρὸς εὐπρόσδεκτος, ἰδοὺ νῦν ἡμέρα σωτηρίας.

[218] The quotation – once again – is from Isa. 49:8 which, although originally referring to the Servant, Paul unhesitatingly applies to himself and his co-workers. He had employed the same device, with respect to Isa. 49:6, in his speech in Pisidian Antioch (Galatia) (cf. Acts 13:47), an exegetical stance supported by the author of 11QMelch, who interprets the "mountains" of Isa. 52:7 as signifying the prophets (cf. 11QMelch 2:17).

[219] If the δι᾿ ἀποκαλύψεως (di apokalypseōs; lit.: "by revelation") of verse 12 is taken as generic, the incident on the way to Damascus constitutes a primary instance. For the possible significance of Damascus, see below.

[220] Cf. Ex. 4:22; Dt. 32:6; 2 Sam. 7:14; Ps. 2:7, 89:26f; Prov. 30:4; Mt. 16:16, 26:63; Lk. 4:41; Jn. 11:27, 20:31; 1 En. 105:2; 4 Ez. 7:28f, 13:32, 37, 52, 14:9.

whom God warns to serve His Son to order to avoid being destroyed (cf.
Le Cornu and Shulam: 507-8).[221]

If the echo of Melchizedek is still making its presence felt, Paul's
thought here may also be reflected in the passage presenting the "new
priest" in the seventh jubilee, a priest who will be glorified by all the
nations:

> And then the Lord will raise up a new priest to whom all the
> words of the Lord will be revealed. He shall effect the judgment
> of truth over the earth for many days. And his star shall rise in
> heaven like a king; kindling the light of knowledge as day is
> illumined by the sun. And he shall be extolled by the whole
> inhabited world. This one will shine forth like the sun in the
> earth; he shall take away all darkness from under heaven, and
> there shall be peace in all the earth. The heavens shall greatly
> rejoice in his days and the earth shall be glad; the clouds will be
> filled with joy and the knowledge of the Lord will be poured out
> on the earth like the water of the seas. And the angels of glory of
> the Lord's presence will be made glad by him. The heavens will
> be opened, and from the temple of glory sanctification will come
> upon him, with a fatherly voice, as from Abraham to Isaac. And
> the glory of the Most High shall burst forth upon him. And the
> spirit of understanding and sanctification shall rest upon him [in
> the water]. For he shall give the majesty of the Lord to those who
> are his sons in truth forever. (Test.Levi 18:2-8)[222] (cf. Shulam and
> Le Cornu: 138f, 447f)

The question of whether or not Paul grasped the full implications of
his calling at the moment of revelation has long been debated (cf.
Longenecker, Road). The passage from Isaiah 42:1 (see above) appears to
constitute much of the scriptural support on which Paul bases his
commission (cf. Kim, Paul: 101-27, and for the following discussion).[223]
God's pleasure in Isaiah 40f is to "call (קראתיך; ἐκάλεσα)" His Servant and
to "set him apart (cf. בחר; ἐκλέγω/ἀφορίζω/ἁγιάζω)" to preach God's
judgment/righteousness (משפט; mishpat) and to be a "covenant to the

---

[221] Paul also quotes Psalm 2 in his homily in the synagogue in Antioch (cf. Acts
13:33). Similar imagery appears in Daniel 7, where the Son of man is said to receive
"dominion, glory and a kingdom, that all the peoples, nations, and *men of every
language* might serve him שלטן ויקר ומלכו וכל עממיא אמיא ולשניא לה יפלחון" (Dan.
7:14).

[222] Cf. Jn. 1:9, 8:12; 2 Cor. 4:4f; Rev. 21:23f; Test.Jud. 24:5; 1Q28b 4:27f (cf. Hays,
Echoes: 70-73). For Melchizedek, see verses 1f.

[223] For the centrality of Scripture for Paul, see Introduction, **Theological pointers**;
2:15-21, 3:1ff, 4:1-7, 21-31, and verses 13-14 (n187).

people, as a light to the Gentiles" (לברית עם לאור גוים; εἰς διαθήκην γένους εἰς φῶς ἐθνῶν) in the strength of the Spirit (cf. Acts 26:16-18).

This account corresponds to the attitude articulated in 11QMelchizedek wherein the heavenly figure brings judgment/salvation (see verses 1f), Paul acting "according to the order of Melchizedek" as a representative on behalf first of his own people – "a covenant to the people" – and then to the Gentiles (here in contrast to 11QMelch?) in fulfilment of God's promise of future justice and salvation in the earth (cf. Isa. 42:4, 49:6) (see also 3:22-25).[224] It would appear on this reading that Paul interpreted his calling in Damascus (cf. 2 Cor. 4:4-6) in the light of the Servant motif, charged with opening the eyes of the blind and delivering them from the power of evil (see 2:1-10, 3:10-14, 4:1ff, 6:17, verses 1-5, 21-24, and above).[225]

Paul's later self-descriptions clearly and unambiguously confirm this calling: An "apostle of Gentiles (ἐθνῶν ἀπόστολος)" (Rom. 11:13) from Jesus "through whom we have received grace and apostleship to bring about *the* obedience of faith among all the Gentiles, for his name's sake (δι' οὗ ἐλάβομεν χάριν καὶ ἀποτολὴν εἰς ὑπακοὴν πίστεως ἐν πᾶσιν τοῖς ἔθνεσιν ὑπὲρ τοῦ ὀνόματος αὐτοῦ)" (Rom. 1:5); "a minister of the Messiah Jesus to the Gentiles, ministering as a priest the gospel of God, that *my* offering of the Gentiles may become acceptable, sanctified by the Holy Spirit"[226] (Rom. 15:16); "to me, the very least of all saints, this grace was given, to preach to the Gentiles the unfathomable riches of the Messiah ('Εμοι τῷ ἐλαχιστοτέρῳ πάντων ἁγίων ἐδόθη ἡ χάρις αὕτη, τοῖς ἔθνεσιν εὐαγγελίσασθαι τὸ ἀνεξιχνίαστον πλοῦτος τοῦ Χριστοῦ)" (Eph. 3:8).[227]

---

[224] This accords well with the idea of Jesus as a "representative" figure in facilitating, as it were, redemption for those who are faithful to him through his own faithfulness (cf. Hays, Faith) (see Introduction, **Theological pointers** [Faithfulness]; 2:15-21, 3:1ff, 4:1f, 21-31). For Jesus and the Son of man/enochic tradition in Rom. 2:16, cf. Shulam and Le Cornu: 94-95.

[225] Kim reinforces his claim that Paul understood his calling to the Gentiles immediately upon his encounter with Jesus with the suggestion that Kedar and Sela in Isa. 42:11 both refer to Arabia, the former giving its name to the Nabateans, the latter being translated in the LXX as Πέτρα (Petra): "If Paul went to Arabia 'immediately,' his interpretation of his call in the light of Isa 42 must have been equally immediate!" (Paul: 104) (see also verses 16c-17 [n254]).

[226] λειτουργὸν Χριστοῦ 'Ιησοῦ εἰς τὰ ἔθνη, ἱερουργοῦντα τὸ εὐαγγέλιον τοῦ θεοῦ, ἵνα γένηται ἡ προσφορὰ τῶν ἐθνῶν εὐπρόσδεκτος, ἡγιασμένη ἐν πνεύματι ἁγίῳ.

[227] Cf. Acts 9:15, 13:46, 18:6, 22:15, 21, 26:17-20, 28:28; Col. 1:23; 1 Tim. 2:7; 2 Tim. 4:17. Nanos has done much to demonstrate that the long tradition of Christian commentators who, like Betz, assume that "Paul's commission to preach is clearly limited to the Gentiles. The formulation 'among the Gentiles' suggests that Paul's mission includes the entire world population apart from the Jews" (p. 72) should be

The fact that Paul so clearly and directly associates his calling as one to the Gentiles – at such an early date – may well serve as a witness to contemporary Jewish outreach to the nations. Had the task been unknown or unintelligible in the current climate Paul would not only have failed to fathom its meaning himself but would also presumably have needed to explain the idea of an "apostle to the Gentiles" to others.[228]

Verses 16c-17:

. . . I did not immediately consult with flesh and blood, nor did I go up to Jerusalem to those who were apostles before me; but I went away to Arabia, and returned once more to Damascus.

These verses constitute Paul's physical proof of his divine commissioning. In relation to his post-revelatory experience, the evidence that his gospel is "not according to man" is to be found in the fact that he did not "consult with flesh and blood (οὐ προσανεθέμην σαρκὶ καὶ αἵματι)."[229] The adverb "immediately (εὐθέως)" is characteristic of miraculous and supernatural phenomena[230] and "call narratives" alike (cf. Mt. 4:20, 22; Mk. 1:18). To the extent that the three clauses in these verses clarify Paul's response to the call, it makes little difference whether the adverb should be referred to its immediate object or (also) to the "affirmative action" of travelling to Arabia (cf. Longenecker, Galatians: 33).[231]

The compound verb προσανατίθημι (prosanatithēmi) occurs only here and in 2:6. In the middle voice (as found in both instances), it denotes "betake oneself to," that meaning being extended to signify "consult," "confer," "communicate with" (ibid). The two instances present complementary aspects of the same action: Here, Paul denies that he

---

revised (a long overdue step) to recognise Paul's "two-step" pattern – "to the Jew first and also the Greek" – as characteristic of his whole ministry (cf. Irony: 238-88) (see 3:10-14 and 4:1f). Cf. also Hays' wonderfully-wrought witness in Echoes. For the view that the "mystery" to which Paul repeatedly returns constitutes the redemption of the Gentiles prior to the final restoration of Israel, cf. Kim, Paul: 242f; Shulam and Le Cornu: 125ff, 303-13, 325-92; Le Cornu and Shulam: 751-55, 994-97.

[228] In this sense, the current reading of Galatians itself suggests the presence of people who, if not proselytes themselves nor wishing to be so, yet promote conversion to Judaism (see Introduction, **Occasion and circumstances** and 2:15-21 [n269]).

[229] Betz's mystification (p. 72) over the "negativity" of this statement seems in itself mysterious: Not only has Paul consistently employed negative terms to define his gospel (cf. verses 1, 11-12) but these clauses cite the central causes whereby he excludes the human element in its transmission. Paul's "obedience" is not the issue under investigation here.

[230] Cf. Mt. 8:3, 20:34; Mk. 10:52; Lk. 8:44, 13:13; Jn. 5:9; Acts 3:7, 9:18, 12:23; 16:18.

[231] εὐθέως is, in fact, a pauline hapax (only occurrence). The affirmation which commentators seek (cf. Burton: 53-54) is contained in the negative: What Paul did was "not consult." For negative arguments, see verses 1-5 (verse 1).

sought advice; in 2:6 he denies that he received it.[232] In rabbinic terms, Paul is asserting that, with respect to his gospel to the Gentiles, he intepreted his own teacher's dictum: "Rabban Gamaliel said: Appoint a teacher for thyself and avoid doubt רבן גמליאל אומר: עשה לך רב והסתלק מן הספק (PA 1:16) – not in reference to a human guide but with respect to a directly divine source.[233]

The Greek σαρκὶ καὶ αἵματι (sarki kai haimati) is a literal rendering of the Hebrew בשר ודם (basar va-dam), an expression which signifies human beings in contrast to heavenly bodies.[234] The generic identification is significant in that Paul's point pertains to human beings in general rather than to specific individuals. In other words, *contra* many commentators, his "defence" of his gospel is not against charges that he is dependent upon the Jerusalem Apostles but an affirmation of its divine – rather than human – source (see verses 1-5, 11-12) (cf. Nanos, Inter: 402-3). This view is supported by the fact that immediately following reference to Jesus' revelation in him Paul speaks of the Apostles as specific instances of "flesh and blood."

The Apostles are important as those who were commissioned like Paul, as "those who were before me (τοὺς πρὸ ἐμοῦ ἀποστόλους)" – sharing the same calling as his own "untimely" one (the preposition being temporal rather than indicative of status). Their location in Jerusalem adduces an added element of *human* authority, Jerusalem constituting the "navel of the earth [טבּור הארץ]," lying at the "center of the nations," the "chief of the mountains" to which "many peoples will come" and from which will go forth "the word of the LORD [דבר-יהי]"[235] (cf. Poorthuis and Safrai).[236]

In keeping with Jerusalem's elevated status (both topographical and "typological"), people are normally said to "go up" to the city and to

---

[232] For the precise understanding of this verse, see 2:1-10.

[233] Many commentators apply this saying to one who is himself a Sage, the import being that a person should choose another scholar whom he (*sic*) respects as a greater authority with whom to consult in cases of difficulty and doubt before giving a legal decision. For Paul, this figure is God as communicated through His son, Jesus. For Rabban Gamaliel, see Appendix, **Gamaliel**.

[234] Cf. Mt. 16:17; 1 Cor. 15:50; Eph. 6:12; Heb. 2:14; Sir. 14:18, 17:31; Naz. 9:5; Sot. 8:1; Tos.Ber. 7:18; Tos.Sot. 14:4.

[235] Cf. Isa. 2:2f; Ezek. 5:5, 38:12; Mic. 4:2.

[236] The LXX speaks of "the faithful metropolis Zion (μητρόπολις πιστὴ Σιὼν)" (Isa. 1:26), and ancient Jewish cartographical schemes place Jerusalem geographically at the centre of the whole world, the orientation of lands and peoples all being linked to the city (cf. Dt. 32:8; LXX Ps. 87:5; 1 En. 26:1; 4 Ez. 10:17; Philo, *In Flac.* 45-46; *Leg.* 281-83; *Conf.Ling.* 77-78; Ex.R. 23:10) (cf. Gill and Gempf: 483ff). Paul is not detracting from Jerusalem's divine and eschatological status (cf. 4:26) here but merely emphasising that he did not receive counsel even from the highest of earthly authorities.

"come down" from it, even when they are geographically as high or higher.[237] The psalms record a tradition of the "songs of ascent [שיר המעלות] " sung by pilgrims on the way to the holy city (cf. Psalms 120-134) (cf. Le Cornu and Shulam: 18-21, 397-98).

Jerusalem

Two Hebrew forms – ירושלם (Yerushalem) and ירושלים (Yerushalayim) (cf. Jer. 26:18) – occur in the biblical texts and most scholars concur that the former is more original (cf. NBD: 615). This is substantiated by the abbreviation to שָׁלֵם (Salem) in Psalm 76:2 (cf. Gen. 14:18) and by the Aramaic ירושלם (Yerushlem) (cf. Ezra 5:14). If the name is indeed compound, שלם (shalam) represents "peace,"[238] the first part possibly designating "possession" or "foundation" (cf. ירש [yarash]). The Assyrian inscriptions referring to the city long before David captured it (see below) as Ursalim (Ur-sa li-im-mu) suggest that the name is not Hebrew but derives from the cognate Assyrian meaning "city of peace."

The Greek Ἰερουσαλήμ (Ierousalēm) (cf. Mt. 23:37) transliterates the Hebrew ירושלןים. The hellenised formation –Ἱεροσόλυμα [Hierosolyma – neut.pl.] (cf. Mt. 2:1) – appears to represent an attempt to give the city a Greek etymology. The designation is compounded of ἱερός (hieros – "sacred") and Σόλυμοι (Solymoi) – a nation of Asia Minor with whom some gentile historians fancied the Jews were connected.[239] The adjective "sacred" recalls Jerusalem's title as the "holy city [עיר הקודש],"[240] presumably in allusion to the Temple (cf. הר הקדוש [har ha-kadosh] – "the holy mountain."[241] The difference between the two forms possibly reflects a gentile and Jewish atmosphere respectively (cf. Bruce, Acts: 101).

The city lies between the two major ancient highways in the Middle East, the so-called *Via Maris* ("Way of the Sea [דרך הים]" [cf. Isa. 9:1]) and the King's Highway (דרך המלך; derekh ha-melekh) (cf. Num. 20:17, 21:22), as well as dissecting the north-south route of the land of Israel (see also below). It is possibly first mentioned in connection with Abraham and Melchizedek, King of Salem.[242] A Jebusite city when David first captured it, it was known as ציון (Zion) and later called after David ("David's city").[243] The appellation "city of David [עיר דוד]" carries messianic connotations, the

---

[237] Cf. Ex. 34:24; 2 Sam. 8:7; 1 Kings 12:27; Ezra 1:3; Mt. 20:17-18; Mk. 10:32-33; Lk. 2:42; Jn. 5:1, 11:55; Acts 11:2, 13:31, 15:2, 18:22, 21:[4], 12, 15, 24:1, 11, 22, 25:9; Gal. 2:1-2; 1 Esd. 2:5; 1 Macc. 4:36-37; 3 Macc. 3:16.

[238] Cf. Heb. 7:2; Gen.R. 56:10.

[239] Cf. Jos.*CA* 1.173; Tac.*Hist.* 5.2; Juv.*Sat.* 6.544.

[240] Cf. Neh. 11:1, 18; Isa. 48:2, 52:1.

[241] Cf. Isa. 27:13; Jer. 31:23; Zech. 8:3.

[242] Cf. Gen. 14:18; [Ps. 76:2, 110:1-4].

[243] Cf. 2 Sam. 5:7; Jos.*Ant.* 7.65f.

Messiah being expected to be a scion of the house of David[244] who was to deliver his people out of Zion.[245] Both the Messiah and Jerusalem are also said to bear God's name.[246]

Jewish devotion to Jerusalem was first and foremost due to the Temple where God's presence resided and which was the only sanctuary where the worship of God was performed as laid down in the Torah.[247] The half-shekel for its upkeep and the obligatory sacrifices, plus tithes and dues, first fruits, and other priestly gifts, were sent from all the diaspora communities, whose members also brought these on regular pilgrimages to the feasts.[248] The diaspora communities further depended on Jerusalem for the intercalation of the moon and the regulation of the intercalary month (Adar II).[249] Proselytes were also required to bring a sacrifice to the city to complete their conversion.[250]

During the Second Temple period, the establishment of the Great Sanhedrin further increased the city's status as the country's civic and halakhic centre, the Sanhedrin also serving as a major source of Torah education. Herod's royal court also played an influential part in the city's importance. The gymnastics, musical performances, dramatic spectacles, and chariot races which Herod arranged in the city's hippodrome, gymnasium, and theatre, together with considerable game-hunting, constituted a powerful attraction to the city both among the local hellenised population and to foreign visitors (cf. Jos.*Ant.* 15.268ff). Many writers and other educated Greeks were guests at the court and the numerous connections which the royal house maintained brought ambassadors, messengers, and bodyguards to the city.

The city gained a reputation amongst non-Jews in the last decades before its destruction, its fame spreading through the entire civilised world (cf. Safrai and Stern: 344). Polybius identified the Jews as those "who live near the Temple of Jerusalem (οἱ περὶ τὸ ἱερὸν τὸ προσαγορευόμενον Ἱεροσόλυμα κατοικοῦντες)" – concerning whose "renown (ἐπιφανείας)" he desired to elaborate (Jos.*Ant.* 12.136), while Pliny described Jerusalem as the "most renowned among the towns of the East, and not only of Judaea (longe clarissima urbium orientis, non Iudaeae modo)" (*Nat.Hist.* 5.15.70).

---

[244] Cf. 2 Sam. 7:11-16; Psalm 89; Isa. 9:6-7, 11:1, 10; Mt. 9:27, 12:23; Mk. 12:35; Num.R. 13:11-12; Suk. 52b; Sot. 48b.

[245] Cf. Isa. 41:27, 52:7; Gen.R. 63:8; Lev.R. 30:16; Mid.Ps. 110:4; Pes. 5a; Meg. 17b.

[246] Cf. Mid.Ps. 21:1-2; Lam.R. 1.16.51.

[247] Cf. 1 Kings 8:12ff; 2 Chron. 6:4ff; Philo, *In Flac.* 45; *Leg.* 279; Sif.Dt. 154, 352; Kel. 1:6-9.

[248] Cf. Neh. 10:33; Jos.*Ant.* 14.112, 18.312-13; Philo, *Spec.Leg.* 1.69ff; *Leg.* 156; Meg.Ta'anit, beg.; Naz. 5:4; Ta'anit 4:2; Shek. 3:1-4; Tos.Shek. 2:3; ARN^a 20:1; Cicero, *Pro Flac.* 28.67, 69; Tac.*Hist.* 5.5.1.

[249] Cf. Sifra, Emor 9; JShevi. 10, 2, 39c.

[250] Cf. Ker. 2:1; Ker. 8b-9a (see Introduction, **Occasion and circumstances**).

Despite Pompey's earlier victory, the inscription to Titus set up subsequent to the Temple's destruction depicts it as a city which had never before been captured ("urbem Hierosolymam omnibus ante se ducibus regibus gentibusque aut frustra petitam aut omnino intemptatam delevit").

Verse 17: Following his two "negative actions," Paul now says what he *did* do: "I went away to Arabia (ἀπῆλθον εἰς ᾿Αραβίαν)." Much commentorial effort has been expended in ascertaining both the precise location of "Arabia" and the character and motive of Paul's visit. On the majority supposition that Arabia signifies the Nabatean kingdom – which presumably did not include Damascus during this period – many scholars have suggested that Paul engaged in a "Nabatean mission" (cf. Riesner: 75-89, 256-63). None of the varied explanations provide conclusive arguments – understandably so in light of the dearth of evidence. Given the importance which this "positive action" carries in Paul's argument here, the speculation may perhaps be entertained that the reference to Arabia should be taken in conjunction with Paul's second allusion to the location in the letter. Without breaking the rules of the "allegory" in which Paul explicitly warns his readers he is engaging, Paul clearly locates Mount Sinai in Arabia in 4:25 (Σινᾶ ὄρος ἐστὶν ἐν τῇ ᾿Αραβίᾳ; Sina oros estin en tē Arabia).[251]

In the context of Paul's claim that his gospel is "prophetic," its source coming directly from God Himself, an assertion that he went to the place of מתן תורה (matan Torah – the "giving of the Torah") carries the greatest possible weight (cf. Schwartz).[252] A midrashic tradition associates Mount Sinai with God's offering of the Torah to all nations: "*The Lord came from Sinai and rose from Seir unto them, He shined forth from Mount Paran* (Dt. 33:2). And it is also written, *God cometh from Teman* (Hab. 3:3). What did He seek in Seir, and what did He seek in Mount Paran? – R. Johanan says: This teaches us that the Holy One, blessed be He, offered the Torah to every nation and every tongue, but none accepted it, until He came to Israel who received it"[253] (AZ 2b).[254] "The Israelites were inquiring: 'Whence cometh

---

[251] Although the inclusion of the Sinai Peninsula within Arabian territory is normally undisputed, it remains unclear whether Sinai was understood during this period to lie in this region or beyond the Gulf of Akaba (cf. Riesner: 258; Schwartz). For the function of Mount Sinai in the allegory itself, see 4:21-31.

[252] Lightfoot grasped something of this conjecture in asking whether Paul did not acquire his understanding of the law through meditation on the Damascus-event during a pilgrimage to Sinai (cf. pp. 87-90). For the suggestion that here again Paul is reliant on Isaiah 42, both Kedar and Sela in verse 11 apparently alluding to Arabia, cf. Kim, Paul: 103-4 (see verses 15-16b [n227]).

[253] ויאמר: ה' מסיני בא וזרח משעיר למו. וכתיב: אלוה מתימן יבוא וגו'. מאי בעי בשעיר ומאי בעי בפאראן?אמר ר' יוחנן: מלמד שההחזירה הקדוש ברוך הוא על כל אומה ולשון ולא קבלוה עד שבא אצל ישראל וקבלוה.

the Lord, from the east or south?' as it is said: *The Lord came from Sinai, and rose* [in the east] *from Seir unto them* (Dt. 33:2), and it is written *God cometh from Teman* [the south] (Hab. 3:3). It says: *And all the people perceived the thunderings* (Ex. 20:18). Note that it does not say 'the thunder' but '*the thunderings*'; wherefore R. Johanan said that God's voice, as it was uttered, split up into seventy voices, in seventy languages, so that all the nations should understand"[255] (Ex.R. 5:9) (cf. Le Cornu and Shulam: 58-62).[256]

While it appears true that Jerusalem remained central to Paul's sense of his calling to the Gentiles (cf. Rom. 15:19), the fact that the latter occurred on the "road to Damascus" – whence he returns following his visit to Arabia – may possess significance of its own. Paul explicitly identifies his calling as being "to preach him [Jesus] among the Gentiles (ἵνα εὐαγγελίζομαι αὐτὸν ἐν τοῖς ἔθνεσιν)." Some twenty years later, he apparently alludes back to this experience in terms which recall the light of creation: "For God, who said, 'Light shall shine out of darkness,' is the One who has shone in our hearts to give the light of the knowledge of the glory of God in the face of the Messiah"[257] (2 Cor. 4:6).[258] The allusions in this text also include the Messiah's light shining in the darkness in which the Gentiles were considered to walk according to Isaiah 9:2: "The people who walk in darkness will see a great light; those who live in a dark land, the

---

[254] Cf. Lam.R. 3.1.1. Seir frequently represents Edom in rabbinic literature, a further synonym for Rome (see 4:21-31). Paran symbolises Ishmael's descendants (cf. Gen. 21:21).

[255] והיו ישראל אומרים: מהיכן הקדוש ברוך הוא בא - מן המזרח או מן הדרום, שנאמר: ה' מסיני בא וזרח משעיר למו; וכתיב: אלוה מתימן יבא; ואומר: וכל העם רואים את הקולות. "הקולי" אין כתיב כאן אלא "הקולות". אמר ר' יוחנן: היה הקול יוצא ונחלק לע' קולות לע' לשון כדי שישמעו כל האומות.

[256] Cf. Tanh.Shmot 25; Dev. 2; Mid.Ps. 92:3; Ex.R. 5:9; Sot. 7:5; Tos.Sot. 8:6; JSot. 31a; Shab. 88b. In its role as a "wilderness" (cf. Ex. 19:1; Num. 1:1), Sinai also constitutes a refuge, the wilderness being, at times, a place in which God bestows His presence and reveals Himself (cf. Jer. 2:2f; Hos. 9:10, 11:1f, 13:5; Amos 2:10; Heb. 13:12f; Rev. 12:6) – as to Hagar (cf. Gen. 16:7), to Moses (cf. Ex. 3:1f; Num. 3:14; Acts 7:30f), to Elijah (cf. 1 Kings 19:4-18), to John the Baptist (cf. Mt. 3:1, 11:7); and to Jesus (cf. Mt. 4:11; Mk. 1:35; Lk. 5:16; Jn. 11:54) (Jesus alternatively ascending a mountain [cf. Mt. 5:1ff, 14:23, 17:1ff; Lk. 6:12]) (cf. Pritz, oral communication). Paul follows in this prophetic tradition (see verses 15-16b). The "theology of mountains" reflected in these passages reappears, in different form, in the allegory of 4:22-31 (see 4:21-31).

[257] ὅτι ὁ θεὸς ὁ εἰπών· ἐκ σκότους φῶς λάμψει, ὃς ἔλαμψεν ἐν ταῖς καρδίαις ἡμῶν πρὸς φωτισμὸν τῆς γνώσεως τῆς δόξης τοῦ θεοῦ ἐν προσώπῳ ['Ιησοῦ] Χριστοῦ.

[258] Gen. 1:3; Acts 26:18; 1 Pet. 2:9. The reference to Genesis here may well underlie Paul's understanding of the "new creation" and the "new things" (cf. Rom. 6:4; 2 Cor. 5:17; Gal. [3:28], 6:15; – with their biblical allusions: Isa. 42:9, 43:18-19) (see 5:26-29 and 6:12-16).

העם ההלכים בחשך ראו אור גדול ישבֵי בארץ צלמות אור will shine on them light
נגה עליהם."²⁵⁹

The Messiah's light/glory is "a light of the nations so that My salvation may reach to the end of the earth- ונתתיך לאור גוים להיות ישועתי עד קצה הארץ" (Isa. 49:6).²⁶⁰ This light is linked with the "stem (חֹטר; choter)/ branch (נצר; netzer)/root (שֹרש; shoresh)" of Jesse, to whom "the nations will resort ידרשו" "אליו גוים who "will stand as a signal for the peoples עמד לנס עמים" (Isa. 11:1, 10). It is also associated with the "star" which shall "come forth from Jacob דרך כוכב מיעקב" (Num. 24:17), and thence with the "scepter from Judah/Israel שבט מיהודה/מישראל" to whom shall be the "obedience of the peoples ולו יקהת עמים" (Gen. 49:10; Num. 24:17).²⁶¹

Contemporary Jewish literature attributes messianic connotations to the "north [צפון]" – the land of the Gentiles.²⁶² A midrash interprets the reference to the "north" in Isaiah 41:25 with regard to the Messiah: ". . . the Messianic King whose place is in the north will come and rebuild the Sanctuary which is situated in the south. This is [indicated by] what is written: *I have roused up one from the north, and he is come* (Isa. 41:25) מלך המשיח שנתון בצפון יבא ויבנה בית המקדש הנתון בדרום, הדא הוא דכתיב: העירותי מצפון ויאת ממזרח שמש" (Lev.R. 9:6).²⁶³ Josephus also maintains that Damascus lay within the territory of the tribe of Naphtali, which Isaiah associates with "the people who walk in darkness will see a great light; those who live in a dark land, the light will shine on them העם ההלכים בחשך ראו אור גדול ישבי בארץ צלמות אור נגה עליהם" (Isa. 9:1) (cf. *Ant.* 5.86).

On the basis of such texts, it is possible that Paul's perception of the eschatological ingathering of the Gentiles in proximity to Damascus may not have been fortuitous (cf. Riesner: 237-41; Le Cornu and Shulam: 480-81).²⁶⁴ As a bearer of the Messiah's light to the Gentiles, Paul's phrase "that I might preach him (ἵνα εὐαγγελίζομαι αὐτὸν)" may – once again – allude

---

²⁵⁹ Cf. Isa. 9:1 (LXX): ὁ λαὸς ὁ πορευόμενος ἐν σκότει, ἴδετε φῶς μέγα· οἱ κατοικοῦντες ἐν χώρᾳ καὶ σκιᾷ θανάτου, φῶς λάμψει ἐφ' ὑμᾶς.

²⁶⁰ Cf. Isa. 42:6, 51:4, 60:1f.

²⁶¹ Cf. 1Q28b 5:23-29; CD-A 7:18-21; 1QM 11:6-7; 4QTest 1:12-13; 4Q161 ff8-10:11-25; [4Q522 f9ii:3-11]; 11Q14 f1i:7-14; Gen.R. 2:5, 85:1, 97 [NV], 99:8; Lev.R. 31:11; Dt.R. 1:20; Lam.R. 1.16.51.

²⁶² Cf. 1 En. 13:7ff; Test.Levi 2:3ff; CD-A 7:14f; Lev.R. 9:6; Num.R. 13:2; Cant.R. 4.8.2.

²⁶³ Cf. Num.R. 13:2; Cant.R. 4.16.1. The association may have arisen from the dual meaning of the Hebrew צפון (zaphon), which also signifies "hidden" or "laid up." The latter motif is a well-known messianic motif (cf. 1 En. 62:7; 4 Ez. 7:26-[44]; Ex.R. 2:4; Num.R. 11:2; [Dt.R. 1:19]; Ruth R. 5:6; Eccl.R. 1.9.1; PRK 5:8; Mid.Sam. 14).

²⁶⁴ The difficulty attendant upon Paul's restraint from going up to Jerusalem – which, on an eschatological reading, (Mount) Zion replaces Sinai as the place of God's dwelling – presumably indicates, as we have suggested, a modification of the Apostles' location in the city rather than any depreciation of Jerusalem's centrality and holiness – the Apostles, again, representing a specific species of "flesh and blood."

to the Servant's task in Isaiah 42:1-7 of preaching the good news of God's righteousness for the establishment of justice and salvation throughout the earth (cf. Kim, Paul: 108) (see 2:1-10, 3:10-14, 4:1ff, 6:17, and verses 15-16b).

Damascus

Damascus is one of the oldest, continuously inhabited cities of the world (cf. McRay, Archaeology: 232). First serving as the capital of the Persian satrapy, the Seleucids later transferred this seat to Antioch. Although Damascus fell under Roman rule with Pompey's conquest of the region (64 B.C.E.), Pompey allowed the ruling Nabatean kingdom to continue to govern until Antony gave the city to Cleopatra in 34 B.C. (cf. ABD: 2:8). It apparently remained in Roman hands until 34 C.E., when scholars conclude on the basis of 2 Corinthians 11:32-33 that it numbered among the cities of the east side of the Jordan, being given by Gauis Caligula to the Nabatean king Aretas IV (cf. Jos.Ant. 13.392, 414). As the northernmost city of the Decapolis it nevertheless enjoyed municipal freedom within the latter's loose federation (cf. Bruce, Acts: 233). The city lay on two great ancient highways: The so-called *Via Maris* – the coastal highway running through the Jezreel valley down to Ashkelon and Gaza and continuing to Egypt through the Sinai desert – and the King's Highway which ran southwards across Trachonitis, Batanaea, and Bostra and then across to Rabbat Ammon through the cities of Moab and Edom until it crossed over the Negev and Sinai from Eilat into Egypt. It was also connected to the trade routes southwards to Mecca and east to Baghdad.

Although lesser in importance than Antioch, the Jewish community in Damascus apparently numbered in the thousands. Luke indicates that there were several synagogues in the city (cf. Acts 9:20) and, despite the dubious historical accuracy of the figures, Josephus reports that 10,500 (or 18,000) were massacred during the outbreaks leading up to the Revolt in 66 (cf. War 2.561, 7.368). He also indicates that the women of Damascus were so drawn to Judaism that when their husbands were plotting to massacre the Jews in 66 they had to hide their plans from their wives (cf. War 2.561).

It is also possible that members of the Dead Sea Scrolls community sought refuge from the high priestly persecution in "the land of Damascus [ארץ דמשק]."[265] The messianic/eschatological convictions held by such communities may have constituted fruitful ground for faithfulness to Jesus as the Messiah. Luke's description of Ananias as "a man who was devout by the standard of the Torah (ἀνὴρ εὐλαβὴς κατὰ τὸν νόμον)" (Acts 22:12) possibly suggests that Ananias was connected to a "Jewish-Christian-ascetic splinter group with an Essenic background" (ibid: 87) – an idea

---

[265] Cf. CD-A 6:5, 8:21; CD-B 19:34, 20:12.

perhaps corroborated by his laying on of hands to heal Paul, a practice known from Qumran[266] (cf. Flusser, Judaism: 21-22).

The messianic community in Damascus may have been established by pilgrims who had came to Jerusalem for Shavuot (Pentecost) and, having heard the proclamation of the gospel, returned to Damascus. Although the list in Acts 2:9 does not explicitly mention Syria, Pontus and Asia Minor are included, and the reference to the scattering of the believers "throughout the regions of Judea and Samaria" in Acts 8:1 may not exclude further reaches, as Acts 11:19 indicates. Once these new believers had returned home, together with those who may have later fled from Jerusalem, they may well have established their own community to which others were then attracted. (Interestingly, Luke speaks of the "disciples [τῶν μαθητῶν/οἱ μαθηταὶ]" in Damascus [cf. Acts 9:19, 25] rather than of a unified "congregation" [cf. Acts 8:3, 9:31].) A network of communication was already operating between Jerusalem and Damascus since the believers in Damascus had heard of Paul's persecution of the community in Jerusalem. Ananias indicates that "many (πολλῶν)" people had brought reports about Paul's activities to Damascus (cf. Acts 9:13, 21; Gal. 1:22f) – although it is difficult to ascertain whether or not these were believers.

Arabia

As a noun, the biblical ערב (Arav) simply signifies "desert," the substantive apparently referring to "nomads" – i.e., the bedouin peoples of North Arabia, Syria, and Sinai (cf. Isa. 13:20; Jer. 3:2, 25:24). From Herodotus onwards'Αραβία was applied by Greek writers to the peninsula between the Red Sea and the Persian Gulf, extending to the ocean on the southeast and including the Sinaitic peninsula on the northwest (cf. Herodotus 2.11, 3.107-113, 4.39) (cf. Burton: 57).

Whether or not an actual Arab tribe ever existed is unknown, "Arabia" itself being a Greek coinage. The earliest extant reference to Arabs alludes to a certain Gindibu' who supplied a thousand camel riders to Ahab's coalition forces. The Mishnah mentions Jewish women from Arabia [ערביות] (cf. Shab. 6:6). The walled city of Taima and the kingdom of Dedan were regarded in biblical times as part of Edom.[267] The latter was apparently followed by the Lihyan, a people unknown in the Tanakh although many foreigners, including Nabateans, Taimanites, Greeks, and Jews resided in al-'Ula, the capital of the former kingdom of Dedan.

Despite their relatively late appearance, the Nabateans are well documented in the later biblical books and Josephus, the assertion of their Arab identity being supported by the Arabic names carried by many of the people and gods. During the third century and the first half of the second

---

[266] Cf. 1QapGen 20:22, 29; [Jos.*War* 2.136]; Gen.R. 33:3.
[267] Cf. Isa. 21:13; Ezek. 25:13, 27:20.

century B.C.E., the nomadic Nabatean tribes spread from Petra to the Gulf of Aqaba, where they took to piracy, and established themselves in south Transjordan and the Negev. They eventually became an organised kingdom at the end of the second century B.C.E. during the seleucid struggle between Egypt and Syria, and broke out into open war with Judaea over disputed territory when Alexander Jannai (Jannaeus) (103-76 B.C.E.) was looking to expand his kingdom.[268] Josephus speaks of the Nabatean kings as "king[s] of the Arabs" (e.g., 'Αρέτας ὁ 'Αράβων βασιλεύς; Aretas ho Arabōn basileus) (cf. *Ant.* 13.360). The strained relations continued into the herodian period, war erupting again in Augustus' reign. While Augustus appointed Aretas IV king (cf. Jos.*Ant.* 16.355), who enjoyed a highly prosperous reign, the Nabatean kingdom finally lost its independence to Rome in the early second century C.E.

While Jewish communities are attested in Arabia (cf. 2:11; Shab. 6:6), there is no other mention of Arabian congregations in the New Testament. Likewise, nothing is known of any communities in the region of Petra prior to the constantinian period, although scholars suggest that Nabatean as a language was fairly well known amongst Eretz Israel Jews (cf. Safrai and Stern: 1027). The country is mentioned in other sources as a place of travel and/or of refuge: R. Akiva states that he went to Arabia, but gives no reason for the visit (cf. RH 26a); Artapanus says that Moses fled to Arabia from an Egyptian plot (cf. 3.27.17); and Sesostris was also reputed to have sojourned there (cf. Diodorus 1.53.5).

The major chronological schemes for understanding Paul's itinerary during this period appear to be as follows:

a) that Paul encountered Jesus on the road to Damascus; went straight to Arabia (for an unspecified period of time) (cf. 1:17); returned to Damascus (cf. 1:17); spent three years there (cf. 1:18) before being forced by pressure from the Jewish community (with the cooperation of the Nabatean ethnarch) to escape (cf. Acts 9:23f; 2 Cor. 11:32-33); whereupon he went up to Jerusalem for his first return trip following his calling (cf. Acts 22:17?) and met Peter and James (cf. 1:18).

b) that he encountered Jesus on his way to Damascus; entered and stayed in the city, becoming acquainted with the believers (cf. Acts 9:8ff); at some (unspecified) point went to Arabia (for an undefined period of time); was forced to flee back to Damascus (cf. Jos.*Ant.* 16.271-355); stayed there three years (cf. Gal. 1:18); went back up to Jerusalem for the first time (cf. Acts 22:17?; Gal. 1:18); and thence went into the regions of Syria and Cilicia (cf. Gal. 1:21), possibly as a result of harassment (cf. Acts 9:29-30).

---

[268] Cf. 1 Macc. 5:25, 9:35; Jos.*Ant.* 1.221, 12.335, 13.10-11, 179, 14.31, 46, 48, 103; *War* 1.178.

c) that he encountered Jesus on his way to Damascus; entered and stayed in the city, becoming acquainted with the believers (cf. Acts 9:8ff); at some (unspecified) point went to Arabia (for an undefined period of time) and returned to Damascus (cf. Gal. 1:17); spent three years there (cf. Gal. 1:18); was then forced to flee from a Jewish plot on his life (with the collusion of the Nabatean authorities) (cf. Acts 9:23-25); went back up to Jerusalem for the first time after his calling (cf. Acts 22:17?; Gal. 1:18); and thence went into the regions of Syria and Cilicia (cf. Gal. 1:21), possibly as a result of harassment (cf. Acts 9:29-30).

d) that he encountered Jesus on the road to Damascus; entered and stayed in the city, becoming acquainted with the believers (cf. Acts 9:8ff); was forced to flee due to pressure from the Jewish community (with the cooperation of the Nabatean ethnarch) (cf. Acts 9:23-25; 2 Cor. 11:32-33); went into Arabia (for an unspecified period of time) (cf. Gal. 1:17); returned to Damascus after the crisis had blown over and stayed in the city for a further three years (cf. Gal. 1:17-18); went up to Jerusalem to visit the community and Peter (cf. Acts 9:26, 22:17?) (cf. Gal. 1:18); was forced to flee from a further plot there (cf. Acts 9:29); and was sent away via Caesarea to Tarsus (cf. Acts 9:30; Gal. 1:21?).

The first option cannot be supported by the text of either Acts or Galatians, both of which indicate that Paul immediately entered Damascus following his encounter with Jesus. (The possibility that Paul does not mean that he actually entered Damascus in 1:17 is outweighed by the evidence of Acts.)

The second alternative explicitly contradicts 2 Corinthians 11:32-33 and, at least implicitly, Acts 9:23-25 in referring the harassment of the Nabatean authorities to Arabia rather than to Damascus. The third option likewise demands an explanation both for the visit to Arabia – an element common to all the options and thus not decisive – and for the fact that the Jewish community and/or Nabatean authorities instigated a persecution against Paul after he had been in the city for three years.

The difficulties which (a) and (b) raise are sometimes explained in terms of Paul being marked as a dangerous man because of the political circumstances of the Nabatean hostilities with Herod. It is assumed in this respect that Paul's preaching (in Arabia) must have drawn a violent response, "otherwise there would have been no point in drawing the authorities into the affair and painting him in such colors that he was remembered as dangerous three years later (2 Cor. 11:32-33)" (Murphy-O'Connor, Arabia: 736). Since this interpretation is not necessary to account for Paul's reference to the ethnarch, it would seem to introduce superfluous/irrelevant complications.

The last option (d) must reconcile Luke's implication that Paul fled from Damascus to Jerusalem (cf. Acts 9:25-26) with the view that he went to Arabia and returned to Damascus for three years. Luke merely states "and when he had come to Jerusalem (παραγενόμενος δὲ εἰς Ἰερουσαλὴμ)" (Acts 9:26) – without creating any causal link with the previous verses. Nor would Paul have had any (known) cause not to return to Damascus if he had not engaged in any "Nabatean outreach."

Should the claim that Peter's travel episodes actually began following his escape from prison (cf. Acts 12:1ff) rather than where Luke places them (cf. Acts 9:32ff) – with the consequence that Paul could only have met him there following his return to Jerusalem after Agrippa I's death (43/44 C.E.) – be accepted, it merely establishes the *terminus a quo* for Peter's imprisonment in 37/38, the year of Agrippa's accession. Similarly, while an earlier visit to Arabia may better suit verse 17 here, Acts suggests that Paul left Damascus (for Jerusalem) because of the plot against his life (cf. Acts 9:23-25).

On the balance of these arguments, options (c) and (d) both seem possible schemes. The question of why Paul should not only have returned to Damascus (if he did) but have also been allowed to witness freely after being hounded out of the city is dependent upon indeterminable circumstances – including the length of his sojourn in Arabia, the political and social climate in Damascus which might have allowed him to go back, and his motivation for returning. The verdict that it is not possible to know what Paul did in Arabia appears to be the most valid conclusion – although it may seem preferable to allocate a relatively short time to Paul's preaching in Damascus, as well as to his visit to Arabia, and to assign the three years in Damascus to the period following his return from Arabia.[269]

Verses 18-20:

Then three years later I went up to Jerusalem to become acquainted with Cephas, and stayed with him fifteen days. But I did not see any other of the apostles except James the Lord's brother. (Now in what I am writing to you, I assure you before God *that* I am not lying.)

Although the section from here to 2:10/21 is clearly governed by the three temporal ἔπειτα (epeita – "then") markers which indicate successive events, the present reference to "three years (ἔτη τρία)" is complicated by the fact that it is virtually impossible to determine whether Paul is referring to *consecutive* or *concurrent* periods of time for his first and second visits to Jerusalem – i.e., whether the "three years" of this verse are included within or are independent of the "fourteen years" of 2:1. If this visit is to be identified with Acts 11:30, the chronological framework only

---

[269] As is frequently pointed out, the allusion to Damascus here confirms Luke's account of Paul's experience in Acts (cf. 9:3, 22:6, 26:12f).

permits the concurrent option, seventeen years (the 14 of 2:1 plus these 3) being too long for the interval between Paul's calling and his first return to Jerusalem (see Introduction, **Date and destination**).

The first "then" contrasts Paul's "immediate" step in not going back up to Jerusalem in verse 17, signifying that the first time he returned to the city was after an interval of three years (μετὰ ἔτη τρία; meta etē tria).[270] Despite the widely diverse proposals which have been offered regarding Paul's visits to Jerusalem – their number and their dating – no substantial reason excludes understanding verses 18f in terms of Acts 9:26. While Acts suggests Paul escaped from Damascus for his life, Jerusalem was the natural (in terms of verses 11-17, the "human") place to which Paul would turn.[271] According to Romans 15:19, Paul perceived Jerusalem as the true point of departure for his outreach to the Gentiles (cf. Isa. 2:3; Mic. 4:2) (see verses 16c-17).

Although the sentence lacks an explicit purpose clause, the infinitive indicates that Paul's acquaintance with Peter served as a focal point of the brief visit. In its classical sense, the verb ἱστορέω (historeō) means "to interview, make inquiry of" (cf. Bruce, Galatians: 98). While it signifies "report, record" in the LXX (cf. 1 Esd. 1:33, 42), substantial evidence exists in hellenistic literature for the sense of "making someone's acquaintance"[272] (cf. ibid).

From the witness of Acts, Peter served as the spokesperson for the believing community from its earliest days.[273] He had been in the "inner circle" of Jesus' disciples (with James and John) from the beginning[274] and was the first Apostle to whom Jesus appeared following his resurrection.[275] The early community may well have accorded him authority on the basis of Jesus' declaration: "And I also say to you that you are Peter, and upon

---

[270] Calculating precise dates on such temporal notations is notoriously difficult, given the uncertainty of the calendrical system employed and the likelihood that the first year is likely not to have been full (cf. Fung: 73; Burton: 59). While not constituting any causal connection, it is interesting to note that this interval constitutes the period of ערלה (orlah) during which the fruit of new trees may not be consumed: "'And when you enter the land and plant all kinds of trees for food, then you shall count their fruit as forbidden. Three years shall it be forbidden to you; *it* shall not be eaten. But in the fourth year all its fruit shall be holy, an offering of praise to the LORD" (Lev. 19:23-24). The levitical tithe is likewise to be brought "at the end of every third year . . . in order that the LORD your God may bless you in all the work of your hand which you do" (Dt. 14:28-29). (In mishnaic law, uninterrupted possession of property for three years also establishes ownership [cf. BM 5:3; BB 3:1].)

[271] For Paul's association with the city, see Appendix, **Education**.

[272] Cf. Jos.*War* 6.81; Plut.*Pompey* 40.1; Epict.*Diss.* 2.14.28, 3.7.1.

[273] Cf. Acts 2:14f, 3:12f, 4:8f. For his possible "zealot" tendencies, see 2:11-14.

[274] Cf. Mt. 17:1f, 26:37f; Mk. 5:37, 9:2f, 14:33; Lk. 9:28f, 22:8, 31f; Acts 8:14.

[275] Cf. Lk. 24:34; 1 Cor. 15:5.

this rock [petra] I will build My community . . . and I will give you the keys of the kingdom of heaven"[276] (Mt. 16:18-19) (see 2:1ff).[277]

With the exception of 2:7-8, Paul employs the Aramaic form of Peter's name – כיפא (Keifa), the Greek supplying a case ending Κηφα (Kēfa[s]).[278] Although the wordplay between Peter's name and his task is assumed to derive from the Greek, it is possible that Πέτρος (Petros) represents a Hebrew rather than a Greek name (cf. Bockmuehl, Simon; Bivin: 34, and for the following discussion). A Yose ben Petros [יוסי בן פיטרס] is known from the third century, putting his father a generation earlier[279] and the spelling פיטרוס (Pitros) in the fragment 4QM130, in a list which includes Magnus, Malkiah, Hyrcanus, Yannai, Aquila, and others, may represent the same name. The existence of the name in Hebrew may perhaps be further confirmed by the fact that the Greek loanword פֶּי(י)טְרָא/ה (Petra/pitra) seems to have entered post-biblical Hebrew at some stage in replacement of the biblical צור (tzur – "rock").[280]

Jewish sources witness to the use of "rock" to signify not only the foundation for a building[281] but also metaphorically to designate a "dependable person" on which a sure construction could be erected: "When, however, the Holy One, blessed be He, saw Abraham, he said, 'Here I have found solid rock on which I can build and upon which I can lay the world's foundation', כיון שצפה הקדוש ברוך הוא באברהם שעתיד לעמוד, אמר: הרי מצאתי פטרא לבנות עליה וליסד את העולם" (Yalk.Num. 766).[282] According to Jesus' statement, Peter's task is to be the foundation stone upon which other stones – i.e., a community – could be constructed into "living stones, [which] are being built up as a spiritual house for a holy priesthood, to offer up spiritual sacrifices acceptable to God through Jesus the Messiah"[283] (1 Pet. 2:5).[284]

If the vision which Paul describes in Acts 22:17 relates to the present visit, Paul may have wished to spend at least two weeks in Jerusalem in order to be able to enter the Temple. Anyone going up to Eretz Israel (the land of Israel) from foreign countries required purification from the

---

[276] κἀγὼ δέ σοι λέγω ὅτι σὺ εἶ Πέτρος, καὶ ἐπὶ ταύτῃ πέτρᾳ οἰκοδομήσω μου τὴν ἐκκλησίαν . . . δώσω σοι τὰς κλεῖδας τῆς βασιλείας τῶν οὐρανῶν.

[277] Cf. Gal. 2:9; 1QHᵃ 14:24-27; 4Q522 f9ii:4; Yalk.Num. 766.

[278] For the irregular usage in 2:7-8, see 2:1-10.

[279] Cf. Gen.R. 94:5; Ex.R. 52:3; J MK 3, 5, 82d; J AZ 3, 1, 42c.

[280] Cf. JShevi. 5, 2, 36a; JKil. 1, 9, 27b.

[281] Cf. Mt. 7:24f; 1QHᵃ 15:8-9; 4Q429 f2ii:5-12; Lev.R. 20:4.

[282] Cf. Isa. 28:16; Zech. 4:9; 1QHa 14:25-26; Tanh.Tol. 14; Gen.R. 75:11; Ex.R. 15:7, 41:6; Lev.R. 20:4; Num.R. 12:4; [Mid.Ps. 1:15, 136:5]; San. 26b; Yoma 38b; [Git. 61a]. For "pillars," see 2:1-10.

[283] λίθοι ζῶντες οἰκοδομεῖσθε οἶκος πνευματικὸς εἰς ἱεράτευμα ἅγιον ἀνενέγκαι πνευματικὰς θυσίας εὐπροσδέκτους [τῷ] θεῷ διὰ Ἰησοῦ Χριστοῦ.

[284] Cf. Isa. 28:16-18; Mt. 3:9; Rom. 12:1-2; 1 Cor. 3:16-17; 2 Cor. 6:16; Eph. 2:18-22; 1QS 5:2ff, 8:4ff, 9:3ff; 4QFlor f1i:1ff; 4QpIsaᵈ 1:1f; Yalk.Num. 766.

uncleanness of the land of the Gentiles before being allowed entry into the Temple[285] (cf. Alon, Jews: 152f, 186). Luke's reference in Acts 21:27 to "seven days" suggests that Paul was required to undergo the seven-day purification period prescribed in the Torah for those defiled by uncleanness when he returned to Jerusalem from Corinth through gentile territory[286] (cf. Le Cornu and Shulam: 1187). While worship in the Temple was daily (cf. Acts 2:46, 3:1, 5:42), Paul may also specifically wished to have been present in Jerusalem on shabbat (the sabbath).[287]

References in Paul's letters indicate familiarity with Peter which may have come from personal acquaintance.[288] Peter on his part speaks of Paul as "our beloved brother (ὁ ἀγαπητὸς ἡμῶν ἀδελφὸς Παῦλος)," alluding to Paul's correspondence, in which "are some things hard to understand" (2 Pet. 3:15-16). The two men presumably shared conversation and discussions about their common faith, Paul learning much from Peter's personal experience with Jesus during his lifetime. While such interaction does not necessarily violate Paul's assertion that he received his gospel from no "flesh and blood," it is difficult conversely to accept that he failed to communicate his calling as the apostle to the Gentiles either to Peter or to James (*pace* Howard, Crisis) (see Introduction, **Occasion and circumstances**).

Verse 19 provides another mitigation in Paul's assertion that he received the gospel not from "flesh and blood" but directly from God (cf. verses 15-17). Although he did see Peter when he first returned to Jerusalem, he did not "see (εἶδον)" - presumably "visit" on the analogy of ἱστορῆσαι (historēsai) in verse 18 - any other of the apostles (ἕτερον δὲ τῶν ἀποστόλων; heteron de tōn apostolōn). Whoever Paul regards as "apostles" here evidently hold the same stature as Peter, the ἕτερον (heteron - "other") indicating people of the same class. The much-debated question is whether Paul intends to include or exclude James from this group. Although grammatically, the εἰ μὴ (ei mē - "except") may govern either the verb - "I did not see" - or the whole clause - "I did not see any of the other apostles" - its force derives most naturally from the "other," which carries "apostles" with it, giving the most natural meaning as "The only other apostle whom I saw was James" (cf. 1 Cor. 1:14) (cf. Lightfoot, Galatians: 84-85; Bruce, Acts: 101). Had Paul wished to indicate that "apart from the apostles, I saw no one but James" he could have done so

[285] Cf. Ohal. 18:6; Naz. 7:3.
[286] Cf. Num. 19:11ff; Ezek. 44:26; Naz. 7:3; Ohal. 18:6; JShab. 1, 4, 3c; Shab. 14b (see previous note).
[287] Prayer and visions in the Temple are well documented in Jewish sources: cf. 1 Sam. 3:3f; [1 Kings 3:4-5]; Isa. 6:1f; Lk. 1:8ff, 18:10; Eccl.R. 5.6.1; Ta'anit 20a; Sot. 33a.
[288] Cf. 1 Cor. [1:12, 3:22], 9:5, 15:5.

unequivocally in good Greek. Being under oath here (cf. verse 20), ambiguity is surely not an attribute to which Paul would have aspired.[289]

The grammatical discussion clearly arises from the ostensible difficulty of identifying James as one of the twelve Apostles. While both Acts and Paul indicate James' position as (one of the) leader(s) of the Jerusalem community during Paul's lifetime, he is nowhere explicitly identified as an Apostle.[290] Notwithstanding, Paul's references to the "rest of the apostles (οἱ λοιποὶ ἀπόστολοι)"in 1 Corinthians 9:5, which is inserted in addition to both "the brothers of the Lord" and to "all the apostles (τοῖς ἀποστόλοις πᾶσιν)" in 1 Corinthians 15:5-7, which cites James and Peter independently, both suggest that his usage of the term apostle is not exclusive to the Twelve. Since in both passages in 1 Corinthians Paul equates apostleship with witness of Jesus, his point here may be that, like his own case, James' calling only occurred following Jesus' resurrection.

James

James (יעקב; Ya'akov) is named as Jesus' brother in the gospels, along with Joseph (Joses), Simon, and Judah - all popular Hebrew names in Eretz Israel during this period, James being rather less common - and an unspecified number of unnamed sisters (cf. Mt. 13:55-56; Mk. 6:3; 1 Cor. 9:5) (cf. Bauckham, Acts: 86ff; Jude). The precise manner in which James came to occupy a leading role in the Jerusalem community is hard to trace. Many commentators identify Acts 12:17 as a significant transition point, the void left by Peter's departure to "another place (εἰς ἕτερον τόπον)" being filled - in unspecified fashion - by James' rise to prominence (cf. Bauckham, Acts: 433-41).[291] His familial connection with Jesus, his personal qualities, and his davidic descent may all have contributed to his prestige (cf. Longenecker, Galatians: 39).[292]

---

[289] The matter may in fact move in the opposite direction - the oath being meant to mitigate any possible ambiguity. Dunn suggests that "Paul leaves the status of James ambiguous ... perhaps unwilling to recognize as an apostle one who seems to have remained throughout in Jerusalem" (Theology: 23).

[290] He is not chosen to replace Judas, that position being filled by Matthias (cf. Acts 1:21-26). It is also doubtful whether Luke's report that Barnabas "brought him [Paul] to the apostles and described to them ... (ἤγαγεν πρὸς τοὺς ἀποστόλους καὶ διηγήσατο αὐτοῖς)" (Acts 9:27) includes James at such an early date - although it does witness to a plurality of personages. (For theories regarding the early community's failure to replace James the son of Zebedee [cf. Acts 12:2], cf. Riesner: 120-21.)

[291] For his description/role as a "pillar," see 2:1-10.

[292] For the much-disputed question of Jesus' "brothers," cf. Bauckham, Jude: 19-32; for the importance of davidic descent in the early community, cf. ibid: 376; Liebes, Horn/Tosefet. Early patristic sources assert that James was the first bishop of Jerusalem (cf. Eus.*EH* 2.1.2; Clem.*Hypot.* 6).

Christian tradition has long held that James represented the "law-observant" stream of early Christianity in contrast to Paul's "law-free" gospel, the "certain men from James (τινας ἀπὸ Ἰακώβου)" in 2:12 – perhaps also synonymous with "the party of the circumcision (τοὺς ἐκ περιτομῆς)" and the "false brethren (ψευδαδέλφους)" (2:4) – being identified with "certain ones of the sect of the Pharisees (τινες τῶν ἀπὸ τῆς αἱρέσεως τῶν Φαρισαίων)" in Acts 15:5 (cf. Schoeps: 67f, 74f).[293] Although his views indicate clear pharisaic affinities (cf. Acts 15:13-29, 21:18-25) and he presumably held similar views to Peter – to whom the gospel to the circumcised was entrusted (cf. 2:7-8) – little hard evidence exists to prove that he was actually a Pharisee.[294]

Even Eusebius' description of James – based on Hegesippus – supplies no definite certification of James' pharisaic status, his most outstanding characteristic – his nazirite existence – being a commitment made by many different people, as also his ascetic lifestyle and dedication to prayer: "The charge of the Church passed to James the brother of the Lord, together with the Apostles. He was called the 'Just' by all men from the Lord's time to ours, since many are called James, but he was holy from his mother's womb. He drank no wine or strong drink, nor did he eat flesh; no razor went upon his head; he did not anoint himself with oil, and he did not go to the baths. He alone was allowed to enter into the sanctuary, for he did not wear wool but linen, and he used to enter alone into the temple and be found kneeling and praying for forgiveness for the people, so that his knees grew hard like a camel's because of his constant worship of God, kneeling and asking forgiveness for the people. So that from his excessive righteousness he was called the Just and Oblias, that is in Greek, 'Rampart of the people and righteousness,' as the prophets declare concerning him"[295] (Eus.*EH* 2.23.4-7).

---

[293] This is not an identification with which we concur. For the "false brethren," see 2:1-10; for the identity of the "men of James," see 2:11-14.

[294] It is not, of course, hard to imagine that those teaching circumcision should be Pharisees (cf. Acts 15:5, 21:20-24). Divergent attitudes towards the Gentiles existed within the pharisaic party, Beit Hillel generally being regarded as more lenient and Beit Shammai more stringent, the latter regularly demanding circumcision and conversion (cf. Safrai, Literature: 192-93; Le Cornu and Shulam: 804-8, 1221-23) (see 2:1-10 [Circumcision]). For Peter's attitude, see 2:11f; for the present identification of the various groups represented in Galatians, see 2:1f.

[295] Διαδέχεται τὴν ἐκκλησίαν μετὰ τῶν ἀποστόλων ὁ ἀδελφὸς τοῦ κυρίου Ἰάκωβος, ὁ ὀνομασθεὶς ὑπὸ πάντων δίκαιος ἀπὸ τῶν τοῦ κυρίου χρόνων μέχρι καὶ ἡμῶν, ἐπεὶ πολλοὶ Ἰάκωβοι ἐκαλοῦντο, οὗτος δὲ ἐκ κοιλίας μητρὸς αὐτοῦ ἅγιος ἦν, οἶνον καὶ σίκερα οὐκ ἔπιεν οὐδὲ ἔμψυχον ἔφαγεν, ξυρὸν ἐπὶ τὴν κεφαλὴν αὐτοῦ οὐκ ἀνέβη, ἔλαιον οὐκ ἠλείψατο, καὶ βαλανείῳ, οὐκ ἐχρήσατο. τούτῳ μόνῳ ἐξῆν εἰς τὰ ἅγια εἰσιέναι· οὐδὲ γὰρ ἐρεοῦν ἐφόρει, ἀλλὰ σινδόνας. καὶ μόνος εἰσήρχετο εἰς τὸν ναὸν ηὑρίσκετό τε κείμενος ἐπὶ τοῖς γόνασιν καὶ αἰτούμενος ὑπὲρ τοῦ λαοῦ ἄφεσιν, ὡς ἀπεσκληκέναι τὰ γόνατα αὐτοῦ δίκην

According to Josephus – an apparently impartial witness in this regard – James' death was the result of further sadducean antagonism towards the early community, the sadducean high-priestly element having played a central role in Jesus' execution (cf. Flusser, Jesus: 146, 195-206). The high priest Ananus illicitly convened the Sanhedrin and accused "James, the brother of Jesus who was called the Christ, and certain others . . . of having transgressed the law and delivered them up to be stoned"[296] (*Ant.* 20.200). Eusebius preserves two accounts of James' death, one based on Hegesippus, the other unattributed.[297] Hegesippus ascribes James' death to pharisaic and scribal retaliation at James' failure to respond to their request to persuade the people from following Jesus and attributes to his death – thrown from the battlement and clubbed to death – Vespasian's siege of Jerusalem.[298] Eusebius' immediately preceding report, on the other hand, suggests that the petition was made directly to James to deny his faith, such testimony to Jesus not being tolerable because James "was by all men believed to be most righteous (δικαιότατον αὐτὸν παρὰ τοῖς πᾶσιν . . . πιστεύεσθαι)" (*EH* 2.23.2).

Verse 20 constitutes an additional source of legitimation – here not directly of Paul's commission (cf. verses 1, 11f) but of his account of it. The reference to "writing (ἃ δὲ γράφω)" would seem to indicate that the oath applies to Paul's preceding argument – the whole of his affirmation of his authority (verses 11ff).[299] In biblical law, God's oath is His expression of ultimate truth (cf. Gen. 22:16-18; Ps. 110:4). It thence commonly occurs whenever a statement is intended to solemnly convey a truthful purpose or relate true facts (cf. Elon: 615f, and for the following discussion). Ancient oaths frequently took the form either of lifting one's hand (cf. Isa. 49:22) or of putting one's hand under the adjurer's thigh (the latter being a euphemism for the sexual organ) (cf. Gen. 24:9, 47:29). While granting power to one's words, false or vain swearing by God constitutes a criminal

---

καμήλου, διὰ τὸ ἀεὶ κάμπτειν ἐπὶ γόνυ προσκυνοῦντα τῷ θεῷ καὶ αἰτεῖσθαι ἄφεσιν τῷ λαῷ. διά γέ τοι τὴν ὑπερβολὴν τῆς δικαιοσύνης αὐτοῦ ἐκαλεῖτο ὁ δίκαιος καὶ ὠβλίας, ὅ ἐστιν Ἑλληνιστὶ περιοχὴ τοῦ λαοῦ, καὶ δικαιοσύνη, ὡς οἱ προφῆται δηλοῦσιν περὶ αὐτοῦ.

[296] τὸν ἀδελφὸν Ἰησοῦ τοῦ λεγομένου Χριστοῦ, Ἰάκωβος ὄνομα αὐτῷ, καὶ τινας ἑτέρους, ὡς παρανομησάντων κατηγορίαν ποιησάμενος παρέδωκε λευσθησομένους.

[297] The latter is not based on Josephus, since Eusebius proceeds to cite the passage from *Antiquities* 20 – with an additional quote which does not appear in the extant texts of Josephus.

[298] Cf. Eus.*EH* 2.1.5, 23.4-19; Orig.*Con.Cel.* 1.47.

[299] For the present reading of chapters 1-2 as Paul's laying out of the authority on which he rebukes his disciples and calls them to recommit themselves to his gospel, see Introduction, **Form**; **Argument**.

offence carrying severe penalties.[300] Only the person who has never sworn deceitfully is worthy to "ascend into the hill of the LORD" to stand in His holy place (Ps. 24:3-4).[301]

While Paul resorts to similar oaths on other occasions,[302] the forensic element may here be stronger than elsewhere. Roman legal practice could employ the oath to conclude a trial short of its full course or to warn the second party that one was prepared to stand before a court of inquiry on the matter (cf. Sampley). In the latter context, Paul's statement may perhaps serve as a veiled intimation of the lengths to which he is prepared to go, as it were, in asserting his authority.[303] Paul may anticipate that his readers will question the plausibility of a visit to Jerusalem during which he met only with Peter and James and/or that he had received a direct commission from God through Jesus, which had not been augmented, or even possibly steered in a particular direction, by the Jerusalem leaders.[304]

Although many commentators take the *narratio* to extend from verse 11 through to 2:14, the consecutive "thens" (verses 18, 21, 2:1) indicating successive autobiographical episodes in Paul's ministry (see above), the insertion of the oath appears to interrupt the sequence. On this reading, while the following section - to the end of chapter 2 - represents autobiographical information, its purpose is less prescriptive than descriptive. Rather than embodying similar apologetic intentions, it shifts into a sketch of Paul's subsequent career, the climax - in terms of relevance to the Galatians - being Peter's visit to Antioch (see 2:10f).[305]

---

[300] Cf. Ex. 20:7; Lev. 19:12; Dt. 5:11.

[301] מי-יעלה בהר-ה' ומי-יקום במקום קדשו: נקי כפים ובר-לבב אשר לא-נשא לשוא נפשו ולא נשבע למרמה.

[302] Cf. Rom. 9:1; 2 Cor. 1:23, 11:[10], 31; 1 Tim. 2:7.

[303] For Galatians' halakhic "rebuke-request" structure, see Introduction, **Form**; **Argument**; for the implications of the oath for Pauline chronology, see Introduction, **Date and destination**.

[304] No intrinsic reason exists to assume that another account of Paul's career was being disseminated - a report which represented him as having gone to Jerusalem to receive authority to exercise his own ministry (see Introduction, **Occasion and circumstances**). For the possibility that the oath is designed to remove any ambiguity regarding James' apostleship, see above.

[305] It may be more accurate to say that Paul's polemical tone starts to pale, since the immediately following verses still present a somewhat defensive stance (see 2:15-21). For the presently-proposed structure of Galatians, see Introduction, **Argument**.

Verses 21-24:
Then I went into the regions of Syria and Cilicia. And I was *still* unknown by sight to the communities of Judea which were in the Messiah; but only, they kept hearing, "He who once persecuted us is now preaching the faith which he once *tried* to destroy." And they were glorifying God because of me.

According to Acts 9:30, Paul's departure from Jerusalem is occasioned by a plot against his life in that city also – a fact which Paul appears to gloss over here.[306] While Luke specifies Paul's destination as Tarsus (cf. Acts 11:25), Paul states more generally here "the regions of Syria and Cilicia" – Tarsus being the capital of the latter (see Appendix, **Citizenship** and below). The Greek τὰ κλίματα (ta klimata) conveys the non-political sense of "territories" or "districts" – in contradistinction to Roman provincial "regions" (cf. Rom. 15:23; 2 Cor. 11:10) (cf. Ramsay, Galatians: 278f). The unusual attribution of the article (τῆς; tēs) to both names may suggest that Paul is referring to Syria and Cilicia as separate locales (cf. Longenecker, Galatians: 40).[307] Since Judaea constituted part of the Roman province of Syria, its independent status here (cf. verse 22) would also seem to indicate that by Syria Paul has in mind the region around Antioch, Cilicia referring to the environs of his hometown of Tarsus.

While Tarsus may have been a natural destination for Paul once Jerusalem also became dangerous, he was theoretically at liberty to choose any location as his place of "refuge" (cf. Riesner: 264f, and for the following discussion). Given the Nabatean control of the east- and south-bound caravans (cf. 2 Cor. 11:32-33), he may have turned northwards rather than eastward, the southwest being excluded by his principle of not encroaching on other people's territory (cf. Rom. 15:20; 2 Cor. 10:15-16). If he was influenced by Isaiah 66:18-21, that passage both precluded east- and south-bound directions and spoke specifically of Tarsus (verse 19) – identified with Tarsus in Cilicia in the New Testament period.[308]

Verse 23 and Acts 15:41 – the latter presupposing the existence of local communities prior to the council – both suggest that Paul was occupied

---

[306] For the "Then," see verses 18-20.

[307] Josephus and the New Testament alike elsewhere regularly use the phrase without the second article (cf. Burton: 62). Cilicia was in fact a double province (Syria-Cilicia), Antioch being the capital of the combined area before the creation of an independent Cilicia in 72 (cf. Hemer, Acts: 172, 179) (see Introduction, **Date and destination**). This understanding is perhaps reflected in ℵ, which omits the second article (τὴν; tēn) both here and in Acts 15:41 (cf. Riesner: 266). For Paul's usage of provincial names, see Introduction, **Date and destination**.

[308] Here again, Paul may have perceived himself in a similar role to Jonah (cf. Jos.*Ant.* 9.208) (see verses 15-16b). Interestingly, the book of Judith associates Φουδ καὶ Λουδ (Foud kai Loud – the masoretic Pul [Put]) not with Libya/Cyrene but with Cilicia, the "Rassis" mentioned in the same context possibly referring to Tarsus (cf. Jud. 2:23) (cf. Riesner: 251). For Paul and the "table of nations," cf. Scott.

with outreach during the extended period (cf. Acts 11:25) which he spent in Tarsus. With a population of perhaps around 500,000, the city apparently possessed a sizable Jewish population by the first century – one which was still vibrant in the fourth century when the patriarch sent an envoy there to collect contributions from the Jewish community – among whom are listed archisynagogoi, priests, elders, and chazanim (cf. Epiph.*Adv.Haer*. 30.11). As a free city under Augustus – who confirmed the privileges won by its citizens' pro-Caesarean sympathies – it enjoyed self-government and tax-exempt status (cf. Pliny, *Nat.Hist*. 5.22.92).

The word *tarseus* early became synonymous with "linen-weaver," the word λινουργός (linourgos) meaning any industrial worker in the first century (cf. Dio Chrys.*Orat*. 34.21). There was a synagogue of *tarsiim* in Jerusalem (cf. Meg. 26a) and Tarsean artisans are found working in Judaea (cf. JShek. 11a). It is consequently not surprising that Paul and Aquila (who originated from Pontus) should both be tent-makers (cf. Acts 18:2-3), or that Paul should have made contact with Lydia, a seller of purple goods in Philippi (cf. Acts 16:14f). Not only would have Paul's dual citizenship served him well in such a city but its proximity to the sea and to the Cilician Gates (cf. Cicero, *Att*. 5.20.2) gave him easy access to both north and west if seeking to enlarge his sphere of influence.[309]

While the claim that Cilicia's appearance – as Put – in Isaiah 66:19 "would be yet another factor making it more comprehensible that he concentrated his efforts so long in this area before a pneumatic experience called him to a different task" (Riesner: 268) is rather obscure, it raises the possibility – built primarily around chronological reconstructions – that the revelation which Paul describes in 2:2 may correspond to 2 Corinthians 12:2ff.[310] While the content of the vision is unfortunately "inexpressible," it is significant that Paul has, for around eleven years, been working independently and in isolation in Syria and Cilicia, whence – whether in response to a revelation or not – he transfers to Antioch, there becoming a co-worker with Barnabas, with whom he is subsequently commissioned by the Antiochian community (cf. Acts 13:1ff) (cf. ibid: 272) (see verses 1-5).

---

[309] The suggestion has been made that Paul may have travelled as far as Cappadocia and Greece during this period, although in distancing himself from Jerusalem he might have been expected to mention the extent of his journeying here (cf. Riesner: 267-71). This time framework is also frequently proposed as the occasion for many of the experiences Paul describes in 2 Cor. 11:23ff. For Paul's status, see Appendix, **Citizenship**.

[310] Although Riesner makes this point, he associates Gal. 2:1-10 with Acts 15 rather than with Acts 11:30 (cf. pp. 320-21). The present volume assumes a correspondence with the latter date (see Introduction, **Date and destination**).

Syria and Cilicia

Together with Phoenicia, Syria was a major Jewish centre in the Second Temple period. Its proximity to Eretz Israel meant that Jewish life there closely resembled that in the Land, the Syrian Jewish community acting as good allies and partners (cf. Hal. 4:11). Jewish settlement in Syria in general was very ancient and was probably augmented by further immigration following the seleucid conquest of Judaea shortly after 200 B.C.E. (cf. Jos.*Ant.* 12.119; *War* 7.43). The Book of Obadiah (vs. 20) witnesses to the colonisation of Jews as military settlers in Syria, possibly subsequent to the annexation of Judaea by Antiochus III (d. 187 B.C.E.). Josephus asserts that Syria possessed the largest percentage of Jewish inhabitants in the diaspora and that both Jews and "judaisers (ἰουδαΐζοντας)" were to be found in every city (cf. *War* 2.463, 7.43). Rabbinic literature records the existence of Jewish tenants (cf. Hal. 4:7), the mortgaging of land to Jews by Gentiles (cf. Tos.Ter. 2:10-11), and various types of tenures on Jewish land – suggesting that some Jews might have held large estates (cf. Tos.Ter. 2:13).

Cilicia consisted of two major regions on the southeast Anatolian coast: Cilicia Tracheai (or Aspera) in the mountainous region west of the Lamus River reaching to Pamphylia, and Cilicia Campestris (or Pedias), the fertile plain south of the Taurus and west of the Amanus range (cf. ABD: 1:1022f, and for the following discussion). The province is mentioned in the book of Judith, Nebuchadnezzar dispatching Holofernes at the head of his army to punish the inhabitants for insubordination (cf. Jud. 1:12, 2:21-25). A further rebellion is recorded in 1 Maccabees 11:14.

The region having become so infested with bandits that "Cilician" became a virtual synonym for "pirate," Pompey was forced to action against the plague. In consequence of the piratical defeat, Cilicia Tracheia was incorporated into the Roman empire, both Cilician districts being joined to the already-existing province, which consisted of Pamphylia and Isauria. Tarsus became the capital of Cilicia under Pompey in 66 B.C.E., the provincial territory initially extending from the Chelidonian Isles to the Gulf of Issus, with Cyprus being added in 58 B.C.E. (cf. Bruce, Acts: 73). While constituting a distinct administrative unit, Cilicia Pedias constituted a dependency of the Legate of Syria in the early principate, Cilicia Aspera being joined to the province of Lycaonia.

Verse 22 retains the polemical edge of Paul's appeal to his personal encounter with Jesus as the source of his apostleship to the Gentiles, in the course of which he maintains his "non-assocation" with the Jerusalem leadership (see verses 11f). While he speaks of Jerusalem in verse 17 due to the Apostles' presence there, here he broadens the location to include "the congregations of Judea which were in the Messiah (ταῖς ἐκκλησίαις τῆς Ἰουδαίας ταῖς ἐν Χριστῷ)." Not only when Paul returned to the city and visited with Peter (and James) but also during his extended stay in Syria and Cilicia, he remained – the periphrastic imperfect ἤμην (ēmēn) indicating a continuing state – "unknown by sight (δὲ ἀγνοούμενος τῷ προσώπῳ)."

It is difficult to ascertain whether Paul's emphasis is expressed in verse 22 or in verses 23-24 – in other words, whether the latter is dependent on the former or vice versa. While the contrast is obviously between sight and hearing, either one may form the focus of Paul's point.[311] In favour of the latter is the fact that the Judaean communities accept Paul without argument – even praising God on his account – without causing Paul the pain which the Galatians have prompted. While this reading must find an adequate explanation for Paul's introduction of the Judaeans' lack of acquaintance of him in person,[312] verse 24 characterises Paul's commissioning in its echo of Isaiah 49:3: "And He said to me, 'You are My servant, Israel, in whom I will show My glory' ויאמר לי עבדי-אתה ישראל אשר-בך אתפאר"[313] (cf. Lightfoot: 86).[314]

The context of Isaiah 49 is constrained by the Servant's calling from the womb (cf. Isa. 49:1, 5; verse 15) – "to raise up the tribes of Jacob, and to restore the preserved ones of Israel; I will also make you a light of the nations so that My salvation may reach to the end of the earth להקים את-שבטי יעקב ונצירי ישראל להשיב ונתתיך לאור גוים להיות ישועתי עד-קצה הארץ" (49:6).[315] Since this text – and the Servant Songs in general – are pivotal to

---

[311] *Contra* Burton, who states categorically that "the whole sentence μόνον . . . ἐν ἐμοί [only . . . in me] is a momentary digression [from Paul's assertion of his independence]" (p. 66).

[312] Burton's argument that "ἡμᾶς ["we"] refers, of course, not directly to those to whom he was unknown by face, but to Christians in general" (p. 64) surely violates the literal signification of the text.

[313] LXX: καὶ εἶπέν μοι Δοῦλός μου εἶ σύ, Ισραηλ, καὶ ἐν σοὶ δοξασθήσομαι.

[314] The use of ἐν (ev – "in") here is usually taken to indicate that which constitutes the ground or basis of an action (cf. Rom. 1:24, 9:7; 1 Cor. 7:14) (cf. Burton: 65). For Isaiah 42, see verses 15-16b; for the isaianic Servant as Paul's model, see 2:1-10, 3:1-5, 4:8f, 21-31, 6:17, and verses 15-16c.

[315] The introductory section of this chapter is central to Paul's self-understanding and teaching (cf. Acts 13:47; 2 Cor. 6:2; Gal. 1:15; Phil. 2:16). It is interesting to note that the Hebrew נתתיך ל- (netatikha – lit.: "I have given you for") appears elsewhere in connection with Gentiles. In Gen. 17:5-6, God tells Abraham that He is going to "make you the father of a multitude of nations/make nations of you אב-המון גוים נתתיך" (cf. Gen. 48:4). To Jeremiah he declares that He has "appointed you a prophet to the nations נביא לגוים נתתיך" (Jer. 1:5) (see verses 15-16c). The same form, in the imperfect (אתנך; etenkhah), occurs in Isa. 42:6 and 49:8 in reference to the Servant. The association of Galatians with both Abraham and Jeremiah is clearly evident (cf. verse 15, 3:6-4:31). For Paul's calling as modelled on Abraham, cf. Le Cornu and Shulam: 1219; for the Servant motif, see 2:1-10, 3:10-14, 4:1ff, 6:17, and verses 1-5, 15-16b, 21-24.

Paul's thinking,[316] verse 24 may prove to be the point of Paul's depiction here: Paul's agency was explicitly confirmed in the acknowledgement of his task as God's "Servant."[317] That God should be glorified through Paul is the paramount affirmation of the fulfilment of Paul's commission.[318]

Verse 22 has caused some discomfort to commentators concerned to reconcile Acts and Galatians, stating as it does – at some apparent variance with the implication of Luke's account of Paul's persecution[319] – that Paul was unknown to those whom he was persecuting. The difficulties arise from the reference in Acts 26:11 to "foreign [or: outlying] cities (τὰς ἔξω πόλεις)"; Galatians' insinuation that the persecution was confined to Jerusalem; and Paul's claim that he proclaimed the gospel "throughout all the region of Judea (πᾶσάν τε τὴν χώραν τῆς 'Ιουδαίας)" following his calling (Acts 9:28?, 26:20). Thus while Luke indicates that Paul was found outside of Jerusalem as both a persecutor and a believer, Paul asserts that, as both, he was "unknown."[320]

Paul's persecutorial activities necessarily took place before he (almost) arrived in Damascus, not logically having occurred following his call –

---

[316] Cf. Betz, Vision; Kim, Paul: 101-27. For the Teacher of Righteousness' adoption of the same office, cf. Dupont-Sommer: 360-67.

[317] "In 2 Corinthians 5:11-21 – which closely parallels Galatians 1:13-16 in its invocation of his Damascus experience – Paul's line of apologetic may have arisen from "his opponents' insinuation of his past as a persecutor of the church and as an enemy of Jesus Christ and God as well as their rejection of his claim to apostleship on the basis of the Damascus revelation of Christ (cf. 1 Cor. 9:1, 15:8-10)" (Kim, Paul: 230-231). Although this theory is difficult to sustain on the current supposition that the Galatians "influencers" are not themselves believers, the reference may be accounted for if Paul's oath in verse 20 marks a transition point, following which Paul goes on to present internal community debates (cf. 2:1-21). While these opponents/accusations are not the same as those in Galatia, on the present reading (Paul also specifically appeals here to his Damascus experience to validate his commission – precisely the event he defends in 2 Corinthians 5), Peter's "enticement" serves as the springboard for Paul's "surprise" that the Galatians have been bewitched, like Peter, into confusing the identity of the "sons of the promise" with that of the "sons of the covenant" (see Introduction, **Argument**). (For the rhetoric of surprise, see verses 1-5.)

[318] The same glorifying is evident in the Jerusalem community's response to Peter's account of Cornelius' household's receipt of the Spirit (cf. Acts 11:18, [13:48]). For the suggestion that glorifying God specifically refers to gentile turning to God in such contexts as can bear the meaning (cf. Mt. 5:16; 1 Pet. 2:12), cf. Hvalvik: 325.

[319] Cf. Acts 8:1-3, 9:1-3, 22:4-6, 26:10-12.

[320] Paul's speech in Acts 26 being before Agrippa II in 59, sufficient time has elapsed to allow for pauline travels throughout Judaea (cf. Acts 18:22 [implying a visit to Jerusalem], 21:15?), his reference to the Gentiles indicating that he has already, as Acts witnesses, wound his way through the diaspora. (For the chronology assumed here, cf. Le Cornu and Shulam: xxiii-xxv.)

when he claims, to the contrary, that he witnessed to Jesus' name.[321] Possibly, non-Jewish towns are meant by "foreign cities," the plural presumably being accounted for by Paul's pre-empted intention to proceed beyond Damascus. On such a northward route – an overland journey being presupposed – Paul could have passed through Samaria and Galilee, both being part of provincial Judaea (cf. Acts 9:31) (see below).

The thesis that the persecution did not affect the environs of Jerusalem may find some corroboration from the witness of 1 Thessalonians 2:14. Not only does this verse echo verbatim Paul's present phrase, "the congregations of God in the Messiah Jesus that are in Judea" (cf. Acts 9:31); it also addresses the persecution which those communities suffered at the hands of "the Jews (τῶν Ἰουδαίων)." Is Paul there referring to the campaign against the early community in Judaea – without mentioning his involvement because he did not himself participate in any measures outside Jerusalem?[322]

The grammatical difficulty in Acts 26:20 caused by the lack of any preposition before πᾶσάν τε τὴν χώραν τῆς Ἰουδαίας (pasan te tēn chōran tēs Ioudaias – "throughout all the region of Judea") – which scholars have suggested reflects a semitism (cf. Dt. 1:19) – may further indicate that, in contrast to those to whom Paul directly witnessed in Damascus and Jerusalem (both of which places are governed by a preposition), the communities in Judaea only received news of him – and his gospel – indirectly, as they had also not experienced his persecutory campaign firsthand (cf. Bruce, Acts: 502f).[323]

Paul presents the reports which reached the Judaean communities (cf. Acts 9:28?, 31, [10:37], 11:1, 29) – quite likely through those who were "scattered" in the wake of Paul's campaign in Jerusalem (cf. Acts 8:1) – in the form of direct speech, as though the Judaeans were present.[324] The fact that τὴν πίστιν (tēn pistin – "the faith") (cf. Acts 14:22, 16:5) occurs here absolutely does not necessarily indicate an early "Jewish-Christian" and non-pauline usage (*contra* Bammel). Despite the heated controversy over

---

[321] For the persecution, see Appendix, **Persecutor** and verses 13-14.

[322] This suggestion carries clear ramifications regarding the extent of the persecution – whether it was a personal "crusade" or an organized, official campaign (cf. Le Cornu and Shulam: 460-64) (see Appendix, **Persecutor**). The association of 1 Thess. 2:14 with this event would imply the latter. For "ekklēsia," see verses 1-5.

[323] If this proves an inadequate explanation, the emendation "and in every country, to Jews and Gentiles (εἰς πᾶσάν τε χώραν Ἰουδαίοις καὶ τοῖς ἔθνεσιν)" (Acts 26:20) (cf. Acts 22:21) may be commended.

[324] In similar fashion, the masculine form of the participle "hearing (ἀκούοντες)" – which should strictly agree with the feminine "congregations (ταῖς ἐκκλησίαις)" – represents a construction *ad sensum*, implying that it was the communities' members who heard the reports (cf. Bruce, Galatians: 104).

the issue, Paul may be using πίστις (pistis) in reference to Jesus himself in 3:23-25.[325] The new era, principle, or power which Jesus inaugurates corresponds to the "gospel (message)" in 3:2, 5 (see 3:1-5).[326] Since our present verse parallels verse 13, the same verbs (διώκω [diōkō] and πορθέω [portheō]) occurring there with the "congregation of God (τὴν ἐκκλησίαν τοῦ θεοῦ)" as the object, Paul appears to easily associate "the faith" (Jesus) with the "gospel" and with believers themselves ("us") (cf. Longenecker, Galatians: 42).[327] The absolute, moreover, gives an impression of unity – also geographical and temporal – which characterizes the gospel. Opposition to Paul's attitude towards the Gentiles – such as evidenced in 2:3f – may have surfaced only at the date indicated by the "false brethren who had sneaked in (ψευδαδέλφους, οἵτινες παρεισῆλθον)" in Jerusalem (2:4) (cf. Burton: 65) (see 2:1-10).[328]

Judaea

The Roman province of Judaea was established in 6 C.E. when Augustus removed Archelaus from his position as ethnarch of Judaea, Samaria, and Idumea[329] (cf. Safrai and Stern: 78ff, 308ff, and for the following discussion). Since Archelaus' territories were too small to warrant the creation of an independent province they were annexed to the neighbouring province of Syria, whose governors had supervised Judaean

---

[325] Attentive readers may have already anticipated that we follow Hays' argument that πίστις Χριστοῦ (pistis Christou) refers to Jesus' faithfulness rather than to faith in him – although Hays himself does not regard "the faith" in 3:23-25 as an allusion to Jesus (see 3:10-14, 21-25 and 4:1-7).

[326] 3:23-25 is paralled by 4:1-10, wherein Paul reiterates the two "aeons" – one of slavery, one of "faithfulness in the Spirit."

[327] The participation of Jesus' followers in what he wins for them through his faithfulness constitutes a central focus in Hays' argument.

[328] These are not, on the present reading, those who are troubling the Galatians, the latter being currently identified as non-believing local godfearing Gentiles (see Introduction, **Occasion and circumstances**). The traditional tendency to see the roots of the "later anti-Pauline opposition" in these communities – in many cases combined with the claim that "From there the invaders in Galatia must have come" (Betz, Galatians: 80) – is tendentious, especially in light of Nanos' determination that the autobiographical material in Galatians 1-2 can only be adduced as *indirect* proof for the Galatian circumstances (cf. Irony: 62-72). Some of the problems may be perceived from the contradictory statements of such scholars as Betz and Dunn: While the former claims that the "Judean Christians would hardly have approved of" Paul's preaching "the gospel free from the Law" (p. 80), the latter considers that it was precisely the Judaean communities' embrace of the Gentiles without circumcision which occasioned Paul's persecution (cf. Theology: 68, 70). (It is difficult to escape the impression – reinforced by the chronological anachronism which seems to lie behind Dunn's argument – that the "must" which carries the force of both arguments conceals a lack of convincing historical knowledge.)

[329] Cf. Jos.Ant. 17.311ff; War 2.90f.

affairs even during Herod's reign. Like Egypt, it belonged to a class of imperial provinces exceptional for their rulers' equestrian ranking. Such provinces normally hosted no legionary forces and were considered unworthy, as it were, of a senatorial governor, either because of their special character or for economic reasons (cf. Safrai and Stern: 310). They frequently appear to have been a function either of a "tenacious and individual culture" or a semi-barbarous population – both of which categories caused serious difficulties in the implementation of ordinary regulations (cf. Schürer: 1:357f).

Despite the initial decision concerning Judaea – which was grounded on the peculiar character of its population – the Roman authorities did not deviate from the normal custom and consider it necessary to station a legionary force in the province, making do instead with auxiliary troops. While various methods of government were employed in the different areas of Syria and adjacent Asia Minor – including Judaea – and the latter could be referred to as separate provinces, combined they were considered to constitute part of the single great eastern *provincia* assigned to Augustus by the various settlements of his power in 27 B.C.E. (cf. Sherwin-White: 11). Since the latter term (province) is relevant to the person rather than to the territory, Judaea was properly Augustus' *provincia*, sharing the same status and conditions as other early equestrian administrations (cf. ibid).

The governor of Judaea was directly appointed by the Emperor (cf. Safrai and Stern: 31). The length of his office was affected by various factors, including a given Emperor's general policy with regard to terms of service and his interest in promoting favourites in the administrative hierarchy outside Judaea, the governor's personal connections at court, and his ability in maintaining peace and security in his territory without unreasonable tyranny and cruelty. Generally speaking, the average term appears to have been two years.

At the same time, the province's administrative division continued to follow the herodian system. Judaea proper was divided into eleven toparchies which Josephus enumerates as Jerusalem, Gophna, Acrabeta, Thamna, Lydda, Emmaus, Pella, Idumaea (excluding Gaza), Engedi, Herodium, and Jericho, plus Jamnia and Joppa.[330] (Although Pliny's list [cf. *Nat.Hist.* 5.14.70] is slightly different – he omits Idumaea and Engaddi [Engedi], assigns Joppa to Judaea with no mention of Jamnia, and replaces Pella with Bethleptephene – neither source is later than the herodian period since they both refer to the fortress of Herodium.)

The toparchies appear to have followed the division of the country according to the twenty-four priestly courses, although the latter were not

---

[330] Cf. Jos.*War* 3.54f; Pliny, *Nat.Hist.* 5.15.70.

confined to Judaea but covered the whole of Eretz Israel[331] (cf. Jeremias, Jerusalem: 71f). While most priests apparently lived in Judaea they did not by any means all reside in Jerusalem. Zechariah lived in the hill country of Judah (cf. Lk. 1:39), Mattathias dwelt in Modi'in (cf. 1 Macc. 2:1), and the Mishnah rules that wherever a priest resides he must receive the heave-offering (cf. Ter. 2:4).

Although Jerusalem served as Judaea's permanent administrative capital as well as that of Idumaea, its control over the whole country ceased when it became a Roman province, whereupon the governor's seat was transferred to Caesarea. (Caesarea was attached to Samaria, both territories being incorporated into the province of Judaea [cf. Jos.*Ant.* 19.351].) Jerusalem nevertheless remained the province's largest city and the chief focus of its political, social, and religious life, due to the presence of both the Temple and the Sanhedrin (see verses 16c-17[excursus]). (A committee of the Sanhedrin seems in fact to have been in charge of finances in the eleven toparchies, and the Jerusalem/Temple authorities in Judaea were at least partly responsible for policing Judaea [cf. Jeremias, Jerusalem: 71, 74].) The province as a whole officially continued to be called Judaea up until the reign of Hadrian (117-138).

Acts 5:16 refers to "the cities in the vicinity of Jerusalem (τῶν πέριξ πόλεων Ἰεροψσαλὴμ)" - which may include Jericho, Mizpeh, Beit Choron, and Emmaus, all of which were strictly towns or large villages (cf. Safrai and Stern: 83). Without making a hard and fast distinction between πόλεις (poleis - "cities") and κῶμαι (kōmai - "villages"), Judaea contained many more villages[332] (cf. ibid: 99).

---

[331] Cf. Lk. 1:5f, 39; Jos.*Ant.* 7.363f; [*CA* 2.108]; *Life* 2; Ta'anit [3:6], 4:2; San. 11:2; Bik. 3:2; Par. 3:11; JPes. 4, 1, 30c.
[332] Cf. [1 Thess. 2:14]; Jos.*Ant.* 17.254; *War* 2.43, 4.241; 1QpHab 12:9.

GALATIANS
2

Verses 1-10: *Narratio II*

THEN after an interval of fourteen years I went up again to Jerusalem with Barnabas, taking Titus along also. And it was because of a revelation that I went up; and I submitted to them the gospel which I preach among the Gentiles, but I did so in private to those who were of reputation, for fear that I might be running, or had run, in vain. But not even Titus who was with me, though he was a Greek, was compelled to be circumcised. But *it was* because of the false brethren who had sneaked in to spy out our liberty which we have in the Messiah Jesus, in order to bring us into bondage. But we did not yield in subjection to them for even an hour, so that the truth of the gospel might remain with you. But from those who were of high reputation (what they were makes no difference to me; God shows no partiality)—well, those who were of reputation contributed nothing to me. But on the contrary, seeing that I had been entrusted with the gospel to the uncircumcised, just as Peter with *the gospel* to the circumcised (for He who effectually worked for Peter in *his* apostleship to the circumcised effectually worked for me also to the Gentiles), and recognizing the grace that had been given to me, James and Cephas and John, who were reputed to be pillars, gave to me and Barnabas the right hand of fellowship, that we might go to the Gentiles, and they to the circumcised. *They* only *asked* us to remember the poor—the very thing I also was eager to do.

This is the third "Then" following Paul's commissioning, the first constituting his initial return to Jerusalem (cf. 1:18) and the second his journey to Syria and Cilicia (cf. 1:21) (see 1:18-20). The fourteen years may allude to Paul's calling (cf. 1:15; "immediately" in 1:16), his first visit back (cf. 1:18), or the last "then" (cf. 1:21), it being unclear whether the ἔπειτα (epeita – "then") simply structures the narrative or serves as a historical connection (cf. Betz, Galatians: 83).[1]

Paul frames this second return visit in terms of the first both in the phrase "I went up again (πάλιν ἀνέβην)" and in allusion to a further revelation (cf. 1:16) (see below).[2] On the chronological scheme adopted here, this visit corresponds to Acts 11:30, the timeline – beginning from Paul's commissioning – thus demanding that the fourteen years *include* the three Paul spent in Damascus (cf. 1:18).[3]

Barnabas

Luke introduces Barnabas – born Joseph – as a Cypriot levite (cf. Acts 4:36). Joseph (Ἰωσήφ; יהוסף/יוסף – "May [God] add [other children]") being the second most popular Jewish name of the Second Temple period (cf. Bauckham, Acts: 89; Hachlili: 189), his nickname may have been necessary to distinguish him from the numerous others bearing the same name (cf. Hachlili: 195ff). Luke interprets the Aramaic "Barnabba [בר נבא]" as meaning "son of consolation" (cf. Acts 11:23), perhaps on the analogy of בר נבא ("bar nabba[s]" – son of the prophet). The actual derivation of the name seems to be בר נבו ("son of Nebo [Nabu]") in reference to a pagan god – despite which it was frequently used as a first name in semitic circles (cf. Bauckham, Acts: 101).

While it is difficult to ascertain the precise biblical relation between levites and prophets (cf. 2 Chron. 20:14ff), the fact that the New Testament places Barnabas among the "prophets and teachers (προφῆται καὶ διδάσκαλοι)" in the Antiochian community (cf. Acts 13:1) and implies that he was a gifted "evangelist"[4] may reflect his education as a levite (cf. Vermes, Dead: 96). His freedom to travel may likewise support the suggestion that levitical service in the Temple was not compulsory (cf. Jeremias, Jerusalem: 213) and that some (many?) levites could be town teachers (cf. Mulder: 23). Despite the social standing of craftspersons (cf. Sir. 38:26ff), the scribal profession was not considered lucrative (cf. Pes. 50b), most scribes beginning their apprenticeship at a comparatively late age when their families could afford to forego their potentially decreased income. Since ordinary priests appear to have been considered rich, it seems reasonable to conclude that the scribal class came almost exclusively from wealthy, distinguished families – including levites.

---

[1] For the dating of Paul's chronology and Galatians, see Introduction, **Date and destination** and 1:18-20.

[2] For going up to Jerusalem, see 1:16c-17.

[3] The calculation, in other words, is concurrent rather than consecutive (see 1:18-20).

[4] Cf. Acts 11:24, 14:12, 15:2.

The fact that Barnabas possessed property (cf. Acts 4:37, 12:12) possibly reflects familial wealth in this regard. Despite the biblical stringencies on levitical sale of land (cf. Num. 35:1ff), Jeremiah and Josephus – both from priestly families – apparently owned land (cf. Jer. 32:6f; Jos.*Life* 422). Whether such strictures applied in the diaspora cannot easily be ascertained, although it is stated "*Take heed . . . lest . . . thou forsake the Levite as long as thou livest . . . upon thy land* (Dt. 12:19) – but not in the Diaspora "השמר לך . . . פן תעזוב את הלוי כל-ימיך . . . על אדמתך - ולא בגולה (Sif.Dt. 74) – i.e., the diaspora levite is no different from any other poor person and need not be supported (as a levite).

It cannot be conclusively determined whether Barnabas' estate was in Cyprus or Jerusalem. Some of Barnabas' relatives apparently lived in Eretz Israel, his cousin's mother (Mary, John Mark's mother) possessing a house in Jerusalem (cf. Acts 12:12; Col. 4:10) and Barnabas apparently residing at least semi-permanently in the city (cf. Acts 9:27). If this family was also of levitical ancestry, it is possible that they lived in the priestly quarters of the Upper City. Mnason, a "long standing disciple (ἀρχαίῳ μαθητῇ)," was also a Cypriot living in Jerusalem (cf. Acts 21:15-16).

According to Luke, Barnabas served as Paul's first "mentor" on returning to the city as a follower of Jesus, introducing him to the Apostles and witnessing to the authenticity of his calling (cf. Acts 9:27).[5] Having been sent by the Jerusalem community to Antioch, he in turn sought Paul out in Tarsus in order to join him in "encourag[ing] them all [the new gentile believers] with resolute heart to remain true to the Lord (παρεκάλει πάντας τῇ προθέσει τῆς καρδίας προσμένειν τῷ κυρίῳ)" (Acts 11:23).[6] Having taught the Antiochian community together for a year, the latter commissioned the two men to deliver a contribution "for the relief of the brethren living in Judea" (Acts 11:29).[7]

Titus
A fourth century tradition asserts that Titus was an Antiochian, and even if the opinion may derive from the present scriptural witness, it remains a reasonable option (cf. Riesner: 269). Luke makes no mention of Titus in Acts, and apart from Paul's letter addressed to him, Titus' primary role in the New Testament is confined to the collection made by the Achaian and

---

[5] For the question of which Apostles Paul actually met on his first return visit to Jerusalem, see 1:18-20; for the dating of the visits, see Introduction, **Date and destination**.

[6] The fact that Barnabas is sent to Antioch in the wake of the successful outreach there suggests his high standing among the Jerusalem community, hitherto only John and Peter having been dispatched to Samaria to deal with "diaspora" affairs (cf. Acts 8:14).

[7] For the significance of Barnabas' mention for the dating of Galatians, see Introduction, **Date and destination**.

Macedonian communities and delivered by Paul to Jerusalem.[8] Paul's remarks in his regard demonstrate that he was not Jewish but a "Greek ("Ελλην ὤν)" – his presence with Paul in Jerusalem occasioning a debate over whether, as a gentile believer, circumcision should be required of him (cf. verses 3-5) (see below). While Paul suggests that Titus may have served as an "assistant" (cf. ὑπηρέτης; hypēretēs) at this stage of their co-operation, he later testifies to the trust and responsibility which he placed in him.[9]

The appeal to revelation directly evokes prophetic status – both that of Agabus' standing, if linked to Acts 11, and that of Paul's prophetic precedessors (see 1:1-5, 15-16a). On the chronological grounds adopted here, the revelation may also recall the vision of which Paul speaks in 2 Corinthians 12:2-5.[10] While unlikely to constitute the source of Paul's visit to Jerusalem, this reference may possibly lie behind his transition from Tarsus (Syria and Cilicia) to Antioch (cf. 1:21) (cf. Riesner: 116, 272). The invocation presumably indicates that the return did not constitute part of Paul's regular routine for coming up to Jerusalem. Observance of the feasts – and the tithes and other offerings linked with their celebration – was a customary practice, one which ostensibly required no revelation (cf. Safrai, Pilgrimage: 123-25).[11] Whether the phrase κατὰ ἀποκάλυψιν (kata

---

[8] Cf. Acts 20:3-24:17; 2 Cor. 2:13, 7:6-14, 8:6, 16-23, 12:18; 2 Tim. 4:10.

[9] Cf. 2 Cor. 2:13, 7:6-14, 8:6, 16-23, 12:18; 2 Tim. 4:10; Tit. 1:4f. Stirewalt's analysis of Paul's prepositional usage of σύν (syn) and μετά (meta) leads him to the conclusion that "Titus is Paul's colleague at the Jerusalem meeting [sic] . . . , while Barnabas accompanies them independently" (p. 99n71).

[10] While not prepared to consider this passage as an account of Paul's calling based on an identification of this vision with his "conversion," as does Segal, the latter's understanding of Paul's Damascus experience in the light of Ezekiel 1 and mystical/apocalyptic aspects of Second Temple Judaism has its instructive moments. As Bruce notes, "The relation between the time-note here and 2 Cor. 12:2 ('fourteen years ago') is fortuitous" (Galatians: 107).

[11] As with the earlier three years (cf. 1:18), while equally lacking historical significance, fourteen carries symbolic significance as a multiple of seven, the latter being a sacred number in many ancient civilizations (cf. Frankel and Teutsch: 149-150). Perhaps most striking is the association of seven with the jubilee (49 years) in the "weeks of years" in which some eschatological literature – including 11QMelchizedek – calculates world history (cf. Kobelski: 49f) (see 1:1-5). Sets of two sevens also occur in Jacob's labour for Leah and Rachel (cf. Gen. 29:18-30), Pharaoh's dream (cf. Gen. 41:26-30), and the years of conquest and division of the land when the tabernacle was at Gilgal (cf. BM 89a; Zev. 118b). Ezekiel also experienced a vision in the fourteenth year (itself calculated to be a jubilee year) after Jerusalem's capture in which the hand of the Lord "brought me into the land of Israel . . . So He brought me there; and behold, there was a man whose appearance was like the appearance of bronze ויביא אותי שמה . . . ויביאני אל-ארץ ישראל

apokalypsin) suggests that it was "according to" or "because of" or "through" (as the "method" by which he obtained the knowledge) the revelation, Paul creates the impression that without this specific instruction he had no plans to return to the city.[12]

Also difficult to establish is whether the conjunctive καὶ (kai – "and") constitutes the cause or the effect of the revelation. Did Paul understand that he was being bidden to "submit his gospel" – or did he merely take the opportunity to do so, the revelation relating to an independent matter? While the association with Agabus may imply that the revelation was linked to delivery of relief monies ahead of an anticipated famine, the tenor of this section tends towards a more personal communication, making the conjunctive more likely to be elaborative (causative). In light of the fact that up until this point Paul has pressed his claim that his commission (in the sense of both his status and the task he was called to perform) originates directly with God/Jesus (cf. 1:1, 11ff), the revelation may have been necessary in order to convince him to now seek the Jerusalem leaders' approval.[13] Further appeal to revelation will, of course, also add more weight to the authority which he intends to exert over his disciples in Galatia.[14]

The "gospel which was preached by me (τὸ εὐαγγέλιον τὸ εὐαγγελισθὲν ὑπ' ἐμοῦ)" (1:11) is the same proclamation which Paul is continuing (ὃ κηρύσσω – present tense) to make.[15] As in 1:16, Paul presents it as focused upon the Gentiles (see 1:15-16b). Although the "among (ἐν)" here may contrast with the εἰς τὰ ἔθνη (eis ta ethnē –"to the Gentiles") in verse 8, suggesting that Paul's preaching covered all those living in gentile

---

והנה-איש מראה כמראה נחשת (Ezek. 40:1-3) (cf. Zev. 118b) – the vision being of the future Temple. For Paul's Jewish identity, see Appendix.

[12] Similar divine interventions, either in the form of visions or direction by the Spirit, continued to play a role in Paul's subsequent ministry – cf. Acts [11:28]; 13:2, 16:6f, 18:9-10, 19:21?, 20:22-23, 21:10-14, 23:11, 27:23-24. For 2 Cor. 12:2ff, see above. Precisely why Paul should have required a revelation to understand the importance of visiting the Jerusalem leaders is also rather enigmatic – especially if he is not portrayed as asserting his independence (see Introduction, **Argument** and below).

[13] If due weight is given to the "eschatological" element of "revelation," the latter may perhaps also signify "the fulness of time" – i.e., an "eschatological realisation" that, in a chronological sense, it was the proper interval at which to go, as well as an insight regarding the nature of the period in which he was preaching. In this sense, the "agreement" reached in verses 7-9 was grounded upon the revelation (cf. Nanos, Inter: 402).

[14] For the assessment of Paul's "defence" of his apostleship – interpreted here rather in terms of an affirmation of his authority over the Galatians – see Introduction, **Argument** and 1:1-5.

[15] Like εὐαγγελίζω (euangelizō), the Greek κηρύσσω (kēryssō – "to proclaim") is a "technical" term closely related to the pronouncer of "good news" (cf. Isa. 61:1) (see 1:1f, 3:1ff, 26-29, and 4:1f).

lands – thus including Jews as well as Greeks (cf. Longenecker, Galatians: 48) – the phrase "among the Gentiles הגוים [מ]בין" is a common designation for Gentiles in Jewish literature (cf. 1:16).[16] The parallel to Paul's phraseology here in Philippians 2:16 – "because I did not run in vain nor toil in vain (οὐκ εἰς κενὸν ἔδραμον οὐδὲ εἰς κενὸν ἐκοπίασα)" – indicates that Paul continues to perceive his calling in terms of the Servant Songs: "But I said, 'I have toiled in vain, I have spent my strength for nothing and vanity' ואני אמרתי לריק יגעתי לתהו והבל כ'חי כליתי"[17] (Isa. 49:4) (see 1:1-5, 15-16a, 4:8f, and 6:17).[18]

The correspondence between this verse and Paul's express concern in 4:11 that he has "labored over you in vain (εἰκῇ κεκοπίακα εἰς ὑμᾶς)" may signify that he is thinking already here in terms of "fathering."[19] He does not wish to think that he has failed to bring forth ("raise up") disciples (cf. PA 1:1) – if they are not recognised as such by the community

---

[16] Cf. Ezek. 37:21; Nid. 7:3; BK 38b. Whether or not Paul continued to work within the Jewish community is a point of contention amongst "Old" and "New Pauline" scholars, the former asserting – in what should be considered as a flagrant misreading of the (con)texts – that "From all the available data, on the contrary [to the claim that Paul continued working among the Jews], one could even speak of Paul systematically avoiding Jerusalem and Judea while concentrating on the mainly gentile world" (Kim, Paul: 253). While Kim uses this argument to ask in the next sentence, "How could he, a "zealous" Pharisee, do this [i.e., forget his Jewish past]," Kim is in general of the "Old" school.

[17] LXX: καὶ ἐγὼ εἶπα Κενῶς ἐκοπίασα καὶ εἰς μάταιον καὶ εἰς οὐδὲν ἔδωκα τὴν ἰσχύν μου.

[18] Cf. Ps. 31:9-13, 38:1-22; 1QHᵃ 12:8-11, 13:22-39. The metaphor of "running" is a favourite of Paul's, most commentators assuming its derivation from the athletic imagery of the day (cf. 1 Cor. 9:24; Gal. 5:7; Phil. 3:14; 2 Tim. 4:7; Hell.Syn.Pray. 2:8(3); Philo, *De Agr.* 177). At the same time, it is tempting to link Paul's thought here with Habakkuk, one of Paul's central texts (see 3:10-14, 26-29, and verses 15-21 [nn267, 271]). God commands that the vision be written "that the one who reads it may run בו קורא ירוץ למען" (ὅπως διώκῃ ὁ ἀναγινώσκων αὐτά) (Hab. 2:2). The LXX text subsequently understands the vision to refer to a "Coming One" who will "arrive and will not linger; if he draws back, my soul will have no pleasure in him; but the Righteous One shall live by my faithfulness (ὅτι ἐρχόμενος ἥξει καὶ οὐ μὴ χρονίσῃ ἐὰν ὑποστείληται, οὐκ εὐδοκεῖ ἡ ψυχή μου ἐν αὐτῷ· ὁ δὲ δίκαιος ἐκ πίστεώς μου ζήσεται)" (Hab. 2:[3]-4) (see 2:15-16b, 3:10-14, 19f, and 4:1-7). Pesher Habakkuk (7:4) applies the "running" to the spiritual insight bestowed upon the Teacher of Righteousness. A similar understanding occurs in Rom. 9:16: "So then it *does* not *depend* on the man who wills or the man who runs, but on God who has mercy (ἄρα οὖν οὐ τοῦ θέλοντος οὐδὲ τοῦ τρέχοντος ἀλλὰ τοῦ ἐλεῶντος θεοῦ)." In such a context, Paul is potentially pondering whether he has properly comprehended his "profession." This meaning is also possible in 5:7 (see 5:2-12).

[19] The same verb conveying "labor (κοπιάω)" occurs here and in Phil. 2:16. For the suggestion that it belongs to "missionary language," see 4:8-11 (n114).

and its leaders (see 4:12-20).[20] It is not coincidental, in this regard, that the same expression occurs in a text in Isaiah which speaks of the "new creation" of heaven and earth: "For behold, I create new heavens and a new earth; and the former things will not be remembered or come to mind. But be glad and rejoice forever in what I create; for behold, I create Jerusalem *for* rejoicing and her people *for* gladness. I will also rejoice in Jerusalem and be glad in My people; and there will no longer be heard in her the voice of weeping and the sound of crying . . . They shall not labor in vain, or bear *children* for calamity; for they are the offspring of those blessed by the LORD, and their descendants with them"[21] (Isa. 65:17-19, 23).[22]

Whether in response to the revelation or not, Paul's desire to "set out (ἀνεθέμην)"[23] his gospel stems from a certain apprehension that he has fallen short of his commission – or that it has failed to bring the anticipated results. Paul possibly has in mind the "success" of his priestly "ministering of the Gentiles": ". . . the grace that was given me from God, to be a minister of the Messiah Jesus to the Gentiles, ministering as a priest the gospel of God, that *my* offering of the Gentiles might become acceptable, sanctified by the Holy Spirit"[24] (Rom. 15:15-16) (cf. Phil. 2:17).[25]

---

[20] A hint of Paul's sense of rejection on the part of his disciples may also be traced here, in that the vanity of his labouring is caused by the transference of their allegiance to another (the influencers): "For I have been rejected by them, and they do not esteem me when you made yourself great through me; for they drive me from my land like a bird from its nest; all my friends and my acquaintances have been driven away from me, and rank me like a broken jug כי נמאס(ת)י למו ולא יחשבוני "בהגבירכה בי כי̇ ידיחני מארצי כצפור מקנה וכול רעי ומועדי נדחו ממני ויחשבוני לכלי אובד (1QHᵃ 12:8-9). See also below, on "spying." Paul makes the link with the Galatians direct in verses 5: "so that the truth of the gospel might remain with you" (see below).

[21] כי-הנני בורא שמים חדשים וארץ חדשה ולא תזכרנה הראשנות ולא תעלינה על-לב: כי-אם-שישו וגילו עדי-עד אשר אני בורא כי הנני בורא את-ירושלם גילה ועמה משוש: וגלתי בירושלם וששתי בעמי ולא-ישמע בה עוד קול בכי וקול זעקה . . . לא ייגעו לריק ולא ילדו לבהלה כי זרע ברוכי ה' המה וצאצאיהם אתם.

[22] Despite the dual meaning of "labour" in English, the Hebrew here does not constitute a verb customarily associated with childbirth. At the same time, the Isaiah text exhibits close affinities with those which describe Jerusalem and her "sons and daughters" as being birthed anew in the eschaton (see 4:21-31 and 6:12-16).

[23] While unknown in classical Greek, the meaning of "to communicate (with a view to consultation)" for ἀνατίθημι (anatithēmi) is attested in later Greek writings (cf. LXX Mic. 7:5; Acts 25:14; 2 Macc. 3:9) (cf. Longenecker, Galatians: 47).

[24] τὴν χάριν τὴν δοθεῖσάν μοι ὑπὸ τοῦ θεοῦ εἰς τὸ εἶναί με λειτουργὸν Χριστοῦ Ἰησοῦ εἰς τὰ ἔθνη, ἱερουργοῦντα τὸ εὐαγγέλιον τοῦ θεοῦ, ἵνα γένηται ἡ προσφορὰ τῶν ἐθνῶν εὐπρόσδεκτος, ἡγιασμένη ἐν πνεύματι ἁγίῳ.

[25] It should be noted that this sentiment has to do with the specifics of the collection for Jerusalem (cf. Acts 24:17; 1 Cor. 16:1; 2 Cor. 8:1ff).

While "There are three things which the Holy One, blessed be He, Himself proclaims, namely, famine, plenty, and a good leader" (Ber. 55a),[26] the appointment of public officials requires "democratic" confirmation: "'A good leader', as it is written: *And the Lord spoke unto Moses, saying, See I have called by name Bezalel, the son of Uri* (Ex. 31:2). R. Isaac said: We must not appoint a leader over a Community without first consulting it, as it says: *See the Lord hath called by name Bezalel the son of Uri* (Ex. 35:30). The Holy One, blessed be He, said to Moses: Do you consider Bezalel suitable? He replied: Sovereign of the Universe, if Thou thinkest him suitable, surely I must also! Said [God] to him: All the same, go and consult them. He went and asked Israel: Do you consider Bezalel suitable? They replied: If the Holy One, blessed be He, and you consider him suitable, surely we must!"[27] (Ber. 55a)."[28]

In such a context the generic αὐτοῖς (autois - "to them") possibly refers to the whole community - hoping that they will affirm his commission. It is perhaps better taken, however, as anticipatory of "those who were of reputation (τοῖς δοκοῦσιν)" (cf. verse 2). These are presumably the same as those named in verse 6, whom Paul subsequently identifies in verse 9 as "James and Cephas and John, who were reputed to be pillars (Ἰάκωβος καὶ Κηφᾶς καὶ Ἰωάννης, οἱ δοκοῦντες στῦλοι εἶναι)." The standing of these men makes them competent to assuage Paul's apprehensions that his present work - including all he has achieved up until this point (ἔδραμον - 2 aor. ind.) - has been of no value (cf. 4:11).[29]

The restrictive nature of the consultation (κατ᾽ ἰδίαν [kat idian] - "in private") (cf. verse 2) may relate either to the small leadership group and/or to Paul's desire not to be embarrassed in public. The expression οἱ δοκοῦντες (hoi dokountes) carries a politically rhetorical force possessed of potentially complimentary, derogatory, or ironic meaning, its "ostensibility" (δοκέω = to think, consider) being true, false, or imputed according to the context (cf. BAGD: 202). While the references here and in verse 9 appears to be commendatory, many commentators perceive an element of disparagement in verse 6. This connotation may be modified, if the participle in the latter verse is understood in the same substantive sense as it carries here and in verse 9. The meaning then becomes "those of

---

[26] Note the proximity between leadership and the presence/absence of victuals (cf. Acts 11:27-30).

[27] אמר רבי יוחנן : שלשה דברים מכריז עליהם הקדוש ברוך הוא בעצמו ואלו הן : רעב ושובע ופרנס טוב . . . פרנס טוב, דכתיב: (ויאמר) ה' אל משה לאמר ראה קראתי בשם בצלאל וגו'. אמר רבי יצחק: אין מעמידין פרנס על הצבור אלא אם כן נמלכים בצבור, שנאמר: ראו קרא ה' בשם בצלאל. אמר לו הקדוש ברוך הוא למשה: משה, הגון עליך בצלאל? אמר לו: רבונו של עולם, אם לפניך הגון, לפני לא כל שכן!! אמר לו: אף על פי כן לך אמור להם. הלך ואמר להם לישראל: הגון עליכם בצלאל? אמרו לו : אם לפני הקדוש ברוך הוא ולפניך הוא הגון, לפנינו לא כל שכן!!

[28] Cf. Rom. 13:1f; Jos.*War* 2.140; Philo, *Virt.* 55-65.

[29] For Paul's assessment of the three leaders, see below.

reputation, being pillars" (see verse 9). Whether τρέχω (trechō) should be understood as a present indicative – "I am running" – or as a future subjunctive – "I should run" – makes little practical difference, Paul's intention being to gain confirmation that he should continue his present course.[30]

Why he should have doubted its validity, having not only worked independently for many years but also been sought out by Barnabas to help teach in Antioch, remains enigmatic.[31] Although Acts gives no hint of such circumstances (cf. Acts 11:19-30), it is perhaps possible that Paul was experiencing some antagonism which he hoped could be halted through the leaders' intervention.[32] The addition of the aorist "or had run" carries some import for this point. Reference to the past would seem to indicate that Paul is seeking an approval without which all that he has accomplished will be proved futile and any future work preempted. Had he anticipated receiving help from the Apostles against opposition to his work, on the other hand, his trepidation would presumably not have related to what he had already achieved but to the threat to his continued ministry.[33]

---

[30] Burton's grammatical exegesis notwithstanding, the question of whether verse 2 actually describes two meetings – one discreetly with the leaders, the other with the community at large – is largely a function of integrating verses 1-10 with Acts 15. Other divisions between verses 7-8 (Paul's first return to Jerusalem) and verse 9 (the "council" – second visit) (cf. Kim, Paul: 253-56) clearly break with the chronology of Acts. For the dating of the visits presumed here, see Introduction, **Date and destination**.

[31] The difficulties in interpreting this passage on the assumption that Paul is defending the independence of his "apostleship" are numerous. Even when he emphasises that his visit is occasioned by a revelation, he is nonetheless explicitly seeking the Apostles' approval of his ministry. If his apprehension derives from the fact that he had previously kept his distance from Jerusalem, what role does the revelation – previously employed to justify his autonomy – play? Some of these problematics at least may be mitigated on the assertion that following his oath (1:20) Paul's polemical purpose recedes into a more descriptive mode, culminating in the projection of Peter's "bewitchment" onto the Galatians (see Introduction, **Argument**; 1:21-24 and 3:1-5).

[32] No good historical reason precludes, at this early stage, the possible presence of such persons as the "men from Judea" who insisted that gentile believers become proselytes (cf. Acts 15:1, 5). Whether the appellation "Christians" (Acts 11:26) may be related in any way to this issue is difficult to ascertain.

[33] While these verses constitute part of the autobiographical/narrative section of the letter and therefore should not form evidence for the "situational discourse" of Galatians (cf. Nanos, Irony: 62-72), it is evident that had Paul been proved to have been "running in vain" he would not have reached Galatia with the gospel (cf. verse 5).

Verse 3: Whether or not Paul has brought Titus with him as a "living piece of evidence" for Paul's gospel – as a deliberate "test case" – Paul adduces the fact that Titus is not circumcised as testimony of the confirmation he received from the Jerusalem leaders.[34] Despite the difficulties attendant upon Timothy's case (cf. Acts 16:1-3), Titus clearly falls into a different category. While Timothy is Jewish (according to the matrilinear line), Paul's remark that Titus is "a Greek ("Ελλην ὤν)" determines that no doubt existed regarding Titus' gentile status.[35] The concessive force of the participle ὤν (ōn – "though being") derives from the resistance to Paul's presentation of the gospel: Despite his gentile status, Titus was not compelled to be circumcised by those whom Paul designates as "false brethren (ψευδαδέλφους)" (cf. verse 4).[36] Although the issue which lies at the heart of Paul's letter thus enters the discussion indirectly, Titus serves as a precedent – an act possessed of legal standing upon which future halakhah (judicial rulings) may be built (cf. Elon: 110-17). It is at least partly on the basis of this event that Paul can tell the Galatians "that the truth of the gospel might remain with you (ἵνα ἡ ἀλήθεια τοῦ εὐαγγελίου διαμείνῃ πρὸς ὑμᾶς)" (verse 5).[37]

Verse 4: This reading interprets the prepositional phrase διὰ . . . (dia) as explaining the compulsion. In contrast to many commentators, Paul's confrontation here is not understood to be with the Apostles (who are impelled to concede the force of his argument) but with those who have "sneaked into" the Jerusalem community (see below). On analogy with 4QMMT's three-group structure, this visit to Jerusalem encompassed a meeting with the "pillars" – James, John, and Peter – during which time a group of believers endeavoured to institute Titus' circumcision, an attempt which was rebuffed both by the leaders and by Paul.[38] There seems little reason to argue that "It is thus clearly implied that they who in person urged the circumcision of Titus (οἱ δοκοῦντες [i.e., those of reputation]) did not themselves regard it as necessary except as a matter of expediency,

---

[34] This is the force of the οὐδὲ – "not even."
[35] For the issue of Timothy's circumcision, cf. Le Cornu and Shulam: 859-63; for the view that Titus was in fact circumcised – partially based on the reading of verse 5 which drops the "to whom [we did] not" – cf. Burton: 79-85.
[36] While the "with me (ὁ σὺν ἐμοί)" is also concessive, indicating a fact already known, some of its import may derive from the fact that Titus is Paul's companion – i.e., not even Paul's associate falls subject to foreign demands.
[37] For the incident with Cornelius as a מעשה (ma'aseh – "legal precedent"), cf. Le Cornu and Shulam: 588, 609, 831-32; for forced conversion in general, cf. Feldman, Jew: 324-26.
[38] The three groups are composed of the initiators (Paul/MMT community); those whom they wish to persuade, being close in outlook to the first party (the Apostles/the addressees); and the "opponents." For Galatians as a "halakhic letter" along the lines of 4QMMT, see Introduction, **Form**; **Argument**.

as a concession to the feelings of convictions of those whom Paul designates as false brethren" (Burton: 77).

The "false brethren (τοὺς ψευδαδέλφους)" are – in contrast to the Galatian influencers – part of the early believing community yet possessed of a tendency which Paul designates as "false" (cf. 2 Cor. 11:26; Phil. 3:2).[39] (This attribute is reinforced by behaviour characterised by stealth and craftiness.) The essence of their exaction is evidently that gentile believers must be circumcised – quite likely along the lines of the "men from Judea" whose teaching in Antioch was directed towards Gentiles who, in the Judaeans' eyes, would not be saved "unless you are circumcised according to the custom of Moses (ἐὰν μὴ περιτμηθῆτε τῷ ἔθει τῷ Μωϋσέως, οὐ δύνασθε σωθῆναι)" (Acts 15:1). Although the epithet does not occur in precisely this form in other contemporary texts, the attitude displayed by the Qumran community towards "those looking for flattering things/easy interpretations [דורשי החלקות]" and their "fraudulent teaching and lying tongue and perfidious lip תלמוד שקרם ולשון כזביהם ושפת מרמה" may perhaps serve as a good parallel.[40] The designation of this group may indicate that it included proselytes – people who believed themselves to be true members of the Jewish community. It is precisely the integrity, motives, and status of such perpetrators, both in Jerusalem and in Galatia (each for their own reason), which Paul calls into question.[41]

Circumcision

Circumcision is the sign of the people's covenant with God (cf. Gen. 17:9f; Lev. 12:3; Jub. 15:28). Its centrality within Judaism is signified – among other things – by its inclusion in the list of acts for which a Jew must suffer martyrdom rather than violate the commandment: "For even if an enemy

---

[39] Paul's meaning quite likely parallels that in Phil. 3:2-3, wherein he contrasts the "false circumcision [mutilation]" with the "*true* circumcision [mutilation]", who worship in the Spirit of God and glory in the Messiah Jesus and put no confidence in the flesh (βλέπετε τὴν κατατομήν. ἡμεῖς γάρ ἐσμεν ἡ περιτομή, οἱ πνεύματι θεοῦ λατρεύοντες καὶ καυχώμενοι ἐν Χριστῷ Ἰησοῦ καὶ οὐκ ἐν σαρκὶ πεποιθότες)." For "boasting in the flesh," see 5:2f and 6:1f.

[40] Cf. 4QpNah ff3-4i:2ff, ii:2-12, iii:3ff; CD-A 1:14-21; 1QHᵃ 10:32f; 4QpIsaᶜ f23ii:10. The Scrolls also repeatedly denounce those who are false to God's covenant and to the community who cling to it, including those who fall away (cf. 1QpHab 9:9ff, 10:9f; 1QS 4:9-19, 5:11-13, 9:8-10; CD-A 1:1-3:13, 5:6-6:1, 8:1-21; CD-B 19:13-35; 4Q501 1:4). For pharisaical hypocrisy, see 6:1-11 and verses 15-21.

[41] The fact that circumcision is the only point at issue here may indicate that in (all) other respects, Titus' behaviour was of such a status as to satisfy the sensibilities of the "false brethren" (cf. Dunn, Incident: 227). For the severity of the language employed in the Qumran texts – albeit more extreme than Paul's, who still regards those opposed to his views as brethren – cf. the references in the previous note; for the pesher style of Paul's "allegory" in 4:22-31, see 4:21-31.

decrees that they [Israel] should desecrate the Sabbath, abolish circumcision, or serve idols, they suffer martyrdom rather than be assimilated with them שאפילו שונא גוזר עליהם לחלל השבת ולבטל את המילה או לעבוד עבודה זרה הן נהרגים ואין מתערבין בהן" (Ex.R. 15:7).

Both Jews and non-Jews recognised circumcision as a distinguishing mark of Judaism.[42] A mishnah lists some of circumcision's greatest attributes: "R. Ishmael says: Great is circumcision, whereby the covenant was made thirteen times [cf. Genesis 17]. R. Jose says: Great is circumcision which overrides even the rigour of the Sabbath. R. Joshua b. Karha says: Great is circumcision, which even for the sake of Moses, the righteous, was not suspended so much as an hour [cf. Ex. 4:24ff]. R. Nehemiah says: Great is circumcision which overrides the laws of leprosy-signs [cf. Neg. 7:5]. Rabbi says: Great is circumcision, for despite all the religious duties which Abraham our father fulfilled, he was not called 'perfect' until he circumcised himself, as it is written, *Walk before me, and be thou perfect* (Gen. 17:1). After another fashion [it is said], Great is circumcision: but for it, the Holy One, blessed is he, had not created his world, as it is written, *Thus saith the Lord, but for my covenant day and night, I had not set forth the ordinances of heaven and earth* (Jer. 33:25)"[43] (Ned. 3:11).

While circumcision can be applied to the heart,[44] the physical act can never be abolished: "R. Elazar of Modim said: One who profanes things sacred, and one who slights the festivals, and one who causes his fellow-man's face to blanch in public, and one who nullifies the covenant of our father Abraham [i.e., removes his circumcision], peace be upon him, and he who exhibits impudence towards the Torah, even though he has to his credit [knowledge of] the Torah and good deeds, he has not a share in the life of the world to come"[45] (PA 3:11).

---

[42] Cf. Ex. 12:44, 48; Josh. 5:2-7; Acts 10:45, 11:2f; Gal. 2:7; Phil. 3:4-5; 1 Macc. 1:15, 48, 60, 2:46; 2 Macc. 6:10; Jub. 15:23ff; Jos.*Ant.* 1.192, 13.318; *CA* 2.137, 140f; Philo, *Spec.Leg.* 1.1-11; *Mig.Abr.* 92; Strabo, *Geog.* 16.2.37; Ex.R. 30:12; Eduy. 5:2; Pes. 8:8; Yev. 47b; Diodorus 1.55.5; Horace, *Sat.* 1.9.60f; Petronius, *Satyr.* 102.13-14; Juv.*Sat.* 14.96ff; Persius, *Sat.* 5.184; Mart.*Epig.* 7.35.3-4, 82.5, 11.94; Tac.*Hist.* 5.5.2; Suet.*Dom.* 12.2.

[43] רבי ישמעאל אומר: גדולה מילה שנכרתו עליה שלש עשרה בריתות. רבי יוסי אומר: גדולה מילה, שדוחה את השבת החמורה. רבי יהושע בן קרחה אומר: גדולה מילה, שלא נתלה לו למשה הצדיק עליה מלא שעה. רבי נחמיה אומר: גדולה מילה, שדוחה את הנגעים. רבי אומר: גדולה מילה, שכל המצות שעשה אברהם אבינו לא נקרא שלם עד שמל, שנאמר: התהלך לפני והיה תמים. דבר אחר, גדולה מילה, שאלמלא היא, לא ברא הקדוש ברוך הוא את עולמו, שנאמר: כה אמר ה' אם-לא בריתי יומם ולילה, חקות שמים וארץ לא שמתי.

[44] Cf. Dt. 10:16, 30:6; Jer. 4:4, 9:25f; Rom. 2:25f; Jub. 1:22-23; Odes Sol. 11:1-3; 1QS 5:5; 1QpHab 11:13; 4Q177 2:16; 4Q434 1:4; PRE 29; Gen.R. 46:5; Lev.R. 25:6; Ber. 29a.

[45] רבי אלעזר המודעי אומר: המחלל את הקדשים והמבזה את המועדות והמלבין פני חברו ברבים והמפר בריתו של אברהם אבינו עליו השלום והמגלה פנים בתורה שלא כהלכה, אף על פי שיש בידו תורה ומעשים טובים, אין לו חלק לעולם הבא.

This attitude also demonstrates how central the covenant is to the Jewish community's identity in the purity of its descent – and thus to God's promises of redemption: "*At that time thy people shall be delivered* (Dan. 12:1). Through whose merit? ... R. Samuel bar Nahmani said: Through the merit of their lineage, for it is said *Bring My sons from far, and My daughters from the end of the earth; every one that is called by My name* (Isa. 43:6b-7). R. Levi said: Through the merit of circumcision. For the verse of this comment says that *At that time thy people shall be delivered*, and in another place it is written *At that time the Lord said unto Joshua: 'Make thee knives of flint, and circumcise ... the children of Israel* ' (Josh. 5:2)"[46] (Mid.Ps. 20:3).

The claim made of gentile believers by the Judaeans who arrived in Antioch that "unless you are circumcised according to the custom of Moses, you cannot be saved (ἐὰν μὴ περιτμηθῆτε τῷ ἔθει τῷ Μωϋσέως, οὐ δύνασθε σωθῆναι)" (Acts 15:1) (cf. Mt. 5:20) fits the attitude of those "zealous for the law"[47] – for whom the "godfearer *versus* proselyte" debate was decided in favour of the latter. In this context, the verb σωθῆναι (sōthēnai - "to be saved") appears to refer to the "righteousness" through which a person merits עולם הבא (olam ha-ba) or "the world to come," both godfearers and proselytes being characterisable according to their righteousness (cf. גר צדק/גוי צדיק [goi tzadik/ger tzedek]).[48]

The acceptance of proselytes was a subject of debate between Beit Shammai and Beit Hillel.[49] The dispute between R. Eliezer and R. Joshua (c. 80-110) directly relates to the necessity of circumcision: "Our Rabbis taught: If a proselyte was circumcised but had not performed the prescribed ritual ablution, R. Eliezer said, 'Behold he is a proper proselyte; for so we find that our forefathers were circumcised and had not performed ritual ablution'. If he performed the prescribed ablution but had not been circumcised, R. Joshua said, 'Behold he is a proper proselyte ...' ת"ר: גר שמל ולא טבל, ר' אליעזר אומר: הרי זה גר שכן מצינו באבותינו שמלו ולא טבלו. "טבל ולא מל, ר' יהושע אומר: הרי זה גר ..." (Yev. 46a).[50]

When interpreted in the context of Beit Shammai's zealot tendencies, this dispute may be read as emphasising the fact that the Gentile is unclean *per se*. He is forbidden to study Torah until he has been circumcised, since circumcision is not merely a commandment but symbolises entry into the

---

[46] ובעת ההיא ימלט עמך. בזכות מי? ... ר' שמואל בר נחמני אמר: בשביל ייחסיהון, שנאמר: כל הנקרא בשמי. ר' לוי אמר: בזכות המילה, כתיב הכא: ובעת ההיא ימלט עמך וכתיב התם: בעת ההיא אמר ה' אל יהושע.

[47] Cf. Acts 21:20, 22:3; Rom. 10:2; Gal. 1:14; Jos.*Ant.* 20.43f.

[48] Cf. [Ps. 146:9]; Isa. 26:2; Ex.R. 15:29; Num.R. 8:9; Sifra, Acharei mot 13; Be-har 5; Mekh.Nez. 19; Tos.Arak. 5:9; Yev. 48b; San. 59a; BK 38a, 113b.

[49] Cf. ARNᵃ 15:3; ARNᵇ 29; Shab. 31a.

[50] Cf. Sifre, Shall. 107; Pes. 8:8; Ker. 9a.

covenant people.[51] Only full conversion – embodied in the blood drawn
through circumcision – fits a person to study what God gave to Israel
alone. Significantly, those responsible for the dicta prohibiting Gentiles
from studying Torah[52] also seem to have been those who insisted that they
become full proselytes (cf. Ben-Shalom: 164f).

Scholars have attempted to link the controversy between R. Eliezer
and R. Joshua with the opposing arguments put forward by Ananias and
Eleazer in Josephus' record of the "conversion" of the royal house of
Adiabene:

> Now during the time when Izates resided at Charax Spasini, a
> certain Jewish merchant named Ananias visited the king's wives
> and taught them to worship after the manner of the Jewish
> tradition. It was through their agency that he was brought to the
> notice of Izates, whom he similarly won over with the co-
> operation of the women . . . When Izates learned that his mother
> was very much pleased with the Jewish religion, he was zealous
> to convert to it himself; and since he considered that he would
> not genuinely be a Jew unless he was circumcised, he was ready
> to act accordingly. When his mother learned of his intention,
> however, she tried to stop him by telling him that . . . if his
> subjects should discover that he was devoted to rites that were
> strange and foreign to themselves, it would produce much
> disaffection and they would not tolerate the rule of a Jew over
> them . . . He, in turn, reported her arguments to Ananias. The
> latter expressed agreement with the king's mother . . . the king
> could, he said, worship God even without being circumcised if
> indeed he had fully decided to be a devoted adherent of Judaism,
> for it was this that counted more than circumcision. He told him,
> furthermore, that God Himself would pardon him if, constrained
> thus by necessity and by fear of his subjects, he failed to perform
> this rite. And so, for the time, the king was convinced by his
> arguments. Afterwards, however, since he had not completely
> given up his desire, another Jew, named Eleazar, who came from
> Galilee and who had a reputation for being extremely strict when
> it came to the ancestral laws, urged him to carry out the rite. For
> when he came to pay him his respects and found him reading the
> law of Moses, he said: "In your ignorance, O king, you are guilty
> of the greatest offence against the law and thereby against God.
> For you ought not merely to read the law but also, and even
> more, to do what is commanded in it. How long will you

[51] Cf. Ex.R. 30:12; Hipp.*Ref.Omn.Her.* 9.21.
[52] Cf. [Ex.R. 33:7]; Hag. 13a; San. 59a.

continue to be uncircumcised? If you have not yet read the law concerning this matter, read it now, so that you may know what an impiety it is that you commit." Upon hearing these words, the king postponed the deed no longer ... It was God who was to prevent their fears from being realized. For although Izates himself and his children were often threatened with destruction, God preserved them, opening a path to safety from desperate straits. God thus demonstrated that those who fix their eyes on Him and trust in Him alone do not lose the reward of their piety.[53] (Jos.Ant. 20.34-35, 38-39, 41-46, 48)

Despite its immediate relevance to the issue of godfearers and converts, the identification of this dispute with Beit Shammai and Beit Hillel[54] remains speculative, Ananias' claim that devotion to Jewish ancestral laws counts more than circumcision being best understood as an argument for the omission of circumcision in cases of physical danger. (While it closely resembles Paul's view in Romans 2:28f, it possesses a

---

[53] Καθ' ὃν δὲ χρόνον ὁ 'Ιζάτης ἐν τῷ Σπασίνου χάρακι διέτριβεν 'Ιουδαῖός τις ἔμπορος 'Ανανίας ὄνομα πρὸς τὰς γυναῖκας εἰσιὼν τοῦ βασιλέως ἐδίδασκεν αὐτὰς τὸν θεὸν σέβειν, ὡς 'Ιουδαίοις πάτριον ἦν, καὶ δὴ δι' αὐτῶν εἰς γνῶσιν ἀφικόμενος τῷ 'Ιζάτῃ κἀκεῖνον ὁμοίως συνανέπεισεν μετακληθέντι ... Πυθόμενος δὲ πάνυ τοῖς 'Ιουδαίων ἔθεσιν χαίρειν τὴν μητέρα τὴν ἑαυτοῦ ἔσπευσε καὶ αὐτὸς εἰς ἐκεῖνα μεταθέσθαι, νομίζων μὴ ἂν εἶναι βεβαίως 'Ιουδαῖος, εἰ μὴ περιτέμοιτο, πράττειν ἦν ἕτοιμος. μαθοῦσα δ' ἡ μήτηρ κωλύειν ἐπειρᾶτο ... λέγουσα ... καταστήσειν εἰς πολλὴν δυσμένειαν τοὺς ὑπηκόους μαθόντας, ὅτι ξένων ἐπιθυμήσειεν καὶ ἀλλοτρίων αὐτοῖς ἐθῶν, οὐκ ἀνέξεσθαι τε βασιλεύοντος αὐτῶν 'Ιουδαίου ... ὁ δ' εἰς τὸν 'Ανανίαν τοὺς λόγους ἀνέφερεν. τοῦ δὲ τῇ μητρὶ συμφάσκοντος ... δυνάμενον δ' αὐτὸν ἔφη καὶ χωρὶς τῆς περιτομῆς τὸ θεῖον σέβειν, εἴγε πάντως κέκρικε ζηλοῦν τὰ πάτρια τῶν 'Ιουδαίων· τοῦτ' εἶναι κυριώτερον τοῦ περιτέμνεσθαι· συγγνώμην δ' ἕξειν αὐτῷ καὶ τὸν θεὸν φήσαντος μὴ πράξαντι τὸ ἔργον δι' ἀνάγκην καὶ τὸν ἐκ τῶν ὑπηκόων φόβον, ἐπείσθη μὲν τότε τοῖς λόγοις ὁ βασιλεύς. μετὰ ταῦτα δέ, τὴν γὰρ ἐπιθυμίαν οὐκ ἐξεβεβλήκει παντάπασιν, 'Ιουδαῖός τις ἕτερος ἐκ τῆς Γαλιλαίας ἀφικόμενος 'Ελεάζαρος ὄνομα πάνυ περὶ τὰ πάτρια δοκῶν ἀκριβὴς εἶναι προετρέψατο πρᾶξαι τοὖργον. ἐπεὶ γὰρ εἰσῆλθεν ἀσπασόμενος αὐτὸν καὶ κατέλαβε τὸν Μωυσέος νόμον ἀναγινώσκοντα, "λανθάνεις," εἶπεν "ὦ βασιλεῦ, τὰ μέγιστα τοὺς νόμους καὶ δι' αὐτῶν τὸν θεὸν ἀδικῶν· οὐ γὰρ ἀναγινώσκειν σε δεῖ μόνον αὐτούς, ἀλλὰ καὶ πρότερον τὰ προστασσόμενα ποιεῖν ὑπ' αὐτῶν. μέχρι τίνος ἀπερίτμητος μένεις; ἀλλ' εἰ μήπω τὸν περὶ τούτου νόμον ἀνέγνως, ἵν' εἰδῇς τίς ἐστιν ἡ ἀσέβεια, νῦν ἀνάγνωθι." ταῦτα ἀκούσας ὁ βασιλεὺς οὐχ ὑπερεβάλετο τὴν πρᾶξιν ... θεὸς δὲ ἦν ὁ κωλύσων ἄρα τοὺς ἐκείνων φόβους ἐλθεῖν ἐπὶ τέλος· πολλοῖς γὰρ αὐτόν τε τὸν 'Ιζάτην περιπεσόντα κινδύνοις καὶ παῖδας τοὺς ἐκείνου διέσωσεν ἐξ ἀμηχάνων πόρον εἰς σωτηρίαν παρασχών, ἐπιδεικνὺς ὅτι τοῖς εἰς αὐτὸν ἀποβλέπουσιν καὶ μόνῳ πεπιστευκόσιν ὁ καρπὸς οὐκ ἀπόλλυται ὁ τῆς εὐσεβείας.

[54] Cf. Tos.Shab. 15:9; JShab. 19, 2, 17a; JYev. 8, 1, 9a; Shab. 31a.

different halakhic implication.[55]) The account nevertheless reflects the framework of the debate and its discussion within a broad spectrum of Second Temple Judaism. [56]

Godfearers

Despite the fact that some scholars doubt whether "godfearers" actually existed as a category during the New Testament period,[57] Acts clearly identifies them as people who attached themselves to the synagogue in their local town and adopted some Jewish customs – such as Sabbath observance and dietary laws – without fully converting (being circumcised).[58] The frequency with which shabbat was observed among godfearers is illustrated by documents testifying to the profuse diffusion of the name Sambathion, deriving from "shabbat" (*CPJ* Sect. 13) (cf. Feldman, Jew: 359f). Juvenal's satire of Jewish customs includes the instructive gibe that once the father starts observing shabbat and refraining from pork the son is ready to circumcise himself and become a full proselyte (cf. Juv.*Sat.* 14.96f).[59]

---

[55] For Romans 2, see 5:2f and verses 15-21.

[56] The debate between R. Eliezer the Shammaite [ר' אליעזר השמתי] and R. Joshua indicates that Jewish attitudes towards Gentiles could be both complimentary and dismissive: "R. Eliezer says: All Gentiles – they have no share in the world to come, as it is said *The wicked will return to Sheol, even all the nations who forget God* (Ps. 9:17) ... R. Joshua said to him ... Since the verse says *who forget God* – this means that there are righteous among the nations who have a share in the world to come ר' אליעזר אומר: כל גוים אין להם חלק לעולם הבא, שנאמר: ישובו רשעים לשאולה כל גוים שכחי אלהים ... אמר לו ר' יהושע ... עכשיו שאומר הכתוב: שכחי אלהים - הא יש צדיקים באומות שיש להם חלק לעולם הבא." (Tos.San. 13:2). Beit Shammai's promulgation of the "Eighteen Decrees" – which prohibited the Gentiles' food, offerings, language, testimony, and sons and daughters – seems to have occurred as an expression of anti-gentile sentiments, exacerbated by the war against Rome, scholars suggesting that Beit Shammai aligned itself with zealot tendencies in the lead-up to the Revolt in 70 C.E. (cf. Ben-Shalom; Hengel, Zealots: 200f).

[57] The literature on this subject is enormous: cf. Feldman, Omnipresence; Stern, Greek: 103f; Goodman; McKnight; Levinskaya; Nanos, Romans: 50f, 166f, Irony: 91-96; Segal: 187-223; Kraabel; Hemer: 177n37; Donaldson; Finn; Lieberman, Greek: 68-90.

[58] Cf. 13:16, 26, 17:1-4, 17; Jos.*Ant.* 14.110; *CA* 2.282; [Philo, *Vit.Mos.* 2.21]; Mid.Ps. 22:29; TBE p. 49; Tert.*Ad Nat.* 1.13; Juv.*Sat.* 14.96-106.

[59] Quidam sortiti metuentem sabbata patrem/ nil praeter nubes et caeli numer adorant,/ nec distare putant human carne suillam,/ qua pater abstinuit, mox et praeputia ponunt;/ Romanas autem soliti contemnere leges/ Iudaicum ediscunt et servant ac metuunt ius,/ tradidit arcano quodcumque volumine Moyses:/ non monstrare vias eadem nisi sacra colenti,/ quaesitum ad fontem solos deducere verpos./ Sed pater in causa, cui septima quaeque fuit lux,/ ignava et partem vitae non attigit ullam.

Josephus witnesses that godfearers went to great lengths – both geographically and spiritually – to show their respect for the God of Israel:

> Only recently certain persons from beyond the Euphrates, after a journey of four months, undertaken from veneration of our temple ... having offered sacrifices, could not partake of the victims, because Moses had forbidden this to any of those not governed by our laws nor affiliated through the customs of their fathers to ourselves. Accordingly some without sacrificing at all, others leaving their sacrifices half completed, many of them unable so much as to gain entrance to the temple, they went their way, preferring to conform to the injunctions of Moses rather than to act in accordance with their own will, and that from no fear of being reproved in this matter but solely through misgivings of conscience.[60] (Jos.Ant. 3.318-19) (cf. Pes. 3b)

While participation in obligatory offerings – e.g., sin- and guilt-offerings, women following childbirth, etc. – was prohibited to Gentiles, the latter could offer all the voluntary sacrifices which fell under the categories of נדיבות (nedivot – free-will offerings or "donations") and נדרים (nedarim – vows). The halakhah ruled that "if a gentile sent his Whole-offering from a region beyond the sea and sent the drink-offerings also, these are offered; but if he did not, they are to be offered at the charges [expense] of the congregation - נכרי ששלח עולתו ממדינת הים ושלח עמה נסכים קרבין משלו, ואם לאו - קרבין משלצבור" – it being understood that the foreigner was ignorant of the requirement that a burnt offering be accompanied by libations (Shek. 7:6)[61] (cf. Safrai and Stern: 199f). Josephus attests to the practice in noting that one of the first steps taken on the outbreak of the Revolt was the announcement that gentile sacrifices were no longer acceptable (cf. War 2.408-21). Those who protested the move "produced priestly experts on the traditions, who declared that all their ancestors had accepted the sacrifices of aliens (παρῆγον τοὺς ἐμπείρους τῶν πατρίων ἱερεῖς, ἀφηγουμένους ὅτι πάντες οἱ πρόγονοι τὰς παρὰ τῶν ἀλλογενῶν θυσίας ἀπεδέχοντο)" (Jos.War 2.417) (cf. Lev. 22:25).

Prominent Greek and Roman personages are numbered among those who brought or sent offerings to the Temple. Josephus mentions Alexander

---

[60] ἤδε δέ τινες καὶ τῶν ὑπὲρ Εὐφράτην μηνῶν ὁδὸν τεσσάρων ἐλθόντες κατὰ τιμὴν τοῦ παρ᾽ ἡμῖν ἱεροῦ ... θύσαντες οὐκ ἴσχυσαν τῶν ἱερείων μεταλαβεῖν, Μωυσέος ἀπηγορευκότος ἐπί τινι τῶν οὐ νομιζομένων οὐδ᾽ ἐκ τῶν πατρίων ἡμῖν αὐτοῖς συντυχόντων. Καὶ οἱ μὲν μηδὲ θύσαντες, οἱ δὲ ἡμιέργους τὰς θυσίας καταλιπόντες, πολλοὶ δ᾽ οὐδ᾽ ἀρχὴν εἰσελθεῖν εἰς τὸ ἱερὸν δυνηθέντες ἀπίασιν, ὑπακούειν τοῖς Μωυσέος προστάγμασι μᾶλλον ἢ ποιεῖν τὰ κατὰ βούλησιν τὴν ἑαυτῶν προτιμῶντες, καὶ τὸν ἐλέγχοντα περὶ τούτων αὐτοὺς οὐ δεδιότες, ἀλλὰ μόνον τὸ συνειδὸς ὑφορώμενοι.

[61] Cf. TBE pp. 34-35; Men. 73b.

the Great (probably legendarily), Ptolemy III, Antiochus VII Sidetes, Marcus Agrippa, and Vitellius[62] (cf. Schürer: 2:309f). Cornelius may have sent offerings to the Temple or even brought them himself, living in close proximity to Jerusalem. (A centurion's salary was apparently sufficiently high to enable him to make generous donations.) Contributions or dedications could be received from Gentiles towards the Temple's maintenance and decoration, although gifts for the Temple service were only accepted after strict examination (cf. Arak. 6a). Contemporary sources also witness to the number of votive offerings (sacrifices vowed on a voluntary basis) brought by foreign rulers.[63]

While the term ἐλεημοσύνη (eleēmosunē – "charitable deed") originally denoted a "kind deed" it later came to refer specifically to almsgiving, frequently being used with the verb ποιεῖν (poien) – "to do charity."[64] Godfearers commonly expressed their commitment to the synagogue by serving as benefactors and patrons to the Jewish community.[65] In the gospel, Luke speaks of another well-respected centurion who built a synagogue for the people of Capernaum, perhaps as its main benefactor (cf. Lk. 7:2ff), and other people dedicated candlesticks or lamps (cf. Arak. 6b).

Verses 4-5: The adjective παρεισάκτους (pareisaktous), carrying the sense of "smuggled in," attributes to the "false brethren (τοὺς ψευδαδέλφους)" an element of spying and infiltration (cf. 2 Pet. 2:1; Jude 4).[66] The atmosphere corresponds in many ways to the incident reflected in 4Q171, wherein the writer applies Psalm 37 to the fate of the Qumran community: "*Ps 37:32-33* The wicked person spies on the just person and tries [to kill him. YH]WH [will not relinquish him into his hand,] n[or] let him be condemned {and} when he is judged. Its interpretation concerns the Wicked [Pri]est, who sp[ie]s on the ju[st man and wants to] kill him [. . .]

---

62 Cf. *Ant.* 11.329f, 13.242f, 16.14, 18.122; *War* 4.262, 5.17; *CA* 2.48; Philo, *Leg.* 157; Tert.*Apol.* 26.3.

63 Cf. Ep.Arist. 42, 51-82; 2 Macc. 3:2, 5:16; Jos.*Ant.* 12.40-77, 13.74ff, 14.488; *War* 2.412f, 4.181, 5.562f; *CA* 2.48f.

64 Cf. Mt. 6:2f; Acts 9:36, 24:17; Tob. 1:3, 16, 4:7f; Sir. 7:10. For "doing good" as *gmilut chasadim* ["deeds of lovingkindness"], see 5:19-23 and 6:1-11.

65 Cf. Lk. 7:2ff; Tos.Meg. 3[2]:5; JMeg. 3, 1, 74a; BB 10b.

66 Despite its passive construction, the adjective need not signify an initiative on the part of others who introduced the intruders, implying that the infiltrators' views were already supported by some within the community. "That they are alien to the body into which they have come is what the term both etymologically and by usage suggests" (Burton: 78). If, as Betz suggests, as in 1:7 Paul indulges here in "the language of political demagoguery, that is, military language turned into political metaphors" (Betz, *Galatians*: 90), his framework remains scriptural on this reading (see Introduction, **Theological pointers** [Scripture]). For "false brethren," see above.

and the law which he sent him; but God will not re[linquish him] nor [let him be condemned when] he is judged . . ."[67] (4Q171 4:7-9).

If Paul has such a verse as Psalm 37:32 ("the wicked spies on the righteous") in mind, the association may have arisen in connection with Isaiah 49:4 (see above), the "wicked who prosper" of the Psalm eventually being destined to be cut off: "But the salvation of the righteous is from the LORD; He is their strength in time of trouble. And the LORD helps them, and delivers them; He delivers them from the wicked, and saves them, because they take refuge in Him"[68] (Ps. 37:39-40) (see also 4:21-31 [verse 29]).[69]

The theme of bondage is central to the letter as a whole. It first appears in 1:4, in reference to "deliverance from the present evil age," the allusion possibly being linked to the forgiveness of debts in the jubilee/sabbatical year (cf. Lev. 25:10; Isa. 61:1) (see 1:1-5). As there, the liberty (τὴν ἐλευθερίαν; tēn eleutherian) here is also a function of Jesus' redeeming role – the Exodus being the other preeminent model of the "yoke of slavery" (cf. Lev. 26:13; Gal. 5:1) (see 4:21-31). In the terms of 11QMelchizedek, those who share Jesus' faithfulness belong to his "lot [גורל]" and "inheritance [נחלה]," it being to them that "liberty will be proclaimed . . . to free them from [the debt of] all their iniquities דרור לעזוב להמה [משא] כול עוונותיהמה" (11QMelch 2:5-6) (see 3:21-25, 4:1-7, and 6:1-11). The prepositional phrase ἐν Χριστῷ Ἰησοῦ (en Christō Iēsou) – one through which Paul repeatedly characterises the believer's faithfulness to Jesus' own obedience – is both local and instrumental, Jesus being the agent and locus of deliverance alike (cf. Longenecker, *Galatians*: 52).[70]

The fact that Paul warns the Galatians against *resubmitting* themselves ("again [πάλιν]") to bondage in 5:1 supports the view that the bondage is not to the Torah but to sin (see 1:1-5 and 4:1f).[71] On the assumption that the

---

[67] צופה רשע לצדיק ומבקש [להמיתו יי]יי [לוא יעזבנו בידו ו]ל[וא י]רשיענו [ו]בהשפטו פשרו על [הכו]הן הרשע אשר צ[ו]פ[ה הצד]יק ומבקש ל[המיתו]. . .[ן והתורה אשר שלח אליו ואל לוא יע[ו]זבנו] ולוא [ירשיענו ב]השפטו . . .

[68] ותשועת צדיקים מה׳ מעוזם בעת צרה: ויעזרם ה׳ ויפלטם יפלטם מרשעים ויושיעם כי-חסו בו.

[69] For the suggestion that the "law" sent to the Wicked Priest is to be identified with 4QMMT, see Introduction, **Form** (n146). For Galatians as a "halakhic letter" along the lines of 4QMMT, see Introduction, **Form; Argument**.

[70] For Jesus' "representative" role, see Introduction, **Theological pointers** and verses 15-21.

[71] Cf. Rom. 6:11-23, 8:2-22; Gal. 4:1-10; Heb. 2:15. Although the "yoke of the Torah" עול התורה is a favourite rabbinic designation, it is never used derogatorily (cf. PA 3:5; Tanh.Ve-zot ha-bracha 5; TBE p. 8; Num.R. 19:26; San. 94b). This simile apart, the image of the yoke is frequently associated with slavery in general (cf. Gen. 27:40; Dt. 28:48; 1 Kings 12:4f; 2 Chron. 10:4ff; Isa. 9:4; 1 Tim. 6:1; 1 Macc. 8:18, 31, 13:41; Sir. 28:19). Significantly, Paul sums up the freedom from sin to which the Gentiles are called in 5:13 as "the whole Torah (πᾶς νόμος)" – serving one

relapse refers to the Galatians' wish to be circumcised in accordance with Jewish norms (cf. 5:2f), the present reading of the circumstances proposes that Paul's propaganda is not directed towards Torah-observance *per se* but towards circumcision as a necessary act for admission into the Jewish community.[72] Specifically, the "bondage (καταδουλώσουσιν)" relates to the "subjection (τῇ ὑποταγῇ)" (verse 5) which Paul feels is being improperly sought by the false brethren.[73] The article before the latter noun restricts its significance, denoting the particular conformity which these brethren demanded (cf. Burton: 84).[74]

Paul affirms to the Galatians that – in direct relevance to their current standing – he did not comply "for a second" with the claims exercised for Titus' circumcision – the Hebrew שעה (sha'ah) designating a "moment, while" as well as a strict "hour" (cf. Jastrow: 1609). While the temporal notation is rather strange – a quantitative/conceptual measurement perhaps rather being anticipated – it may mark the episodic element involved in the physical act of circumcision. The meaning is clearly that at no point did Paul ever consider circumcising Titus.[75] Although Paul may not have had the Galatians specifically in mind during this incident, he acknowledges that his "standing firm" was motivated – at least in part – by a desire to continue preaching the same gospel, maintaining its integrity in the face of all opposition, past, present, and anticipated. Now that he is

---

another/faithfulness working through love (cf. Lev. 19:18) (see 5:2f and 6:1-11). For the Galatians' "return" in 4:9 as a resubmission to bondage under Belial, see 4:8-11.

[72] To this extent we would concur with Gager's claim that Paul is exclusively addressing Gentiles, not Jews, in speaking of Torah-observance, the current conclusion being based on identification of the influencers as godfearers who do not accept Jesus' death and resurrection as a valid or legitimate means for achieving Jewish status (see Introduction, **Occasion and circumstances**). For Gager's argument, see Introduction, **Author**.

[73] This is further suggested by the aorist subjunctive active of the textus receptus (καταδουλώσωνται), which understands the purpose clause to mean that these brethren wished to impose their will upon Paul and his party (cf. Longenecker, Galatians: 52). While in so doing they would naturally also demand circumcision from gentile believers, the bondage which results is not equivalent to circumcision *per se*. Although not wishing to transpose elements from the episode in Jerusalem onto the situation in Galatia, Paul evidently considers the influence of both the "false brethren" and the "troublers" as leading to bondage to sin. For the proper criteria for the influencers' identification, see Introduction, **Occasion and circumstances**.

[74] It is probably also not coincidental that from a halakhic perspective slaves and converts possess parallel status, the slave being in many respects a convert-in-the-making and, once emancipated, by definition a proselyte (cf. Jub. 15:13; Bik. 1:5; Yev. 47a-b) (cf. Cohen, Rabbinic: 186n19) (see also 4:21-31 and below).

[75] For the variants which omit the οὐδέ (oude – "not"), suggesting that Paul *did* submit, cf. Metzger: 591-92.

directly addressing the Galatians he can include them among those for
whom he had acted with regard to Titus.[76]

The "truth of the gospel (ἡ ἀλήθεια τοῦ εὐαγγελίου)" (cf. verse 14;
[5:7]) may reflect the biblical association between God's truth and His
salvation: "O God, in the greatness of Thy lovingkindness, answer me with
the truth of Thy salvation אלהים ברב-חסדך ענני באמת ישעך"[77] (Ps. 69:13) (see
below).[78] It may also express the heart of Paul's attitude towards
circumcision *as a voluntary act* within the context of the early community.[79]
The origin of the "conversion ceremony" in the mid-second century C.E.
can be traced, at least in part, to the attempt to ensure that circumcision
(and immersion) are undertaken with the correct intent (cf. Kulp; Cohen,
Rabbinic: 195ff, and for the following discussion).[80] The belief that the
circumcision rite (as a symbol of conversion) is efficacious *ex opere operato*
(in and of itself) is reflected in the fact that rabbinic law permits both the
conversion of children – who are assumed to be subject to paternal
authority – and of slaves against their will.[81]

---

[76] This helps confirm the thesis that the Galatians are seeking circumcision – and
that they are, therefore, Gentiles (see excursi above and verses 11-14).

[77] Cf. Ps. 85:10, 98:3; Eph. 1:13; 2 Thess. 2:13.

[78] The Qumran texts frequently speak of "joining God's Truth" in a manner in
which Truth parallels the New Testament "gospel": "All those who submit freely to
his truth will convey all their knowledge, their energies, and their riches to the
Community of God in order to refine their knowledge in the truth of God's decrees
and marshal their energies in accordance with his perfect paths and all their riches
in accordance with his just counsel וכול הנדבים לאמתו יביאו כול דעתם וכוחם והונם ביחד
(1QS 1:11-13) "אל לברר דעתם באמת חוקי אל וכוחם לתכן כתם דרכיו וכול הונם כעצת צדקו
(cf. 1QS 2:26, 3:7, 5:5, 9:3; 1QM 13:10, 17:8) (cf. Le Cornu and Shulam: 153-62, 259-
67).

[79] This in distinction to his argument regarding the Galatian influencers – who are
not themselves believers according to the present reading. Paul's opposition to the
latter derives from the fact that they resist Jesus' death and resurrection by insisting
that, if they wish Jewish identity, the gentile believers become full members of the
Jewish community. To the extent that conversion is dependent upon circumcision,
Paul would presumably have objected to any proselytism not conducted לשם שמים
(le-shem shamayim – "for the sake of heaven") – i.e., out of pure motives and with
intent to fulfil the covenant's conditions. Under the latter circumstances, he
perceives it as a proper procedure (cf. Acts 16:1-3).

[80] The first intent is that circumcision be performed in order to bring the child into
God's covenant with Abraham (cf. Tos.AZ 3:13).

[81] Cf. Ket. 1:2, 3:1, 4:3; JKid. 4, 1, 65b; JYev. 8, 1, 8d; Ket. 11a; Yev. 48a, 60b. Cohen
also appeals to the forced conversion of the Idumaeans and Ituraeans (cf. Jos.*Ant.*
13.257-58, 318-19) in demonstrating that "the physical fact of circumcision, no
matter what the circumstances were under which it was perpetrated, sufficed for
conversion" (p. 193). Paul's language here certainly reflects the notion of "forced
conversion."

Paul's conviction – on the contrary – is that *intention* is the axis around which obedience to God revolves (see 3:6ff and verses 15-21). In line with the prophetic critique, the Qumran literature, and Ananias' assertion to Izates, he wishes to declare – to Jews and Gentiles alike – that circumcision is an act first and foremost of the heart: "The king could, he [Ananias] said, worship God even without being circumcised if indeed he had fully decided to be a devoted adherent of Judaism, for it was this that counted more than circumcision"[82] (*Ant.* 20.41).[83] "No-one should walk in the stubbornness of his heart in order to go astray following his heart and his eyes and the musings of his inclination. Instead he should circumcise in the Community the foreskin of his tendency and of his stiff neck in order to lay a foundation of truth for Israel, for the Community of the eternal covenant"[84] (1QS 5:4-6).[85] "But he is a Jew who is one inwardly; and circumcision is that which is of the heart, by the Spirit, not by the letter . . . If therefore the uncircumcised man keeps the requirements of the Torah, will not his uncircumcision be regarded as circumcision?"[86] (Rom. 2:29, 26) (see verses 15-21).[87]

"Truth" serves as an expression both of God's faithfulness and of the propriety of Paul's teaching with regard to the Gentiles – which he

---

[82] δυνάμενον δ᾽ αὐτὸν ἔφη καὶ χωρὶς τῆς περιτομῆς τὸ θεῖον σέβειν, εἴγε πάντως κέκρικε ζηλοῦν τὰ πάτρια τῶν Ἰουδαίων· τοῦτ᾽ εἶναι κυριώτερον τοῦ περιτέμνεσθαι.

[83] It is possible that Eleazar's rebuke of Izates, which is based on the argument that "you ought not merely to read the law but also, and even more, to do what is commanded in it (οὐ γὰρ ἀναγινώσκειν σε δεῖ μόνον αὐτούς, ἀλλὰ καὶ πρότερον τὰ προστασσόμενα ποιεῖν ὑπ᾽ αὐτῶν)" represents an emphasis on the rite *qua* rite – in contradistinction to Ananias' claim that *intention* is the ground upon which Jewishness is founded (cf. Jos.*Ant.* 20.34-48) (cf. Paul's claim in Rom. 2:13). For the controversy over intent between Beit Hillel and Beit Shammai, cf. Safrai, Literature: 190-91.

[84] לוא ילך איש בשרירות לבו לתעות אחר לבבו ועינוהו ומחשבת יצרו (כ)יא אם למול ביחד עורלת יצר ועורף קשה ליסד מוסד אמת לישראל ליחד ברית עולם.

[85] For Qumran and "spiritual sacrifices," cf. Gärtner.

[86] ἀλλ᾽ ὁ ἐν τῷ κρυπτῷ Ἰουδαῖος, καὶ περιτομὴ καρδίας ἐν πνεύματι οὐ γράμματι, οὗ ὁ ἔπαινος οὐκ ἐξ ἀνθρώπων ἀλλ᾽ ἐκ τοῦ θεοῦ . . . ἐὰν οὖν ἡ ἀκροβυστία τὰ δικαιώματα τοῦ νόμου φυλάσσῃ, οὐχ ἡ ἀκροβυστία αὐτου εἰς περιτομὴν λογισθήσεται;

[87] Cf. Dt. 10:16, 30:6; Isa. 1:10-17; Jer. 4:4, 7:21f, 31:33-34; Ezek. 36:26-27; Hos. 6:4-6; Amos 5:21-27; Mic. 6:6-8; Rom. 2:13-16, 12:1; Col. 2:11f; [Heb. 13:15]; Jub. 1:22-23; Odes Sol. 11:1-3; 1QS 9:3-6; 1QHᵃ 10:18-19; 1QpHab 11:13; 4QFlor f1i:1-8; Philo, *Spec.Leg.* 1.8f; *Somn.* 2.25; PA 5:19; TBE pp. 140-41; Gen.R. 46:5; Lev.R. 25:6; Ber. 29a. For Paul as prophet, cf. Sandnes. It is critical to remember, once again, that – as reflected also in Philo's dismay with regard to people who neglect the physical form in refining the psyche (cf. *Mig.Abr.* 89f) – Paul's objection is not to circumcision *per se* (nor to conversion) but to these acts when performed without intent or conviction (cf. 5:3, in at least one of its implications).

immediately contrasts with the infiltrators' falsehood. The fact that Paul feels no necessity here to define the gospel – as "his" or that of "another" (cf. 1:6-7) – may reflect his ironic attribution of gospel status to the influencers' message, although the Jerusalem brethren are not to be confused with the group in Galatia (see 1:6-10).[88] The prepositional πρός (pros), which regularly signifies "with" in association with people in Paul (cf. 1:18, 4:18, 20), here also carries the sense of "for you."[89]

Verse 6: Despite the suggestion that Paul deliberately requested Titus' presence with him as a way of attesting the Jerusalem leaders' viewpoint, Paul's resumption of thought from verse 2 indicates – as his very language insinuates – that the false brethren created a crisis. On this understanding, those responsible for the incident were infiltrators into the community – not "those who were of reputation" (the pillars). Verse 6 thus represents Paul's reading of the leaders' response as to whether or not he was "running in vain" (verse 2). While the traditional exegesis of this verse interprets Paul's thought as part of his continuing defence of his independence, in the three places which speak of "those of reputation," "irony" can only potentially be detected in the last (cf. verse 9). It is, moreover, highly unlikely that Paul would call God's impartiality to witness to a sarcasm, the phrase consequently requiring a circumstance in which Paul is not denigrating the leaders' status.[90] Under such conditions, the most logical sense is the literal: These were indeed men of eminence, from whom Paul sincerely wished to receive affirmation of his gospel.

On such a reading, the modificatory clause "what they were makes no difference to me; God shows no partiality (ὁποῖοί ποτε ἦσαν οὐδέν μοι διαφέρει· πρόσωπον [ὁ] θεὸς ἀνθρώπου οὐ λαμβάνει)" reflects not so much a belittling of the pillars' present standing (whereby Paul can assert his equality/superiority) as a reference to their unpretentious past.[91] Paul is intimating that Peter's, John's, and James' previous standing is unimportant to him and that he is happy to acknowledge their authority.[92]

---

[88] For the influencers' identity, see Introduction, **Occasion and circumstances**.
[89] Cf. 2 Jn. 2; 2 Esd. 7:33. Cf. the Hebrew אצל (etzel), comparable to the French *chez*.
[90] While the sarcasm does not necessarily attach to the leaders' current position (see following note), it is difficult to understand why Paul is questioning their *former* status if he accepts their present reputation. In this light, the irony tends to extend over onto the pillars' current eminence.
[91] The first half of the sentence – "from those who were of high reputation" – stands as its own clause, the verb being present and translated as past merely to suit the narrative of a completed event. Its modification relates to the past, the most satisfactory meaning of ποτέ (pote) being "once, formerly" (cf. Burton: 87-88) (cf. 1:13). The contrast is thus between the pillars' present and past standing.
[92] While God's impartiality is usually regarded – in human terms – as serving to defend the weak against the strong (those with a reputation against those without), it theoretically also defends the "eminent" against discrimination favouring the

While this is a much more difficult thesis to sustain than that Paul feels himself to be an "untimely" apostle in relation to Peter, the community's earliest spokesperson; John, one of Jesus' closest disciples; and James, Jesus' brother (cf. 1 Cor. 15:5-10), the remark seems to function as an explanation of how the three pillars, with the weight of their present status and authority, had nothing to "add" ("contribute") to Paul's ministry.[93] While the notion of נשא פנים (nosei panim – lit.: "lifting the face") is regularly associated with God's non-discriminatory judgment,[94] the precise judicial connotation is difficult to establish here.[95]

The verb προσανατίθεμαι (prosanatithemai – middle) – translated as "consult" in 1:16 – literally conveys the senses of "to offer, dedicate beside" and "to lay upon oneself in addition, undertake besides," the simpler compound προστίθημι (prostithēmi) meaning "to add" (cf. Burton: 89). The fact that Paul here employs a variant of the verb which he uses in his original "submission (ἀνεθέμην)" in verse 2 may reinforce this as the answer he received to his apprehension. His definition of the opposite in verse 7 – "but on the contrary (ἀλλὰ τοὐαντίον)" – also gives an indication of how the meaning of verse 6 should be assessed. The presence of the ἀπό (apo – "from") in verse 6 indicates that Paul originally intended to specify that he had not "received anything" – whatever that may have been – from the leaders.[96] The most probable sense of the thought is that the Jerusalem leaders "imparted" no viewpoint to Paul with which he was not (already) in line, or imposed upon him no additional requirements.[97] In other words,

---

lowly. Although Peter, John, and James are now recognised as the community's leaders, they are human in the same way as are all of its other members (cf. Mt. 26:31-75; Mk. 8:33; Jn. 7:5) (cf. Bauckham, Jude: 46f; Betz, Galatians: 93-94). The thought here may parallel 1 Cor. 15:10, wherein Paul asserts that he did not "run" in vain, "but I labored even more than all of them [those to whom Jesus appeared], yet not I, but the grace of God with me (ἀλλὰ περισσότερον αὐτῶν πάντων ἐκοπίασα, οὐκ ἐγὼ δὲ ἀλλὰ ἡ χάρις τοῦ θεοῦ [ἡ] σὺν ἐμοί)." Whether or not this reference may be associated with the use of "Peter" in verses 7-8 – in contrast to "Cephas" throughout the rest of the letter – remains speculative. For the name, see below.

[93] For the use of προστίθημι (prostithēmi – "add") in 3:19, see 3:19-20.

[94] Cf. Lev. 19:15; Dt. 10:17-18, 16:19; 2 Chron. 19:7; Job 13:10; Ps. 82:1-4; Mal. 2:9; Acts 10:34; Rom. 2:11; Eph. 6:9; Col. 3:25; Jub. 5:16f; Ex.R. 14:3, 30:16; Mid.Ps. 5:10.

[95] Cf. Burton: 90, for a critique of Zahn. Paul's allusion is possibly influenced by the anticipated reference to Peter's duplicity, hypocrisy reflecting in some measure God's impartiality in treating all alike as falling short of His glory, the limitations of human nature preventing people from fulfilling His purposes (cf. Rom. 2:17-3:31; TBE p. 82) (see verses 15-21).

[96] To the extent that Paul is arguing a lack in the leaders' previous status, the concept of *adiaphora* – "matters of indifference" – cannot be appealed to here as a technique to relativise their authority (*pace* Betz, Galatians: 94).

[97] The most well-known biblical idea of "addition" relates to Scripture: "You shall not add to the word which I am commanding you, nor take away from it, that you

in giving him their backing they asked nothing further of him, nor complemented his teaching in any lack it may have demonstrated.[98]

Verses 7-8: Verse 7 constitutes the "positive" aspect of the leaders' response.[99] The emphatic adversative – the ἀλλά (alla – "but") being reinforced by the τοὐναντίον (tounantion – "on the other hand") (cf. 2 Cor. 2:7; 1 Pet. 3:9) – stresses the fact that far from demanding concessions, the leaders in fact extended their approbation. The "seeing (ἰδόντες)" presumably relates to Paul's outline of his work, which either he, or possibly the leaders themselves, conceive in terms of being "entrusted with the gospel (πεπίστευμαι τὸ εὐαγγέλιον)." This expression further articulates Paul's awareness of his calling,[100] here defined in terms corresponding to Israel's collective stewardship of God's word, the gospel being (by extension) part of the "oracles of God (τὰ λόγια τοῦ θεοῦ)" (Rom. 3:2).[101]

In this light, the claim that such phraseology as the "gospel of the un/circumcision" is unpauline (cf. Betz, Galatians: 96-98) seems hardly justified.[102] The genitive construction ("of"), which most obviously implies

---

may keep the commandments of the LORD your God which I command you לא תֹסְפוּ על-הדבר אשר אנכי מצוה אתכם ולא תגרעו ממנו לשמר את-מצות ה' אלהיכם אשר אנכי מצוה אתכם" (Dt. 4:2) (cf. Dt. 12:32; Rev. 22:18). An interpretation of this injunction established that the performance of a commandment not at its proscribed time constitutes a transgression against the prohibition of adding to the commandments (cf. Eruv. 96a). The hazards in adding a "fence" to the Torah in order to further remove the possibility of violating its commandments are also noted at times: "As soon as the serpent heard Eve's words ["neither shall you touch it (the fruit of the tree)" (Gen. 3:3) – which God had not mentioned], he found the weak spot in her argument כיון ששמע הנחש את דבריה של חוה מצא פתח ליכנס בו" (ARN[b] 1). An alternative view considered it the Sages' task to "develop" the Torah through explication/application of its ordinances (cf. TBE [EZ] p. 172) (cf. Flusser, Judaism: 379-80).

[98] Paul's purpose in going to Jerusalem was precisely to procure such approval (cf. verse 2).

[99] For arguments *via* the negative, see 1:1-5, 16c-17, 5:2-12, and verses 15-21 (n286).

[100] Cf. 1 Cor. 9:17; 1 Thess. 2:4; 1 Tim. 1:11.

[101] Cf. Acts 7:58; Tit. 1:3; Heb. 5:12. In Romans, such entrustment constitutes a sign of God's faithfulness to His people. For Paul's repeated allusions to his Damascus experience, see 1:15f and above (verse 2). The fact that Paul identifies himself in this way with the people of Israel as a steward of God's covenant makes it very difficult to sustain the argument that he had פרש מדרכי צבור (parash mi-darkei tzibor – "separated himself from the community"), thus removing himself from כלל ישראל (klal Israel – the Jewish collective) (cf. PA 2:4; Tos.San. 13:5; Ta'anit 11a) (cf. Flusser, Some). His identity remains – first and foremost – Jewish, whence he can also preach the Jewish Messiah to the nations (see Appendix).

[102] Paul repeatedly speaks of himself as an "apostle" – and an apostle of the Gentiles. Nor do these verses contradict 1:6-7 if Paul's irony is recognised there, removing any "gospel status" from the message promoted by the influencers. For

belonging, gives the sense of "to the Gentiles," the Greek possibly reflecting a Hebrew construction (cf. Isa. 49:6: נתתיך לאור גוים).[103] Literally signifying the foreskin, "uncircumcised (τῆς ἀκροβυστίας)" is a Jewish metonymical *terminus technicus* for the Gentiles (heathen), who still possess the item and have thus not entered into covenant with God, "the circumcision" correspondingly functioning to designate Israel.[104] Paul hereby describes his calling as an "apostle to the Gentiles (ἐθνῶν ἀπόστολος)"[105] (see 1:15-16b).

The pillars' perceived by a "theological insight" – indicated by ἰδόντες (idontes – "seeing") – that Paul's ministry was constituted on the model of Peter's commission to his brethren (cf. Betz, Galatians: 96).[106] Precisely how Peter's task was determined remains obscure, although it may be related to Jesus' declaration: "You are Peter, and upon this rock I will build my community (σὺ εἶ Πέτρος, καὶ ἐπὶ ταύτη τῇ πέτρᾳ οἰκοδομήσω μου τὴν ἐκκλησίαν)" (Mt. 16:18).[107] If this suggestion is correct it may also explain Paul's uncharacteristic usage of "Peter (Πέτρος)" in verses 7-8 (cf. Chapman).[108] While Cephas [כיפא] denotes

---

this section as part of Paul's assertion of his authority as the grounds on which to demand imitation/loyalty from his disciples, see Introduction, **Argument**.

[103] Cf. Isa. 42:6, 51:4.

[104] Cf. Gen. 17:11; Ex. 12:48; Judg. 14:3, 15:18; 1 Sam. 14:6; Isa. 52:1; Jer. 9:25-26; Ezek. 32:19f, 44:7; Acts 10:45, 11:3; Rom. 3:30, 4:9; 1 Cor. 7:18; Eph. 2:11f; Col. 3:11; 1QHᵃ 10:18, 14:20; 4Q429 f2i:9-10; Pes. 28b, 120a; Hag. 4b; Yev. 72b. For circumcision, see above (excursus).

[105] Here again, the genitive is attributive, carrying the sense of "for/to."

[106] This in contrast to the deep division posited by Baur between the petrine and pauline positions within the early community. For petrine/pauline parallels, cf. Le Cornu and Shulam: xxx-xxxi, 775.

[107] The metaphor is closely associated – as are the "pillars" themselves – with the Temple (cf. Flusser, Judaism: 173-46, 227-36; Gärtner) (see below); (for "ekklēsia," see 1:1-5). Peter's position as spokesperson for the early community – in the course of which he frequently addresses his brethren – presumably derives directly from Jesus' declaration. While Acts mentions Peter only in Samaria, Judaea, and Galilee (cf. 8:14f, 9:32-43), Paul suggests that Peter may have traveled quite extensively (cf. 1 Cor. 9:5). Peter's first letter is addressed to "those who reside as aliens (παρεπιδήμοις διασπορᾶς)" (1 Pet. 1:1) – i.e., the diaspora Jewish communities of Pontus, Galatia, Cappadocia, Asia, and Bithynia. For Peter, see above; for the pillars, see below; for Peter's initial repulsion towards preaching to the Gentiles, cf. Le Cornu and Shulam: 562-69.

[108] It would also clarify the point that Paul singles Peter out in these verses, without mentioning James or John, the remainder of the "pillars." Peter is the representative of the "gospel to the circumcision" by virtue of his calling. Peter associates himself with the "early days" in being called to witness to the Gentiles: "Brethren, you know that in the early days God made a choice among you, that by my mouth the Gentiles should hear the word of the gospel and believe (ἄνδρες ἀδελφοί, ὑμεῖς ἐπίστασθε ὅτι ἀφ᾽ ἡμερῶν ἀρχαίων ἐν ὑμῖν ἐξελέξατο ὁ θεὸς διὰ τοῦ στόματός

"rock" it does not present the Greek/Hebrew wordplay from which Jesus' original saying gains its meaning (see 1:18-20).[109]

The grounds on which the model is sustainable are God's unity, expressed in His calling of Peter and Paul to disparate but complementary tasks: "Or is God *the* God of Jews only? Is He not *the* God of Gentiles also – if indeed God is one – and He will justify the circumcised by faith and the uncircumcised through faith"[110] (Rom. 3:29-30).[111] The fact that both verbs are aorist – excluding a present and ongoing ministry – suggests that the allusion is to the individual calling of the two men.[112] The dative is more likely in this sense to be that of advantage (*dativi commodi*), the focus lying on the person rather than on the goal.[113] The same "gift of grace" is evident in both Peter and Paul – "according to the working of His power (τὴν δωρεὰν τῆς χάριτος τοῦ θεοῦ τῆς δοθείσης μοι κατὰ τὴν ἐνέργειαν τῆς δυνάμεως αὐτοῦ)" (Eph. 3:7) (cf. verse 9).[114] The reference here may well be to the Spirit, whose outpouring is immediately linked with Peter in Acts 2 and of whose presence and power Paul is crucially conscious (see 1:15-16b, 3:1ff, 4:1-7, 5:13ff, and 6:1-11).[115]

μου ἀκοῦσαι τὰ ἔθνη τὸν λόγον τοῦ εὐαγγελίου καὶ πιστεῦσαι)" (Acts 15:7). This latter verse appears to play a key role in Paul's reproof of Peter's hypocrisy (see verses 15-21).

[109] For a review of other proposals, cf. Betz, Galatians: 96-98. For the link between Peter as the rock and the "pillars," see below.

[110] ἢ Ἰουδαίων ὁ θεὸς μόνον; οὐχὶ καὶ ἐθνῶν; ναὶ καὶ ἐθνῶν, εἴπερ εἷς ὁ θεὸς ὃς δικαιώσει περιτομὴν ἐκ πίστεως καὶ ἀκροβυστίαν διὰ τῆς πίστεως.

[111] Cf. Rom. 1:16; Eph. 2:11ff, 3:6 (cf. Howard, Crisis: 79; Wright, Climax: 154-55). To the extent that the persons are intimately related to the purpose, no real difference obtains between them. (While we acknowledge the value of both Howard's and Wright's views, ultimately we diverge from them both in perceiving the issue of divine, sovereign unity in reference to sin rather than to Jew versus Gentile [see 3:19f]. Given the present "sociological" contextualisation of Galatians, we would argue the appropriateness of a "promise [which] had to be valid for *all* the 'seed' – not Jews only, but also the Gentiles who share Abraham's faith" [Wright, Climax: 168] in regard to *Romans* rather than to Galatians. The point of difference lies primarily in the fact that, on Wright's reading, the Torah is divisive, excluding Gentiles from God's Kingdom. On the present apprehension of the letter, the Torah speaks to the *sin* which intervenes between humanity and God [see 3:10f].)

[112] This possibly strengthens the connection with Mt. 16:18, if the latter constituted a formal "appointment." "The preposition εἰς expresses not mere reference but purpose or result, 'for or unto the creation of,' *i.e.*, 'so as to make him an apostle'" (Burton: 94).

[113] Cf. the chiasmus in verses 7-8: I/uncircumcised, Peter/circumcised, Peter/circumcised, me/uncircumcised. For other chiastic patterns, see 3:10-14 (verses 11-12), 21-25 (verses 22-23), 4:1-7 (n43), 21-31 (n246), and 5:2-12 (verse 4).

[114] Cf. Rom. 1:5, 15:15f; Eph. 3:2; Col. 1:29; 1 Pet. 4:10.

[115] Cf. also 1 Cor. 9:1, 12:6, 11; Phil. 2:13; Col. 1:29.

Verse 9: The phrase "grace given to me (τὴν χάριν τὴν δοθεῖσάν μοι)" is a pauline "shorthand" for his calling, representing the authority which he received for the fulfilment of his commission (see 1:1-5, 15-16b).[116] The act of "recognizing (γνόντες)" parallels the "seeing (ἰδόντες)" in verse 7, the thought picking up directly from there following the interpolated aside. The expression "right hand (δεξιὰς)" first and foremost alludes to God's right hand – the power which He extends in assistance and aid making proximity to it a position of blessing, redemption, and exaltation (cf. Hay: 52f).[117] The person at one's right hand (cf. the English "right-hand man") is under God's protection (cf. Ps. 80:17, 121:5). The strength and favour ascribed to this hand is then transferred to others, "giving the hand [נותן יד]" representing a pledge of agreement or friendship.[118]

An instructive usage of giving or taking the hand in amity may be found in the (apocryphal) rabbinic story of Elisha and Gehazi (and Jehoshua ben Prachia and Jesus):

> Our Rabbis have taught: Always let the left hand thrust away and the right hand draw near. Not like Elisha who thrust Gehazi away with both his hands (and not like R. Joshua b. Perahiah who thrust one of his disciples away with both his hands). How is it with Elisha? As it is written: *And Naaman said: Be content, take two talents*, and it is written: *And he said unto him, Went not my heart with thee when the man turned again from his chariot to meet thee? Is it a time to receive money, and to receive garments, and oliveyards, and sheep and oxen, and manservants and maidservants?* (2 Kings 5:26). But had he received all these things? Silver and garments were what he had received! – R. Isaac said: At that time Elisha was engaged [in the study of the Law concerning] the eight kinds of [unclean] creeping things; so he said to [Gehazi], 'You wicked person, the time has arrived for you to receive the reward for [studying the law of] the eight creeping things.' *The leprosy therefore of Naaman shall cleave unto thee and unto thy seed for ever* [2 Kings 5:27]. *Now there were four leprous men* (2 Kings 7:3) –

---

[116] Cf. Rom. 1:5, 12:3, 15:15; 1 Cor. 3:10, 9:17, 15:10; Eph. 3:2, 7-8; 2 Tim. 1:9. This point may find confirmation in the fact that Paul speaks exclusively of himself here, only including Barnabas implicitly in the final "we" clause.

[117] Cf. Gen. 48:13f; Ex. 15:6, 12; Dt. 33:2; Ps. 18:35, 21:8, 44:3, 89:13, 98:1, 118:15f; Isa. 48:13, 63:12; Mt. 25:33f, 26:64; Acts 11:21; Odes Sol. 25:2; Test.Job 33:3; Test.Ben. 10:6; 1QS 11:4-5; 1QM 4:7; 1Q34 3:7; Mid.Ps. 18:29; Gen.R. 48:1, 54:4; Ex.R. 21:6; Num.R. 22:9; Lam.R. 1.2.23, 2.3.6; Yalk.Micah 553; Sifre, Pinchas 3; Shab. 63a, 88b.

[118] Cf. Gen. 24:2, 9; 2 Kings 10:15; 1 Chron. 29:24; Ezra 10:19; Ezek. 17:18; Lam. 5:6; 1 Macc. 6:58, 13:50; 2 Macc. 11:26, 13:22 (Greek); Jos.*Ant.* 18.328; for oaths, see 1:18-20. Although not associated with extending the hand in friendship, the laying on of hands springs to mind in this context (cf. Daube, New: 224-46).

R. Johanan said: This refers to Gehazi and his three sons. *And Elisha came to Damascus* (2 Kings 8:7) — why did he go there? — R. Johanan said: He went to induce Gehazi to repent but he refused. He said to him, 'Repent'; but he replied: 'Thus have I received from thee that whoever sinned and caused others to sin is deprived of the power of doing penitence'. What had he done? Some say: He applied a loadstone to the idolatrous image of Jeroboam [cf. 1 Kings 12:28] and suspended it between heaven and earth. Others say: He engraved upon it the Name [of God] so that it used to exclaim, 'I [am the Lord thy God]' and 'Thou shalt have no [other God beside me]' — Still others say: He drove the Rabbis from before him, as it is written: *And the sons of the prophets said unto Elisha, Behold now, the place where we dwell before thee is too strait for us* (2 Kings 6:1) — hence, up to then it had not been too strait.[119] (Sot. 47a)[120]

In light of the implication of submission to a superior in "giving one's hand," the addition of "fellowship (κοινωνίας)" (cf. Phil. 1:5) clarifies the equality of the relationship: "For all shall be in a Community of truth, of proper meekness, of compassionate love and upright purpose, towards each other, in a holy council, associates of an everlasting society כיא הכול יהיו ביחד אמת ועוות טוב ואהבת חסד ומחשבת צדק איש לרעהו בעצת קודש ובני סוד עולמים" (1QS 2:24-25) (cf. Le Cornu and Shulam: 147f).

While it is normally supposed that the agreement represents a personal "co-operation" with Paul and Barnabas, it should not be forgotten that the recognition of Paul's grace to the Gentiles also makes the latter co-partners in the "fellowship." In this sense the accord may be understood to

---

[119] תנו רבנן: לעולם תהא שמאל דוחה וימין מקרבת - לא כאלישע, שדחפו לגחזי בשתי ידיו, ולא כיהושע בן פרחיה שדחפו לאחד מתלמידיו בשתי ידיו. אלישע מאי היא? דכתיב: ויאמר נעמן הואל קח ככרים, וכתיב: ויאמר אליו לא לבי הלך כאשר הפך איש מעל מרכבתו לקראתך העת לקחת את הכסף ולקחת בגדים וזיתים וכרמים וצאן ובקר ועבדים ושפחות. ומי שקיל כולי האי? כסף ובגדים הוא דשקיל. אמר ר' יצחק: באותה שעה היה אלישע עוסק בשמנה שרצים. אמר לו: רשע, הגיע עת ליטול שכר שמנה שרצים וצרעת נעמן תדבק בך ובזרעך לעולם. "וארבעה אנשים היו מצורעים". אמר רבי יוחנן: זה גחזי ושלשת בניו. וילך אלישע דמשק: למה הלך? אמר רבי יוחנן שהלך להחזירו לגחזי בתשובה ולא חזר. אמר לו: חזור בך. אמר לו: כך מקובלני ממך: כל מי שחטא והחטיא את הרבים אין מספיקין בידו לעשות תשובה. מאי עבד? איכא דאמרי, אבן שואבת תלה לו לחטאת ירבעם והעמידו בין שמים לארץ. ואיכא דאמרי, שם חקק לה אפומה והיתה אומרת: אנכי ולא יהיה לך. ואיכא דאמרי: רבנן דחה מקמיה, דכתיב: ויאמרו בני הנביאים אל אלישע הנה נא המקום אשר אנחנו יושבים שם לפניך צר ממנו מכלל: דעד האידנא לא הוה דחיק.

[120] Cf. San. 107b. The point of the story is that a person should always be given the opportunity to repent, thence returning to "fellowship" in the community. The theme is also employed in promoting proselytising. For the suggestion that Gehazi, whom Elisha repelled, represents Paul, cf. Travers Herford, Christianity: 50-54, 97-103. (The "pillar" which Gehazi erected is surely purely accidental to our incident here.)

signify that James, Peter, and John could be expected to act towards the Gentiles along the lines set out by Paul (cf. Romans 14-15).[121]

James may stand at the head of the list, displacing Peter from his primary role in verses 7-8, as the most important contemporary figure in the Jerusalem community, Peter's authority being linked more directly with his envoyship (see verses 7-8). Peter and John are frequently mentioned together – also with James, John's brother – apparently being both close friends and business partners.[122] Paul names these three here as "pillars (στῦλοι)," the "reputed (οἱ δοκοῦντες)" – the designation by which he has twice already referred to his discussants – here possibly modifying the "pillars."[123]

The term στῦλος (stylos; עמוד) is directly associated with the metaphor of the "house," "building," or "temple" by which the New Testament texts frequently describe the community[124] (cf. Gärtner). Scholars have suggested on the basis of Proverbs 9:1 – "Wisdom has built her house, she has hewn out her seven pillars חכמות בנתה ביתה חצבה עמודיה שבעה" – that the pillars constituted a group of leaders within the community, possibly numbering seven (cf. Bauckham, Acts: 441ff).[125] Although it has also been contended that the pillars represented the leaders of "the Jerusalem church's outreach to the Jewish people, most members of which, apart from James, would be travelling missionaries" (ibid: 448) (cf. 1 Cor. 9:5), both the order and a further midrashic tradition would indicate that the allusion is more likely to the pillars which support the whole world.

In line with the exegesis of Proverbs 9:1 which refers the pillars to the seven days of creation,[126] the pillars are also associated with Abraham,

[121] This would naturally form the background to Paul's reproof of Peter in Antioch (see verses 11-14).
[122] Cf. Mt. 17:1ff, 26:37; Mk. 1:20, 5:37, 13:3; Lk. 5:7; [Jn. 20:2]. According to Acts 12:2, John's brother James was executed by Agrippa I. Since the latter died in 43/44, the James mentioned here cannot be a bar Zebedee.
[123] Although rather awkward, Paul's previous usage of the phrase as a substantive noun, as it were ("the eminent ones") may still find traces here, giving the sense of "the reputed ones, being pillars."
[124] Cf. [Rom. 12:1]; 1 Cor. 3:9, 6:19; 2 Cor. 6:14f; [Gal. 2:9]; Eph. 2:19f; 1 Tim. 3:15; Heb. 3:6, 10:21; 1 Pet. 2:4f; Rev. 3:12; 1 En. 1:2, 38:2, 62:8; 1QS 5:6, 8:4f; 9:6, 11:8; CD-A 3:19f; CD-B 20:10; 4QFlor f1i:2ff. See also 4:21-31, 6:1-11 (verse 10), and verses 15-21.
[125] The assertion that the remaining four were composed of Jesus' brothers remains speculative. For the seven "best men of the city שבעה טובי העיר," cf. Le Cornu and Shulam: 313.
[126] Lev.R. 11:1; Yalk.Prov. 943; JSan. 23b; San. 38a. This idea is naturally linked to Torah, identified with Wisdom (cf. Num.R. 10:1; Yalk.Prov. 944). This is then extended to Israel (cf. Cant.R. 7.1.1; Hag. 12b), to the righteous in general (cf. Prov. 10:25; Yoma 38b; San. 26b), and finally to "the righteous man" as representative of

Isaac, and Jacob through whose righteousness the world exists: "When the patriarchs came and showed themselves righteous, God said: 'On these will I establish My world'; as it says: *For the pillars of the earth are the Lord's, and He hath set the world upon them* (1 Sam. 2:8). Hence does it say: *'For from the top of the rocks do I see him* [Israel]' (Num. 23:9)"[127] (Ex.R. 15:7).[128]

The "fellowship" includes both Jews and Gentiles, the two foci being complementary to one another. The conjunction ἵνα (hina) functions similarly to the classical ἐφ᾽ ᾧτε (ef hōte), signifying "on condition that, on the understanding that," replacing, to a certain extent, the elliptical verbs (cf. "go") to be supplied in both halves of the clause (cf. Longenecker, Galatians: 58).[129] At this early stage, outreach amongst the Gentiles may still have been confined to communities in proximity to Eretz Israel, Syria being closely tied to the latter (cf. Acts 11:19ff; Gal. 1:21) (cf. Safrai and Stern: 137f).[130] The emphasis would then lie on the agreement that Paul would develop his ministry amongst the Gentiles, Peter, James, and John (simply) continuing to work within the Jewish community.[131]

Verse 10: The concord is conditioned by a single request – "only that we should remember the poor (μόνον τῶν πτωχῶν ἵνα μνημονεύωμεν)." Here again, the verb is elliptical, the μόνον (monon – "only") placed at the beginning for emphasis, together with "the poor" – the true predicate of the sentence (cf. Longenecker, Galatians: 59, and for the following discussion). While the Greek term πτωχός (ptōchos) denotes the financially impoverished, corresponding to οἱ ἄποροι (hoi aporoi – "the lower classes") (cf. Jos.*War* 5.569-70), the term was adopted by the Qumran community as a designation of its spiritual status before God (cf. Isa. 61:1-

---

all (cf. Hag. 12b). For Peter as rock/foundation, see 1:18-20; for the eschatological function of the Twelve, cf. Le Cornu and Shulam: 44-46; for Torah and Wisdom, see 3:1-5 [n42]; for Jesus' "representative" redemptive role, see verses 15-21.

[127] כיון שבאו האבות וזכו, אמר הקדוש ברוך הוא: על אלו אני מכונן העולם, שנאמר: כי להי מצוקי ארץ וישת עליהם תבל. לכך כתיב, כי מראש צורים אראנו.

[128] Gen.R. 43:8, 68:12, 75:11; Ex.R. 2:6, 15:7; Cant.R. 7.8.1. Prominent figures – such as Jochanan b. Zakkai – are also occasionally called "pillars" (cf. Ber. 28b [1 Kings 7:21]).

[129] Cf. Rom. 4:16; 1 Cor. 1:31; 2 Cor. 8:13.

[130] For the dating of Galatians and Paul's Jerusalem visits, see Introduction, **Occasion and circumstances.**

[131] For Paul's itinerary as determined by Isa. 66:18-21, cf. Riesner: 241-56. It is instructive to recall the factors which appear to constitute Paul's "missionary strategy": a) Employing the local synagogue as his base of operations; b) appeal to the godfearers attached to the synagogue; c) un/favourable travel conditions; d) orientation towards Roman provinces and their centers; e) local welcome or rejection of the gospel; f) work in areas otherwise unreached (not encroaching on others' labours); g) building and nurturing viable communities; and h) submission to God's direction and will (cf. ibid: 255-56).

3, 66:2).[132] A similar attitude being reflected in Jesus' words (cf. Mt. 5:3f), the pillars' appeal to Paul may have been not specifically for economic sustenance but for his continued support of the Jewish believers.[133]

An interesting affinity may perhaps be identified here with the stipulations placed on prospective proselytes (cf. Yev. 47a-b; Ger. 1:1f). Following the presentation of "a few of the commandments מקצת מצות קלות ומקצת מצות חמורות,"[134] the convert is further informed of the injunctions regarding forgotten sheaves, gleanings, the corners of the field, and the (poor) tithe – all forms of "remembrance of the poor."[135] In the tractate on proselytes, Gerim, the reference is articulated in the form of a condition: "[He is informed that is accepted as a proselyte only] on condition that he will give gleanings . . . על מנת שהוא נותן בשכחה" (Ger. 1:3). In this light, the plea made by the pillars may have been less of Paul personally than of the Gentiles who become faithful to Jesus. While the leaders recognise that the circumcision cannot constitute a condition for redemption – for Jews and Gentiles alike – they are concerned that non-Jewish believers acknowledge their responsibility towards the "poor."[136]

Such a perspective may find support in the view which apprehends the collection as an expression of reciprocal blessing: ". . . the Father's will is that we give to all from the gifts we have received . . . Thou shalt not turn away the needy, but thou shalt share everything with thy brother, and shalt not say that it is thine own, for if you are sharers in the imperishable,

---

[132] Cf. 1QHa 6:3, 10:32, 13:15-16; 1QM [11:10], 14:7; 1QpHab 12:3f; 4Q88 9:14; 4QpPsa 3:10; 4Q521 f2ii:12. Cf. Flusser, Judaism: 35-44, 102ff. For Isa. 61:1-3, see 1:1f, 3:1ff, 26-29, and 4:1-7.

[133] For the affinities between the Qumran and early believing communities, cf. Flusser, Judaism: 23-74; Le Cornu and Shulam: 145-62, 261, 302, 481, 505, 815f, 1031f, 1130f, 1141-43; Gärtner.

[134] Cf. מקצת מעשי התורה (miktzat ma'asei ha-Torah – 4QMMT). For Galatians' structure as a "halakhic letter," see Introduction, **Form.**

[135] שכחה, לקט, פיאה, ומעשר (shikcha, leket, pe'ah, and ma'aser) (cf. Lev. 19:9; Num. 18:26f; Dt. 24:19, 26:12f).

[136] The fact that Paul calls for support for himself on precisely the same principle in 4:12f and 6:6 would seem to strengthen this speculation (see 4:12-20, 6:1-11, and below). Such an action on the gentile Galatians' part would evidently not be in the nature of a condition of conversion, since Paul precisely opposes proselytism in the Galatian context. Nor would it necessarily be a literal fulfilment of the specific commandments enumerated in the talmudic texts, these only being obligatory in Eretz Israel. If this reading has any merit, it may additionally contribute to the ongoing debate regarding the "mutual" influence between early "Christianity" and rabbinic thought, the influence here possibly originating in the early believing community and developing in later Jewish thought (represented in the talmudic texts) with direct reference to proselytes.

how much more in the things which perish?"[137] (Did. 1:5, 4:8)[138] (cf. Flusser, Judaism: 163). On this reading, the Gentiles – who have become "sharers in the imperishable"– are indebted to their Jewish brethren and should be expected to return the "blessing of the Messiah (εὐλογίας Χριστοῦ)" (cf. Rom. 15:27-29) in material recompense (cf. Le Cornu and Shulam: 156, 1322).[139] Delivery of such funds would constitute a "validation" of the gentile outreach and a way to bind the two groups together in mutual fellowship (cf. CD-A 6:21) (cf. Bruce, Acts: 480).[140]

Paul's response to the plea is unqualifiedly affirmative, the αὐτὸ τοῦτο (auto touto – "this very thing") being emphatic.[141] Significantly, the aorist verb (ἐσπούδασα; espoudasa) indicates an action which he has been accustomed to take in the past, the tense being normally translated in English as a pluperfect. The phrase thus denotes Paul's regular practice of keeping the Jewish believers' welfare at heart – possibly in the context of gentile participation. The argument that the singular pronominal suffix ("I") is unapposite in the present circumstances, Barnabas also being included in the agreement, ignores Paul's usage of the singular throughout the passage. He is anxious to assure the leaders that their concern has always been on his heart – and will continue to be so as he works with Barnabas.[142]

---

[137] πᾶσι γὰρ θέλει δίδοσθαι ὁ πατὴρ ἐκ τῶν ἰδίων χαρισμάτων . . . οὐκ ἀποστραφήσῃ τὸν ἐνδεόμενον, συγκοινωνήσεις δὲ πάντα τῷ ἀδελφῷ σοῦ καὶ οὐκ ἐρεῖς ἴδια εἶναι· εἰ γὰρ ἐν τῷ ἀθανάτῳ κοινωνοί ἐστε, πόσῳ μᾶλλον ἐν τοῖς θνητοῖς;

[138] Cf. [Lk. 16:10-12; Rom. 11:12, 15ff]; 1 Cor. 9:11; PA 5:10; Ep.Barn. 19:8.

[139] While the Mishnah rules that Gentiles are not to be prevented from benefiting from the poor tithes "for the sake of peace דרכי שלום," the tithes were first and foremost intended for the Jewish community (cf. Git. 5:8).

[140] Paul appeals to precisely the same principle in demanding his disciples' imitation of and loyalty to himself in 4:12f and 6:6 – this section thus constituting a further parallel between Antioch and Galatia, in conjunction with Paul's reproof of Peter (see Introduction, **Argument**, 4:12-20, 6:1-11, and verses 15-21). (For the suggestion that the collection was delivered to the Temple for the general Jewish community in Jerusalem, cf. Shulam and Le Cornu: 501-3; Le Cornu and Shulam: 1320-22.)

[141] The argument that any such condition contradicts Paul's contention that the leaders "contributed nothing to [i.e., placed no additional requirements on]" Paul (verse 6) is more pedantic than essential. Commitment to gentile "remuneration" surely does not constitute a greater stringency ("addition") towards the Gentiles – presumably the force which this claim attributes to (Paul's understanding of) the agreement.

[142] While this past policy may have been expressed in the funds just delivered to Jerusalem if this passage is identified with Acts 11:27-30, both this collection and that from Achaia and Macedonia are, on this reading, but one expression of a wider

Verses 11-14:

But when Cephas came to Antioch, I opposed him to his face, because he stood condemned. For prior to the coming of certain men from James, he used to eat with the Gentiles; but when they came, he *began* to withdraw and hold himself aloof, fearing the party of the circumcision. And the rest of the Jews joined him in hypocrisy, with the result that even Barnabas was carried away by their hypocrisy. But when I saw that they were not straightforward about the truth of the gospel, I said to Cephas in the presence of all, "If you, being a Jew, live like the Gentiles and not like the Jews, how *is it that* you compel the Gentiles to live like Jews?"

Verses 11-14 are traditionally considered the final section of Paul's *narratio* – begun in 1:11 and intended to provide a defence against the Galatian influencers' charge of dependenceupon the Jerusalem Apostles.[143] In contrast to the previous segments (cf. 1:18, 21, verse 1), this account does not open with ἔπειτα (epeita – "then") but with the indeterminate particle ὅτε (hote – "when"). Although some commentators have sought in this divergence also a chronological disruption, the present reading suggests that Paul's *narratio* begins to give way to an autobiographical description in 1:21 and here openly "departs" from the scheme (see 1:21-24). Verse 11 appears in this respect to derive directly from the previous incident, Paul utilizing its point to commence his broadside to his addressees (cf. 3:1).[144]

Antioch

During the seleucid dynasty numerous cities throughout Eretz Israel, Syria, and Pisidia were named in honour of Antiochus. Seleucus Nicator founded Antioch on the Orontes in 300 B.C.E., naming it after his father, whence it served as the seleucid capital (cf. ABD: 1:265f, and for the following discussion). It rapidly became a city of importance and in 165 B.C.E. was already the third largest city in the Roman empire after Rome and Alexandria. Modern scholars estimate its population in the first century C.E. as around 100,000. Following Pompey's reorganisation of the whole region it became a free city in 64 B.C.E., serving as the seat of administration of the Roman province of Syria. Its position on the Orontes encouraged its growth as a commercial centre, the produce of Syria passing through its territory on its way to other mediterranean countries. Enlarged and adorned by Augustus and Tiberius, Herod the Great contributed to the city's glory by paving its main street with marble and lining it on both sides with colonnades.[145]

---

consideration on Paul's part. For an interpretation of the contribution(s) as material gentile appreciation for sharing in the spiritual wealth of the Jewish believers, cf. Le Cornu and Shulam: 1322.

[143] For the conventional arguments, see Introduction, **Occasion and circumstances.**

[144] For the structure of Galatians currently proposed, see Introduction, **Form; Argument.**

[145] Cf. Jos.*Ant.* 16.148; *War* 1.425.

Jews had settled in Antioch since its foundation, being included amongst the military colonists who established the city. In line with the city's political importance, its Jewish community ranked in status with those of Alexandria and Rome (cf. Safrai and Stern: 137ff, and for the following discussion). The growth of the Jewish population was presumably stimulated by the material advantages the city offered, as well as its attractions as a major urban centre. Many Jews appear to have emigrated from Eretz Israel, Jews from Syria itself also tending to congregate in the capital – together with migrants from Babylonia and other parts of the Parthian empire.

Josephus reports that Seleucus I granted civil rights as a *politeuma* ("political state") to the Jews of Antioch, which they retained under the Romans, continuing to play a prominent role in the life of the city.[146] The existence of at least three synagogues is recorded and the suggestion of more is proposed in support of understanding the πολιτεία (politeia) as a "federation" of synagogues such as the gerousia in Alexandria, since two inscriptions refer to gerousiarchs (cf. ibid: 485). According to the sources, both tension and conflict between the general and Jewish populace and pro-Jewish sentiments and proselytism were relatively common in the city. Acts speaks of "Nicolas, a proselyte of Antioch (Νικόλαον προσήλυτον Ἀντιοχέα)," and Josephus writes that in contrast to other Syrian towns, the gentile majority in Antioch, Apamea, and Sidon did not harm the Jewish population until the outbreak of the revolt in 66, and that many were drawn to Judaism (cf. *War* 7.43ff).

The annexation of Eretz Israel by the Seleucids around 200 B.C.E. intensified the contacts between Antioch and Jerusalem. Jewish representatives were frequent visitors in the seleucid capital and Onias III apparently sought refuge from his opponents in the famous temple of Apollo at Daphne near Antioch (cf. 2 Macc. 4:33). Acts witnesses to the traffic between Antioch and Jerusalem, as well as the cosmopolitan character of both, noting that "some prophets came down from Jerusalem to Antioch (κατῆλθον ἀπὸ Ἱεροσολύμων προφῆται εἰς Ἀντιόχειαν)" (Acts 11:27) and that among the "prophets and teachers (προφῆται καὶ διδάσκαλοι)" at Antioch were Simeon Niger – i.e., Simeon the Black, presumably a reference to his origin, Lucius of Cyrene, and Manaen "who had been brought up with Herod the tetrarch (Ἡρῴδου τοῦ τετραάρχου σύντροφος)" (Acts 13:1).

Such members may help clarify how the nascent Antiochian believing community was able to send funds in the early 40's to the Jerusalem community. The city early on became one of the major bases of the messianic community, being the first to bear the name "Christians" (cf. Acts 11:26). The source of the epithet nevertheless remains obscure. No

---

[146] Cf. *Ant.* 12.119; *War* 7.43; *CA* 2.39.

good reason seems to exist to explain why the Roman authorities should have distinguished between Jews and "Christians" at this point, nor does any other party appear to have possessed a reason or need for so doing. Although the only real group with a vested interest in this regard was the mainstream Jewish community, it is difficult to perceive that its members were responsible for turning "Christ" into a proper name. The notation may consequently perhaps be best understood as an "aetiological" remark – i.e., the name which later became (in)famous, particularly in Roman circles, was first coined in Antioch by outsiders, whose identity remains uncertain.

Verse 11: According to the present chronological scheme, Peter's arrival in Antioch occurred following Paul and Barnabas' return to the city from their extended travels in southern Galatia (cf. Acts 13:1-14:25).[147] Luke suggests that the two men "spent a long time with the disciples (διέτριβον δὲ χρόνον οὐκ ὀλίγον σὺν τοῖς μαθηταῖς)" at this point (cf. Acts 14:26-28), during which "some men came down from Judea (τινες κατελθόντες ἀπὸ τῆς Ἰουδαίας)" demanding circumcision from gentile believers (Acts 15:1). Precisely when Peter arrived in Antioch, whence, and for what purpose, remains obscure.[148] While the episode took place *before the council* on this dating (see Introduction, **Date and destination**), Peter appears to have been in the city for some time prior to the appearance of the "men from James." While the notation "When Cephas came to Antioch" may imply "a well-known visit of Cephas to the city . . . a visit known to both Paul and his Galatian addressees" (Longenecker, Galatians: 71), it may also directly relate to Peter's action as a "bewitchment" similar to that of Paul's present readers (see 3:1-5).

The imperfect tense of συνήσθιεν (synēsthien – "he used to eat") in verse 12 indicates that Peter enjoyed fellowship with the Antiochian gentile believers over an extended period. Once Paul has given sufficient time for the transgression to have proven itself as a fact and not as a misrepresentation or misunderstanding of the circumstance, he rebukes Peter for what he considers to constitute errant conduct.[149] In this, he follows the practice regulated by Jesus, of directly confronting the

---

[147] For the proposed dating of Galatians, see Introduction, **Date and destination**.

[148] For Peter, see 1:18-20; for "Peter" in verses 7-8, see verses 1-10. In chronological terms, a period of between 2-4 years elapses between verses 1-10 and verse 11 on the present reading (see Introduction, **Date and destination**).

[149] The suggestion that Paul was absent from Antioch during this period, his sense of propriety otherwise making it impossible for him to have allowed such a situation to develop without confronting Peter earlier (cf. Burton: 101), is perhaps in this respect not as necessary as implied. For the current reading of Galatians as a halakhic "rebuke-request" letter along the lines of 4QMMT, see Introduction, **Form**; **Argument**.

transgressor himself, the κατά πρόσωπον (kata prosōpon – "to his face") constituting a "between you and him alone (μεταξὺ σοῦ καὶ αὐτοῦ μόνου)" meeting (Mt. 18:15).

The same custom was strictly followed in the Qumran community, which adjured its members to fulfil the precept of Leviticus 19:17 – "You may surely reprove your neighbor, but shall not incur sin because of him": "One should reproach one another in truth, in meekness and in compassionate love for one's fellow-man. *Blank* No-one should speak to his brother in anger or muttering, or with a hard [neck or with passionate] spirit of wickedness, and he should not detest him [in the fore]sk[in] of his heart, but instead reproach him on that day so as not to incur a sin because of him. And in addition, no-one should raise a matter against his fellow in front of the Many unless it is with reproof in the presence of witnesses"[150] (1QS 5:24-6:1) (see 6:1-11).[151]

The Greek καταγινώσκω (kataginōskō) signifies "condemnation before God" (cf. Jos.*War* 1.635, 7.327), Paul evidently being convinced that he possessed no recourse but to reprove Peter as acting in contravention of God's volition.[152] Considerable weight thus lies on Peter's action not merely as a violation of human norms or conventions but of divine desire itself (see below).

Verse 12 provides the explanation for the condemnation and the nature of the offence. At this juncture, Paul's reproof of Peter stems from a deficiency in the latter's motives, leading to an unfounded act. The circumstances appear to be such that, in participating in fellowship with the Antiochian community, Peter follows the practice seemingly established in the congregation, of unhesitatingly eating with its gentile members.

Gentiles
During the Second Temple period, Gentiles were characterised in general not only as idolaters but also – and consequently – as violent, dirty, immoral, and impure[153]:

---

[150] להוכיֿ איש את רעהו באמת וענוה ואהבת חסד לאיש vacat אל ידבר אלוהיהי (אל אחיהו) באף או בתלונה או בעורף [קשה או בקנאת] רוח רשע ואל ישנאהו [בעורל]ת[ן] לבבו כיא ביום[יו] יוכיחנו ולוא ישא עליו עוון וגם אל יביא איש על רעהו דבר לפני הרבים אשר לוא בתוכחת לפני עדים.

[151] Cf. Mt. 18:15-17; [Eph. 4:26]; 1 Tim. 5:20; CD-A 7:2-3, 9:2-8. For public remonstration, see below.

[152] The "fact" of Peter's condemnation is affirmed by the imperfect ἦν (ēn – "was") which, joined to the perfect participle (κατεγνωσμένος – "condemned"), gives the sense of a pluperfect, thus sharpening the past existent state (cf. Longenecker, Galatians: 72).

[153] Cf. Zech. 13:1f; [Mk. 14:41; Gal. 2:15; Rev. 18:2]; 1QpHab 13:1; 4Q169 ff3-4iii:1; 4Q171 2:20, 4:10.

Cattle may not be left in the inns of the gentiles since they are
suspected of bestiality; nor may a woman remain alone with
them since they are suspected of lewdness; nor may a man
remain alone with them since they are suspected of shedding
blood. The daughter of an Israelite may not assist a gentile
woman in childbirth since she would be assisting to bring to birth
a child for idolatry . . .[154] (AZ 2:1)[155]

Eating with an uncircumcised person was regarded as tantamount to
eating with a "dog" or consuming the "flesh of abomination": "Why did he
[Abraham] circumcise them [the men of his household]? Because of purity,
so that they should not defile their masters with their food and with their
drink, for whosoever eateth with an uncircumcised person is as though he
were eating flesh of abomination [first editions: as though he were eating
with a dog]. All who bathe with the uncircumcised are as though they
bathed with carrion [first editions: a leper], and all who touch an
uncircumcised person are as though they touched the dead, for in their
lifetime they are like (the) dead; and in their death they are like the carrion
of the beast, and their prayer does not come before the Holy One, blessed
be He, as it is said, 'The dead praise not the Lord' (Ps. 115:17)"[156] (PRE 29).

The question of precisely when the Gentiles first began to be regarded
as levitically unclean is frequently explained in reference to the Eighteen
Decrees enacted by the Shammaites just prior to the outbreak of the War in
66. On this reading, the decrees constituted a political act designed to
prevent contact between Jews and their Roman adversaries (cf. Alon, Jews:
146ff, and for the following discussion). The ascription of impurity to the
Gentiles nevertheless more accurately seems to represent an extension of
the halakhic ruling concerning the uncleanness of idols to include those
who worship them – a tradition which arose much earlier than the
Eighteen Decrees and which the latter reinforced (cf. TBE p. 105).

Josephus' account of Hyrcanus' request of Herod to refrain from
bringing his troops into Jerusalem suggests that he was anxious that the
multitudes should not be defiled.[157] While this implies that the tradition
was already observed in the first century B.C.E., the halakhic ruling does
not seem to have been accepted by everyone, nor did Jews refrain from all

---

[154] אין מעמידין בהמה בפונדקאות שלגוים, מפני שחשודין על הרביעה. ולא תתיחד אשה עמהן,
מפני שחשודין העריות. ולא יתיחד אדם עמהן, מפני שחשודין על שפיכת דמים. בת ישראל לא תילד
את הנכרית, מפני שמילדת בן לעבודה זרה . . .

[155] Cf. Mt. 15:26f; Mk. 7:27f; Rom. 1:18ff; Eph. 4:19; Col. 1:21-22; BB 10b; AZ 22b,
25b; BK 117a.

[156] ולמה מלן אלא? בשביל טהרה שלא יטמאו את אדניהם במאכלו ומשקהו. וכל מי שאוכל עם
ערל כאילו אוכל בשר שקץ וכל הרוחץ עם הערל כאילו רוחץ עם הנבלה וכל הנוגע בערל כאילו נוגע
במת. שהם בחייהם כמתים ובמיתתם כנבלת בהמה ואין תפלתם נכנסת לפני הקדוש ברוך הוא,
שנאמר: לא המתים יהללו-יה.

[157] Cf. Ant. 14.285; War 1.229.

dealings with Gentiles – even in circumstances in which they might contract and convey uncleanness. The Qumran community prohibited all contact with Gentiles on shabbat – "No-one <should stay> in a place close to gentiles on the sabbath אל ישבית (ישבות) איש במקום קרוב לגוים בשבת" (CD-A 11:14-15) – presumably because of the latter's sanctity.

Some Sages were inclined towards leniency and others towards stringency regarding the status of both idols and idolaters. Just as idolatry was considered to possess various degrees of impurity,[158] the Gentiles themselves were regarded as unclean to various degrees. Some considered them as those who have come into contact with a reptile, others as having gonorrhoea (a flux), or – most stringently – as being corpse-unclean.[159] The prevailing view seems to have been that gentile impurity was of gonorrhoeal status:

> Gentiles and a resident alien do not defile by reason of a flux, but although they do not defile because of a flux, they are unclean in all respects like those who suffer a flux, and heave-offering is burnt on their account, but an offering is not incurred on their account for defiling the Temple and its holy things.[160] (Tos.Zav. 2:1)[161]

This degree of impurity conveys uncleanness through a number of degrees: "By five means the Zab [flux] conveys uncleanness to what he lies upon, so that it conveys uncleanness to men and garments: by standing, sitting, lying, hanging, or leaning. By seven means what he lies upon conveys uncleanness to a man so that he conveys uncleanness to garments: if he stands, sits, lies, hangs, or leans upon it, or touches or carries it"[162] (Zav. 2:4) (cf. Ohal. 1:5).

The strongest proof of the attribution of ritual impurity to Gentiles is perhaps reflected in the demand for a proselyte to be immersed upon conversion – together with the prohibition against Gentiles entering beyond the rampart into the inner courts of the Temple. Halakhic prohibitions included doing business with Gentiles for three days preceding their festivals in order to prevent the smallest risk of being involved in their idolatrous practices (cf. AZ 1:1f). It was also argued that

[158] Cf. Isa. 52:1; Jer. 2:7, 3:1ff; [Joel 3:17; Zech. 14:21].
[159] Cf. Gen. 35:2; Lev. 15:1ff; Rom. 1:24; Zav. 2:3; Mikv. 5:4; Eduy. 5:1; Nid. 4:3; [Kel. 1:8]; Shab. 9:1; Pes. 8:8; Shek. 8:1; AZ 3:6; Tos.Yoma 4:20; Shab. 83a; AZ 32b; Hul. 13b.
[160] הגוים והגר והתושב אינן מטמאין בזיבה ואף על פי שאינן מטמאין בזיבה טמאין כזבין לכל דבריהם. ושורפין עליהן את התרומה ואין חייבין עליהן על טומאת מקדש וקדשיו.
[161] Cf. Toh. 5:8, 7:6; Nid. 10:4; Shek. 8:1; Nid. 43a.
[162] הזב מטמא את המשכב בחמשה דרכים, לטמא אדם לטמא בגדים: עומד, יושב, שוכב, נתלה, ונשען. והמשכב מטמא את האדם בשבעה דרכים, לטמא בגדים: עומד, יושב, שוכב, נתלה, ונשען, במגע, ובמשא.

bathing in a public bathhouse could bring about impurity – i.e., put a Jew into a state of uncleanness – because the bathhouse contained a statue of a goddess and a Jew who entered was at risk of participating in idol worship (cf. AZ 1:7, 3:4).

Gentile land (its earth and air together) and gentile houses were alike regarded as אבות טומאה (avot tum'ah – "fathers of uncleanness") – i.e., primary sources of impurity[163] (cf. Danby: 803#19). Three kinds of houses were distinguished regarding idolatry: "If a house was built from the first for idolatry it is forbidden; if it was plastered and bedecked for idolatry, or if aught was done to it anew, one only need remove what was done to it anew; but if a gentile did but bring in an idol and take it out again, such a house is permitted [to a Jew]"[164] (AZ 3:7).

Food (cf. Acts 11:3) was obviously a central issue of discussion with respect to ritual purity, not only because of the danger of idolatry but also because of the independent food and ritual impurity laws.[165] It appears that the peculiar nature of gentile impurity led in this respect to the removal of laws governing relations to Gentiles from the developing system of purity rules, and their integration into other areas of halakhic regulation. The Eighteen Decrees enacted in the "upper room of Hananiah b. Hezekiah b. Gorion" include a list of items prohibited because of their connection with Gentiles:

> On that very day they decreed on their [the Gentiles'] bread, their cheese, their wine, their vinegar, their brine, their muries, their pickles, their stews, their salted foods, their *hilka* [fish-brine], their pounded spices, their *tisni* [barley groats], their language, their testimony, their offerings, their sons, their daughters, their first fruits.[166] (JShab. 1, 4, 3c-d)[167]

---

[163] Cf. Jn. 18:28; Kel. 1:1; Ohal. 18:7, 9; Naz. 7:3; JShab. 1, 4, 3c; Sem. 4:23, 25; Shab. 14b-15a; AZ 8b.

[164] בית שבנוי מתחלה לעבודה זרה - הרי זה אסור; סידו וכיירו לעבודה זרה, וחידש - נטל מה חידש; הכניס לתוכה עבודה זרה, והוציאה - הרי זה מֶתָּר.

[165] The issue of tithing – in this context a dietary regulation, untithed produce also being prohibited for consumption – is also raised in this context (cf. Dunn, Incident: 210). Strictly speaking the regulation applied solely to the Land, only produce being grown therein demanding tithing (cf. Lev. 27:30f; Num. 18:26f; Dt. 12:17, 14:22f; Mt. 23:23; Lk. 18:12; tractacte Demai; Hal. 2:2; Kid. 1:9). Nevertheless, while indications exist that various diaspora communities also practiced the custom (cf. Tob. 1:6-8; Jos.*Ant.* 14.245; Philo, *Leg.* 156; *Spec.Leg.* 1.153), untithed produce could also be tithed immediately before eating, thereby resolving the problem (cf. Dem. 3:1) (cf. Tomson: 229n38).

[166] ביום גזרו על פיתן ועל גבינתן ועל יינן ועל חומצן ועל צירן ועל מורייסן על כבושיהן ועל שלוקיהן ועל מלוחיהן ועל החילקה ועל השחיקה ועל הטיסני ועל לשונן ועל עדותן ועל מתנותיהן על בניהן ועל בנותיהן ועל בכוריהן.

Although prohibitions against being hospitable to Gentiles or lodging at their homes were not accepted as binding, such behaviour was generally considered disgraceful. Some Sages held the opposite attitude and were hospitable to Gentiles and visited them. R. Meir and R. Hiya were both guests of Gentiles and Shimon b. Jochai visited a gentile friend in Tyre.[168] A mishnah relates how it could be perfectly permissible to dine and drink wine with a Gentile even in one's own home:

> If an Israelite was eating with a gentile at a table, and he [the Israelite] put flagons [of wine] on the table and flagons [of wine] on the side-table, and left the other [the Gentile] there and went out, what is on the table is forbidden and what is on the side-table is permitted [i.e., the Gentile would not be suspected of taking wine from the side-table and pouring it as a libation to his idol, although he might pour from what was already open on the table, thus defiling the whole jar] הָיָה אוכל עמו על הַשֻּׁלְחָן, והִנִּיחַ לגִינָה על הַשֻּׁלְחָן ולגִינָה על דֻּלבְּקִי, והִנִּיחוֹ ויצא - מַה שעל הַשֻּׁלְחָן אסור, ומַה שעל הַדֻּלבְּקִי מֻתָר. (AZ 5:5)

Halakhot were also enjoined on Israel to greet Gentiles, to visit their sick, to mourn and bury their dead, and to comfort their mourners "in the interests of peace [דרכי שלום]."[169] It was similarly forbidden to steal from them in order to avoid profanation of God's name (חילול ה'; chilul ha-Shem) (cf. Tos.AZ 9:15). (The Qumran shabbat halakhot – which are stricter than pharisaic halakhot[170] – also include an injunction against any contact with Gentiles on shabbat [cf. CD-A 11:14-15], the basis for the stringency clearly being directly connected with both the special sanctity and purity which the community attributed to the day and their own ritual and moral requirements.)

Despite the respect they frequently gained as benefactors, godfearers were still regarded as Gentiles and thus as a source of levitical impurity: "Whoever undertakes to abstain from idolatry . . . Whoever undertakes not to eat flesh that has not been ritually slaughtered. His spittle, his seat, his couch and his urine are unclean; his bread, his oil and wine are clean [because he is no longer suspected of using them in idolatrous practices] כל שקבל עליו שלא לעבוד עבודה זרה . . . כל שקבל עליו שלא להיות אוכל נבילות רוקו "ומושבו ומשכבו ומי רגליו טמאין ; עיסתו ושמנו וייני טהורים (Ger. 3:1-2).

---

[167] Cf. 4QMMTª ff3-7i:6f; 4QMMTᵇ 1:3f; AZ 2:3ff; Yev. 16:5; Tos.Shab. 1:16-22; Shab. 13b-17b.

[168] Cf. PRK 6:2; Est.R. 2:4; Pes.Rab. 16:6; Mid.Prov. 13.

[169] Cf. Shevi. 4:3, 5:9; Git. 5:8; Tos.AZ 1:3; JDem. 4, 4, 24a; Ber. 17a.

[170] Cf. Jub. 2:29, 50:8, 12; CD-A 10:14f, 11:1ff; 4Q265 f7i:1ff, ii:1f; Jos.*War* 2.147f; Hipp.*Ref.Omn.Her.* 9.20.

While the noachide commandments are traditionally given as seven, their number and identity vary widely according to different sources. The seven regularly include idolatry, blasphemy, bloodshed, sexual offences, theft, and eating from a live animal, together with the injunction to establish a legal system על שבע מצוות נצטוו בני נח: על הדינים ועל עבודה זרה ועל קיללת השם ועל גילוי עריות ועל שפיכות דמים ועל הגזל (cf. Tos.AZ 8[9]:4; San. 56a-b). The prohibition against idolatry was frequently considered to refer only to idolatrous acts and not to theoretical principles since Noachides are not required to "know God" but only to abjure false gods. Given their tendency to be prominent members of their local society (cf. Gill and Gempf: 178-79), godfearers would have been required to participate in public ceremonies and pagan religious ceremonies. Julia Severa, who built a synagogue in Acmonia, served at the same time as the high priestess of the imperial cult (cf. Levinskaya: 123).

Peter's reservations in Acts 10 include both hosting Gentiles and visiting them in their own homes. The issues involved in such "association" included the dietary laws founded on the distinction between clean and unclean animals, the prohibition against eating meat and milk together, slaughtering regulations, benedictions, and purity laws – the latter only being applicable in Eretz Israel.[171]

The severity of food restrictions is attested in numerous early texts. Judith refrained from partaking of Holofernes' food, living instead on the oil, bread, and wine which she brought from her own house (cf. Jud. 10:5, 12:1-4), while Tobit kept himself from eating the "food of the Gentiles (τῶν ἄρτων τῶν ἐθνῶν)" (Tob. 1:11) (cf. Jub. 22:16). Josephus relates that the priests sent by Felix to Rome to plead their cause before Nero subsisted on a diet of nuts and figs in their refusal to compromise Jewish dietary regulations (cf. *Life* 13f). Not only was much of a Gentile's food prohibited but his/her utensils were also considered to be ritually impure: "If a man bought utensils from a gentile, those [of metal or glass and others used for uncooked foods] which it is the custom to immerse [in order to free them from uncleanness before use] he must immerse, those which it is the custom to scald he must scald; those which it is the custom to make white-hot in the fire he must make white-hot in the fire. A spit or gridiron must be made white-hot in the fire; but a knife needs but to be polished and it is then clean הלוקח כלי תשמיש מן הגוי: את שדרכו להטביל - יטביל; להגעיל - יגעיל; ללבן בָּאוּר - ילבן באור. השפוד והאסכלא - מלבנן באור; הסכין - שָׁפָה והיא טהרה (AZ 5:12).[172]

---

[171] Cf. Kel. 1:6; Naz. 7:3.

[172] The centrality claimed by consumption of meals in purity issues is dramatically illustrated in Qumran and the pharisaic "associations [חבורות]." In both of these, strict "hierarchical" rules distinguished between those possessed of different

In addition to the restrictions regulating what food was permitted it was also forbidden to say a blessing over food dedicated to idols. Eating food which a pagan considered to be sanctified to his god was tantamount to co-operating in the deification of created things and hence a blasphemy to the Creator – who would be blessed over the same food. The benediction would consequently become a curse: "R. Simon said: If three have eaten at one table and have not spoken thereat words of the Torah, [it is] as if they had eaten sacrifices [offered] to the dead, for [of such persons] it is said, *For all tables are full of filthy vomit,* [they are] without the All-Present (Isa. 28:8). But, if three have eaten at one table and have spoken thereat words of Torah, [it is] as if they had eaten at the table of the All-Present, blessed be He, as it is said, *This is the table before the Lord* (Ezek. 41:22)"[173] (PA 3:3)[174] (cf. Tomson: 256).

Those who partake of idolatry cannot bless the Creator for their food and therefore are also unworthy to host the presence of the Holy Spirit. This attitude is found in several rabbinic sayings, sometimes based on the example of Hezekiah:

> Among the things a man should keep in mind is taking care not to sit at table with a heathen. For < we find >, as will be set forth concerning Hezekiah, king of Judah, that he sat at table with a heathen, and because he did, consequently had great punishment imposed on him . . . Hence, to conclude as we began: He who sits at table with a heathen is on his way to heathen worship and to eat sacrifices to lifeless idols. If such a man is a disciple of the wise, he belittles his learning in the Torah, profanes the name of his Father [in heaven], wastes his possessions, turns his sons over to his enemies – indeed, fells them by the sword or causes them to be exiled from their Land.[175] (TBE pp. 46, 48)[176]

Verse 12: The problem in Antioch appears to be triggered by the "coming of certain men from James (ἐλθεῖν τινας ἀπὸ 'Ιακώβου)"[177]: Their arrival

---

degrees of purity (cf. 1QS 6:16, 20, 7:3, 16, 8:17; 1Q28a 2:17-22; 4Q274 2i:3; Jos.*War* 2.129, 139, 143, 150; Dem. 2:2-3; Tos.Dem. 2:2ff) (cf. Oppenheimer: 118-69).

[173] רבי שמעון אומר: שלשה שאכלו על שֻלחן אחד, ולא אמרו עליו דברי תורה כאילו אכלו מזבחי מתים, שנאמר: כי כל שלחנות מלאו קיא צואה בלי מקום. אבל שלשה שאכלו על שֻלחן אחד ואמרו עליו דברי תורה כאילו אכלו משֻלחנו של מקום ברוך הוא, שנאמר: וידבר אלי זה השֻלחן אשר לפני ה'.

[174] Cf. Mt. 18:20; PRE 29.

[175] ישמור אדם דברים בלבבו שלא יאכל עם הגוי על השולחן. שכך (מצינו) בחזקיהו מלך יהודה שאכל עם הגוי על השולחן וסוף נענש עליו . . . מיכן אמרו: כל האוכל עם הגוי על השולחן עובד עבודה זרה ואוכל זבחי מתים. אם תלמיד חכם (הוא) מזלזל תורתו ומחלל שם אביו ומבזבז את ממונו ומוסר את בניו ומפיל אותם בחרב ומגלה אותם מארצם.

[176] Cf. Jub. 22:16; Tos.AZ 4:6; ARNᵃ 26:4; AZ 8a; San. 104a.

[177] Although the singular ἦλθεν (elthen – "he came") is supported by a combination of good and ordinarily reliable witnesses, the τινά (tina – "someone")

creates a change in Peter's conduct, which Paul attributes to "fear of the party of the circumcision (φοβούμενος τοὺς ἐκ περιτομῆς)."[178] Thus while Peter uninhibitedly sits down to eat together with gentile believers when he first reaches Antioch, he subsequently removes himself from their companionship.[179] What is difficult to determine here is whether this conduct reflects his fundamental conviction that this is the right course of action (cf. Acts 10:28, 34-35); whether he is persuaded by the attitude of the Antiochian community (against his original sentiment); or whether he is perhaps "ambivalent" – wishing simultaneously to accept gentile believers *qua* Gentiles and to retain the distinctives of Jewish identity.[180]

The indication given in verse 12 is inept, providing only the information that Paul regarded Peter's act of separation as motivated not by sincerity but by an expediency which exhibited an inhibition in the face of "superior forces."[181] If the "zealot" theory were historically plausible, it would be possible to plead the imposition of power-politics on Peter: "The action of one whose convictions were proper, but who became confused under pressure . . . Fearing the reaction of zealot-minded Jews and the difficulties they could make for the Jewish Christian mission when it was

---

appears to have originated along with this singular reading and is easily explicable in terms of scribal oversight. While not necessarily a reference to James himself (cf. Origen), no intrinsic reason prohibits an allusion to a single "person from James," even where it is suggested that "the sense of the passage seems to demand the plural" (Metzger: 592).

[178] This suggests that Nanos' question, "was their arrival, although ultimately consequential – at least from Paul's point of view – actually otherwise incidental and the resultant events in no way anticipated or intended? Were they perhaps simply traveling through Antioch or there for something that had nothing to do with the events that unfolded?" (Galatians: 286) should indeed be answered affirmatively (cf. ibid: 291-92) (see further below).

[179] While some commentators propose a distinction between general "table fellowship" and the Lord's supper, the latter would in fact provide a greater test than the former, gentile wine (and bread) being one of the most problematic aspects of gentile contact due to its immediate association with idolatry (see above). The distinction itself is of very doubtful validity during this period.

[180] The issue of gentile participation in an essentially Jewish entity is fundamentally fraught with friction. While Jewish believers may wholeheartedly concur that the effects of Jesus' death and resurrection reach beyond Israel to the nations, the practical aspects of gentile inclusion have direct implications for Jewish identity. The tension is exhibited in the demand for gentile conversion on the one hand, whereby any threats to Jewish sensitivities are precluded, and an openness (such as that which acknowledges godfearing status) which may, ultimately, lead to the dissipation of all Jewish distinctives.

[181] This factor would seem to preclude any perception that Peter purposely breached the "Jerusalem agreement" (cf. Esler). If such were the case, Paul's accusation would surely not have been one of hypocrisy but of something far weightier.

known back in Palestine that one of the 'pillars' of the Jerusalem church ate
with Gentiles at Antioch in an unrestricted manner, Cephas 'began to draw
back and separate himself' from Gentile believers. He had no theological
difficulties with such table fellowship himself" (Longenecker, Galatians:
75).[182]

Better evidence in fact appears to point in the converse direction,
relating the zealot constituent to Peter himself. Peter's immediate response
to the suggestion that he "associate with a foreigner or . . . visit him" is that
it is "unlawful . . . for a man who is a Jew (ἀθέμιτόν ἐστιν ἀνδρὶ 'Ιουδαίῳ
κολλᾶσθαι ἢ προσέρχεσθαι ἀλλοφύλῳ)"(Acts 10:28).[183] While this reaction
appears rather extreme on the part of a Galilean whose contact with
Gentiles might normally have been assumed, the Galilean population was
also noted for its revolutionary (zealot) fervor[184] (cf. Hengel, Zealots: 56f). If
Peter's "surname" masks a "nickname," Bar-Jona ("son of Jo[cha]na[n]")
may allude to "Baryona (Βαριωνᾶ)" [בַּרְיוֹנָא] (cf. Mt. 16:17) – meaning
"rebel" or "bandit" – a name applied to the Zealots (cf. Git. 56a).[185]

Peter's arrest by Agrippa I prior to the latter's death (c. 43/44) (cf.
Acts 12:1ff) may possibly reinforce such a view (cf. Le Cornu and Shulam:
637ff). While neither James and Peter, nor any other members of the early
community, are thought to have participated in riots or social disorder (cf.
Riesner: 196f, in a slightly different context), the leaders of "social

---

[182] This reading distinguishes "the party of the circumcision" from the "men from
James," the former representing the source of the pressure being exerted on the
latter to refrain from gentile contact, stimulating the Jerusalem community to
engage in a "nomistic campaign among their fellow Christians in the late forties and
early fifties" (Jewett, Agitators: 205/341). For the zealot thesis, which Longenecker
adopts from Jewett, see Introduction, **Occasion and circumstances**.

[183] The Greek ἀθέμιτος (athemitos – "unlawful") occurs in the LXX only in
Maccabees, both there and in Josephus referring to things prohibited according to
the Torah: "The altar also was filled with profane things, which the law forbiddeth
(τὸ δὲ θυσιαστήριον τοῖς ἀποδιεσταλμένοις ἀπὸ τῶν νόμων ἀθεμίτοις
ἐπεπλήρωτο)" (2 Macc. 6:5) (cf. 2 Macc. 7:1; Jos.War 1.650, Life 26). In apposition to
"Jew," the term ἀλλόφυλος (allofylos – "foreigner") designates a heathen or Gentile
(cf. Jos.Ant. 4.183). The LXX regularly uses this word to translate פלשת (peleshet –
"Philistine") – i.e., the uncircumcised (cf. Judg. 3:3, 10:6, 14:1f; 1 Kings 4:1ff, 6:1ff,
14:1ff; Isa. 2:6; Ezek. 16:27; Zech. 9:6).

[184] Cf. Mt. 10:4; Acts 5:37; Jos.War 2.108, 3.41f; Life 39; JKet. 29b.

[185] Cf. also James and John's nickname Boanerges (Βοανηργές – "sons of thunder")
(Mk. 3:17), which bears zealot overtones (cf. Hengel, Zealots: 53ff), while Simon, one
of the twelve, is explicitly identified with the Zealots (cf. Mt. 10:4). The Apostles'
question to Jesus before his ascension as to whether this was the time when he
would "restore the kingdom to Israel" would similarly appear to demonstrate that
they were occupied with "national(ist)" issues in some sense. For the possible
"nationalistic" tendency of subsequent figures within the community, cf. Liebes,
Tosefet: 341f.

movements" may have been particularly suspect during periods of unrest, being the natural object of opposition on the part of those wishing to maintain the *status quo*.[186]

At the more radical end of zealot attitudes towards Gentiles – one which highlighted their idolatrous nature and practices – the observation, touching, and carrying of a coin bearing the emblem of an idolatrous cult were all forsworn for fear of violating the prohibition against worshipping foreign gods.[187] Such persons also refused to enter a city through a gate surmounted by statues, some even enduring such "paroxysms" on hearing an uncircumcised person speaking about God and His commandments that they sought an opportunity to corner him alone and threaten to kill him if he refused to be circumcised[188] (cf. Ben-Shalom: 162f). On this reading, Peter's proclivities – in their original form – would have been vigorously "pro-Jewish" and "anti-gentile," his native predisposition being to observe purity, dietary, and other related regulations. Such conduct also suits his assignation as "apostle to the circumcised" (cf. verse 8).[189]

If Peter's withdrawal from fellowship is consequently to be regarded as representing his "natural" tendency (cf. verse 15), the event which appears to have enabled him to fellowship with gentile believers in Antioch is most likely to have been his meeting with Cornelius (cf. Acts 10-11).[190] While evidently effecting a modification of substantial magnitude in Peter's perception – one which was also acknowledged in Jerusalem by those of a similar temperament (cf. Acts 11:18) – it is difficult to ascertain how significantly this "revolution" was subsequently reinforced in Peter's life, his ensuing whereabouts and concerns being largely unknown (cf. Acts 12:17).[191] A relevant pointer may perhaps be found below, in verses

---

[186] It has been suggested that the disturbances connected with zealot activity during this period may have been associated in some form with the food shortages experienced during the period (cf. Acts 11:28) (cf. Le Cornu and Shulam: 627f, 641). For the difficulty in understanding the extremity of Peter's reaction to associating with Gentiles, cf. ibid: 563-68.

[187] Cf. AZ 50a; Hipp.*Ref.Omn.Her.* 9.21 (cf. Hengel, Zealots: 70, 190f).

[188] Cf. [Ex.R. 30:12, 33:7]; AZ 3:8; Tos.Shab. 17:1; J AZ 3, 8, 43b; Hipp.*Ref.Omn.Her.* 9.21.

[189] While it is tempting to add that such a situation may be easily comprehended when pressure arose from the presence of other Jews, whose conviction would have reinforced Peter's natural sensibilities, it must be stressed that such influence did not necessarily derive from the "men from James." The source more probably lay in the non-Jesus-believing Jewish element associated with the Galatian communities (see below).

[190] Under the present chronology, the current incident is datable to 48, immediately prior to the "council." While Cornelius' dating is difficult to definitively determine, that episode would appear to have occurred some 8-10 years previously.

[191] Although Peter's subsequent appearance is at the "council" in Jerusalem (cf. Acts 15:7), the current chronological scheme establishes Antioch as the foreground

15-16. To the extent that these verses open the letter's *propositio* – in which are laid out first the points of agreement and subsequently the grounds of controversy – they constitute "commonly held knowledge" or items widely affirmed in the circles under discussion (cf. Longenecker, Galatians: 82-83). If this assessment is correct, Peter was privy to this "consensus" and subscribed to its tenets.[192]

From this perspective, it might be imagined that Peter was considerably conflicted when confronted by the circumstances current in Antioch. While his natural inclinations may have been dictated by his concern to preserve and promote Jewish identity – his own and that of others in general – he was now faced with a firmly-formulated standard according to which Jewish and gentile believers were engaged in mutual fellowship. Since the transformation which he had undergone was the result of a divine vision (cf. Acts 10-11), the principle contained in which could not be ignored without rejecting God's direct intervention, Paul's accusation of hypocrisy addresses the fact that Peter has allowed people's – rather than God's – standards to steer his conduct.

The issue closely resembles the principles of fellowship which Paul lays out in Romans 14-15: "It is good not to eat meat or to drink wine, or *to do anything* by which your brother stumbles. The faith which you have, have as your own conviction before God. Happy is he who does not condemn himself in what he approves. But he who doubts is condemned if he eats, because *his eating* is not from faith; and whatever is not from faith is sin"[193] (Rom. 14:21-23) (cf. Jas. 4:17).[194] While the two verbs for

---

to this visit (see Introduction, **Date and destination**). At the same time, if Peter is not in Jerusalem he is presumably resident in the diaspora, whether in a settled or itinerant capacity (cf. 1 Cor. 9:5), suggesting that, at the very least, he is in some contact with Gentiles.

[192] Even if the rhetorical argument is not sustained (see the argument in verses 15-21), Paul's inclusive language ("we") indicates Peter's concurrence with the stated conviction. For the *propositio*, see verses 15-21; for Paul's pronominal usage, see 3:10-14 and 4:1f.

[193] καλὸν τὸ μὴ φαγεῖν κρέα μηδὲ πιεῖν οἶνον μηδὲ ἐν ᾧ ὁ ἀδελφός σου προσκόπτει. σὺ πίστιν [ἣν] ἔχεις κατὰ σεαυτὸν ἔχε ἐνώπιον τοῦ θεοῦ. μακάριος ὁ μὴ κρίνων ἑαυτὸν ἐν ᾧ δοκιμάζει· ὁ δὲ διακρινόμενος ἐὰν φάγῃ κατακέκριται, ὅτι οὐκ ἐκ πίστεως· πᾶν δὲ ὃ οὐκ ἐκ πίστεως ἁμαρτία ἐστίν.

[194] Here again, the issue of intention (כוונה; kavannah) arises (see verses 1-10, in connection with circumcision). It seems far from incidental that, "faith" representing "intention" in Romans 14-15, the "justification" of which Paul speaks of in Galatians may be understood as "justification by intention" (see Introduction, **Argument; Theological pointers** and verses 15-21). For the link between intention and love (cf. Rom. 14:15), see 5:2ff and 6:1-11; for Paul's use of ἐκ πίστεως (ek pisteōs – "on the basis of faithfulness"), see 3:10ff. (While the latter phrase carries a different significance in immediate terms in Romans, the fact that it occurs both

"condemnation" differ here and in Romans, they are directly linked through a passage in Sirach, which uses Paul's term from Galatians in a passage closely parallel to that in Romans: "Blessed is he whose conscience hath not condemned him, and who is not fallen from his hope in the Lord (μακάριος οὗ οὐ κατέγνω ἡ ψυχὴ αὐτοῦ, καὶ ὃς οὐκ ἔπεσεν ἀπὸ τῆς ἐλπίδος αὐτοῦ)" (Sir. 14:2).[195]

On this understanding, Peter's "hypocrisy" is both an expression of expediency – acting to please others – and a violation of his conviction that God has cleansed the Gentiles of idolatry through His gift of the Holy Spirit in Jesus (cf. Nanos, Stake: 283).[196] Idolatry constituting one of three acts for which death was desirable rather than submission,[197] it is quite reasonable that Peter – and any other Jewish believers – would have retained a reluctance to enter a potentially idolatrous circumstance and/or been inclined to firmly remove themselves from any such situation, notwithstanding their conviction that the Gentiles had now been made privy to God's righteousness in Jesus (see below). These dual tendencies are also reflected in the language of "withdrawal (ὑπέστελλεν)" and "holding aloof (ἀφώριζεν)" (verse 12). The first, literally signifying "to draw back," suggests a retreat or shrinking due to caution (see also below).

---

here and in Romans 14 permits, at the least, notification of the juxtaposition of meanings in the two contexts.)

[195] While describing the "happy man," Sirach's opening statement also addresses the work of the tongue ("Blessed is the man that hath not slipped with his mouth") (Sir. 14:1). It is that organ, above all others, to which James attributes responsibility for hypocrisy, not only in its "boasting of great things (μεγάλα αὐχεῖ)" but also in its duplicity in issuing "both blessing and cursing (ἐκ τοῦ αὐτοῦ στόματος ἐξέρχεται εὐλογία καὶ κατάρα)" (Jas. 3:5, 10). For blessing and cursing, see 1:6-9, 3:1ff, 4:12-20, and 6:12f.

[196] This point is clarified in Paul's reproof, wherein he indicts Peter for "compelling" gentile believers to assume that they must convert to Judaism, Peter himself knowing that his own status – being a "born Jew" – is itself dependent upon faithfulness to Jesus (cf. Nanos, Stake: 310) (see verses 15-21 and below). The fact that Paul's argument in Romans 14-15 revolves around respect for others reinforces the indication that the issue at hand here is status/identity rather than conduct (see below).

[197] "R. Johanan said in the name of R. Simeon b. Jehozadak: By a majority vote it was resolved in the upper chambers of the house of Nithza in Lydda that in every [other] law of the Torah, if a man is commanded: 'Transgress and suffer not death' he may transgress and not suffer death, excepting idolatry, incest, and murder אמר רבי יוחנן משום רבי שמעון בן יהוצדק: נימנו וגמרו בעליית בית נתזה בלוד: כל עבירות שבתורה, אם אומרין לאדם "עבור ואל תהרג" - יעבור ואל יהרג, חוץ מעבודת כוכבים וגילוי עריות ושפיכות דמים" (San. 74a) (cf. Yalk.Lev. 588; Yalk.Dt. 838) (see also 5:19-23).

The second is specific to purity issues as relating to Israel's status as being "set apart"[198] (cf. Longenecker, *Galatians*: 75).[199]

While many commentators assume a correspondence with the "men from James," the phrase "party of the circumcision (τοὺς ἐκ περιτομῆς)" (verse 12) most commonly delineates "Jews" from the "mainstream" Jewish community (i.e., non-Jesus-believing Jews)[200] (cf. Nanos, *Stake*: 287f). Given the difficulties attendant on the "zealot theory," the reference may in fact be to (a part of) the Jewish community in Antioch itself. On this reading, Peter's apprehension arises specifically from a *Jewish* – not a *Jesus-believing* – presence, his withdrawal being triggered by persons whose views coincided with more stringent Jewish attitudes towards Gentiles (cf. Acts 16:3?) (cf. ibid: 291-92).[201] In other words, while it was the former's arrival which sparked Peter's retreat, the immediate impetus for his "retraction" may have derived not from pressure applied by the "men from James" but from some overt reaction on the part of the *Jewish element*.[202]

If "the ones from James also joined in these mixed meals," this act may have served as "the last straw for the ones for circumcision, who had been opposing this behavior for some time but now saw clearly that it was even supported by the Judean leaders of this coalition" (ibid: 292).[203] Peter's action, under these circumstances, represents a response to real or

---

[198] The verb can thus translate בדל (badal), חרם (charam), פרד (parad), עבר ('avar) and סגר (sagar) in the LXX, amongst other meanings (cf. Gen. 10:5; Ex. 13:12; Lev. 13:4ff, 20:25-26, 27:21; Isa. 56:3; Ezek. 45:1f; 4 Macc. 3:20; Sir. 47:2).

[199] Although not an historical parallel in any form, it is instructive to note that the regulations ordering the life of the pharisaic חבר (chaver – "associate"), some more stringent, some more lenient, are at times based on hypocrisy: "If they regret becoming associates, they can never again be accepted. So claims R. Meir. R. Judah says: If they regret publicly, they can be accepted; but if clandestinely [i.e., if they disregard the ordinances in private but behave as associates in public] they are not to be accepted [due to their hypocrisy] כולן שחזרו בהן, אין מקבלין אותן עולמית - דברי ר' "מאיר. ר' יהודה אומר: חזרו בהם בפרהסיא, מקבלין אותן; ובמטמוניות, אין מקבלין אותן (Tos.Dem. 2:9) (see also 5:2-12 [n18]). For pharisaical hypocrisy, see 6:1-11 and verses 15-21.

[200] Cf. [Acts 10:45, 11:2]; Rom. 3:30, 15:8; Ex.R. 1:15; PRK 28:1 (see verses 1-10 [excursus]).

[201] For an examination of the "Zealot theory," see Introduction, **Occasion and circumstances**.

[202] On this reading, the phrase τοὺς ἐκ περιτομῆς (tous ek peritomēs) is understood as an allusion to "an interest group specifically distinguished from other groups of circumcised Jews as *advocates* of circumcision" (Nanos, *Stake*: 288; original emphasis).

[203] Paul's text nowhere associates Peter with the "men from James." On the contrary, it makes his hypocrisy directly dependent upon the "party of the circumcision."

implied pressure on the part of a Jewish group associated with the Galatian communities, whose presence exerted on him an influence to assert his Jewish identity. The occasion for this "manipulation" was the arrival of certain "men from James" who – contrary to traditional exegesis – did not demand separation from the gentile brethren but, in line with the halakhic ruling shortly to be adopted at the "council," practiced their conviction that, through their participation in Jesus' faithfulness and righteousness, Gentiles had now gained entrance to God's Kingdom *qua* Gentiles (see Introduction, **Argument**). Peter, caught between two conflicts of interest, was compelled to choose between two courses of conduct. In electing to withdraw from gentile fellowship, he was in danger of placing his natural tendencies over principles revealed to him by God Himself. Moreover, he was holding "fleshly" concerns of Jewish identity higher than love of one's brother – in effect, denying the Gentiles the possibility of redemption through God's sending of his faithfulness (see below).[204]

Verse 13: The verb ὑποκρίνομαι (hypokrinomai) literally designates an "answering from under," the action demanded by the mask worn by an actor (= ὑποκριτής; hypokritēs) (cf. BAGD: 845).[205] Out of this sense of "playing a part" developed the meaning of concealment of true character or intent, specifically in an attempt to present oneself in a better light. The attribution takes on special significance in the light of the accusation of withdrawal, the Hebrew חנפים (chanafim – "hypocrites") appearing in

[204] It should be clear from this reading that the present volume does not perceive in the Antioch incident an issue of table-fellowship with its attendant motifs of ritual im/purity, kashrut, and/or tithing. As Paul's rebuke makes evident, the question at stake is one of *status*: Are gentile believers to be considered part of God's Kingdom through participation in Jesus' death and resurrection – or do they need also (or first) to become members of the Jewish community? Peter's withdrawal indicates the latter – a hypocrisy on the scale of misrepresenting the basis of his own redemption (equally through Jesus) as well as on that of surrendering to the pressure of others and betraying his own sense of God's favour.

[205] In its non-prejudicial sense, the verb simply denotes the act of answering, interpreting, or explaining. Although a NT hapax, the compound indicates joint participation, without modifying the sense (cf. Ep.Arist. 267; Jos.*War* 1.569, 5.321; Polybius 3.31.7, 3.52.6, 3.92.5; Plut.*Marius* 14.8, 413A, 17.3, 415B). Epictetus (as quoted by Arrian) asks of the godfearer: "Why do you act the part of a Jew when you are a Greek? ... whenever we see a man halting between two faiths we are in the habit of saying, 'He is not a Jew, he is only acting the part.' But when he adopts the attitude of mind of the man who has been baptized and has made his choice, then he both is a Jew in fact and is called one. So we also are counterfeit baptists, ostensibly Jews but in reality something else (τί ὑποκρίνῃ Ἰουδαῖον ὢν Ἕλλην; ... ὅταν τινὰ ἐπαμφοτερίζοντα ἴδωμεν, εἰώθαμεν λέγειν «οὐκ ἔστιν Ἰουδαῖος. ἀλλ' ὑποκρίνεται.» ὅταν δ' ἀναλάβῃ τὸ πάθος τὸ τοῦ βεβαμμένου καὶ ἡρημένου, τότε καὶ ἔστι τῷ ὄντι καὶ καλεῖται Ἰουδαῖος. οὕτως καὶ ἡμεῖς παραβαπτισταί, λόγῳ μὲν Ἰουδαῖοι, ἔργῳ δ' ἄλλο τι)" (*Diss.* 2.19-21) (see also below).

some versions of birkat ha-minim, the so-called benediction against heretics (cf. Flusser, Some, and for the following discussion). In its original biblical form the Hebrew term seems to have denoted a specific sense of "godlessness."[206] The inclusion of "transgressors" in birkat ha-minim is apparently due to the fact that the biblical signification of the root as "wickedness" was gradually replaced by the modern concept of "hypocrisy." Those who "separate themselves from the community פרשו מדרכי ציבור" could in this sense include those known for their hypocrisy (cf. SOR 3).[207]

Paul designates "the rest of the Jews (οἱ λοιποὶ ᾿Ιουδαῖοι)" as co-defenders to the charge. Since Barnabas is carried along through/with their conduct, there can be little doubt that these others are Jewish believers.[208] Both the result (ὥστε; hōste) and the "even (καὶ)" emphasise how Barnabas' dissimulation in particular pained Paul. This was a personal anguish, Barnabas having been Paul's initial mentor and subsequently his close companion and colleague (see verses 1-10).[209] The linguistic distinction between συνυποκρίνομαι (synypokrinomai) and συναπάγω (synapagō) is due to Paul's peculiar distress over Barnabas' duplicity, the latter verb frequently carrying an aura of irrationality in koine Greek.[210] It is a measure of Paul's esteem for Barnabas that he is unwilling to believe anything but that Barnabas has been swayed by an influential group.[211]

Verse 14: At some unspecified point, Paul recognises that this prevailing conduct, which contravenes the integrity of the gospel, must be

---

[206] Cf. LXX Job 34:30, 36:13; Isa. 9:17, 10:6, 32:6, 33:14; Jer. 23:11; Dan. 11:32; Sir. 16:6, 40:15, 41:10. The Hebrew root denotes uncleanness, pollution, profaneness (cf. BDB: 337-38), an aspect of which may also be present here in the context of gentile idolatry (see above [excursus]).

[207] Delitzsch reflects a similar understanding in translating וכבאם היה מתרחק ופורש מהם מיראתו את בני המילה, although he prefers the root כחש (kachash) to designate the hypocrisy, the latter signifying both flattery and deceit (falsity) (cf. Jastrow: 629).

[208] For the identification of "those of the circumcision," see above.

[209] If the congregations to whom Paul is writing are in south Galatia, they were also personally acquainted with Barnabas (cf. Acts 13:2-14:26). For Barnabas' "role" in determining the chronological setting of Galatians, see Introduction, **Date and destination**.

[210] Cf. Rom. 12:16; 1 Cor. 12:2; 2 Pet. 3:17; Jos.*Ant.* 18.344; *War* 1.493.

[211] Paul presents Barnabas here as the subject of seduction, expressed in the aorist passive ("was carried away"), the attribution of hypocrisy being again leveled against the larger group – αὐτῶν τῇ ὑποκρίσει (autōn tē hyposkrisei – "by their hypocrisy"), the dative either being instrumental or of accompaniment ("along with") (cf. Burton: 109). For various theories regarding Paul's relationship with Barnabas as indicated here and in Acts, cf. Bauckham, Barnabas.

confronted.[212] In claiming that "they were not straightforward about the truth of the gospel (οὐκ ὀρθοποδοῦσιν πρὸς τὴν ἀλήθειαν τοῦ εὐαγγελίου)" Paul understands "hypocrisy" in the sense of "bending or declining from the right path" (Jastrow: 484).[213] The language of "orthopedia (ὀρθοποδοῦσιν)" is reminiscent of the "two ways" between which a person must choose to walk – either to follow God or to follow his/her own inclination: "These are their paths in the world: [The Spirit of Truth is] to enlighten the heart of man, [to] straighten out in front of him all the paths of true justice [righteousness] . . . However, to the spirit of deceit belong greed, sluggishness in the service of justice, wickedness, falsehood, pride . . . ואלה דרכיהן בתבל להאיר בלבב איש ולישר לפניו כול דרכי צדק "אמת . . . ולרוח עולה רחוב נפש ושפול ידים בעבודת צדק רשע ושקר גוה (1QS 4:2, 9) (see 5:13ff).[214] Peter is not walking according to the path of God's truth and righteousness as it is expressed in the gospel, his lack of conviction here (see above) impugning its integrity – its reliability and true expression of God's intention (cf. Rom. 14:17, 20).[215]

Paul's perception of the seriousness of the problem is reflected in his decision to challenge Peter publicly. The procedure for reproving one's neighbour calls for an initial face to face meeting (cf. Lev. 19:17; verse 11), followed by an assembly with witnesses (see above).[216] Only if the matter cannot thus be resolved is recourse to the whole community called for (cf. Mt. 18:17), the grounds adduced in 1 Timothy 5:20 being those of deterrence: "Those who continue in sin, rebuke in the presence of all, so that the rest also may be fearful *of sinning* (Τοὺς ἁμαρτάνοντας ἐνώπιον πάντων ἔλεγχε, ἵνα καὶ οἱ λοιποὶ φόβον ἔχωσιν)" (see 6:1-11).[217] Were it not for this reason, the injunction against shaming one's neighbour in public (המלבין פני חברו ברבים; ha-malbin pnei chavero be-rabim) would hold

---

[212] This εἶδον (eidon – "saw") parallels the ἰδόντες (idontes – "seeing") in verse 7. Although the precise circumstances of the confrontation remain unclear (see above), Paul intervenes at a certain point to interrupt the ongoing pattern of behaviour suggested by the imperfect verbs of verse 12.

[213] Paul works out this theme in 5:13f.

[214] Cf. Mt. 6:24, 7:13f; Rom. 6:6ff; Sir. 5:8-11; Test.Asher 1:3-6:5; 1QHᵃ 10:10, 15:14, 20:34; 4QPsᵃ 3:17; [4Q259 3:5]; Did. 1:1ff.

[215] The matrix of "truth," "righteousness," and "uprightness/straightness" is frequently found in ancient texts (cf. 1 Kings 3:6; Prov. 8:6-8; Isa. 59:14; 1QS 4:2ff; 4Q286 f1ii:7f). To the extent that the idea of "walking" represents the idea of halakhah (הלכה – "walking"), Paul's reproof is also of a halakhic nature, proving that Peter's conduct is unbecoming in God's sight (see 5:2f). For Galatians as a halakhic "rebuke-request" letter along the lines of 4QMMT, see Introduction, **Form; Argument**.

[216] Cf. Mt. 18:16; 1 Tim. 5:19; CD-A 9:2-3.

[217] The fact that "the rest of the Jews" were carried away and joined Peter here indicates the wisdom of Paul's caution to Timothy.

force, constituting an offence whose gravity removes one from the world to come.[218]

The rebuke is formulated in "an elegant though complex enthymeme, 'a brief and pointed argument drawn from contraries' that could be used to expose logical inconsistencies in a ridiculing manner" (Nanos, Stake: 310, and for the following discussion).[219] Paul's charge is that Peter's withdrawal from gentile fellowship constitutes a logical compulsion of the Gentiles to correct their (mis)understanding that they have become full members of the people of Israel. Having been assured that they have acquired God's righteousness in the Messiah, Peter is now invalidating this recognition and demonstrating that equality comes rather through circumcision and conversion. His conduct requires gentile believers to apprehend that their acceptance before God through Jesus' death and resurrection is insufficient in Jewish eyes and that the Jewish community – as represented by the "party of the circumcision" whose views Peter, Barnabas, and the "rest" have (temporarily) adopted – will not recognize them unless they formally join its ranks.[220]

In this sense, the compulsion is *logical* in nature. Peter is (ὑπάρχων; hyparchōn) Jewish.[221] At the time at which Paul takes him to task for his behaviour, he is living according to "normative" Jewish codes, having distanced himself from the gentile believers.[222] Paul's accusation is

---

[218] Cf. PA 3:11; Ber. 43b. For the warning against speaking in anger, cf. Mt. 5:32; 1QS 5:25-26; CD-A 9:4-6.

[219] For the current reading of Galatians as a halakhic "rebuke-request" letter along the lines of 4QMMT, see Introduction, **Form**; **Argument**.

[220] The distinction between conduct and status seems at first glance rather arbitrary. To "live Jewishly" must be expressed in some form, and issues of purity and kashrut constitute obvious examples in the context of table fellowship. At the same time, the issue is not one of *degree* – the extent to which gentile believers conformed to Jewish standards – but of *right*: the prerogative (in its "positive" sense) or obligation (in its "negative" expression) of observing the Torah. Are the Gentiles privileged/obligated to perform the commandments, or are they not?

[221] This recalls Epictetus' "being a Greek" (ὢν Ἕλλην; ōn Hellēn) (see above). Epictetus' accusation is, *mutis mutandis*, an excellent parallel to Romans 2, giving a description of persons who claim a particular identity but who, in reality, are "something else, not in sympathy with our own reason, far from applying the principles which we profess, yet priding ourselves upon them as being men who know them (ἄλλο τι, ἀσυμπαθεῖς πρὸς τὸ λόγον, μακρὰν ἀπὸ τοῦ χρῆσθαι τούτοις ἃ λέγομεν, ἐφ᾽ οἷς ὡς εἰδότες αὐτὰ εηπαιρόμεθα)" (Arrian, *Diss.* 2.9.21). For Romans 2, see 5:2f and verses 15-21.

[222] While not present in Galatia, the claims of this "party" - composed of the "party of the circumcision" who have exerted their influence on Peter, Barnabas, and the "rest of the Jews" - are precisely represented in the Galatians' circumstances in the persons of the godfearers, who are making peculiarly the same claims as the group in Antioch. It is particularly on these grounds that Paul points to Peter's hypocrisy

consequently a theoretical query: If Peter is himself willing to "live like the Gentiles (ἐθνικῶς)" – i.e., to put himself on a par with them, to regard his status as equal to theirs – how can he stop doing so and thereby imply that his Jewish identity is innately superior, consequently "compelling" the gentile believers to look to conversion for equality in standing? On this reading, the verb ἰουδαΐζειν (ioudaïzein) signifies "living as a Jew" in the sense of becoming a proselyte, since Paul's point revolves around identity (status) rather than around conduct (how or what you eat).[223] Peter, Paul argues, is demanding by his current action that gentile believers convert in order to find redemption.

Verses 15-21: [*Propositio*]

"We *are* Jews by nature, and not sinners from among the Gentiles; nevertheless knowing that a man is not justified by the works of the Law but through faith in the Messiah Jesus, even we have believed in the Messiah Jesus, that we may be justified by faith in the Messiah, and not by the works of the Law; since by the works of the Law shall no flesh be justified. But if, while seeking to be justified in the Messiah, we ourselves have also been found sinners, is the Messiah then a minister of sin? May it never be! For if I rebuild what I have *once* destroyed, I prove myself to be a transgressor. For through the Law I died to the Law, that I might live to God. I have been crucified with the Messiah; and it is no longer I who live, but the Messiah lives in me; and the *life* which I now live in the flesh I live by faith in the Son of God, who loved me, and delivered Himself up for me. I do not nullify the grace of God; for if righteousness *comes* through the Law, then the Messiah died needlessly."

---

as the issue facing the Galatians. For the presently-proposed reading of the Galatian situation, see Introduction, **Argument**.

[223] While the verb (a NT hapax) is regularly understood to describe an attachment to Judaism expressed in various ways and to various degrees, normally *exclusive* of circumcision/conversion, the latter is not precluded from its purview. The term occurs in conjunction with "circumcision" (cf. Jos.*War* 2.454; Eus.*Praep.Ev.* 9.22.5) where it may also modify the noun. As Nanos contends, "the context of the interests at stake in Antioch does not support this interpretation [i.e., of " a range of possible degrees of assimilation to Jewish customs" without actually arriving at circumcision] for the case in hand" (Stake: 306). Despite the appearance of tautology – the term must denote conversion because this is the matter at hand – the verb itself can bear the distinction between "assimilation" and "conversion" and therefore requires definition. Its appearance – rather than περιτμηθῆναι (peritmēthēnai – "to be circumcised") – may further be attributable to the fact that it follows Paul's usage of ᾿Ιουδαῖος (Ioudaios – "Jew") and ᾿Ιουδαϊκῶς (Ioudaïkōs – "Jewishly") earlier in the same sentence (cf. Esler: 278). The significance of the issue is discernible from the fact that Dunn's argument turns precisely on the distinction in the *reverse direction* – i.e., that the incident at Antioch represents a case of degree of Jewish practice (cf. Incident). (What should be noted is that the reflexive verbal form does exclude the traditional understanding of persuading *others* to "act Jewishly" [in the sense of "judaising"].)

The long-standing debate over the function and placement of these verses has sought to determine whether they are to be regarded as the continuation of Paul's rejoinder to Peter or as an independent theological "excursus" directed towards Paul's Galatian addressees (cf. Longenecker, Galatians: 80). Recent rhetorical studies applied to Paul's letters have persuaded some commentators to place the epistles within the context of apologetic letters (cf. Betz, Galatians).[224] Under the rubric of such a genre, ancient epistolary practice customarily calls for the inclusion of a *propositio*, this constituting a brief statement of the consensual points drawn from the *narratio*. The *propositio* is followed by an equally concise summary of the controversial items to be demonstrated in the *probatio* or "proof" of the argument (cf. 3:1-4:11).[225]

On this reading, verses 15-16 represent the "commonly held knowledge" of the early Jewish segment of the believing community and verses 17-20 the matters of disagreement, namely "legalism" and "nomism." Finally, verse 21 provides a direct statement refuting the charge laid against Paul, combined with an explicatory sentence identifying the "crux" of the issue. This scheme is viewed as particularly helpful not merely as making sense of a frequently under-interpreted passage but also in clarifying the role of the subsequent sections. Having identified the two primary points with which Paul is preoccupied, 3:1-18 can be understood as an elaboration of the first ("legalism") and 3:19-4:7 an amplification of the second ("nomism").

The presently proposed reading of Galatians places the epistle, alternatively, within the halakhic model exemplified by 4QMMT – the so-called "halakhic letter" (see Introduction, **Form**). With all due respect to the epistolary conventions of the ancient Greek world – and Paul's place in it – Paul remains first and foremost a Jewish author.[226] While he evidently employs contemporary cultural structures and frameworks, his worldview is governed by Scripture. It is the exegesis of the biblical text which undergirds and informs his thought patterns, hermeneutical methods, arguments, and imperatives (halakhah).[227] Most particularly at this juncture, the argument of verses 15-21 makes best sense as an explanation of the grounds on which Paul perceives Peter as in need of reproof. In

---

[224] Not all rhetorically-oriented commentaries follow Betz's identification of the epistle as an apologetic letter. For an instructive critique of Galatians as an example of this genre, cf. Longenecker, Galatians: cviii-cxi.

[225] The *propositio* is consequently inserted following the *narratio* and preceding the *probatio*. For the *narratio*, see 1:11-12 (verses 11-14).

[226] For a critique of the failure of Betz's rhetorical/epistolary approach to account for the letter's Jewish character, cf. Daube, New: 172-88.

[227] See Introduction, **Theological pointers**; Appendix, 3:1-5, and 4:1-7.

similar fashion, Peter's example constitutes the platform and model from which Paul launches into his appeal to the Galatians.[228]

The strongest proof of this claim may perhaps derive from the fact that verses 15-21 – in which Paul introduces the motif of justification – constitute Paul's denunciation of Peter's hypocrisy. Rabbinic literature abounds with condemnation of persons whose practice is at odds with their teaching: "... Good are the commands which come out of the mouth of those who perform them ... There are some who preach well but do not act well, others act well but do not preach well אין דברים כשהן יוצאין מפי "עושיהן ... יש נאה דורש ואין נאה מקיים, נאה מקיים ואין נאה דורש (Tos.Yev. 8:4; Hag. 14b) (cf. Weinfeld, *Hypocrisy:* 52ff, and for the following discussion).[229]

This theme is directly associated in many passages with arguments that Torah-study without piety is valueless: "*Within and without shalt thou overlay it* (Ex. 25:11). Raba said: Any scholar whose inside is not like his outside, is no scholar. Abaye, or, as some say, Rabbah b. 'Ulla said: He is called abominable, as it is said: *How much less one that is abominable and impure, man who drinketh iniquity like water* (Job 15:16). R. Samuel b. Nahmani, in the name of R. Jonathan: What is the meaning of the scriptural statement: *Wherefore is there a price in the hand of a fool, to buy wisdom, seeing he hath no understanding* (Prov. 17:16), i.e., woe unto the enemies of the scholars [i.e., the scholars themselves], who occupy themselves with the Torah, but have no fear of heaven! R. Jannai proclaimed: Woe unto him who has no court, but makes a gateway for his court! Raba said to the Sages: I beseech you, do not inherit a double Gehinnom!"[230] (Yoma 72b)[231] (see 5:2-12 [verse 6]).

---

[228] See 3:1-5 and 5:13f. This appraisal precedes any assessment of the theological content of verses 15-21. It should be evident that neither "legalism" nor "nomism" are terms/concepts appropriate to a Jewish writer such as we view Paul. For the linguistic links between verses 11-14 and 15-21, see below.

[229] Cf. Gen.R. 34:14; TBE p. 140; Yalk.Gen. 61; Yalk.Num. 688; Tos.Hag. 2:1; JHag. 9a; Yev. 63b (see 5:2-12 [verse 6]). The parallel with Mt. 23:3 should be obvious: "Therefore all that they tell you do and observe, but do not do according to their deeds; for they say *things*, and do not do *them* (πάντα οὖν ὅσα ἐὰν εἴπωσιν ὑμῖν ποιήσατε καὶ τηρεῖτε, κατὰ δὲ τὰ ἔργα αὐτῶν μὴ ποιεῖτε· λέγουσιν γὰρ καὶ οὐ ποιοῦσιν)."

[230] מבית ומחוץ תצפנו : אמר רבא : כל תלמיד חכם שאין תוכו כברו אינו תלמיד חכם. (אמר) אביי ואיתימא רבה בר עולא [אמר] : נקרא נתעב, שנאמר : אף כי נתעב ונאלח איש שתה כמים עולה. אמר רבי שמואל בר נחמני אמר רבי יונתן : מai דכתיב "למה זה מחיר ביד כסיל לקנות חכמה ולב אין"?! - אוי להם לשונאיהן של תלמידי חכמים שעוסקין בתורה ואין בהן יראת שמים. מכריז רבי ינאי : חבל על דלית ליה דרתא ותרעא לדרתיה עביד. אמר להו רבא לרבנן : במטותא מינייכו - לא תירתון תרתי גיהנם.

[231] A person's inside and outside should both reflect the same "golden character" as that belonging to the ark. 'Ulla interprets the verse from Job to say that one may drink the water of the Torah and yet have iniquity in one, while Samuel applies

The lack of concord between saying and doing represents a deeper division. It also reflects the incapacity of human beings to act with the proper intention. This disparity between deed and thought, so frequently expressed in form without substance (ritual observance rather than from the heart) disturbs God's unity and sovereignty.[232] "Hypocrisy" in this sense represents the human bondage to sin and Belial which impedes humanity's intimacy with God: "But your iniquities have made a separation between you and your God, and your sins have hid His face from you כי אם-עונתיכם היו מבדלים ביניכם לבין אלהיכם וחטאותיכם הסתירו פנים מכם" (Isa. 59:2). As a midrash relates of Exodus 34:30: "After they [Israel] sinned, they could not gaze even upon the face of God's intermediary. Of their fear it is written *They were afraid to come nigh him* (Ex. 34:30) כיון שחטאו ישראל אפילו פני (השליט) [השליח] הסרסור לא היו יכולין להסתכל, הדא הוא דכתיב: וייראו מגשת אליו" (Pes.Rab. 15:3) (see 1:1-5, 3:19-20, and 4:1-7).[233] Human sinfulness is directly associated with lack of possession of the keys to God's Kingdom: "Because of his sinfulness man has not the power to comprehend the Form on high; otherwise he would have been entrusted with the keys [of knowledge] and discover how heaven and earth had been created אין ספק לאדם לידע מה דמות למעלה ואלמלא כן היו מוסרין לו מפתחות ויודע במה נבראו שמים וארץ" (ARNᵃ 39:1) (cf. Mk. 4:11).[234]

"wisdom" to knowledge of the Torah and "understanding" to the fear of heaven. R. Jannai suggests that the court is the goal, to be entered *via* learning; study without reverence is hypocritical and sinful. Raba's dictum assumes that the person who engages in Torah-study without possessing the fear of heaven suffers not only in this world, where he denies himself pleasure for the sake of his study, but also in the world to come where, because he had no fear of heaven, his reward will be replaced by punishment.

[232] This may be seen most clearly in the Shema: "Hear O Israel, the LORD is our God, the LORD is one! And you shall love the LORD your God with all your heart and with all your soul and with all your might את ואהבת :אחד 'ה אלהינו 'ה ישראל שמע ובכל-לבבך בכל 'ה אלהיך" (Dt. 6:4-5) (see 3:19-20 [n262]).

[233] Cf. Gen. 3:10. Paul develops this theme in relation to sin in 3:19f and in relation to the Spirit in 5:13ff (see there). Peter's hypocrisy is paradigmatic for Paul precisely because it points up the sin which intervenes between wo/man and God – for the Jew and also for the Gentile. For the theme of bondage, see 1:1-5, 3:10ff, 4:1f, 5:13f, and verses 1-10.

[234] Cf. R. Jochanan's statement in praise of Eleazar b. Arakh's learning: "Blessed be the Lord God of Israel who gave a son to our father Abraham who knows how to study and to understand the glory of our Father in heaven. There are those who preach well but who do not practice well ... Happy are you Abraham, our father, that Eleazar b. Arakh descended from you and knows and understands to preach the glory of his Father in heaven לדרוש שיודע אבינו לאברהם בן שנתן ישראל אלהי 'ה ברוך דורש נאה ואין מקיים נאה יש נאה דורש ואין מקיים, נאה מקיים ... שבשמים אבינו בכבוד ולהבין שבשמים אבינו בכבוד ולהבין לדרוש שיודע מחלציד, יצא ערך בן שאלעזר אבינו אברהם אשריך" (Tos.Hag. 2:1). In other words, Eleazar b. Arakh's ability to comprehend the "work

This idea, which reflects Jesus' bestowal of the "keys of the kingdom of heaven (τὰς κλεῖδας τῆς βασιλείας τῶν οὐρανῶν)" to Peter (Mt. 16:19), is elaborated in a statement made by Rabbah bar Rav Huna: "Every man who possesses learning without the fear of Heaven is like a treasurer who is entrusted with the inner keys but not with the outer: how is he to enter? R. Jannai proclaimed: Woe to him who has no courtyard yet makes a gate for the same! Rab Judah said, The Holy One, blessed be He, created His world only that men should fear [reverence] Him, for it is said, *and God hath done it, that men should fear before Him* (Eccl. 3:14)"[235] (Shab. 31b).[236] Without the fear of heaven – the beginning of wisdom – a person's knowledge is of no benefit to him/her.[237] Paul's rebuke of Peter may be understood, in this context, as the reproof of a person to whom the keys have indeed been given but who refuses to acknowledge their efficacy. Before such a person, the doors of the Kingdom of heaven will be shut (see also 3:10-14).[238]

---

of the chariot [מעשה מרכבה]" which he was studying was built upon the foundation of his proper daily living. The reference to Abraham is, of course, not coincidental and accords with the theme of Galatians (see 3:1ff and below).

[235] אמר רבה בר רב הונא: כל אדם שיש בו תורה ואין בו יראת שמים דומה לגזבר שמסרו לו מפתחות הפנימיות ומפתחות החיצונות לא מסרו לו. בהי עייל? מכריז רבי ינאי: חבל על דלית ליה דרתא ותרעא לדרתא עביד. אמר רב יהודה: לא ברא הקדוש ברוך הוא את עולמו אלא כדי שייראו מלפניו, שנאמר: והאלהים עשה שייראו מלפניו.

[236] Cf. Mt. 16:19, 23:13; Lk. 11:52; PA 3:17; ARN[a] 39:1. The weight carried by the "fear of heaven" can be seen from the fact that it is precisely this with which R. Jochanan b. Zakkai blesses his disciples on his deathbed, having acknowledged his uncertainty of whether he will inherit the Garden of Eden or gehinnom (cf. Ber. 28b) (see 5:19-23) (verse 21). Peter's connection with the "keys" of the Kingdom makes Paul's denunciation of his hypocrisy the more severe. For this verse in connection with Peter in verses 7-8, see verses 1-10. Paul engages in a similar admonition against hypocrisy in Romans 2, where intention (faithfulness) again forms the central theme.

[237] Cf. Ps. 111:10; Prov. 1:7, 9:10, 15:33; 1 Cor. 1:17-2:16, 3:18-20; Jas. 3:13-18. The discussion in Shabbat 31b immediately follows the "debate" between Hillel and Shammai over the grounds on which a proselyte is to be admitted (cf. Shab. 31a), indicating that the "fear of the Lord" as representative of the person's intention may have constituted an element of concern regarding proselytes. For conversion and intention, see verses 1-10.

[238] Cf. 4:17, where Paul uses the same verb as in Mt. 23:13, the language of "seeking (ζηλοῦσιν)" (lit., "zealing") also possibly reflecting Jesus' charge that the Pharisees "travel about on sea and land to make one proselyte (περιάγετε τὴν θάλασσαν καὶ τὴν ξηρὰν ποιῆσαι ἕνα προσήλυτον)" (Mt. 23:15) (Mt. 23:14 breaking the natural connection between these two verses) (see 4:12-20, 6:1-11, and below). The link with hypocrisy is further reinforced in Acts 15, where Peter speaks of the prohibition against testing God by "placing upon the neck of the disciples a yoke which neither our fathers nor we have been able to bear (ἐπιθεῖναι ζυγὸν ἐπὶ τὸν τράχηλον τῶν μαθητῶν ὃν οὔτε οἱ πατέρες ἡμῶν οὔτε ἡμεῖς ἰσχύσαμεν βαστάσαι)" (Acts 15:10)

Paul's censure of Peter derives a major part of its force from the fact that Peter is "naturally (φύσει)" Jewish (cf. Rom. 2:14, 27) (cf. Nanos, Stake: 310). As Paul later sets forth in Romans, this circumstance is assumed to bestow a particular advantage, Israel not merely being beloved, in R. Akiva's words, "in that they were called children of the All-Present" but receiving "superabundant love [in that] it was made known to them that they were called children of the All-Present, as it is said: *Ye are children of the Lord your God* (Dt. 14:1). Beloved are Israel in that a desirable instrument [the Torah] was given to them. [It was a mark of] superabundant love [that] it was made known to them that the desirable instrument, wherewith the world had been created, was given to them, as it is said: *For I give you good doctrine; forsake not My teaching* (Prov. 4:2)"[239] (PA 3:14).[240] Paul's most striking presentation of Israel's election is found in Romans 11, wherein he describes the people as the root and "natural *branches*" of a cultivated (domesticated) olive tree – into which the Gentiles are grafted "contrary to nature"[241] (Rom. 11:24).

Although many commentators read the elliptical first half of verse 15 as a relative clause – "We *who are* Jews by birth . . . *who* know that (Ἡμεῖς φύσει Ἰουδαῖοι καὶ οὐκ ἐξ ἐθνῶν ἁμαρτωλοί)" – the primary comparison is between Jews and Gentiles as a matter of nature, rather than one of knowing. Jews are not "sinners" – as is the natural status of the Gentiles (see verses 1-10, 11-14 [excursi]).[242] Paul's thought here may parallel Josephus' description of the Essenes as those who are "of Jewish birth" –

(cf. Acts 15:28: "no greater burden [πλέον . . . βάρος]") (see 6:1-11). This language is reminiscent of Mt. 23:4, part of Jesus' same condemnation of pharisaic hypocrisy, and gives the impression – together with Peter's "quote" of Gal. 2:16 in Acts 15:11 – that Peter is referring in the council to Paul's recent reprobation, the subject in both cases being the status to be accorded to the Gentiles (see 6:1-11 and below). Significantly, the matthean context establishes a Kingdom context for justification – where commentators traditionally speak rather in terms of relational-behavioural and forensic frameworks (see 5:19-23). For this argument in relation to "works of the Torah," see 3:10-14.

[239] חביבין ישראל, שנקראו בנים למקום; חבה יתרה נודעת להם שנקראו בנים למקום, שנאמר: בנים אתם לה' אלהיכם. חביבין ישראל שניתן להם כלי חמדה; חבה יתרה נודעת להם שניתן להם כלי חמדה שבו נברא העולם, שנאמר: כי לקח טוב נתתי לכם תורתי אל-תעזובו.

[240] Cf. Rom. 2:17f, 3:1f, 9:4-5, 11:12, 15f, 28.

[241] εἰ γὰρ σὺ ἐκ τῆς κατὰ φύσιν ἐξεκόπης ἀγριελαίου καὶ παρὰ φύσιν ἐνεκεντρίσθης εἰς καλλιέλαιον, πόσῳ μᾶλλον οὗτοι οἱ κατὰ φύσιν ἐγκεντρισθήσονται τῇ ἰδίᾳ ἐλαίᾳ.

[242] Cf. Rom. 1:18-32; Gal. 4:8f; Eph. 2:1-12, 4:17-19, 5:8; Col. 2:13, 3:7; Num.R. 2:16; Cant.Zuta 1; Mekh.Ba-chod. 5; TBE p. 146; PRK 2:5; BB 10b; AZ 2b f; BK 38b. The most obvious Jewish demonstration of self-recognition is the morning blessing – much maligned in non-Jewish quarters – for having been born Jewish: "Blessed are you, O God, King of the Universe, for not having made me a Gentile ברוך אתה ה' אלהינו מלך העולם אשר לא עשני גוי" (JBer. 63b).

an epithet which, otherwise self-evident, appears to directly relate to their "reputation for cultivating peculiar sanctity" and the fact that they "show a greater attachment to each other than do the other sects (ὃ δὴ καὶ δοκεῖ σεμνότητα ἀσκεῖν, Ἐσσηνοὶ καλοῦντες, Ἰουδαῖοι μὲν γένος ὄντες, φιλάλληλοι δὲ καὶ τῶν ἄλλων πλέον)" (*War* 2.119).[243]

The "advantage of the Jew" – which removes him/her from the status of "gentile sinners" – is to be found first of all, as Akiva notes, in Israel's entrustment with the oracles of God (cf. Rom. 3:1-2). On the basis of their bearing God's name and covenant, to them also belong "the adoption as sons and the glory and the covenants and the giving of the Torah and the *temple* service and the promises, whose are the fathers, and from whom is the Messiah according to the flesh"[244] (Rom. 9:4-5). Notwithstanding these benefits (δὲ; de), precisely such a heritage may make hypocrisy a danger (cf. Rom. 2:17-29).[245] Paul is assured that Peter now knows that, despite his (their) common Jewish birthright – including custody of the "oracles" – his (their) status before God is determined not by (observance of) these but through God's faithfulness in sending His Messiah.[246]

Despite being Jewish by birth, Peter – as also Paul himself – cannot perform God's will by nature.[247] It is only Jesus' obedience to God's will, expressed in his death and resurrection, which gives wo/mankind[248] the means to "comprehend the Form on high" through impartation of the "keys of knowledge." The piety or "intention" (faithfulness) which must accompany learning, and which is thwarted because of sinful nature, is gained first and foremost not through Torah-study but through

---

[243] For the purposes of the present argument, precisely how the parameters of Jewish identity are determined is immaterial. For a discussion of the principles, cf. Cohen, Timothy/Crossing.

[244] . . . ἡ υἱοθεσία καὶ ἡ δόξα καὶ αἱ διαθῆκαι καὶ ἡ νομοθεσία καὶ ἡ λατρεία καὶ αἱ ἐπαγγελίαι, ὧν οἱ πατέρες καὶ ἐξ ὧν ὁ Χριστὸς τὸ κατὰ σάρκα.

[245] The particle δὲ (de) is sufficiently well attested for the committee to have felt justified in bracketing it into the text.

[246] Paul makes the argument regarding the Torah's role in 3:10-14, 19ff (see there). His argument in verses 18-19 speaks more to human inability to find favour with God than to the Torah's function (see below). Paul's quarrel with the influencers who are drawing away his disciples' allegiance to the gospel is precisely that their concept of Jewish identity relates to social standing – not to that which is important in God's eyes.

[247] This idea lies at the root of the Qumran texts, which reinforce the concept of man's sinfulness in comparison to God's purity in their dualist scheme (see below).

[248] Paul reinforces his point that "all flesh" follow the same rules in speaking of ἄνθρωπος (anthrōpos – "a man"), a usage similar to rabbinic exegesis of the expression שיא שיא (ish ish – lit.: "man man"), understood to indicate all persons – Jew, Gentile, male, female, slave and free (cf. San. 56a f).

participation in Jesus' faithfulness – in dying with him in order to be raised from the dead with him (cf. Romans 6) (see below).[249]

The "justification (δικαιοῦται)" of which Paul speaks here may thence be understood in terms of overcoming the evil inclination which prohibits concord between saying/wishing and doing – of entering, in other words, not only into the outer but also into the inner court of God's Kingdom.[250] On this reading, what has traditionally been interpreted as Paul's diatribe against "works" is in fact merely a warning – however strict it may be – that Torah-observance *alone*, without the proper intention, is insufficient to gain entrance into God's Kingdom (cf. Kvasnica: 23-24).[251] Although the Jewish community does possess God's oracles, it cannot be assumed that

---

[249] Although the literature – and the debate – concerning the merits of the subjective and objective genitives in understanding the meaning of "faith (in)" have grown substantially over the years, the main lines of argument remain constant. In our estimation, Hebert and Torrance's assertion that the Hebrew אמונה (emunah – "faithfulness") lies behind the Greek – thus preferring the element of "faithfulness" over "belief" – still serves as the major primary "linguistic" basis. Hays' "representative" construction – developed within a narrative framework – builds upon this foundation, alike deepening and broadening it: "*A story about Jesus Christ is presupposed by Paul's argument in Galatians, and his theological reflection attempts to articulate the meaning of that story* . . . the story *is* the word of God, and we know God in no other way than as the God who has acted through the faithfulness of Jesus Christ to 'rescue us from the present evil age' (Gal 1:4)" (Faith: xxiv, xxvi; original emphasis).

[250] In many respects, this parallels the emphasis Paul places in other passages on intention: Faith as faithfulness is a mark of (human) intent – the will to please God which brings to Torah-observance its real life. For "intention," cf. Higger; for the Kingdom context, see 5:19-23 and above.

[251] This understanding can be derived linguistically from the ἐὰν μὴ (ean = ei + an). Although this expression is properly exceptive in force, it may either qualify the whole of the preceding statement or merely its principal part (cf. Longenecker, Galatians: 83f). On the former reading, the meaning signifies that "a person is not justified even by Torah-observance – **but only** through Jesus' faithfulness." The latter reading yields the sense that "one may not be justified by Torah-observance – **unless** the latter is accompanied by intention." The fact that the second half of the verse appears to state that Torah-observance *per se* does *not* bring justification need not be taken as "pushing a qualification on covenantal nomism into an outright antithesis" (irrespective of whether or not one accepts that the "works of the law" refer exclusively to the "badges of covenantal nomism") (Dunn, New: 112-13). Apprehended within a discussion of piety and Torah-study, justification here represents the intention and capacity to perform God's will. The context consequently calls for a *conjunction* of Torah-observance and faithfulness/intention rather than a contradiction. In this light, the second half of the clause implies "by works of the law **alone**" (cf. Jas. 2:24).

Torah-study and observance are sufficient in and of themselves to enable human nature to know His will *and to do it*.[252]

The citation of Psalm 143:2 (the ὅτι [hoti] representing a "quotation formula") – "For in Thy sight no man living is righteous כי לא-יצדק לפניך כל-חי" (cf. 3:11) – again places the emphasis on God's righteous faithfulness: "Answer me in Thy faithfulness, in Thy righteousness! And do not enter into judgment with Thy servant, for in Thy sight no man living is righteous באמֻנתך עֵנני בצדקתך: ואל-תבוא במשפט את-עבדך כי לא-יצדק לפניך כל-חי" (Ps. 143:1b-2).[253] In adding the phrase "works of the Torah" and interpreting "living" as "flesh (σάρξ)," Paul includes both Jews and Gentiles as subject to the same circumstances, "flesh" indicating in both cases the basis of the blemish.[254] It is hypocritical to declare that Jews are "by nature" better than

---

[252] Paul's argument here closely corresponds to his later assertion in Romans 4, as Hays demonstrates: ". . . the fact that Abraham was reckoned righteous while he was still uncircumcised has symbolic – or typological – significance: he can thereby be the father of Gentiles as well as Jews. Paul spells this out explicitly in verses 11-12: 'And he received a sign of circumcision, a seal of the righteousness of the faith which is in the uncircumcision *in order that* that he might be: (a) the father of all who believe while uncircumcised in order that righteousness might be reckoned to them; (b) the father of circumcision to those who are not only circumcised but also walk in the footsteps of the faith which our father Abraham had while he was uncircumcised' . . . Jews (at least those with circumcised hearts) have found Abraham to be their father not according to the flesh but according to promise. Paul has developed this reading of the story directly through exegesis of Scripture, without any appeal to the language of Christian confession. This reading intends to be and is a Jewish theological interpretation of the significance of Abraham" (Hays, Echoes: 56-57; original emphasis).

[253] Paul also appeals to Psalm 143 in Rom. 3:20 (cf. διότι; dioti), as the climax to his "jackhammer indictment of human sinfulness." As Hays argues, the catena preceding this verse is composed of scriptural citations whose purpose is to demonstrate "that 'those in the Law' (Jews) are addressed by the Law (Scripture) in such a way that their own culpability before God should be inescapable . . . The psalm provides Paul not only with the language for a blanket indictment of humankind but also with the expectant language of prayer that looks to God's righteousness as the source of salvation. Thus, when Paul writes in Rom. 3:21 that 'now, apart from the Law, the righteousness of God has been manifested, *witnessed by the Law and the Prophets*,' he is making a claim that anyone who had ever prayed Psalm 143 from the heart would instantly recognize: God's saving righteousness, for which the psalmist hoped, has at last appeared. The witness of the Law and the Prophets to the righteousness of God is not merely, as Christians have sometimes strangely supposed, a witness concerning a severe retributive justice; rather, it is a witness concerning God's gracious saving power, as Psalm 143 demonstrates" (Hays, Echoes: 50, 52; original emphasis).

[254] LXX Ps. 142:2: ὅτι οὐ δικαιωθήσεται ἐνώπιόν σου πᾶς ζῶν. Hays, following Martyn, suggests that Paul is "perhaps subtly anticipating the argument he will make later in the letter against 'those who want to make a good showing *in the flesh'*

gentile "sinners" – because possession of the Torah does not guarantee its performance:

"For he is not a Jew who is one outwardly; neither is circumcision that which is outward in the flesh. But he is a Jew who is one inwardly; and circumcision is that which is of the heart, by the Spirit . . ."[255] (Rom. 2:28-29) (cf. Rom. 9:6ff).[256] "[«Zi]on» i[s] [the congregation of all the sons of justice, those] who establish the covenant, those who avoid walking [on the pa]th of the people מלכת הסרים הברית מקימ[י] הצדק המה] [עדת כול בני צי]ון ה[ויאה] [נבד[רך העם" (11QMelch 2:23-24).[257]

"Whoever possesses these three things, he is of the disciplesof Abraham, our father; and [whoever possesses] three other things, he is of the disciples of Balaam, the wicked. The disciples of Abraham, our father, [possess] a good eye, an humble spirit and a lowly soul. The disciples of Balaam, the wicked, [possess] an evil eye, a haughty spirit and an over-ambitious soul. What is [the difference] between the disciples of Abraham, our Father, and the disciples of Balaam, the wicked? The disciples of Abraham, our father, enjoy [their share] in this world, and inherit the world to come, as it is said: *That I may cause those that love Me* [i.e., Abraham – cf. Isa. 41:8] *to inherit substance and that I may fill their treasuries* (Prov. 8:21).[258] But the disciples of Balaam, the wicked, inherit gehinnom, as it is said: *But thou, O God, wilt bring them down to the nethermost pit; men of blood*

---

by compelling the Galatians to be circumcised (6:12)" (Galatians: 241; original emphasis) (see 5:13f).

[255] οὐ γὰρ ὁ ἐν τῷ φανερῷ ᾽Ιουδαῖός ἐστιν οὐδὲ ἡ ἐν τῷ φανερῷ ἐν σαρκὶ περιτομή, ἀλλ᾽ ὁ ἐν τῷ κρυπτῷ ᾽Ιουδαῖος, καὶ περιτομὴ καρδίας ἐν πνεύματι . . .

[256] While not concurring with Dunn's overall thesis regarding justification, we apprehend Paul to obviously perceive that Israel may become "hypocritical" in relying on the "badges of ethnic identity" (circumcision, dietary rules, etc.) in Romans 2 – an act which might otherwise be denoted as claiming soteriological privilege on the basis of covenantal distinctiveness, a form of ethnic exclusiveness (cf. Dunn, New/Works, etc.) (see also 3:6-9).

[257] In this sense it is surely significant that Paul employs a variant of "works of the Torah" in relation to the Gentiles' status before God in Rom. 2:14-15: "these, not having the Torah, are a law to themselves, in that they show the **work of the Torah** written in their hearts . . . (οὗτοι νόμον μὴ ἔχοντες ἑαυτοῖς εἰσιν νόμος· οἵτινες ἐνδείκνυνται τὸ ἔργον τοῦ νόμου γραπτὸν ἐν ταῖς καρδίαις αὐτῶν)." For 11QMelchizedek, see 1:1-5, 3:21-25, and 4:1-7; for Galatians' affinities with 4QMMT, wherein the author urges his addressees to separate themselves from general society, see Introduction, **Form**; **Argument**.

[258] "To inherit substance" – in this world; "that I may fill their treasuries" – in the world to come. For Paul's link of Abraham's disciples with the "fruit of the Spirit," see 5:19-23.

and deceit shall not live out half their days; but as for me, I will trust in Thee (Ps. 55:23)"[259] (PA 5:19).[260]

The clearest basis for this view is found, once again, in the Qumran literature, which reiterates the poverty of the human condition and God's undeserved yet generous compassion: "As for me, to God belongs my judgment; in his hand is the perfection of my behaviour with the uprightness of my heart; and with his just acts he cancels my iniquities . . . I belong to evil humankind, to the assembly of unfaithful flesh; my failings, my iniquities, my sins, {. . .} with the depravities of my heart, belong to the assembly of worms and of those who walk in darkness. For to man (does not belong) his path, nor can a human being steady his step; since the judgment belongs to God, and from his hand is the perfection of the path . . . if I stumble, the mercies of God shall be my salvation always; and if I fall in the sin of the flesh, in the justice of God, which endures eternally, shall my judgment be . . . he will judge me in the justice of his truth, and in his plentiful goodness always atone for all my sins; in his justice he will cleanse me from the uncleanness of the human being and from the sin of the sons of man, so that I can give God thanks for his justice and The Highest for his majesty"[261] (1QS 11:2-3, 9-12, 14-15).[262]

Without God's help, human beings lack the capacity to be faithful to him out of their own resources.[263] The aorist here then indicates: "When we

---

[259] כל מי שיש בו שלושה דברים הללו מתלמידיו של אברהם אבינו - ושלושה דברים אחרים מתלמידיו של בלעם הרשע: עין טובה ורוח נמוכה ונפש שפלה – מתלמידיו של אברהם אבינו. עין רעה ורוח גבוה ונפש רחבה - מתלמידיו של בלעם הרשע. מה בין תלמידיו של אברהם אבינו לתלמידיו של בלעם הרשע? תלמידיו של אברהם אבינו אוכלין בעולם הזה ונוחלין לעולם הבא, שנאמר: להנחיל אוהבי יש ואוצרותיהם אמלא. אבל תלמידיו של בלעם הרשע יורשין גיהינום ויורדין לבאר שחת, שנאמר: ואתה אלהים תרידם לבאר שחת אנשי דמים ומרמה לא יחצו ימיהם ואני אבטח בך.

[260] Cf. Mt. 3:8f; Jn. 8:31ff; [2 Pet. 2:15-16]; PRK 3:2; Ned. 31a. The same idea may lie behind the midrash in Ex.R. 46:5 (see 4:1-7 and 6:1-11). Although it may seem tedious to emphasise the point yet again, Paul's critique is not of Judaism *per se* but of what action makes one truly Jewish (see 3:1ff and 4:21-31).

[261] כיא אני לאל משפטי ובידו תום דרכי עם ישור לבבי ובצדקותו ימח פשעי . . . ואני לאדם רשעה ולסוד בשר עול עוונותי פשעי חטאתי { . . . } עם נעוות לבבי לסוד רמה והולכי חושך כיא לוא לאדם דרכו ואנוש לוא יכין צעדו כיא לאל המשפט ומידו תום הדרך . . . ואני אם אמוט חסדי אל ישועתי לעד ואם אכשול בעוון בשר משפטי בצדקת אל תעמוד לנצחים . . . בצדק אמתו שפטני וברוב טובו יכפר בעד כול עוונותי ובצדקתו יטהרני מנדת אנוש וחטאת בני אדם להודות לאל צדקו ולעליון תפארתו.

[262] Cf. 1QS 11:2-15; 1QHᵃ 5:19-26, 9:21-33, 11:19-36, 12:29-38, 15:16-18, 29-30, 35, 17:13-19, 19:7-14, 18, 20:29-40. The object of deliverance is to know God and to declare His praises.

[263] In correspondence with the noun as "faithfulness," the verb πιστεύω (pisteuō) also most properly signifies "being faithful," perhaps especially in conjunction with the preposition εἰς (eis – "unto, towards"). This understanding most significantly combines three intertwined, and thus intelligent, features of the story-word, in Hays' terms: It is God's faithfulness which forms the story from its beginning to its end, a faithfulness expressed first and foremost to Israel, and climaxing in the

became faithful to Jesus" – an act which Paul associates in Romans 6 with baptism into his death and resurrection.[264] While Torah-study and observance constitute the keys to the "inner court," they are acts which a person performs from his own wherewithal. They do not possess the living force of the example lived out by a righteous person, no wo/man being without sin before God. It is only Jesus' righteousness, through his faithfulness to God, which actually embodies – and makes available to those who participate in his death and resurrection – the piety (justification/intention) which can transform human nature into that which is pleasing to God, in thought, word, and action (see 3:10-14, 19f).

Paul's repeated return to the "works of the Torah" in these verses indicates the prevalence of the conviction – prior to the Messiah's advent – that Torah-study and observance had in fact represented the keys of knowledge which would open up God's Kingdom.[265] It is only now that people can know God through Jesus' faithfulness and obedience, constituting the "new covenant" written on the heart of flesh, that the shortcomings of Torah-study have become apparent. The tenor of Paul's words here echoes the Dead Sea Scrolls' ascription – and mediation – of righteousness to the "Interpreter of the Torah" upon whom the "keys of heaven" had, in their estimation, been bestowed:

> You support my soul by strengthening my loins and increasing my strength; you made my steps sturdy on the frontier of evil, so that I became a trap for offenders, but a medicine for all who turn away from offence, a wit for simple folk, and a staunch purpose for the timorous at heart. You have set me as a reproach and a mockery of traitors, a foundation of truth and of knowledge for those on the straight path ... you have set me like a banner for the elect of justice [cf. Isa. 11:(1-)10], like a knowledgeable mediator of secret wonders. *Blank* To put to the test [the men of] truth, to refine those who love learning. I have become a man of

---

fulfilment of the promise to Abraham in His raising Jesus from the dead. Jesus' obedience to the Father is that which gains not only Israel but also all "Abraham's sons" entry into God's glory, an access which human beings appropriate in turn through their faithfulness to God through Jesus, on the basis of his perfect performance of God's will. In becoming obedient to Jesus, people thus become obedient to the Father, living out their lives in the here and now in God's continuing faithfulness to His promises through Jesus and the indwelling of His Spirit.

[264] For Paul's reference to baptism in 3:27, see 3:26-29 [4:1-7].

[265] Cf. Wright's apt remark: "Israel's peculiar plight is that, through the exile, she has been, in one sense, still inside the covenant and, in another, outside it. Gentiles simply come in, from nowhere; Jews have their membership renewed, brought back to life, by sharing the death and resurrection of their Messiah" (Climax: 155). For the Kingdom context, see 5:19-23 and above.

contention to the mediators of error, [but a man of] [pea]ce to all
who view truth … For, at the judgment you pronounce guilty all
those who harass me, separating the just from the wicked
through me [cf. Mal. 3:18] … Its interpretation [Hab. 2:4]
concerns all observing the Law in the House of Judah, whom God
will free from the house of judgment on account of their toil and
of their loyalty to the Teacher of Righteousness.[266] (1QH[a] 10:7-10,
13-15, 15:12; 1QpHab 8:1-3)[267]

The allusion to Malachi 3 in the psalm recalls God's condemnation, in
the context of the LORD coming to His Temple, of His people for robbing
Him in tithes and heave offerings (cf. Mal. 3:1ff). This charge arises again
in Jesus' reproach of the Pharisees for tithing mint and dill and cumin but
neglecting "the weightier provisions of the law: justice and mercy and
faithfulness" – things which should have been observed "without
neglecting the others"[268] (Mt. 23:23).[269] These "weightier" matters – which

----

[266] ותסמוך נפשי בחזוק מותנים ואמוץ כוח ותעמד פעמי בגבול רשעה ואהיה פח לפושעים ומרפא
לכול שבי פשע ערמה לפתיים ויצר סמוך לכול נמהרי לב ותשימני חרפה וקלס לבוגדים סוד אמת
ובינה לישרי דרך . . . ותשימני נס לבחירי צדק ומליץ דעת ברזי פלא vacat לבחון [אנשי] אמת ולנסות
אוהבי מוסר ואהיה איש ריב למליצי תעות [ובעל] [של]וֹם לכול חוזי נכוחות . . . כי כול גרי למשפט
תרשיע להבדיל בי בין צדיק לרשע . . . פשרו על כול עושי התורה בבית אשר יצילם אל מבית המשפט
בעבור עמלם ואמנתם במורה הצדק.

[267] The motif of Hab. 2:4 runs not only through Galatians but also through Romans
(cf. Rom. 1:17) (cf. Hays, Faith: xxxvii and passim) (see 3:10ff, 4:1-7, 5:2f [nn45, 53,
119], 6:1-11, verses 1-10 [n18], and below [n271]).

[268] Οὐαὶ ὑμῖν, γραμματεῖς καὶ Φαρισαῖοι ὑποκριταί, ὅτι ἀποδεκατοῦτε τὸ
ἡδύοσμον καὶ τὸ ἄνηθον καὶ τὸ κύμινον καὶ ἀφήκατε τὰ βαρύτερα τοῦ νόμου,
τὴν κρίσιν καὶ τὸ ἔλεος καὶ τὴν πίστιν· ταῦτα [δὲ] ἔδει ποιῆσαι κἀκεῖνα μὴ
ἀφιέναι.

[269] The logic deriving from accumulative association between this account and Acts
15:10) and Matthew 23 (cf. also Gal. 4:17) suggests that Paul's interlocutors in
Galatians should be identified as pharisaic, in some shape or form. Not only are
Jesus' words directed against the latter but it is an argument made by "certain ones
of the sect of the Pharisees (τινες τῶν ἀπὸ τῆς αἱρέσεως τῶν Φαρισαίων)" (Acts
15:5) which directly occasions the council's convention. McKnight, who argues
against the existence of a "Jewish mission" (i.e., Judaism as a proselytising religion),
claims that both Matthew and Galatians (together with Romans) inveigh against
"Torah-proselytization" – i.e., the (a) pharisaic demand that gentile godfearers "go
the whole way" and assume the "yoke" of the Torah (pp. 104ff) (cf. Levinskaya: 36-
38). Despite the fact that basing the negation of proselytism *per se* on the distinction
between godfearers and full conversion seems rather frail ground, the similarities
between the gospel and Paul – the latter almost indubitably addressing prospective
gentile proselytes – weaken the claim that as a "non-technical term" *proselytos* could
"quite easily be applied to Jews" (Goodman: 73). Goodman's need to modify this
assertion by suggesting that such usage may have been "metaphorical" is
suggestive of the difficulties which the original claim bears, not the least being the
assertion that Jewish "proselytes" were, in some way, akin to gentile "godfearers"

include faithfulness – constitute the piety which gives learning its "punch": "A man should not say to himself: 'I am willing to love Heaven and fear Heaven,' provided I am free to transgress any one of the Commandments of Torah. If this is his stipulation, it is an evil omen for him; an evil portion will be his, and harsh judgments will befall him. Rather should a man say: I am going to love Heaven and fear Heaven and will not transgress any one of the Commandments of Torah. If such is his intention, it is a good omen for him; a good portion will be his, and sin will not come into his hand"[270] (TBE p. 132)[271] (see also below).

(cf. ibid). Against both views, Gal. 4:17 seems to *substantiate* Jewish proselytism, the present passage additionally helping to place the interpretation of Matthew 23 in the proper context of hypocrisy. At the same time, their apparently non-local status, the source of the "persecution," and Paul's claim that they themselves are not Torah-observant all – to various degrees – mitigate against identifying the influencers as Pharisees (see Introduction, **Occasion and circumstances**). The most serious challenge to this scenario lies in configuring precisely who could have been pressurising a group of Pharisees, their putative presence in Galatia establishing, as it were, the existence of diaspora Pharisaism – the claim of their non-observance concurrently being open to the interpretation of hypocrisy which Paul raises here (see below). As the "strictest" Jewish sect (cf. Acts 26:5), they can simultaneously be imagined to constitute the most "authoritative" Jewish presence in any diaspora locale and to have found it difficult to live in such an environment (cf. Dunn, Incident: 211). The conclusion to which we are consequently drawn is that while Gal. 4:17 certainly reinforces the possibility/probability of pharisaic proselytism, it does not in itself constitute proof of this phenomenon in Galatia. Paul may well adopt language with which he is familiar (cf. his own pharisaic background), applying it to persons who, from his perspective, were engaged in precisely the same (hypocritical) pursuit of proselytes, producing very similar results – although under different circumstances and for diverse reasons. See also below [n287]. For the discussion of whether Judaism was a "proselytising religion" during this period, see Introduction, **Occasion and circumstances** and 1:15-16b (end).

[270] אל יאמר האדם בלבו לעצמו : אני אהיה ירא שמים ואוהב את הקדוש ברוך הוא על ממת שאעבור על אחת מכל המצות האמורות בתורה. כי זהו סימן רע וחלק רע וגזירות קשות באות עליו. אלא כך יאמר אדם בלבו : אני אהיה ירא שמים ואוהב את הקדוש ברוך הוא על מנת שלא אעבור אפילו על אחת מכל מצות האמורות בתורה. וזהו סימן טוב וחלק טוב לו ואין חטא בא על ידו.

[271] The same idea is expressed in the various midrashim which distinguish between those who serve God out of fear and those who love Him – the first being designated "servants/slaves," the second as "sons" (cf. TBE pp. 82, 140-41) (see 3:1-5 and 4:1-7). While the parallels with Gal. 4:1f should be evident, the reference to "faithfulness" may already be a hint towards Hab. 2:4, a verse which serves Paul so centrally in chapter 3 (cf. Flusser, Judaism: 496n10) (see 3:10f and 4:1-7). Malachi interprets the robbery as a form of "testing" God (cf. Mal. 3:10, 15) – a motif which Peter picks up in Acts 15:10, a verse which we have suggested demonstrates verbal affinities with this passage (see above [n238]). In saying that "we believe that we are saved through the grace of the Lord Jesus, in the same way as they also are (ἀλλὰ διὰ τῆς χάριτος τοῦ κυρίου Ἰησοῦ πιστεύομεν σωθῆναι καθ' ὃν τρόπον κἀκεῖνοι)" (Acts 15:11), Peter as it were directly recalls Paul's proof to him here in

The appearance of the phrase מעשי התורה (ma'asei ha-Torah – "works of the Torah") in 4QMMT from Qumran, which has been much publicised in connection with Galatians, actually occurs in conjunction with an appeal to David's piety (cf. 4QMMTᵉ ff14-17ii:1-7).[272] The first directive is to "Remember David, who was a man of the pious ones, [and] he, too, [was] freed from many afflictions and was forgiven זכור [את] דויד שהיא איש חסדים [ו]אף היא [נ]צל מצרות רבות ונסלוח לו." Following this charge, the writer then adds: "And also we have written to you some of the works of the Torah which we think are good for you and for your people, for we s[a]w that you have intellect and knowledge of the Law ואף אנחנו כתבנו אליך מקצת מעשי התורה שחשבנו לטוב לך ולעמך שר[א]ינו עמך ערמה ומדע תורה." According to this author, piety, aligned with knowledge, form the basis upon which "it shall be reckoned to you as justice when you do what is upright and good before him, for your good and that of Israel ונחשבה לך לצדקה בעשותך הישר והטוב לפנו לטוב לך ולישראל."[273]

Verse 17 addresses the implications of the source of the righteousness which is to be found in the Messiah.[274] As in verse 16, Paul includes himself, together with Peter, in understanding what Jesus' faithfulness

---

Antioch. See also Introduction, **Date and destination**. On the analogy of Mt. 23:23, Paul is asking of his Galatians disciples to seek "justice and mercy and faithfulness" (cf. Mic. 6:8; Hab. 2:4) in the Messiah (whilst Jewish believers are to do the same, "without neglecting the others [i.e., Torah-observance]"). In 5:16f, Paul speaks to the same issue in the language which he later employs in Romans: "For the kingdom of God is not eating and drinking, but righteousness and peace and joy in the Holy Spirit (οὐ γάρ ἐστιν ἡ βασιλεία τοῦ θεοῦ βρῶσις καὶ πόσις ἀλλὰ δικαιοσύνη καὶ εἰρήνη καὶ χαρὰ ἐν πνεύματι ἁγίῳ)" (Rom. 14:17) (see 5:13f). (For an appreciation of the significance of "in the same way," cf. Nanos, Stake: 312.)

[272] Cf. 2 Bar. 57:2. For a discussion of the semantic fields, cf. Kvasnica; for Galatians as a "halakhic letter" along the lines of 4QMMT, see Introduction, **Form**; **Argument**.

[273] Cf. 1QS 1:2. While Abegg has suggested that the last clause is an echo of Ps. 106:31 rather than Gen. 15:6, thus possibly implying a zealot association (cf. 4QMMTᵉ ff14-17ii:7-8), the allusion to the "upright and the good" derives from such deuteronomic passages as Dt. 6:18, 12:28; 2 Chron. 14:2, 31:20; Ps. 125:4. The association with David is not only strengthened by the attribution of "the upright and good" to David in 1 Sam. 29:6 but also through the "reckoning" to which David appeals in Ps. 32:1-2. Paul himself gives us the connection between this latter verse and Gen. 15:6 in Rom. 4:3-9. On this reading, the Qumran appeal is for the addressees to act in the spirit of David, "a man of the pious ones [א]יש חסדים" who was "freed from many afflictions and was forgiven [נ]צל מצרות רבות ונסלוח לו." Cf. the deliverance from the "house of judgment," which is effected by a conjunction of faithfulness and "toil" (cf. 1QpHab 8:1-3). See also 3:10-14 and 5:13-18.

[274] Since Paul's focus here is upon Jewish believers who accept Jesus' faithfulness, his remarks – contrary to Gager's claims – relate directly to Jews and not to Gentiles. For Gager, see Introduction, **Author**.

means for Jewish believers.[275] The Greek ζητοῦντες (zētountes – "seeking") reflects a semitism, the Hebrew verb בִּקֵּשׁ (bikesh) regularly being conative and denoting the attempt behind an action and/or the method by which the aim is achieved.[276] The terminology of being "found (εὑρέθημεν)"quite likely reflects the legal language of proof, the evidence having been weighed and the verdict then given (cf. Acts 23:9) (cf. Le Cornu and Shulam: 1252f). Here, the sentence is one of guilt: Without the Torah, Jews are no different than Gentiles.[277] But if the Messiah's faithfulness puts Jews on a par with Gentiles – "sinners by nature" – does he, in making God's righteousness accessible to the Gentiles also, lose the uniqueness of his calling as a "servant to the circumcision on behalf of the truth of God to confirm the promises *given* to the fathers"[278] (Rom. 15:8)? Does Jesus become no different from the Torah itself – which, being "holy and righteous and good," cannot help but highlight the weakness and unrighteousness which characterises those who are "sinners by nature"?[279] If the Messiah is himself also an agent of sin – just as the Torah is designed to "increase" sin – what then has anyone, Jew or Gentile, gained?

---

[275] Peter's echo of Paul's words in Acts 15:11 constitutes one of the grounds upon which we are currently suggesting that the Antioch incident – and the letter's composition itself – occurred prior to the "council" (see Introduction, **Date and destination** and above).

[276] Cf. Ex. 2:15, 4:24; Dt. 13:10; 1 Macc. 6:3, 11:10, 16:22.

[277] Commentators have traditionally found the logic of this verse extremely troublesome (cf. Burton: 127-30). Dividing the thought into three distinct statements – a) we are seeking to be justified in the Messiah; b) we have been found sinners; c) the Messiah is a minister of sin – they are in disagreement over whether the emphatic denial includes not merely c) but extends also to b). The present reading countenances no logical differentiation between a) and b), regarding the latter as an integral part of the premise, Paul's problem being identified as one of God's faithfulness to Israel (i.e., theodicy). Burton's objections to the view, most of which turn on the detachment of the argument from the incident at Antioch, seem to have been met in full if it is agreed that understanding ἁμαρτωλοί (hamartōloi – "sinners") in reference to Gentiles is acceptable.

[278] Χριστὸν διάκονον γεγενῆσθαι περιτομῆς ὑπὲρ ἀληθείας θεοῦ, εἰς τὸ βεβαιῶσαι τὰς ἐπαγγελίας τῶν πατέρων.

[279] "But though our fathers received the Law, they did not keep it, and did not observe the statutes; yet the fruit of the Law did not perish – for it could not, because it was yours. Yet those who received it perished, because they did not keep what had been sown in them. And behold, it is the rule that, when the ground has received seed, or the sea a ship, or any dish food or drink, and when it happens that what was sown or what was launched or what was put in is destroyed, they are destroyed, but the things that held them remain; yet with us it has not been so. For we who received the Law and sinned will perish, as well as our heart which received it; the Law, however, does not perish but remains in its glory" (4 Ez. 9:32-37).

Paul makes the same argument, somewhat more clearly because laid out in greater length, to the Roman communities: "And the Torah came in that the transgression might increase; but where sin increased, grace abounded all the more, that, as sin reigned in death, even so grace might reign through righteousness to eternal life through Jesus the Messiah our Lord. What shall we say then? Are we to continue in sin that grace might increase? May it never be! How shall we who died to sin still live in it?"[280] (Rom. 5:20-6:2) (cf. Rom. 3:8f).[281]

The Sages were equally aware that the emphasis of sin-fearing and piety over knowledge could carry one not into stringency but into leniency leading, ultimately, into libertinism: "R. Ulla expounded: Why is it written, *Be not much wicked* (Eccl. 7:17)? Must one not be much wicked, yet he may be a little wicked! But if one has eaten garlic and his breath smells, shall he eat some more garlic that his breath may [continue to] smell? [i.e., having sinned a little, do not think that you must go on sinning]"[282] (Shab. 31b).[283] "Ben Azzai said: Run to [perform] an easy precept as [you would] in [the case of] a difficult one, and flee from transgression; for [one] precept draws [in its train another] precept, and [one trangression draws [in its train another] transgression בן עזאי אומר: הוי רץ למצוה קלה כבחמורה ובורח מן העבירה שמצוה גוררת מצוה ועבירה עבירה" (PA 4:2).[284]

Verse 18: The emphatic μὴ γένοιτο (mē genoito) of verse 17 represents the Hebrew חלילה (chalila) – "God forbid, heaven forfend, may it never be!"[285] The refutation is normally followed by an explanation elaborating the grounds on which the proposal must be dismissed. Here, Paul appears to first present a negative argument, followed by the positive aspect in verse 19.[286] For the first, he employs the metaphor of building and destroying. If, as has been proposed, 4QMMT's addressees are to be

---

[280] νόμος δὲ παρεισῆλθεν, ἵνα πλεονάσῃ τὸ παράπτωμα· οὗ δὲ ἐπλεόνασεν ἡ ἁμαρτία, ὑπερεπερίσσευσεν ἡ χάρις, ἵνα ὥσπερ ἐβασίλευσεν ἡ ἁμαρτία ἐν τῷ θανάτῳ, οὕτως καὶ ἡ χάρις βασιλεύσῃ διὰ δικαιοσύνης εἰς ζωὴν αἰώνιον διὰ Ἰησοῦ Χριστοῦ τοῦ κυρίου ἡμῶν. Τί οὖν ἐροῦμεν; ἐπιμένωμεν τῇ ἁμαρτίᾳ, ἵνα ἡ χάρις πλεονάσῃ; μὴ γένοιτο. οἵτινες ἀπεθάνομεν τῇ ἁμαρτίᾳ, πῶς ἔτι ζήσομεν ἐν αὐτῇ;

[281] Paul takes up this theme in 3:10-14, 19ff (see there).

[282] דרש ר' עולא: מאי דכתיב: אל תרשע הרבה וגו'. הרבה הוא דלא לירשע הא מעט לירשע! אלא מי שאכל שום וריחו נודף, יחזור ויאכל שום אחר ויהא ריחו נודף?!

[283] This statement immediately follows a discussion over the relative merits of piety and learning. It also forms the continuation of the section in which the conditions under which proselytes were to be accepted is debated (cf. Shab. 31a) (see above).

[284] The motif of major ("weighty") and minor ("light") commandments is directly associated with hypocrisy, as Matthew 23 elaborates (see 5:2f and below).

[285] Or חלילה וחס (chalila ve-chas); likewise, חס ושלום (chas ve-shalom – lit.: "forbearance and peace"; i.e., God forfend) (cf. Gen. 18:25; 2 Sam. 20:20; Job 27:5; Lk. 20:16; Rom. 3:4, 6, 9, 31, 6:2, 15, 11:1; Eduy. 5:6; Ber. 12b, 19a; Shab. 138b; BM 85b).

[286] For arguments *via* the negative, see 1:1-5, 16c-17, 5:2-12, and verses 1-10 (n99).

identified as Pharisees (cf. Kampen and Bernstein: 53-80), other Qumran texts further demonstrate the attitude of contempt which the community displayed towards pharisaic hypocrisy (cf. Flusser, Jesus: 69-70).[287] Jesus' accusation that the Pharisees "shut off the kingdom of heaven from men; for you do not enter in yourselves, nor do you allow those who are entering to go in (κλείετε τὴν βασιλείαν τῶν οὐρανῶν ἔμπροσθεν τῶν ἀνθρώπων· ὑμεῖς γὰρ οὐκ εἰσέρχεσθε οὐδὲ τοὺς εἰσερχομένους ἀφίετε εἰσελθεῖν)" (Mt. 23:13) (cf. Lk. 11:52) closely corresponds to the description of the pharisaic party in the Dead Sea Scrolls as "builders of the wall [בוני החיץ]."[288]

This latter phrase appears to relate to the Qumran community's dislike of the pharisaic claim to be the "builders" of Judaism – the scholars through whom knowledge of the Torah was disseminated.[289] In essene

---

[287] The original reference of the term Pharisee (פרוש; parush) was to religious hypocrisy (cf. Sot. 22b). Rather than presuming that Paul is engaging in anti-pharisaic polemic here (see above [n268]), it should be recognised that his language is taken from such vitriolics simply because the Pharisees constituted the example *par excellence*, in contemporary eyes, of hypocrisy. Notwithstanding, Christian identification of "Pharisaism" as hypocrisy in such a way as to make Judaism into a "legalistic" religion represents a gross distortion of reality. (The question regarding whether Paul could have employed this motif precisely out of a sense of personal guilt – one of Christian commentators' common explanations of Paul's behaviour as a "former Pharisee" – is not one to which this passage can provide an answer. While he may have been particularly sensitive to the issue of hypocrisy, it should be evident to the reader that the present authors do not perceive Paul either as having "left/abandoned" Judaism, established a "new religion," or been personally tormented by his "Jewish past" – but to have retained and remained loyal to and proud of his Jewish heritage [see Introduction, **Author**; Appendix, and above (beginning)].)

[288] Cf. CD-A 4:19, 8:12, 18; CD-B 19:24, 31. See also 3:21-25.

[289] "*And great shall be the peace of thy children* (Isa. 54:13); read not *banayik* (thy children) but *bonayik* (thy builders) (Est.R. 10:15) (cf. TBE [EZ] S p. 21; Yalk.Isa. 479; Ber. 64a; Ker. 28b). Schiffman has proposed that the "wall" epithet rather alludes to pharisaic exegetical methods, whereby the Sages endeavoured to "fence" the Torah around with additional commandments (traditions) in order to prevent violation of the original biblical ordinances (cf. PA 1:1, 3:13; Num.R. 10:8; Yev. 90b; Nid. 3b) (cf. Reclaiming: 249-52). Despite the conceptual affinity, it seems rather a long linguistic stretch from סייג (siag – "fence") to בונים (bonim – "builders"). Once the association was made, however, the fence may have played a further part, tradition displaying a tendency to usurp the priority (authority) of the biblical injunction (cf. Num.R. 14:4; Sif.Dt. 154; Pes.Rab. 3:2; San. 11:3; Hor. 1:3; Eruv. 21b; Yev. 20a). The fact that the serpent is identified as the first person to make a breach in the world's fence, in seducing Eve to sin (cf. Lev.R. 26:2; PRE 13; ARNᵇ 1), may possibly, in this context, lie behind the association of the Pharisees with vipers in both Qumran and the New Testament texts (cf. Mt. 3:7, 12:34, 23:33; CD-A 5:14). For the wall as a symbol of

eyes, the Pharisees were "mediators of fraud and seers of deceit" who "have plotted a devilish thing against me {. . .} to change your Law, which you engraved on my heart, for flattering teachings for your people; they have denied the drink of knowledge to the thirsty, but for their thirst they have given them vinegar to drink . . . they, hypocrites, plot intrigues of Belial, they search you with a double heart, and are not firmly based in your truth . . . For they have not chosen the path of your [heart] nor have they listened to your word. For they said of the vision of knowledge: It is not certain! And of the path of your heart: It is not that!"[290] (1QH[a] 12:9-14, 17-18) (see also 4:12f and 6:1-11).[291]

Paul projects the impression here that he is presenting himself as a personal example, commentators variously stressing the fact that the shift to the first person singular reflects a rhetorical feature by which he presents himself as an exemplary or representative (cf. Betz, Galatians: 121n74).[292] Restoring something which he has taken pains to dissemble is an act demonstrative of regression, of repenting of the evil which he previously ascribed to a deed (thought or word). If he encourages what he thinks should be demolished, he does indeed display his unrighteousness. But it is his – not Jesus' – work which demonstrates his own sinfulness.

The Greek οἰκοδομέω (oikodomeō) frequently carries the metaphorical (moral) meaning of building up as "edification" or "benefit"

---

ethnic exclusivity, cf. Eph. 2:14f; Ep.Arist. 139 (see also 3:6-9 [n80] and above [n251]).

[290] והמה מליצי כזב וחוזי רמיה זממו עלי {בי} בליעל להמיר תורתכה אשר שננתה בלבבי בחלקות לעמכה ויעצורו משקה דעת מצמאים ולצמאים ישקום חומץ למען) הבט אל תעותם ... והמה נעלמים זמות בליעל יחשובו וידרשוכה בלב ולב ולא נכונו באמתכה ... כי לא בחרו בדרך]לב[כה ולא האזינו לדברכה כי אמרו לחזון דעת לא נכון ולדרך לבכה לא היאה ...

[291] Cf. 1QH[a] 15:34-35; 4QpNah ff3-4ii:8-11, iii:5-8; 4QpHos[a] 2:3-19; 4QpHosea[b]. The identification is firmly grounded on the information provided in Pesher Nahum, that this group extended an invitation to Demetrius to attack Israel (cf. 4QpNah ff3+4i:2), an event which Josephus independently attributes to the Pharisees (cf. Ant. 13.377-83) (see also 4:21-31 and 5:2-12). The link with Lk. 11:52 – the lukan version of Mt. 23:13 – is clear: "Woe to you lawyers! For you have taken away the key of knowledge; you did not enter in yourselves, and those who were entering in you hindered (Οὐαὶ ὑμῖν τοῖς νομικοῖς, ὅτι ἤρατε τὴν κλεῖδα τῆς γνώσεως· αὐτοὶ οὐκ εἰσήλθατε καὶ τοὺς εἰσερχομένους ἐκωλύσατε)." See also 5:1-12 (n70).

[292] For Paul's heritage, see Appendix, **Pharisaic background**; for his "former life in Judaism," see 1:13-14. His "defence" of his apostleship as a whole (cf. 1:1, 15ff) represents, in the present reading, the laying out of Paul's authority as the basis on which he addresses his rebuke-request to the Galatians (see Introduction, **Argument**). For further appeals to his personal example, see 1:1-5, 15-16b, 21-24, 3:1-5 (nn14, 28), 4:12-20, 5:2-12 (verse 11), 24-26, 6:1f (verses 11, 15, 17), and verses 1-10 (n136); for Galatians as a "halakhic letter" along the lines of 4QMMT, see Introduction, **Form**; **Argument**.

(cf. BAGD: 558).²⁹³ The same is true of καταλύω (katalyō), which can also signify abolishment in the sense of "annulment" (cf. ibid: 414). The latter suggests that Paul has in mind here the validation of what should in fact be repealed, this being, of course, the language of law (cf. Mt. 5:17). In essence, Paul is defining "sin" here, and we may merely be diverted into distractions if we press this to a particular example.²⁹⁴ Yet if this is his own action, he cannot charge Jesus with being the commissioner of sin. It is he himself who does not avail himself of the messianic righteousness – the key to the "inner court" – and thereby shuts himself out of the kingdom of heaven by disenabling the transformation of his evil inclination.²⁹⁵ Such is the negative circumstance of the ideal which he proposes in Romans 2:27: "... you who though having the letter *of the Torah* and circumcision are a transgressor of the Torah (... τὸν νόμον τελοῦσα σὲ τὸν διὰ γράμματος καὶ περιτομῆς παραβάτην νόμου)."²⁹⁶

Verse 19: Paul reinforces the rebuttal with a further rewording, clarifying how and what he has "destroyed."²⁹⁷ The parallel repudiation in

---

²⁹³ Cf. LXX Ps. 27:5; Jer. 40:7; Acts 9:31, 20:32; 1 Cor. 10:23; 1 Thess. 5:11; Test.Ben. 8:3. For the metaphor as descriptive of the early community, see 6:1-11 (verse 10), verses 1-10 (n124), and below.

²⁹⁴ "The term παραβάτης ('violator of the law,' 'lawbreaker') ... has to do with not just breaking a specific statute of the law but with setting aside the law's real intent (cf. Rom 2:25, 27; Jas 2:9, 11; Jos.*Ant*. 3.318; 5.112; 8.129)" (Burton: 131). The fact that it thus also signifies "apostasy" indicates the force of Paul's argument. In the context of hypocrisy, however, the "rebuilding (οἰκοδομῶ)" may refer to Paul's proclivity towards promoting Torah-observance above the piety gained through Jesus' righteous faithfulness, the fault attributed in Romans 2 being that of those who, being obedient to the ordinances, yet miss their real purpose (cf. ibid) (see above). This is, of course, precisely the charge of compelling the Gentiles to seek circumcision/conversion by his action which Paul has just brought against Peter (see verses 11-14 and above).

²⁹⁵ To use Paul's imagery from 2 Cor. 5:1, he is tearing down the "building from God, a house not made with hands, eternal in the heavens (οἰκοδμὴν ἐκ θεοῦ ... οἰκίαν ἀχειροποίητον αἰώνιον ἐν τοῖς οὐρανοῖς)" in favour of "the earthly tent which is our house (ἡ ἐπίγειος ἡμῶν οἰκία τοῦ σκήνους καταλυθῇ)." Similar language appears in Rom. 14:20, although there the warning is against "tearing down" God's work "for the sake of food" (μὴ ἕνεκεν βρώματος κατάλυε τὸ ἔργον τοῦ θεοῦ). For Romans 14 and hypocrisy, see 5:19-23 and verses 11-14; for "shutting up," see 3:22-25.

²⁹⁶ The same word "transgressor" appears in both verses (cf. Jas. 2:9, 11), Paul's point in Romans 2 being that "he is a Jew who is one inwardly (ὁ ἐν τῷ κρυπτῷ Ἰουδαῖος)" (Rom. 2:29) (see above). Paul's point may be summed up in the statement that the Torah demands of human beings not only that they "do good" but that they "be good" (cf. Saphir, Church: 144) (see 5:13f). For "doing good," see 6:1-11.

²⁹⁷ The expressed ἐγὼ (egō – "I"), together with the direct assertion, indicate Paul's personal experience (cf. Burton: 132).

Romans 6:2 states: "How shall we who died to sin still live in it (οἵτινες ἀπεθάνομεν τῇ ἁμαρτίᾳ, πῶς ἔτι ζήσομεν ἐν αὐτῇ;)?" The Torah points through its ordinances to the need for – and thus an actual absence of – the human capacity to perform God's will with true intention: "For I did not speak to your fathers, or command them in the day that I brought them out of the land of Egypt, concerning burnt offerings and sacrifices. But this is what I commanded them, saying, 'Obey My voice, and I will be your God, and you will be My people; and you will walk in all the way which I command you, that it may be well with you'"[298] (Jer. 7:22-23) (see 3:19-20).[299]

"Even though you offer up to Me burnt offerings and your grain offerings, I will not accept *them*; and I will not *even* look at the peace offerings of your fatlings. Take away from Me the noise of your songs; I will not even listen to the sound of your harps. But let justice roll down like waters and righteousness like an ever-flowing stream" (Amos 5:22-24)[300] (cf. Hos. 6:6; PRE 16).[301]

"Is this not the fast which I chose, to loosen the bonds of wickedness, to undo the bands of the yoke, and to let the oppressed go free, and break every yoke? Is it not to divide your bread with the hungry, and bring the homeless poor into the house; when you see the naked, to cover him; and not to hide yourself from your own flesh? Then your light will break out like the dawn, and your recovery will speedily spring forth, and your righteousness will go before you; the glory of the LORD will be your rear guard"[302] (Isa. 58:6-8) (cf. Isa. 61:1-3).[303] "Do not judge according to

---

[298] כי לא-דברתי את-אבותיכם ולא צויתים ביום הוציא אותם מארץ מצרים על-דברי עולה וזבח: כי-אם-את-הדבר הזה צויתי אותם לאמׂר שמעו בקולי והייתי לכם לאלהים ואתם תהיו-לי לעם והלכתם בכל-הדרך אשר אצוה אתכם למען ייטב לכם.

[299] Cf. Mic. 6:6-8 – the verses underlying Mt. 23:23. The last clause of Jer. 7:23 – "that it may be well with you" parallels "that you may live" (cf. Dt. 4:40; Jer. 38:20), and may also lie behind 4QMMT[e] ff14-17ii:7-8 (see 3:10-14 and above).

[300] כי אם-תעלו-לי עלות ומנחׂתיכם לא ארצה ושלם מריאיכם לא אביט: הסר מעלי המון שריך וזמרת נבליך לא אשמע: ויגל כמים משפט וצדקה כנחל איתן.

[301] Jesus employs the verse from Hos. 6:6 in reference to himself, on both occasions in reference to atonement and forgiveness (cf. Mt. 9:13, 12:7) (see below [n304]).

[302] הלוא זה צום אבחרהו פתח חרצבות רשע התר אגֻדות מוטה ושלח רצוצים חפשים וכל-מוטה תנתקו: הלא פרׂס לרעב לחמך ועניים מרודים תביא בית כי-תראה ערׂם וכסיתו ומבשרך לא תתעלם: אז יבקע כשחר אורך וארֻכתך מהרה תצמח והלך לפניך צדקך כבוד ה' יאספך:

[303] Cf. Mt. 25:34-46; Jas. 1:27; Mid.Ps. 118:17. Jesus' parable in Mt. 25 is evidently based on Isa. 58:6f, and addresses the hypocrisy of those thinking that they have performed God's pleasure yet have ignored the basic acts of lovingkindness (gmilut chasidim) (cf. Lachs: 394) (see 5:19-23 and 6:1-11 [verse 10]). Liberty from the bondage of sin is precisely one of Paul's overarching themes in Galatians, one form of hypocrisy being the limitations of human nature which dis-enable intimacy with God (see 1:1-5, 3:21-25, 4:1f, 5:13ff, verses 1-10, above, and below).

appearance, but judge with righteous judgment (μὴ κρίνετε κατ᾽ ὄψιν, ἀλλὰ τὴν δικαίαν κρίσιν κρίνετε)" (Jn. 7:24).[304]

"When these exist in Israel in accordance with these rules in order to establish the spirit of holiness in truth eternal, in order to atone for the guilt of iniquity and for the unfaithfulness of sin, and for approval for the earth, without the flesh of burnt offerings and without the fats of sacrifice – the offering of the lips in compliance with the decree will be like the pleasant aroma of justice and the perfectness of behaviour will be acceptable like a freewill offering – at that moment the men of the Community shall set apart a holy house for Aaron in order to form a most holy community, and a house of the Community for Israel, those who walk in perfection"[305] (1QS 9:3-6).[306]

"R. Hiyya acted within the 'margin of the judgment,' on the principle learnt by R. Joseph: '*And shalt show them* means the source of their livelihood; *the way* means deeds of lovingkindness; *they must walk* means the visitation of the sick; *wherein* means burial, *and the work* means the law; *which they must do* means within the margin of the judgment'"[307] (BK 99b-100a).[308]

---

[304] This verse – as also Jesus' quote of Hos. 6:6 in Mt. 12:7 – occurs in the context of circumcising on shabbat, Jesus' assertion being that Torah's purpose is not "ritual" observance of the commandments but life and love – of God, expressed through concern for one's neighbour (see 5:2f and above).

[305] בהיות אלה בישראל ככול התכונים האלה ליסוד רוח קודש לאמת עולם לכפר על אשמת פשע ומעל חטאת ולרצון לארץ מבשר עולות ומחלבי זבח ותרומת שפתים למשפט כניחוח צדק ותמים דרך כנדבת מנחת רצון בעת ההיאה אנשי היחד בית קודש לאהרון להיחד קודש קודשים ובית יחד לישראל ההולכים בתמים.

[306] Cf. Ps. 50:14, 23, 141:2; Rom. 12:1; 2 Cor. 2:14-16; Eph. 5:2; 1 Pet. 2:5; Test.Levi 3:5-6; Odes Sol. 20:1-5; 1QS 5:5ff, 8:3ff; 4QFlor f1i:2-7 (cf. Gärtner).

[307] רבי חייא לפנים משורת הדין הוא דעבד, כדתני רב יוסף: והודעת להם: זה בית חייהם. את הדרך: זו גמילות חסדים. ילכו : זו ביקור חולים. בה: זו קבורה. את המעשה: זו הדין. אשר יעשון : זו לפנים משורת הדין.

[308] Cf. Mekh.Amalek 4; BM 24b, 30b, 83a; Ket. 97a. R. Hiyya went "beyond the letter of the law" by acting over and above the legal requirements imposed by the explicit commandments. Based here on the verse in Ex. 18:20 (cf. also Prov. 2:20), the latter's enumerated items are first related to specified ordinances, until the final injunction – "which they must do" – which is interpreted as a form of "extra" observance (cf. Shulam and Le Cornu: 109-10). "This could mean that it is sometimes necessary to go beyond the law, which in itself is right and good, in order to do what is right and good" (Berkovits: 27). Rabbinic sources indicate that some Sages considered this principle to constitute part of the Torah itself, while others regarded it as "independent." "The Babylonian view, however, is: All due respect to the law of damages, but there are cases when it is overruled by a superior ethical principle which, in those cases, becomes itself the supervising law" (ibid: 28). The Sermon on the Mount may be seen in its entirety as an exposition of the principle of "within the margin of the judgment" (see 5:13-18). For "work" and

"Woe to you, scribes and Pharisees, hypocrites! For you tithe mint and dill and cummin, and have neglected the weightier provisions of the law: justice and mercy and faithfulness; but these are the things you should have done without neglecting the others"[309] (Mt. 23:23) (see also 3:10-14, 6:1f, verses 1-10, and above).

Paul's point here closely resembles his buttressing of his commission in 1:1, 15-16, wherein he reflects the knowledge that "there is no agent in wrongdoing דאין שליח לדבר עבירה" (Kid. 42b-43a) (see 1:1-5). Where a principal commands his agent to commit an unlawful act, the agent – not the principal – is liable under criminal law: "[When] the words of the master [God] and the words of the pupil [are in conflict], whose are obeyed? דברי הרב ודברי תלמיד - דברי מי שומעים?" (Kid. 42b). Obviously – the master's. If a person is unable to serve both masters – his/her own inclination and God, the two being in conflict – s/he must "anger" one by obeying the other: "R. Simon said: . . . . 'And the servant is free from his master' (Job 3:19) – he who performs the will of his creator (*yozer*) angers his evil inclination (*yezer*), but once he is dead he emerges into freedom, as it is said, 'And the servant is free from his master' אמר ר' סימון . . . ועבד חפשי מאדניו "הוא שעושה רצון יוצרו מכעיס את יצרו. מת, יצא לחירות, שנאמר: ועבד חפשי מאדניו (Ruth R. 3:1) (see 1:6-10 and 5:13-18).[310]

In relation to the Torah, God's words being true and effective, it is only human nature which can be in error of God's will.[311] The Torah simultaneously declares God's ideal, the perfection of His will as it should be performed on earth (cf. Mt. 6:10), and demonstrates how short human capacities fall of this glory (cf. Rom. 3:23).[312] In so doing, it effectively

---

"works," including a discussion of Ex. 18:20, cf. Kvasnica; for "strict justice," see 3:10-14 (n150).

[309] Οὐαὶ ὑμῖν, γραμματεῖς καὶ Φαρισαῖοι ὑποκριταί, ὅτι ἀποδεκατοῦτε τὸ ἡδύοσμον καὶ τὸ ἄνηθον καὶ τὸ κύμινον καὶ ἀφήκατε τὰ βαρύτερα τοῦ νόμου, τὴν κρίσιν καὶ τὸ ἔλεος καὶ τὴν πίστιν· ταῦτα [δὲ] ἔδει ποιῆσαι κἀκεῖνα μὴ ἀφιέναι.

[310] Cf. Ruth R. 8:1; Yalk.Job 886; Ber. 61a; Eruv. 18a (cf. Shulam and Le Cornu: 24, 211ff).

[311] "R. Samuel b. Nahmani said: R. Jonathan pointed out the following contradiction: It is written, *The precepts of the Lord are right, rejoicing the heart* (Ps. 19:8), but it is also written: *The word of the Lord is tried* (Ps. 18:30)? If he is meritorious, it rejoices him; if not it tries him. Resh Lakish said: From the body of the same passage this can be derived: If he is meritorious, it tests him unto life; if not, it tests him unto death רבי שמואל בר נחמני רבי יונתן רמי: כתיב: פקודי ה' ישרים משמחי לב, וכתיב אמרת ה' צרופה. זכה - משמחתו, לא זכה - צורפתו. ריש לקיש אמר: מגופיה דקרא נפקא: זכה - צורפתו לחיים, לא זכה - צורפתו למיתה" (Yoma 72b) (see also 3:21-25).

[312] Here too are hints of Kingdom language, Jesus' prayer being "Thy kingdom come, Thy will be done, on earth as it is in heaven (ἐλθέτω ἡ βασιλεία σου· γενηθήτω τὸ θέλημά σου, ὡς ἐν οὐρανῷ καὶ ἐπὶ γῆς)" (Mt. 6:10) (see 5:2-12, 19-23).

"binds" this nature, reigning it in and controlling it in strict governance – the root אסר (asar), which denotes "fettering," also signifying the prohibitions given in the Torah and their application in rabbinic tradition (cf. Lichtenstein, Studies: 103).[313] The only way to be free to perform the Torah's commandments is to suppress that which obstructs their fulfilment, dying to the nature which they arouse and the fruitless attempt to keep the latter under control:

> A woman is acquired [in marriage] in three ways and acquires her freedom in two ... "She acquires her freedom by divorce or by her husband's death." As for divorce, it is well, since it is written, *then he shall write her a bill of divorcement* (Dt. 24:1); but whence do we know [that she is freed by] her husband's death? – It is logic: he [the husband] bound her; hence he frees her ... thus death is compared to divorce: just as divorce completely frees [lit. 'permits'] her, so does death completely free her. (Kid. 13b)[314]

Torah-study and observance demonstrates that the Torah demands conduct which goes beyond its "strict measures": "With what shall I come to the LORD and bow myself before the God on high? Shall I come to Him with burnt offerings, with yearling calves? Does the LORD take delight in thousands of rams, in ten thousand rivers of oil? Shall I present my first-born *for* my rebellious acts, the fruit of my body for the sin of my soul? He has told you, O man, what is good; and what does the LORD require of you but to do justice, to love kindness, and to walk humbly with your God?"[315]

---

[313] Cf. Mt. 18:18; Kil. 3:4; Shevi. 8:7; Eruv. 10:10 (cf. Le Cornu and Shulam: 741-42) (see 3:19f and 6:1-11 [n39]). (This idea may possibly lie behind Paul's mashal ["allegory"] in 4:22f.)

[314] This reasoning lies behind Paul's statement in Rom. 7:1ff, "the Torah has jurisdiction over a person as long as he lives." The halakhah is based on a סברא (svara) or "logical deduction" from the biblical text. The rabbinic regulation (מדרבנן; mi-de-rabbanan) makes the husband's death, which is not explicitly denoted by the biblical text, equally as binding as the biblically-ordained (דאורייתא; de-oraita) precept of divorce. Although the Torah only permits a married woman to have relations with another man if her husband has given her a bill of divorce (cf. Dt. 24:1-4), the Sages ruled that a woman who remarries following the death of her husband is not guilty of adultery. His death being as legally effective as divorce, restoring her status as an unmarried woman, it also frees her from the penalties for committing adultery in remarriage. For the combined motifs of chalitza (release from levirate marriage), serving two masters, and the "spirit of the Torah," cf. Shulam and Le Cornu: 235-41; for chalitza in Galatians, see 1:1-5. It bears emphasising that it is not the *Torah* which becomes ineffective – "dies" – but the human nature which inhibits its observance with intention (כוונה; kavannah).

[315] במה אקדם ה' אכף לאלהי מרום האקדמנו בעולות בעגלים בני שנה: הירצה ה' באלפי אילים ברבבות נחלי-שמן האתן בכורי פשעי פרי בטני חטאת נפשי: הגיד לך אדם מה-טוב ומה-ה' דורש ממך כי אם-עשות משפט ואהבת חסד והצנע לכת עם-אלהיך.

(Mic. 6:6-8) (see above).[316] In making this point, the Torah itself highlights the necessity of transforming one's human nature by dying to one's self in order to become truly free to serve God.[317] Then it truly comes into its own holiness, righteousness, and goodness, being performed according to God's desire, with true intention and concordant action, free from interference or weakness on the part of human nature.[318]

Verse 20: Jesus' faithfulness in his obedience to the Father's will – even unto death (cf. 1:4) – has now provided the sole recourse whereby a person wishing to die to his/her own self may find new life to serve God (cf. 3:23f).[319] Where the person has died, the Messiah may live in his/her place

---

[316] For the centrality of Mic. 6:6-8 in Galatians as a whole, see Introduction, **Argument**; for Jer. 9:23-26, paralleling Rom. 2:17-29 on boasting and hypocrisy, see Introduction, **Argument** and 6:1f; for Romans 2, see Introduction, **Argument**, 5:13-18, 6:1-11 (n152), and above.

[317] 4 Maccabees contains a parallel statement, presented from the perspective of קדוש ה' (kiddush ha-Shem – martyrdom): "With these words the mother of the seven exhorted each one and persuaded them to die rather than transgress the commandment of God, and they knew full well themselves that those who die for the sake of God live unto God, as do Abraham and Isaac and Jacob and all the patriarchs (Διὰ τούτων τῶν λόγων ἡ ἑπταμήτωρ ἕνα ἕκαστον τῶν υἱῶν παρακαλοῦσα ἀποθανεῖν ἔπεισεν μᾶλλον ἢ παραβῆναι τὴν ἐντολὴν τοῦ θεοῦ, ἔτι δὲ καὶ ταῦτα εἰδότες ὅτι οἱ διὰ τὸν θεὸν ἀποθνήσκοντες ζῶσιν τῷ θεῷ ὥσπερ Αβρααμ καὶ Ισαακ καὶ Ιακωβ καὶ πάντες οἱ πατριάρχαι)" (4 Macc. 16:24-25).

[318] "'*This stumbling block* [the Torah] *is under thy hand*' (Isa. 3:6). A man does not fully understand the words of the Torah until he has come to grief [lit.: been tripped up] over them והמכשלה הזאת תחת ידיך : אין אדם עומד על דברי תורה אלא אם כן נכשל בהן" (Git. 43a) – i.e., it is only by transgressing the commandments that a person understands what is takes to fulfil them and what they fully demand of him/her. "Why is it that in [the] law God gives them [Israel] priests, gives them a tabernacle, and gives them sacrifice? God says, I will forgive your sins, and I will make you draw near to me. How is it that none of the prophets ever, for a single moment, thought that the covenant with Abraham had been set aside, or that they were living under the curse, or that they did not know the grace of God, God forgiving and God sanctifying them? It was necessary that it should be made plain to Israel that the law had this aspect: 'You are all guilty in the sight of God, and if I were to deal with you according to that which is required by the corresponding part on your side to the law, I should have nothing more to do with you. You depend entirely upon sovereign mercy, upon grace.' The law itself thus mocks, so to speak, at its own utter insufficiency, and points us to that covenant of grace which is rooted in the eternal love of God. It was with the Jews as it is with you [Gentiles]" (Saphir, Unity: 271).

[319] "*In a mysterious way, Jesus has enacted our destiny, and those who are in Christ are shaped by the pattern of his self-giving death. He is the prototype of redeemed humanity* ... The greatest strength of the exegesis set forward [here] ... is that it explains how Paul's understanding of the πίστις [pistis – "faith/fulness"] of Jesus is integrally related to his understanding of δικαιοσύνη [dikaiosynē – "righteousness"] ... the

(cf. Rom. 8:1ff). The idea of dying in order to live is well-expressed in numerous rabbinic texts: "Rabbi Judah the Prince says: Do His will as though it were your will so that He may do your will as though it were His will; undo your will for the sake of His will so that He may undo the will of others for the sake of your will [PA 2:4]. He used to say: If you have done His will as though it were your will, you have not yet done His will as He wills it. But if you have done His will as though it were not your will, then you have done His will as He wills it. Is it your wish not to die? Die, so that you will not need to die. Is it your wish to live? Do not live, so that you may live. It is better for you to die in this world, where you will die against your will, than to die in the age to come, where, if you wish, you need not die"[320] (ARN[b] 32).

"He [Alexander of Macedon] said to them [the Rabbis]: . . . What shall a man do to live? They replied: Let him mortify himself [lit. 'kill himself,' with study and hard work]. What should a man do to kill himself? They replied: Let him keep himself alive [i.e. indulge in luxuries] מה יעביד איניש (Tamid 32a) "ויחיה? אמרו לו: ימית עצמו. מה יעביד איניש וימות? יחיה את עצמו (see 5:24-26).[321]

The significance of Jesus' righteousness, available to all those who share in his obedience, is due to its present proportions: "the *life* which I now live in the flesh." It informs current-day, daily living as that is lived out "in the flesh." In other words, participating in Jesus' righteous faithfulness – and his faithful righteousness – enables one to live for God, His own son living in place of sin and unrighteousness.[322] Here we are

---

expression 'the faith of Jesus Christ' signals that the death of Jesus is *simultaneously* an act of human fidelity to God and an act of divine fidelity to humanity" (Hays, Faith: xxix, xxxi; original emphasis). It is precisely the exemplary character of Jesus' life, death, and resurrection which enables the participatory element of the one faithful to God through him. Without Jesus' precedent, there could be no partaking on the part of the believer. This constitutes much of the force of the "representative" understanding of Jesus' faithfulness, human faithfulness being patterned on and structured according to Jesus' obedience. For the argument sustaining the subjective genitive, cf. ibid.

[320] ר' יהודה הנשיא אומר: עשה רצונו כרצונך כדי שיעשה רצונך כרצונו. בטל רצונך מפני רצונו כדי שיבטל רצון אחרים מפני רצונך. הוא היה אומר: אם עשית רצונו כרצונך [לא עשית רצונו כרצונך] ואם עשית רצונו שלא כרצונך, עשית רצונו כרצונו. רצונך שלא תמות? מות, עד שלא תמות. רצונך שתחיה? אל תחיה, עד שתחיה. מוטב לך למות מיתה בעולם הזה שעל כרחך אתה מת, מלמות מיתה לעתיד [לבא]. שאם תרצה אי אתה מת.

[321] Cf. Mt. 16:25; Lk. 17:33; Jn. 12:25-26; Sif.Dt. 32; Ber. 61b. The presence of this motif here serves as an element in the argument that 1:6-4:11 functions as the "rebuke section" of the letter, setting the background for Paul's "request section" in 4:12-6:10/11 – "Become as I am" (see Introduction, **Form**; **Argument**, 4:12-20, and 6:12-16).

[322] The parallelism between "it is no longer I who live, but the Messiah who lives in me" and "the life which I now live in the flesh I live by the faith of the Son of God"

returned, once again, to Paul's initial argument against "wrongdoing in agency." The believer's agency is made so complete in Jesus that s/he is identified with his/her principal without sin and without blemish, Jesus' faithfulness delivering those who partake in it from the bonds and debt of sin: "[Its interpretation] for the last days refers to the captives, who ... are the inherita[nce of Melchize]dek, who will make them return. And liberty will be proclaimed for them, to free them from [the debt of] all their iniquities ... This [...] is the day of [peace about whi]ch he said [... through Isa]iah the prophet, who said: [*Isa 52:7* How] beautiful upon the mountains are the feet [of] the messen[ger who] announces peace, the mess[enger of good who announces salvati]on, [sa]ying to Zion: your God [reigns.»] ... For, you heal us of madness, /blindness/ and confusion [of heart ... Behold, for] our [in]iquities were we sold, but in spite of our sins you did call us [...] and you freed us from sinning against you"[323] (11QMelch 2:4-6, 15-16; 4Q504 ff1-2ii:14-16) (see 1:1-5 and 4:1-7).[324]

The messianic motivation is composed entirely of love, expressed most manifestly in Jesus' obedience to death, even death on a cross (cf. Phil. 2:8).[325] "It is taught ... that in the month of Nisan [Passover] the Patriarchs will arise and say to the Messiah: Ephraim, our true Messiah, even though we are thy forbears, thou art greater than we because thou

---

promotes a reading of the subjective genitive in the second clause, since it is the *Messiah* who lives in the believer in both expressions.

[323] [פשרו] לאחרית הימים על השבויים אשר . . . והמה נחל[ת מלכי צ]דק אשר ישיבמה אליהמה
וקרא להמה דרור לעזוב להמה [משא] כול עוונותיהמה . . . הואה יום ה[שלום א]שר אמר [. .] ביד
ישע[יה הנביא אשר אמר [מה] נאוו על ההרים רגל[י] מבש[ר מ]שמיע שלום מב[שר טוב משמיע
ישוע[ה א]ומר לציון [מלך] אלוהיך . . . כיא תרפאנו משגעון ״עורו]ן״ ותמהון [לבב . . . הן בע[וונותינו
נמכרנו ובפשעינו קרתנו [. .] . . . והצלתנו מחטוא לכה.

[324] Paul's reference to Jesus' crucifixion constitutes a primary marker in the narrative "recapitulation" around which Galatians is constructed: "The cross is not an isolated religious symbol; instead, it is the climactic event in the story of Jesus Christ, who was sent forth by God, who enacted the obedience of faith by giving himself up in order to free humanity from the power of sin and death ... This act of obedience, which according to Romans 5 stands in typological antithesis to Adam's disobedience, is a representative action, in which the fate of humanity is carried, or, to use a key term of Irenaeus, 'recapitulated.' Thus, Jesus' faith is not merely exemplary, as in nineteenth-century liberal theology, but vicariously efficacious" (Hays, Faith: 210). In a significant sense, Melchizedek plays the same role of "subject" in the Qumran story as Jesus does in the New Testament. More than simply the correspondence between the two figures, the parallel "narrative" structure is also of important note: "The fixed order was precisely the state of slavery under the στοιχεῖα [stoicheia – "elemental forces"], whose power has now been broken, according to Paul's gospel story, by Christ's intervention; the new order thus created is one in which Christians live by the power of the Spirit" (ibid: 225) (see 1:1-5, 3:21-25, 4:1f, and 5:13f).

[325] For the language of "delivering," closely linked to the akedah (the binding of Isaac) (cf. Rom. 4:25, 8:32) and Isaiah 53, see 1:1-5.

didst suffer for the iniquities of our children, and terrible ordeals befell thee . . . – all these afflictions on account of the iniquities of our children, all these because of thy desire to have our children benefit by that goodness which the Holy One, blessed be He, will bestow in abundance upon Israel . . . He will reply: O Patriarchs, all that I have done, I have done only for your sake and for the sake of your children, for your glory and for the glory of your children, that they benefit from that goodness which the Holy One, blessed be He, will bestow in abundance upon them – upon Israel. The Patriarchs will say to him: Ephraim, our true Messiah, be content with what thou hast done, for thou hast made content the mind of thy Maker and our minds also"[326] (Pes.Rab. 37:1).[327]

Verse 21 comes to refute the charge, reflected in verse 17, that Jesus' faithfulness does not bring righteousness but sin. Part of this claim is the assertion that Jesus' righteousness – accomplished through his obedience even unto death, in which both Jew and Gentile participate in corresponding faithfulness – can only be gained at the expense of deprecating His word in the Torah (see above).[328] The fact that the Torah itself demands behaviour "within the margin of the judgment" – i.e., above and beyond its (legal) requirements – indicates that it looks for the human ability to observe "justice and mercy and faithfulness." Not finding that capacity, God, in faithfulness to His own promises, provided the means in Jesus who, "being found in appearance as a man, he humbled himself by becoming obedient to the point of death, even death on a cross" so that those who are faithful to him – crucifying themselves with him in his death and rising with him in his resurrection – may "work out your salvation with fear and trembling; for it is God who is at work in you, both to will and to work for *His* good pleasure"[329] (Phil. 2:8, 12-13) (see 3:26-29 and

---

[326] מלמד שעתידים אבות העולם לעמוד בניסן ואומרים לו: אפרים משיח צדקנו, אף על פי שאנו אבותיך אתה גדול ממנו מפני שסבלת עונות בנינו ועברו עליך מדות קשות . . . כל אילו מפני עונות בנינו, רצונך יהנו בנינו מטובה זו שהשפיע הקדוש ברוך הוא לישראל . . . אומר להם: אבות העולם, כל מה שעשיתי לא עשיתי אלא בשבילכם ובשביל בניכם ולכבודכם ולכבוד בניכם שיהנו בניכם מטובה זו שהשפיע הקדוש ברוך הוא להם לישראל. (אמרו) [אומרים] לו אבות העולם: אפרים משיח צדקנו, תנוח דעתך שהנחת דעת קונך ודעתינו.

[327] Cf. Rom. 8:35-39; Eph. 3:17-19; 1 Tim. 1:14; 2 Tim. 1:13. The play between God's love for wo/man as expressed in His giving of His son is again reflected in the akedah, wherein God asks of Abraham to "Take now your son, your only son, whom you love קח-נא את-בנך את-יחידך אשר-אהבת" (Gen. 22:1) (see 3:1-5).

[328] The verb ἀθετέω (atheteō) carries strong legal connotations with regard to the nullification or invalidation of a covenant (cf. 3:15; 1 Macc. 11:36; 2 Macc. 13:25), reinforcing the idea that the abrogation – or lack thereof – relates to God's covenant in the Torah (cf. Longenecker, Galatians: 94).

[329] σχήματι εὑρεθεὶς ὡς ἄνθρωπος ἐταπείνωσεν ἑαυτὸν γενόμενος ὑπήκοος μέχρι θανάτου, θανάτου δὲ σταυροῦ . . . μετὰ φόβου καὶ τρόμου τὴν ἑαυτῶν σωτηρίαν κατεργάζεσθε· θεὸς γάρ ἐστιν ὁ ἐνεργῶν ἐν ὑμῖν καὶ τὸ θέλειν καὶ τὸ ἐνεργεῖν ὑπὲρ τῆς εὐδοκίας.

5:24-26).[330] God's grace is not thereby stymied by human factors, but fully expressed in the forgiveness and atonement conveyed through Jesus' death and resurrection.[331]

---

[330] Hays points out the "deft wordplay" at work in Paul's statement, having already paralleled verse 20 with Rom. 5:15 to demonstrate that no one attempts to translate "the *grace of God* and the gift by the *grace of the one Man*, Jesus the Messiah (ἡ χάρις τοῦ θεοῦ καὶ ἡ δωρεὰ ἐν χάριτι τῇ τοῦ ἑνὸς ἀνθρώπου Ἰησοῦ Χριστοῦ)" as objective genitives: the grace which one attributes to God (cf. Faith: 154). The adverb δωρεὰν (dōrean) is formed from the noun (δωρεά; dōrea) meaning "gift," the adverb thereby conveying the sense of "gratuitously."

[331] The flaw in the contention that "just as 'the works of the law' and 'the faith/faithfulness of Christ' are to be seen as antithetically related (2:16), also 'through the law' and 'Christ crucified' are non-complementary. To affirm the one is to deny the other, and vice versa" (cf. Longenecker, Galatians: 95) is brought out most clearly in Hays' discussion of the meaning of "justification by faith": "The Reformation theme of justification by faith has so obsessed generations of readers (Protestant readers, at least) that they have set Law and Gospel in simplistic antithesis, ignoring the sign of coherence in Rom. 3:1-26 [as also in our passage]; consequently, they have failed to see that Paul's argument is primarily an argument about theodicy, not about soteriology. The driving question in Romans is not 'How can I find a gracious God?' but 'How can we trust in this allegedly gracious God if he abandons his promises to Israel?'" (Hays, Echoes: 53). Nullifying God's grace in the Torah is a specific instance of questioning God's faithfulness to His people, so that "When he [Paul] says that his message confirms the Law, he refers not to the specific commandments of the Pentateuch but to the witness of Scripture, read as a *narrative* about God's gracious election of a people. That is why the Abraham story becomes for Paul the crucial test case. If he can show, as he sets out to do in Romans 4 [and Galatians 3], that the story of Abraham supports his reading of God's Gentile-embracing grace, then he will have demonstrated, to his own satisfaction at least, the unity of Gospel and Law" (ibid: 53-54). See 3:1ff and 5:12-21.

GALATIANS
3

Verses 1-5: [*Probatio* (3:1-4:11)]

YOU foolish Galatians, who has bewitched you, before whose eyes Jesus the Messiah was publicly portrayed *as* crucified? This is the only thing I want to find out from you: did you receive the Spirit by works of the Law, or by hearing with faith? Are you so foolish? Having begun by the Spirit, are you now being perfected by the flesh? Did you suffer so many things in vain – if indeed it was in vain? Does He then, who provides you with the Spirit and works miracles among you, do it by the works of the Law, or by hearing with faith?

Rhetorical analysis represents this section (3:1-4:11) as Paul's presentation of the "proofs" of his argument – those points designed to persuade his audience to return to their senses (cf. Betz, Galatians: 128-130).[1] In a defence speech, this section determines whether or not the case will succeed.[2] Paul has immediately reproved Peter for the hypocrisy explicit in

---

[1] The term *probatio* is thence also known rhetorically as the *argumentatio* or *confirmatio* (cf. Longenecker, Galatians: 97).

[2] We have already expressed reservations regarding the overall rhetorical structure into which Betz wishes to place Galatians (see Introduction, **Form**, 1:11-12 [n165], and 2:15-21). A large part of the objection stems from the well-noted difficulty of fitting the present extended segment into such a framework. Betz's rhetorical approach clearly detracts from Paul's Jewish perspective, which is prevailingly scriptural. Paul is first and foremost always bound to/by the (biblical) text, his points derived from it, interpretative, and expository of it, and framed in Jewish exegetical forms and frameworks (cf. Shulam and Le Cornu; Hays, Echoes) (see Introduction, **Form**; **Theological pointers** [Hermeneutics], 2:15-21 [beginning], 4:21-31, and below). It is rhetorical regard for these chapters (3-4) which appears, in large

his withdrawal from fellowship with the gentile believers in Antioch, his action insinuating both that redemption must be primarily sought through Torah-observance and that Jesus' death is insufficient for gentile access to God's Kingdom. He now turns directly to his Galatian disciples in the same spirit and with similar purpose: "Who has bewitched *you* - as Peter was seduced?"[3]

Rather than alluding to any "national characteristic," the epithet "foolish (ἀνόητοι)" (cf. verse 3) is better understood as referring to the course of action which Paul's disciples are presently proposing to follow. In writing to Titus, Paul attributes such an attitude to those who are rebellious towards God: "disobedient, deceived, enslaved to various lusts and pleasures, spending [their] . . . life in malice and envy, hateful, hating

---

part, to create the "confusion" of the ostensible "frequent interruption of the argumentative sections by dialogue, examples, proverbs, quotations, etc." (Betz, Galatians: 129). The understanding of Galatians as a "halahkic letter" along the lines of 4QMMT places the rhetorical and epistolary features which are evident throughout the letter at various points in a Jewish framework which, so we would argue, is more proper to Paul (see Introduction, Form; Argument). Paul's opening expression in verse 1 is typical of letters of rebuke, as is the expression of distress ("I fear for you") with which the section closes, enclosed within which are two further reproving questions (the present verses and 4:8-10) (cf. Longenecker, Galatians: 97). For the *interrogatio*, see below.

[3] Having noted the shortcomings of Betz's approach, Longenecker rather mystifyingly reverts to rhetorical language, arguing that "Thematically, the *probatio* of 3:1-4:11 sets out the proofs or arguments introduced by the *propositio* of 2:15-21" (ibid). The awkwardness of this analysis is immediately apparent in Longenecker's division of the *probatio* into two parts, the second beginning - for reasons determined by the *propositio* - in verse 19. (For the present evaluation of the *propositio*, see 2:15-21. Our reservations with regard to rhetorical analysis are noted in the brackets into which we have placed their notation throughout the letter.) The link between this section and 2:15-21 is further evident in the allusion to "works of the Torah" (cf. 2:16, verses 2, 5) (cf. Hays, Galatians: 251). On the present reading, 2:15-21 serves as the springboard for Paul's extended address to the Galatian communities, functioning as the model for the "bewitchment" which he perceives them to be facing, the "influencers" seducing them into thinking that their faithfulness to God through participation in Jesus' death and resurrection cannot and does not obtain Jewish status for them. Rejecting the gospel as a means for achieving Jewish identity, the influencers are attempting to convince the gentile Galatian believers that their only "salvation" is in seeking normative social standing through the conventional means available - circumcision/conversion in order to become full and recognised members of the Jewish community. In Paul's eyes, this is double hypocrisy: Not only does it replace God's principles with human norms but it leaves his disciples locked out of the Kingdom of heaven and enslaved under the dominion of Belial and sin (see Introduction, **Occasion and circumstances;** **Argument,** 2:15-21, 4:1-7, and 5:13f [verses 21-25]).

one another"⁴ (Tit. 3:3).⁵ A close link obtains between sin and futility: "The fool has said in his heart, 'There is no God.' They are corrupt, they have committed abominable deeds; there is no one who does good אמר נבל בלבו אין אלהים השחיתו התעיבו עלילה אין עשה-טוב" (Ps. 14:1).⁶

The accompanying association between sin and sickness - "For, you heal us of madness, /blindness/ and confusion [of heart . . .] כיא תרפאנו "משגעון "עירוו ותמהון [ולבב] (4Q504 ff1-2ii:14-15) - may indicate that Paul's reference to "bewitchment (ἐβάσκανεν)" alludes to the giving of the evil eye, a concept used to express envy in Jewish and other ancient texts⁷ (see 1:6-10, 4:12-20, and 5:19f).⁸ The Greek verb βασκαίνω (baskainō) - a New

---

⁴ ἀπειθεῖς, πλανώμενοι, δουλεύοντες ἐπιθυμίαις καὶ ἡδοναῖς ποικίλαις, ἐν κακίᾳ καὶ φθόνῳ διάγοντες, στυγητοί, μισοῦντες ἀλλήλους.

⁵ The fact that various ancient authors alluded to the Gauls as a fickle and superstitious people (cf. Caesar, *BG* 2.1, 4.5, 6.16; Cicero, *Div.* 1.5, 2.36-37) has formed part of some commentators' claim that Paul's addressees are ethnic Galatians, thereby predisposing them to a North Galatian perspective (cf. Lightfoot). (Cf. also the parallelism with βαρβάροις [barbarois - "barbarians"] in Rom. 1:14.) It is no coincidence that the motif of slavery occurs in relation to foolishness and disobedience, its relation to sin forming Paul's central focus in Galatians (see 1:1-5, 2:1-10, 15-21, 4:1f, 5:1ff, and verses 21-25). For such "vices" as "deeds of the flesh," see 5:19-23.

⁶ For the Gentiles as "sinners," see 2:15-21.

⁷ Cf. Dt. 28:60f; Ps. 41:4, 107:17-20; Isa. 19:19f, 53:4-5; Jer. 3:22, 14:19, 30:14ff; Hos. 6:1f, 7:1f; Mal. 4:2; Mt. 9:2; Mk. 2:5, 17; Lk. 5:20; Jn. 9:2; Wis.Sol. 17:8; Sir. 14:6-10; 4QpHosᵃ 1:8-9; 4Q387a 3ii:4-5; Ned. 41a; Amidah no. 8 (cf. Le Cornu and Shulam: 172-73).

⁸ "Appeal to the evil eye belief system is at the center of Paul's most pointed rebuke (3:1-5), and that around which his friendship appeal turns (4:12-20). Paul apparently believed it provided a meaningful explanation for the situation of the addressees, one that they could plausibly project onto the motives and actions of the influencers. His approach suggests that the addressees' experiences were those that would normally raise suspicion of such a force at work among themselves, that they have been experiencing a new level of good fortune, yet at the same time a new kind of suffering (3:4-5). Such a development would provoke the question: whose 'gaze' upon their good has led to this harm? However, it is most important for the interpreter to observe that Paul's delivery of this news in ironic rebuke indicates that Paul believes the addressees had not themselves considered an envious 'gaze' to be the cause of their present dilemma; rather, Paul is the one who raises this concern, blaming the influencers specifically" (Nanos, Social: 5). Despite substantial work on the issue - and without intending to minimise the importance of irony in Galatians - we prefer to read Paul's rebuke here as first, springing from his reprimand of Peter's hypocrisy and, secondly, as grounded in a biblical framework - authoritative for both himself and his disciples - rather than by a device which he considers his disciples might understand. In social theory terms themselves, Paul's opposition is to "social mobility" (crossing boundaries by accepted conventions) and his claim is "social creativity" - or, more precisely, "scriptural creativity": exegeting the biblical text in the creation of an "interpretative community" (cf.

Testament hapax – was commonly used to convey the figurative meaning of bewitching (cf. Betz, Galatians: 131).[9] In this sense, Paul is asserting that the "troubling" (1:7, 5:10) instigated by the influencers through the casting of spells is causing confusion, the folly of fools.[10]

Paul does appeal to the organs of sight (κατ' ὀφθαλμούς; kat ofthalmous – "before [whose] eyes") in countering the "spell" – the influencers' endeavour to engage the gentile Galatian believers in "fleshly," normative status and standing in place of the good and righteousness of Jesus (cf. 4:17).[11] The choice of προγράφω (prografō – lit.: "to write in front of") as verb suits Paul's purposes very well, simultaneously contributing locative and temporal dimensions. In the context of seeing, the prefix (προ; pro) indicates a setting forth in a public display: "Another interpretation of, *And unto him shall the obedience (yikhat)*

Fish). Moreover, while acknowledging the evil eye terminology in 4:12-14, the present volume understands 4:12f in the specifically halakhic framework of the master-disciple relationship. This section itself provides the background for the "allegory" (mashal) in 4:22-31 in which Paul forcefully instructs his gentile disciples to remove the injurious influence from their midst – on the basis of a thoroughly scriptural argument (see Introduction, **Argument** and 4:21-31). For the possible appearance of the concept in the influencers' jealousy, however, see 6:1-11, 12-16 (n152); for the reference to "spitting" in 4:14, see 4:12-20; for "troubling," see 1:6-10.

[9] This would appear to account for the appearance of the additional phrase τῇ ἀληθείᾳ μὴ πείθεσθαι (tē alētheia mē peithesthai – "not to obey the truth") which has evidently crept into some manuscripts, presumably under the influence of 5:7. While a correct interpretation, its obviousness makes it superfluous (cf. Longenecker, Galatians: 100). The LXX employs the verb to render תרע (tēra – "be evil") in Dt. 28:54 (also in connection with eyes) (see also 4:12-20). For the use of the singular "bewitcher (τίς ὑμᾶς ἐβάσκανεν)," see 5:2-12 (verse 10).

[10] The New Testament passage which most closely parallels Paul's direct address to his "foolish listeners" here is Lk. 24:25, the epithet there emphasizing the disciples' lack of perception of the scriptural references to the Messiah (see below). Here again, scriptural grounds appear more pertinent to Paul's argument than that of the evil eye – although such an understanding does not preclude the plausibility of Paul's presenting the influencers' operations in terms of a spell or charm by which his disciples, like Barnabas, have been "carried away (συναπήχθη)" (2:13) (cf. 2 Pet. 3:17). Likewise, the possible presence of sin (if folly/sickness is linked to iniquity) in his disciples surely constitutes a weightier concern for Paul than mere imputation of a system whereby he may gain their attention (see above). For the "suffering" which is adduced as proof of the presence of the evil eye motif here, see below.

[11] Here again, while Paul does elsewhere speaks in terms of shame and of boasting (cf. Rom. 11:18; 1 Cor. 1:17ff, 4:14, 6:5, 15:34; Gal. 6:4; 2 Thess. 3:14), he does so almost exclusively by way of contrasting the ways of the world with those of God – not in the context of "agonistic societies." Rather than employing the "evil eye" as a means of communicating their foolishness to his disciples, he censures boasting/jealousy (as well as "sorcery") and advocates "shame" – on the basis of scriptural standards (see 5:19-23 and 6:1f). For boasting and the evil eye, see 6:1-11.

of the peoples be (Gen. 49:10) – him to whom the nations of the world will flock (*mitkahalin*), as it says, *The root of Jesse, that standeth for an ensign of the peoples, unto him shall the nations seek* (Isa. 11:10)"[12] (Gen.R. 99:8).[13]

How, having seen Jesus' death and resurrection so graphically portrayed – in Scripture, as Paul laid it out for them, and in Paul's own life, as he acted it out in person (cf. Keener: 524) – could his disciples so easily be allowing themselves to be drawn away from it, he puzzles.[14]

Equally significantly, this story was foreshown in Scripture.[15] Being "written beforehand," when subsequent events occurred they could be

---

[12] דבר אחר: ולו יקהת עמים - מי שאומר הכתוב: מתקהלין עליו,שנאמר: שורש ישי אשר עומד לנס עמים אליו גוים ידרשו.

[13] Cf. Acts 10:40; Rom. 3:25; Col. 2:15; [Jos.*Ant.* 12.33]; Gen.R. 97 [NV]. Cf. also the motif of the raised serpent (cf. Num. 21:9; Jn. 3:14). For publicity, cf. Le Cornu and Shulam: 598, (1385), 1415.

[14] Cf. [Rom. 8:17]; Gal. 2:20, 6:14, 17; Phil. 2:17, 3:10; Col. 1:24. The significance of (eye-)witnesses lies in great part in the fact that their testimony is valid only when and if it relates to events which they themselves have witnessed (cf. Lev. 5:1; Acts 22:5, 26:5; *Yad*, Evidence 17:1, 5) (cf. Le Cornu and Shulam: 117, 234, 598, 1385, etc). On this reading, this verse sets the scene for Paul's "request" in 4:12: "I beg of you, brethren, become as *I am*" – an imitator of the Messiah (see 4:12-20). The present verse additionally links the "request" section of the letter (4:12-6:18) with Peter's hypocrisy through 2:20: "I have been crucified with the Messiah . . ." (see above). For Paul's presentation of his personal example, see 1:1-5, 15-16b, 21-24, 2:1-10 (n136), 15-21 (n292), 4:12-20, 5:2-12 (verse 11), 24-26, 6:1f (verses 11, 15, 17), and below (n28); for the presently-proposed structure of Galatians, see Introduction, **Argument**.

[15] Cf. Mt. 1:22f, 2:15, 4:14, 8:17, 26:54f; Mk. 14:49, 15:28; Lk. 4:21, 21:22f, 24:26, 44f; Jn. 12:38, 13:18, 15:25, 19:24; Acts 1:16, 3:18, 13:27f; Rom. 15:4; 1 Pet. 1:10-12; Rev. 17:17; [Jos.*Ant.* 11.283, 12.30] (cf. Le Cornu and Shulam: 38, 735). "Is it possible that by selecting this verb Paul implies that his story of Christ crucified was told through interpretation of scriptural texts? If so, the reference would be not to the gospel passion narrative – which had not yet been written at this time – but to the lament psalms, interpreted as prefigurations of Christ's crucifixion" (Hays, Galatians: 250-51). "Who has converted you, pagans, into worshippers of God and Christ? Have you not derived everything from the apostles? Are you not built upon the foundation of the apostles? And how did the apostles preach? 'That Christ died according to the Scriptures.' Not a single syllable of the New Testament was written then. And they preached that Christ rose again, 'According to the Scriptures.' And when people came to believe in Jesus, how did the apostles teach them? They taught them from Daniel about the man of sin, the Antichrist that was to come. They taught them from the history of the Jews in the wilderness, that all these things had happened to us for an example. They referred them to the whole of prophecy that had gone before, saying that by the consolation which the Scriptures give us, and by patiently waiting for the fulfilment of the Scripture, we should have the hope, namely, of Christ's second advent" (Saphir, Unity: 59).

understood through what had already been explained.[16] The "Messiah crucified" constitutes Paul's encapsulated form of the gospel, "death" and the "cross" metonymically representing God's good news in Jesus (cf. Longenecker, Galatians: 101).[17] Jesus embodies and fulfils all of which Scripture speaks,[18] the Galatians (as Paul himself) having found their redemption in him, through their corresponding obedience to his faithfulness to God. Here again, Paul recalls his argument to Peter, in which he appeals to his personal participation in Jesus' crucifixion (cf. 2:19-20, 6:14).[19] Moreover, it is specifically through the *crucifixion* – Jesus' hanging on a tree, over which lies a curse (cf. verse 13) – that Abraham's blessing comes to the Gentiles (cf. verse 14) (see verses 10-14).[20]

---

[16] In this sense, the verb sets Scripture as the scene for all Paul's ensuing assertions, occurring twice in different forms in verse 8. The allusion to Isaiah 53 in 2:20 may already invoke Abraham, whose sacrifice of Isaac was manifestly discernible (cf. Gen. 22:4, 13: "On the third day Abraham raised his eyes and saw the place from a distance . . . Then Abraham raised his eyes and looked, and behold, behind *him* a ram caught in the thicket by his horns . . . את- בַּיּוֹם הַשְּׁלִישִׁי וַיִּשָּׂא אַבְרָהָם אֶת-עֵינָיו וַיַּרְא אֶת . . . הַמָּקוֹם מֵרָחֹק . . . וַיִּשָּׂא אַבְרָהָם אֶת-עֵינָיו וַיַּרְא וְהִנֵּה-אַיִל אַחַר נֶאֱחַז בַּסְּבַךְ בְּקַרְנָיו . . ."). To the extent that the Hebrew ראה (ra'ah) also signifies "provision" (cf. Gen. 22:14), Abraham "(fore)saw" that God would supply a lamb for atonement (cf. Ps.-Philo, *Bib.Ant.* 18:5-6, 32:1-4; Mekh.Be-shall. 4; Ber. 62b) (cf. Pritz, oral communication).

[17] Cf. 1 Cor. 1:13, 17-18, 23, 2:2, 15:3; 2 Cor. 13:4; Gal. 5:11, 24, 6:12, 14; Phil. 2:8, 3:18; Col. 1:20, 2:14-15; Heb. 9:15-17. In the present context, Scripture, which has already been made "public," may serve as a source of evidence in its own right. The objection that the phrase "before whose eyes" excludes a reference to the biblical text is countered by the fact that, in James' words, "Moses from ancient generations has in every city those who preach him, since he is read in the synagogues every shabbat (Μωϋσῆς γὰρ ἐκ γενεῶν ἀρχαίων κατὰ πόλιν τοὺς κηρύσσοντας αὐτὸν ἔχει ἐν ταῖς συναγωγαῖς κατὰ πᾶν σάββατον ἀναγινωσκόμενος)" (Acts 15:21). For an outworking of Hays' contention that "the cross is the dramatic climax of the Jesus-story, and Paul uses the expression πίστις Ἰησοῦ Χηριστοῦ ['the faithfulness of Jesus the Messiah'] by *metonymy* to suggest that focal moment of the narrative" (Faith: xxx; original emphasis), see Introduction, **Argument**, 4:1-7, and verses 10-14; for crucifixion itself, cf. Le Cornu and Shulam: 106-7.

[18] Cf. Lk. 24:25-27, 44; Jn. 1:45, 5:39-47, 6:45, 7:42, 12:34; Acts 3:18, 10:43, 13:26f, 17:2f, 26:22f, 28:23; Rom. 3:21, 16:26; Col. 1:15ff; 2 Tim. 3:15; 1 Pet. 1:10f; Heb. 1:1ff; 1QHa 12:8-9, 16:27-29; 4QFlorilegium; 4QTestimonia; 4Q471b; 4Q491c f1:6-16; Gen.R. 97 [NV], 98:8; Mid.Ps. 2:9; ARNb 43. It is possible that "Jesus the Messiah crucified" also represents a shorthand for the biblical passages which portray the Messiah's suffering and trials before his glorification (see 2:11-12, 15-16b).

[19] See n3. For πίστις (pistis) as "faithfulness," see 2:15-21 and verses 10ff; for the form of human faithfulness in response to God's faithfulness in Jesus ("self-crucifixion"), see verses 26-29.

[20] Col. 2:15 may be read to say that it was specifically Jesus' crucifixion whereby God "disarmed the rulers and authorities, [and] made a public display of them (ἀπεκδυσάμενος τὰς ἀρχὰς καὶ τὰς ἐξουσίας ἐδειγμάτισεν ἐν παρρησίᾳ,

Verse 2: Since the Galatians constitute, in a real sense, witnesses to the gospel - certainly in Paul's original declaration of it to them - he may "interrogate" them regarding what has happened in its regard.[21] What Paul desires to know - the only point of importance to him - is this: Have they gained entry to God's Kingdom to do the Father's will through Jesus' faithfulness in his death and resurrection?[22] Or - reflecting the influencers' "troubling/bewitchment" - have they been "carried away" by the persuasion that admittance to God's people can be obtained exclusively through the conventional norms of circumcision/conversion?[23] Are they allowing "fleshly" standards of social status to set the circumstances of "salvation" - or will they hold fast to the Messiah through God's Spirit, whose outpouring on the basis of Jesus' death and resurrection has brought them access to the Kingdom of heaven?

Paul *begins* from the fact that the Galatians have "received the Spirit (τὸ πνεῦμα ἐλάβετε)." Bestowal of the Spirit - reflecting the same terminology[24] - is likened in rabbinic texts to study and practice: "R. Aha said: He who learns with the intention of practicing will be privileged to receive the Holy Spirit אמר ר׳ אחא: הלומד על מנת לעשות זוכה להקביל רוח הקדש" (Lev.R. 35:7) (see 2:15-21 and 5:2-12).[25] The Spirit's outpouring on

---

θριαμβεύσας αὐτοὺς *ἐν αὐτῷ*)" - triumphing over the bondage in which they held wo/mankind thrall.

[21] The *interrogatio* serves as a rhetorical device designed to elicit information, Paul here presenting six rhetorical questions in the space of five verses to provocatively and forcefully press his claim against the influencers' (cf. Longenecker, Galatians: 99). Interestingly, the first query is left suspended, losing its force in confrontation of the more substantial issues (cf. ibid: 107). Paul only delivers the consequences of which the influencers are deserving in 5:12: "Would that those who are troubling you would even mutilate themselves" (see 5:2-12).

[22] It is precisely here that Jesus' representative identity takes on full force, Paul's point being that God has been faithful to His promises in bringing the Messiah's blessing (cf. Rom. 15:29), and that all those who participate in Jesus' own faithfulness to God can thereby become part of His people (see verses 26-29).

[23] The central question with which Paul is therefore dealing throughout Galatians is the nature of the real "sons of Abraham": The "disciples of Abraham" are not primarily those who are Jews by birth but those whose circumcision is of the heart. Are his gentile disciples in Galatia going to stand firm in their status as "sons of promise," effected through their participation in Jesus' death and resurrection - or will they admit the influencers' claim that Jewish identity is only to be sought in the "sons of the covenant" - embodied in circumcision? (For the present understanding of the Galatian situation, see Introduction, **Occasion and circumstances**; **Argument**.)

[24] Cf. Jn. 14:17, 20:22; Acts 19:2.

[25] The Hebrew להקביל (le-hakbil) contains the nuances both of receiving and of welcoming - i.e., of being fit for or worthy of (cf. Lev.R. 23:13, 31:11; Cant.R. 8.9.3; PRK 27:2; Yalk.Ps. 833; JSot. 45b; Suk. 28a). The same word is used by those who

the Gentiles is a concrete sign of the advent of the Messiah's righteousness, an expression of the fact that they are now called by God's name, together with Israel (cf. Acts 15:17). Receipt of the Spirit is the essential witness whereby gentile believers can know that, once "no-people," "having no hope and without God in the world," they are now found in Jesus' righteousness through his faithful sacrifice (cf. Eph. 2:11f; Col. 2:10-15) (see 4:1f and verses 10-14).[26]

Paul phrases his first question in such a way as to pre-empt the answer, the language of "receiving" being typical of God's free gifts and His lovingkindness towards His people: "The Spirit of the Lord GOD is upon me, because the LORD has anointed me, to bring good news to the afflicted; He has sent me to bind up the brokenhearted, to proclaim liberty to captives, and freedom to prisoners; to proclaim the favorable year of the LORD, and the day of vengeance of our God"[27] (Isa. 61:1-2).[28] If the believer is faithful to Jesus' obedience, he will also share in the Spirit which God pours upon His servants, Paul's "logic" closely following Cornelius' example in Acts 10 (cf. Hays, Galatians: 251).

The Spirit's presence is as palpable as Jesus' crucifixion was visible, "a datum so vivid as to be undeniable. Paul does not seek to convince the Galatians that they have really received the Spirit. He argues from the indisputable empirical fact that they have received the Spirit in order to

---

"greet" the King when, in their love for Him, they overcome all difficulties to find their way into His presence (cf. TBE pp. 82) (cf. Mt. 22:1-14; Lk. 14:16-24, 19:11-27; TBE pp. 140-41; [EZ] p. 171; Shab. 152b-153a). For the correspondence between "faithfulness," "intention," "walking in the Spirit," and "love," see Introduction, **Argument**, 2:15-21, and 5:13ff.

[26] Cf. Ps. 96:7; Isa. 2:2-4, 45:14, 22-24, 49:6, 12, 23, 55:5, 60:4ff, 66:19f; Hos. 1:9-10, 2:23; Zech. 2:11, 14:16-21; Acts 10:24-25, 15:14-18; Rom. 4:16-25, 15:9-13; Eph. 2:12ff; Ps.Sol. 17:31; 4Q504 ff1-2iv:8f; Cant.R. 4.8.2. For the working out of the concept, see 2:11-14 and verses 6f, 26-29.

[27] רוח ה' עלי יען משח ה' אתי לבשר ענוים שלחני לחבש לנשברי-לב לקרא לשבוים דרור ולאסורים פקח-קוח: לקרא שנת-רצון לה' ויום נקם לאלהינו . . .

[28] Cf. Neh. 9:20; Ezek. 11:19, 36:26; Lk. 11:13; Jn. 3:34, 7:39; Acts 5:32; Rom. 5:5, 8:5-11; 1 Cor. 2:12; 1 Jn. 3:24, 4:13; 1QHª 4:26, 8:19-20, 15:7. The question is sharpened in verse 5. For the importance of Isaiah 61, which here establishes a connection between "justification" and the Spirit, see 1:1f. It is possible that Paul's appeal to the Spirit relates not simply to the Galatians' experience but also to his own – upon which the Galatians' is grounded (cf. 4:19). To the extent that he understands his apostolic/prophetic role on the basis of the Servant in Isaiah, he is aware that God has anointed him too with His Spirit (see 1:15-16b, 2:1-10, 4:8f, and verses 10-14). In this respect, his calling to the Gentiles is intimately linked in dual form to the outpouring of the Spirit (cf. Kim, Paul: 101ff) (see 1:15-16b and verses 10-14). For the Spirit and sonship, see 4:1-7 and verses 26-29; for Paul's "exemplary" role, see 1:1-5, 15-16b, 24-26, 2:1-10 (n136), 15-21 (n292), 4:12-20, 5:2-12 (verse 11), 6:1f (verses 11, 15, 17), and above.

convince them that no further validating action is required to ensure their status as God's children" (ibid). As Paul reiterates later, in Romans: "If anyone does not have the spirit of the Messiah, he does not belong to him. And if the Messiah is in you, though the body is dead because of sin, yet the spirit is alive because of righteousness. But if the Spirit of Him who raised Jesus from the dead dwells in you, He who raised the Messiah Jesus from the dead will also give life to your mortal bodies through His Spirit who indwells you"[29] (Rom. 8:9-11) (see verses 26-29).[30]

Paul assumes a directly causal relation between the act which initiated the Galatians' standing and their receipt of the Spirit, casting his query concerning the manner in which the process manifested itself in the language of "beginning" and "completion."[31] He evidently presupposes that what was bestowed at the outset also guarantees the goal,[32] making

---

[29] εἰ δέ τις πνεῦμα Χριστοῦ οὐκ ἔχει, οὗτος οὐκ ἔστιν αὐτοῦ. εἰ δὲ Χριστὸς ἐν ὑμῖν, τὸ μὲν σῶμα νεκρὸν διὰ ἁμαρτίαν τὸ δὲ πνεῦμα ζωὴ διὰ δικαιοσύνην. εἰ δὲ τὸ πνεῦμα τοῦ ἐγείραντος τὸν Ἰησοῦν ἐκ νεκρῶν οἰκεῖ ἐν ὑμῖν, ὁ ἐγείρας Χριστὸν ἐκ νεκρῶν ζῳοποιήσει καὶ τὰ θνητὰ σώματα ὑμῶν διὰ τοῦ ἐνοικοῦντος αὐτοῦ πνεύματος ἐν ὑμῖν.

[30] A corresponding parallel may be adduced from a midrash on the Song of the Sea, wherein the ground of the people's trust in God lies in their own experience: *"This Is My God and I will Glorify Him* (Ex. 15:2). R. Eliezer says: Whence can you say that a maidservant saw at the sea what Isaiah and Ezekiel and all the prophets never saw? It says about them: 'And by the ministry of the prophets have I used similitudes' (Hos. 12:11). And it is also written: 'The heavens were opened and I saw visions of God' (Ezek. 1:1). To give a parable for this, to what is it like? To the following: A king of flesh and blood enters a province surrounded by a circle of guards; his heroes stand to the right of him and to the left of him; his soldiers are before him and behind him. And all the people ask, saying: 'Which one is the king?' Because he is of flesh and blood like those who surround him. But, when the Holy One, blessed be He, revealed Himself at the sea, no one had to ask: 'Which one is the king?' But as soon as they saw Him they recognized Him, and they all opened their mouths, and said: 'This is my God and I will glorify Him' זה אלי ואנוהו. רבי אליעזר אומר: מנין אתה אומר שראתה שפחה על הים מה שלא ראו ישעיה ויחזקאל וכל שאר הנביאים, שנאמר בהם (הושע י״ב): וביד הנביאים אדמה, וכתיב (יחזקאל א'): נפתחו השמים ואראה מראות אלהים. מושלו משל, למה הדבר דומה? למלך בשר ודם שבא למדינה ועליו צפירה מקיפתו וגבוריו מימינו ומשמאלו וחיילות מלפניו ומלאחריו. והיו הכל שואלין לומר: איזה הוא המלך? מפני שהוא בשר ודם כמותם. אבל כשנגלה הקדוש ברוך הוא על הים לא נצרך אחד מהם לשאול: איזה המלך? אלא כיון שראוהו הכירוהו ופתחו כלן ואמרו: זה אלי ואנוהו" (Mekh.Shir. 3) (see also n160). For the use of Canticles to interpret other parts of Scripture, see 4:21-31; for "flesh and blood," see 1:16c-17.

[31] This is also implicit in the priority Paul ascribes to Scripture in "foreseeing" and "preaching beforehand" (cf. verse 8), an idea which emphasises the precedence (in all its nuances) of faithfulness – and God's unchanging nature, both throughout human history and in its anticipation.

[32] Cf. Isa. 41:4, 44:6; Rev. 1:8, 17, 2:8, 21:6, 22:13; Gen.R. 63:8; Ex.R. 15:1.

any other constituents extraneous.[33] While the gentile Galatians may have been godfearers when Paul first shared the gospel with them, it is yet immediately obvious that they were not Torah-observant, in the sense of having achieved the status of full proselytes (see Introduction, **Occasion and circumstances**). If they have indeed received the Spirit, the basis (ἐξ; ex) on which they therefore must have done so is evidently the "message which elicits faithfulness (ἀκοῆς πίστεως)" (cf. Hays, Galatians: 252; Faith: 124-32, and for the following discussion).[34]

Although the ambiguities apparent in this phrase are awkward, they are not irremediably insoluble. The Greek first confronts us with the same objective/subjective genitive conundrum as that posed by that of "the faith/fulness of Jesus" (see 2:15-21), the present nouns complicating the case due to the fact they both bear various possible significances. As an act of "hearing," ἀκοή (akoē) usually renders the second noun, "faith," either as a similar performative - "hearing by faith" - or as the hearing of "the faith," πίστις (pistis) then signifying the gospel.[35] Alternatively, the noun may be taken not as a performative but as a substantive - "that which is heard," i.e., the report, message.[36] This calls forth the substantive also in πίστις, the whole phrase then denoting "the proclamation of the faith (the gospel)" - or, πίστις (pistis) retaining a performative sense, "the message

---

[33] It is not particularly that any supplementary measures are superfluous but rather that Jesus is both the "means" and the "end." In constituting the goal and purpose, nothing else, whether chosen as a substitute from the beginning or intervening at some point in the process, can act in his stead.

[34] Hays perceptively apprehends that receipt of the Spirit already constitutes in and of itself a proof of the scriptural promise, realized in the latter's preaching: ". . . the *purpose* of Paul's appeal to experience is to establish his claim that the foundation for this experience was the gospel message (ἀκοή). The Galatians were enabled to have these experiences because of one and only one thing: Paul's proclamation of the gospel message, whose content is precisely the story to which 3:1b alludes: Jesus Christ crucified . . . The Spirit that the Galatians have received is not just a self-authenticating religious experience; rather, the experience is significant for Paul's argument because he interprets it, in light of scripture, as the fulfillment of God's promise to Abraham [cf. verse 14]" (Faith: 168, 183; original emphasis). For the latter argument, see verses 10-14; for Paul's association of the Spirit directly with Jesus, see 4:1-7.

[35] One of the strongest objections to this - the traditional - interpretation derives from the fact that God's gift of His Spirit becomes dependent upon another human act - even one of believing: "Paul's primary intention is not at all to juxtapose one type of human activity ('works') to another ('believing-hearing') but rather to juxtapose human activity to God's activity, as revealed in the 'proclamation'" (Hays, Faith: 130).

[36] Cf. Isa. 53:1; Rom. 10:16-17; 1 Thess. 2:13. The significance of this usage is perhaps most evident in Paul's application of Hab. 2:4 to Jesus as "the faithful one" (see verses 10ff).

which is to do with faithfulness."[37] Paul's propensity for presenting Jesus as God's promise, the fulfilment of all His good words, suggests the propriety of the latter reading.[38]

These dual aspects of hearing and faithfulness reflect the twin promises of Israel's response to God's gift of the Torah: "Then he [Moses] took the book of the covenant and read *it* in the hearing of the people; and they said, 'All that the LORD has spoken we will do, and we will be obedient [hear]' ויקח ספר הברית ויקרא באזני העם ויאמרו כל אשר-דבר ה׳ נעשה ונשמע" (Ex. 24:7).[39] Here - as in his rebuke of Peter, albeit with a different purpose - Paul cautions his gentile Galatian disciples that, equally with Israel, their access to the "keys to the Kingdom" is to be found in participation in Jesus' faithfulness (see 2:15-21 and 4:1f).[40] Having once entered God's court, why should anyone wish to seek for an alternative form of admittance?[41]

---

[37] The distinction between these two latter options is perhaps more grammatical than real, "the faith-message (gospel)" and "the message which evokes faithfulness" ultimately both being expressions of God's working. On the most logical of bases, the question "How did you receive the Spirit?" must be answered "Through the preaching of the gospel" - this being Paul's prevalent practice, of proving all things on the basis of Scripture (see above). Moreover, it is only the Spirit as the fulfilment of Abraham's blessing - as Paul immediately sets forth - which bestows upon Gentiles the status of true "sons of Abraham," the uncircumcision of the one "keeping the requirements of the Torah" being regarded as circumcision (cf. Rom. 2:26) (see Introduction, **Argument** and 2:15-21).

[38] Paul's question follows immediately upon his insistence that Jesus has been "publicly portrayed *as* crucified," a statement which, however interpreted, at least includes the sense of preaching. The association with Rom. 10:16-17 may therefore be reinforced through reference to the preceding verses: "How then shall they call upon Him in whom they have not believed? And how shall they believe in Him whom they have not heard? And how shall they hear without a preacher? (Πῶς οὖν ἐπικαλέσωνται εἰς ὃν οὐκ ἐπίστευσαν; πῶς δὲ πιστεύσωσιν οὗ οὐκ ἤκουσαν; πῶς δὲ ἀκούσωσιν χωρὶς κηρύσσοντος;)" (Rom. 10:14). (For a review of the subjects/objects of Rom. 10:12-21, cf. Shulam and Le Cornu: 352-56.)

[39] Literally: "We shall do and we shall hear" - the anticipated natural order, of hearing and then doing, being reversed. In the context of hypocrisy, the "hearing of the Torah" must be performed in "faithfulness." As Paul has indicated to Peter, Torah-observance ("works of the law") lacks reality as mere "ritual": To be effective, it must be accompanied by "intention" (see 2:15-21). For the implications of the commitment involved in this declaration, see verses 10-14.

[40] "Hearing" is related to the study of Torah, "doing" to its performance (cf. Num.R. 14:10). For the form of human faithfulness to God's working in Jesus, see verses 26-29; for the current reading of Galatians as a halakhic "rebuke-request" letter along the lines of 4QMMT, see Introduction, **Form; Argument**.

[41] "These Gentiles have apparently begun to accept the 'influencers' [*sic*] demand to define their status according to the membership norms of the larger Jewish community ... Paul's addressees may well regard completion of the ritual process

Verse 3: Here, Paul sharpens his first question, adding degrees to the Galatians' gullibility: οὕτως (houtōs) carries the comparative sense of "that/so foolish" (cf. BAGD: 598). The Spirit is most evidently associated with beginnings in Genesis: "In the beginning God created the heavens and the earth . . . and the Spirit of God was moving over the surface of the waters בראשית ברא אלהים את השמים ואת הארץ . . . ורוח אלהים מרחפת על-פני המים" (Gen. 1:1-2).[42] Jesus speaks of this creation in terms of receiving a new birth as introduction into God's Kingdom: "Truly, truly, I say to you, unless one is born of water and the Spirit, he cannot enter into the Kingdom of God. That which is born of the flesh is flesh; and that which is born of the Spirit is spirit"[43] (Jn. 3:5-6).[44] Most importantly, the Torah's point and purpose in and of itself is to lead to the Messiah's righteousness: "For the Messiah is the goal of the Torah for righteousness to everyone who believes (τέλος γὰρ νόμου Χριστὸς εἰς δικαιοσύνην παντὶ τῷ πιστεύοντι)" (Rom. 10:4) (see also 2:15-21, 5:13-18, and verses 21-25).

The Greek ἐπιτελέω (epiteleō) – an intensified form of τελέω (teleō), whence τέλος (telos –"goal") – combines the idea of this same "purpose" with that of being "completed" or "perfected," including the added nuance of accomplishment (cf. BAGD: 302). The Galatians' foolishness in Paul's

---

of circumcision as a small price to pay, for the 'rights' of membership that they previously considered theirs exist only to the degree that they are recognized . . . Paul insists, to the contrary, that the benefits held out to them necessarily subvert the foundational principles of their faith in Christ, just as had been implied earlier at Antioch, when Peter's withdrawal because of 'fear' of 'the ones for circumcision' there threatened to undermine the meaning of the death of Christ (2:14-21)" (Nanos, Inter: 404-5). Paul elaborates the content of "beginning in the Spirit" in 5:13, the latter verse structurally paralleling the present one (see 5:13-18).

[42] The association of this verse with the Messiah's spirit is well known, as is also the Wisdom tradition which links the word of God's creativity with the Torah (cf. Jn. 1:1f; Sir. 24:8-29): "*And the spirit of God hovered*: this alludes to the spirit of Messiah, as you read, *And the spirit of the Lord shall rest upon him* (Isa. 11:2). In the merit of what will [this spirit] eventually come? [For the sake of that which] hovered over the face of the waters, i.e. in the merit of repentance which is likened to water, as it is written, *Pour out thy heart like water* (Lam. 2:19)" (Gen.R. 2:4) (see also 97f, 139, 311f, 359).

[43] ἀμὴν ἀμὴν λέγω σοι, ἐὰν μή τις γεννηθῇ ἐξ ὕδατος καὶ πνεύματος, οὐ δύναται εἰσελθεῖν εἰς τὴν βασιλείαν τοῦ θεοῦ. τὸ γεγεννημένον ἐκ τῆς σαρκὸς σάρξ ἐστιν, καὶ τὸ γεγεννημένον ἐκ τοῦ πνεύματος πνεῦμά ἐστιν.

[44] Cf. Ps. 51:10-13; Ezek. 36:25-27; Rom. 8:5ff; Tit. 3:5; 1 Jn. 5:7-8. "Flesh" in this context represents "human effort" not so much in the sense of Torah-observance (although converts would be obligated to the commandments once circumcised – see 5:2-12) as with regard to "social conventions" – i.e., bowing to "social" identity pressure (membership within the Jewish community) at the expense of the righteous living which this identity is to embody (see Introduction, **Occasion and circumstances**; **Argument**). For Paul's play on the significations of "flesh," see 5:13f.

eyes is in perceiving the goal in terms of its beginning, of working towards something already completed, of seeking to add to that which is already whole in itself (cf. Phil. 1:6).[45] The contrast is reflected grammatically between the aorist participle, "having begun," which indicates an absolute point in the past, and the νῦν (nyn –"now"), which marks a time after the initial "fact" and suggests that the Galatians are attempting to revise their origin – "reinventing the wheel" as it were.[46] Righteousness always having been a matter of the "circumcision of the heart,"[47] why, puzzles Paul, are the Galatians coveting its impartation by means of a physical sign in their own flesh?[48]

Verse 4: Paul's final question refers yet again to the Galatians' experience. The ambiguity in this verse stems from the dual connotations of the Greek πάσχω (paschō), one negative (a "bad" experience), one

---

[45] Jewish claims certainly comprehend the idea that circumcision was a form of "perfection": "Rabbi says: Great is circumcision, for despite all the religious duties which Abraham our father fulfilled, he was not called 'perfect' until he circumcised himself, as it is written, *Walk before me, and be thou perfect* (Gen. 17:1) רבי אומר: גדולה מילה, שכל המצות שעשה אברהם אבינו לא נקרא שלם עד שמל, שנאמר (בראשית יז): התהלך לפני והיה תמים" (Ned. 3:11) (see 2:1-10 [excursus]). This notwithstanding, the interpretation that the influencers are not opposed to Paul *per se* but merely wish to "bring his converts to perfection" is not demanded (cf. Longenecker, *Galatians*: 106). The contrast between flesh and Spirit is not one of degree but of kind – even when the present view perceives the issue as that of non-believing godfearing pressure on the gentile Galatian believers to fully join the Jewish community along conventional, legitimate proselyte lines (see Introduction, **Occasion and circumstances**, 4:1f, 5:2f, and above).

[46] Cf. the description of Balaam: "It is like the case of a man who was walking with a king when he saw a robber, and, forsaking the king, he walked with the robber. When he returned to the king the latter said to him: 'Go with the person with whom you have been walking, for you cannot possibly walk with me.' It was the same with Balaam. He had been attached to the Holy Spirit and had returned to be a diviner as at first, a fact that can be inferred from the text, *Balaam also the son of Beor, the soothsayer* (Josh. 13:22) משל למי שמהלך עם המלך. ראה ליסטין, הניח את המלך וטייל עם הליסטין. כשחזר אצל המלך אמר לו המלך: לך עם אותו שטיילת עמו, שאי אפשר לך שתלך עמי. "כך בלעם נזקק לרוח הקדש וחזר להיות קוסם כבתחלה, שנאמר: ואת בלעם בן בעור הקוסם (Num.R. 20:19). For the "disciples of Balaam," see 2:15-21; for "returning," see 4:1f.

[47] Cf. Dt. 10:16, 30:6; Jer. 4:4, 9:25f; Rom. 2:25f; Jub. 1:22-23; Odes Sol. 11:1-3; 1QS 5:5; 1QpHab 11:13; 4Q177 2:16; 4Q434 1:4; PRE 29; Gen.R. 46:5; Lev.R. 25:6; Ber. 29a (see also verses 26-29).

[48] "A non-Jew who lives according to certain fundamental moral laws, without following the whole Mosaic law, is blessed. The proselyte, the Gentile who has converted to Judaism, however, is bound by the whole law. If a proselyte fails to fulfill the whole law, which formerly did not obligate him, his conversion to Judaism is itself the cause of his becoming a child of hell {Mt. 23:15}. Quite needlessly he has thrown away his blessedness" (Flusser, *Jesus*: 76) (cf. Howard, *Crisis*: 16) (see 5:1f). For Mt. 23:15, see verses 21-25 (verse 22).

"neutral" (experience *per se* – not in and of itself necessarily "hurtful"). Most translations render the first, signifying a certain (albeit unspecified) "suffering" on the Galatians' part. On this reading, the allusion may refer to the "shame" to which they have ostensibly been exposed in their contacts with the general Jewish community, the latter scorning the claim that Gentiles are, here and now, *as Gentiles*, participating in the eschaton promised in Scripture – i.e., without becoming full-fledged, legitimate members of Israel (cf. Nanos, Inter; Irony: 106-9, 189-91).[49]

While both Galatians and Acts indicate a degree of "persecution" in relation to the Galatian communities (cf. Acts 14:22; Gal. 4:29, [5:11, 6:12]) – tying in with the previous verse by linking it to the communities' external relations – nothing excludes a forward reference, to the Spirit and miracles of verse 5.[50] Paul's question then queries whether the Galatians' "experience of God's working in their lives" holds no further validity for them. If this situation be true, he himself has "run in vain (εἰς κενὸν)" in maintaining "the truth of the gospel" on their behalf (cf. 2:2, 5).[51]

---

[49] The Galatian believers' interpretion, as it were, of the correction of their assumption as "shame" becomes translated as "persecution," in other words. It bears repetition here that our disagreement with Nanos lies largely in identifying the influencers' identity, Nanos asserting that they are proselytes who, having themselves found status within the Jewish community, are seeking to resolve the gentile Galatians' residual sense of marginalisation by the mainstream Jewish community. This identification itself appears to be largely grounded on the theory of "agonistic societies" in which shame, envy, and the evil eye play a significant role (see 4:12-20). Rather than recognizing the believers' Jewish standing in the Messiah, the Jewish community actually calls it into question. To the extent that the present contribution diminishes the importance of this framework it finds less reason to see the influencers as proselytes. Likewise, seeing no historical basis for proselytes as "social control agents," it rather views the influencers, partially on the basis of Acts 13-14, as godfearers who do not accept messianic claims to Jewish status and insist that those who seek Jewish status gain it by normative, conventional means – i.e., circumcision/conversion (see Introduction, **Occasion and circumstances; Argument**). Likewise, the present authors minimise the function of the evil eye in Paul's "explanation" of his disciples' misapprehension of the influencers' interests (see above). These divergences notwithstanding, the theses share a consensus concerning the criteria according to which the controversy is conducted, namely the grounds upon which Jewish identity/status are predicated: "Has the age to come dawned in Jesus Christ, or not?" (Nanos, Inter: 402).

[50] Cf. Longenecker, who suggests that the phrase "should probably be taken as a recollection of the Galatian believers' past, positive spiritual experiences – perhaps even should be translated 'have you had such remarkable experiences' (so BAGD), or at least understood as 'the great experiences through which the Galatians had already passed in their lives as Christians' (so Burton, *Galatians*, 149 . . .)" (Galatians: 104).

[51] εἰκῆ and εἰς κενὸν being synonymous, Paul employing the former also in 4:11, he clearly establishes a connection between the Galatians' present "experience" and

This understanding appears preferable to the former, the so-called "suffering" being, to all intents and purposes, a direct consequence of the Galatians' response to the influencers' persuasion.[52] Paul's point relates most immediately to any mitigation of their life in Jesus. He is suggesting that if they take the proposed step and commit themselves to circumcision and conversion – all their prior experience will have been to no avail.[53] The conditional sentence allows for the hope that Paul will be able to convince them of the error of following such a course.[54]

Verse 5: If verse 4 alludes to the Galatians' experience in the Messiah, rather than to their "shame," Paul's final question follows naturally, closing the circle of interrogatives which comprise these five verses and

---

his struggle to retain their loyalty to his gospel. The apprehension regarding both sets of "vanity" is the potential loss of the efficacy of Jesus' death and resurrection in obtaining gentile access to God's Kingdom (see 2:1-10, 4:12-20, and below [n54]). Although Paul elsewhere also links the joy of the Spirit with the experience of suffering (cf. [Acts 13:52]; Rom. 8:14-25; 1 Thess. 1:6) – and suffering with the Kingdom of God (cf. Acts 14:22; 2 Thess. 1:4-5), we are presently suggesting that, apart from his own "campaign," none of the various references to "persecution" in Galatians (cf. 4:29, 5:11, 6:12) in fact necessarily allude to any "literal" harassment (see 4:21-31, 5:2-12, and 6:12-16). (For Galatians and the Kingdom of God, see 5:13-18; for Paul's explicit reference to the "persecution" of the Galatian communities, see 4:21-31 [verse 29].)

[52] This intepretation mitigates, in the present opinion, against understanding the Galatians' "suffering" as "proof" of the exercise of the influencers' evil eye (see above).

[53] Here, too, an anticipation of Abraham may possibly be discerned, Abraham's righteousness frequently being associated with his testing/trial/temptation: "... when he was proved, he was found faithful (ἐν πειρασμῷ εὑρέθη πιστός)" (Sir. 44:20). "Was not Abraham found faithful in temptation, and it was imputed to him for righteousness? (Αβρααμ οὐχὶ ἐν πειρασμῷ εὑρέθη πιστός, καὶ ἐλογίσθη αὐτῷ εἰς δικαιοσύνην;)" (1 Macc. 2:52) (cf. Heb. 11:17; Jub. 17:18, 19:8). (According to a midrashic tradition, God tested Abraham with ten trials [cf. Jub. 19:8; Ex.R. 15:27, 30:16, 44:4; Num.R. 18:21; PRE 26-31; PA 5:3].) Are the Galatians not going to follow in the wake of Abraham's archetype and prove *their* faithfulness to Paul in the Messiah (cf. 4:14)? (see 4:12f).

[54] While it appears more natural to place the question mark at the end of the complete sentence, it may also be inserted following the first "in vain," thus reading: "Did you experience so many things in vain? If so, it really was in vain!" (Betz, Galatians: 134-35). Paul's character – and the communication itself – would in fact seem to anticipate the extension of hope rather than the confirmation of hopelessness. The futility is in a measure also Paul's, for the Galatians' faithfulness in Jesus constitutes proof of his calling and the fruit of his labour (cf. 1 Cor. 15:2; Gal. 2:2, 4:11). The εἰκῇ (eikē – "in vain") further recalls the δωρεὰν (dōrean – "gratuitously") in 2:21, again suggesting a link with Paul's "gentile gospel" (see 2:15-21 and above [n51]).

summarising (cf. verse 2) their heart.⁵⁵ The Greek syntax is elliptical in the
extreme, literally reading: "Therefore, the one who supplies the Spirit to
you and works miracles among you – from works of the Torah or from the
message of faithfulness?"⁵⁶ Here, Paul focuses the Galatians' attention on
the source of the benefits they have received, detailing for the first time the
"working of miracles (ἐνεργῶν δυνάμεις)" as a direct expression of the
Spirit in their midst.

While directed towards the Galatians' experience, the question in fact
goes to the origin – the person responsible – for their circumstances.⁵⁷ The
fact that the source is animate is indicated by the masculine article/relative
pronoun ὁ (ho), in contrast to a possible neuter (or feminine) form. Such a
structure is customary of benedictions, rendering the Hebrew מי ש- (mi
she- – "who . . ."), -ש ברוך (baruch she- – "Blessed [be He] who") or simply
ברוך (baruch – "Blessed [be He who] . . .") (cf. Stone: 551ff), reinforcing the
fact that God is the subject here.⁵⁸ Is, then, Paul wishes to know, God's
provision of the Spirit accomplished in response to Torah-observance or in
acceptance of the message of faithfulness, in the Galatians' case?⁵⁹

Phrased in this way, it is evident that Paul anticipates the answer: God
gives His Spirit through His proclamation of "the faithfulness" – "the
gospel of God, which He promised beforehand through His prophets in
the holy Scriptures, concerning His son . . . among whom you also are the
called of Jesus the Messiah"⁶⁰ (Rom. 1:2-3, 6).⁶¹ The fact that God alone is

---

⁵⁵ The postpositive οὖν (oun – "therefore") points to a concluding précis. To the
extent that this verse recaps verses 2-4, it too corroborates the reading of
"experience" in verse 4, the reference to the Spirit paralleling verses 2-3 and that to
miracles the "remarkable experiences" of verse 4.

⁵⁶ For the latter clause, see above.

⁵⁷ For Paul's shift between the plural (cf. 1:7, 6:12-13) and the singular (cf. verse 1,
5:10), see 5:2-12.

⁵⁸ Cf. 2 Cor. 1:21-22, 9:10; Tos.Ber. 3:7, 4:5, 5:22. The Greek ἐνεργέω (energeō) is
customarily employed in relation to God's working in power (cf. 1 Cor. 12:6, 11;
Gal. 2:8).

⁵⁹ Yet again, the reader is reminded that Paul is not speaking in absolute terms. His
objection to Torah-observance arises here only to the extent that the influencers are
persuading his disciples that, if they are seeking status and standing in Jewish eyes,
the sole means of achieving this is through the conventional norm of
circumcision/conversion. Where the influencers do not accept Jesus' death and
resurrection as imparting the "keys of the Kingdom" also to the Gentiles *qua*
Gentiles, Paul protests with his full power against their persuasion, perceiving their
preaching as tantamount to imprisonment under the dominion of Belial (see 4:1f).
For a full account of the Galatian situation, see Introduction, **Occasion and
circumstances; Argument.**

⁶⁰ εὐαγγέλιον θεοῦ, ὃ προεπηγγείλατο διὰ τῶν προφητῶν αὐτοῦ ἐν γραφαῖς
ἁγίαις περὶ τοῦ υἱοῦ αὐτου . . . ἐν οἷς ἐστε καὶ ὑμεῖς κλητοὶ Ἰησοῦ Χριστοῦ.

responsible for the gift of the Spirit means not only that His presence cannot dwell with the Galatians on the basis of their Torah-observance – but also, by the same token, that it cannot rest on their "believing" (see above).[62] Both acts, in this context, belong to the "flesh" – which has no correspondence with the Spirit: "For to man (does not belong) his path, nor can a human being steady his step; since the judgment belongs to God, and from his hand is the perfection of the path כיא לו(א לאדם דרכו ואנוש לוא יכין צעדו כיא לאל המשפט ומידו תום הדרך" (1QS 11:10-11) (see 2:15-21).

The "miracles" which attend the Spirit are those which Jesus demonstrates in his own life and which he promises to those who follow him in faithfulness: "'Are you the Coming One, or shall we look for someone else?' And Jesus answered and said to them, 'Go and report to John the things which you hear and see: *the* BLIND RECEIVE SIGHT and *the* lame walk, *the* lepers are cleansed and *the* deaf hear, and *the* dead are raised up, and *the* POOR HAVE THE GOSPEL PREACHED TO THEM [Isa. 35:5f, 61:1]'"[63] (Mt. 11:3-5).[64] "Truly, truly, I say to you, he who believes in me, the works that I do shall he do also; and greater *works* than these shall he do; because I go to the Father"[65] (Jn. 14:12).[66]

---

[61] Cf. Lk. 1:35, 54-55, 68-79. Compare the correspondence between the "promised beforehand (προεπηγγείλατο)" of Rom. 1:2 and the "displayed beforehand/publicly" of verse 1 and the "foreseeing" and "preaching beforehand" in verse 8. Once "faith" is (re)interpreted as Jesus' faithfulness in his death/resurrection, as embodied in the gospel, the traditional dichotomy between "faith" and "works" begins to lose much of its cogency. For "faithfulness" as a messianic title, see 4:1-7 and verses 10-14, 21-25.

[62] The fact that the Galatians have not, up until now, been observing the Torah (cf. verse 2; 5:2-3) indicates that Paul is not speaking of "works of the Torah" in a "legalistic" sense of "works *versus* faith," but rather of a means of membership within Israel. In the same way, he is also not saying that Torah-observance *cannot* bring the Spirit – only that, in the Galatians' case, it *has* not (see Introduction, **Occasion and circumstances**; **Argument**). This is, at least partially, the significance of Peter's statement: "Surely no one can refuse the water for these to be baptized who have received the Holy Spirit just as we *did*, can he? (μήτι τὸ ὕδωρ δύναται κωλῦσαί τις τοῦ βαπτισθῆναι τούτους, οἵτινες τὸ πνεῦμα τὸ ἅγιον ἔλαβον ὡς καὶ ἡμεῖς;)" (Acts 10:47).

[63] εἶπεν αὐτῷ· σὺ εἶ ὁ ἐρχόμενος ἢ ἕτερον προσδοκῶμεν; καὶ ἀποκριθεὶς ὁ Ἰησοῦς εἶπεν αὐτοῖς· πορευθέντες ἀπαγγείλατε Ἰωάννῃ ἃ ἀκούετε καὶ βλέπετε· τυφλοὶ ἀναβλέπουσιν καὶ χωλοὶ περιπατοῦσιν, λεπροὶ καθαρίζονται καὶ κωφοὶ ἀκούουσιν, καὶ νεκροὶ ἐγείρονται καὶ πτωχοὶ εὐαγγελίζονται.

[64] For Isa. 61:1-3, see 1:1-5, 4:1f, verses 6f, 26-29, and above; for the "Coming One," see 4:1-7 and verses 10-14, 19f.

[65] Ἀμὴν ἀμὴν λέγω ὑμῖν, ὁ πιστεύων εἰς ἐμὲ τὰ ἔργα ἃ ἐγὼ ποιῶ κἀκεῖνος ποιήσει καὶ μείζονα τούτων ποιήσει, ὅτι ἐγὼ πρὸς τὸν πατέρα πορεύομαι.

[66] While the Spirit forms a predominant theme throughout the letter, Paul fails to pick up the theme of the "working of miracles" in the continuation. Since there is presumably only "one Spirit," whose various functions Paul addresses at specific

When Jesus returns to his Father, the Spirit takes his place in the world, to witness to and to glorify Jesus, to guide wo/men into all truth and knowledge, and to provide "rivers of living water" for those faithful to him.[67] Paul's own witness is of that which Jesus had "accomplished through me, resulting in the obedience of the Gentiles by word and deed, in the power of signs and wonders, in the power of the Spirit; so that from Jerusalem and round about as far as Illyricum I have fully preached the gospel of the Messiah"[68] (Rom. 15:18c-19).[69]

Verses 6-9:
Even so Abraham BELIEVED GOD, AND IT WAS RECKONED TO HIM AS RIGHTEOUSNESS. Therefore, be sure that it is those who are of faith that are sons of Abraham. And the Scripture, foreseeing that God would justify the Gentiles by faith, preached the gospel beforehand to Abraham, *saying* "ALL THE NATIONS SHALL BE BLESSED IN YOU." So then, those who are of faith are blessed with Abraham, the believer.

As commentators frequently point out, following his rhetorical barrage in verses 1-5, Paul now appeals directly to Scripture to prove his point (see verses 1-5, 10f).[70] It is Scripture which circumscribes the argument, and on whose basis Paul asserts that the Galatians "know (γινώσκετε ἄρα)" that "it is those who are of faithfulness who are sons of Abraham (οἱ ἐκ πίστεως, οὗτοι υἱοί εἰσιν ᾿Αβραάμ)" (verse 7).[71] This is the decisive

junctions in the epistle (cf. verses 10-14, 4:1-7, and 5:16-24), his neglect of such further reference may indicate that the miracles are to be primarily attributed here to God's working in the Galatians' lives, rather than to miracles which they themselves are performing (see also 5:19-23 [n269]). It should be evident that reading πίστις (pistis) as indicating "faithfulness" renders the most convincing and appropriate signification also of the verb (πιστεύω; pisteuō), in most instances, as "trust" (see 2:15-21 [n263]).

[67] Cf. Jn. 7:38-39, 15:26, 16:7-15. For the power of the Spirit, cf. Le Cornu and Shulam: 596-97. Paul picks up this theme again in 5:13ff.
[68] εἰς ὑπακοὴν ἐθνῶν, λόγῳ καὶ ἔργῳ, ἐν δυνάμει σημείων καὶ τεράτων, ἐν δυνάμει πνεύματος [θεοῦ]· ὥστε με ἀπὸ ᾿Ιερουσαλὴμ καὶ κύκλῳ μέχρι τοῦ ᾿Ιλλυρικοῦ πεπληρωκέναι τὸ εὐαγγέλιον τοῦ Χριστοῦ.
[69] A clear linkage exists in this verse between preaching the word and signs and wonders, other passages (cf. Acts 2:43; Heb. 2:4) also suggesting that "the introduction of the gospel to new territories was regularly accompanied by miraculous healings and other 'signs and wonders'" (Bruce, Galatians: 151). This may correspond to Paul's testimony of the "signs of a true apostle" - "signs and wonders and miracles (σημεῖα τοῦ ἀποστόλου . . . σημείοις τε καὶ τέρασιν καὶ δυνάμεσιν)" (2 Cor. 12:12) - which he performed "among you (ἐν ὑμῖν)" (verse 5).
[70] To say that he "now" turns to a scriptural argument is an inaccuracy, given the centrality which Scripture claims in Paul's questioning concerning the Galatians' standing in Abraham's blessing through the Spirit (see verses 1-5). For this section as Paul's *probatio* and for the *interrogatio*, see verses 1-5.
[71] For Galatians' epistolary characteristics, see Introduction, **Form**.

answer – to which in all his haste and urgency, Paul has left his readers with no room to reply – to his initial interrogative inquiry. The gentile Galatians have no need of circumcision, as the symbol of Jewish membership, because Jewish identity is ultimately based as much on behaviour as on birth.[72]

The measure of the present reading of the situation in Galatia is well taken by its divergence here from that major exegetical tradition which sees in verse 6 a "decided shift in his [Paul's] argumentation," the whole section (verses 6-14) being "only rather tenuously related thematically to 3:1-5" (Longenecker, *Galatians*: 109).[73] If Paul regards the Gentiles as aspiring after a social status whose attribution thereby detracts from what they have already acquired through the Messiah, an appeal to Abraham as their "forefather in faithfulness" constitutes the natural and logical step in his proof.[74]

---

[72] While the reader's patience may be tried by such repetition, it still bears reiterating that Paul is not seeking an abolition of Judaism *per se*, nor expressing contempt for/of Torah-observance in and of itself (see Introduction, **Author**; Appendix). His critique is along the lines of the prophetic denunciation of practices performed without intention, rituals repeated out of routine – here applied to the covenant as a whole, symbolic of the nation's relationship with God, and thus of their status (identity) as His people (see 2:15-21 and verses 19-20). For the importance of Mic. 6:6-8 for Galatians in this respect, see Introduction, **Argument**.

[73] Longenecker's admission that "Paul brings the arguments of vv 6-14 to a climax not by way of an appeal to justification by faith, *as one would expect* . . . but by a renewed focus on the Spirit and the Galatians' experience" (*Galatians*: 109; emphasis added) tacitly signifies the difficulty in the normal "expectation." The discrepancy in anticipation is closely linked to the argument that "much of what appears in this section was undoubtedly influenced by Paul's desire to meet the arguments of the Judaizers and outclass them on their own grounds" (ibid). If the "influencers" are not Judaizers, Paul's argument is less directly polemical in force than primarily scriptural in function (see verses 1-5). His assertions take the form of proof-texts for an independent affirmation, rather than a refutation of the Judaizers' claims. At dispute here is not that the fact that the influencers are arguing for circumcision as the symbol of conversion but the store which is put by this demand. To the extent that the Galatians' persuaders are deemed to be people insistent on Torah-observance, arguments regarding "justification by faith" will appear to constitute a logical component. If, on the other hand, the controversy is over Jewish status, promoted by those with a stake in social convention, Paul will rather focus attention on issues of identity. For the influencers' identity, see Introduction, **Occasion and circumstances**; for the structure of Galatians, see Introduction, **Form**; **Argument**; for the centrality of Scripture for Paul, see **Theological pointers**, 1:13f, 2:15-21, 3:1ff, 4:1-7, 21-31, and verses 1-5, 10ff.

[74] His concern, in other words, is to demonstrate that as "sons of the promise," having found access to God's Kingdom through Jesus' death and resurrection, gentile believers do not need to become "sons of the covenant." If they are now seeking also to become "sons of Abraham" through circumcision/conversion, this

The adverb καθὼς (kathōs), in combination with γέγραπται (gegraptai – "it is written"), frequently serves in the New Testament as a formula introducing a scriptural prooftext – "as it is written."[75] While its absolute occurrence (lacking the verb) is a New Testament hapax, it evidently precedes Paul's citation of Genesis 15:6. More recent attempts to read it as an "*exemplum* reference" have led to such translations as "consider Abraham," "take Abraham, for example" (cf. Longenecker, Galatians: 112).[76] While this approach ameliorates the ostensible rupture between verses 1-5 and 6-14, where such a break is conspicuous for its absence, such an understanding mitigates the force of Paul's appeal precisely to Abraham. The latter is not merely exemplary; he is the model *par excellence*.[77]

Verse 7: Paul now tells his disciples precisely how he reads Genesis 15:6 – in this particular context, in its peculiar circumstance, and for his

---

status can only represent – for them – a social standing which, in representing "fleshly" standards, returns them to the bondage of "the elemental things of the world" under the dominion of Belial (see Introduction, **Argument** and 4:1f). For a possible anticipation of Abraham in verses 1-5, see n16.

[75] Cf. Mt. 26:24; Mk. 1:2, 14:21; Lk. 2:23; Acts 15:15; Rom. 1:17, 3:10, 4:17, 8:36. The Hebrew/Aramaic equivalents are numerous: שנאמר [כמה] ([ke-ma] she-nēamar); דכתיב (di-khtiv), etc.

[76] It is a measure, yet again, of Christian commentators' contempt for most forms of Judaism that has led them to see in Paul's argumentation "une fantaisie ingénieuse" (cf. Betz, Galatians: 137, the latter phrase belonging to Loisy). Unfortunately, these grounds are in reality more the attributable cause for the "highly arbitrary" exegetical mode perceived than the modern historical-critical tradition itself. Although the latter certainly has not been predisposed towards Jewish hermeneutical traditions, the discontent and dismissal of these far precedes contemporary interpretative systems. Significantly, a degree of rapprochement has been achieved of late in the intertextual approach reflected within literary criticism; cf. Handelman; Boyarin, Intertexuality. While Hays' *Echoes* might have been expected to favour such a tack, he ultimately takes his *opus magnum* in another direction.

[77] "But it is to be doubted that Paul uses Abraham only as an example. His emphasis on the sons of Abraham (vss. 7, 29) and the blessing of Abraham (vs. 14) suggests that Abraham, rather than being merely an example of justification by faith, is part of a salvific faith-process which works for the salvation of the Gentiles. This point is made clearer in Romans 4 where Abraham is said to be an heir of the cosmos (vs. 13) and a father of many nations (vs. 17). In Gal. 3:8 ('In thee will all the nations be blessed') and 3:14 ('that the blessing of Abraham might come unto the Gentiles') the same idea is present. The idea is that the Gentiles are blessed not simply like Abraham but because of Abraham ... [The quotation of Gen. 15:6] serves as a transitional statement with the primary function of giving an answer in the form of an analogy to the question stated in vs. 5 ... [Its] point is: As God 'supplies' and 'works' to and among the Galatians, so he 'reckoned' to Abraham" (Howard, Crisis: 54-55).

present purpose.[78] Abraham serves as the "faithful forefather" of those who exhibit a similar faithfulness to God – through Jesus.[79] The point is carefully played up, in the "punning" and word-play so much part and parcel of midrashic exegesis (cf. Braude and Kapstein: 585-93). What is at stake is the status – and thus the definition – of "Abraham's sons."[80]

The phrase is a well-known and characteristic self-epithet in Jewish texts.[81] Paul appeals to Genesis 15:6 in its regard because the latter verse clearly designates the source of Abraham's standing with God: It is God who "imputes" righteousness to human beings.[82] To the extent that

---

[78] The inferential particle ἄρα (ara) defines this statement as a consequence deriving logically from the preceding quote (cf. Burton: 155).

[79] Not only does Paul wish the Galatians to "see their experience prefigured in the story of Abraham; in both cases the blessing of God comes as sheer grace" (Hays, Galatians: 255), but Abraham also functions as the *scriptural warrant* for gentile inclusion in God's people. This is the force of the "foreseeing" and "preaching beforehand" which Paul attributes to Scripture in verse 8. The fact that the "sons of Abraham" argument is two-edged gives Paul equal leverage with the influencers' insistence on circumcision: Just as they may cite conversion as an incontrovertible demand, so too, and on the same basis, Paul can claim intention, without which the physical act is voided of its validity (see 2:1-10, 15-21).

[80] "The whole question at issue between Paul and his opponents is clearly: to whom do the promises really belong? Who are the children of Abraham? Paul argues this point from scripture not because he is appealing to an authority which stands outside the argument but because scripture is where the promises, the foundations of the covenant whose terms are the point at issue, are to be found" (Wright: Climax: 144). (On a minor note, while it is not automatically obvious that Paul here is addressing his opponents, since he may just as well be clarifying the issue for his disciples, the point is ultimately moot, since the matter at hand remains constant: What is the true definition of the "sons of Abraham"? It should also be remarked that the present reading of Galatians does not follow Wright's and Dunn's boundary-marker theory of "doing the things that mark Israel out" [cf. ibid: 150].) For "those who are of faith," Paul's unique coinage, see below; for Wright, see also below (n120).

[81] Cf. Isa. 51:2, [63:16]; Mt. 3:9; Lk. 1:73, 3:8; Jn. 8:39, 53; Acts 7:2; Rom. 4:12f; Jas. 2:21; Jub. 15:30; Ps.Sol. 18:3; Tanh.Ki tetzei 5; Ex.R. 3:16; PRK 3:2; ARNᵃ 4:1; BK 8:6; BM 7:1; Pes. 87a (see also below [n85]).

[82] The force of the verb (-ל חשב [chashav le-]/λογίζομαι [logizomai]) derives from the fact that, whether it takes an item or a person as its object, it represents God's prerogative in prescribing a value to something, whether the latter holds such esteem naturally or not. Here, it supplements the ἐπιχορηγῶν (epichorēgōn – "provide richly") and ἐνεργῶν (energōn – "working") in verse 5, the Spirit and miracles embodying in the Galatians' lives the power which God also displayed in relation to Abraham (see above). Howard argues that "In Paul's mind 'to reckon' (λογίζεσθαι), used in the absolute state as in Gen. 15:6, apparently means 'to reckon according to grace' (λογίζεσθαι κατὰ χάριν), his reasoning being that Scripture would have stated explicitly 'to reckon according to debt' (λογίζεσθαι κατὰ ὀφείλημα) if obligation had been involved. Paul considered λογίζεσθαι by itself to

Scripture has "preached the gospel beforehand to Abraham (προευηγγελίσατο τῷ 'Αβραάμ)" (verse 8), the καθώς (kathōs) posits a direct analogy between "our father Abraham" and the Galatians' "sonship" (cf. Hays, Echoes: 108) (see verses 26-29).[83]

This strategy is familiar from the declarations of John the Baptist (cf. Mt. 3:9//), Jesus (cf. Jn. 8:39), and numerous rabbinic texts: "[In commenting on God's command to remember Amalek], R. Tanhum bar Hanila'i began his discourse by citing the following verse: *Your acts of remembering [Amalek, followed by repentance for your sins] will be like 'ashes'; but when you deserve visitation [for sin], visitation in 'clay' shall be your punishment* (Job 13:12). The Holy One said to Israel: My children, I inscribed in Torah two references to Amalek that you are to remember – heed them: *Thou shalt blot out the remembrance of Amalek* (Dt. 25:19); *I will entirely blot out the remembrance of Amalek* (Ex. 17:4). But let *your acts of remembering [be followed by repentance for your sins so that you] will be like 'ashes'* – that is, if through repentance you gain merit, you will be true children of Abraham who spoke of himself as 'ashes,' saying 'I am . . . but dust and ashes' (Gen. 18:27)"[84] (PRK 3:2) (see 5:19f).[85]

---

be equivalent to 'give freely' (χαρίζεσθαι) . . . Abraham had righteousness *reckoned* to him and this means that it was by grace" (Crisis: 56).

[83] The Spirit serves as a further link in the fact that it functions as the spokesperson of Scripture, as it were – the medium through whom God converses with wo/men: "And it came about that when the Spirit rested upon them, they prophesied ויהי כנוח עליהם הרוח ויתנבאו" (Num. 11:25). "For no prophecy was ever made by an act of human will, but men moved by the Holy Spirit spoke from God (οὐ γὰρ θελήματι ἀνθρώπου ἠνέχθη προφητεία ποτέ, ἀλλὰ ὑπὸ πνεύματος ἁγίου φερόμενοι ἐλάλησαν ἀπὸ θεοῦ ἄνθρωποι)" (2 Pet. 1:21) (cf. Num. 24:2; 1 Sam. 10:10; Isa. 40:5, 58:14; Jer. 1:2, 9, 2:1, 5:14, 23:16ff; Ezek. 1:3; Hos. 1:1; Joel 1:1; Amos 3:7-8; Lk. 1:70; Mk. 12:36; Acts 1:16, 3:18, 21f, 4:25, 28:25; Eph. 3:5; 1 Tim. 4:1; Heb. 1:1; 2 Pet. 3:2; Wis.Sol. 11:1; Sir. 36:14-16; 1QS 8:16; CD-A 2:12-13; 1QHᵃ 6:25; Gen.R. 85:2; Lev.R. 1:3; Cant.R. 2.1.3; Pes.Rab. 35:1; PRE 32) (cf. Le Cornu and Shulam: 38-39, [250], 1521).

[84] ר' תנחום בר' חנילאי פתח: זכרוניכם משלי אפר לגבי חומר גביכם. אמר הקדוש ברוך הוא לישראל: בניי אותן שתי זכירונות שהכתבתי לכם בתורה היו זהירין בהן: תמחה את זכר עמלק ; כי מחה אמחה את זכר עמלק. משלי אפר, משולי באפר: אם זכיתם הרי אתם בניו של אברהם, אותו שהמשיל את עצמו באפר: ואנכי עפר ואפר.

[85] Cf. Romans 2, 9:6-29; 4 Macc. 9:21, 18:23; Philo, *Virt*. 195-97; Tanh.Ki teztei 5; Ex.R. 46:4-5; Yalk.Dt. 938; Yalk.Job 906; PA 5:19 (see 2:15-21, 4:21-31, and verses 26-29). Does Rom. 9:6ff possibly reflect the influence of the "clay [חומר]" in Job 13:12? (see 4:1-7, 21-31 [n211]). The imagery of dust and clay (cf. Gen. 3:19) is common currency in the Qumran scrolls, together with an emphasis on God's saving grace: "You have opened the ear of dust . . . [. . . to an]nounce from his knowledge to a creature, to mediate these matters to dust such as me. You have opened a spr[ing] to rebuke the path of the fashioned from clay, the guilt of the one born of woman according to his deeds, to open the sp[rin]g of your truth to the creature whom you have supported with your power, to [be,] according to your truth, a herald [. . .] of

Verse 8: While the issue of conduct and identity is obviously an internal Jewish affair, Paul is concerned here not so much with deciding an in-house debate but with applying the principles on which it is conducted also with respect to *Gentiles*.[86] He consequently appeals once again to Scripture to provide proof of his proposition. The δὲ (de) here may serve in this respect as an explicative conjunctive (cf. BAGD: 171), the quotation demonstrating the grounds on which the "sons of Abraham" are to be properly understood.[87]

If by "Scripture (ἡ γραφή)" a particular passage is frequently understood to be meant (cf. Rom. 9:17, 10:11, 11:2), the reference here is evidently to Genesis 15:6. This notwithstanding, the "personification" of

---

your goodness, to proclaim to the poor the abundance of your compassion, [. . .] . . . from the spring [. . . the bro]ken of spirit, and the mourning to everlasting joy ותגל אוזן עפר . . . [לה]שמיע ליצר מבינתו ולמליץ באלה לעפר כמוני ותפתח מק[ור] להוכיח ליצר חמר דרכו ואשמות ילוד אשה כמעשיו ולפתח מ[ן]קו[ר] אמתכה ליצר אשר סמכתה בעוזכה ל[ה]יות] כאמתכה מבשר [. . .] טובכה לבשר עוים לרוב רחמיכה [. . .] . . . ממקור [. . .] . . . דכ]אי רוח ואבלים לשמחת עולם (1QHᵃ 23:4, 11-15) (cf. 1QS 11:21-22; 1QHᵃ 9:21-23, 11:23-25, 12:29-35, 19:11-12, 20:24-35, 21:6-16, 22:7-11; 4Q511 ff28+29:3-4; Philo, *Quis Rerum* 57f; PA 3:1) (see 2:15-21 and 4:1-7). For Isa. 61:1-3, see 1:1f, 4:1f, and verses 1f, 26-29; for "born of a woman," see 4:1-7.

[86] "Paul wants to argue that Judaism, rightly understood, claims its relation to Abraham not only by virtue of physical descent from him (*kata sarka*) but equally by virtue of sharing his trust in the God who made the promises. In that sense, the gospel, which invites all people, including Gentiles, into right relation with God through faith, confirms the Law; it is consistent with the real substance of the Law's teaching. This is the proposition that Paul sets out to demonstrate through his exposition of Genesis" (Hays, Echoes: 54-55). Hays' following clarification also has rare rivals: "This reading of the text will appear odd only if we are committed to the presupposition that Paul is expounding a message that stands in antithetical relation to Judaism. If we do not hold such a view a priori, it will be clear that Paul means precisely what he says: the gospel confirms the Torah ... Paul, speaking from *within* the Jewish tradition, contends that the Torah itself provides the warrant for a more inclusive theology that affirms that the one God is God of Gentiles as well as Jews and that Abraham is the forefather of more than those who happen to be his physical descendants" (ibid: 55; original emphasis) (cf. Howard, Crisis: 46-65). For God's unity, see verses 19f.

[87] As Hays points out, "The odd expression *hoi ek pisteōs* (literally, 'those out of faith') is a *Vorklang* of Hab. 2:4, *ho dikaios ek pisteōs zēsetai* (the righteous one shall live by faith), not yet cited in the discussion, but soon to appear in 3:11" (Echoes: 108) (see below). (We have, in fact, suggested the possible presentiment of the verse in 2:15-21 [see nn267, 271], as well as, potentially, in 1:10 [see 1:6-10 (n163)].) The phrase is additionally set in some contrast to οἱ ἐκ περιτομῆς (hoi ek peritomēs – "those of the circumcision") (cf. 2:12), although not in as theologically a dichotomous manner as is usually maintained. For ὅσοι ἐξ ἔργων νόμου (hosoi ex ergōn nomou – "those who are from works of the Torah"), see verses 10-14.

Scripture is common in contemporary sources,[88] and scriptural unity – the availability of all texts to interpret one another – is an *a priori* Jewish exegetical assumption (see 4:21-31).[89] While the Greek προευαγγελίζομαι (proeuangelizomai) is a New Testament hapax, Philo's use of the verb indicates its "typological" tendencies, both of his examples coming from nature: "Do you not often see how the fledgling, before it actually [s]oars its way in the air, likes to flutter or shake its wings, thus *giving a welcome promise* of ability to fly hereafter?"[90] (*Mut.Nom.* 158). "These barriers [between darkness and light] are evening and dawn. The latter, gently restraining the darkness, *anticipates* the sunrise *with the glad tidings* of its approach"[91] (*Opif.Mun.* 34).

To the extent that the gospel – "promised beforehand through His prophets in the holy Scriptures" – concerns God's son, "born of the seed of David according to the flesh, who was declared with power *to be* the Son of God by the resurrection from the dead, according to the Spirit of holiness, Jesus the Messiah, our Lord"[92] (Rom. 1:1-4), Jesus himself could say: "Your father Abraham rejoiced to see my day; and he saw *it*, and was glad (᾿Αβραὰμ ὁ πατὴρ ὑμῶν ἠγαλλιάσατο ἵνα ἴδῃ τὴν ἡμέραν τὴν ἐμήν, καὶ εἶδεν καὶ ἐχάρη)" (Jn. 8:26).[93] In this sense, the phrase indicates that God's promise to Abraham constitutes the blessing of the Messiah to the Gentiles

---

[88] Cf. Gen.R. 96:2, 3; Lev.R. 7:3, 9:6; PA 3:7, 8; Ber. 13a, 15a; RH 10a. While the language is temporal it appears not to be contrastive here, the latter element applying only in relation to the Torah. Paul's point is that, right from the beginning, God purposed to call the Gentiles by His name, providing the means through Abraham's "seed" (see verses 15-18). For Paul's understanding of the Torah's role and function, see verses 10-14, 19f.

[89] Cf. Boyarin, Intertextuality; Handelman: 27-50; Rojtman. This is reflected in the Talmud adage "there is no early and late in the Torah אין מוקדם ומאוחר בתורה" (cf. Tanh.Ter. 8; JShek. 25b; JSot. 37a; Pes. 6b) – i.e., chronology is irrelevant in the interpretation of texts. While Paul *is* evidently making a temporal distinction here, the fact that he describes Abraham's knowledge in terms of the "gospel" implies such a scriptural unity as may link the later with the earlier. For the centrality of Scripture for Paul, see Introduction, **Theological pointers**; 1:13f, 2:15-21, 4:1-7, 21-31, and verses 1f, 15f.

[90] ἢ τὸν νεοττὸν οὐχ ὁρᾷς, ὅς, πρὶν ἀέρι ἐπινήχεσθαι, πτερύσσεσθαι καὶ τοὺς ταφοὺς διασείειν φιλεῖ, τὴν ἐλπίδα τοῦ πέτεσθαι δυνήσεσθαι προευαγγελιζόμενος;

[91] οὗτοι δ' εἰσὶν ἑσπέρα τε καὶ πρωΐα, ὧν ἡ μὲν προευαγγελίζεται μέλλοντα ἥλιον ἀνίσχειν, ἠρέμα τὸ σκότος ἀνείργουσα.

[92] ὃ προεπηγγείλατο διὰ τῶν προφητῶν αὐτοῦ ἐν γραφαῖς ἁγίαις περὶ τοῦ υἱοῦ αὐτοῦ τοῦ γενομένου ἐκ σπέρματος Δαυὶδ κατὰ σάρκα, τοῦ ὁρισθέντος υἱοῦ θεοῦ ἐν δυνάμει κατὰ πνεῦμα ἁγιωσύνης ἐξ ἀναστάσεως νεκρῶν, ᾿Ιησοῦ Χριστοῦ τοῦ κυρίου ἡμῶν.

[93] Cf. "All the prophets prophesied only for the days of the Messiah כל הנביאים כולן לא נתנבאו אלא לימות המשיח" (Ber. 34b) (cf. 1 Pet. 1:10-12; Yalk.Dt. 898; Yalk.Isa. 508; Shab. 63a; San. 99a).

(cf. Rom. 15:29).[94] As Paul later says in Romans, the "righteousness of God is revealed from faithulness to faithfulness; as it is written, 'BUT THE RIGHTEOUS man SHALL LIVE BY FAITHFULNESS' (δικαιοσύνη γὰρ θεοῦ ἐν αὐτῷ ἀποκαλύπτεται ἐκ πίστεως εἰς πίστιν, καθὼς γέγραπται· ὁ δὲ δίκαιος ἐκ πίστεως ζήσεται)" (Rom. 1:17): God proves His faithfulness from before the foundation of the world in planning His salvation for all.[95]

Not surprisingly, Paul prefers the reference to the "nations of the land [גויי הארץ]" in Genesis 18:18 and 26:4 over the alternative "families [משפחת]," given the explicit allusion to the "Gentiles" (גוים; goyim) in the former verses.[96] The direct address to Abraham puts him at the focus, demonstrating that he serves as the source of the scriptural argument. Rather than appealing to a text which also includes Abraham's "seed," however – as he does in verse 16 – Paul appears to make his argument here *via* Genesis 18:18, which speaks of Abraham indirectly (בו; ἐν αὐτῷ – "in him"), to Psalm 72:17 (LXX 71). Psalm 72 is davidic, and hence also messianic: "May his name endure forever; may his name increase as long as the sun *shines*; and let *men* bless themselves by him; let all nations call him blessed יהי שמו לעולם לפני-שמש ינון שמו ויתברכו בו כל-גוים יאשרוהו" (Ps. 72:17) (cf. Rom. 15:29) (see also verses 10f).[97]

---

[94] "Preaching the gospel (εὐαγγελίζω)" is, of course, common New Testament terminology for testimony to Jesus' death and resurrection (cf. [Mk. 16:15]; Lk. 4:18; Rom. 1:15f, 10:15, 15:20; 1 Cor. 1:17; Gal. 1:8-9, 2:2; Rev. 14:6). See 1:6-10.

[95] It is possible that Paul also has "revelation" in mind in the "preaching beforehand of the gospel," the former element being a theme which runs throughout Scripture: "The LORD has made known His salvation; He has revealed His righteousness in the sight of the nations. He has remembered His lovingkindness and His faithfulness to the house of Israel; all the ends of the earth have seen the salvation of our God הודיע ה' ישועתו לעיני הגוים גלה צדקתו : זכר חסדו ואמונתו לבית ישראל ראו כל-אפסי-ארץ את ישועת אלהינו" (Ps. 98:2-3). "The LORD has bared His holy arm in the sight of all the nations; that all the ends of the earth may see the salvation of our God חשף ה' את-זרוע קדשו לעיני כל-הגוים וראו כל-אפסי-ארץ את ישועת אלהינו" (Isa. 52:10) (cf. Hays, Echoes: 36f).

[96] The blessing is repeated throughout Genesis and referred to in other places: cf. 18:18, 26:4, 28:14; Ps. 72:17; Acts 3:25-26. The LXX uniformly renders ἐνευλογηθήσονται (eneulogēthēsontai – future passive) in all five biblical passages, disguising the divergent Hebrew niphal/hitpael constructions. (The niphal occurs in 18:18 and 28:14, the hitpael in 26:4. The distinction between "earth" and "land" is marginal, reflected in the fact that Paul omits the phrase altogether.) The fact that Peter appeals to Abraham's blessing in Acts 3:25-26 to demonstrate *Israel's* status mitigates against the argument that Paul is here countering the influencers' claims for Abraham's circumcision.

[97] "Another comment on *Give the king Thy judgments O God, and Thy righteousness* (Ps. 72:1): here *king* means the King Messiah, of whom it is said *And there shall come forth a shoot out of the stock of Jesse . . . And the spirit of the Lord shall rest upon him . . . And he shall not judge after the sight of his eyes, neither decide after the hearing of his ears;*

Verse 9 succinctly sums up Paul's assertion: Scripture's "foresight" is, within this framework, not merely historical but, as it were, cosmological: Both the Torah and the Messiah are pre-existent, prior to the creation of the world – and instruments of its construction (see 4:1-7).[98] This "foreknowledge" could then also be transmitted to Abraham who, while living post-creation, certainly preceded the Messiah's appearance – not to speak of the Galatians' (re)generation.[99] God's plan from the beginning of creation was to choose a people to carry His name, to witness to Him – and, in the fulness of time, to bless not just those with whom He had made His covenant but all the nations of the world.[100] In his standing as one who

---

but with righteousness shall he judge the poor, and decide with equity for the meek of the land (Isa. 11:1a, 3b-c, 4a) . . . *His name shall endure for ever* (Ps. 72:17) – that is, the king Messiah will never know the taste of death. *Before the sun was, his name existed* (ibid). Seven things existed before the world was created: the throne of glory, the name of the Messiah, Torah, Israel, the Garden of Eden, Gehenna, repentance, and the Temple יהי ... וגו׳ ישי מגזע חוטר ויצא :שנאמר המשיח, מלך זה :תן למלך משפטיך :אחר דבר העולם׃ שנבראה קודם היו דברים שבעה :שמו ינון שמש לפני .מיתה טעם יטעום שלא :לעולם שמו המקדש ובית ותשובה, וגהינם, עדן גן וישראל, ותורה, משיח, ושם כבוד, כסא" (Mid.Ps. 72:3, 6) (cf. Mid.Ps. 93:3; Gen.R. 1:4; Lam.R. 1.16.51; PRK 22:5; PRE 3; TBE p. 160; Tanh.Naso 11; Mid.Prov. 8, 19; San. 98b; Pes. 54a). As the midrashim from Proverbs indicate, those things which were created "before the foundation of the world" are linked through the nature of and role played by Wisdom, a tradition articulated in the New Testament in reference to Jesus (cf. [Lk. 11:49]; Jn. 1:1ff, [8:58], 17:24; 1 Cor. 1:24, 30; Eph. 2:10; Col. 1:15-18; Heb. 9:26; 1 Pet. 1:20) (cf. Schechter: 127f; Schoneveld; Skarsaune: 325-33) (see also nn42, 139, 311f).

[98] Cf. Prov. 8:22ff; Dan. 7:13; Mic. 5:2 (+ LXX); Jn. 1:1f, 8:56-58, 17:5, 24; Eph. 1:4; Col. 1:15f; Sir. 24:9; Targ.Jon. to Mic. 5:1 (2), Zech. 4:7; Lev.R. 24:9; Pes.Rab. 33:6, 36:1; Mid.Ps. 72:6, 90:12, 93:3; DEZ 1:18.

[99] In a certain sense, Paul is presenting Abraham as a prophet (cf. Gen. 20:7; PRE 28). For Paul's later argument regarding the precedence of the promise over the covenant, see verses 15f.

[100] For the Thomist/Scotist debate over God's purpose to send Jesus into the world as determined (or not) by Adam's sin, cf. Soulen: 44-45, 51. Soulen deals marvelously with the mysterious relationship between Jew and Gentile, suggesting that "when the canon's unity [the "Old" and New Testaments together] is grasped in light of God's economies of difference and mutual dependence, the distinction between Israel and the nations cannot be viewed as a mere instrument God employs to overcome conflict with creation, an instrument that becomes obsolete once the conflict is decisively resolved. Rather, the distinction of Israel and the nations, of Jew and of Gentile, is intrinsic to God's overarching purpose and work as Consummator of the world . . . As attested by the Scriptures, God's work as Consummator engages the human family in a historically decisive way in God's election of Israel as a blessing to the nations. The resulting distinction and mutual dependence of Israel is the fundamental form of the economy of consummation through which God initiates, sustains, and ultimately fulfills the one human family's destiny for life with God. So conceived, God's economy of consummation

embodied the faithfulness to be exhibited *par excellence* by his "seed," Abraham represents the forefather of faithfulness to Israel and to the nations alike.[101] It was his trust in God's promise which supported him through the test of losing the very son, whose existence itself was an inconceivable thought, through whom the blessing would come; his trust in God's power to "resurrect" which formed the basis upon which those who were not a nation were called into being (cf. Shulam and Le Cornu: 159ff).[102] In his assurance is the Gentiles' hope fulfilled (cf. Rom. 4:18; 1 Pet. 2:4-10).[103]

---

is essentially constituted as *an economy of mutual blessing* between those who are and who remain different" (pp. 117, 111).

[101] "At the beginning you were the father of Aram; and now you are the father of the whole world בתחלה הרי אתה אב על ארם ועכשיו הרי אתה אב לכול באי העולם (Tos.Ber. 1:15) (cf. Gen. 17:4f; Isa. 51:2; Rom. 4:11f; Sir. 44:19; 2 Bar. 78:4; Tanh.B.Lekh lekha 6; Sif.Dt. 32; Gen.R. 14:6, 39:2, 43:7; Ex.R. 21:8, 23:5; Dt.R. 6:5; Cant.R. 1.3.3; Mid.Ps. 110:1; PRK 23:8; Yalk.Dt. 837; Ber. 13a). Luke portrays Paul himself along the model of Abraham in Acts: "And he said to me, 'Go! For I will send you far away to the Gentiles' (πορεύου, ὅτι ἐγὼ εἰς ἔθνη μακρὰν ἐξαποστελῶ σε)" (Acts 22:21) – the resonances with "Go forth ולך-לך" clearly ringing in the background (cf. Le Cornu and Shulam: 1219) (see also 4:12-20 [nn131, 156, 186] and 5:24-26).

[102] Cf. Hos. 1:9-10, 2:23; Rom. 4:17; Eph. 2:11ff. "The story of Abraham is told as it is told (or, as Paul would say, these things happened to Abraham in the order in which they happened) in order that Abraham might fitly serve as the archetype for Gentile believers as well as Jewish believers. He is said to be the father of both groups not because they are descended from him *kata sarka* [according to the flesh] but because their faith mirrors his and because their destiny is prefigured in him: they are included vicariously in the blessing pronounced by God, a blessing which is specifically said to apply to 'all the nations [panta ta ethnē]'" (Hays, Echoes: 56). (Although Hays rather surprisingly refrains from phrasing "faith" as "faithfulness" here, his own *Faith* indicates that it bears this meaning – or, at least, "trust.") Or, in the words of the midrash: "The Holy One, blessed be He, said to him, 'Abraham, what can I say to you, or what blessing can I bestow upon thee? That thou mayest be perfectly righteous before Me, or that Sarah your wife may be righteous before Me? Thou art righteous and Sarah thy wife is righteous before Me. Or that all the children of thy household may be righteous? They are, indeed, righteous before Me. What blessing, then, can I bestow upon thee? Only that all the progeny that is destined to spring from thee may be like thee.' How do we know this? For so it is written, *'And He said unto him: So shall thy seed be'* (Gen. 15:5) [i.e., as perfect as Abraham himself] אמר לו הקדוש ברוך הוא: אברהם, מה יש לי לומר לך ומה יש לי לברכך? שתהא שלם צדיק לפני או שתהא שרה אשתך צדקת לפני? צדיק אתה, שרה אשתך צדקת לפני. או שיהיו כל בני ביתך צדיקים? צדיקים הם לפני. מה יש לי לברכך אלא כל בנים שעתידים לעמוד ממך יהיו כמותך. מנין שכן כתיב: ויאמר לו כה יהיה זרעך" (Num.R. 2:12).

[103] Cf. "R. Joshua of Siknin said in R. Levi's name: The Holy One, blessed be He, took the words used by the Patriarchs and made them a key for the redemption of their descendants רי יהושע דסכנין בשם רי לוי: נטל הקדוש ברוך הוא שיחתן של אבות ועשאן מפתח לגאולתן של בנים" (Gen.R. 70:6) (cf. Yalk.Isa. 409; Yalk.Zech. 585).

God first displays His faithfulness (a), to Abraham – who responds himself in faithfulness.[104] Through Abraham's seed, the Messiah himself was designated to embody God's continuing faithfulness (b), reflected in Jesus' total obedience to his Father.[105] Through participation in the Messiah's faithfulness (c), the Gentiles are now entering into possession of the blessing promised to them through Scripture, that all the families of the earth would use Abraham as a byword for blessing, Paul understanding this verse as meaning "in him [Abraham/the Messiah] all the nations would receive God's blessing"[106] (see verses 26-29).

---

[104] Here again, no justification exists for rendering τῷ πιστῷ ᾿Αβραάμ (tō pistō Abraham) as "Abraham, the believer" rather "the faithful Abraham" (cf. Hays, Galatians: 256).

[105] This is illustrated not only through Psalm 72 but also in Genesis 22 (which further calls up Isaiah 53). In the latter passage, God's blessing to Abraham is explicitly cited as a reward for his willingness and obedience in "not withholding your son, your only son את-בנך את-יחידך" (Gen. 22:16). In Rom. 8:32, Paul alludes to this in demonstrating how God's faithfulness to Israel cannot be annulled by the objections of others, since "He who did not spare His own son, but delivered him up for us all, how will he not also with him freely give us all things? (ὅς γε τοῦ ἰδίου υἱοῦ οὐκ ἐφείσατο ἀλλὰ ὑπὲρ ἡμῶν πάντων παρέδωκεν αὐτόν, πῶς οὐχὶ καὶ σὺν αὐτῷ τὰ πάντα ἡμῖν χαρίσεται;)" (cf. Hays, Echoes: 61-63; Shulam and Le Cornu: 303-13). In both cases, God's faithfulness is displayed in "resurrecting" the person condemned to die. For the implicitly explicit allusion to Isaiah 53 through the "seed" in verse 16, see verses 15-18; for reflections of the akedah in verses 10-14, cf. Bruce, Galatians: 167.

[106] Although the LXX disguises the passive niphal and reflexive hitpael form of the Hebrew, the former may emphasise God's initiative, the latter the Gentiles' taking hold of the initiative extended to them in the Messiah. It is rather disingenuous to claim that Paul has reinterpreted the text to indicate a blessing given to and for Abraham's seed, when Gen. 28:4 itself speaks of God giving "the blessing of Abraham ברכת אברהם" to Jacob and his descendants – with specific reference to the land (see verses 15-18 and below). For Hab. 2:4 – on which Jesus' faithfulness is predicated, and that of the Gentiles' also in turn – see 4:1-7 and verses 10-14, 26-29; for the identification of the blessing with receipt of the Spirit, see verses 10-14, 26-29. The blessing is life (cf. Dt. 30:19) – in the specific case of the Gentiles, a calling into being from non-existence – and in that sense corresponds to "justification" (see also 5:2-12). Such a reading seems to make far better sense of Paul's argument than the claim that the reason why he "here says 'blessed with . . . Abraham' instead of 'justified' is doubtless due to the fact that he is still using the language of his opponents" (Burton: 162).

Chapter 3

Verses 10-14:
For as many as are of the works of the Law are under a curse; for it is written, "CURSED IS EVERY ONE WHO DOES NOT ABIDE BY ALL THINGS WRITTEN IN THE BOOK OF THE LAW, TO PERFORM THEM." Now that no one is justified by the Law before God is evident; for, "THE RIGHTEOUS MAN SHALL LIVE BY FAITH." However, the Law is not of faith; on the contrary, "HE WHO PRACTICES THEM SHALL LIVE BY THEM." The Messiah redeemed us from the curse of the Law, having become a curse for us – for it is written, "CURSED IS EVERY ONE WHO HANGS ON A TREE" – in order that in the Messiah Jesus the blessing of Abraham might come to the Gentiles, so that we might receive the promise of the Spirit through faith.

At this point, Paul's address shifts its focus from his disciples to those who are "troubling" them (cf. 1:7, 5:12).[107] As he has already invoked upon the influencers (cf. 1:9), anyone preaching contrary to Paul's gospel – Abraham's blessing to the Gentiles through his seed – is calling a curse upon him/herself. The blessing conveyed through Abraham is logically contrasted with a potential curse, the ὅσοι (hosoi - "as many as") who are "of Torah works (ἐξ ἔργων νόμου)" standing opposite the οὗτοι (houtoi - "those [of faithfulness]") of verse 7.[108] The former phrase denotes those who have committed themselves to God's covenant: "Then he [Moses] took the book of the covenant and read *it* in the hearing of the people; and they said, 'All that the LORD has spoken we will do, and we will be obedient [hear]!' ויקח ספר הברית ויקרא באזני העם ויאמרו כל אשר-דבר ה' נעשה ונשמע" (Ex. 24:7). The latter has its rewards (for fulfilment) and its punishments (for violations): "But it shall come about, if you will not obey the LORD your God, to observe to do all His commandments and His statutes which I charge you today, that all these curses shall come upon

---

[107] While commentators recognize that the γάρ (gar - "for") marks a further stage in the argument (cf. Betz, *Galatians*: 144n50), most maintain that this section represents a second proof from Scripture that "those who are not 'men of faith' must be 'men of [the] Torah' (οἱ ἐκ νόμου), and they must be 'under a curse'" – this conclusion already being contained in the *propositio* of 2:15-21 (ibid). The present reading substantially diverges from this interpretation, both with respect to the *propositio* itself (see 2:15-21) and to the present passage. Where it is asserted that the influencers are not themselves believers and are insisting that gentile believers seeking Jewish status must undergo circumcision/conversion (see Introduction, **Occasion and circumstances**), Paul's references to Torah-observance may be perceived as directed primarily towards the influencers. In pointing out the implications of proselytism, Paul is hereby attempting to demonstrate to his disciples the severity of the step which they are contemplating in conversion. For for the epistle as a "halakhic letter" along the lines of 4QMMT, see Introduction, **Form; Argument;** for other indirect addresses to the influencers, see 4:12f, 5:2-12, and 6:1-11.

[108] Although Gen. 12:3 speaks of both blessing and curse, Paul appears to introduce the topic thematically rather than textually. The curse related to Abraham lacks any direct connection to Torah-observance.

you and overtake you -כל-את לעשות לשמֹר אלהיך י׳ בקול תשמע לא-אם והיה
(Dt. "מצותיו וחֻקֹתיו אשר אנכי מצוך היום ובאו עליך כל-הקללות האלה והשיגוך
28:15).[109]

Paul pertinently brings a passage which directly invokes the curse upon transgression of the covenant, conflated from Deuteronomy 27:26 and 30:10, the latter elaborating the "this law התורה-הזאת" of the former as "the book of the law התורה הזה ספר."[110] Those who insist on status according to Torah-observance – urging the gentile Galatian believers to join the Jewish community legitimately, thereby also taking upon themselves the "yoke of the Torah and commandments" – are, by that very fact, susceptible to the curses which descend upon breach of commitment (cf. ARN[a] 2:3). Having taken an oath to "do and obey," they are liable to the castigation consequent upon contravention (cf. Yoma 73b) (see 5:2-12). Logically, "those who are of faithfulness" cannot be those who live *solely* on the basis of obedience to the Torah because "in Thy sight no man living is righteous" – and the penalty for transgression precludes God's blessing.[111]

---

[109] A tradition following the disaster of the golden calf proposes that it was this incident which occasioned the writing of the second set of tablets: "Wherever we find '*dibber'*, '*debarim'*, and '*ha'debarim'*, it signifies adjurations and rebukes דבר, "דברים, הדברים - אלות ותוכחות הם (Ex.R. 47:3) – i.e., wherever the biblical text mentions "He spoke," "words," or "the words" it alludes to the second set of the Decalogue, which had to be reinforced by oaths and curses in the event of disobedience, the first tablets having received their authority from the fact that the people had been freed from their inclination to sin (Radal) (cf. Ex.R. 41:5, 42:5; Eccl.R. 1.13.1, 3.10.1; Tanh.Ki tavo 4; Ned. 22b) (see also verses 15-18 [n237]). (For the Torah of the Messiah, see 1:11-12 and 6:1-11.)

[110] ארור אשר לא-יקים את-דברי התורה-הזאת לעשות אותם. LXX: Ἐπικατάρατος πᾶς ἄνθρωπος, ὃς οὐκ ἐμμενεῖ ἐν πᾶσιν τοῖς λόγοις τοῦ νόμου τούτου τοῦ ποιῆσαι αυτούς· (Dt. 27:26). The thought is expressed very clearly in Jer. 11:2-8, where "life" is equated with acceptance as God's people: "Hear the words of this covenant, and speak to the men of Judah and to the inhabitants of Jerusalem; and say to them, 'Thus says the LORD, the God of Israel, "Cursed is the man who does not heed the words of this covenant which I commanded your forefathers in the day that I brought them out of the land of Egypt, from the iron furnace, saying, 'Listen to My voice, and do according to all which I command you; so you shall be My people, and I will be your God'"' שמע את-דברי הברית הזאת ודברתם אל-איש יהודה ועל-ישבי ירושלם: ואמרת אליהם כה-אמר ה׳ אלהי ישראל ארור האיש לא ישמע את-דברי הברית הזאת: אשר צויתי את- אבותיכם ביום הוציאי-אותם מארץ-מצרים מכור הברזל לאמֹר שמעו בקולי ועשיתם אותם ככל אשר- "אצוה אתכם והייתם לי לעם ואנכי אהיה לכם לאלהים (see also 5:24-26).

[111] The meaning is not that "those who observe the Torah are cursed" – like the blessings, the curses are all *conditional* – but that the Torah regulates a system of rewards and punishments whose satisfaction lies outside human capability. The Torah's strength being mitigated by human weakness, and the curse and the blessing being mutually exclusive – the blessing life, the curse death – Torah-observance alone, without the intention which gives it its meaning, cannot bring life

Verse 11: In hinting once again at Psalm 143:2, Paul picks up the same argument as he made to Peter at Antioch in 2:15-21.[112] The associative phrase "works of the Torah" which he employs both there and here is found in 4QMMT, in a text which may shed light on the present passage.[113] In addressing the "en[d] of days, the blessing [and the] curse אחרי[ת] הימים [וה]קללא הברכה" (ff14-17i:6-7), the author appeals to the example of David,

---

even where it is designed to point to it (cf. Jas. 2:24) (see 2:15-21 and verses 19f). Wright's point that the curses apply to the nation as a whole – as the threat of exile presupposes – is well taken, particularly in light of the present claim that Paul's dispute is over obtaining status as part of the Jewish people: "Genesis 15 . . . is one of the great covenantal chapters in the Jewish scriptures, and describes how Israel's God came to make the initial and fundamental covenant with Abraham and his family, his 'seed.' Paul is well aware of this overall context, and is working within it from beginning to end. His use of the Abraham story is fundamental to his theology, not brought in merely for polemical purposes or because Genesis 15 happens to contain, juxtaposed, the ideas of righteousness and faith . . . Paul's use of the 'curse' terminology here belongs exactly with this overall covenantal exposition, since it comes from one of the other great covenantal sections, Deuteronomy 27-8. We are here faced, once again, with echoes of scripture which exegesis will show to be intentional on Paul's part . . . The blessing and curse are not merely 'take-it-or-leave-it' options: Deuteronomy declares that Israel will in fact eventually make the wrong choice, and, as a result, suffer the curse of all curses, that is exile (Deuteronomy 28.15-29.29). But that will not be the end of the story, or of the covenant. Deuteronomy 30 then holds out hope the other side of covenantal failure, a hope of covenantal renewal, of the regathering of the people after exile, of the circumcision of the heart, of the word 'being near you, on your lips and in your heart' (30.1-14). In other words, Deuteronomy 27-30 is all about exile and restoration, *understood as* covenant judgment and covenant renewal" (Climax: 140; original emphasis) (see also nn187f). It is perhaps not surprising that Wright acknowledges a debt to Hays – as does Hays to Wright.

[112] This remark may further reinforce the argument that the reference to "works of the Torah" is to be related to the influencers' rhetoric, and only indirectly to the Galatians themselves (see above). For Paul's rebuke of Peter as central to the structure of Galatians, see Introduction, **Argument**.

[113] A rabbinic midrash on Isaiah 3:11 speaks, in the context of blessings and curses, of a similar distinction to that which Paul later makes between "work" and "fruit": "You find that the blessing bears fruit and that the curse does not bear fruit, as is said Woe unto the wicked! It shall be ill with him; for the work of his hands shall be done to him (Isa. 3:11). Note that the verse does not say "fruit of his hands" but work of his hands, because the curse does not bear fruit את מוצא את הברכה עושה פירות והקללה אינה עושה פירות, שנאמר: אוי לרשע רע כי גמול ידיו ישיב לו. יכפרי׳ אינו אומר אלא ״כגמולי׳ - ללמדך שאין עושה פירות (Mid.Ps. 118:2). The idea of "bearing fruit" appears to be related here to the "reward" for one's actions which one receives already in this world. The point is thus made that the wicked are *not* punished here and now but only receive full recompense for their iniquities in the world to come. In contrast, good deeds are remunerated both here and in the world to come (see 5:19-23).

"a man of the pious ones דויד שהיא איש חסדים" who was "freed from many afflictions and was forgiven לו ונסלוח רבות מצרות נ]צל[" (ff14-17ii:1-2).[114]

In his psalms, David declares that his forgiveness has come directly from God, rejoicing in the blessing of imputed righteousness: "How blessed is he whose transgression is forgiven, whose sin is covered! How blessed is the man to whom the LORD does not impute iniquity - אשרי נשוי פשע כסוי חטאה: אשרי אדם לא יחש̇ב ה' לו עון" (Ps. 32:1-2) (cf. Rom. 4:6-8).[115] If and when 4QMMT's addressees "turn to him with all your heart [and with al]l [your] soul [at the en]d [of time] ושבתה אלו בכל לבבך]ובכ[ל נפשך[באחרי]ת [העת]" (ff14-17i:7-8), declares its author, like David "it shall be reckoned to you as justice when you do what is upright and good before him {God} ונחשבה לך לצדקה בעשותך הישר והטוב לפנו" (ff14-17ii:7) (cf. 1QS 3:1).[116] Here, the themes of repentance, love, and the "yoke of the Kingdom" are conjoined (cf. 4Q504 ff1-2ii:13-16) (see verses 19-20).[117]

Having noted the prerequisite of repentance for joining the community, Qumran commentators have suggested that the meaning to be attributed to the phrase "works of the Torah מעשי התורה" in 4QMMT is that of "the [particular] interpretation of the Law which the men of holy perfection live by" (CD-B 20:6-7) (cf. Abegg, 4QMMT: 144). In other words, "Paul was reflecting a theology [in 4QMMT] that was established on 'an

---

[114] The allusion appears to be based on a complex of texts which link David with God's lovingkindness (חסד; chesed), perhaps most specifically Isa. 55:3 (cf. 2 Sam. 22:51; 1 Kings 3:6, 8:23-24; Ps. 18:50, 52:8, 59:17, 89:49, Isa. 16:5).

[115] The blessing is immediately linked with the reckoning also here. God's lovingkindness is likewise also an expression of His faithfulness and righteousness (cf. Ps. 36:5-9, 40:10, 88:11, 89:24, 33, 49, 92:2, 98:3, 100:5).

[116] In conjunction with the clause of the final verse – "for your good and the good of Israel לטוב לך ולישראל" – the thought seems to be influenced by Jer. 32:39 (36-44): "I will give them one heart and one way, that they may fear Me always, for their own good, and for *the good of* their children after them ונתתי להם לב אחד ודרך אחד ליראה אותי כל-הימים לטוב להם ולבניהם אחריהם" (cf. Isa. 44:3; Acts 2:39). The Qumran community evidently saw itself as living in the time of the "new covenant," which its own members embodied and performed (cf. CD-A 6:19, 8:21; CD-B 20:12) (see 6:12-16 [verse 15]). For Galatians as a "halakhic letter" along the lines of 4QMMT, see Introduction, Form; **Argument**.

[117] The text of Gen. 18:19 – immediately following God's confirmation of His oath/blessing – plainly states the way in which the latter will be fulfilled: "For I have chosen him [Abraham], in order that he may command his children [sons] and his household after him to keep the way of the LORD **by doing righteousness and justice**; in order that the LORD may bring upon Abraham what he has spoken about him כי ידעתיו למען אשר יצוה את-בניו ואת-ביתו אחריו ושמרו דרך ה' לעשות צדקה ומשפט למען הביא ה' על-אברהם את אשר-דבר עליו." This may, in fact, constitute a prooftext for the "sons of Abraham" motif, intimately linked as it is with righteousness and God's working. For the link between God's sovereignty and His unity, see verses 19-20; for love as the fulfilment of the Torah, see 5:13-18; for the Kingdom, see 5:2ff.

unconditional commitment to maintain Israel's distinctiveness, to prevent the purity of its covenant set-apartness to God from being adulterated or defiled,' and that this zeal was 'directed not only against the Gentile but against the fellow Jew'" (ibid: 147).[118]

Rather than extrapolate "ethnic markers" from this exegesis – "Paul was not likely reacting against a Judaism that argued that one earned final salvation as a result of works, but rather a Judaism that saw in the law and its interpretation Israel's distinctiveness before God" (ibid: 147) – we are inclined to read the text in the framework of "Torah-study" and "piety," an issue which directly relates to "hypocrisy" (see 2:15-21). The "works of the Torah" in this sense represent the former (Torah-study) – which, to be of value, need to be accompanied by the latter (piety), the keys to the "inner court" of knowledge being matched by those to the "outer court" of the fear of heaven and intention: "Every man who possesses learning without the fear of heaven is like a treasurer who is entrusted with the inner keys but not with the outer: how is he to enter? כל אדם שיש בו תורה ואין בו יראת שמים דומה לגזבר שמסרו לו מפתחות הפנימיות ומפתחות החיצוניות לא מסרו לו. בהי עייל?" (Shab. 31b).[119] Knowledge of the Torah without the intention of putting it into practice – or, even more fundamentally, without the "intention" which goes beyond observance of the law, itself right and good, in order to do what is right and good in the capacity given by the Spirit – is ineffective (see 2:15-21, 5:13f, and 6:1f).[120]

---

[118] "Paul's opponents were prepared to prevent the law and their understanding of it from being defiled by the hands of either Jew or gentile. Thus they were determined to see that the believing gentiles also committed to issues which they understood as indicative of covenant standing, whereas Paul was equally determined to underscore only a knowledge of and faith in God; a position on which in his estimation – although certainly radical – both parties should have been able to agree" (Abegg, 4QMMT: 147). Abegg acknowledges his debt to Dunn (reflected in the quotations), both writers relying heavily on Sanders' concept of "covenantal nomism." While our reading of Galatians does not perceive the issues discussed to revolve around "identity/ethnic markers," we do apprehend Paul's preoccupation to be with the understanding of the "sons of Abraham" as those who "do his deeds" – an attitude which, by definition, opens up membership as "sons of the promise" to those upon whom God bestows His Spirit through Jesus' death and resurrection. For the "Israel of God" in this respect, see 6:12-16; for Abegg's reading of 4QMMT and for the present understanding of Galatians as a "halakhic letter" along the lines of the Scroll, see, Introduction, **Form**; **Argument**; for non-ethnic markers also in Antioch, see 2:11-14; for the "tutor" as custodial guardian until the minor's "release" from restraints, rather than as warden against contamination, see verses 21-25.

[119] For the context of this saying, see 2:15-21.

[120] Deuteronomy 30 provides in itself the language upon which Paul later builds in Romans 2, reflecting the hypocrisy between being called as Israel and failing to act as God's people: "So it shall become when all of these things have come upon you,

Paul presents Habakkuk 2:4 – well known also from Pesher Habakkuk – as his prooftext here precisely because it apportions the "righteousness" posited to Abraham in terms of faithfulness.[121] The phrase is most suitable, because of its textual ambiguity (cf. Hays, Faith: 132-41, and for the following discussion). The masoretic text runs: וצדיק באמונתו יחיה – which may signify either that "the righteous [one] shall live by H/his faithfulness"[122] or that "the one-who-is-righteous-by-H/his-faithfulness shall live."[123] The Hebrew does not determine whether the referent of "his" is that of the righteous (one) or of God, both being grammatical and

---

the blessing and the curse which I have set before you ... and you return to the LORD your God and obey Him with all your heart and soul [cf. Dt. 6:5] according to all that I command you today, you and your sons ... the LORD your God will circumcise your heart and the heart of your descendants, to love the LORD your God with all of your heart and with all of your soul, in order that you may live והיה כי-יבאו עליך כל-הדברים האלה הברכה והקללה אשר נתתי לפניך ... ושבת עד-ה' אלהיך ושמעת בקלו ככל אשר-אנכי מצוך היום אתה ובניך בכל-לבבך ובכל-נפשך ... ומל ה' אלהיך את-לבבך ואת-לבב זרעך לאהבה את ה' אלהיך בכל-לבבך ובכל-נפשך למען חייך" (Dt. 30:1-2, 6). Despite Wright's insights, we suggest that this is the sense in which Paul is employing "covenant theology" in Galatians – rather than "the acting out by Israel of the primeval sin of Adam, coming to its full flowering in 'national righteousness', the meta-sin against which the gospel of the cross struck with its scandalous force, and resulting in Israel's rejection of that gospel" (Climax: 261). Precisely because Paul's "critique" is "based on Torah, Prophets, and Psalms" (ibid: 262) it functions in the prophetic tradition of practice informed by intent. (For Romans 2, see 2:15-21, 5:13-18 [nn145, 163], 6:1-11, and verses 6-9 [n80].)

[121] As Keener notes, in appealing to Gen. 15:6 and Hab. 2:4 "Paul ... has selected the only two texts in the entire Old Testament that speak of both righteousness and faith together" (p. 526). For πίστις (pistis) as "faithfulness" and for the possible anticipation of Hab. 2:4 in chapter 2, see 2:15-21 (nn267, 271).

[122] Cf. 1QpHab 7:17-8:3: "[But the righteous man will live because of their [*sic*] loyalty to him.] Its interpretation concerns all observing the Law in the House of Judah, whom God will free from the house of judgment on account of their toil and of their loyalty to the Teacher of Righteousness [וצדיק באמונתו יחיה] פשרו על כול עושי התורה בבית יהודה אשר יצילם אל מבית המשפט בעבור עמלם ואמנתם במורה הצדק" (The translation here is unfortunate, apparently influenced by the fact that the following exegesis refers the "loyalty" [= faithfulness] to "all," in the plural. The text, notwithstanding, is in the singular. The addition "to him," on the other hand, has no textual justification.) The implication here is clearly that "life" is equivalent to release from the "house of judgment."

[123] As has been well recognised, "life" represents an eschatological category, equivalent to "the world to come" (cf. Lk. 18:18; Targ.Onk./Ps.-Jon. to Lev. 18:5; Pes. 113a) (see verses 26-29). The fact that Paul uses the verb as a virtual synonym for δικαιοῦται (dikaioutai – "justified") both here and in verse 21b strongly suggests that "faithfulness" in fact adverbially modifies the verb and not the noun (as an adjective). As Hays comments, "the meaning of this statement is substantially identical to the affirmation that 'the one who is righteous [= justified]' by faith shall live" (Faith: 133-34). For justification, see 2:15-21.

"theological" possibilities. The majority of LXX manuscripts, in addition to interpreting the difficult initial clauses of the verse, clarify this issue by replacing "his faithfulness" with "My faithfulness (ἐκ πίστεώς μου)": "The righteous one shall live by My faithfulness."[124] A third tradition is reflected in two LXX texts and in Hebrews 10:38: "But My righteous one shall live by faith (ὁ δὲ δίκαιός μου ἐκ πίστεως ζήτεσαι)."[125]

Paul – both here and in Romans 1:17 – chooses a text which provides a place for all the potential possibilities: "The righteous one shall live by (God's/the Messiah's/the believer's own) faithfulness (ὁ δίκαιος ἐκ πίστεως ζήσεται)."[126]

While the reference to "the righteous one" has traditionally been regarded as carrying generic significance – anyone who is righteous shall live by faithfulness – ὁ δίκαιος (ho dikaios) is also patently a messianic title (cf. Longenecker, Christology: 46-47; Hays, Righteous).[127] This is corroborated by the LXX text of Habakkuk itself, wherein the (masculine) object (αὐτόν; auton – lit.: "him") awaited for in its delay in 3b lacks a grammatical correspondence with the (feminine) "vision (ὅρασις)." In like fashion, the participle ἐρχόμενος (erchomenos – "coming") is also masculine (cf. Heb. 10:37: ὁ ἐρχόμενος). The rendering of 4a – which interprets הנה עפלה לא-ישרה נפשו בו ("behold, as for the proud one, his soul

---

[124] No theological assumptions are present here, merely an orthographical confusion between ׳ and ׳ – the former (yod) signifying the first person and the latter (vav) the third person possessive suffix.

[125] This reading possibly arises from a wish to clarify personal in contrast to divine faithfulness – both of which may be derived from the Hebrew; or to emphasise the messianic significance of the personage (cf. Hays, Faith: 139). Targum Jonatan reads: צדיקיא על קושטהון יתקימון ("the righteous will be preserved on [the basis of] his truth").

[126] For God's faithfulness, see 2:15-21 (footnotes) and above (n105). While the Hebrew אמונה (emuna) certainly applies to God's steadfast commitment to His covenant and to His promises, such an attribute is not an exclusively divine property. Thus both the Hebrew and the Greek (πίστις; pistis) describe with equal aptness both God's faithfulness to His people and their trusting and obedient response (cf. Hays, Faith: 139-40).

[127] Cf. 2 Sam. 23:3; Isa. 9:7, 11:4, 16:5, 53:11; Jer. 23:6; Zech. 9:9; Mt. 27:19; Lk. 23:47; Acts 3:14, 7:52, 22:14; Jas. 5:6; 1 Pet. 3:18; 1 Jn. 2:1; 1 En. 38:2f, 46:3f, 48:1-50:5; 53:6; Ps.Sol. 17:26ff, 18:7-8; Odes Sol. 8:5; Test.Jud. 24:1f; 1QIsaᵃ 1:11, 51:5; 4Q252 5:3f; Targ. to Jer. 23:5, 33:15; Num.R. 18:21; Lam.R. 1.16.51; Mid.Ps. 21:2; Tanh.Kor. 12. For "Joseph the righteous" (as a messianic prototype), cf. Gen.R. 93:7, 11; Num.R. 14:3, 6; Tanh.Vayetzei 7; ARNᵃ 16:2; Yoma 35b; Mak. 23a (cf. Le Cornu and Shulam: 200-1, 1214); for the Teacher of Righteousness as a messianic figure, cf. Dupont-Sommer: 358-67; Flusser, Judaism: 93-99; for Melchizedek, see 1:1f; for the so-called Self-Glorification Hymn, cf. Knohl.

is not right within him") as "if he draws back,[128] my soul will have no pleasure in him" (cf. Isa. 42:1, 53:10) – further suggests that the participle signifies "a Coming One."[129]

This reading leaves all the possible options open. Underlying them all is God's faithfulness to His promises, His oaths, His covenants – to all concerned (cf. Ps. 105:8f).[130] The means by which God's blessing is conveyed is the faithfulness of His Messiah – the Righteous One who died, the just for the unjust, in order to bring wo/men to God (cf. 1 Pet. 3:18).[131] Finally, the epithet "out of faithfulness (ἐκ πίστεως)" – which appears to function as a "theological abbreviation" (cf. Betz, Galatians: 27-28) – may form the basis on which Paul coins the phrase οἱ ἐκ πίστεως (hoi ek pisteōs – "those who are of faithfulness") in verses 7, 9.[132] It is through

---

[128] This is the same word with which Paul describes Peter's "withdrawal" at Antioch (cf. 2:12). Since it also carries the meaning of "to keep silence" (cf. BAGD: 847), it immediately recalls the muteness of Isa. 53:7. The associations with the latter text are broadened through its reference to the same title and task (Righteous One/justify), the "soul" (either his or God's), "knowledge בדעתו" substituting for "faithfulness" (cf. 53:11). For the "seed" (also singular) (cf. 53:10), see verses 15-18. Isaiah 53 is, of course, a description of the Servant's obedience to the point of death.

[129] Cf. Ps. 40:7; Mt. 11:3; Jn. 1:9f, 6:14, 11:27; Heb. 10:5f, 37; 1QS 9:11; CD-A 12:23; CD-B 20:1. The LXX consequently speaks of the Messiah as the Righteous One who will live because of God's faithfulness. A messianic reading of Hab. 2:4 is also supported by Isa. 11:5: "Also righteousness will be the belt about his loins, and faithfulness the belt about his waist והיה צדק אזור מתניו והאמונה אזור חלציו" (cf. 1Q28b 5:26) (see verses 21-25). (Jn. 6:14 indicates that the Coming One and the prophet like Moses [cf. Dt. 18:15f] were at times associated [cf. 1 Macc. 4:46, 14:41] [see 4:1-7 (nn46, 79), 21-31, and verses 19-20 (nn246, 264)].) For the "hope of righteousness" in 5:5 as a possible allusion to Hab. 2:4, see 5:2-12.

[130] Cf. the apparent gloss on Hab. 2:4 in 1QM, speaking of the eschatological battle: "And in their positions they shall bless the God of Israel and all the deeds of his truth and they shall damn there Belial and all the spirits of his lot. They shall begin speaking and say: «Blessed be the God of Israel for all his holy plan and for all the deeds of his truth, and blessed be all who serve him in justice [righteousness], who know him in faith» וברכו על עומדם את אל ישראל ואת כול מעשי אמתו וזעמו שם את בל[י]על ואת כול רוחי גורלו וענו ואמרו ברוך אל ישראל בכול מחשבת קודשו ומעשי אמתו ובר[וכים כול משרתיו בצדק יודעיו באמונה" (1QM 13:1-3) (cf. 1QpHab 8:1-3; 1QHᵃ 4:14). According to this text, "serving in righteousness" is to "know God in faithfulness" (the reverse being equally true).

[131] The idea that the Messiah verifies God's faithfulness is well illustrated in Rom. 15:8: "The Messiah has become a servant to the circumcision on behalf of God's truthfulness to confirm the promises *given* to the patriarchs, and for the Gentiles to glorify God for His mercy (Χριστὸν διάκονον γεγενῆσθαι περιτομῆς ὑπὲρ ἀληθείας θεοῦ, εἰς τὸ βεβαιῶσαι τὰς ἐπαγγελίας τῶν πατέρων, τὰ δὲ ἔθνη ὑπὲρ ἐλέους δοξάσαι τὸν θεόν)" (see 4:1-7 and below).

[132] Cf. verses 13-14, 22. In this sense, the designation is equivalent to "those who are of the Righteous One/Messiah" – both as belonging to him and as partaking of

Jesus' faithful obedience to God's will (cf. Mt. 26:39-44), to the point of death, that the person who is faithful to this death will also obtain life: "The life which I now live I live by the Son of God's faithfulness, namely his love which led him to deliver himself up for me" (2:20).[133]

Although interesting, the suggestion – legitimately supportable grammatically – that verse 11 should be read: "Now because no one is justified by the Law, it is clear that 'The righteous one will live by faith'" (Wright, Climax: 149n42), is ultimately less likely. The more traditional rendering links the expression with the preceding rather than with the following clause: "Now[,] that no one is justified by the Law before God is clear; for ..." (NASB). This reading understands Habakkuk 2:4 as a prooftext, the Greek δῆλον (dēlon – "it is clear") occurring elsewhere as an exegetical tool, justifying its use as introducing the following quotation (cf. Betz, Galatians: 146). The alternative reading comprehends the first ὅτι (hoti) as causal ("because") rather than as descriptive ("that"), the first clause thereby establishing the warrant for Habakkuk 2:4 – rather than the reverse.[134]

(trusting in) his example: "And if you belong to the Messiah, then you are Abraham's seed, heirs according to promise (εἰ δὲ ὑμεῖς Χριστοῦ, ἄρα τοῦ Ἀβραὰμ σπέρμα ἐστέ, κατ' ἐπαγγελίαν κληρονόμοι)" (verse 29). Hays suggests: "those who are given life on the basis of [Christ's] faith" (Faith: 172). (Again, "faith" here is equivalent to "faithfulness.") Perhaps most significantly, this theme resurfaces, as it were, in 5:6 and 6:10, wherein Paul defines the community of those who are faithful to God in Jesus, serving one another in love (see 5:2f and 6:1-11).

[133] This definition is particularly important with respect to Paul's argument in this chapter as a whole: "Paul, as we have repeatedly emphasized, does regard Christ's people as 'believers'; those who receive life 'out of' Christ's faith in turn trust him (cf. 3:22) and live their lives also in a manner characterized by faith (cf. 2 Cor. 5:7) ... However, this is not the exclusive or even primary meaning demanded by the context; Paul is not concerned here with developing the parallelism between Abraham's faith and the faith of Christians ... Christ is not the object of Abraham's faith; rather, Abraham's faith is a foreshadowing of Christ's ... The idea that only Christ is the heir of the promises to Abraham (3:16) clashes with the idea that all who believe are Abraham's sons (3:7). Likewise, the mystical-sacramental language of verses 26-29 appears to comport oddly with the 'justification by faith' teaching found in verses 6-9 [whose traditional interpretation] clashes not only with the latter part of Galatians 3 but also with verse 8, which depicts Abraham not as an exemplary paradigm for faith but as a representative figure in and through whom others are blessed" (Hays, Faith: 172-73, 168, 177).

[134] While it is true that much of Paul's hermeneutic is guided by his knowledge of what the Messiah has accomplished – in other words, reflects a *post facto* determinative – his exegesis remains dependent upon the priority (in both temporal and conceptual terms) and authority of Scripture. On these grounds – together with a strong proviso regarding the absolute rejection of the Torah – we would diverge from Hays' declaration, based on an adoption of the alternative punctuation, that

In this context, δῆλον may reflect affinities with the talmudic פשיטא (pshita), an expression used in the gemara to express astonishment at what has just been stated because it appears self-evident (cf. Steinsaltz, Talmud: 137).[135] The doubt it raises is customarily answered either by demonstrating that the statement was not as obvious as assumed, or that it was necessary in order to avoid misunderstandings. We might read Paul to say in this framework: "No one is justified by Torah-observance (alone) before God. But that's obvious!" – the following quote providing the prooftext (see 5:13-18 [n180]). Verse 12 would then stand as an elaboration of the possible misunderstanding (see below).[136]

Verse 12: While numerous commentators recognise that verses 11 and 12 are linked on the basis of a גזירה שוה (gzerah shavah – verbal analogy), the common word linking Habakkuk 2:4 and Leviticus 18:5 being "live (ζήσεται),"[137] the precise relationship between them is frequently less succinctly grasped (cf. Hays, Faith: 184-94; Steinsaltz, Talmud: 150). In contrast to their discernment as conflictual passages, calling for a third text to resolve the contradiction between them (cf. Dahl, Studies: 159ff), these two verses may perhaps be better read as a form of chiasmus (cf. Drake):

"Paul rejects the Law not because of an empirical observation that no one can do what it requires but because its claim to give life . . . is incompatible with the gospel story, which says that Christ had to die in order to give life to us" (Faith: 179). Hays otherwise customarily acknowledges Scripture's claim on Paul, asserting the fact that "unless the Law and the Prophets really do witness to the gospel there is no gospel at all" (Echoes: 64). For the centrality of Scripture in Paul's writing, see Introduction, **Theological pointers**, 1:13f, 2:15-21, 4:1-7, 21-31, and verses 1f, 15f.

[135] The caution required in appealing to amoraic material in exegesis of the New Testament texts is duly noted here.

[136] Wright well perceives the issue of identity which Paul is hereby pursuing here: "Habakkuk, faced with the imminent destruction of Israel, had seen the covenant community being redefined in terms of faith: the δίκαιος [righteous] will now be the one who believes, and will be vindicated in the eschatological deliverance . . . [His] use of Habakkuk, it then appears, is neither as odd nor as arbitrary as it is sometimes made out to be. Of course in one sense the verse is used as a prooftext, but its wider context is the same as that which Paul – and Deuteronomy 27-30 – envisions: the redefinition of the covenant community by means of divine judgment. Paul's point, in using Habakkuk in this way, is that *when* that redefinition comes about, the demarcating characteristic of the covenant people is to be precisely their faith, their belief in Israel's God; and this, obviously, enables him to align Habakkuk, in his redefinition of the covenantal people, with the promise to Abraham, and its initial definition of that people as 'those of faith' (3.6-9)" (Climax: 149-49).

[137] MT: יחיה (yechiyei) and וחי (va-chai) respectively.

A   Now that no one is justified by the Torah before God is evident;
B   FOR THE RIGHTEOUS MAN SHALL LIVE BY FAITHFULNESS;
B'   However the Torah is not of faithfulness;
A' On the contrary [for], He WHO PRACTICES THEM SHALL LIVE BY THEM[138]

The first clause repeats the point established by Habakkuk: It is the "righteous person" who lives by faithfulness – not "(those who are of) the Torah."[139] That faithfulness is the sum and total of the Torah is clear from rabbinic treatments of Habakkuk.[140] In a discussion of karet (being "cut off" from one's people through punishment at the hands of heaven [God]), R. Simlai gives the following interpretation of the thought expressed in Leviticus 18:5: "[Therefore gave He them Torah (teachings) and many commandments . . .] [Mak. 3:15]. R. Simlai when preaching said: Six hundred and thirteen precepts were communicated to Moses . . . David came and reduced them to [encapsulated them in] eleven [principles], as it is written [citing the 'virtues' listed in Psalm 15] . . . Isaiah came and reduced them to six [principles] [quoting from Isa. 33:15-16, the first being 'He that walketh righteously' – in reference to Abraham, on the basis of Gen. 18:19] . . . Micah came and reduced them to three [principles], as it is written, *It hath been told thee, O man, what is good, and what the Lord doth require of thee: [i] only to do justly, and [ii] to love mercy and [iii] to walk humbly before thy God* [Mic. 6:8] . . . Again came Isaiah and reduced them to two [principles], as it is said, *Thus saith the Lord, [i] Keep ye justice and [ii] do righteousness* [etc.] [Isa. 56:1]. Amos came and reduced them to one [principle], as it is said, *For thus saith the Lord unto the house of Israel, Seek ye Me and live* [Amos 5:4]. To this R. Nahman b. Isaac demurred, saying: [Might it not be taken as,] Seek Me by observing the whole Torah and live? But it is Habakkuk who came and based them all on one [principle], as it is said, *But the righteous shall live by his faith* (Hab. 2:4) "[141] (Mak. 24a) (see also below).[142]

---

[138] This framework is equally as conceptual as it is structural (see below).

[139] The repetition of the catchword ἐκ πίστεως (ek pisteōs – "by faithfulness") links this clause directly with the previous one. Paul's exegesis of Lev. 18:5 in Rom. 10:6 by way of a midrash on Moses' death (cf. Shulam and Le Cornu: 347-50) associates Torah-observance with the search for Wisdom – again personified in Jesus (see nn42, 97f, 311f).

[140] Although of merely speculative value, it is worth noting that the haftarah (prophetic portion) for the parasha in which Lev. 18:5 appears (Acharei mot) is Ezek. 22:1-19 (MT), which speaks of Jerusalem's sin and punishment. For the haftarah, see 4:21-31.

[141] ולפיכך הרבה להם תורה ומצות]: דרש ר' שמלאי: שש מאות ושלש עשרה מצות נאמרו לו
למשה . . . בא דוד והעמידן על אחת עשרה . . . בא ישעיהו והעמידן על שש . . . בא מיכה והעמידן על
שלש, דכתיב: הגיד לך אדם מה טוב ומה ה' דורש ממך כי אם עשות משפט ואהבת חסד והצנע לכת

While the δὲ (de) may be contrastive (NASB: "However"), it is not necessarily so and may function here more as a simple conjunctive or even explanative (cf. BAGD: 171). In similar fashion, the normally adversative ἀλλά (alla – "but") serves on this reading not to indicate a dichotomy (NASB: "on the contrary") but rather acts as an explicative formula defining the first clause through a further prooftext (Lev. 18:5): "It is clear" that Torah-observance is not based on faithfulness – because, according to this text, "life" (the Kingdom of God) is gained through "keeping God's statutes and judgments (אֶת־חֻקֹּתַי וְאֶת־מִשְׁפָּטַי; et-chukotai ve-et mishpetai)."[143] This is precisely the distinction which R. Nahman demonstrates: "Amos came and reduced them to one [principle], as it is said, *For thus saith the Lord unto the house of Israel, Seek ye Me and live* [Amos 5:4]. To this R. Nahman b. Isaac demurred, saying: [Might it not be taken as,] Seek Me by observing the whole Torah and live? But it is Habakkuk

---

עם (הי) אלהיך . . . חזר ישעיהו והעמידן על שתים, שנאמר: כה אמר הי שמרו משפט ועשו צדקה.
בא עמוס והעמידן על אחת, שנאמר: כה אמר הי לבית ישראל דרשוני וחיו. מתקיף לה רב נחמן בר
יצחק: אימא דרשוני בכל התורה כולה. אלא בא חבקוק והעמידן על אחת, שנאמר: וצדיק באמונתו
יחיה.

[142] Cf. Tanh.Shof. 9; Mid.Ps. 17:18-25; Ex.R. 23:5; Eccl.R. 3.9.1. Apart from R. Nachman's explicit clarification, the whole passage is clearly based on the "weightier provisions of the Torah (τὰ βαρύτερα τοῦ νόμου)" – "justice and mercy and faithfulness," which things Jesus declares "you should have done without neglecting the others (ταῦτα [δὲ] ἔδει ποιῆσαι κἀκεῖνα μὴ ἀφιέναι)" (Mt. 23:23). Significantly, the demand to "go beyond the margin of the judgment," which clearly links hypocrisy to the definition of the true "sons of Abraham," is also based on Mic. 6:8 (cf. Suk. 49b; Mak. 24a), such that "living" is equated with the "faithfulness" which is embodied in doing justice, loving mercy, and walking humbly with God (see Introduction, **Argument**, 2:15-21, 5:13f, 6:1-11, 12-16 [n179], and verses 19-20). This confirms the link between Mt. 23:23 and both Mic. 6:8 and Hab. 2:4, Jesus' words constituting an early conceptual link between the two passages (see 2:15-21 [nn267, 271] and 6:1f). Paul's exegesis demonstrates the further influence of Lk. 11:42 (// Mt. 23:23), in which Jesus "paraphrases" Mic. 6:8 as "justice and the love of God (τὴν κρίσιν καὶ τὴν ἀγάπην τοῦ θεοῦ)." In "reducing" the Torah to one principle, Hab. 2:4 is aligned with love *via* Mic. 6:8, Paul making this correspondence explicit in 5:6 – "faithfulness working through love (πίστις δι᾽ ἀγάπης ἐνεργουμένη)" – and in speaking of love as the כלל גדול בתורה (klal gadol ba-Torah – the "great principle of the Torah") in 5:14 (see 5:2f). (For an association of Isaac with Mic. 6:7, cf. Gen.R. 55:5.)

[143] The MT Hebrew makes the correspondence here clearer than does the Greek, the two grounds – of living by practicing and living by faithfulness – both being designated by the preposition בְּ (be – "in/through"). While Paul disguises this in the Greek, he presumably does so in preferring the advantages which the ἐκ (ek – "out of") of the LXX rendering of Hab. 2:4 provides in permitting an identification of persons (those who "belong to") (cf. Rom. 1:17, 3:30; verses 7-9, 11-12, 22, 24).

who came and based them all on one [principle], as it is said, *But the righteous shall live by his faith* (Hab. 2:4) "[144] (Mak. 24a) (see above).[145]

Although verse 12 therefore retains the disparity between the two modes of living, it is not antithetical to verse 11 but a reiteration of its thought. In the words of Deuteronomy 30:19: "I call heaven and earth to witness against you today, that I have set before you life and death, the blessing and the curse. So choose life in order that you may live, you and your descendants העידתי בכם היום את-השמים ואת-הראץ החיים והמות נתתי לפניך הברכה והקללה ובחרת בחיים למען תחיה אתה וזרעך."[146]

Verse 13: When verses 11-12 are read chiastically, this verse picks up verse 10 and provides both its proof and its explanation. The curse, which is invoked and imposed on the person who violates his/her commitment to the covenant, has been removed through Jesus' crucifixion (cf. verse 1). The titular usage of Habakkuk 2:4 (the Righteous One) – cited directly in verse 11 and indirectly in verse 12 – affords an immediate transition to Jesus' redemptive act in verses 13-14 – a shift which otherwise appears abrupt and unfounded (cf. Hays, Faith: 179) (see below). Paul describes Jesus' action in terms of "buying back" or "delivering" (ἐξηγόρασεν; exēgorasen).[147] While this root occurs only once in the LXX, and is only found, again, in connection with "time" in the New Testament (cf. Eph. 5:16; Col. 4:5), it appears to relate in this context to the removal of just punishment from those who deserve it (cf. 4:5) (see also 4:1-7). The "curse of the Torah" – the constructive here, in contrast to "Jesus' faithfulness," being objective and not subjective[148] – is the penalty due to transgression: "You chose our fathers and gave their descendants your truthful regulations and your holy precepts, so that man could carry them out and live. And you established frontiers for us, and you curse those who cross

---

[144] בא עמוס והעמידן על אחת, שנאמר: כה אמר ה׳ לבית ישראל דרשוני וחיו. מתקיף לה רב נחמן בר יצחק: אימה דרשוני בכל התורה כולה. אלא בא חבקוק והעמידן על אחת, שנאמר: וצדיק באמונתו יחיה.

[145] In other words, while the verse in Amos allows for the prospect that "life" is found through Torah-observance, Habakkuk excludes that possibility.

[146] This, too, is a verse which speaks of the "seed" (singular) (see verses 15-18).

[147] "The meaning [of the verb] here is evidently the same as in 4:5, 'to deliver, to secure release for one,' probably with the implication conveyed in the etymological sense of the word (the simple verb ἀγοράζω means 'to buy,' and is frequently used in this sense in the LXX) that such deliverance involves cost of some kind (effort, suffering) to him who effects it" (Burton: 168). For other "metaphorical" descriptions of Jesus' vicarious death, see 1:1-5; for the narrative relation between verses 13-14 and 4:3-6, cf. Hays, Faith: 95-111.

[148] The Torah is not accursed (it is holy, righteous, and good) – nor are those who obey its commandments. Rather, the curses are invoked to regulate its observance and are a consequence of its violation (cf. Lev. 26:14ff; Dt. 27:13-26, 28:15-68; 1QS 2:16-17, 5:12-13; ARNª 2:3). For the Torah's "addition" because of transgressions, see verses 19f.

them. And we are the people of your nd the flock of your pasture. You curse those who cross them but us you have raised up"[149] (4Q266 f11:11-14) (cf. Jn. 7:49).[150]

The idea lying behind "ransoming" is one of exchange or substitution – the release of captured prisoners on payment of a stipulated price.[151] Paul understands that Jesus' death on the "tree" invoked upon him the curse promised by God for those who hang in capital punishment for a "sin worthy of death חטא משפט-מות" (cf. Dt. 21:22-23).[152] All the curses which are due to human beings for their displeasing of God fell upon him: "Surely our griefs he himself bore, and our sorrows he carried; yet we ourselves esteemed him stricken, smitten of God, and afflicted. He was pierced through for our transgressions, he was crushed for our iniquities; the chastening for our well-being *fell* upon him, and by his scourging we are healed. All of us like sheep have gone astray, each of us has turned to his own way; but the LORD has caused the iniquity of us all to fall on him"[153] (Isa. 53:4-6) (see also verses 19-20).[154]

---

[149] ובאבותינו בחרתה לזרעם נתתה חוקי אמתכה ומשפטי קודשכה אשר יעשה האדם וחיה וגבולות הגבלתה לנו אשר את עובריהם ארותה ואנו עם פדותכה וצון מרעיתך^ה אתה ארותה את עובריהם ואנו הקימונו.

[150] The "frontiers" here apparently designate the commandments, violation of which brings down judgment upon trangressors שורת הדין (shurat ha-din – "according to strict justice") (cf. Dt.R. 4:1; Mekh.Amalek 4; Git. 4:4; Tos.Ter. 2:3; Git. 40b, 41a, 54b) (see Introduction, **Argument**). Those whom God blesses He has, as it were, "ransomed" from condemnation: "Its interpretation concerns all observing the Law in the House of Judah whom God will free from the house of judgment on account of their toil and of their loyalty to the Teacher of Righteousness פשרו על כול "עושי התורה בבית יהודה אשר יצילם אל מבית המשפט בעבור עמלם ואמנתם במורה הצדק (1QpHab 8:1-3) (cf. Mic. 6:4) (see 2:15-21 and above). It is evident that Psalm 95 (cf. Psalm 100), with its warning against unfaithfulness, is to be read in the background of this passage (cf. Ex.R. 25:12) – quite possibly in conjunction with Isa. 53:7 (see 1:1-5). For the motif of bondage, see 1:1-5, 2:1-10, 4:1f, 5:13ff, and verses 19f.

[151] Cf. Ex. 30:12; Num. 3:46f; Ps. 49:7; Isa. 43:3; Mt. 20:28; Mk. 10:45; 1 Cor. 6:20 , 7:23; 1 Tim. 2:6; 4Q504 ff1-2ii:15-16. "In 3:13 Christ acts as a representative figure, taking the curse upon himself in order to set his people free from it. The 'logic' of this transaction may appear puzzling to us, but it is central to Paul's understanding of the Christ-event. A clear parallel is to be found in 2 Cor 5:21: '[God] made him who knew no sin to be sin for us, in order that we might become the righteousness of God in him.' The logic of such a transformation must be a narrative logic: it depends upon a 'pattern of exchange,' to use Hans Frei's phrase, which can be made intelligible only in terms of a sequence of events in which a hero/protagonist acts on behalf of others" (Hays, Faith: 179, citing Frei: 74-84).

[152] For the importance of Scripture for Paul, and its use in his argumentation, see Introduction, **Theological pointers**, 2:15-21, 4:1-7, and verses 1f.

[153] אכן חֳלָיֵנוּ הוּא נָשָׂא וּמַכְאֹבֵינוּ סְבָלָם וַאֲנַחְנוּ חֲשַׁבְנֻהוּ נָגוּעַ מֻכֵּה אֱלֹהִים וּמְעֻנֶּה: וְהוּא מְחֹלָל מִפְּשָׁעֵנוּ מְדֻכָּא מֵעֲוֹנֹתֵינוּ מוּסַר שְׁלוֹמֵנוּ עָלָיו וּבַחֲבֻרָתוֹ נִרְפָּא-לָנוּ: כֻּלָּנוּ כַּצֹּאן תָּעִינוּ אִישׁ לְדַרְכּוֹ פָּנִינוּ וַה' הִפְגִּיעַ בּוֹ אֵת עֲוֹן כֻּלָּנוּ.

The Hebrew construction allows for multiple interpretations of the biblical text (Dt. 21:23).[155] While the phrase may be taken as objective – "he who is hanged is accursed of God" – it may also be understood as "he that is hanged is a curse against God" (cf. San. 6:4), or as "he is hanged [because of] a curse [which he made] against God."[156] Paul chooses to employ an adjective derived from the Greek root (καταράομαι; kataraomai: "cursed"), which modifies or is the predicate of "everyone (πᾶς)" – although he refrains from specifying that the curse derives directly from God. In this way, he argues that Jesus' crucifixion represents God's punishment for Jesus' (implied) sin – not because he himself cursed God but because sin and death are both anathema to God.[157] The curse in this sense is constituted by death itself: It is death which is accursed (cf. Gen. 3:17-19).[158]

---

[154] Here is the converse "imputation," of human reckoning of sin to the Messiah ("cursing"), whereby – so sovereignly and so graciously – God reckons righteousness to wo/mankind.

[155] The practice of leaving a corpse hanging had as its purpose either the increase of insult or public warning/deterrent (cf. Num. 25:4; Josh. 10:26-27; 2 Sam. 21:6-9). The form of execution was later adopted in the custom of crucifixion (cf. 11QTemp 64:6-13) (cf. Fitzmyer). (Again, the fact that it is the *land* which is defiled – that which is promised to Abraham – is hardly irrelevant [see below].)

[156] Cf. Ex.R. 30:5; Sif.Dt. 221; Yalk.Dt. 930; JSan. 29a; San. 45b-46a. The LXX renders the verse: κεκατηραμένος ὑπὸ θεοῦ πᾶς κρεμάμενος ἐπὶ ξύλου ("cursed by God is [pf.] everyone who is hanging on a tree). Targum Onkelos removes the curse to avert the ambiguity: אֲרֵי עַל דְּחָב יְיָ קדָם יְיָ אִצְטְלַב – "For he was hanged because he sinned before the Lord." 11QTemp 64:12 pronounces that "those hanged on a tree are cursed by God and man מקוללי אלהים ואנשים תלוי על העץ."

[157] "God is holy, and that which cannot stand before a holy God is twofold – namely, sin and death. Sin and everything pertaining to it, death and everything leading up to it; these two are excluded from the presence of God; for God is the living One, and God is of purer eyes than to behold iniquity [Hab. 1:13]; and both these ideas are included in that which includes everything, namely that God is holy, or God is God" (Saphir, Unity: 287). The link with the Spirit is made clear in 1 Cor. 12:3: ". . . no one speaking by the Spirit of God says, 'Jesus is accursed'; and no one can say, 'Jesus is Lord,' except by the Holy Spirit (οὐδεὶς ἐν πνεύματι θεοῦ λαλῶν λέγει· Ἀνάθεμα Ἰησοῦς, καὶ οὐδεὶς δύναται εἰπεῖν· Κύριος Ἰησοῦς, εἰ μὴ ἐν πνεύματι ἁγίῳ)." For the meaning of the "anathema" – Jesus as an "accursed thing" – see 1:6-10.

[158] Cf. Rom. 5:12-21, 7:24, 8:2ff; 1 Cor. 15:21ff. This is the import of Hebrews' "gloss" on Rom. 8:15 – "For you have not received a spirit of slavery leading to fear again, but you have received a spirit of adoption as sons by which we cry out, 'Abba! Father!' (οὐ γὰρ ἐλάβετε πνεῦμα δουλείας πάλιν εἰς φόβον ἀλλὰ ἐλάβετε πνεῦμα υἱοθεσίας ἐν ᾧ κράζομεν· αββα ὁ πατήρ)": "and might deliver those who through fear of death were subject to slavery all their lives (καὶ ἀπαλλάξῃ τούτους, ὅσοι φόβῳ θανάτου διὰ παντὸς τοῦ ζῆν ἔνοχοι ἦσαν δουλείας)" (Heb. 2:15). Both these texts may in turn be read in the light of 1 Jn. 4:18: "There is no fear in love; but perfect love casts out fear, because fear involves punishment, and the one

By the same token, the accusation applies to anyone who has committed an act "worthy of death" (see above).[159] In his death on the cross, Jesus has consequently taken the place of everyone who deserved such a curse on account of his/her sin.[160]

Verse 14: Paul takes the object of the action as being "us (ἡμᾶς)" ("redeemed us/for us") which, if his pronounal usage is consistent and significant, further confirms that in this passage Paul is pursuing issues posed to Jewish believers.[161] His logic leads directly here to the purpose which God's redemptive act possesses in relation to Israel: It begins with Israel, extends itself to include the Gentiles, and finally, in completed circle, applies itself to Israel in full (see below).

Paul's establishment of Jesus' representative function becomes clear here in the fact that it is through ("in") him that Abraham's blessing is conveyed to the Gentiles.[162] To the extent that the redemption of verse 13 is related to those within the covenant, the purpose clause constitutes an immediate conclusion to Jesus' removal of the curse. It is because he "became a curse (κατάρας . . . γενόμενος)" that – his sacrificial ransom

---

who fears is not perfected in love (φόβος οὐκ ἔστιν ἐν τῇ ἀγάπῃ ἀλλ' ἡ τελεία ἀγάπη ἔξω βάλλει τὸν φόβον, ὅτι ὁ φόβος κόλασιν ἔχει, ὁ δὲ φοβούμενος οὐ τετελείωται ἐν τῇ ἀγάπῃ)" (see 4:1f and verses 19-20 [n248]). (For affinities between the pauline literature and Hebrews, see 1:1-5 [nn99f] and 4:1-7, 21-31.)

[159] Cf. Dt. 28:58-59: "If you are not careful to observe all the words of this Torah which are written in this book, to fear this honored and awesome name, the LORD your God, then the LORD will bring extraordinary plagues on you and your descendants - אִם־לֹא תִשְׁמֹר לַעֲשׂוֹת אֶת־כָּל־דִּבְרֵי הַתּוֹרָה הַזֹּאת הַכְּתֻבִים בַּסֵּפֶר הַזֶּה לְיִרְאָה אֶת־הַשֵּׁם הַנִּכְבָּד וְהַנּוֹרָא הַזֶּה אֵת ה' אֱלֹהֶיךָ: וְהִפְלָא ה' אֶת־מַכֹּתְךָ וְאֵת מַכּוֹת זַרְעֶךָ מַכּוֹת גְּדֹלֹת." The literal rendering of the second half of this passage runs: "The Lord will make wonderful your stripes/blows and the stripes of your seed [singular]." Here, the "seed" is identified not with the blessing but with the curse, the "wonder," as it were, resulting from the blessing that this curse ultimately achieves (cf. Isa. 28:29; Joel 2:26). (This text is recited during a judicial flogging, to remind the offender of his felony [cf. Mak. 3:14].)

[160] The Tosefta interprets the verse as if God's own face is disfigured in the hanging of a human person: "R. Meir used to say: What does the verse 'he who is hanged is accursed of God' come to teach us? [It is compared to] two twins, brothers, who resembled one another, one a king over the whole world, the other who became a brigand. After some time, the one who became a brigand was caught and crucified on a cross. All those who passed by said: This looks like the king being crucified! This is why it is written, 'he who is hanged is accursed of God [ki kililat elohim talui]' הָיָה רִ' מֵאִיר אוֹמֵר: מַה תַּלְמוּד לוֹמַר "כִּי קִלְלַת אֱלֹהִים תָּלוּי"? לִשְׁנֵי אַחִים תְּאוֹמִים דּוֹמִין זֶה לָזֶה, אֶחָד מֶלֶךְ עַל כָּל הָעוֹלָם כּוּלוֹ, וְאֶחָד שִׁיצָּא לְלִיסְטְיָיא. לְאַחַר זְמַן נִתְפַּס זֶה שִׁיצָּא לְלִיסְטְיָא וְהָיוּ צוֹלְבִים אוֹתוֹ עַל הַצְּלוּב וְהָיָה כָל עוֹבֵר וָשָׁב אוֹמְרִים: דּוֹמֶה שֶׁהַמֶּלֶךְ צָלוּב! לְכָךְ נֶאֱמַר: כִּי קִלְלַת אֱלֹהִים תָּלוּי" (Tos.San. 9:7) (see also n30).

[161] For Paul's pronounal usage ("we/us" and "you"), see 4:1f and below (verse 14).

[162] Cf. Ps. 72:17; Rom. 15:29. See above (verse 8).

being acceptable to God[163] – the blessing is communicated "in him."[164] Significantly, Paul's argument regarding Torah-observance leads him directly and immediately to Jesus' role with regard to the *Gentiles*. Were it not for the fact that Jesus has "paid the price" of the curse invoked by transgression of God's covenant, thus robbing it of its power – no blessing could come to *them* (see verses 26-29).[165]

As Paul shortly elaborates, God's promise to Abraham is fulfilled in Abraham's seed (singular) – the Messiah (see verses 6-9, 15-18).[166] It is God's faithfulness to his people, "from whom is the Messiah according to the flesh (ἐξ ὧν ὁ Χριστὸς τὸ κατὰ σάρκα)" (Rom. 9:5), which has redeemed them "in the eyes of all the nations": "For you are a living God, you alone, and there is no other apart from you. You remembered your covenant, for you redeemed us in the sight of the nations[167] and did not desert us among the nations. You did favours to your people Israel among all {the} countries amongst whom you had exiled them, to place upon their heart to turn to you and to listen to your voice {cf. Dt. 30:8}, [in agreement] with all that you commanded through the hand of Moses, your servant. [Fo]r you have poured your holy spirit upon us, [to be]stow your blessings to us, so that we would look for you in our anguish ... [... You have thrown awa]y f[r]om us all ou[r] failings and have [pu]rified us from our sin, for yourself. To you, to you, /Lord,/ belongs the justice, for you are the one who has done all this ..." (4Q504 ff1-2v:8-16, vi:2-4)"[168] (see also verses 26-29).

---

[163] Cf. Isa. 41:8ff, 42:1ff, 49:1ff, 53:2ff; Mt. 3:17, 12:18, 17:5.

[164] Jesus' representative role is reinforced here in his "becoming" first the curse (γενόμενος; genomenos) and then the blessing (γένηται; genētai), the "in the Messiah Jesus (ἐν Χριστῷ Ἰησοῦ)" merely making the becoming specific (see also 4:1-7). For the "representation," see above.

[165] "Christ, as the representative Messiah, has achieved a specific task, that of taking on himself the curse which hung over Israel and which on the one hand prevented her from enjoying full membership in Abraham's family and thereby on the other hand prevented the blessing of Abraham from flowing out to the Gentiles. The Messiah has come where Israel is, under the Torah's curse (see 4.4), in order to be not only Israel's representative but Israel's *redeeming* representative" (Wright, Climax: 151). For the Torah as condescending to human nature – an understanding which must modify Wright's view – see [2:15-21], verses 19f.

[166] Dahl notes that this clause "already presupposes the messianic interpretation of 'the offspring of Abraham'" (Studies: 131) (quoted in Hays, Faith: 180).

[167] Cf. n95.

[168] אל חי לבדכה ואין זולתכה ותזכור ברית^{כה} אשר הוצאתנו לעיני הגוים ולוא עזבתנו בגוים ותחון את עמכה ישראל בכול [ה]ארצות אשר הדחתם שמה להשיב אל לבבם לשוב עודך ולשמוע בקולכה [כ]כול אשר צויתה ביד משה עבדכה [כי]א יצקתה את רוח קודשכה עלינו [לה]ביא ברכותיכה לנו ל[מ]{פ}קודכה בצר לנו ... [. ... ותשלי[ך] מ[ע]לינו כול פשעינו[ן] ות[ט]הרנו מחטתנו למענכה לכה אתה ' הצדקה כיא אתה עשיתה את כול אלה.

Because God has displayed His faithfulness to His own people, He can also be trusted to redeem those who were "not-a-people," His chosen means being through the blessing of His Messiah – to Israel first and subsequently to the Gentile.[169] As Hays judiciously remarks in relation to Paul's argument with respect to Abraham in Romans: "Thus, Rom. 3:21-4:25 asserts openly what the biblical echoes earlier in the letter only suggested: Scripture (the Law and the Prophets) bears witness to the gospel in such a way that the continuity of God's grace is upheld. Despite the subsequent protests of Marcion and his seed, the God whose righteousness is shown forth in Jesus Christ is Israel's God, the God of Abraham, who paradoxically affirms his unwavering faithfulness to his covenant with Israel precisely by electing to embrace the Gentiles among his people" (Echoes: 57).

Although the first consequence of redemption from the curse is conveyance of the blessing to the Gentiles, its consummation lies in *Israel's* receipt of the promise through faithfulness.[170] Here again, Paul's thought is apparently dominated by the motif of the "seed" – the thread which ties Abraham to the Gentiles, through the Messiah (see verses 15-18). The prooftext which lies in the background at this point appears to be Isaiah 44:3, in which the blessing and the Spirit are correlated: "For I will pour out water on the thirsty *land* and streams on the dry ground; I will pour out My Spirit on your offspring, and My blessing on your descendants כי אצק-מים על-צמא ונזלים על-יבשה אצק רוחי על-זרעך וברכתי על-צאצאיך."[171] While the "descendants" are referred to in the plural, the "seed" is singular, thus linking up by way of verbal analogy (גזרה שווה; gzerah shavah) with other instances of such occurrence in Scripture[172] (cf. Hays, Faith: 136f, 181f).[173]

The dual purpose clauses of verse 14 recall the thought expressed in Romans 15:8-9: "For I say that the Messiah has become a servant to the circumcision on behalf of the truthfulness of God to confirm the promises *given* to the fathers [patriarchs], and for the Gentiles to glorify God for His

---

[169] Cf. Rom. 1:16, 2:9, 3:1-2, 9:23-29, 11:25-26, 28.

[170] Paul clearly establishes a correspondence between "the blessing of Abraham" in 14a and "the promise of the Spirit" in 14b. (The reference to the "promise" serves as the transition to the following section.)

[171] Cf. Ps. 42:1f, 63:1f, 143:6f; Isa. 41:17f, 55:1f; Jer. 2:13; Ezek. 37:2ff; Jn. 4:10f, 7:37-39; 4Q504 ff1-2v:2; Test.Jud. 24:2. LXX: ἐπιθήσω τὸ πνεῦμά μου ἐπὶ τὸ σπέρμα σου καὶ τὰς εὐλογίας μου ἐπὶ τὰ τέκνα σου.

[172] Cf. Gen. 3:15; 2 Sam. 7:12-14, 22:51; 1 Kings 2:33; Ps. 18:50, 89:4, 36; Isa. 53:10; Jer. 33:22, 26.

[173] For similar usage of the blessing imparted by the Spirit in 4Q504, see above. For Paul's use of the singular, see verses 15-18; for the "outgrowths" of this motif, see the "fruit" in 5:19-23, and the "sowing" in 6:1-11.

mercy . . .[174]."[175] Following this declaration Paul cites a catena of prooftexts affirming God's dealings with the Gentiles, culminating in the prayer that "the God of hope fill you with all joy and peace in being faithful, in order that you may abound in hope in the power of the Holy Spirit"[176] (Rom. 15:13).[177] While some commentators shrink from understanding the two clauses as sequential, claiming that "it is difficult to see how the reception of the Spirit by the Jews could be conditioned upon the Gentiles obtaining the blessing of Abraham" (Burton: 176), the thought corresponds to Paul's argumentation elsewhere, notably in Romans.[178] Most striking, perhaps, is Romans 8:15, which reiterates Paul's thought here in 4:5-6 almost verbatim: "For **you** have not received a spirit of slavery leading to fear again, but **you** have received a spirit of adoption as sons by which **we** cry out, 'Abba! Father!' (οὐ γὰρ *ἐλάβετε* πνεῦμα δουλείας πάλιν εἰς φόβον ἀλλὰ *ἐλάβετε* πνεῦμα υἱοθεσίας ἐν ᾧ *κράζομεν*· αββα ὁ πατήρ)" (see 4:1-7).

Characteristically, Paul inverts the order of redemption most common in the biblical texts[179]: "For I do not want you, brethren, to be uninformed of this mystery, lest you be wise in your own estimation, that a partial

---

[174] λέγω γὰρ Χριστὸν διάκονον γεγενῆσθαι περιτομῆς ὑπὲρ ἀληθείας θεοῦ, εἰς τὸ βεβαιῶσαι τὰς ἐπαγγελίας τῶν πατέρων, τὰ δὲ ἔθνη ὑπὲρ ἐλέους δοξάσαι τὸν θεόν . . .

[175] Cf. Isa. 42:6, 49:6-8 (cf. Kim, Paul: 110-15). The same thought recurs in 4:6, that passage constituting a more complex section because Paul adds a further step to the "you"-to-"we" dynamic in verse 7 – which then returns to the "you" (see 4:1f).

[176] Ὁ δὲ θεὸς τῆς ἐλπίδος πληρώσαι ὑμᾶς πάσης χαρᾶς καὶ εἰρήνης ἐν τῷ πιστεύειν, εἰς τὸ περισσεύειν ὑμᾶς ἐν τῇ ἐλπίδι ἐν δυνάμει πνεύματος ἁγίου.

[177] Cf. Isa. 42:4; Mt. 12:21; Rom. 5:2, 8:24-25; Eph. 2:12f; 1 Thess. 4:13 (cf. Kim, Paul: 109). For Abraham's trust in God's life-giving capacities and the implications for the Gentiles, see verses 6-9. Paul frequently associates "hope" (as a promise) with the resurrection (cf. Acts 23:6, 24:15, 26:6-8, 28:20; Gal. 5:5) (cf. Le Cornu and Shulam: 1387f).

[178] "Paul's quotation of Hab. 2:4 – the climax of his proclamatory introduction ([Rom.] 1:17) . . . speaks directly to the theological problem of God's faithfulness to Israel . . . By showcasing this text – virtually as an epigraph – at the beginning of the letter to the Romans, Paul links his gospel to the Old Testament prophetic affirmation of God's justice and righteousness. Like Habakkuk long before him and like Milton long after, Paul undertakes in his own way to 'justify the ways of God to men' by proclaiming that the righteousness of God is now definitively manifest in the gospel . . . Paul is not ashamed in relation to the gospel precisely because the gospel is God's eschatological vindication of those who trust in him – and consequently of God's own faithfulness" (Hays, Echoes: 38, 40, 39).

[179] While the biblical order frequently foresees Israel's redemption as preceding that of the Gentiles (cf. Isa. 45:14-17, 20-25, 59:19-20; Mic. 4:1-8; Zech. 2:10-13, 14:4ff) (cf. Kim, Paul: 243), it is also evident from the not-insignificant number of texts to which Paul appeals that his "triadic" understanding is a direct consequence of scriptural exegesis (see below). For Paul's use of Scripture, see Introduction, **Theological pointers**, 1:13f, 2:15-21, 4:1-7, 21-31, and verses 1f, 15f.

hardening has happened to Israel until the fulness of the Gentiles has come in; and thus all Israel will be saved; just as it is written . . ."[180] (Rom. 11:25-26).[181] If it is acknowledged that the scriptural bases for this mystery lie predominantly in Isaiah 6 and 42 (cf. Kim, Paul: 239ff), the present text may in fact serve as further evidence of Paul's own calling as an apostle to the Gentiles (see 1:15-16b).[182] On this reading, Israel's heart has been hardened (cf. Rom. 11:7; 2 Cor. 3:14) for a time (cf. Rom. 11:25), in order to permit room for the Gentiles' "creation" as part of God's people (cf. Eph. 2:12ff) – to which task Paul is directly called on the model of the Servant (cf. ibid: 241-42).[183] Isaiah 49:5-8 demonstrates that the Servant is appointed to be both a "light to the nations [אור לגוים]" and a "covenant of the people [Israel] [ברית עם]."[184]

The same assertion recurs in Romans 15. The complex of citations there, in verses 9-12, all combine allusions to the Gentiles with the element of God's mercy (cf. Rom. 9:15).[185] Moreover, they each speak, in their

---

[180] Οὐ γὰρ θέλω ὑμᾶς ἀγνοεῖν, ἀδελφοί, τὸ μυστήριον τοῦτο, ἵνα μὴ ἦτε [παρ'] ἑαυτοῖς φρόνιμοι, ὅτι πώρωσις ἀπὸ μέρους τῷ Ἰσραὴλ γέγονεν ἄχρι οὗ τὸ πλήρωμα τῶν ἐθνῶν εἰσέλθῃ καὶ οὕτως πᾶς Ἰσραὴλ σεθήσεται, καθὼς γέγραπται·

[181] Rom. 11:12, 15 are obviously influenced by such texts as Zech. 8:13: "And it will come about that just as you were a curse among the nations, O house of Judah and house of Israel, so I will save you that you may become a blessing והיה כאשר הייתם קללה בגוים בית יהודה ובית ישראל כן אושיע אתכם והייתם ברכה."

[182] Verses 18-19 of Isaiah 42 speak of a person (LXX: persons/community) who is blind and deaf. Kim argues that "guided by the LXX, Paul could have seen Israel's obduracy or God's hardening of them also in Isa 42:18-20 (see further vv. 21-25)" (Paul: 124).

[183] The relevance of Romans 9 here is surely significant. That chapter not merely picks up the theodicy theme from 3:1 but also resumes the "sons of Abraham" discussion of chapter 2 (cf. Shulam and Le Cornu: 15-16). If Hab. 2:4 sounds the keynote of theodicy and God's faithfulness, Hos. 1:10 and 2:23 resonate with the Gentiles' "regeneration," the potter exercising his prerogative to have mercy on whom He will. But Paul's argument here is precisely that God's word has not failed – to Israel – because "it is not the children of the flesh who are children of God, but the children of the promise are regarded as descendants (οὐ τὰ τέκνα τῆς σαρκὸς ταῦτα τέκνα τοῦ θεοῦ ἀλλὰ τὰ τέκνα τῆς ἐπαγγελίας λογίζεται εἰς σπέρμα)" (Rom. 9:8) (cf. Ned. 31a) (see 2:15-21 and verses 1ff). May Paul's employment of λογίζεται (logizetai – "they are reckoned") here not represent an echo of Gen. 15:6?

[184] "The hope for the eventual salvation of Israel can also be explained in the combined light of Isa 6:13 (MT and Tg) and Isa 49:5-6 . . . When the 'mystery' is taken together with Rom 11:11, 13-14 and 15:15-16, 19, 23, it appears to involve a self-understanding on Paul's part as the gentiles' apostle who was, first, responsible to bring in 'the full number of the gentiles' but then also responsible to bring about the eventual salvation of Israel thereby" (Kim, Paul: 242).

[185] Cf. Dt. 32:43; 2 Sam. 22:50; Ps. 18:49; 117:1; Isa. 11:10. Hays rightly recognises that the quotations (evidence from the Torah, Prophets, and Writings) demand a

original context, of Israel and the Gentiles joined together.[186] The final text - from Isaiah 11 - envisions Israel and the Gentiles gathering around the Messiah: "And He will lift up a standard for the nations, and will assemble the banished ones of Israel, and will gather the dispersed of Judah from the four corners of the earth ונשא נס לגוים ואסף נדחי ישראל ונפצות יהודה יקבץ מארבע כנפות הארץ" (Isa. 11:12).[187] Paul carries the catena to its climax in verse 29, assuring his gentile disciples that he knows "that when I come to you, I will come in the fullness of the blessing of the Messiah (οἶδα δὲ ὅτι ἐρχόμενος πρὸς ὑμᾶς ἐν πληρώματι εὐλογίας Χριστοῦ ἐλεύσομαι)." This blessing recalls Psalm 72:17, attributed in rabbinic literature to the Messiah: "May his name endure forever; may his name increase as long as the sun *shines*; and let *men* bless themselves by him; let all nations call him blessed

---

fuller reading than the precise passage cited, a regular mode of Jewish exegesis (cf. Hays, Echoes: 70f; Boyarin, Intertextuality).

[186] Although Psalm 117 might be regarded as an exception to this claim, the "us" in verse 2 presumably refers to Israel. With respect to Dt. 32:43, Paul is clearly utilizing the LXX text which understands the masoretic text's "Gentiles, praise His people הרנינו גוים עמו" by repointing it as "Rejoice, Gentiles, with His people (εὐφράνθητε, ἔθνη, μετὰ τοῦ λαοῦ αὐτοῦ)" (cf. Hays, Echoes: 72).

[187] Such a reading, which gives the pronouns their due weight, enriches a text which, without such attention to detail, would be sorely impoverished (see 4:1f). The "we" may, notwithstanding, also be perceived inclusively, Paul's point being not merely that God's faithfulness to Israel is proved by His "creation" equally of the Gentiles, but that His method of doing so establishes a parity between the two derived from the Messiah's faithfulness, in which they both participate and which they both enjoy (see 4:12-20 and verses 26-29). It is in this context that we would place Wright's summary: "The thought which drives Paul into this paragraph [verses 10-14], then, has to do with the question of what happens to the promises of Abraham, *granted the plight of the Jews which is brought about by the Torah.* The thought is as follows: God promised Abraham a worldwide family, characterized by faith. The promises were entrusted to Israel, the people whose life was lived ὑπὸ νόμου [under the law]. The Torah, however, held out over this people, the agents of promise, the curse which had in fact come true, and was still being proved true, in the events of the exile and its strange continuance right up to Paul's day and beyond. How could the promises, the blessings promised to Abraham, now reach their intended destination? The Torah looks as though it might render the promise to Abraham, and to his worldwide family, null and void ... He [Paul] does not deny the premises of the argument: Abraham's promises of blessing remain the vital thing, and the Torah really does place a valid interdict on those promises. He shows that the problem has been dealt with. The covenant has reached its climax in the death of the Messiah ... the death of Christ means that now the blessing of Abraham can come upon the Gentiles, and that 'we' [Jewish Christians] may receive the blessing of the Spirit through faith" (Climax: 142-43; emphasis added). The problematic involved in this reading becomes clearer in verses 19f, where Paul's question regarding "Why the Torah then?" demands a more positive answer than Wright provides (see verses 19f).

יהי שמו לעולם לפני-שמש ינון שמו ויתברכו בו כל-גוים יאשרוהו" (see verses 6-9, 15-
18).[188]

The thought is admirably expressed in the Testament of Judah,
evidently composed as a "Christian" text: "And after this there shall arise
for you a Star from Jacob in peace: And a man shall arise from my posterity
[Judah] like the Sun of righteousness, walking with the sons of men in
gentleness and righteousness, and in him will be found no sin. And the
heavens will be opened upon him to pour out the spirit as a blessing of the
Holy Father. And he will pour out the spirit of grace on you. And you shall
be sons in truth, and you will walk in his first and final decrees. This is the
Shoot of God Most High; this is the fountain for the life of all humanity.
Then he will illumine the scepter of my kingdom, and from your root will
arise the Shoot, and through it will arise the rod of righteousness for the
nations, to judge and to save all that call on the Lord" (Test.Jud. 24:1-6) (see
verses 26-29).[189]

Verses 15-18:
Brethren, I speak in terms of human relations: even though it is *only* a man's covenant,
yet when it has been ratified, no one sets it aside or adds conditions to it. Now the
promises were spoken to Abraham and to his seed. He does not say, "AND TO SEEDS,"
as *referring* to many, but *rather* to one, "AND TO YOUR SEED," that is, the Messiah.
What I am saying is this: the Law, which came four hundred and thirty years later, does
not invalidate a covenant previously ratified by God, so as to nullify the promise. For if
the inheritance is based on law, it is no longer based on a promise; but God has granted
it to Abraham by means of a promise.

Paul's direct address to his "Brethren (Ἀδελφοί)" marks a pause in the
argument and the introduction of a new sub-unit (cf. Longenecker,
Galatians: 126).[190] At this juncture, Paul adopts another tack, this one

---

[188] "As in Romans 9-11, these scriptures project an inversion of the order suggested
by Paul's earlier claim that the gospel is the power of salvation to the Jew first and
then subsequently to the Greek. Here the Gentiles seem to come in first; that is the
anomaly that Paul must explain. Isaiah sings in the background, however. If
Gentiles come, can Israel be far behind?" (Hays, Echoes: 73). It is surely in no wise
incidental that these texts speak of the return from Exile and the restoration to the
Land – an integral element of Abraham's blessing (cf. Gen. 15:18, 17:8, 26:2-3, 28:13-
14) (see below). For the exile motif, see 1:1-5 (nn80, 90), 4:21-31, and 5:2-12 (n37).

[189] Cf. Num. 24:17; Ps. 2:9, 45:4 (LXX); Isa. 11:2, 53:2ff, 61:11; Joel 2:28; Test.Levi 18:3;
Ps.Sol. 17:21ff, 18:5f. As commentators have recognised, verse 14 closes the
"hermeneutical circle" in answering the question of verse 2, the Spirit being the
fulfilment of God's promise to Abraham (cf. Hays, Faith: 183) (see verses 1-5 [n34]).

[190] This is, in fact, the first occasion on which Paul employs the term, although it
recurs frequently throughout the rest of the letter (cf. 4:12, [19], 28, 31, 5:11, 13, 6:1,
18); for the epithet, see 1:1-5. For the argument that Paul's abstinence from
designating the "influencers" by name contributes to the likelihood that they are

elaborating the point by way of a "human" analogy, as it were.[191] The phrase κατὰ ἄνθρωπον λέγω (kata anthrōpon legō – lit.: "I speak in a human way") reflects the quasi-legal terminology of rabbinic literature designed to mitigate the force of anthropomorphisms attributed to God.[192] The Hebrew term כביכול (ki-vyakhol – "as it were/as if it were possible") signals that the description projects human qualities onto God and must not be taken literally: "R. Meir said: When a man is sore troubled, what says the Shekinah [God's Presence]? (As it were) My head is ill at ease, my arm is ill at ease. If God is sore troubled at the blood of the ungodly that is shed, how much more at the blood of the righteous?"[193] (San. 6:5) (cf. Frank: 118).[194]

---

not believers, see Introduction, **Occasion and circumstances**. For Galatians' epistolary characteristics, see Introduction, **Form**.

[191] The rendering "Let me take an example from everyday life" reflects the rabbinic terminology of learning from "the ways of the world": "A Cuthean asked R. Meir, 'Do the dead live again'?" He answered, 'Yes.' He then asked, ['Do they come back to life] secretly or in public?' He answered, 'In public.' 'How can you prove it to me?' he asked, to which R. Meir replied: 'Not from Scripture nor from the Mishnah, but from everyday life I will answer you ... כותי שאל לר׳ מאיר. אמר לו: חיין מתייא? אמר לו: אין. אמר לו: בחשאי או בפרהסיא? אמר לו: בפרהסיא. אמר לו: מאן את מחמי לי? אמר לו: לא ממקרא ולא ממשנה אלא מדרך ארץ אני מששיבך" (Eccl.R. 5.10.1) (cf. Tanh.Tzav 13; TBE p. 30; Pes.Rab. 21:6). The importance of the form of testament and will with which the Galatians would have been familiar – or which Paul himself would have adduced as an example – increases when the human is taken to be the model for the divine. The converse is true in the reverse direction.

[192] For the phrase in relation to Paul's apostleship, see 1:1-5, [11-12]. Daube suggests that the principle דברה תורה בלשון בני אדם (dibra Torah bi-leshon bnei adam – "the Torah speaks in the language of men") remains the most likely source of Paul's phrase. Since its usage in a manner parallel to Paul's only occurs in the middle ages, Daube submits that Paul represents the original meaning, subsequently transferred by R. Ishmael into a somewhat more restricted exegetical principle to explain the "common language" of double verbs (cf. ראה ראיתי) in the biblical text. Such usage is characteristic of the latter's debate with R. Akiva, who insisted that the phrase constituted an "amplificatory expression" whence halakhic inferences may be drawn. It may then have been a natural process for the expression to have expanded, around the ninth century, to denote biblical anthropomorphisms (cf. Daube, New: 399; Steinsaltz, Talmud: 151). For the term's relation to divine condescendence, see verses 19f. Paul may take pains to emphasise that this constitutes a human example because he does not generally deviate from scriptural proof as his primary authority (see verses 1ff); for his use of "allegory," see 4:21-31.

[193] אמר רבי מאיר: בזמן שאדם מצטער, שכינה מה הלשון אומרת? כביכול קלני מראשי, קלני מזרועי. אם כן המקום מצטער על דמם שלרשעים שנשפך, קל וחמר על דמם שלצדיקים.

[194] Cf. Rom. 3:5, [6:19]; Dt.R. 3:8, 10:3; Sif.Dt. 311, 346; JSan. 49a; ARNᵃ 37:12; DEZ 9:12; Tanh.Mishp. 15; Naso 4. For Rom. 6:19, see verses 19-20.

Given the following comparison, the ὅμως (homōs - "nevertheless") is better understood as influenced by ὁμῶς (homōs - accented differently = "likewise"). Rather than setting up an antithesis ("Although I am speaking in human terms, what follows is nonetheless true"), Paul is drawing a comparison - adducing the attributes of God's covenant with Abraham (cf. Gen. 15:18, 17:4) from a human illustration.[195] While the previous verses have addressed the Gentiles' status in relation to the curse and the blessing, here Paul speaks to the legal form of inheritance.[196]

At the most basic level, the analogy is given linguistically: While the Greek διαθήκη (diathēkē) customarily serves to signify a person's last will and testament, the LXX employs it regularly to render the Hebrew ברית (brit - "covenant"),[197] together with תורה (Torah) (cf. Dan. 9:13) (cf. Hays, Galatians: 263). Paul identifies the Greek term with the "will and testament" made by a dying person by turning it into a "human (ἀνθρώπου)" covenant.[198] It is characteristic of the latter, so goes his claim, that, once it has been ratified, it cannot be altered, amended, or annulled (by a third party) (cf. Rom. 4:14, 11:29).

Biblical law stipulates that "If a man dies and has no son, then you shall transfer his inheritance to his daughter. And if he has no daughter, then you shall give his inheritance to his brothers. And if he has no brothers, then you shall give his inheritance to his father's brothers. And if his father has no brothers, then you shall give his inheritance to his nearest

---

[195] On this basis, Longenecker appears to interpret Paul's thought as an *a minori ad maius* (קל וחומר; kal va-chomer) proposal - "that is, an argument from what occurs in the human sphere to what is true in the divine economy" (Galatians: 127). This is rather disingenuous exegesis, even if it captures some of the sense.

[196] Paul's discussion comes full circle here to where it began in verse 1 with an astonished question that the gentile Galatian believers should have allowed themselves to become as "bewitched" as Peter - to the point of being persuaded that social identity markers could take precedence over - to the point of eclipsing - the spiritual content which they signify (see Introduction, **Occasion and circumstances**). Paul's reproof of Peter (cf. 2:14f) indicates tha tthe issue at stake is the nature of Jewish identity: What are the true criteria according to which the "sons of Abraham" are to be defined? For the argument that verses 10ff address the *influencers'* concerns, see above; for the structure of Galatians as a whole, see Introduction, **Form; Argument**.

[197] Cf. Gen. 9:9ff, 15:18, 17:2ff; Ex. 34:10; Lev. 2:13; Dt. 4:13, 23, 31.

[198] Josephus consistently refers the Greek term to a testament/will to the exclusion of the meaning of "covenant" (cf. *Ant.* 13.349, 17.53, 78, 146; *War* 1.451, 573, 588, 600). דיתיקי/דיאתיקי (diatiki) in fact serves as a rabbinic loanword signifying "testament" (cf. BM 1:7; BB 8:6; MK 3:3; BB 135b), Delitzsch employing precisely the term to render "covenant" in his Hebrew translation.

relative in his own family, and he shall possess it"[199] (Num. 27:8-11).[200] In this context, a will constitutes the disposition of a person's property in favour of someone who is *not* a legal heir (cf. Elon: 445ff, and for the following discussion).[201] A person desiring to make a gift of his estate must in this sense divest himself of it during his lifetime, in order to prevent it from naturally devolving upon his heirs (cf. Heb. 9:15-17). The act of gifting the body of his property during his lifetime, while retaining its usufruct until his death, is known as מתנת בריא (matnat bari) (cf. BB 8:7).[202] In promising to transfer the property to the legatee "from today [מהיום]," the legator may not afterwards retract his will, even though the legatee's entitlement to the usufruct only becomes valid subsequent to the legator's death. Upon demise, the estate passes automatically and immediately into the heir's ownership, being unrenounceable by refusal due to the impossibility of waiving what is already in one's possession.[203]

---

[199] איש כי-ימות ובן אין לו והעברתם את-נחלתו לבתו: ואם-אין לו בת ונתתם את-נחלתו לאחיו: ואם-אין לו אחים ונתתם את-נחלתו לאחי אביו: ואם-אין אחים לאביו ונתתם את-נחלתו לשארו הקרׄב אליו ממשפחתו וירש אׄתה.

[200] Cf. Mt. 21:33-38; Lk. 12:13, 15:11-32. In other words, the right of inheritance devolves on all the deceased's kin in the agnate (paternal) line of descendancy and ascendancy, the firstborn son receiving a double portion of the estate, equal to the portions of two ordinary heirs (cf. Dt. 21:15-17). Since the birthright is determined according to the inheritance at the time of its devolution, it is neither diminished by the birth of an additional son following the father's demise nor increased by the subsequent death of a son (cf. BB 142b). According to Graeco-Roman law, a will may be altered at any moment (cf. Betz, Galatians: 155).

[201] It is significant that, save for isolated hints (cf. Num. 27:1ff; Job 42:15), the Tanakh makes no provision for wills or testaments, succession necessarily following the closest (paternal) relative. Personal disposition of property represents, in this respect, a post-biblical development. It is possible that Paul's thought here is influenced by the regulation that "If a man has two wives, the one loved and the other unloved [hated], and *both* the loved and the unloved have borne him sons, if the first-born son belongs to the unloved, then it shall be in the day he wills what he has to his sons, he cannot make the son of the loved the first-born before the son of the unloved, who is the first-born. But he shall acknowledge the first-born, the son of the unloved, by giving him a double portion of all that he has, for he is the beginning of his strength; to him belongs the right of the first-born כי-תהיין לאיש שתי נשים האחת אהובה והאחת שנואה וילדו-לו בנים האהובה והשנואה והיה הבן הבכׄר לשניאה: והיה ביום הנחילו את-בניו את אשר-יהיה לו לא יוכל לבכֵּר את-בן-האהובה על-פני בן-השנואה הבכׄר: כי את-הבכׄר בן-השנואה יכיר לתת לו פי שנים בכל אשר-ימצא לו כי-הוא ראשית אׄנו לו משפט הבכֹרה" (Dt. 21:15-17) (see 4:21-31 [nn202, 228]).

[202] Cf. JPe'ah 18a; BM 19a; BB 135b; Git. 59a.

[203] If it is allowed that the "universal understanding of a διαθήκη [diathēkē] as able to be revoked or emended" is an accurate assessment (cf. Tos.BB 8:11; BB 152b), Paul's usage appears rather inexact (cf. Longenecker, Galatians: 130). We would concur that the resolution of the problem may reflect a "lack of sufficient data" on our part at this point, the suggestion that Paul "felt no compulsion to speak in precise legal parlance" clouding the precise point he is attempting to convey.

The "ratification (κεκυρωμένην)" of the will refers to its signature, this event intended to be conducted in public and testified by witnesses (cf. BB 40b).[204] The Greek κυρόω (kyroō) signifies the confirmation or validation of an agreement, the idea of ratification in general being the giving of formal approval or consent to a matter (cf. LXX Gen. 23:20).[205] In arguing that no human will or testament may be "annulled (ἀθετεῖ)," Paul recalls with this verb his assertion in 2:21 that God's working in Jesus does not in any way "nullify (ἀθετῶ)" His grace (cf. Hays, *Galatians*: 263f).[206] In similar fashion, the verb ἐπιδιατάσσομαι (epidiatassomai) – "to add a codicil/condition" – prepares for the "ordination (διαταγείς)" of which Paul speaks in verse 19 (cf. ibid).[207]

Verse 16 begins to unpack the analogy invoked in verse 15. The reference to the "promises (ἐπαγγελίαι)" resumes the theme of verse 14, where the "promise of the Spirit (τὴν ἐπαγγελίαν τοῦ πνεύματος)" parallels "the blessing of Abraham (ἡ εὐλογία τοῦ ᾽Αβραάμ)."[208] Paul employs a common principle of biblical exegesis in reading Scripture in its most precise detail to make a halakhic ruling: "Whence do we learn of a garden-bed, six handbreadths square, that five kinds of seed may be sown therein, four on the sides and one in the middle? Because it is written, *For as the earth bringeth forth her bud and as the garden causeth the seeds sown in it to spring forth* (Isa. 61:11). It is not written [said] *Its seed*, but the *seeds sown in it*"[209] (Shab. 9:2) (cf. San. 4:5).[210] The same principle is also applied

---

[204] For the implications of the "precedence" contained in προκυρόω (prokyroō – "ratify previously"), see the discussion of προγράφω (prografō) in verse 1 and προοράω (prooraō) and προευαγγελίζομαι (proeuangelizomai) in verse 8.

[205] Although it is tempting to adduce Abraham as Paul's pattern here, the reference in Gen. 23:20 relates to purchase of property rather than to the inheritance of estate.

[206] While Hays picks up on the allusion, his discernment of its denotation diverges from ours.

[207] The fact that ἐπιδιατάσσομαι (epidiatassomai) is a koine Greek hapax (only occurrence) makes it all the harder to verify Paul's precise reference. Isaac's blessing of Jacob which, despite being given through deception, could not be taken back and given instead to Esau (cf. Gen. 27:18-41), is an indication how immutable a blessing was, once bestowed.

[208] The plural here may signify the complex nature of God's guarantees to Abraham (Num.R. 11:2 enumerates them as seven) on the one hand, and their repetition on the other. 4Q393 speaks of God's promises to Abraham in relation to the "remnant": "You are YHWH, you have chosen our fathers long ago. May you raise us up to be their remnant, to give us what you established with Abraham, with Israel . . . אתה הוא ה' בחרתה באבותינו למקדם תעמידנו לשארית להם לתת לנו הקימות לאברהם לישראל" (4Q393 3:6-7). See below for the specific quotations.

[209] מנין לערוגה שהיא ששה על ששה טפחים, שזורעין בתוכה חמשה זרעונין, ארבעה בארבע רוחות הערוגה ואחד באמצע? שנאמר: כי כארץ תוציא צמחה וכגנה זרועיה תצמיח. "זַרְעָהּ" לא נאמר, אלא "זֵרוּעֶיהָ".

aggadically, where the interpretation tends more frequently to constitute a "re-reading" of the text in order to render a certain point: "The Rabbis said: She [Eve] began weeping aloud (*be-kolah*) over him; hence it is written, *And unto Adam he said: Because thou hast hearkened unto the voice* (be-kol) *of thy wife* (Gen. 3:17): It is not written, 'To the *words* of thy wife,' but '*to the* voice *of thy wife*'"[211] (Gen.R. 20:8).[212]

The point which Paul wishes to depict, in his meticulous reading of Genesis 15:6, is that the singular signifies a specific person – the Messiah.[213] The first hint of Paul's exegesis may lie in his repetition of the "spoken to (ἐρρέθησαν τῷ)." In the first occurrence, the address is that of God to Abraham: "the promises were spoken to Abraham" – the obvious allusion being to Genesis 12:1-3, etc. The second, however, implies that God spoke to Abraham's "seed." While this is evidently so, on the biblical witness – most prominently in Genesis 28:14 in God's reiteration of the promise to Jacob – it is possible that Paul is employing the phrase ("[spoken] to") in this instance in a more restricted, specific sense. Here, rather than indicating "direct speech" he may be suggesting that God's promises were "in respect of" or "have as their object" the "seed" to come (cf. Test.Levi 8:15).[214]

As commentators have noted, a complex of "seed" passages exists within the biblical texts, through whose juxtaposition/verbal analogy

---

[210] As with Paul's example – although with the singular and plural reversed – the mishna wishes to adduce that the presence of the plural indicates the sowing of (at least) two kinds of seeds, not one, which the singular would have signified. (The gemara clarifies the number five: "bringing forth" – one; "her bud" – one, making two; "seeds sown" – [at least] two more; "causeth to sprout forth" – one; making five in all.) It is difficult to discern why commentators should assume that the impersonal (οὐ λέγει; ou legei) refers to God rather than to Scripture (cf. Longenecker, Galatians: 131). For the relation of this passage to the fruit of the Spirit, see 5:24-26.

[211] רבנן אמרין: התחילה מיללת עליו בקולה, הדא הוא דכתיב: ולאדם אמר כי שמעת לדברי אשתך - אין כתיב כאן אלא "לקולי" אשתך וגוי.

[212] Here, attention to the singular – rather than to the possible plural – as well as to the specific noun, allows the midrash to understand that Eve was weeping rather than speaking. For Paul's focus on Scripture, see Introduction, **Theological pointers**, 2:15-21, and verses 1ff.

[213] In other words, it is in and through this designated person that Abraham's blessing will be communicated.

[214] The English idiom that a passage "speaks to" a certain subject may convey the sense here. The most basic Hebrew structure would probably be indicated by a preposition: נאמר ב- (ne-amar be-) (cf. Gen. 18:19). The most explicit association between the Messiah and God's blessing occurs in Ps. 72:17: "May his name endure forever; may his name increase as long as the sun *shines*; and let *men* bless themselves by him; let all nations call him blessed יהי שמו לעולם לפני-שמש ינון שמו "ויתברכו בו כל-גוים יאשרוהו" (see verses 6f [n97]).

Abraham's seed becomes associated with that of David, the latter's seed (descendant) being the scion to whom God promises a seat on David's throne forever (cf. Hays, Faith: 136-38, and for the following discussion).[215] In 2 Samuel 7:12-14, God reassures David that "I will raise up your descendant [seed] after you, who will come forth from you, and I will establish his kingdom ... I will be a father to him and he will be a son to Me והקימתי את-זרעך אחריך אשר יצא ממעיך והכינתי את-ממלכתו ... אני אהיה-לו לאב והוא יהיה-לי לבן."[216] This association is further linked to the "seed" spoken of in Isaiah 53: "He will see *his* offspring [seed], He will prolong *his* days, and the good pleasure of the LORD will prosper in his hand. As a result of the anguish of his soul, he will see *it* and be satisfied; by his knowledge the Righteous One, My Servant, will justify the many, as he will bear their iniquities"[217] (Isa. 53:10-11) (see also below).[218]

---

[215] The topic is determined according to the principle of גזרה שוה (gzerah shavah – verbal analogy) – "seed (זרע/σπέρμα)" (in the singular) being common to all the passages. 4QBer[b] contains what appears to be a tantalisingly fragmentary allusion to a similar thought: "[. . . a mul]titu[de] of nations to gi[ve to them the earth] [. . .] [. . .] their families [. . .] [. . .] in your righteous truth when [your kingdom] is exal[ted . . .] [. . . and to bless] your [glor]ious [name] all of them together. Amen. A[men . . .] [. . .] coming [near] to you and the se[ed (?) . . .] [. . .] the families of the earth to be באמת [. . .] [. . .] משפחותמה ב]. [. . .] גויים לתת להמה את ארץ ... [. . .] ה[מון]ן . . .] צדקכה בהנש]א מלכותכה . . .[. . .] ולברך את שם כבו]דכה ביחד כולמה אמן א[מן . . .] [. . .] משפחות האדמה להיות [. . .] . . .] קרו[נ]בי]ם אליכה וזר[ע . . .] [. . .]"]. . .[" (4Q287 f5:8-13) (see also verses 26-29).

[216] Cf. 2 Sam. 22:51, 23:5; 1 Kings 2:4, 8:24f; 2 Chron. 6:15f, 7:18; Ps. 18:50, 89:20ff; 132:11; Isa. 9:7; Jer. 33:15; Hos. 3:5; Amos 9:11; Mic. 4:8, 5:1f; Lk. 1:32f; 1 Jn. 3:9. This was early understood as a messianic text (cf. Ps.Sol. 17:21ff, 18:1ff; Test.Jud. 24:1f; 1QH[a] 16:4ff; 4QpIsa[a] ff8-10:11f; 4QFlor f1i:10f; 4QPat.Bless. 3; 4Q252 5:1f; 4Q285 5:2f; Targ.Jon. to Isa. 11:1f, 16:1; Pes.Rab. 33:6, 36:1f, 37:1f; Mid.Ps. 16:10; 21:1, 42/43:5, 60:3, 87:6; Lam.R. 1.16.51; JBer. 2, 3, 5a; San. 93b, 96b ff; Suk. 52a-b; Sot. 48b). The rubric of "I will be" is clearly reminiscent of God's promises to Israel to be their God: "I will be their God, and they shall be My people והייתי להם לאלהים והמה יהיו-לי לעם" (cf. Gen. 17:8; Jer. 7:4, 24:7, 31:33, 32:38; Ezek. 11:20, 36:28, 37:23, 27; Zech. 8:8).

[217] והי' חפץ דכאו החלי אם-תשים אשם נפשו יראה זרע יאריך ימים וחפץ ה' בידו יצלח: מעמל נפשו יראה ישבע בדעתו יצדיק צדיק עבדי לרבים ועונתם הוא יסבל.

[218] Cf. also Gen. 3:15, 4:25. The LXX perhaps creates an even firmer reading for Paul in its rendering of "inherit (κληρονομήσει)" in place of "apportion (אחלק" in verse 12. For the Messiah as the "Righteous One" of Hab. 2:4, see verses 10-14. Cf. "Gen 49:10 The scepter shall [no]t depart from the tribe of Judah. While Israel has the dominion, there [will not] be cut off someone who sits on the throne of David. For «the staff» is the covenant of royalty, [and the thou]sands of Israel are «the standards». Blank Until the Messiah of righteousness comes, the branch of David. For to him and to his descendants has been given the covenant of the kingship of his people for everlasting generations לוא] יסור שליט משבט יהודה בהיות לישראל ממשל]לוא י]כרת יושב כסא לדויד כי המחקק היא ברית המלכת]וא[לפי ישראל המה הדגלים ... עד בוא משיח הצדק צמח דויד כי לו ולזרעו נתנה ברית מלכות עמו עד דורות עולם" (4Q252 5:1-4). "Ps

Both Mary and Simeon understood Jesus' birth in terms of God's promise to Abraham: "'For the Mighty One has done great things for me; and holy is His name. AND HIS MERCY IS UPON GENERATION AFTER GENERATION TOWARDS THOSE WHO FEAR HIM . . . He has given help to Israel His servant, in remembrance of His mercy, as He spoke to our fathers, to Abraham and his seed forever' . . . Blessed *be* the Lord God of Israel, for He has visited us and accomplished redemption for His people, and has raised up a horn of salvation for us in the house of David His servant – as He spoke by the mouth of His holy prophets from of old – salvation FROM OUR ENEMIES AND FROM THE HAND OF ALL WHO HATE US; to show mercy toward our fathers, and to remember His holy covenant, the oath which He swore to Abraham our father, to grant us that we, being delivered from the hand of our enemies, might serve Him without fear, in holiness and righteousness before Him all our days"[219] (Lk. 1:49-55, 68-74).

Verse 17: A further association with the motif of the "seed" may almost certainly be supposed on the basis of Paul's chronology in this verse (cf. Daube, New: 438f, and for the following discussion). The number of "430 years" as the interval between God's promise of the land to Abraham and מתן תורה (matan Torah – the giving of the Torah) (cf. Ex. 12:40) diverges from the "four hundred years" during which, God informs Abraham, his descendants will be enslaved and oppressed as strangers in a land not theirs[220] in Genesis 15:13.[221] Rabbinic texts account the disparity by

---

37:25-26 I have [been young] and am old now; yet [I have] not [seen a just person] deserted or his offspring begging for bre[ad. Daily] he has compassion and lends, and [his] off[spring is blessed. The interpretation] of the word concerns the Teac[her of Righteousness]. [נער היי]תי וגם זקנתי ולוא [ראיתי צדיק] נעזב וזרעו מבקש לח[ם כו]ל היום] "חונן ומלוה וזר[ע]ו לברכה פשר] הדבר על מו[נ]רה הצדק] (4QpPsª 3:17-19). The "many" which features so prominently in Isaiah 53 is taken up in verses 19f.

[219] ὅτι ἐποίησέν μοι μεγάλα ὁ δυνατός. καὶ ἅγιον τὸ ὄνομα αὐτοῦ, καὶ τὸ ἔλεος αὐτοῦ εἰς γενεὰς καὶ γενεὰς τοῖς φοβουμένοις αὐτόν. Ἐποίησεν κράτος ἐν βραχίονι αὐτοῦ, διεσκόρπισεν ὑπερηφάνους διανοίᾳ καρδίας αὐτῶν· καθεῖλεν δυνάστας ἀπὸ θρόνων καὶ ὕψωσεν ταπεινούς, πεινῶντας ἐνέπλησεν ἀγαθῶν καὶ πλουτοῦντας ἐξαπέστειλεν κενούς. ἀντελάβετο Ἰσραὴλ παιδὸς αὐτοῦ, μνησθῆναι ἐλέους, καθὼς ἐλάλησεν πρὸς τοὺς πατέρας ἡμῶν, τῷ Ἀβραὰμ καὶ τῷ σπέρματι αὐτοῦ εἰς τὸν αἰῶνα . . . Εὐλογητὸς κύριος ὁ θεὸς τοῦ Ἰσραήλ, ὅτι ἐπεσκέψατο καὶ ἐποίησεν λύτρωσιν τῷ λαῷ αὐτοῦ, καὶ ἤγειρεν κέρας σωτηρίας ἡμῖν ἐν οἴκῳ Δαυὶδ παιδὸς αὐτοῦ, καθὼς ἐλάλησεν διὰ στόματος τῶν ἁγίων ἀπ' αἰῶνος προφητῶν αὐτοῦ, σωτηρίαν ἐξ ἐχθρῶν ἡμῶν καὶ ἐκ χειρὸς πάντων τῶν μισούντων ἡμᾶς, ποιῆσαι ἔλεος μετὰ τῶν πατέρων ἡμῶν καὶ μνησθῆναι διαθήκης ἁγίας αὐτοῦ, ὅρκον ὃν ὤμοσεν πρὸς Ἀβραὰμ τὸν πατέρα ἡμῶν, τοῦ δοῦναι ἡμῖν ἀφόβως ἐκ χειρὸς ἐχθρῶν ῥυσθέντας λατρεύειν αὐτῷ ἐν ὁσιότητι καὶ δικαιοσύνῃ ἐνώπιον αὐτοῦ πάσαις ταῖς ἡμέραις ἡμῶν.

[220] ויאמר לאברם ידע תדע כי-גר יהיה זרעך בארץ לא להם ועבדום וענו אתם ארבע מאות שנה.
[221] Josephus and the LXX solve the chronological difficulty by including the patriarchal wanderings in Canaan within the 430 years (cf. Jos.*Ant.* 2.318). As Daube notes, Josephus' troublesome dates do not affect the present calculations.

identifying the reference to the (singular) "seed" in this text with Isaac: "It was said to our father Abraham at the covenant of the pieces: *Know for certain that your descendants will be strangers*, etc. (Gen. 15:13). Who is the seed? – Isaac, as it is written, *for through Isaac your descendants [seed] will be named* (Gen. 21:12)"[222] (SOR 3).[223] In other words, the "four hundred years" commenced only following Isaac's birth: "The Holy One, blessed be He, said this to Abraham only at the hour when he had seed, as it is said, 'Thy seed shall be a stranger in a land that is not theirs' (Gen. 15:13). From the time when Isaac was born until Israel went forth from Egypt 400 years (elapsed)"[224] (PRE 48).[225]

The determination of this chronology is enabled by specific identification of the singular seed in Genesis 21:12 with Isaac – the son of the promise.[226] Paul evidently sets up Isaac as the node according to which the timing of the giving of the Torah on Sinai is established. His point "is this (τοῦτο)": Isaac's birth allows us to firmly date תורה מתן (matan Torah), whereby we know it to have been given four hundred and thirty years subsequently.[227] The conjunction of the irrevocability of a human will with this time framework leads Paul's argument to the conclusion that God's covenant with Abraham constitutes His permanent agreement, which anything consequent must acknowledge and affirm.[228]

---

[222] נאמר לאברהם אבינו בברית בין הבתרים : ידוע תדע כי גר יהיה זרעך וגו׳. ואי זה זרעי – יצחק, שנאמר : כי ביצחק יקרא לך זרע.

[223] Cf. Josh. 24:3: "I took your father Abraham . . . and multiplied his descendants and gave him Isaac ואקח את-אביכם את-אברהם . . . וארבֶ את-זרעו ואתן-לו את-יצחק."

[224] לא אמר לו הקדוש ברוך הוא לאברהם אלא משעה שהיה לו זרע, שנאמר : כי גר יהיה זרעך בארץ לא להם, וכתיב : כי ביצחק יקרא לך זרע. ומשנולד יצחק עד שיצאו ישראל ממצרים ארבע מאות שנה.

[225] The midrash understands 60 years from Isaac's birth to that of Jacob, 130 until Jacob stood before Pharaoh, and a total of 210 years of bondage (cf. SOR 3; Tanh.Shmot 4; Gen.R. 44:18).

[226] Isaac is also associated with the Messiah through the akedah (Isaac's binding/sacrifice) (see 1:15-16b and 4:21-31).

[227] The phrase τοῦτο δὲ λέγω (touto de legō) in such a hermeneutical context may presage the usage later adopted in such rabbinic formulas as אימא (eima – "say!") (cf. Suk. 32b), זאת אומרת (zot omeret – "this says") (cf. Shab. 21b), מכלל ד- (mikhlal de- – "[this proves] by implication that . . .") (cf. Hul. 37b), שמע מינה (shma mina – "conclude from this") (cf. Ber. 13a), אלמא (alma – "consequently") (cf. Yoma 14b) (cf. Steinsaltz, Talmud: 102, 115, 131, 104, 141).

[228] Significantly, Paul later uses the same verb (καταργέω; katargeō – "to nullify") in Rom. 3:31 in claiming the reverse: Just as the Torah cannot nullify the promise by coming later, so faithfulness cannot nullify the Torah but only establish it (cf. Rom. 3:3). Although the rabbinic principle "he who precedes in Scripture also precedes in reality כל הקודם במקרא קודם במעשה" is normally brought not to support but to rebut an assertion (cf. Sifre, Be-he'al. 73; Mekh.Pischa 1; Ba-chod. 8), that which was earlier is generally conceived to possess greater authority (cf. Jos.*Ant*. 16.44; *CA* 1.7). The talmudic *locus classicus* wherein the Torah is contrasted with previous

Verse 18 clarifies the same point yet again, this time bringing out the force of the inheritance.[229] Israel's descent – the people's national identity – is not based (exclusively) on their commitment to "do and hear נעשה ונשמע" (Ex. 24:7) (see verses 1-5).[230] It possesses a prior foundation, upon which the giving of the Torah is inherently, innately, and irrevocably founded – namely, God's covenant with Abraham through his "seed": "For from the beginning of our forefather Abraham's laying claim to the way of truth, You led (him) by a vision, having taught (him) what at any time this world is. And his faith traveled ahead of his knowledge, but the covenant was the follower of his faith" (Hell.Syn.Pray. 2:14-15). On the analogy of human wills and testaments, which are immutable, two covenants cannot remain simultaneously valid if their terms diverge.[231] In this context of inheritance

---

covenants is at pains to demonstrate that none of the former commandments are stricter or more demanding than the latter, thereby safeguarding – in theory if not in practice – Israel's superior moral conduct (cf. San. 59a f).

[229] Although the promises are indeed spoken to Abraham and to his offspring, the actual passage which Paul quotes refers specifically – and exclusively – to the gift of the land (cf. Gen. 13:15, 15:18, 17:8, 24:7) (cf. Daube, New: 438ff). "This is not to deny that, in the eyes of both Paul and the Rabbis, the promise of the land and that of becoming a blessing to all the earth are frequently one and the same thing. They are obviously one and the same thing in Galatians. Still, the actual verse Paul invokes is one where the land is promised" (ibid: 439) (see below). Paul's "spiritualisation" of the inheritance may reflect the thought expressed in Heb. 11:9-10, wherein the author perceives Abraham as "an alien in the land of promise, as in a foreign *land* . . . looking for the city which has foundations, whose architect and builder is God (παρῴκησεν εἰς γῆν τῆς ἐπαγγελίας ὡς ἀλλοτρίαν . . . ἐξεδέχετο γὰρ τὴν τοὺς θεμελίους ἔχουσαν πόλιν ἧς τεκνίτης καὶ δημιουργὸς ὁ θεός)" – an idea which may also lie in the background of Paul's allegory in 4:22-31 (see 4:21-31).

[230] While this constitutes Paul's linguistic introduction of the concept of inheritance into the discussion (cf. Longenecker, Galatians: 134), the theme underlies not only the immediately preceding verses but also Paul's charge of Peter's hypocrisy in 2:14ff. The fact that this is "disguised"(as it were) under the rubric of the "sons of Abraham" should not distract modern readers from observing its central role in these passages. Failure to acknowledge its presence poses serious exegetical problems to the understanding of Paul's text. Not only has the tendency of Christian thought to "spiritualise" biblical truths led to a traditional anti-Jewish reading of Galatians, but remarks such as "'inheritance' had become thoroughly spiritualised" when Paul was himself penning these passages are themselves symptomatic of such a trend.

[231] Here again, Paul employs the phrases ἐξ ἐπαγγελίαν (ex epangelian – "on the basis of a promise") (parallel to ἐκ πίστεως [ek pisteōs – "on the basis of faithfulness"]) and ἐκ νόμου (ek nomou – "on the basis of the Torah") to indicate the ways in which God covenants Himself with His people (see verses 6f). For "doing" and "hearing" as the two necessary aspects of Torah-observance, see 2:15-21 and verses 1-5 (n39).

- which Paul specifically states to be the framework - it is obvious that there cannot be two heirs.[232] One will leaves the inheritance to a certain person, the other to a second, a situation which is legally invalid and unviable since the proper heir is divided.[233] At the same time, the relationship of matan Torah to Abraham's promise is not retrospective but prospective: What the Torah cannot, nor is designed to, do is to annul or replace what is to take place *in the future*, as guaranteed by the promise.

Philo well articulates the way in which God's covenant with Abraham was predicated on Abraham's (and God's own) faithfulness - and his example for others, most essentially and fully in his own "seed": "God, marveling at Abraham's faith in Him, repaid him with faithfulness by confirming with an oath the gifts which He had promised ... He [Abraham] did them [obeyed the divine commands], not taught by written words, but unwritten nature gave him the zeal to follow where wholesome and untainted impulse led him. And when they have God's promises before them what should men do but trust in them most firmly? Such was the life of the first, the founder of the nation, one who obeyed the law, some will say, but rather, as our discourse has shown, himself a law and an unwritten statute"[234] (*De Abr.* 273, 275-76) (cf. Rom. 2:14-15; TBE p. 35).[235]

---

[232] See above, on Dt. 21:15-16 (n201).

[233] While it is evidently true that God's covenant with His people on the basis of מתן תורה (matan Torah - the giving of the "Law") is divisive, in the sense that it creates a distinct people who carry His name, we do not consider this point to be at the focus of Paul's argument here. Our disagreement with Dunn over "ethnic markers/boundaries" and with Wright over the Torah's role has already been noted (see verses 1f [n80, 111, 118]) - as has our regard for Soulen's solution (see verses 6-9 [n100]).

[234] ὃς τῆς πρὸς αὐτὸν πίστεως ἀγάμενος τὸν ἄνδρα πίστιν ἀντιδίδωσιν αὐτῷ, τὴν δι' ὅρκου βεβαίωσιν ὧν ὑπέσχετο δωρεῶν ... τὸν θεῖον νόμον καὶ τὰ θεῖα προστάγματα πάντα ἐποίησεν ὁ ἀνὴρ οὗτος, οὐ γράμμασιν ἀναδιδαχθείς, ἀλλ' ἀγράφῳ τῇ φύσει σπουδάσας ὑγιαινούσαις καὶ ἀνόσοις ὁρμαῖς ἐπακολουθῆσαι· περὶ δὲ ὧν ὁ θεὸς ὁμολογεῖ, τί προσῆκεν ἀνθρώπους ἢ βεβαιότατα πιστεύειν; τοιοῦτος ὁ βίος τοῦ πρώτου καὶ ἀρχηγέτου τοῦ ἔθνους ἐστίν, ὡς μὲν ἔνιοι φήσουσι, νόμιμος, ὡς δ' ὁ παρ' ἐμοῦ λόγος ἔδειξε, νόμος αὐτὸς ὢν καὶ θεσμὸς ἄγραφος.

[235] Apart from the obvious substantive relevance of this passage (cf. Rom. 2:12-14), Hays aptly observes that "Philo refers several times to 'faith in God,' using the construction ἡ πρὸς θεὸν πίστις (see also [§§] 268, 271), *not* πίστις θεοῦ and - more importantly - because he uses πίστις in two different senses in the same sentence: it refers first to Abraham's faith/trust towards God and then, immediately thereafter, to God's faithfulness in keeping his promise to Abraham. This example nicely illustrates the multivalence of πίστις and the need to interpret it contextually. If Philo can pivot about in this way in a single sentence, we should hardly be surprised that Paul can similarly speak in the same breath both of our faith in God (καὶ ἡμεῖς εἰς Χριστὸν Ἰησοῦ ἐπιστεύσαμεν) and of the faithfulness of Jesus

Verses 19-20:
Why the Law then? It was added because of transgressions, having been ordained through angels by the agency of a mediator, until the seed should come to whom the promise had been made. Now a mediator is not for one *party only*; whereas God is *only* one.

Having elaborated the source of the inheritance – the criteria upon which identity as God's people within His Kingdom is predicated – as being God's promise to Abraham, Paul is now compelled to explain the role of the Torah in God's purposes.[236] The Greek προστίθημι (prostithēmi – "to add") reinforces Paul's presentation of the Torah as "post-promise" and consequently not of primary validity for the establishment of Jewish identity (see verses 15-18).[237] The preposition χάριν (charin –

Christ (διὰ πίστεως 'Ιησοῦ Χριστοῦ . . . ἐκ πίστεως Χριστοῦ; Gal. 2:16)" (Faith: xlvi). For Jesus' "representative" role and the "faithfulness of Jesus," see Introduction, **Theological pointers** (Faithfulness); for the discrepancy between "hearing" and "doing" (represented in the notion of "hypocrisy") as the sin which separates God from His creation, see Introduction, **Argument**; (for Paul's hermeneutical divergence from Philo [on the present reading], see 4:21-31).

[236] Cf. Rom. 3:1, 19-31, 5:12-21, 7:1-25, 9:31-10:21. Although he has not quoted directly from Scripture in the immediately preceding argument, Paul follows the logic of justifying his use of a "verse" (or thought) for a particular purpose when its explanation seemingly either contradicts another "verse" or renders the latter superfluous (cf. ומה אני מקיים [u-ma ani mekayyem] – "and how do I establish/explain") (cf. Kid. 36a) (cf. Steinsaltz, Talmud: 128); for verses 15-18 as representing a divergence from Paul's customary argument from Scripture, see there. With this in mind, we may concur with Betz's rhetorical thesis that "3:19-25 is an extremely concise 'digression' (*digressio*). It does not add a new argument to the defense, but prevents a wrong conclusion the readers might reach on the basis of the preceding" (Galatians: 163).

[237] Cf. the similar verb παρεισῆλθεν (pareisēlthen – "came in") in Rom. 5:20. The thought resonates with the midrashic tradition that the second set of tablets were given only once Israel had sinned with the golden calf and deserved punishment (cf. Ex. 32:19): "R. Adda son of R. Hanina said: Had Israel not sinned, only the Pentateuch and the Book of Joshua would have been given them, [the latter] because it records the disposition of Eretz Israel [among the tribes]. Whence is this known? *For much wisdom proceedeth from much anger* (Eccl. 1:18) [i.e., God's wrath at Israel's disobedience caused Him to send the prophets, whose teaching is wise – the fact that human beings learn through error causing sin to become the occasion for a fuller revelation] אמר רב אדא ברבי חנינא: אלמלא (לא) חטאו ישראל לא ניתן להם אלא חמשה "חומשי תורה וספר יהושע בלבד שערכה של ארץ ישראל הוא. מאי טעמא? כי ברוב חכמה רב כעס (Ned. 22b) (cf. Eccl.R. 1.13.1) (see also verses 10-14 [n109]). It must be reiterated here, once again, that Paul is not dismissing Torah-observance (and/or Judaism) out of hand, as so frequently contended by Christian commentators. Here he is merely defining the criteria upon which Jewish identity is properly predicated: observance of the "weighty provisions of the Torah: justice and mercy and faithfulness" (see Introduction, **Argument** and below).

predominantly following the word it governs) indicates either reason or goal (cf. BAGD: 877). Since it appears here as part of Paul's explication, it asserts that the Torah was given "for the purpose of/on account of" transgressions.[238] Most importantly for understanding this phrase, it needs to be recognised as dependent upon the final clause of the verse. In other words, in answering the question "Why the Torah then?" Paul's response is governed by the quasi-purpose clause "until the seed should come to whom the promise had been made (ἄχρις οὗ ἔλθῃ τὸ σπέρμα ᾧ ἐπήγγελται)."[239]

Paul argues in Romans that "until the Torah sin was in the world; but sin is not imputed when there is no law (ἄχρι γὰρ νόμου ἁμαρτία ἦν ἐν κόσμῳ, ἁμαρτία δὲ οὐκ ἐλλογεῖται μὴ ὄντος νόμου)" (Rom. 5:13). The blessings and curses invoked by the commitment to observe God's covenant mean that "the Torah brings about wrath, but where there is no law/Torah, neither is there violation (ὁ γὰρ νόμος ὀργὴν κατεργάζεται· οὗ δὲ οὐκ ἔστιν νόμος οὐδὲ παράβασις)" (Rom. 4:15).[240] Because it is "through the Torah [that] the knowledge of sin [comes] (διὰ γὰρ νόμου ἐπίγνωσις ἁμαρτίας)" (Rom. 3:20) (cf. Rom. 7:7), Paul concludes that "the Torah came in that the transgression might increase (νόμος δὲ παρεισῆλθεν, ἵνα πλεονάσῃ τὸ παράπτωμα)" (Rom. 5:20).

If Paul is still thinking in terms of the previous "parable," it is possible that he has in mind here the principle of "accommodation." In this sense, his question anticipates the question and answer given by R. Meir: "A Tanna taught in the name of R. Meir: Why was the Torah given to Israel? Because they are impetuous [and required discipline] תנא משמיה דר׳ מאיר: מפני מה נתנה תורה לישראל? מפני שהן עזים" (Betza 25b) (cf. Tanh.Ki tavo 4; [Ex.R. 42:5, 9]) (cf. Skarsaune, Proof: 313-20). The notion that the Torah was given as a form of discipline is directly related to God's "condescension," as it were, to the level of human beings: "I am speaking in human terms because of the weakness of your flesh (Ἀνθρώπινον λέγω διὰ τὴν

---

[238] A number of textual witnesses read πράξεων (praxeōn - "deeds") here in place of παραβάσεων (parabaseōn) (cf. Metzger: 594).

[239] This reliance on a forthcoming event gives to the Torah a positive role which most commentators deny it by dissociating it from the advent of faithfulness, common Christian comprehension commanding a clear dichotomy between "works" and "grace" (faith).

[240] In an era during which the Torah has no jurisdiction, not yet having been implemented, sin cannot rightly be judged or punished. In this sense, Abraham's righteousness could only be "reckoned" since he could not rightly be accused of sinning. While rabbinic texts ascribe Torah-observance to Abraham and to all the patriarchs (cf. Gen.R. 56:11, 61:1, 95:3; Lev.R. 2:10; Kid. 4:14; Yoma 28b) in order that they may benefit from its rewards, the implication of this view, even if remaining unexpressed, is that the Torah also introduced punishments.

ἀσθένειαν τῆς σαρκὸς ὑμῶν)" (Rom. 6:19) (see also 4:12-20).[241] In speaking of the freedom from sin achieved through the indwelling of the Spirit, Paul says in the same letter: "For what the Torah could not do, weak as it was through the flesh, God *did*: sending His own son in the likeness of sinful flesh and *as an offering* for sin, He condemned sin in the flesh"[242] (Rom. 8:3).[243]

Here, Paul appeals to the Torah's "weakness" primarily in reference to the fact that it has been "mediated (μεσίτου/μεσίτης)" – "accommodated."[244] In this sense, the allusion to the "angels" appears to be subsumed under the issue of divine unity/sovereignty (see below).[245] Not

---

[241] Accommodation or divine condescension as a hermeneutical principle may be summed up as follows: "1. That God's revelation came to us, not only couched in human language, but also taking into consideration the thought-patterns and customs related to it; 2. that God did not at any time reveal to man everything he was capable of notionally apprehending, but only what he was able to effectively assimilate on account of his weakness and sinfulness; 3. that some divine dispositions were given unwillingly, out of consideration for human waywardness, with a view towards him fulfilling the Divine will more perfectly in the long run; 4. that those pagan elements (rites, customs and institutions) which found their way into the Mosaic Law from the existing cultural background must be understood and explained in this perspective" (Drefyus: 74-75). One of the most commonly cited New Testament examples is Mt. 19:8: "He [Jesus] said to them, 'Because of your hardness of heart, Moses permitted you to divorce your wives; but from the beginning it has not been this way' (λέγει αὐτοῖς ὅτι Μωϋσῆς πρὸς τὴν σκληροκαρδίαν ὑμῶν ἐπέτρεψεν ὑμῖν ἀπολῦσαι τὰς γυναῖκας ὑμῖν, ἀπ' ἀρχῆς δὲ οὐ γέγονεν οὕτως)." The Odes of Solomon speak of the Lord who "became like me, that I might receive him. In form he was considered like me, that I might put him on" (Odes Sol. 7:4).

[242] Τὸ γὰρ ἀδύνατον τοῦ νόμου ἐν ᾧ ἠσθένει διὰ τῆς σαρκός, ὁ θεὸς τὸν ἑαυτοῦ υἱὸν πέμψας ἐν ὁμοιώματι σαρκὸς ἁμαρτίας καὶ περὶ ἁμαρτίας κατέκρινεν τὴν ἁμαρτίαν ἐν τῇ σαρκί.

[243] God's accommodation to human nature, as it were, in giving the Torah embodies the idea of sin as "hypocrisy" – people's inability to "do" what they "say/hear" (see Introduction, **Argument**; **Theological pointers** [Justification]). Paul relates to Jesus' role in verses 22f, where he also develops the idea of the tutor as a "pedagogue" (see verses 22-25). For the freedom of/in the Spirit, see [2:15-21], 4:1-7 and 5:13ff; for "sending," see 4:1-7.

[244] It is difficult to ascertain here whether the clauses in this verse are independent or explicative of one another. The Greek order suggests that Paul's thought is still dominated by a chronological purpose, the "until the seed" forming its focus, and the condensed clause διαταγεὶς δι' ἀγγέλων ἐν χειρὶ μεσίτου (diatageis di angelōn en cheiri mesitou) serving as a modification of "added."

[245] Cf. the attributes ascribed to Wisdom: "For wisdom . . . . is the breath of the power of God, and a pure influence flowing from the glory of the Almighty . . . she is the brightness of the everlasting light, the unspotted mirror of the power of God, and the image of his goodness. And being but one, she can do all things: and remaining in herself, she maketh all things new: and in all ages entering into holy

only does the Greek link these beings immediately with the mediator, but Paul pays them no independent attention in verse 20.

Rabbinic texts contain the tradition that both Moses and the angels played a mediating role in the giving of the Torah on Sinai:

> "The Torah which the Holy One, blessed be He, gave to Israel was given solely through Moses, as it is stated, *Between him and the children of Israel* (Lev. 26:46). Thus Moses was worthy to become the intermediary between Israel and the All-present תורה
> שנתן הקדוש ברוך הוא לישראל לא נתנה אלא על ידי משה, שנאמר: ביני לבין
> בני ישראל. זכה משה להיות שליח בין בני ישראל למקום" (ARNa 1:2) (see also below)[246]

> *Let him kiss me with the kisses of his mouth* (Cant. 1:1). R. Johanan said: An angel carried the utterances [at Mount Sinai] from before the Holy One, blessed be He, each one in turn, and brought it to each of the Israelites and said to him, 'Do you take upon yourself this commandment? So-and-so many rules are attached to it, so-and-so many penalties are attached to it, so-and-so many precautionary measures are attached to it, so many precepts and so many lenient and strict applications are attached to it; such-and-such a reward is attached to it.' The Israelite would answer

---

souls, she maketh them friends of God, and prophets (σοφία . . . ἀτμὶς γάρ ἐστιν τῆς τοῦ θεοῦ δυνάμεως καὶ ἀπόρροια τῆς τοῦ παντοκράτορος δόξης εἰλικρινής . . . ἀπαύγμασμα γάρ ἐστιν φωτὸς ἀϊδίου καὶ ἔσοπτρον ἀκηλίδωτον τῆς τοῦ θεοῦ ἐνεργείας καὶ εἰκὼν τῆς ἀγαθότητος αὐτοῦ. μία δὲ οὖσα πάντα δύναται καὶ μένουσα ἐν αὐτῇ τὰ πάντα καινίζει καὶ κατὰ γενεὰς εἰς ψυχὰς ὁσίας μεταβαίνουσα φίλους θεοῦ καὶ προφήτας κατασκευάζει)" (Wis.Sol. 7:24-27). For Wisdom as identified with the Torah and the Logos, see verses 6-9.

[246] Cf. Ass.Mos. 1.14; Philo, *Vit.Mos.* 2.166. Moses responded to the people's request to put a distance between them and God – "Speak to us yourself, and we will listen; but let not God speak to us, lest we die דבר-אתה עמנו ונשמעה ואל-ידבר עמנו אלהים פן-נמות" (Ex. 20:19) (cf. Dt. 5:5) – by promising that God would "raise up a prophet like me from among you, from your countrymen, you shall listen to him נביא מקרבך מאחיך כמני יקים לך ה' אלהיך אליו תשמעון" (Dt. 18:15) (cf. Jer. 30:21) (see 4:1-7 [nn46, 79], 21-31 and verses 10-14 [n129]). In the words of a midrash: "R. Ishmael taught: As long as a man refrains from sin, he is an object of fear and awe. The moment he sins, he is himself subject to fear and awe . . . after they [Israel] sinned, they could not gaze even upon the face of God's intermediary. Of their fear it is written *They were afraid to come nigh him* (Ex. 34:30) ר' ישמעאל: עד שלא יחטא אדם נותנים לו אימה וייראה. וכיון שהוא חוטא נותנים עליו אימה וייראה . . . כיון שחטאו ישראל אפילו פני (השליט) [השליח] הסרסור לא היו יכולין להסתכל, הדא הוא דכתיב: ויראו מגשת אליו" (Pes.Rab. 15:3). For sin and mediation, see below. (The dictum "Just as [Scripture] was given through a mediator so we too must deal with it through a mediator כשם שנתנה על-ידי סרסור כך אנו צריכין לנהוג בה על- ידי סרסור" [JMeg. 4, 1, 74d] refers to the necessity of a translator: Since Scripture was, as it were, being given anew when read, it must be given indirectly [cf. Safrai and Stern: 931].)

him, 'Yes.' He then said, 'Do you accept the divinity of the Holy
One, blessed be He?' and he answered, 'Yes, yes.' Thereupon he
kissed him on the mouth; hence it says, *Unto thee it was shown that
thou mightest know* (Dt. 4:35), namely, by an [angelic]
messenger.[247] (Cant.R. 1.2.2)[248] (see 1:6-10)

The "seed" is evidently the Messiah, as Paul has established in verse
16 – the singular being specific (see verses 13-18). Possibly here Paul is
again influenced by the LXX of Habakkuk 2:3-4, where the "vision" is
understood as a person: "If **he** delays, wait for him, because a Coming One
will arrive and will not linger ... The Righteous One shall live by My
faith"[249] (see verses 10-14). The seed is not so much the recipient of the
promise ("to whom [it] had been made") as its embodiment – the "one to
come" for (concerning) whom the promise was given, the one in whom it
finds its fulfilment (see 4:1-7).[250]

Verse 20: Having identified the "mediator" in verse 19 with Moses,
Paul develops the idea of mediation as that which "comes between" people
– and between people and the Holy One, blessed be He.[251] The deficiency
of the Torah's regulation from this perspective lies in the fact that it
disturbs God's sovereignty/unity.[252] The Torah's ordinances – ordained by
angels through Moses' hand – represent an intervention between God and

---

[247] ישקני מנשיקות פיהו: אמר רבי יוחנן: מלאך היה מוציא הדיבור מלפני הקדוש ברוך הוא על כל
דיבור ודיבור ומחזירו על כל אחד ואחד מישראל ואומר לו: מקבל אתה עליך את הדיבור הזה? כך
וכך דינין יש בו כך וכך עונשין יש בו, כך וכך גזרות יש בו, וכך מצות, וכך קלים וחמורים יש בו. כך
וכך מתן שכר יש בו. והיה אומר לו ישראל: הן. וחוזר ואומר לו: מקבל את אלהותו של הקדוש
ברוך הוא? והוא אומר לו: הן והן. מיד היה נושקו על פיו הדא הוא דכתיב: אתה הראת לדעת על
ידי שליח.

[248] Cf. Lev. 26:46; Num. 36:13; Dt. 33:2; 2 Chron. 33:8; Neh. 9:14; Acts 7:38, 53; Heb.
2:2; Jos.*Ant.* 15.136; Cant.R. 1.2.2 [Dt. 4:35]; TBE pp. 119-120; Mekh.Ba-chod. 9; Sifra,
Be-chuk. 8; ARNᵃ 1:2.

[249] ὅτι ἐρχόμενος ἥξει καὶ οὐ μὴ χρονίσῃ ... ὁ δὲ δίκαιος ἐκ πίστεώς μου
ζήσεται.

[250] Cf. "Abraham was *only* one, yet he possessed [inherited] the land אחד היה אברהם
וייֿרש את-הארץ" (Ezek. 33:24) (see verses 26-29). "Therefore, also, there was born of
one man ... AS THE STARS OF HEAVEN (διὸ καὶ ἀφ᾽ ἑνὸς ἐγεννήθησαν ... καθὼς
τὰ ἄστρα τοῦ οὐρανοῦ) ..." (Heb. 11:12) (cf. Rom. 5:15-19).

[251] This may be the meaning of the Qumran texts which speak of a mediator: "For
you have brought [your truth and] your [glo]ry to all the men of your council and
in the lot, together with the angels of the face, without there being a mediator
between [your holy ones ...] לכול אנשי עצתכה ובגורל יחד עם מלאכי פנים ואין מליץ בנים
[...לקןֿדושיכה" (1QHᵃ 14:13-14) (cf. 1QHᵃ 26:11-12//4Q427 f7ii:18-20?).

[252] Cf. Ex. 8:10, 9:14; Dt. 4:35, 39, 6:4, 33:26; Ps. 96:5; Isa. 44:8, 45:21f, 46:9; Zech. 14:9;
Acts 10:36; Rom. 3:29-30, 10:12; 1 Cor. 8:4f. For the unity of the human community,
derived from Abraham, see verses 26-29.

human beings.[253] To the extent that the Torah serves as an accommodation
to human weakness, God "did not speak to your fathers, or command
them in the day that I brought them out of the land of Egypt, concerning
burnt offerings and sacrifices. But this is what I commanded them, saying,
'Obey My voice, and I will be your God, and you will be My people; and
you will walk in all the way which I command you, that it may be well
with you'"[254] (Jer. 7:22-23) (cf. Ezek. 20:25).[255]

What comes "between" people and God is their sin: "But your
iniquities have made a separation between you and your God, and your
sins have hid His face from you, so that *He* does not hear כי אם-עונׂתיכם היו
מבדלים ביניכם לבין אלהיכם וחטאותיכם הסתירו פנים מכם משמוע" (Isa. 59:2) (see
2:15-21 and verses 26-29).[256] "After they [Israel] sinned, they could not gaze

---

[253] Various texts witness to the belief that angels were at times held to mediate
between God and man: "If trouble should come upon a man, he first goes to his
patron's house and calls his servant or son, saying: so-and-so is standing at your
gate. He may let him in or he may leave him outside. But God is not like that. If a
person encounters trouble he should not call upon Michael, or Gabriel, to intercede
for him; but he should turn immediately to Me and I will immediately answer him,
as it is written *Whosoever shall call on the name of the Lord shall be delivered* (Joel 2:32)
אם באת לו עת צרה אינו נכנס אצלו פתאום אלא בא ועמד לו על פתחו של פטרונו וקורא לעבדו או
לבן ביתו והוא אומר: איש פלוני עומד על פתח חצירך. שמא מכניסו ושמא מניחו. אבל הקדוש ברוך
הוא אינו כן. אם בא על אדם צרה, לא יצווח לא למיכאל ולא לגבריאל אלא לי יצווח ואני עונה לו
מיד. הדא הוא דכתיב: כל אשר יקרא בשם ה' ימלט" (JBer. 63a).
[254] כי לא-דברתי את-אבותיכם ולא צויתים ביום הוציא אותם מארץ מצרים על-דברי עולה וזבח:
כי אם-את-הדבר הזה צויתי אותם לאמר שמע בקולי והייתי לכם לאלהים ואתם תהיו-לי לעם
והלכתם בכל-הדרך אשר אצוה אתכם למע ייטב לכם.
[255] This verse is, of course, frequently included amongst the matrix of prophetic
passages which denounce the cultus when practiced without intention (cf. Ps. 50:7-
23; Isa. 1:10ff, 66:3; Hos. 6:6; Amos 5:21-27) (see 2:15-21 and verses 6-9 [n72]). (For
the suggestion that Jeremiah may be following a tradition which understands the
deuteronomic legislation to have been delivered shortly before Moses' death, on the
plains of Moab [cf. Dt. 1:5, 29:1], cf. Dreyfus: 84, citing M. Weinfeld, "Jeremiah and
the Spiritual Metamorphosis of Israel," *ZAW* 88 [1976], 17-56 [54].) Paul picks up
here the idea of "hypocrisy" introduced in his reproof of Peter, asserting that
without piety or "faithfulness/intention" neither Jew nor Gentile gains access to the
"outer chamber" of the Kingdom – despite Israel having, in the Torah, the keys to
the inner chamber (see 2:15-21). He expands on this idea of sin as the grounds of
"hypocrisy" in speaking of the "deeds of the flesh" in 5:16f, the fruit of the Spirit
having "no law against them" (see 5:13f and below).
[256] It is no coincidence that Isaiah 59 ends with God's promise that "'a Redeemer
will come to Zion, and to those who turn from transgression in Jacob,' declares the
LORD. 'And as for Me, this is My covenant with them,' says the LORD: 'My Spirit
which is upon you, and My words which I have put in your mouth, shall not depart
from your mouth, nor from the mouth of your offspring [seed], nor from the mouth
of your offspring's offspring,' says the LORD, 'from now and forever' ובא לציון גואל
ולשבי פשע ביעקב נאם ה': ואני זאת בריתי אותם אמר ה' רוחי אשר עליך ודברי אשר-שמתי בפיך
לא-ימושו מפיך ומפי זרעך ומפי זרע זרעך אמר ה' מעתה ועד-עולם" (Isa. 59:20-21).

even upon the face of God's intermediary. Of their fear it is written *They were afraid to come nigh him* (Ex. 34:30) (השליט) כיון שחטאו ישראל אפילו פני
"[השליח] הסרסור לא היו יכולין להסתכל, הדא הוא דכתיב: ויראו מגשת אליו
(Pes.Rab. 15:3) (see above).[257]

God's sovereignty is most explicitly expressed in His unity – which, in turn, demands from human beings their all: heart, soul, and strength (cf. Dt. 6:5). "But what is the text that proves to us we should love God? It is a weighty commandment, the most weighty of the Torah, the command to love God, *Thou shalt love the Lord thy God* (Dt. 6:5) being conjoined with the verse which affirms His sovereignty, *Hear O Israel: the Lord is our God, the Lord alone* (Dt. 6:4)"[258] (TBE p. 140) (see 5:13-18). Love for God – and for one's neighbour – is that which ascribes to God His true nature. It is therefore love which God most seeks of wo/man: "'YOU SHALL LOVE THE LORD YOUR GOD WITH ALL YOUR HEART, AND WITH ALL YOUR SOUL, AND WITH ALL YOUR MIND.' This is the great and foremost commandment. And a second like it is, 'YOU SHALL LOVE YOUR NEIGHBOR AS YOURSELF.' On these two commandments depend the whole Law and the Prophets"[259] (Mt. 22:37-40) (see 5:13f). "He has told you, O man, what is good; and what does the LORD require of you but to do justice, to love kindness, and to walk humbly with your God"[260] (Mic. 6:8) (cf. Jer. 9:23-24) (see Introduction, **Argument**).[261]

This stance represents Israel's central covenantal declaration in the Shema – what God wishes of His people's commitment: "Hear O Israel, the

---

[257] If the people were too terrified to approach Moses, all the more so were they afraid to approach God, lest they die (cf. Gen. 3:10; Ex. 20:18-20). (The events of Ex. 34:30f occurred subsequent to the making of the golden calf – to which incident the midrash presumably refers in relation to Israel's sinning, the "literal" signification pertaining to the glory of Moses' face.) For sin in relation to hypocrisy, one of Paul's guiding motifs in Galatians, see Introduction, **Argument; Theological pointers** (Justification), and 2:15-21.

[258] אהבת אדם למקום מנין? אלא אהבת אדם למקום היא מצוה חמורה מן התורה, דהא עיל
מלכות שמים כתיב בצד האהבה, שנאמר: שמע ישראל ה' אלהינו ה' אחד.

[259] ἀγαπήσεις κύριον τὸ θεόν σου ἐν ὅλῃ τῇ καρδίᾳ σου καὶ ἐν ὅλῃ τῇ ψυχῇ σου καὶ ἐν ὅλῃ τῇ διανοίᾳ σου· αὕτη ἐστὶν ἡ μεγάλη καὶ πρώτη ἐντολή. Δευτέρα ὁμοία αὐτῇ· ἀγαπήσεις τὸν πλησίον σου ὡς σεαυτόν. ἐν ταύταις ταῖς δυσὶν ἐντολαῖς ὅλος ὁ νόμος κρέματι καὶ οἱ προφῆται.

[260] הגיד לך אדם מה-טוב ומה-ה' דורש ממך כי אם-עשות משפט ואהבת חסד והצנע לכת עם-אלהיך.

[261] This contrast of "love" with "sin" represents the hypocrisy with which Paul is concerned throughout Galatians. What God desires from wo/man is performance of the "weightier provisions of the Torah" – "justice and mercy and faithfulness" (cf. Mt. 23:23). Love is the "intention" which enables God's will to be carried out in human lives, or "go[ing] beyond the law, which in itself is right and good, in order to do what is right and good" (Berkovits: 27) (see 2:15-21, 5:2ff, verses 10-14 [n142], 5:2ff, and below).

LORD is our God, the LORD is one! And you shall love the LORD your God
with all your heart and with all your soul and with all your might שמע
"ישראל ה' אלהינו ה' אחד : ואהבת את ה' אלהיך בכל-לבבך ובכל-נפשך ובכל-מאדך"
(Dt. 6:4-5).[262] The manner in which this love is expressed is demonstrated
in the following verse: "And these words, which I am commanding you
today, shall be on your heart והיו הדברים האלה אשר אנכי מצוך היום על-לבבך"
(Dt. 6:6).[263] God promises that the commandment is "not too difficult for
you, nor is it out of reach לא-נפלאת הוא ממך ולא רחקה הוא" (Dt. 30:11), and
that He will "put My Torah within them, and on their heart I will write it;
and I will be their God, and they shall be My people נתתי את-תורתי בקרבם
ועל-לבם אכתבנה והייתי להם לאלהים והמה יהיו-לי לעם" (Jer. 31:33) (see 5:13-
18).[264] As John later writes in one of his letters: "The Son of God appeared
for this purpose, that he might destroy the works of the devil. No one who
is born of God practices sin, because His seed [Seed?] abides in him . . . any
one who does not practice righteousness is not of God, nor the one who
does not love his brother" (1 Jn. 3:8-10) (see 5:13-18 [n116]).

In a certain sense, Jesus' representative "oneness" is that also which
counters the "multiplicatory" aspect of sin, that which "adds" or
"increases" transgression among all wo/mankind: "Surely **our** griefs **he
himself** bore, and **our** sorrows **he** carried; yet **we ourselves** esteemed **him**
stricken, smitten of God, and afflicted. But **he** was pierced through for **our**
transgressions, **he** was crushed for **our** iniquities; the chastening for **our**
well-being *fell* upon **him**, and by **his** scourging **we** are healed. All of us like
sheep have gone astray, each of us has turned to his own way; but the
LORD has caused the iniquity of **us all** to fall on **him** . . . Yet he himself bore

---

[262] Cf. Zech. 14:9, where God's unity is explicitly associated with His sovereignty –
when everything is subject to His will: "And the LORD will be king over all the
earth; in that day the LORD will be *the only* one, and His name *the only* one והיה ה'
למלך על-כל-הארץ ביום ההוא יהיה ה' אחד ושמו אחד" (the English translation altering the
sense of the literal meaning) (see 2:15-21 [n232]). For the universality of God's
oneness, see verses 26-29.

[263] Cf. the clear association between loving God and obeying His commandments:
"You shall therefore love the LORD your God, and always keep His charge, His
statutes, His ordinances, and His commandments ואהבת את ה' אלהיך ושמרת משמרתו
וחקתיו ומשפטיו ומצותיו כל-הימים" (Dt. 11:1) (cf. Ex. 20:6; Dt. 13:4, 19:9, 30:6; Josh. 22:5;
Jn. 15:10, 15:14; 1 Jn. 2:3ff, 3:24) (see 5:13f and 6:1-11).

[264] Cf. also the theme of "today, if you would hear His voice, do not harden your
hearts . . . היום אם-בקלו תשמעו : אל תקשו לבבכם" (Ps. 95:7-8) which, in certain
midrashic texts, is associated with the coming of the Messiah (cf. Heb. 5:5-10; Ex.R.
25:12; [PRK 24:12]; Yalk.Zech. 576; San. 98a). Cf. also the verbal association between
בקרבם (be-kirbam) in Jer. 31:33 and מקרבך (mi-kirbekha) in Dt. 18:15 (cf. Ezek. 36:26-
27). For the relation between the "one and the many," see verses 26-29; for Dt.
18:15f, see 4:1-7 (nn46, 79), 21-31 and verses 10-14 (n129); for the commandment to
love, see 5:13f and 6:1-11.

the sin of **many**, and interceded for the **transgressors**"[265] (Isa. 53:4-6, 12). "So then as through **one** transgression there resulted condemnation to **all men**, even so through **one** act of righteousness there resulted justification of life to **all men**. For as through the **one man's** disobedience the **many** were made sinners, even so through the obedience of the **One** the **many** will be made righteous"[266] (Rom. 5:18-19).[267]

The idea of mediatorship is derived from the repeated expression בין (beyn - "between"), present in Leviticus 26:46 as in Isaiah 59:2 (cf. ARN[a] 1:2; ARN[b] 1).[268] As expressed by the midrash, "the eye and the heart are the two go-betweens of sin חטאה סרסורי תרין ועינא "ליבא (JBer. 1, 4, 3c).[269] The Torah was "added (προσετέθη)" to God's original, unmediated relationship with wo/man - in order to regulate human sin through reward and punishment, the idea of an intercessor/intermediary being logically dependent upon the presence of transgression: "R. Simeon said: For what purpose does a sin-offering come? — [You ask,] 'for what purpose does a sin-offering come?' Surely in order to make atonement! — Rather, [the question is:] Why does it come before the burnt-offering? [Because it is] like an intercessor who enters [to appease the King]: When the intercessor has appeased [him], the gift follows אמר ר' שמעון: חטאת, למה באה? למה באה?! לכפר! אלא למה באה *לפני עולה?* לפרקליט שנכנס [ריצה פרקליט, נכנס], דורון אחריו" (Zev. 7b) (cf. Longenecker, Galatians: 142-43).[270]

---

[265] אכן חֳלָיֵנוּ הוּא נָשָׂא וּמַכְאֹבֵינוּ סְבָלָם וַאֲנַחְנוּ חֲשַׁבְנֻהוּ נָגוּעַ מֻכֵּה אֱלֹהִים וּמְעֻנֶּה: וְהוּא מְחֹלָל מִפְּשָׁעֵנוּ מְדֻכָּא מֵעֲוֹנֹתֵינוּ מוּסַר שְׁלוֹמֵנוּ עָלָיו וּבַחֲבֻרָתוֹ נִרְפָּא-לָנוּ . . . חֵטְא-רַבִּים נָשָׂא וְלַפֹּשְׁעִים יַפְגִּיעַ.

[266] Ἄρα οὖν ὡς δι' ἑνὸς παραπτώματος εἰς πάντας ἀνθρώπους εἰς κατάκριμα, οὕτως καὶ δι' ἑνὸς δικαιώματος εἰς πάντας ἀνθρώπους εἰς δικαίωσιν ζωῆς· ὥσπερ γὰρ διὰ τῆς παρακοῆς τοῦ ἑνὸς ἀνθρώπου ἁμαρτωλοὶ κατεστάθησαν οἱ πολλοί, οὕτως καὶ διὰ τῆς ὑπακοῆς τοῦ ἑνὸς δίκαιοι κατασταθήσονται οἱ πολλοί.

[267] The point to be made here being the multiplicity of sin - both in the number of transgressions and in the number of transgressors - on the one hand, and the messianic unity on the other. The ἑνὸς οὐκ ἔστιν (henos ouk estin - "[a mediator] is not one") picks up and contrasts with the ἀλλ' ὡς ἐφ ἑνός (all hōs ef henos - "[it says] as to one") of verse 16, tying Jesus to God's unity. See also verses 26-29.

[268] While the Torah "comes between" God and wo/man, it is not, like sin itself, counter to God's purposes (see verses 21-25). The reader should already be aware that the present picture of Paul as remaining faithful to his Jewish heritage precludes the prejudice which Christian theology has traditionally maintained against Judaism (see Introduction, **Author**; Appendix).

[269] Cf. Num.R. 17:6; Yalk.Dt. 836 (see also 4:12-20).

[270] R. Simeon's question is along the lines of Paul's: "What does the Torah come for?" For Moses' intervention between the people and God's direct address, see 4:1-7 (nn46, 79), 21-31 (nn211, 239), verses 10-14 (n129), and above (nn246, 264).

Verses 21-25:

Is the Law then contrary to the promises of God? May it never be! For if a law had been given which was able to impart life, then righteousness would indeed have been based on law. But the Scripture has shut up all men under sin, that the promise by faith in Jesus the Messiah might be given to those who believe. But before faith came, we were kept in custody under the law, being shut up to the faith which was later to be revealed. Therefore the Law has become our tutor *to lead us* to the Messiah, that we may be justified by faith. But now that faith has come, we are no longer under a tutor.

By the force of his own argument, Paul turns, again and again, to defending the Torah as an expression of God's will.[271] Even if the "addition" (cf. verse 19) of the Torah can be explained as an accommodation to human weakness – can that idea itself not be perceived as implying that the Torah actually runs contrary (κατά; kata) to the promises which God first made to Abraham (see verses 15f)? Or, as Paul asks in Romans: "What shall we say then? Is the Torah sin? (Τί οὖν ἐροῦμεν; ὁ νόμος ἁμαρτία;)" (Rom. 7:7).[272]

As in the other places in which Paul repudiates such a claim, here too he invokes the strongest denial: "God forbid (μὴ γένοιτο)."[273] The present refutation is logical rather than chronological, and indicates that the "contrariness" to which he is referring relates to an obstruction in the gift of life.[274] While the nouns signifying "law (νόμος)" are anarthrous, enabling them to be understood as signifying a general principle, Paul does not mean a "legal structure" but, as the parallel to "Scripture (ἡ γραφή)" substantiates in verse 22, God's covenant as embodied in the Torah.[275] The negation thus contains within it the true purpose: the giving of a covenant competent to bestow life/righteousness.[276]

---

[271] This would, of course, constitute an entirely superfluous necessity if his primary concern – as conceived by so many Christian commentators – is to disclose the Torah's supercession.

[272] It is but a short step – as Christian tradition again witnesses - from acknowledging that God condescends to the human level of human beings to asserting that the Torah itself is a source of sin, given against God's better judgment and original intention; that the Torah itself is a curse, opposed to all God's blessings. 2 Peter 2:19 very clearly demonstrates that bondage occurs in relation to sin - not to the Torah: "they themselves are slaves of corruption; for by what a man is overcome, by this he is enslaved (αὐτοὶ δοῦλοι ὑπάρχοντες τῆς φθορᾶς· ᾧ γάρ τις ἥττηται, τούτῳ δεδούλωται)."

[273] Cf. Rom. 3:4, 6, 31, 6:2, 15, 7:7, 13, 11:1, 11; Gal. 2:17 (see 2:15-21).

[274] The sentence "For if . . ." is formulated as a second class "contrary to fact" condition, which assumes the condition to be incorrect. "Such a sentence is often used to prove the falsity of the hypothesis from the unreality of the apodosis" (Burton: 194).

[275] Although "Scripture [מקרא; הכתוב]" is broader than the Torah, including not just the Pentateuch but also the Prophets and Writings, the term regularly denotes a

It is this power which the Torah lacks – not in its inherent character, which is of God, but in consequence of its conditionality,[277] its accommodation to human beings and the level of their ability to observe its statutes (cf. 1 Tim. 1:8-11) (see 2:15-21 and verses 10-14, 19-20).[278] Paul's proof here is almost tautological: It is only if you assume that the Torah is meant to grant life that you mistakenly deem it dissimilar to the promises. Had it been intended to convey righteousness, it would have done so![279]

Verse 22: This argument, too, is merely provisional – not strictly having proved the point.[280] Paul now provides the full exposition of the Torah's role. The governing metaphor through verse 25 is protective custody – imprisonment to ensure the prevention of harm.[281] The Greek

---

passage from the Torah (cf. Lev.R. 19:5; Num.R. 6:1, 14:4; Dt.R. 1:1; Ber. 21b; Yev. 4b, 63b; Sot. 2b).

[276] For the parallelism between life and righteousness, see verses 10-14; for Paul's argumentation *via* the negative, see 1:1-5 and 6:1-11.

[277] "And I gave them My statutes and informed them of My ordinances, by which, if a man observes them, he will live ואתן להם את-חֻקותי ואת-משפטי הודעתי אותם אשר יעשה אותם האדם וחי בהם" (Ezek. 20:11).

[278] While the Torah is frequently adduced as the antidote to sin (cf. [1QHᵃ 10:8ff, 15:12]; BB 16a; Kid. 30b), at least one midrashic tradition understands that the Torah contains within it not merely the ointment of life but also the poison of death: "Why are the words of the Torah compared to a prince? To tell you: just as a prince has power of life and death, so have the words of the Torah [potentialities] of life and death. Thus Raba said: To those who go to the right hand thereof it is a medicine of life; to those who go to the left hand thereof it is a deadly poison למה נמשלו דברי תורה כנגיד? לומר לך: מה נגיד! זה יש בו להמית ולהחיות -. אף דברי תורה, יש בם להמית ולהחיות. היינו דאמר רבא: למיימינין בה סמא דחיי, למשמאילים בה סמא דמותא" (Shab. 88b) (cf. Mt. 25:31-46; [Lk. 2:34]; 1QHᵃ 10:8-10, 13-15; Shab. 63a; Yoma 72b) (see also 2:15-21).

[279] "In that case, the Law would offer a rival system of salvation as an alternative to the promise. Paul insists, however, that the Law had no such power (cf. Rom 8:3) and was never intended for such a purpose. He has already argued emphatically that righteousness is ἐκ πίστεως (ek pisteōs), not ἐν νόμῳ (en nomō, vv. 11-12). Consequently – and this is the point of v. 21 – the Law, understood rightly, is not in a relation of competition or opposition to the promise. Thus, by denying the life-giving power of the Law, Paul is not opposing the Law but affirming its true purpose" (Hays, Galatians: 268).

[280] Paul is nonetheless possibly (still) thinking along the lines of divine condescension here. In the (perhaps unexpected) words of Chrysostom, some of God's ordinances were given with a view towards avoiding a greater evil and in anticipation of an eventual greater good. He therefore "countenanced sacrifices which He did not want, in order to assure the success of what He really wanted" (*On Isa.* 1.4) (cf. *Adv.Jud.* 4.3; *On Gen.* 18.3; *On Mt.* 26.39; *On Col.* 4.3; *On Tit.* 3.2; *On Heb.* 18.1).

[281] This is precisely the circumstance of the minor, who is under the guardianship of his father until he attains his majority (cf. Elon: 444) (see 4:1-7).

συγκλείω (syngkleiō) signifies "closing up together" (cf. LXX Ps. 30:9).[282] Paul employs precisely the same verb in Romans 11:32: "For God has shut up all in disobedience that He might show mercy to all (συνέκλεισεν γὰρ ὁ θεὸς τοὺς πάντας εἰς ἀπείθειαν, ἵνα τοὺς πάντας ἐλεήσῃ)."[283] Had wo/men not been so "guarded," they would have not have had access to God's grace, His anger having destroyed them long before.[284] This thought resembles God's "handing over (παρέδωκεν)" of wo/men to do "what is right in their own eyes" (cf. Rom. 1:24-32 [Judg. 17:6]), and thus recalls God's הסתר פנים (hester panim – "hiding His face").[285]

The LXX and DSS texts understand the presence of that motif in Isaiah 64:7 to signify that by hiding His face from them, God effectively hands people over to their evil inclination: "For Thou hast hidden Thy face from us, and hast delivered us into the power of our iniquities כי-הסתרת פניך ממנו ותמוגנו ביד-עוננו."[286] The midrashic tradition explicates on this theme in demonstrating how "sin croucheth at the door לפתח חאטת רבץ" (Gen. 4:7): "A parable. If a man leads a beast up to the top of the roof, it recoils, but a child runs (forward) to fall from the roof. When he is close to a fire, he runs to fall in the middle of it. When he is close to glowing coals, he stretches out his hand to grasp a handful. Why? Because the evil impulse has been cast into him"[287] (ARN[b] 30).[288]

A similar idea lies behind the association of sin and debt in 11QMelchizedek, where release is obtained in the jubilee year:

---

[282] The LXX employs the word most commonly to translate the Hebrew root סגר (sagar), "to close, shut."

[283] For the idea of God's "attribute of mercy" overcoming his "attribute of judgment," cf. Gen.R. 26:6, 73:3; Ex.R. 3:6; Lev.R. 29:3f; Ber. 7a.

[284] For the motif of "shutting out" – which links up with that of "hypocrisy" *via* Matthew 23 – see 2:15-21 and 4:12-20 (verse 17).

[285] Cf. Dt. 31:17-18, 32:20f; Ps. 27:9, 30:7, 44:23-24, 69:17, 88:14f, 102:2, 143:7; Isa. 8:17, 54:8; Jer. 33:5; Ezek. 39:29; Mic. 3:4; 4Q387a f3iii:4-5; 4Q389 f1ii:4-5; 4Q390 f2i:6f; 11QTemp 59:7. One aspect of the concept, at least, suggests that God withdraws in order to give people the opportunity (space) to exercise their own free will. At the same time, separation/bondage is tantamount to death (see verses 26-29).

[286] The LXX reads the MT מוג (mug – "to melt") as representing the root גנן (ganan – "to cover, defend") (cf. ותמגננו) (cf. Gen. 14:20; Prov. 4:9; Hos. 11:8), indicated by its usage of παραδίδωμι (paradidōmi – "to hand over").

[287] אם יעלה אדם את הבהמה לראש הגג היא סוללת אחריה (את) (אבל) התינוק הוא רץ ליפול ממנה. סמוך למדורה הוא רץ ליפול בתוכה. סמוך לגחלים הוא פושט ידו לקומצן. מפני מה? מפני יצר הרע נורק בו.

[288] Cf. Mid.Ps. 9:5; PRK S 3:2; Pes.Rab. 9:2; ARN[a] 16:2-3; ARN[b] 16; San. 91b; Ber. 61a; Suk. 52b. For the motif of serving two masters - God or one's evil inclination ("if you do not do well, sin is crouching at the door; and its desire is for you, but you must master it [אם לא תיטיב לפתח חטאת רבץ ואליך תשוקתן ואתה תמשל-בו]") (Gen. 4:7) - see 2:15-21 and 5:13-18. Paul brings out the "echo" of Romans 6 in these verses explicitly in verse 27, in speaking of baptism (see verses 26-29).

And as for what he said: *Lev 25:13* «In [this] year of jubilee, [you shall return, each one to his respective property», concerning it he said: *Deut 15:2* «Th]is is [the manner of the release:] every creditor shall release what he lent [to his neighbour. He shall not coerce his neighbour or his brother, for it has been proclaimed] a release for G[od». Its interpretation] for the last days refers to the captives ... And liberty will be proclaimed for them, to free them from [the debt of] all their iniquities. And this [wil]l [happen] in the first week of the jubilee which follows the ni[ne] jubilees. And the d[ay of aton]ement is the e[nd of] the tenth [ju]bilee in which atonement shall be made for all the sons of [light and] for the men [of] the lot of Mel[chi]zedek ... accor[ding to] a[ll] their [wor]ks, for it is the time for the «year of grace» [Isa. 61:2] of Melchizedek ...[289] (11QMelch 2:1-4, 6-9) (see 1:1-5, 2:1-10, and 4:1-7)[290]

The purpose of this protective custody is in order to ensure survival until such time as freedom can be obtained – as through the "forgiveness of debts" in the jubilee year. Perhaps most instructively, Paul may be seen here to be playing with the idea of "shutting out" which he makes explicit in 4:17 and which appears to underlie the argument in 2:15-21.[291] Jesus warns against making hypocritical demands on proselytes, arguing that

---

[289] ‏ואשר אמר בשנת היובל [הזאת תשובו איש אל אחוזתו ועליו אמר וז]ה [דבר השמטה] שמוט כול‎
‏בעל משה יד אשר ישה [ברעהו לוא יגוש את רעהו ואת אחיו כיא קרא] שמטה לא[ל פשרו] לאחרית‎
‏הימים על השבויים ... וקרא להמה דרור לעזוב להמה [משא] כול עוונותיהמה ו[כן יהי]ה הדבר‎
‏הזה בשבוע הראישון אחר תש[ע]ת ה[יו]בלים וי[ו]ם הכפ[ו]רים הו[א]ה ס[וף] ה[יו]בל העשירי‎
‏לכפר בו על כול בני [אור ו]אנש[י] גורל מל[כי] צדק ... כיא הואה הקץ לשנת הרצון למלכי צדק ...‎

[290] The text closely corresponds to Paul's thought, moreover, in that the "spiritual captives/slaves" are considered to be Melchizedek's "inheritance/lot" (cf. 11QMelch 2:5, 8) (see 1:1ff, 4:1-7). Melchizedek is also directly linked with Abraham, the story in Genesis 14 revolving around Abraham's deliverance of Lot and his possessions from captivity under the four kings. If 11QMelch forms part of an extended pesher on the Periods of History (cf. 4Q280), at least one section of the latter source addresses the angelic appearances to Abraham and the akedah (Isaac's binding) (cf. Kobelski: 51). The theme of bondage runs throughout Galatians (see 1:1-5, 2:1-10, 15-21, 4:1f, 21-31, and 5:13ff); for the motif of binding/prohibiting, see 2:15-21. Affinities with Melchizedek are also apparent via Heb. 7:11-12: "Now if perfection was through the Levitical priesthood (for on the basis of it the people received the Torah), what further need *was there* for another priest to arise according to the order of Melchizedek ... For when the priesthood is changed, of necessity there takes place a change of law also (Εἰ μὲν οὖν τελείωσις διὰ τῆς Λευιτικῆς ἱερωσύνης ἦν, ὁ λαὸς γὰρ ἐπ' αὐτῆς νενομοθέτηται, τίς ἔτι χρεία κατὰ τὴν τάξιν Μελχισέδεκ ἕτερον ἀνίστασθαι ἱερέα ... μετατιθεμένης γὰρ τῆς ἱερωσύνης ἐξ ἀνάγκης καὶ νόμου μετάθεσις γίνεται)."

[291] 4:17 uses ἐκκλείω (ekkleiō – "to shut out"), another compound of the root κλείω (kleiō – "to shut, lock") (see 4:12-20). For "hindering," see 5:2-12.

such stringency "shut[s] off the kingdom of God from men" with the result that they become "sons of gehinnom"[292] (Mt. 23:13, 15) (see 2:15-21, 4:12-20, 5:2-12, and verses 1ff).[293]

In parallel to the Melchizedek text, Paul envisions redemption as accomplished through the person of the Messiah - and thus made available to all (see verses 10-14, 26-29). The various translations witness to the awkwardness of rendering πίστις (pistis) here as "faith" rather than "faithfulness."[294] The expression ἐκ πίστεως 'Ιησοῦ Χριστοῦ (ek pisteōs Iēsou Christou) most obviously modifies the verb (δοθῇ [dothē - "might be given"]) (cf. 2:16, verses 8, 11, 14, 24). When the expression is taken to modify the noun ("promise") the meaning, very strangely, becomes "what was promised through faith in Jesus the Messiah" (cf. NRSV). Even when it is understood to modify the verb, the denotation "faith" requires some such interpolation as found in the NIV, which inserts a redundant "being given" ("so that what was promised, being given through faith in Jesus Christ, might be given to those who believe") absent from the Greek text. Even more violent in its mistreatment of the text is the RSV, which converts the ἐκ (ek - "out of") into its very opposite: "that what was promised *to* faith in Jesus Christ might be given to those who believe" (cf. Hays, Galatians: 269; Faith: 141f).

Hays sets out the theological - and textual - defects in this position with typical clarity: "We would do well to begin by asking whether it is more intelligible to suppose that 'believing in Jesus Christ' is the basis upon which 'the promise' is given to those who believe. Is this traditional view entirely satisfactory as an account of Paul's thought? If this is the correct reading of Paul, what sense does it make for him to invoke the example of Abraham, whose faith was, after all, not directed towards Jesus? Indeed, the apparent appeal to Abraham as the prototype of the justified believer has always created considerable difficulties for Christian theology and exegesis precisely because his faith was *not* directed toward Christ as object . . . (Gal. 3:6, quoting Gen. 15:6). This is one of the causes of the difficulty described by G. Ebeling, that the doctrine of justification by

---

[292] Οὐαὶ δὲ ὑμῖν . . . ὑποκριταί, ὅτι κλείετε τὴν βασιλείαν τῶν οὐρανῶν ἔμπροσθεν τῶν ἀνθρώπων· ὑμεῖς γὰρ οὐκ εἰσέρχεσθε οὐδὲ τοὺς εἰσερχομένους ἀφίετε εἰσελθεῖν . . . ὅτι περιάγετε τὴν θάλασσαν καὶ τὴν ξηρὰν ποιῆσαι ἕνα προσήλυτον, καὶ ὅταν γένηται ποιεῖτε αὐτὸν υἱὸν γεέννης διπλότερον ὑμῶν.

[293] Cf. 4Q286 f7ii:3f; RH 17a (בני גיהנם). The term closely resembles בני בליעל (bnei Belial - "the sons of Belial") - those whom Melchizedek comes to free from captivity to sin, who are contrasted with the "sons of God בני אל" (cf. 11QMelch 2:14) (see above). Rabbinic literature also employs the term בנים לגהינום (banim le-gehinnom), indicating that the Greek in Mt. 23:15 may signify "sons destined for gehinnom" (cf. Cant.R. 1.5.3; Yalk.Isa. 477; Ber. 10a).

[294] For the objective genitive, the "faithfulness of Jesus," see 2:15-21 and verses 10-14[f]).

faith, as usually understood, is not integrally linked with Christology. If we are justified by believing in Jesus Christ, in what sense is Abraham's faith a precedent for ours, or in what sense is our christocentric faith analogous to his? If Abraham could be justified by trusting God, why should we need to believe in *Christ* to be justified? Why not simply put our trust in God, as Abraham did?" (Faith: 150-51).[295]

On such a reading, the facileness of the construal "that, on the ground of faith in Jesus, the promise might be given to those who believe" (cf. Burton: 196) is resolvable by attributing the noun to Jesus' own faithfulness. Paul proposes simply to say that God's faithfulness to His people (in essence, to wo/mankind) is made available through Jesus' act of faithfulness to the Father: "That the promise, embodied in Jesus the Messiah's faithfulness, might be given to those who are faithful (to God through Jesus)."[296]

Verse 23 repeats the thought of verse 22, creating another chiastic pattern (see verses 10-14).[297] The correspondence between these two verses helps to clarify the meaning of "faith" also here. While it is frequently acknowledged that πίστις (pistis) is virtually synonymous in this context with "the faith" – i.e., the gospel, or the "Christian message" – Paul has consistently throughout this chapter been playing on Habakkuk 2:4 (see verses 10f).[298] The fact that he alludes to the LXX text in verse 19 – as it were, "the coming seed" – suggests that the same combination of "faith" and "coming" derives from Habakkuk (LXX) here also (see 4:1-7 and verses 19-20).[299] This ties in well with the language of "revelation

---

[295] The reference to Ebeling is presumably to G. Ebeling, *Word and Faith* [Philadelphia: Fortress, 1963], although Hays provides no page marker.

[296] Cf. Rom. 5:1-2, 19; Eph. 3:11-12; Phil. 2:8; Heb. 12:2. Paul has already established that the "promise" was addressed to the Messiah (verse 16), the same promise being the "blessing" promised through Abraham to all the nations of the earth (cf. verse 8). While commentators reserve weighty judgment against rendering the verb πιστεύω (pisteuō) as anything other than "to believe," usually in the sense of "mental assent," in this verse at least the verb functions as a substantive noun. On this reading – which accords an equality of denotation to the verb and noun alike – the simple meaning is "the faithful." Such usage fits Paul's general attribution of the shorthand phrase ἐκ πίστεως (ek pisteōs – "based on faithfulness") to the same subject (people) (cf. verses 7, 11-12, [14]) (cf. Hays, Faith: 141-53).

[297] The parallelism here is not quite as precise as that in verses 11-12. For other chiastic patterns, see 2:1-10 (n113), 4:1-7 (n43), 21-31 (n246), 5:2-12 (verse 4), and verses 10-14 (verses 11-12).

[298] "Here, 'the faith' cannot possibly refer to human subjective believing, because it is something that comes by revelation, and Paul has insisted from the beginning of the letter that revelation is not a matter of human responsibility; rather, it is a matter of divine action and divine disclosure (see, e.g., 1:11-12)" (Hays, Galatians: 270).

[299] Faithfulness is said to be "the belt about his [the Messiah's] waist האמונה אזור חלציו" in Isa. 11:5 (in parallel to the belt of righteousness around his loins) (cf. Jer.

(ἀποκαλυφθῆναι)," this theme being picked up from 1:15-16: "He who had set me apart ... was pleased to reveal His son in me (εὐδόκησεν ὁ ἀφορίσας με ... ἀποκαλύψαι τὸν υἱὸν αὐτοῦ ἐν ἐμοί)" (see 1:15-16b).[300]

Although Paul alters the verb at this point, from κλείω (kleiō) to φρουρέω (froureō), to signify the "watch" under which wo/men have been put by the Torah, he reverts once again to συγκλείω (syngkleiō) in relation to the revelation of faithfulness.[301] The play on this verb in these two verses indicates that the Torah's stewardship is not simply to put people behind bars but – more constructively – to protect them to ensure their survival until their release ("protective custody") (see above).[302]

Verse 24: This leads Paul to the metaphor of the "tutor (παιδαγωγός)."[303] Since this whole passage is dependent on verse 15 (cf. verse 19), the idea of the tutor may naturally be read into the continued context of God's "condescension" to human nature (see verses 19-20). While the design of such dicta as "to prevent our being perverted by contact with others or by mixing with bad influences, he hedged us in on all sides with strict observances [purities] connected with meat and drink and touch and hearing and sight, after the manner of the Law" (Ep.Arist. 142)[304] is regularly considered as intended to guard Israel from contamination, the purpose of the commandments can also be interpreted as "pedagogical":

2:21). Cf. also the midrashim which associate "Amana" (a mountain, but derived from the root for "faithfulness") with the Messiah, at times in conjunction with Hab. 2:4 itself (cf. Ex.R. 23:5; Cant.R. 4.8.2); for Paul's use of mountain metaphors, see 4:21-31. The very thought of Hab. 2:4 expresses the "coming" of someone/something anticipated but long awaited: "For the vision is yet for the appointed time; it hastens toward the goal, and it will not fail. Though it tarries, wait for it; for it will certainly come, it will not delay" (MT)/"Because the vision still awaits its time, and will rise to fulfilment and not be in vain. If he delays, wait for him, because a Coming One will arrive and will not linger" (LXX) (see 4:1-7).

[300] Cf. Pes.Rab. 15:10, 36:1-2; Yalk.Cant. 992; PRK 5:8, S 6:5; Perek Ha-Shalom 12.
[301] The former verb only occurs in the LXX in apocryphal texts (cf. Wis.Sol. 17:15; 1 Macc. 11:3).
[302] The modern concept of custody is very apt to Paul's perception, denoting on the one hand the act of keeping safe, especially the guardianship of a minor, and on the other, police arrest (cf. the "dominion of Belial" – see 4:1-7).
[303] The ὥστε (hōste) is a mark of consequence or purpose – "for this reason, therefore, so that" (cf. BAGD: 899). "The πεδαγωγός [pedagogos], though usually a slave, was an important figure in ancient patrician households, being charged with the supervision and conduct of one or more sons in the family. He was distinguished from the διδάσκαλος [didaskalos – "teacher"], for he gave no formal instruction but administered the directives of the father in a custodial manner, though, of course, indirectly he taught by the supervision he gave and the discipline he administered" (Longenecker, Galatians: 148).
[304] Cf. Ep.Arist. 139f; [Jos.CA 2.173-74].

"R. Phinehas in the name of R. Levi said: The matter[305] may be compared to the case of a king's son who thought he could do what he liked and habitually ate the flesh of *nebeloth* and *terefoth* [types of meat ritually unfit for consumption]. Said the king: 'I will have him always at my own table and he will abstain of his own free will.'[306] Similarly, because Israel were passionate followers of idolatry in Egypt and . . . used to offer their sacrifices in the forbidden high places, on account of which punishments used to come upon them, the Holy One, blessed be He, said: 'Let them offer their sacrifices to Me at all times in the Tent of Meeting, and thus they will separate themselves from idolatry and be saved from punishment'. Hence it is written, *What man soever there be of the house of Israel that killeth an ox . . . and hath not brought it unto the door of the Tent of Meeting,* etc. (Lev. 17:3-4).[307] (Lev.R. 22:8)[308]

---

[305] The discussion occurs in a debate between R. Ishmael and R. Akiva over the law permitting the consumption of meat (cf. Hul. 17a). R. Akiva's opinion is that Scripture comes only to forbid ritually unclean slaughter, the eating of meat itself being permissible, R. Ishmael contends that the law of slaughter is rather a permissive law which allows consumption – on condition that the meat is properly slaughtered. This debate forms the context of R. Phinehas' illustration, thus establishing that it is brought to demonstrate the purpose of the commandment (cf. Lev. 17:3-4).

[306] The text varies at significant points in the available versions. Here, it may be read either as נדור (nadur – "vowed") or as גדור (gadur – "hedged around") (the palaeographical difference being very slight between the initial letters in Hebrew). On the first reading, the meaning is that permitting the son to eat his fill will promptly lead him to lose his taste for what is forbidden. Some of the variants also read "let him **eat them** always at my table" in place of "let him always **be** at my table" (cf. Dreyfus: 81).

[307] ר' פנחס בשם ר' לוי אמר: משל לבן מלך שגס לבו עליו והיה למוד לאכול בשר נבלות וטרפות. אמר המלך: זה יהיה תדיר על שֻׁלחני ומעצמו הוא נדור [גדור]. כך לפי שהיו ישראל להוטין אחרי עבודה זרה ... והיו מקריבין קרבניהן באיסור במה ופורעניות באות עליהן. ואמר הקדוש ברוך הוא: יהיו מקריבין לפני בכל עת קרבנותיהן באוהל מועד ויהיו נפרשים מעבודה זרה והם ניצולים, הדא הוא דכתיב: איש איש מבית ישראל וגו'.

[308] In other words, the commandment to bring sacrifices to the *Tent of Meeting* represents a permissive law, designed to avert punishment by allowing the performance – under supervised conditions – of something in essence forbidden. While God would have preferred, as it were, no sacrifices at all, offerings too closely resembling pagan practices, if they were to be made at all, should be conducted in a manner and place which He instituted and administered. For the purpose of the cultic commandments, see verses 19-20.

The educational purpose of this action is, while acknowledging their human tendencies, to wean people away from their idolatrous habits and to bring them closer to God's true will.[309] The "imprisonment" constitutes a form of "accommodation" of/to human weakness which does not aspire to change the latter but merely to improve it – limiting itself to the bounds of human capacities.[310]

Paul's thought reflects the Hebrew wordplay on the root אמן (aman), whence are derived the nouns אמונה (emunah – "faithfulness") and אָמוֹן (amon – an artist or craftsman). Read as אָמוּן (amun), the signification denotes "guarded, nursed,"whence, in a transposition of the letters (אוֹמֵן; omēn), also "tutor": "R. Oshaya commenced [his exposition thus]: *Then I was by Him, as a nursling* (amon); *and I was daily all delight* (Prov. 8:30).[311] '*Amon*' means tutor; '*amon*' means covered; '*amon*' means hidden; and some say, '*amon*' means great. '*Amon*' is a tutor, as you read, *As an* omen (*nursing-father*) *carrieth the sucking child* (Num. 11:12). '*Amon*' means covered, as in the verse, Ha'emunim (*they that were clad* – i.e. covered) *in scarlet* (Lam. 4:5). '*Amon* ' means hidden, as in the verse, *And he concealed* (omen) *Hadassah* (Est. 2:7). '*Amon*' means great, as in the verse, *Art thou better than No-amon* (Nah. 3:8)? which is rendered, Art thou better than Alexandria the Great, that is situate[d] among the rivers? Another

---

[309] Cf. Jerome, *On Ezek.* to 20:25: "It was not good in itself and yet by no means bad, since they [the sacrifices] were offered to God. Nevertheless, it was not good because they offended the author of the good (non erat per se bonum et nequaquam malum quia Deo offerebantur, et tamen non bonum quia boni auctorem offenderant)" (cf. Wis.Sol. 16:21, 25; Iren.*Adv.Haer.* 4.38.1; Jerome, *On Jer.* to 7:22; Clem.*Rec.* 1.35-37; Just.*Dial.* 40, 46). If the Torah does not actually "prepare the way" for Jesus, Jesus nonetheless embodies what God seeks among human beings: The person in whom they attain maturity, "the measure of the stature which belongs to the fulness of the Messiah (μέτρον ἡλικίας τοῦ πληρώματος τοῦ Χριστοῦ)" (Eph. 4:13) (cf. Rom. 10:4).

[310] The classical description of this attitude is provided by Maimonides: "What was there to prevent Him [God] from causing the inclination to accomplish acts of obedience willed by Him . . . to be a natural disposition fixed in us? God does not change at all the nature of human individuals by means of miracles . . . It is because of this that there are commandments and prohibitions, rewards and punishments . . . We do not say this because we believe that the changing of the nature of any individual is difficult for Him . . . Rather it is possible and fully within His capacity. But according to the foundations of the Law, of the Torah, He has never willed it, nor shall He ever will it. For if it were His will that the nature of any human individual be changed because of what He wills from that individual, the sending of prophets and all giving of the Law would have been useless" (*Guide* 3:32). For the fruit of the Spirit as those actions "against which there is no law" – which are not accommodations to human limitations – see 5:19-23 (verse 23).

[311] The original reference of the biblical quotation is to Wisdom, extrapolated by the Sages to allude to the Torah (see verses 1f and below).

interpretation: *'amon'* is a workman (*uman*). The Torah declares: 'I was the
working tool of the Holy One, blessed be He'[312] (Gen.R. 1:1).[313]

A midrash on Proverbs 8:30 applies the verse in assertion of the claim
that God as it were "set wo/man up" by establishing the Torah – and its
punishments – before He even created the world:

> *Now Joseph had been taken down to Egypt* (Gen. 39:1). This refers to
> what is written: *Come and see the works of God, who is awesome in
> His deeds towards the sons of men* (Ps. 66:5). R. Joshua b. Korcha
> said: Even the awesome things which You bring upon us with
> craftiness [trickery], it is You who bring them. Come and see:
> When the Holy One, blessed be He, created the world, from the
> first day He created the Angel of Death. How do we know this?
> Said R. Berakhiah: Because it is written *And darkness was over the
> surface of the deep* (Gen. 1:2) – this is the Angel of Death who
> makes the face of the creatures dark. And man was created on the
> sixth day – as if God had planted a trick on him, because he
> brought death into the world, as it says *In the day that you eat from
> it you shall surely die* (Gen. 2:17). To what is this to be compared?
> To a man who wished to divorce his wife. When he went to go
> home he wrote out a bill of divorce and was armed with it when
> he arrived at the house. He sought to give it to his wife by
> tricking her. He said to her: Pour me a cup that I may drink. She
> poured him a cup and when he took the cup out of her hand he
> said to her: This is your bill of divorce. She asked him: What
> wrong have I done? He replied: Get out of my house, because
> you poured me a tepid cup. She responded: You already knew
> that I was going to pour you a tepid cup because you prepared
> the bill of divorce and brought it ready-written with you. Thus
> did Adam say to the Holy One, blessed be He: Sovereign of the
> Universe, before You had even created the world You had hidden
> the Torah with You for four thousand years, as it is written *Then I
> was beside him as concealed and I was daily His delight* (Prov. 8:30).

---

[312] רבי הושעיה רבה פתח: ואהיה אצלו אמון ואהיה שעשועים יום יום וגו'. אמון - פדגוג; אמון -
מכוסה; אמון - מוצנע; ואית דאמרי: אמון - רבתא. אמון פדגוג, היך מה דאת אמר: כאשר ישא
האומן את היונק. אמון מכוסה, היאך מה דאת אמר: האמונים עלי תולע וגו'. אמון מוצנע, היך מה
דאת אמר: ויהי אומן את הדסה. אמון רבתא - כמה דתימא: התיטבי מנא אמון - ומתרגמינן האת
טבא מאלכסנדריא רבתא דיתבא בין נהרותא. דבר אחר: אמון - אומן. התורה אומרת: אני הייתי
כלי אומנתו של הקדוש ברך הוא.

[313] R. Oshaya's exposition is of Gen. 1:1. "Hidden" is a reference to the fact that the
Torah (Wisdom personified in Proverbs 8) was not merely reared, as it were, by
God but was also concealed from the foundation of the world (see nn42, 97f, 139).
While Mordechai "raised" Hadassah, he also hid her from public gaze, according to
this interpretation. For the relation between the nursing/foster father and guardian,
see 4:1-7; for Paul's "fathering" role, see 2:1-10, 4:12-20, and 6:1-11.

Four thousand years – and it is written in it *This is the law when a man dies in a tent* (Num. 19:14). Had You not already established that man would die, would You have written this? But You determined to trick and play craftily with him, (as it says) *awesome in His deeds towards the sons of men*.[314] (Tanh.Vayeshev 4)[315]

On this reading, while the Torah – as a form of "tutor" – remains "holy and righteous and good," God knew before promulgating it that He meant it for a limited purpose. Its power was predefined by the capacities of human beings – among these being the choice of obedience and disobedience. In the same sense, the Torah's function was "chronologically" restricted, its role extending to the point in time when God decided to intervene in human history (again). The period of "confinement" comes to an end with the coming/revelation of faithfulness.[316] This is the most appropriate force of the εἰς (eis – "to") in verse 24, indicating a temporal ("until") rather than a spatial purpose.[317] Jesus is God's ultimate revelation of faithfulness, disclosing His compassion and love in not "sparing His own son, but delivering him up

---

[314] ויוסף הורד מצרימה. זה שאמר הכתוב: לכו חזו מפעלות אלהים נורא עלילה על בני אדם. אמר ר' יהושע בן קרחה: אף הנוראות שאתה מביא עלינו, בעלילה את מביאן. בא וראה: כשברא הקדוש ברוך הוא את העולם, מיום הראשון ברא מלאך המות. מנין? אמר ר' ברכיה: משום שנאמר: וחושך על פני תהום. זה מלאך המות המחשיך פניהם של בריות. ואדם נברא בששי ועלילה נתלה בו שהוא הביא את המיתה לעולם, שנאמר: כי ביום אכלך ממנו מות תמות. למה הדבר דומה? למי שמבקש לגרש את אשתו. כשבקש לילך לביתו כתב גט. נכנס לביתו והגט בידו ; מבקש עלילה ליתנו לה. אמר לה: מזגי לי את הכוס שאשתה. מזגה לו. כיון שנטל הכוס מידה אמר לה: הרי זה גיטך. אמרה לו : מה פשעי? אמר לה: צאי מביתי שמזגת לי כוס פשור. אמרה לו: כבר היית יודע שאני עתידה למזוג לך כוס פשור, שכתבת הגט והביאתו בידך! אף כך אמר אדם לפני הקדוש ברוך הוא: רבונו של עולם! עד שלא בראת עולמך קודם שני אלפים שנה היתה תורה אצלך אמון, שכך כתיב: ואהיה אצלו אמון ואהיה שעשועים יום יום. ב' אלפים שנה וכחיב בה: זאת התורה אדם כי ימות באהל. אלולי שהתקנת מות לבריות, היית כותב בה כך? אלא באת לתלות בי את העלילה – "יהוי נורא עלילה על בני אדם".

[315] The midrash's point of departure is the negative connotations inherent in the Hebrew נורא (nora – translated in English as "awesome"), which frequently signifies "awful" in the sense of "terrible." As something hidden, the Torah is here given the function of assigning to wo/men a "predetermined fate" – without, as it were, allowing people to prove their worth.

[316] The English word is felicitous here, signifying in contemporary language "imprisonment" and, residually, the period of pregnancy during which the woman's movements are restricted. For Paul's "creation" language, see 6:12-15 and verses 26-29.

[317] The spatial interpretation understands the preposition (in both verses 23-24) in the sense of "leading to the Messiah" – although the verb must be supplied. Despite the principle of accommodation, Paul does not present the Torah in any progressively educative function. Its tutelage is not designed to bring people to the Messiah but to protect and safeguard them from the effects of sin – until the Messiah is revealed. It is only the Messiah's faithfulness which releases wo/men from its protective custody (cf. Hays, Galatians: 270).

for us all (οὐκ ἐφείσατο ἀλλὰ ὑπὲρ ἡμῶν πάντων παρέδωκεν αὐτόν)"
(Rom. 8:32), Jesus himself "giving himself for our sins (τοῦ δόντος ἑαυτὸν
ὑπὲρ τῶν ἁμαρτιῶν ἡμῶν)" (1:4) (see 1:1-5).

Once again, Paul picks up the key phrase from Habakkuk 2:4 to point
out that it is through the "Righteous One" – in his faithfulness – that
wo/men find approval before God (see verses 10-14).[318] When the
"Coming One" has appeared – the fulness of time being the time
appointed, which will surely arrive (cf. 4:2-4) – God is no longer
constrained to accommodate Himself to human nature or to condescend to
human weakness (see 4:1-7).[319] He can fully redeem all humanity, as a free
gift graciously granted, removing debts and releasing people to liberty in
the day of His good pleasure (cf. 11QMelch 2:13-25; 4Q**504** ff1-2ii:13-17)
(see 1:1-5 and above).[320]

---

[318] Although a late midrash, the following nicely illustrates the faithfulness which
the Messiah embodies as a gift from God: "Whence do we know that the Holy One,
blessed be He, entrusted his faithfulness to Israel? As it says *He has remembered His
lovingkindness and His faithfulness to the house of Israel* (Ps. 98:3). And all Israel opened
their mouth and sang the Song before the Holy One, blessed be He at that time, as it
is written *O Lord, Thou art my God; I will exalt Thee, I will give thanks to Thy name; for
Thou hast worked wonders, plans formed long ago, with perfect faithfulness* (Isa. 25:1) [cf.
Ex. 15:1]. If it says *omen* [perfect], why add *emuna* [faithfulness]? And if it says
emuna, why add *omen* [i.e., why do you need two nouns to say the same thing,
although grammatically the expression simply indicates intensity]? But it teaches
that the Holy One, blessed be He, entrusted two sets of faithfulness to Israel on Mt.
Sinai: one to Israel and one to the Messiah. One to Israel – as it is said *He has
remembered His lovingkindness and His faithfulness to the house of Israel*. Whence one to
the Messiah? As it is said *Also righteousness will be the belt about his loins, and
faithfulness the belt about his waist* (Isa. 11:5)! מנין שהפקיד הקדוש ברוך הוא אמונתו לישראל?
שנאמר: זכר חסדו ואמונתו לבית ישראל. והיו כל ישראל פותחים את פיהם ואומרים שירה לפני
הקדוש ברוך הוא באותה שעה, שנאמר: ה' אלהי אתה ארוממך אודה שמך כי עשית פלא עצות
מרחוק אמונה אומן. אם נאמר "אומן" למה נאמר "אמונה"? ואם נאמר "אמונה" למה נאמר
"אומן"! אלא מלמד ששתי אמונות הפקיד הקדוש ברוך הוא לישראל על הר סיני: אחד לישראל
ואחד למשיח. אחד לישראל מנין! שנאמר: זכר חסדו ואמונתו לבית ישראל. ואחד למשיח מנין!
שנאמר: והיה צדק אזור מתניו והאמונה אזור חלציו" (Otiot d-R. Akiva 1:1). (R. Akiva and
his school subsumed grammatical principles under God's intention, thus assigning
an exegetical significance to what the school of R. Ishmael, on the other hand,
regarded as "ordinary [human] language.")

[319] "R. Hanina [or, Hinena] b. Isaac said: There are three incomplete phenomena:
the incomplete experience of death is sleep; an incomplete form of prophecy is the
dream; the incomplete form of the next world is the Sabbath. R. Abin added another
two: the incomplete form of the heavenly light is the orb of the sun; the incomplete
form of the heavenly wisdom is the Torah רבי חנינא בר יצחק אמר: ג' נובלות הן: נובלת
מיתה - שינה; נובלת נבואה - חלום; נובלת העולם הבא - שבת. רבי אבין מוסיף עוד תרתין: נובלת
אורה של מעלה - גלגל חמה; נובלת חכמה של מעלה - תורה" (Gen.R. 17:5, 44:17).

[320] Hays' narrative structural formulation leads him to identify "faithfulness" in the
role of the "Helper" in the Sender-Object-Subject[2] actantial model (cf. Faith: 105).
Within this scheme, the Helper is the figure or force that aids the Subject in carrying

Verse 25: Having hidden His face for a while, so as not to see the people's sins, and treated them as enemies because of their transgressions, God returns to them in Emmanuel – God with us, the Prince of peace.[321] While Paul declares that "we are no longer under a tutor (οὐκέτι ὑπὸ παιδαγωγόν ἐσμεν)," this statement is regularly understood to mean that the Torah itself has been invalidated and become obsolete (see also 2:15-21).[322] The present reading of Galatians (as of all Paul's writings) attributes the sentence's significance to the fact that human beings are no longer subject to its supervision.[323] Jesus' faithfulness in bringing forgiveness of sins and the restoration of God's presence is not the "end" but the "purpose" to which the Torah's custody was intended (cf. Rom. 10:4).[324]

Human participation in Jesus' faithfulness reflects the outpouring of the Spirit through whom those living in him walk pleasing to God: "And if the Messiah is in you, though the body is dead because of sin, yet the spirit is alive because of righteousness. But if the Spirit of Him who raised Jesus from the dead dwells in you, He who raised the Messiah Jesus from the dead will also give life to your mortal bodies through His Spirit who indwells you ... For all who are being led by the Spirit of God, these are sons of God"[325] (Rom. 8:10-11, 14) (see 4:1-7, 5:19f, and verses 26-29).

---

out his/her mandate, the latter being established by the Sender with the Subject. The Helper is in many instances summoned to overcome the otherwise all-powerful dominion of the Opponent (cf. ibid: 90-91).

[321] Cf. Isa. 7:14, 9:6; Ezek. 39:29; Mt. 1:23; Rom. 5:1; 2 Cor. 5:14-21; Gen.R. 42:3; Lev.R. 11:7; Est.R.Proem 11.

[322] While primarily theologically based, this view also appears to have the textual support of the adverb οὐκέτι (ouketi – "no longer"), the latter at times serving Paul as a logical rather than as a temporal marker (cf. Rom. 7:17, 20; verse 18) (cf. BAGD: 592).

[323] With Jesus' coming, they have, as Paul says in 4:1f, reached maturity and become heirs/sons rather than minors/slaves (see 4:1-7).

[324] In this sense, the τέλος (telos) of the Torah serves as the "teleological" time framework denoted by the εἰς (eis) as "until" in verses 23-24. See also 5:13-18 and verses 1-5.

[325] εἰ δὲ Χριστὸς ἐν ὑμῖν, τὸ μὲν σῶμα νεκρὸν διὰ ἁμαρτίαν τὸ δὲ πνεῦμα ζωὴ διὰ δικαιοσύνην. εἰ δὲ τὸ πνεῦμα τοῦ ἐγείραντος τὸν Ἰησοῦν ἐκ νεκρῶν οἰκεῖ ἐν ὑμῖν, ὁ ἐγείρας Χριστὸν ἐκ νεκρῶν ζῳοποιήσει καὶ τὰ θνητὰ σώματα ὑμῶν διὰ τοῦ ἐνοικοῦντος αὐτοῦ πνεύματος ἐν ὑμῖν ... ὅσοι γὰρ πνεύματι θεοῦ ἄγονται, οὗτοι υἱοὶ θεοῦ εἰσιν.

Verses 26-29:
For you are all sons of God through faith in the Messiah Jesus. For all of you who were baptized into the Messiah have clothed yourselves with the Messiah. There is neither Jew nor Greek, there is neither slave nor free man, there is neither male nor female; for you are all one in the Messiah Jesus. And if you belong to the Messiah, then you are Abraham's offspring, heirs according to the promise.

The effect of participating in Jesus' faithfulness – his obedience to death on the cross – is to make all, without distinction, "sons of God (υἱοὶ θεοῦ)."[326] The expression picks up the theme of the "sons of Abraham" with which Paul has engaged throughout this chapter (see 2:15-21 and verses 6-9). Here, he clarifies that those who inherit Abraham's blessing, through God's faithfulness displayed in Jesus' delivering up of himself on our behalf, are God's children.[327]

Since Abraham's blessing is fulfilled in the bestowal of the Spirit (cf. verse 14), an intimate connection is established between sonship and receipt of the Spirit: "For all who are being led by the Spirit of God, these are sons of God . . . The Spirit himself bears witness with our spirit that we are children of God, and if children, heirs also, heirs of God and fellow-heirs with the Messiah"[328] (Rom. 8:14, 16-17a) (see 4:1-7 and below).[329] Here, too, Paul may have Abraham in mind as the source of both Spirit and sonship. A midrash in the name of R. Shimon b. Lachish relates two verses speaking of Abraham so as to suggest that the blessing of the Spirit is fulfilled precisely in the multiplication of offspring:

---

[326] Significantly, Paul changes pronouns here all at once – from the "we/our" which has characterised the discussion of the Torah's role (a Jewish issue), to "you (pl.)." The switch indicates – in like manner to verse 14 – that the grounds upon which the Gentiles' status are based have now been established and Paul can apply the conclusions. For Paul's pronominal usage, see 2:15-21, 4:1f, and verses 10-14; for Jesus' representative death, as an expression of his faithfulness, see 2:15-21 and verses 10f. As Hays points out, the expression "in the Messiah Jesus" serves to modify the verb rather than the noun ("faith"), the more adequate translation thus being "for in the Messiah Jesus you are all sons of God through [his/your] faithfulness" (Galatians: 271).

[327] As the sources reflect, the Hebrew בנים (banim – the plural of בן [ben]) indicates not merely "sons" or "children" in the strict familial sense but also those who partake of the same nature/attitude – belong to the same "species" of thought, etc. (see 2:15-21 and verses 6-9).

[328] ὅσοι γὰρ πνεύματι θεοῦ ἄγονται, οὗτοι υἱοὶ θεοῦ εἰσιν . . . αὐτὸ τὸ πνεῦμα συμμαρτυρεῖ τῷ πνεύματι ἡμῶν ὅτι ἐσμὲν τέκνα θεοῦ. εἰ δὲ τέκνα, καὶ κληρονόμοι· κληρονόμοι μὲν θεοῦ, συγκληρονόμοι δὲ Χριστοῦ.

[329] The Spirit, too, is one (cf. 1 Cor. 12:4ff), as also are its fruit (cf. 5:22-23) (see 5:19-23). For God's unity, see verses 19-20 and below.

This [the story of the tower of Babel] is what the Scripture refers to: *But not one has done so who has a remnant of the Spirit. And what did that one do while he was seeking a godly offspring* [seed]? (Mal. 2:15).[330] R. Shimon b. Lachish said: *But not one has done* – that is Abraham, who was unique in the world in his deeds and God separated him from idolatry, as it is said *When he was one I called him* (Isa. 51:2). *Who has a remnant of the Spirit* – (these are the) sons and their sons which the Holy One, blessed be He, gave him, as it is said *Then I blessed him and multiplied him* (ibid).[331] (BM, Yelamdenu Lech 34)[332]

A similar thought is expressed in a text from Qumran which, in citing Isaiah 61, exhibits affinities with Malachi 2:5-6: "My covenant with him was *one of* life and peace, and I gave them to him *as an object of* reverence; so he revered Me, and stood in awe of My name. True instruction was in his mouth, and unrighteousness was not found on his lips; he walked with Me in peace and uprightness, and he turned many back from iniquity"[333] (cf. Isa. 53:11; Rom. 5:15ff; Heb. 9:28):

For the Lord will consider the pious, and call the righteous by name, and his spirit will hover upon the poor {cf. Gen. 1:2}, and he will renew the faithful with his strength. For he will honour the pious upon the throne of an eternal kingdom, freeing

---

[330] The Hebrew of this verse is very awkward. The English rendering here is taken from the NASB, which gives the alternative marginal reading of: "Did He not make one, although He had the remnant of the Spirit? Why one? He sought a godly offspring." The JPS version more closely approximates the midrashic understanding: "And did not God make of you one flesh? So that one should have a spiritual kin? A godly seed."

[331] זה שאמר הכתוב: ולא אחד עשה ושאר רוח לו וגו'. אמר רבי שמעון בן לקיש: ולא אחד עשה - זה אברהם, שהיה יחידי בעולם במעשיו והפרישו הקדוש ברוך הוא מעבודה זרה, שנאמר: כי אחד קראתיו. ושאר רוח לו - בנים ובני בנים שנתן לו הקדוש ברוך הוא, שנאמר: ואברכהו וארבהו.

[332] Cf. Ezek. 33:24; Heb. 11:12. Abraham (who is called "your father [אביכם]" in the same verse in Isa. 51:2) is identified as being unique ("one") in comparison to the confusion of the languages at Babel, as well as being "called out" – from Ur, whose inhabitants were consumed by idolatry (as explained in the following text). (The linguistic correspondence recalls the fact that the outpouring of the Spirit on Shavuot [cf. Joel 2:28f] should be considered as a "restoration" of the unity of human speech, while the Gentiles are further expected to receive a purified speech with which to call on the name of the Lord [cf. Zeph. 3:9; Tanh.B.Vayera 38] [cf. Le Cornu and Shulam: 85, 601-2] [see also below].) The word for "remnant" here is one of the regular terms employed to express the concept in the biblical texts. R. Shimon identifies it with Abraham's (immediate and direct) descendants – who are his blessing "in the Spirit" (see verses 1-5, 10-14).

[333] בריתי היתה אתו החיים והשלום ואתנם-לו מורא וייראני ומפני שמי נחת הוא: תורת אמת היתה בפיהו ועולה לא-נמצא בשפתיו בשלום ובמישור הלך אתי ורבים השיב מעון.

prisoners, giving sight to the blind, straightening out the
twis[ted] {cf. Ps. 146:7-8} . . . he will heal the badly wounded and
will make the dead live, he will proclaim good news to the poor
[Isa. 61:1] and [. . .] . . . [. . .] he will lead the [. . .] . . . and enrich
the hungry . . ."[334] (4Q521 f2ii:5-8, 12-13)[335]

This concept recurs in the characteristic language of the Dead Sea
literature in the Aramaic Visions of Amram, which associates the righteous
with the "sons of light " – who are also the "sons of blessing": ". . . from
their healer . . . [. . .] [. . .] [up]on you, sons of the blessing, and . . . [. . .] [. . .]
all generations of Israel for all [centuries . . .] [. . .] [. . .] . . . rejoice in me,
because the sons of ri[ghteouness . . .] you will be ca[lled . . .] your [. . .]
sons of lie [*sic*] and not son[s of truth . . .] I will [tea]ch you the desirable
[way,] I would let [you] know [the truth. For the sons of light] will be
brilliant, and [all the sons of] darkness will be dark"[336] (4Q548 1:3-10).

One of the most illuminating passages, composed of a mosaic of
prooftexts, is found in the Testament of Judah which, despite its clear
christianizing tendencies, reflects direct biblical influences:

And after this there shall arise for you a Star from Jacob in peace
[cf. Num. 24:17]: And a man shall arise from my posterity [Judah]
like the Sun of righteousness [cf. Mal. 1:2], walking with the sons
of men in gentleness and righteousness, and in him will be found
no sin. And the heavens will be opened upon him to pour out the
spirit as a blessing of the Holy Father [cf. Joel 2:28-29; Mt. 3:16].
And he will pour out the spirit of grace on you [cf. Joel 2:28-29;
Zech. 12:10]. And you shall be sons in truth, and you will walk in
his first and final decrees. This is the Shoot of God Most High [cf.
Isa. 11:1, 53:2; Jer. 23:5]; this is the fountain for the life of all
humanity [cf. Ps. 36:9; Prov. 14:27]. Then he will illumine the
scepter of my kingdom [cf. Gen. 49:10], and from your root will
arise the Shoot, and through it will arise the rod of righteousness
for the nations [cf. Ps. 2:9], to judge and to save all that call on the

---

[334] כי אדני חסידים יבקר וצדיקים בשם יקרא ועל ענוים רוחו תרחף ואמונים יחליף בכחו כי יכבד
את חסידים על כסא מלכות עד מתיר אסורים פוקח עורים זוקף כ[פופים . . .] . . . ירפא חללים
ומתים יחיה ענוים יבשר ו[. . . .] . . . ש[. . . .]ושים ינהל ורעבים יעשר . . .

[335] The influence of Isa. 61:1-3 on this passage is clear, setting it within the
framework of the messianic bestowal of life and salvation in the anointing of the
Spirit (see 1:1f, 4:1f, and verses 1ff). For the "many," see below; for the "spirit of the
Messiah hovering," see below.

[336] מן אסיאנהון . . . .] . . .[.].[.].[.] [ע]ליכון בני ברכתא וש[.].[.] כל דרי ישראל לכל [עולמין . . .]
[. .].י חדא בי די בני צ[דקתא . . .] תתקר[און . .].כון בני שקר ולא בנ[י קשוט . . .] אנא מ[נ]קר[ ]ה לכ[ון
ארח]א יצבתא אנה מודע ל[כון קשטא ארו כל בני נהורא] נהרין להוון [וכל בני] חשוכא חשיכין
להוון.

Lord [cf. Joel 2:32]. (Test.Jud. 24:1-6) (cf. Ps.Sol. 17:21-46, 18:5-9) (see also verses 10-14)

Verse 27 extends the explanation of verse 26 (cf. γὰρ [gar] – "for").[337] If the motif behind verse 26 is in fact the Spirit, it is presumably this which prompts Paul's reference to baptism. God's Spirit "clothes" people specifically in order to give them strength, indicating the close association between the Holy Spirit and power.[338] The metaphor of "putting on (ἐνεδύσασθε)" derives from the Isaiah passages which speak of God clothing Himself with garments of salvation in order to redeem His people through His Messiah:

> When the Messiah appears, God will put on the sixth garment: He will be clothed in righteousness, as is said *He put on righteousness as a coat of mail, and a helmet of salvation upon His head* (Isa. 59:17) ... The splendor of the garment He puts on the Messiah will stream forth from world's end to world's end, as implied by the words *As a bridegroom putteth on a priestly diadem* (Isa. 61:10). Israel will live in his radiance and say: Blessed is the hour in which the Messiah was created![339] (PRK S 6:5)[340]

---

[337] This γὰρ (gar) and that in the previous verse make both clauses dependent on, or clarificatory, of verse 25. Most strikingly, the expression "sons of God בני אל" appears in 11QMelch, a text which identifies those who have become captives/debtors/slaves with Melchizedek's "lot גורל" – those whom he rescues from the dominion of Belial as his "inheritance נחלה" (cf. 11QMelch 2:5, 8) (see 1:1ff, 4:1-7, and verses 21-25).

[338] Cf. Judg. 6:34, [14:19]; 1 Chron. 12:18; 2 Chron. 24:20; Isa. 11:2; Acts 1:5, 8; 2 Tim. 1:7; Ps.Sol. 17:37. Clothing and power both appear as metaphors for God's attributes, some of which are personified (cf. Ps. 93:1, 104:1; Isa. 51:9, 59:17, 61:10, 63:1-2; Gal. 3:27; Eph. 4:24, 6:11; 1 Thess. 5:8; Ps.Sol. 11:7; Odes Sol. 7:4, 20:7; Ap.Bar. 5:1-3; Test.Levi 18:14; 4Q161 ff8-10:16; 4Q381 f15:9f; 4Q437 ff3+4:6; 4Q438 f4ii+5:3; PRK 22:4-5, S 6:5; Gen.R. 1:6, 20:12; Num.R. 14:3; Nid. 25a).

[339] לבוש השישי בשעה שמשיח יגלה ילבש צדקה, שנאמר: וילבש צדקה כשריון וכובע ישועה בראשו . . . והלבוש שהלביש למשיח יהיה הולך ומבהיק מסוף העולם ועד סופו, שנאמר: כחתן יכהן פאר. וישראל משתמשים לאורו ואומרים למשיח: אשרי השעה שמשיח נברא.

[340] Cf. [Job 29:14]; Ps. 93:1, 104:1; Isa. 11:5, 51:9-10, 59:17, 63:1-2; [Dan. 7:9]; Rom. 13:14; 4Q438 f4ii+5:3; PRK 22:5; Pes.Rab. 36:2, 37:1f; Yalk.Hamakiri on Isa. 61:10. The LXX (Septuagint) renders the Hebrew לבש (lavash – "to put on") by the verb ἐνδύναμοō (endynamoō – "to strengthen") (cf. LXX Ps. 51:7), a term which recalls the Greek ἐνδύω (endyō – "to clothe") (cf. Mic. 3:8; Lk. 1:15, 4:14; Rom. 1:4, 15:19; 1 Cor. 2:4). In 4Q521, God's spirit "hovering upon the poor ועל ענוים רוחו תרחף" is parallel to His "renewing the faithful with his strength ואמונים יחליף בכחו" (and "calling the righteous by name וצדיקים בשם יקרא") (4Q521 f2ii:5-6).

Having spoken throughout the chapter of Jesus' faithfulness as the fulfilment of God's promise to Abraham, Paul now advises his disciples of the form which *human* faithfulness takes in response.[341] Those – "all of you (ὅσοι)" – who are "buried" with Jesus in his death, will God also raise with Jesus, whom He proclaimed "with power *to be* the Son of God by the resurrection from the dead, according to the Spirit of holiness (υἱοῦ θεοῦ ἐν δυνάμει κατὰ πνεῦμα ἁγιωσύνης ἐξ ἀναστάσεως νεκρῶν)" (Rom. 1:4).[342]

In this respect, the idea of baptism is introduced through the metaphor of "putting on" the Messiah through participation in his death. In its "putting to death" of sin, baptism-burial as a "metaphorical" event enacts the "angering" of one's evil inclination in order to be able to serve the one true Master: ". . . knowing this, that our old self was crucified with *him*, that our body of sin might be done away with, that we should no longer be slaves to sin . . . Even so consider yourselves to be dead to sin, but alive to God in the Messiah Jesus"[343] (Rom. 6:6, 11)[344] (cf. Shulam and Le Cornu: 209ff).[345] To "put on the Messiah" is to receive through the Spirit a "new self" – one which displays the Messiah's own character: ". . . Put on the Lord Jesus the Messiah, and make no provision for the flesh in regard

---

[341] Here, Paul speaks not of ἐκ πίστεως (ek pisteōs – "on the basis of faithfulness") but of τῆς πίστεως ἐν (tēs pisteōs en – "the faithfulness in"), marking believers' participation in Jesus' faithfulness; (for the latter, see 2:15-21 and verses 10ff). For Galatians as a "halakhic letter" along the lines of 4QMMT, see Introduction, **Form**; **Argument**.

[342] Cf. Rom. 6:3ff; Col. 2:12.

[343] τοῦτο γινώσκοντες ὅτι ὁ παλαιὸς ἡμῶν ἄνθρωπος συνεσταυρώθη, ἵνα καταργηθῇ τὸ σῶμα τῆς ἁμαρτίας, τοῦ μηκέτι δουλεύειν ἡμᾶς τῇ ἁμαρτίᾳ . . . οὕτως καὶ ὑμεῖς λογίζεσθε ἑαυτοὺς [εἶναι] νεκροὺς μὲν τῇ ἁμαρτίᾳ ζῶντας δὲ τῷ θεῷ ἐν Χριστῷ Ἰησοῦ.

[344] A passage in the Odes of Solomon links the metaphor of "putting on" with God's condescension: "He [God] became like me, that I might receive him. In form he was considered like me, that I might put him on" (Odes Sol. 7:4). For condescension/accommodation, see verses 19-20.

[345] Cf. Rom. 8:9-11. The "echoes" of this verse resonate with numerous aspects of the motifs with which Paul has been playing in this passage. Thus, the verb "consider (λογίζεσθε)" recalls the "reckoned (ἐλογίσθη)" of Gen. 15:6 in verse 6. The "doing away with (καταργηθῇ)" of sin is the same action (verb) of which Paul speaks in verse 17 in indicating the (non)invalidation of the original covenant. And the "life (ζῶντας)" picks up Paul's citation of Hab. 2:4 (verse 11), which verse runs as a theme throughout the chapter (see verses 10f). The "life" is the embodiment of Abraham's blessing. Bondage to sin is tantamount to death – and it is only through voluntary renunciation of the "body of sin" that we may win freedom for ourselves in dying and being buried with the Messiah. For the motif of "angering one's inclination," see 1:6-10, 2:15-21, and 5:13-18; for the presentiment of Hab. 2:4 in chapter 2, see 2:15-21 (nn267, 271).

to *its* lusts . . . be renewed in the spirit of your mind, and put on the new self, which in *the likeness of* God has been created in righteousness and holiness of the truth[346] (Rom. 13:14; Eph. 4:23-24) (see also below).[347]

Here, Paul pulls together all the strands of his argument in demonstration of the claim that Abraham's sons according to God's purpose are those whose hearts have been circumcised to remove the foreskin of their evil inclination, and thus received a new heart and self to "hear and to do" God's commandments. Through their faithfulness to the Messiah and in the Spirit with which God has blessed them in him they are enabled to put piety into practice (see 2:15-21):

> And the Lord said to Moses, "I know their contrariness and their thoughts and their stubbornness. And they will not obey until they acknowledge their sin and the sins of their fathers. But after this they will return to me in all uprighteousness and with all of (their) heart and soul. And I shall cut off the foreskin of their heart and the foreskin of the heart of their descendants. And I shall create for them a holy spirit, and I shall purify them so that they will not turn away from following me from that day and forever. And their souls will cleave to me and to all my commandments. And they will do my commandments. And I shall be a father to them, and they will be sons to me. And they will all be called 'sons of the living God.' And every angel and spirit will know and acknowledge that they are my sons and I am their father in uprightness and righteousness. And I shall love them." (Jub. 1:22-25)

> My heart was pruned and its flower appeared, then grace sprang up in it, and it produced fruits for the Lord. For the Most High circumcised me by his Holy Spirit, then he uncovered my inward being toward him, and filled me with his love. And his circumcising became my salvation, and I ran in the Way in his peace, in the Way of truth. (Odes Sol. 11:1-3) (see also 5:13-18)[348]

---

[346] ἀλλὰ ἐνδύσασθε τὸν κύριον Ἰησοῦν Χριστὸν καὶ τῆς σαρκὸς πρόνοιαν μὴ ποιεῖσθε εἰς ἐπιθυμίας . . . ἀνανεοῦσθαι δὲ τῷ πνεύματι τοῦ νοὸς ὑμῶν καὶ ἐνδύσασθαι τὸν καινὸν ἄνθρωπον τὸν κατὰ θεὸν κτισθέντα ἐν δικαιοσύνῃ καὶ ὁσιότητι τῆς ἀληθείας.

[347] Cf. Rom. 13:12; 2 Cor. 4:16; Eph. 6:10f; 1 Thess. 5:8. As Paul says in 1 Corinthians, Jesus, the "power of God and the wisdom of God (Χριστὸν θεοῦ δύναμιν καὶ θεοῦ σοφίαν)" has become to us, in him, "wisdom from God, and righteousness and sanctification, and redemption (ὃς ἐγενήθη σοφία ἡμῖν ἀπὸ θεοῦ, δικαιοσύνη τε καὶ ἁγιασμὸς καὶ ἀπολύτρωσις)" (1 Cor. 1:24, 30).

[348] Cf. Dt. 10:16, 30:6; Jer. 4:4, 9:25f; Rom. 2:25f; Jub. 1:22-23; Odes Sol. 11:1-3; 1QS 5:5; 1QpHab 11:13; 4Q177 2:16; 4Q434 1:4; PRE 29; Gen.R. 46:5; Lev.R. 25:6; Ber. 29a.

Verse 28: The distinctions which Paul presents as having disappeared being so culturally and socially laden, discussion of this verse has largely centred upon the dichotomies themselves.[349] While such a focus may obviously serve as a legitimate operation in its own right, and should not be neglected, Paul's point appears to rest in fact not on the differences but on the *Messiah's oneness* (see verses 19-20).[350] God's sovereignty and unity is expressed in the fact that in the end of days He will "give to the peoples purified lips, that all of them may call on the name of the LORD, to serve Him with one shoulder אהפך אל-עמים שפה ברורה לקראֹ כֻלם בשם ה׳ לעבדו שכם אחד" (Zeph. 3:9) – because then "the LORD will be king over all the earth; in that day the Lord will be *the only* one, and His name *the only* one והיה ה׳ למלך על-כל-הארץ ביום ההוא יהיה ה׳ אחד ושמו אחד" (Zech. 14:9) (see also above). God's oneness is reflected in – and expressed by – the unity of mankind (cf. Rom. 3:29-30) (see verses 26-29).[351]

Just as God is one – and His Messiah is one with Him – so in Jesus all wo/mankind are also shaped anew in the image of the One and Only, in whom there is "no variation, or shadow of turning (παρ᾽ ᾧ οὐκ ἔνι παραλλαγὴ ἢ τροπῆς ἀποσκίασμα)" (Jas. 1:17).[352] Paul later plays on the

---

[349] The three categories recall those which appear in the morning prayer: "Blessed be Thou who hast not made me a Gentile . . . an ignoramus . . . a woman ברוך שלא עשאני גוי, ברוך שלא עשאני בור, ברוך שלא עשאני אשה" (JBer. 63b) (cf. Men. 43b; Diog.Laert.*Vit.Phil.* 1.33; Plut.*Marius* 46.1; Lact.*Inst.* 3.19.17) (cf. Bruce, Galatians: 187).

[350] It is perhaps significant that Paul does not speak here in terms of "no longer" (cf. verses 18, 25) (*pace* Hays, Galatians: 272). He is not contrasting a time "before and after" but describing a present situation "in the Messiah." This is reflected most clearly in the fact that, in contrast to the other items, the male/female distinction constitutes not a binary opposition but a pairing – "there is no male **and** female (οὐκ ἔνι ἄρσεν *καὶ* θῆλυ)." Likewise, while the Jew/Gentile distinction may be "the element of the formula which Paul particularly wants to emphasize in the present context" (ibid: 272-73), its adducement together with other categories suggests that it, too, is subservient to an aspect of even greater importance. Not only has the slave/freedman division played a key role in Paul's argument so far but it continues to do so in chapter 4 (see 4:1f).

[351] In this sense, God's oneness dissolves all binary oppositions (cf. Leach: 11). One reading of Gen. 3:7 suggests that wo/man's guilt found its expression in an awareness of plurality (separation): "Then the eyes of both of them were opened, and they knew that **they were** naked . . . ותפקחנה עיני שניהם וידעו כי עירמים הם" (cf. Irwin: 34). Although not agreeing with Boyarin's reading of Paul as on a par with Philo, his emphasis on "oneness" certainly possesses a certain validity (cf. Boyarin, Radical).

[352] Cf. Isa. 45:5f, 14, 22, 46:9. We may find here further echoes of Mal. 2:15: "And did not God make of you one flesh? So that one should have a spiritual kin? And what does that one flesh seek? A godly seed" (JPS), the זרע אלהים (zera elohim) being equivalent to "son of God" (see above). Peter expresses a similar thought to

relation between the "one and the many" explicitly in Romans 5: "But the free gift is not like the transgression. For if by the transgression of the one the many died, much more did the grace of God and the gift by the grace of the one man, Jesus the Messiah, abound to the many"[353] (Rom. 5:15) (see verses 19-20).[354] The ultimate effect of being found in the One and in His Messiah is being sinless – lacking all and every need for an external intercessor: ". . . until we all attain to the unity of the faithfulness and knowledge of the son of God, to a mature man, to the measure of the statute which belongs to the fulness of the Messiah . . . to grow up in all *aspects* into him, who is the head, *even* the Messiah"[355] (Eph. 4:13, 15).[356]

Whoever is found in God in His Messiah is being formed into the image of the Father, "from whom every family in heaven and on earth derives its name" (Eph. 3:15): ". . . you laid aside the old self with its *evil* practices, and have put on the new self who is being renewed to a true knowledge according to the image of the One who created him, – *a renewal* in which there is no *distinction between* Greek and Jew, circumcised and uncircumcised, barbarian, Scythian, slave and freeman, but the Messiah is all, and in all"[357] (Col. 3:9-11) (cf. 1 Cor. 12:13) (see also 4:12-20).[358]

Cornelius: "The word which He sent to the sons of Israel, preaching peace through Jesus the Messiah (he is Lord of all) (τὸν λόγον [ὃν] ἀπέστειλεν τοῖς υἱοῖς ᾽Ισραὴλ εὐαγγελιζόμενος εἰρήνην διὰ ᾽Ιησοῦ Χριστοῦ, οὗτός ἐστιν πάντων κύριος)" (Acts 10:36) (cf. Rom. 3:22[f], 29-30, 10:12).

[353] ᾽Αλλ᾽ οὐχ ὡς τὸ παράπτωμα, οὕτως καὶ τὸ χάρισμα· εἰ γὰρ τῷ τοῦ ἑνὸς παραπτώματι οἱ πολλοὶ ἀπέθανον, πολλῷ μᾶλλον ἡ χάρις τοῦ θεοῦ καὶ ἡ δωρεὰ ἐν χάριτι τῇ τοῦ ἑνὸς ἀνθρώπου ᾽Ιησοῦ Χριστοῦ εἰς τοὺς πολλοὺς ἐπερίσσευσεν.

[354] Cf. Isa. 53:4-12; Mal. 2:6; Acts 17:31; Rom. 5:16ff; Heb. 9:28. Daube suggests that, despite any explicit allusion to Jesus as the Second Adam in Galatians, the theme may be implicitly contained in the motif of the creation (cf. New: 443). For Dunn's allusion to this language, see 4:1-7 (n46).

[355] μέχρι καταντήσωμεν οἱ πάντες εἰς τὴν ἑνότητα τῆς πίστεως καὶ τῆς ἐπιγνώσεως τοῦ υἱοῦ τοῦ θεοῦ, εἰς ἄνδρα τέλειον, εἰς μέτρον ἡλικίας τοῦ πληρώματος τοῦ Χριστοῦ . . . αὐξήσωμεν εἰς αὐτὸν τὰ πάντα, ὅς ἐστιν ἡ κεφαλή, Χριστός.

[356] This accords with those passages which speak of God Himself forgiving, without the aid of intermediators: "And He saw that there was no man, and was astonished that there was no one to intercede; then His own arm brought salvation to Him, and His righteousness upheld Him וירא כי-אין איש וישתומם כי אין מפגיע ותושע לו זרעו וצדקתו היא סמכתהו" (Isa. 59:16). Jesus' intercession is effective precisely because he entered the holy of holies and sits at God's right hand (cf. Heb. 9:11ff, 10:12f).

[357] ἀπεκδυσάμενοι τὸν παλαιόν ἄνθρωπον σὺν ταῖς πράξεσιν αὐτοῦ καὶ ἐνδυσάμενοι τὸν νέον ἀνακαινούμενον εἰς ἐπίγνωσιν κατ᾽ εἰκόνα τοῦ κτίσαντος αὐτόν, ὅπου οὐκ ἔνι ῞Ελλην καὶ ᾽Ιουδαῖος, περιτομὴ καὶ ἀκροβυστία, βάρβαρος, Σκύθης, δοῦλος, ἐλεύθερος, ἀλλὰ [τὰ] πάντα καὶ ἐν πᾶσιν Χριστός.

This "new creation" – which surpasses even the natural order of male and female, and their ways of procreation – is a restoration of the original event: "*And the Spirit of God hovered* (Gen. 1:1): this alludes to the spirit of Messiah, as you read, *And the spirit of the Lord shall rest upon him* (Isa. 11:2). In the merit of what will [this spirit] eventually come? [For the sake of that which] *hovered over the face of the waters*, i.e. in the merit of repentance which is likened to water, as it is written, *Pour out thy heart like water* (Lam. 2:19)"[359] (Gen.R. 2:4) (see 6:12-16).[360]

Verse 29: In this one verse, Paul summarises his whole argument to his Galatian disciples: If you belong to the Messiah, you are Abraham's seed, heirs (of the blessing of life) according to promise. You do not need to be "bewitched" into thinking that you must undergo circumcision and conversion in order to be accepted as members of the Jewish community. Your participation in the Messiah makes you part of the real "sons of Abraham" who are distinguished by their "circumcised hearts." The Messiah's faithfulness in his obedience unto death has brought righteousness and life to those who put to death their evil inclination. Being buried with Jesus, those who have received newness of life, being led by the Spirit live as God's "seed" (see 5:13f).[361]

---

[358] Paul should not be taken as prescribing a dissolution of exclusivity, an abolishment of ethnic, social, or physiological differences. It is rather that in light of God's unity, these distinctions fade in significance. For "male and female," cf. Daube, New: 441-44.

[359] ורוח אלהים מרחפת: זה רוחו של מלך המשיח, היאך מה דאת אמר: ונחה עליו רוח ה'. באיזו זכות ממשמשת ובאה? המרחפת על פני המים - בזכות התשובה שנמשלה כמים, שנאמר: שפכי כמים לבך.

[360] Cf. 4Q521 f2ii:5 (see n42 and above). A hint at the inclusion of the Gentiles may also be found in Gen. 4:25, wherein Eve declares that "God has appointed me another offspring [seed] in place of Abel; for Cain killed him שת-לי אלהים זרע אחר תחת הבל כי הרגו קין." The midrash associates this verse with that in Ruth 4:12: "*And she called his name Seth: For God hath appointed me another seed*, etc. R. Tanhuma said in the name of Samuel Kozith: [She hinted at] that seed which would arise from another source, viz. the king Messiah רבי ותקרא את שמו שת כי שת לי אלהים זרע אחר וגו'. רבי תנחומא בשם רבי שמואל אמר: נסתכלה אותו זרע שהוא בא ממקום אחר. ואי זה? זה מלך המשיח" (Gen.R. 23:5) – "another source" being understood as from gentile stock, i.e., Ruth (cf. Gen.R. 51:8; Ruth R. 8:1) (cf. Daube, New: 27ff, 444). For other messianic understandings of the "seed," see verses 15-18.

[361] The reading of Galatians proposed here perceives the influencers as gentile non-believers who are pressuring the gentile Galatian believers to fully convert in order to gain acceptance within the Jewish community (see Introduction, **Occasion and circumstances**). Paul's argument has therefore been to assert that the correct and proper criteria for Jewish identity are just as much spiritual as physical/biological. If the Gentiles display the qualities of Abraham, Paul regards them as "heirs according to God's promise" (see 2:11-14). For the motif of hypocrisy as dominant in Galatians, see Introduction, **Argument**, 2:15-21, 5:13-18, and 6:1-11.

GALATIANS
4

Verses 1-7:

Now I say, as long as the heir is a child, he does not differ at all from a slave although he is owner of everything, but he is under guardians and managers until the date set by the father. So also we, while we were children, were held in bondage under the elemental things of the world. But when the fulness of the time came, God sent forth His son, born of a woman, born under the Law, in order that He might redeem those who were under the Law, that we might receive the adoption as sons. And because you are sons, God has sent forth the Spirit of His son into our hearts, crying "Abba! Father!" Therefore you are no longer a slave, but a son; and if a son, then an heir through God.

Having established that the true "heirs" of God's promise are those – Gentiles as well as Jews – who emulate Abraham's faithfulness and participate, through baptism, in Jesus' own obedience in his death and resurrection (see 3:1ff), Paul proceeds to elaborate this statement through the example of sons (heirs) and slaves.[1]

---

[1] In confronting the circumstance that his gentile disciples in Galatia are seeking Jewish status and are being persuaded that to gain it they must undergo circumcision/conversion, Paul argues that in Jesus, Gentiles are legitimately "sons of promise." To the extent that they wish to become "sons of the covenant" they will replace God's criteria for identity with human norms. Here, he forcefully asserts that such action binds those taking it under the "elemental things of the world" – the "dominion of Belial" and sin. Verses 1-7 in fact closely recapitulate the thought of 3:23-29 (cf. Dunn, Galatians: 210; Hays, Galatians: 281). This circumstance establishes a pronounal usage in these verses consistent with that of 3:13-14, 19ff – the "we/us" referring to Jewish believers, the "you" to gentile believers (see 3:10-14, 19ff). The λέγω δέ (legō de – "Now I say") picks up the same phrase from 3:17, serving as an epistolary marker to indicate the opening of a new

While inheritance is dependent first of all on the demise of the benefactor (father), it is also conditioned by the age of the heir.[2] Although a minor – a son under the age of thirteen full years – is legal heir of his father's estate, he may not inherit it until he has become an adult (cf. Elon: 457f).[3] Guardianship automatically terminates at this point, since guardians are generally appointed only over minors (cf. BM 39a). The responsibility includes directing one's ward's upbringing and education, determining his/her place of residence, and generally taking care of him/her – all in accordance with the ward's best interests.

A child is recognized as an adult from the onset of puberty, when s/he becomes responsible for the observance of the precepts and the discharge of communal obligations.[4] (Young) adults are held accountable for all ritual, civil, and criminal matters, being held punishable by the court for transgressions or breaches of contract – although only those above the age of twenty were originally liable for military service (cf. Num. 1:3) or obligated to pay the half-shekel (cf. Ex. 30:14).[5] In consequence, before this age, the minor has no halakhic (legal) standing in relation to these matters. As such he "does not differ at all from a slave (οὐδὲν διαφέρει δούλου)" – even though the estate will eventually fall to him and he may technically be considered an "owner (κύριος)" or "householder" (to be).[6]

Slaves, minors, and women are frequently associated as common groups with regard to whom certain things are impermissible (cf. ibid: 231ff, and for the following discussion).[7] While they can act as agents for

---

(sub)-section in a continued explication of that argument. For Galatians' epistolary structure, see Introduction, **Form**.

[2] For the rules governing inheritance, see 3:15-18.

[3] A mother possesses no legal standing as guardian of her children, unless she is explicitly appointed to the task. Despite the fact that νήπιος (nēpios – lit. "one without understanding," "child") is not attested as a technical term for "minor," this is evidently Paul's meaning. The Greek term may suit his purpose in its nuance of intellectual and moral immaturity (cf. 1 Cor. 13:11; Eph. 4:14) (cf. Burton: 212).

[4] This is expressed in Jewish tradition in the bar mitzvah ceremony, the event designating the point at which a boy becomes responsible for his observance/violation of the commandments, being thought capable of controlling his desires (cf. Mid.Ps. 9:5; ARN[b] 16:2). Although originating in a later period, mishnaic sources reflect the fact that a father was responsible for his son's deeds until the latter reached the age of thirteen (cf. Nid. 5:6).

[5] At the same time, heavenly punishment was not considered to be forthcoming for sins committed before the age of twenty (cf. Shab. 89b; BB 121b).

[6] The latter would have at least one, if not a number of, slaves in his possession as a matter of course (cf. Mt. 13:27, 24:45f, 25:14f; Lk. 7:2f, 14:16f; Suk. 2:9; BB 10:7; Ket. 96a; Ber. 16b).

[7] Cf. Shek. 1:5, 6; Ber. 3:3; Pes. 8:7; Suk. 2:8; Men. 43b-44a; Hag. 4a. For the purposes of Paul's argument, the question of whether he was thinking of Hebrew or alien slaves is irrelevant (cf. Elon: 231f).

their masters they are themselves mortgageable chattle, being fundamentally regarded either as immovable objects – likened to land as regards acquisition (money, deed, possession) and not subject to theft, wrongdoing, or bailment – or as movables.[8] Although slaves could hold property of their own, they could not dispose of it at will.[9] At the same time, as members of the family household they both enjoyed the benefit of and were liable to the duty of observing shabbat (the sabbath) (cf. Ex. 20:10, 23:12; Dt. 5:14-15) and festivals (cf. Dt. 12:18, 16:11-14). Since they were bound to be circumcised (cf. Gen. 17:2-14), they were also obligated to celebrate Pesach (Passover) (cf. Ex. 12:44). Where no direct issue existed, slaves could inherit a master's estate – possibly even in cases where the latter had offspring of his own (cf. Prov. 17:2).

Verse 2: As a slave could not enjoy the rights of a freedperson until s/he was manumitted, a minor was also unable to benefit from bequests or inheritance until the age of majority (cf. Lk. 15:19).[10] The Greek ἐπίτροπος (epitropos) serves as a Hebrew loanword (אפיטרופוס), adopted in rabbinic literature to designate the "father" of minors and the "guardian/custodian" of another's affairs (cf. ibid: 441f).[11] The οἰκονόμος (oikonomos) – another loanword (איקונומוס) – signifies a steward or manager (frequently a slave) in a household context.[12]

The reference to "until the date set by the father (ἄχρι τῆς προθεσμίας τοῦ πατρός)" suggests that Paul has in mind the appointment of a guardian by the father, indicative of his incapacity, for whatever reason, to take care of his son(s): "If orphans were supported by a householder, or if their father appointed a guardian for them, he must give Tithe from the produce that belongs to them. If a guardian was appointed by the orphans' father he must take an oath [that he has not impaired their property]; if he was appointed by the court he need not take an oath"[13] (Git. 5:4).[14]

---

[8] Cf. Lev. 22:11; Git. 4:4; Kid. 1:3; BM 4:9, 8:3; Eruv. 7:6; Yev. 66a; BK 11b-12a; BM 96a, 99a; BB 68a, 150a.

[9] Cf. 2 Sam. 9:10, 16:4, 19:28; Tos.BK 11:1; San. 105a; Pes. 88b.

[10] He could benefit from bequests if they were assigned to a third party, appointed for that purpose on his behalf (cf. Elon: 458).

[11] Cf. Philo, *Quod omnis* 35; Ex.R. 46:5; Tos.Ter. 5:7. The term also renders the office of Roman "procurator" in Judaea, the official responsible for administering the province (cf. Tanh.Re'eh 10; Shab. 121a). As with most of such loanwords, the Hebrew is variously spelt.

[12] Cf. LXX 3 Kings 4:6, 18:3; Rom. 16:23; 1 Esd. 4:47; Lk. 12:43, 16:1; Tos.BM 9:14; J BM 9, 1, 12a; J BB 4, 7, 14c.

[13] יתומים שסמכו אצל בעל הבית, או שמינה להן אביהן אפוטרופוס - חייב לעשר פירותיהן. אפטרופוס שמינהו אבי יתומים, ישבע; מינהו בית דין - לא ישבע.

[14] Cf. Jos.*War* 1.556; Philo, *Jos.* 74; P. Oxy. 491.8-10. Orphans are naturally ready subjects for guardianship although, with reference to legal standing, only the child who has lost his/her *father* is recognised as an orphan (cf. Elon: 438). If a man dies

Like ἐπίτροπος (epitropos) and οἰκονόμος (oikonomos), the Greek προθεσμία (prothesmia) is also a rabbinic loanword (פרותיזמיה), signifying an "appointed day" or "limited time."[15] While the natural date for release from guardianship was the age of majority (thirteen for boys, twelve for girls), the father (or court) might appoint a guardian for a set period of time in light of specific circumstances, separate guardians being put in charge of the ward's person and property respectively, for example (cf. ibid: 443).[16]

This passage – once again – displays clear echoes of 11QMelchizedek (see 1:1ff). Melchizedek is represented in the Qumran scroll as the eschatological "herald (מבשר)" who is also the "anointed of the spirit משיח הרוח" of Daniel 9:25. His task is to rescue those who have fallen into spiritual "debt" and "slavery" and to release them into his inheritance as heirs of God's lot in the year of jubilee:

> And as for what he said: Lev 25:13 «In [this] year of jubilee, [you shall return, each one to his respective property», concerning it he said: Deut 15:2 «[Th]is is [the manner of the release:] every creditor shall release what he lent [to his neighbour. He shall not coerce his neighbour or his brother, for it has been proclaimed] a release for G[od». Its interpretation] for the last days refers to the captives, who [...] ... and they are the inherita[nce of Melchize]dek, who will make them return. And liberty will be

---

leaving his minor offspring without a guardian, the court is responsible for appointing one in its role as "father of orphans אביהן של יתומין" (cf. BK 37a). Children orphaned of both parents become wards of the court (cf. Git. 37a). It is possible that the reference to the "father (πατρός)" here includes the court, although in light of the continuation it is more likely that Paul is alluding to God (cf. Dan. 8:19, 11:35; Mk. 13:32; Acts 1:7, 17:31; Eph. 1:10; 1 Tim. 2:6; Tit. 1:3; 4 Ez. 4:36-37; Philo, Vit.Mos. 2.238; Sot. 9:15) (see also below). Burton suggests that Paul may have the case of Lysias in mind, appointed steward of his royal affairs and guardian of his son by Antiochus Epiphanes (cf. 1 Macc. 3:32f, 6:17; 2 Macc. 11:1, 13:2). If so, the two terms which he employs designate not different persons but two functions of one official, the plural constituting a qualitative plural (cf. Burton: 214). The lengthy debate over which legal system of guardianship Paul is alluding to becomes less relevant the more emphasis is placed on the scriptural basis of his argument(s) (cf. Davies, Jewish: 176ff) (see Introduction, **Theological pointers** [Scripture], 2:15-21, 3:1-5, [15-18], and verses 21-31). For adoption, see below.

[15] Cf. Jos.Ant. 12.201; War 2.633; Philo, Spec.Leg. 1.251, 2.142; Mekh.Be-shall. 2; PRK 12:11. The fact that Greek terminology abounds in the context of guardianship does not necessarily indicate that the concept should be understood in light of Graeco-Roman customs. When appropriated to a Jewish legal setting, such principles were governed by halakhic principles (cf. Le Cornu and Shulam: 1283ff).

[16] The court may also appoint a guardian to serve together with the father when the latter is considered incapable of fully discharging his duties towards his child(ren) (cf. Elon: 443). The "until (ἄχρι)" picks up the theme from 3:19, 23 (see above).

proclaimed for them, to free them from [the debt of] all their
iniquities. And this [wil]l [happen] in the first week of the jubilee
which follows the ni[ne] jubilees. And the d[ay of aton]ement is
the e[nd of] the tenth [ju]bilee in which atonement shall be made
for all the sons of [light and] for the men [of] the lot of
Mel[chi]zedek ... accor[ding to] a[ll] their [wor]ks, for it is the
time for the «year of grace» {Isa. 61:2} of Melchizedek ...
Melchizedek will carry out the vengeance of Go[d's] judgments,
[and on that day he will fr]e[e them from the hand of] Belial and
from the hand of all the sp[irits of his lot] ... This [. . .] is the day
of [peace about whi]ch he said [. . . through Isa]iah the prophet,
who said: [*Isa 52:7* How] beautiful upon the mountains are the feet
[of] the messen[ger who] announces peace, the mess[enger of
good who announces salvati]on, [sa]ying to Zion: your God
[reigns.»] Its interpretation: The mountains [are] the prophet[s
. . .] ... And the messenger i[s] the anointed of the spir[it] as
Dan[iel] said [about him: *Dan 9:25* «Until an anointed, a prince, it is
seven weeks.»] ... [«Zi]on» i[s] [the congregation of all the sons
of justice, those] who establish the covenant, those who avoid
walking [on the pa]th of the people. And «your God» is [. . .
Melchizedek, who will fr]e[e them from the ha]nd of Belial.[17]
(11QMelch 2:2-9, 13, 15-18, 23-25)[18] (see 1:1-5, 3:21-25, and
below)[19]

---

[17] ואשר אמר בשנת היובל [הזאת תשובו איש אל אחוזתו ועליו אמר וז]ה [דבר השמטה] שמוט כול
בעל משה יד אשר ישה] ברעהו לוא יגוש את רעהו ואת אחיו כיא קרא] שמטה לא]ל פשר[ה לאחרית
הימים על השבויים אשר . . . והמה נחל]ת מלכי צ]דק אשר ישיבמה אליהמה וקרא להמה דרור
לעזוב להמה [מסא] כול עוונותיהמה ו]כן יהי]ה הדבר הזה בשבוע היובל הראישון אחר תשׁ]עת
ה]יובלים וי]ום הכפ]ורים ה]וא]ה סו]ף] ה]יו]בל העשירי לכפר בו על כול בני [אור ו]אנש]י] גורל
מלכ]י] צדק . . . לפ]נ]י] כו]ל עש]ות]מה כיא הואה הקץ לשנת הרצון למלכי צדק . . . ומלכי צדק יקום
נקם משפטי א]ל וביום ההואה יצי]ל]מה מיד] בליעל ומיד כול ר]וחי גורלו] . . . הזאת הואה יום
ה]שלום א]שר אמר [. . . ביד ישע]יה הנביא אשר אמר [מה] נאוו על ההרים רגל]י] מבש]ר מ]שמיע
שלום מב]שר טוב משמיע ישוע]ה [א]ומר לציון [מלך] אלוהיך פשרו ההרים [המה] הנביאי]ם] המה
. . . והמבשר הו]אה] משיח הרו]ח] כאשר אמר דנ]יאל עליו עד משיח נגיד שבועים שבעה] . . . [צי]ו]ן
ה]יאה] [עדת כול בני הצדק המה] מקימ]י] הברית הסרים מלכת [בד]רך העם ואל]ו]היך הואה [. . .
מלכי צדק אשר יצי]ל]מה מי]ד בליעל.

[18] Cf. Heb. 5:10-7:28; 1QH[a] 23:13-15; 4Q504 ff1-2ii:16, vii:2; 4Q521 f2ii:7-13 (see 1:1f
and 3:21-25).

[19] Melchizedek is the agent of the release from bondage and the forgiveness of
"debts" (cf. Flusser, Judaism: 186-92, 256-60; Kobelski). As with Paul's present
passage, the action derives from God, who Himself sets the time for the jubilee (cf.
Lev. 23:2f; Ezra 3:5; Ezek. 44:24; Num.R. 21:25). [A similar passage is ascribed to
Cyrus' role as God's servant: "'I have aroused him in righteousness, and I will make
all his ways smooth (cf. Isa. 40:3); he will build My city, and will let My exiles go
free, without any payment or reward,' says the LORD of hosts -אנכי העירֹתֵהו בצדק וכל
דרכיו אישר -צבאות .(Isa. 45:13).] For "דרכיו אישר הוא-יבנה עירי וגלותי ישלח לא במחיר ולא בשֹׁחד אמר ה' צבאות
Paul's use of such pesher language, applying Scripture to contemporary events, see
verses 21-31.

Verse 3: Paul now applies the principles of inheritance to his present argument (see 3:15ff).[20] To all legal extents and purposes – and these, of course, are the criteria for inheritance – while the heir is still a minor he is merely the *potential* heir. He has not received his father's estate and is not even considered eligible to do so – until he reaches the age of majority. Under such circumstances, his status corresponds to that of a slave (in the broad sense). Until he attains legal maturity, the minor cannot exercise his rights of inheritance. He is not the heir.[21]

This understanding lies behind Paul's provocative declaration that – as "minors" – Jews, like Gentiles, are "held in bondage under the elemental things of the world (ὑπὸ τὰ στοιχεῖα τοῦ κόσμου ἤμεθα δεδουλωμένοι)" (cf. verse 9).[22] While it is tempting to assume that Paul's reference here must be to *Gentiles* – no self-respecting Jewish author being capable of claiming that Jews were held in such bondage – the parallelism with 3:23-29 suggests that Paul's pronounal usage remains consistent.[23] When the theme of "bondage (δεδουλωμένοι)" is perceived to continue from 3:21ff, the "elemental things of the world" correspond to wo/men being handed over into "the power of sin."[24]

---

[20] For Israel as God's inheritance, cf. Dt. 9:26, 32:9; 1 Sam. 10:1; Ps. 78:71, 94:14; Isa. 19:25; Jer. 10:16, 51:19; 4Q504 ff1-2iii:4ff; Philo, *Spec.Leg.* 4.179-80; Ex.R. 32:7; Num.R. 20:19.

[21] Theologically speaking, as "heir-in-waiting," as it were, the minor is in the care of the Torah as his tutor who is in charge of him until the Messiah comes, this advent both signaling and effecting the ward's maturity (cf. 3:19ff). Whether Paul has any thought here of Jesus' death serving to bring the minor into full heirship is doubtful, unless that idea reflects the blood necessary to establish a covenant (cf. Ex. 24:8; Heb. 9:11ff). (For parallels between Hebrews and Galatians, see 1:1-5 [nn99f], verses 21-31, and below [n82].)

[22] At least four independent meanings are offered for the significance of the phrase: a) fundamental learning principles (cf. Heb. 5:12; CD-A 10:6) – an extension of the initial alphabetical usage of letters placed side by side; b) the elemental substances out of which the world is formed – earth, water, fire, air (cf. 2 Pet. 3:10f). This usage is the only meaning attested when the phrase is conjoined to the modifier "of the world (τοῦ κόσμου)"; c) elementary spirits associated by syncretistic religions with the physical elements. The sources for this denotation are generally later than Paul; d) heavenly bodies. These are frequently associated with the spirits of (c), conjuring connotations of "demonic entities of cosmic proportions and astral powers which are hostile towards man" (Martyn, *Galatians*: 394-95; Betz, *Galatians*: 205).

[23] See n1.

[24] The tendency to associate these obviously negative phenomena with the Torah misperceives the argument of 3:21f, for Paul is not charging the Torah with criminality but highlighting the weakness of human nature in the hands of the evil inclination (see 3:21-25). It is significant that Paul's other reference to the "cosmos (κόσμος)" in Galatians alludes to the fact that it has "been crucified to me, and I to the world (δι' οὗ ἐμοὶ κόσμος ἐσταύρωται κἀγὼ κόσμῳ)" (6:14), an "echo" of Romans 6 (cf. Col. 2:20) (see 3:21f and 5:24-26).

Here again, the Qumran texts may prove instructive in defining a Jewish context for such "elemental principles." The scrolls' governing conceptual framework is that of captivity by the forces of Belial during a certain time period , the bondage being equated with the debt of sin, and the release - into heirship - effected in the year of jubilee, associated with the Day of Atonement.[25] The bondage expresses the "dominion of Belial and his spirits" - or the Angel of Darkness under whose rule all the earth lies: ". . . in the hand of the Angel of Darkness is total dominion over the sons of deceit; they walk on paths of deceit. From the Angel of darkness stems the corruption of all the sons of justice, and all their sins, their iniquities, their guilts and their offensive deeds are under his dominion in compliance with the mysteries of God, until his moment; and all their afflictions and their periods of grief are caused by the dominion of his enmity"[26] (1QS 3:20-23).[27]

This is the world as it appears in all its "raw state," as it were - representing the realm of Belial as "prince of this world." According to Paul's statement in Romans, the earth "was subjected to futility, not of its own will, but because of Him who subjected it, in hope that the creation itself also will be set free from its slavery to corruption into the freedom of the glory of the children of God"[28] (Rom. 8:20-21). In a sense similar to that in which he speaks of the risk of the "false brethren" bringing people into bondage (cf. 2:4) - in the sense of sin (see 2:1-10) - Paul clearly understands that, before the Messiah came to release wo/men from the bonds of their human nature, Jews as well as Gentiles were under custodianship: "Among them [the sons of disobedience] we [Jews] too all formerly lived in the lusts of our flesh, indulging the desires of the flesh and of the mind,

---

[25] Both the jubilee year and Yom Kippur are referred to as מועדים (mo'adim) - "set times" determined by God to be celebrated by the people (cf. Lev. 23:2, 4, 37; Dt. 31:10). See also verses 8-11 (n99).

[26] וביד מלאך חושך כול ממשלת בני עול ובדרכי חושך יתהלכו ובמלאך חושך תעות כול בני צדק וכול חטאתם ועוונותם ואשמתם ופשעי מעשיהם בממשל֯תו לפי רזי אל עד קצו וכול נגועיהם ומועדי צרותם בממשלת משטמתו.

[27] Cf. Jn. 12:31, 14:30, 16:11; 1 Cor. 2:6-8; 2 Cor. 4:4; Eph. 2:2, 6:12; 1 Jn. [4:4], 5:19; Jub. 1:20; Test.Dan 1:7, 3:6, 4:7; [Test.Asher 1:3f]; Test.Ben. 6:1, 7:1f; 1QS 1:18, 4:9f, 23; CD-A 12:2, 16:5; 1QM 4, 11-12; 14:9; 4Q177 4:12; 4Q286 f7ii:5-7; 4Q390 f2i:4; Ber. 16b; BB 16a.

[28] τῇ γὰρ ματαιότητι ἡ κτίσις ὑπετάγη, οὐχ ἑκοῦσα ἀλλὰ διὰ τὸν ὑποτάξαντα, ἐφ' ἐλπίδι ὅτι καὶ αὐτὴ ἡ κτίσις ἐλευθερωθήσεται ἀπὸ τῆς δουλείας τῆς φθορᾶς εἰς τὴν ἐλευθερίαν τῆς δόξης τῶν τέκνων τοῦ θεοῦ.

and were by nature children of wrath, even as the rest [i.e., the Gentiles]"[29] (Eph. 2:3).[30]

1QH^a 20:8 describes God's ordering of the world in the change of light to dark, season to season, "the births of time, **the foundations of the period** מולדי עת יסודי קץ." The same Hebrew term also denotes the "principle of creation [ויסוד הבריאה]" (male and female) (cf. CD-A 4:21). In the context of the community's teaching, the word signifies the "principles of the covenant [יסודי הברית]" (cf. CD-A 10:6), the singular יסוד (yesod) also designating the community itself or, perhaps, its secret teaching.[31] It thus parallels several of the meanings attributed to Paul's Greek phrase here. Given its array of significance and the Hebrew tendency to play on meanings, Paul may consequently be indirectly alluding to various denotations simultaneously.[32]

Verse 4: The phrase "the fulness of the time (τὸ πλήρωμα τοῦ χρόνου)" - parallel in meaning to "the date set by the father" - bears connotations firstly in respect to the "filling" of years.[33] In this sense, it denotes the minor's coming of age, his attaining the age of majority - at the

---

[29] ἐν οἷς καὶ ἡμεῖς πάντες ἀνεστράφημέν ποτε ἐν ταῖς ἐπιθυμίαις τῆς σαρκὸς ἡμῶν ποιοῦντες τὰ θελήματα τῆς σαρκὸς καὶ τῶν διανοιῶν, καὶ ἤμεθα τέκνα φύσει ὀργῆς ὡς καὶ οἱ λοιποί.

[30] The pronouns in Ephesians are equally as crucial as in Galatians (cf. McRay, Paul: 340-48). The role of the cosmic powers can be interpreted in similar fashion, these constituting, on the present reading, Paul's reference in "the elemental things of the world." The significance of the past tense - the periphrastic construction being pluperfect ("while we *had been* held in bondage") - indicating that this period has now passed, is evident in verses 6-11 (see verses 8-11 and below).

[31] Cf. 1QS 7:17f, 8:10, 9:3; 1Q28a 1:12-13. The basic meaning of the word is "foundation," the extension to knowledge reflecting the fact that the community was grounded upon God's revelation of His mysteries to its members through the Teacher of Righteousness. The Hebrew is also phonetically very close to סוד (sod), which in turn signifies both "council" and "secret" (cf. CD-B 19:35; 1QS 2:25, 4:6, 6:19).

[32] It does not seem unreasonable to speculate that such texts as this form part of the development of the "elements of the world" into spiritual forces and principles. The significance of this is brought out clearly in Rev. 21:7-8: "He who overcomes shall inherit these things, and I will be his God and he will be My son. But for the cowardly and unbelieving and abominable and murderers and immoral persons . . . their part *will be* in the lake that burns with fire and brimstone, which is the second death (ὁ νικῶν κληρονομήσει ταῦτα καὶ ἔσομαι αὐτῷ θεὸς καὶ αὐτὸς ἔσται μοι υἱός. τοῖς δὲ δειλοῖς καὶ ἀπίστοις καὶ ἐβδελυγμένοις καὶ φονεῦσιν καὶ πόρνοις . . . τὸ μέρος αὐτῶν ἐν τῇ λίμνῃ τῇ καιομένῃ πυρὶ καὶ θείῳ, ὅ ἐστιν ὁ θάνατος ὁ δεύτερος)" (see also 5:19-23).

[33] The verb מלא (malē) is used in conjunction with years in order to signify the passing of time (cf. Lev. 25:30; Acts 7:23, 30, 24:27).

time set by the father.[34] The expression is, in fact, frequently employed in the papyri to indicate contractual termination.[35] It then marks the date on which the guardianship concludes. In its association with καιρός (kairos), the notation acts as a chronological signifier of particular periods of history.

In this sense, Paul's thought closely parallels his later speech before the Areopagus in Athens: "Therefore having overlooked the times of ignorance, God ... has fixed a day in which He will judge the world in righteousness through a man whom He has appointed ... "[36] (Acts 17:30-31).[37] The time which has now been "filled" is also a "fulfilment" of God's promises – the redemption which He assured and which the prophets both foretold and sought.[38] Most obviously in the context of 3:10f, this is also the time which Habakkuk envisioned, the "appointed time [מוֹעֵד]" which "hastens toward the goal, and it will not fail. Though it tarries, wait for it; for it will certainly come, it will not delay -וְיָפֵחַ לַקֵּץ וְלֹא יְכַזֵּב אִם-יִתְמַהְמָהּ חַכֵּה לוֹ כִּי-בֹא יָבֹא לֹא יְאַחֵר" (Hab. 2:4).[39]

---

[34] On the analogy of the Melchizedek text (see above), the set time is the jubilee year, when all slaves must be released and property returned to its owner (cf. Leviticus 25). This jubilee is itself the tenth jubilee, associated thereby with the Day of Atonement (cf. Lev. 16:29, 23:27) (see 1:1-5 and above).

[35] Cf. BAGD: 706 [s.v. προθεσμία].

[36] τοὺς μὲν οὖν χρόνους τῆς ἀγνοίας ὑπεριδὼν ὁ θεός ... ἔστησεν ἡμέραν ἐν ᾗ μέλλει κρίνειν τὴν οἰκουμένην ἐν δικαιοσύνῃ, ἐν ἀνδρὶ ᾧ ὥρισεν.

[37] Cf. Eph. 1:10; 1 Tim. 2:6; Tit. 1:3; 4 Ez. 4:36-37; Tob. 14:5; 1QpHab 7:1ff; 1QS 3:16, 4:18ff; 1QM 1:8f, 4:7, 11:10f; 13:14f, 17:5; 1QHª 17:24; 2 En. [J] 55:1; Ex.R. 25:12; San. 96b ['Ulla]. Although the "ignorance (ἀγνοίας)" may be influenced by the "unknown God (Ἀγνώστῳ θεῳ)" whose identity Paul is now revealing (cf. Acts 17:23), the phrase otherwise describes the period when wo/men were shut up under sin in rather more positive terms. For a discussion – and narrative re-reading – of the christological formulas in verses 3-6 and 3:13-14, cf. Hays, Faith: 95ff ("Galatians 3:13 and 4:4-5 are two summarizations of the same story, and the action of 'redemption' alluded to in 4:5 has already been more fully related in the earlier passage" [ibid, Galatians: 284]); for the recent dating of Galatians, see Introduction, **Date and destination**.

[38] Cf. Mt. 1:22f, 2:15; Mk. 1:15, 14:49; Lk. 4:21, 22:22f; Jn. 12:38, 15:25; Acts 1:16, 3:18; 1 Pet. 1:10-12; Yalk.Dt. 898; Yalk.Isa. 508; Ber. 34b; Shab. 63a; San. 99a.

[39] Cf. Prov. 12:17; Cant. 2:17, 4:6 (Hebrew). This is God's "faithfulness" which He embodies in His Messiah, the Righteous One, whose coming in his own faithfulness accomplishes human inheritance (see above). The inclusion of ἦλθεν (ēlthen – "come"), which serves as the verb in the phrase ("when the fulness of time **came**"), further recalls the Coming One of LXX Hab. 2:4: "If he delays, wait for him, because a Coming One will arrive and will not linger ... The Righteous One shall live by My faith" (see 3:10-14, 19f). Such echoes mitigate against seeing in these verses "'confessional formulae' or 'sayings' statements drawn from the early church" (Longenecker, Galatians: 166) (see also below [n41]) – as does also the parallelism between verses 1-7 and 3:23-29 (see above).

At this time God "sent forth His son (ἐξαπέστειλεν ὁ θεὸς τὸν
υἱὸν)."[40] Here, the significance of the compound ἐξ (ex – "out of") may
reflect both locative and "temporal" aspects of God's redemption through
His Messiah. Although the idea of agency is linked to commissioning in
general – peculiarly of the prophets and apostles (cf. Jer. 7:25; Acts 22:21) –
the present context suggests that the Messiah was "with God" (cf. Jn. 1:1)
from before the foundation of the world, God sending him "forth" on the
appointed day.[41] Being with God, he left the heavenly abode and "came
into the world."[42]

In this framework, Paul describes the Messiah's human qualities:
"born of a woman, born under the Torah (γενόμενον ἐκ γυναικός,
γενόμενον ὑπὸ νόμον)."[43] The first expression denotes the biological
nature peculiar to human beings (cf. verse 23).[44] In the Qumran literature, it

[40] For the role of the "sender" in narrative structures, cf. Hays, Faith: 73-117, who
also applies narrative logic to explain the relationship between 3:13-14 and verses 4-
5. We would beg to diverge from referring to the Torah the role of "opponent."
While theoretically parallel to the "elemental things of the world," the Torah is not
part of these. It rather accommodates to the weakness of the flesh, which lies under
the governance of these forces (see above). The real opponent is the "stoicheia
(elemental things)."

[41] Cf. Mt. 13:35, 25:34; Jn. 3:17; Rom. 8:3; Eph. 1:4; Heb. 4:3; 1 Pet. 1:20; 1 Jn. 4:9-10;
Rev. 13:8 [?]; 1QH^a 11:7ff. For the Messiah's preexistence, see 3:6-9. If the idea of
agency lies at the source of the "sending" motif (see 1:1-5), the question of whether
it represents a hellenistic Jewish formula or Paul's own articulation, "drawn from
his Damascus-road experience" (cf. Longenecker, Galatians: 161) may be answered
in favour of the latter, Paul evidently modeling his commissioning on the Servant in
Isaiah (see 1:1-5, 15f, 21-24, 2:1-10, 3:10-14, and verses 1ff). For Hays' narrative
construction of these verses, cf. Faith: 95ff.

[42] Cf. Ps. 40:7; Jn. 1:9; Heb. 10:5 (see 3:21-25). Hays clarifies the implications
embedded in perceiving the participial phrases either as "'qualifications' of the
Subject, i.e., statements that describe a state of being; or as expressions of narrative
action. In the former case, they simply provide additional information about the
Subject. In the latter, they rather suggest a change in the Subject's circumstances
("being born of a woman, becoming subject to the Law"). On this second reading,
they may be taken [to indicate that] ... the Son of God leaves his heavenly
environment (disjunction) and enters the network of earthly relations
(conjunction)" (Faith: 96).

[43] The chiastic structure of these verses is clearly visible:
    A   God sent His Son
      B   born under the Torah
      B'   to redeem those under the Torah
    A'   that we might receive the adoption as sons
(cf. Longenecker, Galatians: 166) (see also 2:1-10 [n113], 3:10-14 [verses 11-12], 21-25
[verses 22-23], 5:2-12 [verses 11-12], and verses 21-31 [n246]).

[44] It may not be coincidental that Paul speaks here literally of "out of a woman (ἐκ
γυναικός)." While reflecting the natural physical process (cf. Rom. 1:3), the phrase
also parallels the ἐκ πίστεως (ek pisteōs – "out of faithfulness") which characterises

frequently takes on the corrupt traits of the "flesh" characteristic of the "sons of disobedience" who live in opposition to the Spirit of Truth and God's will: "What, indeed, is the son of man, among all your marvelous deeds? As what shall one born of woman be considered in your presence? Shaped from dust has he been, maggots' food shall be his dwelling; he is spat saliva, moulded clay, and for dust is his longing. What will the clay reply and the one shaped by hand? And what advice will he be able to understand?"[45] (1QS 11:20-22).[46]

"Born under the Torah" further denotes Jesus' Jewish birth, the expression corresponding to Paul's description of Jesus' role as a "servant to the circumcision on behalf of God's truthfulness to confirm the promises given to the patriarchs (διάκονον γεγενῆσθαι περιτομῆς ὑπὲρ ἀληθείας θεοῦ, εἰς τὸ βεβαιῶσαι τὰς ἐπαγγελίας τῶν πατέρων)" (Rom. 15:8) (cf. Flusser: Judaism: 621; Hays, Galatians: 283).[47] Paul possibly presents these two attributive participles to signal Jesus' faithfulness in the act of

---

Jesus' obedience/righteousness (see 3:10-14). This passage is certainly perceivable as demonstrative of Jesus' "representative quality" – that very attribute which informs Hays' reading of Jesus' "faithfulness" (cf. Faith: xxix-xxxiii, 203f, and passim) (see 2:15-21 and 3:10f).

[45] ומה אף הואה בן ‏ֹ‏אדם במעשי פאלכה וילוד אשה מה י(ח)שב לפניכה והואה מעפר מגבלו ולחם רמה מדורו והואה מצירוק חמר קורץ ולעפר תשוקתו מה ישיב חמר ויוצר יד ולעצת מה יבין.

[46] Cf. Job 14:1, 15:14, 25:4; Mt. 11:11; Lk. 7:28; 1QHᵃ 5:20, 21:1, 8-9, 23:12-13; 4Q501 1:5; Lev.R. 35:2; ARNᵃ 2:3; Shab. 88b; Nid. 13a. (For the phrase "flesh and blood," see 1:16b-17.) At the same time, a midrashic tradition attaches the phrase to Moses when he ascended to receive the Torah from God (cf. Pes.Rab. 20:4; Yalk.Num. 752; Yalk.Ps. 641; Shab. 88b). Flusser suggests that in so referring to John the Baptist (cf. Mt. 11:11), Jesus was implying that John was a type of "second Moses" (cf. Jesus: 261n8). May Paul have a similar thought in mind – as in his later association of Jesus with Moses through a midrash on Job 28 (Wisdom) in Rom. 10:6-11 (cf. Shulam and Le Cornu: 348-50)? Dunn (Christology: 39f) further suggests that these verses reflect the language of the Second Adam, which concept Daube (New: 443) already adduces for 3:26-28 (n354) – even if Dunn dismisses the preexistent element in the Torah-Wisdom-Logos motif. If these allusions are present, they affirm this section's integral propriety – contrary to the suggestion that it represents "part of the pre-Pauline material, taken up here by Paul in full and without regard to its usability in the argument" (Betz, Galatians: 207). (For Dt. 18:15f, see 3:10-14 [n129], 19-20 [nn246, 264], verses 21-31 [nn211, 239], and below; for the motif of clay, see 3:6-9 [n85] and verses 21-31 [n211].)

[47] The term γίνεσθαι ὑπό (ginesthai hypo – "to be under") "defines the conditions of existence of a human being" (Betz, Galatians: 207). This latter verse encapsulates God's faithfulness to His promises to His people, fulfilled in the sending of His son who, in his faithfulness to his Father, delivered himself in order to redeem humanity from this present evil age (cf. 1:4) (see 1:1-5, 3:10-14, and verses 21-31 [end]). The Greek phrase also anticipates the description of those to whom Jesus was sent, in verse 5, and Paul's request of the Galatians in verse 12 (see verses 12-20). For Galatians as a "halakhic letter" along the lines of 4QMMT, see Introduction, Form; Argument.

"learning obedience from the things which he suffered [experienced] (ἔμαθεν ἀφ' ὧν ἔπαωεν τὴν ὑπακοήν)" (Heb. 5:8).[48]

Evidence of the Torah's status as Israel's unique possession is abundant in both Jewish and non-Jewish writings: "Beloved are Israel in that a desirable instrument [the Torah] was given to them. [It was a mark of] superabundant love [that] it was made known to them that the desirable instrument, wherewith the world had been created, was given to them, as it is said: *For I give you good doctrine; forsake not My teaching* (Prov. 4:2)"[49] (PA 3:14) (cf. Montefiore and Loewe: 58f, 119ff)[50] (see 2:15-21). Josephus quotes Hecataeus on the Torah: "In another passage Hecataeus mentions our regard for our laws, and how we deliberately choose and hold it a point of honour to endure anything rather than transgress them . . . 'for these laws, naked and defenceless, they face tortures and death in its most terrible form, rather than repudiate the faith of their forefathers'"[51] (Jos.CA 1.190-91) (cf. Stern, Greek; Safrai and Stern: 1101ff; Feldman: 84-177). Even non-sympathetic Romans recognised its compass: ". . . the customs of this accursed race have gained such influence that they are now received throughout all the world. The vanquished have given laws to their victors"[52] (Seneca, *De Sup., apud* Aug.CD 6.11).[53]

Verse 5 serves as the parallel to 3:24, the purpose clause signaling the principle and point of Jesus' commission (see above).[54] The "redemption (ἐξαγοράσῃ)" is, in the literal signification of the verb, a "leading/bringing out" - in this context, an emancipation from slavery or bondage.[55] The verb

---

[48] Cf. Rom. 5:19; Phil. 2:8. Hebrews' contrast of Jesus' obedience with his sonship – "despite being a son . . ." carries echoes of Paul's distinction between son and heir here. (For affinities between the pauline literature and Hebrews, see 1:1-5 [nn99f], 3:10-14 [n158], verses 21-31, and above.)

[49] חביבין ישראל, שנקראו בנים למקום; חבה יתרה נודעת להם שנקראו בנים למקום, שנאמר: בנים אתם לה' אלהיכם. חביבן ישראל שניתן להם כלי חמדה; חבה יתרה נודעת להם שניתן להם כלי חמדה שבו נברא העולם, שנאמר: כי לקח טוב נתתי לכם תורתי אל-תעזובו.

[50] Cf. Jos.CA 2.184ff; Ex.R. 47:3; Eccl.R. 1.4.4; Zev. 116a.

[51] εἶτα Ἑκαταῖος δηλοῖ πάλιν πῶς ἔχομεν πρὸς τοὺς νόμους, ὅτι πάντα πάσχειν ὑπὲρ τοῦ μὴ παραβῆναι τούτους προαιρούμεθα καὶ καλὸν εἶναι νομίζομεν . . . ἀλλὰ γεγυμνωμένως περὶ τούτων καὶ αἰκίαις καὶ θανάτοις δεινοτάτοις μάλιστα πάντων ἀπαντῶσι, μὴ ἀρνούμενοι τὰ πατρῷα.

[52] usque eo sceleratissimae gentis consuetudo convaluit, ut per omnes iam terras recepta sit; victi victoribus leges dederunt.

[53] When Paul's meaning is acknowledged here, Christian abuse of the Torah becomes highly visible. It is difficult to ascribe such negative attributes as those assigned to the Torah ("under the Torah" = "under sin") when they also define Jesus.

[54] For the parallelism between verses 1-7 and 3:23-29, see above.

[55] [Cf. Gen. 40:14; Ps. 141:8 (LXX); Isa. 42:7; Acts 5:19, 12:17, 16:37, 39]. For the Servant motif in Galatians, see 1:1-5, 15f, 21-24, 3:10-14, verses 8f, and below. Under the narrative scheme which Hays propounds, Melchizedek plays the role of Subject/rescuer, in parallel to Jesus' position in the New Testament: "The activity of

also serves in the sense of "redeeming time."[56] The fact that this verb picks up that in 3:13 may indicate that Paul is thinking here in terms of release from the "curse of the Torah" (cf. Hays, Galatians: 284) (see 3:10-14).[57] It is precisely as one who was himself obedient to God's will and fulfilled His covenant (the Torah) – being "made like his brethren in all things, that he might become a merciful and high priest in things pertaining to God, to make propitiation for the sins of the people"[58] – that Jesus embodies God's promise to the "seed of Abraham (σπέρματος 'Αβραὰμ)" (Heb. 2:16-17).[59]

The correlative consequence of Jesus' redemptive activity is that "we might receive the adoption as sons (ἵνα τὴν υἱοθεσίαν ἀπολάβωμεν)."[60] Here, the parallelism between "those under the Torah" and "we" is suggested not merely by Paul's consistent pronounal usage (see above) but also because the first designation logically describes Jews (see 2:15-21 and above).[61] The term "adoption (υἱοθεσίαν)" appears rather odd in this context, Israel consistently being identified as God's (natural) "sons" throughout the Tanakh.[62] The idea directly associates with the "orphans"

Mechizedek as a redeemer figure in 11QMelch is described in the same general language as the work of Jesus in Hebrews: each defeats the enemies of God (11QMelch 2:9-15; Heb 2:14-15) and brings salvation for humanity (11QMelch 2:13-25; Heb 9:11-12; 9:15) ... These similarities suggest at the very least that the descriptions of the redemptive activity of Jesus in Hebrews and Melchizedek in 11QMelch were part of a complex of ideas associated with the common understanding of salvation and the heavenly redeemer figure. In terms of a salvation that was yet to come, 11QMelch presents Melchizedek as a figure who 'embodied' the people's hopes for a definitive release from the bondage of evil; in terms of a salvation that has been accomplished, Hebrews presents Jesus as the one who actually brought about this release" (Kobelski: 128-29) (cf. Hays, Faith: 73-117, 224f).

[56] Cf. LXX Dan. 2:8; Eph. 5:16; Col. 4:5 (cf. BAGD: 271).

[57] Jesus' advent constitutes the "redemption of time," in the sense of 3:23, as the "fulfilment" of an age and its "deliverance" from the dominion of Belial.

[58] ὤφειλεν κατὰ πάντα τοῖς ἀδελφοῖς ὁμοιωθῆναι, ἵνα ἐλεήμων γένηται καὶ πιστὸς ἀρχιερεὺς τὰ πρὸς τὸ θεὸν εἰς τὸ ἱλάσκεσθαι τὰς ἁμαρτίας τοῦ λαοῦ.

[59] Cf. Rom. 4:25, 8:3; 2 Cor. 5:21; Phil. 2:7; Heb. 2:9ff, 4:14-15, 5:7-10; 1 Pet. 2:22; 1 Jn. 3:5. For the theme of the "sons of Abraham," see 2:15-21, 3:6ff.

[60] Cf. Rom. 8:15, 23, 9:4; Eph. 1:5. The parallel with Ephesians suggests that the "fulness of time" is linked in some way to "predestination (προορίσας)."

[61] Most telling in this regard is the fact that in Rom. 8:15, Paul repeats the thought of verses 4-5 here almost verbatim – retaining the pronounal usage: "For **you** have not received a spirit of slavery leading to fear again, but **you** have received a spirit of adoption as sons by which **we** cry out, 'Abba! Father! (οὐ γὰρ *ἐλάβετε* πνεῦμα δουλείας πάλιν εἰς φόβον ἀλλὰ *ἐλάβετε* πνεῦμα υἱοθεσίας ἐν ᾧ *κράζομεν* αββα ὁ πατήρ)" (see 3:10-14). Concealed in this statement is Paul's claim, expressed explicitly elsewhere, of "to the Jew first" (cf. Mt. 15:24; Jn. 4:22; Acts 3:26, 13:46, 18:6; Rom. 1:16, 2:9; 1 Cor. 1:24) (cf. Betz, Galatians: 208).

[62] Cf. Ex. 4:22; Dt. 1:31, 14:2, 32:5f; Jer. 31:9; Hos. 1:10, 11:1.

who are perhaps most frequently the wards of guardians (see above). Jewish law (halakhah) does not in fact recognise any legal relationship of personal status between a child and anyone but his/her natural parents (cf. Elon: 440, and for the following discussion). While the act of taking a child into one's home and raising him/her is highly esteemed – "Whoever brings up an orphan in his home, Scripture ascribes it to him as though he had begotten him כל המגדל יתום בתוך ביתו מעלה עליו הכתוב כאילו ילדו" (San. 19b) – the child remains a ward and the "adopter" a guardian.

Here, the phrase "under the Torah (ὑπὸ νόμον)" indicates that the Torah has, until this point, constituted the guardian appointed to take care of the child (see 3:21-25). With Jesus' "coming," and the redemption which his faithfulness effects, those in Israel who become obedient to God through Jesus are transposed back into their original relationship of sons to their Father. This concept is well-illustrated in rabbinic literature, several midrashim explicating how sonship is defined not by birth but by behaviour: "'Ye are sons of the Lord your God' (Dt. 14:2): when you behave as sons you are designated as sons; if you do not behave as sons, you are not designated sons בנים אתם לה׳ אלהיכם: בזמן שאתם נוהגים מנהג בנים, אתם קרוים בנים. אין אתם נוהגים מנהג בנים, אין אתם קרוים בנים" (Kid. 36a). "You are called both sons and servants. When you carry out the desires of the Omnipresent you are called 'sons', and when you do not carry out the desires of the Omnipresent, you are called 'servants'"[63] (BB 10a) (see 2:15-21).[64]

A similar idea is reflected in a midrashic tradition which interprets Isaiah 42:7 in the light of Isaiah 43:8, differentiating "sons" who serve God out of love from "slaves" who serve Him only out of fear:

"The Holy One said to those of Israel [who remained standing in the courtyard and lane leading to a wide space in which they could pay their respects to the King]: My children, why though I came to pay My respects to you, do you not come to pay your respects to Me? Even though, *Some of you choose to dwell in courtyards* [*outside the open ground before My palace*], *nevertheless, just as companions* [*who, having made their way into the open ground before Me,*] *hearken eagerly for your utterance* [*of regard for Me,*] *I, too, would have you make Me hear such utterance* (Cant. 8:13). [Thus God in speaking of companions is referring to those authors who in the Writings and the Books of the Prophets teach Torah. For

---

[63] אתם קרוים בנים וקרוים עבדים. בזמן שאתם עושין רצונו של מקום, אתם קרוין בנים. ובזמן שאין אתם עושין רצונו של מקום, אתם קרוין עבדים.

[64] Cf. Yalk.Dt. 891; Yalk.Jer. 273; Kid. 36a. The same idea lies behind Jesus' admonition in Jn. 8:31-47, that "if you are Abraham's children, do the deeds of Abraham (εἰ τέκνα τοῦ Ἀβραάμ ἐστε, τὰ ἔργα τοῦ Ἀβραάμ ἐποιεῖτε)" (Jn. 8:39) (see 2:15-21, 3:1ff, and 5:19f). For Paul's "fathering" of the Galatians as his "sons/disciples," see verses 12-20.

example, speaking through Isaiah, God says]: *Let there be brought forth [into the open ground before Me] people who are blind though they have eyes* (Isa. 43:8) – that is, men unlettered in Torah who are obedient to the precepts of right conduct and to other precepts, and, it goes without saying, stay far away from unchastity and any other kind of indecency. And let also be brought *They who are deaf, though they have ears* (ibid): these may even be Sages and their disciples who give themselves utterly to Scripture, to Mishnah, to Midrash of Halakot and 'Aggadot, [but still fail to comprehend them]. With regard to blind and deaf such as these, Isaiah quotes God as saying: *I have taken hold of thy hand . . . to open the blind eyes, to bring out . . . them that sit in darkness out of the prison house* (Isa. 42:7) – [out of the confining courtyards into the open *ground* beyond]."[65] (TBE p. 82) (see 2:15-21)[66]

The definition of a father as the person who rears the child rather than as the physical progenitor is also recognised in a midrash on the expression "Abraham our father" in Isaiah:

"Another explanation of *'But now, O Lord, Thou art our father'* (Isa. 64:7). The Holy One, blessed be He, said: 'You have ignored your own fathers, Abraham, Isaac, and Jacob, and Me do you call father?' To which they replied: 'Thee do we recognise as our Father.' It can be compared to an orphan who was brought up with a guardian that was a good and trustworthy man, and brought her up and looked after her most carefully. Later he wished to marry her, and when the scribe came to write the marriage document he asked her: 'What is your name?' to which she replied: 'So-and-so'; but when he asked her: 'What is the

---

[65] כך אמר להם הקדוש ברוך הוא לישראל: בני, מה עשיתם? באתי אני להקביל פניכם ואתם לא באתם להקביל פני, שנאמר: היושבת בגנים וגו'. ואומר: הוציא עם עור ועינים יש וחרשים ואזנים למו. הוציא עם עור ועינים יש - אלו עמי הארץ, שיש בהם דרך ארץ ושאר מצות ומרחיקין את עצמם מן הגזל ומן כל דבר מכוער. וחרשים ואזנים למו - אלו תלמידי חכמים, שמסרו את עצמן למקרא למשנה להלכות ולאגדות. ועל אלו הוא נאמר: לפקוח עינים עורות להוציא ממסגר אסיר מבית כלא יושבי חשך.

[66] Cf. Isa. 6:1-13; Mal. 1:6; Mt. 25:31-46; Lk. 1:74-75; TBE p. 140. The midrash clearly demonstrates that a person's status – whether unlettered (an am aretz, not considered to perform the Torah strictly) or educated (the Sage, who is the paradigm of Torah-observance) – does not necessarily ensure that s/he serves God out of love (intention), making of all "hypocrites" (see Introduction, **Argument** and 2:15-21). In speaking of both in terms of the deaf and blind, the tradition implies that human beings are "slaves to sin" (Rom. 6:6). This may also be the sense in which Jesus exegetes Isa. 6:9-10 in Mt. 13:10-17//. This latter isaianic passage appears to form one of Paul's prooftexts for the "mystery" of Israel's salvation reflected in the dual purpose clauses of Mt. 13:14 (see 3:10-14) – another parallel between those verses and the present text. For Isaiah 42 (cf. Isa. 61:1-3) and the motif of bondage, see 1:1f, 2:1-10, 3:1ff, 26-29, and above.

name of your father?' she was silent. Whereupon her guardian said to her: 'Why are you silent?' and she replied: 'Because I know of no other father save you, for he that brings up a child is called a father, and not he that gives birth' ... Similarly, the orphan is Israel, as it says, *We are become orphans and fatherless* (Lam. 5:3). The good and faithful guardian is the Holy One, blessed be He, whom Israel began to call 'Our father', as it says, *'But now, O Lord, Thou art our father'*. God said: 'You have ignored your own father, and now call Me your father'; as it says, *Look unto Abraham, your father*, etc. (Isa. 51:2). They replied: 'Lord of the Universe! He who brings up children is called the father, not he who gives birth,' as it says, *For Thou art our Father; for Abraham knoweth us not* (Isa. 63:16)."[67] (Ex.R. 46:5)[68]

The fact that Paul speaks of the "spirit of adoption (πνεῦμα υἱοθεσίας)" in Romans 8:15 seems to indicate that it is – as he has emphasized here in 3:2ff – receipt of the Spirit which effects the adoption. Here, 11QMelchizedek's interpretation of the jubilee through Isaiah 52:7 may once again help in explaining Paul's thought. In the jubilee year, all those who have been reduced to slaves are restored to their "own property" and "own family"[69] (cf. Lev. 25:8f). While the biblical texts do not speak in terms of "adoption," Paul may possibly be thinking of the believers' "release" through the herald of salvation, anointed by God's Spirit to "proclaim the favorable year of the Lord" (Isa. 61:2), as a "restoration" of sonship interrupted by slavery.[70] The Spirit's presence and indwelling not only brings the remnant of Israel to life – having been "dead in their sins" – but presents them alive before God in righteousness as they walk according to the Spirit, condemning sin in the flesh (cf. Rom. 6:3-23, 8:2-27).[71]

---

[67] דבר אחר "ועתה ה' אבינו אתה": אמר להם הקדוש ברוך הוא: הנחתם אבותיכם, אברהם יצחק ויעקב ולי אתם קוראים אב? אמרו לו: לך אנו מכירים כאב. משל ליתומה שהיתה מתגדלת אצל אפוטרופוס והיה אדם טוב ונאמן, גדלה ושמרה כראוי. בקש להשיאה. עלה הלבלר לכתוב הכתובה, אמר לה: מה שמך? אמרה: פלנית. אמר לה: ומה שם אביך? התחילה שותקת. אמר לה אפוטרופוס שלה: למה את שותקת? אמרה לו: מפני שאיני יודעת לי אב, אלא אותך שהמגדל נקרא אב ולא המוליד. כך היתומים - אלו ישראל, שנאמר: יתומים היינו ואין אב. אפוטרופוס שלהם הטוב הנאמן - זה הקדוש ברוך הוא, התחילו ישראל קורין אותו אבינו, שנאמר: ועתה ה' אבינו אתה. אמר הקדוש ברוך הוא: הנחתם את אבותיכם ולי אתם קוראים אבינו, שנאמר: הביטו אל אברהם אביכם. אמרו לו: רבון העולם, המגדל אב ולא המוליד, שנאמר: כי אתה אבינו כי אברהם לא ידענו.

[68] Cf. Rom. 8:15; 1QHᵃ 15:20-21, 17:29-36. David speaks of his deliverance and salvation in terms of God's "taking him up" when his mother and father have forsaken him (Ps. 27:10: כי-אבי ואמי עזבוני וה' יאספני).

[69] ושבתם איש אל-אחזתו ואיש אל-משפחתו תשבו.

[70] For Isa. 61:1-3, see 1:1-5, 3:1ff, 26-29, verses 8-11, and below.

[71] "... Paul's adoption metaphor may have another nuance as well. In contrast to God's own Son, all other human beings, including Jewish believers, enter God's family only by adoption. Augustine saw this point clearly in commenting on this passage: 'He says *adoption* so that we may clearly understand that the Son of God is

Verse 6: As in 3:14, the argument here is dialectical. Paul perseveres in proposing that Israel receives God's promise of the Spirit through the Gentiles (see 3:10-14).[72] Abraham's blessing that "all the families of the earth shall be blessed" specifically includes – is addressed to – the gentile nations (see 3:6-9). It is only once this promise has been fulfilled in Jesus' coming, his faithfulness providing the Gentiles with a way to God through his death on the cross, that Israel also partakes of the same blessing (cf. Rom. 11:25-36).[73] Paul may be expressing this thought in 2 Corinthians 1:21-22: "Now He who establishes us with you in the Messiah and anointed us is God, who sealed us and gave *us* the Spirit in our hearts as a pledge."[74]

Although the Greek does not necessitate positing any precedence to the Gentiles, such a signification is not precluded. The passage itself has been taken as an allusion to Paul's commissioning, an experience which he models on the Servant anointed for his task with the Spirit, perhaps especially here with respect to Isaiah 42 (cf. Kim, Paul: 117-21) (see 1:15-16b).[75] In this context, Paul might naturally identify the Spirit with Jesus as "the Spirit of His Son (τὸ πνεῦμα τοῦ υἱοῦ αὐτοῦ)."[76] Such a text as Isaiah

---

unique. For we are sons of God through his generosity and the condescension of his mercy, whereas he is Son by nature, sharing the same divinity with the Father'" (Hays, Galatians: 284). By participating in Jesus' faithfulness as a son, those who are obedient to him share the same status.

[72] This reading obviates any need for a discussion of the theological implications of the narrative sequence – whether or not the sending of the Spirit should be considered an action dependent and consequent upon adoption.

[73] This scheme should not be considered to challenge Israel's general precedence – "to the Jew first" (see above). As Paul says in Romans, "what advantage has the Jew? Or what is the benefit of circumcision? . . . Great in every respect. First of all, that they were entrusted with the oracles of God . . . to whom belongs the adoption as sons and the glory and the covenants and the giving of the Torah and the *temple* service and the promises, whose are the fathers and from whom is the Messiah according to the flesh (Τί οὖν περισσὸν τοῦ Ἰουδαίου ἢ τίς ἡ ὠφέλεια τῆς περιτομῆς· πολὺ κατὰ πάντα τρόπον. πρῶτον μὲν [γὰρ] ὅτι ἐπιστεύθησαν τὰ λόγια τοῦ θεοῦ . . . ὧν ἡ υἱοθεσία καὶ ἡ δόξα καὶ αἱ διαθῆκαι καὶ ἡ νομοθεσία καὶ ἡ λατρεία καὶ αἱ ἐπαγγελίαι, ὧν οἱ πατέρες καὶ ἐξ ὧν ὁ Χριστὸς τὸ κατὰ σάρκα)" (Rom. 3:1-2, 9:4-5). It was only because God chose Israel that He could subsequently call another, "not-My-people," into existence (cf. Soulen: 109ff).

[74] ὁ δὲ βεβαιῶν ἡμᾶς σὺν ὑμῖν εἰς Χριστὸν καὶ χρίσας ἡμᾶς θεός, ὁ καὶ σφραγισάμενος ἡμᾶς καὶ δοὺς τὸν ἀρραβῶνα τοῦ πνεύματος ἐν ταῖς καρδίαις ἡμῶν.

[75] In this sense, the "our" here possesses a personal aspect particular to Paul himself. Kim's argument, designed to demonstrate Paul's self-perception in terms of Isaiah 42, simultaneously mitigates against the traditional thesis that 2 Cor. 1:21-22 represents a baptismal formula.

[76] Cf. Acts 16:7; Rom. 8:9; 2 Cor. 3:17; Phil. 1:19. The same verb (ἐξαπέστειλεν; exapesteilen) describes God's sending forth of His Son and the sending forth of the

61:1-3, moreover, combines the Spirit's role with deliverance from bondage: "The Spirit of the Lord GOD is upon me, because the LORD has anointed me . . . to proclaim liberty to captives, and freedom to prisoners; to proclaim the favorable year of the LORD, and the day of vengeance of our God : רוח ה׳ עלי יען משח ה׳ אותי . . . לקרא לשבוים דרור ולאסורים פקח-קוח "לקרא שנת-רצון לה׳ ויום נקם לאלהינו (see 1:1f, 3:1ff, and above).[77]

The action of sending the Spirit "into our hearts (εἰς τὰς καρδίας ἡμῶν)" is evidently based on such passages as Ezekiel 18:31, 36:26, where God replaces the heart of flesh with His Spirit: "I will give you a new heart and put a new spirit within you ונתתי לכם לב חדש ורוח חדשה אתן בקרבכם."[78] This is the "purpose (τέλος)" of the Torah (cf. Rom. 10:4), that all God's people should know Him and do His will: "And I will put My Spirit within you and cause you to walk in My statutes, and you will be careful to observe My ordinances ואת-רוחי אתן בקרבכם ועשיתי את אשר-בחקי תלכו ומשפטי תשמרו ועשיתם" (Ezek. 36:27) (see 2:15-21 and 3:19-20 [end]).[79]

Abba (אבא) – the emphatic form of both the Hebrew and Aramaic אב (av – "father") – reflects Jesus' own usage (cf. Mk. 14:36).[80] The freedom to approach God which the "spirit of adoption as sons" gives derives from the removal of the "spirit of slavery leading to fear" – enabling those

---

Spirit of His Son. Jesus' own birth exemplifies most clearly the connection between the Spirit and sonship: "The Holy Spirit will come upon you, and the power of the Most High will overshadow you; and for that reason the holy offspring shall be called the Son of God (πνεῦμα ἅγιον ἐπελεύσεται ἐπὶ σὲ καὶ δύναμις ὑψιστου ἐπισκιάσει σοι· διὸ καὶ τὸ γεννώμενον ἅγιον κληθήσεται υἱὸς θεοῦ)" (Lk. 1:35).

[77] Cf. 1QHª 23:12-15; 11QMelch 2:15-25; 4Q521 f2ii:5f; Gen.R. 2:4 (see 1:1f, 2:1-10, 3:26-29). For Isa. 42:7, see above. On an "exegetical" level, the combination of Jesus with the Spirit marks the juxtaposition of Jesus' coming (cf. 3:11, 25) and the coming of Abraham's blessing on the Gentiles through the Spirit (cf. 3:2f, 14).

[78] Cf. Isa. 59:21; Jer. 24:7, 31:31f, 32:38f; Ezek. 11:19-20; Lk. 22:20; Rom. 5:5; 1 Cor. 11:25; 2 Cor. 1:22, 3:6; Heb. 9:15; CD-A 6:19, 8:21; CD-B 19:33-34, 20:12; 1QpHab 2:3; 4Q504 ff1-2ii:7-18, v:15-16, vi:2-4.

[79] The proximity between the בקרבכם (be-kirbekhem – "in your midst") in these passages and the מקרבך (mi-kirbekha – "from your midst") in Dt. 18:15 (cf. Dt. 18:18) suggests the association of the Prophet as one of Israel – מאחיך (me-achekha – "from your brethren"). Jesus comes "to his own" (Jn. 1:11) because "'their [his] ruler shall be one of them, and their ruler shall come forth from their [his] midst; and I will bring him near, and he shall approach Me; for who would dare to risk his life to approach Me?,' declares the LORD והיה אדירו ממנו ומשלו מקרבו יצא והקרבתיו ונגש אלי כי מי הוא-זה ערב את-לבו לגשת אלי נאם ה׳" (Jer. 30:21) (see 3:19-20 [nn246, 264]). Rabbinic literature applies the last part of the verse in Jeremiah to the Gentiles, as those whom God accepts when they call upon Him, having Himself called Israel on His own initiative (cf. Yalk.Jer. 312; Kid. 70b).

[80] The epithet is one of honour, given to esteemed personages (cf. Gen. 45:8; Judg. 17:10; Kil. 2:3; Mid. 2:6; JNed. 5, 6, 39b) (cf. Safrai, Literature: 263f; Flusser, Jesus: 32, 115f; Jeremias, Abba/Lord's). As such the name was not bestowed on slaves, such people being considered unworthy of the title (cf. Ber. 16b).

baptised into Jesus' death and resurrection to "cry out, 'Abba! Father!'"[81] (Rom. 8:15).[82] The action of "crying out (κράζων)" may reflect the "calling on the name of the Lord," although the regular Greek verb used in the latter expression is (ἐπι)καλέω ([epi]kaleō).[83] The example of Choni (Onias) the Circlemaker, who was known as a member of God's family (בן בית; ben beit – lit.: "son of the house"), provides an excellent illustration of sonship: "thou [Choni] importunest God and he performeth thy will, like a son that importuneth his father and he performeth his will אתה מתחטא לפני המקום ועושה לך רצונך כבן שהוא מתחטא על אביו ועושה לו רצונו" (Ta'anit 3:8).[84] This suggests that Paul's context here is likely to be that of prayer.[85]

Verse 7: To call a person "father" is the most definitive sign of sonship.[86] Paul therefore sums up his argument here by repeating the logical sequence: Once Jesus has come in faithfulness, those obedient to him have reached the age of majority, when sin no longer has power or

---

[81] οὐ γὰρ ἐλάβετε πνεῦμα δουλείας πάλιν εἰς φόβον ἀλλὰ ἐλάβετε πνεῦμα υἱοθεσίας ἐν ᾧ κράζομεν· αββα ὁ πατήρ.

[82] Cf. Lk. 1:74-75; Heb. 2:15. It is evident that Paul's thought here strongly resembles both Romans and Hebrews, such that the two verses recalled above may stand, in some respects, as summaries of Galatians as a whole (see also verses 8-11). For Hebrews, see 1:1-5 (nn99f), 3:10-14 (n158), verses 21-31, and above.

[83] In this sense, Paul's thought resembles Jn. 1:12: "But as many as received him, to them he gave the right [power] to become children of God, even to those who believe in his name (ὅσοι δὲ ἔλαβον αὐτόν, ἔδωκεν αὐτοῖς ἐξουσίαν τέκνα θεοῦ γενέσθαι, τοῖς πιστεύουσιν εἰς τὸ ὄνομα αὐτοῦ)." The Greek ἐξουσία [exousia], translated here as "right," also carries the meaning of "capability" (cf. BAGD: 278), while believing and calling on Jesus' name are virtually synonymous (cf. Rom. 10:9-12). For the association between the Spirit and power, cf. Judg. 6:34, [14:19]; 1 Chron. 12:18; 2 Chron. 24:20; Acts 1:8 (cf. Le Cornu and Shulam: 11).

[84] Cf. Tanh.Ki tavo 4; Mid.Ps. 126:1-2; Yalk.Ps. 880; JTa'anit 16b; Ta'anit 23a; Ber. 19a. For Choni, cf. Le Cornu and Shulam: 193ff, 244f, 275, 375f.

[85] Cf. LXX Ps. 3:5, 106:13. Jesus teaches his disciples to pray to "Our Father in heaven (Πάτερ ἡμῶν ὁ ἐν τοῖς οὐρανοῖς)" (Mt. 6:9), such a designation being quite commonly employed in Second Temple Judaism (cf. Mt. 7:11, 23:9; Yalk.Gen. 117; Yalk.Ps. 733; Sot. 9:15) (cf. Jeremias, Lord's). He also declares that he will not leave his followers as "orphans (ὀρφανούς)" by promising to send the Spirit to abide with them as a type of "guardian" (cf. Jn. 14:16-18). To the extent that a guardian may also be a tutor (see 3:21-25), the Spirit may perhaps be thought of here as a "nursing/foster father" – the person who "rears" the believer into the knowledge of the Messiah (cf. Num. 11:12; Ruth 4:16; 2 Kings 10:1; Isa. 49:23; Col. 2:2-3; 1 Jn. 4:20, 27; 1QHᵃ 17:29-36). (אומן [omēn] also signifying "hidden," the Spirit's tutorship may be linked with Col. 3:3: "For you have died [in baptism] and your life is hidden with the Messiah in God (ἀπεθάνετε γὰρ καὶ ἡ ζωὴ ὑμῶν κέκρυπται σὺν τῷ Χριστῷ ἐν τῷ θεῷ)" (see 3:26-29).

[86] If the doubling of the invocation reflects the "bilingual character of the early church," the latter also includes Gentiles as well as Jews, both, in different languages, crying "Father" (cf. Betz, Galatians: 211). The epithet further intimates intimacy.

bondage over them. At this point, the child is neither a slave nor a minor but has entered into the status of heir (see the argument above). Having just made this point in respect of Jews (Israel – verses 3-5, 6b), Paul now makes a dialectical turn and relates the application to the Gentiles.[87]

This brings his argument full circle, closing on the note of the Gentiles' heirship "through God (διὰ θεοῦ)."[88] God's calling of the Gentiles by name is His sovereign act, accomplished through Jesus' faithfulness to death on the cross, whereby God's promise to Abraham to bless all the nations of the earth is fulfilled. It is through this means – and not by any other – that the rest of the world receives access to God, in that, being "separate from the Messiah, excluded from the commonwealth of Israel, and strangers to the covenants of promise, having no hope and without God in the world," they have now been "brought near by the blood of the Messiah"[89] (Eph. 2:12-13).[90]

Verses 8-11:

However, at that time, when you did not know God, you were slaves to those which by nature are no gods. But now that you have come to know God, or rather to be known by God, how is it that you turn back again to the weak and worthless elemental things, to which you desire to be enslaved all over again? You observe days and months and seasons and years. I fear for you, that perhaps I have labored over you in vain.

Paul's immediate and overwhelming concern is that his gentile Galatian disciples are not conducting themselves as befits their standing before God (see Introduction, **Argument**). The disparity between their actions and (spiritual) reality, expressed in their desire to attain Jewish identity as a social status, demonstrates that they are being persuaded away from the (Paul's) teaching of the gospel (see Introduction, **Occasion and circumstances**). In so doing, they are in effect eliminating the "no longer (οὐκέτι)" which defines their current distinction, and "turning back (ἐπιστρέφετε)" to that previous period which was characterised by

---

[87] For Paul's pronounal usage, see above. Even though Paul has employed the analogy of son and slave to illustrate Israel's position, verses 8-11 witness to the fact that Paul goes on to apply it also to the Gentiles.

[88] For Paul's switch from the plural to the singular in verse 7, see 6:1-11 (verse 1).

[89] χωρὶς Χριστοῦ, ἀπηλλοτριωμένοι τῆς πολιτείας τοῦ Ἰσραὴλ καὶ ξένοι τῶν διαθηκῶν τῆς ἐπαγγελίας, ἐλπίδα μὴ ἔχοντες καὶ ἄθεοι ἐν τῷ κόσμῳ . . . ἐγενήθητε ἐγγὺς ἐν τῷ αἵματι τοῦ Χριστοῦ.

[90] Specifically, Paul is persuading the Galatians that inheritance within Judaism – i.e., attainment of Jewish identity – is not a goal to be sought when they have already received access to God through Jesus' death and resurrection. To look, *after receipt of* God's favour, for additional Jewish identity in social terms is not merely superfluous but, to all intents and purposes, nullifies God's act of faithfulness in Jesus, not merely for them but also for Israel (see Introduction, **Argument**). For the importance of the "chronological" periods, see verses 1-7 and below.

bondage and slavery – to whose dominance they thus appear to Paul to wish to resubject themselves.[91]

The Gentiles' position clearly differs from that of Israel, Gentiles never having been called as God's people nor been given His commandments. As naturally "sinners," their "former life" is typically one of idolatry:

> For the devising of idols was the beginning of *spiritual* fornication, and the invention of them the corruption of life. For neither were they from the beginning, neither shall they be for ever . . . But miserable are they, and in dead things is their hope, who called them gods, which are the works of men's hands . . . And so the multitude, allured by the grace of the work, took him now for a god, which a little before was but honored as a man. And this was an occasion to deceive the world: for men, serving either calamity or tyranny, did ascribe unto stones and stocks the incommunicable name.[92] (Wis.Sol. 14:12-13, 13:10, 14:20-21)[93] (see 2:11-14 [excursus])

Verse 9: Paul directly associates the Gentiles' "coming to know God (νῦν δὲ γνόντες θεόν)" with God's "sending His Son (ἐξαπέστειλεν ὁ θεὸς τὸν υἱὸν αὐτοῦ)" (verse 4) to deliver wo/mankind from slavery and bondage (cf. verse 7: διὰ θεοῦ – "through God").[94] The "correction"– "or rather to be known by God (μᾶλλον δὲ γνωσθέντες ὑπὸ θεοῦ)"– contains virtually all of Paul's "theology": It is God who has sought out wo/mankind to bring them back to Himself.[95] Jesus' relation of the attribute to the shepherd who "knows" his sheep – "My sheep hear my

---

[91] For the specific addressees of this, and the subsequent section, see verses 1-7.

[92] Ἀρχὴ γὰρ πορνείας ἐπίνοια εἰδώλων, εὕρεσις δὲ αὐτῶν φθορὰ ζωῆς. οὔτε γὰρ ἦν ἀπ' ἀρχῆς οὔτε εἰς τὸν αἰῶνα ἔσται ... Ταλαίπωροι δὲ καὶ ἐν νεκροῖς αἱ ἐλπίδες αὐτῶν, οἵτινες ἐκάλεσαν θεοὺς ἔργα χειρῶν ἀνθρώπων ... τὸ δὲ πλῆθος ἐφελκόμενον διὰ τὸ εὔχαρι τῆς ἐργασίας τὸν πρὸ ὀλίγου τιμηθέντα ἄνθρωπον νῦν σέβασμα ἐλογίσαντο. καὶ τοῦτο ἐγένετο τῷ βίῳ εἰς ἔνεδρον, ὅτι ἢ συμφορᾷ ἢ τυραννίδι δουλεύσαντες ἄνθρωποι τὸ ἀκοινώνητον ὄνομα λίθοις καὶ ξύλοις περιέθεσαν.

[93] Cf. Rom. 1:18-32; 1 Cor. 12:2; Gal. 2:15; Eph. 2:1-2, 11-12, 4:17-19, 5:3-8; Col. 1:21, 2:13, 3:5-7; Philo, *Virt.* 102. The "by nature (φύσει)" plays in part on the fact that idols are frequently composed of natural elements, this being also their "nature" (definition/character). For "Jews by nature," see 2:15-21; for the motif of bondage, see 1:1-5, 2:1-10, 15-21, 3:19ff, 5:13f, 6:1-11, and verses 1-7.

[94] Worship of idols constituted a clear indication that people did not know God (cf. Ex. 5:2; Ps. 79:6; Jer. 10:25; 1 Thess. 4:5; 2 Thess. 1:8). The biblical form of "knowing God" is not merely to know *that* He is God (cf. Ex. 6:7, 16:12; Dt. 4:39, 7:9; 1 Kings 8:60; Ps. 46:10, 100:3) but also to be acquainted with His person and nature – as Adam "knew" Eve – and to acknowledge Him as sovereign (cf. Gen. 4:1; 1 Chron. 28:9; Dan. 11:32; Hos. 8:2, 13:4; Joel 2:27, 3:17; Eph. 3:19; 1 Jn. 4:8, 16, 5:20; 4QFlor f1ii:3).

[95] Cf. Mt. 18:11f; Lk. 15:3f, 32, 19:10; Jn. 15:16, 19.

voice, and I know them, and they follow me; and I give eternal life to them, and they shall never perish; and no one shall snatch them out of my hand"⁹⁶ (Jn. 10:27-28) – establishes "being known" as an element of election: Those whom God has chosen and brought into a community of obedience – Gentiles as well as Jews.⁹⁷

Now – having experienced the promise of the Spirit, communicated through Jesus' obedience to death – how is it (πῶς; pōs) that the gentile believers are, as it were, turning the clock backwards and seeking to live as though Jesus had never "come" (see 3:1-5 and verses 1-7)? The difficulty of this verse has long been noted by commentators, for whom the claim that the Gentiles' desire for circumcision and proselyte status constitutes a return to "weak and worthless elemental things (τὰ ἀσθενῆ καὶ πτωχὰ στοιχεῖα)" is preposterous.⁹⁸ The verse otherwise implies that, at the same time as the gentile Galatians are seeking full Jewish identity, they are also reverting to pagan worship – an equally puzzling phenomenon (see also below, on verse 10).

While ἐπιστρέφω (epistrefō) quite regularly indicates "conversion" and "repentance," the conundrum can most effectively be understood by apprehending the "turning back" not in terms of a deterioration back to former practices of worship but of a reversion to a former "chronological period" – when the world, including both Jews and Gentiles, was under the dominion of Belial (see verses 1-7).⁹⁹

---

⁹⁶ τὰ πρόβατα τὰ ἐμὰ τῆς φωνῆς μου ἀκούουσιν, κἀγὼ γινώσκω αὐτὰ καὶ ἀκολουθοῦσίν μοι, κἀγὼ δίδωμι αὐτοῖς ζωὴν αἰώνιον καὶ οὐ μὴ ἀπόλωνται εἰς τὸν αἰῶνα καὶ οὐχ ἁρπάσει τις αὐτὰ ἐκ τῆς χειρός μου.

⁹⁷ Cf. Isa. 19:24-25, 56:1-8, 66:7-24; Jn. 10:14f; Acts 10:34-35; Rom. 9:6-33, 10:6-21; 1 Cor. 8:3; Odes Sol. 8:12f. See 4:21-31 (verses 26-28).

⁹⁸ "It is not hard to see how Paul could associate the worship of pagan deities, in the Galatians' former life, with slavery to celestial powers. The difficulty for this reading, however, emerges in vv. 9-10, when Paul describes the Galatians' turning to observance of Jewish law as a return to slavery under the *stoicheia*. How could Law-observant worship of the God of Israel possibly be categorized as slavery to the principalities and powers? ... Paul is suggesting that Judaism's holy observances are, in effect, no different from paganism's worship of earthly elements" (Hays, Galatians: 282, 287).

⁹⁹ Here again the idea of the jubilee contributes to Paul's argument, the "inheritance" of a slave being impermanent – whereas that of a son is irrevocable: "'Thus says the Lord GOD, "If the prince gives a gift *out of* his inheritance to any of his sons, it shall belong to his sons; it is their possession by inheritance. But if he gives a gift from his inheritance to one of his servants, it shall be his until the year of liberty; then it shall return to the prince. His inheritance *shall be* only his sons'; it shall belong to them. And the prince shall not take from the people's inheritance, thrusting them out of their possession; he shall give his sons inheritance from his own possession so that My people shall not be scattered, anyone from his possession'" כה-אמר אדני ה' כי-יתן הנשיא מתנה לאיש מבניו נחלתו היא לבניו תהיה אחזתם היא בנחלה : וכי-יתן מתנה מנחלתו לאחד מעבדיו והיתה לו עד-שנת הדרור ושבת לנשיא אך נחלתו

Paul speaks in similar terms in Romans 8:15, declaring to his (gentile) Roman readers that they have not "received a spirit of slavery leading to fear again (πάλιν εἰς φόβον)" (cf. Lk. 1:74-75), the "again" there corresponding to the "turning back (ἐπιστρέφετε πάλιν)" to the "weak and worthless elemental things" here (cf. 5:1).[100] Although the latter are evidently to be equated with the "elemental things" of verse 3, they nonetheless designate a time-framework as much as a substantive entity. In seeking social status within the Jewish community, through circumcision/conversion, the gentile believers are in effect removing their heirship by restoring themselves to an age of minority.[101]

While such an action evidently places Torah-observance (as the concomitant of circumcision) *within the sphere of* the "elemental things," the former is not thereby *equated* with the latter.[102] Although Paul has himself acknowledged that before the coming of the Righteous One, even Israel was subject to the powers of sin and evil (see 3:19f and verses 1-7), he never says that the Torah itself is a "weak and worthless elementary thing." On the contrary, the commandment is "holy and righteous and good (ἁγία καὶ δικαία καὶ ἀγαθή)" (Rom. 7:12), while it is the flesh which is weak (see 3:19f). To the extent that the Gentiles' status-seeking returns them to Belial's dominion by dismissing Jesus' act of faithfulness which overcomes the fear of death, which is the wage of sin, that it is to which Paul so forcefully objects.[103]

בניו להם תהיה: ולא-יקח הנשיא מנחלת העם להונתם מאחזתם מאחזתו ינחל את-בניו למען אשר לא-יפצו עמי איש ממאחזתו" (Ezek. 46:16-18) (cf. Rom. 11:29). For the jubilee, see 1:1-5 and verses 1-7; for the Gentiles' idolatry, see 2:11-14 (excursus) and 5:19-23 (n192).

[100] The πάλιν (palin) denotes "back" and "again" in equal measure, relating to a previous period which recurs, as it were – "often used when the repetition involves return to a previous state or position (Mk. 2:1, 3:1); but also (like the English 'again') when the action is a return to a previous state through reversal, not, strictly speaking, repetition" (Burton: 231-32).

[101] We would remind the reader that the present volume reads the influencers as endeavouring to persuade Paul's gentile disciples that, having become "sons of the promise" through Jesus' death and resurrection, this does not make them "sons of the covenant." If they wish the latter status, they must undergo circumcision in order to join the Jewish community according to normative conventions. Paul is here arguing that if his disciples take this step they will be "severing" themselves from the Messiah and becoming enslaved all over again to the "elemental things of the world." See Introduction, **Occasion and circumstances; Argument.**

[102] Although this may appear to be an over-refined distinction, the history of Christian commentary on Galatians calls for a scrupulously careful reading of the text. Once the Torah and Torah-observance have been defined as "legalistic/legalism" and/or "nomism," it is all too easy to dismiss Judaism as a whole as displeasing before God – and thence to reject Israel as God's people, replaced by the Church (cf. Soulen).

[103] Cf. Lk. 1:74-75; Rom. 6:23; Heb. 2:15.

The gentile believers' "desire to be enslaved (δουλεύειν θέλετε)" is Paul's apprehension of the situation, his disciples clearly intending a positive and beneficial outcome, to which they appear to have been persuaded by the influencers (see Introduction, **Occasion and circumstances**).[104] In submitting to the latters' persuasion, they are, in Paul's eyes, placing themselves in subjection to the powers of the world, remaining slaves – rather than continuing to enjoy the release from debt which Jesus' death and resurrection have obtained for them as the measure of God's faithfulness to Abraham (see 3:6ff).[105] In contrast to God's life-giving and creative act in Jesus, the powers of the world, despite their dominion, are "weak and worthless."[106] "Insofar as they have any power at all, it is the power of illusion. They have already been defeated by the Son of God's victorious incursion" (Hays, Galatians: 288).

Verse 10: Paul's reference to the gentile believers' observance of "days and months and seasons and years (ἡμέρας παρατηρεῖσθε καὶ μῆνας καὶ καιροὺς καὶ ἐνιαυτούς)" has long been debated with respect to its Jewish or gentile address. Does it point to pagan practices to which the gentile believers are returning, or to the adoption of Jewish tradition? Both alternatives pose certain difficulties.[107] Why, on the one hand, should Gentiles seeking to be recognised as full and legitimate members of the Jewish community simultaneously be drawn to pagan practices? If, on the

---

[104] The Greek θέλετε (thelete – "desire") corresponds to the Hebrew מבקש (mevakesh – "seek"), frequently employed in the biblical text in the sense of "looking to" (see 2:15-21 [verse 17]).

[105] "And when you were dead in your transgressions and the uncircumcision of your flesh, He made you alive together with him, having forgiven us all our transgressions, having cancelled out the certificate of debt consisting of decrees against us *and* which was hostile to us; and He has taken it out of the way, having nailed it to the cross. When He had disarmed the rulers and authorities, He made a public display of them, having triumphed over them through him [or: it – the cross] (καὶ ὑμᾶς νεκροὺς ὄντας [ἐν] τοῖς παραπτώμασιν τῇ ἀκροβυστίᾳ τῆς σαρκὸς ὑμῶν, συνεζωοποίησεν ὑμᾶς σὺν αὐτῷ, χαρισάμενος ἡμῖν πάντα τὰ παραπτώματα. ἐξαλείψας τὸ καθ᾽ ἡμῶν χειρόγραφον τοῖς δόγμασιν ὃ ἦν ὑπεναντίον ἡμῖν, καὶ αὐτὸ ἦρκεν ἐκ τοῦ μέσου προσηλώσας αὐτὸ τῷ σταυρῷ· ἀπεκδυσάμενος τὰς ἀρχὰς καὶ τὰς ἐξουσίας ἐδειγμάτισεν ἐν παρρησίᾳ θριαμβεύσας αὐτοὺς ἐν αὐτῷ)" (Col. 2:13-15). For Paul's pronounal usage (reflected also here), see verses 1-7.

[106] In this respect, they resemble the pagan idols – images which are "no gods," which possess "no life," are "weak" and "dead," and in "need of help" (cf. 2 Chron. 13:9; Isa. 37:19, 44:9-17, 46:5-7; Jer. 2:11; Wis.Sol. 13:1-19). For the Torah's condescension to human "weakness," see 3:19f.

[107] The literature on the subject is enormous, the text having also given rise to a "two-front hypothesis" according to which Paul makes not one but two accusations against the Galatians (cf. 1:6-9: another gospel of "circumcision" *versus* 4:8-11: reversion to "paganism") (cf. Martin).

other hand, the notation relates to Jewish festivals, why not employ Jewish terms (shabbat, new moon, feasts, jubilees)? (cf. Col. 2:16; 1 Macc. 10:34)[108]

The problem may perhaps be mitigated if the verse is understood as a descriptive statement of fact rather than as a consequence of the influencers' affect.[109] On this reading, no direct causal relation obtains between the Gentiles' aspirations and their actual, present-day practice.[110] Paul's indictment at this point is that they are behaving as though still under the power of the previous "regime."[111]

The fact that Paul's gentile Galatian disciples are likely to have been godfearers (see Introduction, **Occasion and circumstances**) would not necessarily have precluded performance of pagan practices. It is known that Julia Severa, who built a synagogue in Acmonia, served at the same time as the high priestess of the imperial cult in the city (cf. Levinskaya: 123).[112] The prohibition against idolatry was frequently considered to refer

---

[108] This does not represent the sole problem. The caution with which commentators have seen fit to see verse 10 as a reference to the "Jewish law" reflects its appalling implications, as conveyed in Hays' summary: "This is perhaps the most stunning sentence in this entire confrontational letter. Paul is suggesting that Judaism's holy observances are, in effect, no different from paganism's worship of earthly elements . . . When one strips away the specific terminology of the Jewish festivals, Paul suggests, one sees that they are in essence just another kind of nature religion!" (Galatians: 287-88). One should indeed be extremely wary of allowing this as Paul's meaning – in any way, shape, or form.

[109] While Hays also terms the verse a "descriptive statement," he appears in fact to understand it as explicative: "The Galatians show themselves to be coming back under the sway of the *stoicheia* **by adopting** a pattern of life governed by fixed calendrical observances" (Galatians: 288) (emphasis added).

[110] The verb is, indeed, a simple present (middle) construction – "you are observing," indicative of a descriptive statement (the active and middle carrying the same meaning). P[46] well demonstrates the attempt to make the connection causal by reading παρατηροῦντες (paratērountes; present modal – "by observing") in place of παρατηρεῖσθε (paratēreisthe). The verb itself occurs nowhere else in the LXX or NT in a religious sense (cf. Longenecker, Galatians: 182).

[111] The point to be made is that any contradiction caused by their concern for circumcision is obviated, their current observance simply constituting a natural rite in a pagan framework. For the proposed view of the influencers' identity and purpose with respect to the gentile Galatian believers, including the (unlikely) possibility that they are endeavouring to avoid Roman persecution for non-participation in pagano-civic rites, see Introduction, **Occasion and circumstances**.

[112] Latin and Greek writers on Jews and Judaism reflect the tendency of godfearers to progress from that status forward into full proselytism – rather than *backwards*, towards paganism again: "Some who have had a father who reveres the Sabbath, worship nothing but the clouds, and the divinity of the heavens, and see no difference between eating swine's flesh, from which their father abstained, and that of man; and in time they take to circumcision (Quidam sortiti metuentem sabbata patrem/ nil praeter nubes et caeli numen adorant,/ nec distare putant humana carne suillam,/ qua pater abstinuit, mox et praeputia ponunt)" (Juv.*Sat.* 14.96-99).

only to idolatrous acts and not to theoretical principles, Noachides not being required to "know God" but only to abjure false gods (cf. San. 56a ff). Given the fact that they tended to be prominent members of their local society, godfearers presumably continued to participate in public and pagan religious ceremonies at the same time as attaching themselves to the synagogue (cf. Gill and Gempf: 178-79) (see 2:11-14 [excursus]).

In this context, the calendar expressive of such bondage was presumably constituted by popular and civic cultic culture alike, including the demands imposed by the imperial cult (cf. Ferguson, Backgrounds: 111ff, and for the following discussion). Sacrifices – onè of the three principal acts of worship in the ancient world – were offered according to fixed, annual times in tune with the natural cycle of the seasons, being accompanied by public banquets, entertainment, and processions. These activities were incorporated into the imperial cult, the sacrifices being transferred to the emperor and offered at altars in temples dedicated to him throughout the empire. The emperor was identified with a god, festivals were renamed in his honour, games were instituted in his commemoration, and months named after him. The high priest – who simultaneously served as president of the local assembly – manifested provincial devotion to the emperor through public honors, religious ceremonies, games, and feasts (cf. Nanos, Irony: 267; Martin).[113]

Verse 11: Such behaviour on the part of Paul's gentile disciples causes him great distress. While Paul's expression of apprehension immediately

---

(Rabbinic texts, on the other hand, often speak of the proselyte falling back into his/her former customs [cf. TBE p. 146; Num.R. 8:2; Yev. 47b; AZ 3b; BM 59b].) For the presently-proposed understanding of the influencers' non-Torah-observance, see Introduction, **Occasion and circumstances; Argument** and 6:12-16.

[113] Nanos attempts to resolve the problem posed by a simultaneous seeking after circumcision and adoption of pagan practices by suggesting that "the addressees are in some way beginning to return (or at least contemplate returning) to pagan public cult practices that they had abandoned completely as inappropriate to their standing as righteous ones according to Paul's gospel ... [in reaction] to the status ambiguity that has resulted from the response of the influencers to their [the gentiles'] claims of identity in the absence of proselyte conversion ... The addressees are thus informed that they are not protected from their pagan civic responsibilities by the authority of Jewish communal identity because they are not proselytes or candidates" (Irony: 268). While this theory purports to explain the pressure exerted on the influencers – being, as members of the Jewish community, anxious to deflect potential Roman persecution for possible infringement of Judaism's legal standing by, as it were, sheltering pagans under its umbrella – the paradox seems more historically amenable to resolution by understanding the "turning back" as a "chronological" reversion of "turning the clock back" rather than relating to a change in conduct. For the nature of the persecution feared by the influencers presently proposed, see Introduction, **Occasion and circumstances** and 6:12-16.

follows his reference to the Galatians' observance of festivals, the latter is more a symptom of the disease than its root. Paul's concern is not immediately occasioned by his disciples' participation in pagan practices in and of themselves – although it can be presumed that this would surely displease him – but by their desertion of Jesus and of he himself as Jesus' representative and example and teacher of his gospel by submitting to the persuasion of those seeking social standing. Such behaviour is, to Paul, tantamount to a voluntary return to bondage to sin (see 5:2-12 and verses 1-7).

The cause of Paul's distress is his sense of having "fathered" his disciples' new status – of having brought them into fellowship with Jesus as the Messiah. As had the Thessalonians, the Galatians have turned to God through Paul's preaching (cf. 1 Thess. 1:9).[114] The concept of fathering is known from contemporary Jewish sources, the relationship between a master and his disciples being described in (halakhic) terms as that of "a father and his son [ואב ובנו]" (cf. Le Cornu and Shulam: 448, 858) (see 2:1-10 and verses 12-20).[115] Paul's expression here (cf. verse 19) explicitly recalls Isaiah 49:4 (LXX)[116]: "But I said, 'I have toiled in vain, I have spent my strength for nothing and vanity' ואני אמרתי לריק יגעתי לתהו והבל כ'חי"[117] (see 1:15-16b, 2:1-10, and verses 12-20). The Servant motif directly links this passage with Isaiah 61:1-3, thereby indicating that Paul's trepidation lies in his concern that, despite Jesus' having proclaimed liberty to the captives and freedom to the prisoners, the gentile Galatians are not availing themselves of this release from bondage.[118] Having rebuked his disciples for deserting him and the gospel he preaches, Paul now proceeds to assert his authority and request that they restore themselves in allegiance to himself and to the "good news of God concerning His son" (Rom. 1:1, 3).[119]

---

[114] Betz suggests that κοπιάω (kopiaō – "to labour") "is taken from missionary language" (Galatians: 219) (see 2:1-10 [verse 2]). For κερδαίνω (kerdainō – "to win/gain"), see verses 12-20.

[115] Cf. 1 Cor. 4:15; 1 Thess. [2:7], 11; 1 Tim. 1:2, 18; 2 Tim. 1:2, 2:1; Tit. 1:4; Phlm 10; 1 Pet. 5:13; CD-A 13:9; 1QHᵃ 15:20; 4Q267 f9iv:6; [11QPsᵃ 21:14]; Sif.Dt. 34; TBE p. 80; BM 2:11; Eruv. 73a (see also verses 12-20). Hence the Galatian believers are also *Paul's* "sons" – and no longer slaves (see 2:1-10 and verses 1-7, 12-20). For Galatians as a "halakhic letter," along the lines of 4QMMT, see Introduction, **Form**; **Argument** and verses 12-20.

[116] καὶ ἐγὼ εἶπα Κενῶς ἐκοπίασα καὶ εἰς μάταιον καὶ εἰς οὐδὲν ἔδωκα τὴν ἰσχύν μου.

[117] Cf. Ps. 126:1 (LXX); Isa. 65:23; 1 Cor. 15:10; Phil. 2:16; Col. 1:29; 1 Thess. 5:12; 1 Tim. 4:10.

[118] For Isa. 61:1-3, see 1:1-5, 3:1ff, 26-29, and verses 1f.

[119] For Galatians' halakhic rebuke-request structure, see Introduction, **Form**; **Argument**.

Verses 12-20:
I beg of you, brethren, become as *I am*, for I also *have become* as you *are*. You have done me no wrong; but you know that it was because of a bodily illness that I preached the gospel to you the first time; and that which was a trial to you in my bodily condition you did not despise or loathe; but you received me as an angel of God, as the Messiah Jesus *himself*. Where then is that sense of blessing you had? For I bear you witness, that if possible, you would have plucked out your eyes and given them to me. Have I therefore become your enemy by telling you the truth? They eagerly seek you, not commendably, but they wish to shut you out, in order that you may seek them. But it is good always to be eagerly sought out in a commendable manner, and not only when I am present with you. My children, with whom I am again in labor until the Messiah is formed in you – but I could wish to be present with you now and to change my tone, for I am perplexed about you.

The epistolary conventions clustered in this section, signifying most usually a break in a writer's thought, suggest that this passage stands as a significant turning point in the letter (cf. Longenecker, Galatians: 184, and for the following discussion).[120] Paul's "pleading (δεόμαι)" serves here in the role regularly played by verbs of amazement or astonishment (cf. 1:6) (see 1:6-10). In epistolary terms, verse 12 consequently concludes the first half of the letter, introducing, with Paul's first use of an imperative ("be/come like me"), a rhetorical shift which transfers the tone to that of deliberative rhetoric. Deliberative rhetoric seeks to exhort or to dissuade an audience from pursuing a certain course of action by demonstrating the

---

[120] The petition with which the segment opens represents a request formula. Verses 13, 15 contain two disclosure formulas ("you know that"/"I testify that"). Paul addresses the Galatians directly in verse 19 ("my children"), and expresses a wish to visit in verse 20. An expression of distress appears in verse 11, and a transitional usage of a verb of saying ("tell me") in verse 21 (cf. Longenecker, Galatians: 184). Although not following his "theological" interpretation of the letter, Longenecker's epistolary-structural analysis seems to us to represent the most fruitful framework for its understanding – especially when Galatians is understood as a "halakhic letter" along the lines of 4QMMT (see Introduction, **Form**; **Argument**). We would adapt Longenecker's scheme to read as follows (cf. Hansen): The "rebuke section" of 1:6-4:11 serves as the background for the request in this verse, Paul preparing the way for the latter by setting forth his authority and recounting his personal history (1:1-2:21). The substantive climax of this segment is his rebuke of Peter, which forms the model and springboard for his reproof of his Galatian disciples. Having argued for the Gentiles' status according to Scripture (chapter 3), proving that that they are heirs ("sons of promise") and not slaves if they become faithful to God through Jesus, he subsequently calls on them to continue to walk in the Spirit of adoption – and to remove those troubling them from their field of influence. The "request section" – 4:12-6:18 – deals with Paul's continued efforts to gain these dual aims – a) restoration of his disciples' loyalty; b) by segregation from the influencers (see Introduction, **Form**; **Argument**). For epistolary conventions in Galatians in general, see Introduction, **Form**; for critiques of Betz's attempt to read Galatians in its entirety in terms of forensic rhetoric, cf. Longenecker, Galatians: 184f; Davies, Jewish: 176ff; for "brethren," see 1:1-5.

latter's expedient or injurious nature. What follows – including the "perplexing" allegory (mashal) – forms part of Paul's appeal for proper halakhic conduct – appropriate to the "messianic age" in which his readers are now living (see 6:1-11 and verses 1f).

Since the Servant's role is evidently somewhere present in Paul's apprehension, it is perhaps possible to posit that his plea to his Galatian disciples that they "become as *I am*, for I also *have become* as you are (Γίνεσθε ὡς ἐγώ, ὅτι κἀγὼ ὡς ὑμεῖς)" indicates not merely a simple request that they imitate him but also reflects Paul's sense that he himself is a model of the Messiah. The character of the latter is embodied in the fact that he "emptied himself, taking the form of a bondservant, *and* being made in the likeness of men. And being found in appearance as a man, he humbled himself by becoming obedient to the point of death, even death on a cross"[121] (Phil. 2:7-8).[122] In 1 Corinthians 4:15-16, Paul directly links the fact of his "fathering" with a demand from his readers to "be imitators of me (μιμηταί μου γίνεσθε)."[123] This reflects the rabbinic definition of the disciple as a "son," Paul thus further applying the status which the Galatians have received in the Messiah in relation to himself as their "teacher/master."[124]

---

[121] ἀλλὰ ἑαυτὸν ἐκένωσεν μορφὴν δούλου λαβών, ἐν ὁμοιώματι ἀνθρώπων γενόμενος· καὶ σχήματι εὑρεθεὶς ὡς ἄνθρωπος ἐταπείνωσεν ἑαυτὸν γενόμενος ὑπήκοος μέχρι θανάτου, θανάτου δὲ σταυροῦ.

[122] Cf. Jn. 1:14; Rom. 8:3; Gal. 4:4; Heb. 2:14-18, 4:15 (cf. Hays, Christology: 280f). For Paul's use of the Servant model, see 1:15-16b, 2:1-10, 3:1-5 (n28), 10-14, and verses 8-11; for Jesus' (representative) example, see 2:15-21 and 3:1ff.

[123] Cf. 1 Cor. 11:1; Phil. 3:17, 4:9; 1 Thess. 1:6; 2 Thess. 3:7-9. When verses 8-11 are not taken to refer to Torah-observance, the sense that "The apostle desires the Galatians to emancipate themselves from bondage to law, as he had done, and appeals to them to do this on the ground that he, who possessed the advantages of the law, had foregone them and put himself on the same level, in relation to law, with them" (Burton: 236) becomes even less feasible. The "twist" which Hays claims Paul here gives to his normal usage of the imitation motif – embodied in "his own decision to reject the practices of Torah observance and live like a Gentile" – is, likewise, non-existent. This passage is in fact finely consistent with other imitation passages, in which Paul "urges his readers to be conformed to Christ's example of self-sacrificial suffering for the sake of others, as reflected in the apostle's own conduct" (Galatians: 293). For Paul's Jewish identity, see Introduction, **Author**; Appendix.

[124] "[You shall teach them diligently] unto thy children [sons] (Dt. 6:7): This refers to the disciples [of the wise], for you find that disciples are always referred to as children, as in the verse *And the sons of the prophets that were at Bethel came forth to Elisha* (2 Kings 2:3) – were they the children of the prophets? Were they not the disciples? Hence we learn that disciples are called children . . . Just as the disciples are called sons so the teacher is called father, as it is said: *And Elisha saw it, and he cried, 'My father, my father, the chariots of Israel and the horsemen thereof,' and he saw him no more* (2 Kings 2:12) לבניך : אלו תלמידיך, וכן אתה מוצא בכל מקום שהתלמידים קרוים

Paul's request represents a variation on a "missionary maxim" which he adopts elsewhere: "I have become all things to all men, that I may by all means save some (τοῖς πᾶσιν γέγονα πάντα, ἵνα πάντως τινὰς σώσω)" (1 Cor. 9:22) (cf. Daube, New: 227ff).[125] This idea appears to be based on such maxims as "When you enter a town, follow its customs עלת לקרתא הלך בנימוסה" – employed in an "evangelistic" context: "A man should not rejoice among people who weep or weep when among those who rejoice. He should not stay awake among people who sleep or sleep when among those who are awake . . . This is the general rule: A man should not deviate from the custom of his companions or from society"[126] (DER 7:7).[127]

His disciples having already shared in the good news of the gospel, this rule is equally applicable to the "imitation" demanded by discipleship.[128] In this sense, Paul's request is not that the gentile Galatians refrain from taking upon themselves observance of the commandments, in the same manner as he has divested himself of this burden and become like them.[129] If his appeal is based on the Servant model, he is rather asking them to "have this attitude in yourselves which was also in the Messiah Jesus . . . work[ing] out your salvation with fear and trembling"[130] (Phil. 2:5, 12).[131] Just as he has taken Jesus' example and humbled himself, so he

---

בנים, שנאמר: ויצאו בני הנביאים. וכי בני הנביאים היו? והלא תלמידים היו? אלא מכאן לתלמידים שהם קרוים בנים . . . וכשם שהתתלמידים קרוים בנים כך הרב קרוי אב, שנאמר: "ואלישע רואה והוא מצעק אבי אבי וגו'" (Sif.Dt. 34) (cf. Yalk.Dt. 841).

[125] The likelihood that this constitutes the context of this section increases when verse 19 is apprehended as a reference to proselytising activity. The allusion to "they" in that verse – with no prior mention – indicates that such persons' presence has probably precipitated this passage *in toto*. The idea of imitation also appears to be concealed in Paul's reference to the Galatians' "zeal" (see below, on verse 19).

[126] לא ישמח בין הבוכים ולא יבכה בין השמחים. ולא יהא ער בין הישנים ולא ישן בין הערים . . . כללו של דבר: אל ישנה אדם דעתו מדעת חביריו ובני אדם.

[127] Cf. Rom. 12:15f; 1 Cor. 9:19ff; [Ep.Arist. 257]; Gen.R. 48:14; Ex.R. 47:5; Tos.Ber. 2:21; DEZ 5:5; [BM 86b]. For Roman concepts of friendship, cf. Betz, Galatians: 222f.

[128] Denial to Paul of any use of the concept of discipleship (cf. Betz, Galatians: 221n19) appears to constitute a very shortsighted claim. If "imitation" is to be considered a form of this concept – a completely natural assumption in a Jewish context – Paul treats of discipleship throughout his letters (cf. "Not surprisingly, the language [of 'zeal'] can also describe the relationship between the teacher and his student" [ibid: 229]!). It is surely understanding this section as an "ode to friendship" which has, at least partially, given rise to its exegetical awkwardness – as Betz himself recognises (ibid: 220).

[129] "He became like me, that I might receive him. In form he was considered like me, that I might put him on" (Odes Sol. 7:4) (see 3:19-20 [n241]). For Paul's Jewish identity, see Appendix.

[130] Τοῦτο φρονεῖτε ἐν ὑμῖν ὃ καὶ ἐν Χριστῷ Ἰησοῦ . . . μετὰ φόβου καὶ τρόμου τὴν ἑαυτῶν σωτηρίαν κατεργάζεσθε.

[131] The import of this section, on this reading, is that the Galatians regard Paul and the influencers as competitive sources of identity-conferral, the influencers having at this point gained over Paul among at least some of his gentile Galatian disciples.

is asking the Galatians to also become like the Messiah.[132] No greater proof of one's being "in the Messiah" exists than imitating his conduct, taking on his character, putting on his qualities, and growing up in "all *aspects* into him, who is the head, *even* the Messiah (εἰς αὐτὸν τὰ πάντα, ὅς ἐστιν ἡ κεφαλή, Χριστός)" (Eph. 4:15) (see 3:1-5 and 6:1-11).[133]

Coming "out of the blue" as it seems to, the notation "you have done me no wrong (οὐδέν με ἠδικήσατε)" is perhaps best taken with Paul's evident allusion to the Galatians' apprehensiveness towards him when he first visited. Understanding ἐκπτύω (ekptyō) as an act of "spitting" to ward off the evil eye, Paul appears to be speaking in this passage of the way in which his disciples overcame their natural fears and welcomed him as an apostle and mentor (cf. 2 Cor. 7:2). On this reading, Paul's reference to the lack of harm done to him (cf. verse 12) and his "weakness of flesh" both relate to elements which his gentile disciples might have originally interpreted in terms of the "evil eye" system, thereby taking immediate steps to remove themselves from his malevolent influence: "The point then is, in spite of the fact that Paul's fleshly condition when he was present – or their own – gave them pause, tempting them to suspect him, neither did they conclude to 'despise' him as though a dangerous possessor of the evil eye, perhaps a victim himself now filled with this malevolent force, nor did they protect themselves by way of one of the almost universal expressions when confronted by this threat: they did not 'spit.' This they were indeed 'tempted' to do, yet they concluded otherwise, in fact the opposite,

---

The exhortation to imitate emphasises Paul's perception of himself as the "father of proselytes" (an epithet usually attributed to Abraham), and follows directly on the heels of his discussion of heirship because the influencers are exercising themselves in the attempt to convince the Galatians that they should become part of the Jewish community in order to be considered "sons of the covenant." If they are to imitate anyone, Paul counters, *he* is to be their model – and through/in him, the Messiah himself, thus assuring their status as "sons of the promise." For Abraham, see 3:6ff; for Abraham as Paul's model, see 3:6-9 (n101) and verses 12-20 (n186); for the present reading of the Galatian situation, see Introduction, **Argument**.

[132] The imperative picks up the participles of verse 4, which may themselves be understood either as qualifications or as expressions of narrative action (see verses 1-7). The exhortation is not only for the sake of the Galatians, but also for Paul himself, constituting proof that he has not "run in vain" (see 2:1-10). The question of whether the gnomic paradox should be translated as "become as I am, because I have become as you are" or "be as I am, because I am also as you are" (cf. Betz, *Galatians*: 221-22) is not only a moot issue on the grounds that "It is, however, not necessary to choose between these translations, for it is the nature of a gnome that it can be understood in several ways" (ibid: 222) – but also because Paul's ultimate aim is imitation.

[133] Paul has, in rather paradoxical logic, become what he is asking the Galatians to be – an imitator of the Messiah. For Num. 11:11f in the context of fathering, see 6:1-11.

receiving him instead as though an agent of good will" (Nanos, Social: 5) (see below).[134]

Verse 14: The attitude which his disciples refrain from demonstrating towards Paul is one of "despising and spitting (ἐξουθενήσατε οὐδὲ ἐξεπτύσατε)." The Greek ἐξουθενέω (exoutheneō) is employed several times to describe the contemptuous treatment bestowed upon Jesus during his execution – as well as Paul's own speech, which his detractors characterise as "contemptible (ἐξουθενημένος)" (cf. 2 Cor. 10:10). In Jeremiah 6:14, the LXX employs the verb to render the deceptive healing attempted by the false prophets, who endeavour to pacify the people by proclaiming "peace, peace" when there is no peace.[135]

Much attention has been devoted to the "magical" context of the second verb, ἐκπτυω (ekptyō), in relation to Galatians, spitting constituting a common form of protection against the evil eye (cf. Nanos, Irony: 184-91, 279-80, and for the following discussion).[136] As Nanos lays out the theory, "The process and participants may be simply set out as follows. An evil eye action involves a gazer (actual or suspected) who is feared to have the evil eye, an envious response to a gazee, a person fearing the effects of the eye upon themselves or their possessions, or a gazee detector. The detector is someone who suspects the gaze may be leveled at some other person or thing within their sphere of responsibility (like a child, animal, or thing), such as is the case in the letter to the Galatians for Paul with regard to his "children." The gazee detector thus functions in the role of patron and protector. The gazee or gazee detector moves to protect the threatened person(s) or item(s) in advance of or during any attack, for example, by displaying a sign, or gesturing in a manner believed to offer protection, such as cursing or spitting (the elements of gazee protection). If however, the person or thing suffers damage, the gazee or gazee detector will seek to

---

[134] A similar dynamic is reflected in Acts 28:1-6, the Maltese assuming that Paul was a murderer who, despite having been saved from the sea, was now to receive his punishment at the hands of a snake and, when Paul failed to fall dead, then began to consider him a god. For such "divine retribution," cf. Miles and Trompf. The precise nature of Paul's "sickness" remains unknown. (For his "thorn in the flesh," see Appendix, **Status**.)

[135] וירפאו את־שבר עמי **עַל־נְקַלָּה** לאמֹר שלום שלום ואין שלום. LXX: καὶ ἰῶντο τὸ σύντριμμα τοῦ λαοῦ μου *ἐξουθενοῦντες* καὶ λέγοντες Εἰρήνη εἰρήνη.

[136] In ancient Jewish culture, expectoration in front of another was regarded as a sign of high offence and contempt, punishable at the hands of heaven, the fine for so shaming a person being a hefty 400 *zuz* (cf. Num. 12:14; Isa. 50:6; BK 8:6; Tos.BK 9:31f). A student who spits before his teacher is also considered to have committed a sin (cf. Eruv. 99a). For the motif of eyes, see 3:1-5, [6:1-11].

restore or repair the affected person or item, and perhaps exact revenge upon the gazer as well" (pp. 9-10) (see 1:6-10 and above).[137]

While Paul's language certainly appears to reflect the evil eye idea (see above), he quite evidently integrates this concept into a halakhic framework.[138] In legal contexts, spitting constituted part of the ceremony of חליצה (chalitza), whereby a man's childless widow released his successive brother(s) from the obligation of marrying her in order to continue the family line (cf. Dt. 25:5-10) (see 1:1-5). Paul may be utilising this metaphor – a public humiliation of the man unwilling to marry his sister-in-law – to convey the shame accompanying lack of commitment.[139] On this reading, he wishes to stress just how fully the Galatians accepted him and devoted themselves to the Gospel when he first visited them.

If verse 17 relates to the influencers' attempt to gain converts (see below), Paul's meaning here may be that the Galatians had accepted him as their "father" or mentor and considered themselves to be his disciples.[140] Disciples not merely studied with a Sage but also learnt from his behaviour by "serving" him – a task which included performing for him all the duties a slave performs for his master[141] (cf. Safrai, Master; Alon, Land: 2:476-78).[142] By submitting to their master's teaching and conduct-by-example, they became proper vessels to receive his spiritual wisdom and thereby fit to be his true and faithful successors (cf. Ket. 96a; Yoma 28b). This concept corresponds to Paul's exhortation to the Galatians to "imitate" him – as disciples in relation to their master (see also verses 8-11).[143]

Paul may have in mind here a concept similar to that expressed in Sirach: "If thou wouldst get a friend, prove him first, and be not hasty to

---

[137] Spitting not only constituted both a common method of warding off the evil eye but also a healing charm – especially for eyes (cf. Mk. 8:23; Jn. 9:6; Lev.R. 9:9) (cf. Preuss: 85f, 277).

[138] In this sense we diverge from Nanos' use of the concept, in which he perceives the influencers' proselyte status causing them envy of the Galatians' standing in the Messiah, in a zero-sum situation (cf. Nanos, Social). For the present understanding of "bewitchment" in 3:1 – frequently also adduced as an "evil eye" marker – see Introduction, **Argument** and 3:1-5.

[139] For the motif of marriage in relation to the Galatian circumstances, see 5:2-12 (verse 4) [verses 21-31].

[140] For an interesting parallel to Paul's thought here, cf. Gen. 16:5: "And Sarai said to Abram, 'May the wrong done me be upon you עליך חמסי אל-אברם שרי ותאמר." (The LXX renders the Hebrew חמסי [chamasi – "my wrong"] by ἀδικοῦμαι [adikoumai] – the verb which Paul employs here.) In asserting that the Galatians have "done him no wrong," Paul may be implying that he is not willing to return the wrong upon them. It is not coincidental that Genesis 16 lies behind Paul's "allegory" in verses 22-31 (see verses 21-31).

[141] Cf. TBE pp. 37, 127; Yalk.Dt. 830; PA 6:6; DEZ 8:9; Kal.Rab. 8:6; Sot. 22a.

[142] See also 5:13-18 (n117).

[143] For the teacher as an "angel of the Lord," see below.

credit him (εἰ κτᾶσαι φίλον, ἐν πειρασμῷ κτῆσαι αὐτὸν καὶ μὴ ταχὺ ἐμπιστεύσῃς αὐτῷ)" (Sir. 6:7). The Greek of Sirach literally says "get a friend in testing" – i.e., prove that he is a true friend by testing his commitment.[144] On this reading, Paul is indicating that notwithstanding the particular circumstances of his visit, the Galatians had approved him as their mentor.[145]

The verb κατάομαι (kataomai – "to procure") regularly translates the Hebrew קנה (kana) in the LXX, and Sirach's advice closely resembles the mishnaic dictum, "Appoint for yourself a teacher and acquire for thyself a companion עשה לך רב וקנה לך חבר" (PA 1:6).[146] The concept of "acquiring" was understood to involve struggle and hardship, as interpreted through God's command to Moses in response to Moses' request for a successor: "Take Joshua the son of Nun לך את יהושע בן נון" (Num. 27:18). In the midrashic tradition, the verb קח (kach) is taken to signify "to pay for": "Take thee: One can do this only by seizing [a technical terms for possession], for one cannot acquire a friend except by great effort, as the Sages have said: One should acquire a friend for oneself, to study Torah with him, to drink with him, and to reveal his secrets to him, as it is said, Two are better than one (Eccl. 4:9) and A threefold cord is not quickly broken (Eccl. 4:12)"[147] (Sif.Dt. 305)."[148]

In yet another rabbinic development, the verbs קנה (kana) and כנס (kanas), which originally denoted "to buy" or "to acquire wealth" (cf. Eccl. 2:8, 3:5), are both extended to the "gathering" of men (cf. Daube, New: 352ff, and for the following discussion). In addition to bringing a child into the covenant in circumcision (cf. Shab. 137b), "getting" is also specifically applied to the making of proselytes: "R. Eleazar also said: The Holy One, blessed be He, did not exile Israel among the nations save in order that proselytes might join them, for it is said: And I will sow her unto Me in the

---

[144] We have suggested that a trace of Abraham's prototype may be found in this reference: ". . . when he was proved, he was found faithful (ἐν πειρασμῷ εὑρέθη πιστός)" (Sir. 44:20). "Was not Abraham found faithful in temptation, and it was imputed to him for righteousness? (Αβρααμ οὐχὶ ἐν πειρασμῷ εὑρέθη πιστός, καὶ ἐλογίσθη αὐτῷ εἰς δικαιοσύνην;)" (1 Macc. 2:52) (cf. Heb. 11:17; Jub. 17:18, 19:8) (see 3:1-5 [n53]). Here again, Paul's framework ultimately appears to be dictated by Scripture/halakhah rather than by the "evil eye" (see 3:1-5).

[145] Ultimately, Paul's reference here remains intelligible only to the Galatians themselves at the time.

[146] Cf. TBE [EZ] S p. 6; ARNᵃ 8:1f, 22:1.

[147] קח לך : אין לך אלא לקיחה, לפי שאין חבר נקנה אלא בקשי קשיין. מכאן אמרו : יקנה אדם חבר לעצמו, להיות קונה קורא עמו ושונה עמו ואוכל עמו ושותה עמו וגולה לו סתריו וכן הוא אומר : טובים השנים מן-האחד ו : החוט המשולש לא במהרה ינתק.

[148] Cf. Yalk.Num. 776. The source in Sifre quotes Avot de Rabbi Natan, itself a commentary on Pirkei Avot. In other places, the idea of "taking" is interpreted in terms of a financial transaction (cf. TBE [EZ] S p. 6).

land (Hos. 2:23): surely a mans sows a *se'ah* in order to harvest many *kor!*"[149] (Pes. 87b).[150] Jesus' dictum, "For what will a man be profited, if he gains [i.e., wins] the whole world, and forfeits his soul? Or what will a man give in exchange for his soul?"[151] (Mt. 16:26) carries a similar significance (see 6:1-11 and below).[152]

In such a context, Paul may be apprehended as praising the Galatians for the welcome with which they originally received him, having made a concerted effort to accept him "as an angel of the Lord (ὡς ἄγγελον θεοῦ)." This description of the Galatians' greeting of Paul directly relates to the motif of imitation. In demonstrating that a Sage's life and character were meant to instill in his disciples a desire to study Torah and to learn God's ways, the teacher is depicted as an angel of the Lord: ". . . if the teacher is like an angel of the Lord of hosts, they should seek the Law at his mouth, but if not, they should not seek the Law at his mouth! אם דומה הרב למלאך ה׳ צבאות - יבקשו תורה מפיהו. ואם לאו - אל יבקשו תורה מפיהו" (Hag. 15b) (cf. MK 17a). In considering Paul to be a true apostle and mentor, the Galatians had initially exhibited their trust in him and their acceptance of his authority.[153] In this sense, the "reception" which they had extended to Paul was not merely of his person but also of the gospel: "And for this reason we also constantly thank God that when you received from us the word of God's message, you accepted *it* not *as* the word of men, but *for* what it really is, the word of God, which also performs its work in you who believe"[154] (1 Thess. 2:13).[155]

The tradition of "receiving angels" most likely derives from Abraham's encounter with the three men at the oaks of Mamre and their

---

[149] אמר ר׳ אלעזר: לא הגלה הקדוש ברוך הוא את ישראל לבין האומות אלא כדי שיתוספו עליהם גרים, שנאמר: וזרעתיה לי בארץ. כלום אדם זורע סאה אלא להכניס כמה כורין.

[150] Cf. 1QS 5:7-8, 8:19; 1Q28a 1:1; CD-A 13:11; Yalk.Hos. 519 (cf. Le Cornu and Shulam: 153). Cf. Prov. 11:30: "The fruit of the righteous is a tree of life, and he who is wise wins [lit.: takes] souls פרי-צדיק עץ חיים ולקח נפשות חכם" (see 6:1-11 [Monobaz]).

[151] τί γὰρ ὠφεληθήσεται ἄνθρωπος ἐὰν τὸν κόσμον ὅλον κερδήσῃ τὴν δὲ ψυχὴν αὐτοῦ ζημιωθῇ; ἢ τί δώσει ἄνθρωπος ἀντάλλαγμα τῆς ψυχῆς αὐτοῦ;

[152] For κοπιάω (kopiaō – "to labour") as a "missionary" term, see verses 8-11 (n114).

[153] For Paul's earlier reference to "an angel from heaven," see 1:6-10; for chapters 1-2 as Paul's setting out of his authority in the present context, see Introduction, **Argument**. The description of Paul as sometimes possessing "the face of an angel (aliquando sicut figuram angeli habens)" (Acts of Paul and Thecla [2:3]) is possibly based upon this passage (see Appendix, **Status**).

[154] Καὶ διὰ τοῦτο καὶ ἡμεῖς εὐχαριστοῦμεν τῷ θεῷ ἀδιαλείπτως, ὅτι παραλαβόντες λόγον ἀκοῆς παρ' ἡμῶν τοῦ θεοῦ ἐδέξασθε οὐ λόγον ἀνθρώπων ἀλλὰ καθώς ἐστιν ἀληθῶς λόγον θεοῦ, ὅς καὶ ἐνεργεῖται ἐν ὑμῖν τοῖς πιστεύουσιν.

[155] Paul also links acceptance of the gospel here with imitation (cf. 1 Thess. 2:14).

sojourn with Lot (cf. Genesis 18-19).[156] Jesus takes up this theme, precisely
in the context of "gaining one's soul": "He who has found his life shall lose
it, and he who has lost his life for my sake shall find it. He who receives
you receives me, and he who receives me receives Him who sent me"[157]
(Mt. 10:39-40) (see above).[158] This idea also appears in the Didache, in a
passage addressing false apostles whose language closely resembles the
rabbinic dictum regarding teachers' appearances: ". . . if his [the true
apostle's] teaching be for the increase of righteousness and knowledge of
the Lord, receive him as the Lord (εἰς δὲ τὸ προσθεῖναι δικαιοσύνην καὶ
γνῶσιν κυρίου, δέξασθε αὐτὸν ὡς κύριον)" (Did. 11:2) (see 1:1-5 and 6:1-
11).

   Verse 15: Having recalled the Galatians' initial warm reception of him
and of his gospel (cf. 1:6f), Paul pointedly asks what has happened to their
"blessing (ὁ μακαρισμὸς ὑμῶν)." In the only other place in which this
word occurs in the New Testament, Paul employs it in speaking of the
"blessing upon the man to whom God reckons righteousness apart from
works"[159] (Rom. 4:6) (cf. Rom. 4:9).[160] This use derives from Psalm 31:1f, the
"blessed (μακάριοι)" representing אשרי (ashrei – "blessed") – the key word
of the beatitudes (cf. Mt. 5:3-11). The first three beautitudes appear to be
dependent on Isaiah 61:1-2 (cf. Flusser, Judaism: 102-25).[161] This text can be

----

[156] In explicating how the three personages could first be called "men" and then
"angels," R. Tanhuma comments: "They may be likened to a man who received a
governorship from the king. Before he reaches the seat of his authority, he goes like
an ordinary citizen. Similarly, before they performed their mission, they are called
men; having performed it, they assumed the style of angels אמר ר' תנחומא: לאחר
שנטל הגמוניא מן המלך עד שלא הגיע לבית אורייו שלו, היה מהלך כפגן. כיון שהגיע לבית אורייו
שלו, היה מהלך כאלמין. כך עד שלא עשו שליחותן, קראן אנשים. כיון שעשו שליחותן, קראן
מלאכים" (Gen.R. 50:2). Midrashic texts frequently associate God's appearance to
Abraham here with his ability to make proselytes (cf. Gen.R. 48:2, 8) (see 3:6-9
[n101] and below [n186]).
[157] ὁ εὑρὼν τὴν ψυχὴν αὐτοῦ ἀπολέσει αὐτήν, καὶ ὁ ἀπολέσας τὴν ψυχὴν
αὐτοῦ ἕνεκεν ἐμοῦ εὑρήσει αὐτήν. Ὁ δεχόμενος ὑμᾶς ἐμὲ δέχεται, καὶ ὁ ἐμὲ
δεχόμενος δέχεται τὸν ἀποστείλαντά με.
[158] Cf. Mt. 18:5, 25:40; Mk. 9:37; Lk. 10:16; Jn. 13:20. For Jesus' commission, see
verses 1-7; for agency in general, see 1:1-5, 15-16b.
[159] τὸν μακαρισμὸν τοῦ ἀνθρώπου ᾧ ὁ θεὸς λογίζεται δικαιοσύνην χωρὶς
ἔργων.
[160] Cf. "Blessed is he who keeps from stumbling over me (μακάριός ἐστιν ὅς ἐὰν
μὴ σκανδαλισθῇ ἐν ἐμοί)" (Mt. 11:6). For this theme in connection with Abraham,
see 3:6ff.
[161] If Luke's allusion to the laughter which will replace the present weeping (cf. Lk.
6:21) is numbered among the original beatitudes (cf. Flusser, Judaism: 113), their
affinity with Eccl. 3:3ff becomes quite striking. The latter text serves as the basis of
Hillel's principle of conforming one's conduct to others' in order to gain converts
(see above). When placed in the context of Hillel's numerous sayings concerning a
person's presence representing the Shekhina (cf. Mekh.Ba-chod. 11; Sif.Zuta,

discerned as one of Galatians' *leitmotivs*, presenting Jesus' deliverance of wo/mankind from the bondage of sin (see 1:1f, 2:[1-10], 15-21, 3:1-5, 10-14, and verses 1-7).[162]

Paul's usage in Romans argues for reading this blessing not as a "feeling of blessedness" but as a concretely pronounced blessing – with which the Galatians had originally greeted him (cf. Hays, Galatians: 294).[163] Benedictions spoken to people are well known in Jewish circles, and are recited over Sages, kings, wise men, and friends (cf. Mt. 9:8; Ber. 58a) (cf. Flusser, Judaism: 535ff).[164] Paul is very willing to testify – himself act as a witness – to the Galatians' devotion to his person, to the extent of plucking out their eyes to give to him. Such an action, when performed in the service of preventing sin, serves to gain people access to the Kingdom of Heaven (see also 5:2f).[165]

Here, Paul seems to be thinking of the "good eye [עין טובה]" which signifies generosity in rabbinic literature. A midrash on Proverbs 23:26 states: "The eye and the heart are the two go-betweens of sin, as it says *Give me your heart, my son, and let your eyes delight in my ways* (Prov. 23:26). God says: If you give me your heart and your eyes, I know that you are Mine"[166] (JBer. 1, 4, 3c).[167] The attribute of a "good eye" is said to be one of the qualities definitive precisely of the "sons of Abraham": "Whoever possesses these three things, he is of the disciples of Abraham, our Father . . . a good eye, an humble spirit and a lowly soul כל מי שיש בו שלושה דברים

Pinchas 1; PA [1:14], 3:6; Tos.Suk. 4:3; Suk. 53a), the idea of God's promise is reinforced: "In every place where I cause My name to be remembered, I will come to you and bless you ובברכתיך אליך אבוא את-שמי אזכיר אשר בכל-המקום" (Ex. 20:24) (cf. Flusser, Judaism: 509-25). If the beatitudes are further intimately linked with the woes (cf. Lk. 6:25f) (cf. ibid: 113, 116f) – the blessings against the curses – we find an additional link with Jesus' condemnation of hypocrisy which obstructs entry into God's Kingdom (see 2:15-21 and 5:2-12, 16-23 [6:12f]) and the curse invoked by transgression of the covenant (see 3:10-14 and 6:17).

[162] We may thus find here a conjunction of the *topoi* of Abraham's blessing and Jesus' anointing – the Righteous One whose obedience constitutes God's blessing by releasing those who become faithful to him – Jews and Gentiles alike – from slavery to the elementary things of the world (see verses 1f). For the beatitudes/Sermon on the Mount as a lying behind the motif of the "fruit of the Spirit," see 5:13-18 [n148].

[163] Such an active, transitive sense is representative of the word in general (cf. BAGD: 487).

[164] For greetings in general, see 1:1-5 and 6:12f.

[165] Cf. Num. 15:39; Mt. 5:29, 18:9; Mk. 9:47; DEZ 1:4; Sot. 8a.

[166] ברוך הקדוש אמר. תצרנה דרכי ועיניך לי לבך בני : דכתיב דחטאה, סרסורין תרין ועינא ליבא לי. דאת ידע אנא ועיניך לבך לי יהבת אי : הוא

[167] The delimitator "if possible (εἰ δυνατόν)" signifies that Paul has a metaphor, rather than a concrete action, in mind. For the "bad eye" (envy), see 1:6-10, 3:1-5, 5:19f, and below (n179). Biblical texts also make much use of the expression "apple of the eye [אישון [בת] עין" to denote that which is precious and dearest to a person – such as Israel before God (cf. Dt. 32:10; Ps. 17:8; Prov. 7:2; Ep.Barn. 19:9).

"הללו מתלמידיו של אברהם אבינו... עין טובה ורוח נמוכה נפש שפלה (PA 5:19)[168]
(see 2:15-21, 3:6ff, and below).[169]

Verse 16: Against this background, Paul now notes the Galatians' changed attitude towards him.[170] While the majority of commentators apprehend the force of ὥστε (hōste) as "therefore," this verse is traditionally posed as a question. Linguistically, it may be better presented as an indignant exclamation: "So [now] I have become your enemy because I am telling the truth?!" (cf. Longenecker, *Galatians*: 193). Although the "now" is lacking, Paul clearly means that his present "truth telling (ἀληθεύων)" – his rebuke – appears to have transposed their friendship and discipleship into hostility (ἐχθρός; echthros).[171] While various theories have been mooted regarding Paul's inability/unwillingness to speak "the truth, the whole truth" on his initial visit, the contrast to which he is pointing is not best understood as between a previous "falsehood" and a present veracity. In view of verses 17-18, which relate to the influencers' activities in seeking the Galatians as converts, and Paul's assertion that it was right for him to be zealous for his disciples even in his physical absence, the "truth-telling" rather appears to refer to Paul's unequivocal rebuff of the Galatians' expressed desire to obtain social status and standing within the Jewish community as proselytes.[172] To the extent to which his disciples have been persuaded by the influencers and have joined their campaign, as it were, they have sided against Paul.[173]

Verse 17: Even if it is not assumed that verse 16 "reflects a direct accusation of the Missionaries" (Hays, *Galatians*: 295), the seamlessness of the transition indubitably implies that the influencers' activity has

---

[168] Cf. Ex.R. 47:3 [Hebrew]; PA 2:9; JSan. 8b; ARNᵃ 40:6; Kal.Rab. 5; DEZ 3:1.

[169] In ascribing this characteristic to the Galatians, Paul is indirectly acknowledging that when they accepted the gospel through his teaching they marked themselves as true disciples of Abraham – and do not, therefore, need to seek additional social status (see Introduction, **Occasion and circumstances**; **Argument**). Plucking out one's eyes on behalf of a friend is so frequently found as a motif in Graeco-Roman literature as to bestow upon it almost proverbial status (cf. Betz, *Galatians*: 227-28). (For the influencers' jealousy/boasting, see 6:1f.)

[170] Here, Paul picks up the theme of 1:10, wherein he speaks of the influencers as seeking to "please men" – and denies that his conduct matches such behaviour (see 1:6-10). Paul is in effect accusing his disciples of confusing things to the point of identifying him as their "troubler" – and accepting the influencers as their true instructors.

[171] Cf. 2 Cor. 7:2, 13:1-10. The change in outlook is signified by the perfect γέγονα (gegona –"I have become").

[172] See Introduction, **Occasion and circumstances** and 2:11f.

[173] The antagonism is consequently more a matter of their having been swayed by the influencers than by Paul's truth telling, although the need to choose allegiances has been directly generated by Paul's response to his disciples' shift of commitment.

generated Paul's communication in this section (see above).[174] His meaning in these two verses (17-18) is nonetheless much disputed, due primarily to the reference ascribed to the verb ἐκκλείω (ekkleiō). Since its normal signification is "to shut out," some commentators have assumed that the influencers' intent is to lock the gentile Galatians believers away from Paul. Given the violence this interpretation imposes on the Greek syntax, others have proposed that Paul's complaint is that the gentile believers have been shut out of fellowship by the Jewish believers' withdrawal (cf. 2:11f).[175]

ἐκκλείω is, however, a compound of the same verb which appears in Matthew 23:13. In these verses, Jesus, addressing the Pharisees' hypocrisy, claims that they "shut off the kingdom of heaven from men; for you do not enter in yourselves, nor do you allow those who are entering to go in."[176] In the matthean context, the reference is evidently to proselytising efforts, verse 15 speaking of the "zeal" with which the group's members "travel about on sea and land to make one proselyte (περιάγετε τὴν θάλασσαν καὶ τὴν ξηρὰν ποιῆσαι ἕνα προσήλυτον)."[177] Paul's thought here demonstrates close similarities to Matthew's text. In effect, he is denouncing the "hypocrisy" which derives from a zealous courting of converts – promising privileges and advantages in their new position, when the benefit of these is, in light of the Messiah's advent, valueless (see also 5:2-12, 6:1-11, and verses 21-31).[178]

---

[174] If it is insisted that the force of γέγονα (gegona – "I have become") demands a present state as the result of a past action, some form of communication otherwise unindicated in the New Testament texts is implied – either an intermediate visit or a previous letter (cf. Burton: 245). Verses 17-18 – together with 1:7-9, 5:7, 12, 6:12-13 – are the sole "direct" references from which details concerning the influencers' identity may be obtained (cf. Nanos, Irony: 67ff) (see Introduction, **Occasion and circumstances**).

[175] The first reading demands rendering "shut out" as "alienate," together with the interpolation of the phrase "from us." The second assumes that the influencers are in fact members of the community, a proposal which the present commentary does not adopt (see Introduction, **Occasion and circumstances**).

[176] ὅτι κλείετε τὴν βασιλείαν τῶν οὐρανῶν ἔμπροσθεν τῶν ἀνθρώπων· ὑμεῖς γὰρ οὐκ εἰσέρχεσθε οὐδὲ τοὺς εἰσερχομένους ἀφίετε εἰσελθεῖν.

[177] Verse 14 obviously intervenes between two interconnected verses (cf. Metzger: 60). For the nature of the hypocrisy, see Introduction, **Argument**; **Theological pointers** and 2:15-21. The verb ζηλόω (zēloō) means variously "to desire earnestly" and "to be zealous" (among other denotations). Here, "it is likely that Paul is making a clever play [on these two significations]. The primary meaning is the first sense: The Missionaries are 'courting' the Galatians to win them over (the NIV supplies this idea). At the same time, Paul's choice of the verb *zēloō* is ironically appropriate, because the Missionaries ... would probably describe their courtship of the Galatians as an expression of their religious zeal" (Hays, Galatians: 295).

[178] Such hypocrisy is evident from the condemnations of those endeavouring to "please men" (see 1:6-10). For the implications of this view for the existence, nature, and prevalence of Jewish proselytism in the Second Temple period, see

This is evident in the description of the "uncommendable (οὐ καλῶς)" (literally: "not good") way in which Paul maintains that the influencers are making their presence known. It is possible to apprehend this declaration as a proverbial statement, running along the lines of "good is always to be courted in a good way" (cf. Longenecker, Galatians: 194). At the same time, the "good" may here pick up the "good eye" which Paul is invoking from the Galatians.[179] In a Jewish context, good is one of God's characteristics: "Let the good come and receive the good from the Good for the good. 'Let the good come' – that is, Moses, as it is written, *And she saw that he was good* (Ex. 2:2). 'And receive the good' – that is, the Torah, as it is written, *For I give you good doctrine* (Prov. 4:2). 'From the Good' – that is, the Holy One, blessed be He, as it is written, *The Lord is good to all* (Ps. 145:9). 'For the good' – that is, Israel, as it is written, *Do good, O Lord, unto the good* (Ps. 125:4)" (Men. 53b) (see 6:1-11).[180]

The influencers' persuasion is to the effect that the Galatians may become as zealous in their conduct as are they themselves. In this respect, the Galatians' "seeking (ζηλοῦτε)" represents the "imitation" which Paul has asked of them in regard to *himself* (cf. verse 12) (see above).[181] Whereas Paul attributes to the influencers a "wish (θέλουσιν)" which will bring them no good, his own claims on the Galatians as disciples *are* legitimate.[182]

Verse 18: Despite the influencers' conduct, Paul indicates that seeking disciples ("converts") is not, in and of itself, a dishonourable activity – his own opportuning being indeed "for the good." Such is true also now, in

---

Introduction, **Occasion and circumstances** (nn72, 89) and 2:15-21 (n269); for Jesus' shammaite views on proselytism, cf. Flusser, Jesus: 75f; for Paul's hillelite views, see Appendix, **Persecutor**. Once again, it should be stressed that Paul is not dismissing Judaism out of hand, nor declaring Torah-observance or circumcision *per se* as defunct. In the specific context of the "messianic age" which Jesus' death and resurrection have inaugurated, the Gentiles have become "children of the promise." Under such circumstances, seeking social standing as "sons of the covenant" is not only superfluous but detrimental to the Galatians' spiritual status, replacing the latter with human, fleshly conventions and bondage under the dominion of Belial (see Introduction, **Argument** and verses 4:1f).

[179] This attribute, it will be remembered, is one of the three which constitute the "disciples of Abraham" (see above). Its antitype is the "evil eye" – i.e., envy (see 1:6-10, 3:1-5, 5:19f, and above). Paul appears to pick up this theme again in relation to the influencers in 5:26 and 6:4 (see 5:24-26 and 6:1-11).

[180] Doing the good in the right way is a central theme of the Testament of Asher, which strongly denounces the hypocrisy of those who "express good for the sake of evil, but the outcome of the action leads to evil" (Test.Asher 2:1). For "doing good" in a "missionary" sense, see 6:1-11.

[181] This may be derived from the verb's signification of "striving, exerting oneself earnestly" – an attitude which easily exhibits itself as emulation.

[182] For the scriptural grounds on which Paul makes this claim – rather than those of the evil eye system – see 3:1-5.

his absence. "Out of sight" should not be "out of mind" – and Paul asserts his steadfastness in continuing his zeal for his disciples even when removed from them.[183] While the most effectual and profound form of imitation is direct observation and the development of an intimate relationship (see above), the notion that a letter represents its sender, substituting for an address by the author in person, was widespread in antiquity (cf. Stone: 584f) (see Introduction, **Form** and 1:1-5). Paul is thus claiming that, despite his absence, he retains the right to ask for conformation on his disciples' part – the more so when they are vulnerable to persuasion from rival sources (cf. Phil. 1:27) (see also below).[184]

Verse 19: In his devotion to them, Paul addresses his disciples directly, changing the familiar "brethren (ἀδελφοί)" – equals in the Messiah's body (cf. verse 12) – to that into which he is striving to turn them, his "children (τέκνα μου)" (i.e., those whom he has fathered/discipled) (cf. 1 Cor. 4:14-15; 1 Thess. 2:7) (see above).[185] The emphasis in this verse lies – as so frequently in chapter 4-5 – on the πάλιν (palin -"again"), although Paul is presently expressing the requirement the Galatians have imposed on him of "birthing" them all over again by their turning to others for their model (see above).[186] Here, Paul specifically states that the "new birth" constitutes the "formation of the Messiah" in those who are faithful to his death and resurrection (see 3:26-29).[187]

---

[183] The clear implication here is that, in imitating him, the Galatians also keep faith with Paul – in his absence as in his presence. The degree of Paul's zeal in his previous persecution of the early community is now matched by that in endeavouring to preserve his disciples in the Messiah. For Paul's campaign, see Appendix, **Persecutor**.

[184] The implications also run the other way, as Paul signifies in 1 Cor. 4:18 – that his absence has encouraged some of the Corinthian believers to become arrogant.

[185] The variant τεκνία (teknia – "little children") is better suited to the vocative, as well as nicely fitting the context of Paul's "birthing" disciples. For "brethren," see 1:1-5.

[186] For the other "again"s, see 5:1 and verses 1f. Here too, Abraham may serve as a pattern for Paul. In remarking the strange linguistic form in Gen. 12:5 – "And Abram took Sarai his wife and ... the souls which they had made in Haran ויקח" "אברם את-שרי אשתו . . . ואת-הנפש אשר-עשו בחרן" – the midrash states: "R. Leazar observed in the name of R. Jose b. Zimra: If all the nations assembled to create one insect they could not endow it with life, yet you say, *And the souls that they had made!* [a verb parallel to "creating"]. It refers, however, to the proselytes [which they had made]. Then let it say, 'That they had converted'; why *that they had made?* That is to teach you that he who brings a Gentile near [to God] is as though he created him ואת הנפש אשר עשו בחרן. אמר רבי אלעזר בן זימרא: אם מתכנסין כל באי העולם לברוא אפילו יתוש אחד אינן יכולין לזרוק בו נשמה - ואת אמר "ואת הנפש אשר עשו"! אלא אלו הגרים שגיירו. ואם כן שגיירו, למה הוא אמר "עשו"?! אלא ללמדך שכל מי שהוא מקרב את העובד כוכבים ומגיירו כאלו בראו" (Gen.R. 39:14) (see 3:6-9 [n101], 5:24-26, and above [n131]).

[187] Cf. Jn. 3:3; Rom. 6:4, 7:6; 2 Cor. 5:17; Eph. 4:13, 24; Phil. 3:9-10; Col. 2:2-3, 3:3-17; 1QHᵃ 19:10-14; Cant.R. 8.2.1, 8.5.1. The "until (μέχρις)" serves here as a form of

If the plural "in you (ἐν ὑμῖν)" is best translated as "among you," "in your midst" – in the sense that the community as a whole takes on the Messiah's character – we are returned to Exodus 20:24: "In every place where I cause My name to be remembered, I will come to you and bless you בכל-המקום אשר אזכיר את-שמי אבוא אליך וברכתיך" (see above).[188] Both Hillel's dictum and Jesus' saying in Matthew 18:20 – "For where two or three have gathered together in my name, there am I in their midst (οὗ γάρ εἰσιν δύο ἢ τρεῖς συνηγμένοι εἰς τὸ ἐμὸν ὄνομα, ἐκεῖ εἰμι ἐν μέσῳ αὐτῶν)" – reflect this text, interpreting it to define the smallest unit (מנין; minyan – "quorum") within which God's presence resides (cf. Flusser, Judaism: 515ff; Le Cornu and Shulam: 603).[189] Here again, Paul is urging his disciples to be renewed, through imitation of his own example, in their "new selves" "to a true knowledge according to the image of the One who created him . . . the Messiah is all, and in all"[190] (Col. 3:10-11).[191]

Verse 20: The awkwardness of the transition between verse 19 and this verse reflects the vagaries of Greek syntax, the δὲ (de) demanding either the linking of verses 18 and 19 or the assumption of a anacoluthon (*non sequitur*) in verse 20 (cf. Burton: 248).[192] In effect, the first half relates back to verse 18 while the last clause anticipates the "allegory" with which Paul attempts to resolve his perplexity regarding his disciples. In desiring to be physically present in the Galatian communities Paul may be reflecting the perception that proximity would permit him to "change his voice (ἀλλάξαι τὴν φωνήν μου)."[193] On this reading, Paul is possibly desirous of exchanging the written language of the letter for a personal conversation

---

purpose clause. For halakhic purposes, proselytes are considered to be "new born babes" (cf. Yev. 22a, 48b; San. 58a; Kid. 17b). While verses 1ff speak in terms of "cosmic" periods, the halakhic context of "fathering" seems more immediately pertinent here than that of eschatological "birthpangs" (cf. Mk. 13:8; Rom. 8:22-23; 1 Thess. 5:3; Rev. 12:2; 1 En. 62:4; 2 Bar. 56:6) – although the latter are not be entirely excluded (cf. Hays, Galatians: 296).

[188] For blessing, see 1:6-10, 3:10-14, and 6:12ff.

[189] This idea may constitute a partial backdrop to Paul's concept of the "Messiah's body" (cf. Rom. 12:4ff; 1 Cor. 10:16-18, 12:12ff) (cf. Hays, Galatians: 296).

[190] . . . τὸν νέον τὸν ἀνακαινούμενον εἰς ἐπίγνωσιν κατ᾽ εἰκόνα τοῦ κτίσαντος αὐτόν . . . πάντα καὶ ἐν πᾶσιν Χριστός.

[191] For further appeals to Paul's personal example, see 1:1-5, 15-16b, 21-24, 2:1-10 (n136), 12-15 (n292), 3:1-5 (nn14, 28), 5:2-12 (verse 11), 24-26, and 6:1f (verses 11, 15, 17).

[192] The NASB represents the latter, signified by the m-dash at the end of verse 19. The absence of the particle would allow understanding verse 20 as the natural completion of verse 19.

[193] The ἄρτι (arti), a more sharply defined allusion to the present than νῦν (nyn), signifies "at this very moment" – as though the direct encounter would have an immediate impact. Alternatively, the two purposes are independent – to be present and to change his "tone."

(cf. 2 Cor. 3:1ff, 7:8). It is otherwise likely that the reference is to softening – or otherwise modulating – his tone, his presence mediating the confrontation and emphasising his paternal propriety (cf. Hays, Galatians: 296).[194]

The "perplexity (ἀπορoῦμαι)" which plagues Paul with respect to the Galatians (ἐν ὑμῖν; en hymin) probably also functions as part of Paul's aspiration to be present amongst them (cf. Burton: 250). If imitation is most effectively achieved through personal example, Paul obviously wishes to gain the optimal conditions by not being absent, thus bringing his disciples into greater conformity to the image of the Messiah he represents and whom he is endeavouring to be formed in them (see 3:1-5 and above). Absence of one's model – especially where a competitive source is active – naturally contributes to uncertainty and ambivalence. This state Paul endeavours to dispel by proffering an "allegorical" resolution, designed to demonstrate the true pattern of replication.[195]

---

[194] Cf. 1 Cor. 2:3f; 2 Cor. 10:1ff. The contrast with 1 Cor. 4:14-21 is very instructive, not merely as to the spirit in which Paul addresses his readers but also as to the Galatian circumstances. Whereas Paul expresses the intention of arriving in Corinth in the near future, which occasion will permit him to "find out, not the words of those who are arrogant, but their power (γνώσομαι οὐ τὸν λόγον τῶν πεφυσιωμένων ἀλλὰ τὴν δύναμιν)" (1 Cor. 4:19), here in Galatians he makes no mention of any anticipated visit. It would appear reasonable to assume, in consequence, that he was prevented from thinking of a subsequent journey (the imperfect ἦλθον [ēlthon] representing a "potential" or "voluntative" – "how I wish that I could") – although the reason for this must remain obscure (see Introduction, **Occasion and circumstances**).

[195] On this reading of verses 12-20, the text runs comprehensibly and coherently, belying any need to appeal to Paul's pathos, employed in place of clear argumentation (cf. Longenecker, Galatians: 188, citing Mussner, Schlier, and Betz). At the same time, the notion of imitation/discipleship is a halakhic concept rather than an "emotional appeal" – and would seem far more profound a matter than "personal loyalty" and the argument that "If they have any decency, Paul implies – if they are not fickle friends – they will stand with Paul in this controversy" (Hays, Galatians: 297). Paul is asking of his readers not mere allegiance to his own person but conformity to the Messiah's image (cf. Rom. 8:29) (see verses 12-20). For Galatians as a "halakhic letter," see Introduction, **Form; Argument**.

Verses 21-31:
Tell me, you who want to be under law, do you not listen to the law? For it is written that Abraham had two sons, one by the bondwoman and one by the free woman. But the son by the bondwoman was born according to the flesh, and the son by the free woman through the promise. This contains an allegory: for these *women* are two covenants, one *proceeding* from Mount Sinai bearing children who are to be slaves; she is Hagar. Now this Hagar is Mount Sinai in Arabia, and corresponds to the present Jerusalem, for she is in slavery with her children. But the Jerusalem above is free; she is our mother. For it is written, "REJOICE, BARREN WOMAN WHO DOES NOT BEAR; BREAK FORTH AND SHOUT, YOU WHO ARE NOT IN LABOR; FOR MORE ARE THE CHILDREN OF THE DESOLATE THAN OF THE ONE WHO HAS A HUSBAND." And you brethren, like Isaac, are children of promise. But as at that time, he who was born according to the flesh persecuted him *who was born* according to the Spirit, so it is now also. But what does the Scripture say? "CAST OUT THE BONDWOMAN AND HER SON, FOR THE SON OF THE BONDWOMAN SHALL NOT BE AN HEIR WITH THE SON OF THE FREE WOMAN." So then, brethren, we are not children of a bondwoman, but of the free woman.

Having strongly remonstrated with his Galatian disciples over their apparent willingness to shift their allegiance away from Jesus towards conversion and Torah-observance, ostensibly in order to gain Jewish status, Paul pointedly asks if they fully understand the implications of such action.[196] Here, the "wishing (θέλοντες)" represents the Galatians' genuine desire – in contrast to the aspirations which he imputes to the influencers in verse 17 (see verses 12-20). The force of the "under law (ὑπὸ νόμον)" derives primarily from verses 1-10, wherein Paul describes the bondage under which the Gentiles have laboured all this time, prior to the Messiah's advent (see verses 1f).[197]

The question "do you not listen to the law (τὸν νόμον οὐκ ἀκούετε;)" is pregnant with meanings. It recalls, most immediately, the Shema: "Hear O Israel . . . שמע ישראל" (Dt. 6:4) (see 3:19-20). Equally strikingly, it echoes Israel's promise of commitment at מתן תורה (matan Torah – the giving of the Torah at Sinai): "All that the LORD has spoken we will do, and we will

---

[196] For the nature of the Galatians' situation, see Introduction, **Occasion and circumstances**; **Argument**. The question here thus parallels, both formally and substantively, Paul's warning in 5:2f. The latter passage culminates, in verse 13, in a repetition of the admonition: If you wish to observe the Torah, listen to what it says – look not to the flesh (circumcision) but to the Spirit, as the fulfilment of the Torah through "faithfulness working through love" (see 5:2f).

[197] This passage is in turn intimately linked to 3:19-29, although that section primarily addresses Israel rather than the Gentiles (see 3:19ff). The fact that Paul speaks here of "law" does not necessitate understanding verses 9-10 in reference to Jewish festivals, since the present appeal is a direct outcome of Paul's protest against the Galatians' adoption of an alternative "role model" – Jewish identity over the Messiah. For verses 9-10 as referring to a time period rather than to a resumption of old practices, see verses 8-11; for the influencers' identity and their persuasion of the gentile Galatians believers, see Introduction, **Occasion and circumstances**; **Argument**, and verses 12-20.

hear ונשמע נעשה חי אשר-דבר-הי נעשה ונשמע "כל" (Ex. 24:7) (see 3:1-5). It also resonates with Deuteronomy 18:15, where God commands the people to "listen" to the prophet like Moses whom He will raise up "from among your countrymen נביא מקרבך מאחיך כמני יקים לך הי אלהיך אליו תשמעון." [198] On the basis of this latter verse, Jesus declares that "If they do not listen to Moses and the Prophets, neither will they be persuaded if someone rises from the dead" [199] (Lk. 16:31) – Moses "being read in the synagogues every shabbat (ἐν ταῖς συναγωγαῖς κατὰ πᾶν σάββατον ἀναγινωσκόμενος)" (Acts 15:21). The question repeats that which Paul has previously asked in inquiring whether the Galatians received the Spirit "by the works of the Law, or from the message (hearing) of the gospel (ἐξ ἔργων νόμου τὸ πνεῦμα ἐλάβετε ἢ ἐξ ἀκοῆς πίστεως;)" (3:2) (see 3:1-5). [200] It receives its "practical" answer in verse 30, and its formal and substantive "explanation" in 5:13 (see 5:13-18).

Verse 22: The straightforward signification of the listening is to Scripture, Paul appealing immediately to the biblical story of Sarah and Hagar. [201] According to the triennial cycle of scripture reading, the portions read on at least two shabbatot (sabbaths) signal the exceptional birth of great men. Genesis 16f marks Ishmael's birth, its haftarah or prophetic portion being Isaiah 54:1f – which Paul quotes in verse 27. [202] Genesis 21:1f,

---

[198] See 3:10-14 [n129], 19-20 [nn246, 264], verses 1-7 [nn46, 79], and below [n239]). All these passages emphasise the people's obedience – in contrast to the Galatians' disinclination to "heed" Paul (and his gospel). There is definite irony in the fact that while the Galatians are oscillating towards conversion, they are ignorant of the Torah's deepest meaning (see 5:13-18).

[199] Εἰ Μωϋσέως καὶ τῶν προφητῶν οὐκ ἀκούουσιν, οὐδ' ἐάν τις ἐκ νεκρῶν ἀναστῇ πεισθήσονται.

[200] The motif of listening also directly picks up the biblical story of Hagar, at the conclusion of which God directs Abraham not to be "distressed because of the lad and your maid; whatever Sarah tells you, listen to her, for through Isaac your descendants shall be named כל ויאמר אלהים אל-אברהם אל-ירע בעיניך על-הנער ועל-אמתך יקרא לך זרע "אשר תאמר אליך שרה שמע בקלה כי ביצחק (Gen. 21:12) (cf. Gen. 16:6) (see below [n268]).

[201] "This type of interrogation is familiar to us from the diatribe literature. It also presupposes the Apostle's allegorical hermeneutic: to understand the Torah means to understand its allegorical meaning. In this sense his call is different from the prophet's call in the Old Testament to 'hear the word of the Lord' ... [which] was the call to obey[,] while Paul refers to the meaning of the scriptural tradition" (Betz, Galatians: 241). For a different perception of Paul's purpose here, see Introduction, **Argument** and below.

[202] In the seven-shabbat cycle of consolation, Isa. 54:1-10 constitutes the haftarah for Ki Tetzei (Dt. 21:10-25:19), the fifth Shabbat following Tisha B'Av, the latter commemorating the destruction of the first and second Temples (cf. PRK 20) (cf. Mann: 122-24, 562) (see below [n228]). It is noteworthy that most of the interpretations of Isa. 54:1 in PRK – a collection of discourses for special shabbatot and festivals based on the prescribed biblical portions – refer to Jerusalem. Ki Teztei

which describes Isaac's birth (cf. verse 30), is read together with 1 Samuel 2:21f, which contains the account of Samuel's calling (cf. Mulder: 157).[203]

Paul specifically depicts the homily as an "allegory (ἀλληγορούμενα)" (verse 24). Although much ink has been spilt in discussion of the meaning both of the form and content of this verb, and consequently of verses 22-31 as a whole, most efforts have contextualised both in a hellenistic framework.[204] When reading Paul in a Jewish setting, other options immediately become available. Given the centrality of Scripture for ancient Jewish writers, we may look to the biblical text as the primary pattern according to which Paul may build his argument (see Introduction, **Theological pointers**, 1:13f, 2:15-21, 3:1ff, and verses 1-7).

Rabbinic literature frequently perceives the משל (mashal) as a hermeneutic key to the unlocking of the Torah, in particular the book of Canticles, the latter being considered, in its entirety, as a "symbol" (cf. Boyarin, Intertextuality: 105ff, and for the following discussion).[205]

---

opens the portion "When you go out to battle against your enemies כי-תצא למלחמה על-איביך" – a fitting text for Paul's warning to his disciples, engaged in a struggle with the influencers. For the issue of inheritance (Dt. 21:15-17), see below.

[203] While Paul's combination of the first two readings, with a further reference to Gen. 21:10, may point towards a certain "magnetising" of prophetic passages to the Torah portions, it is difficult to claim Galatians as direct proof of the triennial cycle. That these texts, combined, may have already formed an established subject for teaching and homily is, on the other hand, a more reasonable assumption.

[204] For a brief bibliography of the literature on allegory, cf. Longenecker, Galatians: 197. The ramifications of this approach for Christian theology have been profound – if not tragic. As Nanos judiciously remarks: "Interpreters understand Paul's reference to 'present Jerusalem,' characterized as 'in slavery with her children,' to signify a profoundly negative valuation of the Judaism of his time, although some attempt to limit his target to the Christian Judaism of the Jerusalem Church. The language is allegorical; nevertheless, the implications derived from it play a significant role in Pauline theology ... Understanding Paul to be engaged in allegorically linking text instead of oppositional columns moves away from the implications of the opposition of Judaism and Christianity, Jews and Christians, and so on, that is structurally characteristic of the prevailing approach" (Present: 1, 16).

[205] To the objection that משל (mashal) is not an accurate rendering of ἀλληγορία (allegoria) it is contended that, while writing in Greek, Paul retained "rabbinic" thought patterns and exegetical modes (see above). In this context, although allegory was a familiar genre (cf. Philo), the mashal ("likeness") serves as a specifically rabbinic (intertextual) hermeneutical mode which enabled the Sages to connect texts with the ultimate Text: "The way in which the Writings were comprehended as interpretation was by relating the more or less vague situations of various poetic texts to specific parts of the Torah. The reading method was accordingly not allegorical – relating signifier to signified – but intertextual – relating signifier to signifier. But it is indeed possible for midrashic intertextual readings to be substantially the same thematically as allegorical readings (e.g., to relate to the love of God for Israel), since the Torah-texts to which the Song of Songs

Solomon, the author of Canticles, is described as the master of mashalim, and thereby the comprehender of the Torah's wisdom *par excellence*:

> *The proverbs of Solomon son of David king of Israel; to know wisdom and instruction*, etc. (Prov. 1:1): through the proverbs [or parables] of Solomon he [Solomon] mastered the words of the Torah. Our Rabbis say: Let not the parable be lightly esteemed in your eyes, since by means of the parable a man can master the words of the Torah. If a king loses gold from his house or a precious pearl, does he not find it by means of a wick worth a farthing? So the parable should not be lightly esteemed in your eyes, since by means of the parable a man arrives at the true meaning of the words of the Torah.[206] (Cant.R. 1.1.8)[207]

While Paul's text in Galatians ostensibly carries no connection with Canticles, a striking parallel to Paul's thought may be found in a midrashic treatment of Canticles 8:2: "I would lead you *and* bring you into the house of my mother, who used to instruct me": "*I would bring thee into my mother's house*: this is Sinai. R. Berekiah said: Why is Sinai called *my mother's house*? Because there Israel became like a new-born child"[208] (Cant.R. 8.2.1) (see below).[209] Here, we suggest, is the first indication of Paul's "allegory": It

---

was understood to refer describe the relationship of Israel to God ... This kind of midrash, the mashal, does its hermeneutic work by recasting diverse texts into a narrative, which then frames and contextualizes the verse to be interpreted ... The mashal gives to the Torah narrative a clear ideological value, without reducing the vitality and vividness of the representation of character and event in it. Both the complication and interest of the narrative surface and the clarity of meaning of the narrative deep-structure are combined and embodied in one textual system" (Boyarin, Intertextuality: 115-16, 80, 85) (cf. Hays, Echoes: 163-64) (see also below [n273]). For the present passage's relation to Canticles, see below.

[206] משלי שלמה בן דוד מלך ישראל. על-ידי משלותיו של שלמה עמד על דברי תורה. ורבנן אמרין: אל יהי המשל הזה קל בעיניך, שעל-יד המשל הזה אדם יכול לעמוד בדברי תורה. משל למלך שאבד זהב מביתו או מרגליות טובה: לא על-ידי פתילה כאיסר הוא מוצא אותה? כך המשל הזה לא יהיה קל בעיניך, שעל-ידי המשל אדם עומד על דברי תורה.

[207] By employing the genre of the mashal in this sense, Paul's intention appears to be to provide his disciples with a "true" interpretation of the hidden wisdom concealed in the Torah, discernible only through applying the symbolism of Canticles (Isaiah) (see below). For the allegory's affinities with the pesher genre, see below.

[208] אביאך אל בית אמי - זה סיני. אמר ר' ברכיה: למה קוראין לסיני "בית אמי"? שמשם נעשו ישראל כתינוק בן יומו.

[209] Cf. Ex.R. 30:5; Cant.R. 2.3.4; TBE pp. 21-22. While the allusion to the Torah might be considered natural in consequence of the תלמדני (telamdeni – "who used to instruct me") (cf. Prov. 1:8), the identification of the "mother" with Sinai remains a "reworking" or deepening of the Torah through the text of Canticles. In light of Ben Azzai's dictum in Yalk.Num. 776, the metaphor of the child reflects a purity derived from cleansing from sin. Although deviating from Hays' circumstantial argument, we would concur here with his suggestion that the point here is "a matter of two

constitutes a "mashal" by means of which one biblical text interprets another.

In such a context, the formula "it is written (γέγραπται)" here introduces not a prooftext but, more unusually, a "narrative."[210] Paul's recounting of the story is evident in his signification of Sarah as "the free woman (ἐλευθέρας)." While the biblical text regularly depicts Hagar as a "bondwoman (παιδίσκης)" (cf. Gen. 16:1ff, 25:12), Sarah's status is merely implied. The fact that he makes this status explicit marks the issue with which Paul's exegesis is concerned.[211] A midrash describing the ten trials with which Abraham was tested states: "Abraham! Dost thou not know that Sarah was appointed to thee for a wife from her mother's womb? She is thy companion, and the wife of thy covenant; Sarah is not called thy handmaid, but thy wife; neither is Hagar called thy wife, but thy handmaid"[212] (PRE 30).[213]

Verse 23 adds the second detail important for Paul's argument – couched in terms resumed from 3:16f – in respect of the sons' progeniture.[214] Here again, while Isaac is known from the biblical text to be a son by promise,[215] Ishmael's birth is noted as nothing but an ordinary

---

rival interpretations of Israel's heritage" (Galatians: 302; original emphasis) (although both are not, on our understanding, "being promulgated by Jewish *Christians*," as he claims). Strictly speaking, Paul's "metaphorical" text may in fact be Isa. 54:1 (see below).

[210] For introductory scriptural formulae, see 3:6-9.

[211] The fact that Paul chooses an episode focusing upon motherhood indicates that the "allegory" (mashal) is meant to elucidate the element of imitation/discipleship (see verses 12-20). In connection with Isa. 54:1, this discipleship is of "sons of the promise" (children born "supernaturally," from a "barren woman"). In this light, Paul is declaring to the Galatians that they should not strain against his ways – but listen (through Scripture) to his voice: "If you do not gain such merit, however, [because when you remembered Amalek you did not repent of your own sins], then a deserved *visitation, visitation in 'clay' shall be your punishment* (Job 13:12). You will have to prepare yourselves for another servitude like that in Egypt. What is written of the servitude in Egypt? The Egyptians 'made their lives bitter with hard service, in clay,' etc. (Ex. 1:4). [Hence, *Remember what Amalek did unto thee* (Dt. 25:17).] אם לאו, לנגי חומר גביכם: התקינו עצמיכם לשיעבודה של מצרים. מה כתוב במצרים? וימררו את חייהם "בעבודה קשה בחמר וגי' (PRK 3:2) (see 3:6-9 and below). (For Dt. 18:15f, see verses 1-7 and below [n239].)

[212] אברהם אין אתה יודע שהיית לך שרה ראויה לאשה ממעי אמה והיא חברתך ואשת בריתך? לא נקראת שרה "שפחה" אלא "אשתך"; לא נקראת הגר "אשתך" אלא "שפחתך".

[213] The expression "wife of your covenant" signifies that Sarah was Abraham's first wife (cf. Mal. 2:14). Paul may be suggesting here that he is the Galatians' "first" father – calling for a renewal of their loyalty.

[214] This picks up the theme of sonship in verses 1-7. Abraham's other sons by Keturah (cf. Gen. 25:1-6) are irrelevant to Paul's allegory, although some midrashim identify Hagar and Keturah (cf. PRE 30).

[215] Cf. Gen. 15:4, 17:16, 21, 18:10, 21:1, 12; Rom. 9:9; Heb. 11:11 (see 3:15-18).

event, albeit the offspring of a maidservant. This fact – as Hays puts it "the 'fleshly' stratagem of having Abraham impregnate Hagar" (Galatians: 301) – plays directly into Paul's hands, his argument regarding those influencing his disciples focusing on the fact that they are concerned with social identity and convention (see Introduction, **Occasion and circumstances; Argument**).

Verse 24: The "allegory" properly begins in this verse, the motif of "birthpangs" in verse 19 leading Paul to an exposition of "motherhood." The passive participle ἀλληγορούμενα (allēgoroumena – "interpreted allegorically") signifies the character of the interpretation to be given by the reader – rather than any symbolism native to the text itself (cf. ibid).[216] The notation is of immediate importance, since it marks the transition from purely scriptural exegesis to its application in present circumstances.[217] Paul has already provided the tools with which he is about to reveal the "latent sense" of Sarah and Hagar's relationship, having emphasized over and again that God's first and original covenant is with Abraham.[218] Any covenant made subsequent to that with Abraham must correspond to the conditions of the first contract (see 3:15-18). The "two sons" are, therefore, two definitions of the "disciples of Abraham" – in an extension of the theme which Paul has been pursuing since 2:15-21 (see also below).[219]

---

[216] Cf. "Of them [the Israelites standing before the Sea, with Pharaoh's forces at their heels] it is **interpreted** in the traditional sacred writings [Prophets and Writings]: 'O my dove that art in the clefts of the rock, let me hear thy voice' (Cant. 2:14) יונתי בחגוי הסלע וגו' :עליהם **מפורש** בקבלה" (Mekh.Be-shall. 3). "R. Akiba interpreted the verse as applying to Israel at the time when they stood before Mount Sinai. *My dove in the cleft of the rock*: so called because they were hidden in the shadow of the mountain ר' עקיבא **פתר** קרייה בישראל בשעה שעמדו לפני הר סיני. "יונתי בחגוי הסלע" - שהיו חבויין בסתרו של סיני" (Cant.R. 2.14.4).

[217] This represents the pesher aspect of Paul's allegory – the interpretation of Scripture in the light of contemporary events, wherein the latter takes on greater weight than the former (cf. Horgan) (see below).

[218] Paul may well still have the idea of "testament/will"– rather than "covenant" – in mind here, the former idea fitting the context of heirs more closely than that of the covenant. Even less can his comparison be between Judaism and Christianity if this is so (see above [n204]). As Hays correctly points out, "Rather, Paul claims that the covenant of promise and freedom is what the Law itself, rightly understood, teaches" (Galatians: 302). The concept of the "covenant" itself represents the commitment demanded in obedient "imitation" of its institutor: "Speak to all the congregation of the sons of Israel and say to them, 'You shall be holy, for I the LORD your God am holy' דבר אל-כל-עדת בני-ישראל ואמרת אלהם קדשים תהיו כי קדוש אני ה' אלהיכם" (Lev. 19:2).

[219] The force of Paul's language here – on which many commentators have remarked, even when not particularly perturbed by Paul's alleged disparagement of Judaism – derives from the fact that he is presenting the "allegory" not merely as an exegetical type but as an example of conduct: "But what does the Scripture say? Cast out the bondwoman and her son . . ." (verse 30). Once this is understood as the

Hagar here "represents" Mount Sinai.[220] Paul employs here the Greek term συστοιχέω (sustoicheō), whose root meaning is "to stand in line" with something. Rather than indicating a "representation," however, his parallels are best understood as reflecting intertextual "correspondences" (cf. Nanos, Present: 6). Since Hagar was Sarah's maidservant, she is associated with servanthood.[221] Hagar is repeatedly described as an "Egyptian" (cf. Gen. 16:1, 3, 21:9, 25:12), while Ishmael's descendants are said to have lived "east of Egypt [על-פני מצרים]" (Gen. 25:18). In this sense, Hagar directly represents the exile and bondage in Egypt, symbolising, as it were, the prohibition against returning to Egyptian slavery[222] – Sarah standing, on the other hand, as the model for God's great redemption to come, in the new Exodus (cf. Jer. 16:14-21).[223]

The (quasi-)purpose clause "for slavery (εἰς δουλείαν)" indicates that this is the point on which Paul wishes to focus in the mashal. Hagar's "sons" – those not only born to her physically but who also belong to her as "disciples" – are designates of her status as a slave.[224] This is the reverse of the midrashic association of Sinai with freedom: "R. Berekiah said: Why is Sinai called *my mother's house?* Because there Israel became like a newborn child" (Cant.R. 8.2.1) (see above).

---

point of the allegory, its assumed anti-Jewishness is further mitigated. Moreover, it takes on features known from the pesharim at Qumran in which radical and extreme epithets were attributed to the groups with whom the community was in internecine conflict (cf. Flusser, Pharisees) (see 2:15-21 and below).

[220] (The fact that the verb picks up on the στοιχεῖα [stoicheia] of verses 3, 9 is hardly accidental [see 5:24-26, 6:12-16, and verses 1f].) For a critique of the approach which sees the allegory in terms of a pythagorean tables of opposites (cf. LXX Ezek. 42:3), cf. Nanos, Present: 5f, 16.

[221] According to Philo, Hagar herself was a proselyte – "an Egyptian by birth, but a Hebrew by her rule of life (γένος μὲν Αἰγυπτίαν, τὴν δὲ προαίρεσιν Ἑβραίαν)" (*De Abr.* 251). (Philo's own allegorical reading of Isaac and Ishmael sees the story as a depiction of the soul's [Abraham's] transcendence of sensory perception and sophistry [Hagar/Ishmael] to the plane of wisdom and knowledge [Sarah/Isaac] [cf. *De Cher.* 8-10; *De Sob.* 7-9].) Bondage to sin is, of course, the enemy against which Paul has been exerting his energy throughout the letter (see 1:1-5, 2:1-10, 15-21, 3:19f, 5:13f, and verses 1f). It is presumably not uncoincidental that Canticles' reinterpretation of Scripture is primarily related to the Exodus (cf. Boyarin, Intertextuality: 105-16).

[222] Cf. Ex. 13:17, 14:13; Dt. 17:16; Hos. 11:5; Est.R. Proem 3; JSuk. 55b. For the development of Israel's "slave mentality" in Egypt, cf. Leibowitz: 240-47.

[223] For "returning to bondage," see verses 1-7.

[224] The offspring of a person's slaves were themselves naturally slaves (cf. Gen. 14:14, 17:12-13; Ex. 23:12; Lev. 22:11; JKid. 41b) (cf. Elon: 232). For the meanings attributed in Hebrew to בנים (banim – "sons"), see 3:6-9, 26-29 (n293). Hagar's function here is analogous to that of Balaam's role as the "father of the wicked" in PA 5:19 (see 2:15-21 and 3:1-5).

In the context of imitation and discipleship in which Paul brings the "allegory," the image of childbearing may well stand as a metaphor of proselytising – gaining converts (cf. Martyn, Galatians: 451ff) (see verses 12-20).[225] Paul is attributing "slavery" to those who are persuading the gentile Galatian believers towards conversion. Identified with Hagar, the influencers' wish to tie his disciples to a social standing/identity rather than allow them access to God's Kingdom through Jesus' faithfulness (their "childbearing") leads, as a natural consequence, to bondage to the "flesh" and to the "elemental things of the world" (see 3:19f and verses 1f).[226]

Although we do not see Paul as following in the allegorical tradition of Philo in *Quis Rerum Divinarum Heres* (Who is the Heir of Divine Things), the Alexandrian similarly employs the motif of two women to describe two of the "three kinds of life, one looking Godwards, another looking to created things": "The God-regarding life has never come down to us, nor submitted to the restraints of the body. The life that looks to creation has never risen at all nor sought to rise, but makes its lair in the recesses of Hades and rejoices in a form of living, which is not worth the pains ... Now Moses while he gives the crown of undisputed victory to the Godward kind of life, brings the other two into comparison by likening them to two women, one of whom he calls the beloved [Pleasure] and the other the hated [Prudence]. These names are very suitable, for who does not look with favour on the pleasures and delights that come through the eyes, or the ears, or through taste and smell and touch? Who has not hated the opposites of these? – frugality, temperance, the life of austerity and knowledge, which has no part in laughter and sport, which is full of anxiety and cares and toils, the friend of contemplation, the enemy of ignorance, which puts under its feet money and mere reputation and pleasure, but is mastered by self-restraint and true glory and the wealth which is not blind but sees ... This life of the senses, then, which he [Moses] calls Masek [Eliezer of Damascus, who is Abraham's heir prior to

---

[225] Whereas the LXX consistently employs τίκτω (tiktō) in rendering the act of childbearing, Paul prefers γεννάω (gennaō) here. Signifying both "bearing" and "begetting," Paul uses the latter verb to describe his "fathering" in 1 Cor. 4:15 (see verses 12-20). For Sarah as the mother of proselytes, see below (n248).

[226] Presumably, Paul perceives these disturbers as in bondage themselves and casting a similar net also over his disciples (cf. 2 Pet. 2:19-20; [Wis.Sol. 17:8]) (see 5:2-12). Halakhah frequently attributes to proselytes a status similar to women, female converts also being associated with the "harlot אשה זנה וחללה" of Lev. 21:7 (cf. Yev. 6:5; Sot. 38a; Zev. 103a; Men. 43a). Only a slave is lower in rank than a proselyte (cf. Jeremias, Jerusalem: 345-51), slaves and women also frequently being comparable in legal standing (see 2:1-10 [n74] and verses 1-7). For the theme of bondage in Galatians, see 1:15, 2:1-10, 15-21, 3:19f, 5:13f, 6:1-11, and verses 1f; for the influencers' identity and objectives, see Introduction, **Occasion and circumstances**; for the requirements devolving from conversion, see 5:2-12.

the births of Ishmael and Isaac – Gen. 15:2], has for her son each one among us who honours and admires the nurse and foster-mother of our mortal race, that is Sense, on whose just-fashioned form the earthly mind, called Adam, looked and gave the name of what was his own death to her life. 'For Adam,' it says, 'called the name of his wife "Life," because she is the mother of all things living' (Gen. 3:20), that is doubtless of those who are in truth dead to the life of the soul. But those who are really living have Wisdom for their mother, but Sense they take for a bond-woman, the handiwork of nature made to minister to knowledge"[227] (*Quis Rerum* 45-48, 52-53).[228]

---

[227] Ζωῆς δὲ τριττὸν γένος, τὸ μὲν πρὸς θεόν, τὸ δὲ πρὸς γένεσιν, τὸ δὲ μεθόριον, μικτὸν ἀμφοῖν. τὸ μὲν οὖν πρὸν θεὸν οὐ κατέβη πρὸς ἡμᾶς οὐδὲ ἦλθεν εἰς τὰς σώματος ἀνάγκας. τὸ δὲ πρὸς γένεσιν οὐδ' ὅλως ἀνέβη οὐδ' ἐζήτησεν ἀναβῆναι, φωλεῦον δὲ ἐν μυχοῖς ῞Αιδου τῷ ἀβιώτῳ βίῳ χαίρει ... Μωυσῆς δὲ τὸ τῆς πρὸς θεὸν ζωῆς γένος ἀκονιτὶ στεφανώσας εἰς ἐπίκρισον τὰ λοιπὰ ἄγει δυσὶν ἀπεικάζων γυναιξίν, ὧν τὴν μὲν ἀγαπωμένην, τὴν δὲ μισουμένην καλεῖ προσφυέστατα θεὶς ὀνόματα. τίς γὰρ οὐ τὰς δι' ὀφθαλμῶν, τίς δ' ὤτων, τίς δ' οὐ τὰς διὰ γεύσεως ὀσφρήσεώς τε καὶ ἀφῆς ἡδονὰς καὶ τέρψεις ἀποδέχεται; τίς δ' οὐ τὰ ἐναντία μεμίσηκεν, ὀλιγοδείαν, ἐγκράτειαν, αὐστηρὸν καὶ ἐπιστημονικὸν βίον, γέλωτος καὶ παιδιᾶς ἀμέτοχον, συννοίας καὶ φροντίδων καὶ πόνων μεστόν, φίλον τοῦ θεωρεῖν, ἀμαθίας ἐχρόν, χρημάτων μὲν καὶ δόξης καὶ ἡδονῶν κρείττω, ἥττω δὲ σωφροσύνης καὶ εὐκλείας καὶ βλέποντος οὐ τυφλοῦ πλούτου ... ταύτης οὖν τῆς κατ' αἴσθησιν ζωῆς, ἣν καλεῖ Μασέκ, υἱὸς ἕκαστος ἡμῶν ἐστι τιμῶν καὶ θαυμάζων τὴν τροφὸν καὶ τιμήνην τοῦ θνητοῦ γένους, αἴσθησιν, ἣν καὶ ὁ γήινος νοῦς, ὄνομα Ἀδάμ, ἰδὼν διαπλασθεῖσαν τὸν ἑαυτοῦ θάνατον ζωὴν ἐκείνης ὠνόμασεν. "ἐκάλεσε" γάρ φησιν " Ἀδὰμ τὸ ὄνομα τῆς γυναικὸς αὐτοῦ ζωή, ὅτι αὕτη μήτηρ πάντων τῶν ζώντων," τῶν πρὸς ἀλήθειαν τὸν ψυχῆς τεθνηκότων δήπου βίον. οἱ δὲ ζῶντες ὄντως μητέρα μὲν ἔχουσι σοφίαν, αἴσθησιν δὲ δούλην πρὸς ὑπηρεσίαν ἐπιστήμης ὑπὸ φύσεως δημιουργηθεῖσαν.

[228] Cf. *Leg.All.* 2.48; *De Sac.* 19ff; *De Sob.* 21ff. The "third kind of life" appears to be the "mixed life (τὸ μικτόν)" composed of the two others, represented by the ordinary virtuous (ascetic) person. Despite the affinities which appear to exist between Paul and Philo on the basis of the passage, Paul's scriptural exegesis does not fall into the allegorical category of Philo's system. Whereas Philo associates the two women with two philosophical qualities – Prudence and Pleasure – whose respective cultivation and rejection he promotes, Paul wishes his disciples to "listen to Scripture" and to obey its directive to "Cast out the bondwoman and her son" who are persecuting God's chosen community (see below). It is, nonetheless, striking that Philo's text is based on Dt. 21:15-17, whose haftarah according to the seven-shabbat cycle is Isa. 54:1-10 (see above [n202]). The passage in Deuteronomy deals with the case of a man whose first, "hated" wife gives birth before his second, "beloved" wife, the first, less-loved son consequently inheriting the birthright (see 3:15-18 [n201]). Both Paul (cf. Rom. 9:6ff) and Philo invoke the principle of the "older will serve the younger" in order to ensure that the son of the beloved in fact receives the inheritance. For a philonic interpretation of Paul, see Boyarin, *Paul*; for the doctrine of the "Two Ways/Spirits," see 5:13f.

Verse 25: In the light of the Qumran pesharim, this verse takes on the character of a "quotation" – along the lines of the interpretation given of Isaiah 52:7 in the Melchizedek text: "[*Isa 52:7* «Saying to Zi]on: your God rules». [«Zi]on» i[s] [the congregation of all the sons of justice, those] who establish the covenant, those who avoid walking [on the pa]th of the people. And «your God» is [. . . Melchizedek, who will fr]e[e them from the ha]nd of Belial"[229] (11QMelch 2:23-25) (see 1:1-5 and verses 1-7).[230] Paul's use of the neuter definite article (τό; to) before Hagar's name indicates that he is referring to "Hagar" as a word appearing in a field of elements to be allegorically interpreted: "Now «Hagar» is Sinai the mountain in Arabia" (cf. Hays, Galatians: 302).[231]

Paul in fact appears to be playing with several elements simultaneously, causing his thought to appear to jump from one association to another. Having begun with Hagar, he is reminded of his argument of God's promise of an heir to Abraham. This (re-)introduces the theme of the covenant, which naturally calls to his mind מתן תורה (matan Torah) and Sinai. In verse 25 he conjoins, slightly awkwardly, these two figures – Hagar and Sinai.[232]

At this point, he obliquely introduces the text which governs the mashal (inter)textually – Isaiah 54:1 (see above). Because his starting point is the mother who gives birth supernaturally, the "allegorical" contrast is with an "earthly" mother.[233] With respect to the latter, Hagar corresponds to Sinai, the fashioner of Israel (see 2:15-21, 5:2-12, and verses 1-7). She thence comes to correspond to "the present Jerusalem (τῇ

---

[229]]אומר לצי]ו[ן מלך אלו]היך [צי]ו[ן ה]ני]אה] [עדת כול בני הצדק המה] מקימ]י[ן הברית הסרים מלכת]בד]רך העם ואל]ו]היך הואה]. . . מלכי צדק אשר יצי]ל]מה מי]ד בליעל.

[230] For the textual variants omitting "Hagar," and the concomitant exegeses, cf. Longenecker, Galatians: 211f.

[231] This is an adaptation of Hays' comment, utilizing the marking system of Martínez's and Tigchelaar's study edition of the Scrolls. On this reading, Paul's reversal of the usual order (Mount Sinai) does not appear particularly significant, although it tends to emphasise Arabia (see 1:16c-17 and below).

[232] For the connection between the two figures *via* Esau, see below.

[233] A certain *Min* [heretic] said to Beruriah [R. Meir's wife]: It is written: *Sing, O barren, thou that didst not bear* (Isa. 54:1). Because she did not bear is she to sing [what has she to rejoice over]? She replied to him: You fool! Look at the end of the verse, where it is written, *For the children of the desolate shall be more than the children of the married wife, saith the Lord.* But what then is the meaning of '*a barren that did not bear*'? Sing, O community of Israel, who resemblest a barren woman, for not having born children like you for Gehenna. אמר לה ההוא]צדוקי] לברוריא: כתיב: רני עקרה ילדה. משום דלא ילדה רני! אמרה ליה: שטיא! שפיל לסיפיה דקרא, דכתיב: כי רבים בני שוממה מבני בעולה אמר ה'. אלא מאי עקרה לא ילדה! רני כנסת ישראל שדומה לאשה עקרה שלא ילדה בנים לגיהנם" (Ber. 10a). Bruria may have been thinking of Rome as the "married wife" and Jerusalem as "the desolate."

νῦν Ἰερουσαλήμ)."[234] While it is possible that Paul has in mind here Jerusalem's current occupation by the Romans – which adds an even greater poignancy to his *mashal* – the slavery to which he is primarily referring remains that of the "flesh" (cf. Rom. 9:8; Targ.Isa. to 54:1) (cf. Hays, Galatians: 303-4) (see 2:15-21 and 3:19ff).[235]

A misrashic interpretation of the King of Tyre's splendid attire in the garden of Eden conjoins a reference to Adam's mortality with access to the "heavenly Jerusalem": "*Thou wast in Eden the garden of God . . . . the gold, the work of thy timbrels and holes* (Ezek. 28:13) . . . Thus said [the Holy One, blessed be He], 'I looked upon thee and decreed the penalty of death over Adam.' What is implied by, *and over her assemblies*? – Rabbah said in the name of R. Johanan: Jerusalem of the world to come will not be like Jerusalem of the present world. [To] Jerusalem of the present world, anyone who wishes goes up, but to that of the world to come only those invited will go"[236] (BB 75b).[237]

Hebrews 12 likewise reflects a tradition in which Mount Zion will, in the end times, take precedence over Mount Sinai: "For you have not come to *a mountain* that may be touched and to a blazing fire, and to darkness and gloom and whirlwind . . . But you have come to Mount Zion and to the

---

[234] This rather tortuously-wrought analogy may account for Paul's description of Mt. Sinai as being "in Arabia," no natural logic tying Sinai to Jerusalem. For "Arabia," see 1:16c-17; for Sinai in Jewish tradition, cf. Schwartz, Sinai; for Jerusalem, see 1:16c-17.

[235] Since Esau married Machalat, Ishmael's daughter, Ishmael is also associated with Esau, the latter later being identified with Edom (= Rome = Christianity) (cf. Gen. 28:9, 36:1, 8, 43; Obad. 8; Gen.R. 16:4, 65:11, Gen.R. 67:8; Ex.R. 27:1; Num.R. 11:1; Sif.Dt. 41; Tanh.Ter. 3) (cf. EJ: 6:857-58). Esau and his descendants settled in the region of Seir, Mount Seir being given to Esau as a possession (cf. Gen. 36:8; Dt. 2:4-5; Josh. 24:4). According to Dt. 33:2, Seir and Sinai are synonymous. (For Paul's image of marriage to sin, cf. Rom. 7:1ff; for being "cut off" from the Messiah through divorce, see 5:2-12 [verse 4].)

[236] בעדן גן אלהים היית . . . בך נסתכלתי וקנסתי מיתה על אדם הראשון. מאי "ועל מקראיה"?!
אמר רבה אמר יוחנן : לא כירושלים של עולם הזה ירושלים של עולם הבא. ירושלים של עולם הזה –
כל הרוצה לעלות ; של עולם הבא - אין עולין אלא המוזמנין לה.

[237] The reference to "timbrels and holes [וְתֻפֶּיךָ וּנְקָבֶיךָ]" in this verse is understood as an allusion to the grave. The Hebrew translated as "her assemblies" can also mean "invited guests." This midrash suggests that Paul's contrast between Jerusalem "above" and the "present" Jerusalem – which commentators frequently point out as diverging from the anticipated "Jerusalem below" – reflects the common rabbinic expressions of "this world" and the "world to come," synonyms for "earthly" and "heavenly."

city of the living God, the heavenly Jerusalem, and to myriads of angels"[238] (Heb. 12:18, 22).[239]

The genre in which this type of exegesis belongs is best known from the Qumran pesharim (cf. Flusser, Pharisees, and for the following discussion).[240] The Qumran community conceived itself as a "house" or "temple" or "city" – all these metaphors being based on the Temple in Jerusalem which housed God's presence.[241] It was a natural consequence that Jerusalem itself should also constitute a vital part of the community's self-designation. So, for example, the Isaiah Pesher applies the prophet's description of the eschatological temple in 54:11-12 – the same chapter from which Paul quotes in verse 27 – to the community, in similar fashion to the Melchizedek Scroll's ascription of "Zion" to the Qumran sectarians: "*Isa 54:11* And I will found you [Jerusalem] in sapphi[res. Its interpretation:] they will found the council of the Community, [the] priests and the peo[ple . . .] the assembly of their elect, like a sapphire stone in the midst of stones. [*Isa 54:12* I will make] all your battlements [of rubies]. Its interpretation concerns the twelve [chiefs of the priests who] illuminate with the

---

[238] Οὐ γὰρ προσεληλύθατε ψηλαφωμένῳ καὶ κεκαυμένῳ πυρὶ καὶ γνόφῳ καὶ ζόφῳ καὶ θυέλλῃ ... ἀλλὰ προσεληλύθατε Σιὼν ὄρει καὶ πόλει θεοῦ ζῶντος, Ἰερουσαλὴμ ἐπουρανίῳ, καὶ μυριάσιν ἀγγέλων.

[239] Cf. Jub. 1:28, 4:26, 8:19; Gen.R. 99:1 (cf. Flusser, Judaism: 88f, 265, 271, 464; Le Cornu and Shulam: 58ff). Flusser suggests that "The comparison between the two covenants and Mounts Zion and Sinai is in the Epistle to Galatians built upon a contrast, while the author of the Epistle to the Hebrews wants to show that the new excels the old. I venture that here – and not only here – the conception of the Epistle to the Hebrews is more archaic than Paul, who from his theological views creates a contrast" (Judaism: 265n52). It would seem equally – if not more – likely, to us, that the contrast is in fact a factor of Paul's *sociological polemic* with the influencers within the Galatian communities (see Introduction, **Occasion and circumstances; Argument**). For the people's reluctance to approach Sinai as a cause of God's raising of a "prophet like Moses," see 3:10-14 (n129), 19-20 (nn246, 264), verses 1-7 (nn46, 79); for Hebrews and Galatians, see 1:1-5 and verses 1-7.

[240] The hermeneutical proximity between pesharim and the Christian concepts of allegory/typology can be perceived from such definitions of typology as point out the latter's interpretation of "historical material commonly used in primitive Christianity. Persons, events, and institutions of Scripture and tradition are taken as prototypes of present persons, events, and institutions, which are explained as their fulfillment, repetition, or completion within a framework of salvation history" (Betz, Galatians: 239). "In fact, it is more helpful to recognize that typology is nothing other than a particular type of allegory, in which the latent sense of a narrative is to be found in later events rather than in 'higher' spiritual concepts" (Hays, Galatians: 301).

[241] Cf. 1 Kings 8:12ff; 2 Chron. 6:4ff; [Rom. 12:1]; 1 Cor. 3:9, 6:19; 2 Cor. 6:14f; [Gal. 2:9]; Eph. 2:19f; 1 Tim. 3:15; 1 Pet. 2:4f; 1 En. 1:2, 38:2, 62:8; 1QS 5:6, 8:4f; 9:6, 11:8; CD-A 3:19f; CD-B 20:10; 4QFlor f1i:2ff; Philo, *In Flac.* 45; *Leg.* 279; Sif.Dt. 154, 352; Kel. 1:6-9 (see 2:1-10, 15-21 and 6:1-11 [verse 10], 12-16 [n186]).

A Commentary on the Jewish Roots of Galatians

judgment of the Urim and the Thummim . . . *Isa 54:14* And a[ll your gates of glittering stones.] Its interpretation concerns the chiefs of the tribes of Israel in the l[ast days . . . of] its lot"[242] (4QpIsaᵈ 1:1-8) (cf. 11QMelch 2:23-24).[243]

The enmity between the members of the Qumran community – who removed themselves into the desert to create a pure and undefiled community – and the Pharisees and Sadducees alike would, according to the Scrolls, finally end in a recognition of the community's status as members of the "new covenant": "And when the glory of Judah [the community] is re[ve]aled the simple people of Ephraim [i.e., those now allied with the Pharisees] will flee from among their [the pharisaic] assembly and desert the ones who misdirected them and will join the [majori]ty of I]srael. *Nah 3:7* They shall say: Nineveh is laid waste, who will be sorry for her? Where shall I find comforters for you? *Blank* Its interpretation [concerns] those looking for easy interpretations [the Pharisees], whose council will die and whose society will be disbanded; they shall not continue misdirecting [the] assembly and simple [folk] shall no longer support their council"[244] (4QpNah ff3-4iii:4-8).[245]

Verses 26-27 provide the prooftext through which Paul is "decoding" the story of Abraham, Sarah, and Hagar – being, in effect, the verses which control the whole mashal.[246] The fact that the symmetry of the parallelism is broken – Paul failing to identify the heavenly Jerusalem explicitly with

---

[242] ‏ויסדתיך בספני[רים פשרו] [אש]ר יסדו את עצת היחד [ה]כוהנים והע[ום . . .] עדת בחירו כאבן‎
‏הספיר בתוך האבנים [ושמתי כדכוד] כל שמשותיך פשרו על שנים עשר [ראשי הכוהנים אשר]‎
‏מאירים במשפט האורים והתומים [. . . ולוא] הנעדרות מהמה כשמש[ל] בכול אורו וכו]ל שעריך‎
‏לאבני אקדח] פשרו על ראשי שבטי ישראל לא[חרית הימים . . .] גורלו.‎

[243] Just as the author of this Qumran text understands the passage in Isaiah in relation to the community's organisational structure – the priests and the lay community – that of Pesher Habakkuk perceived the actual, present-day Temple as occupied by evil, wicked priests (cf. 1QpHab 8:3ff, 9:3f, 10:5f, 12:6f). In the same fashion, Revelation 21 describes the heavenly Jerusalem as the Lamb's bride/wife (cf. 2 Esd. 10:25-27; 4 Ez. 9:38-10:28). For 11QMelch, see 1:1-5 and verses 1-7.

[244] ‏ובה[ג]לות כבוד יהודה ידודו פתאי אפרים מתוך קהלם ועזבו את מתעיהם ונלוו על [רו]ב‎
‏[י]שראל ואמרו שודדה נינוה מי ינוד לה מאין אבקשה מנחמים לך *vacat* פשרו [על] דורשי החלקות‎
‏אשר תובד עצתם ונפרדה כנסתם ולא יוסיפו עוד לתעות [ה]קהל ופתא[ים] לא יחזקו עוד את עצתם.‎
[245] «Nineveh» functions here as a "code" for the pharisaic party. For pharisaic hypocrisy, see 2:15-21, 6:1-11, and verses 12-20.
[246] This should not be taken as breaking the chiastic structure of verses 25-26:

A   Hagar
      B   Mount Sinai
          C   slavery
             D   present Jerusalem
             D′   heavenly Jerusalem
          C′   freedom
      B′   (Mount Zion)
A   our mother (Sarah)
(cf. Longenecker, *Galatians*: 213). For other chiastic patterns, see 2:1-10 (n113), 3:10-14 (verses 11-12), 21-25 (verses 22-23), 5:2-12 (verse 4), and verses 1-7 (n43).

Sarah – indicates Paul's assumption of the biblical passage's presence, which he forgets to properly introduce and mark. The image of Jerusalem as a "mother of sons" is widespread.[247] What is special about the "heavenly" Jerusalem is precisely the fact that her children are born "from above," since she – like Sarah – is barren and is given the capacity to bear by God Himself (cf. Gen. 11:30, 16:1; Isa. 51:2).[248] While her own sons are "no longer" – scattered in exile, destroyed in God's wrath, turned away in rebellion – in the end days the city, once empty and desolate, will be filled with inhabitants, the noise and bustle of the redeemed filling it with singing and joy.[249] Not only will Jerusalem's "sons" (children) return to her, but they will be restored together with those who formerly were "not-a-people," over whom God will also call His name, taking them out of the nations and bringing them to His holy mountain.[250]

The LXX explicitly identifies Zion as the "mother-city (μητρόπολις; metropolis)" in rendering Isaiah 1:26: "After that you will be called the city of righteousness, a faithful city אחרי-כן יקרא לך עיר הצדק קריה נאמנה."[251]

---

[247] Cf. Ps. 87:5, 113:9; Isa. 62:4-5, 66:7ff; 2 Esd. 10:7; 4 Ez. 10:7, 25ff. Sarah is explicitly linked to these texts (cf. Gen.R. 53:5; Pes.Rab. 43:4).

[248] Isa. 51:2-3 in fact links Sarah directly with Zion: "'Look to Abraham your father, and to Sarah who gave birth to you in pain; when *he was* one I called him, then I blessed him and multiplied him.' Indeed, the LORD will comfort Zion; He will comfort all her waste places. And her wilderness He will make like Eden, and her desert like the garden of the LORD; joy and gladness will be found in her, thanksgiving and sound of a melody הביטו אל-אברהם אביכם ואל-שרה תחוללכם כי-אחד קראתיו ואברכהו וארבהו כ- נחם ה' ציון נחם כל-חרבתיה וישם מדברה כעדן וערבתה כגן-ה' ששון ושמחה ימצא בה תודה וקול זמרה." For Sarah as the "mother of proselytes," cf. Tanh.B. Vayera 38; Gen.R. 39:14; Cant.R. 1.3.3; Pes.Rab. 43:4; ARN[b] 26; for the theme of barren women giving birth, cf. Rebekah (Gen. 25:21); Rachel (Gen. 29:31), Manoach (Judg. 13:2-3), Chana (1 Sam. 2:5), Elizabeth (Lk. 1:7-17) (cf. also Ex. 23:26; Dt. 7:14; Ps. 113:9).

[249] Cf. [Dt. 30:1-10]; Isaiah 52-66; Jeremiah 30-33; Ezekiel 36-39; Micah 4-7; Zechariah 12-14. The rejoicing – which is common to so many of these texts – also recalls Isaac, whose name signifies "laughter" (cf. Gen. 21:6). An even more elusive allusion may echo in the "joy and gladness, thanksgiving and the voice of song" in Isa. 51:3 which recalls the "Song of Songs" – whose own text calls up the "Song of the Sea" in Exodus 15 (picked up again in the Song of Moses re/cited in Revelation 15 in the song of the Lamb).

[250] Cf. Isa. 14:1ff, 19:18ff, 49:22f, 55:5, 56:3ff, 60:3ff, 66:7ff; Hos. 1:9f, 2:23; Zech. 2:10-13, 8:22-23; Acts 15:15f; Eph. 2:12f; 4Q504 ff1-2iv:8f. For the motif of exile, see 1:1-5 (nn80, 90), 3:15-18 (n188), and 5:2-12 (n37).

[251] καὶ μετὰ ταῦτα κληθήσῃ Πόλις δικαιοσύνης, μετρόπολις πιστὴ Σιων (cf. 1 En. 26:1; Philo, *In Flac.* 45-46; *Leg.* 281-83; Ex.R. 23:10) (see 1:16c-17). Jerusalem is also located geographically at the centre of the whole world, the orientation of lands and peoples all being linked to the city (cf. Dt. 32:8) (cf. Gill and Gempf: 483ff; Le Cornu and Shulam: 18f). Rabbinic midrashim speak of the city as the "metropolis מטרפולין/" to whom all the nations will stream in the eschaton (cf. Mid.Ps. 36:6; Ex.R. 23:10; Est.R. 1:9; Cant.R. 1.5.3; Yalk.Ezek. 383). Both the epithets used of

Rabbinic midrashim speak in similar terms in an interpretation of Ezekiel 16:60-61: "'Nevertheless I will remember My covenant with you in the days of your youth, and I will establish an everlasting covenant with you. Then you will remember your ways and be ashamed when you receive your sisters, *both* your elder and your younger; and I will give them to you as daughters, but not because of your covenant":

> *O ye daughters of Jerusalem* (Cant. 1:5). R. Johanan said: Jerusalem will one day become the metropolis of all countries, and draw people to her in streams to do her honour, as we read, *Ashdod, its towns* (benotheha), *and its villages, Gaza, its towns* (benotheha) *and its villages until Lesha* (Josh. 15:47). This is the opinion of R. Johanan, who said: It is written, *And I will give them unto thee for daughters, but not because of thy covenant* (Ezek. 16:61). What is meant by daughters? Towns. *'But not because of thy covenant'*: that is, not as part of thy contract [dowry], but as a gift from me [as bridegroom]. R. Bibi said in the name of R. Reuben: It is written, *Sing, O barren* (Isa. 54:1). What song can there be for barrenness? What it means, however, is, 'Sing, O barren one, that hast not born children for Gehinnom.'[252] (Cant.R. 1.5.3)[253]

> What is meant by *daughters of Jerusalem* (Cant. 1:5)? [God] calls the [gentile] nations "daughters of Jerusalem." R. Jochanan said: In the future the Holy One, blessed be He, will make Jerusalem a metropolis for the whole world, as it is said *And I will give them unto thee for daughters, but not because of thy covenant* (Ezek. 16:61).[254] (Tanh.B.Dev. 2:3)[255]

Jerusalem – righteous and faithful – constitute keynotes of Paul's arguments throughout Galatians (see Introduction, **Argument; Theological pointers**).

[252] בנות ירושלים: אמר רבי יוחן: עתידה ירושלים להעשות מטרפולין לכל המדינות ולהמשיך כנהר אליה לכבודה, כדאמר: אשדוד בנותיה וחצריה עזה בנותיה וחצריה עד לשע. היא דעתיה דרבי יוחן, דאמר ר' ייוחן: כתיב: ונתתי אתהן לך לבנות ולא מבריתך. מהו "לבנות" – לכופרנין. "ולא מבריתך"? - לא מן פרניך אלא מן פרנין דידי. רבי ביבי משום רבי ראובן אמר: רני עקרה. הא רנה עקרותא היא אלא רני עקרה שלא ילדה בנים לגיהנם.

[253] Cf. Yalk.Ezek. 383. It is evidently uncoincidental that Isa. 54:1 becomes linked to this motif. R. Bibi's comment is designed to explain why barrenness is linked with *joy* and may indicate either that the person who does not give birth does not undergo the grief of knowing that her children will die – or, possibly, that the "children of the barren woman" are not subject to sin and death as are natural offspring (cf. Isa. 65:23 [17-25]) (see also 6:12-16). For "sons of hell," see 3:21-25 (n293).

[254] מהו "בנות ירושלים"? קורא לאומות "בנות ירושלים." אמר ר' יוחן: עתיד הקדוש ברוך הוא לעשות ירושלים מטרופוליא לכל העולם, שנאמר: ונתתי אתהן לך לבנות ולא מבריתך.

[255] Here, the midrashist explicitly associates "Jerusalem" with "the nations" – not with Israel. R. Jochanan also appears to understand ברית (brit) in its more common sense of "covenant" rather than as "dowry," leading him to suggest that God has

Since the heavenly Jerusalem is God's "gift," Paul easily associates it with liberty from human limitation, with a "non-natural" birth - the bestowal of life where death is all that can be expected. The heavenly Jerusalem is relieved of her barrenness and filled with the promise of life, thus being equated with the Garden of Eden: "Or do you think that this is the city of which I said: *On the palms of my hands I have carved you* [Isa. 49:16]? It is not this building that is in your midst now; it is that which will be revealed, with me, that was already prepared from the moment that I decided to create Paradise. And I showed it to Adam before he sinned. But when he transgressed the commandment, it was taken away from him - as also Paradise. After these things I showed it to my servant Abraham in the night between the portions of the victims [Gen. 15:12f]. And again I showed it also to Moses on Mount Sinai when I showed him the likeness of the tabernacle and all its vessels. Behold, now it is preserved with me - as also Paradise" (2 Bar. 4:2-6) (see 3:10ff).[256]

Verse 28 supplies the climax to verses 1-11 - wherein Paul has demonstrated that the gentile Galatian believers have become God's heirs through Jesus' act of deliverance from the domination of the "elementary things of the world."[257] This brings Paul back full circle to his central argument concerning Jewish identity (see 2:15-21 and 3:1ff). As he states in Romans 9: "THROUGH ISAAC YOUR DESCENDANTS WILL BE NAMED [Gen. 21:12]. That is, it is not the children of the flesh [who walk according to the flesh] who are children of God, but the children of the promise are regarded as descendants"[258] (Rom. 9:7-8) (cf. Ned. 31a) (see 2:15-21 and above).[259] The NASB rendering "like Isaac" in this verse is misleading,

---

"another people" not constituted by the Torah (cf. Ps. 72:10f; Isa. 2:2-4, 14:1f, 56:8, 60:3ff, 66:18f; Mic. 4:1-8; Zech. 2:11; Jn. 10:16; Ps.Sol. 17:31; Tob. 13:11; 4Q504 ff1-2iv:8f; Cant.R. 4.8.2; Yalk.Ps. 438). The rabbinic expression "what is meant by [מהו]" here functions similarly to the "pesher" terminology ("its interpretation is [פשרו]") of the Qumran texts. For the use of Canticles to interpret the rest of Scripture, see above.

[256] Cf. 1 En. 53:6, 90:28-29; 2 En. [J] 55:2; Ps.Sol. 17:33; 4 Ez. 7:26, 8:52, 10:25-28; 2 Bar. 32:2, 59:4; 1QM 12:1-2; 4Q400-405; Tanh.Pkudei 1; Gen.R. 55:7, 69:7; Num.R. 4:13; Cant.R. [3.11.2]; Pes.Rab. 40:6; Mid.Ps. 30:1, 122:4; Ta'anit 5a; Hag. 12b. For the motif of life, see 3:10-14.

[257] "One question inevitably raised by this analysis [of Isaiah's prophetic paraclesis] is the role of Isa. 52:13-53:12 in Paul's vision. If the citation in Gal. 4:27 evokes echoes of Isaiah 51-54, is the Suffering Servant figure - who 'opened not his mouth' - to be seen standing silently behind the text?" (Hays, Echoes: 215n92). For the Servant motif, see 1:1-5, 15f, 21-24, 2:1-10, 3:10-14, and verses 1ff.

[258] ἐν Ἰσαὰκ κληθήσεταί σοι σπέρμα. τοῦτ᾽ ἔστιν, οὐ τὰ τέκνα τῆς σαρκὸς ταῦτα τέκνα τοῦ θεοῦ ἀλλὰ τὰ τέκνα τῆς ἐπαγγελίας λογίζεται εἰς σπέρμα.

[259] In Romans, Paul counters the gentile claim to have "replaced" Israel, an idea which has nevertheless persisted throughout Christian history, gentile believers in their majority having dismissed Paul's warning and forgotten the "true end of what

since the Gentile believers are not merely *also* children of promise in the same way as was Isaac (see 3:15-18). They are in fact "after the order of Isaac (κατὰ [τὴν τάξιν] 'Ισαάκ)," as it were - possessed of the same status or pattern (cf. Hays, Galatians: 305).²⁶⁰ If they are truly Paul's disciples (see verses 12-20), they will understand that they are, in truth, heirs of God's promise to Abraham, in whose seed they, as part of "all the nations," have been blessed (see 3:6ff).²⁶¹

Verses 29-30: The point of Paul's mashal is a *practical* one: It is designed to demonstrate to his disciples the mode of conduct which they should adopt.²⁶² Not merely does Abraham have two sons - Jerusalem in

---

they denominate the Gentile dispensation; instead of recollecting what God declared by his servant Moses, that because the Jews moved him to jealousy by that which was not God, he would move them to jealousy by those who were not a people, - and forgetting James' declaration, that God would visit the Gentiles, to take *out* of them a people for his name, and that *after this* he would return and build again the tabernacle of David, - they magnified this visitation of the Gentiles into the ultimate purpose of God" (Herschell: 17; original emphasis).

²⁶⁰ Cf. verse 29: according to the flesh/spirit (κατὰ σάρκα/πνεῦμα). The allusion is to Ps. 110:4: "The Lord has sworn and will not change His mind, 'Thou art a priest forever, according to the order of Melchizedek נשבע ה' ולא ינחם אתה-כֹהן לעולם על-." (For Melchizedek, see 1:1-5, 3:21-25, and verses 1-7.) It might be noted, in light of the "bondage of Egypt" and the Exodus as God's great redemption, that Isaac is considered to have been born at Pesach (Passover) (cf. RH 11a) and so represents, on a symbolic level, God's passing over of human sin. For the akedah, see 3:10ff.

²⁶¹ Paul's mashal can itself be instructively viewed through the lens of Hebrews 11, wherein the author speaks of all those who died trusting the fulfilment of God's promises (including Abraham and Sarah), "confess[ing] that they were strangers and exiles on the earth ... desir[ing] a better *country*, that is a heavenly one. Therefore God is not ashamed to be called their God; for He has prepared a city for them (ὁμολογήσαντες ὅτι ξένοι καὶ παρεπίδημοί εἰσιν ἐπὶ τῆς γῆς ... κρείττονος ὀρέγονται, τοῦτ' ἔστιν ἐπουρανίου. διὸ οὐκ ἐπαισχύνεται αὐτοὺς ὁ θεὸς θεὸς ἐπικαλεῖσθαι αὐτῶν· ἡτοίμασεν γὰρ αὐτοῖς πόλιν)" (Heb. 11:13, 16) (cf. 2 En. 55:2). Here, the "city" appears to represent "peoplehood" - God being willing to acknowledge as His people those who affirm Him to be their God (cf. Lev. 26:12; Jer. 7:23, 11:4, 24:7, 30:22, Ezek. 37:23; Zech. 8:8; Heb. 11:10; Rev. 21:2).

²⁶² One of the pauline passages which most corresponds to this occurs in 1 Cor. 10:1ff where, having interpreted the Exodus "typologically" (midrashically), Paul specifically tells his readers that "Now these things happened as examples to us, that we should not crave evil things, as they also craved ... and were written for our instruction, upon whom the ends of the ages have come. Therefore let him who thinks he stands take heed lest he fall (Ταῦτα δὲ τύποι ἡμῶν ἐγενήθησαν, εἰς τὸ μὴ εἶναι ἡμᾶς ἐπιθυμητὰς κακῶν κἀκεῖνοι ἐπεθύμησαν ... ἐγράφη δὲ πρὸς νουθεσίαν ἡμῶν, εἰς οὓς τὰ τέλη τῶν αἰώνων κατήντηκεν)" (1 Cor. 10:6, 11) (cf. Rom. 4:23-25, 15:4; Gal. 5:1; 2 Tim. 3:16; Gen.R. 70:6). It may not be coincidental that the key verse in 1 Cor. 10:1-13 also revolves around the word "play" - which appears to lie behind Paul's reference in verse 29 here (see below). "Paul's quotation

an earthly and a heavenly aspect – but the two are in disagreement, the son "born according to the flesh" troubling the son "born according to the Spirit."[263] While this practical application relates to the Galatians' immediate circumstances, it is based upon a textual element within the Abraham story itself. In a play on Genesis 21:9, Ishmael's "mocking [מצחק]" – which is sandwiched between Isaac's weaning and Sarah's plea to Abraham to banish Hagar and Ishmael – is interpreted midrashically to mean that Abraham's "natural" son behaved maliciously and immorally, peculiarly towards Isaac:

> Thus R. Akiba lectured: *And Sarah saw the son of Hagar the Egyptian, whom she had borne unto Abraham, making sport* (Gen. 21:9). Now *making sport* refers to nought else but immorality, as in the verse, *The Hebrew servant, whom thou hast brought unto us, came in unto me to* make sport *of me* (Gen. 39:17). Thus this teaches that Sarah saw Ishmael ravish maidens, seduce married women and dishonour them. R. Ishmael taught: This term *sport* refers to idolatry, as in the verse, *And rose up to* make sport (Ex. 32:6). This teaches that Sarah saw Ishmael build altars, catch locusts, and sacrifice them. R. Eleazar said: The term *sport* refers to bloodshed, as in the verse, *Let the young men, I pray thee, arise and sport before us* (2 Sam. 2:14). R. 'Azariah said in R. Levi's name: Ishmael said to Isaac, 'Let us go and see our portions in the field'; then Ishmael would take a bow and arrows and shoot them in Isaac's direction, whilst pretending to be playing. Thus it is written, *As a madman who casteth fire-brands, arrows, and death; so is the man that deceiveth his neighbour, and saith: Am not I in sport* (Prov. 22:18f)? But I say: This term sport [mockery] refers to inheritance. For when our father Isaac was born all rejoiced, whereupon Ishmael said to them, 'You are fools, for I am the firstborn and I receive a double portion.' You may infer this from Sarah's protest to Abraham: *For*

---

from Exodus, by coaxing the reader to recall the golden calf story, links the present Corinthian dilemma (whether to eat meat offered to idols) to the larger and older story of Israel in the wilderness. This metaphorical act creates the imaginative framework within which Paul judges – and invites his readers to judge – the proper ethical response to the problem at hand" (cf. Hays, Echoes: 91ff) (see Introduction, **Theological pointers**).

[263] Paul's direct association of Isaac with the "Spirit" is a natural extension of his argument of 2:15ff – "It is written, *for in Isaac shall thy seed be called* (Gen. 21:12). But there is Esau [i.e., is *Esau the wicked* one of Isaac's offspring]? — 'In *Isaac*', but not *all* [the descendants of] Isaac והאיכא ישמעאל? כי ביצחק יקרא לך זרע כתיב. והאיכא עשו? "ביצחק - ולא כל יצחק (Ned. 31a). (For Paul's hermeneutic methods, see **Theological pointers**.) Since children are regarded as the "fruit of the womb" (cf. Gen. 30:2; Dt. 7:13; Ps. 127:3; Isa. 13:18; Hos. 9:16), this passage may also anticipate the argument of 5:16ff (see 5:2-12 [n107]).

the son of this bondwoman shall not be heir with my son, with Isaac
(Gen. 21:10). *With my son,* even if he were not Isaac; or *with Isaac,*
even if he were not my son; how much the more, *with my son,*
with Isaac![264] (Gen.R. 53:11)[265]

The "persecution (ἐδίωκεν)" reflects Paul's extrapolation of the
biblical story to current circumstances, the verb not occurring in the
original passage. In the fashion of pesher exegesis, it represents
contemporary events interpreted in the light of biblical texts – "so it is now
(οὕτως καὶ νῦν)."[266] In a more literal reflection of Genesis 21, Paul could
have claimed – on the present reading of the mashal – that the influencers
were "playing around" with his disciples.[267] On this basis, Paul employs
Scripture to give his disciples direct instruction: "Cast out the bondwoman
and her son (ἔκβαλε τὴν παιδίσκην καὶ τὸν υἱὸν αὐτῆς)." Twice-over –
through Sarah's voice and Scripture's which records it – comes the
command to remain faithful to God's promises and not to rely on the
"flesh."[268]

---

[264] דרש רבי עקיבא: ותרא שרה וגו': אין מצחק אלא גלוי עריות, היך מה דאת אמר: בא אלי העבד
העברי אשר הבאת לנו לצחק בי. מלמד שהיתה אמנו שרה רואה אותו לישמעאל מכביש גנות וצד
נשי אנשים ומענה אותן. תני רבי ישמעאל אומר: אין הלשון הזה של צחוק אלא עבודת כוכבים,
שנאמר: וישב העם לאכול ושתו ויקומו לצחק. מלמד שהיתה אמנו שרה רואה את ישמעאל בונה
בימוסיות וצד חגבים ומקריב עליהם. רבי אלעזר בנו של רבי יוסי הגלילי אומר: אין הלשון הזה
צחוק אלא לשון שפיכות דמים, היך מה דאת אמר: יקומו נא הנערים וישחקו לפנינו. רבי עזריה
משום רבי לוי אמר: אמר ליה ישמעאל ליצחק: נלך ונראה חלקינו בשדה והיה ישמעאל נוטל קשת
וחצים ומורה כלפי יצחק ועושה עצמו כאילו מצחק, הדא הוא דכתיב: כמתלהלה היורה זקים וגו',
כן איש רמה את רעהו ואומר הלא מצחק אני. ואומר אני: אין לשון הזה של צחוק של לשון ירושה,
שבשעה שנולד אבינו יצחק היו הכל שמחים. אמר להם ישמעאל: שוטים אתם! אני בכור ואני נוטל
פי שנים - שמתשובת אמנו שרה לאברהם כי לא יירש בן האמה הזאת עם בני אתה למד כי לא יירש
"עם בני" - אפילו שאינו יצחק; "ישם יצחק" - אף על פי שאינו בני; קל וחומר "עם בני עם יצחק".

[265] Cf. Philo, *De Sob.* 8; PRE 30; Ex.R. 1:1; [41:7; Tanh.Shmot 1; Ki tissa 20; Pes.Rab.
48:2; Tos.Sot. 6:6]. For the traditional antagonism ascribed to the two siblings'
relationship, cf. Longenecker, *Galatians*: 200ff (see also below).

[266] "Hermeneutical principles and techniques play an important role in the
Pesharim due to their specific purpose: to read historical and eschatological events
into the biblical prophecies. Since there is a gap between the literal sense and the
desired sense, a series of hermeneutical devices were employed in order to extract
the latter from the former" (Stone, *Jewish*: 505) (see also above).

[267] This is, in fact, the LXX's rendering of מצחק (metzachek): ἰδοῦσα δὲ Σαρρα τὸν
υἱὸν Αγαρ . . . παίζοντα μετὰ Ισαακ (idousa de Sarra ton huion Agar . . . paizonta
meta Isaak) – interpolating "with Isaac," who is not mentioned by name in the
masoretic text. Paul's "deliberate" change would appear to signify his evaluation of
the influencers' activity in seeking to draw his disciples away (see 6:1-11 and verses
12-20). Apart from the reference to Paul's persecution of the early community in
1:13, none of the other uses of the root διώκω (diōkō) in Galatians appear to relate to
a literal, physical persecution (see Introduction, **Argument**, 5:2-12 and 6:12-16).

[268] "The words he quotes from Gen 21:10 are actually Sarah's demand to [sic]
Abraham, but Paul lifts them out of that context and treats them as a command
spoken by Scripture directly to the hearers of this letter . . . In order to achieve this

Those who are disturbing his disciples are, like Ishmael, pretenders to the inheritance, and their claims must be rebutted: "He [Ishmael] saw Isaac sitting by himself, and he shot an arrow at him to slay him. Sarah saw (this), and told Abraham. She said to him: Thus and thus has Ishmael done to Isaac, but (now) arise and write (a will in favour) of Isaac, (giving him) all that the Holy One has sworn to give to thee and to thy seed. The son of the handmaid shall not inherit with my son, with Isaac, as it is said, 'And she said unto Abraham, Cast out this bondwoman and her son' (Gen. 21:10)"[269] (PRE 30).[270] Paul may in this sense be thinking in terms of the "persecution" of the righteous by the wicked – as in Psalm 37:32, a verse which may already underlie 2:4: "The wicked person spies upon the righteous, and seeks to kill him צופה רשע לצדיק ומבקש להמיתו" (see 2:1-10).[271]

---

effect, he has to modify the wording of the quotation just slightly, most notably by replacing 'my son Isaac' (Gen 21:10) with 'the son of the freewoman.' This change is necessary if Scripture, rather than Sarah, is to be heard as the speaker" (Hays, Galatians: 306 + note). Gen. 21:12 hovers here in the background: "But God said to Abraham, 'Do not be distressed because of the lad and your maid; whatever Sarah tells you, listen to her, for through Isaac your descendants shall be named' ויאמר אלהים אל-אברהם אל-ירע בעיניך על-הנער ועל-אמתך כל אשר תאמר אליך שרה שמע בקלה כי ביצחק יקרא לך זרע" (cf. Gen. 16:6) (see above, on verse 21). It should be remembered that, on the present reading, the influencers are considered to be godfearing gentiles who reject the Gospel and are insistent that the Galatians convert if they truly wish to claim status as part of the Jewish community (see Introduction, **Occasion and circumstances**).

[269] פעם אחת ראה את יצחק יושב לבדו, וירה עליו חץ להרגו. ראתה שרה והגידה לאברהם, כזה וכזה עשה ישמעאל ליצחק. אלא עמוד וכתוב ליצחק כל מה שנשבע הקדוש ברול הוא לתן לך ולזרעך. חייך, שאין בן-האמה הזה יורש עם בני יצחק, שנאמר: ותאמר לאברהם גרש האמה הזאת ואת בנה וגו'.

[270] The question of inheritance here becomes that of the gentile Galatians' as against the influencers', the "birthright" of the latter, as it were, as promoters of Jewish status (themselves being godfearers on the present reading), being made subject to Sarah's will regarding God's promises. The consequences of this "conflict" are apparent in the midrash's continuation, wherein Ben Tema says: "Sarah said to Abraham, Write a bill of divorce, and send away this handmaid and her son from me and from Isaac my son, in this world and from the world to come אמרה שרה לאברהם: כתוב גט גרושין ושלח את האמה הזאת ובנה מעלי ומעל בני, מן העולם הזה ומן העולם הבא." In this sense, Paul's language of "severance" in 5:4 may reflect the motif of marriage which, in the biblical texts, so frequently characterises God's relationship with His people (cf. Canticles; Isa. 54:6, 61:10, 62:4-5; Jeremiah 2-3; Hosea) (see 5:2-12 [n28]).

[271] The element of theodicy here combines with that evident in Habakkuk, thus retaining the theme of faithfulness even in the "allegory," on this reading. For Habakkuk and theodicy, cf. Hays, Echoes: 34ff. For the possibility that the Galatian communities are experiencing physical persecution, see Introduction, **Occasion and circumstances** and 3:1-5.

Verse 30 constitutes the specific answer to Paul's original question in verse 21: "do you not listen to the law (τὸν νόμον οὐκ ἀκούετε;)?"[272] If the gentile Galatian believers wish to follow the influencers' persuasion and engage in Torah-observance to gain Jewish status, they are – on an "allegorical" level – violating the Torah's own clear ordinance.[273] Genesis 21:10 works for Paul's purposes not merely because it constitutes an immediate directive – "have nothing to do with those attempting to draw your allegiance away from Jesus" – but also because it reiterates the point which underlies the whole epistle: God's "heirs" are those who have been

---

[272] For Paul's previous use of Scripture with regard to the Galatians, see 3:1f. While 4QMMT is not pesher in genre, certain affinities are again apparent here between Galatians and this "hakakhic letter." 4QMMT's author appeals directly to his addressees, "quoting" Scripture, that they should adopt his advice and conduct themselves according to it: "And also we have written to you some of the works of the Torah which we think are good for you and for your people, for we s[a]w that you have intellect and knowledge of the Law. Reflect on all these matters and seek from him that he may support your counsel and keep far from you the evil scheming{s} and the counsel of Belial, so that at the end of time, you may rejoice in finding that some of our words are true. And it shall be reckoned to you as justice when you do what is upright and good before him, for your good and that of Israel ואף אנחנו כתבנו אליך מקצת מעשי התורה שחשבנו לטוב לך ולעמך שר[א]ינו עמך ערמה ומדע תורה הבן בכל אלה ובקש מלפנו שיתקן את עצתך והרחיק ממך מחשב[ו]ת רעה ועצת בליעל בשל שתשמח באחרית העת במצאך מקצת דברינו כן ונחשבה לך לצדקה בעשותך הישר והטוב לפנו לטוב לך" וישראל (4QMMTᵉ ff14-17ii:2-8). For Galatians as a halakhic "rebuke and request" letter along the lines of 4QMMT, see Introduction, **Form**; **Argument** and verses 12-20; for Paul's previous anathema on the influencers, see 1:6-10. In the continuation of the letter, Paul repeatedly reiterates this command (cf. 5:9, [26], 6:3-5) (see Introduction, **Argument**, 5:2-12, 24-26, and 6:1-11). For 5:13 as a formal and substantive parallel to verse 21, see 5:13-18.

[273] Paul's insistence that this section is an "allegory" safeguards him against the objection that he cannot make use of Scripture in such an arbitrary or subjective fashion – or in a manner which makes its application ridiculous. While some of the Qumran pesharim may seem ludicrous to moderns steeped in the historical-critical tradition, they represent a specific literary genre whose hermeneutic rules and principles should be respected (see Introduction, **Theological pointers**). As Boyarin states in respect of midrash: "Ben Azzai does not speak of having achieved the original meaning or inner meaning or hidden meaning of Torah, but only of having read in such a way that he reconstituted the original *experience* of revelation. He did what he did, not by linking texts with their meanings but by linking texts with texts, that is, by revealing the hermeneutic connection between the Prophets and Writings and the Torah. For the midrash the correspondences are not between things seen and their hidden or inner meanings, but between texts and the historical contexts in which they were produced or to which they apply, between signifiers and signifiers, not between signifiers and signifieds. In midrash, emotional and axiological context is released in the process of generating new strings of language out of the beads of the old" (Intertexuality: 110) (see also above [n205]). For precisely the same argument, in terms of "love" being the fulfilment of the Torah, see 5:13-18 (verse 14).

released from the bondage of sin into the freedom of the Spirit.[274] Although "casting (ἔκβαλε)" is regularly used in an ordinary sense, it may here reflect the technical usage of "banishment" – as perhaps in John 9:34f and 3 John 10 (cf. Betz, Galatians: 250n122). Paul cannot tolerate his disciples' commitment to others when such following detracts from their standing in the Messiah, a loss of all that which they have gained in their deliverance through Jesus' death and resurrection from "the elemental things of the world" (see verses 1f).

Verse 31: Here, Paul pulls together all the strands of the argument he has asserted into a rhetorical climax. The "we" stands here – in contrast to Paul's previous usage in 3:14 and verses 1-7 – as inclusive of all the "brethren."[275] While the phrase "of the free woman (τῆς ἐλευθέρας)" recalls verse 22 ("by the free woman [ἐκ τῆς ἐλευθέρας]"), Paul's presentation of Jesus as "representative" of the faithful suggests that it is better read in conjunction with 5:1: "the Messiah set us free with/through the freedom of the free woman" (see 5:1).[276] The "free woman" is the mother of Isaac, through whom God's promise to Abraham that all the nations of the earth would be blessed was fulfilled: "Who then shall be the heir? Not that way of thinking which abides in the prison of the body of its own will, but that which released from its fetters into liberty has come forth outside the prison walls, and if we may say so, left behind its own

---

[274] It is important to note the "theological" implications of this interpretation of Paul's mashal. To the extent that it addresses the rivalry between himself and the influencers for the gentile Galatian believers' commitment (imitation), it possesses little if any theological import. On this reading, it says nothing about Judaism and Christianity, or about "works" and "grace." Since the influencers are not presently conceived to be believers (nor even Jewish), the allegory does not even constitute a polemic against Torah-observance (cf. Nanos, Present: 1, 12f). Essentially, it speaks to the Galatian believers about their proper *action* – not about their proper *belief*. Paul's intention is to warn his disciples not to be persuaded towards devoting themselves to someone else – an act which in effect will draw them away from imitation of the Messiah (see verses 12-20). In its actual textual exegesis, the mashal stays firmly within the bounds of reasonable interpretation, the only "exaggeration" or "distortion" deriving from its application – the latter simply serving as a function of its genre. This is not to say that it gives no rise to theological significance – simply that the latter only comes later, as Paul unpacks it in chapter 5.

[275] Such inclusive language does not contradict Paul's regular distinction between "us" and "you" (see 3:10-14 and verses 1f). As a summary statement, the condition of freedom from sin applies to both Jews and Gentiles (see verse 1f). For "brethren," see 1:1-5; for the influencers' identity, see Introduction, **Occasion and circumstances**.

[276] As Hays points out, "this [the traditional] division of the text obscures the role of this verse as the culmination of the freedom/slavery antithesis which has dominated chap. 4" (Galatians: 306). It is slightly surprising that Hays misses the textual opportunity to indicate Jesus' representative role here (cf. Faith: xxix-xxxiii, 203f, and passim) (see 2:15-21, 3:1ff, and verses 1f).

self. For 'he who shall come out of thee,' it says, 'shall be thy heir' (Gen. 15:4). Therefore, my soul [Abraham], if thou feelest any yearning to inherit the good things of God, leave not only thy land, that is the body, thy kinsfolk, that is the senses, thy father's house (Gen. 12:1), that is speech, but be a fugitive from thyself also and issue forth from thyself. Like persons possessed and corybants, be filled with inspired frenzy, even as the prophets are inspired"[277] (Philo, *Quis Rerum* 68-69) (see 3:15-18 and 5:24-26).[278]

While not adopting Philo's allegorical interpretation, Philo is asking – and answering – the same question as Paul: Who is Abraham's true heir? Although Philo and Paul both understand this inheritance in terms of "freedom from the self," Paul's exegesis is that inheritance/entrance into God's Kingdom comes through participation in Jesus' death and resurrection, and the bestowal of the Holy Spirit on those who are obedient to his faithfulness to death on a cross (see 3:10f, 5:13f, and verses 1-7).[279] Just as the Messiah is designated as the "righteous one" (see 3:10-14) he is thus also known as the one who brings freedom (see 1:1-5, 5:13f, and verses 1-7).[280]

---

[277] τίς οὖν γενήσεται κληρονόμος; οὐχ ὁ μένων ἐν τῇ τοῦ σώματος εἱρκτῇ λογισμὸς καθ᾽ ἑκούσιον γνώμην, ἀλλ᾽ ὁ λυθεὶς τῶν δεσμῶν καὶ ἐλευθερωθεὶς καὶ ἔξω τειχῶν προεληλυθὼς καὶ καραλελοιπώς, εἰ οἷόν τε τοῦτο εἰπεῖν, αὐτὸς ἑαυτόν. "ὃς γὰρ ἐξελεύσεται ἐκ σοῦ" φησίν, "οὗτος κληρονομήσει σε." πόθος οὖν εἴ τις εἰσέρχεταί σε, ψυχή, τῶν θείων ἀγαθῶν κληρονομῆσαι, μὴ μόνον "γῆν," τὸ σῶμα, καὶ "συγγένειαν," <τὴν> αἴσθησιν, καὶ "οἶκον πατρός," τὸν λόγον, καταλίπῃς, ἀλλὰ καὶ σαυτὴν ἀπόδραθι καὶ ἔκστηθι σεαυτῆς, ὥσπερ οἱ κατεχόμενοι καὶ κορυβαντιῶντες βακχευθεῖσα καὶ θεοφορηθεῖσα κατά τινα προφητικὸν ἐπιθειασμόν.

[278] The omission of the article before παιδίσκης (paidiskēs) in Paul's text here imparts to the term a qualitative emphasis – "not of *a* maidservant" – in contrast to the articled, and thus specified, "*the* freewoman" (cf. Burton: 267).

[279] For Philo's allegorical exegesis, see above on verse 24.

[280] Cf. verse 4, where Jesus' birth "of a woman, under the law" is now brought to completion in his birth of promise, as Abraham's seed through Isaac, born of the freewoman Sarah (see verses 1-7).

GALATIANS
5

Verse 1: [*Exhortatio* (5:1-6:10)][1]
It was for freedom that the Messiah set us free; therefore keep standing firm, and do not be subject again to a yoke of slavery.

Reading this verse as the "hortatory conclusion to the whole train of argument so far," it forms a continuation of 4:31 rather than opening a new section (cf. Hays, Galatians: 306) (see 4:21-31).[2] This is even truer when the

---

[1] Betz's epistolary characterisation of 5:1-6:10 as an *exhortatio* or paraenetic section (cf. Galatians: 14ff, 253ff) causes difficulty for his own definition of Galatians as an "apologetic letter," since Graeco-Roman rhetoric provides no precedent for the inclusion of an *exhortatio* in the structure of an apologetic speech, juries presumably not being accustomed to receiving moral advice from defendants. On this epistolary model, chapters 5 and 6 awkwardly intrude and impinge on the epistle's structure. Equally damaging from a "theological" perspective is the fact that while Betz attempts to demonstrate that the letter should be read as an apology in defense of the Spirit, he also argues that the norms and guidelines which Paul sets forth to instruct the Galatians in their walk in the Spirit derive from no more than prevailing ethical standards, leaving the Spirit's working completely on the plain of the moral conduct typical of the surrounding society (cf. Hays, Christology: 269-70). For the current reading of Galatians as a halakhic "rebuke and request" letter along the lines of 4QMMT, see Introduction, **Form, Argument**.
[2] While the final two chapters of Galatians evidently constitute exhortatory – halakhic – material, Betz's assessment that "The beginning of the paraenetical section (5:1-6:10) is marked by an abrupt new start" (Galatians: 255) ignores the transitional nature of verse 1 when read in conjunction with 4:31. The argument that "these words are not to be attached to 4:31 ... but constitute an independent sentence in which, the allegory of 4:21-31 being left behind, the apostle expresses himself in language akin to that of 4:4-11" (Burton: 270) misleads both with regard

emphasis is placed not so much on the contrast between the free sons and those who were enslaved, but on Jesus as the one who has effected redemption and release from bondage to sin in this world (see 1:1-5, 2:[1-10], 15-21, 3:19f, and 4:1-7).[3]

Jesus' deliverance constitutes the grounds upon which Jews and Gentiles – alike – obtain liberty from the "elemental things of the world" (see 4:1f). It is therefore "in him" that they must continue to stand, as sons, in order not to become slaves to sin and death once again (see 3:26-29). The injunction to "stand firm (στήκετε)" thus correlates with the instruction to "cast out the bondwoman and her son" (4:30), the "again (πάλιν)" – as so often throughout the letter – emphasising once more the watershed which has occurred in the Galatians' lives (as in human history as a whole) through Jesus' death and resurrection (see 3:19f and 4:1f).[4]

In the passive and carrying the dative, the verb ἐνέχω (enechō) bears connotations of "loaded" or "burdened" with – corresponding to the metaphor of the "yoke (ζυγῷ)" of slavery. While many commentators have found it felicitous to ascribe such an overbearing weight to the Torah, speciously reading this significance into the rabbinic expression "the yoke of the Torah [עול התורה]," the latter epithet in fact goes hand in hand with that of the "yoke of the Kingdom [עול המלכות]" – signifying acceptance of

---

to the allegory and with respect to the purpose of the present passage. On the presently proposed reading, this section constitutes a direct continuation of the allegory's admonition (cf. especially verses 7-12 below) (see Introduction, Argument, 4:21-31, and verses 2-12). Hays' suggestion that "the narrative model also helps to account for the logic of Paul's movement from indicative (proclamation) to imperative (exhortation) ... Christ's victory ... is the necessary precondition that enables those who are redeemed to complete the story by carrying out their own mandate, by becoming active subjects who fulfill God's original purpose by loving one another" (Faith: 223) facilitates an understanding of the relationship between pauline theology ("aggadah") and ethics (halakhah – as the "wisdom of the feasible" [Berkovits]) (cf. Hays, Christology).

[3] This reading is not mutually exclusive "theologically" of freedom as the purpose for which Jesus' sacrifice was made (cf. Rom. 8:21, 24), to which extent Betz's assertion that "The whole sentence states in a very concise form both the 'indicative' and the 'imperative' of Christian salvation in the Pauline sense" (Betz, Galatians: 256) may be admitted. Paul may have in mind such a wordplay as that contained in the Passover Haggada on "slavery": "Originally our fathers were slaves of strange slavery [lit.: "worshippers of strange worship" – the technical designation of idolators], but now the Omnipresent has brought us near to His slavery [service] מתחלה עובדי עבודה זרה היו אבותינו. ועכשיו קרבנו המקום לעבודתו." (The root עבד [avad – "to work"] extends to both slavery and worship [cf. Daube, New: 282].)

[4] Cf. 1 Cor. 16:13; Phil. 1:27, 4:1; 1 Thess. 3:8; 2 Thess. 2:15. Paul's usage of the term "again" reflects the two periods of which he is speaking – that of the "elemental things of the world" and that of the "coming of Faith" (see 3:10-14, 19f, and 4:1f). This verse in essence recapitulates 4:1-31 – as clearly recognised when conjoined with 4:31.

God's reign.[5] While most readings of Galatians further assume that "slavery (δουλείας)" is – again – subjection to the Torah and commandments, Paul's argument from 3:19 onwards demonstrates an equivalence rather with sin (see 3:19f, 4:1f, 6:1-11, and verses 2-12).[6] Here, since he has the influencers still in mind, the bondage links into the "allegory" of Sarah/Isaac and Hagar/Ishmael (see 4:21-31). In this sense, the "yoke" is a play on which sovereignty (kingdom) the Galatians should take upon themselves – that of God or that of men (see 1:1-5, 2:15-21, and verses 13f).[7]

Verses 2-12:
Behold I, Paul, say to you that if you receive circumcision, the Messiah will be of no benefit to you. And I testify again to every man who receives circumcision, that he is under obligation to keep the whole Law. You have been severed from the Messiah, you who are seeking to be justified by law; you have fallen from grace. For we through the Spirit, by faith, are waiting for the hope of righteousness. For in the Messiah Jesus neither circumcision nor uncircumcision means anything, but faith working through love. You were running well; who hindered you from obeying the truth? This persuasion *did* not *come* from Him who calls you. A little leaven leavens the whole lump of *dough*. I have confidence in you in the Lord, that you will adopt no other view; but the one who is disturbing you shall bear his judgment, whoever he is. But I, brethren, if I still preach circumcision, why I am still persecuted? Then the stumbling block of the cross has been abolished. Would that those who are troubling you would even mutilate themselves.

Paul's emphasis on his identity – "I, Paul" – highlights his exercise of authority over those who are his disciples, who are in danger of transferring their commitment and loyalty to others (see 4:12f).[8] Here, for

---

[5] Cf. Mt. 11:29-30; Tanh.Ve-zot ha-bracha 5; TBE p. 8; Num.R. 19:26; Ber. 2:2; PA 3:5; Tos.Sot. 14:4; JBer. 13b; JKid. 11b; San. 94b; Ber. 13a-b; San. 94b (cf. Le Cornu and Shulam: 823).

[6] It is generally accepted that the Galatians are *in the process* of seeking conversion and have not, as yet, taken the final step, Paul urgently writing to dissuade them from doing so (see Introduction, **Occasion and circumstances; Argument**). This understanding makes little sense of any identity between the "yoke of slavery" and Torah-observance. For the meaning of the "again" in 4:9, see 4:8-11.

[7] The former is, of course, the faithfulness Jesus exhibited in his death and resurrection; the latter, the elemental things of the world which, before God sent His Messiah, reigned in His place, as it were. The link with the Kingdom becomes explicit in verse 21 (see verses 19-24 and below).

[8] The idiomatic Ἴδε (Ide) – properly the imperative of εἶδον (eidon – "see, look") – serves as an opening particle, signifying some such exclamation as "mark my words" (cf. Longenecker, Galatians: 225). "Structurally, the *exordium* of 1:6-10 and the hortatory statements of 5:1-12 form an *inclusio* for Paul's whole treatment of the judaizing threat in the body of his letter, for in both tone and expression they serve as the frame for all that he says regarding the threat" (Longenecker, Galatians: 221). A large part of this appeal may rest on Paul's own strong Jewish identity (see

the first time, Paul identifies the immediate issue: namely, circumcision, as a sign and symbol of conversion.[9]

The source of Paul's authority derives from his obedience to the Messiah – that being what permits him to demand the Galatians' equally faithful response (see 4:12-20 and below).[10] The influencers' demand that the gentile Galatian believers undergo circumcision in order to find acceptance within the local mainstream Jewish community is not merely ill-advised, but directly injurious to their standing in the Messiah.[11] To prefer social status in the eyes of wo/men over approval in God's eyes is to obey wo/men rather than God (see 1:1-5). It is to seek the things of the flesh rather than those of the Spirit; to remain in bondage to the powers of this world in the face of life and righteousness in the Messiah; to (hypocritically) seek the "lighter" commandments of men in preference to the "justice and mercy and faithfulness" of which God has told His people (cf. Mic. 6:8; Mt. 23:23) (see 2:15-21, 3:1ff, 4:1f, verses 13f, and below).[12]

Appendix). If I, Paul – who would in other circumstances firmly advocate circumcision – am warning you against taking such a step, you should heed the caution's gravity. For Paul's "preaching of circumcision," see below; for chapters 1-2 as setting out Paul's affirmation of his authority, on the basis of which he proceeds to rebuke his disciples for turning away from his gospel and then request their renewed loyalty, see Introduction, **Argument**. (While the present volume concurs with Longenecker's structural apprehension of Galatians, it does not follow his "theological" position.)

[9] It should be remembered that, on the present reading, the influencers are gentile godfearers who reject the gospel and are insistent that the gentile Galatian believers convert if they truly wish to find status as part of the Jewish community (see Introduction, **Occasion and circumstances; Argument**).

[10] The "saying (λέγω)" is a form of legal testimony, as Paul makes clear in verse 3: "I testify again (μαρτύρομαι)." While we do not concur with Betz's assessment of the epistle as a an "apologetic letter," Paul is certainly speaking in halakhic (legal) terms at this point – almost in "anticipation" of the beit din (court) before whom proselytes were later required to make their "profession of faith," as it were (cf. Yev. 47a) (see 2:1-10).

[11] The clause ἐὰν περιτέμνησθε (ean peritemnēsthe) represents a third class conditional construction which implies that the act was still pending at the time of Paul's writing, the subjunctive also being conative in force (cf. Longenecker, Galatians: 225-26).

[12] In the terms in which Paul has presented the issue so far, the Galatians are faced with a choice between two dominions/domains – that of the elemental things of the world and that of the Coming/Righteous One. There exists no option of living in both, since one is bondage to sin and death, the other life-giving freedom. To the extent that the gentile Galatian believers have been persuaded that Jesus' death and resurrection is insufficient to gain them official standing within the Jewish community they will compromise both Jesus' and Paul's work if they now seek to obtain such social status (see 2:11-14 and 4:12-20). Again, we find it expedient to repeat here that the dichotomy is *not* between Judaism and Christianity or "Christ

Verse 3: The lack of "benefit (ὠφελήσει)" of which the Galatians will be the beneficiaries derives, Paul posits, from the fact that "every man who receives circumcision [i.e., converts] . . . is under obligation to keep the whole Torah (παντὶ ἀνθρώπῳ περιτεμνομένῳ . . . ὀφειλέτης ἐστὶν ὅλον τὸν νόμον ποιῆσαι)."[13] While the conversion ceremony envisioned in Yevamot includes only provisional instruction "in some of the minor and some of the major commandments מודיעין אותו מקצת מצוות קלות ומקצת מצוות חמורות," it is evident that the issue of intention (responsibility) was uppermost in the proselytising process: "Be it known to you that before you came to this condition, if you had eaten suet [forbidden fat] you would not have been punishable with *kareth*, if you had profaned the Sabbath you would not have been punishable with stoning; but now were you to eat suet you would be punished with *kareth*; were you to profane the Sabbath you would be punished with stoning"[14] (Yev. 47a) (cf. San. 56a ff) (see also 3:10-14, 6:1-11, and verses 13-18).[15]

While a Jew is not consulted concerning his willingness to observe the covenant, the proselyte voluntarily takes such performance upon himself, binding himself to obedience.[16] "A non-Jew [godfearer] who lives

---

and the Law." This point is brought out more clearly still when it is posited that the influencers are not themselves Jesus' followers but godfearers wishing to convince other Gentiles that they must join the Jewish community in order to gain Jewish identity. On this reading, Paul's argument carries *social* rather than primarily *religious* connotations, and it is striking that he in fact only addresses the "theological" aspects of conversion at this late point in the epistle.

[13] Paul is evidently playing on the homophony of ὠφέλεια (ōfeleia) (cf. ὄφελος [ofelos]) in verse 2 and ὀφείλω (ofeilō – "to owe/be obligated to") – the ostensible "benefit" in fact constituting a "responsibility" (see also below [verse 12]). The latter verb indeed reflects the nuances of rabbinic usage represented by חייב (chayav), this signifying the "obligation" involved in an oath ("bound") (cf. Mt. 23:16, 18) as well as, in the noun (חוב; chov), the commission of a transgression (cf. Lk. 11:4) (cf. BAGD: 599) (see 1:1-5). The verbal and substantive analogy with Rom. 2:25 is significant, as is also the "anticipation" of the "profit" accruing from love in verse 14 (see verses 13-18). For ὄφελον (ofelon – "would that"), see below; for the further play on "bound [אסור]," see 2:15-21 (n313) [6:1-11 (n39)]; for Romans 2, see verses 13-18 and below.

[14] הוי יודע שעד שלא באת למדה זו אכלת חלב, אי אתה ענוש כרת; חללת שבת, אי אתה ענוש סקילה. ועכשיו, אכלת חלב, ענוש כרת, חללת שבת, ענוש סקילה.

[15] For the development of such a ceremony only in the second century, see Introduction, **Occasion and circumstance**; for karet ("cutting off"), cf. Le Cornu and Shulam: 265f.

[16] This is perhaps most clearly evident in the Qumran scrolls, which describe the intertwined commitment and responsibility required from the initiate: "All those who submit freely to his [God's] truth will convey all their knowledge, their energies, and their riches to the Community of God in order to refine their knowledge in the truth of God's decrees and marshal their energies in accordance with his perfect paths and all their riches in accordance with his just counsel. They

according to certain fundamental moral laws, without following the whole Mosaic law, is blessed. The proselyte, the Gentile who has converted to Judaism, however, is bound by the whole law. If a proselyte fails to fulfill the whole law, which formerly did not obligate him, his conversion to Judaism is itself the cause of his becoming a child of hell [cf. Mt. 23:15]. Quite needlessly he has thrown away his blessedness" (Flusser, Jesus: 76).[17]

The δὲ (de) being a postpositive particle, it establishes a connective rather than an adversial relation with the preceding (cf. Longenecker, Galatians: 226). Paul's re-testification (πάλιν – "again") may reflect his custom of explaining the ramifications of circumcision to all those, both actually and potentially, standing before such a step. Such an elaboration was later given to proselytes, in order to confirm their intentions and commitment (see 2:1-10).[18] Paul would presumably have made use of much

---

shall not stray from any one of all God's orders concerning their appointed times; they shall not advance their appointed times nor shall they retard any one of their feasts. They shall not veer from his reliable precepts in order to go either to the right or to the left. And all those who enter the Rule of the Community shall establish a covenant before God in order to carry out all that he commanded ... And the priests and the levites shall continue, saying: «Cursed by the idols which his heart reveres whoever enters this covenant, and places the obstacle of his iniquity in front of himself to fall over it ... May God's anger and the wrath of his verdicts consume him for everlasting destruction. May stick fast to him all the curses of this covenant. May God separate him for evil, and may he be cut off from the midst of all the sons of light because of his straying from following God on account of his idols and obstacle of his iniquity. May he assign his lot with the cursed one forever» כול הנדבים

לאמתו יביאו כול דעתם וכוחם והונם ביחד אל לברר דעתם באמת חוקי אל וכוחם לתכן כתם דרכיו וכול הונם כעצת צדקו ולוא לצעוד בכול אחד מכול דברי אל בקציהם ולוא לקדם עתיהם ולוא להתאחר מכול מועדיהם ולוא לסור מחוקי אמתו ללכת ימין ושמאול וכול הבאים בסרך היחד י{א}עברו בברית {א}לפני אל לעשות ככול אשר צוה ... והוסיפו הכוהנים והלויים ואמרו ארור בגלולי לבי לעבור הבא בברית ומכשול עוונו ישים לפניו להסוג בו ... אף אל וקנאת משפטיו יבערו בו לכלת עולמים ידבקו בו כול אלות הברית הזות ויבדילהו אל לרעה ונכרת מתוך כול בני "אור בהסוגו מאחרי אל בגלוליו ומכשול עוונו יתן גורלו בתוך ארורי עולמים (1QS 1:11-17, 2:11-12, 15-17) (see also 1:6-10 and 3:10-14).

[17] For godfearers, see 2:1-10 (excursus); for Mt. 23:13, 15, see 2:15-21 and 4:12-20; for the consequences of violation of the covenant, see 3:10-14; for the negative argument ("not"), see 1:1-5, 16c-17 and 2:1f (nn99, 286).

[18] A similar process, dating from Paul's period, is known concerning the pharisaic associates: "Our Rabbis taught: If one is prepared to accept the obligation of a *haber* [associate, pharisaic] except one religious law, we must not receive him as a *haber*. If a heathen is prepared to accept the Torah except one religious law, we must not receive him [as an Israelite] ... One who desires to accept the obligations of a *haber* is required to accept them in the presence of three *haberim*, and even a *talmid hakam* [a scholar] is required to accept the obligations in the presence of three *haberim* : ת"ר הבא לקבל דברי חבירות חוץ מדבר אחד, אין מקבלין אותו. עובד כבבים שבא לקבל דברי תורה חוץ מדבר אחד, אין מקבלין אותו ... הבא לקבל דברי חבירות, צריל לקבל בפני ג' חבירים ואפילו תלמיד חכם צריך לקבל בפני שלשה חבירים (Bek. 30b) (cf. Tos.Dem. 2:4-5) (see 2:11-14 [n199]). These texts clearly reflect the potential for hypocrisy, substituting the

the same subject matter in addressing the issue of conversion with godfearers.[19] The testimony here (see also above) is urgent, in that upon taking an oath upon themselves, those seeking circumcision are binding themselves to observance of "the truth, the whole truth, and nothing but the truth."[20]

Scholars have recognised in this statement a proselytising maxim which speaks to the convert's obligation in regard to Torah-observance (cf. Tomson: 68, 88f). A clear tannaitic tradition supports the view, evidently in existence also during Paul's period, that converts were expected to perform all the commandments: "A proselyte came to him and said: Can I be accepted amongst you? . . . as a citizen. Who is a citizen? – He who accepts upon himself all the words of the Torah. In the same way, a proselyte accepts upon himself all the words of the Torah. From here they said: A proselyte who accepts upon himself all the words of the Torah except for one precept – he is not accepted. R. Jose b. R. Judah says: Even a minor precept from the ordinances of the Scribes"[21] (Sifra, Ked. 8:3) (see also verses 13-18).[22]

"traditions of men" for God's desires. For this as a dominant theme of Galatians, see Introduction, **Argument** and below.

[19] For other interpretations of the reference of "again," cf. Burton: 274-75. It would seem more reasonable to suppose that Paul had spoken of circumcision to the gentile Galatian believers on his initial visit(s), in explaining to them the nature and value of Jesus' death and resurrection in their regard, than to assume that "When he was with them there was probably no occasion to mention circumcision. The occasion to mention it had only recently arisen" (Bruce, Galatians: 229). The likelihood that they were, in large part, themselves already godfearers would indicate a basic knowledge of Judaism amongst them – including the rite of circumcision and conversion. While no beit din (court) appears to have existed during this period before whom a proselyte was required to appear, the influencers may well exemplify those people who were willing to "teach" Torah to prospective converts (cf. Kulp: 442-43).

[20] "The remarkable repetition of content between these two sentences [verses 2-3] is balanced by a difference in form: the first is a personal statement and refers to Christ, whereas the second is an impersonal statement of principle. This gives the impression that the second sentence states some accepted rule. This is confirmed by comparison with rabbinic literature. In the first place the introductory phrase μαρτύρομαι, 'I testify', parallels a technical term in Hebrew: העיד, 'testify', which means to quote formally an oral tradition, usually a halakha [e.g. mEd 1:3; 2:1, 3] . . . Thus it seems that Paul quotes and applies a halakha regarding proselyting [sic] in his polemic against circumcision of gentile Christians" (Tomson: 88-89). (The biblical usage of witnessing sets a tone of warning, without which punishment may not be meted out [cf. Dt. 8:19, 17:6, 19:15, 30:19; Jer. 11:7; 2 Cor. 13:1; San 8b].)

[21] בא ואמר לו: גר אני, יכול יקבלנו . . . כאזרח. מה אזרח. מה שקיבל עליו את כל דברי התורה: אף גר שקיבל עליו כל דברי התורה. מיכן אמרו: גר שקיבל עליו את כל דברי התורה חוץ מדבר אחד אין מקבלין אותו. רבי יוסי ברבי יהודה אומר: אפילו דבר קטן מדקדוקי סופרים.

[22] Cf. [Rom. 2:25-29]; Jas. 2:10; Yalk.Lev. 617; Mekh. de-R. Shimon bar Jochai, Yitro 20; Tanh.Vayikra 2; [Mak. 3:15]; Tos.Dem. 2:4-5; JDem. 9a; Shab. 31a; Bek. 30b; [Hul.

The same attitude is reflected in other statements in Second Temple Jewish literature which assert that violation of one commandment is tantamount to transgression of the whole Torah: "Minor sins are just as weighty as great sins, for in each case the Law is despised" (4 Macc. 5:20-21).[23] "It is written, *He that doeth these things shall never be moved* (Ps. 15:5). Whenever R. Gamaliel came to this passage he used to weep, saying: [Only] one who practiced all these shall not be moved; but anyone falling short in any of these [virtues] would be moved!"[24] (Mak. 24a).[25] Likewise, while the admonition "It is not incumbent upon you to undertake to finish the whole of the Torah, yet you are not free to keep aloof from it לא כל התורה כולה אתה מקבל עליך לגומרה ואי אתה בן חורין לפרוש הימנה" (ARN[a] 27:2) exempts a person from absolute observance, this remains the ideal.

Verse 4: Paul sums up the consequences of the Galatians' seeking of social status in a chiastic sentence (ABA) which focuses on the fact that this act will cut them off from the Messiah.[26] The idea of "severance (κατηργήθητε)" (cf. Rom. 7:2; verse 11 [Greek]) speaks both to the acceptance which the Galatians wish to gain within the Jewish community by means of conversion and their entry into the "messianic age" inaugurated by Jesus' coming (see 3:10ff and 4:1f).[27] The two aorists –

4b]. Paul brings out the point of this ordinance in verse 14, where he refers to another rabbinic tradition which sees the purpose of the Torah as summed up in the commandment to love (see verses 13-18). (In point of fact, the Sages' ordinances were frequently considered more binding than scriptural injunctions [cf. Num.R. 14:4; Sif.Dt. 154; Pes.Rab. 3:2; San. 11:3; Hor. 1:3; Eruv. 21b; Yev. 20a].)

[23] The injunction to be diligent in observing "minor" as well as "major" commandments forms part of the development of the Decalogue tradition (see 6:1-11 [n30] and verses 13-18).

[24] כתיב: עושה אלה לא ימוט לעולם. כשהיה רבן גמליאל מגיע למקרא הזה היה בוכה. אמר: מאן דעביד להו לכולהו - הוא דלא ימוט; הא חדא מינייהו - ימוט.

[25] Cf. Jas. 2:10; Pes.Rab. 21:17; PA 4:2; San. 81a. For the phrase "the whole Torah כל התורה]," cf. 4QFlor f1ii:2; Kid. 4:14; [1Q22 2:9; 11QTemp 59:9-10]; Tos.Dem. 2:4-5; ARN[a] 6:2, 11:2, 27:2; Shab. 31a; Ned. 25a.

[26] The situating of the two verbs (severing/falling) at the beginning and end of the sentence signals the emphasis which they carry, both positions frequently being reserved in Greek sentences for items to be stressed (cf. Longenecker, Galatians: 228). For other chiastic patterns, see 2:1-10 (n113), 3:10-14 (verses 11-12), 21-25 (verses 22-23), and 4:1-7 (n43), 21-31 (n246).

[27] This verb regularly appears in the context of annulment (cf. בטל [batel]), thus bearing legal (halakhic) connotations (cf. Rom. 3:31; Gal. 3:17; Eph. 2:15), as well as denoting closure, such as the end of a period/power (cf. 1 Cor. 15:24; 2 Thess. 2:8; 2 Tim. 1:10) (cf. Hays, Echoes: 133f). While Paul is at pains in chapter 3 to demonstrate that the Torah, coming after God's covenant with Abraham, does not annul God's promise in the latter (see 3:15-18), here he strongly cautions that seeking social status *will* void the Galatians' acceptance before God through the Messiah. Although the verb does not render כרת (karet – "to [be] cut off") in the LXX, this meaning – the theme of which appears in the "conversion ceremony" – is

"severed" and "fallen" – together with the conative δικαιοῦσθε (dikaiousthe – "seeking to be justified") highlight the dichotomous relationship between being "in the Messiah" and everything which lies within the realm of this world.[28] As Paul declares to the Philippians, "If anyone else has a mind to put confidence in the flesh, I far more ... But whatever things were gain to me, those things I have counted as loss for the sake of the Messiah. More than that, I count all things to be loss in view of the surpassing value of knowing the Messiah Jesus my Lord ... being conformed to his death in order that I may attain to the resurrection from the dead"[29] (Phil. 3:4, 7-8, 10-11) (see below).[30]

---

highly appropriate (see above). In an ironical reversal of normal procedure, Paul intimates that the gentile believer who *does* circumcise himself shall be cut off from the Messiah (cf. Gen. 17:14); for Paul's view of circumcision, see 2:1-10. (Hays' warning that "a pun on 'cutting' the flesh ... is not present in the text" [Galatians: 313] is nonetheless timely [see n69].) (In the present circumstances, it is the Galatians' wish to be accepted as members of the Jewish community which constitutes a betrayal of their acceptance in the Messiah's righteousness, in effect implying that Jesus' death and resurrection are inadequate and insufficient for their needs. This says nothing either about circumcision or about Judaism *per se*.)

[28] "Severance" is the complete antithesis of "being in the Messiah" – the choice of the curse rather than of the blessing, of death rather than of life (see 3:10-14). It is tempting to think that Paul may have the motif of marriage in mind here. While the LXX does not employ καταργέω (katargeō) to render גרש (garash) or a similar verb, the allegory in 4:22-31, of which this section is an explanatory continuation, speaks (in)directly of God's "divorce" of His "bride/wife" (see 4:21-31 [n270]). If so, Paul may be thinking of God having cut off intimate relations with His rebellious children, who have gone adultering/idolatoring after strange gods: "'And I saw that for all the adulteries of faithless Israel, I had sent her away and given her a writ of divorce ... Surely, as a woman treacherously departs from her lover, so you have dealt treacherously with Me, O house of Israel וארא כי על-כל-אדות אשר נאפה משבה ישראל שלחתיה ואתן את-ספר כריתתיה אליה ... אכן בגדה אשה מרעה כן בגדתם בי בית ישראל" (Jer. 3:8, 20) (see 1:1-5 [n91]). Such a speculation is supported by the fact that the biblical expression ספר כריתות (sefer kritut – "bill of divorce") derives from the same root, כרת (karat). Paul may thus be playing on the significances of "making a covenant" (כריתת ברית – kritat brit), כריתה (krita) as "cutting off" – both of the foreskin and from the community, and כריתות (kritut) as "divorce" (cf. Rom. 11:11ff). (For הסתר פנים [hester panim], the "hiding of God's face," see 3:21-25.)

[29] καίπερ ἐγὼ ἔχων πεποίθησιν καὶ ἐν σαρκί. Εἴ τις δοκεῖ ἄλλος πεποιθέναι ἐν σαρκί ... ['Αλλὰ] ἅτινα ἦν μοι κέρδη, ταῦτα ἥγημαι διὰ τὸν Χριστὸν ζημίαν. ἀλλὰ μενοῦνγε καὶ ἡγοῦμαι πάντα ζημίαν εἶναι διὰ τὸ ὑπερέχον τῆς γνώσεως Χριστοῦ Ἰησοῦ τοῦ κυρίου μου ... συμμορφιζόμενος τῷ θανάτῳ αὐτοῦ, εἴ πως καταντήσω εἰς τὴν ἐξανάστασιν τὴν ἐκ νεκρῶν.

[30] While the correspondences which Philippians 3 demonstrates with Galatians have long been recognised, the circumstances of the two letters must be carefully distinguished. Yet here, too, Paul is deprecating neither circumcision nor Judaism, simply acknowledging that being in the Messiah places everything in true perspective.

"Falling (ἐξεπέσατε)" – here lying in chiastic parallel with being "cut off" in the first part of the clause – relates literally to falling off/from, and metaphorically to "losing" (cf. BAGD: 243-44).[31] The LXX employs ἐκπίπτω (ekpiptō) in Isaiah 6:13 to render the Hebrew בשלכת (be-shalekhet): "Whose stump remains when it is felled אשר בשלכת מצבת בם."[32] If Paul understood the "mystery of Israel's hardening" in the light of Isaiah 6:9-10 (cf. Acts 28:25-28), verse 13 also serves him as a source for the "holy root" in Romans 11 (cf. Kim, Paul: 124f, 239-57; Shulam and Le Cornu: 371).[33] In this context, he warns his gentile readers that Israel have not stumbled "so as to fall (μὴ ἔπταισαν ἵνα πέσωσιν)" (Rom. 11:11) because "there has also come to be at the present time a remnant according to *God's* choice of grace (ἐν τῷ νῦν καιρῷ λεῖμμα κατ᾽ ἐκλογὴν χάριτος γέγονεν)" (Rom. 11:5).[34]

Here is the reverse of Paul's later argument in Romans, where he counters the Roman gentile believers' understanding of the grace which God had extended towards them to mean that God had forsaken and abandoned Israel, His סגולה (sgula – "treasured possession"). In the present letter, Paul is arguing that his gentile Galatian disciples are risking "stumbling so as to fall" in seeking acceptance within the Jewish community by conventional procedures.[35] They have "lost" all benefit of Jesus' act of redemption and resurrection on their behalf – if they continue to seek earthly approval.[36] The notation of "grace (τῆς χάριτος)" serves in a virtual locative sense, designating "a sphere from which the Galatians will exile themselves if they go forward with the action they are contemplating" (Hays, Galatians: 313).[37] At the same time, it also suggests

---

[31] The idea of "falling" fits Paul's presentation of Jesus' coming as the advent of a new mode of existence, out of which it is possible to fall – back into the bondage of the elemental things of the world (see 4:1f). It also corresponds to his initial warning at the beginning of this section: "Stand firm!" (verse 1).

[32] ὅταν ἐκπέσῃ ἀπὸ τῆς θήκης αὐτῆς – lit. "[like a terebinth or an oak] whenever it falls from its sheath."

[33] Kim suggests that "Isa 6 was actually one of the texts in the light of which he [Paul] interpreted his Damascus experience" (Paul: 248) (see 1:1-5 [n104]).

[34] "The hope for the eventual salvation of Israel can also be explained in the combined light of Isa 6:13 (MT and Tg) and Isa 49:5-6 . . . When the 'mystery' is taken together with Rom 11:11, 13-14 and 15:15-16, 19, 23, it appears to involve a self-understanding on Paul's part as the gentiles' apostle who was, first, responsible to bring in 'the full number of the gentiles' but then also responsible to bring about the eventual salvation of Israel thereby" (Kim, Paul: 242). For Paul's dialectical redemptive argument, see 3:10-14 and 4:1f.

[35] For Paul's understanding of "justification," see 2:15-21.

[36] Cf. also Paul's association of "grace" with his calling to the Gentiles: ". . . because of the grace that was given me from God, to be a minister of the Messiah Jesus to the Gentiles (διὰ τὴν χάριν τὴν δοθεῖσάν μοι ὑπὸ τοῦ θεοῦ εἰς τὸ εἶναί με λειτουργὸν Χριστοῦ Ἰησοῦ εἰς τὰ ἔθνη)" (Rom. 15:15-16).

[37] For the motif of exile, see 1:1-5 (nn80, 90), 3:15-18 (n188), and 4:21-31.

a titular sense – in much the same way as "faith(fulness)" functions as a messianic designation in 3:23 (see 3:10-14, 21-25 and 4:21-31 [end]).[38]

Verse 5: Paul explains why the Galatians cannot seek to please both men *and* God (see verses 13-18 and above). In contrast to earlier chapters, the language here appears inclusive, the "we" covering in its scope all those who are influenced by the Spirit and participate in the Messiah's faithfulness (see 2:15-21, 3:10-14, and 4:1f).[39] Paul picks up here the themes which have sustained the epistle until this point: the gift of the Spirit and faithfulness (see especially 3:10-14 and 4:1-7).[40] These he now elaborates specifically in relation to the "hope of righteousness (ἐλπίδα δικαιοσύνης)."[41] While the precise phrase is unique, Paul elsewhere speaks abundantly of the "hope and resurrection of the dead (ἐλπίδος καὶ ἀναστάσεως νεκρῶν)"[42] (Acts 23:6) (cf. Le Cornu and Shulam: 1387f).

The well-known chasid (pious one) Pinchas b. Jair, in his "saint's progress," speaks of the role of the Holy Spirit in bringing about resurrection: "Heedfulness leads to cleanliness, and cleanliness leads to purity, and purity leads to abstinence, and abstinence leads to holiness, and holiness leads to humility, and humility leads to the shunning of sin, and the shunning of sin leads to saintliness, and saintliness leads to [the gift of] the Holy Spirit, and the Holy Spirit leads to the resurrection of the dead"[43] (Sot. 9:15)[44] (see also verses 19-23). This "hope of righteousness" is

---

[38] The parallel with 2:21 is often cited, and there too, combined with "righteousness," the "Messiah" stands for "the grace of God": "I do not nullify the grace of God; for if righteousness *comes* through the Torah, then the Messiah died needlessly" (see 2:15-21). As Paul makes clear in chapter 3, God's faithfulness to His people Israel is demonstrated in the sending of His son, whose own obedience to death enables them to receive their inheritance as "sons" – a status also bestowed upon the Gentiles (see 3:10-14 and 4:1f).

[39] The reference to "circumcision and uncircumcision" in verse 6 corroborates this claim. The "you" in the subsequent verses is simply a direct address, with no relevance to any distinction with "we/us." Standing at the head of the sentence, the "we (ὑμεῖς)" is emphatic. For Paul's pronominal usage, see 3:10-14 and 4:1f.

[40] Most strikingly, he returns to the expression ἐκ πίστεως (ek pisteōs – "of faithfulness") which informs his discussion of the Gentiles' status as sons of Abraham in chapter 3 (see 3:10-14). Given Paul's previous use of the phrase, it is reasonable to understand him as meaning here: "For we who are of faithfulness wait for the hope of righteousness through the Spirit" (see below). As Burton notes, "The contrast with the flesh which in 5:16, 18, 25 is expressed is probably latent here" (p. 278).

[41] For righteousness, see 3:10-14.

[42] Cf. Jer. 14:8, 17:13, [50:7]; Acts 23:6, 24:15, 26:6-8, 28:20; Eph. 1:18, 2:12.

[43] רבי פנחס בן יאיר אומר: זריזות מביאה לידי נקיות, ונקיות מביאה לידי טהרה, וטהרה מביאה לידי פרישות, ופרישות מביאה לידי קדֻשה, וקדֻשה מביאה לידי ענוה, וענוה מביאה לידי יראת חטא, ויראת חטא מביאה לידי חסידות, וחסידות מביאה לידי רוח הקדש. ורוח הקדש מביאה לידי תחית המתים.

the same promise of life of which Paul speaks in 3:11f, in his explication of Habakkuk 2:4 (see 3:10-14).[45] In this sense, the "hope of righteousness" may actually refer to Jesus through Hab. 2:4 (see 3:10-14). In the resurrection of the Righteous One himself, those who are faithful to his death find "new birth/creation" – the overcoming of fear, sin, and death (cf. 3:26-29, 6:15) (see 3:19ff and 4:1f).

Verse 6: In a consecutive explanation (cf. the γάρ [gar – "for"] here and in verse 5), Paul resumes his arguments from previous chapters.[46] Jesus' place at the head of the sentence marks the emphasis. When a person – Jew or Gentile – becomes faithful to God through Jesus, being found in his righteousness, all other distinctions lose their significance (cf. 3:28, 6:15).[47] The principle which informs the Kingdom of God is, with the Messiah's advent, not merely God's covenant with His people Israel but His faithfulness in His Messiah in whom the Torah's purpose is fulfilled (cf. Rom. 10:4).[48] Here, Paul comes back full circle to his opening argument, in

---

[44] Cf. Cant.R. 1.1.9; Yalk.Dt. 933; Yalk.Isa. 503; Mid.Prov. 15; JShek. 14b; JShab. 1, 3, 3c; AZ 20b.

[45] In this sense, Paul's allusion is more to the resurrection than to a "dialectical eschatology [which] continues to insist that *dikaiosynē* [righteousness] is a future state of affairs . . . insofar as 'rectification' refers to God's final establishment of justice, it remains a future hope" (Hays, Galatians: 313). At the same time, Hays correctly takes us back to the context of Hab. 2:4, suggesting that "the righteous will live in a posture of trustful expectation, waiting for God to bring the promised deliverance. That is precisely the stance Paul describes in v. 5" (ibid: 314) (see below). For the believer's "faithfulness," see 3:26-29.

[46] See most specifically 3:26-29.

[47] It is important to note, as we have remarked throughout, that this is not a general statement concerning circumcision, reducing it to an obsolete hindrance *per se*. Its "irrelevance" arises only in the context of "being in the Messiah" – in which state his obedience unto death calls forth the corresponding faithfulness of all wo/men. Just as male and female do not disappear, neither do Jew and Gentile (see 3:26-29). To the extent that Paul elsewhere associates this state with "keeping the commandments of God (τήρησις ἐντολῶν θεοῦ)" (1 Cor. 7:19), he here anticipates the argument of verses 14f, Jesus having stated: "If you love me, you will keep my commandments ('Εὰν ἀγαπᾶτέ με, τὰς ἐντολὰς τὰς ἐμὰς τηρήσετε)" (Jn. 14:15) (cf. Jn. 15:10, 14; 1 Jn. 2:3ff, 3:24) (cf. Burton: 281) (see also 3:19-20 and verses 24-26). For "circumcision/ uncircumcision," see 2:1-10 (excursus). 1 Cor. 7:19, on this reading, becomes the *locus classicus* of "intention" (faithfulness/love) *versus* social identity/standing (see Introduction, **Argument** and 2:15-21).

[48] For the significance of "faithfulness" (God's/Jesus'/the believer's), see 3:10-14, 26-29. As there, the "love" of which Paul speaks here can be understood first as God's concern for His creatures, out of which He sent His son so that they might not perish (cf. Jn. 3:16); subsequently as Jesus' own love (cf. 2:20); and finally as the love enjoined on those who are faithful to God through Jesus (cf. Jn. 15:9ff; 1 John).

respect of Peter (see 2:15-21).[49] Even within Israel, Torah-study (observance) without intention ("love") is inadequate: ". . . when a man is not loving in the give-and-take of his daily life – in his going about in the marketplace and in his dealing with men – even if he reads Scripture and recites Mishnah, people, seeing him say: 'Alas for So-and-so who has studied Torah! Blessed be my father who did not teach me Torah! So-and-so has studied Torah, yet see how evil are his deeds, how corrupt his ways!'"[50] (TBE p. 140) (see 2:15-21 and verses 13-18).

Torah-study – as one set of keys to the Kingdom – must be accompanied by the "fear of heaven" as the other set.[51] One without the other leaves a person locked outside the Kingdom of Heaven (see 2:15-21, 6:1-11, and verses 13f).[52] It is the enablement of this intention which God provides through Jesus' faithfulness – placing Jews and Gentiles, circumcised and uncircumcised, on equal footing in their access to the Kingdom (see 2:15-21, 3:26-29, 6:12-16, and verses 13f).[53] As Paul shortly elaborates, rather than seeking social status through Torah-observance and conversion, the Galatians should be seeking the intention/faithfulness which enables persons – Jews and Gentiles alike – to fulfil God's "weightiest" commandments: "justice and mercy and faithfulness" working through love (see verses 13-18).

---

[49] For Galatians as a "halakhic letter" along the lines of 4QMMT and for the centrality of Paul's rebuke of Peter, see Introduction, **Form; Argument**.

[50] בזמן שאין אדם יודע משאו ומתנו והוליכו בשוק ועסקו עם בני אדם וקורא ושונה, בני אדם שרואין אותו אומרים: אוי לו לפלוני שלמד תורה; אשרי אבא שלא לימדני תורה. פלוני, שלמד תורה, ראו כמה רעים מעשיו! כמה מקולקלין דרכיו!

[51] For this definition of hypocrisy, God's Kingdom being represented by two courts, the outer and inner, see Introduction, **Argument; Theological pointers** (Justification), and 2:15-21.

[52] While ἰσχύω (ischyō) is regularly translated "avail, have meaning," its basic meaning of strength connects this statement with Rom. 1:16: "For I am not ashamed of the gospel, for it is the *power of God* for salvation to everyone who believes . . . (Οὐ γὰρ ἐπαισχύνομαι τὸ εὐαγγέλιον, δύναμις γὰρ θεοῦ ἐστιν εἰς σωτηρίαν παντὶ τῷ πιστεύοντι . . .)."

[53] "The love of the Son of God is shown by his action of self-giving for our sake; this self-giving in turn is understood as the enactment of his faith. Thus Gal 2:20 provides a paradigmatic picture of 'faith working through love.' What does it look like? It looks like Jesus on the cross. That, Paul says, is the only thing that matters in the new creation. The church is called to embody this faith working through love in a way that corresponds to the story of the cross" (Hays, Galatians: 314). To the outworking of this love Paul devotes the final, paraenetical (exhortatory) section of the letter – as an expression of his request of Jesus' imitation from his disciples: "Therefore be imitators of God . . . and walk in love, just as the Messiah also loved you and gave himself up for us (Γίνεσθε οὖν μιμηταὶ τοῦ θεοῦ . . . καὶ περιπατεῖτε ἐν ἀγάπῃ, καθὼς καὶ ὁ Χριστὸς ἠγάπησεν ἡμᾶς)" (Eph. 5:1-2) (see 4:12-20 and 6:1-11). For "faithfulness" as based on Hab. 2:4, see 2:15-21 (nn267, 271), 3:10f, and 6:1-11 (n114).

Here, James complements and completes Paul's thought in his depiction of the "law of liberty": "So speak and so act, as those who are to be judged by *the* law of liberty. For judgment *will be* merciless to one who has shown no mercy; mercy triumphs over judgment. What use is it, my brethren, if someone says he has faith, but he has no works? Can that faith save him? If a brother or sister is without clothing and in need of daily food, and one of you says to them, 'Go in peace, be warmed and be filled,' and yet you do not give them what is necessary for *their* body, what use is that? Even so faith, if it has no works, is dead, *being* by itself. But someone may *well* say, 'You have faith and I have works; show me your faith without the works, and I will show you my faith by my works'"[54] (Jas. 2:12-18) (cf.) (see 6:1-11 and verses 13-18).[55]

A rabbinic midrash similarly equates intention with putting one's learning into practice, whence one is worthy of receiving the Holy Spirit: "He who learns with no intention of practising had been better unborn . . . R. Aha said: He who learns with the intention of practising will be privileged to receive the Holy Spirit. What is his reason? Because it says, *That thou mayest observe to do according to all that is written therein; for then thou shalt make thy ways prosperous, and then thou shalt have good wisdom –* taskil (Josh. 1:8), and 'taskil' cannot but allude to the Holy Spirit; as may be inferred from the text, *Maskil of Ethan the Ezrahite* (Ps. 89:1)"[56] (Lev.R. 35:7) (see 2:15-21 and verses 13f).[57] This is the import of James' statement

---

[54] Οὕτως λαλεῖτε καὶ οὕτως ποιεῖτε ὡς διὰ νόμου ἐλευθερίας μέλλοντες κρίνεσθαι. ἡ γὰρ κρίσις ἀνέλεος τῷ μὴ ποιήσαντι ἔλεος· κατακαυχᾶται ἔλεος κρίσεως. Τί τὸ ὄφελος, ἀδελφοί μου, ἐὰν πίστιν λέγῃ τις ἔχειν ἔργα δὲ μὴ ἔχῃ; μὴ δύναται ἡ πίστις σῶσαι αὐτόν; ἐὰν ἀδελφὸς ἢ ἀδελφὴ γυμνοὶ ὑπάρχωσιν καὶ λειπόμενοι τῆς ἐφημέρου τροφῆς εἴπῃ δέ τις αὐτοῖς ἐξ ὑμῶν· ὑπάγετε ἐν εἰρήνῃ, θερμαίνεσθε καὶ χορτάζεσθε, μὴ δῶτε δὲ αὐτοῖς τὰ ἐπιτήδεια τοῦ σώματος, τί τὸ ὄφελος; οὕτως καὶ ἡ πίστις, ἐὰν μὴ ἔχῃ ἔργα, νεκρά ἐστιν καθ' ἑαυτήν.

[55] Cf. [1 Thess. 1:3]; Jas. 1:22-27;1QS 10:11; PA 6:2. James is evidently addressing that well-known form of hypocrisy – the discrepancy between "hearing" and "doing" (see 2:15-21 and 3:1-5). For the motif of "benefit," see above. To the extent that "faithfulness" represents a messianic title (see 3:10-14, 21-25), Paul can be understood here as saying that it is God who works in human lives through (their participation in) Jesus' faithfulness (see also verses 13-18 ["fulfilment"]). Paul frequently employs the Greek ἐνεργέω (energeō) to describe the working of an external power – most strikingly the Holy Spirit – within human beings (cf. 1 Cor. 12:6, 11; Gal. 2:8, 3:5; Phil. 2:13; Col. 1:29; 1 Thess. 2:13) (cf. Hays, Galatians: 318).

[56] הלמד שלא לעשות, נוח לו שלא נברא . . . אמר ר' אחא: הלמד על מנת לעשות זוכה להקביל רוח הקדש. מה טעם? למען תשמור לעשות בכל הכתוב בו כי אז תצליח דרכיך ואז תשכיל – ואין "תשכילי" אלא רוח הקדש, כמה דאמר: משכיל לאיתן האזרחי.

[57] Cf. Mt. 7:12-27, 23:1ff; Rom. 2:12-29; Jas. 1:22-27, 2:14-26; Ps.Sol. 4:1ff; Gen.R. 34:14; Yalk.Gen. 61; Yalk.Num. 688; PA 1:17, 3:9, 17, 4:5, 5:14, 6:5; Tos.Yev. 8:4; JHag. 9a; Hag. 14b; Yev. 63b (cf. Shulam and Le Cornu: 77-124 for references) (see also verses 13-18 [n153]).

concerning Abraham's faithfulness – which was "perfected" in works: "Was not Abraham our father justified by works, when he offered up Isaac his son on the altar? You see that faithfulness was working with his works, and as a result of the works, faith was perfected"[58] (Jas. 2:21-22).[59]

Verse 7: Having identified the principle according to which the Galatians ought to be "living," Paul now turns his attention to those who are interfering with its proper exercise among them.[60] This verse reiterates the concern he expressed previously in 4:11, reminding his readers again of their responsibility as his disciples (see 4:8f and 6:1-11).[61] The theme of "running (ἐτρέχετε)" is associated in Jewish literature with following a pious life to gain the world to come. On leaving the house of study, people recite the following prayer: "I give thanks to Thee, O Lord my God, that Thou hast set my portion with those who sit in the Beth ha-Midrash and Thou hast not set my portion with those who sit in [street] corners, for I rise early and they rise early, but I rise early for words of Torah and they rise early for frivolous talk; I labour and they labour, but I labour and receive a reward and they labour and do not receive a reward; I run and they run, but I run to the life of the future world and they run to the pit of destruction"[62] (Ber. 28b).[63] In this sense the term is synonymous with "walking" – the mode of living in the Spirit which Paul sets out in verses 14ff.[64] It also carries connotations of properly interpreting Scripture (cf. Hab. 2:2; Rom. 9:16) (see 2:1-10).

Paul's notation concerning those who are "hindering [the Galatians] from obeying the truth (ἐνέκοψεν [τῇ] ἀληθείᾳ μὴ πείθεσθαι)" is one of

---

[58] 'Αβραὰμ ὁ πατὴρ ἡμῶν οὐκ ἐξ ἔργων ἐδικαιώθη ἀνενέγκας 'Ισαὰκ τὸν υἱὸν αὐτοῦ ἐπὶ τὸ θυσιαστήριον; βλέπεις ὅτι ἡ πίστις συνήργει τοῖς ἔργοις αὐτοῦ καὶ ἐκ τῶν ἔργων ἡ πίστις ἐτελειώθη.

[59] James thus echoes Paul's declaration of "faithfulness working through love" here, also playing on the themes of "fulfilment" and "perfection" (cf. verse 14). He then goes on to say that "just as the body without *the* spirit is dead, so also faith without works is dead (ὥσπερ γὰρ τὸ σῶμα χωρὶς πνεύματος νεκρόν ἐστιν, οὕτως καὶ ἡ πίστις χωρὶς ἔργων νεκρά ἐστιν)" (Jas. 2:26) – indicating, in pauline terms, that the Spirit is he who enables a person to exercise his/her faithfulness through love.

[60] For the singular, see below (verse 10).

[61] For the Graeco-Roman background, cf. TDNT 8:226-35.

[62] מודה אני לפניך ה' אלהי ששמת חלקי מיושבי בית המדרש ולא שמת חלקי מיושבי קרנות. שאני משכים והם משכימים. אני משכים לדברי תורה והם משכימים לדברים בטלים. אני עמל והם עמלים. אני עמל ומקבל שכר והם עמלים ואינם מקבלים שכר. אני רץ והם רצים. אני רץ לחיי העולם הבא והם רצים לבאר שחת.

[63] Cf. Rom. 9:16; PA 4:2; ARNᵃ 2:2; DEZ 2:1, 7. The καλῶς (kalōs – "well") further picks up the theme from 4:17-18, reminding Paul's readers yet again of their loyalty to him.

[64] "Walking" ("progression") is the *technicus terminus* for the regulation of הלכה (halakhah – Jewish law) (cf. 1QS 1:8, 13f, 3:9f, 18, 4:6f, 8:13; 1QM 7:18; PA 2:1, 9) (cf. Strack: 6f; Safrai, Literature: 121ff; Berkovits) (see verses 13f).

the letter's rare "direct" allusions to the "influencers" (see Introduction, **Occasion and circumstances**). While little enough about their identity can be ascertained from the reference, the circumstances indicate a group of people intervening between Paul and his disciples and seeking to draw the latter away (see 4:12f).[65] Signally, Paul relates here not to his authority but to the Galatians' obedience to "[the] truth" – specifically, to the gospel (cf. Rom. 2:8; Gal. 2:5, 14).[66] The language of truth and obedience is reminiscent of the Qumran literature, much of which is characterised by conflict and friction between the three main "schools" of Second Temple Jewish life in Eretz Israel.[67] 4QMMT particularly addresses a situation in which a specific group have isolated themselves from the majority, whom they regard as opponents. The letter is addressed to a third group, with whom the community associated with 4QMMT is in some affinity, and functions as an appeal for this group to sever themselves from the perverted mainstream community (cf. 11QMelch 2:24).[68]

In the context of "running," the verb ἐγκόπτω (engkoptō), which ordinarily signifies some sort of hindrance or thwarting, may perhaps carry the connotation of being "cut in on" – an act which impedes the runner's progress (cf. Longenecker, Galatians: 230).[69] If it is established that this verb parallels κωλύω (kōlyō – "to prevent"), Paul's thought further recalls the hindrance placed in the way of people entering the Kingdom of God, however.[70]

---

[65] For other character passages, see 1:6-10, 4:12-20, 6:12-16, and below. The variants which read 7b as a paronomatic maxim – "Obey no one in such a way as to disobey the truth (τῇ ἀληθείᾳ πείσεσθαι μηδενὶ πείσεσθε)" – recall the rabbinic dictum governing an agent: "[When] the words of the master and the words of the pupil [are in conflict], whose are obeyed? דברי הרב ודברי תלמיד - דברי מי שומעים?" (Kid. 42b) (see 1:1-5 and 2:15-21).

[66] The anarthrous use of "truth" may possibly suggest an adjectival force – "truthfully." For "Paul's gospel," see 1:6-10.

[67] Cf. 1QS 1:5, 11, 2:26, 5:3f, 7:18, 1QM 13:12f; 1QHᵃ 6:15, 13:9, 15:20.

[68] Cf. Flusser, Pharisees; Kampen and Bernstein: 67ff (see Introduction, **Form** and 2:15-21). The proximity of the phrase to the "truth of the gospel" in 2:5, 14 further returns us in this section to Paul's reproof of Peter (see 2:15-21). For the current reading of Galatians as a halakhic "rebuke-request" letter along the lines of 4QMMT, see Introduction, **Form**; **Argument** and above.

[69] The nuance of "cutting ([ἐγ]κόπτω)" may be connected – here – to the subsequent "cutting off" of flesh (cf. verse 12), Hippocrates employing the verb to signify the making of an incision (cf. Hays, Galatians: 314-15; Burton: 282) (see above [n27]).

[70] Cf. Mt. 19:14; Mk. 10:14; Lk. 11:52. The latter passage is the lukan parallel of Mt. 23:13, which idea seems to underlie Paul's argument to Peter with respect to justification: "Woe to you lawyers! For you have taken away the key of knowledge; you did not enter in yourselves, and those who were entering in you hindered (Οὐαὶ ὑμῖν τοῖς νομικοῖς, ὅτι ἤρατε τὴν κλεῖδα τῆς γνώσεως· αὐτοὶ οὐκ εἰσήλθατε καὶ τοὺς εἰσερχομένους ἐκωλύσατε)" (see 2:15-21). The

Verse 8: This obstruction is a "persuasion (ἡ πεισμονή)," Paul playing on the Greek πείθω (peithō – "to obey"), the noun homophonically recalling the verb.[71] Presumably somewhat ironically, Paul suggests here that the Galatians' obedience has turned into dissuasion from the gospel.[72] Their loyalty, in other words, is not to God who called them but to those who are turning them away from their calling (see 1:6-10).[73]

Verse 9 – a proverbial statement (cf. 1 Cor. 5:6) – serves Paul as a cautionary warning to his disciples: It takes but little to influence the whole community.[74] Leaven (ζύμη; zymē) traditionally signified a corrupting power in the ancient world: "R. Alexandri on concluding his prayer used to add the following: Sovereign of the Universe, it is known full well to Thee that our will is to perform Thy will, and what prevents us? The yeast in the dough and the subjection to the foreign Powers. May it be Thy will to deliver us from their hand, so that we may return to perform the statutes of Thy will with a perfect heart!"[75] (Ber. 17a).[76] Jesus employs the same metaphor to describe the Pharisees' hypocrisy.[77] Hypocrisy represents a major theme in Galatians, Paul being at pains to demonstrate to his gentile

---

correspondence is further suggested in the parallelism between Rom. 1:13 and 15:22, the former employing κωλύω (kōlyō), the latter ἐγκόπτω (engkoptō). We have already suggested that the present section resumes the argument from 2:15-21 (see above [n68]).

[71] The noun – not only a NT hapax but also appearing in Greek literature here for the first time – appears to derive from πεῖσμα (peisma), a ship's cable, although when associated with πείθω it signifies "persuasion, confidence" (cf. Liddell and Scott: 1355-56). The restrictive article identifies "**this** persuasion" with the hindrance just spoken of. Paul picks up the same root in verse 10, speaking of his own "confidence." The Talmud says of persuasion: "Persuasion [in Scripture] never means with words [but only by actions] אין הסתה בדברים" (Hul. 4b).

[72] For Galatians' ironic structure, see 1:6-10.

[73] This passage demonstrates close affinities with 1:6-9, constituting as it does the second (third) section in which Paul comes closest to revealing the influencers' identity (see Introduction, **Occasion and circumstances** and above).

[74] In this sense, verse 9 represents a direct continuation of 4:30 (see 4:21-31). Paul's reiterated warnings to his disciples (cf. verse 26, 6:3-5) not to entertain the influencers and their views serves as the complement to his "request" that his disciples renew their loyalty to his person – by refusing to be persuaded into following "another gospel" (see Introduction, **Argument**, 4:112f, 6:1-11, and verses 24-26).

[75] ר' אלכסנדרי בתר דמצלי אמר הכי: רבון העולמים, גלוי וידוע לפניך שרצוננו לעשות רצונך, ומי מעכב? שאור שבעיסה ושעבוד מלכויות. יהי רצון מלפניך שתצילנו מידם ונשוב לעשות חוקי רצונך בלבב שלם.

[76] Cf. 1 Cor. 5:6f; Philo, *Spec.Leg.* 1.293, 2.183; Tanh.B.Noach 4; Gen.R. 34:10; JBer. 4, 2, 7d; 1 Clem. 5:6; Ignat.*Mag.* 10.2; Just.*Dial.* 14.2.3; Ps.-Clem.*Hom.* 8:17; Plut.*Quaest.Rom.* 109 [2.289F]. For the (unlikely) possibility that the influencers were Pharisees, see 2:15-21 (n269).

[77] Cf. Mt. 16:6, 11f; Mk. 8:15; Lk. 12:1. For leaven as an image of the Kingdom itself, cf. Mt. 13:33; Lk. 13:21; Gos.Thom. 96.

Galatian disciples that both Jews and Gentiles acquire the keys to God's Kingdom through their participation in Jesus' faithfulness (see Introduction, **Argument** and 2:15-21 [6:1-11]).

Paul utters this statement as a warning to the Galatians against allowing the godfearers' influence to take root within the community and so draw them away from the gospel.[78] This is a more subtle reiteration of his prior direct command, the latter albeit dressed in scriptural language, in 4:30: "Cast out the bondwoman and her son" (see 4:21-31). Paul employs the same sentiment in enjoining the Corinthians to avoid all association with immoral people (cf. 1 Cor. 5:6f) – with precisely the same view in mind: "Remove the wicked [man] from among yourselves (ἐξάρετε τὸν πονηρὸν ἐξ ὑμῶν αὐτῶν)" (1 Cor. 5:13 [Dt. 17:7]) (see 6:1-11 and below). The "other view (ἄλλο φρονήσετε)" against which Paul cautions his disciples is anything which has not Jesus as its goal (cf. 1:6-8). As Paul writes, in a similar context, to the Philippians: "I press on toward the goal for the prize of the upward call of God in the Messiah Jesus. Let us therefore, as many as are perfect [mature], **have this attitude** [think this way]; and if in anything you have a **different attitude,** God will reveal that also to you"[79] (Phil. 3:14-15).[80]

Verse 10: While in 1:6-8 Paul has scolded his disciples for "so quickly deserting Him who called you" for "another gospel," and expressed his apprehension in 4:11 lest he has consequently laboured over them in vain, he now demonstrates a "confidence in the Lord (ἐγὼ πέποιθα εἰς ὑμᾶς ἐν κυρίῳ)" (cf. 2 Cor. 3:4; 2 Thess. 3:4) (see 1:6-10 and 4:12-20). Precisely what grounds undergird Paul's optimism remain unclear, although the verbal association with πείθω (peithō – "to obey, be confident") may indicate rather more "wishful thinking" than assurance.[81] It is, in any case, his trust

[78] 2 Pet. 2:18-19 provides a striking parallel to Paul's dictum here: "For speaking out arrogant *words* of vanity they entice by fleshly desires, by sensuality, those who barely escape from the ones who live in error, promising them freedom while they themselves are slaves of corruption; for by what a man is overcome, by this is he enslaved (ὑπέρογκα γὰρ ματαιότητος φθεγγόμενοι δελεάζουσιν ἐν ἐπιθυμίαις σαρκὸς ἀσελγείαις τοὺς ὀλίγως ἀποφεύγοντας τοὺς ἐν πλάνῃ ἀναστρεφομένους, ἐλευθερίαν αὐτοῖς ἐπαγγελλόμενοι, αὐτοὶ δοῦλοι ὑπάρχοντες τῆς φθορᾶς· ᾧ γάρ τις ἥττηται, τούτῳ δεδούλωται)" (see verses 19f).
[79] κατὰ σκοπὸν διώκω εἰς τὸ βραβεῖον τῆς ἄνω κλήσεως τοῦ θεοῦ ἐν Χριστῷ Ἰησοῦ. Ὅσοι οὖν τέλειοι, τοῦτο *φρονῶμεν* καὶ εἴ τι ἑτέρως *φρονεῖτε,* καὶ τοῦτο ὁ θεὸς ὑμῖν ἀποκαλύψει.
[80] Cf. "For those who are according to the flesh **set their minds on** the things of the flesh, but those who are according to the Spirit, the things of the Spirit (οἱ γὰρ κατὰ σάρκα ὄντες τὰ τῆς σαρκὸς *φρονοῦσιν,* οἱ δὲ κατὰ πνεῦμα τὰ τοῦ πνεύματος)" (Rom. 8:5). For love as "perfection," see verses 19-23 (end).
[81] The verbal play sets the influencers' persuasion against Paul's confidence "in the Lord" – the latter lending the greater weight and force to Paul's side. The perfect πέποιθα (pepoitha) reflects Paul's pre-existent attitude towards his disciples, its

in God (ἐν κυρίῳ; en kyriō) which supports his conviction that, in the end, his disciples will remain loyal to him and to the gospel.[82]

The admonitory aspect of these verses becomes obvious when Paul openly threatens the people who are "disturbing (ὁ δὲ ταράσσων)" his disciples.[83] The verbal link with 1:7 – "there are some who are disturbing you (οἱ ταράσσοντες ὑμᾶς)" – identifies this figure, here alluded to in the singular, with the original group of antagonists (see 1:6-10 and 6:1-11).[84] In light of the plural not only in 1:7 but also following, in verse 12, Paul appears at this point to be specifying a particular person.[85] Precisely who this figure might be is virtually impossible to ascertain, more than that he appears to have possessed a position of some importance.[86] While the reference may be taken as a collective/generic singular, the modifier, "whoever he is (ὅστις ἐὰν ᾖ)" both further strengthens the singular and suggests a person of authority (see also 6:1-11).[87]

present significance signalling his current anticipation. The emphatic ἐγὼ (egō – "I") likewise signals the personal, subjective character of his confidence (cf. Longenecker, Galatians: 231).

[82] Cf. 2 Cor. 2:3, 7:4,16, 8:22, 10:2; Phlm 21. Given the ironic nature of much of the letter, it is even possible that the "confidence" masks a veiled threat – of God's visitation on the Galatians as it will come upon the influencers, if the former prove unwilling to "obey the truth" (see also 6:17). For Paul's request of the "spiritual" in the communities to restore those who have been persuaded, see 6:1-11.

[83] It is precisely the reproach which provides this passage with a structural composition whose alleged lack has otherwise caused commentators to remark on its "abruptness of expression and sudden changes of thought" (Burton: 284). While Paul's language is indeed concise, the thought is not disarranged.

[84] For a full discussion of the Galatian situation, see Introduction, Occasion and circumstances.

[85] Several explanations are offered in explication of the singular: a) Paul may be thinking – along the lines of 4QMMT – of the group's leader; b) There may be a particular person at work in each of the Galatian communities (cf. 1:2) (cf. Hays, Galatians: 316). In fact, Paul has already spoken in the singular in 3:1 – "who has bewitched you (τίς ὑμᾶς ἐβάσκανεν)" and in verse 7 – "who hindered you (τίς ὑμᾶς ἐνέκοψεν)." Even if Paul picks out a specific individual, he evidently expects the punishment to fall on all those responsible (cf. verse 12) (see below).

[86] Here again 4QMMT may serve as an example, the "main, halakhic, part of the text [B] being addressed to a group denoted by the second person plural" while the final section (C) is directed to "a ruler of the Jewish people" who is "reminded of examples from Israel's biblical past and exhorted to heed the Law properly" (Kampen and Bernstein: 77-78). For 4QMMT and Galatians, see Introduction, Form.

[87] Betz suggests that "Parallels from other Pauline letters make it probable that Paul is thinking of Satan [cf. Rom. 15:22; 1 Cor. 9:12; 1 Thess. 2:18]" (Galatians: 264, 267). The more compelling context would appear to be that of hypocrisy (see above). Although no compelling reason exists to assume that had Paul had a particular person in mind he would have shrunk from identifying him, being willing to name names elsewhere (cf. Hays, Galatians: 316), it is indeed striking that Paul nowhere directly addresses the influencers. This contrast with other believers, whose actions

Despite his status, and perhaps also the recognition which the Galatians might wish to naturally accord him, this person will not escape God's justice. Paul's language may in fact be influenced here by the story of Achar/Achan in Joshua 7 (cf. 1 Chron. 2:7) (see 1:6-10). Not only Achan himself – the actual "troubler" – but his entire family with him were killed in reprisal for his individual act: "And Joshua said: 'Why have you troubled us? The LORD will trouble you this day.' And all Israel stoned them [him] with stones; and they burned them with fire after they had stoned them with stones"[88] (Josh. 7:25).[89] Paul may be attributing similar circumstances to the "representative" disturber – who may further receive the consequences ascribed to other "troublers": "The merciful man does himself good [lit.: good to his own soul], but the cruel man does himself harm [lit.: troubles his flesh] . . . He who troubles his own house will inherit wind, and the foolish will be servant to the wisehearted"[90] (Prov. 11:17, 29).[91]

Verse 11: Paul now brings himself as a counter-example, the "But I ('Εγὼ δέ)" standing emphatically at the head of the sentence.[92] If the ἄρα (ara – "then") is consequential, explaining the first two clauses of the verse, Paul appears to be claiming that if the influencers' persuasion is successful, Jesus' crucifixion as "to Jews a stumbling block ('Ιουδαίοις μὲν

---

he does denounce, has been appealed to in support of the thesis that the influencers were not in fact believers (see Introduction, **Occasion and circumstances**). (Whether or not Paul was personally acquainted with the influencers is also a virtually unanswerable question [cf. Nanos, Irony: 174-78].) For Paul's reproof of Peter, see 2:14f; for Paul's disregard of the pillars' status, see 2:1-10.

[88] ויאמר יהושע מה עכרתנו יעכרך ה' ביום הזה וירגמו אֹתו כל-ישראל אבן וישרפו אֹתם באש ויסקלו אֹתם באבנים.

[89] Achan was of the household of Zavdi, of the family of Zerach, and a representative of the tribe of Judah (cf. Josh. 7:16-18) (cf. Ex.R. 48:2; San. 44a-b. In this respect, the modifier "whoever he may be" may be inclusive – covering all those involved rather than simply the "leader," as reflected in the singular/plural Hebrew usage. For the biblical command to place anything associated with a false prophet under a ban, see 1:6-9 [nn125, 132]); for the grammatical switch between plural and singular, see 6:1-11.

[90] גמל נפשו איש חסד ועכר שארו אכזרי . . . עכר ביתו ינחל-רוח ועבד אויל לחכם-לב.

[91] Cf. Prov. 15:6. "Troubling the flesh" is certainly what Paul has in mind in verse 12 (see below). For the present identification of the influencers as godfearers insisting that the gentile Galatian believers cannot find Jewish identity through Jesus, see Introduction, **Occasion and circumstances**; for Paul's warning to the influencers in 6:3-5, see 6:1-11; for Prov. 11:30, see 4:12-20 and 61-:11; for "merciless," see Jas. 2:13 (above).

[92] "I," Paul in effect says, "am no 'troubler'." The appeal to his "brothers (ἀδελφοί)" reminds them, once again, of their loyalty as his disciples (see 1:1-5 and 4:12-20). The fact that Paul returns to the influencers' visitation in verse 12 confirms the reading of verse 11 as relating to the consequences of Paul's conduct.

σκάνδαλον)" (1 Cor. 1:23) will have been annulled (in their case).[93] To the extent that the "preaching of the Messiah crucified (κηρύσσομεν Χριστὸν ἐσταυρωμένον)" (1 Cor. 1:23) challenges Jewish sensibilities, it must remain in place. To remove it is tantamount to denying that, as God's Messiah, Jesus "became . . . the power of God and the wisdom of God . . . and righteousness and sanctification, and redemption"[94] (1 Cor. 1:24, 30).[95] Those without these "keys to the Kingdom," in substituting circumcision for Jesus' faithfulness, are those "severed (κατηργήθητε)" from the Messiah (cf. verse 4) (see above).[96]

If Paul himself were advocating conversion to his Galatian disciples, he himself would be annulling Jesus' atonement on the cross.[97] Even less, under such circumstances, would he have grounds for insisting that the

---

[93] To the Gentiles, it constitutes "foolishness (μωρίαν)" (1 Cor. 1:23) (cf. 1 Cor. 1:18, 21, 25, 2:14). The Greek σκάνδαλον (skandalon) originally denotes a trap or snare (cf. LXX Josh. 23:13; Ps. 68:23, 140:9; Isa. 8:14 [Symm./Theod.]; Rom. 11:9; 1 Macc. 5:4). It was thence extended to signify the cause of offense, revulsion, or opposition (cf. Sir. 7:6, 27:23; Jud. 5:20). For καταργέω (katargeō), see below.

[94] αὐτοῖς δὲ τοῖς κλητοῖς . . . Χριστὸν θεοῦ δύναμιν καὶ θεοῦ σοφίαν . . . δικαιοσύνη τε καὶ ἁγιασμὸς καὶ ἀπολύτρωσις.

[95] Cf. Lev. 19:14; Isa. 8:14, 28:16; Lk. 2:34; Rom. 1:16, 9:33; 1 Cor. 1:18; 2 Cor. 13:4; 1 Pet. 2:8; Yoma 77b (see 3:1-5). The original reference, in Lev. 19:14, carries overtones of hypocrisy in its assumption that a person considers it permissible to curse the person who cannot hear him do so, or to deliberately cause someone to fall by putting in their path that which they cannot perceive. In this sense, it is said: "One should expose hypocrites to prevent the profanation of the Name [i.e., so that people should not imitate their conduct], as it is said: *Again, when a righteous man doth turn from righteousness, and commit iniquity, I will lay a stumbling-block before him* מפרסמין את החנפין מפני חילול השם, שנאמר : ובשוב צדיק מצדקו ועשה עול ונתתי (Ezek. 3:20) מכשול לפניו" (Yoma 86b). For hypocrisy as a dominant theme in Galatians, see Introduction, **Argument**, 2:15-21, verses 13-18, and above (nn18, 51, 55).

[96] Paul favours the use of καταργέω (katargeō) (cf. 3:17; verse 4) (see 3:15-18 and above). (Out of a total of 27 occurrences, only two are in fact non-pauline [including Ephesians].) Although "severed" carries no nuance of "cut off" in the Greek, Paul may be playing on the verb's association with annulment of the covenant (see 3:15-18). For the play on cutting, see above/below; for the keys to the Kingdom – "justice and mercy and faithfulness" – see Introduction, **Argument**; **Theological pointers**, 2:15-21, and above.

[97] The "preaching of circumcision (περιτομὴν ἔτι κηρύσσω)" appears to be pauline coinage, standing against the "preaching of the crucifixion (κηρύσσομεν Χριστὸν ἐσταυρωμένον)" in 1 Cor. 1:23. In this sense, it represents one of Paul's designations of the influencers. The standard inference regards Paul's claim to be that he has ceased to promote conversion for gentile believers – and is consequently not deserving of harassment. He could understand such treatment if he were so preaching – but he is no longer doing so. The persecution therefore constitutes proof that he has discarded his proselytising perspective. (For Paul's personal example, see 1:1-5, 15-16b, 24-26, 2:1-10 [n136], 15-21 [n292], 3:1-5 [nn14, 28], 4:12-20, 6:1f [verses 11, 15, 17], and verses 24-26.)

Galatians interpret the influencers' message as "a gospel contrary to that which we have preached to you" - or for invoking upon them a curse (cf. 1:6-9). On this reading, the first conditional clause - "if I still preach circumcision" - refers to a hypothetical circumstance: If Paul was proselytizing, he would not be opposing the influencers. 'Evidently, I do not preach circumcision.'

This requires a different understanding of the apodosis, "why am I still persecuted? (τί ἔτι διώκομαι;)," than is customarily adopted.[98] While Paul is evidently the subject of the action, the verb being passive, its more proper meaning here may be "driven out" (cf. BAGD: 201). Paul is saying to his gentile disciples in Galatia: 'You are opening yourselves to the influence of people desirous of giving you social status. If I am preaching the same message as theirs, why are you **driving me away**? Do you not understand that in pledging your allegiance to those who "preach circumcision," you and they alike are directly dismissing and deprecating "the Messiah crucified"?'[99]

---

[98] It should be obvious that the present authors do not concur with the more traditional interpretation of these verses: "It seems that in coming to an end of his treatment of the judaizing threat he [Paul] feels it necessary to add something further - something evidently occasioned by a false claim made by his opponents - that Paul evidently did believe in circumcision and preached it elsewhere in his missionary activity and/or earlier in his ministry activity and/or early in his ministry, though withheld from the Galatians in order to win their approval (cf. 1:10) . . . The inferential particle ἄρα ("so," "then," "therefore") may here conclude 5:1-11 (so, e.g., Betz, *Galatians*, 269) or be the reason for what is stated in 5:11a (so, e.g., Mussner, *Galaterbrief*, 360). But in that it is used elsewhere in Galatians to conclude entire sections (cf. 2:21; 3:29; 6:10), it should probably also be seen as signalling Paul's conclusion to his entire discussion of the 'judaizing threat' in 1:6-5:11, paralleling ἄρα in 6:10, which concludes his treatment of 'libertine tendencies' in 5:13-6:10 - with v 12 then thrown in as an additional sarcastic comment" (Longenecker, Galatians: 323-33) (see Introduction, **Argument**, 6:1-11, and verses 13-18).

[99] Cf. "For I have been rejected by them, and they do not esteem me when you made yourself great through me; for they drive me from my land like a bird from its nest; all my friends and my acquaintances have been driven away from me, and rank me like a broken jug כי נמאס(ת)י למו ולא יחשבוני בהגבירכה בי כיˣ ידיחני מארצי כצפור מקנה וכול רעי ומועדי נדחו ממני ויחשבוני לכלי אובד" (1QHᵃ 12:8-9) (see 2:1-10 [n20]). The problem of the double ἔτι (eti - "still") in verse 11 has long been recognised. While the present reading radically differs from traditional explanations, the latter frequently assign a "logical" status to the second adverb (cf. Burton: 286-87). On the present reading, the first calls for such a logical connotation while the second carries the force of a question regarding the future: What further need is there of driving me away? (the Greek διώκω [diōkō] carrying the sense both of "persecuting" and "driving out") (cf. Mt. 26:65; Mk. 5:35b, 14:63; Lk. 22:71; Rom. 6:2) (cf. BAGD: 201, 315-16).

Verse 12 returns yet again to a denunciation of the influencers (see 1:6-10, 4:21-31, and above). "Those troubling you (οἱ ἀναστατοῦντες ὑμᾶς)" parallel "some who are disturbing you" in 1:7 – whose representative Paul appears to designate in verse 10 (see above).[100] The ὄφελον (ofelon – "would that") picks up the ὠφελήσει (ōfelēsei – "benefit") in verse 2 and the ὀφειλέτης (ofeiletēs – "under obligation") in verse 3 (see above).[101] Paul adopts the typical Jewish precept of מדה כנגד מדה (meida ke-neged meida – "measure for measure") in invoking punishment on the influencers:

> *That the Waters May Come Back upon the Egyptians, upon Their Chariots and upon Their Horsemen* (Ex. 14:26). Let the wheel [of fortune] turn against them and bring back upon them their own violence. For with the same device with which they planned to destroy Israel I am going to punish them. They planned to destroy My children by water, so I will likewise punish them only by water. For it is said: "He hath digged a pit, and hollowed it, and is fallen into the ditch which he made" (Ps. 7:15). "He that diggeth a pit shall fall into it; and whoso breaketh through a fence, a serpent shall bite him. Whoso quarrieth stones shall be hurt therewith; and he that cleaveth wood is endangered thereby" (Eccl. 10:8-9). And it also says: "His mischief shall return upon his own head" (Ps. 7:16).[102] (Mekh.Be-shall. 7)[103]

Here, Paul desires that the "troubling (ἀναστατοῦντες)" of the influencers' demand that the gentile Galatian believers be circumcised if they wish to be recognised as part of the Jewish community return upon their "members" in the same fashion as they are seeking to impose on the Galatians' "parts."[104] Early Greek commentators consistently translated the

---

[100] Cf. the rabbinic dictum: "Whoever causes the many to sin, they do not afford him the faculty to repent . . . Jeroboam, the son of Nebat, sinned and caused others to sin, [therefore] the sin of the many was [considered] dependent on him . . . כל המחטיא את הרבים אין מספיקין בידו לעשות תשובה . . . ירבעם חטא והחטיא את הרבים, חטא חטאו הרבים תלוי בו" (PA 5:18) (cf. [Mt. 5:19]; Sem. 8:13; Yoma 87a).

[101] The form probably arose as the first person singular second aorist of ὀφείλω (ofeilō – "to owe"), subsequently turning into a *technicus terminus* for a wish – unattainable with an imperfect or aorist indicative and potentially attainable with a future indicative verb (cf. Longenecker, Galatians: 234).

[102] וישובו המים על מצרים על רכבו ועל פרשיו. יחזור עליהם הגלגל ויחזיר עליהם זדונם. שבמחשבה שחשבו מצרים לאבד את ישראל בה אני דן. הם חשבו לאבד את בני במים, אף אני לא נפרע מהם אלא במים, שנאמר: בור כרה ויחפרהו ויפול בשחת יפעל: חופר גומץ בו יפול ופורץ גדר ישכנו נחש מסיע אבנים יעצב בהם ובוקע עצים יסכן בם. ואומר: ישוב עמלו בראשו וגי'.

[103] Cf. Judg. 1:7; Obad. 15; Wis.Sol. 11:15-16, 12:23; Test.Gad 5:10. See also verses 13-18 (n127).

[104] Cf. Phil. 3:2f, where – in parallel to περιτομή (peritomē – "circumcision") in verse 3, Paul expresses the idea of "false circumcision" by the derogatory term κατατομή (katatomē – "mutilation"). For "troubling one's flesh," see above (n91) (see also 6:1-11). It seems unlikely that any inference may be drawn from this

verb ἀποκόπτω (apokoptō) in terms of "self-mutilation" (cf. Longenecker, Galatians: 234).[105] Josephus, who designates self-mutilators as γάλλοι (galloi) after the Gallic-Phrygian Cybelian priests who castrated themselves, cautions against keeping company with such people "who have deprived themselves of their virility and of those fruits of generation, which God has given to men for the increase of our race" – and, in a fashion similar to Paul's exhortation here (cf. 4:22-31), urges society to "expel them even as infanticides who withal have destroyed the means of procreation"[106] (*Ant.* 4.290-91).[107]

---

comment regarding the issue of whether or not the influencers were themselves circumcised (i.e., were born-Jews or proselytes) (see Introduction, **Occasion and circumstances** and 6:12-16). Although it is possible that Paul may imply that the knife might slip slightly further than intended, turning circumcision into castration, castration is a sufficiently independent "punishment" to serve as its own reason.

[105] Paul is evidently playing here on the root of κόπτω (koptō – "to cut"), having used ἐγκόπτω (engkoptō) in verse 7 (see above). While circumcision removes the foreskin of the male member, castration removes the testicles, effectively emasculating the male. Although the custom was well known in ancient Egypt, Ethiopia, Media and Persia, and Babylon, the biblical injunction clearly prohibits such "mutilation": "No one who is emasculated, or has his male member cut off, shall enter the assembly of the LORD . . . anything *with its testicles* bruised or crushed or torn or cut, you shall not offer to the LORD, or sacrifice in your land, nor shall you accept any such from the hand of a foreigner for offering as the food of your God; for their corruption is in them, they have a defect, they shall not be accepted for you לא-יבא פצוע-דכא וכרות שפכה בקהל ה' . . . ומעוך וכתות ונתוק וכרות לא תקריבו לה' ובארצכם לא תעשו: ומיד בן-נכר לא תקריבו את-לחם אלהיכם מכל-אלה כי משחתם בהם מום בם לא ירצו לכם" (Dt. 23:1; Lev. 22:24-25) (cf. LXX Dt. 25:12). Tannaitic literature interprets the prohibition in a very general sense: "Anyone who castrates a human being or a domesticated or wild animal or bird, whether large of small, male or female, is punishable המסית את האדם ואת הבהמה ואת החיה ואת העופות בין גדולים בין קטנים בין זכרים ביו נקבות עובר בלא תעשה" (Tos.Mak. 5:6) (cf. Shab. 110b-111a; San. 56b) (cf. Preuss: 222-24).

[106] Γάλλους ἐκτρέπεσθαι καὶ σύνοδον φεύγειν τὴν μετ' αὐτῶν ἀφελομένων αὐτοὺς τὸ ἄρρεν καὶ τὸν τῆς παιδοποιίας καρπόν, ὃν ἀνθρώποις ἐπ' αὐξήσει τοῦ γένους ὑμῖν ὁ θεὸς παρέσχεν, ἐλαύνειν δὲ οὕτως ὡς ἐπὶ τέκνων σφθαγῆ καὶ πρὸς τούτῳ ἀπολλύντας τὸ ἐκείνων αἴτιον.

[107] Josephus' instruction also reflects the banishment of eunuchs from the community, in the sense of being "cut off [כרת]" from the midst of the people (see above). Attribution of this latter meaning to Paul's statement reflects the interpretation followed by many of the early Latin commentators, who understood the injunction in terms of withdrawal from the congregations or self-imposed excommunication (cf. Longenecker, Galatians: 234); for karet ("excommunication"), cf. Le Cornu and Shulam: 265f. The context of procreation invoked by eunuchs evidently forms part of the background to Paul's following discussion of the "fruit of the Spirit," the latter being the "offspring" of a life lived before God in the performance of His will (see 4:21-31 [n263] and verses 19-23). Whatever its actual

Verses 13-18:

For you were called to freedom, brethren; only *do* not *turn* your freedom into an opportunity for the flesh, but through love serve one another. For the whole Law is fulfilled in one word, in the *statement,* "YOU SHALL LOVE YOUR NEIGHBOR AS YOURSELF." But if you bite and devour one another, take care lest you be consumed by one another. But I say, walk by the Spirit, and you will not carry out the desire of the flesh. For the flesh sets its desire against the Spirit, and the Spirit against the flesh; for these are in opposition to one another, so that you may not do the things that you please. But if you are led by the Spirit, you are not under the Law.

This verse – together with the following section – has led many commentators to categorise Paul's Galatians offensive as two-pronged.[108] While in verses 1(2)-6 he attacks the Galatians' tendency towards Torah-observance, he here polemicises against libertine licenses (cf. Betz, Galatians: 258).[109] Despite the scholarly view which considers verse 13 as the opening of Paul's paraenetical conclusion, however, no compelling reason exists to separate it from verse 12.[110] Continuing the thought

---

significance, the remark represents a vicious invocation – on a par with the invective employed in the Psalms (cf. Ps. 137:8-9) (cf. Hays, Galatians: 319).

[108] Burton's remarks exemplify this approach: "On this word [monon – 'only'], as on a hinge, the thought of the epistle turns from freedom to a sharply contrasted aspect of the matter, the danger of abusing freedom. So far he [Paul] has strenuously defended the view that the Gentile is not under obligation to keep the statutes of the law . . . To men who have been accustomed to think of law as the only obstacle to free self-indulgence, or to those who, on the other hand, have not been accustomed to high ethical standards, such language is (despite the contrary teaching of vv. 5, 6) easily taken to mean that for the Christian there is nothing to stand in the way of the unrestrained indulgence of his own impulses. Of this danger Paul is well aware (cf. Rom. 6:1ff; Phil. 3:17ff; Col. 3:1ff), and beginning with this v. addresses himself vigorously to meeting and averting it" (pp. 291-92). Structurally, verse 13 parallels 3:2: "This is the only thing I want to find out from you: did you receive the Spirit by the works of the Torah, or by the hearing of the gospel" (see 3:1-5).

[109] The identification of libertinism works in a directly dichotomous direction to the body of the letter, in which, framed in traditional terms, Paul has been opposing the Galatians' tendency towards putting themselves "under the Law" – *enlarging their observance of, rather than shunning, the Torah and commandments* – by means of undergoing circumcision. In attempting to reconcile these two conflicting phenomena, two major exegetical proposals have arisen within Christian commentary on Galatians. On the one hand, Ropes, followed by Lütgert, has suggested a two-fold opposition to Paul, one party composed of a gentile judaizing group, the other of "pneumatics" who, in reaction to the first party, exaggerated the idea of freedom. In response, Schmithals has argued for a unified opposition, whose members he characterises as "Jewish Christian gnostics" – who, though being Jewish, interested themselves exclusively in the "magical" ritual aspects of circumcision, otherwise being "libertines."

[110] The ὑμεῖς (hymeis – "you"), standing at the head of the sentence, immediately follows the ὑμᾶς (hymas – direct object) of verse 12: "You, whom they are troubling,

expressed in 4:31 and verse 1 (reading these as conjoined), Paul repeats his caution to his gentile disciples, on this reading.[111] The "only thing (μόνον)" he wishes them to do is to avoid giving "an opportunity for the flesh (εἰς ἀφορμὴν τῇ σαρκί)" – by/in seeking social status within the Jewish community.[112]

The Greek syntax – lacking a verb – parallels "freedom (τὴν ἐλευθερίαν)" with "opportunity (ἀφορμὴν)," making of the former a pretext or occasion for the "working of the flesh" instead of for "faithfulness working through love" (cf. verse 6).[113] Here, Paul plays – perhaps ironically – on the demands for Torah-observance entailed in

---

were called for freedom" (Burton: 291). The γάρ (gar – "for") also functions as an explanatory conjunction.

[111] In effect, verse 13 functions as the response to 4:21. In answer to the question posed there, "Tell me, you who want to be under the Torah, do you not listen to the Torah?" Paul now informs his disciples (having already warned them of the implications of circumcision/conversion in verses 2f) that that which the Torah speaks of is love. If they are seeking Torah-observance, he says here, they should know that it is contained in "one word, in the *statement*, YOU SHALL LOVE YOUR NEIGHBOR AS YOURSELF" (verse 14) (see below). (While Hays understands Paul to justify his call for removal of the influencers on the grounds that the Galatians were called to freedom, he nevertheless still considers this section in terms of Paul's response to the challenge: "Does the freedom given by Christ leave us without moral guidance" [Galatians: 320].) For the relationship between Paul and his readers, see 4:12-20; for "calling," see verses 2-12 (verse 8); for "brethren," see 1:15; for the Galatian situation as assumed here, see Introduction, **Occasion and circumstances**; **Argument**; for Galatians' structure as a "halakhic letter" along the lines of 4QMMT, see Introduction, **Form**; **Argument**.

[112] Paul is, in this sense, using "the flesh" as a literal reference to circumcision (see also below). As in 1:23 and 2:10, the μόνον (monon – "only") delimits the freedom, "fencing" it, as it were, by constraining its employment: While this liberty is for the Galatians' benefit, they may not misuse it by accepting what is being offered to them as "another gospel" (cf. 1:6f). On this reading, Paul does not address the issue of libertinism at all here, verses 19f rather representing a halakhic prescription for "walking in the Spirit" by "angering one's inclination" (see verses 19-23). Removing the libertine issue from this passage dramatically simplifies the understanding of the epistle as a whole (see Introduction, **Argument** and 6:12-16 [n126]).

[113] The Greek ἀφορμή (aformē) originally signified a staging area or base for military operations (cf. BAGD: 127). With the possible further military metaphors in the following section (cf. verses 17, 25), Paul may have this meaning in mind. In light of the present reading of Galatians as a "halakhic letter," however, he may not be thinking so much in the sense that "The Galatians have been caught up in a cosmic conflict, and they must take care not to let the territory won for them by Christ become a staging ground for a counterattack by the hostile power of the flesh" (Hays, Galatians: 321) as engaging in a struggle with the influencers and their persuasion of his disciples towards social status and away from loyalty to his teaching concerning the Messiah (see Introduction, **Argument** and below).

proselytism (see verses 2-12 and below).[114] If his disciples are being persuaded that they will only find acceptance in the eyes of the Jewish community if they "officially" join it, he will demonstrate to them that the true property of Torah-observance is in fact love – for God, through love for one's neighbour (see below).[115]

On the present reading, "love" is synonymous with the "intention/faithfulness" which enables Jew and Gentile alike to "go beyond the law, which in itself is right and good, in order to do what is right and good" (Berkovits: 27). Since Gentiles do not even possess the more "lenient" commandments, they require Jesus' faithfulness to gain entrance to God's Kingdom wherein they are given the capacity, through the Spirit, to practice the "weightier provisions of the law: justice and mercy and faithfulness" (cf. Mt. 23:23) (see Introduction, **Argument; Theological pointers** and 2:15-21). "'The love of God is shed abroad in our hearts by the Holy Ghost, which is given to us' [Rom. 5:5]. The love whereby we dwell in God, and God in us, is His Spirit. God is love; and this is the blessing of the new covenant in Christ the incarnate Son, that He hath given us the Spirit in whom is bestowed the love which is the fulfilling of the law [cf. Gal. 5:13-14, 6:2]" (Saphir, Church: 148).[116]

Verse 14: In explaining his charge, Paul expresses a Second Temple adage which he reiterates in Romans 13:8 with words which he could have used here, picking up the theme of benefit/obligation (cf. verses 2-3):

---

[114] The irony may disappear if Paul's statement is compared with Jas. 2:7f. James argues that fulfilling the minor as the major commandments is a function of the "law of liberty (νόμου ἐλευθερίας)," the latter insisting that the judgment received by the merciless will itself be merciless (see 6:1-11 [nn35, 86] and below). On this account, anticipated by Jas. 1:25 – "But one who looks intently at the perfect law, the *law* of liberty, and abides by it, not having become a forgetful hearer but an effectual doer, this man shall be blessed in what he does (ὁ δὲ παρακύψας εἰς νόμον τέλειον τὸν τῆς ἐλευθερίας καὶ παραμείνας, οὐκ ἀκροατὴς ἐπιλησμονῆς γενόμενος ἀλλὰ ποιητὴς ἔργου, οὗτος μακάριος ἐν τῇ ποιήσει αὐτοῦ ἔσται)" – the law of liberty approximates the Golden Rule and the principle of לפנים משורת הדין (lifnim mi-shurat ha-din – "within the margin of the judgment") (cf. Flusser, Judaism: 494ff) (see 2:15-21, 3:10-14 [n142], 6:1-11, and below [nn131, 133, 148, 163]). It should be evident that a direct link obtains between this verse and verse 6.

[115] For the Gentiles' status within the early community, see 2:10f. The incongruence ostensibly generated by the command to "serve one another" when Paul might have been expected to reiterate his decree that the Galatians "cast out the bondwoman and her son" (4:30) may be mitigated when the service is conceived as a modifier of "love." Paul works out this theme fully in 6:1ff (see 6:1f).

[116] Love is the antithesis of sin, in that it affirms God's unity through His sovereignty, and overcomes the "hypocrisy" of not being able to perform what one wishes: "No one who is born of God practices sin, because His seed abides in him . . . any one who does not practice righteousness is not of God, nor the one who does not love his brother" (1 Jn. 3:9-10) (see 2:15-21 and 3:19-20). For the "seed," see 3:15-18.

"Owe nothing to anyone except to love one another; for he who loves his neighbor has fulfilled *the* Torah (Μηδενὶ μηδὲν ὀφείλετε εἰ μὴ τὸ ἀλλήλους ἀγαπᾶν· ὁ γὰρ ἀγαπῶν τὸν ἕτερον νόμον πεπλήρωκεν)" (see below).[117] The perception that love of one's neighbour represents the כלל גדול בתורה (klal gadol ba-Torah) – the highest and most central principle of the Torah, that which is its nature, that in which it is brought to fulfilment – is well documented in rabbinic literature: "Ben Azzai said: *This is the book of the descendants of Adam* (Gen. 5:1) is a great principle of the Torah. R. Akiba said: *But thou shalt love thy neighbour as thyself* (Lev. 19:18) is even a greater principle"[118] (Gen.R. 24:7).[119] Paul reinforces this conception by speaking of the Torah as fulfilled in "one word (ἑνὶ λόγῳ)." He hereby parallels love with the דברות/דיבורים (diburim/dibrot – "words") by which the Decalogue are designated.[120] His thought at this point corresponds with

---

[117] Paul's exhortation in Romans follows upon a halakhic section providing ethical guidelines for living in the Messiah (Romans 12), including the exhortation: "if service, [let him exercise his gift] in his serving (εἴτε διακονίαν ἐν τῇ διακονίᾳ)" (Rom. 12:7). "Serving the Sages [חכמים וְשָׁמֵשׁ]" constitutes a central rabbinic principle whereby, in performing for him all the tasks which a slave was bound to perform for his master and submitting to his master's teaching and conduct-by-example, a disciple became a proper vessel to receive his master's spiritual wisdom and, eventually, his true and faithful successor (cf. EJ: Talmudic Discipleship [CD-Rom]) (see 4:12-20). For Galatians as a "halakhic letter" along the lines of 4QMMT, see Introduction, **Form; Argument**.

[118] בן עזאי אומר: זה ספר תולדות אדם - זה כלל גדול בתורה. ר' עקיבא אומר: ואהבת לרעך כמוך - זה כלל גדול בתורה.

[119] Cf. Mt. 22:34-40; Mk. 12:28-34; Lk. 10:25-28; 1 Corinthians 13; Jas. 2:8; Test.Iss. 5:2; Sifra, Ked. 4:12; TBE p. 140; Gen.R. 24:7; Lev.R. 24:5; Yalk.Gen. 40; Yalk.Lev. 613; JNed. 30b. As the parallel in Sifra, Ked. 4:12 indicates – wherein the order is reversed – the two Sages are concerned to determine the basis for the sanctity of human life. Whereas a person put to shame may retaliate, on Akiva's ruling, since he is not bidden to love his neighbour *more* than himself, Ben Azzai asserts that the dignity of human life derives from being created in God's image. Both dicta flow from the notion of God's universal fatherhood, which implies the unity and brotherhood of wo/man. For Hab. 2:4 as the Torah's "summation," thereby equating "faithfulness" and "love," see 3:10-14; for Hab. 2:4 as determinative of those who exercise their identity in the Messiah in faithfulness working through love, see 2:15-21 (nn267, 271), 3:10ff, 6:1-11, and verses 2-12.

[120] Cf. Ex.R. 28:3; Tanh.Ter. 10; Ekev 9; Mekh.Ba-chod. 4; Shevu. 39a. Since the Torah maintains the world (cf. PA 1:2; Shab. 88a), even the smallest portion cannot be neglected without endangering human existence (cf. Mt. 5:17-20; Lk. 16:17; PA 2:1, 4:2). Despite its emphasis on the "Ten Commandments," the New Testament does not refer to them by this name, and in fact focuses on the final five – those dealing with inter-human relationships (cf. Flusser, Decalogue). Contrary to centuries of Christian dissociation from Judaism – largely based on a biased reading of Paul – he himself speaks here in terms of the Torah's summation, not of its supercession; (for Paul's Jewish identity, see Introduction, **Author**; Appendix). As the embodiment of God's "word (Λόγος)" (cf. Jn. 1:1f), Jesus is its "purpose" and

James 2:8-11, both texts reflecting a tradition which understands that violating one of these commandments is equivalent to contravention of them all (cf. verse 3):

> You might have thought that a person is not guilty unless he transgresses all these commandments. Therefore the Torah says, "You shall not murder, you shall not commit adultery . . ." (Ex. 20:13f) in order to make one liable for each commandment separately. That being so, why does Deuteronomy join all these commandments together, saying, "You shall not murder *and* you shall not commit adultery *and* etc." (Dt. 5:17f)? It is to teach us that they are all interrelated. When a person breaks one of them, he will end up by breaking them all."[121] (Mekh. de-R. Shimon bar Jochai, Yitro 20)[122]

This tradition developed in conjunction with the "Golden Rule" – as illustrated in Hillel's well-known dictum: "On another occasion it happened that a certain heathen came before Shammai and said to him, 'Make me a proselyte, on condition that you teach me the whole Torah while I stand on one foot.' Thereupon he repulsed him with the builder's cubit which was in his hand. When he went before Hillel, he said to him, 'What is hateful to you, do not to your neighbour: that is the whole Torah, while the rest is the commentary thereof; go and learn it'"[123] (Shab. 31a)[124] (cf. Flusser, Judaism: 469-89, and for the following discussion).[125]

---

fulfilment/completion (cf. Rom. 10:4) (see 3:1-5, 21-25 [end], 4:1-7, 6:1-11 [verse 9], and below).

[121] יכול לא י]הא חיי]ב עד שיעבור על כולן. תלמוד לומר: לא תרצח לא תנאף לא תגנב לא תענה לא תחמוד - לחייב על כל אחד ואחד בפני עצמו. אם כן, למה נאמר להלן: לא תרצח <ו>לא תנאף ולא תגנב ולא תענה ולא תחמוד? מגיד שכולן תפוסין זה בזה. פרץ אדם באחד מהן, סופו לפרוץ בכולן.

[122] Cf. Dt. 27:26; Mt. 5:17ff; 4 Macc. 5:19-20; TBE p. 132; PA 2:1, 4:2; DEZ 3:3; Mak. 24a [R. Gamaliel]; Did. 3:1-6. See also above (n114).

[123] מעשה בנכרי אחד שבא לפני שמאי. אמר לו: גיירני על מנת שתלמדני כל התורה כולה כשאני עומד על רגל אחת. דחפו באמת הבנין שבידו. בא לפני הלל גייריה. אמר לו: דעלך סני לחברך לא תעביד: זו היא כל התורה כולה ואידך פירושה; הוא זיל גמור.

[124] Cf. Mt. 7:12; Tob. 4:15; Ep.Arist. 207; [Test.Naph. 1:6 (Heb.)]; Sir. 31:15; Philo, *Hypothetica*; Targ.Jon. to Lev. 19:18; PA 2:10; ARNᵃ 15:1, 16:1; ARNᵇ 26; Did. 1:2; Eus.*Praep.Ev.* 8.6; Isocrates, *Nicocles* 61; Herodotus 3.142.

[125] "What he [Hillel] meant by 'explication' is that the remaining commandments simply spell out or interpret the Golden Rule. Of course, those who held with Hillel and Akiva that there is but one all-inclusive principle – love of one's neighbor – believed that the whole Torah was derived from that principle. From this doctrine emerges the literature which stresses the importance of the second half of the Ten Commandments, linked to the verse 'You shall love your neighbor as yourself' . . . [the] New Testament passages say two things about the command to love one's neighbor. On the one hand, 'You shall love your neighbor as yourself' is presented as a summary of the whole Torah; and on the other hand, it is called a summary of the second half of the Decalogue" (Flusser, Decalogue: 7) (see also 3:19-20). (Note,

Paul's thought demonstrates evidence of an exegetical tradition of Leviticus 19:18 according to which reward and punishment are predicated not on awe of God but on love for one's fellow beings. If a person loves his neighbour, s/he may expect compensation; if s/he fails to love others, condemnation is assured: "He that revengeth shall find vengeance from the Lord, and he will surely keep his sins [in remembrance]. Forgive thy neighbor the hurt that he hath done unto thee, so shall thy sins also be forgiven when thou prayest. One man beareth hatred against another, and doth he seek pardon from the Lord? He showeth no mercy to a man, which is like himself: and doth he ask forgiveness for his own sins? If he that is but flesh nourish hatred, who will intreat for pardon of his sins? Remember thy end, and let enmity cease"[126] (Sir. 28:1-6).[127]

To the extent that Jesus is the "goal/aim (τελός) of the Torah" (cf. Rom. 10:4), he is the one in and through whom the command of love is observable.[128] It is his faithfulness to God, in his obedience to the point of death, that has overcome the dominion of Belial and the "elemental things of the world," thereby releasing human beings from captivity to sin (see 1:1-5, 2:1-10, 15-21, 3:19f, and 4:1f).[129] God's purpose in so sending His son

---

too, that Hillel's dictum is directed towards a potential proselyte [see 6:1-11 and verses 2-12].)

[126] ὁ ἐκδικῶν παρὰ κυρίου εὑρήσει ἐκδίκησιν, καὶ τὰς ἁμαρτίας αὐτοῦ διατηρῶν διατηρήσει. ἄφες ἀδίκημα τῷ πλησίον σου, καὶ τότε δεηθέντος σου αἱ ἁμαρτίαι σου λυθήσονται. ἄνθρωπος ἀνθρώπῳ συντηρεῖ ὀργήν, καὶ παρὰ κυρίου ζητεῖ ἴασιν; ἐπ᾽ ἄνθρωπον ὅμοιον αὐτῷ οὐκ ἔχει ἔλεος, καὶ περὶ τῶν ἁμαρτιῶν αὐτοῦ δεῖται; αὐτὸς σὰρξ ὢν διατηρεῖ μῆνιν, τίς ἐξιλάσεται τὰς ἁμαρτίας αὐτοῦ; μνήσθητι τὰ ἔσχατα καὶ παῦσαι ἐχθραίνων.

[127] Cf. Mt. 7:1f; Lk. 6:36f; Rom. 2:1f; 1 Jn. 4:21; Jub. 20:2; Test.Zev. 8:1; DEZ 3:1; Shab. 127a; RH 16b; BK 93a. For the principle of "measure for measure" and James 2, see verses 2-12.

[128] Cf. Jn. 14:15f, 15:12ff, 17:23-26; 1 Jn. 2:7f, 3:1ff, 4:16-21, 5:1f. Paul's use of πληρόω (plēroō) plays on the idea of "fulfilment" – in the sense of "completion" (both temporal and conceptual) and "summation" (encapsulating) (cf. ἀνακεφαλαιόω in Rom. 13:9; τελειόω in 1 Jn. 4:17-18). The correspondence of his thought here with that in Rom. 8:3-4 indicates a close affinity with Gal. 3:19f and 4:1-7. The Christian casuistry countenanced in the distinction between "doing" the Torah – which Paul ostensibly never requires from his readers – and its "fulfilling," of which he does speak, yet only while "describing its results" and never in "prescribing Christian conduct" (cf. Longenecker, Galatians: 242-43) is ironically misplaced here. While such nuances should be characteristic of exegesis of the New Testament, properly recognised as a Jewish text, they here rather appear to derive from an *indisposition* to the Torah – an attitude which Paul himself fails to manifest but which Christians of all colours intractably continue to ascribe to him (see Introduction, **Author**; Appendix).

[129] In this respect, the sense of surprise demonstrated by some commentators that Paul should introduce love at this point, rather than exhort his disciples to "resist sinful desires with all of your might" (cf. Eph. 6:13; Jas. 4:7; 1 Pet. 5:9), may reflect a

(cf. 4:4) is "In order to seek God with [all (one's) heart and] with a[ll (one's) soul;] {cf. Dt. 6:5} in order to do what is good and just in his presence, as he commanded by the hand of Moses and by the hand of all his servants the Prophets; in order to love everything which he selects and to hate everything that he rejects; in order to keep oneself at a distance from all evil, and to become attached to all good works; in order to do truth and justice and uprightness on earth and not to walk any more in the stubbornness of a guilty heart and of lecherous eyes performing every evil"[130] (1QS 1:1-7).[131]

In juxtaposing slavery to God – through His Messiah – and bondage to the flesh, Paul is playing on a well-founded tradition known as the "Two Ways":

These are their [the two Spirits'] paths in the world: to enlighten the heart of man, straighten out in front of him all the paths of true justice, establish in his heart respect for the precepts of God; it is a spirit of meekness, of patience, generous compassion, eternal goodness, intelligence, understanding, potent wisdom which trusts in all the deeds of God and depends on his abundant mercy; a spirit of knowledge in all the plans of action, of enthusiasm for the decrees of justice, of holy plans with firm purpose, of generous compassion with all the sons of truth, of magnificent purity which detests all unclean idols, of careful behaviour in wisdom concerning everything, of concealment concerning the truth of the mysteries of knowledge. *Blank* These are the foundations of the spirit of the sons of truth (in) the world. And the reward of all those who walk in it will be healing, plentiful peace in a long life, fruitful offspring with all everlasting blessings, eternal enjoyment with endless life, and a crown of glory with majestic raiment in eternal light. However, to the spirit of deceit belong greed, sluggishness in the service of justice, wickedness, falsehood, pride, haughtiness of heart, dishonesty, trickery, cruelty, much insincerity, impatience, much foolishness,

---

misconstrual of context, the passage being viewed rather as a fresh section than as a further explication of 4:1ff (cf. 1:4, 3:19ff). The significance of this passage for verses 19f should be immediately evident.

[130] לדרוש אל ב]כול לב ו]כב]ול נפש] לעשות הטוב והישר לפניו כאשר צוה ביד מושה וביד כול עבדיו הנביאים ולאהוב כול אשר בחר ולשנוא את כול אשר מאס לרחוק מכול רע ולדבוק בכול מעשי טוב ולעשות אמת וצדקה ומשפט בארץ ולוא ללכת עוד בשרירות לב אשמה ועיני זנות לעשות כול רע.

[131] 1QS 5:8f; CD-A 15:9f; 4QMMT[e] ff14-17i:7-8; 11QTemp 54:12-14, 59:9-10. Herein, with the echoes of Gen. 18:19; Dt. 6:5, 12:28; Jer. 9:24; Mic. 6:8, love of God and love of one's neighbour are conjoined with the principles of לפנים משורת הדין (lifnim mi-shurat ha-din – "within the margin of the judgment") (see 2:15-21 and below) and the resistance of evil which leads to observance of the minor commandments equally with the major ones (see above and below).

impudent enthusiasm for appalling acts performed in a lustful passion, filthy paths in the service of impurity, blasphemous tongue, blindness of eyes, hardness of hearing, stiffness of neck, hardness of heart in order to walk in all the paths of darkness and evil cunning. And the visitation of all those who walk in it will be for an abundance of afflictions at the hands of all the angels of destruction, for eternal damnation by the scorching wrath of the God of revenges, for permanent terror and shame without end with the humiliation of destruction by the fire of the dark regions. And all the ages of their generations (they shall spend) in bitter weeping and harsh evils in the abysses of darkness until their destruction, without there being a remnant or survivor for them.[132] (1QS 4:2-14) (cf. Flusser, Sources: 235ff) [133]

---

[132] ואלה דרכיהן בתבל להאיר בלבב איש ולישר לפניו כול דרכי צדק אמת ולפחד לבבו במשפטי אל
ורוח ענוה וא'רך אפים ורוב רחמים וטוב עולמים ושכל ובינה וחכמת גבורה מאמנת בכול מעשי אל
ונשענת ברוב חסדו ורוח דעת בכול מחשבת מעשה וקנאת משפטי צדק ומחשבת קודש ביצר סמוך
ורוב חסדים על כול בני אמת וטהרת כבוד מתעב כול גלולי נדה והצנע לכת בערמת כול וחבא לאמת
רזי דעת *vacat* אלה סודי רוח לבני אמת תבל ופקודת כול הולכי בה למרפא ורוב שלום באורך ימים
ופרות זרע עם כול ברכות עד ושמחת עולמים בחיי נצח וכליל כבוד עם מדת הדר באור עולמים *vacat*
ולרוח עולה רחוב נפש ושפול ידים בעבודת צדק רשע ושקר גוה ורום לבב כחש ורמיה אכזרי ורוב
חנף קצור אפים ורוב אולת וקנאת זדון מעשי תעובה ברוח זנות ודרכי נדה בעבודת טמאה ולשון
גדופים עורון עינים וכבוד אוזן קושי עורף וכובד לב ללכת בכול דרכי חושך וערמת רוע ופקודת כול
הולכי בה לרוב נגועים ביד כול מלאכי חבל לשחת עולמים באף עברת אל נקמ[ו]ת לזעות נצח
וחרפת עד עם כלמת כלה באש מחשכים וכול קציהם לדורותם באבל יגון ורעת מרורים בהויות
חושך עד כלותם לאין שרית ופליטה למו.

[133] Cf. Dt. 30:15-20; Ps. 1:6; Prov. 4:10-19; Mt. 7:13f; Phil. 4:8; Sib.Or. 8:399;
Test.Asher 1:3f; Test.Abr. 11:1f; 1QS 3:18ff, 4:1ff; 1QH[a] 3:13ff, 4:17, 26, 9:9, 12:31,
15:7, 20:11f; CD-A 1:13, 2:6; 4Q473; Philo, *Quis Rerum* 45ff; Ex.R. 30:20; Tanh.Mishp.
7; PA 2:1, 9, 3:5; Ber. 28b (Jochanan b. Zakkai); Ep.Barnabas 18-21; Did. 1:1f, 5:1f. The
Didache makes the connection particularly clear: "There are two Ways, one of Life
and one of Death, and there is a great difference between the two Ways. The Way of
Life is this: 'First, thou shalt love the God who made thee, secondly, thy neighbour
as thyself; and whatsoever thou wouldst not have done to thyself, do not thou to
another.' Now the teaching of these words is this ... the second commandment of
the teaching is this: 'Thou shalt do no murder; thou shalt not commit adultery ...
(Ὁδοὶ δύο εἰσί, μία τῆς ζωῆς καὶ μία τοῦ θανάτου, διαφορὰ δὲ πολλὴ μεταξὺ
τῶν δύο ὁδῶν. Ἡ μὲν οὖν ὁδὸς τῆς ζωῆς ἐστιν αὕτη· πρῶτον ἀγαπήσεις τὸν
θεὸν τὸν ποιήσαντά σε, δεύτερον τὸν πλησίον σου ὡς σεαυτόν· πάντα δὲ ὅσα
ἐὰν θελήσῃς μὴ γίνεσθαί σοι, καὶ σὺ ἄλλῳ μὴ ποίει. Τούτων δὲ τῶν λόγων ἡ
διδαχή ἐστιν αὕτη ... Δευτέρα δὲ ἐντολὴ τῆς διδαχῆς· οὐ φονεύσεις, οὐ
μοιχεύσεις ...)" (Did. 1:1-3, 2:2). The parallels between Did. 3:1-6 and Mt. 5:17-48,
both being based on the second half of the Decalogue, further establish a link back
to the "hypocrisy" of which Paul accuses Peter in 2:13f, the underlying idea
between these passages being that of לפנים משורת הדין (lifnim mi-shurat ha-din –
"within the margin of the judgment") (see 2:15-21, 6:1f, above, and below [nn148,
163]). For arguments against Paul's use of the doctrine of the Two Ways/Spirits, see
verses 19-23 (n185).

This theme of the "Two Ways/Spirits" goes hand in hand with that of serving two masters: You must either choose to serve God, or choose to serve your own (evil) inclination. Since in giving loyalty to one, you inevitably frustrate the designs of the other, simultaneous service of both is impossible: "'*And the servant is free from his master*' (Job 3:19): he who performs the will of his creator (*yozer*) angers his evil inclination (*yezer*), but once he is dead he emerges into freedom, as it is said, '*And the servant is free from his master*' ועבד חפשי מאדוניו : זה הוא שעושה רצון יוצרו מכעיס את יצרו. "מת - יצא לחירות, שנאמר : ועבד חפשי מאדוניו" (Ruth R. 3:1).[134]

Verse 15: In a quasi-chiastic parallel (verses 13-15), Paul warns that any fulfilment of the Torah other than through love will allow the "flesh" to express itself, with the result that, "biting and devouring one another (ἀλλήλους δάκνετε καὶ κατεσθίετε)," the members of the community will be "consumed by one another (ὑπ' ἀλλήλων ἀναλωθῆτε)."[135] "Biting" frequently serves as a metaphor for usury in rabbinic texts, the Hebrew root נשך (nashakh) conveying the sense that interest "bites into" the debtor.[136] The action is regularly attributed to the snake, whose bite is deadly. To the extent that the serpent is associated with sin and punishment, biting may also, by extension, represent both transgression and its penalty: "Flee from sin as from the face of a serpent: for if thou comest too near it, it will bite thee. The teeth thereof are as the teeth of a lion, slaying the souls of men"[137] (Sir. 21:2).[138]

The parallel verb of "devouring (κατεσθίετε)" - a compound form of the regular verb "to eat" - carries the basic sense of eating up, strengthened to the point of being "swallowed up" to destruction: "R. Hanina, the vice-high priest, said: Pray for the welfare of the government, for were it not for the fear thereof, one man would swallow up alive his

---

[134] Cf. Mt. 6:24; Lk. 16:13; Rom. 12:9; [2 Cor. 6:14f]; 1 Thess. 5:21-22; Test.Dan 4:7; Ruth R. 8:1; Gen.R. 14:4; Yalk.Job 886; Ber. 61a; Eruv. 18a; Haggada (see n3) (cf. Shulam and Le Cornu: 24, 209-33; Flusser, Judaism: 169-72) (see also 1:6-10 and 2:15-21). For the association between this theme and hypocrisy, see 2:11-14.

[135] It is at this juncture that Paul appears to move into a more explicitly paraenetical mode, shifting from a denunciation of the influencers and the admonition to "cast them out" into a direct address of the behaviour demanded from those who "fulfil the great commandment of the Torah" in the Spirit (see also 6:1-11). For this reading of Galatians, see Introduction, **Argument**.

[136] Cf. 2 Cor. 11:20; Ex.R. 31:5-6, 13; BM 5:1.

[137] ὡς ἀπὸ προσώπου ὄφεως φεῦγε ἀπὸ ἁμαρτίας· ἐὰν γὰρ προσέλθῃς δήξεταί σε· ὀδόντες λέοντος οἱ ὀδόντες αὐτῆς ἀναιροῦντες ψυχὰς ἀνθρώπων.

[138] Cf. Gen. 3:1ff; Num. 21:6; Dt. 32:24; Eccl. 10:8; Jer. 8:17; Amos 5:19, 9:3; Ex.R. 3:12; Lev.R. 22:4, 26:2; Num.R. 18:22, 19:2, 22; Eccl.R. 1.18.1, 5.8.4, 10.11.1; Mekh.Amalek 1; RH 3:8; Tos.Ber. 3:20; J RH 18a; Ber. 33a P; Sot. 8b; Ket. 30b; San. 37b. Laypeople are also warned not to associate too closely with the Sages, on account of the "bite" of their teaching (cf. Gen.R. 52:4; Num.R. 3:1; PA 2:10). For fleeing from sin, cf. 1 Cor. 6:18, 10:14; 1 Tim. 6:11; 2 Tim. 2:22.

רבי חנינא סגן הכהנים אומר: הוי מתפלל בשלומה של מלכות שאלמלא fellow-man
מוראה איש את רעהו חיים בלעו" (PA 3:2).[139] The final verb (ἀναλίσκω;
analiskō) is also regularly used of consumption, attended in many
instances by conflagration – God commonly being described as a
"consuming fire."[140] The final destruction of all this activity being death,
love constitutes the countering power of life: "Just as love wants to bring
the dead back to life and to recall those under sentence of death, so hate
wants to kill the living and does not wish to preserve alive those who have
committed the slightest sin. For among all men the spirit of hatred works
by Satan through human frailty for the death of mankind; but the spirit of
love works by the Law of God through forbearance for the salvation of
mankind" (Test.Gad 4:6-7).[141]

The force of Paul's warning derives from the fact that in yielding to
the influencers' persuasion, his disciples are placing themselves once again
under the "elemental things of the world" – delivering themselves, once
again, into the hands of their own inclination (see 4:1-7).[142] In so doing,
they may, first and foremost, be displaying their "enmity" to Paul himself,
shifting from a willingness to pluck out their eyes on his behalf towards
the acceptance of "another gospel," "contrary to that which we have
preached to you" (1:6, 8) (cf. 4:15-16) (see 1:6-10 and 4:12-20).[143] If his

---

[139] Cf. LXX Ps. 13[14]:4; Isa. 9:11[12]. The same verb also denotes a form of usury
(cf. Mk. 12:40; Lk. 20:47; 2 Cor. 11:20). R. Hanina is also the author of a dictum
which exegetes Lev. 19:18 in terms of the right and wrong deeds a person does to
another – "as yourself" being interpreted as "one like you" (cf. ARN[b] 26).

[140] Cf. Ex. 24:17; Dt. 4:24, 9:3; 2 Thess. 1:7; Heb. 10:27, 12:29.

[141] 1 Cor. 3:3 suggests that "consumption" is a direct expression of the "desire of
the flesh": "For since there is jealousy and strife among you, are you not fleshly, and
are you not walking according to man (ὅπου γὰρ ἐν ὑμῖν ζῆλος καὶ ἔρις, οὐχὶ
σαρκικοί ἐστε καὶ κατὰ ἄνθρωπον περιπατεῖτε;)?" (see also 6:1-11 and verses 19-
23).

[142] In a parallel admonition to John the Baptist's warning to his pharisaic and
sadducean audience that "God is able from these stones to raise up children to
Abraham (δύναται ὁ θεὸς ἐκ τῶν λίθων τούτων ἐγεῖραι τέκνα τῷ Ἀβραάμ)" (Mt.
3:9), Paul is cautioning his gentile disciples that they must demonstrate themselves
to be "Abraham's sons" by bringing forth "fruit in keeping with repentance
(ποιήσατε οὖν καρπὸν ἄξιον τῆς μετανοίας)" (Mt. 3:8) (cf. Eph. 4:1) (see 2:15-21
and verses 19f). For Paul's argument regarding the Galatians as "sons of promise,"
see Introduction, **Argument** and 3:1ff.

[143] On this reading of the text, this verse relates to a spirit of strife and dissension
within the community generated by the influencers' activities. While the presumed
paraenetic character of the section has inclined many commentators to understand
the "one another (ἀλλήλους/ἀλλήλων)" to refer to the ethical conduct of the
community's own members, the Greek does not intrinsically demand an inner
community dispute and may as logically allude to people outside – such as the
influencers (see 6:1-11). In reference to Paul, the "another" includes himself, an

disciples do not observe the Torah through loving God and their neighbour – Paul himself perhaps being the prime example – their acceptance of the influencers' persuasion will in fact bring them to destruction, not to status (see also 6:1-11 and verses 24-26).[144]

Paul's conclusion at this point *may* be rather surprising. In the light of contemporary interpretations of Leviticus 19:18 in terms of the second half of the Decalogue, we might have expected to find here a reference to a lack of forgiveness from God – rather than a caution against mutual devouring. Yet, Paul has expressed his confidence that his disciples will adopt the "narrow path" – and, in keeping with the inter-personal context of the second half of the Decalogue, this is displayed in human relationships as much as God's reward of good conduct. Since this section constitutes his exhortation not to give "opportunity to the flesh," it naturally gives preference to human conduct as that which demonstrates love for God (cf. Rom. 14:17) (see verses 19-23).[145]

---

indirect self-allusion. The second half of the verse may then constitute a veiled threat: If you treat me this way, such will be the consequences (see 6:17).

[144] Cf. Mt. 23:15: "Woe to you, scribes and Pharisees, hypocrites, because you travel about on sea and land to make one proselyte; and when he becomes one, you make him twice as much a son of hell as yourselves (Οὐαὶ ὑμῖν, γραμματεῖς καὶ Φαρισαῖοι ὑποκριταί, ὅτι περιάγετε τὴν θάλασσαν καὶ ξηρὰν ποιῆσαι ἕνα προσήλυτον, καὶ ὅταν γένηται ποιεῖτε αὐτὸν υἱὸν γεέννης διπλότερον ὑμῶν)" (see 2:15-21, 3:21-25 [verse 22], and 4:12-20 [6:1-11]). The hypocrisy of such conduct becomes clear in a "favourite saying of Raba": "The goal of wisdom is repentance and good deeds, so that a man should not study Torah and Mishnah and then despise his father and mother and teacher and his superior in wisdom and rank, as it says, *The fear of the Lord is the beginning of wisdom, a good understanding have all they that do thereafter* (Ps. 111:10). It does not say, 'that do [or: learn]', but 'that do thereafter', which implies, that do them for their own sake and not for other motives [cf. criticism and quarrelling]. If one does them for other motives, it were better that he had not been created מרגלא בפומיה דרבא : תכלית חכמה תשובה ומעשים טובים, שלא יהא אדם קורא ושונה ובועט באביו ובאמו וברבו ובמי שהוא גדול ממנו בחכמה ובמנין, שנאמר : ראשית חכמה יראת ה' שכל טוב לכל עושיהם. "לעושים" לא נאמר אלא "לעושיהם" - לעושים לשמה ולא לעושים שלא לשמה. וכל העושה שלא לשמה, נוח לו שלא נברא" (Ber. 17a) (see verses 2-12 [n57]). (For conclusions drawn from the precise wording of Scripture, see 3:15-18.)

[145] Paul is merely focusing on the human side of the "equation," in this respect – that which constitutes love of one's neighbour. Not only will lack of such brotherly respect and acknowledgement destroy the community's fabric; it will also bring its members into disrepute with God. If they so act, they will inherit neither this world nor the world to come: "Do not complain, brethren, against one another, that you yourselves may not be judged; behold, the Judge is standing right at the door (μὴ στενάζετε, ἀδελφοί, κατ' ἀλλήλων ἵνα μὴ κριθῆτε· ἰδοὺ ὁ κριτὴς πρὸ τῶν θυρῶν ἕστηκεν)" (Jas. 5:9) (cf. Mt. 7:1ff; Rom. 2:1ff). For the link between Romans 14 and hypocrisy and the Kingdom of God, see 2:15-21 and verses 19-23; for Romans 2 and hypocrisy – creating a clear connection between chapter 5 and chapter 2, on the one hand, and chapters 2, 5, and 6, in this respect – see 6:1-11, verses 2-12, and below (n163).

Verse 16: The epistolary phrase "I say (Λέγω δὲ)" marks the transition from one sub-section to another (cf. Longenecker, Galatians: 244).[146] In directing his disciples to "walk by the Spirit (πνεύματι περιπατεῖτε)," Paul directly marks his words as lying in the realm of halakhic instruction, the Greek περιπατέω (peripateō – "to walk") embodying the Hebrew concept of הלכה (halakhah – "walking/progression")[147] (cf. Strack: 6f; Safrai, Literature: 121ff; Berkovits).[148]

The rather abrupt reference to the "Spirit" is, in fact, a logical derivation from Paul's argument up until this point. Where "love" is the Torah's summation – its goal and purpose – it corresponds to the intention by which a person is enabled to avoid the "hypocritical" conduct generated when, wishing to obey God's commands, a person is obstructed by his/her nature from practicing what they say: "Good are the commands which come out of the mouth of those who perform them נאין דברים כשהן יוצאין מפי עושיהן" (Tos.Yev. 8:4).

God's foremost requirement is love – for Himself and, equally importantly, between human beings: "For the kingdom of God is not eating and drinking, but righteousness and peace and joy in the Holy Spirit. For he who in this *way* serves the Messiah is acceptable to God and approved by men. So then let us pursue the things which make for peace and the building up of one another"[149] (Rom. 14:17-19) (see 3:19-20).[150] This

---

[146] For Galatians' epistolary structure, see Introduction, **Form**.

[147] Cf. Lk. 1:6; 1QS 1:8, 13f, 3:9f, 18f, 4:6f; PA 2:1, 9 (see verses 19-23 [verse 22]).

[148] "The essence of the Oral Torah is the Halakha. As the root of the word indicates (*Halokh*, to walk, to go), Halakha teaches the way along which the Jew is required to walk in accordance with the Torah. Halakha is the application of the Torah to life. But since there is no such thing as life in general, since it is always a certain form of life at a specific time in history, in a specific situation, Torah application means application to a specific time in a specific situation" (Berkovits: 1-2). (While this is evidently Paul's understanding, the LXX consistently renders the Hebrew הלך by πορεύομαι [poreuomai] rather than with περιπατέω [peripateō].) Paul has already intimated the halakhic sphere of this section in verse 3 (see verses 2-12), and his discussion of the "fruit" of the Spirit is further conducted in a linguistic and conceptual halakhic framework (see verses 19-23). While the "I say" is epistolary, it also directly recalls Jesus' proper interpretation of Scripture ("fulfilment") in the Sermon on the Mount, the latter representing a striking example of the principle of לפנים משורת הדין (lifnim mi-shurat ha-din – "within the margin of the judgment") (see 2:15-21, verses 2-12 [verse 6], 4:12-20 [verse 15] and below). For Galatians as a "halakhic letter" along the lines of 4QMMT, see Introduction, **Form**; **Argument**.

[149] οὐ γάρ ἐστιν ἡ βασιλεία τοῦ θεοῦ βρῶσις καὶ πόσις ἀλλὰ δικαιοσύνη καὶ εἰρήνη καὶ χαρὰ ἐν πνεύματι ἁγίῳ· ὁ γὰρ ἐν τούτῳ δουλεύων τῷ Χριστῷ εὐάρεστος τῷ θεῷ καὶ δόκιμος τοῖς ἀνθρώποις. Ἄρα οὖν τὰ τῆς εἰρήνης διώκωμεν καὶ τὰ τῆς οἰκοδομῆς τῆς εἰς ἀλλήλους.

[150] "In another comment on *Thou shalt love the Lord thy God* (Dt. 6:5), [*we-'ahabta*, 'thou shalt love,' is read *we-he-'ehabta*, 'thou shalt cause to be loved'] – that is, you are to cause the name of heaven to be loved by mankind. Hence you are to be

declaration concerning the Kingdom, in which Paul juxtaposes love with the Spirit, closely corresponds to Micah 6:8, the text which underlies Matthew 23:23: "What does the LORD require of you but to do justice, to love kindness, and to walk humbly with your God? - ומה-ה' דורש ממך כי אם-עשות משפט ואהבת חסד והצנע לכת עם-אלהיך"[151] (Mt. 23:23). These verses, together with others of a similar nature, form the basis for the rabbinic principle of לפנים משורת הדין (lifnim mi-shurat ha-din) – acting "within the margin of the judgment" or "according to the spirit of the law": "R. Hiyya acted within the 'margin of the judgment,' on the principle learnt by R. Joseph : '*And shalt show them* means the source of their livelihood; *the way* means deeds of lovingkindness; *they must walk* means the visitation of the sick; *wherein* means burial, *and the work* means the law; *which they must do* means within the margin of the judgment'"[152] (BK 99b-100a) (see 2:15-21).[153]

The "spirit of the law" becomes, in consequence of the believer's participation in Jesus' death and resurrection, the indwelling and guidance of God's Spirit. Paul's injunction here constitutes, in this respect, an outworking of God's promise to His people in Ezekiel 36: "Moreover, I will give you a new heart and put a new spirit within you; and I will remove the heart of stone from your flesh and give you a heart of flesh. And I will

---

loving in the give-and-take of everyday life – in your going about in the marketplace and in your dealing with men. For when a man is loving in the give-and-take of daily life ... people seeing him say ... 'See how comely are the deeds, how beautiful are the ways of this who one who studied Torah' ... Thus, through such a man, is the name of Heaven hallowed שאתה : ואהבתה את ה' אלהיך מאהב על הבריות שם שמים. שתהא יודע משאך ומתנך והוליכך בשוק ועסקך עם בני אדם. ובזמן [שאדם] יודע משאו ומתנו והוליכו בשוק ועסקו עם בני אדם ... הרואים אותו אומרים : ... ראו כמה נאים מעשיו, כמה יפין דרכיו ... ונמצא מתקדש שם שמים על ידו" (TBE p. 140). For the hypocritical behaviour which is the opposite of this conduct, see verses 2-12 (verse 6).

[151] Walking in the Spirit, in love, is the antithesis of sin and hypocrisy: "Woe to you, scribes and Pharisees, hypocrites! For you tithe mint and dill and cummin, and have neglected the weightier provisions of the law: justice and mercy and faithfulness; but these are the things you should have done without neglecting the others (Οὐαὶ ὑμῖν, γραμματεῖς καὶ Φαρισαῖοι ὑποκριταί, ὅτι ἀποδεκατοῦτε τὸ ἡδύοσμον καὶ τὸ ἄνηθον καὶ τὸ κύμινον καὶ ἀφήκατε τὰ βαρύτερα τοῦ νόμου, τὴν κρίσιν καὶ τὸ ἔλεος καὶ τὴν πίστιν· ταῦτα [δὲ] ἔδει ποιῆσαι κἀκεῖνα μὴ ἀφιέναι)" (Mt. 23:23) (see 2:15-21, 3:19-20, and above [n116]). Both here and in Romans 14, pleasing God is predicated on love of one's fellow, as a commandment "higher" even than observance of those which He requires in His covenant (Torah). For hypocrisy as the context of "justification" in Galatians, see Introduction, **Argument; Theological pointers** (Justification), 3:1-5, 19-20, verses 2-12, and below.

[152] רבי חייא לפנים משורת הדין הוא דעבד, כדתני רב יוסף : והודעת להם - זה בית חייהם. את הדרך - זו גמילות חסדים. ילכו - זו ביקור חולים. בה - זו קבורה. את המעשה - זו הדין. אשר יעשון - זו לפנים משורת הדין.

[153] "This could mean that it is sometimes necessary to go beyond the law, which in itself is right and good, in order to do what is right and good" (Berkovits: 27). The principle is based (here) on Ex. 18:20 (see 2:15-21).

put My Spirit within you and cause you to walk in My statutes, and you will be careful to observe My ordinances"[154] (Ezek. 36:26-27) (see also 6:1-11).[155] As Paul later states in 1 Corinthians, the Spirit's presence gives the assurance of liberty: "Now the Lord is the Spirit; and where the Spirit of the Lord is, *there* is liberty (ὁ δὲ κύριος τὸ πνεῦμά ἐστιν· οὗ δὲ τὸ πνεῦμα κυρίου, ἐλευθερία)" (2 Cor. 3:17). This liberty is release from the power of sin which prevents entry to God's Kingdom, through the outpouring of His Spirit – upon those, both Jews and Gentiles, who have turned "from darkness to light and from the dominion of Satan to God, in order that they may receive forgiveness of sins and an inheritance among those who have been sanctified by faithfulness to me [Jesus]"[156] (Acts 26:18)[157] (cf. Col. 1:12-14; 1 Thess. 2:12).[158]

---

[154] ונתתי לכם לב חדש ורוח חדשה אתן בקרבכם והסרֹתי את-לב האבן מבשרכם ונתתי לכם לב בשר: ואת-רוחי אתן בקרבכם ועשיתי את אשר-בחֻקי תלכו ומשפטי תשמרו ועשיתם.

[155] Cf. Isa. 44:3, 59:21; Jer. 31:31f, 32:39; Ezek. 11:19-20, 18:31, 37:14, 39:29; Joel 2:28; 1QS 4:2ff, 5:5, 11:2; 1QHa 4:26, 8:15, 21:12f; 4Q381 f15:1; 4Q393 ff1-2ii:5-6; 4Q435 f1i:1f; 4Q436 f1i:4f, ii:1f; 4Q444 1:1f; 4Q504 ff1-2ii:13-18, v:11-16, vi:2-4, f4:4-14; 4Q511 ff48, 49 + 51:1f. The fact that the promise is made first and foremost to Israel does not exclude the Gentiles, as the passage in Joel 2:28 makes clear ("I will pour out My Spirit on all mankind אשפוך את-רוחי על-כל-בשר"). The association between loving one's neighbour and the presence of the Spirit is made clear in 1 Jn. 4:12-13: "No one has beheld God at any time; if we love one another, God abides in us, and His love is perfected in us. By this we know that we abide in Him and He in us, because He has given us of His Spirit (θεὸν οὐδεὶς πώποτε τεθέαται. ἐὰν ἀγαπῶμεν ἀλλήλους, ὁ θεὸς ἐν ὑμῖν μένει καὶ ἡ ἀγάπη αὐτοῦ ἐν ὑμῖν τετελειωμένη ἐστίν. Ἐν τούτῳ γινώσκομεν ὅτι ἐν αὐτῷ μένομεν καὶ αὐτὸς ἐν ἡμῖν, ὅτι ἐκ τοῦ πνεύματος αὐτοῦ δέδωκεν ἡμῖν)." 1 John may in fact be read as a "commentary" on Gal. 5. For the Gentiles' receipt of the Spirit, see 3:10-14 and 4:1f.

[156] τοῦ ἐπιστρέψαι ἀπὸ σκότους εἰς φῶς καὶ τῆς ἐξουσίας τοῦ σατανᾶ ἐπὶ τὸν θεόν, τοῦ λαβεῖν αὐτοὺς ἄφεσιν ἁμαρτιῶν καὶ κλῆρον ἐν τοῖς ἡγιασμένοις πίστει τῇ εἰς ἐμέ.

[157] R. 'Awira or, as some say, R. Joshua b. Levi, made the following exposition: The Evil Inclination has seven names. The Holy One, blessed be He, called it Evil, as it is said, *For the imagination of man's heart is evil from his youth* (Gen. 8:21). Moses called it the Uncircumcised, as it is said, *Circumcise therefore the foreskin of your heart* (Dt. 10:16). David called it Unclean, as it is said, *Create [in] me a clean heart, O Lord* (Ps. 51:10), which implies that there is an unclean one. Solomon called it the Enemy, as it is said, *If thine enemy be hungry, give him bread* [Torah] *to eat and if he be thirsty give him water to drink. For thou wilt heap coals of fire upon his head, and the Lord will reward thee* (Prov. 25:21-22); read not, 'will reward thee' but 'will cause it to be at peace with thee.' Isaiah called it the Stumbling-Block, as it is said, *Cast ye up, Cast ye up, clear the way, take up the stumbling-block out of the way of my people* (Isa. 57:14). Ezekiel called it Stone, as it is said, *And I will take away the heart of stone out of your flesh and I will give you a heart of flesh* (Ezek. 36:26). Joel called it the Hidden One, as it is said, *But I will remove far off from you the hidden one* [MT: northern] (Joel 2:20) דרש רבי עירא ואיתימא רבי יהושע בן לוי: שבעה שמות יש לו ליצר הרע: הקדוש ברוך הוא קראו 'רע,' שנאמר: כי יצר לב האדם רע מנעוריו. משה קראו 'ערל,' שנאמר: ומלתם את ערלת לבבכם. דוד קראו 'טמא,' שנאמר: לב טהור ברא לי אלהים - מכלל דאיכא טמא. שלמה קראו 'שונא,' שנאמר: אם רעב שנאך האכילהו

The conjunction καὶ (kai - "and") in verse 16 may serve as a promise or, perhaps, function causally - the latter mode indicating the consequence of walking in the Spirit: "so that you will not carry out the desire of the flesh (ἐπιθυμίαν σαρκὸς οὐ μὴ τελέσητε)" (cf. verse 17).[159] The verb τελέω (teleō - "carry out") recalls the "fulfilment (πεπλήρωται)" of the Torah in love (cf. verse 14) (cf. 1 Jn. 4:12).[160] The Greek root functions in the LXX to render the Hebrew roots שלם (shalem) and תמם (tamam), both signifying "perfection, completeness, wholeness."[161] Paul later employs the same verb in Romans in describing how gentile believers become acceptable before God through circumcision of the heart: "And will not he who is physically uncircumcised, if he keeps [fulfils] the Torah, will he not judge you who though having the letter *of the Torah* and circumcision are a transgressor of the Torah?"[162] (Rom. 2:27).[163]

The expression "the desire of the flesh (ἐπιθυμίαν σαρκὸς)" denotes the shift which Paul now makes from a literal usage of "flesh" to a quasi-personification of the "Flesh" as equivalent to "sin." Up to this point, Paul has employed "flesh" in pertinence to bodily parts - i.e., circumcision, the

---

לחם ואם צמא השקהו מים כי גחלים אתה חותה על ראשו וה' ישלם לך. אל תקרי 'ישלם לך' אלא 'ישלימנו לך'. ישעיה קראו 'מכשול,' שנאמר: סולו סולו פנו דרך הרימו מכשול מדרך עמי. יחזקאל קראו 'אבן,' שנאמר: והסרתי את לב האבן מבשרכם ונתתי לכם לב בשר. יואל קראו 'צפוני,' שנאמר: ואת הצפוני ארחיק מעליכם" (Suk. 52a).

[158] These verses indicate the breadth of Paul's employment of "Kingdom language" - a usage which has traditionally been marked as rather sparse in contrast to the gospels (cf. Wenham: 71ff). His so-called preference for the terminology of "righteousness" should not obscure the fact that, in dealing here in Galatians with sin as "hypocrisy" - that behaviour which places importance on the "minor" commandments, restricts the commandments by the "traditions of men," and fails to see love as the Torah's purpose - Paul is speaking directly about the "keys" to God's Kingdom, which is/are "righteousness and peace and joy in the Holy Spirit (ἡ βασιλεία τοῦ θεοῦ ... δικαιοσύνη καὶ εἰρήνη καὶ χαρὰ ἐν πενύματι ἁγίῳ)" (Rom. 14:17) (see Introduction, **Theological pointers** (Justification), 2:15-21, 3:1-5, 19-20, verses 2-12, and above).

[159] In effect, the grammatical distinctions (including reading the verb either as an imperative or as an aorist subjunctive expressive of emphatic negation of a future possibility) are moot in light of Paul's claim that subjection to dual masters constitutes an impossibility (cf. verse 18) (see above).

[160] Rabbinic texts speak not of "fulfilling [למלא]" all the commandments of the Torah but of "making it stand/exist [לקיים]" - or, in other words, confirming its true meaning by properly interpreting it (cf. Mekh.Be-shall. 7 [R. Pappias]) (cf. Flusser, Judaism: 378f).

[161] Cf. Gen. 6:9; Ex. 12:5; Dt. 18:13; 2 Kings 22:26; 3 Kings 8:61; 2 Chron. 8:16; Mt. 5:48, 19:21; 1 Cor. 14:20; Col. 4:12; Sir. 44:17. For Jesus as the Torah's fulfilment, see verses 2-12 (n48) and above.

[162] καὶ κρινεῖ ἡ ἐκ φύσεως ἀκροβυστία τὸν νόμον *τελοῦσα* σὲ τὸν διὰ γράμματος καὶ περιτομῆς παραβάτην νόμου.

[163] For the significance of Romans 2 for Galatians, embodying as it does the ideas of "within the margin of the judgment" and hypocrisy, see 2:15-21, 6:1f and above.

Galatians' desire being for social status through acceptance by the Jewish community on the customary terms of full conversion.[164] Here, however, he begins to treat "Spirit" and "flesh" more as "ethical" terms, in a fashion particularly reminiscent of the Qumran literature: "To the spirit of deceit belong greed, sluggishness in the service of justice, wickedness, falsehood, pride, haughtiness of heart, dishonesty, trickery, cruelty, much insincerity, impatience, much foolishness, impudent enthusiasm for appalling acts performed in a lustful passion, filthy paths in the service of impurity, blasphemous tongue, blindness of eyes, hardness of hearing, stiffness of neck, hardness of heart in order to walk in all the paths of darkness and evil cunning"[165] (1QS 4:9-11).[166]

Rather than seeking after the flesh/circumcision, God looks for the circumcision of the heart: "My heart was pruned and its flower appeared, then grace sprang up in it, and it produced fruits for the Lord. For the Most High circumcised me by his Holy Spirit, then he uncovered my inward being toward him, and filled me with his love. And his circumcising became my salvation, and I ran in the Way in his peace, in the Way of truth" (Odes Sol. 11:1-3)[167] (see 3:24-26, below, and verses 19-23).[168] In terms which portray the irreparable dichotomy between the "flesh" – as a physical entity and/or convention – and God's pleasure, Paul later tells the Corinthians: "Now I say this, brethren, that flesh and blood cannot inherit the kingdom of God; nor does the perishable inherit the imperishable"[169] (1 Cor. 15:50).[170]

---

[164] See Introduction, **Occasion and circumstances**; **Argument**, 6:1-11, and verses 2f. This section may consequently be seen as an elaboration on the "narrative" (or "historical") handling of the issue in 3:19f and 4:1f (see there).

[165] ולרוח עולה רחוב נפש ושפול ידים בעבודת צדק רשע ושקר גוה ורום לבב כחש ורמיה אכזרי ורוב חנף קצור אפים ורוב אולת וקנאת זדון מעשי תעובה ברוח זנות ודרכי נדה בעבודת טמאה ולשון גדופים עורון עינים וכבוד אוזן קושי עורף וכובוד לב ללכת בכול דרכי חושך וערמת רוע.

[166] The singular ("desire of the flesh") here may reflect the Hebrew יצר בשר (yetzer basar – "inclination of the flesh") found in the Qumran literature (cf. 1QHᵃ 18:23, 24:5; 4Q418 2:8), a parallel phrase to the "spirit of flesh רוח בשר" (cf. 1QHᵃ 4:25, 5:19; 4Q416 1:12; 4Q418 81:1-2). The author of the Self-glorification Hymn designates his lack of "desire according to the flesh" as a mark of his divine stature: "I am counted among the gods and my dwelling is in the holy congregation; [my] des[ire] is not according to the flesh, [but] all that is precious to me is in (the) glory (of) [. . .] the holy [dwel]ling אני עם אלים את[תי]חשב ומכוני בעדת קודש לוא כבשר תאותי "כיא] כול יקר לי בכבוד [. . . מעוון הקודש (4Q491c f1:7-8).

[167] Cf. Dt. 10:16, 30:6; Jer. 4:4, 9:25-26; Rom. 2:25f; Jub. 1:22-23; Odes Sol. 11:1-3; 1QS 5:5; 1QpHab 11:13; 4Q177 2:16; 4Q434 1:4; PRE 29; Gen.R. 46:5; Lev.R. 25:6; Ber. 29a (see 2:1-10 [Circumcision] and 3:1-5 [verse 3], 26-29).

[168] For the uncircumcision of the Gentiles, see 2:11-14 (excursus).

[169] Τοῦτο δέ φημι, ἀδελφοί, ὅτι σάρξ καὶ αἷμα βασιλείαν θεοῦ κληρονομῆσαι οὐ δύναται οὐδὲ ἡ φθορὰ τὴν ἀηφθαρσίαν κληρονομεῖ.

[170] While Paul is not playing, in Corinthians, on "flesh" in the sense of circumcision, his declaration to that community lends itself to such an

Verse 17: The "two spirits" are in opposition to one another, and cannot be reconciled, it being impossible to serve two masters – one unclean and the other holy – simultaneously: "[What is] the spirit of flesh to understand all these matters and to have insight in [your wondrous] and great counsel? What is someone born of a woman among all your awesome works? He is a structure of dust fashioned with water, his counsel is the [iniquity] of sin, shame of dishonor and so[urce of] impurity, and a depraved spirit rules over him ... Only by your goodness is man acquitted, [purified] by the abundance of [your] compa[ssion.] You embellish him with your splendour, you install [him over an abun]dance of pleasures, with everlasting peace and length of days. For [you are the truth, and] your word does not depart ... What is flesh compared to this? What creature of clay can do wonders? He is in iniquity from his maternal womb, and in guilt of unfaithfulness right to old age. But I know that justice does not belong to man nor to a son of Adam a perfect path. To God Most High belong all the acts of justice, and the path of man is not secure except by the spirit which God creates for him to perfect the path of the sons of Adam so that all his creatures come to know the strength of his power and the abundance of his compassion with all the sons of his approval" (1QHᵃ 5:19-24, 12:29-33)[171] (cf. Shulam and Le Cornu: 209-90) (see 3:1-5, 19f, 4:1-7, and above).[172]

Rabbinic texts reflect a similar idea in explaining why the slave's *ear* was bored: "Why was the ear singled out from all the other limbs of the body? The Holy One, blessed be He, said, This ear, which heard my Voice

---

interpretation when read in the light of Galatians. Although Paul only mentions the "Kingdom" explicitly here in Galatians (cf. verse 21), we have suggested that the motif of hypocrisy, as demonstrated in Peter's behaviour in 2:12-13, is a dominant one in the letter. In the light of the fact that hypocrisy is expressed in "Kingdom language" in rabbinic literature, Galatians may be read as informed by the theme of God's Kingdom (see Introduction, **Argument**; **Theological pointers**, 2:15-21, verses 2-12, and above).

[171] ‏נומה אף ה[ו]א רוח בשר להבין בכול אלה ולהשכיל בסו[ד] פאל[ך ה]גדול ומה ילוד אשה בכול מעשיך הנוראים והוא מבנה עפר ומגבל מים א[שר עוון חטא]ה סודו ערות קלן ומ[קור] נדה ורוח נעוה משלה בו ... רק בטובך יצדק איש וברוב רח[מי]ך יטהר] בהדרך תפארנו ותמשילה[נ] בר[ו]ב עדנים עם שלום עולם ואורך ימים כי [אמת אתה ו]דברך לא ישוב אחור ... מי בשר כזאת ומה יצר חמר להגדיל פלאות והוא בעוון מרחם ועד שבה באשמת מעל ואני ידעתי כי ל[א לאנוש צדקה ול]א לבן אדם תום דרך לאל עליון כול מעשי צדקה ודרך אנוש ל[א תכון כי אם ברוח יצר אל לו להתם דרך לבני אדם למען ידעו כול מעשיו בכוח גבורתו ורוב רחמיו על כול בני רצונו.‏

[172] Cf. Jn. 3:6; Rom. 7:7ff, 8:3f; Test.Reuv. 2:1-3:9; Test.Jud. 18:6, 20:1f; Test.Asher 1:3-9. The postpositive conjunction γάρ (gar – "for") both confirms the opposition between the Spirit and flesh stated in verse 16 and elaborates its nature (cf. Longenecker, Galatians: 245). It is no coincidence that the Qumran community conceived their constitution as a warring faction against the "sons of darkness" – such warfare yielding the context of the struggle between the "Two Ways." For bondage to sin, see 1:1-5, 2:1-10, 15-21, 3:19f, and 4:1f; for "born of a woman," see 4:1-7.

on Mount Sinai when I proclaimed, *For unto me the children of Israel are servants, they are my servants* (Lev. 25:55), and not servants of servants, and yet this [man] went and acquired a master for himself — let it be bored!"[173] (Kid. 22b).[174] Once a person becomes part of God's people, s/he becomes His slave – and that of none other, be it an idol or another human being. Rather than an anticipated consequence, Paul inserts a more awkward purpose clause here: "so that you may do not the things that you please (ἵνα μὴ ἃ ἐὰν θέλητε ταῦτα ποιῆτε)" – as if to say, the opposition between flesh and Spirit is for the purpose of preventing you from doing what/as you wish/will.

Since the purpose cannot be God's, it is best understood as that of the flesh and Spirit independently: "*Thus you are to be holy to Me, for I the Lord am holy* (Lev. 20:26): Just as I am holy, so you are to be holy. *And I have set you apart from the peoples to be Mine* (ibid). If you are separated from the nations you are for my sake. If not, you belong to Nebuchadnezzar, king of Babylon, and his company. R. Eleazar b. Azariah said: Whence do we know that a man should not say: It is impossible [not] to wear *shatnetz* or not to eat pork or to come into unchastity? He should rather say: It *is* possible – what shall I do?! For thus my Father in Heaven has decreed. This comes to teach us that 'I have set you apart from the peoples to be Mine' means that a man distances himself from transgression and takes upon himself the yoke of the kingdom"[175] (Sifra, Ked. 9:11-12). To the extent that human nature is embroiled in a war between pleasing one master and angering another, those wishing to please God are also constrained – not their own will – to fight the enemy's forces (cf. PA 4:22) (cf. Hays, Galatians: 326).[176]

Verse 18: Paul reiterates his imperative from verse 16, the expression being "led (ἄγεσθε)" by the Spirit (cf. Rom. 8:14) paralleling "walking in the Spirit (πνεύματι περιπατεῖτε)," being "under the Torah (ὑπὸ νόμον)"

---

[173] מה נשתנה אזן מכל אברים שבגוף? אמר הקדוש ברוך הוא: אזן ששמעה קולי על הר סיני בשעה שאמרתי "כי לי בני ישראל עבדים", ולא עבדים לעבדים - והלך זה וקנה אדון לעצמו: ירצע.

[174] Cf. Ex. 21:6; BK 116b; BM 10a; Haggada (n3).

[175] והייתם לי קדושים כי קדוש אני ה': כשם שאני קדוש כך אתם היו קדושים. כשם שאני פרוש כך אתם היו פרושים: ואבדיל אתכם מן העמים להיות לי: מובדלים אתם מן העמים הרי אתם לשמי ואם לאו - הרי אתם של נבוכדנצר מלך בבל וחבריו. רבי אלעזר בן עזריה אומר: מנין שלא יאמר אדם: אי איפשי ללבוש שעטנז, אי איפשי לאכול בשר חזיר, אי איפשי לבוא על הערוה - אבל איפשי - מה אעשה ואבי שבשמים גזר עלי כך? תלמוד לומר: ואבדיל אתכם מן העמים להיות לי: נמצא פורש מן העבירה ומקבל עליו מלכות שמים.

[176] In this sense, the significance is not simply of "wishing to do good yet transgressing instead" but of having no choice in whether to engage in the conflict. Once embroiled a war, one is committed to its close (cf. PA 2:16) (cf. Hays, Galatians: 326). Here too, traces of Paul's previous argument against the influencers may still be reflected. As representatives of the "flesh," the influencers lust against the Spirit. The Galatians cannot do as they wish and become circumcised because in doing so they disown the Spirit's working in them.

corresponding in parallel to the "desire of the flesh (ἐπιθυμίαν σαρκὸς)."[177] Having depicted the Torah's custody in terms of an accommodation to human weakness (see 3:19f), the latter constituting the domain of the "elemental things of the world" (see 4:1-7), it is evident that receipt of the Spirit characterises the life of one living in the Messiah.[178] Once a person has died to him/herself by putting on the Messiah in baptism, s/he cannot obey the "prince of this world" except by forfeiting his/her inheritance (see 2:15-21 and 4:1-7). In seeking to find social status within the Jewish community through circumcision/conversion, with the demand for full Torah-observance which the latter entails, Paul's Galatian disciples are, he warns, in danger of putting themselves under the bondage of sin all over again: "By what a man is overcome, by this he is enslaved (ᾧ γάρ τις ἥττηται, τούτῳ δεδούλωται)" (2 Pet. 2:19). Paul cannot allow such an act – for "It was for freedom that the Messiah set us free" (verse 1).[179]

Verses 19-23:
Now the deeds of the flesh are evident, which are: immorality, impurity, sensuality, idolatry, sorcery, enmities, strife, jealousy, outbursts of anger, disputes, dissensions, factions, envying, drunkenness, carousings, and things like these, of which I forewarn you, just as I have forewarned you that those who practice such things shall not inherit the kingdom of God. But the fruit of the Spirit is love, joy, peace, patience, kindness, goodness, faithfulness, gentleness, self-control; against such things there is no law.

Paul tells his disciples that the "deeds of the flesh" with which they are at war are "evident (φανερὰ δέ ἐστιν)." This expression pre-empts Paul's declaration in Romans that "that which is known about God is evident within them [the Gentiles]; for God made it evident to them (τὸ γνωστὸν τοῦ θεοῦ φανερόν ἐστιν ἐν αὐτοῖς· ὁ θεὸς γὰρ αὐτοῖς ἐφανέρωσεν)" (Rom. 1:19) – such that people are "without excuse" for refusing to honour God.[180] The opposite of this recognition is represented by those things

---

[177] For "living" in the Spirit, see verses 24-26. Begging over-repetition, the reader is reminded, once again, that Paul does not equate Torah or Torah-observance ("works of the law") with sin, but with the need to "go beyond the law, which in itself is right and good, in order to do what is right and good" (Berkovits: 27). Sin is bondage to the "elemental things of the world" – to which the Torah merely "accommodates" itself in condescending to the limitations of human nature, resulting in the "hypocrisy" of not "doing" what one "says/hears" (see Introduction, **Argument; Theological pointers** (Justification), 2:12-15, 3:1-5, 19f, 4:1f, verses 2-12, and above).

[178] For Jesus' "representative" role, see 2:15-21, 3:1ff, and 4:1f.

[179] For this verse, see 4:21-31 (end) and verse 1.

[180] The Greek word also calls attention to the talmudic term פשיטא (pshita – "it is obvious!"). The latter expresses some astonishment that a statement, so manifest in its significance, should have necessitated expression, being followed in such a case by a demonstration that its clarity was less evident than assumed, or that it was necessary to avoid misunderstanding (cf. Ber. 20b). When employed at the

which rabbinic literature considers to be injunctions which, despite not being explicitly stated in Scripture, should be understood as "natural law": "Our Rabbis taught: *Mine ordinances shall ye do*, i.e., such commandments which, if they were not written [in Scripture], they should by right have been written and these are they: [the laws concerning] idolatry, immorality and bloodshed, robbery and blasphemy"[181] (Yoma 67b).[182]

While in "stating the obvious" here Paul may wish to encourage his disciples, giving them to understand that the enemy is easily identifiable, passages from the Qumran texts suggest that "evidence" provides the ground for punishment: "And thus is the judgment of everyone who enters the congregation of the men of perfect holiness and is slack in the fulfilment of the instructions of the upright. This is the man who is melted in the crucible. *Blank* When his deeds are evident, he shall be expelled from the congregation ... But when his deeds are evident, according to the explanation of the law in which the men of perfect holiness walked, no-one should associate with him ..."[183] (CD-B 20:1-3, 6-7).[184]

The "deeds of the flesh (ἔργα τῆς σαρκός)" themselves represent the "fruit" of a "mind set on the flesh (τὸ φρόνημα τῆς σαρκὸς)" (Rom. 8:7).[185]

---

beginning of a sentence, it may introduce a question indicating that while some issues possess obvious answers, others remain to be resolved: "It is clear what the ruling is in case A; but what about case B?" (cf. Ber. 12a) (cf. Steinsaltz, Talmud: 137) (see 3:10-14 [n135]).

[181] ת"ר: את משפטי תעשו - דברים שאלמלא (לא) נכתבו, דין הוא שיכתבו. ואלו הן: עבודת ככבים וגלוי עריות ושפיכות דמים וגזל וברכת השם.

[182] Cf. Apoc.Abr. 8:1-6; Philo, *De Abr.* 6; Sifra, Acharei mot 13; Tanh.Mishp. 7; Yalk.Lev. 587f; Gen.R. 39:1, 61:1; Lev.R. 2:10; Num.R. 14:2; [ARNᵃ 4:5]; San. 74a; Eruv. 100b (cf. Shulam and Le Cornu: 91-95; Le Cornu and Shulam: 783, 837f).

[183] וכן המשפט לכל באי עדת אנשי תמים הקדש ויקוץ מעשות פקודי ישרים הוא האיש הנתך בתוך כור: {ה} *vacat* בהופע מעשיו ישלח מעדה ... ובהופע מעשיו כפי מדרש התורה אשר יתהלכו בו אנשי תמים הקדש אל {ית} יאות איש עמו ...

[184] For the principle of non-association, see 6:1-11.

[185] For the "Two Ways," see verses 13-18. The reservations expressed by commentators regarding Paul's reflection of this concept are less than convincing. The present discussion has attempted to demonstrate its traces already in verses 13-18, where it forms part of a complex tradition concerning Torah-observance through love rather than fear (see there). This fact mitigates against the claim that the doctrine can only be identified when expressly invoked by the word "two" (ways, spirits, angels) (cf. Longenecker, Galatians: 251-52). Flusser, moreover, asserts a "literary affinity" between 1QS and Gal. 5: "In the list of the 'fruit of the spirit', ἀγαπή corresponds to אמת בני כול על חסדים רוב = χαρά ;שמחת עולמים = εἰρήνη = רוב ;שלום; μακροθυμία = אפים אורך ;ἀγαθωσύνη = עולמים טוב ;ὅσιος = אמאנת מאמנת גבורה חכמת ... טהרת כבוד מתעב כול גלולי נדה = ἐγκράτεια ;רוח ענוה = πραΰτης ;צדקת = בכול מעשי אל (?) There is no term corresponding to χρηστότης" (Judaism: 262n157). (In translation: "love" is aligned with "generous compassion with all the sons of truth"; "grace" with "eternal enjoyment"; "peace" with "plentiful peace"; "longsuffering" with the

While the "sinful passions" bear "fruit for death," dying to one's human nature through Jesus' death enables the bearing of "fruit for God"[186] (Rom. 7:4-5). The "deeds of the flesh" parallel here "the works of the Torah (ἔργων νόμου)" (cf. 2:16, 3:1, 5, 10) to the extent that the latter accommodate the "weakness of the flesh" and leave a person in the "hypocritical" position of not being able to perform the "weighty provisions" of "justice and mercy and faithfulness."[187]

Paul now sets out before his Galatian disciples the two "spirits," of practice and intention/faithfulness, and their "ways" – in direct parallel to the description in 1QS 4:1ff (see verses 2f).[188] The list opens with three terms designating sexual offences, continues with idolatry and sorcery, contains an extended catalogue of eight forms of strife and dissension in the middle, and concludes with transgressions devolving from self-indulgence (cf. Hays, Galatians: 327). The first group refers to dishonouring of the physical body, the second relates to dishonouring of God, the third to the dishonouring of one's fellow, and the last to lack of personal respect.[189]

---

same; "goodness" with "eternal goodness"; "faithfulness" with "potent wisdom which trusts in all the deeds of God" (?); "gentleness" with a "spirit of meekness"; and "self-control" with "magnificent purity which detests all unclean idols." Only "goodness" has no parallel in 1QS.)

[186] ἐθανατώθητε τῷ νόμῳ διὰ τοῦ σώματος τοῦ Χριστοῦ ... ἵνα καρποφορήσωμεν τῷ θεῷ. ὅτε γὰρ ἦμεν ἐν τῇ σαρκί, τὰ παθήματα τῶν ἁμαρτιῶν τὰ διὰ τοῦ νόμου ἐνηργεῖτο ἐν τοῖς μέλεσιν ἡμῶν, εἰς τὸ καρποφορῆσαι τῷ θανάτῳ.

[187] See Introduction, **Argument; Theological pointers** (Justification), 2:15-21, 3:1-5, 19f, and verses 2f. Here again, we would emphasise that Paul's diatribe is not against the Torah but against the human weakness which frustrates its designs (see 3:19f).

[188] Such lists are commonplaces in contemporary Jewish literature on the "two ways" (cf. Mk. 7:21-23; Rom. 1:29-32; 1 Cor. 6:9-10; 2 Cor. 12:20; Eph. 5:3-5; Col. 3:5-10; 1 Tim. 6:11; 2 Tim. 2:22; Rev. 21:8; Test.Ben. 7:2-3; 1 Enoch 94-104; 2 En. [J] 10:4-5 ; 2 Bar. 73:4; 3 Bar. 8:4, 13:3; Lev.R. 9:9; PA 2:7, 9, 11). As the omission of money and theft – such an anathema to the Qumran community, for example – suggests, the list is not comprehensive but serves as a selection of practices which characterise the "sons of darkness."

[189] The list thus covers both halves of the Decalogue and involves sins between wo/man and wo/man and wo/man and God, including "thoughts" and "actions." While πορνεία (porneia) frequently also designates idolatry in the Tanakh ("whoring after other gods") (cf. Isa. 57:3ff; Jer. 3:1ff; Ezek. 16:6ff; Hosea; Jn. 8:41; Rev. 2:20f), the following two sexual terms suggest that Paul is employing the term in its predominant sense of fornication – i.e., any unlawful sexual intercourse, whether involving a married person or not (cf. Gen. 38:24; Hos. 1:2; Mt. 5:32; Acts 15:20, 29). For the Decalogue, see verses 13-18; for Jewish characterisation of gentile behaviour, see 2:11-14 (excursus).

While idolatry is considered to be a sin against the whole Torah,[190] certain rabbinic traditions regard interpersonal sins as deserving of greater punishment:

> When Israel disregarded *Thou shalt have no other gods before Me* (Ex. 20:3), He forgave them, for in idolatry there is only jealousy, as it says, *They roused Him to jealousy with strange gods, with abominations did they provoke Him* (Dt. 32:16), and it also says, *Thus they exchanged their glory for the likeness of an ox* (Ps. 106:20). When Israel, however, sinned in Shittim with immorality, twenty-four thousand of them fell [cf. Num. 25:1-9] ... What benefit does Israel have from worshipping idols, that neither see, hear, nor speak, as it says, *They that make them shall be like unto them* (Ps. 115:8)? But for immorality, which is a tangible sin, they were punished. For idolatry, therefore, were they forgiven, but concerning the laws and the commandments God warned them, as it says, *Keep My commandments and live* (Prov. 7:2), and also, *Write them upon the table[t] of thy heart* (Prov. 7:3).[191] (Ex.R. 30:21)[192]

The Greek ἀκαθαρσία (akatharsia) signifies both ritual and moral impurity in the LXX.[193] While it also appears in the first sense in the New Testament texts (cf. Mt. 23:27), its use as a moral term denoting the uncleanness which separates a person from God is confined to the pauline literature, where it overwhelmingly occurs in conjunction with other words denoting sexual vices[194] (cf. Longenecker, Galatians: 254, and for the following discussion).

Although the etymology of ἀσέλγεια (aselgeia) is doubtful, ancient Greek authors employ it to describe "wantonness" or "violence." Josephus associates the word, among other things, with conduct that on the one hand offends ascetic sensibilities and on the other expresses passionate "zeal."[195] Paul links it elsewhere with words expressive of sensuality.[196]

---

[190] Cf. Yev. 9a; Kid. 40a; Ned. 25a.

[191] כיצד בטלו ישראל לא יהיה לך ומחל להם, שאין בעבודת כוכבים ממש אלא קנאה, שנאמר: יקניאוהו בזרים בתועבות יכעיסוהו. וכן כתיב: וימירו את כבודם בתבנית שור. וכשחטאו ישראל בשטים בזנות נפלו מהן כ״ד אלף ... כן ישראל: מה נהנו מעבודת כוכבים שלא רואה ולא שומעת ולא מדברת, שנאמר: כמוהם יהיו עושיהם. אבל הזנות שהוא דבר של ממש לקו עליו ונמחל להם על עבודת כוכבים. אבל על הדינין ועל המצות האלו הזהירן הקדוש ברוך הוא, שנאמר: שמור מצותי וחיה וכן: כתבם על לוח לבך.

[192] The frequency with which the motif of idolatry occurs in this section is striking – and may reflect the fact that this is precisely the background out of which Paul's disciples have come, a relapse into which constitutes a rejection of God Himself. (For the presently-proposed understanding of the Gentiles' "return" in 4:9, see 4:8-11.)

[193] Cf. Lev. 5:3, 18:19, 20:25, 22:3; 2 Chron. 29:5, 16; Prov. 6:16; Ezek. 9:9; 1 Esd. 1:42.

[194] Cf. Rom. 1:24, 6:19; Eph. 5:3; Jos.*War* 4.562.

[195] Cf. *War* 2.121, 4.562. For "zeal," see below.

Sexual misconduct, as represented by incest, constitutes one of the three "cardinal sins" which a Jew must not commit even if his/her life is at stake: "R. Johanan said in the name of R. Simeon b. Jehozadak: By a majority vote it was resolved in the upper chambers of the house of Nithza in Lydda that in every [other] law of the Torah, if a man is commanded: 'Transgress and suffer not death' he may transgress and not suffer death, excepting idolatry, incest [which includes adultery], and murder"[197] (San. 74a) (see also 2:10-14).[198]

Φαρμακία (farmakia – "sorcery"), deriving from φάρμακον (farmakon – a "drug"), signifies the general usage of any drug, for therapy or in its poisonous capacity. The New Testament texts employ it, in continuation of the LXX usage, to designate witchcraft or enchantment, an activity strongly condemned in Jewish literature.[199]

The "enmity," "hostility," or "hatred" which ἔχθραι (echthrai [pl.]) expresses is a common notion in classical Greek writings, the LXX, and the New Testament.[200] Whereas ancient cultures understood its antonym to be "friendship," this is replaced with ἀγάπη (agapē – "love") in the latter texts (cf. verse 22). Jewish sources make hatred as serious as the three cardinal sins together, baseless hatred being considered the cause of the destruction of the Second Temple: "Why was the second Sanctuary destroyed, seeing that in its time they were occupying themselves with Torah, [observance of] precepts, and the practice of charity [gmilut chasadim]? Because therein prevailed hatred without cause. That teaches you that groundless hatred is considered as of even gravity with the three sins of idolatry, immorality, and bloodshed together [the latter being the cause of the destruction of the First Temple]"[201] (Yoma 9b).[202]

---

[196] Cf. Rom. 13:13; 2 Cor. 12:21; Eph. 4:19. "Like ἀκαθαρσία [akatharsia], less specific than πορνεία [porneia], and referring to an indecent conduct, whether involving violation of the person or not, ἀσέλγεια [aselgeia] differs from ἀκαθαρσία [akatharsia] in that the latter emphasises the grossness, the impurity of the conduct, the former its wantonness, its unrestrainedness" (Burton: 306).

[197] אמר רבי יוחנן משום רבי שמעון בן יהוצדק: נימנו וגמרו בעליית בית נתזה בלוד: כל עבירות שבתורה אם אומרין לאדם יעבור ואל תהרג' - יעבור ואל יהרג, חוץ מעבודת כוכבים וגילוי עריות ושפיכות דמים.

[198] Cf. CD-A 4:12-5:11; Wis.Sol. 3:13ff; Sir. 9:1-9, 23:16-28; Test.Reuv. 2:8-9, 4:1-6:5; Test.Jud. 15:1f, 18:2; Pes. 25a-b; Yoma 82a.

[199] Cf. Ex. 7:11, 22; Isa. 47:9, 12; Rev. 9:21, 18:23; 1QS 5:26; Wis.Sol. 12:4; 2 En. 10:4; 3 Bar. 8:4; San. 10:1; San. 56b, 65b. The verb, φαρμάσσω (farmassō), means "to poison." For Paul's possible reference to the "evil eye" motif, see 3:1-5 and 4:12-20.

[200] The prevalence of plurals in the list points to Paul's emphasis upon the communal aspect of such behaviours, the items constituting phenomena carried out in the context of community, rather than being purely personal reprehensions.

[201] אבל מקדש שני שהיו עוסקין בתורה ובמצות וגמילות חסדים, מפני מה חרב? מפני שהיתה בו שנאת חנם - ללמדך ששקולה שנאת חנם כנגד שלש עבירות: עבודה זרה גלוי עריות ושפיכות דמים.

[202] Cf. Test.Gad 3:1-5:6; Tos.Men. 13:22; JYoma 4b; Kal.Rab. 1:12, 8:10; DEZ 6:5; Shab. 32b; Arak. 16b. For gmilut chasadim, see 6:1-11.

ἔρις (eris) denotes "strife," "discord," "contention" both in the LXX and Josephus.[203] The nine New Testament usages are all pauline.[204] Sirach admonishes: "Abstain from strife, and thou shalt diminish thy sins; for a furious man will kindle strife. A sinful man disquieteth friends and maketh debate among them that be at peace . . . An hasty contention kindleth a fire and an hasty fighting sheddeth blood. If thou blow the spark, it shall burn"[205] (Sir. 28:8-9, 11-12).[206]

In its sense of "envy" – which Paul adds separately (φθόνοι; fthonoi [pl.]) – ζῆλος (zēlos) denotes the negative aspect of "jealousy" and "anger" generated by devotion to another person or thing – and thence either a desire to appropriate what lies in the other's possession and/or a resentment over their tenure of it. According to Proverbs, envy eats at a person's body: "It is written, *But envy is the rottenness of the bones* (Prov. 14:30): he who has envy in his heart, his bones rot away כל : ורכב עצמות קנאה מרכיבים עצמותיו בלבו, קנאה לו שיש מי" (Shab. 152b). Envy is easily associated with strife: "R. Simeon b. Gamaliel said: . . . whoever brings jealousy and strife into his house, Scripture ascribes it to him as though he brought these among Israel"[207] (ARN[a] 28:3).[208]

As with zeal, the positive or negative meaning of θυμοί (thumoi [pl.]) is also established according to the context. While in the first sense it denotes "disposition" or "courage," in the second it signifies "anger" or "rage" – frequently occurring with ὀργή (orgē – "wrath").[209] Here too, anger is considered as tantamount to idolatry: "Rabbah son of R. Huna said: He who loses his temper, even the Divine Presence is unimportant in his eyes, as it is written, *The wicked, through the pride of his countenance, will not seek God; God is not in all his thoughts* (Ps. 10:4).[210] R. Jeremiah of Difti said: He forgets his learning and waxes ever more stupid, as it is written, *For anger resteth in the bosom of fools* (Eccl. 7:9); and it is written, *But the fool layeth open his folly* (Prov. 13:16). R. Nahman b. Isaac said: It is certain that

---

[203] Cf. Ps. 138:20 [B]; Sir. 28:11, 40:5, 9-10; Jos.*Ant.* 3.96, 7.17, 9.240; *War* 4.109, 5.71.

[204] Cf. Rom. 1:29, 13:13; 1 Cor. 1:11, 3:3; 2 Cor. 12:20; Phil. 1:15; 1 Tim. 6:4; Tit. 3:9.

[205] Ἀπόσχου ἀπὸ μάχης, καὶ ἐλαττώσεις ἁμαρτίας· ἄνθρωπος γὰρ θυμώδης ἐκκαύσει μάχην, καὶ ἀηνὴρ ἁμαρτωλὸς ταράξει φίλους καὶ ἀνὰ μέσον εἰρηνευόντων ἐμβαλεῖ διαβολήν ... ἔρις κατασπευδομένη ἐκκαίει πῦρ, καὶ μάχη κατασπεύδουσα ἐκχέει αἷμα. ἐὰν φυσήσῃς εἰς σπινθῆρα ἐκκαήσεται.

[206] Cf. Ex.R. 30:17; Num.R. 18:4; San. 7a, 32b.

[207] רי שמעון בן גמליאל אומר: . . . המטיל קנאה ותחרות בתוך ביתו מעלה עליו הכתוב כאילו מטיל קנאה ותחרות בישראל.

[208] Cf. 4Q416 f2ii:11-12; Test.Reuv. 3:5; Test.Sim. 3:1ff, 4:5f; Test.Gad 4:5; Sib.Or. 3.662; PA 4:21; Gen.R. 49:8.

[209] Cf. Lk. 4:28; Acts 19:28; Rom. 2:8; 2 Cor. 12:20; Eph. 4:31; Col. 3:8; Heb. 11:27; Rev. 12:12, 14:10, 16:19, 19:15.

[210] NASB: "The wicked, in the haughtiness of his countenance, does not seek *Him*. All his thoughts are, 'There is no God.'"

his sins outnumber his merits, as it is written, *And a furious man aboundeth in transgressions* (Prov. 29:22)"[211] (Ned. 22b).[212]

While ἐριθεῖαι (eritheiai [pl.]) represents a fairly rare word in ancient Greek literature, its cognate ἔριθος (erithos) – signifying a "wage earner" (cf. Tob. 2:11) – lent to it the meaning of "self-seeking." In this sense of selfish ambition and serving one's own interests, it is widely found in the biblical texts.[213] "R. Eleazar Ha-Kappar said: Jealousy, cupidity and [the desire for] honour put a man out of the world"[214] (PA 4:21).

In urging the seriousness of interpersonal disputation, Paul adds διχοστασίαι (dichostasiai [pl.]) – a common political term for "dissensions" or "seditions" (cf. Rom. 16:17). Together with this goes αἱρέσεις (haireseis [pl.]), whose basic meaning of "choice" or "seizure" was extended to signify a "school of thought" – the latter, when denoted in a pejorative sense, conveying the idea of a "faction" or "heresy" (cf. 1 Cor. 11:19; 2 Pet. 2:1). In Jewish tradition, dissension was particularly associated with Korah: "[A controversy] that is not in the name of heaven, the end thereof is not [destined] to result in something permanent . . . Which is the [kind of] controversy that is not in the name of heaven? Such as was the controversy of Korah and all his congregation [cf. Num. 16:1ff]"[215] (PA 5:17) (cf. PA 4:11).

The two final vices are associated with drink. μέθαι (methai [pl.]) signifies both "strong drink" and "drunkenness" in the LXX. In later Jewish writings, the latter sense prevails almost exclusively.[216] Such a state was frequently induced by and expressed in κῶμοι (kōmoi [pl.]) – "orgies," "carousing," or "revelling" – particularly those linked to the honouring of Dionysus (Bacchus) in the Greek world, although warnings against similar effects are found in the LXX.[217]

As with the strong warnings against and graphic descriptions of overindulgence found throughout Jewish literature[218], the latter abounds in admonitions that engaging in the vices listed here will "put a man out of the world":

---

[211] אמר רבה בר רב הונא: כל הכועס אפילו שכינה אינה חשובה כנגדו, שנאמר: רשע כגובה אפו בל ידרוש אין אלהים כל מזמותיו. ר' ירמיה מדיפתי אמר: משכח תלמודו ומוסיף טיפשות, שנאמר: כי כעס בחיק כסילים ינוח, וכתיב: וכסיל יפרוש אולת. ר' נחמן בר יצחק אמר: בידוע שעונותיו מרובין מזכיותיו, שנאמר: ובעל חימה רב פשע.

[212] Cf. Test.Dan 3:1-4:7; PA 2:10; Eruv. 65b.

[213] Cf. Rom. 2:8; 2 Cor. 12:20; Phil. 1:17, 2:3; Jas. 3:14, 16.

[214] רבי אלעזר הקפר אומר: הקנאה והתאוה והכבוד מוציאין את האדם מן העולם.

[215] [כל-מחלוקת] שאינה לשם שמים אין סופה להתקיים . . . ושאינה לשם שמים? זו מחלוקת קרח וכל עדתו.

[216] Cf. Jud. 13:15; Jos.Ant. 1.177; War 5.21, 23; CA 2.195, 204.

[217] Cf. Rom. 13:13; 1 Pet. 4:3; Wis.Sol. 14:23; 2 Macc. 6:4; Jos.Ant. 11.66, 17.65; War 1.570, 2.29.

[218] Cf. Prov. 20:1, 23:29f; Lk. 21:34; Rom. 13:13; 1 Cor. 5:11; Eph. 5:18; 1 Thess. 5:7; 1 Pet. 4:3; 1 Esd. 3:17-24; Sir. 26:8; Lev.R. 12:1f; Num.R. 10:3, 8; Eruv. 65a-b.

He [R. Jochanan further] said unto them: Go forth and observe which is the evil way from which a man should remove himself far? R. Eliezer said, An evil eye [envy]; R. Joshua said, An evil associate; R. Jose said, An evil neighbour . . . R. Eleazar said, An evil heart. Said he [R. Jochanan] unto them: I prefer the words of Eleazar b. Arach to your words, for within the comprehensive character of his words are your words [included].[219] (PA 2:9)[220]

R. Joshua said: An evil eye, the evil inclination, and hatred for [one's fellow-]creatures put a man out of the world.[221] (PA 2:11)[222]

R. Dosa ben Harkinas said, Morning sleep, (and) midday wine, (and) children's talk, and sitting in the houses of assembly of the ignorant drive a man from the world.[223] (PA 3:10)[224]

Although commentators frequently remark on the relative paucity of Paul's reference to the Kingdom of God, sometimes suggesting that this section constitutes "a portion of the catechetical instruction of the early church given by Paul to his converts when he was with them" (Longenecker, Galatians: 258), Paul's rebuke of Peter – which we have suggested forms the heart of the letter – appears to revolve precisely around the ways in which it is possible to "enter the kingdom of heaven."[225] Here, in parallel to the hypocrisy of neglecting the "weightier provisions" of the Torah such as "justice and mercy and faithfulness" in favour of "lighter" commandments (Mt. 23:23),[226] Paul speaks in the language which he later adopts again in Romans: "For the kingdom of God is not eating and drinking, but righteousness and peace and joy in the Holy Spirit"[227] (Rom. 14:17) (see 2:15-21, verses 13-18, and below).[228]

---

[219] אמר להם : צאו וראו איזוהי דרך רעה שיתרחק ממנה האדם. רבי אליעזר אומר : עין רעה. רבי יהושע אומר : חבר רע. רבי יוסי אומר : שכן רע . . . רבי אלעזר אומר : לב רע. אמר להם : רואה אני את דברי אלעזר בן ערך מדבריכם, שבכלל דבריו דבריכם.

[220] For the evil eye, see 3:1-5 and 4:12-20.

[221] רבי יהושע אומר : עין הרע, ויצר הרע, ושנאת הבריות, מוציאין את האדם מן העולם.

[222] See also the tradition of "keeping far from" the evil [person] (cf. Dt. 13:5, 17:7; Rom. 16:17; 1 Cor. 5:9-13; 2 Cor. 6:14-18; 2 Thess. 3:6; PA 1:7) (see 6:1-11).

[223] רבי דוסא בן הרכינס אומר : שינה של שחרית, ויין של צהרים, ושיחת הילדים, וישיבת בתי כנסיות של עמי הארץ, מוציאין את האדם מן העולם.

[224] Cf. PRE 13; TBE p. 61; ARN[a] 16:1f, 40:1; ARN[b] 30 (see verses 13-18). For the correspondence between this list and 1QS 4:2f, see above (n185).

[225] See Introduction, **Form**; **Argument**, and 2:15-21.

[226] ἀφήκατε τὰ βαρύτερα τοῦ νόμου, τὴν κρίσον καὶ τὸ ἔλεος καὶ τὴν πίστιν· ταῦτα [δὲ] ἔδει ποιῆσαι κἀκεῖνα μὴ ἀφιέναι.

[227] οὐ γάρ ἐστιν ἡ βασιλεία τοῦ θεοῦ βρῶσις καὶ πόσις ἀλλὰ δικαιοσύνη καὶ εἰρήνη καὶ χαρὰ ἐν πνεύματι ἁγίῳ.

[228] Hardly a better parallel can be found than that of the words of John the Baptist: "Now in those days John the Baptist came preaching in the wilderness of Judea, saying, 'Repent, for the kingdom of heaven is at hand' . . . But when he saw many of

The term "inherit (κληρονομήσουσιν)" relates directly to the Kingdom of Heaven, Paul being at pains to establish for his Galatian disciples the fact that, in Jesus, they have become "sons of the promise" and do not need to look further for status as "sons of the covenant" (see 2:15-21, 3:1ff, and 4:1-7, 21-31). As in the other places in the letter where Paul uses the concept (cf. 3:18, 29, 4:1, 30), it has to do with gaining the "world to come": "One of them, a lawyer, asked him a question, testing him, 'Teacher which is the great commandment in the Torah' ... And behold, a certain lawyer stood up and put him to the test, saying, 'Teacher, what shall I do to inherit eternal life?'"[229] (Mt. 22:35-36; Lk. 10:25).[230]

When on his deathbed, R. Jochanan b. Zakkai was asked by his disciples why he wept – to which he replied: "When there are two ways before me, one leading to Paradise and the other to Gehinnom, and I do not know by which I shall be taken, shall I not weep? They said to him: Master, bless us. He said to them: May it be [God's] will that the fear of heaven shall be upon you like the fear of flesh and blood. His disciples said to him: Is that all? He said to them: If only [you can attain this]!"[231] (Ber. 28b).[232]

---

the Pharisees and Sadducees coming for baptism, he said to them, 'You brood of vipers, who warned you to flee from the wrath to come? Therefore bring forth fruit in keeping with *your* repentance; and do not suppose that you can say to yourselves, 'We have Abraham for our father'; for I say to you, that God is able from these stones to raise up children to Abraham ('Εν δὲ ταῖς ἡμέραις ἐκείναις παραγίνεται 'Ιωάννης ὁ βαπτιστὴς κηρύσσων ἐν τῇ ἐρήμῳ τῆς 'Ιουδαίας [καὶ] λέγων· μετανοιοεῖτε· ἤγγικεν γὰρ ἡ βασιλεία τῶν οὐρανῶν ... 'Ιδὼν δὲ πολλοὺς τῶν Φαρισαίων καὶ Σαδδουκαίων ἐρχομένους ἐπὶ τὸ βάπτισμα αὐτοῦ εἶπέ αὐτοῖς· γεννήματα ἐχιδνῶν, τίς ὑπέδειξεν ὑμῖν φυγεῖν ἀπὸ τῆς μελλούση· ὀργῆς; ποιήσατε οὖν καρπὸν ἄξιον τῆς μετανοίας καὶ μὴ δόξητε λέγειν ἐν ἑαυτοῖς· πατέρα ἔχομεν τὸν 'Αβραάμ. Λέγω γὰρ ὑμῖν ὅτι δύναται ὁ θεὸς ἐκ τῶν λίθων τούτων ἐγεῖραι τέκνα τῷ 'Αβραάμ)" (Mt. 3:1-2, 7-9). Here, we find the Kingdom of God linked to acting as "Abraham's disciples/sons of Abraham" through the producing of the "fruit" of repentance (see 2:15-21, 3:1ff, and verses 2ff, 24-26). For pharisaic hypocrisy, see 2:15-21 and 4:21-31.

[229] καὶ ἐπηρώτησεν εἷς ἐξ αὐτῶν [νομικὸς] πειράζων αὐτόν· διδάσκαλε, ποία ἐντολὴ μεγάλη ἐν τῷ νόμῳ; ... Καὶ ἰδοὺ νομικός τις ἀνέστη ἐκπειράζων αὐτὸν λέγων· διδάσκαλε, τί ποιήσας ζωὴν αἰώνιον κληρονομήσω;

[230] Cf. Mt. 19:16, 29, 25:34; Mk. 12:28f; Lk. 18:18; Acts 20:32; 1 Cor. 6:9, 15:50; Eph. 5:5; Rev. 21:7; 1 En. 40:9; 2 En. 50:1; Ps.Sol. 14:10; 1QS 2:1, 11:7; 1QM 1:13, 13:5-6; 1QHᵃ 6:19, 14:8, 13; 4Q418 55:6; Num.R. 9:17; PA 5:19; Ber. 4b, 51a; Kid. 40b; Pes. 113a; AZ 35b; Sot. 7b.

[231] שיש לפני שני דרכים, אחת של גן עדן ואחת של גיהנם, ואיני יודע באיזו מוליכים אותי ולא אבכה? אמרו לו: רבינו ברכנו. אמר להם: יהי רצון שתהא מורא שמים עליכם כמורא בשר ודם. אמרו לו תלמידיו: עד כאן? אמר להם ולואי.

[232] Rabban Jochanan's answer to his own question regarding which path would bring him to inherit the world to come was thus the "fear of heaven" – the highest possible aspiration: "From our earliest forebears we learn that it was fear of the Holy One which preceded all their subsequent acts, as is said, *Israel saw the great*

Since Paul does not appear to have previously given a similar caution against the practices which he here lists, it is suggested that the reference to a prior "forewarning (προεῖπον)" alludes to his initial visit, perhaps as part of his "prebaptismal ethical teaching" (cf. Did. 7:1) (cf. Longenecker, Galatians: 258).[233] To the extent that the issue *has* arisen – albeit indirectly in Paul's reproof of Peter – a possibility exists that this latter is the occasion which Paul has in mind.[234] The import, in either case, is that "inheritance" – the Kingdom of God – is obtained through God's promise to Abraham, the blessing coming, in Jesus, to Jews and Gentiles alike (see Introduction, **Argument,** 2:15-21, 3:1ff, 4:1-7, and verses 2f).

Verse 22: Paul now presents the proper path according to which those faithful to God in His Messiah should walk (see verses 13-18 [verse 16]). The "fruit (ὁ καρπός)" stand in contrast to the "deeds of the flesh" (verse 19). In such a halakhic setting as this, the term primarily denotes the interest on capital: "Merit has a capital value and also bears fruit [interest], as it is stated, *Say ye of the righteous, that it shall go well with him, for they shall eat* the fruit *of their doings* (Isa. 3:10). Transgression has a capital value but bears no fruit, as it is stated, *Woe unto the wicked! it shall be ill with him* [*for* the work of his hands *shall be done to him*]. Some say that transgression also

---

work which the Lord did upon the Egyptians, and the people feared the Lord (Ex. 14:31). You may conclude, therefore, that as a reward for Israel's awe of their Father in heaven and as a reward for Israel's trust in their Father in heaven, the Holy One will come and deliver Israel from among the peoples of the world and bring them the days of the Messiah and the days of redemption וכן למדנו מאבותינו הראשונים שבתחלת מעשיהם היה להם יראה מלפני הקדוש ברוך הוא, שנאמר: וייראו העם את ה' וגו'. הא למדת שבשכר היראה שיראו אבותינו הקדושים אברהם יצחק ויעקב מן הקדוש ברוך הוא ובשכר האמונה שהאמינו ישראל בהקדוש ברוך הוא יהיה לעתיד שיבא הקדוש ברוך הוא ויפדה את ישראל "מבין העובדי כוכבים ויביא להם ימות בן דוד וימות גאולתנו (TBE p. 129) (cf. Mekh.Be-shall. 7) (see 2:15-21).

[233] The προ (pro) of the verb προλέγω (prolegō) may signify either "*foretelling*" or "telling forth *publicly*" (cf. προγράφω in 3:1). Since Paul elsewhere employs the verb in predictive fashion (cf. 2 Cor. 13:2; 1 Thess. 3:4), it would seem best to understand it here also as an admonition of future consequences attendant upon certain courses of action (cf. Longenecker, Galatians: 258) (see 6:17). For the language of halakhic testimony, see verses 2-12 (verse 3); for Galatians as a "halakhic letter" of rebuke-request along the lines of 4QMMT, see Introduction, **Form**; **Argument** and verses 2f.

[234] This hypothesis may be strengthened if Peter's reprimand is perceived to constitute a direct complaint against the Galatians: "Who has bewitched *you* – in the same way as was Peter?" (see Introduction, **Argument,** 2:15-21, and 3:1-5). For the motif of hypocrisy as occurring throughout this chapter, see verses 2f; for its function in defining "justification," see Introduction, **Theological pointers** (Justification). (The motif of crucifixion [cf. 2:20, 6:14] also recurs in verse 24.) Paul may possibly also be referring to his statement in verse 16.

bears fruit, as it is stated, *Therefore shall they eat of the fruit of their own way, and be filled with their own devices* (Prov. 1:31)"[235] (ARNª 40:2).[236]

Another comment on the same passage directly contrasts the "work of the hands" with the "fruit of blessing": "In another comment the verse is read *Say ye unto the righteous, that it shall be well with him; for they shall eat the fruit of their doings* (Isa. 3:10): You find that the blessing bears fruit, and that the curse does not bear fruit, as is said *Woe unto the wicked! It shall be ill with him; for the work of his hands shall be done to him* (Isa. 3:11). Note that the verse does not say 'fruit of his hands' but *work of his hands*, because the curse does not bear fruit"[237] (Mid.Ps. 118:2) (see 3:10-14).[238]

Halakhah – "walking" with God – constitutes the "wisdom of the feasible" which applies God's written commands in Scripture to daily life in order to please Him out of love for one's fellow: "The rabbis in the Talmud were guided by insight: God forbid that there should be anything

---

[235] זכות יש לה קרן ויש לה פירות, שנאמר: אמרו צדיק כי טוב כי פרי מעלליהם יאכלו. עבירה יש לה קרן ואין לה פירות, שנאמר אוי לרשע רע וגו'. ויש אומרים: יש להם לעבירות פירות, שנאמר: ויאכלו מפרי דרכם וממועצותיהם ישבעו.

[236] Cf. Ex.R. 25:12; Num.R. 3:1; Mid.Ps. 62:4; Yalk.Dt. 946; Yalk.Isa. 395; Pe'ah 1:1; Tos.Pe'ah 1:2-3; JPe'ah 5a; BB 11a. The "capital" in this instance is the reward stored up for the world to come, the "fruits" being enjoyed by the righteous (and wicked, on one view) in this world. (The discrepancy in views with respect to whether transgression bears fruit is due precisely to the fact that in some biblical texts the word "fruit" appears in relation to the reward of the wicked.) According to Paul, the Spirit, who functions as it were as the "down payment" of the Kingdom, constitutes the source from which the interest arises (cf. 2 Cor. 1:22, 5:5; Eph. 1:14 – the Greek ἀρραβών [arrabōn] being a semitic loanword [ערבון; eravon]). For "fruit" as linked to the inheritance of the "disciples of Abraham" (cf. PA 5:19), see below.

[237] דבר אחר: אמרו צדיק כי טוב כי פרי מעלליהם יאכלו. את מוצא את הברכה עושה פירות והקללה אינה עושה פירות, שנאמר: אוי לרשע רע כי גמול ידיו ישיב לו. "כפריי" אינו אומר אלא "כגמולי" – ללמדך שאין עושה פירות.

[238] Although this represents a midrash on the same verse in Isa. 3:10, it is difficult to determine whether the phrase "bears fruit" carries the same significance. The context suggests, first of all, that the verse is read differently, and secondly, that the theme of blessings and curses takes over that of capital and interest. Whatever the conclusion, the midrashist is clearly contrasting "fruit" and "work." For blessings and curses, see 1:6-10, 3:10-14, and 6:12f. Christian commentators also point out the contrast between the plural of deeds and the singular of fruit of a unified community, achieved by natural growth rather than by concerted effort (cf. Gen. 3:17-19), and produced by God in place of flesh and blood (cf. Longenecker, Galatians: 259). It might also be noted that the "vices" constitute premeditated rather than unwitting sins (or "sins of commission" rather than "sins of omission"), thereby implying not only a measure of intention but also a deliberate exercise of will. Their "wages" are earnt – in contrast to God's imputation of righteousness (see 3:6-9). Isa. 57:19 uses the phrase "fruit of the lips [נוב שפתים]" to denote healing and peace – i.e., "salvation" (although rabbinic texts frequently understand the reference to be to prayer [cf. Lev.R. 16:9; Num.R. 11:7; Ber. 34b]). For the Spirit himself as the "first fruit," cf. Rom. 8:23; [1 Cor. 15:20-23; 2 Cor. 1:22; Jas. 1:18].

in the application of the Torah to the actual life situation that is contrary to the principles of ethics. What are those principles? They are Torah principles, like: 'And thou shalt do that which is right and good in the sight of the Eternal One' (Dt. 6:18); or, 'Her ways are ways of pleasantness, and all her paths are peace' (Prov. 3:17) (according to talmudic teaching, those are the ways and the paths of the Torah); or, 'That thou mayest walk in the way of good men, and keep the paths of the righteous' (Prov. 2:20) (which is commanded for every Jew). In summation of such principles the Talmud would say: 'The Torah in its entirety exists for the ways of peace' (Git. 59b). Quite clearly, these principles and such an understanding of the meaning and purpose of the Torah give priority to the ethical demand" (Berkovits: 19) (cf. Travers Herford, Talmud: 109ff).[239]

While the inventory of iniquities may be categorised into groups, that of the Spirit's fruit simply constitutes an exemplary of the qualities which characterise the Kingdom of God.[240] As with catalogues of "trangressions," lists of "good deeds" likewise abound in Jewish literature:

> Whoever possesses these three things, he is of the disciples of Abraham, our Father; and [whoever possesses] three other things, he is of the disciples of Balaam, the wicked. The disciples of Abraham, our father, [possess] a good eye, an humble spirit and a lowly soul.[241] (PA 5:19)[242]

> In [. . .] [. . .] you have [re]moved from me, and in stead of it you have given a pure heart; the evil inclination [you have] remo[ved . . .] [. . .] you have placed in my heart; lewdness of eyes you have removed from me, and you have looked at [. . .] [. . . st]ubbornness you sent away from me, and you turned it into humility; angry rage you removed [from me and you gave] [me a spirit of pa]tience; arrogance and haughtiness you discarded

---

[239] It is not coincidental that Paul later adopts the same principle of acting in "the ways of peace/pleasantness דרכי שלום/נועם" in his discursus on "building up one's brother in love" in Romans 14-15, stressing, as Jesus before him, that "the kingdom of God is not eating and drinking, but righteousness and peace and joy in the Holy Spirit (οὐ γάρ ἐστιν ἡ βασιλεία τοῦ θεοῦ βρῶσις καὶ πόσις ἀλλὰ δικαιοσύνη καὶ εἰρήνη καὶ χαρὰ ἐν πνεύματι ἁγίῳ)" (Rom. 14:17) (see 2:10-14, 6:1-11, verses 2f, and below [n251]). For "walking," see verses 13-18.

[240] Notwithstanding the possible categorisation of the vices, both groups constitute a representative rather than a comprehensive listing (see above [n188]).

[241] כל מי שיש בו שלושה דברים הללו מתלמידיו של אברהם אבינו - ושלושה דברים אחרים מתלמידיו של בלעם הרשע: עין טובה ורוח נמוכה ונפש שפלה – מתלמידיו של אברהם אבינו.

[242] See 2:15-21. This theme is the constant thread through Paul's argument (see Introduction, **Argument**). In chapter 3, he identifies the "heirs" and "inheritance" to God's Kingdom, carried over in 4:1-7 and picked up here in the motif of "eating [the fruit] ואוכלין]" of deeds pleasing to God in this life and "inheriting נוחלין]" the world to come.

from me [. . . to me, the spirit of] [deceit you destroyed . . .] . . . you gave to me … … compassionate [lo]ve and with just judgment and to behave seemly in the paths of God, and [you have removed . . .] you have wiped out, and with the spirit of salvation you have clothed me.[243] (4Q436 f1i:10-ii:4; 4Q438 f4ii:2-3)[244]

"Heedfulness leads to cleanliness, and cleanliness leads to purity, and purity leads to abstinence, and abstinence leads to holiness, and holiness leads to humility, and humility leads to the shunning of sin, and the shunning of sin leads to saintliness, and saintliness leads to [the gift of] the Holy Spirit, and the Holy Spirit leads to the resurrection of the dead."[245] (Sot. 9:15) (see verses 2-12 [verse 5])[246]

Not only does Paul place "love" at the head of the list, but the attributes which follow are all subsumed under its character as Paul later sets it out in 1 Corinthians 13: "Love is patient, love is kind, *and* is not jealous; love does not brag *and* is not arrogant, does not act unbecomingly; it does not seek its own, is not provoked, does not take into account a wrong *suffered*, does not rejoice in unrighteousness, but rejoices with the

---

[243] ב]. .]. .[. .].ג[ערתה ממני ותשם לב טהור תחתיו יצר רע גע]רתה . . . .[.]. . .[ש שמתה בלבבי זנות עינים הסירותה ממני ותבט א]. . .[.]. . .[ע]ורף קשה שלחתה ממני ותשמו ענוה זעף אף הסירותה ממני ותשם]]לי רוח אר]וך אפים גבה לב ורום עינים התנשיתה ממני]. . . לי רוח]]שקר אבדתה . . .]ה נתתה לי מ.]. .[.].

[244] For 1QS 4:2-8, see verses 13-18. The central messianic passage of Isaiah 61 which has resonated in Paul's thought throughout the letter has obvious parallels here too, tying together the motifs of clothing and sowing (cf. 3:27, 6:7-9): "I will rejoice greatly in the LORD, my soul will exult in my God; for He has clothed me with garments of salvation, He has wrapped me with robes of righteousness, as a bridegroom decks himself with a garland, and as a bride adorns herself with her jewels. For as the earth brings forth its sprouts, and as a garden causes the things sown in it to spring up, so the Lord GOD will cause righteousness and praise to spring up before all the nations שוש אשיש בה' תגל נפשי באלהי כי הלבישני בגדי-ישע מעיל צדקה יעטני כחתן יכהן פאר וככלה תעדה כליה: כי כארץ תוציא צמחה וכגנה זרועיה תצמיח כן יצמיח ה' יצמיח צדקה ותהלה נגד כל-הגוים אדני" (Isa. 61:10-11). See 1:1f, 3:1f, 26-29, 4:1f.

[245] רבי פנחס בן יאיר אומר: זריזות מביאה לידי נקיות, ונקיות מביאה לידי טהרה, וטהרה מביאה לידי פרישות, ופרישות מביאה לידי קדשה, וקדשה מביאה לידי ענוה, וענוה מביאה לידי יראת חטא, ויראת חטא מביאה לידי חסידות, וחסידות מביאה לידי רוח הקדש. ורוח הקדש מביאה לידי תחית המתים.

[246] Cf. Cant.R. 1.1.9; Yalk.Dt. 933; Yalk.Isa. 503; Mid.Prov. 15; JShek. 14b; JShab. 1, 3, 3c; AZ 20b. These qualities are among those designated in rabbinic literature as being "great" – a variant on the theme of the "great principle": "Great is peace because . . ." (cf. Num.R. 11:7; Lev.R. 9:9; Eccl.R. 3.14.1; Cant.R. 2.5.3; BB 10a; Ber. 19b, 33a; Ned. 32a) (see verses 13-18). It is striking that all the attributes which Paul lists as fruit here are also to be found elsewhere in Scripture as commandments (cf. Lev. 19:18; Dt. 6:5; Ps. 34:14; Mt. 5:44, 22:36-39; Phil. 4:4; Col. 3:12; 1 Tim. 4:12; Tit. 1:8-9; Jas. 5:8; 2 Pet. 1:5-7) (cf. Pritz: personal communication).

truth; bears all things, believes all things, hopes all things, endures all things"[247] (1 Cor. 13:4-7).[248] According to the Wisdom of Solomon, "the care of discipline is love; and love is the keeping of her [wisdom's] laws; and the giving heed unto her laws is the assurance of incorruption; and incorruption maketh us near God: therefore the desire of wisdom bringeth to a kingdom"[249] (Wis.Sol. 6:17-20) (cf. Rom. 5:2-5).[250]

As in Paul's declaration to the believers in Rome (cf. Rom. 14:17), "joy (χαρά)" is directly associated with the Holy Spirit in rabbinic texts: "The Holy Spirit only rests upon a joyful heart . . . The Holy Spirit does not come to rest . . . but only in the midst of joy . . . שאין רוח הקודש שורה אלא על לב שמח . . . שאין רוח הקודש שורה . . . אלא מתוך דבר שמחה" (JSuk. 22b; Mid.Ps. 24:3).[251]

Like love, "peace (εἰρήνη)" is considered to be one of the qualities most expressive of God's ways: "R. Simeon b. Yohai said: Great is peace, since all blessings are comprised therein, as it is written, *The Lord will give strength unto His people; the Lord will bless His people with peace* (Ps. 29:11)" (Lev.R. 9:9).[252]

"Patience (μακροθυμία)"is most commonly attributed to God, who is "slow to anger ארך אפים" (Ex. 34:6) and thereby gives human beings time to repent: "'*Slow to anger*' (Ps. 103:8) – He was patient with them [Israel], turning towards lovingkindness and looking upon their good deeds rather than upon the evil ones they were destined to do ארך אפים: שהאריך אף עמהם שהוא מטה כלפי חסד ונסתכל בטוב ולא ברע שהיו עתידין לעשות" (Ex.R. 2:1).[253]

---

[247] Ἡ ἀγάπη μακροθυμεῖ, χρηστεύεται ἡ ἀγάπη, οὐ ζηλοῖ, [ἡ ἀγάπη] οὐ περπερεύεται, οὐ φυσιοῦται, οὐκ ἀσχημονεῖ, οὐ ζητεῖ τὰ ἑαυτῆς, οὐ παροξύνεται, οὐ λογίζεται τὸ κακόν, οὐ χαίρει ἐπὶ τῇ ἀδικίᾳ, συγχαίρει δὲ τῇ ἀληθείᾳ· πάντα στέγει, πάντα πιστεύει, πάντα ἐλπίζει, πάντα ὑπομένει.

[248] For love as the summation of the Torah, see verses 13-18. While classical Greek literature neglects the noun ἀγάπη (agapē) in favour of φιλία (filia - intimate friendship), ἔρως (erōs - physical love), and στοργή (storgē - familial love), the LXX employs agapē and erōs indiscriminately. At the same time, it consistently renders God's love by the former (cf. Longenecker, Galatians: 260). James attributes the same fruit to "wisdom" (cf. Jas. 3:17-18).

[249] φροντὶς δὲ παιδείας ἀγάπη, ἀγάπη δὲ τήρησις νόμων αὐτῆς, προσοχὴ δὲ νόμων βεβαίωσις ἀφθαρσίας, ἀφθαρσία δὲ ἐγγὺς εἶναι ποιεῖ θεοῦ· ἐπιθυμία ἄρα σοφίας ἀνάγει ἐπὶ βασιλείαν.

[250] In the context of possession of the keys to enter the Kingdom of Heaven through observance of the "weighty commandments" (see 2:15-21), this reference to a "kingdom" is perhaps not coincidental.

[251] Cf. Ps. 51:11-12; [Jn. 7:38-39]; Acts 13:52; Rom. 14:17, 15:13; Shab. 30b. For Paul's possible precipitation of Rom. 14:17 in this letter, see above; for Romans 14-15 and Galatians with regard to hypocrisy in general, see 2:15-21, 6:1-11, and above (n239).

[252] Cf. Mt. 5:9; Jn. 14:27, 16:33; Rom. 12:18, 14:17; Phil. 4:7; Col. 3:15; Jub. 1:16, 25:20, 31:20; 1 En. 5:7f, 58:4; Test.Dan 5:11; Gen.R. 38:6, 18, 100:8; Num.R. 11:7, 21:1; Dt.R. 5:12, 15; PA 1:11, 17, 2:7.

[253] Cf. Acts 17:30; Rom. 2:4, 3:25, 9:22; 2 Pet. 3:9, 15; Sir. 18:11-12; 1 En. 60:5, 25; Philo, Leg.All. 3.106; Mid.Ps. 77:1; Pes.Rab. 11:2; PRK 24:11; PA 5:2.

Patience is also enumerated in the attributes which describe those who will
find blessing in God's Kingdom: "On that day, they shall lift up one voice,
blessing, glorifying, and extolling in the spirit of faith, in the spirit of
wisdom and patience, in the spirit of mercy, in the spirit of justice and
peace, and in the spirit of generosity. They shall all say in one voice,
'Blessed (is he) and may the name of the Lord of the Spirits be blessed
forever and evermore'" (1 En. 61:11).[254] In this sense, wo/men are required
to be forgiving of others, while on their own account they are to endure
sufferings and trials with steadfastness, accompanied by joy and hope.[255]

"Kindness (χρηστότης)" – the Greek denoting "goodness," "honesty,"
or "kindness" in relation to people – is a further attribute of God, a sign of
His concern for the welfare of His people. As a quality which they also
imitate it constitutes one of the three things upon which the world rests:
"Simeon the Righteous was one of the last of the men of the Great
Synagogue. He used to say: The world is based on three things: the Torah,
divine service [the Temple], and the practice of kindliness"[256] (PA 1:2).[257]

"Goodness (ἀγαθωσύνη)" appears in the LXX as a synonym of
"kindness" and characterises God's favour to His people: "Let the good
come and receive the good from the Good for the good. 'Let the good
come' — that is, Moses, as it is written, *And she saw that he was good* (Ex.
2:2). 'And receive the good' — that is, the Torah, as it is written, *For I give
you good doctrine* (Prov. 4:2). 'From the Good' — that is, the Holy One,
blessed be He, as it is written, *The Lord is good to all* (Ps. 145:9). 'For the
good' — that is, Israel, as it is written, *Do good, O Lord, unto the good* (Ps.
125:4)" (Men. 53b).[258]

"Faithfulness (πίστις)" is the quality of obedience which Paul has
been urging throughout the letter as the proper response to God's
faithfulness in freely sending His son to effect deliverance from the
bondage to the power of sin in this world (see 1:1-5, 2:1-10, 15-21, 3:6ff, 4:1f,
and verses 2f). The fact that Paul includes it in the "fruit of the Spirit"
indicates that it constitutes a way of life ("walk") characterized by

[254] Cf. Col. 3:12; 1 Thess. 5:14; Jas. 5:7f; Test.Jos. 2:7, 10:1, 17:2; 2 En. 50:2; 1QS 4:3;
4Q436 f1ii:3; Ex.R. 19:4. The parallels between these qualities and those of Mic. 6:8
are striking, emphasizing, once again, the link between "walking" and producing
fruit "in the Spirit" and acting "beyond the law, which in itself is right and good, in
order to do what is right and good" (see 2:15-21, verses 2f, and above).
[255] Cf. Ex. 34:6; Rom. 2:4, 5:3-5, 9:22; 2 Cor. 6:6; Eph. 4:2; Col. 1:11, 3:12; 1 Tim. 1:16; 2
Tim. 3:10, 4:2; Heb. 6:12.
[256] שמעון הצדיק היה משירי כנסת הגדולה. הוא היה אומר: על שלושה דברים העולם עומד: על
התורה ועל העבודה ועל גמילות חסדים.
[257] Cf. Ps. 89:3 [Hebrew]; PRE 12, 16; Pe'ah 1:1; Tos.Pe'ah 4:21; Suk. 49b; AZ 5b; Kid.
40a. For "kindliness" (gmilut chasadim), see 6:1-11.
[258] Cf. Ps. 34:8, 135:3, 145:9; Jer. 33:11; Lam. 3:25; Nah. 1:7; Mt. 19:17; 1 En. 61:11,
81:4, 91:17, 92:3-4; Test.Naph. 2:4; Test.Asher 3:1; Test.Ben. 8:1; Ps.Sol. 5:20, 8:33,
9:14, 17:51, 18:6; 1QS 4:3, 11:14; 1QHᵃ 5:22, 15:30, 19:6f; 4Q418 81:6-7; PA 5:15.

obedience in all human relationships – both those between wo/man and wo/man and between wo/man and God (cf. 4Q418 81:6): "*'The faithful God'* (Dt. 7:9). The Rabbis say: You can best learn the faithfulness of God from the faithfulness of man. It is related of R. Phinehas ben Jair that when he was living in a city in the South some men came there to seek a livelihood. They had with them two *se'ahs* of barley which they deposited with him, but they forgot about it and went away. R. Phinehas b. Jair sowed the barley year by year and harvested it and stored it. After the lapse of seven years those men returned to that place to claim back their grain. As soon as R. Phinehas b. Jair recognised them he said to them: 'Come and take these your storehouses [full of grain].' Lo, from the faithfulness of man you can best learn the faithfulness of God"[259] (Dt.R. 3:3).[260]

"Gentleness (πραΰτης)" represents the biblical "meekness" which constitutes that humility and submission to God's will which He seeks: ". . . saintliness leads to the [possession of] the holy spirit, the holy spirit leads to life eternal, and saintliness is greater than any of these, for Scripture says, *Then Thou didst speak in vision to Thy saintly ones* (Ps. 89:19). This, then, differs from the view of R. Joshua b. Levy. For R. Joshua b. Levy said: Meekness is the greatest of them all, for Scripture says, *The spirit of the Lord God is upon me, because the Lord hath anointed me to bring good tidings unto the meek* (Isa. 61:1). It does not say, 'unto the saints', but '*unto the meek'*,

---

[259] ״הָאֵל הַנֶּאֱמָן״: רבנין אמרי: מאמונתו של בשר ודם אתָ יודע אמונתו של הקדוש ברוך הוא. מעשה ברבי פנחס בן יאיר שהיה דר בעיר אחת בדרום והלכו אנשים להתפרנס שם והיו בידו שתי סאין של שעורים והפקידו אצלו ושכחו אותן והלכו להן. והיה רבי פנחס בן יאיר זורע אותן בכל שנה ועושה ואותן גורן וכונסן. אחר שבע שנים הלכו אותן החברים לשם לתבוע אותן ליתן להן. מיד הכיר אותן ר׳ פנחס בן יאיר. אמר להם: בואו וטלו אוצרותיכם. הרי מאמונתו של בשר ודם אתה יודע אמונתו של הקדוש ברוך הוא.

[260] It is important to note that this example portrays faithfulness as reliability and trustworthiness in doing what is "right and good" (cf. Dt. 6:18) – not merely as doctrinal affirmation. This is precisely the halakhic sense in which Paul speaks of "faithfulness working through love" (verse 6), enabled through the Spirit's indwelling: "Some porters [negligently] broke a barrel of wine belonging to Rabbah son of R. Huna. Thereupon he seized their garments; so they went and complained to Rab. 'Return them their garments,' he ordered. 'Is that the law?' he enquired. 'Even so,' he rejoined: '*That thou mayest walk in the way of good men*' (Prov. 2:20). Their garments having been returned, they observed, 'We are poor men, have worked all day, and are in need: are we to get nothing?' 'Go and pay them,' he ordered. 'Is that the law?' he asked. 'Even so,' was his reply: '*and keep the path of the righteous*' (ibid) רבה בר רב חנן תברו ליה הנהו שקולאי חביתא דחמרא. שקל לגלימייהו. אתו אמרו לרב. אמר ליה: הב להו גלימייהו. אמר ליה: דינא? הכי, אמר ליה, אין למען תלך בדרך טובים. יהיב להו גלימייהו אמרו ליה: עניי אנן וטרחינן כולה יומא וכפינן, ולית לן? מידי אמר ליה: זיל הב אגרייהו. אמר ליה: דינא? הכי, אמר ליה, אין וארחות צדיקים תשמר (BM 83a) (see Introduction, **Argument**; **Theological pointers**, 2:15-21, 3:10-14 (n142), 6:1f, and verses 2f).

from which you learn that meekness is the greatest of all these"[261] (AZ 20b).[262] The due response to God's mercies is recognition of one's insignificance and worthlessness: "The Holy One, blessed be He, said to Israel, I love you because even when I bestow greatness upon you, you humble yourselves before me. I bestowed greatness upon Abraham, yet he said to Me, *I am but dust and ashes* (Gen. 18:27). Upon Moses and Aaron, yet they said: *And we are nothing* (Ex. 16:8); upon David, yet he said: *But I am a worm and no man* (Ps. 22:6)"[263] (Hul. 89a) (see also 6:1-11).[264]

The last in the list – "self-control (ἐγκράτεια)" – sums up the "angering of the evil inclination" in which a person must engage in order to please God – together with the "giving preference to one another in honour" which constitutes the devotion of brotherly love (cf. Rom. 12:10) (see verses 13-18). While it stands in parallel to "drunkenness and carousings" of verse 21, rabbinic texts again link the lack of self-control with turning to strange gods: "He who tears his clothes in anger or breaks his vessels in his rage, will in the end worship idols; for such is the device of the evil inclination: to-day it bids man, 'Tear your clothes' and to-morrow it bids him, 'Worship idols'"[265] (ARN[a] 3:2) (cf. Shab. 105b).

Verse 23b: The characteristic of "such things" which constitute the fruit of the Spirit is that "against them there is no law" (κατὰ τῶν τοιούτων οὐκ ἔστιν νόμος; kata tōn toioutōn ouk estin nomos). The κατὰ (kata – "against") with the genitive picks up the same opposition as the flesh demonstrates against the Spirit and the Spirit against the flesh in verse 17 (cf. Longenecker, Galatians: 263). In the possible sense conveyed by the Hebrew מול (mul – "opposite"), Paul may be indicating that these attributes do not stand against any corresponding negative force, but are all positive qualities which flow naturally from their source in the Spirit, uninhibited by antagonistic intervention or disturbance.[266]

---

[261] . . . קדושה מביאה לידי רוח הקודש ורוח הקודש מביאה לידי תחיית המתים וחסידות גדולה
מכולן, שנאמר: אז דברת בחזון לחסידיך. ופליגא דרבי יהושע בו לוי, דאמר ר' יהושע בו לוי: ענוה
גדולה מכולן, שנאמר: רוח ה' אלהים עלי יען משח ה' אותי לבשר ענוים. 'חסדים' לא נאמר אלא
'ענוים'. הא למדת שענוה גדולה מכולן.

[262] Cf. Num. 12:3; Ps. 37:11; Mt. 5:5; 1QS 3:8, 4:3; Num.R. 11:7; Kid. 71a; Ta'anit 16a; San. 88b; Did. 3:7 (see also 6:1-11). For the exegetical method, see 3:15-18; for Isa. 61:1-3, see 1:1f, 3:1ff, 26-29, and 4:1f.

[263] אמר להם הקדוש ברוך הוא לישראל: חושקני בכם שאפילו בשעה שאני משפיע לכם גדולה,
אתם ממעטין עצמכם לפני. נתתי גדולה לאברהם. אמר לפני: ואנכי עפר ואפר; למשה ואהרן,
אמרו: ונחנו מה; לדוד, אמר: ואנכי תולעת ולא איש.

[264] Cf. 1QS 11:9-22; 1QH[a] 4:18-28, 5:19-26, 7:14-28, 9:21-33 . For Abraham, see 3:6-9.

[265] הקורע את בגדיו בחמתו והמשבר כליו בחמתו סוף שיעבוד עבודת כוכבים, שכך אומנתו של יצר
הרע: היום אומר לו: קרע את בגדיך, ולמחר אומר לו: עבוד עבודת כוכבים.

[266] Cf. Mt. 7:16ff, 12:33; Jas. 3:12; Sir. 27:6; Gen.R. 16:3, 30:6. This is the sense in which Paul speaks of God "condescending" to human limitations, the Torah regulating, but not changing, human nature (see 3:19f and below). Paul picks up the verb στοιχέω (stoicheō – "in line with") again in verse 25 (see 4:1-7, 21-31 and 6:17). Cf. 4 Ez. 9:32-33: "Yet the fruit of the Law did not perish – for it could not, because it

In its more literal signification ("down"), κατά (kata) may actually reflect the "condescension" or "accommodation" which the Torah constitutes in its role as "pedagogue/tutor" to human nature (see 3:19f).[267] In this sense, those who, walking in the Spirit, do not naturally seek to sin do not need to add "fences" in order to keep far from transgressing.[268] The commandments of the Torah fail to apply when a person is not apt to sin – just as the rules of kashrut (against mixing meat with milk) are irrelevant to a vegetarian. To the extent that they carry the risk of punishment equally with the promise of reward, their observance is linked to fear. Love, on the other hand, has in it no fear and even casts such out, "because fear involves punishment, and the one who fears is not perfected in love (ὅτι ὁ φόβος κόλασιν ἔχει, ὁ δὲ φοβούμενος οὐ τετελείωται ἐν τῇ ἀγάπῃ)" (1 Jn. 4:18) (cf. Lk. 1:74-75).

Most significantly, in this respect, the fruit of the spirit represent qualities which fulfil God's purposes in and of themselves, embodying in their nature and action the "law of love" in the Messiah (cf. verse 14, 6:2) (see 6:1-11 and verses 2-12). The assertion stands as an indirect allusion to the fact that if the Galatians follow the Spirit, Paul will not have to caution them against being swayed by the influencers (see also verses 24-26).[269]

---

was yours. Yet those who received it perished, because they did not keep what had been sown in them."

[267] The anarthrous νόμος (nomos - "law") signals the qualitative sense of "legal jurisdiction," indicating a system for regulating whatever is unruly and disorderly. It is this aspect of the the "Law" - alone - by which Paul appears to designate the Torah here. He is not hesitant, in other places, to designate the Spirit as "law" - as in Rom. 8:2 where, as here, the term takes on overtones of a "(guiding) principle": "I will put the fear of Me in their hearts so that they will not turn away from Me -ואת ירָאתי אתן בלבבם לבלתי סור מעלי" (Jer. 32:40) (see also 2:15-21). In this sense, the fruit constitute the "natural" phenomena of the Spirit in the same way as robbery, bloodshed, and blasphemy represent the "natural laws" of the human condition and did not need the Torah to be known (see above [verse 19]). (For the "curse" devolving from disobedience, see 3:10-14 [6:17].)

[268] Cf. PA 1:1, 3:13; ARNa 1:5; ARNb 1; Yev. 20a. The very use of a fence can lead to sin, as in Eve's claim that she was forbidden also to *touch* the fruit of the tree of good and evil (cf. Gen. 3:3; ARNb 1).

[269] Cf. 1:6-9, 4:12f, 30, verses 2ff, 6:7-8. See also Paul's use of ὑπὸ νόμον (hypo nomon - "under the law") (cf. 3:23, 4:5, 21, verse 18). Appeal to Aristotle's maxim "there can be no law dealing with such men as those described who are equal in birth and ability, for they are themselves a law (κατὰ δὲ τῶν τοιούτων οὐκ ἔστι νόμος αὐτοὶ γάρ εἰσι νόμος)" (*Pol.* 8.2) (cf. Longenecker, Galatians: 263-64) in justification of the saying's proverbial status seems rather forced (see 3:15-18 [end]). It is striking that this passage - like 4:1f - contains no allusion to the "receipt of the Spirit" and "miracles" which God was working in the Galatians of 3:5, although it is to be assumed that there is only "one Spirit" (see 3:1-5). This circumstance may be explained by the fact that Paul is addressing divergent aspects of the Spirit's

Verses 24-26:
Now those who belong to the Messiah Jesus have crucified the flesh with its passions
and desires. If we live by the Spirit, let us also walk by the Spirit. Let us not become
boastful, challenging one another, envying one another.

Verse 24 brings Paul's point full circle, Paul turning to address his gentile
Galatian disciples yet again with regard to their loyalty. Here, once more,
he reiterates his warning to his disciples not to be persuaded by the
"influencers."[270] At this point, he remains with an impersonal reference,
only speaking in the first person plural in the following statement. His
audience being found among "those who belong to the Messiah (οἱ δὲ τοῦ
Χριστοῦ 'Ιησοῦ)," they are consequently bound by the conditions of this
status. The allusion to the Messiah picks up from verse 1: "With the
freedom of the free woman the Messiah set us free (τῇ ἐλευθερίᾳ ἡμᾶς
Χριστὸς ἠλευθέρωσεν)."[271]

When combined with a possessive genitive ("of the Messiah Jesus"),
the substantival plural article οἱ (hoi – "those") signifies "those who
belong to" or are "in the Messiah" (cf. 3:29) (cf. Longenecker, Galatians:
264).[272] Paul identifies these as those who have "crucified the flesh with its
passions and desires (ἐσταύρωσαν σὺν τοῖς παθήμασιν καὶ ταῖς
ἐπιθυμίαις)." In this sense, he indirectly marks them as his disciples,
himself having set the example in "dying to the Torah" when "crucified
with the Messiah (νόμῳ ἀπέθανον . . . Χριστῷ συνεσταύρωμαι)" (2:19-20)
(see 2:15-21).[273] The use of the past tense (aorist) indicates that this act has
occurred previously, quite likely having been one definitive of identity.[274]
Paul later employs the language of "dying" and "crucifixion" in
elaborating how it is impossible for those who have been "baptized into

---

working in the believers' lives in the various sections of the letter – as, for example,
linked to Abraham's blessing in 3:1-14, and sonship/slavery in 4:1-7 (see 3:1-5 and
4:1-7).

[270] For the present reading of the situation in Galatia, see Introduction, **Occasion
and circumstances**. The repetition directly follows verses 13-15, which section itself
is an extension of verses 1ff, chapter 5 as a whole being dependent on 4:12 (see
Introduction, **Argument**). The δὲ (de) is connective and continuative here rather
than contrastive (cf. Longenecker, Galatians: 264). For the structure of Galatians as a
"halakhic letter" of rebuke-request along the lines of 4QMMT, see Introduction,
Form; Argument and verses 2f.

[271] For this interpretation of the verse, linking it to 4:31, see 4:21-31 (end).

[272] The unusual combination τοῦ Χριστοῦ 'Ιησου (tou Christou Iēsou) (cf. Eph.
3:1) marks a titular usage, "they that belong to the Messiah, Jesus" (cf. Burton: 319).

[273] For his readers' relationship to Paul as disciples, see 4:12-20; for Paul's personal
example, see 1:1-5, 15-16b, 21-24, 2:1-10 (n136), 15-21 (n292), 3:1-5 (nn14, 28), 4:12-20,
6:1f (verses 11, 15, 17), and verses 2-12 (verse 11).

[274] The parallel in verse 13 speaks of being "called to freedom (ἐπ' ἐλευθερίᾳ
ἐκλήθητε)."

his death" to continue to sin (cf. Rom. 6:1ff).[275] In this sense, verse 24 parallels 3:27: "For all of you who were baptized into the Messiah have clothed yourselves with the Messiah (ὅσοι γὰρ εἰς Χριστὸν ἐβαπτίσθητε, Χριστὸν ἐνεδύσασθε)" – baptism representing the way in which a person participates in Jesus' faithful obedience to the Father's will (see 3:26-29).[276]

Numerous rabbinic texts echo the idea of "denying your will before His will":

> No-one should walk in the stubbornness of his heart in order to go astray following his heart and his eyes and the musings of his inclination. Instead he should circumcise in the Community the foreskin of his tendency and of his stiff neck in order to lay a foundation of truth for Israel, for the Community of the eternal covenant.[277] (1QS 5:4-6)

> Rabbi Judah the Prince says: Do His will as though it were your will so that He may do your will as though it were His will; undo your will for the sake of His will so that He may undo the will of others for the sake of your will [PA 2:4]. He used to say: If you have done His will as though it were your will, you have not yet done His will as He wills it. But if you have done His will as though it were not your will, then you have done His will as He wills it. Is it your wish not to die? Die, so that you will not need to die. Is it your wish to live? Do not live, so that you may live. It is better for you to die in this world, where you will die against your will, than to die in the age to come, where, if you wish, you need not die.[278] (ARNᵇ 32)

---

[275] While Romans 6 evidently comes to answer a charge of libertinism – "Are we to continue in sin that grace might increase?" – we have suggested that this is not the issue which Paul has been countering here (see verses 13-18). The likelihood that he is referring to baptism at this point does not, in and of itself, demand an accompanying concern with libertinism. Paul appears to have treated the matter here in terms of the choice between the "Two Ways" (see verses 13f).

[276] In a sense, the crucifying performed by the believer is "borrowed" from Jesus' own act, the latter being the ultimate expression of his submission to God's will and thus that whereby he achieved victory over death – the wages of sin – when God raised him from the dead. In partaking of Jesus' representative act, believers exhibit their trust in Jesus' death and resurrection by re-enacting it in their own life. For Jesus' representative role, see Introduction, **Theological pointers** (Faith), 2:15-21, 3:1ff, and 4:1f.

[277] לוא ילך איש בשרירות לבו לתעות אחר לבבו ועינוהו ומחשבת יצרו (כ)יא אם למול ביחד עורלת יצר ועורף קשה ליסד מוסד אמת לישראל ליחד ברית עולם.

[278] הוא היה אומר: עשה רצונו כרצונך, כדי שיעשה רצונך כרצונו. בטל רצונך מפני רצונו, כדי שיבטל רצון אחרים מפני רצונך. הוא היה אומר: אם עשית רצונו כרצונך לא עשית רצונו כרצונו. ואם עשית רצונו שלא כרצונך עשית רצונו כרצונו. רצונך שלא תמות - מות עד שלא תמות. רצונך

He [Alexander of Macedon] said to them [the Rabbis] . . . What shall a man do to live? They replied: Let him mortify himself [lit. 'kill himself']. What should a man do to kill himself? They replied: Let him keep himself alive [i.e. indulge in luxuries] אמר להם : מה יעביד איניש ויחיה? אמרו ליה : ימית עצמו. מה יעביד איניש וימות? יחיה את עצמו. (Tamid 32a)[279]

Thou shalt love the Lord thy God (Dt. 6:5): Perform (God's commandments) out of love. Scripture makes a distinction between one who performs out of love and one who performs out of fear . . . *With all thy heart*: With both your Inclinations, the Inclination to good and the Inclination to evil. Another interpretation: *With all thy heart*: With all the heart that is within you; your heart should not be divided in regard to God. *And with all thy soul*: Even if God takes away your soul, as it is said, *For thy sake are we killed all the day; we are accounted as sheep for the slaughter* (Ps. 44:22). R. Simeon b. Menasya says: How can a man be slain all the day? Rather, the Holy One, blessed be He, credits the righteous as if they were slain daily. R. Simeon b. Azzai says: *With all thy soul*: love Him until the last drop of life is wrung out of you.[280] (Sif.Dt. 32)[281] (cf. Shulam and Le Cornu: 209ff) (see 2:15-21)[282]

Verse 25: "Crucifixion" of the flesh by "angering one's evil inclination" and choosing the "right path" in which one should walk is the way to life: "I call heaven and earth to witness against you today, that I have set before

---

שתחיה - אל תחיה עד שתחיה. מוטב לך למות מיתה בעולם הזה שעל כרחך אתה מת מלמות מיתה לעתיד לבא, שאם תרצה, אי אתה מת.

[279] Cf. Mt. 16.25; Lk. 17:33; Jn. 12:25; Mid.Prov. 9; Ber. 61b.

[280] ואהבת את ה' אלהיך : עשה מאהבה, הפריש בין העושה מאהבה לעושה מיראה . . . בכל לבבך : בשני יצריך, ביצר טוב וביצר רע. דבר אחר: בכל לבבך : בכל לב בך, שלא יהיה לבך חלוק על המקום. ובכל נפשך : אפילו הוא נוטל את נפשך. וכן הוא אומר: כי עליך הורגנו כל היום נחשבנו כצאן טבחה. ר' שמעון בן מנסיא אומר: וכי היאך איפשר לו לאדם ליהרג בכל יום? אלא מעלה הקדוש ברוך על הצדיקים כאילו הם נהרגים בכל יום.

[281] For serving out of fear or love, see 2:15-21 and 4:1-7; for love as the fulfilment of the Torah, see 6:1-11 and verses 13-18. It should come as no surprise that the motive behind denying one's self lies in full and complete devotion to obeying God's commandments, for "If you love me, you will keep my commandments ('Εὰν ἀγαπᾶτέ με, τὰς ἐντολὰς τὰς ἐμὰς τηρήσετε)" (Jn. 14:15) (cf. 1 Jn. 5:2) (see verses 2-12 [n47]). The Greek παθήμασιν (pathēmasin), as a morally neutral term, may signify the Hebrew יצר (yetzer), denoting a "disposition" or "inclination" which may be swayed towards good or towards evil (cf. Test.Jud. 20:1-5; Test.Asher 1:3-9).

[282] It is not fortuitous that these passages constitute interpretations of the Shema: "Thou shalt love the Lord thy God with all thy heart and with all thy soul and with all thy might ואהבת את ה' אלהיך בכל-לבבך ובכל-נפשך ובכל-מאדך" (Dt. 6:5) – love being the "fulfilment of the Torah" whose performance Paul urges upon his disciples (cf. 4Q504 ff1-2ii:13; 11QTemp 59:9-10) (see 6:1-11 and verses 13-18).

you life and death, the blessing and the curse. So choose life in order that you may live, you and your descendants, by loving the LORD your God, by obeying His voice, and by holding fast to Him; for this is your life and the length of your days ..."[283] (Dt. 30:19-20).[284] Having received life – righteousness – through participation in Jesus' death and resurrection in baptism, Paul wishes his disciples to maintain their discipline and to continue to "walk" in the Spirit: To consistently put the "deeds of the body to death," and in all things, "being led by the Spirit," not let themselves be "overcome" by their own inclination – for "by what a man is overcome, by this he is enslaved (ᾧ γάρ τις ἥττηται, τούτῳ δεδούλωται)" (2 Pet. 2:19).[285]

In place of the regular πορεύομαι (poreuomai) or περιπατέω (peripateō) ("to walk"), Paul speaks here of "keeping in step with (στοιχῶμεν)" the Spirit. In so doing, he appears to be playing on his previous assertion that through God's sending of His Spirit into their hearts, the Galatians have been delivered from their bondage to the "elemental things of the world (τὰ στοιχεῖα τοῦ κόσμου)" (4:3).[286] Having received the Spirit, he now tells them to "walk in line with" its liberty – refraining from "carrying out the desire of the flesh" (cf. verses 16-18, 6:16).[287] In the sense in which he employs the same verb in relation to

---

[283] העד̇תי בכם היום את-השמים ואת-הארץ החיים והמות נתתי לפניך הברכה והקללה ובחרת בחיים למען תחיה אתה וזרעך : לאהבה את-ה' אלהיך לשמע בקלו ולדבקה-בו כי הוא חייך וארך ימיך . . .

[284] "For "life," see 3:10-14, 21-25; for the "flesh," see verses 13f; for blessing/cursing, see 1:6-10, 3:10-14, and 6:17. The aphoristic and gnomic structure of this verse closely parallels verses 1, 13 (cf. Longenecker, Galatians: 265).

[285] Cf. Rom. 6:1ff, 8:13-14. While the verbs "walk" and "be led" are virtually synonymous, "living" here appears to designate a "state" rather than an action, perhaps to be identified with the "sending forth of the Spirit of His son into our hearts" (4:6) in baptism, effecting new life in the person: "These are the foundations of the spirit of the sons of truth (in) the world. And the reward of all those who walk in it will be healing, plentiful peace in a long life, fruitful offspring with all everlasting blessings, eternal enjoyment with endless life, and a crown of glory with majestic raiment in eternal light אלה סודי רוח לבני אמת תבל ופקודת כול הולכי בה למרפא ורוב שלום באורך ימים ופרות זרע עם כול ברכות עד ושמחת עולמים בחיי נצח וכליל כבוד עם מדת עולמים הדר באור עולמים" (1QS 4:6-8) (see 3:10-14, 26-29 and above).

[286] The "elemental things" are formed of the "inherent components" which are "members in a rank," whence the noun derives, denoting "standing in a row" (see 4:1-7).

[287] Cf. the author of Jubilee's description of God's renewal of human nature following the Flood: "And he made for all his works a new and righteous nature so that they might not sin in their nature forever, and so that they might all be righteous, each in his kind, always. And the judgment of all of them has been ordained and written in the heavenly tablets without injustice. And (if) any of them transgress from their way with respect to what was ordained for them to walk in, or

Abraham in Romans 4:12,[288] Paul brings his readers back full circle to his argument in chapter 3, reasserting that they are Abraham's heirs – who do not, consequently, need to seek any further social status (see 3:1ff).

It is in Abraham's footsteps, as elaborated and exemplified before them by Paul, that they must walk – not in those of the influencers (see 3:1-5).[289] Paul's further association of the verb in 6:16 with "this rule (τῷ κανόνι τούτῳ)" which is the "new creature (καινὴ κτίσις)" (cf. 6:15) further ties it to the "whole law fulfilled in one word (πᾶς νόμος εην ἐνὶ λόγῳ πεπλήρωται)" (verse 14) – namely, love (see 6:1f and verses 13-18).[290] In this way he establishes the halakhah of the Kingdom of God – the "fruit" of the "repentance" which constitutes people as true "children of Abraham" (cf. Mt. 3:7-10), thereby gaining them access to God's Kingdom (see verses 19f).

Verse 26: Having turned directly to the Galatians in verse 25, Paul now reasserts his original caution against "biting and devouring" (cf. verse 15), although he now includes himself ("let us . . .") (cf. 6:14). While "boasting (κενόδοξοι)," "challenging one another (ἀλλήλους προκαλούμενοι)," and "envying (φθονοῦντες)" all come under the rubric of the "desire/deeds of the flesh," Paul may here be specifically addressing the Galatians' situation in relation to the influencers.[291] In 6:13, Paul charges the influencers with "boasting in the flesh (σαρκὶ καυχήσωνται)," an attitude which closely

---

if they do not walk in it, the judgment for every (sort of) nature and every kind has been written" (Jub. 5:12-12) (cf. Eph. 2:10).

[288] "The father . . . [of those] who also follow in the footsteps of the faithfulness of our father Abraham (πατέρα . . . καὶ τοῖς *στοιχοῦσιν* τοῖς ἴχνεσιν τῆς . . . πίστεως τοῦ πατρὸς ἡμῶν ᾿Αβραάμ)" (cf. Shulam and Le Cornu: 165f).

[289] For Abraham as Paul's model, see 3:6-9 (n101) and 4:21-31 (nn131, 156, 186).

[290] Cf. Acts 21:24; Phil. 3:16. Where "keeping line" also implies "agreement with," this verse also recalls Rom. 7:16: "But if I do the very thing I do not wish *to do*, I agree with the Torah, *confessing* that it is good (εἰ δὲ ὃ οὐ θέλω τοῦτο ποιῶ, σύμφημι τῷ νόμῳ ὅτι καλός)." The sense of "instruction" may also lie in the background here, the Spirit enabling the believer to know and to follow God's will (cf. Jn. 14:26, 16:13; 1 Jn. 2:20, 27; 1QHᵃ 6:13f, 25-26, 20:11f; 1QS 4:2f, 9:3; 4Q504 f4:5) (see 1:11f).

[291] While we deem the connection with 6:1ff to be substantially tighter and far less accidental, Longenecker's statement is well taken: "In effect, what follows in 6:1-10 is Paul's 'going off at a word' from the general statement of 5:26, and so spelling out certain specific directives in elaboration of that general statement. It is, therefore, to the directives of 6:1-10 that we must turn to 'unpack' what Paul had in mind here in v26 in speaking of 'conceited' or 'boastful people' (κενόδοξοι) who 'are provoking one another' (ἀλλήλους προκαλούμενοι) and 'are envying one another' (ἀλλήλοις φθονοῦντες)" (Galatians: 266). The present reading mitigates the difficulties involved in understanding the connection which exists between verse 25 and the immediately preceding and following verses (cf. ibid: 265, 269f) (see Introduction, **Argument** and 6:1-11).

parallels "conceit" (cf. Burton: 324).[292] Both these attributes are staple elements of "provocation" or "challenging." In seeking "knowledge" in human terms – social status, approval, and identity – the Galatians are in danger of becoming arrogant, in place of promoting the edification which is the consequence of love (cf. 1 Cor. 8:1).[293]

---

[292] Cf. 3:1, where the Galatians' "foolishness" reappears, as it were, in Titus in a list of people designated as "disobedient, deceived, enslaved to various lusts and pleasures, spending ... life in malice and envy, hateful, hating one another (ἀπειθεῖς, πλανώμενοι, δουλεύοντες ἐπιθυμίαις καὶ ἡδοναῖς ποικίλαις, ἐν κακίᾳ καὶ φθόνῳ διάγοντες, στυγητοί, μισοῦντες ἀλλήλους)" (Tit. 3:3) (see 3:1-5). In its antonymous relationship with σωφρονέω (sōfroneō – "to be of sound mind"), the noun anticipates 6:3f (cf. Rom. 12:3) (see 6:1-11).

[293] The fact that Paul speaks in inclusive language may corroborate the supposition that he is admonishing his disciples for turning away and pledging their allegiance to another "Master" (see 4:12-20 and verses 2-12). Softer in its tone, the verse essentially repeats Paul's directive expressed in 4:30 and verses 1, 9, 13, 16, and anticipates the strictures against his errant disciples – and the influencers – in chapter 6 (see Introduction, **Argument** and 6:1-11).

GALATIANS
6

Verses 1-11: [*Exhortatio*]

Brethren, even if a man is caught in any trespass, you who are spiritual, restore such a one in a spirit of gentleness; looking to yourselves, lest you too be tempted. Bear one another's burdens, and thus fulfill the law of the Messiah. For if anyone thinks he is something when he is nothing, he deceives himself. But let each one examine his own work, and then he will have *reason for* boasting in regard to himself alone, and not in regard to another. For each one shall bear his own load. And let the one who is taught the word share all good things with him who teaches. Do not be deceived, God is not mocked; for whatever a man sows, this he will also reap. For the one who sows to his own flesh will from the flesh reap corruption, but the one who sows to the Spirit will from the Spirit reap eternal life. And let us not lose heart in doing good, for in due time we shall reap if we do not grow weary. So then, while we have opportunity, let us do good to all men, and especially to those who are of the household of the faith. See with what large letters I am writing to you with my own hand.

Paul's direct address to his disciples marks an epistolary signification in the text, indicating a new subunit.[1] Following his caution against boastful provocation and envy in 5:26, this section represents Paul's instructions as to how to deal with those within the Galatian communities who are being swayed by the influencers (see 5:24-26).[2] Paul appears here to be appealing

---

[1] For the epistolary character and halakhic structure of Galatians, see Introduction, Form; for "brethren," see 1:1-5.

[2] In recollection of the argument presently being asserted, it is herein proposed that the influencers – non-believing godfearers – are exercising their efforts on Paul's gentile Galatian disciples in the direction of circumcision/conversion, not being willing to acknowledge that, in Jesus' death and resurrection, Gentiles may find

to members of the Galatian communities who have not been persuaded by the influencers' arguments, requesting of them a sense of responsibility for the community's welfare.[3] These persons he describes as "spiritual (πνευματικοί)," the epithet in this context apparently relating to the "walking in the Spirit" according to which they are living (cf. 5:16, 18, 25) (see 5:13ff).[4]

The actuality of the circumstances is reinforced by the καὶ (kai) which, in this context, is intensive, serving to emphasise the subsequent verb: If anyone is found.[5] In this sense, Paul's stress is laid upon the reality of the transgression – not merely its theoretical potential. The verb (προλημφθῇ; prolēmfthē) carries the dual nuances of being "caught" by someone in a transgression and of being "entrapped" by some sin.[6] παραπτώματι

---

legitimate Jewish identity. To the extent that Paul's disciples are accepting the persuasion, they are placing themselves once again under the "elemental things of the world," returning themselves to the dominion of Belial and sin – and thus turning their backs on the freedom from sin and access to God's Kingdom which Jesus' redemption has effected. See Introduction, **Occasion and circumstances**; **Argument**. For the connection of this segment with 5:26, Paul maintaining his injunction to the Galatians not to yield to the influencers' persuasion, see 5:24-26 and below. The most telling argument against this reading, and in support of the majority of commentators who perceive this passage as a general paraenetic (exhortatory) segment, is the presence of the τινι (tini – "any"), giving to the transgression a generic, non-specific property. The inclusive language nevertheless does not *exclude* the particular, and by extending the reference Paul can provide a principle applicable to other circumstances. Likewise, "while there is something of an indefinite tone to the first part of this sentence, there is also the suggestion in the use of the third class 'future more probable' conditional construction that such a circumstance will almost certainly take place" (Longenecker, Galatians: 273). For indications linking 6:12-13 – generally recognised as identifying the influencers – with verses 1-10, see below.

[3] For the current reading of Galatians as a halakhic "rebuke-request" letter along the lines of 4QMMT, see Introduction, **Form**; **Argument**, and 4:12-20.

[4] This reading is in distinction, on the one hand, to that which sees in this segment a situation "hypothetical and general in character," the reference being to "all members of the community, not to a select group of spiritual leaders" (Hays, Galatians: 332); and, on the other, to that which perceives in the "pneumatics" a party of libertines (cf. Lütgert) and/or gnostics (cf. Schmithals) (see 5:13-18).

[5] As commentators note, the exhortation contains "three parts: (1) a protasis cast in the form of a third class 'future more probable' condition (ἐάν with a subjunctive verb in the protasis, with almost any form of the verb appearing in the apodosis) that states the circumstance addressed; (2) an apodosis that gives a directive as to what should be done; and (3) an added concessive statement introduced by the adverbial participle σκοπῶν ("though watch") that gives pointed warning to those who carry out the directive" (Longenecker, Galatians: 272).

[6] The literal sense of προλαμβάνω (prolambanō) – "to take beforehand" – subsequently came to imply "to anticipate, forestall" in the active voice and "be

(paraptōmati) signifies a "false step" or "falling beside," Paul's choice of precisely this term perhaps reflecting the influence of the στοιχέω (stoicheō – "walk in line") in 5:25. If so, it serves as a further indicator of the close links between these two sections (see 5:24-26).

Under such circumstances, Paul says, those who have not fallen into the trap laid out are liable to "restore (καταρτίζετε)" the person who has so stumbled.[7] Paul appears here to be oscillating between two principles regarding wickedness. On the one hand the instruction is expulsion: "So you shall purge the evil [the wicked man] from your midst ובערת הרע מקרבך" (Dt. 17:7).[8] On the other, the command is to "surely reprove your neighbor, but [you] shall not incur sin because of him לא-תשנא את-אחיך בלבבך הוכח תוכיח את-עמיתך ולא-תשא עליו חטא" (Lev. 19:17).[9] The tension between the two attitudes is evident in 2 Thessalonians 3:14-15, wherein Paul directs the community: "And if anyone does not obey our instruction in this letter, take special note of that man and do not associate with him, so that he may be put to shame. And *yet* do not regard him as an enemy, but admonish him as a brother"[10] (cf. 2 Cor. 5:5-8).

To the extent that the concessive statement relates to sinning, Paul may be placing the Galatians' conduct at the centre of his injunction. Such an interpretation of Leviticus 19:17 is well illustrated in the Qumran scrolls, which understand the biblical text to say that a person sins if s/he delays in reproving another: "One should reproach one another in truth, in meekness and in compassionate love for one's fellow-man *Blank* No-one should speak to his brother in anger or muttering, or with a hard [neck or with passionate] spirit of wickedness, and he should not detest him [in the fore]sk[in] of his heart, but instead reproach him that day so as not to incur a sin because of him"[11] (1QS 5:24-6:1) (see 2:11-14).[12]

---

taken by surprise, overtaken" in the passive (cf. BAGD: 708). For the motif of bondage to sin, see 1:1-5, 2:1-10, 3:10-14, 19ff, 4:1f, and 5:13f.

[7] Cf. the rabbinic adage: "All Israel are sureties for one another כל ישראל ערבים זה בזה" – bearing the responsibility for one another's sins (cf. Shevu. 39a).

[8] Cf. Dt. 13:5; Mt. 18:17; 1 Cor. 5:1-5; 2 Cor. 2:5-6; [Eph. 5:11]; 1QS 1:4, 5:1f, 10ff; CD-A 6:14-15; CD-B 20:7 (see also 5:19-23).

[9] Cf. Mt. 18:15; 2 Cor. 5:7-8; Eph. 4:2; 1 Tim. 5:20; 2 Tim. 4:2; Heb. 12:7ff; Jas. 5:19-20; 1QS 5:24-6:1; CD-A 6:20-7:4, 9:2ff.

[10] Εἰ δέ τις οὐχ ὑπακούει τῷ λόγῳ ἡμῶν διὰ τῆς ἐπιστολῆς, τοῦτον σημειοῦσθε μὴ συναναμίγνυσθαι αὐτῷ, ἵνα ἐντραπῇ· καὶ μὴ ὡς ἐχθρὸν ἡγεῖσθε, ἀλλὰ νουθετεῖτε ὡς ἀδελφόν.

[11] להוכיꞏ איש את רעהו באמת וענוה ואהבת חסד לאיש *vacat* אל ידבר אלוהיהי (אל אחיהו) באף או בתלונה או בעורף [קשה או בקנאת] רוח רשע ואל ישנאהו [בעור]ל[ת] לבבו כיא ביום{יו} יוכיחנו ולוא ישא עליו עוון.

[12] Cf. CD-A 6:20-7:4, 9:2ff. Here again, Paul has set himself as the example for reproving others, having done so – on a very similar issue – with Peter. For 2:14-21 as one of the letter's central motifs, see Introduction, **Argument** and below; for Paul's personal example as the grounds for his rebuke/request of his disciples, see

It is equally possible, however, to understand Paul's injunction as alluding to the temptation to fall into the same transgression rather than to the sin engendered by failure to reprove. On this latter reading, he wishes to encourage those who are truly walking in the Spirit to act responsibly towards those who have "slipped," in the proper spirit of gentleness; at the same time, "watching out (σκοπῶν)" to make sure that they are not themselves pulled into the same net – spread by the influencers.[13]

Noticeably, Paul switches at this point to the singular (σκοπῶν σεαυτόν, μὴ καὶ σὺ πειρασθῇς; skopōn seauton, mē kais sy peirasthēs) "each one" requiring a personal warning against the possibility of him/herself "stumbling."[14] Such a switch, in mid-sentence, between first person singular and plural is a fairly common biblical structure (although one which the English translations tend to obscure): "You [pl.] are the sons of the LORD your God; you [pl.] shall not cut yourselves nor shave your forehead for the sake of the dead. For you [s.] are a holy people to the LORD your God; and the LORD has chosen you [s.] to be a people for His own possession . . . you [s.] shall not eat any detestable thing"[15] (Dt. 14:1-3).[16]

On noting this fact, a midrash suggests that it speaks to a person's responsibility: " At times He [God] addresses them [Israel] as one speaking to a multitude, at other times . . . as though speaking to each of them individually . . . [And because each man is thus directly addressed by Him], every one in Israel should ask himself, When will my deeds match the deeds of Abraham, Isaac, and Jacob, who came to own this world and the world-to-come only because of their good deeds and study of Torah?"[17] (TBE p. 127).

The verb καταρτίζω (katartizō) signifies "putting in order, repairing" in a physical context and, in an ethical framework, "completing" or "perfecting" (cf. BAGD: 417-18).[18] It suggests here that those caught have

---

Introduction, **Argument**, 1:1-5, 15-16b, 21-24, 2:1-10 (n136), 15-21 (n292), 4:12-20, 5:2-12 (verse 11), and verses 12f. In this sense, the present section serves as the outworking of Paul's plea for imitation in 4:12ff (see there and below).

[13] For the possibility that some of Paul's disciples have already undergone circumcision/conversion, see Introduction, **Occasion and circumstances** (n51).

[14] For the same device, employed in a positive direction, cf. 4:7.

[15] בנים **אתם** לה' אלהיכם לא **תתג'דדו** ולא-**תשימו** קרחה בין עיניכם למת: כי עם קדוש **אתה** לה' אלהיך **ובך** בחר ה' להיות לו לעם סגלה... לא **תאכל** כל-תועבה.

[16] Cf. Dt. 4:3-4, 12:4-8, 30:19. Paul evidences a similar usage in 4:1-7, switching to the singular in verse 7. For the singular as "representative," see 5:2-12 (verse 10).

[17] לפעמים הוא מדבר עמהם כמו שהוא מדבר עם הרבים ולפעמים הוא מדבר עמהם כמו שהוא מדבר עם היחיד ... לפיכך הייתי אומר שכל אחד ואחד מישראל חייב לומר: מתי יגיע מעשי למעשה אבותי, אברהם יצחק ויעקב - שלא קנו האבות העולם הזה והעולם הבא וימות בן דוד אלא בשביל מעשיהם הטובים ותלמוד תורה.

[18] Cf. 1 Cor. 1:10; 1 Thess. 3:10; Heb. 13:21; 1 Pet. 5:10. πειράζω (peirazō) represents the regular verb for "temptation" or "testing" (cf. Jas. 1:13-16) – here in the resistance of the influencers' persuasion. Delitzsch translates פן-תבא לידי נסיון (pen

merely "stumbled" and need to be restored to their rightful place – in liberty rather than under bondage to sin (and the flesh) (see 5:13-18 [verse 16] and verses 12-16).[19]

The "spirit of gentleness (πνεύματι πραΰτητος)" is itself one of the fruit of the Spirit (cf. 5:23): "One should reproach one another in truth, in meekness and in compassionate love for one's fellow man להוכי' איש את רעהו באמת וענוה ואהבת חסד לאיש" (1QS 5:24-25). If the quality parallels the "spirit of meekness רוח ענוה" in the Qumran texts,[20] it involves a measure of humility, on which theme Paul expands in verses 2f – in relation to the influencers. While Paul himself is prepared to use the harshest of words in reprimanding his disciples and calling them back to their "first love" (cf. 1 Cor. 4:21; Gal. 1:6, 3:1), he is anxious that those in the community act compassionately in remonstrating with and restoring their brethren (cf. Mt. 18:15).

Such conduct is the mark of those who are "wise and understanding," who demonstrate their good behaviour in the "gentleness of wisdom," a wisdom which is "not that which comes down from above, but is earthly, natural, demonic. For where jealousy and selfish ambition exist, there is disorder and every evil thing. But the wisdom from above is first pure, then peaceable, gentle, reasonable, full of mercy and good fruits, unwavering, without hypocrisy. And the seed whose fruit is righteousness is sown in peace by those who make peace"[21] (Jas. 3:13-18).[22]

Verse 2: In exercising this responsibility, those indeed walking in the Spirit demonstrate that they are "bearing one another's burdens (ἀλλήλων τὰ βάρη βαστάζετε)." The phrase originates from Moses' grievance before God of carrying responsibility for the people alone: "Why hast Thou been so hard on Thy servant? And why have I not found favor in Thy sight, that Thou hast laid the burden of all this people on me?" (Num. 11:11). God responds to Moses' complaint by declaring: "I will take of the Spirit who is

---

tavo li-day nisayon), a phrase which directly recalls Jesus' words in Mt. 6:13: "Do not lead us into temptation, but deliver us from evil (μὴ εἰσενέγκῃς ἡμᾶς εἰς πειρασμόν, ἀλλὰ ῥῦσαι ἡμᾶς ἀπὸ τοῦ πονηροῦ)" (cf. Mt. 26:41; Mk. 14:38; Lk. 11:4, 22:40, 46; 1 Tim. 6:9).

[19] The verb may also anticipate verse 2, where Paul indicates that "bearing one another's burdens" realizes the "law of the Messiah" (see below).

[20] Cf. 1QS 3:8, 4:3; Did. 3:7.

[21] Τίς σοφὸς καὶ ἐπιστήμων ἐν ὑμῖν; δειξάτω ἐκ τῆς καλῆς ἀναστροφῆς τὰ ἔργα αὐτοῦ ἐν πραΰτητι σοφίας ... οὐκ ἔστιν αὕτη ἡ σοφία ἄνωθεν κατερχομένη ἀλλὰ ἐπίγειος, ψυχική, δαιμονιώδης. ὅπου γὰρ ζῆλος καὶ ἐριθεία, ἐκεῖ ἀκαταστασία καὶ πᾶν φαῦλον πρᾶγμα. ἡ δὲ ἄνωθεν σοφία πρῶτον μὲν ἁγνή ἐστιν, ἔπειτα εἰρηνική, ἐπιεικής, εὐπειθής, μεστὴ ἐλέους καὶ καρπῶν ἀγαθῶν, ἀδιάκριτος, ἀνυπόκριτος. καρπὸς δὲ δικαιοσύνης ἐν εἰρήνῃ σπείρεται τοῖς ποιοῦσιν εἰρήνην.

[22] The affinities of this passage with the present chapter should be readily evident – continuing Paul's thought from 5:13ff.

upon you, and will put *Him* upon them; and they shall bear the burden of
the people with you, so that you shall not bear *it* all alone"[23] (Num. 11:17).[24]
Here, the bearing of burdens is specifically associated with God's bestowal
of His Spirit, whose presence is designed to enable the leaders to "carry
them [the people] in your bosom as a nurse carries a nursing infant שאהו
בחיקך כאשר ישא האמן את-הינק" (Num. 11:12).[25]

The parallel passage in Exodus 18:18 indicates that the issue
concerned the appointment of judges: "The Rabbis say: Come and see.
When Moses was appointed over Israel he said to them: 'I am not able
alone to bear your burden; appoint therefore judges who shall judge you,'
as it is said, *Get you wise men* (Dt. 1:13)"[26] (Dt.R. 1:10).[27] In this sense, Paul's
injunction appears to reiterate the responsibility of the "spiritual," being

---

[23] למה הרעת לעבדך ולמה לא-מצתי חן בעיניך לשום את-משא כל-העם הזה עלי . . . ואצלתי מן-
הרוח אשר עליך ושמתי עליהם ונשאו אתך במשא העם ולא-תשא אתה לבדך.

[24] Cf. Ex. 18:13-26; Dt. 1:9-15. The association between the Spirit and bearing
burdens should not need emphasis. The LXX translates here with
συναντιλήμψονται (synantilēmpsontai), from συναντιλαμβάνομαι
(syantilambanomai – "come to the aid of"), a verb which Paul adopts in Rom. 8:26
("the Spirit also helps our weakness [τὸ πνεῦμα συναντιλαμβάνεται τῇ ἀσθενείᾳ
ἡμῶν]"). Paul's later use of this motif in Rom. 15:1 suggests that it relates to a
willingness to extend oneself on behalf of those in difficulty. The situation in
Romans 14-15 pertains to Galatians not in the sense that one's conviction of God's
strength is greater than that of another, the "weaker" being convinced that His
commandments must be observed as He has given them (cf. Shulam and Le Cornu:
455ff), but in relation to Paul's reproof of Peter in 2:11ff, wherein Paul reprimands
Peter for not standing in his confidence that the sufficiency of God's grace means
that Gentiles together with Jews can now come to Him equally in the Messiah (see
Introduction, **Argument; Theological pointers** [Jewish-gentile relations] and 2:11f).
See also below.

[25] Although Paul does not speak of himself as a "nurse" in 4:12f, the motif of
"fathering/mothering" bears close affinities with that of the "omēn" in whose role
Moses becomes exhausted: "'Was it I who conceived all this people? Was it I who
brought them forth, that Thou shouldst say to me, "Carry them in your bosom as a
nurse carries a nursing infant . . ."?' -כי האנכי הריתי את כל-העם הזה אם-אנכי ילדתיהו
תאמר אלי שאהו בחיקך כאשר ישא האמן את-הינק . . ." (Num. 11:12). Paul is now asking
his faithful disciples to further imitate him in "fathering" those who have fallen (see
4:12-20 and below). For the omēn as tutor, see 3:21-25.

[26] רבנין אמרי: בוא וראה: בשעה שנתמנה משה על ישראל אמר להן: איני יכול לישא את משאכם
לעצמי. אלא מנו לכם דיינים שיהיו דנין אתכם, שנאמר: הבו לכם אנשים חכמים ונבנים.

[27] Judges were required to be men of quality: "Judges must possess seven qualities
and of these [three] are: They must be wise men, and understanding and full of
knowledge. And the other four are as enumerated elsewhere in Scripture. *Moreover,
thou shalt provide out of all the people able men, such as fear God, men of truth, hating
unjust gain* (Ex. 18:21). צריכין הדייניו שיהא בהן שבע מדות ואלו הן: חכמים ונבונים וידועים.
 וארבע, כמה שכתוב להלן: ואתה תחזה מכל העם וגו'" (Dt.R. 1:10).

endowed with the Spirit, to guide and lead those who have been "hindered from obeying the truth" (5:7).[28]

The resonances in this verse with Leviticus 19:17 may extend further to include the "incurring of sin" – the Hebrew expression ישא חטא (yisa chet) literally signifying the "bearing of sin" (cf. Lev. 22:9; Num. 9:13; Heb. 9:28). A passage in the Damascus Document associates the role of the judges with adjudicating the people's sins: "If the judges adju[re] (someone) by the curses of the covenant *Blank* If he transgresses, he will be guilty and will have to confess and make emends, and (then) he shall not be liable to sin [and] die"[29] (CD-A 15:4-5). Possibly, Paul is proposing that the sin or "burden" (cf. verse 5) which the leaders should "bear" (be liable for incurring) is that of not restoring the people to the proper path (see above).[30]

The direct consequence of following Paul's proposals is the "fulfilment of the law of the Messiah (ἀναπληρώσετε τὸν νόμον τοῦ Χριστοῦ)."[31] It is difficult to determine, first of all, whether this "law" is a set or body of teachings to which Paul is advocating adherence, or whether the phrase is descriptive of the sort of behavior which befits that which Paul is promoting amongst the Galatians.[32] What is common to both

---

[28] The traditional interpretation of the clause refers it, largely under the influence of Rom. 15:1, to living in "a relationship of interdependence," a "costly matter because our common sinfulness gives us the capacity to inflict pain upon one another and place heavy loads upon each other" (Hays, Galatians: 333). Some scholars have attempted to associate the burden with the idea of financial support for Jerusalem (cf. 2:10) (cf. Strelan).

[29] ואם באלות הברית ישב]יעו[השפטים *vacat* אם עבר אשם הוא והתודה והשיב לו ולא ישא חטאה [וי]מות.

[30] His emphasis on "gentleness" thence reflects the *proper manner* in which such "judges" should carry out their task. The command to love one's neighbour as oneself is explicitly related to the injunction against bearing a grudge: "*But if any man hate his neighbor, and lie in wait for him, and rise up against him* (Dt. 19:11): Hence the Sages have said: If a person transgresses a minor commandment, he will eventually transgress a major commandment. If he transgresses *Thou shalt love thy neighbor as thyself* (Lev. 19:18), he will eventually transgress *Thou shalt not take vengeance, nor bear any grudge* (Lev. 19:18), *Thou shalt not hate thy brother* (Lev. 19:17), and *That thy brother may live with thee* (Lev. 25:36), until he ends up shedding blood ולא ישפך דם נקי בקרב ארצך אשר ה' אלהיך נתן לך נחלה. כי יהיה איש שונא לרעהו וארב לו וקם עליו. מכאן אמרו : עובר אדם על מצוה אחת קלה, סופו לעבור על מצוה חמורה. עבר על : ואהבת לרעך כמוך - סופו לעבור על : לא תשנא, ועל : לא תקום, ועל : לא תטור. וסופו לעבור על : וחי אחיך עמך - עד שבא לידי שפיכות דמים" (Sif.Dt. 186/87) (see 5:13-18 and below [n86]).

[31] "The adverb οὕτως ("in this manner," "thus," "so") with the conjunction καί ('and') correlates what follows with what has immediately preceded, thereby setting out a logical connection between the two" (Longenecker, Galatians: 275).

[32] Or, in other words, whether they are putting into practice a "body of rules" given by Jesus or acting according to a "regulative principle or structure of existence" in his spirit (Spirit) (cf. Hays, Christology: 276). The idea of a "messianic

understandings is the Messiah's authority in directing the conduct of those who follow him. In this sense, the governing motif is – unsurprisingly in the light of 4:12 – that of imitation (cf. Hays, Christology: 275).[33] If the Messiah is responsible for redeeming human beings from the bondage of sin, Paul has been responsible for preaching this gospel – and now he is calling "those who are spiritual" to bear _their_ responsibility, in restoring to their proper liberty those who have "relapsed" (see 4:1-7).

To the extent that Jesus speaks of the "burden" which the Pharisees place on those whom they lead, it is possible that Paul is indirectly referring back to the motif of hypocrisy against which he has been inveighing throughout the letter (see above). As those who "have seated themselves in the chair of Moses (ἐπὶ τῆς Μωϋσέως καθέδρας ἐκάθισαν)" – i.e., claiming his inheritance and authority – rather than bearing responsibility for the people's weakness, the Pharisees lay on them a greater "weight/burden" (cf. Mt. 23:1ff).[34] Rather than performing the "major commandments" of "justice and mercy and faithfulness," they "strain out a gnat and swallow a camel (διϋλίζοντες τὸν κώνωπα, τὴν δὲ κάμηλον καταπίνοντες)" (Mt. 23:24) (see 2:15-21 and 4:12f). Paul may possibly be alluding to Jesus' words in this respect, contrasting Jesus' "law" with that of the Pharisees.[35] Rather than acting in the spirit of the

---

Torah" (cf. Acts 1:2?) has been variously proposed, among others, by Davies (Torah; Paul: 142-44) and Dodd (134-48) (see 1:11-12). While it was not generally assumed that the Messiah's advent would alter the nature or extent of the Torah, some midrashic traditions indicate that in addition to gathering the exiles and delivering Israel from the yoke of foreign kingdoms, the Messiah would also give commandments to the Gentiles (cf. Gen.R. 98:9; [JMeg. 1, 4, 70d]) (cf. Urbach, Sages: 308f) (see verses 12-16 and also below).

[33] See 4:12-20. Paul's return to the theme of imitation here would appear to reinforce the importance of 4:12 for both the structure and the argument of the letter in general. We have argued that 4:12f directly informs first of all the immediately-following allegory, whose message Paul reaffirms and repeats throughout chapter 5. Since we also predicate an express continuation between 5:26 and verses 1ff, it is possible to see the present verses as directly proceeding from 4:12. In a very significant sense, the issue of imitation also lies behind Paul's reproof of Peter which, we have argued, constitutes one of the guiding themes of the letter (see Introduction, **Argument**).

[34] For the (unlikely) possibility that the influencers are themselves Pharisees, see 2:15-21 (n269).

[35] Paul's thought here also closely resembles that of James' warning against hypocrisy as unfitting to the "law of liberty": "So speak and so act, as those who are to be judged by _the_ law of liberty. For judgment _will be_ merciless to one who has shown no mercy; mercy triumphs over judgment. What use is it, my brethren, if someone says he has faith but he has no works? Can that faith save him? If a brother or sister is without clothing and in need of daily food, and one of you says to them, 'Go in peace, be warmed and be filled,' and yet you do not give them what

Pharisees – whose "followers" the influencers are demonstrating themselves to be – he asks that those who are "spiritual" serve the community as leaders who bear responsibility for their flock.[36]

To the degree to which Paul calls his disciples to order, as it were, in 4:12, reminding them of their loyalty to him as their "spiritual father" and mentor, being himself Jesus' representative and example, the context remains that of ensuring that they remain his disciples (see 4:12-20). In his "labouring" over them (cf. 4:11) (in both senses of the word), he has indicated how, by participating in Jesus' death and resurrection, these former Gentiles have been delivered from bondage to the "elemental things of the world" and been transferred into the Messiah's domain (see 4:1f). As both his own disciples and as those of the Messiah, they are "called to freedom" (5:13).[37]

This dimension is characterised by life in the Spirit, the "life" demanding also a continued "walking in the Spirit" (see 5:24-26). It is consequently possible to see in the "law of the Messiah" a designation parallel to "walking in the Spirit."[38] In this sense, the Torah of the messianic age is "vanity" in comparison with that of the world to come, for while people "forget" the Torah on earth (cf. Jas. 1:21-27), in the world to come God promises that "I will put My law within them, and on their

---

is necessary for *their* body, what use is that? Even so faith, if it has no works, is dead, *being* by itself. But someone may *well* say, 'You have faith and I have works; show me your faith without the works, and I will show you my faith by my works' (Οὕτως λαλεῖτε καὶ οὕτως ποιεῖτε ὡς διὰ νόμου ἐλευθερίας μέλλοντες κρίνεσθαι. ἡ γὰρ κρίσις ἀνέλεος τῷ μὴ ποιήσαντι ἔλεος· κατακαυχᾶται ἔλεος κρίσεως. Τί τὸ ὄφελος, ἀδελφοί μου, ἐὰν πίστιν λέγῃ τις ἔχειν ἔργα δὲ μὴ ἔχῃ; μὴ δύναται ἡ πίστις σῶσαι αὐτόν; ἐὰν ἀδελφὸς ἢ ἀδελφὴ γυμνοὶ ὑπάρχωσιν καὶ λειπόμενοι τῆς ἐφημέρου τροφῆς εἴπῃ δέ τις αὐτοῖς ἐξ ὑμῶν· ὑπάγετε ἐν εἰρήνῃ, θερμαίνεσθε καὶ χορτάζεσθε, μὴ δῶτε δὲ αὐτοῖς τὰ ἐπιτήδεια τοῦ σώματος, τί τὸ ὄφελος; οὕτως καὶ ἡ πίστις, ἐὰν μὴ ἔχῃ ἔργα, νεκρά ἐστιν καθ' ἑαυτήν)" (Jas. 2:12-18) (see 5:2f).

36 The "weighty commandments (מצוות חמורות)" constitute the qualities associated with acting הדין (לפנים משורת (lifnim mi-shurat ha-din – "within the margin of the judgment") or "walking in the Spirit/faithfulness working in love" (see 2:15-21, 3:10-14 [n142], 5:13-18, verses 12-16 [nn152, 179], and below [nn86, 91]). A further link with Peter, whose actions serve as Paul's springboard for the charge of hypocrisy, may perhaps be found in Peter's reference to "testing God" by placing a "yoke" on the Gentiles (cf. Acts 15:10) (see 2:15-21 [n238] and below [nn57, 73]). This notwithstanding, we do not see the necessity of identifying the influencers as Pharisees (see 2:15-21 [n269] and above).

37 See 1:1-5, 2:1-10, 15-21, 3:10-14, 19ff, 4:1f, and 5:13f.

38 Cf. "the law of the Messiah (ἔννομος Χριστοῦ)" in 1 Cor. 9:21, the "law of faith (νόμου πίστεως)" in Rom. 3:27, the "law of the Spirit of life in the Messiah Jesus (ὁ νόμος τοῦ πνεύματος τῆς ζωῆς ἐν Χριστῷ Ἰησοῦ)" in Rom. 8:2, and "faith working through love (πίστις δι' ἀγάπης ἐνεργουμένη)" in 5:6.

heart I will write it נתתי את-תורתי בקרבם ועל-לבם אכתבנה" - where it will remain, God being their God and they His people (Jer. 31:33)[39] (see [3:19-20], 5:13-18).

The use of the verb "fulfill (ἀναπληρώσετε)" affirms such an interpretation by recalling the "fulfilment of the whole Torah (πᾶς νόμος . . . πεπλήρωται)" which is identified with loving one's neighbour in 5:14 (see 5:13-18). It is in this way that the Galatians will properly realize their desire to observe the Torah, the latter being summed up in love (see 5:13-18). The "law of the Messiah" may in this sense also be another way of expressing 5:13, "through love become slaves of one another (διὰ τῆς ἀγάπης δουλεύετε ἀλλήλοις)."[40] Rather than serving sin and the elemental things of the world, those in the Messiah are to become God's slaves, seeking the good of one another - most fundamentally, in ensuring that they remain in the Messiah.[41]

Verse 3: While the γάρ (gar -"for") is commonly acknowledged as introducing the reason for the preceding injunction (cf. Burton: 330), Paul is predominantly thought of here as addressing, in general terms, the Galatian communities. Given his consistent appeal throughout the latter part of the letter (cf. 4:12 onwards), it is possible, however, that verses 3-5 relate not to the Galatians' behaviour but to that of the *influencers*.[42] This is suggested by the theme of "boasting (καύχημα)" (cf. verse 4), which characterises the influencers' activity (cf. verse 13) (see verses 12-16).

---

[39] Cf. Lev.R. 9:7; Eccl.R. 2.1.1, [12.1.1]; Shab. 151b. While the commandments are not to be abolished in the days of the Messiah, their observance being presumed in numerous biblical texts (cf. Isa. 66:23; Ezek. 36:27, 37:24, 45:17; Zech. 14:18-19), there will be no more need of commandments to restore God's light to its fulness following the resurrection, when human nature will no longer possess the tendency to sin (cf. Nid. 61b) (cf. Lichtenstein, Studies: 101f; Flusser, Judaism: 173f) (see also 2:15-21 [n313] and 5:2-12 [n13]).

[40] Cf. Rom. 3:27: "Where then is boasting? It is excluded. By what kind of law? Of works? No, but by a law of faith (Ποῦ οὖν ἡ καύχησις; ἐξεκλείσθη. διὰ ποίου νόμου; τῶν ἔργων; οὐχί, ἀλλὰ διὰ νόμου πίστεως)" - the law which governs the "aeon" of the Messiah (see also verses 12-16).

[41] An element of imitation may also be present here, Jesus having "borne our griefs and carried our sorrows חלינו הוא נשא ומכאבינו סבלם," "bearing the sin of many והוא חטא-רבים נשא" (Isa. 53:4, 12). If so, Paul is recalling his earlier appeal that his disciples imitate Jesus in respecting his authority and in their proper walk in life (see 4:12-20, verse 17, and below).

[42] The shift from directly addressing his disciples ("bear one another's burdens . . .") to an indirect allusion to the influencers follows the pattern of 5:7-9, whose content it also immediately reflects (cf. Mt. 18:15-17; 1 Cor. 16:22). This reading of the text corroborates the suggestion above that acting in love to bring erring brothers back into line (cf. 5:25) constitutes the imitation of the Messiah, Paul moving from the Galatians' responsibility to restore the brethren to a further condemnation of the influencers themselves.

Perhaps most significantly, the apparent contradiction between verses 2 and 5 – the first claiming that one person is responsible for another, the second that each person is responsible for himself – is resolved by reading verse 5, again on analogy with 5:8-12, as a form of "curse" (cf. 1:8-9) (see 1:6-10, 5:2-12, and verses 12f).[43]

Paul's condemnation of those "troubling" his disciples takes the initial form of putting them in their place. The expression "thinks he is something (δοκεῖ τις εἶναί τι)" indicates a false presumption – as in the case of Theudas, who "rose up, claiming to be somebody (ἀνέστη Θευδᾶς λέγων εἶναί τινα ἑαυτόν)" (Acts 5:36), his claim being to prophetic/messianic status. Paul's judgment is that the influencers are in fact "nothing (μηδὲν ὤν)" – presumably because, on the present reading of the situation, they most prominently refuse to acknowledge Jesus (see Introduction, **Occasion and circumstances; Argument**).[44] Quite possibly, Paul is also hereby indicating to the Galatians that he considers the influencers to lack the very status which the Galatians are seeking from them.[45]

The fact that this concessive phrase is unusually harsh for Paul (cf. Rom. 12:3; Phil. 2:3-4) (cf. Longenecker, Galatians: 276) may reflect its address here to unbelievers.[46] The same phenomenon possibly explains his use of a verb (φρεναπατάω; frenapataō – "to deceive") which otherwise occurs nowhere else in the New Testament – although the substantive appears in Titus 1:10 in a description of "rebellious men, empty talkers and deceivers, especially those of the circumcision (ἀνυπότακτοι, ματαιολόγοι καὶ φρεναπάται, μάλιστα οἱ ἐκ τῆς περιτομῆς)."[47]

Verse 4 continues Paul's indirect address to the influencers, warning them to "each one examine his own work (τὸ δὲ ἔργον ἑαυτοῦ

---

[43] The verbal affinities are particularly pronounced in 5:10, where Paul speaks of "bearing his judgment (βαστάσει τὸ κρίμα)" – a very close parallel to "bear his own load (φορτίον βαστάσει)."

[44] On Paul's own witness, the Messiah is "all in all" (cf. 1 Cor. 1:18-31; 2 Cor. 1:20; Phil. 1:21, 3:7-8; Col. 1:13-20). While δοκέω (dokeō) in 2:2, 6 signifies the imputation of importance by others, here it signals thinking of *oneself* as possessed of stature/status.

[45] In this sense, they neither hold the social position they are insisting that the Galatians obtain nor can they provide it – even were it to be of worth to the Galatians. For the influencers as godfearers exploiting the Galatians' seeking after social standing by advocating full conversion (in dismissal of Jesus' death and resurrection), see Introduction, **Occasion and circumstances**.

[46] For the conjecture that Paul's failure to speak to the influencers directly may indicate their position as non-believers, see Introduction, **Occasion and circumstances**. The idea of thinking oneself something as referred to the community's members is prevalent in 1 Corinthians (cf. 1 Cor. 3:18, 8:2, 10:12, 14:37).

[47] See also 5:24-26 (n292). For "of the circumcision," see 2:11-14.

δοκιμαζέτω)" in order to confine his "boasting (τὸ καύχημα)" to his individual status.[48] While observation of one's own deeds is frequently advised as a means of repentance,[49] the hint of punishment is perhaps uppermost here: "Take these words to heart: Know whence you came, and whither you go, and before Whom you are destined to give an account and reckoning. Eye not [enviously] another's wealth because it undermines the gates of heaven"[50] (DEZ 4:5).[51] Their "boasting" is evidently related to what the influencers consider to be their status, the thought here in many ways anticipating that of Romans 2 where, being Jewish, Paul's addressees present themselves as "somebodies" in relation to others of inferior position (see verses 12-16).[52] The noun καύχημα (kauchēma – "boasting") refers primarily to "exultation" or "gratulation" – here of the self, the article and neuter particle μόνον (monon –"alone") both serving as restrictive emphases indicating the "ground" or "basis" of boasting (cf. Longenecker, Galatians: 277).

Paul's point derives from the fact that this self-aggrandizement is at the expense of others. Perhaps more than anything else, this verse suggests the influencers as the subject – most particularly in the light of verses 12-13, in which Paul charges them with wishing to "make a good showing in

---

[48] For boasting as a sign of the influencers' identity, see above. Paul elaborates on the theme in verses 12-13. Like those in verses 2-3, the verb here displays the form of a command or directive (cf. Longenecker, Galatians: 276).

[49] Cf. 1 Cor. 11:28; 2 Cor. 13:5; Test.Jud. 20:3-5; PA 2:1, 22. The more common biblical concept is that of God examining one's heart and thoughts (cf. Ps. 26:2; Jer. 11:20, 17:10, 20:12; Rom. 2:16; 4 Ez. 16:63f; Sib.Or. 8:368f; 2 Bar. 83:2; 1QH^a 15:13) (cf. Shulam and Le Cornu: 94-95). It was the task of the Qumran "Instructor/Inspector" to examine the novitiate/sectarian's heart to make certain of his commitment to God's will (including reproaching one another "in truth, in meekness and in compassionate love") (cf. 1QS 5:23-24, 6:14f; CD-A 13:11f).

[50] דברי אלו יהיו על לבבך : דע מאין באת ולאן אתה הולך ולפני מי אתה עתיד ליתן דין וחשבון. אל תתן עיניך בממון שאינו שלך, שהן משקעות שערי הרקיע.

[51] Cf. PA 3:1; ARN^a 19:1f; ARN^b 32. While the present reading of Galatians does not equate "deeds" with Torah-observance *per se*, the link between "work" here and the "works of the Torah" (cf. 2:16, 3:2, 5, 10) may recall the fact that, in Paul's eyes, the influencers are walking according to the flesh (see 4:21-31, 5:13-18, and verses 12-16). Paul as it were works out the "theological" basis of this argument in reverse here, the grounds appearing in verse 7; (for the structure of verses 7-9, cf. Longenecker, Galatians: 279). Interestingly, the "undermining" of the gates of heaven literally signifies their "sinking" – a metaphor which recalls the weight of hypocritical burdens, whose imposition on others obstructs the latters' entrance into God's Kingdom (see 2:15-21 and above). For jealousy, see verses 12-16 (n152).

[52] Cf. Matthew 23. The issue of hypocrisy therefore comes to the forefront here also – as we have suggested it in fact runs throughout Galatians from Paul's initial rebuke of Peter (see Introduction, **Argument**; **Theological pointers**, 2:15-21, 3:1-5, 10-14, 21-25, 5:2f, and below). (For the dating of Galatians, see Introduction, **Date and destination**.)

the flesh [. . . and] desire to have you [the Galatian believers] circumcised, that they may boast in your flesh."⁵³ His warning is directly to the influencers' persuasion of others towards circumcision, cautioning them that they will be judged not according to what influence they may wield "in regard to another (οὐκ εἰς ἕτερον)" but on the basis of their own deeds and status.⁵⁴ "Make sure that *you* are right before God," Paul admonishes, "for your boasting in *others* constitutes no grounds for approval."⁵⁵

Verse 5: Paul brings the warning to a climax by directly invoking judgment on sin. While some commentators understand the statement to reflect a traditional maxim, its affinities with Jesus' reprimand of (pharisaic) hypocrisy – a dominant theme throughout Galatians – suggests that Paul has the same issue in mind here (see verses 12-16 and above).⁵⁶ Not only does he employ the same verb (βαστάζω; bastazō –"to bear") in relation to "sin" in verse 2 (see above), but the Greek φορτίον (fortion – "burden") of which he speaks here regularly renders the Hebrew משא (masa), as in the phrase ישא חטאו (yisa chet'o – "bear his sin") (see above).⁵⁷ This verse consequently repeats Paul's previous warning in 5:10: "the one

---

⁵³ εὐπροσωπῆσαι ἐν σαρκί . . . θέλουσιν ὑμᾶς περιτέμνεσθαι ἵνα ἐν τῇ ὑμετέρα σαρκὶ καυχήσωνται.

⁵⁴ The double ἕκαστος (hekastos – "each," "every one"), which emphasises the influencers' individual responsibility, parallels the responsibility of the "spiritual" within the community to "restore" those who have been persuaded (see above).

⁵⁵ "The day of judgment is decisive and displays to all the seal of truth. Just as now a father does not send his son, or a son his father, or a master his servant, or a friend his dearest friend, to be ill or asleep or eat or be healed in his stead, so no one shall ever pray for another on that day, neither shall anyone lay a burden on another; for then everyone shall bear his own righteousness or unrighteousness" (4 Ez. 7:[104-105]).

⁵⁶ The awkwardness of this interpretation is overtly acknowledged: "Paul, however, uses the maxim in general support of his directive that 'each one should test his own actions' in v 4, with ἕκαστος ('each one,' 'everyone') as the subject both of the directive and the maxim, tying these two statements together and the content of the maxim being generally confirmatory, though admittedly used out of context" (Longenecker, Galatians: 278).

⁵⁷ Cf. Mid.Ps. 25:3. Nor is it likely to be coincidental that the idea of the "burden" informs Matthew 23, where it signifies a "heavy commandment [מצווה חמורה]," with the implication of punishment for its violation – in the context of being "noticed by men" (Mt. 23:5). It is, moreover, precisely such a "yoke (ζυγὸν)" which the "council" in Acts refused to make the Gentiles "bear (βαστάσαι)" (Acts 15:10). For the possible link between verse 7 and Acts 15:10, see above (n36) and below; for the relationship between the "council" and Galatians, see Introduction, **Date and destination**. In contrast to those who demonstrate that they are "walking in the Spirit" by taking responsibility for those who stumble, the influencers' interest is restricted to their own wellbeing (see verses 12-16).

who is troubling you shall bear his judgment" (cf. Ezekiel 18) (see 5:2-12, above, below, and verse 17).[58]

Verse 6: The exhortation in this verse is frequently considered to constitute "the most puzzling of all Paul's directives in 6:1-10 – or for that matter elsewhere in the Galatian letter" (Longenecker, Galatians: 278). The present reading may help mitigate its difficulty, making as it does this section of the letter dependent on 4:12f (see above). Having indirectly warned the influencers of their accountability, Paul turns back once again to his own disciples, over whom he fears he has laboured in vain (cf. 4:11), and admonishes them as to *their* right conduct. The "comparison" here is between s/he who is taught and the one teaching, the former being responsible for "sharing all good things (κοινωνείτω ... ἐν πᾶσιν ἀγαθοῖς)" with the latter.

Paul's reference here to the "good things" may directly pick up the theme of 4:12f in which he associates the "good" with his "fathering" (cf. 4:18).[59] In urging his disciples to share with him as the one who has taught them, he is calling upon them to confirm their commitment to him – and not to any other.[60] Paul's directive is known from other sources from the general period: ". . . the Father's will is that we give to all from the gifts we have received . . . Thou shalt not turn away the needy, but thou shalt share everything with thy brother, and shalt not say that it is thine own, for if you are sharers in the imperishable, how much more in the things which perish?"[61] (Did. 1:5, 4:8).[62] If Paul has "fathered" the gentile Galatians in faithfulness, it is upon them to acknowledge their "debt" by proving their discipleship to him: "If we sowed spiritual things in you, is it too much if

---

[58] On this reading, the troublesome "contradiction" between this verse and verse 2 is dissolved, Paul not speaking to one group – even with different objectives in mind – but in the first to those who are spiritual and here to those who have caused others to stumble.

[59] For the associated idea of envy there, see 4:12-20.

[60] The Greek κατηχούμενος (katēchoumenos) is frequently associated with instruction in Scripture (cf. Acts 18:25; Rom. 2:18). Here again, Paul provides the exemplar, having demonstrated his eagerness to "remember the poor" in Jerusalem – perhaps on the same principle of material remuneration for spiritual blessings (see 2:1-10 [verse 10]).

[61] πᾶσι γὰρ θέλει δίδοσθαι ὁ πατὴρ ἐκ τῶν ἰδίων χαρισμάτων . . . οὐκ ἀποστραφήσῃ τὸν ἐνδεόμενον, συγκοινωνήσεις δὲ πάντα τῷ ἀδελφῷ σοῦ καὶ οὐκ ἐρεῖς ἴδια εἶναι· εἰ γὰρ ἐν τῷ ἀθανάτῳ κοινωνοί ἐστε, πόσῳ μᾶλλον ἐν τοῖς θνητοῖς;

[62] Cf. [Lk. 16:10-12]; Rom. 11:12, 15ff; 1 Cor. 9:11; PA 5:10; Ep.Barn. 19:8 (cf. Le Cornu and Shulam: 155, 1322). Flusser argues that John's dictum with regard to letting "the man who has two tunics share with him who has none (ὁ ἔχων δύο χιτῶνας μεταδότω τῷ μὴ ἔχοντι)" (Lk. 3:11) constitutes an adaptation of the essene ideal of the "community [sharing] of goods" which Josephus defines as τὸ κοινωνικόν (to koinōnikon) (cf. War 2.122) (cf. Judaism: 162f).

we should reap material things from you? (εἰ ἡμεῖς ὑμῖν τὰ πνευματικὰ ἐσπείραμεν, μέγα εἰ ἡμεῖς ὑμῶν τὰ σαρκικὰ θερίσομεν;)" (1 Cor. 9:11).[63]

While "all good things (πᾶσιν ἀγαθοῖς)" may seem rather a vague reference, its first echoes are of the Torah itself, given by the Good, to the good, as their good, to do good[64] (see 5:19-23). In this sense, Paul is encouraging the Galatians to read Scripture as he has taught them, the "word (τὸν λόγον)" also calling forth Jesus' status as the "Logos" (cf. Jn. 1:1ff; 1 Jn. 1:1f) and his presence with people gathered together in study (cf. Mt. 18:20; PA 3:3).[65] Paul extends the instruction from discipleship in this verse to "doing good" in general in verses 9-10 (see below).[66]

Verse 7: While verse 6 speaks to Paul's disciples' responsibility to him, this verse addresses both sides of the conflict – Galatians and influencers alike – since both need to be careful how they act.[67] Although the "deception (πλανᾶσθε)" first recalls the influencers' behaviour (cf. verse 3), the metaphor of reaping and sowing encompasses all human activity.[68]

---

[63] Paul later speaks of this debt as that of love (cf. Rom. 13:8) – the very thing to which he has called them in chapter 5 (see 5:13-18 and above). If Paul is speaking also in terms of material support the weight of this instruction lies in comparison with his regular policy of *not* accepting remuneration for teaching (cf. 1 Cor. 9:6ff; 1 Thess. 2:9) (cf. Le Cornu and Shulam: 682, 674, 693, 932, 1141) (see 1:1-5 [n46]). τὰ πνευματικὰ (ta pneumatika – "spiritual things") picks up, as it were, the "spiritual (οἱ πνευματικοὶ)" disciples whom Paul is addressing (cf. verse 1). For the motif of sowing/reaping, see below.

[64] Cf. Gen.R. 99:10; Ex.R. 1:16; PA 3:14, 6:3; Men. 53b; Ber. 5a, 48b; AZ 19b.

[65] See also 4:12-20 (verse 19) and 5:13-18. The emphasis in this verse lies on *mutual* recognition and respect. The singular "he who teaches" can most properly be referred to Paul himself on this reading – rather than to a "class of teachers" whom Paul either appointed to the task on his departure or who emerged from the community to fill the office (cf. Martyn, Galatians: 552; Longenecker, Galatians: 279). This statement may have constituted a common introductory formula to an admonitory statement (cf. Longenecker, Galatians: 279). For Paul's use of Scripture with respect to the Galatians, see Introduction, **Theological pointers**, 3:1ff, and 4:1f, 21-31.

[66] No intrinsic reason exists to exclude financial support on the Galatians' behalf. For Paul's welcoming of the idea that the gentile believers help provide for their Jewish brethren, see 2:1-10.

[67] While 1 Corinthians is later than Galatians according to the chronology currently proposed, the present passage in Galatians appears to suggest a well-established comprehension on Paul's part of "reaping and sowing" in terms of returning material benefit in exchange for spiritual impartation – an association which presents the logical progression of thought from verse 6 to the following passage. See also below (verse 9).

[68] While the present reading does not sustain all of the particulars of his argument, Longenecker's summation of the structure of this segment is succinctly set forth: "Verses 7-9 comprise a warning with an explication and an appeal. The unit seems to consist of (1) an introductory formula ('do not be deceived'), (2) the warning itself

Paul's injunction recalls verse 4 in cautioning people not to forget before Whom they stand: "Know that all is according to the reckoning. And let not thy [evil] inclination assure thee that the grave is a place of refuge for thee; for without thy will wast thou fashioned, without thy will wast thou born, without thy will livest thou, without thy will wilt thou die, and without thy will art thee of a certainty to give an account and reckoning before the King of the Kings of Kings, blessed be He"[69] (PA 4:22) (see above).[70]

God is not a man, that he should be deceived by human ploys: "Will it be well when he examines you? Or will you deceive Him as one deceives man? הטוב כי-יחקר אתכם אם-כהתל באנוש תהתלו בו" (Job 13:9).[71] God is "the fashioner, the creator, He the discerner, He the judge, He the witness, He the complainant, and . . . He is of a certainty to judge, blessed be He, before whom there is no unrighteousness, nor forgetting, nor respect of persons, nor taking of bribes, for all is His"[72] (PA 4:22).[73] Consequently (γάρ; gar –

---

cast in proverbial form ('God is not mocked'), (3) a traditional maxim given in support of the warning ('whatever a man sows, that he also reaps'), (4) Paul's explication in term of his own 'flesh-Spirit' antinomy ('the one who sows to the flesh, from the flesh shall reap destruction; the one who sows to the Spirit, from the Spirit shall reap life eternal'), (5) Paul's appeal to comply with the warning and his explication to circumstances within Galatia ('let us not become weary in doing good'), and (6) another traditional maxim given in support of the appeal and promising a good outcome when such an appeal is heeded ('at the proper time we shall reap a harvest if we do not give up')" (Galatians: 279).

[69] ודע שהכל לפי החשבון. ואל יבטיחך יצרך שהשאול בית מנוס לך, שעל כרחך אתה נוצר, (ועל כרחך אתה נולד), ועל כרחך אתה חי, ועל כרחך אתה מת, ועל כרחך אתה עתיד לתן דין וחשבון לפני מלך מלכי המלכים הקדוש ברוך הוא.

[70] Cf. Sir. 7:1-3: "Do no evil, so shall no harm come unto thee. Depart from the unjust and iniquity shall turn away from thee. My son, sow not upon the furrows of unrighteousness, and thou shalt not reap sevenfold (Μὴ ποίει κακά, καὶ οὐ μή σε καταλάβῃ κακόν· ἀπόστηθι ἀπὸ ἀδίκου, καὶ ἐκκλινεῖ ἀπὸ σοῦ. υἱέ, μὴ σπεῖρε ἐπ' αὔλακας ἀδικίας, καὶ οὐ μὴ θερίσῃς αὐτὰ ἑπταπλασίως)."

[71] The Greek μυκτηρίζω (myktērizō) - a NT hapax - literally signifies "turning up the nose," the compound ἐκμυκτηρίζω (ekmytērizō) in Lk. 16:14, 23:35 well illustrating the meaning. The LXX and other contemporary Jewish texts employ the verb chiefly in describing the ungodly behaviour of Israel's enemies (cf. Prov. 1:30, 11:12, 12:8; Isa. 37:22; Jer. 20:7; Ezek. 8:17; 1 Esd. 1:49; 1 Macc. 7:34; Sib.Or. 1.171; Ps.Sol. 4:7; Test.Jos. 2:3) (cf. Betz, Galatians: 306).

[72] הוא אל, הוא היוצר, הוא הבורא, הוא המבין, הוא הדין, הוא עד, הוא בעל דין, והוא עתיד לדון. ברוך הוא, שאין לפניו לא עולה ולא שכחה ולא משוא פנים ולא מקח שוחד, שהכל שלו.

[73] There may be in mocking God also an element of testing Him (cf. Mal. 3:15) - which then recalls Peter's words before the "council" in warning against "placing upon the neck of the disciples a yoke which neither our fathers nor we have been able to bear (τί πειράζετε τὸν θεὸν ἐπιθεῖναι ζυγὸν ἐπὶ τὸν τράχηλον τῶν μαθητῶν ὃν οὔτε οἱ πατέρες ἡμῶν οὔτε ἡμεῖς ἰσχύσαμεν βαστάσαι;)" (Acts

"for"), Paul cautions, everyone should know that "whatever a man sows, this he will also reap (ὃ γὰρ ἐὰν σπείρῃ ἄνθρωπος, τοῦτο καὶ θερίσει)." Both the concept and the metaphor are biblical in origin, Paul echoing here such texts as: "He who sows iniquity will reap vanity זוֹרֵעַ עַוְלָה יִקְצָור-אָוֶן" (Prov. 22:8). "According to what I have seen, those who plow iniquity and those who sow trouble harvest it. By the breath of God they perish, and by the blast of His anger they come to an end"[74] (Job 4:8-9).[75]

While rabbinic texts do not develop the agricultural metaphor they repeatedly emphasise the need to acknowledge God's justice in rewarding the righteous and the wicked according to their deeds: "Everything is given against a pledge, and a net is spread out over all the living; the store is open and the storekeeper allows credit, but the ledger is open and the hand writes, and whoever wishes to borrow may come and borrow; but the collectors go round regularly every day and exact dues from man, either with his consent or without his consent, and they have that on which they [can] rely [in their claims], seeing that the judgment is a righteous judgment, and everything is prepared for the banquet"[76] (PA 3:16).[77]

Verse 8: Having provided the scriptural principle supporting his argument, Paul now proceeds to apply it to the Galatians' specific circumstances.[78] The simile of sowing and reaping (action and consequence) picks up the theme of "fruit" from 5:22f, with its correlated references to the "flesh" and "Spirit."[79] As in 5:12-13, Paul appears to be playing here on the metaphorical and physical aspects of the "flesh." A person may literally "sow to his flesh" in "investing" in conversion – "to

---

15:10) (cf. Le Cornu and Shulam: 823f) (see 2:15-21 [Malachi 3] and above [nn36, 57]). For God's impartiality, see 2:1-10.

[74] כאשר ראיתי חֹרשׁי און וזֹרעי עמל יקצרֻהֻו: מנשמת אלוה יאבדו ומרוח אפו יכלו.

[75] Cf. Prov. 11:18, 22:8; Hos. 8:7, 10:12; Mt. 13:18-32; Mk. 4:26-32; Jn. 4:35-36; 2 Cor. 9:6; Jas. 3:18; Test.Levi 13:6; Sir. 7:3; Plato, *Phaed.* 260C; Arist.*Rhet.* 3.3.4 [1406B]; Demos.*Cor.* 159; Cicero, *Orat.* 2.65; Plautus, *Mer.* 71.

[76] הכל נתון בערבון, ומצודה פרוסה על כל החיים. החנות פתוחה, והחנוני מקיף, והפנקס פתוח, והיד כותבת, וכל הרוצה ללות יבוא וילוה, והגבאים מחזירים תדיר בכל יום, ונפרעין מן האדם מדעתו ושלא מדעתו, ויש להם על מה שיסמוכו, והדין דין אמת, והכל מתקן לסעודה.

[77] Cf. Isa. 3:11, 59:18; Jer. 17:10, 32:19; Ezek. 18:30, 24:14; Mt. 16:27; Rom. 2:2ff; 2 Cor. 5:10, 11:15; Rev. 2:23, 20:12-13; Ps.Sol. 2:16, 34, 17:8; 4 Ez. 7:34; PA 2:1, 3:1, 15, 4:16, 6:5; BB 8a (cf. Urbach, Sages: 436-44; Moore: 2:89ff, 287ff).

[78] The severity of Paul's remarks make Hays' comment "The statements of v. 7 are bits of proverbial wisdom that he applies to the Galatian situation" (Galatians: 336) read rather strangely. To the extent that the remark reflects the assumption that verses 1-10 represent diverse and general maxims, the latter presupposition fails in even greater measure to convince.

[79] It also recalls the motif of the "seed" in 3:16 (see 3:15-18).

place one's confidence and hope for the future in the mundane expedient of cutting the flesh, i.e., circumcision" (Hays, Galatians: 336) (see 5:2ff).[80]

If the preposition εἰς (eis – "to") carries the nuance of the Hebrew expression לשם (le-shem – "for the sake of," "for the purpose of"), Paul may be indicating that his wayward disciples are being persuaded to work towards obtaining fleshly status, putting stock in social standing in an attitude which will induce conflict and controversy: "Every [action] which is for the name of heaven [will in] the end thereof become [of] permanent [value]; and every [action] which is not for the name of heaven, [will in] the end thereof not become [of] permanent [value] כל [מעשה] שהו[ן] לשם שמים סופו[ן] להתקיים ושאינו[ן] לשם שמים אין סופו[ן] להתקיים" (PA 4:11) (cf. PA 5:17) (cf. Flusser, Judaism: 516f).

Only sowing "for the purpose of the Spirit" – without an ulterior motive – will gain one life in the world to come: "R. Eliezer ben R. Zadok says: Perform deeds for the sake of doing them, and speak of them for their own sake ... *To love the Lord your God* (Dt. 11:13): You might say, 'I am going to study Torah in order to become rich,' or 'in order to be called Rabbi,' or 'in order to receive a reward in the world-to-come'; therefore Scripture says *To love the Lord your God* – whatever you do should be done out of love"[81] (Sif.Dt. 48, 41).[82]

Our "mortal bodies (τὰ θνητὰ σώματα)" to which the Spirit gives life (cf. Rom. 8:11) are themselves "sown perishable ... in dishonor ... in weakness ... a natural body (σπείρεται ἐν φθορᾷ ... ἐν ἀτιμίᾳ ... ἐν ἀσθενείᾳ ... σῶμα ψυχικόν)" (1 Cor. 15:42-44).[83] Being ruled by sin, the "flesh" constitutes the dominion of Belial, whose desires are opposite to

---

[80] This idea is strengthened by the "own (ἑαυτοῦ)" in reference to the flesh. It is not simply a general warning against "the flesh" but a specific warning to "one's *own* flesh." Those who seek circumcision amongst the Galatians will not find "life" through social status – which leaves them within the bounds and bonds of "fleshly desires." (Again, we wish to stress that Paul is not speaking against circumcision *per se* – see Introduction, **Argument** and 2:1-10.)

[81] ר' אליעזר ברבי צדוק אומר: עשה דברים לשם פעולתם דבר בהם לשמן... לאהבה את ה' אלהיכם: שמא תאמר: הריני למד תורה בשביל שאעשיר, בשביל שאקרא רבי, בשביל שאקבל שכר לעולם הבא. תלמוד לומר: לאהבה את ה' אלהיכם: כל שאתם עושים, לא תהו עושים אלא מאהבה

[82] Here, too, the idea of hypocrisy can easily be discerned in the background (see above).

[83] It is striking that the LXX employs the noun (φθορά; fthora) and a compound of the verb (καταφθείρω; kataftheirō) in rendering נבל (naval) in Ex. 18:18: "You shall surely wear out, both yourself and these people who are with you, for the task is too heavy for you; you cannot do it alone נבל תבל גם-אתה גם-העם הזה אשר עמך כי-כבד ממך הדבר לא-תוכל עשהו לבדך" (see above). (The Hebrew root נבל [naval] itself denotes the drooping or fading of flowers or leaves [cf. Isa. 1:30]. The LXX also renders by φθορά the Hebrew שחת [shachat], which signifies the "pit" of Sheol [cf. Ps. 103 (102):4; Jon. 2:6(7)], השחתה [hashchata – "corruption"] being identified with idolatry and immorality [cf. Dt. 4:16; San. 57a; AZ 23b; Hul. 23a] [see below].)

those of God: The "mind set on the flesh is death ... [and] hostile toward God (τὸ γὰρ φρόνημα τῆς σαρκὸς θάνατος ... ἔχθρα εἰς θεόν)" (Rom. 8:6-7).[84] Paul is here "anticipating" his declaration to the Corinthians, that "flesh and blood cannot inherit the kingdom of God; nor does the perishable inherit the imperishable (σὰρξ καὶ αἷμα βασιλείαν θεοῦ κληρονομῆσαι οὐ δύναται οὐδὲ ἡ φθορὰ τὴν ἀφθορσίαν κληρονομεῖ)" (1 Cor. 15:50).[85]

The "sowing to eternal life" parallels "inheriting the kingdom of God" (5:21), both being expressed in relation to the "fruit of the Spirit" (see 5:19f).[86] Paul's thought reflects a similar sentiment as one attributed to Monobaz of Adiabene:

> It is related of King Monobaz that he dissipated all his own hoards and the hoards of his fathers in years of scarcity. His brothers and his father's household came in a deputation to him

---

[84] Cf., albeit in a different context: "You shall not sow your vineyard with two kinds of seed ... [you shall not plow with an ox and a donkey together. You shall not wear a material mixed of wool and linen together] -לא ... לא-תזרע כרמך כלאים תחרש בשור-ובחמר: לא תלבש שעטנז צמר ופשתים יחדו" (Dt. 22:9-11). For the "Two Ways," see 5:13f.

[85] The Greek φθορά (fthora) underlies both "corruption" here and "that which is perishable" in 1 Cor. 15:42, 50. The verbal analogies between these two passages places them in close substantive proximity. At the same time, the idea may be influenced by that of "sharing in the imperishable" as expressed in the Didache (see above). For the dating of Galatians, see Introduction, **Date and destination**; for "flesh and blood," see 1:16c-17.

[86] Cf. Mt. 3:8: "Therefore bring forth fruit in keeping with *your* repentance (ποιήσατε οὖν καρπὸν ἄξιον τῆς μετανοίας)" (see 5:19f). For righteousness and life, see also 3:10-14, 21-25. A text from the Aramaic Testament of Levi at Qumran indicates how the idea of sowing and reaping may be associated with the "Golden Rule": "The principle of all your deeds should be the truth, and l[e]t justice and tru[th] stay with you for ever, [...] ... upon them a blessed harvest. The [sow]er that sows goodness, harvests good, and whoever sows evil, against him his seed turns עלון ... .[וקושו]טא וקשה צדקה עמכון קאים י]הו[י עלמ]נא[ועד קושטא יהוי עובדיכון ראש זרעה תאיב ביש עלוהי זרע די מהנעל טאב זרע די וזר]עא ברי[כה עללה" (4Q213 1:8-9). The affinities of this sentiment with Mic. 6:8 ("to do justice, to love kindness, and to walk humbly with your God") reinforce the link between the Golden Rule and acting "within the margin of the judgment" – going beyond the law, which in itself is right and good, in order to do what is right and good by "walking in the Spirit." This association links the present passage back to Paul's rebuke of Peter's hypocrisy, which attitude Paul projects onto the gentile Galatians' circumstances in suggesting that they are being persuaded towards the "lighter" commandments (of Torah-observance) and thereby neglecting the "weightier" ones of "justice and mercy and faithfulness" (in Jesus' death and resurrection) (cf. Mt. 23:23) (see Introduction, **Argument**, 2:15-21, 3:10-14 [n142], 5:2ff, verses 12-16 [n179], above [n36], and below).

and said to him, 'Your father saved money and added to the treasures of his fathers, and you are squandering them.' He replied: 'My fathers stored up below and I am storing above, as it says, *Truth springeth out of the earth and righteousness looketh down from heaven* (Ps. 85:11). My fathers stored in a place which can be tampered with, but I have stored in a place which cannot be tampered with, as it says, *Righteousness and judgment are the foundation of his throne* (Ps. 97:2). My fathers stored something which produces no fruits, but I have stored something which does produce fruits, as it is written, *Say ye of the righteous* [zaddik] *that it shall be well with them, for they shall eat of the fruit of their doings* (Isa. 3:10). My fathers gathered treasures of money, but I have gathered treasures of souls, as it is written, *The fruit of the righteous* [zaddik] *is a tree of life, and he that is wise winneth souls* (Prov. 11:30).[87] My fathers gathered for others and I have gathered for myself, as it says, *And for thee it shall be righteousness* [zedakah] (Dt. 24:13). My fathers gathered for this world, but I have gathered for the future world, as it says, *Thy righteousness* [zedakah] *shall go before thee, and the glory of the Lord shall be thy rearward* (Isa. 58:8).'[88] (BB 11a)

Verse 9: While the majority of commentators continue to see in this verse a further general ethical exhortation, it may well be that Paul is reflecting here the development of the tradition whereby צדקה (tzdaka – "righteousness") designates "charity."[89] One of the texts in which צדקה is so interpreted gave rise to a direct association between "sowing" and "doing good (καλὸν ποιοῦντες)" – gmilut chasadim ("deeds of loving-kindness"):

R. Eleazar stated, Greater is he who performs charity than [he who offers] all the sacrifices, for it is said, *To do charity and justice is more acceptable to the Lord than sacrifice* (Prov. 21:3). R. Eliezer further stated, *Gemiluth Hasadim* is greater than charity, for it is said, *Sow to yourselves according to your charity, but reap according to your* hesed (Hos. 10:12); if a man sows, it is doubtful whether he will eat [the harvest] or not, but when a man reaps, he will

---

[87] For this verse, see 4:12-20 (n150).

[88] ת״ר: מעשה במונבז המלך שבזבז אוצרותיו ואוצרות אבותיו בשני בצורת וחברו עליו אחיו ובית אביו ואמרו לו: אבותיך גנזו והוסיפו על של אבותם ואתה מבזבום. אמר להם: אבותי גנזו למטה, ואני גנזתי למעלה, שנאמר: אמת מארץ תצמח וצדק משמים נשקף. אבותי גנזו במקום שהיד שולטת בו, ואני גנזתי במקום שאין היד שולטת בו, שנאמר: צדק ומשפט מכון כסאך. אבותי גנזו דבר שאין עושה פירות, ואני גנזתי דבר שעושה פירות, שנאמר: אמרו צדיק כי טוב כי פרי מעלליהם יאכלו. אבותי גנזו [אוצרות] ממון, ואני גנזתי אוצרות נפשות, שנאמר: פרי צדיק עץ חיים ולוקח נפשות חכם. אבותי גנזו לאחרים, ואני גנזתי לעצמי, שנאמר: ולך תהיה צדקה. אבותי גנזו לעולם הזה, ואני גנזתי לעולם הבא, שנאמר: והלך לפניך צדקך כבוד ה' יאספך.

[89] Cf. Dan. 4:27; Sir. 3:30, 7:10; Tob. 4:7, 12:8-9; AZ 5b.

certainly eat. R. Eleazar further stated, The reward of charity depends entirely upon the extent of the kindness in it, for it is said, '*Sow to yourselves according to charity, but reap according to the kindness*'. Our Rabbis taught, In three respects is *Gemiluth Hasadim* superior to charity: charity can be done only with one's money, but *Gemiluth Hasadim* can be done with one's person and one's money. Charity can be given only to the poor, *Gemiluth Hasadim* both to the rich and the poor. Charity can be given to the living only, *Gemiluth Hasadim* can be done both to the living and to the dead [by attending to their funeral and burial].[90] (Suk. 49b)[91]

Paul appears to be an early tradent (transmitter) of this interpretation, possibly having Hosea 10:12 in mind here.[92] In this sense, this verse repeats Paul's injunctions in verses 1-2 with regard to the restoration of those who

---

[90] אמר רבי אלעזר: גדול העושה צדקה יותר מכל הקרבנות, שנאמר: עשה צדקה ומשפט נבחר לה' מזבח. ואמר רבי אלעזר: גדולה גמילות חסדים יותר מן הצדקה, שנאמר: זרעו לכם לצדקה וקצרו לפי חסד. אם אדם זורע - ספק אוכל, ספק אינו אוכל. אדם קוצר - ודאי אוכל. ואמר רבי אלעזר: אין צדקה משתלמת אלא לפי חסד, שבה שנאמר: זרעו לכם לצדקה וקצרו לפי חסד. תנו רבנן: בשלשה דברים גדולה גמילות חסדים יותר מן הצדקה: צדקה בממונו - גמילות חסדים בין בגופו בין בממונו; צדקה לעניים - גמילות חסדים בין לעניים בין לעשירים; צדקה לחיים - גמילות חסדים בין לחיים בין למתים.

[91] Cf. Yalk.Prov. 959; Mid.Prov. 21; Eccl.R. 11.3.1-5; [J MK 18b; J RH 2b; JShek. 11b; JBer. 13a]; BB 10a; BK 17a; AZ 5b. This statement forms part of the principle of לפנים משורת הדין (lifnim mi-shurat ha-din – "with the margin of the judgment"), thereby picking up, once again, Paul's argument from 2:15f that a person must have both the "fear of heaven" and Torah-study in order to enter God's Kingdom (see above and below). "Deeds of loving-kindness" constitute in this regard one of the defining features of the Jew: "Only he who cultivates these three characteristics [mercy, bashfulness, and benevolence] is fit to join this nation [Israel] כל שיש בו שלושה סימנים הללו ראוי להדבק באומה זו" (Yev. 79a), since "our brethren [are] bestowers of lovingkindness, sons of bestowers of lovingkindness, who hold fast to the covenant of Abraham our father אחינו גומלי חסדים, בני גומלי חסדים המחזיקים בבריתו של אברהם אבינו [cf. Gen. 18:19]" (Ket. 8b) (see 2:15-21). Gmilut chasadim is also numbered among those things "for which no measure is prescribed [and . . .] whose fruit a man enjoys in this world while the capital is laid up for him in the world to come אלו דברים שאין להם שעור: . . . : גמילות חסדים . . . אלו דברים שאדם אוכל פרותיהן בעולם הזה והקרן קימת לו לעולם הבא" (Pe'ah 1:1) – a person thus benefiting from its rewards both in this life and in the hereafter (see 5:19-23).

[92] See the link between verses 6 and 7 above. Although the Greek ποιῶν τὸ καλὸν translates יטב (yatav) in the LXX, no intrinsic reason exists to exclude it as a rendering of גומל חסדים טובים (gomel chasadim tovim), the singular perhaps representing the more common Hebrew phrase גמילות חסדים (gmilut chasadim). Rabbinic texts associate the performance of gmilut chasadim with mastery over the evil inclination: "When they [Israel] occupy themselves with Torah and acts of kindness their inclination is mastered by them, not they by their inclination בזמן שעוסקין בתורה ובגמילות חסדים יצרם מסור בידם ואין הם מסורים ביד יצרם" (AZ 5b) (cf. ARNa 4:5).

are being influenced, together with his encouragement of his disciples to keep faith with him in verse 6.[93]

Sowing is already associated with the idea of patience and perseverance in the biblical texts: "*In the morning sow thy seed, and in the evening withhold not thy hand* (Eccl. 11:6). R. Eliezer and R. Joshua discussed this. R. Eliezer said: If you have sown in the early season, sow in the late season, for you do not know which will be successful, whether the early sowing or the late sowing, as Scripture continues, *For thou knowest not which shall prosper, whether this or that, or whether they both shall be alike good* (ibid)."[94] (Gen.R. 61:3).[95] Moreover, the "good" is that which God defines for wo/men in Micah 6:8: "He has told you, O man, what is good; and what does the LORD require of you but to do justice, to love kindness, and to walk humbly with your God - הגיד לך אדם מה-טוב ומה-ה' דורש ממך כי אם- עשות משפט ואהבת חסד והצנע לכת עם-אלהיך."[96]

The fact that Paul appears to include himself in the present injunction may reflect his personal experience and thus his calling as "apostle to the Gentiles." In 2 Corinthians he speaks of himself as "not losing heart" because he has received his ministry in mercy, thus renouncing "the things hidden because of shame" and walking "by the manifestation of truth, commending ourselves to every man's conscience in the sight of God"[97] (2

---

[93] Note also the link between חסד (chesed - "lovingkindness") and "spirit of gentleness (πνεύματι πραΰτητος)" in verse 1. The verb גמל (gamal) literally signifies "to load (good or evil)," hence "to do good to" - possibly also a play on the "burden" of verses 2, 5.

[94] בבקר זרע את זרעך ולערב אל תנח ידך: רבי אליעזר ורבי יהושע: רבי אליעזר אמר: אם זרעת בבכיר זרע באפיל, שאין אתה יודע איזהו יכשר - אם של אפיל אם של בכיר ואם "שניהם כאחד טובים".

[95] Cf. Tanh.Chayei Sara 6; Eccl.R. 11.6.1; PA 2:15; ARNᵃ 3:5-6; Yev. 62b. Included among the acts that one should persevere in performing is that of raising up disciples. The phrase תנח ידך (tanach yadkha - "withhold your hand") may easily be interpreted as miserliness in the giving of charity. It also describes, however, the falling of Moses' hand in staying the forces of Amalek, its "raising" assuring Israel's victory (cf. Ex. 17:11). R. Eliezer and R. Joshua (c. 80-110 C.E.) represent the houses of Hillel and Shammai respectively, the divergences of whose views concerning proselytes are well known (cf. Safrai, Literature: 185ff [192]; Le Cornu and Shulam: 805-8).

[96] Here again, Paul's thought picks up the theme of "going beyond the law, which in itself is right and good, in order to do what is right and good" by walking in the Spirit, the believer's faithfulness working through love in seeking the other person's good (see above). For the importance of Mic. 6:6-8 for Galatians as a whole, see Introduction, **Argument**.

[97] Διὰ τοῦτο, ἔχοντες τὴν διακονίαν ταύτην καθὼς ἠλεήθημεν, οὐκ *ἐγκακοῦμεν* ἀλλὰ ἀπειπάμεθα τὰ κρυπτὰ τῆς αἰσχύνης, μὴ περιπατοῦντες ἐν πανουργίᾳ . . . ἀλλὰ τῇ φανερώσει τῆς ἀληθείας συνιστάνοντες ἑαυτοὺς πρὸς πᾶσιν συνείδησιν ἀνθρώπων ἐνώπιον τοῦ θεοῦ.

Cor. 4:1-2).[98] In this respect, the present statement may allude both to the Galatians' "standing firm" in the gospel (cf. 5:1), those of them "walking in the Spirit" further taking responsibility for restoring those who have opened themselves to influence – and to Paul's original preaching of the gospel to them (as Gentiles), and their continued loyalty to him.[99]

Having warned his readers – so that those who are spreading their "leaven" among them (cf. 5:9) will also hear – that each person will bear his own burden/sin/judgment, Paul again emphasises the need for continuing in "good deeds." Since not "all that is planted takes root," people must be careful and constant in their labour: "For as the husbandman soweth much seed upon the ground, and planteth many trees, and yet the thing that is sown good in his season cometh not up, neither doth all that is planted take root. Even so is it of them that are sown in the world; they shall not all be saved" (2 Esd. 8:41).[100]

Verse 10: Paul now expands the process of "reaping" – whose significance in verse 9 is primarily personal – into a more general application, of reaping "for others."[101] This sense of reaping is also a well-known motif, Jesus speaking of sending out workers to reap the harvest, the latter further representing God's final judgment.[102] The "doing good" is expressed here in seeking the wellbeing and welfare of others, in a "spirit of gentleness" (cf. verse 1) and love: "For among all men the spirit of hatred works by Satan through human frailty for the death of mankind; but the spirit of love works by the Law of God through forbearance for the salvation of mankind" (Test.Gad 4:6-7) (see also 5:13-18).[103] R. Tarfon's

---

[98] For the association of 2 Cor. 3:16-18 with Paul's calling, cf. Kim, Paul: 121-22, 165-213; [Hays, Echoes: 125-53]. (For 2 Cor. 4:4-6 as part of the same experience, see 1:13-14.)

[99] In all these aspects, the ultimate significance of "doing good" is repentance and "salvation."

[100] Cf. Mt. 7:15-27, 13:10-30, 22:14 Lk. 6:39-49; Rev. 14:15; 2 Esd. 8:1-3, 42-45, 9:14f; 4 Ez. 9:14f; Mekh.Nez. 10. Here, too, the "fruit" by which a person is judged is directly linked to hypocrisy – the gap between "saying" and "doing" (cf. 4Q424 1:8-12). For hypocrisy as a central motif of Galatians, see Introduction, **Argument**; **Theological pointers** (Justification), 2:15-21, 3:1-5, 19-20, 5:2ff, and above.

[101] The inferential particle ἄρα (ara), strengthened here by the transitional particle οὖν (oun – "therefore"), frequently signals the conclusion or main point of a pauline discussion (cf. Longenecker, Galatians: 282). Rather than recognising this statement as the summation of 5:13ff, however, we are presently suggesting that it forms the climax of Paul's injunction in 4:12 (see above).

[102] Cf. Jer. 51:33; Hos. 6:11; Joel 3:13; Mt. 9:37-38, 13:30; Mk. 4:29; Lk. 10:1-2; Jn. 4:35-38; Rev. 14:14-20; 2 Bar. 70:1f.

[103] Cf. Heb. 10:23-24: "Let us hold fast the confession of our hope without wavering, for He who promised is faithful; and let us consider how to stimulate one another to love and good deeds (κατέχωμεν τὴν ὁμολογίαν τῆς ἐλπίδος ἀκλινῆ,

saying "The day is short, and the work [to be performed] is much; and the workmen are indolent, but the reward is much; and the master of the house is insistent"[104] (PA 2:15) is pertinent here, not only because of urging persistence in good works but also because of the possible play between יום קצר (yom katzar - "the day is **short**") and יום קציר (yom katzir - "the day of the **harvest**") (cf. Abrahams: 100-1).[105]

The reference to "reward [שכר]" here may further support the speculation that Paul has in mind the theme of "winning souls" reflected in 4:12f - a unit on which the present passage is logically dependent (see 4:12-20 and above). Both the noun שכר (sakhar) and the verb נשכר/השתכר (niskhar/histakher) parallel the Greek root κερδαίνω (kerdainō - "to win") (κέρδος [kerdos] - "profit") (cf. Daube, New: 352ff). The adjunctive כנס (kanas - "to gather") is, moreover, found in an exegesis of Hosea 2:23 in the sense of "harvesting" converts: "R. Eleazar also said: The Holy One, blessed be He, did not exile Israel among the nations save in order that proselytes might join them, for it is said: *And I will sow her unto Me in the land* (Hos. 2:23): surely a man sows a *se'ah* in order to **harvest** many *kor*!"[106] (Pes. 87b) (cf. Yalk.Hos. 519) (see 4:12-20).[107]

The "opportunity (καιρὸν)" for so acting to extend God's Kingdom, asserts Paul, will not always be available. The adverbial temporal particle ὡς (hōs) followed by the accusative signifies "as long as" - or possibly "whenever" in a more existential sense (cf. Longenecker, Galatians: 282).[108] In the light of such sayings as R. Tarfon's, the former is more likely, the day being short and the work prolific (see above).[109] Several rabbinic texts speak of this issue precisely in the (implied) context of almsgiving: "He [R. Simeon ben Eleazar] used to say: Act while you are still present, and have

---

πιστὸς γὰρ ὁ ἐπαγγειλάμενος, καὶ κατανοῶμεν ἀλλήλους εἰς παροξυσμὸν ἀγάπης καὶ καλῶν ἔργων)" (cf. 1 Tim. 6:18; Tit. 3:8).

[104] רבי טרפון אומר: היום קצר והמלאכה מרובה והפועלים עצלים והשכר הרבה ובעל הבית דוחק.

[105] In a similar sense, the "in due time (καιρῷ ἰδίῳ)" (lit.: "appropriate time") marks the period between the sowing and harvesting. In its resonances with 4:4, Acts 17:31, Rom. 5:6, and 1 Tim. 2:6, 6:15, the expression may also serve as an allusion to Jesus' death and resurrection.

[106] אמר ר' אלעזר: לא הגלה הקדוש ברוך הוא את ישראל לבין האומות אלא כדי שיתוספו עליהם גרים, שנאמר: וזרעתיה לי בארץ. כלום אדם זורע סאה אלא להכניס כמה כורין.

[107] For a discussion of this midrash, cf. Gafni: 36. Cf. "*But he that soweth righteousness* (Prov. 11:18) alludes to Abraham, of whom it is written, *That they may keep the way of the Lord, to do righteousness and justice* (Gen. 18:19)" (Gen.R. 44:2).

[108] The present indicative ἔχομεν (echomen) and the present subjunctive ἔχωμεν (echōmen) are equally well attested. Between the meanings "we have" or "we might have" little significant difference obtains, although Paul appears to be speaking more of a reality than of a potentiality.

[109] Cf. Rom. 13:11-14; 1 Cor. 7:29; 2 Cor. 6:2; Col. 4:5; Heb. 10:25. The "time" is determined not according to the hours of the day, on this understanding, but on the period before the ripening of the harvest.

the opportunity and the one to whom you can give is still present הוא היה
תתן לאשר ומצוי לך ומצוי שאתה עד עשה :אומר" (ARNb 32).[110] Here again,
Paul emphasises collective responsibility in undertaking the endeavour,
writing not in the impersonal of there "being" occasion but of "our
having" opportunity.[111]

Although the "all (πάντας)" is inclusive – denoting the potential
harvest – Paul modifies it by giving priority to a specific group: "especially
to those who are of the household of the faith (μάλιστα δὲ πρὸς τοὺς
οἰκείους τῆς πίστεως)." Rather than representing a "lapse from the
universalism of concern expressed in 5:13 and immediately previous in
6:10 [sic]" (Longenecker, Galatians: 283), this verse can be read as returning
once again to the injunction of verses 1-2, Paul encouraging the restoration
of erring brethren to the "fold" (see above).

The community's designation as a "house (בית [beit]; οἶκος [oikos])"
or "temple (מקדש [mikdash]; ἱερόν [hieron]/ναός [naos])" is common to
both the Qumran and the New Testament literature (cf. Gärtner).[112] Here,
the slightly different οἰκεῖος (oikeos) – which Paul also uses in Ephesians
2:19 in reference to God – signifies virtually the same, denoting those who
are His "sons" (see 3:26-29 and 4:1-7).[113] This "household" Paul designates
with the catchphrase which has run through the whole letter, based on
Habakkuk 2:4: Those being "of faithfulness ([ἐκ] τῆς πίστεως)" (see 1:13-14,
3:10-14, 4:1-7, and verses 12-16).[114]

---

[110] Cf. Shab. 151b, where the Munich ms. introduces the saying with "Perform
almsgiving." Here, the saying follows the maxim: "Know whence you came" (see
above).

[111] An interesting parallel may exist here with Rom. 12:11 if the latter is read as
"serving the time" rather than "serving the Lord." The former expression, as known
from Qumran, reflects the principle of temporary non-retaliation until the final
victory of the "sons of light" over the "sons of darkness" (cf. 1QS 9:16ff) (cf. Flusser,
Jewish: 397-401; Shulam and Le Cornu: 413ff). See also the references in the
previous note and below.

[112] Cf. [Rom. 12:1]; 1 Cor. 3:9, 6:19; 2 Cor. 6:14-18; [Gal. 2:9]; Eph. 2:14-22; 1 Tim.
3:15; 1 Pet. 2:4f; 1 En. 1:2, 38:2, 62:8; 1QS 5:6, 8:4f, 9:6, 11:8; CD-A 3:19f; CD-B 20:10;
4QFlor f1i:2ff. The primary signifier may perhaps be בית ישראל (beit Israel – "the
house of Israel") (cf. Ex. 16:31, 40:38; Lev. 10:6). See also 2:1-10 (n124), 15-21 (verse
19).

[113] It is noteworthy, however, that the household of the ancient world was more
extensive than strict blood relatives (cf. Acts 11:14, 16:15, 31f, 18:8; 1 Cor. 1:16; 1
Tim. 3:15; 1 Pet. 4:17; 1QapGen 20:28; PRE 10) (cf. Le Cornu and Shulam: 887-88).

[114] This primary marker signifies Paul's confidence (cf. 5:10) that, while his
disciples have been temporarily persuaded away from the gospel, they will return
both to him and to it, in "faithfulness" – being aided in doing so by those who are
truly "walking in the Spirit" and demonstrating their own "faithfulness working
through love" (cf. 5:6, 16). In this sense, the "household of the faithful" are those,
both Jews and Gentiles, who live through God's faithfulness in Jesus, participating

In so doing, he reminds the Galatians of the grounds of their acceptance before God. God's faithfulness in sending His Messiah (cf. 1:4, 4:4) is paralleled in the latter demonstrating his obedience to his Father's will (cf. 1:4), whence both Jew and Gentile gain access to God's Kingdom and release from the bondage of sin into son/heirship through their faithful participation in Jesus' death and resurrection (cf. 1:4, 3:5ff, 23-29, 4:1ff).[115] While Paul calls the Galatians to tend to the spiritual welfare of those around them, as the expression of their "faithfulness working through love," their first responsibility is to those who have strayed and stumbled.[116]

A midrash gives the reason for such action as imitating God's love for Israel: "The Sages taught: Be forbearing toward every man, and more so, in particular, toward the members of your household than toward all others. The reason you can see for yourself: you need only follow the example of the Holy One who was forbearing toward His people not only on one occasion but on two and even three occasions. He did not act toward them as they acted toward Him, nor did He punish them according to their iniquities, but simply showed forbearance"[117] (TBE [EZ] p. 178).[118] The

---

in their own faithfulness in Jesus' obedience, to death on a cross (cf. 1 Tim. 3:15) (see Introduction, **Theological pointers** (Justification), 3:10-14, and verses 12-16).

[115] Paul perhaps has Isa. 58:6-7 in mind here as "faithfulness working through love": "Is this not the fast which I chose, to loosen the bonds of wickedness, to undo the bands of the yoke, and to let the oppressed go free, and break every yoke? Is it not to divide your bread with the hungry, and bring the homeless poor into the house; when you see the naked, to cover him; and not to hide yourself from your own flesh? הלוא זה צום אבחרהו פתח חרצבות רשע התר אגדות מוטה ושלח רצוצים חפשים וכל-מוטה תנתקו: הלא פרס לרעב לחמך ועניים מרודים תביא בית כי-תראה ערם וכסיתו ומבשרך לא תתעלם" (cf. Isa. 61:1-3; Mt. 25:31-46 [1ff]) (see 2:15-21 [n303]). Such a passage appears to lie behind the injunctions in CD-A: ". . . for each to love his brother like himself; to strengthen the hand of the poor, the needy and the foreigner; *Blank* for each to seek the peace of his brother and not to be unfaithful against his blood relation לאהוב איש את אחיהו כמהו ולהחזיק ביד עני ואביון וגר ולדרוש איש את שלום אחיהו ולא ימעל איש בשאר בשרו" (CD-A 6:20-7:1) (cf. CD-A 8:5-6; CD-B 19:15-20; 1QS 5:3-4). (For "reproving," see verses 1-11; for loving one's neighbour, see 5:13-18; for the motif of bondage in Galatians, see 1:1-5, 2:1-10, 15-21, 3:19f, 4:1f, and 5:13f.)

[116] The tradition of judgment beginning with God's people is reflected in 1 Pet. 4:17-18, which intimates the seriousness of the fate of the disobedient: "For *it is* time for judgment to begin with the household of God; and if *it begins* with us first, what *will be* the outcome for those who do not obey the gospel of God? And IF IT IS WITH DIFFICULTY THAT THE RIGHTEOUS IS SAVED, WHAT WILL BECOME OF THE GODLESS MAN AND THE SINNER? (ὅτι [ὁ] καιρὸς τοῦ ἄρξασθαι τὸ κρίμα ἀπὸ τοῦ οἴκου τοῦ θεοῦ· εἰ δὲ πρῶτον ἀφ' ἡμῶν, τί τὸ τέλος τῶν ἀπειθούντων τῷ τοῦ θεοῦ εὐαγγελίῳ;)" (cf. Prov. 11:31; Amos 3:2).

[117] שנו חכמים: הוי עלוב ועניו לכל אדם ולאנשי ביתך יותר מכל אדם. ומנין זה תדע לך שכן הוא? צא ולמד מן הקדוש ברוך הוא, שהיה עלוב ועניו לעמו בכל מקום ולא הלך עמהן כדרכיהן ולא שפט אותם כעונותיהם אלא היה להם במדת ענוה שלו.

analogy, in both Paul and the midrash, is evidently based on God's choice of Israel as His "treasured possession [סגולה עם]": "Even as one's proper treasure is better loved by a man than all else which he may claim to, so are Israel better loved by the Holy One, blessed be He, than all other nations מה הסגולה הזו חביבה על אדם יותר מכל מה שיש לו, כך ישראל חביבין לפני הקדוש ברוך הוא מכל האומות" (Pes.Rab. 11:7) (see 2:15-21).[119]

Verse 11: While many commentators treat this verse as the opening of a new section, the present reading of verses 1-10 as a reiterated rebuke of the influencers and a renewed called for Paul's disciples to keep faith with him suggests that Paul is here drawing attention (cf. ἴδετε [idete] – "see!") to the emotion and passion with which he is making his appeal.[120] Not only does his handwriting prove his authorship of the words so written (in contrast to an amanuensis responsible for its body), but – in contrast to his other letters[121] (as also in his prescript or salutation in 1:1-5) – this "autograph" also carries the added weight of "large letters (πηλίκοις γράμμασιν)."[122] While the Greek γράμμα (gramma), both in the singular and

---

[118] Cf. TBE pp. 139-40; Mekh.Kaspa 1; Tanh.Mishp. 15; DEZ 3:5; Kal.Rab. 5; BM 71a. For God's "condescendence" or "accommodation" to human weakness, see 3:19f.

[119] Cf. Num.R. 2:19, 7:10; Tanh.Be-shall 20; Pkudei 1; Mekh.Vayassa 20; Nez 10; PA 3:14; Hul. 91b. In speaking of the need for humility and respect, these references repeat, virtually verbatim, Paul's injunction in 5:26 – providing additional support for the argument here presented, that verses 1ff directly expand 5:26 (see above). To the extent that the statement appeals to the imitation of God, it also links this section – once again – with 4:12f (see 4:12-20 and above). For this idea in relation to the "Israel of God," see verses 12-16.

[120] "Hellenistic letters in Paul's day usually exhibited two styles of handwriting: a more practiced, carefully constructed script of an amanuensis or secretary in most of the letter and the cruder or more casual style of the sender in the subscription . . . Paul, in fact, seems to have followed the practice of using an amanuensis for the writing of all his letters, though his amanuenses were personal companions or able fellow believers of the various churches rather than professional scribes . . . And here by the phrase τῇ ἐμῇ χειρί, 'in my own hand,' Paul's recipients are alerted to the fact that they are not now reading and/or hearing what an amanuensis has written down on his behalf but Paul's own statements that he has inscribed himself" (Longenecker, Galatians: 289). To the extent that the phrase also signals the opening of the subscription it nevertheless belongs to the latter, verse 11 serving in this respect as a transitional statement. While attention has rightly been drawn to the subscription as reflecting many of any particular letter's essential concerns and issues – that of Galatians also bearing directly on the influencers' identity – the intimate connection between the subscription and the preceding section should neither be overlooked nor underestimated. For this purpose, we have included it as part of the first unit of this chapter. For Paul's use of an amanuensis, see Introduction, **Form**.

[121] Cf. 1 Cor. 16:21; Col. 4:18a; 2 Thess. 3:17; Phlm 19.

[122] This is to be noted in the context of the rarity of such a phrase in extant letters, difference in script being immediately evident to the recipients when reading them

plural, signifies "writing" of any kind (a document, letter, or book) in early
and later Greek,[123] Paul's preference for the designation of an "epistle" is
precisely that word (ἐπιστολή) (again both singular and plural),[124] γράμμα
(gramma) rather serving him as reference to a letter of the alphabet (cf. 2
Cor. 3:7) (cf. Longenecker, Galatians: 289).[125]

Verses 12-16: [*peroratio/conclusio*][126]
Those who desire to make a good showing in the flesh try to compel you to be
circumcised, simply so that they will not be persecuted for the cross of the Messiah.
For those who are circumcised do not even keep the Law themselves, but they desire to
have you circumcised, that they may boast in your flesh. But may it never be that I
should boast, except in the cross of our Lord Jesus the Messiah, through which the
world has been crucified to me, and I to the world. For neither is circumcision
anything, nor uncircumcision, but a new creation. And those who will walk by this
rule, peace and mercy *be* upon them, and upon the Israel of God.

Having signaled the beginning of letter's end (see verses 1-11), Paul in fact
continues his condemnation of those who have been "troubling" his
disciples (cf. 1:7, [4:17], 5:7-12, verses 3-5) and attempting to transfer their
allegiance away from the gospel to a form of social status.[127]

– perhaps even in the case of "circulars" which were read aloud within the various
Galatian communities (see Introduction, **Date and destination** and 1:1-5).

[123] Cf. Est. 8:5, 10; Acts 28:21; 1 Macc. 5:10; Ep.Arist. 43; Jos.*Ant.* 1.13, 7.137, 8.50,
10.210; *CA* 1.54; Philo, *Vit.Mos.* 2.290f; *Praem.* 79; Herodotus 5.14.

[124] Cf. Rom. 16:22; 1 Cor. 5:9, 16:3; 2 Cor. 3:1, 7:8, 10:9-11; Col. 4:16; 1 Thess. 5:27; 2
Thess. 2:2, 15, 3:14, 17.

[125] For other explanations of Paul's large handwriting, including his ostensible poor
penmanship, eye sight (cf. 4:15), or other physical deficiency, cf. Longenecker,
Galatians: 290; for other customary subscriptive characteristics, see verse 18.

[126] For the argument against Galatians as an apologetic letter and for its structure as
a "halakhic letter" of rebuke and request along the lines of 4QMMT, see
Introduction, **Form; Argument**. To the extent that Betz's rhetorico-epistolary
analysis is not presently followed, this section is treated as a subscription rather
than as a *peroratio*. As part of a section of concluding exhortations summing up the
matters discussed within the body (cf. 1 Cor. 16:13-18, 22; 2 Cor. 13:11a), Paul's
subscript in Galatians is significant for containing no emphasis on rejoicing,
similarly neither referencing prayer nor including an (explicit) doxology (cf.
Longenecker, Galatians: 288). For the benedictions, see below; for the "doxology,"
see verse 18.

[127] See Introduction, **Occasion and circumstances; Argument** and verses 1-11. It is
noteworthy that the claim which sees these verses as picking up "on Paul's
arguments and exhortations of 1:6-5:12 against the so-called judaizing threat,
without specifically carrying on his arguments and exhortations of 5:13-6:10 against
the libertine tendencies" demonstrates not only that the latter appear very much out
of place but also that the discursus on the fruit of the Spirit thereby becomes of
secondary significance, Longenecker suggesting that "One obvious indicator of the
shift back to the *major discussion* of the letter is his [Paul's] use of σάρξ ("flesh")"

Verses 12-13 are chiastic in form (A-B-C-C'-B'-A'): The "boasting in the flesh (ἐν τῇ ὑμετέρᾳ σαρκὶ καυχήσωνται)" in verse 13c corresponds to the "desire to make a good showing in the flesh (θέλουσιν εὐπροσωπῆσαι ἐν σαρκί)" in verse 12a; the phrase "compel you to be circumcised (ἀναγκάζουσιν ὑμᾶς περιτέμνεσθαι)" in 12b parallels the "desire to have you circumcised (θέλουσιν ὑμᾶς περιτέμνεσθαι)" in 13b; and the "avoidance of persecution for the cross of the Messiah (τῷ σταυρῷ τοῦ Χριστοῦ μὴ διώκωνται)" in 12c leads into the "lack of observance of the Torah (οὐδὲ γὰρ οἱ περιτεμνόμενοι αὐτοὶ νόμον φυλάσσουσιν)" in 13a.[128]

On the grounds that no concrete "persecution" of believers – as implied in the modifier "for/because of the cross of the Messiah" – is historically plausible, we have concluded on the one hand that the persecution cannot be "literal" and on the other that the influencers are not Jesus' followers.[129] While here too, Paul refrains from calling them by name, he provides further identificatory markers based on the acts in which they are engaged.[130] Although the Greek εὐπροσωπέω (euprosōpeō) – literally signifying a "good face" – is rare, occurring only once elsewhere, the chiastic structure of verses 12-13 place it in correspondence with "boasting (καύχησωνται)." This picks up Paul's accusation in verses 3-4, where he has warned those troubling his disciples that they are deceived if they think they are something when they are, in fact, "nothing," further admonishing them (indirectly) that they must examine their own work, that constituting their only ground for "boasting (τὸ καύχημα)" (see verses 1-11).[131]

(Galatians: 290). For the present reading of 5:13ff as *part* of the "major discussion," see 5:13f.

[128] This structure is also reflected in the purpose clauses of the wish for circumcision, which parallel avoidance of persecution (12c) with boasting in the flesh in 13c.

[129] For the detailed outworking of this argument, see Introduction, **Occasion and circumstances**.

[130] For the argument that Paul's "neglect" to name his antagonists is indicative of their non-believing status, see Introduction, **Occasion and circumstances**.

[131] The relation of boasting/making a good showing to hypocrisy is clear from such texts as Mt. 6:1ff: "When therefore you give alms, do not sound a trumpet before you, as the hypocrites do in the synagogues and in the streets, that they may be honored by men. Truly I say to you, they have their reward in full ('Ὅταν οὖν ποιῇς ἐλεημοσύνην, μὴ σαλπίσῃς ἔμπροσθέν σου, ὥσπερ οἱ ὑποκριταὶ ποιοῦσιν ἐν ταῖς συναγωγαῖς καὶ ἐν ταῖς ῥύμαις, ὅπως δοξασθῶσιν ὑπὸ τῶν ἀνθρώπων· ἀμὴν λέγω ὑμῖν, ἀπέχουσιν τὸν μισθὸν αὐτῶν)" (Mt. 6:2). The "reward" which such people receive is no more than the "bargain" which they have struck: "Look around you and you shall find that those who are said to bestow benefits sell rather than give; and those who seem to us to receive them in truth buy. The givers are seeking praise or honour as their exchange and look for the repayment of the benefit, and thus, under the specious name of gift, they in real truth carry out a sale

Given Paul's prior presentation of the influencers as worthy of self-mutilation (cf. 5:12) and his play on the Galatians' apparent willingness to "indulge the flesh" by undergoing circumcision (cf. 5:13f), it seems reasonable to conclude that the "troublers" are seeking to convince the gentile Galatian believers that their acceptance by God in Jesus does not thereby gain them social standing within the Jewish community – a status upon which they (the influencers) insist for those who wish to be officially identified as Jewish rather than remaining mere "godfearers" (see 2:1f). On the assumption that the Galatians are implicitly seeking or laying claim to such status (whether actively or passively, as a practical step or as an ideal remaining within the realm of wishes), the influencers are promoting their (the Galatians') circumcision.[132]

Identification of the "good showing" with "boasting" further obviates the problem of expediency presented by the former feature, with its implication that the influencers are acting in order to find favour in someone else's eyes.[133] The present reading rather suggests that, in the form of "boasting," their behaviour is motivated by social concerns and status, as embodied in official standing and recognition within/by the Jewish community. According to Paul, the "flesh and its desires" – i.e., circumcision and the seeking after social status – belong to the "elemental things of the world" from whose bondage the Gentiles have been delivered by Jesus' death and resurrection (see 4:1f).[134] To the extent that the wish for status is a "work of the flesh" it returns the Galatians to the position of slaves – when they are already, and should remain, sons, adopted through the Spirit, heirs according to promise (cf. 3:14, 29, 4:1ff).[135]

(εὑρήσεις τοίνυν σκοπῶς ν ἅπαντας καὶ τοὺς λεγομένους χαρίζεσθαι πιπράσκοντας μᾶλλον ἢ δωρουμένους καὶ οὓς οἰόμεθα λαμβάνειν χάριτας πρὸς ἀλήθειαν ὠνουμένους)" (Philo, *Cher.* 122). At the same time, since we do not consider the influencers to be proselytes, no hypocrisy is involved in their failure to observe the Torah – performance of which does not devolve upon godfearers.

[132] The presumptions may be being made on the part of the influencers rather than constituting "factual" declarations on the Galatians' side. Whether or not the Galatians are making such claims, the influencers perceive them to be doing so. Simultaneously, the gentile Galatians are being persuaded by the influencers' argument that *if* they (the Galatians) consider their fellowship in the Messiah to constitute Jewish identity, they are mistaken, such status being obtainable, according to the influencers' argument, only through full conversion (see Introduction, **Occasion and circumstances**). For the influencers' own godfearing standing, see below.

[133] Just whom this "third party" could comprise constitutes one of the crucial complexities in espousing such an interpretation (see Introduction, **Occasion and circumstances**).

[134] For Paul's "literal" signification of "the flesh," see 5:2f.

[135] Yet again, it behoves us to emphasise that circumcision *per se* is not "of the flesh" here – but the *desire* to be circumcised *as a sign of social standing*.

If the "persecution (διώκωνται)" is not literal, precisely what consequences are the influencers endeavouring to avoid, and on what grounds?[136] This question demands the prior definition – as far as is possible under the circumstances – of the persons' identities. The signification of the participle [οἱ] περιτεμνόμενοι ([hoi] peritemnomenoi) has been much debated in this regard (cf. Nanos, Irony: 234f, and for the following discussion).[137] Reading it as a present middle *causative* renders the emphasis upon those who "cause to be circumcised" – otherwise translatable as "the advocates of circumcision." Here, the influencers are those who wish others to be circumcised.

If the causative is substituted with a *reflexive*, the focus shifts to self-motivation – "those who circumcise themselves," i.e., "those who choose to be circumcised." On this reading, the influencers are possibly/probably themselves proselytes – who have had themselves circumcised and converted to Judaism.

As a present middle *permissive*, the passive aspect becomes paramount, indicating a situation in which the subjects are those who "receive circumcision" or "let themselves be circumcised." Their identity here is similar to the previous option.

A *concessive* force focuses on the exception – "even the ones who circumcise/are circumcised," the distinction between active and passive dissolving. This reading obstructs the possibility of determining whether the antagonists promote circumcision or are themselves circumcised.

As a "present middle *circumstances attendant*" the participle is understood in relation to the main verb, indicating that "the ones who are circumcising/the ones circumcising/who get circumcised" do not observe the Torah. Again, this fails to help in clarifying the influencers' Jewish/non-Jewish identity.

While all the above options render the participle as middle, its reading as a *present passive* gives the sense of "the ones who receive circumcision." This clearly defines the influencers as (potential) proselytes.

As a *perfect passive*, a variant construction attested in several important manuscripts, the condition resultant from a prior action becomes

---

[136] For an alternative translation of this verb, see 5:2-12 (verse 11).

[137] Nanos' comment regarding the propriety of inspecting the context in which the participle appears before investigating the weight of the participle itself is timely: "... the explanatory value of any decision on this substantive participle must make sense of its verbal aspect, that is, its relationship to the circumstances under which the verbal action of the main verb takes place ... this kind of variety [of explanation] makes it clear that it [the meaning of the participle] cannot be settled unambiguously on strictly grammatical grounds" (Irony: 235-36 [n42]).

determinative, giving "those who have been circumcised" or "those in a state of circumcision."[138] Here, too, proselytes are assumed.

Apart from the reading which incorporates the issue as part of the signification, linking the participle directly to the verb, the alternatives which attribute to the participle a reflexive or passive denotation – emphasising their own proselyte status – face the difficulty of explaining how, according to Paul's claim, these same persons do not observe the Torah.[139] Since 13a is a descriptive statement – despite corresponding to the purpose clause in 12c – the relation between its verb and the participle should be recognised as simple. Having established that, no persecution of believers being historically plausible, the influencers cannot, virtually by default, be regarded as believers, this conjunction most logically also excludes them from being *Jewish* (even as proselytes).[140]

On the present reading of the Galatian circumstances, the most feasible reading of the participle understands it as a *present middle causative* – i.e., "the advocates of circumcision."[141] To the extent that the influencers are not believers, in the absence of a literal persecution, they appear to be *non-believing gentile godfearers* who – without seeking favour with or being under obligation to a third party, and hence also not in the grip of any expediency, promoting an attitude and code of conduct to which they themselves are uncommitted – believe that persons wishing to be considered Jewish should undergo the official rite and process prescribed for obtaining Jewish identity.[142] In this case, Paul's "gibe" that they are not themselves Torah-observant is simply a statement of fact: As godfearers, they are not *obliged* to perform the commandments. While they perceive

---

[138] Where the tense dominates, the participle may also be understood as middle, etc.

[139] While the reference is not perforce to proselytes, possibly pertaining to Jews by birth, the weight of the point is considerably increased if the element of choice is enlarged.

[140] This is true not so much on the grounds that some Jews cannot be considered to have been "non-religious" during the Second Temple period, but on the internal logic of Galatians, whereby the promotion of Jewish status, expressed in official conversion to Judaism – an act designed almost by definition to determine and maintain Jewish identity – is unlikely to have gone hand in hand with a laxity towards Torah-observance. While it is true that the Jewish community tended to assume that proselytes would relapse, the opposite assumption – that proselytes become more zealous than born Jews – is also to be found (see 4:8-11 [n112]). For the (non-)issue of libertinism in Galatians, see 5:13-18.

[141] Such an understanding most comprehensively fits the tenor of the letter as a whole, in which Paul has been at pains to warn his disciples against the influence to which they have opened themselves up, and his repeated warnings to remove the troublers from their midst (see 4:21-31, 5:2ff, and verses 1-11).

[142] This identification of the influencers as godfearers is based on Acts 13:50 (see Introduction, **Occasion and circumstances** and below).

people wishing Jewish status to be in need of circumcision/conversion, they themselves have not chosen (or chosen not) to take that step. Being godfearers, they presumably *do not* observe all the Torah – correctly considering that exercise to fall, as a privilege and duty, solely upon proselytes.[143]

Their "boasting in the Galatians' flesh" – i.e., in their circumcision – is Paul's evaluation of these gentile godfearers' activity (cf. Phil. 3:18-19). His ire is aroused in particular because the influencers appear to conjoin their persuasion of the Galatians to undergo conversion with a rejection of the gospel itself. In his eyes, the claim that the disciples he has made in Galatia are not equal members with those within the Jewish community who are of the "disciples of Abraham" (both being "sons of promise") is tantamount to dismissing Jesus' work on the cross.[144] Gentiles who have come to God through Jesus – who have been delivered through his death and resurrection from bondage to the "elemental things of the world" – are not only in no need of social standing in the eyes of the Jewish community (not to speak of their estimation by godfearers) but are also liable to forfeit their inheritance in God's Kingdom by accepting worldly standards.

The vehemence of Paul's attack against the influencers is precisely because they will not admit that Jesus' death and resurrection effect the "sonship" of Gentiles. In this context, the best understanding of the "persecution" which the "troublers" are endeavouring to avoid is the attribution to them of acceptance of the gospel. On the assumption that the Galatian communities to whom Paul is writing are those of southern

---

[143] The chiastic correspondence of this description with "avoiding persecution for the cross" suggests that in not wishing to be considered as believers, the godfearers are even more hypocritical in promoting Jewish identity (circumcision leading to a commitment to Torah-observance – see 5:2-12), since they themselves do not wish to convert. While they are unwilling to ascribe Jewish identity to Gentiles in the Messiah, they themselves remain godfearers – without the benefit either of the Messiah or of Jewish status. There is, of course, an added element here of irony: Why, suggests Paul, should his disciples wish to take on an obligation which its promoters are themselves unwilling to make? (To the objection that godfearers would be unlikely to advise a step beyond their willingness to adopt, it can be maintained that people are quite willing to hold a *principle* – in this case, that Jewish identity is only available through conventional, social means – without themselves being committed to its *practice*.)

[144] The language of this section demonstrates close affinities with that of 4:17, which suggests that the influencers' persuasion will shut the Galatians out of God's Kingdom (see 4:12-20). This notwithstanding, Paul is not claiming that the Gentiles are also "sons of the covenant" – a status confined to Israel. It is precisely because the latter status includes the "sons of the promise" that Gentiles can find access to God's Kingdom. Seeking to become – in addition – also "sons of the covenant," on the understanding propounded by the influencers, will forfeit them their standing as "sons of the promise" (see Introduction, **Argument**).

Galatia (cf. Acts 13-14), many of Paul's disciples may have been godfearers prior to receiving the gospel (cf. Acts 13:16, 26, 43). To the extent that Paul was teaching against the necessity of conversion for Gentiles who became faithful to God through Jesus, other local godfearers may have been apprehensive lest they should be considered holders of the same conviction.[145] This circumstance provides an explanation for the chiastic correspondence between 12c and 13a: The influencers do not wish to be associated with the early believing community precisely because they (the influencers) are godfearers and might be thought to possess views similar to those with whom, in practice, they were most in conflict.[146]

Verse 14: Paul responds to this damning description of those troubling his disciples with his personal "credo."[147] This not only constitutes a counterattack against the influencers' persuasion, but further demonstrates that the latter itself represents an impugnation of his own "fathering" of the Galatians (see 4:12-20 and verses 1-11).[148] The emphatic ἐμοὶ (emoi – "as for me") contrasts his behaviour with that of the influencers: Whereas they boast in the flesh, his boast is solely in the cross.[149] That which they reject and despise is for Paul the only thing of worth: "But whatever things were gain to me, those things I have counted as loss for the sake of the Messiah. More than that, I count all things to be loss in view of the surpassing value of knowing the Messiah Jesus my Lord . . . for we are the *true* circumcision, who worship in the Spirit of God and glory [boast] in the Messiah Jesus and put no confidence in the flesh"[150] (Phil. 3:7-8, 3).

---

[145] It was, precisely, their conviction that full adherents of Judaism must undergo circumcision that constituted their opposition to the gospel in the first place.

[146] A comparison of the two purpose clauses, in 12c and 13c, indicates a further correspondence between boasting and avoiding persecution. Here, the boasting may be understood as the influencers' insistence on circumcision as a sign of social status – their demand for which constitutes the reason for their wish not to be identified with the "law-free" gospel. For a situation in which the influencers are being pressured by a third group, see Introduction, **Occasion and circumstances**.

[147] Although it does not refute a putative inference (cf. 2:17), the optative μὴ γένοιτο (mē genoito – "may it never be!") retains the function here of designating an unthinkable proposition (see 2:15-21).

[148] "If Paul's initial request in 4:12 ('Become like me!') is a major concern of Paul, then we should expect that Paul would conclude the letter by presenting his own experience as a paradigm for the Galatians to follow. In fact, this is just what we find" (Hansen, Paradigm: 149) (see verses 1-11). For the current reading of Galatians as a "halakhic letter" of rebuke-request along the lines of 4QMMT, see Introduction, **Form; Argument**.

[149] For "boasting," see verses 1-11; for this motif as linking verses 12-13 with verses 3-5, see verses 1-11. No good reason appears to exist for the attribution of the emphatic to Paul's "perspective now as a Christian" (Longenecker, Galatians: 293).

[150] ἅτινα ἦν μοι κέρδη, ταῦτα ἥγημαι διὰ τὸν Χριστὸν ζημίαν. ἀλλὰ μενοῦνγε καὶ ἡγοῦμαι πάντα ζημίαν εἶναι διὰ τὸ ὑπερέχον τῆς γνώσεως Χριστοῦ Ἰησοῦ

This idea is based on Jer. 9:23-26: "Thus says the LORD, 'Let not a wise man boast of his wisdom, and let not the mighty man boast of his might, let not a rich man boast of his riches; but let him who boasts boast of this, that he understands and knows Me, that I am the LORD who exercises lovingkindness, justice, and righteousness on earth, for I delight in these things,' declares the LORD. 'Behold, the days are coming,' declares the Lord, 'that I will punish all who are circumcised and yet uncircumcised – Egypt, and Judah, and Edom, and the sons of Ammon, and Moab, and all those inhabiting the desert who clip the hair on their temples; for all the nations are uncircumcised, and all the house of Israel are uncircumcised of heart'"[151] (cf. 1 Cor. 1:31; 2 Cor. 10:17; [PA 4:1]).[152]

Paul's inclusive language ("our Lord") is a reminder and reinforcement of the Galatians' initial obedience to the gospel and to Paul's preaching of it. While both are despised by the influencers, Paul emphasises that the Galatians and himself are bound precisely by their common faithfulness to God in Jesus. God's expressed His faithfulness to the Gentiles in His promise to Abraham, fulfilled through Jesus' obedience to the Father, and it is shared by those who participate in his death and resurrection (see 3:1ff). If Paul is to boast, their boast will be the same as his – to know "nothing among you except Jesus the Messiah and him crucified"[153] (1 Cor. 2:2).[154] Under the "law of the Messiah," which governs

---

[151] τοῦ κυρίου . . . ἡμεῖς γάρ ἐσμεν ἡ περιτομή, οἱ πνεύματι θεοῦ λατρεύοντες καὶ καυχώμενοι ἐν Χριστῷ 'Ιησοῦ καὶ οὐκ ἐν σαρκὶ πεποιθότες.

כה אמר ה' אל-יתהלל חכם בחכמתו ואל-יתהלל הגבור בגבורתו אל-יתהלל עשיר בעשרו : כי
אם-בזאת יתהלל המתהלל השכל וידע אתי כי אני ה' עשה חסד משפט וצדקה בארץ כי-באלה
חפצתי נאם ה' : הנה ימים באים נאם-ה' ופקדתי על-כל-מול בערלה : על-מצרים ועל-יהודה ועל-
אדום ועל-בני עמון ועל-מואב ועל כל-קצוצי פאה הישבים במדבר כי כל-הגוים ערלים וכל-בית
ישראל ערלי-לב.

[152] Given the relation of this passage to Mic. 6:6-8 and Hos. 6:6, the issue of "boasting" may be associated with the principle of "within the margin of the judgment," especially *via* Romans 2: "*Maschil of Ethan the Ezrahite* (Ps. 89:1). These words are to be considered in the light of the verse *But let him that glorieth glory in this, that he understandeth (haskel) and knoweth Me, that I am the Lord who exercise mercy, justice, and righteousness in the earth* (Jer. 9:23). When Ethan the Ezrahite said: 'I understand' hence *Maschil [understanding] of Ethan the Ezrahite* – the Holy One, blessed be He, replied: Does thou understand that *In these things I delight* (Jer. 9:23), and that any man who praises Me, must praise Me only with these things? Thus again Scripture says, *For I desire mercy, and not sacrifice* (Hos. 6:6). Ethan the Ezrahite said to God: Thou desirest mercy, and I shall praise Thee with mercy . . . משכיל
לאיתן האזרחי חסדי ה' (לעולם) אשירה : זהו שאמר הכתוב : כי אם בזאת יתהלל המתהלל השכל
וידע אותי. אמר איתן : אני השכלתי - משכיל לאיתן האזרחי. אמר לו הקדוש ברוך הוא : השכלת,
כי באלה חפצתי וכל מי שיקלסני לא יקלסני אלא באלה? וכן הוא אומר : כי חסד חפצתי ולא זבח.
אמר לו : חסד חפצת ובחסד אקלסך" (Mid.Ps. 89:1). See Introduction, **Argument**; **Theological pointers** (Justification), 2:15-21 (n271), 3:11-14, 5:2f, and verses 1-11.

[153] οὐ γὰρ ἔκρινά τι εἰδέναι ἐν ὑμῖν εἰ μὴ 'Ιησοῦν Χριστὸν καὶ τοῦτον ἐσταυρωμένον.

the era of deliverance and redemption from sin/debt, "Where then is boasting? It is excluded. By what kind of law? Of works? No, but by a law of faithfulness (Ποῦ οὖν ἡ καύχησις; ἐξεκλείσθη. διὰ ποίου νόμου; τῶν ἔργων; οὐχί, ἀλλὰ διὰ νόμου πίστεως)" (Rom. 3:27) (see also verses 1-11).

If κόσμος (kosmos) carries overtones of meta-historical forces, Paul may be referring back to the "elemental things of the world (τὰ στοιχεῖα τοῦ κόσμου)" to which wo/men are in bondage unless availing themselves of Jesus' faithfulness to God in his death and resurrection (see 4:1-7). While again presenting himself here as a personal example ("to me"/"I"), Paul is once more reminding his disciples of that which he has already explained to them: "Now those who belong to the Messiah Jesus have crucified the flesh with its passions and desires (οἱ δὲ τοῦ Χριστοῦ [Ἰησοῦ] τὴν σάρκα ἐσταύρωσαν σὺν τοῖς παθήμασιν καὶ ταῖς ἐπιθυνίαις)" (5:24) (see 3:1-5).[155]

Verse 15: At this point Paul provides the ultimate rationale behind the argument he is presenting to his disciples.[156] The immediate association is not merely with the "circumcision" of verses 12-13, but also with the "anything (τί)" which picks up the "something (τι)" of the influencers' boasting in verse 3 (see verses 1-11).[157] While the Galatians are not to be swayed into seeking social standing, neither are they to rely on any other "fleshly" status – "uncircumcision" representing a person's heart given

---

154 Cf. Rom. 5:3ff; 1 Cor. 1:18-31. "The whole difference between an improper 'boasting' and Paul's 'boasting in the Lord' is expressed by the replacement of the emphatic ἐμοί ('to me') in v 14a by the ever more emphatic δι᾽ οὗ ἐμοί ('through which [or: through whom] to me'). This means that for Paul 'my boasting' cannot simply be based upon 'what happened to me,' but must be based upon 'what happened through Christ to me.' Whether δι᾽ οὗ refers to the cross of Christ, or to the person of Christ is of no consequence, since for Paul 'Christ' is always the crucified redeemer Christ" (Betz, *Galatians*: 318).

155 Here again, Paul has set the initial example: "I have been crucified with the Messiah; and it is no longer I who live, but the Messiah lives in me; and the *life* which I now live in the flesh I live by the faithfulness of the Son of God, who loved me, and delivered himself up for me" (2:20). For Paul's personal exemplification, see 1:1-5, 15-16b, 21-24, 2:1-10 (n136), 15-21 (n292), 3:1-5 (nn14, 28), 4:12-20, 5:2-12 (verse 11), 24-26, and verses 1-11 (verse 11), 17; for crucifixion, see 2:15-21, [3:26-29], and 5:24-26; for the "faithfulness of Jesus," see Introduction, **Theological pointers** (Faithfulness).

156 The verse is, in fact, a reiteration of 3:28 and 5:6.

157 Yet again, we wish to emphasise the fact that Paul is not dismissing circumcision out of hand (a view which would also entail outlawing uncircumcision). Circumcision stands here for the Galatians' desire for social status which, their having already received the Spirit of adoption, would effectively relegate them once again to bondage to the elemental things of the world (see 4:1f). For the present reading of the Galatian situation, see Introduction, **Occasion and circumstances; Argument**.

over to sin and Belial in the "foreskin of his tendency and of his stiff neck
עורלת יצר וערף קשה" (1QS 5:5) (see 2:1f [excursi]).

Paul is so enthused with what God has performed in His Messiah that
his sentence structure deserts him, exclaiming in an outburst: "but – new
creation! (ἀλλὰ καινὴ κτίσις)" (cf. Hays, Galatians: 344). The fact that the
Greek κτίσις (ktisis) signifies both "creation" (something created) and
"creature" (someone created) suggests that Paul is thinking of the "new
heavens and a new earth" in which "the former things shall not be
remembered or come to mind כי-הנני בורא שמים חדשים וארץ חדשה ולא תזכרנה
הראשנות ולא תעלינה על- לב" (Isa. 65:17) (cf. ibid: 345; Echoes: 159).[158]

Such a concept is common also to the Qumran community, who saw
themselves as members of the "New Covenant": "For the sake of your
glory you have purified man from offence, so that he can make himself
holy for you from every impure abominations [*sic*] and guilt of
unfaithfulness, to become united wi[th] the sons of your truth and in the
lot with your holy ones, to raise the worms of the dead from the dust, to an
ever[lasting] community and from a depraved spirit, to [your] knowledge,
so that he can take his place in your presence with the perpetual host and
the spirits [. . .], to renew him with everything that will exist, and with
those who know in a community of jubilation"[159] (1QHᵃ 19:10-14).[160]

A similar association between purification and repentance occurs in
rabbinic texts: "R. Lazar from the house of R. Josa said in the name of R.
Josi bar Katzarta: In reference to all the sacrifices it is written *and you shall
present an offering* but here [in reference to New Year's Day] it says *You shall
make* (Num. 29:2). The Holy One, blessed be He, said to them [Israel]: Since

---

[158] In light of 4:22-31, it is not coincidental that the continuation of this passage
speaks of God creating "Jerusalem *for* rejoicing, and her people *for* gladness הנני
בורא את-ירושלם גילה ועמה משש" – the biblical text also lacking a verbal context
("Jerusalem – rejoicing; her people – gladness"). As Hays pertinently notes, in the
similar context of 2 Cor. 5:17, "Individualistic interpretations of Paul's 'new
creation' language are promoted by most English translations of 2 Cor. 5:17a:
'Therefore, if anyone is in Christ, he is a new creation' (RSV). The words 'he is' are
not present in Paul's elliptical sentence ... In view of the fact that Paul
characteristically uses *ktisis* and its cognates in a cosmological frame of reference
(see, e.g., Rom. 8:19-23) and in view of the scriptural subtexts from which Paul
derives this language, it would be far better to complete the ellipsis in a way that
would demonstrate that Paul is speaking here not of individual spiritual renewal
but of the reconciliation of the *world* to God (cf. 2 Cor. 5:19): 'Therefore, if anyone is
in Christ – there is a new creation!'" (Echoes: 223n15).
[159] למען כבודך טהרתה אנוש מפשע להתקדש לכה מכול תועבות נדה ואשמת מעל להיחד עם[ם] בני
אמתך ובגורל עם קדושיכה להרים מעפר תולעת מתים לסוד ע[ולם] ומרוח נעוה לבינת[כה]
ולהתיצב במעמד לפניכה עם צבא עד ורוחי [. . .] להתחדש עם כול נהיה ועם ידעים ביחד רנה.
[160] Cf. CD-A 6:19, 8:21; CD-B 20:12.

you come into My presence for judgment this day and go forth in peace, I regard you as though you had been made a new creation"[161] (J RH 21a).[162]

The "new creation" is also directly associated with the Messiah, his spirit being considered to be that which hovered over the waters when God created the world: *"And the Spirit of God hovered* (Gen. 1:1): this alludes to the spirit of Messiah, as you read, *And the spirit of the Lord shall rest upon him* (Isa. 11:2: ורוח אלהים מרחפת: זה רוח של מלך המשיח, היאך מה דאת אמר: "ונחה עליו רוח ה' (Gen.R. 2:4) (see 3:26-29). A midrash on Psalm 2:7, a well-known messianic psalm, states that "When the time comes, the Holy One, blessed be He, will say: 'I must create the Messiah – a new creation.' As Scripture says, *This day have I begotten thee* – that is, on the very day of redemption, God will create the Messiah"[163] (Mid.Ps. 2:9).

It is this new creation – in the "new creation" of the Messiah – which destroys (the bondage of) this world and its "elemental things," thereby breaking the power of sin and of Belial and establishing God's reign on earth: *"This shall be written for a vergent generation; a people that shall be created shall praise the Lord* [Ps. 102:18] ... in saying *a people that shall be created shall praise the Lord*, he meant that God gives a new life to each man that repents ... The word *This* in *This shall be written for a vergent generation* alludes to the present generations which are on the verge of death. And the words *a people that shall be created shall praise the Lord* mean that the Holy One will give us a new life"[164] (PRK 27:2-3).

Through the Messiah, whom God sent into the world (cf. 4:4), both Jews and Gentiles thus find entrance into God's Kingdom, gaining possession through Jesus to its keys – the ability to perform the weighty commandments, of "justice and mercy and faithfulness" in "lovingkindness and righteousness."[165] Through the adoption of both (one a slave/stranger, one a minor) as "sons," each has been delivered "from

---

[161] ר' לעזר בי ר' יוסה בשם ר' יוסי בר קצרתא: בכל הקרבנות כתיב "והקרבתם" וכאן כתיב "ועשיתם." אמר להן הקדוש ברוך הוא: מכיון שנכנסתם לדין לפני בראש השנה ויצאתם בשלום, מעלה אני עליכם כאילו נבראתם בריה חדשה.

[162] Cf. PRK 23:12; Yalk.Lev. 645; Yalk.Num. 782; [Yalk.Ex. 171; Gen.R. 39:11]; Lev.R. 30:3; Tanh.Lech lecha 3; Mid.Ps. 102:3. The parallel in PRK speaks of the people "going forth free [בדימוס]" and explains the allusion in reference to Isa. 66:22: "For as the heavens [which I have already made] stand before Me as though they were new, and the earth [which I have already made stands before Me] as though it were new, so shall your seed and your name stand before Me [as though they were newly made]."

[163] וכד תיתי שעתיה, אומר הקדוש ברוך הוא: עלי לבראתו ברייה חדשה. וכן הוא אומר: אני היום ילדתיך. הא שעתא בריית ליה.

[164] תכתב זאת לדור אחרון: מכן שהקדוש מקבל את השבים. ועם נברא יהלל יה: שבראם הקדוש ברוך הוא בריה חדשה ... תכתב זאת לדור אחרון: אילו דורות הללו, שהם נטוים למיתה. ועם נברא יהלל יה: שעתיד הקדוש ברוך הוא לבראותן בריה חדשה.

[165] Cf. Jer. 9:24; Mic. 6:8; Mt. 23:23; Eph. 2:12-22 (see Introduction, **Argument**; **Theological pointers** [Justification], and 2:15-21).

darkness to light and from the dominion of Satan to God, in order that they may receive forgiveness of sins and an inheritance among those who have been sanctified by faithfulness towards me"[166] (Acts 26:18) (see 3:19f and 4:1-7).[167]

Verse 16: At this point – at the height of its purpose – Paul begins to bring his letter to its close, invoking a blessing on his readers.[168] The conjunctive καὶ (kai – "and") nonetheless closely relates the blessing to the previous verse, describing the conduct characteristic of the "new creation." Once again, Paul picks up previous threads, reminding his disciples that their "walk" should be "keeping in step with (στοιχήσουσιν)" the Spirit – as he has indicated in 5:25 (see 5:24-26). In place of the Spirit he speaks here of "the rule (τῷ κανόνι)." In light of the fact that "walking" corresponds to הלכה (halakhah) – that which, as the "wisdom of the feasible," applies the Torah to each generation's historical circumstances (see 5:19f) – Paul's choice of a term which designates a rule or standard is appropriate.[169]

While the term κανών (kanōn) came to designate the "rule of faith" by the second century (cf. BAGD: 403), no necessary reason exists to refer it to a new messianic instruction (see verses 1-11) or even to "the Christian teaching" (cf. 4 Macc. 7:21) (Longenecker, Galatians: 297). Serving also to denote a "sphere" (cf. 2 Cor. 10:13, 15-16), it may better be taken as modifying the "new creation" as emblematic of "that same *standard* to which we have attained" in perfection (Phil. 3:16: πλὴν εἰς ὃ ἐφθάσαμεν, τῷ αὐτῷ στοιχεῖν [κανόνι]).[170] The "rule" may also represent Paul's personal instruction (halakhah), adding further weight to his urging that his disciples follow his example by walking in the Spirit (see 5:13f).[171] In

---

[166] ... ἀπὸ σκότου εἰς φῶς καὶ τῆς ἐξουσίας τοῦ σατανᾶ ἐπὶ τὸν θεόν, τοῦ λαβεῖν αὐτοὺς ἄφεσιν ἁμαρτιῶν καὶ κλῆρον ἐν τοῖς ἡγιασμένοις πίστει τῇ εἰς ἐμέ.

[167] The implication of this view suggests that, while gentile believers are "grafted in" to God's Kingdom from a place of alienation, Jewish believers are now enabled to observe the "minor commandments" of Torah without neglecting the "major" ones, having the "fear of heaven" added to study/practice (see Introduction, **Theological pointers** [Jewish-gentile relations]).

[168] In this sense, he as it were returns the blessing which he originally received from the Galatian communities (see 4:12-20 [verse 15]).

[169] "In practice הלכה [halakhah] has the same meaning as ὅρος [oros] (literally 'boundary') which means *regula*" (Lieberman, Hellenism: 83n3). The word may also be a conscious reflection of the idea of line, rank, or order implied in στοιχέω (stoicheō) (see 4:1-7). For Galatians' halakhic status, see Introduction, **Form**.

[170] Cf. 1QS 9:6. Whether or not the inclusion of κανόνι (kanoni) in Phil. 3:16 is under the influence of the present verse, the context there exhibits such close affinities with this passage that an association between στοιχέω (stoicheō) (also present in Phil. 3:16) and κανών (kanōn) may have been "common." See also below.

[171] The statement is strongly reminiscent of those passages in which blessings and curses are pronounced for observance or transgression of the Torah: "Now it shall

this respect, while as a conditional blessing it implies a threat against those who do not comply with its authority (cf. Betz, Galatians: 321),[172] it also stands as a verbal directive to the Galatians to commit themselves to Jesus through acknowledging him, through Paul, as their "master/Sage." In imitating Paul, himself a "bondservant of the Messiah," they will practice that which they observe in his conduct and receive from his teaching (cf. Alon, Land: 476-78), thereby being "filled with the knowledge of His will in all spiritual wisdom and understanding, so that you may walk in a manner worthy of the Lord, to please *Him* in all respects, bearing fruit in every good work and increasing in the knowledge of God; strengthened with all power, according to His glorious might, for the attaining of all steadfastness and patience; joyously giving thanks to the Father, who has qualified us to share in the inheritance of the saints in light. For He delivered us from the domain of darkness, and transferred us to the kingdom of His beloved son, in whom we have redemption, the forgiveness of sins"[173] (Col. 1:9-14) (see 1:1-5, 4:1-7, 12-20, and verses 1-11).

While "peace benedictions" are customarily found in Paul's letters, being absent only in 1 Corinthians, Colossians, the Pastorals, and Philemon,[174] the present example is closely associated with Paul's opening

---

be, if you will diligently obey the LORD your God, being careful to do all His commandments which I command you today, the LORD your God will set you high above all the nations of the earth. And all these blessings shall come upon you and overtake you, if you will obey the LORD your God . . . But it shall come about that if you will not obey the LORD your God, to observe to do all His commandments and His statutes which I charge you today, that all these curses shall come upon you and overtake you והיה אם־שמוע תשמע בקול ה' אלהיך לשמר לעשות את־כל־מצותיו אשר אנכי מצוך היום ונתנך ה' אלהיך עליון על כל־גויי הארץ: ובאו עליך כל־הברכות האלה והשיגך כי תשמע בקול ה' אלהיך (Dt. 28:1-2, 15) (cf. 1 En. 94:6-103:15; 1QS 1:21-2:18). The "rule" may also relate to the סרך (serekh) used of the "discipline[/discipleship]" of the Qumran community (cf. 1QS 1:1, 5:1; CD-A 12:22, 14:12) (see 3:10-14). For Galatians' "rebuke-request" structure, see Introduction, **Form; Argument.**

[172] See also verse 17.

[173] πληρωθῆτε τὴν ἐπίγνωσιν τοῦ θελήματος αὐτοῦ ἐν πάσῃ σοφίᾳ καὶ συνέσει πνευματικῇ, περιπατῆσαι ἀξίως τοῦ κυρίου εἰς πᾶσαν ἀρεσκείαν, ἐν παντὶ ἔργῳ ἀγαθῷ καρποφοροῦντες καὶ αὐξανόμενοι τῇ ἐπιγνώσει τοῦ θεοῦ, ἐν πάσῃ δυνάμει δυναμούμενοι κατὰ τὸ κράτος τῆς δόξης αὐτοῦ εἰς πᾶσαν ὑπομονὴν καὶ μακροθυμίαν. Μετὰ χαρᾶς εὐχαριστοῦντες τῷ πατρὶ τῷ ἱκανώσαντι ὑμᾶς εἰς τὴν μερίδα τοῦ κλήρου τῶν ἁγίων ἐν τῷ φωτί· ὃς ἐρρύσατο ἡμᾶς ἐκ τῆς ἐξουσίας τοῦ σκότους καὶ μετέστησεν εἰς τὴν βασιλείαν τοῦ υἱοῦ τῆς ἀγάπης αὐτοῦ, ἐν ᾧ ἔχομεν τὴν ἀπολύτρωσιν, τὴν ἄφεσιν τῶν ἁμαρτιῶν.

[174] Cf. Rom. 15:33, 16:20a; 2 Cor. 13:11; Eph. 6:23; Phil. 4:9b; 1 Thess. 5:23; 2 Thess. 3:16. Galatians is also notable in this respect for its absence of "greetings" – whether from Paul himself and/or from those with him (cf. Rom. 16:16b, 21-23; 1 Cor. 16:19-20a; 2 Cor. 13:13; Phil. 4:22; Col. 4:10-14; 2 Tim. 4:21b; Tit. 3:15a; Phlm 23), or from addressees acting as agents for conveying Paul's greetings to others (cf. Rom. 16:3-15; Col. 4:15; 1 Thess. 5:26; 2 Tim. 4:19; Tit. 3:15). A corresponding lack occurs only

blessing in 1:3 – that immediately being followed by the invocation of a curse on those who are troubling his disciples (cf. 1:8-9) (see 1:1f).[175] The exegesis of this verse has traditionally been made difficult by its irregular order, in which "peace" uncustomarily precedes "mercy" and by the fact that Paul makes two uses both of the preposition ἐπί (epi) and of the conjunction καί (kai). Given the fact that "mercy and peace" may correspond to two groups, together with a perhaps uncharacteristic Christian reluctance to apply the term "Israel" to Gentiles, some commentators have repunctuated the verse to read: "Peace upon all those who follow this rule, and mercy upon the Israel of God" – thereby bestowing peace on the Gentiles, on the one hand, and mercy on "pious Jews who would yet [later] come to accept the Christian gospel" on the other (Longenecker, Galatians: 297-98).[176]

Despite the claims that Paul's routine order in later blessings is "mercy and peace," he does not invariably employ this practice.[177] The formula itself follows the additional nineteenth blessing of peace in the Shmoneh Esreh (Eighteen Benedictions/Amidah): "Establish peace, goodness, blessing, graciousness, kindness, and compassion upon us and upon all of your people Israel שים שלום, טובה, וברכה, חן, וחסד, ורחמים עלינו

---

in Ephesians (most probably a "circular" letter) and 1 Timothy. Here in Galatians, this circumstance is likely reflective of Paul's agitated and aggressive stance – reinforced by a corresponding absence of thanksgiving in the prescript (see 1:1-5), and any expression of joy, request for prayer, or explicit doxology in the subscription here, together with the insertion of a direct warning (cf. Rom. 16:17-20). For the "doxology," see verse 18.

[175] "One of the special features of Paul's Galatians is that the curse (1:8-9) must be seen in its connection with the conditional blessing in the *peroratio* . . . As a result the entire 'body' of the letter is bracketed by this conditional curse and blessing" (Betz, Galatians: 50). While we do not concur that, on this basis, the epistle should be regarded as assuming "the power of a magical letter," nor with the terminology of "sacred law" (ibid), we hope to have demonstrated the master-disciple halakhic context which frames Galatians – on the one hand in Paul's rebuke of the influencers and on the other in his request of his readers to continue in loyalty to him (see Introduction, Form; Argument, 1:6-9, 4:12-20, 5:2-12, 24-26, and verses 1-11).

[176] Alternatively: "Peace be upon them, and mercy, and upon the Israel of God" – which equally distinguishes between two groups. Notwithstanding Paul's confirmation of Israel's deliverance in Rom. 11:26, appeals to his declaration "all Israel shall be saved" there in assertion of an eschatological context in which "the totality of the Jews will be saved" surely ignore the difference in context for the present purposes, Paul endeavouring in Romans to warn the Gentiles against pride in their acceptance before God while here in Galatians insisting on that very status (cf. Shulam and Le Cornu: 273ff; Hays, Galatians: 346).

[177] Cf. 2 Cor. 13:11; Eph. 6:23-24; 1 Thess. 5:23-28; 2 Thess. 3:16-18.

ועל כל ישראל עמך‎‎."[178] The attributes of God here invoked (cf. Est.R. 10:15) correspond in large part to the fruit of the Spirit which Paul has enumerated as those qualities which characterise the person who "walks in the Spirit"[179] (see 5:19f and verses 1-11).[180]

Peace and mercy/grace also appear in the prayer recited when a person goes out into the public domain: "May it be Thy will, O Lord my God, that Thou conduct me in peace and uphold me in peace; and let me obtain grace, favour and mercy in Thine eyes and in the eyes of all who behold me; bestow lovingkindness upon me, and cause me to return to my house in peace. Deliver me from the hand of every enemy and ambush by the way and from an evil tongue. Let me not become accustomed to sin, transgression or iniquity, and let me not err in a matter of *halakhah* or in any matter whatsoever. Deliver me from all kinds of harm and from all manner of afflictions which break forth and come upon the world that they do not injure me by day or by night. Blessed is He Who bestoweth lovingkindnesses upon His people Israel"[181] (DER 11:18).[182]

---

[178] Cf. Ps. 125:5, 128:6; Isa. 14:1; Ezek. 39:25; 2 Bar. 78:1; 1 En. 5:6; Jub. 22:9; Ps.Sol. 9:11, 10:8, 11:9, 17:45, 18:5; Num.R. 12:1; Dt.R. 5:15; Est.R. 10:15; Sot. 40a; Ket. 50a; Ber. 44a. While the precise date of the Shmoneh Esreh is difficult to determine, the benedictions themselves are of evidently early providence and would surely have been known to Paul (cf. Schürer: 2:454-63; Stone: 552, 571; Flusser, Judaism: 149, 216-17; Liebes).

[179] The last of the benedictions also exhibits dependence on Mic. 6:8, "do justice, love kindness עשות משפט ואהבת חסד‎‎," where the second term is understood as meaning "love and mercy" (cf. Flusser, Judaism: 496). To the extent that it may be presumed that Jesus was quoting Mic. 6:8 in Mt. 23:23, we have here once more a reference to acting within the margin of the judgment = walking in the Spirit (see Introduction, **Argument**, 2:15-21, 3:10-14 [n142], 5:2ff, verses 1-11 [nn36, 86, 91], and above [n152]). For boasting and Jer. 9:23-26, see above (n152).

[180] Cf. 1QM 17:7-9: "He sends everlasting aid to the lot of his [co]venant by the power of the majestic angel for the sway of Michael in everlasting light, to illuminate with joy the covenant of Israel, **peace and blessing to God's lot**, to exalt the sway of Michael above all the gods, and the dominion of Israel over all flesh. Justice will rejoice in the heights and all the sons of his truth will have enjoyment in everlasting knowledge. And you, sons of his covenant, be strong in God's crucible until he shakes his hand and finishes his testings, his mysteries concerning your existence וישלח עזר עולמים לגורל]ב[ריתו בגבורת מלאך האדיר למשרת מיכאל באור עולמים‎ להאיר בשמחה ברית ישראל *שלום וברכה לגורל אל* להרים באלים משרת מיכאל וממשלת ישראל בכול בשר ישמח צדק במרומים וכול בני אמתו יגילו בדעת עולמים ואתם בני בריתו התחזקו‎ במצרף אל עד יניף ידו ומלא מצרפיו רזיו למעמדכם‎" (cf. Jub. 1:29; 1QM 1:9, 12:3; 4Q504 ff1-2iv:13).

[181] יהי רצון מלפניך ה' אלהי שתוליכני לשלום ותסמיכני לשלום ותתנני לחן ולחסד ולרחמים‎ בעיניך ובעיני כל רואי ותגמלני חסדים טובים ותחזירני לביתי לשלום ותצילני מכף אויב ואורב‎ בדרך ותצילני מיד לשון הרע ואל תרגילני לדבר עבירה וחטא ועון ואל אכשל בדבר הלכה ולא בשום‎ דבר בעולם ותצילני מכל מיני מזיקין ומכל מיני פורעניות המתרגשות ובאות לעולם שלא יזיקו בי‎ בין ביום ובין בלילה.]ברוך אתה ה' גומל חסדים טובים לעמו ישראל[‎.

These "parallels" suggest that pleas for such qualities as gmilut chasadim, love, mercy, and peace were made by Israel as the nation's signature – "the house of Israel."[183] This view may be strengthened by the correspondences exhibited in the rabbinic texts which speak of "forbearance first of all towards your household" (see verses 1-11). The "household" there is identified with Israel, whom God loves more than any other nation.[184] In conjunction with the dual "subjects" – "on us and upon all of your people Israel" – in the Shmoneh Esreh, which speak conjointly of Israel, it would appear that Paul is adapting the blessing according to the principle which has informed the whole letter: Those who are Abraham's children are those who exhibit his qualities, who follow faithfully in his footsteps, who have become "sons" and "heirs" through Jesus' deliverance from the bondage of sin, and who, being blessed in Abraham's seed, now walk in God's Spirit (see Introduction, **Argument**).[185] These are the "Israel of God" – composed of both Jews and Gentiles in the "new creation" (verse 15), both meriting the title on the grounds of their faithfulness to Jesus' obedience to his Father's faithfulness (see 2:15-21, 3:1ff, 4:1f, and 5:19f).[186]

---

[182] The last clause does not appear in the Hebrew text but is found in the prayer for washing one's face, whose formula closely resembles this prayer (cf. Ber. 60b). The phrase directly recalls the principle of גמילות חסדים (gmilut chasadim – "deeds of lovingkindness") which we have suggested lies behind Paul's injunction in verse 9 (see verses 1-11). It is hardly surprising that Paul's dicta here resemble the Derekh Eretz literature, both being concerned with the "way of walking" in the world.

[183] For gmilut chasadim as a "national characteristic," see verses 1-11 (n91).

[184] The continuation of the nineteenth blessing runs: "Bless us, our Father, all of us as one, with the light of Your countenance, for with the light of Your countenance You gave us, O Lord our God, the Torah of life and a love of kindness, righteousness, blessing, compassion, life, and peace. And may it be good in Your eyes to bless Your people Israel, in every season and in every hour with Your peace. Blessed be You, O Lord our God, Who blesses His people Israel with peace ברכנו אבינו, כלנו כאחד באור פניך, כי באור פניך נתת לנו, ה׳ אלהינו, תורת חיים ואהבת חסד וצדקה וברכה ורחמים וחיים ושלום. וטוב בעיניך לברך את עמך ישראל, בכל עת ובכל שעה בשלומך. ברוך אתה ה׳, המברך את עמו ישראל בשלום ברכת הכֹהנים" (PB: 117-118). The allusions to ברכת הכֹהנים (birkat ha-cohanim – the priestly blessing) are clear, the six forms of goodness also corresponding to the latter's six blessings and the benediction itself only being recited when the priestly blessing is pronounced. In this sense, Paul's final blessing repeats his initial introductory benediction, with its overtones of the aaronic blessing (cf. 1:3) (see 1:1-5).

[185] Cf. Jub. 31:20. No grammatical difficulty exists in translating the second καὶ (kai –"and") as "even," the phrase "Israel of God" thus modifying "upon them." Paul is likewise unspecific in his address, employing an impersonal "those who" which is not restricted to his gentile Galatian disciples. See also verse 18.

[186] "Evidently both communities [in Qumran and the New Testament] were attracted by the eschatological content of the biblical expression 'New Covenant',

Verse 17:
From now on let no one cause trouble for me, for I bear on my body the brand-marks of Jesus.

Following the implied threat of the previous verse, Paul now adds a further personal warning – presumably to those who are liable not to "walk by this rule" (see verses 12-16).[187] The adverbial genitive expression τοῦ λοιποῦ (tou loipou) may signify either a temporal event ("henceforth," "in the future") or logical sequence ("in addition," "finally"), both being equally attested (cf. Longenecker, Galatians: 299). The second may be marginally preferable here, on the grounds that the present tense of the verb does not easily sustain a future reference (cf. ibid). As a present imperative, παρεχέτω (parechetō) indicates an ongoing activity – "let no one continue to cause trouble."

The noun κόπος (kopos) also carries a dual meaning, indicating both "trouble" or "difficulty" and "work, labour, toil" (cf. BAGD: 443). While the former is regularly assumed to be the obvious denotation – giving rise to immediate associations with those who are "troubling" the Galatians (despite the difference in verbal root) – the idea of "labour" also picks up

---

especially as the prophets says that the New Covenant will be different from the old broken one. Of course both communities did not interpret literally the part of the prophecy which says that the New Covenant will be made 'with the house of Israel and with the house of Judah.' In their opinion this expression could not mean the whole Jewish people; they saw in it a designation of the 'true Israel': these are 'Israel who walk in perfection' according to the Qumran covenanters (DSD [1QS] 9:6) or according to Paul [the] 'Israel of God' (Gal. 6:16)" (Flusser, Judaism: 44). What should be emphasised here is the fact that the epithet "Israel of God" remains first and foremost a Jewish category. It designates initially "who is a disciple of Abraham." Under that definition, and through Jesus' faithful obedience, it now extends to Gentiles who "show the work of the Law written in their hearts (ἐνδείκνυνται τὸ ἔργον τοῦ νόμου γραπτὸν ἐν ταῖς καρδίαις)" (Rom. 2:15). These are consequently "no longer strangers and aliens, but you are fellow-citizens with the saints, and are of God's household, having been built upon the foundation of the apostles and prophets, the Messiah Jesus himself being the corner *stone*, in whom the whole building, being fitted together [cf. Ps. 122:3] is growing into a holy temple in the Lord; in whom you also are being built together into a dwelling of God in the Spirit (οὐκέτι ἐστὲ ξένοι καὶ πάροικοι ἀλλὰ ἐστὲ συμπολῖται τῶν ἁγίων καὶ οἰκεῖοι τοῦ θεοῦ, ἐποικοδομηθέντες ἐπὶ τῷ θεμελίῳ τῶν ἀποστόλων καὶ προφητῶν, ὄντες ἀκρογωνιαίου αὐτοῦ Χριστοῦ Ἰησοῦ, ἐν ᾧ πᾶσα οἰκοδομὴ συναρμολογουμένη αὔξει εἰς ναὸν ἅγιον ἐν κυρίῳ, ἐν ᾧ καὶ ὑμεῖς συνοικοδομεῖσθε εἰς κατοικητήριον τοῦ θεοῦ ἐν πνεύματι)" (Eph. 2:19-22) (cf. 1 Tim. 3:15) (see also 2:1-10 ["pillars"], 15-21, 4:12-21, and verses 1-11 [verse 10]). For the meaning of "brethren," with which address Paul closes the letter, see verse 18.

[187] This may follow the pattern of 5:1-12, where Paul inveighs against the "troublers," inserting a personal note – as here – of "persecution" in verse 11 and a final invective in verse 12 (cf. Longenecker, Galatians: 299) (see 5:2-12).

Paul's apprehension in 4:11, where he employs the same verb (κεκοπίακα; kekopiaka) in indicating his apprehension that he has "labored in vain"[188] (see 2:1-10 and 4:12-20). A similar idea may also be reflected in the motif of sowing in verses 8-9, where the "day is short, and the work [to be performed] is much היום קצר והמלאכה מרובה" (PA 2:15) (see verses 1-11).[189]

The reason behind Paul's present stricture is frequently regarded as being rather cryptic (cf. Longenecker, Galatians: 299). The remark is nonetheless immediately linked to the previous verses by Paul's repetition of βαστίζω (bastizō – "to carry") (cf. verses 2, 5) (see verses 1-11). Whereas at the beginning of this chapter he has urged those truly walking in the Spirit to take "bear responsibility" for the restoration of those who are being persuaded away from the gospel and Paul's example, and indirectly warned the influencers that they would each "bear his own burden/sin" (cf. verses 1-8), Paul, in contrast, is visibly marked as Jesus' bondservant.[190] While the LXX does not render נשא (nasa) in Isaiah 53:4, 12 by βαστίζω, Paul may nevertheless also have had Jesus' role in "bearing sin" in mind (see verses 1-11).[191]

If this be the case, rather than demonstrating "his integrity and the truth of his message" (Hays, Galatians: 346), the physical marks which his body bore from his mistreatment in the Messiah's service[192] more significantly bear witness to his role as God's "Suffering Servant" (see 1:[1-5], 15-16b, 21-24 and 2:1-10). In this sense, Paul's final admonition returns first to the opening of the letter, where he sets out his "credentials" as authoritative to rebuke, and then to 4:12, where he appeals to his disciples to "Become as I am (Γίνεσθε ὡς ἐγώ)" (see 4:12-20 and verses 1-11).[193] In

---

[188] For 4:12f as the transition from the "rebuke section" of the letter to Paul's "request," see Introduction, **Argument**, 4:12-20, and verses 1f. For the current reading of Galatians as a halakhic "rebuke-request" letter along the lines of 4QMMT, see Introduction, **Form; Argument**.

[189] The noun could work for Paul in this respect to warn both the influencers and his disciples (see verses 1-11).

[190] Some commentators have suggested in this regard that, the Greek τὰ στίγματα (ta stigmata) signifying, among other things, the branding of a slave, Paul may be claiming visible evidence of his possession by Jesus (cf. Longenecker, Galatians: 299).

[191] Whether Paul is indirectly presenting himself in a priestly role in this sense is difficult to determine in the context of Galatians, wherein the motif appears to be almost entirely absent. Paul does speak of his apostleship to the Gentiles in priestly terms in Rom. 15:16 (cf. Le Cornu and Shulam: 494, 500, 590, 1215-20, 1319-23). See also verse 18.

[192] Cf. Isa. 44:5; Ezek. 9:4; 2 Cor. 6:4-9, 11:23-30; Rev. 13:16.

[193] For the current reading of Galatians as a halakhic "rebuke-request" letter along the lines of 4QMMT, see Introduction, **Form; Argument**. It is perhaps significant that in 4:14 Paul alludes to the effect of "a bodily illness (ἀσθένειαν τῆς σαρκὸς)" – although its precise nature remains obscure (see 4:12-20).

speaking of the "brand-marks" as those of Jesus, he also reminds his readers of the importance of the crucifixion, by which all wo/mankind has been delivered from the bondage of sin and the fear of death and forms the model whereby, each taking his/her cross and following him, each person crucifies him/herself to the world and the world to themselves, by walking in the Spirit (see 1:1-5, 2:1ff, 3:26-29, 4:1ff, and 5:13ff).

Verse 18:
The grace of our Lord Jesus the Messiah be with your spirit, brethren. Amen.

While Paul customarily concludes his later letters with a "grace benediction,"[194] this one strikingly includes the vocative "brethren (ἀδελφοί)" (cf. Longenecker, Galatians: 300, and for the following discussion). In the context of a letter written with very strong sentiment both towards his addressees and towards those "troubling" them, Paul takes leave of his disciples – as nowhere else in a subscription – as "brethren."[195] Quite likely in doing so he is reinforcing their membership in the "household of faithfulness" and the "Israel of God" (see verses 12f and below).

The "grace (ἡ χάρις)" with which he blesses them is specifically that of Jesus, through whose gracious act of self-sacrifice they have been "called" by God (cf. 1:6) – the same grace which he has received from God for his (priestly) ministry (cf. 1:15, 2:9; Rom. 15:15) (see verse 17).[196] The phrase "with your spirit (μετὰ τοῦ πνεύματος)" (cf. Phil. 4:23; 2 Tim. 4:22; Phlm 25) gives the impression of a semitism, possibly reflecting the biblical עשה חסד עמכם (asah chesed imakhem – lit. "doing mercy with you") (cf. Gen. 24:12). This latter expression occurs in the daily morning prayer: "Our Father, our King, be gracious with us and answer us, though we have no worthy deeds; treat us with charity and kindnesses, and save us בינו מלכנו, חננו ועננו, כי אין בנו מעשים. עשה עמנו צדקה וחסד והושיענו" (PB: 122-23).[197]

While commentators commonly claim that Galatians contains no doxology, the "amen" with which the letter concludes is unusual without the presence of either a prayer or a doxology (cf. 1:5).[198] The significance of its inclusion here lies not merely in its implication of a doxology but also in

---

[194] Cf. Rom. 16:20b, [24]; 1 Cor. 16:23; 2 Cor. 13:14; Eph. 6:24; Phil. 4:23; Col. 4:18b; 1 Thess. 5:28; 2 Thess. 3:18; 1 Tim. 6:21b; 2 Tim. 4:22b; Tit. 3:15b; Phlm 25. For the "peace benediction," see verses 12-16;
[195] for "brethren," see 1:1-5.
[196] For the inclusive language ("our"), see verses 12-16 [verse 14].
[197] Cf. Sof. 14:12. While these passages are late, it is interesting that they are both linked with the "remnant" of Israel – those whom Paul has just described as "the Israel of God" (see verses 12-16). Cf. also 1QHᵃ 10:23: "by your kindness you save my soul, because from you come my steps מצעדי מאתכה כיא נפשי תושיע ובחסדיכה."
[198] It does occur thus in 1 Cor. 16:23-24.

the fact that the utterance of "So be it" asks for the Galatians' concurrence with the preceding. "R. Jose b. Hanina said: 'Amen' implies oath, acceptance of words, and confirmation of words. It implies oath, as it is written: *And the woman shall say, Amen, amen* (Num. 5:22). It implies acceptance of words, as it is written: *Cursed be he that confirmeth not the words of this law to do them, and all the people shall say, Amen* (Dt. 27:26). It implies confirmation of words, as it is written: *And the prophet Jeremiah said, Amen, the Lord do so! The Lord perform thy words!* (Jer. 28:6)"[199] (Shevu. 36a) (see 1:1-5). At the end of a letter of both rebuke and request, Paul's prayer is that his disciples will join with him, accepting his authority, his reprimand, and his request, declaring: "May it be so!"[200]

---

[199] רבי יוסי ברבי חנינא: אמן בו שבועה, בו קבלת דברים, בו האמנת דברים. בו שבועה, דכתיב: ואמרה האשה אמן אמן. בו קבלת דברים, דכתיב: ארור אשר לא יקים את דברי התורה הזאת לעשות אותם ואמר כל העם אמן. בו האמנת דברים, דכתיב: ויאמר ירמיה [הנביא] [אל חנניהו] אמן כן יעשה ה' יקם ה' את דבריך.

[200] Here too Paul may allude to Jesus' representative role, as he later addresses his Corinthian disciples: "For as many as may be the promises of God, in him they are yes; wherefore also by him is our Amen to the glory of God through us (ὅσαι γὰρ ἐπαγγελίαι θεοῦ, ἐν αὐτῷ ναί διὸ καὶ δι' αὐτοῦ τὸ ἀμὴν τῷ θεῷ πρὸς δόξαν δι' ἡμῶν)" (2 Cor. 1:20).

PAUL – A BIOGRAPHY

Name

Paul provides explicit details regarding his Jewish identity, to which can be added the information which Luke attributes to him in Acts.[1] According to his own testimony, he was born into a Jewish, pharisaic family, of the tribe of Benjamin, in Tarsus of Cilicia – facts of which he is proud.[2] He is known by two names in the New Testament texts: Saul (שאול) (Hebrew) and Paul (Latin) (cf. Hachlili: 188ff, and for the following discussion). According to a tannaitic tradition, "A man is called by three names: one which his father and mother call him, a second which other persons call him, and a third by which he is designated in the book of the generations of his creation תני ג': שמות נקראו לאדם הזה: האחד שקראו לו אביו ואמו, ואחד שקראו לו אחרים, ואחד שקרוי לו בספר תולדות ברייתו" (Eccl.R. 7.1.3).[3] It would appear that biblical names – such as Saul – gradually lost their widespread popularity and were replaced with others. Saul ("asked [from God]") nevertheless remains well attested during this period.[4]

---

[1] The material for this Appendix has been adapted from Le Cornu and Shulam: 439ff,1393ff and passim.

[2] Cf. Acts 9:11, 21:39, 22:3; Rom. 11:1; 2 Cor. 11:22; Phil. 3:5.

[3] Cf. Mid.Sam. 23. The last clause perhaps refers to the name which a person gains as a result of her/his conduct in life.

[4] Cf. Jos.War 2.418, 469, 556f; PA 2:8; Shab. 24:5. During the early Second Temple period, the commonest Jewish names were Shimon (Simeon), Joseph, Yehuda (Judah), Yochanan (John), and Eleazar (cf. Hachlili: 188).

Whereas biblical names were frequently chosen for their "emotional content" or their symbolic meaning,[5] it became standard practice in the early Second Temple period to name a child after his grandfather (paponymy) or (more commonly) his father (patronymy) – a custom also known in Greece, Phoenicia, and Egypt. Luke's statement concerning John the Baptist reflects common usage in this regard: ". . . they were going to call him Zacharias, after his father . . . and they said to her, 'There is no one among your relatives who is called by that name'"[6] (Lk. 1:59-61).[7] The designation x בן (ben x – "the son of x") without a personal name also signifies an epithet. In this respect, Saul may have been a familial name, especially since the family was from the tribe of Benjamin (see below, **Ancestry**).[8]

The scholarly consensus asserts that "Paul (Paulus/Παῦλος)" represents a Roman and not a Jewish name. While several midrashim, ascribe Israel's redemption from Egypt, among other things, to their refusal to change their names – ". . . They did not call Judah 'Leon', nor Reuben 'Rufus', nor Joseph 'Lestes', nor Benjamin 'Alexander' לא היו קורין "ליהודה רופא ולא לראובן לוליאני ולא ליוסף לסטיס ולא לבנימין אלכסנדר (Lev.R. 32:5)[9] – the phenomenon was prevalent amongst members of the hasmonean dynasty, whose double names (Jochanan *Hyrcanus*; Judah *Aristobolus*; Shlomtzion *Alexandra*) appear to reflect, in large part, the cosmopolitan influence of hellenism (cf. Jos.*Ant.* 12.239). The fact that non-Jewish names are not clearly forbidden is evident from their widespread use, the lack of criticism of the practice in rabbinic literature, and the recognition that not all names are clearly Jewish or non-Jewish[10] (cf. Stern, Identity: 193).

Since Luke never refers to Paul by his full Roman name (*praenomen, nomen,* and *cognomen*), it is difficult to ascertain from whose patronage his parents had benefited (see below) – an enfranchised person normally taking the *praenomen* (first or given name) and *nomen* (*gens* or clan name) of his patron (cf. Sherwin-White: 152f, and for the following discussion). Although Paul or Paulus is very rarely found as a *praenomen* – usually appearing as a *cognomen* ("nickname" [later family name]) (cf. Sergius

---

[5] Cf. Gen. 17:17f, 29:32-30:24; 1 Sam. 4:21; Isa. 7:3, 14f; Gen.R. 37:7.

[6] καὶ ἐκάλουν αὐτὸ ἐπὶ τῷ ὀνόματι τοῦ πατρὸς αὐτοῦ Ζαχαρίαν . . . καὶ εἶπαν πρὸς αὐτὴν ὅτι οὐδείς ἐστιν ἐκ τῆς συγγενείας σου ὃς καλεῖται τῷ ὀνόματι τούτῳ.

[7] This latter source (cf. also Lk. 2:21) also serves as evidence for the practice of naming sons at their circumcision. Although this custom is not mentioned in rabbinic sources other than in a late midrash, it nonetheless seems to have been prevalent during the first century (cf. Safrai and Stern: 767).

[8] For tribal names as "surnames," see below, **Ancestry**.

[9] Cf. Mekh.Pischa 5; TBE p. 85; Mid.Ps. 114:4.

[10] Cf. Tos.Git. 8[6]:4; JGit. 1, 1, 43b; Git. 11a-b, [14b].

Paulus – Acts 13:7) – a person's *cognomen* was commonly derived from a person's original personal name. If this was Greek it remained unchanged; if barbarian, it was either latinized or translated.

It is suggested in this regard that rather than deriving from a Roman patron, "Paulus" represents the most similar Latin name to Saul, many diaspora second names being of this "user-friendly" variety (cf. Bauckham, Acts: 105n277). It was apparently quite common for Jews to bear a Hebrew/Aramaic name for use in Jewish circles and a Greek/Latin name employed in gentile contexts.[11] On this reading, Paul and Saul could perhaps indeed be considered as synonyms, Paul arguably being a "translation" of Saul, although the literal Greek translation would more likely have been Ἔτητος (Etētos) (cf. Safrai and Stern: 1052). It is alternatively proposed that the choice of "biblical" names amongst diaspora Jews may have been influenced by similar-sounding non-Jewish names fashionable at a given place and period (cf. Stern, Identity: 193n329) – or that either one of the two names may represent a *supernomen* or *signum* ("epithet") (cf. Riesner: 145).

On the strength that Paul means "little" in Latin, Augustine suggested that Paul adopted the name out of modesty (cf. *Serm.* 27.3); (for an early description of Paul's appearance, see below). While הגדול (h-gadol – "the Great/Big") was commoner than הקטן/זעירה (ha-katan/zeira – "the Little/Small") as an epithet during the mishnaic and talmudic period, the latter remains well attested in this period (cf. שמואל הקטן, שמעון בן ננס, ינאי זעירא – Samuel the Little, Shimon son of the Dwarf, Jannai the Small) (cf. Hachlili: 197). Whether "Paul," in the sense of "little" can in any way represent "junior" (Jr.) in respect to his father is nevertheless far from certain.

Luke's sole reference to "Saul, who was also *known* as Paul (Σαῦλος δὲ, ὁ καὶ Παῦλος)" (Acts 13:9) may be understood in terms of distinguishing between two people bearing the same *cognomen*, since the notation occurs precisely where someone else bearing the same name appears – i.e., Sergius Paulus (cf. Rapske: 85f). (Although Luke uses ὁ καὶ [ho kai – "who was also"] in place of the more customary λεγόμενος [legomenos] or καλούμενος [kaloumenos] – which, in parallel to the Hebrew terms הקרוי [ha-karui] and המכונה [ha-mekhunei], designate "nicknames"[12] – it is difficult to ascertain precisely what weight to attribute to the divergence.)

The fact that the New Testament writings overwhelmingly prefer the name Paul should consequently not be overemphasised. The argument that Saul's name was changed to Paul following his "conversion" cannot

---

[11] Cf. Joseph/Justus (cf. Acts 1:23); Dorcas/Tabitha (cf. Acts 9:36); Silas/Silvanus (cf. Acts 15:32; 2 Cor. 1:19).
[12] Cf. Acts 10:5, 13:1; Jos.*Ant.* 15.252, [18.63], 20.200.

be sustained when it is not envisioned that Paul "converted" in the Christian understanding of the term. It is also unnecessary to suggest that "Paul" is used in light of the apostle's calling to the Gentiles. The use of a Latin name is quite natural in gentile contexts – and is particularly appropriate where Paul appeals to his Roman citizenship. Although an argument from silence, it is likely that Paul continued to be known as Saul in Jewish contexts. The fact that Paul uses his Latin *cognomen* freely[13] may indicate that he himself regarded it as a (mere) translation of Saul, especially since the New Testament documents suggest that it effectively served as Paul's *praenomen* (cf. Acts 13:9).[14]

Citizenship

According to Jerome, Paul's family apparently either moved at some point to Gischala (Gush Chalav) in the Galilee (later famous for the John who headed the zealot revolt in Jerusalem), remaining there until the town was taken by the Romans, or migrated/were transferred (*commigravit/fuisse translatos*) from Gush Chalav to Tarsus as a result of war, possibly in the disturbances of 4 B.C.E.[15] Since Jerome's account allows for the possibility that Paul's parents were taken to Tarsus as slaves, it might be inferred that Paul was born there following his father's manumission, thereby gaining Roman citizenship together with his father (cf. Taylor: 115). While the above dating is problematic, several disturbances occurred following Pompey's conquest in 63 B.C.E. during which Galilean Jews might have become Roman slaves (cf. Riesner: 152).

The numerous references to Tarsus (and Cilicia) in the New Testament suggest that the city played a significant function in Paul's life. He himself defines himself in reference to it (cf. Acts 21:39, 22:3), while he is identified to Ananias as "a man from Tarsus (ὀνόματι Ταρσέα)" (Acts 9:11). Both Acts and Galatians indicate that he was resident in Tarsus/Cilicia for some time (cf. Acts 9:30, 11:25; Gal. 1:21), and that Tarsus formed part of his sphere of ministry (cf. Acts 15:23, 41). Paul explicitly claims that he holds Tarsean citizenship (οὐκ ἀσήμου πόλεως πολίτης; ouk asēmou poleōs politēs).

Paul specifically states that he was born into Roman citizenship (Acts 22:28: ἐγὼ δὲ γεγέννημαι [egō de gegennēmai]). Roman citizenship was normally acquired either through inheritance (citizen-born), an *en bloc* grant, completion of military service, manumission, the granting of a

---

[13] Cf. Rom. 1:1; 1 Cor. 1:1, 16:21; Gal. 1:1.

[14] While slaves and free-born provincials took the personal name (*praenomen*) and surname (*nomen*) of the person granting the citizenship and retained their native name as family name (*cognomen*), their children were frequently given a full Roman name (cf. Rapske).

[15] Cf. Jerome, *De Vir.Ill.* 5; Jos.*Ant.* 17.286ff; *War* 2.66ff.

special (imperial) favour, or for financial considerations (cf. Rapske: 86; Sherwin-White: 144ff). As part of a Roman province, Tarsus' citizens were eligible to receive Roman citizenship (cf. Acts 23:34-35?), clear historical evidence existing that some (both hellenised and Torah-observant) Jews of Asia had obtained Roman citizenship in the first century B.C.E. (cf. Jos.*Ant.* 14.228ff; *CA* 2.38f).

While Josephus attests to the existence of Judaeans/Jerusalemites of equestrian rank – "men who, if Jews by birth, were at least invested with that Roman dignity (ἄνδρας ἱππικοῦ τάγματος . . . ὧν εἰ καὶ τὸ γένος Ἰουδαῖον ἀλλὰ γοῦν τὸ ἀξίωμα ʿΡωμαϊκὸν ἦν)" (*War* 2.308) – Galilean Jews may have possessed less opportunity to obtain Roman citizenship. Although Judaea became a Roman province in 6 C.E., Galilee and Peraea only came under direct Roman rule in 43/44 C.E. with Agrippa I's death. If, on the other hand, Paul's claim that he was a "son of Pharisees (υἱὸς Φαρισαίων)" (Acts 23:6) is to be taken literally, his parents (father) were Pharisees – and Judaeans (see below).

The question concerning the manner in which Paul's parents received citizenship possesses implications for Paul's own status. Although Paul "outranked" Lysias since he had been born into citizenship whereas Lysias had bought his status, Paul lay outside the ranks of Roman aristocracy in other respects, presumably not belonging to either of the two most prestigious orders, the senatorial and equestrian, whose ranks were composed – apart from senators and knights – of soldiers and veterans with their children, and holders of municipal offices in towns outside Rome together with their descendants (cf. Carcopino: 52ff). Thus, unless his father had served in the army or held a municipal post in Tarsus – the first perhaps being more probable than the second – he would have ranked among the plebeians (*humiliores*). On the other hand, as a Roman citizen he would have outranked freedpersons and *peregrini* (citizens of any city other than Rome). It is unlikely that he would have been sufficiently wealthy to cross the line into the ranks of the aristocracy. Although the New Testament witnesses to his consistent preference of his Jewish over his Roman identity, Paul was aware of this system and was prepared to use it when forced to – as he was also treated according to its laws by other Romans.[16]

The claim that Paul's father was a Pharisee is difficult to substantiate. Whereas evidence concerning Pharisees in Eretz Israel is abundant, their presence in diaspora communities seems completely lacking – although some scholars have suggested that Gamaliel the Elder's letter to the diaspora communities regarding the intercalation of a month (cf. Tos.San. 2:6; San. 11a) may have been written to Jews of pharisaic allegiance in Babylonia and Media (the named destinations), without being certain just

---

[16] Cf. Acts 16:37f, 22:25ff, 23:27, 25:8f, 16, 21, 25, 26:32, 28:19.

whom they might have been (cf. Neusner: 1:358-89) (see also below, **Pharisaic background**). Perhaps the best support for the view that such communities existed comes from the claim that Matthew 23:15 indicates pharisaic efforts to make (Jewish) converts to their own party, although this interpretation of the verse is not widely accepted (cf. Levinskaya: 35ff).[17] The Ananias and Eleazar who "converted" members of the royal house of Adiabene were also apparently living at least temporarily in the kingdom (cf. Jos.*Ant.* 20.34ff).

The expressions בן פרוש/פרושים (ben parush[im]) or בני חכמים (bnei chakhamim) occur most frequently in the sense of "disciples."[18] Despite the fact that master and disciple were considered like father and son, little evidence seems to exist that the epithets denoted familial relations.[19] Paul's usage here should perhaps thus be taken to refer to his education under Gamaliel and/or as a member of a pharisaic חבורה (havura – "association") (cf. Jeremias, Jerusalem: 252n26). (Some scholars suggest that בן [ben] – like משפחה [mishpacha – "family"] – serves as a reference to the "member [chaver]" of a guild. Given that sons frequently followed their father's profession [see below, **Occupation**], it seems quite likely that the guilds were heavily influenced by familial and dynastic ties [cf. Hachlili: 195]. Pharisaic associates were similarly known as בני חבורה [bnei chavura – lit.: "sons of the fellowship"] and/or בני כנסת [bnei Knesset – lit.: "sons of the assembly].[20]) The fact that Paul uses this particular designation precisely in front of the Sanhedrin, composed of both parties, may confirm this view (cf. also Acts 22:3; Phil. 3:5-6). On the other hand, Paul's description of the designees of his letters as "brethren (ἀδελφοὺς)" (Acts 22:5) should not be made to carry more than its normal usage: They are fellow Jews – as well as Jesus' disciples – and not specifically Pharisees.

Education

The evidence in Acts and Paul's own letters provides a detailed "curriculum vitae." Although Paul was born in Tarsus, he was "brought up in this city [Jerusalem] (ἀνατεθραμμένος δὲ ἐν τῇ πόλει ταύτῃ)" and "educated at the feet of Gamaliel, strictly according to the law of our fathers, being zealous for God (παρὰ τοὺς πόδας Γαμαλιὴλ πεπαιδευμένος κατὰ ἀκρίβειαν τοῦ πατρῴου νόμου, ζηλωτὴς ὑπάρχων

---

[17] This verse does appear to have direct repercussions with regard to proselytism in Galatia, in Paul's verbal recollection of it in 4:17 (see the commentary on 2:15-21 and 4:12-20).

[18] Cf. Mt. 12:27; Lk. 11:19; Tos.San. 7:9; Sem. 3:4; Hor. 13b.

[19] Cf. 1 Cor. 4:15; 1 Thess. [2:7], 11; 1 Tim. 1:2, 18; 2 Tim. 1:2, 2:1; Tit. 1:4; Phlm 10; 1 Pet. 5:13; CD-A 13:9; 1QH[a] 15:20; 4Q267 f9iv:6; 11QPs[a] 21:14f; Sif.Dt. 34; TBE p. 80; BM 2:11; Eruv. 73a.

[20] Cf. Pes. 7:3, 8:4; Zav. 3:2; Tos.Pes. 7:6f; Tos.Meg. 3[2]:1; Kal.Rab. 1:8; Pes. 102a; Eruv. 85b.

τοῦ θεοῦ)" (Acts 22:3). While it is difficult to pinpoint the date of Paul's birth, several indications may be adduced. Luke first introduces him as a "young man (νεανίου)" (Acts 7:58) – a term which denotes an age range between 24-40 (cf. BAGD: 534). The lower limit is roughly confirmed by the discovery of the Gymnasiarchal Law of Beroea, which distinguishes between παῖδες (paides) – children up to age fifteen, ἔφηβοι (efēboi) – ages 15-17, and νεανίσκοι (νέοι) (neaniskoi/neoi) – ages 18-22 (cf. ibid: 330; McRay, *Archaeology*: 372). Although this testimony provides little evidence to determine the upper limit of *neanias* and thus Paul's possible age when Luke first introduces him, Paul speaks of himself in Philemon 9 as πρεσβύτης (presbytēs) – an "old man." On the calculation that Paul wrote to Philemon either around 52/54 or 57-59 and that the remark is appropriate to a man who has attained or just passed his mid-50's (cf. "sixty – for mature age" [PA 5:21; Philo, *Opif.Mun.* 103-5]) and notices that the vigour of his earlier years has begun to decrease, scholars cautiously ascribe Paul's date of birth to the turn of the century (cf. Riesner: 214; Murphy-O'Connor, *Critical*: 4). This would make him approximately the right age for an ordained Sage, if rather young.

Paul's comment that he was "brought up (ἀνατεθραμμένος)" in Jerusalem should probably be understood to refer to the time prior to his discipleship under Rabban Gamaliel (see below, **Gamaliel**). Numerous examples of diaspora Jews coming to study in Eretz Israel and becoming well known Sages exist, Jerusalem being regarded as "the mother city not of one country Judaea but of most of the others (μητρόπολις δὲ οὐ μιᾶς χώρας Ἰουδαίας ἀλλὰ καὶ τῶν πλείστων)" (Philo, *Leg.* 281). It was said: "All may be compelled to go up to the Land of Israel but none may be compelled to leave it. All may be compelled to go up to Jerusalem but none may be compelled to leave it, whether they be men or women הכל מעלין לארץ ישראל, ואין הכל מוציאין. הכל מעלין לירושלים, ואין הכל מוציאין, אחד האנשים ואחד הנשים" (Ket. 13:11).

Hillel the Elder was nicknamed "the Babylonian" because he was descended from a family of Babylonian exiles, and the families of Bathyra and R. Hiyya both originated in Babylon.[21] Towards the end of the Second Temple period, Nahum the Mede and Hanan the Egyptian acted as "judges of civil law [דַּיָּנֵי גְזֵירוֹת]" in Jerusalem – an office apparently under the aegis of the Sanhedrin.[22] Josephus also records that Izates of Adiabene sent "five sons of tender age [to Jerusalem] to get a thorough knowledge of our native language and culture (πεπομφὼς πέντε μὲν τὸν ἀριθμὸν υἱοὺς τὴν ἡλικίαν νέους γλῶτταν τὴν παρ' ἡμῖν πάτριον καὶ παιδείαν ἀκριβῶς μαθησομένους)" (*Ant.* 20.71).

---

[21] Cf. Gen.R. 26:4; Pe'ah 3:6; Suk. 20a; San. 5a; Pes. 66a; Ker. 8a.
[22] Cf. Ket. 13:1; Shab. 2:1; Naz. 5:4; BB 5:2; AZ 7b; Ket. 105a.

The Mishnah states: "Five years [is the age] for [the study of] Scripture, ten – for [the study of] the Mishna, thirteen – for [becoming subject to] commandments, fifteen – for [the study of] Talmud, eighteen – for the [bridal] canopy, twenty – for pursuing [a vocation], thirty – for [full] strength, forty – for understanding, fifty – for [ability to give] counsel, sixty – for mature age, seventy – for a hoary head, eighty [is a sign of superadded] strength, ninety [is the age] for [a] bending [figure], at a hundred, one is as one that is dead, having passed and ceased from the world"[23] (PA 5:21).

While some scholars suggest that Paul originally came on pilgrimage and simply stayed on – as was the custom of many (cf. Safrai and Stern: 193) – no good reason appears to exist to exclude the possibility that Paul was in fact raised in Jerusalem. While his statement in Acts 26:4 that "from my youth up, which from the beginning was spent among my *own* nation and at Jerusalem (ἐκ νεότητος τὴν ἀπ᾽ ἀρχῆς γενομένην ἐν τῷ ἔθνει μου ἐν τε Ἱεροσολύμοις)" may represent two phases – the "beginning" referring to Tarsus and "Jerusalem" later – he might then have been expected to speak of his "birth" rather than his youth. The particle τε (te) not only links clauses or sentences which serve to explain and/or amplify but also connects single parallel nouns and pronouns so that the two combined ideas form a whole (cf. Smyth: 666) – the remark itself failing to indicate when Paul moved to Jerusalem.

It might be speculated that Paul lived with his sister and her family, although his nephew's evident familiarity with Paul does not indicate under what circumstances he was acquainted with his uncle – nor conclusively the family's acquaintance with the nation's leaders. The fact that Paul's nephew is present in Jerusalem when a plot is instituted against Paul's life (cf. Acts 23:16f) provides little evidence regarding the family's residence, especially since the event apparently took place at Shavuot (cf. Acts 20:16). Nor does the τῶν ἰδίων αὐτοῦ (tōn idiōn autou – "his own") of Acts 24:23 necessarily indicate immediate family or relatives if Acts 4:23 is taken as determinative, the latter reference obviously alluding to (members of) the community in general.

Talmudic sources regularly distinguish between the בית ספר (beit sefer) – "house of the book" wherein the סופר (sofer) taught reading of the written Torah – and the בית תלמוד (beit talmud) – the "house of learning" in which the משנה (mashneh) taught Mishnah or Oral Torah (cf. Safrai and Stern: 950ff, and for the following discussion). Children learnt the alphabet and how to read in the former, the teacher writing the letters on a small

---

[23] יהודה בן תימה היה אומר: בן חמש שנים למקרא, בן עשר למשנה, בן שלוש עשרה למצות, בן חמש עשרה לתלמוד, בן שמונה עשרה לחופה, בן עשרים לרדוף, בן שלושים לכוח, בן ארבעים לבינה, בן חמשים לעצה, בן ששים לזקנה, בן שבעים לשיבה, בן שמונים לגבורה, בן תשעים לשוח, בן מאה כאילו מת ועבר ובטל מן העולם.

wax tablet with a stylus and the pupils reciting them aloud (cf. ARNᵃ 6:2). Reading skills were attained through repetition after the teacher and auditive memory since the scriptural text was not vocalized, students being dependent on the teacher's precision in orally transmitting the precise reading for every passage.

Young children were taught how to read and understand the Torah and Prophets, to recite the Shema and the basic blessings over food, and received instruction regarding their future roles in family and communal life (cf. ARNb 13). While the later biblical books, the apocryphal literature, Philo, Josephus, and tannaitic sources all witness to obligatory Torah-study solely for boys, the fact that women were required to recite various blessings and were involved in their children's education indicates that girls received some instruction, although it was normally considered an "ornament."[24] Numerous dicta speak of the interdiction against teaching women Torah, one of the reasons being that study took a wife away from her household duties[25] (cf. Ilan: 191f).

Following five years of Bible study, students moved on to study of the Oral Torah (cf. PA 5:21). These studies were also conducted orally and in the process of committing texts to memory pupils were encouraged to ask and answer questions. According to most Second Temple sources, the school was connected to the synagogue, instruction taking place in a prayer hall or study room (cf. JKet. 13, 1, 35c). Studies began early in the morning on every day of the week, although no new material was learnt on shabbat, and finished around twelve o'clock (cf. Pes.Rab. 43:8).

School studies finished at the age of twelve or thirteen (bar mitzva age) and if a boy was gifted and so inclined he could then enroll at a beit midrash to study Torah with other adults who devoted themselves to Torah-study in their spare time. If he showed further ability and willingness he could go to one of the famous Sages and learn with him for a number of years[26] (cf. Safrai and Stern: 953). No continuous formal educational system seems to have existed past bar mitzva age during this period. A midrash provides "statistics" regarding how many reached the peak of the learning process: "Usually if a thousand men take up the study of Scripture, a hundred of them proceed to the study of Mishnah, ten to Talmud, and one of them becomes qualified to decide decisions of law בנוהג שבעולם אלף בני אדם נכנסין למקרא, יוצאין מהן מאה, יוצאין מהן עשרה. למשנה, יוצאין מהן אחד להוראה, יוצא מהם אחד לתלמוד" (Eccl.R. 7.28.1) (Lev.R. 2:1). Paul may be alluding to this circumstance when he says "I was advancing in Judaism beyond many of my contemporaries among my countrymen (καὶ

---

[24] Cf. Jos.*CA* 2.181; JPe'ah 3a; JSot. 46b; JShab. 34a.
[25] Cf. Sot. 3:4; JSot. 3, 4, 19a; Yoma 66b; Kid. 30a.
[26] Cf. PA 1:4, 6, 16, 5:21; ARNᵃ 3:6, 8:1f; AZ 19a.

προέκοπτον ἐν τῷ Ἰουδαϊσμῷ ὑπὲρ πολλοὺς συνηλικιώτας ἐν τῷ γένει μου)" (Gal. 1:14).[27]

Josephus describes his education in terms similar to Paul's own: "Brought up with Matthias, my own brother by both parents, I made great progress in my education, gaining a great reputation for an excellent memory and understanding. While still a mere boy, about fourteen years old, I won universal applause for my love of letters; insomuch that the chief priests and the leading men of the city used constantly to come to me for precise information on some particular in our ordinances. At about the age of sixteen I determined to gain personal experience of the several sects into which our nation is divided . . ."[28] (*Life* 8-10). The fact that Paul's prestige corresponds to that to which Josephus gained distinguishes him as one of the foremost figures of his age, a person of great distinction and learning, among the best minds and exemplary characters in the rabbinic world of the period.

Pharisaic background

Paul describes himself as "a Pharisee according to the strictest sect of our religion . . . zealous for my ancestral traditions (κατὰ τὴν ἀκριβεστάτην αἵρεσιν τῆς ἡμετέρας θρησκείας ἔζησα Φαρισαῖος . . . ζηλωτὴς ὑπάρχων τῶν πατρικῶν παραδόσεων)" (Acts 26:5; Gal. 1:14).[29] The title "Pharisee [פרוש]" in fact occurs rarely outside of the gospels: Josephus and Paul are the only two men who describe themselves as Pharisees,[30] while Rabban Gamaliel is called a Pharisee only in Acts 5:34 and his son, Simon, is thus designated only in Josephus (cf. *Life* 191) (see above, **Citizenship**; below, **Gamaliel**).

Josephus describes the Pharisees as those "considered the most accurate interpreters of the laws, and hold the position of the leading sect (οἱ μετ' ἀκριβείας δοκοῦντες ἐξηγεῖσθαι τὰ νόμιμα καὶ τὴν πρώτην ἀπάγοντες αἵρεσιν)" (*War* 2.162), being devoted to the "tradition of the

---

[27] Alternatively, he might be referring to a particularly strict observance of ritual purity. In this case it might be posited that Paul had become a חבר (chaver) or "associate."

[28] ἐγὼ δὲ συμπαιδευόμενος ἀδελφῷ Ματθίᾳ τοὔνομα, γεγόνει γὰρ μοι γνήσιος ἐξ ἀμφοῖν τῶν γονέων, εἰς μεγάλην παιδείας προύκοπτον ἐπίδοσιν, μνήμῃ τε καὶ συνέσει δοκῶν διαφέρειν ἔτι δ' ἀντίπαις ὢν περὶ τεσσαρεσκαιδέκατον ἔτος διὰ τὸ φιλογράμματον ὑπὸ πάντων ἐπῃνούμην, συνιόντων ἀεὶ τῶν ἀρχιερέων καὶ τῶν τῆς πόλεως πρώτων ὑπὲρ τοῦ παρ' ἐμοῦ περὶ τῶν νομίμων ἀκριβέστερόν τι γνῶναι. περὶ ἑκκαίδεκα δὲ ἔτη γενόμενος ἐβουλήθην τῶν παρ' ἡμῖν αἱρέσεων ἐμπειρίαν λαβεῖν.

[29] Cf. Mk. 7:3; Acts 22:3, 23:6, 24:14; 2 Cor. 11:6; Phil. 3:6; Jos.*Ant.* 12.271, 13.297; Philo, *Spec.Leg.* 1.186; *Leg.All.* 3.242.

[30] Cf. Acts 23:6, 26:5; Phil. 3:5; Jos. *Life* 12.

fathers"[31] – i.e., the "oral law" whose development was the hallmark of the pharisaic Sages.[32] Their halakhic enactments were generally accepted as authoritative by the people, who expressed their admiration for the Sages and readily performed acts in the Temple contrary to the views of the high priests, a circumstance which at times led to violent clashes.[33]

Although the Pharisees' influence among the people extended to all areas of life through the halakhot (decrees) which they issued regulating property, family matters, agriculture, ritual purity, civil laws, and shabbat and holidays, pharisaic "strictness (ἀκριβεστάτην αἵρεσιν)" was perhaps demonstrated most specifically in the areas of ritual purity and tithing (cf. Oppenheimer). These laws were observed in particular by חברים (chaverim – "associates"). Membership in the חבורה (chavura – "association") involved a probationary period and further preparatory stages before final admission: "They proceed to accept him if he undertakes to observe cleanness of hands, and afterwards he is accepted for the observance of the laws of purity. If he takes upon himself the observance of the cleanness of hands alone, he is accepted. If he takes upon himself the observance of the laws of purity but has not taken upon himself the observance of the cleanness of hands, he is not deemed to be trustworthy even with regard to the laws of purity. How long is the period that has to elapse before he is accepted as a chaver? Beit Shammai say, As regards the purity of liquids, the period is thirty days, and as regards the purity of his garments, the period is twelve months, whereas Beit Hillel say, In both cases the period is thirty days"[34] (Tos.Dem. 2:11-12) (cf. Mk. 7:4f; Bek. 30b).

The conditions of observance are similarly laid out in detail in the tannaitic literature, most particularly with regard to the am ha-aretz, who was considered the antithesis of the associate with regard to the observance of tithing and purity laws: "He who takes upon himself four things is accepted as a haver: that he will not give terumah [heave-offering to the priest] and tithes to an am ha-aretz, that he will not prepare his food in the observance of the laws of ritual purity with an am ha-aretz, and that he will eat his secular food in a state of purity . . . He that undertakes to be

---

[31] Cf. Mk. 7:8ff; Jos.*Ant.* 13.297.

[32] For Paul's hillelite or shammaite background, see below, **Persecutor**.

[33] Cf. 4QpNah ff3-4i:2-6, ii:8-12, iii:3-8; 4QpHos 2:5-6; 4QpPs[a] 3:5-13; Tos.Suk. 3:1; Yoma 71b. The Qumran pesharim not only confirm the triple sectarian character of Second Temple Judaism (Pharisees, Sadducees, and Essenes), but also reflect the widespread influence wielded by the Pharisees over the general populace, whom the Qumran community accused the former of misleading and deceiving *en masse* (cf. Flusser, Pharisees).

[34] והולכין ומקבלין לכנפים ואחר כך מקבלין אתו לטהרות ואם אינו מקבל עליו אלא לכנפים בלבד מקבלין אתו. קיבל עליו לטהרות ולא קיבל עליו לכנפים, אף על הטהרות אינו נאמן. עד מתי מקבלין? בית שמאי אומרים: למשקין שלשים יום ולכסות שנים עשר חודש. ובית הילל אומרים: זה וזה שלשים יום.

an associate may not sell to an am ha-aretz [foodstuff that is] wet or dry, or buy from him [foodstuff that is] wet; and he may not be the guest of an am ha-aretz nor may he receive him as a guest in his own raiment"[35] (Tos.Dem. 2:2; Dem. 2:3).[36] (If Paul was an associate, his travels outside Eretz Israel in the impure "lands of the Gentiles" would not necessarily have disqualified him, it being ruled that "an associate who went outside the Land is not dismissed from his fellowship" [JDem. 2, 3, 23a].)

Acts 15:5 speaks of the "sect of the Pharisees (αἵρεσις τῶν Φαρισαίων)" as a common description for the "school of thought" or philosophy – in Josephus' words – which, alongside the Sadducees, Essenes, and Zealots, formed one of the main parties within Second Temple Judaism.[37] According to Josephus, the Pharisees' moderate living, observance of the commandments, respect of and deference to their elders – together with their acknowledgment of both providence and human will and their belief in resurrection – made them "extremely influential among the townsfolk; and all prayers and sacred rites of divine worship are performed according to their exposition. This is the great tribute that the inhabitants of the cities, by practising the highest ideals both in their way of living and in their discourse, have paid to the excellence of the Pharisees"[38] (*Ant.* 18.15).[39]

Although this portrait has largely provided the basis for the traditional view that the pharisaic movement was exclusively religious – in direct contrast to the political activism of the Sadducees (cf. Alon, Attitude: 54ff) – the involvement of numerous prominent Pharisees in the nation's life, as well as the fact that pharisaic halakhah was designed to regulate and reform all aspects of worldly affairs, including the juridical, civil, and criminal spheres, public and political law, and rulings concerning royalty, indicates that the Pharisees were a broad-based party.

While being known as the "strictest sect of our religion (ἀκριβεστάτην αἵρεσιν τῆς ἡμετέρας θρησκείας)" (Acts 26:5), the Pharisees also frequently served as a synonym for (religious) hypocrisy.[40]

---

[35] המקבל עליו ארבעה דברים מקבלין אותו להיות חבר : שלא יתן תרומה ומעשרות לעם הארץ, ושלא יעשה טהרותיו אצל עם הארץ, ושיהא אוכל חולין בטהרה . . . המקבל עליו להיות חבר - אינו מוכר לעם הארץ לח ויבש, ואינו לוקח ממנו לח, ואינו מתארח אצל עם הארץ, ולא מארחו אצלו בכסותו.

[36] Cf. CD-A 12:15f; 4Q284a; 4QMMTᵃ f8iv:5f; 4QMMTᶜ 2:5f.
[37] Cf. Acts 5:17, 26:5; Jos.*Ant.* 13.171f, 288, 293f, 18.11f; *War* 2.162f; *Life* 10f; Hipp.*Ref.Omn.Her.* 9.23.
[38] τοῖς τε δήμοις πιθανώτατοι τυγχάνουσιν καὶ ὁπόσα θεῖα εὐχῶν τε ἔχεται καὶ ἱερῶν ποιήσεως ἐξηγήσει τῇ ἐκείνων τυγχάνουσιν πρασσόμενα. εἰς τοσόνδε ἀρετῆς αὐτοῖς αἱ πόλεις ἐμαρτύρησαν ἐπιτηδεύσει τοῦ ἐπὶ πᾶσι κρείσσονος ἔν τε τῇ διαίτῃ τοῦ βίου καὶ λόγοις.
[39] Cf. *Ant.* 13.288, 298; *War* 2.166.
[40] Cf. Mt. 23:1ff; Lk. 11:39ff; CD-A 4:19, 8:12; 1QHᵃ 12:6ff; JBer. 67a; JSot. 25a; Sot. 22b.

Among the seven types of Pharisee are listed the "shoulder-Pharisee who lays commandments on men's shoulders שיכמי: טעין מצוותא על כיתפא," the "*nikpi* Pharisee" who walks with exaggerated humility [פרוש נקפי - זה המנקיף] את רגליו, the "*kizai* Pharisee" who knocks his head against the wall in order to avoid looking at a woman (or sets off a bad deed by performing a good one) [פרוש קיזאי ... זה המקיז דם לכתלים], the "pestle Pharisee" whose head is bowed like a pestle in a mortar [פרוש מדוכיא ... דמשפע כי מדוכיא], and the Pharisee who constantly exclaims "what further duty can I perform that I have not already done! מה חובתי תן ואעשנה."[41] Jesus speaks of similar hypocritical behaviour precisely in the language of burdening: ". . . they tie up heavy loads, and lay them on men's shoulders; but they themselves are unwilling to move them with *so much as* a finger (δεσμεύουσιν δὲ φορτία βαρέα καὶ ἐπιτιθέασιν ἐπὶ τοὺς ὤμους τῶν ἀνθρώπων, αὐτοὶ δὲ τῷ δακτύλῳ αὐτῶν οὐ θέλουσιν κινῆσαι αὐτά)" (Mt. 23:4) (cf. Lk. 11:46) (cf. Flusser, Jesus: 68ff).[42]

Gamaliel

Since Gamaliel was such a distinguished teacher it may be presumed that Paul began to study with him only after he had demonstrated great promise and had reached an age whereby he could profit from learning under a great master. Gamaliel (flourished c. 20-40 C.E.) was Hillel's (grand)son (Shabbat 15a implies that his father was Simeon) and according to rabbinic sources acted as נשיא (Nasi – President) of the Sanhedrin during the time of the Emperor Caligula (37-41 C.E.) (cf. Shab. 15a). The house of Hillel constituted a unique example of a family originating from the diaspora, with no priestly connections, which attained the position of hereditary leaders of the nation until, in the time of Rabbi Judah ha-Nasi (170-200 C.E.), its members gained official recognition by the Roman government as Patriarchs. Beit Hillel produced three pre-eminent personalities in succession, Rabban Gamaliel the Elder being the first Sage esteemed with the honorific title of Rabban – "our master."

Gamaliel served as one of the foremost teachers of the בית מדרש (beit midrash – college or "seminary") conducted by the pharisaic leaders within the Sanhedrin.[43] Disciples frequently sat on the floor – or at a lower level – than their master, who sat either on a pillow or on a chair (καθέδρα).[44] Although a baraita claims that "From the days of Moses up to Rabban Gamaliel, the Torah was learnt only standing. When Rabban Gamaliel died, feebleness descended on the world, and they learnt the

---

[41] Cf. Mt. [6:16], 23:4, 15; Lk. 11:46; JBer. 67a; JSot. 25a; Sot. 22b.

[42] For the significance of this concept for Galatians, see Introduction, **Argument**.

[43] Cf. Git. 4:2-3; RH 2:5; Sot. 9:15; Tos.San. 2:6.

[44] Cf. Mt. 23:2; Lk. 2:46, [8:35], 10:39; PRK 1:7; Sifre, Pinchas 140; Yalk.Num. 771; Ex.R. 43:4; PA 1:4; ARNᵃ 6:2; Meg. 21a; Betza 15b; Ber. 27b; San. 107b.

תנו רבנן: מימות משה ועד רבן גמליאל לא היו למדין תורה אלא מעומד. Torah sitting
משמת רבן גמליאל ירד חולי לעולם והיו למדין תורה מיושב" (Meg. 21a) (cf. Yalk.Dt.
831), the practice of sitting had obviously become customary some time
before.[45] Simeon of Mizpeh, Joezer of Ha-Birah, and Nehemiah of Beit Dali
are all said to have consulted and/or studied under Rabban Gamaliel.[46]

Rabban Gamaliel evaluated students according to four categories
based on different types of fish: "As regards disciples Rabban Gamaliel the
Elder discerned four types: the unclean fish, the clean fish, the Jordan fish
and the Great Sea fish. 'The unclean fish' – what is meant by this? [It
describes] the son of poor parents [or: the student of poor intellect] who,
though he has learnt Scripture, Mishnah, *halakoth* and *'aggadoth*, remains
without understanding [i.e., useless]. 'The clean fish' – what is meant by
this? [It describes] the son of wealthy parents [or: the student of rich
intellect] who, when he had learnt Scripture, Mishnah, *halakoth* and
'aggadoth, has understanding [through a combination of wealth and
learning (cf. Prov. 14:24)]. 'The Jordan fish' – what is meant by this? [It
describes] the student who has learnt Scripture, Mishnah, Midrash,
halakoth and *'aggadoth*, but lacks the ability to discuss it [the Jordan fish
being small and narrow, the student is likened to a person with limited
knowledge who cannot develop it through argument]. 'The Great Sea fish'
– what is meant by this? [It describes] the student who has learnt Scripture,
Mishnah, Midrash, *halakoth* and *'aggadoth*, and has the ability to discuss it
[the Great Sea or mediterranean fish being large, this type of disciple is
proficient and discerning and can interpret the Torah correctly through
argumentation]"[47] (ARNa 40:9).

In the initial stages of their studies, young men would usually be
taught by a single distinguished scholar, under whom a student studied
for years, receiving most of his Torah education from him: "Provide
yourself with a teacher. What does this mean? It teaches that a man should
provide himself with a permanent teacher from whom he may learn
Scripture, Mishnah, Midrash, *halakah* and *'aggadoth*. Accordingly, points
which the teacher omitted to tell him in Scripture he can teach him later in
the Mishnah, [what he omitted in the Mishnah he can teach him later in the
Midrash], what he omitted in the Midrash he can teach him later in the
halakoth, and finally what he omitted in the *halakoth* he can teach him in the
'aggadoth. Consequently, this man remains in his place and is replete with
well-being and blessing. R. Meir used to say: He who learns Torah from

---

[45] Cf. Mt. 23:1; Lk. [8:35], 10:39; PA 1:4; Meg. 21a.
[46] Cf. Pe'ah 2:6; Orla 2:12; Yev. 16:7.
[47] לענין תלמידים דרש רבן גמליאל הזקן ארבעה דברים: דג טמא דג טהור דג מן הירדן דג מן הים
הגדול. דג טמא כיצד? בן עניים שלמד מקרא ומשנה הלכות ואגדות ואין בו דעה. דג טהור כיצד? זה
בן עשירים שלמד מקרא ומשנה הלכות ואגדות ויש בו דעה. דג מן הירדן כיצד? זה תלמיד חכם
שלמד מקרא ומשנה מדרש הלכות ואגדות ואין בו דעת להשיב. דג מן הים הגדול כיצד? זה תלמיד
חכם שלמד מקרא ומשנה מדרש הלכות ואגדות ויש בו דעת להשיב.

one teacher, to what can he be compared? To a man who has but one field; he sowed it partly with wheat and partly with barley, in another part he planted olive-trees and in still another fruit-trees. The consequence is that this man is [in one place and is] replete with well-being and blessing"[48] (ARN[a] 8:1-2).[49]

Both in their personal relations and also in the eyes of the halakhah, students frequently forged a deep bond with their teacher, establishing a relationship of love and respect (cf. Steinsaltz, Talmud: 22f, and for the following discussion). In Eretz Israel, this relationship was at times considered to be even more important than that between father and son. The subject matter for study centred around three major areas: Bible, midrash (creative biblical interpretation), and aggadah (narrative elaboration of the biblical text). Although the great, well-known Sages left their imprint on all three disciplines, some teachers specialised in the collection and preservation of halakhot and did not engage in midrash at all, whereas specific study of the bible, including textual problems, exact readings, and similar subjects, was undertaken by specialists [בעלי מקרא] mostly associated with the Sanhedrin. Paul's familiarity with the biblical text is demonstrated, among other ways, by the fact that he quotes (explicitly) from the Tanakh over ninety times in his letters, engaging with the biblical text and interpreting it employing the standard hermeneutical rules both halakhically and aggadically (cf. Shulam and Le Cornu).[50]

Status

A man was considered to be a student (תלמיד; talmid) his whole life unless and until he was ordained (נסמך; nismakh) upon appointment to public office. A late rabbinic source indicates that the "canonical" age for ordination to the Sanhedrin was forty (cf. Sot. 22b), appointment being for life (cf. Safrai and Stern: 390f). In the tannaitic era (to the end of the C2), the Sage of each beit midrash (study house) was authorised to ordain his pupils and would co-opt two of his colleagues. While it seems evident that ordination was a pharisaic custom, regarded as the continuation of the chain of tradition of the Torah through successive generations which granted authority to teach it and to direct the public,[51] it appears in practice

---

[48] עשה לך רב. כיצד? מלמד שיעשה לו את רבו קבע וילמד ממנו מקרא ומשנה מדרש הלכות ואגדות. טעם שהניח לו במקרא - סוף שיאמר לו במשנה. טעם שהניח לו במדרש - סוף שיאמר לו בהלכות. טעם שהניח לו בהלכות - סוף שיאמר לו בהגדה. נמצא האדם ההוא [יושב במקומו] ומלא טוב וברכה: היה רבי מאיר אומר: הלומד תורה מרב אחד, למה הוא דומה? לאחד שהיה לו שדה אחת וזרע מקצתה חטים ומקצתה שעורים ובמקצתה זיתים ובמקצתה אילנות ונמצא האדם ההוא מלא טובה וברכה.

[49] Cf. ARN[a] 3:6; ARN[b] 18; AZ 19a.
[50] See Introduction, **Theological pointers**.
[51] Cf. PA 1:1; Sifre, Pinchas 140; San. 13b.

to have constituted an institutional act conducted by a court of law in the presence of at least three judges (cf. Safrai and Stern: 390f).

Following ordination, some scholars were admitted to the Sanhedrin at a certain rank. The highest order was that of scholars who sat on the בית דין של שבעה (beit din shel shiv'ah) or Court of Seven, which dealt with the intercalation of the year and to which only the most eminent scholars were elected (cf. San. 1:2; San. 10b-11a) (cf. Steinsaltz, Talmud: 23). Rabbinic texts specify the qualifications to be met by those seeking appointment to the Sanhedrin: "R. Johanan said: None are to be appointed to be members of the Sanhedrin, but men of stature, wisdom, good appearance, mature age, with a knowledge of sorcery, and who are conversant with all the seventy languages of mankind, in order that the court should have no need of an interpreter. Rab Judah said in Rab's name: None is to be given a seat on the Sanhedrin unless he is able to prove the cleanness of a reptile from Biblical texts"[52] (San. 17a).[53]

A tannaitic tradition stipulates that in capital cases (cf. Acts 26:10), only those possessed of priestly, levitical, or Israelite status whose daughters were fit to marry into priestly stock were eligible to vote (cf. San. 4:2; Kid. 4:1ff). Although these three groups were permitted to intermarry, priests were subject to strict conditions which in practice led them to prefer marrying into another priestly family (cf. Pes. 49a) (cf. Jeremias, Jerusalem: 214ff, and for the following discussion). According to Scripture, a priest is forbidden to marry a harlot, a woman who has been defiled or seduced, a divorcee, a woman released from levirate marriage (יבמה; yebama), a widow, a proselyte, or a manumitted slave, although with the exception of the high priest the latter ordinance was not generally observed.[54]

This meant that only the (virgin) daughter of a priest or levite qualified to officiate or of a pure-bred Israelite was eligible to marry a priest, and the Sages demanded close scrutiny of the woman's ancestry: "If a man would marry a woman of priestly stock, he must trace her family back through four mothers, which are, indeed, eight: her mother, mother's mother, and mother's father's mother, and this one's mother; also her father's mother and this one's mother, her father's father's mother, and this one's mother. [If he would marry] a woman of levitic or Israelitish stock, he must trace the descent back to one mother more"[55] (Kid. 4:4).

---

[52] אמר רבי יוחנן : אין מושיבין בסנהדרי אלא בעלי קומה ובעלי חכמה ובעלי מראה ובעלי זקנה ובעלי כשפים ויודעים בשבעים לשון, שלא תהא סנהדרי שומעת מפי המתורגמן. אמר רב יהודה אמר רב: אין מושיבין בסנהדרין אלא מי שיודע לטהר את השרץ מן התורה.

[53] Cf. [CD-A 14:9f]; Dt.R. 1:10; Yalk.Ezra 1067; Tos.Shek. 3:27; San. 36b; Men. 65a.

[54] Cf. Lev. 21:7, 13f; Ezek. 44:22; Jos.*Ant.* 3.277; Philo, *Spec.Leg.* 1.107; Sifra, Emor 2; Yev. 6:4-5.

[55] הנושא אישה כהנת צריך לבדוק אחריה ארבע אמהות, שהן שמונה: אמה, ואם אמה, ואם אבי אמה ואמה, ואם אביה ואמה, ואם אבי אביה ואמה. לויה וישראלית - מוסיפין עליהן עוד אחת.

Since no evidence exists to indicate that Paul came from a priestly family – he was a Benjamite (see below) – he must have possessed pure-bred Israelite ancestry in order to be able to serve as a judge. Proof of pure ancestry was required for membership in the Sanhedrin (Great or small): "All [of the family stocks] are qualified to try non-capital cases; but all are not qualified to try capital cases, only priests, levites, and Israelites that may give [their daughters] in marriage to the priestly stock הכל כשרין לדון דיני ממונות ואין הכל כשרין לדון דיני נפשות, אלא כהנים, לוים, וישראלים המשיאין לכהנה" (San. 4:2).[56] A further restriction was imposed on men without sons who, even if their ancestry was pure, were denied membership in the Sanhedrin on the grounds that lack of male issue reflected a blemish and divine punishment.[57]

Since judges were similarly required to be pure from bodily defects, as well as men of stature and imposing appearance (cf. Elon: 564), the interpretation of Paul's "thorn in the flesh (σκόλοψ τῇ σαρκί)" (2 Cor. 12:7) and Paul's insinuation that he was "unskilled in speech (ἰδιώτης τῷ λόγῳ)" (2 Cor. 11:6) (cf. 1 Cor. 1:17; 2 Cor. 10:10) as some form of physical impediment appears invalid. (The apocryphal Acts of Paul and Thecla [2:3] describes Paul as "a man little of stature, thin-haired upon the head, crooked in the legs, of good state of body, with eyebrows joining, and nose somewhat hooked, full of grace; for sometimes he appeared like a man, and sometimes he had the face of an angel"[58] [cf. 1 Cor. 2:1f; 2 Cor. 10:10].)

While as an outstanding pupil of Gamaliel (cf. Acts 22:3; Gal. 1:14) (see above) Paul would presumably have been in very good standing, he never claims in the lists of his other status-positions that he was ordained – a necessary step before becoming eligible to assume a public office (cf. Steinsaltz, Talmud: 23). Much of the evidence of Acts nevertheless suggests that Paul should be regarded as an official representative of the Sanhedrin – whether or not the persecution in which he engaged constituted an "official" initiative. Paul may have been present at Stephen's trial in some official capacity (cf. Acts 7:58) (cf. Le Cornu and Shulam: 381). "Voting" – i.e., being counted (נמנה; nimneh) – was a customary form both of promulgating halakhic decrees[59] and of passing judicial sentences (cf. San. 5:5; Pes. 52a) – the context in Acts 26:10 (see below, **Persecutor**). This factor – together with his access to the high priest, the letters which he procured from the Sanhedrin (cf. Acts 22:5, 26:10), and the fact that envoys (שליחים;

---

[56] Cf. Kid. 4:5; Hor. 1:4f; Kid. 76b.

[57] Cf. Hor. 1:4; Tos.San. 7:5; San. 36b. For Paul's marital status, see below.

[58] statura brevis (pusillus), (at)tonso capite, cruribus scambus, brevibus superciliis (supercilia iuncta), naso aquilino, gratia dei plenus. Aliquando videbatur ut homo, aliquando sicut figuram angeli habens.

[59] Cf. Shab. 1:4; Betza 5a; RH 31b; Hag. 3b; MK 3b; San. 88b.

shlichim) were public officials – all indicate a close association with the Sanhedrin.[60]

Ancestry

Paul further identifies himself by his tribal association (cf. Rom. 11:1; Phil. 3:5). Proof of legitimate ancestry – i.e., families who had not intermarried with Gentiles – formed the cornerstone of Jewish "nationality" following the return from exile (cf. Ezra 9:1-10:44) (cf. Jeremias, *Jerusalem*: 275ff, and for the following discussion). During this period, the names of the patriarchs of the twelve tribes also came to serve as "surnames" – one of the indications that status – in contrast to (Jewish) identity – was determined patrilineally.[61] The evidence suggests that not only the priestly lines but also lay Israelites knew their immediate ancestors and could identify the tribe to which they belonged.[62] It was further claimed that every public official in Jerusalem was of pure ancestry, including such public officers as the seven-member local councils and almoners (cf. Kid. 4:5; Kid. 76b).

The practical implications deriving from lay lineal purity most importantly concerned the right to marry into priestly families.[63] Jews resident in the diaspora were required to present their genealogy for five generations in order to be eligible to marry a daughter into a priestly family (cf. Jos.*CA* 1.33; Kid. 4:5). The priestly genealogies were kept in an archive in the Temple (cf. Sifre, Kor. 116) and whenever wars destroyed the records new ones were composed (cf. Jos.*CA* 1.34f). Lay genealogies were composed on the basis of older documents (cf. Neh. 7:64; Ezra 2:62) which recorded the heads of each family and their ancestors.[64] Since the offices of priest and levite were both hereditary and could only be obtained by inheritance, these classes were generally required to produce their genealogy before being allowed to take office (cf. Mid. 5:4; Kid. 4:5).

The tribe of Benjamin which, with Judah, constituted the core of post-exilic Judaism, is very well documented. Saul and Mordechai were both Benjamites (cf. 1 Sam. 9:21; Est. 2:5), and Chronicles enumerates the Benjamite families of that period.[65] A Benjamite family of high rank named Senaah [הַסְּנָאָה] is well attested before 70 C.E.[66] R. Judah ha-Nasi was descended from Benjamin on his father's side and Judah on his mother's

---

[60] The account of his nephew's activities (cf. Acts 23:16-22) does not necessarily indicate that he was intimate with the Jerusalem leaders.

[61] For patronymy, see above, **Name**.

[62] Cf. Lk. 2:36; Tob. 1:1-2; Jud. 8:1, 9:2; Jos.*Life* 1-2, 6; Ta'anit 4:5; JKil. 9, 4, 32b.

[63] Cf. Kid. 4:1f; San. 4:2; Arak. 2:4.

[64] Cf. Ezra 2:1-67, 8:1-14; Neh. 7:6-69, 11:3-24; 1 Chron. 2:1ff, 3:1ff; Mt. 1:1-17; Lk. 3:23-28; CD-A 4:4-6; Yev. 4:13; Ket. 62b; Eus.*EH* 1.7.14.

[65] Cf. 1 Chron. 7:6-11, 8:1ff, 9:7-9.

[66] Cf. Ta'anit 4:5; Tos.Ta'anit 4[3]:6; Ta'anit 12a.

side[67] – indicating that Rabban Gamaliel, his ancestor, was also from the tribe of Benjamin. A midrashic tradition interprets 1 Chronicles 8:27 to signify that the prophet Elijah – who was associated in his zeal with Pinchas – was a Benjamite,[68] although his identification with Pinchas also led to his representation as a priest (cf. BM 114b).

Persecutor

The issue of the authorisation and initiation of the persecution Paul mentions on numerous occasions[69] and which Luke describes in Acts[70] is complicated and problematic. Paul indicates in Acts 22:5 that his activities were authorised by the πρεσβυτέριον (presbyterion), a term which Luke uses in Luke 22:66 to designate the Sanhedrin. While Luke employs the word "commission (ἐπιτροπή)" in Acts 26:12, it is difficult to know what weight should be attributed to the word, especially since it is a New Testament hapax (only occurrence). Although it may mean no more than "permission," the associated verb (ἐπιτροπεύω; epitropeuō) and substantive (ἐπίτροπος; epitropos) both represent the office and function of the Roman procurator (cf. Jos.*Ant.* 15.406), so that the term can also carry the weight of "full power" (cf. BAGD: 303). Ananias' reference to ἐξουσίαν (exousian – "authority") (cf. verse 14) is similarly a very general term, although obviously one which suggests some official capacity.

The fact that his speech before Agrippa II (cf. Acts 26:1-23) largely constitutes an *apologia pro vita sua* and is not a forensic defence makes it difficult to ascertain how much halakhic weight Paul's assumption of personal responsibility for the persecution carries. Despite his slightly obscure reasoning, he appears in this passage to be speaking primarily in autobiographical terms – and emphasising his own part in the drama not so much as a protagonist but as a "guilty party." On this count, little reason exists to doubt the reliability of his account. As in Acts 22:4f, Paul conveys the clear impression that he made it his personal business to oppose the early community, and is at pains to demonstrate that his actions were approved by his colleagues, operating through the proper legal channels.

A midrash on Numbers 25:7f describing Pinchas' slaying of Zimri may shed light on Paul's actions in this regard: "[*When Phinehas the son of Eleazar, the son of Aaron the priest, saw it,*] *he arose from the midst of the assembly* [NASB: congregation]. Whence did he arise? But they [the "assembly" – i.e., the Sanhedrin] were discussing the case whether or not

---

[67] Cf. Gen.R. 33:3; JKil. 9, 4, 32b.
[68] Cf. Gen.R. 71:9; Ex.R. 40:4; Num.R. 21:3; TBE p. 97, [EZ] p. 199; PRE 47; Yalk.Num. 771.
[69] Cf. 1 Cor. 15:9; Gal. 1:13; Phil. 3:6;·1 Tim. 1:13.
[70] Cf. Acts 8:1-3, 9:1-21, 22:4-21, 26:9-12.

he [Zimri] deserved death. Phinehas arose from the midst of the assembly and dedicated himself [swore an oath to kill Zimri] ויקם מתוך העדה. מהיכן עמד? אלא שהיו נושאין ונותנים בדבר אם הוא חיב מיתה או לאו. עמד פינחס בתוך הקהל ונתנדב" (Tanh.Balak 21).

The "many things hostile (πολλὰ ἐναντία)" (Acts 26:9) which Paul considered fit to institute included a radical programme of execution, during which the believers were flogged and forced to blaspheme.[71] The verb ἀναιρουμένων (anairoumenōn – "being put to death") (Acts 26:10) occurs in Acts 22:20 (cf. the noun in Acts 8:1) with reference to Stephen's death – although overall it seems doubtful that the plural here represents a "generalising" of Stephen's actual and single case (cf. Bruce, Acts: 500).

The reference to "blaspheming (βλασφημεῖν)" in Acts 26:11 appears to serve as a means of confirming the identity of those accused of the crime in question in order that they may receive due punishment (cf. Flusser, Judaism: 636f). Josephus records that the Roman forces tortured the Essenes in order break their resistance and "to induce them to blaspheme their lawgiver or to eat some forbidden thing (ἵν' ἢ βλασφημήσωσιν τὸν νομοθέτην ἢ φάγωσίν τι τῶν ἀσυνήθων) …" (War 2.152). Such blasphemy, he further asserts, is "punished with death (κολάζεται θανάτῳ)" within the community, since "After God they hold most in awe the name of their lawgiver (σέβας δὲ μέγα παρ' αὐτοῖς μετὰ τὸν θεὸν τοὔνομα τοῦ νομοθέτου)" (145). While this "lawgiver" is frequently understood to be Moses, good grounds seem to support the suggestion that it refers to the community's founder[72] (cf. Dupont-Sommer: 31n3, 131, 134).[73] Paul may have adopted some such similar methods, attempting (ἠνάγκαζον [ēnangkazon] – impf. [Acts 26:11]) first, by violent measures, to force people to renounce their adherence to Jesus and – when these failed – incarcerating them to await capital charges.[74]

---

[71] Cf. 8:1f, 9:1f, 13f, 22:3f.

[72] Cf. המחוקק (ha-mechokek) – CD-A 6:7f, [7:18].

[73] It is interesting to speculate whether this reference may allude to a belief that the "Lawgiver" will be resurrected. Since the latter had apparently died (cf. CD-B 19:35-20:1), it is possible that when the text in CD-A 6:8-12 declares that the "nobles of the people [נדיבי העם]" will not obtain full knowledge of the Torah "until there arises he who teaches justice at the end of days עד עמד יורה הצדק באחרית הימים" it describes his reappearance (cf. Dupont-Sommer: 131). This may possibly have formed one of the dissenting "doctrines" over which the original "benediction against heretics" arose – to which Paul's trial in Acts 26 would then exhibit similar traits.

[74] The practice of forcing people to blaspheme is also demonstrated in Pliny's treatment of those who were suspected of being Christians in Bithynia in 112: "Among these I considered that I should dismiss any who denied that they were or ever had been Christians when they had repeated after me a formula of invocation to the gods and had made offerings of wine and incense to your statue … and furthermore had reviled the name of Christ: none of which things, I understand,

The allusion to "voting (αὐτῶν κατήνεγκα ψῆφον)" (Acts 26:10) further corroborates the reliability of Paul's account, the practice being well documented in contemporary and later sources (cf. Schürer: 2:226). A mishnah in Sanhedrin describes the procedure whereby capital sentences were determined: "If they found him innocent they set him free; otherwise they leave his sentence over until the morrow. [In the meantime] they went together in pairs, they ate a little (but they used to drink no wine the whole day), and they discussed the matter all night, and early on the morrow they came to the court … If they [all] found him innocent they set him free; otherwise they decide by vote. If twelve favour acquittal and eleven favour conviction, he is declared innocent; if twelve favour conviction and eleven favour acquittal, or even if eleven favour acquittal and eleven favour conviction and one says, 'I do not know', or even if twenty-two favour acquittal or favour conviction and one says, 'I do not know', they must add to the number of judges. Up to what number may they add to them? By two at a time up to one and seventy. If then thirty-six favour acquittal and thirty-five favour conviction, he is declared innocent; if thirty-six favour conviction and thirty-five favour acquittal, they debate one with another until one of them that favoured conviction approves of the words of them that favour acquittal"[75] (San. 5:5) (cf. San. 4:1).

Whereas in non-capital cases – such as those involving purity laws – the vote was begun with the most experienced member, in capital cases the poll was taken first of all "from the side [הצד מן]" – i.e., beginning with the most junior judge – each man standing to cast his vote (cf. San. 4:2). The students in attendance were permitted to speak in defence of the accused alone and thus spoke among the first, the hearing (of capital cases) opening with defence arguments followed by those for conviction (cf. San. 4:1). Ψῆφος (psēfos) is literally a "small stone" – used for counting, board games, astrological calculations, and magic.[76] Its primary linguistic usage

---

any genuine Christian can be induced to do (Qui negabant esse se Christianos aut fuisse, cum praeeunte me deos adpellarent et imagini tuae . . . ture ac vino supplicarent, praeterea male dicerent Christo, quorum nihil cogi posse dicuntur, qui sunt re vera Christiani dimittendos putavi)" (Pliny, *Ep.* 10.96.5) (cf. 1 Cor. 12:3) (cf. Ferguson, Backgrounds: 473f).

[75] אם מצאו לו זכות, פטרוהו. ואם לאו, מעבירין דינו למחר. היו מזדוגין זוגות זוגות, וממעטין במאכל, ולא היו שותין יין כל היום, ונושאין ונותנין כל הלילה, ולמחרת משכימין ובאין לבית דין ... אם מצאו לו זכות, פטרוהו. ואם לאו, עומדים למנין. שנים עשר מזכין ואחד עשר מחיבין - זכאי. שנים עשר מחיבין ואחד עשר מזכין, ואפילו אחד עשר מזכין ואחד עשר מחיבין, ואחד אומר: איני יודע, ואפילו עשרים ושנים מזכין או מחיבין ואחד אומר: איני יודע - יוסיפו הדיינין. עד כמה מוסיפין? שנים שנים, עד שבעים ואחד. שלשים וששה מזכין ושלשים וחמשה מחיבין - זכאי. שלשים וששה מחיבין ושלשים וחמשה מזכין - דנין אלו כנגד אלו עד שיראה אחד מן המחיבין דברי המזכין.

[76] In Jewish literature the term frequently denotes a mosaic [פְּסֵיפַס/פְּסֵפַס] (cf. Ex.R. 10:3; Dt.R. 1:10; Mid.Ps. 26:7; Tos.San. 5:2; J RH 1, 8, 57c; JShevu. 7, 4, 37d; JShab. 49a; ARN[a] 24:1f; San. 25b) (cf. TDNT: 9:604f).

was for designating the dice employed for voting, the term occurring in rabbinic literature as a loan word for a voting tablet or verdict[77] (cf. Jastrow: 1196).

Despite its divergent motive, the incident with the group of "zealots" who take an oath to kill Paul and turn to the "chief priests and elders" of the Sanhedrin asking for their co-operation is instructive in this regard. There, the Sanhedrin is not only the source to which the band turns for authorisation, but its members are also apparently willing to collude with a band of zealots in order to create the opportunity for a "political" assassination on the one hand, and with the Roman military commander to bring charges against Paul on the other. Even here the issue is nonetheless not clear cut, since it is also possible that the would-be assassins approached "that section which had shown itself most hostile to Paul" (Bruce, Acts: 468) – i.e., the high-priestly faction – rather than the Sanhedrin as the national leadership. Despite the interfactional conflict between various Jewish groups in the period leading up to and during the War, a reasonable explanation likewise needs to be found to clarify why Paul would have found himself the object of zealot hostility. The suggestion that Paul acted as a spy or informer (cf. Bauckham, Acts: 385) does not seem to fit Luke's picture of the scope of Paul's activities.

Extending the Sanhedrin's reaches to diaspora Jewish communities outside Eretz Israel (cf. *Yad*, Sanhedrin 14:14) indicates a campaign of quite serious proportions. While the Romans granted Judaea the right of extraditing Jews from outside Eretz Israel – "We thought it good therefore to write unto the kings and countries, that they should do them [the Jews there] no harm, nor fight against them, their cities, or countries, nor yet aid their enemies against them ... If therefore there be any pestilent fellows that have fled from their country unto you, deliver them to Simon the high priest, that he may punish them according to their law"[78] (1 Macc. 15:19-21) (cf. Jos.*Ant.* 14.192f) – the persecution of the Qumran community may well have led the sect's members to seek refuge in Damascus as out of reach of the high priest, suggesting that the Sanhedrin's authority was limited at least with regard to Damascus.

Evidence for internecine Jewish conflicts is found only slightly later, in Antioch. Josephus records that when war against Rome had been declared and hatred against Jews was high, Antiochus, the son of the city's chief Jewish magistrate, "entered the theatre during an assembly of the people

---

[77] Cf. 4 Macc. 15:26; Jos.*Ant.* 2.163; *CA* 2.265; Philo, *Spec.Leg.* 4.57; *Dec.* 141f; Lam.R. 2.1.3.

[78] ἤρεσεν οὖν ἡμῖν γράψαι τοῖς βασιλεῦσιν καὶ ταῖς χώραις ὅπως μὴ ἐκζητήσωσιν αὐτοῖς κακὰ καὶ μὴ πολεμήσωσιν αὐτοὺς καὶ τὰς πόλεις αὐτῶν καὶ τὴν χώραν αὐτῶν καὶ ἵνα μὴ συμμαχῶσιν τοῖς πολεμοῦσιν πρὸς αὐτούς ... εἴ τινες οὖν λοιμοὶ διαπεφεύγασιν ἐκ τῆς χωχρας αὐτῶν πρὸς ὑμᾶς, παράδοτε αὐτοὺς Σίμωνι τῷ ἀρχιερεῖ, ὅπως ἐκδικήσῃ αὐτοὺς κατὰ τὸν νόμον αὐτῶν.

and denounced his own father and the other Jews, accusing them of a design to burn the whole city to the ground in one night; he also delivered up some foreign Jews as accomplices to the plot"[79] (*War* 7.47). Whereas Paul's zeal was awakened on behalf of the Torah, Antiochus' motivation stemmed from a desire to furnish proof of his hellenization – to the extent of delivering his fellowmen to be killed if they refused to assimilate (cf. Jos.*War* 7.50-51). Likewise, the massacre was executed by their so-called fellow-citizens rather than by Jews. A closer example to Paul might perhaps be found in the treatment meted out to Jonathan the Weaver in Cyrenaica (c. 116), against whose revolutionary activities the local Jewish community encouraged the Roman authorities to take action (cf. Jos.*War* 7.437-46). Whether official or unofficial, Paul's zealousness has biblical predecessors in such figures as Pinchas (cf. Num. 25:1-9), Elijah (cf. 1 Kings 19:10, 14), and on into the maccabean period.[80]

The fact that the Damascene believers believed that Paul had come to bring them "bound before the high priests (δεδεμένους αὐτοὺς ἀγάγῃ ἐπὶ τοὺς ἀρχιερεῖς)" (Acts 9:21) may reflect their recognition of the high priestly power and/or their knowledge that Paul carried the high priest's authority. An example of the possible overlap between priestly and pharisaic authority can perhaps be found in Gamaliel's letter to the diaspora regarding the intercalation of a month (cf. San. 11b), calendrical matters of this kind usually falling under the responsibility of the Temple authorities (cf. Bauckham, *Acts*: 424-25). It would further appear that the high priesthood retained an aura of importance in the diaspora (cf. Schwartz, *Studies*: 10) – in some contrast to Eretz Israel where its reputation had been tarnished through the brutal behaviour of many members of the high priestly families.

Contemporary evidence suggests that the Sadducees (the chief priests) were more actively engaged in political intrigue than the Pharisees (cf. Flusser, *Jesus*: 195-206). Since the high-priestly Sadducees had already demonstrated their continuing antagonism to Jesus' disciples (cf. Acts 4:1ff, 5:17ff, 6:12f), Paul may have presumed on their support – if it was not the sadducean grouping within the Sanhedrin which in fact commissioned him. Here the question arises why Paul – a Pharisee according to his own account – should have aligned himself with sadducean policy regarding the early believers – especially in the face of his teacher's previous opposition to the plan to kill them.

---

[79] εἰς τὸ θέατρον παρελθὼν τόν τε πατέρα τὸν αὐτοῦ καὶ τοὺς ἄλλους ἐνεδείκνυτο, κατηγορῶν ὅτι νυκτὶ μιᾷ καταπρῆσαι τὴν πόλιν ἅπασαν διεγνώκεισαν, καὶ παρεδίδου ξένους Ἰουδαίους τινὰς ὡς κεκοινωνηκότας τῶν βεβουλευμένων.
[80] Cf. 1 Macc. 2:24-26; Jos.*Ant.* 12.271; Philo, *Spec.Leg.* 1.186.

Although in the minority, several pharisaic Sages were also priests. One of Jochanan b. Zakkai's disciples was Jose the Priest [ויוסי הכהן] (cf. PA 2:8). R. Eleazar b. Azariah of Yavneh (50-120 C.E.) was a wealthy priest of distinction who served as head of the college both before and concurrently with Gamaliel II.[81] R. Ishmael was of priestly descent,[82] while R. Joshua b. Chananiah was of levitical descent (cf. PA 2:8; Ket. 1:6f).

The Prefect of the priests (סגן הכהנים; sgan ha-cohanim) was apparently a Pharisee – at least towards the end of the Second Temple period (cf. Safrai and Stern: 875f). It may be speculated in this regard that a Prefect's pharisaic allegiance may have been tempered, to one degree or another, by the fact that he served as deputy to the high priest and was in charge of the Temple priesthood – whose sympathies were generally sadducean. (At the same time, pharisaic leverage over the sadducean Sanhedrin was largely achieved through the Prefect's influence as the high priest's deputy [cf. Yoma 1:5; Suk. 4:9].) While it is true that Paul nowhere indicates that he was from a priestly family (Romans 15:16 is not a literal reference), it appears that he was willing to follow sadducean preferences in persecuting the early believers. Elijah's association with Pinchas – Aaron's grandson – also meant that Elijah, otherwise said to be a Benjamite like Paul, was considered to be a priest (cf. BM 114b) (see above).

Despite the example of the Prefect Eleazar son of Ananias – who was one of the leading Shammaites during the period leading up to the outbreak of the Revolt[83] and an outright political, religious, and social opponent of the sadducean high priesthood – all the New Testament evidence suggests that Paul belonged to Beit Hillel rather than to Beit Shammai. His halakhot – with the possible exception of the legal status of women, an area in which Beit Hillel eventually accepted the more lenient rulings of Beit Shammai[84] – his openness to the Gentiles, his non-literal interpretation of Scripture, and his anthropocentric rather than theocentric emphases (given also the influence of essene theology which his views on human nature display) – all suggest that he was a Hillelite.

The associated suggestion that Paul was a "shammaite zealot" (cf. Wright, What) or was closely allied to those Pharisees who displayed zealot sympathies and persecuted the early community for its "pacifist" stance (cf. Taylor) is problematic. While Paul clearly indicates that the "zeal" with which he observed the commandments of the Torah was the force which motivated him to persecute the early community,[85] his persecution of the latter does not appear to fall under the category of

---

[81] Cf. Sot. 9:15; Yad. 4:2; Maas.Sheni 5:9.
[82] Cf. [3 Enoch]; Kil. 6:4; Ket. 5:8; PA 3:12; Ket. 105b; Hul. 49a; Ber. 7a.
[83] Cf. Jos.War 2.409; Tos.Par. 4:6; Sem. 6:11.
[84] Cf. Yev. 15:2-3; Git. 9:10; Ket. 1:6-9, 8:1.
[85] Cf. 1:13f; Phil. 3:6; 1 Tim. 1:13?

zealot/non-zealot clashes. Nor does it appear likely that as a Zealot he would have "been given special and plenary powers by the high-priest to act against Christians" (Hengel, Zealots: 180). Similarly, little if any evidence suggests that the early community was "pacifist" with regard to the Revolt in 70, not to speak of this early date about which almost nothing is known (cf. Brandon: 180).[86]

Paul's fanaticism has also been attributed at times to his hellenistic diaspora background – on the supposition that the hellenists had close contacts with the high-priestly faction (cf. Acts 6:12-7:1). Despite arguments to the contrary, no good reason appears to require that Paul should primarily be identified with the "hellenists" – and although the sadducean high priests were undoubtedly strongly influenced by the hellenization process (cf. Schürer: 2:136ff), the supposition that hellenistic "immigrants" would have developed an association with the local aristocracy is unproven. (From the reverse perspective, it may appropriately be assumed that the high priestly establishment later turned against its former "protégé," as it were, because he joined the ranks of those whose persecution they had originally sanctioned – even if the traditional Christian comprehension of Paul's "conversion" is highly suspect [see below, **Calling**].) While the presupposition that the hellenist community was "hostile to the temple prerogatives" (Bruce, Acts: 214) may suggest that Paul's anger was roused by such opposition to the Temple, the assumption that Paul advocated so-called "liberal" anti-Torah (and Temple?) views would seem to contradict the fact that he himself was persecuted by the hellenist faction which held views similar to his own.

While Acts 26:9 may seem to indicate that Paul undertook the persecution in Jerusalem on his own initiative – "I thought to myself that I had to do many things hostile to the name of Jesus of Nazareth ... (ἔδοξα ἐμαυτῷ πρὸς τὸ ὄνομα Ἰησοῦ τοῦ Ναζωραίου δεῖν πολλὰ ἐναντία πρᾶξαι)" – this statement is made in the context of an *apologia pro vita sua* and it is doubtful whether it should be taken to mean more than that Paul turned the affair into a "personal crusade." The fact that Paul describes the same events in a similar tone in Acts 22:4f may suggest that the chief priests gave their authorisation to an originally "private" initiative. On this reading, the "vote (κατήνεγκα ψῆφον)" in which Paul participated may represent the Sanhedrin's official approval of the campaign which, as a member of its ranks, also sanctioned Paul's activities on its behalf (see above).

Several other examples of Jewish in-fighting which led to brutal results can be adduced from this general period. During the reign of Alexander Jannai (Jannaeus) (103-76 B.C.E.), relations between the king and

---

[86] Fredrikson's theory that Paul objected to the early community's gentile outreach is presented in the strangest possible way.

the pharisaic party degenerated into a civil war which lasted six years and led to the massacre of fifty thousand Jews, including Jannai's crucifixion of the 800 leaders of the revolt – their wives and children being slaughtered in front of their eyes.[87]

The Qumran scrolls describe how the sect was persecuted by the "Wicked Priest [והכהן הרשע]" – who was apparently responsible for the arrest, judgment, maltreatment, and death of the community's founder, the priestly Teacher of Righteousness [מורה הצדק], on the sect's Day of Atonement.[88] It appears likely that the community originated in a group of חסידים (chasidim) who came to oppose the ruling high priest in Jerusalem when he accepted a position to which he was not entitled as a non-zadokite priest (cf. Vermes, Dead: 54ff, and for the following discussion). Allusions in the Scrolls may also indicate a reference to Jannai's persecution of the Pharisees,[89] suggesting that the Qumran community regarded both Pharisees and Sadducees – designated by the biblical symbols of Ephraim and Menasseh, the two northern tribes – as defectors and apostates.[90]

Following a violent confrontation between the opposing factions within the chasidim in which the "Man of the Lie [איש הכזב]" gained the upper hand, the Teacher of Righteousness and his remaining disciples apparently took refuge in the "land of Damascus" – either the real city or a cryptic/symbolic name for Babylon or Qumran. The persecution which ensued appears to have been grounded in the fact that the sect celebrated the festivals according to their own calendar,[91] a halakhic state of affairs which the high priest was not prepared to tolerate.

Later, a violent conflict broke out between Beit Hillel and Beit Shammai over the issuing of the Eighteen Decrees on the eve of the outbreak of the Revolt in 70. On this occasion, the disciples of Beit Shammai slaughtered a (large?) number of Hillelites in order to prevent the latter from carrying the majority vote (cf. JShab. 1, 4, 3c). Similarly, during the period leading up to the outbreak of the Revolt in 66 numerous political assassinations were carried out, many at the hands of the sicarii[92] (cf. Schürer: 1:463).

While the struggle between Jannai and the Pharisees was both political and religious in nature and the internecine bloodshed between the two pharisaic houses was also influenced by the political climate leading

---

[87] Cf. 4QpNah ff3+4i:6-8; Jos.*Ant.* 13.372ff; *War* 1.88ff, 96f.

[88] Cf. 1QpHab 1:13, 5:9f, 8:8, 16, 9:2, 9f, 11:4f, 12:2f; 4Q171 2:18f, 4:8f.

[89] Cf. 4QpNah ff3+4i:5f; 4QpHos[b] 2:1f.

[90] Cf. 4Q169 ff3-4iv:1f; 4Q171 1:24, 2:18; [4QpNah ff3+4i:5f; 1QH[a] 12:11]. See the commentary on 2:15-21 and 4:21-31.

[91] Cf. 1QpHab 11:2f; 4QpHos[a] 2:16; [1QH[a] 12:9f].

[92] Cf. Jos.*Ant.* 20.161f; *War* 2.254f.

up to the War,[93] marring an otherwise mainly peaceful (if competitive) co-existence,[94] the conflict between the Qumran community and the Pharisees and Sadducees appears to have been primarily "theological" in nature. Pesher Habakkuk speaks of the oppression which the former suffered at the hands of the latter in similar terms to those which Luke uses to describe the persecution of the early community and with which Paul characterises those troubling his disciples:

> *Hab 1:13b* Why do you stare, traitors, and remain silent when a wicked person consumes someone more upright than himself? *Blank* Its interpretation concerns the House of Absalom and the members of their council, who kept silent when the Teacher of Righteousness was rebuked and did not help him against the Man of the Lie, *Blank* who rejected the Law in the midst of their whole Council ... *Hab 2:8b* For the human blood (spilt) and the violence (done) to the country, the city and all /who dwell/ in it. *Blank* Its interpretation concerns the [Wi]cked Priest, whom, for the wickedness against the Teacher of Righteousness and the men of his council, God delivered into the hands of his enemies to disgrace him with a punishment, to destroy him with bitterness of soul for having acted wickedly against his elect.[95] (1QpHab 5:8-12, 9:8-12)

Some scholars have adduced that the expression "House of Absalom" here refers symbolically to the Sanhedrin, and that the Teacher of Righteousness was tried before the Court on the accusation of the Wicked Priest and condemned without any intervention on his part (cf. Dupont-Sommer: 261).

Like the "Wicked Priest," Paul seems to have regarded the early community as a separatist group which must be eliminated. Yet even if Stephen (and the hellenists in Acts 6) did hold anti-Temple sentiments – not an indubitable assumption – no real evidence exists to suggest that the early community ever followed a separate calendar.[96] In the context of

---

[93] Cf. Jos.*War* 2.409f; JShab. 1, 4, 3c.

[94] Cf. Eduy. 4:8; Tos.Yev. 1:10-11; [Yev. 14b].

[95] למה תביטו בוגדים ותחריש בבלע רשע צדיק ממנו *vacat* פשרו על בית אבשלום ואנשי עצתם אשר נדמו בתוכחת מורה הצדק ולוא עזרוהו על איש הכזב *vacat* אשר מאס את התורה בתוך כול עצתם ... מדמי אדם וחמס ארץ קריה וכול *vacat* בה יושבי פשרו על הכהן הר[ש]ע אשר בעוון מורה הצדק ואנשי עצתו נתנו אל בידי אויביו לענ'תו בנגע לכלה במרורי נפש בעבור [א]שר הרשיע על בחירו.

[96] Even if it can be maintained that Jesus' celebration of Pesach followed the essene calendar (cf. Germano), thus taking place on the Wednesday night, this does not conclusively prove that the community retained the same practice (cf. Acts 1:5, 2:1, 18:21 [variant], [19:21], 20:6, 16, 21:26f, 24:17f, 27:9). Other indications in the gospels

isolating oneself from the community, the reference to forcing Jesus' followers to blaspheme (ἠνάγκαζον βλασφημεῖν; ēnangkazon blasfēmein) (cf. Acts 6:11, 26:11) recalls the institution of "birkat ha-minim ברכת המינים" – the benediction against heretics whose determination at the request of Rabban Gamaliel of Yavneh around 80-95 C.E. is normally attributed to Samuel the Little: "For the separatists and for the apostates and for the traitors let there be no hope, and the heretics shall perish in a moment, and the dominion of arrogance do Thou speedily uproot, O Lord, who humblest the arrogant לפרושים ולמשומדים ולבוגדים אל תהי תקוה והמינים כרגע יאבדו ומלכות הזדון מהרה תעקר. ברוך אתה ה' מכניע זדים" (cf. Ber. 28b; [Meg. 17b]).

A more accurate assessment of the history of the benediction reveals that Samuel the Little was actually responsible for combining two already-existing benedictions from the maccabean era – one against "heretics" and one against the "arrogant" gentile government (cf. Flusser, Judaism: 637ff, and for the following discussion). This joint benediction was the second in a series of three sections inserted in the Eighteen Benedictions. The first benediction was apparently directed against the Sadducees, while the third invoked blessings upon the "pharisaic" community – i.e., the pious [וחסידים], the scribes, and the elders of the people.[97] The second "benediction" may thus have originally referred to the Essenes (corresponding to Josephus' three "schools") – considered to be included among the wicked men who separated themselves (הפורשין; ha-porshin) from the Jewish collectivity. In the later context of the increasingly acerbic relations between the early believers and the Jewish community, the purpose of the benediction was to pick out suspected heretics in the synagogue, the assumption being that no one would be willing to curse himself.[98]

Since neither the essene community nor the Sadducees survived the War intact, this set of benedictions apparently originated pre-70 and was very likely in currency during the New Testament period. If, as the variant traditions of the benediction indicate, its original intention was to indict those who severed their ties with the community – in the most extreme case, to ally themselves with Israel's enemies (the Seleucids and then the Romans) – it may be that the early messianic community was considered to be separatist in a sense similar to that of the Qumran community. The fact that the Sadducees were originally included in the imprecation demonstrates that otherwise "mainstream" or "Establishment" groups could also fall under the heading.

---

suggest that Jesus observed the regular dates for the festivals (cf. Mt. 26:2; Mk. 14:1-2; Lk. 22:1ff; Jn. 5:1, 6:4f, 7:2f, 37, 10:22-23, 12:1, 13:1).

[97] Cf. SOR 3; Tos.San. 13:4f; Tos.Ber. 3:25; ARN[a] 16:4; RH 17a.

[98] Cf. [Lk. 6:22]; Jn. 9:22, 12:42, 16:2.

While the references to being "cast out (ἀποσυνάγωγος γένηται)" of the synagogue in John (cf. Acts 9:12, 12:42, 16:2) are usually perceived as anachronistic, the fact that only a few years later Paul punished those faithful to Jesus "in all the synagogues (κατὰ πάσας τὰς συναγωγὰς πολλάκις τιμωρῶν)" would seem to indicate that such activity could have occurred much earlier than the nineties. (Despite the fact that the benediction probably had an early origin, any proof of a direct line of contact between Paul's activities and later circumstances lies beyond reasonable expectation. Paul later describes himself to Timothy as having formerly been "a blasphemer and a persecutor and a violent aggressor [ὄντα βλάσφημον καὶ διώκτην καὶ ὑβριστήν]" [1 Tim. 1:13].)

Luke's notation that Paul pursued the members of the community from "house to house (κατὰ τοὺς οἴκους)" (cf. Philo, *In Flac.* 74) may indicate that the community was continuing to break bread together in various houses – as well as praying daily in the Temple. Both here and in Paul's own letters, Paul's conduct towards the early community is described in violent language. The classical verb λυμαίνομαι (lymainomai) evokes the image of being ravaged by a wild beast (cf. Philo, *Leg.* 134), while πορθέω (portheō) (cf. Acts 9:21; Gal. 1:13, 23) specifically refers to the sacking of cities (cf. Bruce, *Acts*: 215). (The metaphor later became a reality when Christians were sent to their death in the arena.)

Although scholars have questioned the authenticity of Luke's account that Paul's zeal extended not only to arresting and imprisoning the believers but also to executing them (cf. Acts 9:1, 22:4), Paul himself specifically distinguishes between imprisonment and homicide: ". . . not only did I lock up many of the saints in prisons . . . but also when they were being put to death . . . (καὶ πολλούς τε τῶν ἁφίων ἐγὼ ἐν φυλακαῖς κατέκλεισα . . . ἀναιρουμένων . . .)" (Acts 26:10). The fact that Paul suggests that he brought those whom he arrested to Jerusalem for trial (cf. 22:5) would likewise seem to indicate capital cases, the authority to try which rested exclusively in the hands of the Sanhedrin. In his letters he nonetheless never suggests that he was responsible for any believer's death.

Paul's own witness seems to indicate that the scope of his vendetta extended outside Jerusalem "even to foreign cities (ἕως καὶ εἰς τὰς ἔξω πόλεις)" (Acts 26:11). The reference here is apparently to non-Jewish cities, which does not necessarily mean outside the land of Israel since Greek cities such as Caesarea and Tiberias existed in Eretz Israel. Since most of Paul's statements suggest that he first went north to Damascus, Paul could have passed through Samaria and Galilee, both being part of provincial Judaea (cf. Acts 9:31) – plural being accounted for by Paul's pre-empted intention to proceed beyond Damascus. Paul's self-description as a "persecutor of the community . . . beyond measure (διώκαν τῆν ἐκκλησίαν . . . ὑπερβολὴν)" (Gal. 1:13; Phil. 3:6) (cf. 1 Cor. 15:9; Gal. 1:23) may

similarly reflect geographical localities, in addition to the quality of his
zeal.

The statement that "I was *still* unknown by sight to the churches of
Judea which were in the Messiah; but only they kept hearing, 'He who
once persecuted us is now preaching the faith which he once *tried* to
destroy'"[99] (Gal. 1:22) may on this reading indicate a correct assessment.
The fact that "Judaea" is anathrous in Acts 26:20 possibly suggests a
contrast in the manner of Paul's recognition between Jerusalem and
Damascus and the communities of Judaea, the latter only having "heard"
of his teaching activities – as they had also not experienced his persecutory
campaign firsthand. Such a speculation may receive support from 1
Thessalonians 2:14, which echoes Galatians 1:22 almost verbatim in
speaking of "Jewish persecution." Is it possible that Paul is referring
therein to the campaign against the early community in Judaea – without
mentioning his involvement because he did not himself participate outside
Jerusalem?[100]

Calling

Paul's "conversion" or, better named, his calling as an "apostle to the
Gentiles (ἐθνῶν ἀπόστολος)" (Rom. 11:13), has been the subject of
innumerable explanations from all conceivable perspectives (cf.
Longenecker, Road). It is regularly assumed that if, at the time of Luke's
writing of Acts, the early community witnessed exclusively to the Gentiles,
this circumstance was due to the fact that Israel had rejected the gospel and
had therefore been rejected by God (cf. Jervell, Luke: 42). Such a claim is
frequently accompanied by the presupposition that Paul himself either
rejected his Jewish heritage and/or his reverence for the Torah and/or the
Jewish particularism which ostensibly excluded the Gentiles from election,
salvation, and the Kingdom of God (cf. Longenecker, Road: 62-84) –
together with the assertion of a serious discrepancy between the evidence
of Acts and that gathered from Paul's own letters with regard to the notion
that Paul's first priority was to his own people (e.g., Sanders: 181ff).

The fact that Luke's record of Jesus' words to Paul may be modelled
on such a description of a travelling Sage as Ben Sirach gives (cf. Sir. 39:1,
4, 10, Sir. 44:1ff) corroborates the alternative view that Paul remained
within an "orthodox" (pharisaic) Jewish framework throughout his life. In
this sense, Paul may best be understood on the model of such "itinerant
merchant-missionaries" as Ananias, who taught the house of Adiabene's
royal wives to "worship God after the manner of the Jewish tradition

---

[99] ἤμην δὲ ἀγνοούμενος τῷ προσώπῳ ταῖς ἐκκλησίαις τῆς Ἰουδαίας ταῖς ἐν
Χριστῷ. Μόνον δὲ ἀκούοντες ἦσαν ὅτι ὁ διώκων ἡμᾶς ποτε νῦν εὐαγγελίζεται
τὴν πίστιν ἥν ποτε ἐπόρθει.
[100] See the commentary on 1:21-24.

(ἐδίδασκεν αὐτὰς τὸν θεὸν σέβειν, ὡς Ἰουδαίοις πάτριον ἦν)" and Eleazar, who subsequently urged Monobaz' son Izates to be circumcised (cf. Jos.*Ant.* 20.34, 43-46).[101]

While it is true that in his letters Paul makes most of his outreach to the Gentiles, the supposed conflict with Luke's account in Acts is more apparent than real. In all three reports of Paul's revelation on his way to Damascus, both Jews and Gentiles are included and Paul consistently goes first to the synagogue in whatever town or city he visits, making a point of visiting towns with Jewish communities.[102] Paul's statements that he turned to the Gentiles because his Jewish audience rejected his message (cf. Acts 13:46, 28:24ff) are correctly understood in light of the fact that Paul did not consequently abandon the synagogues but continued his practice of going to them first.

Given the nature of the Jewish debate regarding whether Gentiles wishing to attach themselves to Judaism should become proselytes – i.e., full converts – or whether they could remain godfearers, it is difficult to ascertain whether as a Pharisee Paul originally promoted full conversion. Luke mentions in Acts that Paul held lengthy debates about the latter (cf. 15:2 – precisely with pharisaic believers) and gives no indication that these served to change Paul's mind on the issue. The evidence of the New Testament in general conveys the impression that Paul was never persuaded that Gentiles should become more than "godfearers." It is likewise clear that Paul did not apprehend his calling to the Gentiles as exclusive of or in any sense contradictory to sharing the gospel with his fellow countrymen.[103]

Just as Paul set out to persecute those who followed Jesus, so he too was expected to learn from personal experience to suffer for Jesus' sake. The expression "chosen instrument (σκεῦος ἐκλογῆς)" in Acts 9:15 may be drawn in this respect from the biblical motif of the potter,[104] although it is also directly associated with the "Suffering Servant."[105] The latter passages further furnish a "universalistic" context wherein the Servant is presented as being the "light to the nations" (cf. Isa. 42:6, 49:6, 51:4).

---

[101] For the issue of Jewish proselytism during the period, see Introduction, **Occasion and circumstances**.

[102] Cf. Acts 9:20, 13:5, 14ff, 14:1f, 16:13, 16, 17:1f, 10f, 17, 18:4f, 19f, 19:8f.

[103] Cf. Rom. 1:16, 3:29-31, 9:1-11:36; 1 Cor. 9:19-23. For the present interpretation of Gal. 5:11, see the commentary on 5:2-12.

[104] Cf. Jer. 18:1-11, 22:28; Hos. 8:8; Rom. 9:19ff; 2 Cor. 4:7; Sir. 33:10f; 1QS 11:21f.

[105] Cf. Isa. 42:1ff, 44:1f, 49:1ff, 52:13-53:12; Hag. 2:20f; 1QHᵃ 11:6f, 23f, 12:8f, 23, 17:29f. See the commentary on 1:[1-5], 15-16b, 21-24, 2:1-10, and 6:17.

Language

Paul's reference to being a "Hebrew of Hebrews ('Εβραῖος ἐξ 'Εβραίων)" (Phil. 3:5) (cf. 2 Cor. 11:22) may possibly indicate a linguistic allegiance, Eretz Israel believers being distinguished from Greek-speaking hellenists on the basis of their home language.[106] Alternatively, he may be referring to the fact that his parents were Galileans and that his sister and family apparently lived in Jerusalem. He obviously spoke mishnaic Hebrew/Aramaic[107] as well as Greek (cf. Acts 21:37), in addition to possessing a reading knowledge of biblical Hebrew. Jerome witnesses that Paul, "being a Hebrew, wrote Hebrew, that is his own tongue and most fluently (Scripserat ut Hebraeus Hebraice, id est, suo eloquio disertissime)" (*De Vir.Ill.* 5).

The members of the Sanhedrin were required to know seventy languages in order that the court should need no interpreter.[108] The familiarity with the works of Homer which rabbinic literature demonstrates[109] may reflect a broad acquaintance with Greek literature – such as Paul's quotation of the Greek poets (Epimenides, Aratus, Euripides, Menander)[110] displays, although the breadth of Paul's knowledge of Greek literature cannot be clearly ascertained from such limited evidence. The high incidence of Greek words and phrases in talmudic literature indicates that from as early as the later books of the Tanakh Greek was sufficiently widely heard and read that many words were adopted into the native tongue, particularly in the areas of government and legislation. The list of loan words may reach as many as two thousand (cf. Safrai and Stern: 1050; Hengel, Judaism: 60f). Although Paul is perfectly at home in the Septuagint (LXX) (cf. Hays, Echoes), the clarity of his Greek is clearly not as elegant as Philo's, for example, possibly suggesting a moderate education.

Occupation

A boy was normally taught a trade by his father[111] and frequently took up his father's profession.[112] During the second half of the second century it was decreed that a man was obliged to provide instruction for his son until the age of twelve whence he was to teach him a craft and gradually introduce him to work (cf. Ket. 50a) (cf. Safrai and Stern: 952). At times, a

---

[106] Cf. Philo, *Conf.Ling.* 68 [129]; *Mut.Nom.* 71.
[107] Cf. Acts 21:40, 22:2, 26:14.
[108] Cf. [CD-A 14:9f]; San. 17a; Men. 65a.
[109] Cf. Yalk.Ps. 613, 678; Yad. 4:6; JSan. 10, 1, 28a; Hul. 60b.
[110] Cf. Acts 17:22f, 26:14; 1 Cor. 15:32.
[111] Cf. Eccl.R. 9.9.1; Mekh.Pischa 18; Yalk.Gen. 92; Tos.Kid. 1:11; JKid. 19a; Kid. 29a, 82a-b.
[112] Cf. J RH 1, 2, 57b; Arak. 16b.

boy was apprenticed to another craftsman, occasionally going to live in his house for a number of years. Shimon b. Shetach was a flax comber (cf. J BM 2, 4, 8c), Shammai a carpenter (cf. Shab. 31a), and Hillel a day-labourer – at least while he was studying (cf. Yoma 35b). Jochanan b. Zakkai was a merchant (cf. San. 41a) and Abba Saul b. Bitnit a wine merchant (cf. Betza 29a) (cf. Jeremias, Jerusalem: 113).

Many rabbinic dicta reflect the pharisaic estimation of Talmud Torah (studying) combined with manual labour – one of the significations of derekh eretz (דרך ארץ) – a term alternatively used to express courtesy, labour, and the "ways of the world": "Excellent is the study of the Torah together with worldly occupation, for the energy [taken up] by both of them keeps sin out of mind; and [as for study of the] Torah where there is no worldly occupation, the end thereof [is that] it comes to nought and brings sin in its train . . . Where there is no Torah there is no good breeding [derekh eretz]; where there is no good breeding there is no Torah . . . where there is no meal [flour] there is no Torah; where there is no Torah there is no meal"[113] (PA 2:2, 3:17).

Paul himself was committed to not eating "anyone's bread without paying for it" and not "being a burden" on anyone.[114] Although no knowledge exists concerning how and where Paul acquired his profession as a tent-maker (σκηνοποιός; skēnopoios) (Acts 18:3), the craft was apparently common among the Jews of Asia Minor. Aquila, who was also a tent-maker, was from Pontus (cf. Acts 18:3). It is sometimes suggested that Paul and others like him may have employed their trade in the service of the Roman army (cf. Safrai and Stern: 716).

The recently popular explanation that Paul was a weaver of tent cloth made from goat's hair or linen is misleading, leather in fact being the preferred medium.[115] Since a weaver would presumably have required large and awkward tools he would not have found frequent journeying – a hallmark of Paul's ministry – easy. A maker/repairer, on the other hand, might have been able to travel merely with a bag of cutting tools, awls, sharpening stone and such – and thus have been far more mobile (cf. Gill and Gempf: 6-7; Rapske: 107f).

It seems probable that master craftsmen and artisans constituted an organised factor in the larger diaspora communities, craft guilds functioning as a part of the Jewish communal structure (cf. Safrai and Stern: 483). The fact that the Sages did not belong to the aristocracy yet were accorded widespread respect among the general populace reflected a

---

[113] יפה תלמוד תורה עם דרך ארץ, שיגיעת שניהם משכחת עון. וכל תורה שאין עמה מלאכה, סופה בטלה, וגוררת עון . . . אם אין תורה אין דרך ארץ, אם אין דרך ארץ אין תורה . . . אם אין קמח אין תורה, אם אין תורה אין קמח.

[114] Cf. Acts 20:34; 1 Cor. 4:12, 9:1ff; 1 Thess. 2:9; 2 Thess. 3:6f.

[115] Cf. Livy, *Hist.* 5.2.7, 37.39.2.

dissolving of the previously existing class distinctions, at the same time as disdain for the labourer and craftsman also generally dissipated, although certain trades retained a negative stigma (cf. Jeremias, *Jerusalem*: 303ff).

Paul's own class and financial status can be only indirectly adduced from the literary evidence. His payment for the nazirite vow of four men (cf. Acts 21:23-24), his ability to maintain himself for two years in Caesarea (cf. Acts 24:23), Felix's hoped-for bribe (cf. Acts 24:26), possibly his decision to appeal to Caesar (cf. Acts 25:10f), his privileged standing and accompanying entourage as a prisoner to Rome (cf. Acts 27:3), and his occupation of private lodgings in Rome (cf. Acts 28:16) may all indicate a (relatively) financially-privileged position – although all these factors must be assessed in the light of custodial customs and prison life (cf. Rapske: 106). He had access to a secretary (scribe), to whom he dictated his letters (cf. Rom. 16:22), although he himself also commonly added a greeting.[116] He was frequently accompanied by assistants who at times served him and at others were sent by him to serve others,[117] nor was he ashamed of requesting the use of a "guest-room" (cf. Phlm 22), although he "rejoiced in every circumstance" when serving the Lord (cf. Phil. 4:11-12).

Marital status

The question of Paul's marital status has traditionally been a vexing one (cf. 1 Cor. 7:7-8, 9:5). Very few people are known as being unmarried in the world of the Sages. One of the few was Rabbi Eliezer b. Hyrcanus, who lived at the end of the Second Temple period and was still unmarried at twenty-two or twenty-eight, the accepted marriageable age for men being between eighteen and twenty (cf. PA 5:21; ARNb 13). In Eretz Israel, people tended to marry later than in Babylon, it therefore also being more common for students to study before marriage (cf. Steinsaltz, *Talmud*: 23). Late marriage was frequently the reflection of a poor economic situation, the fact that a wife moved into the groom's house requiring that he already possess a house and a means of livelihood (cf. Sot. 44a).

The only Jewish groups which appear to have made an institution of celibacy are the Essenes/Therapeutae – although in some essene communities the members seem to have taken wives[118] (cf. Vermes, *Jesus*: 99ff, and for the following discussion). Since sexual abstinence was included in the biblical ritual purity laws relating to the state of holiness, intercourse was forbidden in connection with all forms of worship because

---

[116] Cf. 1 Cor. 16:21; Gal. 6:11; Col. 4:18; 2 Thess. 3:17; Phlm 19. For the custom of using an amanuensis, see Introduction, **Form**.
[117] Cf. 1 Cor. 16:3; 2 Cor. 1:1; Phil. 2:19f; 2 Tim. 4:11; Tit. 3:12; Phlm 1.
[118] Cf. Jos.*War* 2.120f; Philo, *Hypoth.* 11.14-17; *Vit.Cont.* 68; Pliny, *Nat.Hist.* 5.15.73.

it caused ritual uncleanness lasting until the following evening (as did contact with a menstruating woman).[119]

The Sages also apparently understood prophecy and marriage to be incompatible. Moses is said to have voluntarily renounced relations with his wife on the grounds that if the Israelites – to whom God spoke only once and briefly – were ordered to temporarily abstain from women he, being in continual dialogue with God, should remain permanently chaste.[120] Such an explanation could be adduced by "celibate" Sages in the face of charges that deliberate abstinence was tantamount to murder: "Anyone who does not engage in the propagation of the race is as though he sheds blood כל מי שאין עוסק בפריה ורביה כאילו שופך דמים" (Yev. 63b).[121] Simeon b. Azzai, for example, pleaded unceasing devotion to Torah-study as an excuse for his lack of offspring: ". . . my soul is in love with the Torah; the world can be carried on by others אמר להן בן עזאי : ומה אעשה שנפשי חשקה בתורה? אפשר לעולם שיתקיים על ידי אחרים" (Yev. 63b). The Galilean chasid Pinchas b. Jair seems to include sexual abstinence in his well-known dictum: "Heedfulness leads to cleanliness, and cleanliness leads to purity, and purity leads to abstinence, and abstinence leads to holiness, and holiness leads to humility, and humility leads to the shunning of sin, and the shunning of sin leads to saintliness, and saintliness leads to [the gift of] the Holy Spirit, and the Holy Spirit leads to the resurrection of the dead"[122] (Sot. 9:15).[123]

Although disciples could quite commonly be bachelors, the early age of marriage frequently meant that they possessed a wife and children (cf. Lk. 4:38; 1 Cor. 9:5). Such men required their wife's permission to leave home to study with a Sage for longer than thirty days (cf. Ket. 5:6). Unmarried women are known from contemporary sources. Mary and Martha lived with their brother Lazarus, a fact which may indicate that they resided in their father's house (cf. Lk. 10:38f; Jn. 11:1ff). Neither Susanna nor Mary Magdalene are mentioned in connection with a husband – although any or all of the above may have been widows.[124]

The contemporary evidence overwhelmingly suggests, in consequence, that it would have been highly unusual for Paul to have been unmarried.

---

[119] Cf. Ex. 19:10-15; Lev. 15:18-23; Test.Naph. 8:8; CD-A 12:1-2; Jos.*War* 5.227.

[120] Cf. Philo, *Vit.Mos.* 2.68-69; Sifre, Be-he'al. 99; Shab. 87a.

[121] Cf. Gen.R. 34:14; Yalk.Gen. 61; Yalk.Num. 688.

[122] רבי פנחס בן יאיר אומר : זריזות (זהירות) מביאה לידי נקיות, ונקיות מביאה לידי טהרה, וטהרה מביאה לידי פרישות, ופרישות מביאה לידי קדשה, וקדשה מביאה לידי ענוה, וענוה מביאה לידי יראת חטא, ויראת חטא מביאה לידי חסידות, וחסידות מביאה לידי רוח הקדש. ורוח הקדש מביאה לידי תחית המתים.

[123] Cf. Cant.R. 1.1.9; Yalk.Dt. 933; Yalk.Isa. 503; Mid.Prov. 15; JShab. 1, 3, 3c; JShek. 14b; AZ 20b; Sot. 49b.

[124] Cf. Mt. 27:56, 61, 28:1; Mk. 15:40, 47, 16:1, 9; Lk. 8:2f, 24:10; Jn. 19:25, 20:1, 18.

INDEX OF SOURCES

Division: 1. Tanakh (OT). 2. New Testament. 3. Septuagint. 4. Apocrypha and Pseudepigrapha. 5. Qumran (DSS). 6. Josephus. 7. Philo. 8. Strabo. 9. Targum. 10. Midrash. 11. Mishna. 12. Tosefta. 13. Jerusalem Talmud. 14. Babylonian Talmud. 15. Prayer Book. 16. New Testament Apocrypha and Patristic Authors. 17. Greek and Latin Authors. 18. Maimonides. 19. Papyri and Inscriptions.

1. TANAKH

20:13ff, 14
20:14ff, 82
24:20, 248, 273
30:6, 45
30:9, 45
31:20, 148
33:8, 227

Ezra
1:3, 55
2:1-67, 452
2:62, 452
3:5, 259
4:17, 1
5:7, 1, 16
5:14, 55
7:12, 1, 16
8:1-14, 452
8:35, 18
9:1-10:44, 452
9:11, 4
10:19, 108

Nehemiah
1:9, 26
7:6-69, 452
7:64, 452
9:14, 227
9:20, 170
9:30, 49
10:33, 56
11:1, 55
11:3-24, 452
11:18, 55

Esther
2:5, 452
2:7, 240
8:5, 414
8:10, 414

Job
3:19, 36, 156, 353
4:8-9, 403
13:9, 402
13:10, 104
13:12, 184, 302

14:1, 265
15:14, 265
15:16, 136
25:4, 265
27:5, 151
28, 265
29:14, 248
42:15, 215

Psalms
1:6, 352
2, 50, 51
2:7, 50, 424
2:9, 212, 247
7:15, 343
7:16, 343
8:1, 33
8:4, 33
9:17, 96
10:4, 369
14:1, 165
15, 201
15:5, 328
17:8, 291
18:30, 156
18:35, 108
18:49, 210
18:50, 194, 208, 218
21:8, 108
22:6, 379
22:27, 45
24:3-4, 71
26:2, 398
27:1, 17
27:9, 234
27:10, 270
29:11, 376
30:7, 234
31:1f, 290
31:9-13, 86
31:19, 17
32:1-2, lxxii, 148, 194
34:8, 378
34:14, 376
35:13, 28
36:5-9, 194
36:9, 247

37:11, 379
37:25-26, 218
37:32, lxxii, xcii, 99, 317
37:32-33, 98
37:39-40, 99
38:1-22, 86
40:6-8, 22
40:7, 198, 264
40:10, 194
41:4, 31, 165
41:13, 24
42:1f, 208
44:3, 108
44:9-16, 19
44:22, 383
44:23-24, 234
46:10, 275
49:7, 204
50:7-23, 228
50:14, 155
50:23, 155
51:10, 358
51:10-13, 174
51:11-12, 376
52:8, 194
55:23, 144
59:17, 194
63:1f, 208
66:5, 241
67:1-7, 16
69:13, 101
69:17, 234
71:17, 187
72, 190
72:1, 187
72:10f, 313
72:17, 187, 188, 206, 211, 217
72:19, 24
76:2, 55
78:71, 260
79:6, 275
80:17, 108
82:1-4, 104
85:10, 101
85:11, 406

2. NEW TESTAMENT

496

A Commentary on the Jewish Roots of Galatians

3. SEPTUAGINT

4. APOCRYPHA AND PSEUDEPIGRAPHA

5. QUMRAN

19:7-14, 145
19:10-14, 295, 423
19:11-12, 185
19:18, 145
20:8, 262
20:11-13, 43
20:11f, 385
20:24-35, 185
20:29-40, 145
20:34, 132
21:1, 265
21:6-16, 185
21:8-9, 265
21:12f, 358
22:7-11, 185
23:4, 185
23:10, 48
23:11-15, 185
23:12-13, 265
23:12-15, 272
23:13-15, 20, 259
23:14-15, liv, 48
24:5, 360
26:11-12, 227

1QIsaiah^a
1:11, 197
51:5, 197

1QM
1:8f, 263
1:9, 17, 428
1:13, 371
4:7, 108, 263
7:18, 335
11:6-7, 59
11:10, 112
11:10f, 263
12:1-2, 313
12:3, 17, 428
13:1-3, 198
13:4, 21, 261
13:5-6, 371
13:9-10, 32
13:10, 101
13:10f, 21
13:11-12, 261

13:12f, 336
13:14, 32
13:14f, 263
14:7, 112
14:9, 21, 261
17:5, 263
17:7, 17
17:7-9, 428
17:8, 101

1QpHabakkuk
30
1:6, 31
1:13, 461
2:3, 272
2:9, 5
5:8-12, 463
5:9f, 461
7:1ff, 263
7:4, 86
7:4-6, 42
7:5, 5
7:17-8:3, 196
8:1-3, 146, 149, 198, 204
8:2, 19
8:3ff, 310
8:8, 461
8:11, 31
8:16, 461
9:2, 461
9:3-9, 31
9:3f, 310
9:8-12, 463
9:9f, 461
9:9ff, 91
10:5f, 310
10:9f, 91
11:2f, 462
11:4f, 461
11:13, 92, 102, 175, 250, 360
11:17-12:10, 31
12:2f, 461
12:3f, 112
12:6f, 310
12:9, 80

13:1, 118

1QS
lxx
1:1, 426
1:1-7, 351
1:1-5:22, 48
1:2, 148
1:3, 5
1:4, 389
1:5, 336
1:8, 45, 335, 356
1:11, 336
1:11-13, 101
1:11-17, 326
1:13f, 45, 335, 356
1:18, 21, 261
1:21-2:18, 426
2:1, 371
2:4-5, 34
2:11-12, 326
2:11-18, 34
2:15-17, 326
2:16-17, 203
2:24-25, 109
2:25, 262
2:26, 101, 336
3:1, 194
3:7, 101
3:8, 379, 391
3:9f, 45, 335, 356
3:16, 263
3:18, 335
3:18f, 45, 356
3:18ff, 352
3:20, 32
3:20-23, 261
3:20-24, 21
4:1ff, 352, 365
4:2, 132
4:2-8, 32, 375
4:2-14, 352
4:2f, 370, 385
4:2ff, 132, 358
4:3, 377, 378, 379, 391
4:6, 262

6. JOSEPHUS

7. PHILO

8. STRABO

9. TARGUMIM

10. MIDRASH

Exodus Rabbah
1:1, 316
1:15, 129
1:16, 401
2:1, 377
2:4, 59
2:6, 111
3:6, 234
3:12, 353
3:16, 183
5:9, 58
5:14, 5
10:3, 457
14:3, 104
15:1, liv, 171
15:7, 66, 92, 111
15:27, 177
15:29, 93
19:4, 377
21:6, 108
21:8, 189
23:5, 18, 189, 202, 238
23:10, 54, 311
25:12, 204, 230, 263, 373
27:1, 308
28:1, 33
28:3, 348
29:8, 33
30:5, 205, 301
30:12, xlix, 92, 94, 126
30:16, 104, 177
30:17, 368
30:19, 18
30:20, 352
30:21, 366
31:13, 353
31:17, 31
31:5-6, 353
32:7, 260
33:7, xlix, 94, 126
40:4, 453
41:5, 192

41:6, 66
41:7, 316
42:5, 192, 224
42:9, 224
43:4, 447
44:4, 177
46:4-5, 184
46:5, 144, 257, 270
47:3, 192, 266, 292
47:5, 284
48:2, 340
52:3, 66

Genesis Rabbah
1:1, 241
1:4, 188
1:6, 248
1:15, 26
2:3, 20
2:4, 174, 253, 272, 424
2:5, 59
3:8, 20
14:4, 353
14:6, 189
16:3, 380
16:4, 308
17:5, 243
20:8, 217
20:12, 248
23:5, 253
24:7, 348
26:4, 441
26:6, 234
30:6, 380
33:3, 61, 453
34:10, 337
34:14, 136, 334, 469
37:7, 436
38:6, 376
38:18, 376
39:1, 364
39:2, 189
39:11, 424
39:14, 295, 311

42:3, 6, 244
43:7, 189
43:8, 111
44:2, 410
44:4, 17
44:17, 243
44:18, 220
46:5, 92, 102, 175, 250, 360
48:1, 108
48:2, 290
48:8, 290
48:14, 284
49:8, 368
50:2, 290
51:8, 253
51:9, xxxiii
52:4, 353
53:5, 311
53:11, 316
54:4, 108
55:5, 202
55:7, 313
56:10, 55
56:11, 224
61:1, 224, 364
61:3, 408
63:8, liv, 56, 171
65:11, 308
67:8, 308
68:12, 111
69:7, 313
70:6, 189, 314
71:9, 453
73:3, 234
75:5, lxvii, 1, 16
75:8, 18
75:11, 66, 111
85:1, 59
85:2, 184
93:7, 197
93:11, 197
94:5, 66
95:3, 224
96:2, 186

23:8, 189
23:12, 424
24:11, 377
24:12, 230
26:4, 20
27:2, 169
27:2-3, 424
28:1, 129
S 3:2, 234
S 6:5, 238, 248

Ruth Rabbah
3:1, 36, 156, 353
5:6, 59
8:1, 36, 156, 253, 353

Sifra on
Leviticus
Acharei mot
13, 93, 364

Kedoshim
4:12, 348
8:3, 327
9:11-12, 362
Emor
2, 450
9, 56

Be-Har
5, 93

Be-chukkotai
7, 15
8, 227
13:7, 41

Sifre
Deuteronomy
32, 160, 189, 383
34, 15, 281, 284, 440
41, 41, 308, 404
48, 404
74, 83
154, 56, 152, 309, 328

186/87, 393
188, 10
221, 205
305, 288
311, 213
346, 213
352, 56, 309
354, lxi

Sifre Numbers
Be-he'alotekha
73, 220
99, 469
104, 32

Shallach
107, 93

Korach
116, 452

Pinchas
3, 108
140, 447, 449

Masa'ei
161, 15

Sifre Zuta on
Numbers
Pinchas
1, 291

Seder Olam
Rabbah
3, 131, 220, 463

Tanhuma
Lekh lekha
3, 424

Chayai Sara
6, 408

Toldot
14, 32, 66

Vayetzei
7, 197

Vayishlach
3, 1, 16

Vayeshev
4, 242

Vaychi
10, 42

Shmot
1, 316
4, 220
25, 58

Bo
10, 819

Pkudei
1, 313, 413

Be-shallach
20, 413

Yitro
6, lxii

Mishpatim
7, 352, 364
15, 213, 413

Terumah
3, 308
8, 186
10, 348

Ki tissa
20, 316

837, 189
838, 129
841, 268, 284
891, 268
898, 42, 186, 263
930, 205
933, 332, 375, 469
938, 184
946, 373
951, xlix

Ezra
1067, 450

Job
886, 36, 156, 353
906, 184

Psalms
438, 313
613, 466

641, 265
678, 466
733, 273
880, 273

Proverbs
943, 110
944, 110
959, 407

Canticles
986, 23
992, 238

Isaiah
395, 373
409, 189
477, 236
479, 151
503, 332, 375, 469
508, 42, 186, 263

Jeremiah
273, 268
312, 272

Ezekiel
383, 311, 312

Hosea
519, 289, 410

Zechariah
569, 23
576, 230
585, 189

Yalkut Hamakiri
Isaiah
61:10, 248

11. MISHNA

Abodah Zarah
1:1f, 120
1:7, 120
2:1, 118
2:3ff, 121
2:5, 15
3:4, 120
3:6, 119
3:7, 120
3:8, xlix, 126
5:5, 121
5:12, 123

Arakhin
2:4, 452
8:6, 32

Baba Bathra
3:1, 65

5:2, 441
8:6, 214
8:7, 215
10:7, 256

Baba Kamma
8:6, 183, 286

Baba Mezia
2:8, 41
2:11, 281, 440
3:4-5, 41
4:9, 257
5:1, 353
5:3, 65
6:8, 26
7:1, 183
8:3, 4, 257

Berakoth
2:1, 16
2:2, 323
3:3, 256
5:5, 3

Bikkurim
1:5, 100
3:2, 80

Demai
120
2:2-3, 123
2:3, 446
3:1, 120

Eduyoth
1:3, 327
2:1, 327

12. TOSEFTA

| Yoma (Yom Hakippurim) | 4:20, 119 | Zabim 2:1, 119 |

13. JERUSALEM TALMUD

N.B. This index contains two numbering systems. The three digit notation refers to the Hebrew Academy Jerusalem Talmud (see Abbreviations). The single notation a/b refers to the Bar Ilan data base and is listed at the ending of the relevant tractate.

14. BABYLONIAN TALMUD

15. PRAYER BOOK

16. NEW TESTAMENT APOCRYPHA AND PATRISTIC AUTHORS

17. LATIN AND GREEK AUTHORS

18. MAIMONIDES

19. PAPYRI AND INSCRIPTIONS

INDEX OF AUTHORS

Dunn, J., xli, liv, 18, 68, 78, 91,
120, 134, 142, 143, 147, 183,
195, 222, 252, 255, 265
Dupont-Sommer, A., 76, 197, 456,
463
Ebeling, G., 236, 237
Elon, M., 3, 4, 10, 21, 32, 40, 70,
90, 215, 233, 256, 257, 258, 268,
304, 451
Esler, P., 125, 134
Feldman, L., xxxiii, xlviii, li, lv,
90, 96, 266
Ferguson, E., xlvii, 14, 280, 456
Finn, T., 96
Fish, S., 166
Fitzmyer, J., 205
Flusser, D., 18, 20, 23, 32, 36, 61,
70, 105, 106, 112, 113, 131, 148,
151, 175, 197, 259, 265, 272,
290, 291, 294, 296, 304, 309,
326, 336, 347, 348, 349, 352,
353, 359, 396, 400, 404, 411,
428, 430, 445, 447, 455, 463
Frank, Y., 213
Frankel, E. and Teutsch, B., 84
Fredrikson, P., 460
Frei, H., 204
Fung, R., 65
Gafni, I., 410
Gager, J., xxiv, xxv, xxvi, xliv,
lxvi, lxix, 44, 100, 149
Gärtner, B., 102, 106, 110, 112,
155, 411
Germano, M., 463
Gill, D. and Gempf, C., xxvii,
xxxii, 14, 54, 122, 280, 311, 467
Goodman, M., li, lv, 96, 147
Hachlili, R., 82, 435, 437, 440
Handelman, S., 182
Hansen, G.W., 282, 420
Hay, D., 108
Hays, R., lxviii, lxxxv, lxxxvi, xc,
xci, xcii, 8, 19, 23, 50, 51, 52, 53,
78, 141, 142, 143, 146, 159, 161,

162, 163, 164, 167, 168, 170,
171, 172, 182, 183, 184, 185,
187, 189, 190, 193, 196, 197,
199, 200, 203, 204, 207, 208,
209, 211, 212, 214, 216, 218,
233, 236, 237, 242, 243, 244,
245, 251, 255, 263, 264, 265,
267, 271, 276, 278, 279, 283,
291, 292, 293, 296, 297, 301,
303, 307, 308, 309, 313, 314,
315, 317, 319, 321, 322, 328,
329, 330, 332, 333, 334, 336,
339, 345, 346, 362, 365, 388,
393, 394, 403, 404, 409, 423,
427, 431, 466
Hebert, A., 141
Hemer, C., xxix, xxxi, xxxii,
xxxiv, xxxviii, xl, xli, xlii, 72, 96
Hengel, M., xlviii, 96, 125, 126,
460, 466
Herschell, R., 314
Higger, M., 141
Horgan, M., 303
Howard, G., xxxvii, xlii, xlv, lxv,
lxvi, 67, 107, 175, 182, 183, 185
Hugger, J., lxiv
Hvalvik, R., 76
Ilan, T., 443
Irwin, 251
Jeremias, J., 6, 80, 82, 272, 273,
305, 440, 450, 452, 467, 468
Jervell, J., 453
Jewett, R., xlviii, xlix, l, 125
Kampen, J. and Bernstein, M.,
lxix, lxx, lxxi, lxxii, lxxiii, 44,
151, 336, 339
Keck, L., xc
Keener, C., lxi, 29, 167, 196
Kim, S., xli, lxvi, 22, 24, 41, 42, 43,
44, 47, 49, 50, 51, 52, 53, 57, 60,
76, 86, 89, 170, 209, 210, 271,
330, 409
Knohl, 197

GENERAL INDEX

Shame, 25, 166, 176,
177, 287, 348, 352,
361, 389, 408
Shaming in public,
92, 133
Shammai, 138, 349,
467 *See also* Beit
Shammai
Shavuot (Pentecost),
61, 442
Shekhina, 213, 290,
368
Shema, 137, 229, 298,
384, 443
Shemaiah, lviii
Shepherd, 275
Shikcha ("forgotten
sheaves"), 112
Shimon b. Jochai, 121
Shimon b. Kosibah, 2
Shimon b. Shetach,
467
Shittim, 366
Shmoneh Esreh
(Eighteen
Benedictions/
Amidah), lxxxiv,
427, 428, 429, 463
Shoot of God, 212,
247
Shorthand, lxvii,
lxxxix
Shurat ha-din
(according to strict
justice), 204
Shutting off, 151, 293
Shutting out, lxxxix,
234, 235, 293, 419
Sicarii, xlix
Sick, visiting of
(bikur cholim),
121, 155, 357
Sickness, 31, 165-66
– Paul's, 286

Sidon, 115
Signifieds, 318
Signifiers, 318
Signs and wonders,
10, 32, 41, 180
Signum, 437
Silas, xxxiv, xxxix, lii,
437
Silvanus, 437
Simeon, 219
Simeon Niger, 13,
115
Simeon, Gamaliel's
father, 447
Simon b. Gamaliel,
444
Simon the high
priest, 458
Simon the Zealot, 126
Sin, xxxix, lxii, lxxv,
lxxvi, lxxvii, lxxix,
lxxx, lxxxi, lxxxii,
lxxxvi, lxxxviii, xc,
xciv, xcv, xcvi, 1,
18, 19, 20, 21, 22,
23, 28, 88, 95, 97,
99, 100, 107, 117,
128, 132, 133, 136,
137, 139, 141, 142,
144, 145, 147, 150,
152, 153, 154, 155,
158, 160, 161, 164,
165, 166, 171, 179,
184, 192, 201, 204,
205, 207, 223, 224,
225, 226, 228, 229,
231, 232, 233, 234,
236, 242, 247, 249,
250, 252, 255, 260,
261, 262, 263, 266,
269, 270, 273, 277,
281, 284, 286, 290,
291, 296, 301, 304,
308, 312, 314, 319,

322, 323, 324, 331,
343, 347, 350, 353,
354, 358, 359, 360,
361, 362, 363, 366,
378, 380, 382, 385,
388, 389, 390, 391,
393, 394, 396, 399,
400, 401, 404, 408,
409, 412, 415, 422,
423, 424, 428, 429,
431, 432
– Adam's, 188, 196
– and sickness, 31
– bondage to, lv,
lxii, lxxvi, lxxix,
lxxx, lxxxi, lxxxvi,
xcvi, 17, 18, 19, 21,
22, 24, 99, 100, 137,
155, 160, 164, 165,
169, 178, 182, 204,
220, 232, 234, 235,
242, 259, 260, 261,
262, 266, 267, 269,
272, 274, 275, 280,
281, 283, 291, 294,
298, 304, 305, 314,
319, 322, 323, 324,
330, 351, 362, 363,
378, 384, 386, 389,
391, 394, 395, 412,
416, 419, 422, 424,
429, 432
– fleeing from, 353
– multiplicity of,
230, 231
– offerings, 97, 231
Sinai, xciv, 33, 35, 57,
58, 59, 60, 61, 220,
226, 243, 298, 301,
303, 304, 307, 308,
309, 310, 313, 362
Sinai Peninsula, 61
Singular (collective),
339

— goal of, 174, 211,
244, 272, 328, 338,
349, 350, 356, 332
— interpretation of,
105
— maintains world,
348
— messianic, 394
— narrative role of,
264
— Oral (halakhah),
356, 442
— power of, 233
— pre-existence of,
188, 241
— role of, 223, 224,
242
— speaks in human
language, 213
— supercession of,
232
— violation of, 192,
193, 203, 211
— works of, l, lxix,
lxx, lxxii, lxxiii,
139, 141, 142, 145,
148, 164, 173, 178,
179, 185, 193, 194,
195, 299, 318, 345,
363, 365, 398
Torah-observance,
xliv, l, lvi, lx, lxii,
lxiv, lxvi, lxxviii,
lxxix, lxxx, lxxxi,
lxxxii, lxxxiv,
lxxxviii, xc, 15,
100, 133, 141, 148,
153, 158, 164, 172,
173, 174, 178, 179,
181, 191, 192, 200,
201, 202, 203, 207,
221, 223, 224, 269,
277, 283, 284, 294,
298, 318, 319, 323,

325, 327, 328, 333,
345, 346, 363, 364,
398, 405, 415, 416,
418, 419
Torah-study, lxxvii,
lxxxvii, xcv, 93, 94,
136, 137, 141, 142,
145, 150, 158, 169,
173, 195, 333, 390,
407, 425, 443, 447,
448, 467, 469
Tracheia, 74
Trachonitis, 60
Trades, 440, 466, 467,
468
Tradition, 23, 26, 35,
36, 40, 41, 47, 52,
55
— Jesus tradition,
50
Traditions, ancestral
46, 95
Transgressio, 36, 38
Transitional
passages, xlvi
— seams, xlvi
Transitus, 36
Transjordan, 62
Trials, Abraham's,
177, 288, 302
Tribes, 452, 453
— chiefs of, 310
— twelve, 14
Triennial cycle, 299,
300
Troas, xxxii
Trocmi, xxvii, xxviii
Truth, 38, 101, 102,
109, 117, 132, 144,
146, 149, 152, 155,
166, 176, 180, 184,
197, 198, 212, 218,
221, 227, 247, 250,
265, 292, 306, 325,

335, 336, 339, 351,
360, 361, 365, 376,
384, 389, 391, 393,
398, 399, 405, 408,
423, 428, 431
Truthfulness, God's,
208
Turning back, lv,
lxxx, 274, 276, 277,
280, 366
Tutor, lxxix, 195, 225,
238, 240, 242, 244,
260, 273, 380
Twelve, the, 9, 11, 68,
111 *See also*
Apostles
Two Masters, lxxxii,
36, 156, 323, 353,
359
Two Spirits, 306, 351,
352, 353, 361
Two Ways, lxxxii,
132, 306, 351, 352,
353, 362, 364, 382
Two-front
hypothesis, 278
Typology, 54, 142,
160, 186, 309, 314
Tyre, 121
Uncircumcision,
lxxvii, 102, 142,
173, 331, 358, 359,
360, 421, 423
Unity, of God, lxxix,
xc, 107, 137, 185,
188, 194, 225, 227,
229, 230, 231, 245,
246, 251, 252, 253
— of humanity, 227,
348
— of Scripture, 186
Unwritten law, 222
Ur, 246

BIBLIOGRAPHY

Abegg, M. "Paul, 'Works of the Law' and MMT," *Biblical Archaeology Review* 20 (1994), 52-55, 81.

--------. "4QMMT C27, 31 and 'Works Righteousness'," *Dead Sea Discoveries* 6 (1999), 139-47.

--------. "4QMMT, Paul, and 'Works of the Law'." In P. Flint (ed.), *The Bible at Qumran: Text, Shape, and Interpretation.* Grand Rapids: Eerdmans, 2001:203-216.

Abrahams, I. *Studies in Pharisaism and the Gospels.* First and Second Series. New York: Ktav, 1967.

Alexander, P. "Rabbinic Biography and the Biography of Jesus: A Survey of the Evidence." In C. Tuckett (ed.), *Synoptic Studies.* Sheffield: JSOT Press, 1984:19-50.

Alon, G. *Studies in Jewish History in the Times of the Second Temple, the Mishna and the Talmud.* Tel Aviv: Hakibbutz Hameuchad, 1958. 2 vols. [Hebrew: מחקרים בתולדות ישראל בימי בית שני ובתקופת המשנה והתלמוד].

--------. "The Attitude of the Pharisees to the Roman Government and the House of Herod," *Scripta Hierosolymitana* 7 (1961), 53-78.

--------. *Jews, Judaism and the Classical World.* Jerusalem: Magnes Press, 1977.

--------. *The Jews in their Land in the Talmudic Age.* 2 vols. Jerusalem: Magnes Press, 1984.

Arndt, W. and F. Gingrich. *A Greek-English Lexicon of the New Testament and Other Early Christian Literature.* Chicago: University of Chicago Press, 1972. (BAGD)

Aune, D. *Prophecy in Early Christianity and the Ancient Mediterranean World.* Grand Rapids: Eerdmans, 1983.

Avi-Yonah, J. *The Jews under Roman and Byzantine Rule.* Jerusalem: Magnes Press, 1984.

Bagatti, B. *The Church from the Circumcision.* Jerusalem: Franciscan Printing Press, 1984.

Bamberger, B. *Proselytism in the Talmudic Period.* New York: Ktav, 1968.

Bammel, E. "Galater 1:23," Zeitschrift für die neutestamentliche Wissenchaft 59 (1968), 109-12.

Bauckham, R. "Barnabas in Galatians," *Journal for the Study of the New Testament* 2 (1979), 61-70.

--------. *Jude and the Relatives of Jesus in the Early Church.* Edinburgh: T&T Clark, 1990.

--------. (ed.). *The Book of Acts in its First Century Setting.* Vol. 4: Palestinian Setting. Grand Rapids: Eerdmans, 1995.

Baumgarten, J. "The Pharisaic-Sadducean Controversies About Purity and the Qumran Texts," *Journal of Jewish Studies* 31 (1980), 157-170.

Baur, F.C. *Paulus, der Apostel Jesu Christi.* Stuttgart: 1845.

Ben-Shalom, I. *Beit Shammai and the Zealots' Struggle against Rome.* Jerusalem: Yad Ben-Zvi Institute, 1993. [Hebrew: בית שמאי ומאבק הקנאים נגד רומי].

Berkovits, E. *Not in Heaven: The Nature and Function of Halakha.* New York: Ktav, 1983.

Betz, H.D. "Die Vision des Paulus im Tempel von Jerusalem – Apg 22,17-21 als Beitrag zur Deutung des Damaskuserlebnisses." In O. Böcher and K. Haacker, *Verborum Veritas. Festschrift Gustav Stählin.* Wuppertal: 1970, 113-23.

--------. *Galatians.* Philadelphia: Fortress Press, 1979.

Betz, O. "The Qumran Halakhah Text Miqsat Ma'ase Ha-Torah (4QMMT) and Sadducean, Essene, and Early Pharisaic Tradition." In D. Beattie and M. McNamara (eds.), *The Aramaic Bible: Targums in their Historical Context.* Sheffield: JSOT Press, 1994:176-202.

Bivin, D. "Matthew 16:18: the *Petros-petra* Wordplay – Greek, Aramaic, or Hebrew?," *Jerusalem Perspective* 46/47 (1994), 32-38.

Bockmuehl, M. *Jewish Law in Gentile Churches: Halakhah and the Beginning of Christian Public Ethics.* Edinburgh: T&T Clark, 2000.

--------. "Simon Peter's Names in Jewish Sources," *Journal of Jewish Studies* 55.1 (2004), 58-80.

Boyarin, D. *Intertextuality and the Reading of Midrash.* Bloomington: Indiana University Press, 1990.

--------. *A Radical Jew: Paul and the Politics of Identity.* Berkeley: University of California Press, 1994.

Braude, W. and Kapstein, I. *Pesikta de Rab Kahana.* Philadelphia: Jewish Publication Society, 1975.

Brooke, G. *Exegesis at Qumran*. Sheffield: JSOT Press, 1985.

--------. "Luke-Acts and the Qumran Scrolls: The Case of MMT." In C. Tuckett (ed.), *Luke's Literary Achievement: Collected Essays*. Sheffield: Sheffield Academic Press, 1995:72-90.

Brown, F., Driver, S., and Briggs, C. *A Hebrew and English Lexicon of the Old Testament*. Oxford: Clarendon Press, 1959. (BDB)

Bruce, F.F. *The Book of the Acts*. Grand Rapids: Eerdmans, 1988.

--------. *The Epistle to the Galatians*. Exeter: Paternoster Press/Grand Rapids: Eerdmans, 2002².

Büchler, A. "The Reading of the Law and Prophets in a Triennial Cycle," *Jewish Quarterly Review* 6 (1984), 1-73.

Burton, E. de Witt. *A Critical and Exegetical Commentary on the Epistle to the Galatians*. Edinburgh: T&T Clark, 1921.

Chapman, J. "St. Paul and Revelation to St. Peter, Matt. XVI.17," *Revue Bénédictine* 29 (1912), 133-47.

Charlesworth, J. (ed.). *The Old Testament Pseudepigrapha*. 2 vols. New York: Doubleday and Co., 1985.

Cohen, S.J.D. "Was Timothy Jewish (Acts 16:1-3)? Patristic Exegesis, Rabbinic Law, and Matrilinear Descent," *Journal of Biblical Literature* 105.2 (1986), 251-68.

--------. "Crossing the Boundary and Becoming a Jew," *Harvard Theological Review* 80 (1987), 13-33.

--------. "The Rabbinic Conversion Ceremony," *Journal of Jewish Studies* 41.2 (1990), 177-203.

Cohen, Y. "The Attitude to the Gentile in the Halakhah and in Reality in the Tannaitic Period," *Immanuel* 9 (1979), 32-41.

Culler, J. *The Pursuit of Signs: Semiotics, Literature, Deconstruction*. Ithaca: Cornell University Press, 1981.

Cullmann, O. *The Christology of the New Testament*. London: SCM, 1963).

Dahl, N. *Studies in Paul: Theology for the Early Christian Mission*. Minneapolis: Augsburg, 1977.

--------. "Paul's Letter to the Galatians: Epistolary Genre, Content, and Structure." In M. Nanos (ed.), *The Galatians Debate*. Massachusetts: Hendrickson, 2002:117-142.

Danby, H. *The Mishnah*. Oxford: Oxford University Press, 1933.

Daube, D. "Rabbinic Methods of Interpretation and Hellenistic Rhetoric," *Hebrew Union College Annual* 22 (1949), 239-64.

--------. *The New Testament and Rabbinic Judaism*. Massachusetts: Hendrickson, 1956.

Davies, W.D. *Paul and Rabbinic Judaism*. New York: Harper, 1948.

--------. *Torah in the Messianic Age and/or the Age to Come*. Philadelphia: Society of Biblical Literature, 1952.

--------. *Jewish and Pauline Studies*. London: SPCK, 1984.

578

A Commentary on the Jewish Roots of Galatians

Dodd, C.H. *More New Testament Studies.* Manchester: Manchester University Press, 1968.

Donaldson, T. "Proselytes or 'Righteous Gentiles'? The Status of Gentiles in Eschatological Pilgrimage Patterns of Thought," *Journal for the Study of the Pseudepigrapha* 7 (1990), 3-27.

Drake, H. "The Book of Romans: A Believers' House Church Manifesto?" MA Thesis, Golden Gate Seminary, 1996. (www.hccentral.com/romans)

Dreyfus, F. "Divine Condescendence (SYNKATABASIS) as a Hermeneutic Principle in Jewish and Christian Tradition," *Immanuel* 19 (1984/5), 74-86.

Driver, S. and Neubauer, A. *The Fifty-Third Chapter of Isaiah According to the Jewish Interpreters.* 2 vols. New York: Ktav, 1969.

Dunn, J. *Baptism in the Holy Spirit.* Philadelphia: Westminster Press, 1970.

--------. *Christology in the Making.* London: SCM, 1980.

--------. "The Incident at Antioch (Gal. 2:11-18)," *Journal for the Study of the New Testament* 18 (1983), 3-57. Reprinted in M. Nanos (ed.), *The Galatians Debate.* Massachusetts: Hendrickson, 2002: 199-234.

--------. "The New Perspective on Paul," *Bulletin of the John Rylands Library* 65 (1985), 95-122. Reprinted in *Jesus, Paul, and the Law: Studies in Mark and Galatians.* Louisville: Westminster John Knox, 1990:183-214.

--------. *Jesus, Paul, and the Law: Studies in Mark and Galatians.* Louisville: Westminster John Knox, 1990.

--------. *The Epistle to the Galatians.* Massachusetts: Hendrickson, 1993.

--------. *The Theology of Paul's Letter to the Galatians.* Cambridge: Cambridge University Press, 1993.

--------. "4QMMT and Galatians," *New Testament Studies* 43 (1997), 147-53.

--------. *The Theology of Paul the Apostle.* Grand Rapids: Eerdmans, 1997.

Dupont-Sommer, A. *The Essene Writings from Qumran.* Gloucester, Massachusetts: Peter Smith, 1973.

Ebeling, G. *Word and Faith.* Philadelphia: Fortress, 1963.

Elon, M. (ed.). *The Principles of Jewish Law.* Jerusalem: Keter, 1975.

Encyclopedia Judaica. Jerusalem: Keter, 1974.

Esler, P. "Making and Breaking an Agreement Mediterranean Style: A New Reading of Galatians 2:1-14." In M. Nanos, *The Galatians Debate.* Massachusetts: Hendrickson, 2002:261-81.

Feldman, L. "The Omnipresence of the G-d Fearers," *Biblical Archaeology Review* 12.5 (1986), 58-69.

--------. *Jew and Gentile in the Ancient World.* Princeton: Princeton University Press, 1993.

Ferguson, E. *Early Christians Speak.* Abilene: Abilene Christian University Press, 1981.

--------. *Backgrounds of Early Christianity.* Grand Rapids: Eerdmans, 1987.

Finkelstein, L. *The Pharisees.* 2 vols. Philadelphia: Jewish Publication Society, 1962.

Finn, T. "The Godfearers Reconsidered," *Catholic Biblical Quarterly* 47 (1985), 75-84.

Fish, S. *Is There A Text in This Class?: The Authority of Interpretive Communities.* Cambridge: Harvard University Press, 1980.

Fitzmyer, J. "Paul's Jewish Background and the Deeds of the Law." In *According to Paul: Studies in the Theology of the Apostle.* New York: Paulist Press, 1993:20-35.

--------. *The Semitic Background of the New Testament.* Grand Rapids: Eerdmans, 1997.

Flint, P. (ed.), *The Bible at Qumran.* Grand Rapids: Eerdmans, 2001.

Flusser, D. "Pharisees, Sadducees, and Essenes in Pesher Nahum." In M. Dorman, S. Safrai, and M. Stern (eds.), *Studies in the History of Israel and the Hebrew Language.* Tel Aviv: Hakibbutz Hameuchad, 1970:133-160. [Hebrew: מחקרים בתולדות ישראל ובלשון העברית; English summary in *Immanuel* 1 (1962), 39-41.]

--------. *Jewish Sources in Early Christianity.* Tel Aviv: HaKibbutz HaArtzi HaShomer HaTzair, 1979. [Hebrew: יהדות ומקורות הנצרות].

--------. *Judaism and the Origins of Christianity.* Jerusalem: Magnes Press, 1988.

--------. "The Decalogue and the New Testament," *Jerusalem Perspective* 3.6 (1990), 6-11.

--------. "Some of the Precepts of the Torah from Qumran (4QMMT) and the Benediction Against the Heretics," *Tarbiz* 61 (1992), 333-73. [Hebrew: מקצת מעשי התורה" וברכת המינים].

--------. *Jesus.* Jerusalem: Magnes Press, 1997.

Fox, R.L. *Pagans and Christians.* San Francisco: Harper, 1986.

Fraade, S. "To Whom It May Concern: 4QMMT and Its Addressee(s)," *Revue de Qumran* 76.19 (2000), 507-26.

Frank, Y. *The Practical Talmudic Dictionary.* Jerusalem: Ariel, 1991.

Frankel, E. and Teutsch, B. *The Encyclopedia of Jewish Symbols.* Northvale, NJ: Jason Aronson Inc., 1992.

Fredrikson, P. "Judaism, the Circumcision of Gentiles, and Apocalyptic Hope: Another Look at Galatians 1 and 2." In M. Nanos (ed.), *The Galatians Debate.* Massachusetts: Hendrickson, 2002: 235-60.

Freedman, D. (ed.). *Anchor Bible Dictionary.* New York: Doubleday, 1992. (ABD)

Frei, H. *The Identity of Jesus Christ.* Philadelphia: Fortress, 1975.

Frey, J.B. *Corpus Inscriptionum Iudicarum.* New York: 1975. (CIJ I²)

--------. *Corpus Inscriptionum Iudicarum II.* Rome: 1952.

Fung, R. *The Epistle to the Galatians.* Grand Rapids: Eerdmans, 1988.

Fitzmyer, J. "Crucifixion in Ancient Palestine, Qumran Literature, and the NT," *Catholic Biblical Quarterly* 40 (1978), 493-513.

Gafni, I. *Land, Center and Diaspora.* Sheffield: Sheffield Academic Press, 1997.

Gager, J. *Reinventing Paul.* Oxford: Oxford University Press, 2000.

Gärtner, B. *The Temple and the Community in Qumran and the New Testament.* Cambridge: Cambridge University Press, 1965.

Gathercole, S. *Where is Boasting? Early Jewish Soteriology and Paul's Response in Romans 1-5.* Grand Rapids: Eerdmans, 2002.

Germano, M. "The Last Seder: Unscrambling the Baffling Chronology of the First Christian Passover," *Biblical Archaeology* 4.3 (2001). http//:www.bibarch.com

Gill, D. and Gempf, C. (eds.). *The Book of Acts in its First Century Setting.* Vol. 2: Graeco-Roman Setting. Grand Rapids: Eerdmans, 1994.

Goodman, M. *Mission and Conversion: Proselytizing in the Religious History of the Roman Empire.* Oxford: Clarendon Press, 1994.

Hachlili, R. "Jewish Names and Epithets in the Second Temple Period," *Eretz Israel* 17 (1984), 188-211. [Hebrew: שמות וכינויים אצל היהודים בתקופת הבית השני].

Handelman, S. *The Slayers of Moses: The Emergence of Rabbinic Interpretation in Modern Literary Theory.* Albany: State University of New York Press, 1982.

Hansen, G.W. *Abraham in Galatians: Epistolary and Rhetorical Contexts.* Sheffield: JSOT Press, 1989.

--------. *Galatians.* Downers Grove, Ill.: InterVarsity Press, 1994.

-------- "A Paradigm of the Apocalypse: The Gospel in the Light of Epistolary Analysis." In M. Nanos (ed.), *The Galatians Debate.* Massachusetts: Hendrickson, 2002: 143-54.

Hanson, A. *Studies in Paul's Technique and Theology.* London: SPCK, 1974.

Harink, D. *Paul among the Postliberals.* Grand Rapids: Baker Book House Co., 2003.

Hay, D. *Glory at the Right Hand: Psalm 110 in Early Christianity.* Nashville/New York: Abingdon, 1973.

Hays, R. "Psalm 143 and the Logic of Romans 3," *Journal of Biblical Literature* 99 (1980), 107-15.

--------. "Christology and Ethics in Galatians," *Catholic Biblical Quarterly* 49 (1987), 268-90.

--------. *Echoes of Scripture in the Letters of Paul.* New Haven: Yale University Press, 1989.

--------. "'The Righteous One' as Eschatological Deliverer: A Case Study in Paul's Apocalyptic Hermeneutics." In J. Marcus and M. Soards (eds.), *Apocalyptic and the New Testament: Essays in Honor of J. Louis Martyn.* Sheffield: JSOT, 1989.

--------. *The Letter to the Galatians.* Nashville: Abingdon, 2000.

--------. *The Faith of Jesus Christ: An Investigation of the Narrative Substructure of Galatians 3:1-4:11.* Grand Rapids: Eerdmans, 2002[2].

Hebert, A. "'Faithfulness and 'Faith'," *Theology* 58 (1955), 373-79.

Hemer, C.J. *The Book of Acts in the Setting of Hellenistic History*. Ed. by C. Gempf. Tübingen: J.C.B. Mohr, 1989.

Hengel, M. *Judaism and Hellenism*. 2 vols. London: SCM, 1974.

--------. *The Zealots*. Edinburgh: T&T Clark, 1989.

Herschell, R. *A Brief Sketch of the Present State and Future Expectations of the Jews*. London: J. Unwin, 1937.

Higger, M. *Intention in Talmudic Law*. PhD Thesis, Columbia University, 1927.

Horgan, M. *Pesharim: Qumran Interpretations of Biblical Books*. Washington: Catholic Biblical Association of America, 1979.

Horsely, G. *New Documents Illustrating Early Christianity*. Sydney: Macquarie University, 1981-1992.

Howard, G. "On the 'Faith of Christ'," *Harvard Theological Review* 60 (1967), 459-65.

--------. "The Faith of Christ," *Expository Times* 85 (1974), 212-15.

--------. *Paul: Crisis in Galatia*. Cambridge: Cambridge University Press, 1979.

Hugger, J. *Historical Aspects*. Tel-Aviv: Association of Hebrew Writers and Dvir Co., 1951. [Hebrew: בחינות היסטוריות].

Hvalvik, R. *The Struggle for Scripture and Covenant: The Purpose of the Epistle of Barnabas and Jewish-Christian Competition in the Second Century*. Oslo: Det teologiske Menighetsfakultet, 1994.

Ilan, T. *Jewish Women in Greco-Roman Palestine*. Massachusetts: Hendrickson, 1995.

Jastrow, M. *A Dictionary of the Targumim, the Talmud Babli and Yerushalmi, and the Midrashic Literature*. Israel: Hillel Press [n.d.].

Jeremias, J. *The Lord's Prayer*. Phil.: Fortress Press, 1964.

--------. *Abba. Studien zur neutestamentlichen Theologie und Zeitgeschichte*. Göttingen: 1966.

--------. *Jerusalem in the Time of Jesus*. London: SCM, 1967.

Jervell, J. *Luke and the People of God*. Minneapolis: Augsburg Publishing House, 1972.

Jewett, R. "The Agitators and the Galatian Congregation," *New Testament Studies* 17 (1970/71), 198-212. Reprinted in M. Nanos (ed.), *The Galatians Debate*. Massachusetts: Hendrickson, 2002: 334-47.

--------. *Dating Paul's Life/A Chronology of Paul's Life*. London: SCM/Philadelphia: Fortress Press, 1979.

Kaiser, W. "James' View of the Law," *Mishkan* 1-2 (1988), 9-12.

Kampen, J. and Bernstein, M. (eds.). *Reading 4QMMT*. Atlanta: Scholars Press, 1996.

Keener, C. *The IVP Bible Background Commentary: New Testament*. Downers Grove, Ill.: InterVarsity Press, 1993.

Kim, S. *The Origin of Paul's Gospel*. Grand Rapids: Eerdmans, 1982.

--------. *Paul and the New Perspective*. Grand Rapids: Eerdmans, 2002.

Kittel, F. *Theological Dictionary of the New Testament*. 10 vols. Grand Rapids: Eerdmans, 1964. (TDNT)

Knohl, I. *The Messiah before Jesus*. Berkeley: University of California Press, 2000.

Kobelski, P. *Melchizedek and Melchireša'*. Washington: The Catholic Biblical Association of America, 1981.

Kraabel, A. "The Disappearance of the 'God-Fearers'," *Numen* 28 (1981), 113-26.

--------. "The Roman Diaspora: Six Questionable Assumptions," *Journal of Jewish Studies* 33 (1982), 445-64.

--------. "The God-fearers Meet the Beloved Disciple." In B. Pearson, *The Future of Early Christianity*. Minneapolis: Fortress Press, 1991:276-84.

Kulp, J. "The Participation of a Court in the Jewish Conversion Process," *Jewish Quarterly Review* 94.3 (2004), 437-70.

Kvasnica, B. "The 'Works of the Law' in Paul and the Dead Sea Scrolls." Unpublished paper.

Lachs, S. *A Rabbinic Commentary on the New Testament*. New York: Ktav, 1987.

Leach, E. *Genesis as Myth and Other Essays*. London: Cape, 1969.

Le Cornu, H. and Shulam, J. *A Commentary on the Jewish Roots of Acts*. Jerusalem: Academon, 2003.

Leibowtiz, N. *Studies in Shemot (Exodus)*. Jerusalem: World Zionist Organization, 1981.

Levinskaya, I. *The Book of Acts in its First Century Setting*. Vol. 5: Diaspora Setting. Grand Rapids: Eerdmans, 1996.

Lichtenstein, Y.Z. *Studies in the Prophets*. Berlin: Julius Gittenfeld, 1869. [Hebrew: לימודי הנביאים].

--------. *Geography in the Talmud*. London: R. Mazin & Co., 1912. [Hebrew: שבע חכמות]

--------. *A Commentary on Selected Portions from the New Testament*. Jerusalem: Keren Ahvah Meshihit, 2002². [Hebrew: סוגיות נבחרות בספר הברית החדשה].

Lieberman, S. *Greek in Jewish Palestine*. New York: Jewish Theological Seminary, 1942.

--------. *Hellenism in Jewish Palestine*. New York: Jewish Theological Seminary, 1950.

Liebes, Y. "Mazmiah Qeren Yeshu'ah," *Tarbiz* 3.3 (1983/4), 313-48. [Hebrew: מצמיח קרן ישועה; English summary, v-vii]. [English version (condensed): "Who makes the Horn of Jesus to Flourish," *Immanuel* 21 (1987), 55-67]

--------. "Tosefet l'ma'amari 'Mazmiah Qeren Yeshu'ah'" ("An Addition to My Article 'Mazmiah Qeren Yeshu'ah'"), *Tarbiz* 4.3-4 (1984/5), 341-51. [Hebrew: תוספת למאמרי "מצמיח קרן ישועה"; English summary, xxxiv].

Lightfoot, J. *Saint Paul's Epistle to the Galatians*. London: Macmillan, 1890.

--------. *A Commentary on the New Testament from the Talmud and Hebraica*. Grand Rapids: Baker Book House, 1979. Vol.1: Place Names in the Gospels. Vol. 4: Acts and 1 Corinthians.

Lim, T. *Holy Scripture in the Qumran Commentaries and Pauline Letters*. Oxford: Clarendon Press, 1997.

--------. "The Qumran Scrolls, Multilingualism, and Biblical Interpretation." In J. Collins and R. Kugler (eds.), *Religion in the Dead Sea Scrolls*. Grand Rapids: Eerdmans, 2000:57-73.

Loisy, A. *L'épître aux Galates*. Paris: Nourry, 1916.

Longenecker, R. *The Christology of Early Jewish Christianity*. London: SCM, 1970.

--------. *Galatians*. Dallas, TX: Word Books, 1990.

-------- (ed.). *The Road From Damascus*. Grand Rapids: Eerdmans, 1997.

Lüdemann, G. *Paul, Apostle to the Gentiles: Studies in Chronology*. Philadelphia: Fortress Press, 1984.

Lütgert, W. *Gesetz und Geist*. Gütersloh: Bertelsmann:,1919.

McKnight, S. *A Light Among the Gentiles: Jewish Missionary Activity in the Second Temple Period*. Minneapolis: Fortress Press, 1991.

Mann. J. *The Bible as Read and Preached in the Old Synagogue*. 2 vols. New York: Ktav, 1971.

Martin, T. "Apostasy to Paganism: The Rhetorical Stasis of the Galatian Controversy." In M. Nanos, (ed.), *The Galatians Debate*. Massachusetts: Hendrickson, 2002:73-94.

Martyn, J.L. "Apocalyptic Antinomies in Paul's Letter to the Galatians," *New Testament Studies* 31 (1985), 410-24.

--------. *Galatians*. New York: Doubleday, 1997.

--------. *Theological Issues in the Letters of Paul*. Nashville: Abingdon, 1997.

Metzger, B. *A Textual Commentary on the Greek New Testament*. London: United Bible Societies, 1971.

Miles, G.B. and Trompf, G. "Luke and Antiphon: the Theology of Acts 27-28 in the Light of Pagan Beliefs About Divine Retribution, Pollution, and Shipwreck," *Harvard Theological Review* 69 (1976), 259-67.

Mitchell, S. *Anatolia: Land, Men, and Gods in Asia Minor*. 2 vols. Oxford: Clarendon Press, 1993.

Montefiore, C. and Loewe, H. *Rabbinic Anthology*. New York: Schocken, 1974.

Moore, G.F. *Judaism in the First Centuries of the Christian Era*. 2 vols. Cambridge: Harvard University Press, 1962.

Muddiman, J. "The Anatomy of Galatians." In S. Porter *et al* (eds.), *Crossing the Boundaries: Essays in Biblical Interpretation in Honour of Michael Goulder*. Leiden: Brill, 1994:257-70.

Mulder, M. (ed.). *Mikra*. Philadelphia: Fortress Press, 1990.

Munck, J. *The Acts of the Apostles*. New York: Doubleday, 1967.

Murphy-O'Connor, J. "Paul in Arabia," *Catholic Biblical Quarterly* 55 (1993), 732-37.

--------. *Paul: A Critical Life.* Oxford: Clarendon Press, 1996.

--------. *St. Paul's Corinth: Text and Archaeology.* Wilmington, Del.: Michael Glazier, 2002.

--------. (ed.). *Paul and Qumran.* London: Geoffrey Chapman, 1968.

Mussner, F. *Der Galaterbrief.* Freiburg et al: Herder, 1977.

Nanos, M. *The Mystery of Romans.* Minneapolis: Fortress Press, 1996.

--------. *The Irony of Galatians.* Minneapolis: Fortress Press, 2002.

--------. "What Was at Stake in Peter's 'Eating with Gentiles' at Antioch?" In M. Nanos, (ed.), *The Galatians Debate.* Massachusetts: Hendrickson, 2002:282-318.

--------. "The Inter- and Intra-Jewish Political Context of Paul's Letter to the Galatians." In M. Nanos, (ed.), *The Galatians Debate.* Massachusetts: Hendrickson, 2002:396-407.

--------. (ed.). *The Galatians Debate.* Massachusetts: Hendrickson, 2002.

--------. "The Social Context and Message of Galatians in View of Paul's Evil Eye Warning (Gal. 3:1)." http://mywebpages.comcast.net/nanosmd, 2003.

--------. "What Does 'Present Jerusalem' (Gal 4:25) in Paul's Allegory Have to Do with the Jerusalem of Paul's Time, or the Concerns of the Galatians?" http://mywebpages.comcast.net/nanosmd, 2004.

Neusner, J. *The Rabbinic Traditions about the Pharisees before 70.* 2 vols. Leiden: Brill, 1971.

Nulman, M. *The Encyclopedia of Jewish Prayer.* NJ: Jason Aronson, 1996.

Oppenheimer, A. *The 'Am ha-aretz.* Leiden: Brill, 1977.

Pardee, D et al. *Handbook of Ancient Hebrew Letters.* Chico: Scholars Press, 1982.

Pfann, C. "Who is My Brother?" MA Thesis, The Graduate Theological Union. Berkeley, 1985.

Poorthuis, M. and Safrai, Ch. *The Centrality of Jerusalem.* Kampen: Kok Pharos, 1996.

Preuss, J. *Biblical and Talmudic Medicine.* Northvale, NJ: Jason Aronson, 1993.

Qimron, E. and Strugnell, J. *Qumran Cave 4, V: Miqsat Ma'ase Ha-Torah.* Oxford: Clarendon Press, 1994. (DJD X)

Pritz, R. *Nazarene Jewish Christianity.* Leiden: Brill, 1988.

Ramsay, W. *A Historical Commentary on St. Paul's Epistle to the Galatians.* Grand Rapids: Baker, 1965.

Riesner, R. *Paul's Early Period: Chronology, Mission Strategy, Theology.* Grand Rapids: Eerdmans, 1998.

Rojtman, B. "Sacred Language and Open Text." In G. Hartman and S. Budick (eds.), *Midrash and Literature.* New Haven: Yale University Press, 1986:159-75.

Rokeah, D. *Jews, Pagans and Christians in Conflict.* Jerusalem: Magnes Press, 1982.

Ropes, J. *The Singular Problem of the Epistle to the Galatians.* Cambridge: Harvard University Press, 1929.

Safrai, S. "Master and Disciple," *Jerusalem Perspective* 3.6 (1990), 3-13.

--------. (ed.). *The Literature of the Sages.* Part I: Oral Torah, Halakha, Mishna, Tosefta, Talmud, External Tractates. Philadelphia: Fortress Press, 1987.

Safrai, S. and M. Stern. (eds.). *The Jewish People in the First Century.* 2 vols. Philadelphia: Fortress Press, 1974.

Samet, M. "Conversion in the First Centures C.E." In I. Gafni *et al* (eds.), *Jews and Judaism in the Second Temple, Mishnah, and Talmud Period.* Jerusalem: Yad Yitzhak Ben-Tzvi, 1993:316-43. [Hebrew: יהודים ויהדות בימי בית שני, המשנה והתלמוד].

Sampley, J. "'Before God, I do not lie' (Gal. 1:20): Paul's Self-Defence in the Light of Roman Legal Praxis," *New Testament Studies* 23 (1977), 477-82.

Sanders, E.P. *Paul, the Law, and the Jewish People.* Philadelphia: Fortress Press, 1983.

Sandnes, K. *"Paul – One of the Prophets"? A Contribution to the Apostle's Self-Understanding.* Tübingen: J.C.B. Mohr, 1991.

Sandt, H. van de and Flusser, D. *The Didache.* Assen/Philadelphia: Royal Van Gorcum/Fortress Press, 2002. (Compendia Rerum Iudaicarum ad Novum Testamentum 5).

Saphir, A. *Christ and the Church.* Jerusalem: Keren Ahva Meshihit, 2001.

--------. *The Divine Unity of Scripture.* Jerusalem: Keren Ahva Meshihit, 2001.

Schechter, S. *Aspects of Rabbinic Theology.* Woodstock, Vermont: Jewish Lights Publishing, 1993.

Schiffman, L. *Sectarian Law in the Dead Sea Scrolls.* Chico: Scholars Press, 1983.

--------. *Reclaiming the Dead Sea Scrolls.* Philadelphia: Jewish Publication Society, 1994.

Schlier, H. *Der Brief an die Galater.* Göttingen: Vandenhoeck & Ruprecht, 1971.

Schmithals, W. *Paul and the Gnostics.* Nashville: Abingdon, 1972.

Schoeps, H.J. *Paul: The Theology of the Apostle in the Light of Jewish Religious History.* Philadelphia: Westminster, 1961.

Schoneveld, J. "Torah in the Flesh," *Immanuel* 24/25 (1990), 77-94.

Schürer, E. *The History of the Jewish People in the Age of Jesus Christ.* Rev. and ed. by G. Vermes, F. Millar, and M. Black. 3 vols. Edinburgh: T&T Clark, 1979.

Schwartz, J. "Sinai in Jewish Thought and Tradition," *Immanuel* 13 (1981), 7-14.

Scott, J. *Paul and the Nations.* Tübingen: J.C.B. Mohr, 1995.

Segal, A. *Rebecca's Children: Judaism and Christianity in the Roman World.* Cambridge: Harvard University Press, 1986.

--------. *Paul the Convert*. New Haven: Yale University Press, 1990.

Sherwin-White, A.N. *Roman Law and Roman Society in the New Testament*. Grand Rapids: Baker Book House, 1922.

Shulam, J. and Le Cornu, H. *A Commentary on the Jewish Roots of Romans*. Baltimore: Lederer, 1998.

Skarsaune, O. *The Proof from Prophecy: A Study in Justin Martyr's Proof-Text Tradition: Text-Type, Provenance, Theological Profile*. Leiden: Brill, 1987.

--------. *In the Shadow of the Temple*. Downers Grove, Ill.: InterVarsity Press, 2002.

Smyth, H. *Greek Grammar*. Cambridge: Harvard University Press, 1920.

Soulen, R.K. *The God of Israel and Christian Theology*. Minneapolis: Fortress Press, 1996.

Steinsaltz, A. *The Essential Talmud*. New York: Basic Books, 1976.

--------. *The Talmud: A Reference Guide*. New York: Random House, 1989.

Stern, M. *Greek and Latin Authors on Jews and Judaism*. 3 vols. Jerusalem: Magnes Press, 1980.

Stern, S. *Jewish Identity in Early Rabbinic Writings*. Leiden: Brill, 1994.

Stirewalt, L. *Paul, the Letter Writer*. Grand Rapids: Eerdmans, 2003.

Stone, M. (ed.). *Jewish Writings of the Second Temple Period*. Philadelphia: Fortress Press, 1984.

Stowers, S. *A Rereading of Romans: Justice, Jews, and Gentiles*. New Haven: Yale University Press, 1994.

Strack, H. *Introduction to the Talmud and Midrash*. New York: Atheneum, 1983.

Strack, H. and Billerbeck, P. *Kommentar zum Neuen Testament aus Talmud und Midrasch*. 6 vols. München: C.H. Beck'sche Verlagsbuchhandlung, 1926.

Strelan, J. "Burden-Bearing and the Law of Christ: A Re-Examination of Galatians 6:2," *Journal of Biblical Literature* 94 (1975), 266-76.

Taylor, J. "Why did Paul persecute the church?" In G. Stanton and G. Stroumsa (eds.), *Tolerance and Intolerance in Early Judaism and Christianity*. Cambridge: Cambridge University Press, 1998: 99-120.

Tomson, P. *Paul and the Jewish Law*. Philadelphia: Fortress Press, 1990.

Torrance, T. "One Aspect of the Biblical Aspect of Faith," *Expository Times* 68 (1957), 111-14.

Travers Herford, R. *Christianity in Talmud and Midrash*. New York: Ktav, 1903.

--------. *Talmud and Apocrypha*. New York: Ktav, 1971.

Urbach, E.E. "Halakha u-Nevua [Halakhah and Prophecy]," *Tarbiz* 18 (1947), 1-27. [Hebrew: הלכה ונבואה].

--------. *The Sages*. 2 vols. Jerusalem: Magnes Press, 1979.

Vermes, G. *The Dead Sea Scrolls in English*. Harmondsworth: Penguin, 1975.

--------. *Jesus the Jew*. London: Collins, 1976.

Walter, N. "Paulus und die Gegner die Christusevangeliums in Galatien." In A. Vanhoye (ed.), *L'Apôtre Paul: Personnalité, Style et Conception du Ministére*. Leuven: Leuven University Press, 1986: 351-56. Reprinted (in abridged form) in M. Nanos, (ed.), *The Galatians Debate*. Massachusetts: Hendrickson, 2002:362-66.

Weinfeld, M. "Jeremiah and the Spiritual Metamorphosis of Israel," *ZAW* 88 (1976), 17-56

--------. "The Charge of Hypocrisy in Matthew 23 and in Jewish Sources," *Immanuel* 24/25 (1990), 52-58.

Wenham, D. *Paul: Follower of Jesus or Founder of Christianity?* Grand Rapids: Eerdmans, 1995.

Wright, N.T. *The Climax of the Covenant: Christ and Law in Pauline Theology*. Edinburgh: T&T Clark, 1991.

--------. *What Saint Paul Really Said*. Grand Rapids: Eerdmans, 1997.

Zakovitch, Y. "Jerusalem in the Days to Come – the Second Giving of the Torah (Isa. 2:2-5). Or, the Two Mountains." http://www.pardes.org.il/online_learning/blaustein.

Zahn, T. *Der Brief des Paulus an die Galater*. Leipzig and Erlangen: Deichert, 1922.